AN INTRODUCT
TO POPULATION

AN INTRODUCTION TO POPULATION
Eleventh Edition

John R. Weeks
San Diego State University

WADSWORTH
CENGAGE Learning™

Australia • Brazil • Japan • Korea • Mexico • Singapore • Spain • United Kingdom • United States

WADSWORTH
CENGAGE Learning™

An Introduction to Population, Eleventh Edition International Edition

John R. Weeks

Publisher/Executive Editor: Linda Schreiber-Ganster

Acquisitions Editor: Erin Mitchell

Development Editor: Liana Sarkisian

Assistant Editor: John Chell

Editorial Assistant: Mallory Ortberg

Media Editor: Melanie Cregger

Marketing Manager: Andrew Keay

Marketing Assistant: Dimitri Hagnere

Marketing Communications Manager: Laura Locallio

Content Project Management: PreMediaGlobal

Creative Director: Rob Hugel

Art Director: Caryl Gorska

Print Buyer: Paula Vang

Rights Acquisitions Account Manager, Text: Don Schlotman

Rights Acquisitions Account Manager, Image: Thomas McDonough

Manuscript Editor: Deanna Weeks

Production Service: PreMediaGlobal

Copy Editor: PreMediaGlobal

Cover Designer: Riezebos Holzbaur/ Brieanna Hattey

Compositor: PreMediaGlobal

For product information and technology assistance, contact us at
Cengage Learning Customer & Sales Support, 1-800-354-9706
For permission to use material from this text or product,
submit all requests online at **www.cengage.com/permissions**
Further permissions questions can be emailed to
permissionrequest@cengage.com

International Edition:

ISBN-13: 978-1-111-72221-0

ISBN-10: 1-111-72221-8

Cengage Learning International Offices

Asia
www.cengageasia.com
tel: (65) 6410 1200

Australia/New Zealand
www.cengage.com.au
tel: (61) 3 9685 4111

Brazil
www.cengage.com.br
tel: (55) 11 3665 9900

India
www.cengage.co.in
tel: (91) 11 4364 1111

Latin America
www.cengage.com.mx
tel: (52) 55 1500 6000

UK/Europe/Middle East/Africa
www.cengage.co.uk
tel: (44) 0 1264 332 424

Represented in Canada by
Nelson Education, Ltd.
tel: (416) 752 9100 / (800) 668 0671
www.nelson.com

Cengage Learning is a leading provider of customized learning solutions with office locations around the globe, including Singapore, the United Kingdom, Australia, Mexico, Brazil, and Japan. Locate your local office at: **www.cengage.com/global**

For product information: **www.cengage.com/international**
Visit your local office: **www.cengage.com/global**
Visit our corporate website: **www.cengage.com**

Printed in Canada
1 2 3 4 5 6 7 14 13 12 11 10

To Deanna

BRIEF TABLE OF CONTENTS

DETAILED TABLE OF CONTENTS

PART FOUR
USING THE DEMOGRAPHIC PERSPECTIVE

PREFACE

Growth, transition, and evolution. These are the key demographic trends as we move through the twenty-first century, and they will have huge impacts on your life. When I think about population growth in the world, I conjure up an image of a bus hurtling down the highway toward what appears to be a cliff. The bus is semiautomatic and has no driver in charge of its progress. Some of the passengers on the bus are ignorant of what seems to lie ahead and are more worried about whether or not the air conditioning is turned up high enough or wondering how many snacks they have left for the journey. Other more alert passengers are looking down the road, but some of them think that what seems like a cliff is really just an optical illusion and is nothing to worry about; some think it may just be a dip, not really a cliff. Those who think it is a cliff are trying to figure out how to apply the brakes, knowing that a big bus takes a long time to slow down even after the brakes are put on. Are we headed toward a disastrous scenario? We don't really know for sure, but we simply can't afford the luxury of hoping for the best. The population bus is causing damage and creating vortexes of change as it charges down the highway, whether or not we are on the cliff route; and the better we understand its speed and direction, the better we will be at steering it and managing it successfully. No matter how many stories you have heard about the rate of population growth coming down or about the end of the population explosion (and those stories are true, up to a point), the world *will* continue to add billions more to the current 7 billion before it stops growing. Huge implications for the future lie in that growth in numbers.

The transitions represent the way in which population growth actually affects us. The world's population is growing because death rates have declined over the past several decades at a much faster pace than have birth rates, and as we go from the historical pattern of high birth and death rates to the increasingly common pattern of low birth and death rates, we pass through the demographic transition. This is actually a whole set of transitions relating to changes in health and mortality, fertility, migration, age structure, urbanization, and family and household structure. Each of these separate, but interrelated, changes has serious consequences for the way societies and economies work, and for that reason they have big implications for you personally. Over time, these transitions have evolved in ways that vary from one part of the world to another, and so their path and progress are less predictable than we once thought.

The growth in numbers (the bus hurtling toward what we hope is *not* a cliff) and the transitions and evolutions created in the process (the vortex created by the passing bus) have to be dealt with simultaneously, and our success as a human civilization depends on how well we do in this project. A lot is at stake here and my goal in this book is to provide you with as much insight as possible into the ways in which these demographic trends of growth, transition, and evolution affect your life in small and large ways.

Over the years, I have found that most people are either blissfully unaware of the enormous impact of population growth and change on their lives, or they are nearly overwhelmed whenever they think of population growth because they have heard so many horror stories about impending doom, or, increasingly, they have heard that population growth is ending and thus assume that the story has a happy ending. This latter belief is in many ways the scariest, because the lethargy that develops from thinking that the impact of population growth is a thing of the past is exactly what will lead us to doom. My purpose in this book is to shake you out of your lethargy (if you are one of those types), without necessarily scaring you in the process. I will introduce you to the basic concepts of population studies and help you develop your own demographic perspective, enabling you to understand some of the most important issues confronting the world. My intention is to sharpen your perception of population growth and change, to increase your awareness of what is happening and why, and to help prepare you to cope with (and help shape) a future that will be shared with billions more people than there are today.

I wrote this book with a wide audience in mind because I find that students in my classes come from a wide range of academic disciplines and bring with them an incredible variety of viewpoints and backgrounds. No matter who you are, demographic events are influencing your life, and the more you know about them, the better off you will be.

What Is New in This Eleventh Edition

Every chapter has been revised for readability, relevancy, recency, and reliability, and there has been a considerable amount of fine-tuning following the major overhaul that was done for the tenth edition. Chapter 7 on migration has been substantially revised, especially to incorporate into this chapter the discussion of immigration policy that had previously been hiding in Chapter 12. That chapter has been completely reorganized and rewritten to allow you to reflect on what has already been accomplished in reining in population growth, and to put you in mind of what the next several decades may look like demographically. These revisions reflect the evolution of the book over time, in step with the evolution of our knowledge about the demography of the world.

Special Features of the Book

To help increase your understanding of the basic concepts and issues of population studies, the book contains the following special features.

Short Essays Each chapter contains a short essay on a particular population concept, designed to help you better understand current demographic issues, such as Chapter 1's "The Demography of Conflict in the Middle East" or Chapter 11's "How Big is Your Ecological Footprint." *New for the 11th edition* is that each essay ends with two discussion questions to encourage you to think about the topic in greater depth.

Main Points A list of 10 main points appears at the end of each chapter, following the summary, to help you review chapter highlights.

Questions for Review A set of five questions are provided at the end of each chapter, designed to stimulate thinking and class discussion on topics covered in the chapter.

Websites of Interest At the end of each chapter, I have provided an annotated list of five websites that I have found to be particularly interesting and helpful to students.

Glossary A Glossary in the back of the book defines key population terms. These terms are in boldface type when introduced in the text to signal that they also appear in the Glossary.

Complete Bibliography This is a fully referenced book and all of the publications and data sources I have used are included in the Bibliography at the end of the book.

A Thorough Index To help you find what you need in the book, I have built as complete an index as possible, divided into a Subject Index, and a Geographic Index.

Ancillary Course Material An Instructor's Manual and other ancillary materials are available through the book's home page on the publisher's website: ***http://www.cengage.com/wadsworth/*** and I have created a blog to accompany the book that provides resources for instructors and students: ***http://weekspopulation.blogspot.com/***.

Personal Acknowledgments

Like most authors, I have an intellectual lineage that I feel is worth tracing. In particular, I would like to acknowledge the late Kingsley Davis, whose standards as a teacher and scholar will always keep me reaching; Eduardo Arriaga; the late Judith Blake; Thomas Burch; Carlo Cipolla; Murray Gendell; the late Nathan Keyfitz; and Samuel Preston. Individually and collectively, they have helped me unravel the mysteries of how the world operates demographically. Thanks are due also to Steve Rutter, formerly of Wadsworth Publishing Company, who first suggested that I write this book. Special thanks go to John, Gregory, Jennifer, Suzanne, Amy, and Jim for teaching me the costs and benefits of children. They have instructed me, in their various ways, in the advantages of being first-born, the coziness of the middle child, the joys that immigration can bring to a family, the wonderful gifts (including Andrew, Sophie, Benjamin, Julia, Elizabeth, and Kayla) that daughters and daughters-in-law can bring, and the special place that a son-in-law has in a family.

However, the one person who is directly responsible for the fact that the first, second, third, fourth, fifth, updated fifth, sixth, seventh, eighth, ninth, tenth and now eleventh editions were written, and who deserves credit for the book's strengths, is my wife, Deanna. Her creativity, good judgment, and hard work in reviewing and editing the manuscript benefited virtually every page, and I have dedicated the book to her.

Other Acknowledgments

I would also like to thank the users of the earlier editions, including professors, their students, and my own students, for their comments and suggestions.

Many, many other people have helped since the first edition came out more than 30 years ago, and I am naturally very grateful for all of their assistance.

The essay in Chapter 7 was co-authored by Gregory B. Weeks, University of North Carolina at Charlotte. Marta Jankowska made important contributions to the essay in Chapter 12. Amy J. Weeks and Jeanie Gaudette provided important cartographic assistance. Andrew Weeks provided important input for Chapter 12.

AN INTRODUCTION TO POPULATION

CHAPTER 1
Introduction to Demography

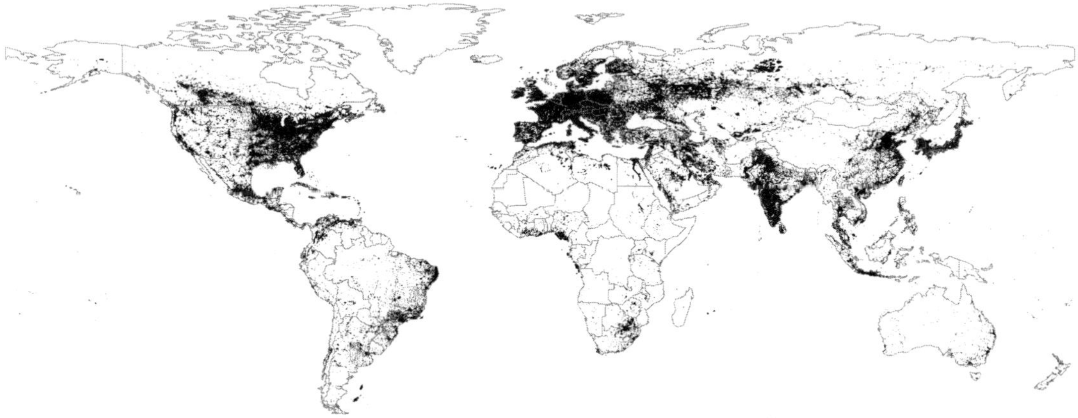

Figure 1.1 The World's Population Distribution Defined by Nighttime Lights
The nighttime light data are reversed in this map, so that the darker areas show where there are the most lights at night, suggestive of population distribution (albeit skewed to the richer countries).

Source: Image and data processing by NOAA's National Geophysical Data Center. DMSP data collected by US Air Force Weather Agency, http://www.ngdc.noaa.gov/dmsp/.

Population growth is the single most important set of events ever to occur in human history—"the most revolutionary phenomenon of our times," as Spanish philosopher Ortega y Gasset (1932:51) put it early in the twentieth century. It has changed—and continues to alter—the way of life in even the most remote corners of the earth. No matter how much you may have heard about declining birth rates, it is still true that the number of people added to the world each day is unprecedented in history and unparalleled in its consequences. We now live in a world crowded not only with people but with contradiction. There are more highly educated people than ever before, yet also more illiterates; more rich people, but also more poor; more well-fed children, but more hunger-ravaged babies whose images haunt us. We have better control over the environment than ever before, but we are damaging our living space in ways we are afraid to imagine.

Our partial mastery of the environment is, indeed, key to understanding why the population is growing, because we have learned how to conquer more and more of the diseases that once routinely killed us. Although the rapid, dramatic drop in mortality all over the world is certainly one of humanity's greatest triumphs, it seems that no good deed goes unpunished, even such an altruistic one as conquering (or at least delaying) death. Because the birth rate almost never goes down in tandem with the decline in the death rate, the result is rapid population growth. This relentless increase in the population has fueled both environmental damage and social upheaval.

Not all demographic change is bad, of course, but population growth does make implacable demands on natural and societal resources. A baby born this year won't create much of an immediate stir, but in a few years she will be eating more and needing clothes, an education, and then a job and place of her own to live.

Population growth is an irresistible force. Virtually every social, political, and economic problem facing the world has demographic change as one of its root causes. Furthermore, I can guarantee you that it is a force that will increasingly affect you personally, in ways both large and small. Population change is not just something that happens to other people. It is taking place all around us, and we each make our own contribution to it. Whether your concern with demography is personal or global, unraveling the "whys" of population growth and change will provide you with a better perspective on how the world works. Understanding these and a wide range of related issues is the business of demography.

What Is Demography?

Demography is the scientific study of human populations. The term itself was coined in 1855 by Achille Guillard, who used it in the title of his book *Éléments de Statistique Humaine ou Démographie Comparée.* The word he invented is a combination of two Greek words: *demos,* which means "people," and *graphein,* which means "to write about" (in this instance, population).

Guillard defined demography as "the mathematical knowledge of populations, their general movements, and their physical, civil, intellectual and moral state" (Guillard 1855:xxvi). This is generally in tune with how we use the term today in that modern demography is the study of the determinants and consequences of population change and is concerned with virtually everything that influences or can be influenced by

- **population size** (how many people there are in a given place)
- **population growth or decline** (how the number of people in that place is changing over time)
- **population processes** (the levels and trends in fertility, mortality, and migration that are determining population size and change and which can be thought of as capturing life's three main moments: hatching, matching, and dispatching)
- **population distribution** (where people are located and why)
- **population structure** (how many males and females there are of each age)
- **population characteristics** (what people are like in a given place, in terms of variables such as education, income, occupation, family and household relationships, immigrant and refugee status, and the many other characteristics that add up to who we are as individuals or groups of people).

It has been said that "the past is a foreign country; they do things differently there" (Hartley 1967:3). Population change and all that goes with it is an integral part of creating a present that seems foreign by comparison to the past, and it will create a future that will make today seem strange to those who look back on it several decades from now. Table 1.1 illustrates this idea, comparing population data for the United States in the year 1900 with that of the year 2000. Although the U.S. population grew considerably during that century, from 76 million to 281 million, it did not keep pace with overall world population growth and so accounted for a slightly smaller fraction of the world's population in 2000 than it had in 1900 (more on this in the next chapter). Mortality levels dropped substantially over the century, leading to a truly amazing 30-year rise in life expectancy, from 47 in 1900 to 77 in 2000 (the reasons for this are laid out in Chapter 5).

Fertility also declined, although by world standards fertility in the United States was already fairly low (3.5 children per woman) in 1900. Still, the drop from 3.5 to 2.1 clearly makes a huge difference in the composition of families, and I discuss this more in Chapters 6 and 10. Americans rearranged themselves considerably within the country over that century, and the westward movement is exemplified by the change in the fraction of the population living in California. It went from only 2 percent in 1900 to 12 percent in 2000. Consider that in 1900 Los Angeles had about the same population as Buffalo, New York, but in 2000 Los Angeles was 35 times more populous than Buffalo.

In the latter part of the twentieth century, much of that growth in Los Angeles was fueled by immigrants from Mexico and Central America, but over the course of the century the composition of international immigrants had shifted substantially. In the decade following the 1900 census, there were about 50,000 Mexican immigrants to the United States, compared to 2 million Italian immigrants in the same time period. By contrast, in the decade prior to Census 2000, the numbers were essentially reversed, with 63,000 Italian immigrants and at least 2.2 million

Mexican immigrants. Yet, as strange as it might seem in an era when there is so much talk about immigrants, the data in Table 1.1 show that the foreign-born population actually represented a greater fraction of the nation in 1900 than it did a century later. We'll explore the reasons for that in Chapter 7.

The past was predominantly rural and the present is predominantly urban (as I discuss in Chapter 9); the past was predominantly pedestrian (there were only 8,000 passenger cars in 1900) and the present is heavily dependent on the automobile (with more than 130 million passenger cars being driven around the country). The past was young, with 34 percent of the population under the age of 15 and only 4 percent aged 65 and older; whereas the present is older, with only 21 percent under 15 and 12 percent aged 65 and older (more on this in Chapter 8). In the past, people lived in households with more people than today (4.76 compared to 2.59), and the average person in each household was considerably less well educated than today, with only 10 percent of those in 1900 achieving a high school education, compared to 80 percent now. These trends are discussed more in Chapter 10.

The world of 1900 was very different from the world of 2000, and the demographics represent an important part of that difference. The future will be different, in its turn, partly because of demographic changes taking place even as you read this page. The study of demography is thus an integral part of understanding human society.

Table 1.1 The Past Is a Foreign Country

	1900	2000
World population (billions)	1.6	6.1
U.S. population (millions)	76	281
U.S. percent of world total	4.8%	4.6%
Life expectancy	47	77
Children per woman	3.5	2.1
% of U.S. population in California	2%	12%
Population of Buffalo, NY, compared to Los Angeles	About the same	LA was 35 times more populous
Immigrants from Italy (1900–1910); (1990–2000)	2 million	63,000
Immigrants from Mexico (1900–1910); (1990–2000)	50,000	2.2 million
% foreign-born	13.6%	11.1%
% urban	40%	80%
Passenger cars	8,000	130 million
% of population under 15	34.4%	21.4%
% of population 65+	4.1%	12.4%
Persons per household	4.76	2.59
% high school graduates	10%	80%

Source: Data for 1900 from http://www.census.gov/prod/99pubs/99statab/sec31.pdf, accessed 2007; data for 2000 from http://www.census.gov, accessed 2010.

Why Is Demography Important?

The demographic foundation of our lives is deep and broad. As you will see in this book, demography affects nearly every facet of your life in some way or another. Population change is one of the prime forces behind social and technological change all over the world. As population size and composition changes in an area—whether it be growth or decline—people have to adjust, and from those adjustments radiate innumerable alterations to the way society operates.

Nearly Everything Is Connected to Demography

It may sound presumptuous, even preposterous, to suggest that nearly everything is connected to demography, but it really is true. This is very different, however, from saying that demography determines everything. Demography is a force in the world that goes hand in hand with every improvement in human well-being that the world has witnessed over the past few hundred years. Children survive as never before, adults are healthier than ever before, women can limit their exposure to the health risks involved with pregnancy and still be nearly guaranteed that the one or two or three babies they have will thrive to adulthood. Having fewer pregnancies and babies in a world where most adults reach old age means that men and women have more "scope" in life; more time to develop their personal capacities and more time and incentive to build a better world for themselves, their children, and everyone else. Longer lives and the societal need for less childbearing by women mean that families and households become more diverse. The changes taking place all over the world in family structure are not the result of a breakdown of social norms so much as they are the natural consequence of societies adapting to the demographic changes of people living longer with fewer children in a world where urban living and migration are vastly more common than ever before. These are all facets of demography affecting your life in important ways.

There is no guarantee, however, about how a society will react to demographic change. That is why it is impossible to be a demographic determinist. Demographic change does demand a societal response, but different societies will respond differently, sometimes for the better, sometimes not. Nonetheless, it turns out that population structures are sufficiently predictable that we can at least suggest the kinds of responses from which societies are going to have to choose. The population of the world is increasing by more than 200,000 people per day, as I will discuss in more detail in the next chapter, but this growth is much more intense in some areas of the world than in others. In those places where societies have been unable adequately to cope, especially with increasing numbers of younger people, the fairly predictable result has been social, economic, and political instability.

Population growth is obviously not the only source of trouble in the world, but its impact is often incendiary, igniting other dilemmas that face human society (Davis 1986). Without knowledge of population dynamics, for example, we cannot fully understand why the world is globalizing at such a rapid pace, nor can we understand the roots of terrorism and conflict from the Middle East to Southeast Asia; nor why there is a simultaneous acceptance of and a backlash against immigrants in the United States and Europe. And we cannot begin to imagine our future without taking into account the fact that the population of the world at the middle of this century is expected to include 2 billion more people than it does now, since the health of the planet depends upon being able to sustain a much larger number of people than are currently alive. Because so much that happens in your life will be influenced by the consequences of population change, it behooves you to understand the causes and mechanisms of those changes. Let's look at some examples.

Globalization

Most broadly, globalization can be thought of as an increasing level of connectedness among and between people and places all over the world. However, the term has taken on a more politically charged dimension since many people interpret it to mean a penetration of less developed nations by multinational companies from the more developed nations. This trend is promoted by the removal of trade barriers that protect local industries and by the integration of local and regional economies into a larger world arena. The pros and cons of this process invite heated debate, but an important, yet generally ignored, element of globalization is that it is closely related to the enormous increase in worldwide population growth that took place after the end of World War II.

Control over mortality, which has permitted the growth of population, occurred first in the countries of Europe and North America, and it was there that population first began to grow rapidly in the modern world. However, after World War II, death control technology was spread globally, especially through the work of various United Nations agencies, funded by the governments of the richer countries. Since declines in mortality initially affect infants more than any other age group, there tends to be a somewhat delayed reaction in the realization of the effects of a mortality decline until those people who would otherwise have died reach an age where they must be educated, clothed, fed, and jobs and homes must be created for them on a scale never before imagined.

As huge new cohorts of young people have come of age and needed jobs in developing countries, their willingness to work for relatively low wages has not gone unnoticed by manufacturers in North America, Europe, and Japan. Nor have big companies failed to notice the growing number of potential consumers for products, especially those aimed at younger people, who represent the bulk of the population in developing countries. Given the demographics, it should not be surprising to us that jobs have moved to the developing countries and that younger consumers in those countries have been encouraged to spend their new wages on products that are popular with younger people in the richer countries, including music, fast food, cars, mobile phones, and electronic games. Globalization exists, in essence, because of the nature of world demographic trends.

Terrorism and Regional Conflict

One reaction to population growth is to accept or even embrace the change and then seek positive solutions to the dilemmas presented by a rapidly growing younger population. Another reaction, of course, is to reject change. This is what the Taliban has been trying to do in Afghanistan—to forcibly prevent a society from modernizing and, in the process, keeping death rates higher than they might otherwise be (you will learn in Chapter 5 that Afghanistan has one of the highest rates of maternal mortality in the world, not to mention the deaths from the violence there), and maintaining women in an inferior status by withholding access to education, paid employment, and the means of preventing pregnancy. The difficulty the Taliban face (besides active military intervention to stop them) is that it is very hard, if not impossible, to put the genie back in the bottle once people have been given access to a longer life and the freedoms that are inherently associated with that. Very few people in the world prefer to go back to the "traditional" life of harsh exposure to disease, oppression, and death.

Throughout the Middle East we can see with special clarity the crucial role that demography has played for several decades now. The migration of poor rural peasants to the cities of Iran, especially Tehran, contributed to the political revolution in that country in 1978 by creating a pool of young, unemployed men who were ready recruits to the cause of overthrowing the existing government (Kazemi 1980), and this pattern has been repeated throughout the region. It has been said that the "dogs of war" (with no disrespect meant to dogs) are young and male (Mesquida and Wiener 1999), and this description applies especially to the Middle East, where large fractions of the population are young, and where males are routinely accorded higher status than females. The impact of the "youth bulge" has been the subject of research for a long time (Moller 1968; Cincotta, Engelman, and Anastasion 2003; Staveteig 2005), but having a large population of young men does not automatically lead to conflict. Rather, the evidence suggests that such a demographic situation is incendiary (Choucri 1984), ripe for exploitation by those who choose to take advantage of it. And, of course, the very existence of Israel is openly threatened by the more rapid growth rate of, and particularly the youth bulge in, the neighboring populations, which are predominantly Muslim. I discuss this in the accompanying essay.

Sub-Saharan Africa is another part of the world where population growth has been increasing faster than resources can be generated to support it—despite the devastation caused by HIV/AIDS—increasing the level of poverty and disease, and encouraging child labor, slavery, despair, and violent ethnonationalist conflict (Wimmer, Cederman, and Min 2009). Throughout sub-Saharan Africa, the large number of children, enmeshed in poverty and often orphaned because their parents have died of AIDS, provides recruits for rebel armies waging warfare against one government or another (Corder 2006). Those children who resist the army recruiters may find themselves sold into slavery, which is part of a larger global problem of child trafficking (International Labour Office 2003). This kind of abuse of children is not caused by demographic trends, but the demographic structure of society contributes to the problem by creating a situation where children are available to be exploited (Bell 2006).

Embracing and Hating Immigration

The youthful age structure produced by high fertility may engender violence, but low fertility is not without its problems. The transition from higher to lower fertility in North America, Europe, and East Asia, as well as Australia and New Zealand, has created a situation in all of these parts of the world in which the younger

THE DEMOGRAPHY OF CONFLICT IN THE MIDDLE EAST

At the end of World War I, the British took control of Palestine from the remnants of the Ottoman empire, which was defunct and had been shrunk back geographically to its origins in Turkey. At that time, Palestine under the British mandate included the territory of modern Israel and Jordan. In 1922, it was divided into the mandates of Transjordan, east of the Jordan River, and Palestine, west of the river. Under the Balfour Declaration of 1917, the British had already agreed to help establish a Jewish national home in Palestine, although later they were sorry they had done so (Oren 2002). In the 1930s and 1940s, European anti-Semitism encouraged the migration of Jews to Palestine and, despite the drop in support from the British, the changing demographics were leading inexorably in the direction of a Jewish state.

Not unexpectedly, this trend was resisted first by Palestinian Arabs, and subsequently by virtually all Arab states. In 1946, at the end of World War II, Transjordan was granted full independence and became the modern state of Jordan, which had in fact been ruled by the great-grandfather of the current King Abdullah II since the end of World War I. Britain handed the decision about Palestine to the United Nations, and in 1947 the UN passed General Assembly Resolution 181. "This provided for the creation of two states, one Arab and the other Jewish, in Palestine, and an international regime for Jerusalem. The Zionists approved of the plan but the Arabs, having already rejected an earlier, more favorable (for them) partition offer from Britain, stood firm in their demand for sovereignty over Palestine in full" (Oren 2002:4). The stage was thus set for the continuing struggle for control of the region. The nascent state of Israel was immediately attacked by armies from all surrounding Arab nations, but managed to prevail, and when hostilities ended in 1949 Israel had claimed more territory than originally allotted to it by the UN. Because as many as 750,000 Palestine's Arabs (who came to be known simply as Palestinians) had fled the area when fighting broke out, the Jewish population emerged as the demographic majority. The Palestinian population was effectively cordoned into the Gaza Strip (controlled by Egypt) and the West Bank (controlled by Jordan), as shown on the accompanying map, with the remainder of what had been Palestine being the state of Israel.

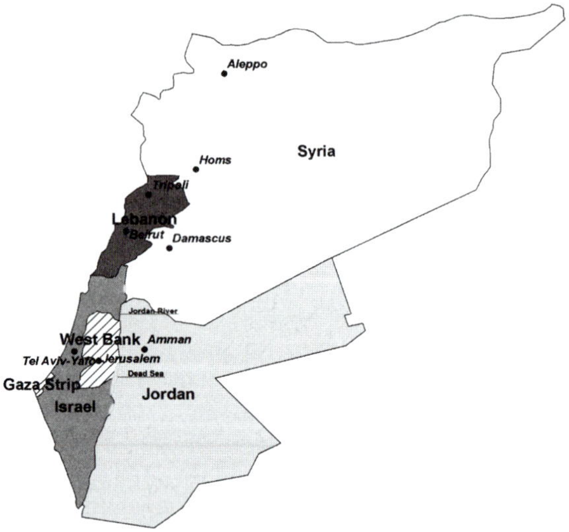

To the north of Israel and Jordan lie Lebanon and Syria. They too had been part of the Ottoman empire for centuries prior to World War I, and at the end of that war they came under the French Mandate of Syria (Salibi 1988). The Maronite Christians in Lebanon lobbied the French for, and were granted, a state of "Greater Lebanon," although nearly half the population in the region was Muslim or Druze (who are neither Christian nor Muslim)—religious/ethnic divisions that continue to plague the country. The remaining territory was divided into four parts, which were later consolidated into modern Syria, and by the mid-1920s Lebanon and Syria were separate republics, although both were under French control. They were granted political independence by France at the end of World War II.

In 1950, the population of Israel accounted for 43 percent of the region's population (excluding Syria for the moment), as you can see in the accompanying table. Israel accepted large numbers of immigrants early in its existence and by 1970, shortly after the 1967 war (the "Six Day War" to Israelis and the "June 1967 War" to Arabs), Israel accounted for 57 percent of the population in the area. After each round of hostilities between Israel and its Arabs neighbors, Jordan received a new flood of Palestinian refugees, which explains why between 1950 and 1970 the population of Jordan was growing much more quickly than the Occupied Palestinian Territory (Gaza and the West Bank). In 1970 a group of Palestinians attempted to overthrow the government of Jordan in order to establish it as the Palestinian state. Jordan is thus a very important part of the picture and, in fact, in 1983, Benjamin Netanyahu, then a member of the Israeli mission to the United States, but later prime minister of Israel, wrote that "the Arabs of Palestine already have a state, called Jordan, in eastern Palestine" (Netanyahu 1983:30). Jordanians do not share that view, of course. This comment came shortly after Israel had twice invaded Lebanon in the early 1980s and had established a "buffer zone" in southern Lebanon, all in response to attacks on Israel by the Palestine Liberation Organization (PLO), which was based at the

(continued)

	Year					
	1950	1970	1990	2010	2030	2050
Total Population						
Israel	1,258	2,898	4,514	7,285	9,219	10,649
Occupied Palestinian Territory	1,005	1,096	2,154	4,409	7,320	10,265
Jordan	472	1,623	3,254	6,472	8,616	10,411
Lebanon	1,443	2,390	2,741	4,255	4,858	5,033
Syria	3,495	6,378	12,843	22,505	30,560	36,911
	7,673	14,385	25,506	44,926	60,573	73,269
Israel as % of nearest neighbors (excluding Syria)	43%	57%	55%	48%	44%	41%
Percent under age 25						
Israel	49	53	49	43	37	32
Occupied Palestinian Territory	63	64	67	64	54	44
Jordan	63	65	69	54	43	33
Lebanon	53	60	55	43	33	29
Syria	60	47	68	55	45	34
Number of children born per woman						
Israel	4.2	3.8	3.0	2.8	2.2	1.9
Occupied Palestinian Territory	7.4	7.7	6.4	5.1	3.1	2.4
Jordan	7.4	7.8	5.9	3.1	2.1	1.9
Lebanon	5.7	4.8	3.3	1.9	1.9	1.9
Syria	7.2	7.5	6.2	3.3	2.2	1.9
Infant mortality rate (per 1,000 live births)						
Israel	41	22	11	5	4	3
Occupied Palestinian Territory	160	82	35	18	10	8
Jordan	145	82	42	19	11	8
Lebanon	87	43	37	22	13	9
Syria	144	83	40	16	10	8

Source: Compiled from the United Nations Population Division, 2009, "World Population Prospects: The 2008 Revision, Population Database," http://esa.un.org/unpp/, accessed 2010.

THE DEMOGRAPHY OF CONFLICT IN THE MIDDLE EAST (CONTINUED)

time in Lebanon. Thus, Lebanon was drawn into the picture, although it was largely Syrian forces, not Lebanese, that the Israelis were worried about.

In the meantime, Yasser Arafat, who had emerged as the primary leader and spokesperson of the Palestinian population through his role as Chairman of the Palestine Liberation Organization, was applauding the high birth rate among Palestinians, calling it their "secret weapon" to beat back the Israeli challenge (Waldman 1991), and he urged women to have babies for the cause (the intifada, or uprising, against Israel) to replace the young male fighters who were being killed fighting the Israelis (Sontag 2000). The evidence suggests that, in fact, Palestinian fertility did increase during the first intifada (1988–1991), although this was mainly because women during this period married and started having children at an earlier age than either before or after (Khawaja and Randall 2006).

To be sure, Palestinians in the region have consistently had fertility rates that are the highest, or close to the highest, of any group in the world. As you can see in the accompanying table, Palestinian women in the occupied territories were averaging nearly eight children each in 1970 and more than six each as recently as 1990. Furthermore, as a result of major public health efforts by UNICEF, infant mortality has dropped dramatically among Palestinian refugees. In 1950, 160 out of every 1,000 babies born died before reaching their first birthday, but by 2010 the mortality rate was almost one-tenth of that figure, at 18 per 1,000.

As we will see throughout this book, the inevitable consequence of high fertility and rapidly declining infant and child mortality is a huge increase in the number of young people. The Arab population in general, but especially the Palestinian population, has experienced an enormous baby boom over the past several decades (Tabutin and Schoumaker 2005). Two out of every three Palestinians is under the age of 25, putting tremendous pressure on all societal resources. The fact that there are

population is declining as a fraction of the total population, creating holes in the labor force and concerns about who will pay the taxes needed to fund the pensions and health care needs of the older population. For a variety of reasons that I will discuss in Chapter 6, women in the richer countries are choosing to have fewer children than are required to replace the population. One solution in the short term is immigration. Canada has been the country most welcoming of immigrants, at least on the basis of immigrants per resident population, with Asians being the largest group entering Canada (a pattern followed also in Australia). The United States has been the most accepting of all countries in the world in terms of absolute numbers of immigrants, including both legal and undocumented, with Mexico leading the list of countries from which immigrants to the U.S. come.

Like it or not, the countries sending migrants have their own demographic issues that complement those of the richer countries. For example, in Mexico, fertility has not declined as quickly as mortality, and the resulting high rates of population growth have made it impossible for the economy to generate enough jobs for each year's crop of new workers. Underemployment in Mexico naturally increases the attractiveness of migrating to where better jobs are. This happens especially to be the United States, not just because the United States is next door, but because low rates of population growth there have left many jobs open, particularly at the lower end of the economic ladder. These positions provide foreign laborers with a higher standard of living than they could have had in Mexico. The North American Free Trade Agreement, passed in 1994, promised new and higher-wage jobs in Mexico that far more young Palestinians each year than there are new jobs being created means that there is a pool of discontent waiting to be tapped by any group interested in overturning the present social order (Fargues 1995, 2000).

Embedded in the demography of the Arab–Jewish conflict is the fact that although the fertility levels in Israel have always been lower than among Palestinians, fertility rates among the ultra-orthodox Jewish population are nearly as high as for Palestinians living in Israel, whereas Christians have the country's lowest fertility rates (Goldscheider 1991; Courbage 2000). Nonetheless, Muslims in Israel average 3.8 children each compared to 2.9 among Jews (Israel Central Bureau of Statistics 2010). In Lebanon, as Christians have migrated out of the area, the demography of the country has begun to merge with its Muslim neighbors, as can be seen in the accompanying table. I should note that none of these population projections for the region takes into account the surge in return migration to both Israel and the West Bank that has occurred in the aftermath of the global economic crisis that began in 2007 (Stub 2009). When times are bad, some of the people who had left home to work elsewhere find themselves out of a job and head back home.

Overall, the high fertility and steadily declining mortality will produce a projected population for the region (including Syria) in 2050 of 73 million—ten times what it was in the middle of the twentieth century. Goldscheider suggests that demography is embedded in the Israel–Palestinian conflict, and the demographics continue to be incendiary, and keep in mind that we haven't even talked about the water scarcity already existing in that part of the world . . .

Discussion Questions: (1) Do you agree or disagree with the idea of trying to manipulate the birth rate (either up or down) to achieve political aims? **(2)** How do you think the status of women in the Middle East might be influencing both demographic and political trends?

---

would eventually reduce the need for Mexicans to leave their country to find work (Cornelius 2002). That promise has been sideswiped, however, by the fact that rising wages in Mexico have led many companies to take their manufacturing businesses to other countries where wages are still low, particularly China, whose population outnumbers Mexico's by a ratio of ten to one. The worldwide recession that began in 2007 has made it harder for immigrants from developing countries to find jobs in richer countries, but the recessions in their own countries have only made the need for a decent job that much more desperate.

Since the terrorist attacks of September 11, 2001, undocumented immigrants have found it more difficult to enter the United States. As a consequence, many Latin American migrants have been going to Europe instead, both legally and illegally (Millman and Vitzthum 2003; Caramés 2004). The open-border policy within the European Union (EU) means that once people enter Europe they are free to travel to any of the other EU countries in search of a job. Not surprisingly, Spain is the largest recipient of predominantly Spanish-speaking immigrants, but Switzerland and Italy as well include growing communities of Latin Americans. There is a certain amount of symmetry, one might say, in the fact that the migration of Spaniards to the New World created "Latin America" from the mixing of Europeans with the indigenous population; now, five centuries later, the current is reversing.

There is, in fact, a bigger vacuum of laborers in Europe than in North America, because European birth rates have been declining for several decades and are now considerably lower than in the United States. There is thus the "sucking sound" of people from developing nations, notably former European colonies, filling the jobs in Europe that would otherwise go begging. The United Kingdom has large immigrant populations from India, Pakistan, and the Caribbean, while France has immigrants from Algeria and Senegal, Germany has immigrants from Turkey (not a former colony, but a sympathizer in both world wars), the Netherlands has immigrants from Indonesia, and Spain has immigrants from Morocco (along with those from Latin America). Europeans, however, are not necessarily in favor of this trend. Caldwell (2009) has documented the rise in anti-foreigner sentiment in Europe, aimed especially at Muslim immigrants, and politicians throughout Europe are increasingly being forced by voters to take a stand on immigration issues.

Given the needs in European countries for laborers and the complementary surplus of laborers in developing countries, we can expect that immigration will quite literally change the face of Europe in your lifetime. The "demographic time bomb" of an aging European population (Kempe 2006) means that these countries may need immigrants in place of the babies that aren't being born, but the problem is always that immigrants tend to be different. They may look different, have a different language, a different religion, and differ in their expectations about how society operates. Furthermore, since the immigrants tend to be young adults, they will wind up contributing disproportionately to the birth rate in their new countries, leading to a rapid and profound shift in the ethnic composition of the younger population. These differences create problems for all societies and create situations of backlash against immigrants.

American history is replete with stories of discrimination against immigrant groups for one or more generations until the children and grandchildren of immigrants finally are accepted as part of mainstream society. This process produces children who would not be recognizable to their ancestors and a society that is in certain ways a foreign country relative to the past. Just as in the United States, European nations have highly visible anti-immigrant groups, but the immigrants have kept coming anyway because jobs have been available and they need the jobs. This is less true in Japan because the level of anti-foreign sentiment is so high. The Japanese simply take it for granted that people from other countries will not become permanent members of Japanese society. This means that Japan has had fewer immigrant workers per person than North America or Europe, and it is not unreasonable to think that the Japanese economy has been moribund for many years now because it has not been invigorated by immigration.

Degradation of the Environment and Natural Disasters

As the human population has increased, its potential for disrupting the earth's biosphere has grown in tandem. We are polluting the **atmosphere** (producing problems such as global warming, acid rain, and holes in the ozone layer); the **hydrosphere** (contaminating the fresh water supply, destroying coral reefs, and fishing out the ocean); and the **lithosphere** (degrading the land with toxic waste and permitting topsoil loss, desertification, and deforestation). This degradation is caused by our intensive use of resources, which has dramatically increased our standard of living over the past 200 years. That very same use of resources has permitted us to bring mortality under control, launching the world on its course of a huge increase in the number of people alive on the planet. The task we will confront in the future is to maintain our standard of living while using many fewer resources per person. Keep in mind that international agencies such as the United Nations and the World Bank have suggested, through the Millennium Development Goals, that long-term sustainability of the planet requires that we lift all people out of poverty so that everyone can be a better steward of the planet. So, the challenge is really to maintain our own standard of living, while increasing that of people everywhere else in the world, and doing so while not using resources in an unsustainable fashion. This is not going to be a simple project, based on data from the United Nations Human Development Report released in 2006 indicating that the richer countries became even richer in the 1990s, but "in 2003, 18 countries with a combined population of 460 million people registered lower scores on the human development index (HDI) than in 1990—an unprecedented reversal" (United Nations Development Programme 2006:3).

The number of people living in extreme poverty has increased nearly in lockstep with population growth, and poverty is one of the major reasons why millions of children in less developed nations are forced to work, jeopardizing their health, their education, and their future. Worldwide, the gap has been increasing between rich and poor countries, especially between the very richest and the very poorest. Reducing poverty is a worthwhile goal in all events, but the Millennium Development Goals do not really reckon with how this can be accomplished, given the huge increase in numbers that the United Nations itself (through its Population Division) projects will be sharing the planet by the middle of this century. Can we reduce worldwide poverty and not further degrade our environment in the face of continued population pressure? No one really knows the answer to that question.

None of the basic resources required to expand food output—land, water, energy—can be considered abundant today. This especially affects the food security of people in less developed countries with rapidly rising food demands and small energy reserves. Even now, in sub-Saharan Africa food production is not keeping pace with population growth, which raises the fear that the world may have surpassed its ability to sustain current levels of food production. Genetically modified foods (GMF) may be the answer, but if we don't like that idea, then some other solutions that we currently don't know about will have to come forth if we are not only to feed 9 billion or more people but also to meet the United Nations Food and Agriculture Organization's goal of reducing malnutrition throughout the world. In other words, we want to feed more people, and feed them better than we are currently doing. It is often argued that there is, in fact, plenty of food in the world, but it is just not properly distributed to the places that need it. However, Jenkins and Scanlan (2001) have argued convincingly that even when these other factors are taken into account, population pressure has undermined the supply of food and the access to food in less developed nations, thus aggravating problems of food security in much of the world.

Keep in mind that every person added to the world's population requires energy to prepare food, to provide clothing and shelter, and to fuel economic life. Each increment in demand is another claim on energy resources (and creates problems of what to do with the by-products of energy use), forcing further global adjustments in the use of energy. Water is also an issue. More than half a billion people already face water scarcity, and an additional 2 to 3 billion live in areas that are water-stressed.

Paradoxically, it turns out that in order to grow enough food for the expected party of 9 billion, we need fewer people in agricultural areas, not more. Humans are poor converters of energy, and machines are required to increase production. This means that cities will be absorbing an increasing fraction of the world's population. A safe and healthy urban environment requires the infrastructure necessary to provide clean water and to treat sewage and waste, and a growing economy requires transportation and communications infrastructure. However, rapidly growing countries routinely find that their "demographic overhead" is too great just to maintain what they already have, much less to keep up with the demand for new infrastructure.

The Danger of Demographic Fatigue

In the face of nearly relentless population pressure, as we continue to add tens of millions of people per year to the world's total, there is the danger that those of us who live in more developed countries will tire of and turn our backs on the less developed countries, where population growth continues to create one problem after another. After all, much of the population news that we hear refers to declining birth rates and laments how low fertility in rich countries creates problems such as the need for immigrants. Our rates of growth may be low, but the "silent explosion" (Appleman 1965) continues in the rest of the world. Although we live in a demographically divided world, we in the rich countries were the ones who lit the fuse on the population bomb, and increasing globalization demands that we remember that there is no such thing as "their" problem—all problems are ours (and theirs) to deal with together.

How Will You Use This Information?

It is my hope that you will use the demographic insights in this book to improve your understanding of how the world works. In that general way, a demographic perspective can be personally empowering for you. But it is also no exaggeration to say that much of what you will glean from the book is potentially very useful in more mundane, but not necessarily less important, ways. **Demographics** is the term that has become associated with practical applications of population information, and this can be a veritable treasure trove for you to mine.

Because you live in a social world, many if not most of the decisions that you have to make about life involve people, and when the issues relate to how many people there are, and where they live and work, and what they are like, demographics become part of the decision-making process, allowing you to lay out a systematic strategy for achieving your own goal whether your challenges relate to business, social, or political planning.

Geodemographics and Spatial Demography

We can talk simply about the numbers and characteristics of people (their "demographic"), but we are more often interested as well in where they live or work or play. When we add this spatial element we are talking about **geodemographics** or **spatial demography**, which is the analysis of demographic data that takes into account the location of the people being studied (Harris, Sleight, and Webber 2005; Wachter 2005). As you will see throughout this book, demography is an inherently spatial science because cultural similarities lead to similarities in demographic behavior and culturally similar people often live close to one another. The advent of high-powered personal computers has revolutionized our ability to analyze massive demographic data sets, and this has allowed the spatial component of demographic analysis to come into its own and further improve our knowledge of how the world works. We will return to this theme throughout the book—where you are matters a great deal demographically and in almost every other way.

Demographics of Politics

Demographics are central to the political process in the United States. The constitutional basis of the Census of Population is to provide data for the **apportionment** of seats in the House of Representatives, and this process reaches down to the local level. Legislators also ask questions about how population growth and distribution influence the allocation of tax dollars. Will the increase in the older population bankrupt the Social Security and Medicare systems? Are undocumented immigrants creating an undue burden on the criminal justice and health care systems? Can we adequately educate the next generation of young people who are increasingly from diverse backgrounds?

Politicians are not completely altruistic, of course, and routinely apply demographics for their own personal use when campaign time rolls around. What are the demographic characteristics of a candidate's supporters and where are these voters located so that they can be encouraged to get to the polls on election day? Marketers track the demographics of voters in each district and help candidates craft messages that fit the voters' characteristics, since people seeking office must either match their election platform to the political attitudes of voters or realize that they will face an uphill battle to convince people to vote for them. "The demography of the voting-age population within a political district is a crucial ingredient in winning an election because demographic characteristics such as age, sex, race, and education are strongly related to the likelihood of voting and, to some extent, to political preferences" (Hill and Kent 1988:2). Data for the United States from the 2008 general election indicate that women are more likely to vote than are men, older people more than younger people (although there was a substantial increase in voting among younger people in 2008), native-born citizens more than naturalized citizens, married people more than single, well educated more than less educated, employed more than unemployed, and higher income more than low income (U.S. Census Bureau 2009). If you know where people with these differing demographics live (and that's part of spatial demography), and you know their political party (which is influenced by demographics), you can improve your chances of winning an election. With respect to political party, in 1969 the political analyst Kevin Phillips used the demographic characteristics of voters in the United States to correctly predict "The Emerging Republican Majority" (Phillips 1969). In 2002, John Judis and Ruy Teixeira took a new look at the demographics of voters and decided that they portended an emerging democratic majority (Judis and Teixeira 2002). The presidential election of 2008 suggested that the demographic tea leaves were again correct on this score.

As noted above, the original purpose of the Census of Population in the United States was to determine how membership in the House of Representatives should be distributed. After each enumeration, which historically takes place every ten years in the month of April, the U.S. Census Bureau is required by law to deliver total population counts for all 50 states to the President on or before December 31st of that year. These data are then sent to the House of Representatives for use in determining the number of representatives to which each state is entitled. Since the 1910 census, the total number of House seats has been fixed at 435, and the Constitution requires that every state get at least one seat. The first 50 House seats are thus used up. The question remains of how to allocate or apportion the remaining 385 seats, remembering that congressional districts cannot cross state boundaries and there can be neither partial districts nor sharing of seats. Since 1940, this number has been based on a formula called the method of equal proportions, which rank-orders a state's priority for each of those 385 seats based on the total population of a state compared with all other states. The calculations themselves are cumbersome (Poston 1990), but they produce an allocation of House seats that is now accepted without much criticism or controversy, except for the issue of whether and how to count overseas Americans, as I discuss in Chapter 4.

Once the number of seats per state has been reapportioned, the real fight begins. This involves **redistricting**, the reconfiguration of congressional districts (geographic areas) that each seat will represent. In the 1960s, a series of Supreme Court decisions extended to the state and local levels the requirement that legislative districts be drawn in such a way as to ensure demographically equal representation ("one person, one vote"). Public Law 94-171 mandates that the Census Bureau provide population counts by age (under 18 and 18 and over) and by race and ethnicity down to the block level for local communities (and, as you will see in Chapter 4, these were the only data collected from everyone in the 2010 Census). These data are then used to redefine legislative district boundaries (Williams 1994).

State legislatures are charged with redistricting congressional seats, and local governments may also use the census data to redistrict city council or other boundaries. In 2004, the U.S. Supreme Court ruled that once the lines are drawn they can be challenged only if racial discrimination is involved. But deciding on which lines make sense can be a messy issue, because the availability of powerful desktop geographic information system software, along with the fact that the Census Bureau makes data available for free on the Internet, means that almost anyone can create their own set of districts and can then lobby their state legislature to choose their plan.

There are very few rules that govern the formation of a district beyond the requirement that, after the census is complete, each state must change its political boundaries to make sure each congressional district is equally populated. Newly drawn districts do not have to take into account existing political boundaries, such as cities and counties, nor do they have to take into account natural geographic boundaries, such as mountains and rivers. They need only be equally populated. When political boundaries are drawn solely for partisan gain, the process is called "gerrymandering," after early-nineteenth-century Massachusetts governor (and later vice president of the United States) Elbridge Gerry. Gerry attempted to draw political districts to favor his own Federalist Party over the opposing Democratic–Republicans. These districts looked like salamanders and so were dubbed "gerrymanders." Since that time, this mix of demography, geography, and politics has become a common weapon that a majority party uses to increase its majority without increasing its share of the vote.

The United States is certainly not alone in the use of demographic data for political campaign work. The Mexican presidential election in 2006 was the most closely contested in that country's modern history and the candidates had campaigned heavily to attract the different demographic groups of Mexico to their cause. The results of the election showed a geodemographic mix reflecting the richer, better educated Mexicans in the northern part of Mexico voting differently than the less well educated, less well off Mexicans dominating the southern part of the country (see Figure 1.2). And, since there are an estimated 4.1 million Mexican expatriates living in the United States who were eligible to vote in the Mexican presidential elections (Prengaman 2006), the candidates sought out their votes as well. For the first time ever, absentee ballots were available for Mexicans living outside the country, although the potential voter had to have gone to Mexico to sign up for a ballot six months before the election, so not many people (indeed, only about 28,000 in the United States) took advantage of that. Those who did vote tended to join the northern Mexicans in voting for the ultimate winner, Felipe Calderón, the more conservative of the major candidates.

Demographics of Social Planning

Even after election day, of course, demographics underlie many of the major social issues that confront national and state legislators, as I will discuss in virtually every chapter of this book. The demographics of the baby boom, for example, helped fuel inflation in the United States during the 1970s. Government policies in that period were oriented toward creating new jobs for the swelling numbers of labor force entrants, directly contributing to inflation through government expenditures and indirectly having an effect because Congress's attention was turned away from combating inflation. This same bulge in the young adult male population also contributed to the ability of the United States to get as involved as it did in the Vietnam War—the "dogs of war" phenomenon mentioned earlier in connection with current issues in the Middle East.

The baby boom is still having an impact on legislative analysis in the new millennium. The big question has become: How will the country finance the retirement and the health care needs of baby boomers as they age and retire? Most of the richest nations, but also China, are facing similar issues, as declining fertility and increased longevity have contributed to the prospect of substantial increases in both the number and percentage of the older population. As the older cohorts begin to squeeze national systems of social insurance, legislative action will be required to make long-run changes in the financing and benefit structure of these systems if they are to survive, because, as we will discuss later in the book, immigration is one solution, but it comes with a lot of other costs attached. Changes will be made, of course,

Figure 1.2 The "blue" and "red" states reflecting the spatial demography of recent presidential elections in the United States and Mexico.

Note: The dark ("blue") states represent those with a majority voting for the liberal candidate in each country's recent presidential election (2008 in the U.S. and 2006 in Mexico); the lighter ("red") states represent a majority voting for the conservative candidate.

even if their exact shape is difficult to forecast. Delaying retirement is probably the easiest change to make, at least in the abstract. At the individual level, of course, few people want to make that choice to keep working for a few more years after spending their working life thinking that they were going to retire at a relatively young age. Increased self-reliance is another proposed solution: requiring people when younger to save for their own retirement, through mandatory contributions to mutual funds and other investment instruments. It may also be that, when the time comes, taxes will be raised on younger people in order to bail out older people who, in fact, did not save enough for their retirement.

Demographics are widely used in American society to chart population movements and plan for social change. When such planning breaks down, as it often does in cities of developing nations where rapid population growth is occurring, the result can be a certain amount of chaos, social foment, and even political upheaval. However, in the United States, regional planning agencies have become commonplace in an effort to coordinate the wide range of public services that maintain a high quality of life. Perhaps most obvious in its need for demographic information is the educational system. Public elementary and secondary school districts cannot readily recruit students or market their services to new prospects; they rise and fall on demographic currents that determine enrollment and the characteristics of students, such as English proficiency, which can affect resource demands. Of course, not every community experiences the national trend; there is variation among and between individual school districts and they all have a need for precise information, because even within a district some geographic areas may be growing while others are diminishing in the number of school-aged children or children of one ethnic group or another.

Do you close some schools and open new ones elsewhere? If so, what do you do with the old schools, and how do you pay for the new ones? Should children be bused from one area to another? If so, how is that to be organized and paid for? Can teachers be retrained to fill classes where demand is growing? These and a host of related questions push school district demographers to pore over questionnaires about the number of younger, preschool-aged siblings reported by currently enrolled students; examine birth records to see where the families are that are having babies; and talk to realtors to assess the potential for home turnover and to evaluate the likely number of children among families moving in and out. From these data, they construct enrollment projections, which are a vital part of public education planning.

Educators must also bear in mind the important influence economic conditions have on job opportunities, and thus on the likelihood that people will be moving in or out of the district. This means that school district demographers increasingly pay attention to regional economic models that are designed to forecast local economic trends on the theory that people follow jobs (and different kinds of people follow different kinds of jobs), so the creation of jobs within a region will influence local demographic trends (Siegel 2002). Demographic conditions can also affect a school district in ways that go beyond the numbers. Adult immigrants to the United States from Latin America tend to have substantially lower levels of education than prevail in the United States, so they may have relatively little experience with schools in their native country, much less in the United States. When their children start attending school, they may be generally unable to help them with schoolwork. Since parental involvement is a key ingredient in student success, school districts are faced with the need to create new policies and programs to educate immigrant parents about what their children are experiencing in school.

Nor are colleges and universities immune to the effects of demographics. The number of high school graduates in the United States declined each year between 1988 and 1992 because of the baby bust that had followed the baby boom. Then it began increasing again in the mid-1990s as the baby boomlet children reached college age, but demand for college has increased more rapidly than population growth because an increasing fraction of high school graduates are now attending college. In California, immigration since the 1960s has brought to the state a large number of young adults who then had children, and those kids began to move through high school and into colleges in the late 1990s. Since then, the number of undergraduates in California's public universities and community colleges has steadily increased, and it is projected to continue climbing at least through 2014 (California Department of Finance 2006), contributing to what some educators have called Tidal Wave II (the first tidal wave, of course, was brought about by the baby boom).

The same age structure changes that influence the educational system also have an impact on the health care industry. Over the years, hospitals and other health care providers have learned that they have to "reposition" themselves in a classic marketing sense to meet the needs of a society that is changing demographically (Rives 1997; Pol and Thomas 2001; Beckett and Morrison 2010). In countries like the United States, health care is less about birthing and coping with childhood illnesses, and more about treating the chronic diseases that beset an older population.

Crime, like health, is closely tied to the age and sex structure of a community. Everybody knows that certain kinds of crimes—especially street crimes and drug-related crimes—are more likely to occur in neighborhoods with particular sociodemographic characteristics (Sampson and Morenoff 2004). Areas where the poverty level and unemployment are high are especially prone to these visible kinds of crime (as opposed to white collar crime, for example) (Short 1997).

"Build it and they will come" may apply to ballparks and it might have once applied to churches in America, but why leave it to chance? Religious organizations and private companies employ demographic researchers to keep track of household preferences in religion so that churches can respond most effectively to the needs of their members and can, in essence, "market" themselves to the demographically appropriate community. For example, the Presbyterian Church (USA) conducts a scientific panel survey of its membership and on the church's website you can discover that the median age of Presbyterians is 60, 46 percent are Republicans, 96 percent are white, and 38 percent have more than $100,000 in household income (Presbyterian Church [USA] 2008). This is the kind of information that can then be used to help locate new sites or expand local membership (Wendelken 1996) and, in fact, the Presbyterian Church website has a geodemographic service that helps you do that. It has even been argued that demographic trends are encouraging a revival in religiosity in the United States. Roof (1999) has suggested that as baby boomers have aged they have become more religious (a not uncommon phenomenon among humans), but that being boomers they have been drawn to new types of Christian Protestant churches, rather than swelling the ranks of the more established denominations.

Demographics of Business

Making a profit in business requires having an edge on your competitors. This may mean that your product or service is better or at least different in some meaningful way, or it may mean that you have been able to find and keep customers that your competition has ignored (using **marketing demographics**, **cluster marketing**, and/or **geodemographics**), or it may mean that you have found a better location for your business than have your competitors based on an analysis of demographic data (**site selection demographics**, a variation of geodemographics) (Harris, Sleight, and Webber 2005; Murdock and Swanson 2008).

Profits are also maximized by investing in the businesses with the greatest opportunities for growth, based on changing demographics (**investment demographics**), as well by being able to employ and keep the best possible labor force (**demographics of human resource management**). In each instance, then, demographic knowledge can be one of the keys to generating higher profits: When it comes to understanding today's consumer marketplace, just about the only thing that's certain is that uncertainty reigns. The speed of technological change, the volatile global economy, the emergence of media-savvy and ever-more-demanding customers have all coalesced into the blur that now seems to characterize business-as-usual. Grappling with uncertainty in business planning requires more than guesswork, warned the late business guru Peter Drucker. It requires looking at "what has already happened that will create the future. The first place to look," said Drucker, "is in demographics" (quoted in Russell 1999:54).

Marketing Demographics One of the first and still very profitable ways in which demographics can be used in business is for marketing. Demographics are employed to segment and target the market for a product, an approach so popular that a television program's demographic base is an important predictor of its commercial success. **Segmentation** refers to the manufacturing and packaging of products or the provision of services that appeal to specific sociodemographically identifiable groups within the population. "Consumer markets are segmented on the basis of such demographic variables as geographic location, rate of product usage, income, age, sex, education, stage in the family life cycle, religion, race, and social class. Industrial markets are segmented demographically according to such variables as geographic location, kind of business, rate of product usage, and size of user" (Levy, Frerichs, and Gordon 1994:177). Automobile manufacturers are especially famous for segmenting the market and producing different cars to appeal to different categories of people. Ford did this very successfully with the original Mustang:

> Our market research showed that the youthful image of the new decade had a firm basis in demographic reality. Millions of teenagers, born in the postwar baby boom, were about to surge into the national marketplace. Here was a market in search of a car. Any car that would appeal to these young customers had to have three main features: great styling, strong performance and a low price (Iacocca 1984:64).

Ford continued that approach when it introduced its Focus as a car aimed specifically at "Echo Boomers (children of the baby boomers) and Gen Xers" (Kranhold 1999:B8).

Closely related to segmenting (sometimes indistinguishable in the literature) is the concept of **targeting**. It involves picking out particular sociodemographic characteristics of people who might purchase what you have to offer, then appealing to the consumer tastes and behavior reflected in those particular characteristics. Throughout this book, I will be emphasizing the ways in which sociodemographic characteristics can influence behavior. It is this relationship that is of interest to business. The kinds of products you buy and how much you will spend on those products is dictated, at least in part, by factors such as your age, gender, education, income, socioethnic identity, household structure and living arrangements, and whether you live in a city and even where in the city you live.

People at different ages have different needs and tastes for products and differing amounts of money to spend. Companies catering to the youngest age group have to keep track of the number of births (their potential market) as well as the characteristics of the parents and grandparents (who spend the money on behalf of the babies). The baby market has seen some wild fluctuations in recent decades in the United States, as you can see in Figure 1.3. The number of babies being born each year plummeted during the 1960s and 1970s, rebounded in the 1980s, peaked in 1990, and slacked off in the early 1990s before rebounding. The U.S. Census Bureau projects the number of births to continue rising steadily for the foreseeable future. It is a dangerous business, however, to be lulled into believing that every company dealing with baby products will necessarily live or die on the peaks and troughs of birth cycles. In 2006, there were 4.3 million births in the United States, virtually the same as at the height of the baby boom in 1958. Yet, in 2006 there were 1.7 million *first* births, compared to only 1.1 million in 1958. If you have hung around new parents and new grandparents, you know that people react differently to first births than to others. In particular, they open their pocketbooks wider to pay for cribs, buggies, strollers, diapers, and every conceivable type of baby toy designed to stimulate and "improve the quality" of the baby's life. Businesses that cater to these needs, then, are as sensitive to birth order as they are to the absolute volume of births.

As the ups and downs in births work their way through the age structure (augmented by people moving in and out and, of course, some people dying), we can see that the age pattern of teenagers (ages 10 to 19) follows a wave that is largely a delayed reaction to the birth wave. Thus, as the baby market dried up in the 1970s (the babies born during this time are popularly known as Generation X), the young adult population was expanding, only to deflate again in the 1980s, but by then the baby market was growing again. Now, in the first part of the twenty-first century, the crop of babies born in the 1990s is moving into and through the teen years.

Marketers have labeled people born from 1977 through 1994 as Generation Y, and in the 1990s the parents of these children were spending money on their education and entertainment. Many of these people (perhaps including you) are now trying to complete their education so that they can compete for well-paying jobs, which in turn will produce discretionary income for which businesses will be competing. The middle age group (represented in Figure 1.3 by people aged 40 to 49) was relatively unchanged in size and essentially unnoticed until the baby boom generation began moving into it in the 1980s. Since then, it has become a new "boom" industry. Laser eye surgery surged, as did sales of walking shoes (running shoe sales slowed to a walk). When not walking, the aging baby boomers have been driving their luxury or near-luxury sport utility vehicles (and are now snapping up hybrid cars). It was the

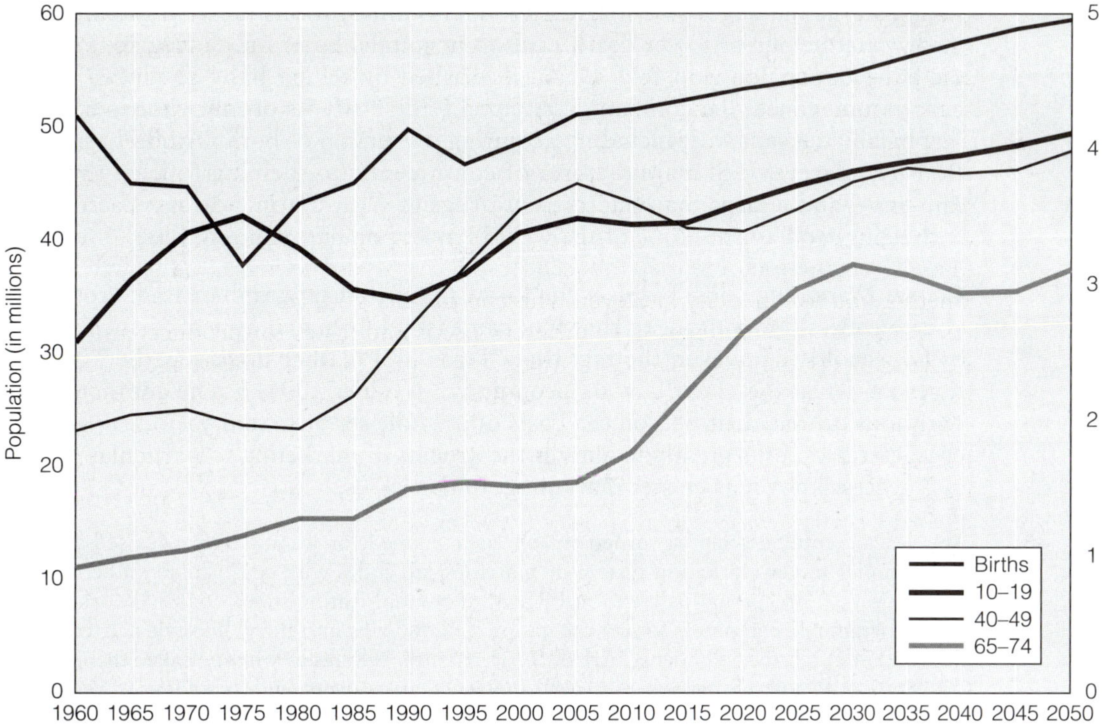

Figure 1.3 Riding the Age Wave: Births and Selected Age Groups in the United States

Sources: Data for births 1960 to 1975 are from U.S. Census Bureau, 1996, Statistical Abstract of the United States (Washington, DC: Government Printing Office); Table 90; births for 1980 to 2000 are from the U.S. National Center for Health Statistics Vital Statistics Reports (various years); age data from 1960 to 2000 are from the United Nations Population Division; age and birth data from 2005 to 2050 are from the U.S. Census Bureau's National Population Projections (updated 2009): http://www.census.gov/population/www/projections/2009projections.html

baby boom reaching middle age that helped to fatten the nonfat market. However, younger people have led the movement toward vegetarian meals, and the demographics of vegetarians are that they are disproportionately college-educated people with higher-than-average incomes (Fetto 2000). They will probably carry those food preferences into their middle ages at a time when the number of people 40 to 49 will dip as the baby boomers are replaced by the smaller cohort of Generation X.

The young-old population (ages 65 to 74) has been steadily increasing in numbers over time and, as you will learn in Chapter 8, has also become increasingly affluent. This segment of the population creates a market for a variety of things, from leisure travel to appliances with larger print, to door handles that are shaped to be used more easily by arthritic fingers. Perhaps most importantly, the aging of the population in North America has spurred the marketing of health services and products aimed at that age group, and the targeting of neighborhoods where people are aging in place (so-called naturally occurring retirement communities—NORC) (Morrison and Bryan 2010).

Johnson & Johnson provides a good example of a company that has kept its eye on the changing demographics not only of the United States but of the world in general. The company got its start in the 1880s when Robert Wood Johnson began selling sterile bandages and surgical products—innovations built on Lister's germ theory that helped to lower death rates in hospitals. Later on, during the years of the baby boom, Johnson & Johnson flourished by selling baby products. As the baby boom waned, the company continued to diversify its product line in a demographically relevant way, including acquiring ownership of both Ortho Pharmaceuticals (the largest U.S. manufacturer of contraceptives—helping to keep the birth rate low—and a large manufacturer of drugs to treat chronic diseases associated with aging) and Tylenol (one of the world's most popular pain relievers).

Cluster Marketing Just because you know the sociodemographic target groups for your business does not mean that you can easily locate and appeal to such people or households. However, the fact that "birds of a feather flock together" (sometimes known as the "First Law of Geography"—Tobler 2004) has meant that neighborhoods can be identified on the basis of a whole set of shared sociodemographic characteristics. This greatly facilitates the process of marketing to particular groups in a process known as cluster marketing. In the 1970s,

> . . . a computer scientist turned entrepreneur named Jonathan Robbin devised a wildly popular target-marketing system by matching zip codes with census data and consumer surveys. Christening his creation PRIZM (Potential Rating Index for Zip Markets), he programmed computers to sort the nation's 36,000 zips into forty "lifestyle clusters." Zip 85254 in Northeast Phoenix, Arizona, for instance, belongs to what he called the Furs and Station Wagons cluster, where surveys indicate that residents tend to buy lots of vermouth, belong to a country club, read *Gourmet* and vote the GOP ticket. In 02151, a Revere Beach, Massachusetts, zip designated Old Yankee Rows, tastes lean toward beer, fraternal clubs, Lakeland Boating and whoever the Democrats are supporting (Weiss 1988:xii).

The PRIZM system has made Robbin's company, Claritas Corporation (now Nielsen Claritas), one of the largest and most successful geodemographics firms in the world. A core principle is that *where* you live is a good predictor of *how* you live (Weiss 2001). It combines demographic characteristics with lifestyle variables and permits a business to home in on the specific neighborhoods where its products can be most profitably marketed. In keeping with the changing demographics of America, Neilsen Claritas adds new clusters as neighborhoods evolve. For example, there is "Latino America," concentrated in Miami, Chicago, and the Southwest and representing middle-class neighborhoods with a high percentage of families that are Hispanic, and "Family Scramble," which is a set of neighborhoods concentrated along the U.S.–Mexico border.

Site Selection Demographics One of the most common uses to which geodemographic data are put is in helping businesses select a site (Siegel 2002). This is an extension of the concept of targeting because businesses that rely on walk-in traffic, for example, naturally prefer a location that is closest to the maximum number of people who are likely to want to buy their goods or services. Demographics do not represent the sole measure of potential success—access to the site and visibility of the location are also important, and a firm has to be able to buy or lease the property for a price that allows it to make a profit, but the population component—proximity to your clientele—is the single most important factor for many retail businesses (Albert 1998; Mendes and Themido 2004).

Demographics of Human Resource Management Manufacturing and service firms also make use of demographics in selecting sites that meet their human resource needs. Knowledge of the optimal sociodemographic characteristics for a firm's workers (for instance, males or females, preferred racial or ethnic groups, required level of education or background) can be crucial in helping a company decide where it should locate a new plant or facility. These decisions can then feed back to influence the community's long-term demographic structure if firms that need similar kinds of employees wind up clustering together in the same geographic region, such as the Silicon Valley in northern California. Of course, these are the same demographic decision tools that convinced some companies to move their manufacturing sites out of the United States into less developed nations.

No matter where a company (or other type of organization) is located, it will have its own culture into which all employees or members of the organization will typically be expected to fit (Weeks 2004c). The organizational culture is not necessarily fixed, of course, and one of the important sources of change may be the changing demographic characteristics of employees. Managing these interactions between demography and culture is an important part of an organization's chances for long-term success (Harrison and Carroll 2005; Clark and Ghent 2010).

Investment Demographics To invest is to put your money to use for the purpose of securing a gain in income. Companies invest in themselves by plowing their profits back into the company in order to develop new products or expand or change markets; individuals (and companies also) invest by buying stocks or bonds of companies viewed as having a profitable future, or by purchasing real property whose value is expected to rise in the future. Clearly, a wide range of factors goes into the decision to invest in one product line, a particular company, or a specific piece of property, but one very important consideration is future demographic change. Companies that plan for demographic shifts have a better chance at success than those that do not. In fact, it has long been said that "demography plays" on Wall Street (Gillies 2004).

Basically, making sound investment decisions (as opposed to lucky ones) involves peering into the future, forecasting likely scenarios, and then acting on the basis of what seems likely to happen. After reading this book, you should have a good feel for the shape of things to come demographically. Most people do not, but those who do have an edge in life. A group of financial investors in the United Kingdom, for example, has established the Life and Longevity Markets Association in an attempt to spur the development of ways to make money from the pension funds into which an increasingly older population is pouring money (*The Economist* 2010). If people die sooner than expected, insurance companies lose money, whereas if they live longer than expected, the insurance companies reap a profit. The flip side of this is that if people live longer than expected, pension funds may be underfunded, whereas the pension funds profit if people die sooner, rather than later. You can see that people are betting one way or the other on your demographic future.

What else do the demographics suggest about current and future investment opportunities? The fact that 90 percent of the world's population growth in the foreseeable future will occur in the less developed nations is, as already noted, an important reason for the globalization of business and the internationalization of investment. Developing nations have millions of babies, and each one needs some kind of diaper.

Procter & Gamble, maker of Pampers disposable diapers, has found a huge market out there. Declining fertility in many developing countries is a very recent phenomenon, and in the meantime much of the world is experiencing a rapid increase in the number of young adults (trends that we will examine in detail throughout the book). How much ketchup do you eat? Heinz has discovered that people in Mexico like ketchup and is increasing its market share there (Brat and Kiernan 2009). More broadly, from Malaysia to Argentina, young adults are buying iPods, cell phones, handheld electronic games, satellite dishes, and the perennial favorites, blue jeans and Coca-Cola. Companies selling in these markets are thus potential investment targets.

International investors have been particularly intrigued by the world's two most populous countries, China and India. General Motors, Chrysler, and Ford all have invested in car manufacturing in China, as have Volkswagen and Peugeot Citroën from Europe. The problem, of course, is that a huge population does not necessarily mean a huge market if most people are poor. Pizza Hut and McDonald's serve up fast food in China, but the average Chinese consumer cannot afford very many expensive goods. Enter Wal-Mart, which opened its first store in China in the mid-1990s, and had 146 stores there by 2009 (Wal-Mart 2009).

India, which is almost as populous, but is less well-off than China, does not yet allow foreign ownership of retail businesses, but the so-called "consuming class" in India (those with at least some discretionary income) is estimated to comprise about 200 million people. This is less than 20 percent of the population, yet may account for the world's eighth-largest retail market (Bellman and Hudson 2006), and thus it represents an opportunity for some people to make money. Yum Brands, Inc., based in Louisville, Kentucky, which owns Pizza Hut, KFC, and Taco Bell (among other fast-food franchises), decided in 2010 that the growing young adult population (the youth bulge) in India represented a good market for Mexican food, and so they opened a Taco Bell in Bangalore (Bellman 2010). We will return repeatedly to this paradox that most people (the "street") have a gut feeling that population growth is a good thing, yet we have no idea if we can sustain it, and if we can't, then what?

What Is the Rest of the Book About?

In order to help you understand how the world works demographically, I have organized the book into four parts, each building on the previous one. This first chapter obviously is designed to introduce you to the field of population studies and illustrate why this is such an important topic. The second chapter reviews world population trends (past, present, and future projections), so that you have a good idea of what is happening in the world demographically, how we got to this point, and where we seem to be heading. The third chapter introduces you to the major perspectives or ways of thinking about population growth and change, and the fourth chapter reviews the sources of data that form the basis of our understanding of demographic trends. In Part Two, "Population Processes," I discuss the three basic demographic processes whose transitions are transforming the world—the health and mortality transition (Chapter 5), the fertility transition (Chapter 6), and the migration transition (Chapter 7). Knowledge of these three population processes and transitions provides you with the foundation you need to understand why changes occur and what might be done about them.

Part Three, "Population Structure and Characteristics," is devoted to studying the interaction of the population processes and societal change that occur as fertility, mortality, and migration change. These include the age transition (Chapter 8), the urban transition (Chapter 9), and the family and household transition (Chapter 10). The fourth and final part of the book, "Using the Demographic Perspective," first explores the relationship between population and the environment (Chapter 11): Can economic growth and development be sustained in the face of continued population growth? There are no simple answers, but we are faced with a future in which we will have to deal with the global and local consequences of a larger and constantly changing population. In Chapter 12 I review the ways in which the world copes politically with these changes as they alter the fabric of human society all across the globe.

Summary and Conclusion

It is an often-repeated phrase that "demography is destiny," and the goal of this book is to help you to cope with the demographic part of your own destiny and that of your community, and to better understand the changes occurring all over the world. Demographic analysis helps you do this by seeking out both the causes and the consequences of population change. The absolute size of population change is very important, as is the rate of change, and of course, the direction (growth or decline).

The past 200 years have witnessed almost nonstop growth in most places in the world, but the rate is slowing down, even though we are continuing to add nearly 9,000 people to the world's total every hour of every day. You may prefer to bury your head in the sand and pretend that there is no world beyond your own circle of family and friends, but everything happening around you is influenced by demographic events. I refer not just to the big things like regional conflict, globalization, global warming, and massive migration movements, but even to little things that affect you directly, like the kinds of stores that operate in your neighborhood, the goods that are stocked on your local supermarket shelf, the availability of a hospital emergency room, and the jobs available to college graduates in your community. Influential decision makers in government agencies, social and health organizations, and business firms now routinely base their actions at least partly on their assessment of the changing demographics of an area. So, both locally and globally, demographic forces are at work to change and challenge your future. In the next chapter, I outline the basic facts of the global demographic picture.

Main Points

1. Demography is concerned with virtually everything that influences or can be influenced by population size, distribution, processes, structure, or characteristics.
2. The cornerstones of population studies are the processes of mortality (a deadly subject), fertility (a well-conceived topic), and migration (a moving experience).
3. Almost everything in your life has demographic underpinnings that you should understand.
4. Examples of global issues that have deep and important demographic components include terrorism and regional conflict, violence in sub-Saharan Africa,

the backlash against immigrants, globalization, and the degradation of the environment.

5. "Local" uses for demographic information, usually labeled "demographics," represent the application of population theory and methods to the solution of practical problems.
6. When we account for the location of the people whose demographic behavior we are studying, we are engaging in spatial demography, or geodemographics.
7. Demographics is the central ingredient in congressional reapportionment and redistricting in the United States, and politicians also find demographics helpful in analyzing legislation and in developing their strategy for their own election to office.
8. Local agencies use demographics to plan for the adequate provision of services for their communities, including education, criminal justice, and health.
9. A major use of demographics is to market products and services in the private sector.
10. Demographics are an important component of site selection for many types of businesses, are key elements of human resource management, and help investors pinpoint areas of potential market growth, because population is a major factor behind social change (and thus opportunity).

Questions for Review

1. When did you first become aware of demography or population issues more broadly, and what were the things that initially seemed to be important to you?
2. Why is the idea that nearly everything is connected to demography, or the companion idea that demography is destiny, not the same as demographic determinism?
3. How do you think the demography of the Middle East will be influenced in the long term by the Iraq war?
4. Discuss the relative advantages and disadvantages of a youth bulge for a population that policy planners might have to deal with.
5. If globalization has an underlying demographic component, how might that affect the investing patterns of someone who uses demography as one of their investment criteria?

Suggested Readings

1. Paul Demeny and Geoffrey McNicoll, eds., 2003, *Encyclopedia of Population* (2 volumes). (New York: MacMillan Reference USA) (Available as an E-book).

   An important reference source for any person (lay or professional) seeking an expert overview of virtually every major topic in the field of demography or population studies. This can be thought of as an update of both the *Dictionary of Demography* (William and Renee Petersen, 1985), and the *International Encyclopedia of Population* (edited by John Ross, 1982).

2. Dudley L. Poston Jr. and Michael Micklin, eds., 2005, *Handbook of Population* (New York: Kluwer Academic/Plenum).

   This volume covers fewer topics, but deals with each in more detail than does the *Encyclopedia of Population.* It is thought of as an update of Hauser and Duncan's 1959 classic, *The Study of Population.*

3. Graziella Caselli, Jacque Vallin, and Guillaume Wunsch, eds., 2006, *Demography: Analysis and Synthesis: A Treatise in Population Studies* (Volumes 1–4) (Amsterdam: Elsevier).

   This is a huge, four-volume, 3,000 page treatise covering nearly every imaginable aspect of demography, written in encyclopedia essay form by various demographers, most of them European.

4. Proceedings of the National Academy of Sciences (PNAS), 2005, *Spatial Demography Special Feature,* PNAS, volume 102, No. 43 (October 25).

   This special issue of the Proceedings of the National Academy of Sciences offers a set of several papers exploring several aspects of the rapidly emerging field of spatial demography.

5. Michael J. Weiss, 2001, *The Clustered World: How We Live, What We Buy, and What It All Means about Who We Are* (New York: Little Brown).

   A journalistic but very detailed description of the PRIZM system of clustering zip codes according to demographic and lifestyle characteristics. Weiss describes the 62 lifestyle clusters and suggests that America is characterized more as a salad bowl than a melting pot.

Websites of Interest

Remember that websites are not as permanent as books and journals, so I cannot guarantee that each of the following websites still exists at the moment you are reading this. You may have to Google the name of the organization to find the current web address.

1. **http://www.census.gov**
   The website of the U.S. Census Bureau has several very useful features, including U.S. and world population information and U.S. and world population clocks (where you can check the latest estimate of the total U.S. and world populations).

2. **http://www.prb.org**
   The Population Reference Bureau (PRB) in Washington, D.C., is a world leader in developing and distributing population information. The site includes regularly updated information about PRB's own activities, as well as links to a wide range of other population-related websites all over the world.

3. **http://www.un.org/esa/population/unpop.htm**
   The Population Division of the United Nations is the single most important producer of global demographic information, which can be accessed at this site. Closely related United Nations data can be accessed through **http://data.un.org**.

4. **http://www.poodwaddle.com/clocks2.htm**
   This website keeps track of a wide range of demographic data from various official sources and then produces estimates that are constantly being updated (thus, they are called "clocks") by extrapolation models.

5. **http://en-us.nielsen.com/tab/product_families/nielsen_claritas**
   The website for Neilsen Claritas (a Latin term for "clarity"), the geodemographics firm that developed the PRIZM cluster marketing approach, includes a feature that allows you to enter the zip code of your choice (such as that of your own neighborhood) to see how that neighborhood would be characterized in demographic terms.

CHAPTER 2
Global Population Trends

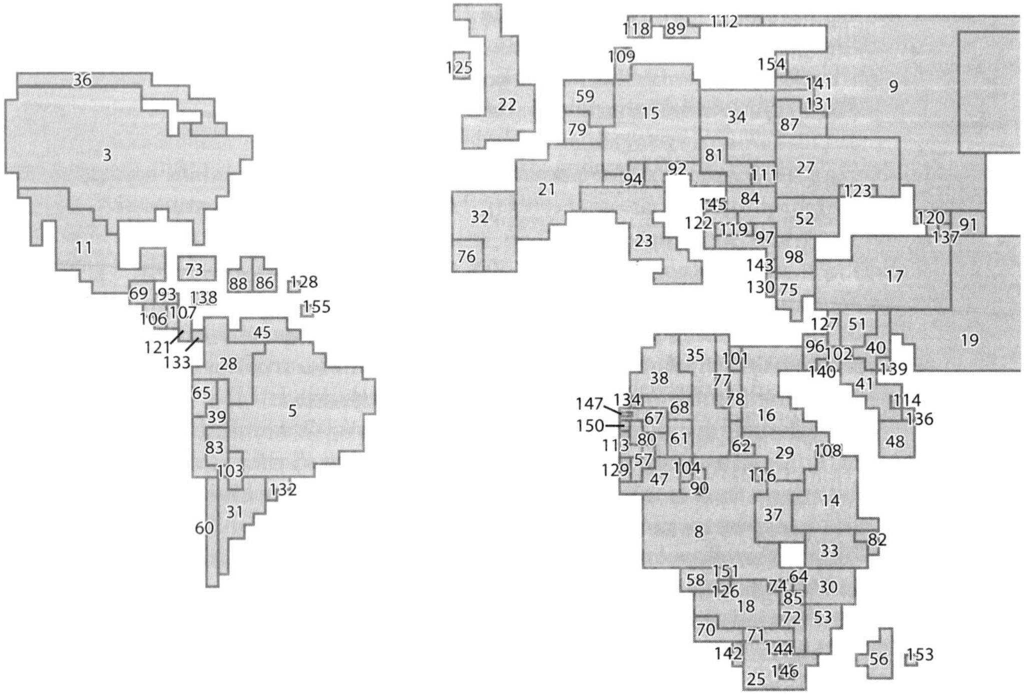

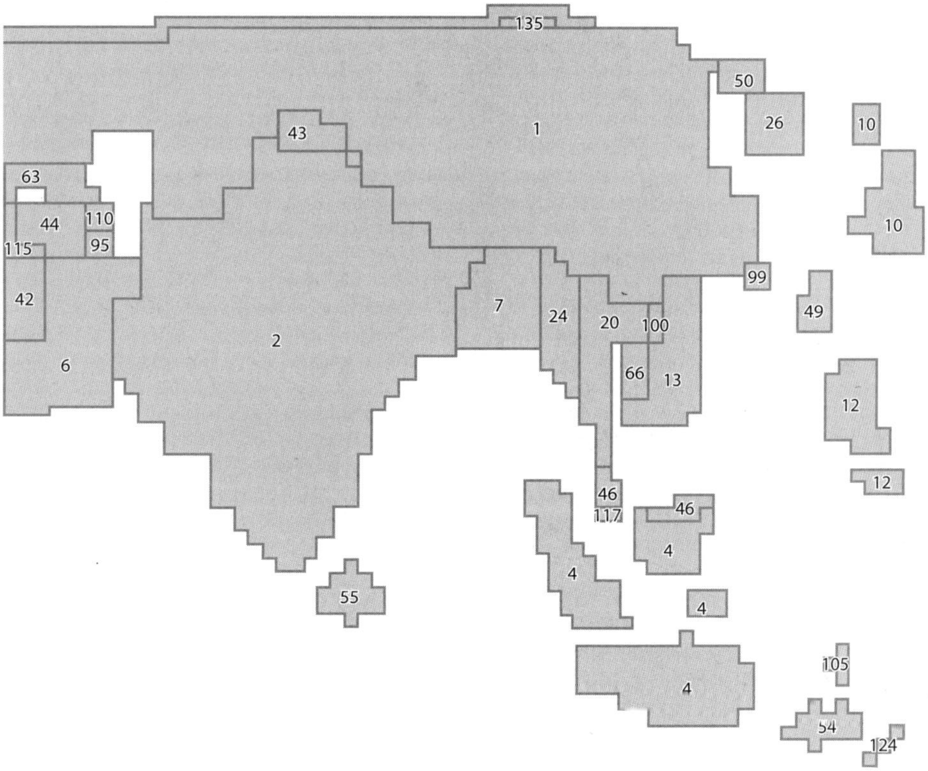

Figure 2.1 Cartogram of Countries of the World by Population Size

Note: The map shows the size of each country of the world according to its population. The number indicates that country's overall ranking in population. The country name associated with each numbers is listed in the Appendix along with additional population data. Each square represents approximately 1.5 million persons.

Source: Prepared by John Weeks and Jeanie Gaudette using data from the U.S. Census Bureau's International Data Base and the United Nations Population Division Online Data Base. Data refer to 2010.

South America
Europe
Northern Africa and Western Asia
Sub-Saharan Africa
East Asia
South and Southeast Asia
Oceania

GLOBAL DEMOGRAPHIC CONTRASTS

ESSAY: Implosion or Invasion? The Choices Ahead for the Low Fertility Countries

At this moment you are sharing the planet, vying for resources, with nearly 7 billion other people, and before the year 2050 yet another 2 billion souls will have joined you at the world's table. This in and of itself is pretty impressive, but it becomes truly alarming when you realize that this is a huge leap up from the "only" 2.5 billion in residence as recently as 1950. This phenomenon is obviously without precedent, so we are sailing in uncharted territory. In order to deal intelligently with a future that will be shared with 2 billion or more people than today, we have to understand why the populations of so many countries are still growing (and why some are not) and what happens to societies as their patterns of birth, death, or migration change. In this chapter, I trace the history of population growth in the world to give you a clue as to how we got ourselves into the current situation. Then I will take you on a brief guided tour through each of the world's major regions, highlighting current patterns of population size and rates of growth, with a special emphasis on the world's 10 most populous nations.

World Population Growth

A Brief History

Human beings have been around for at least 200,000 years (Cann and Wilson 2003), and probably much longer—perhaps a million or more years. For almost all of that time, our presence on the earth was scarcely noticeable. Humans were hunter-gatherers living a primitive existence marked by high fertility, high mortality, and only very slow population growth. Given the large amount of space required by a hunting-gathering society, it seems unlikely that the earth could support more than several million people living like that (Coale 1974; McEvedy and Jones 1978; Biraben 1979), so it is no surprise that the population of the world on the eve of the **Agricultural Revolution** (also known as the **Neolithic Agrarian Revolution**) about 10,000 years ago is estimated at about 4 million (see Table 2.1). Many people argue that the Agricultural Revolution occurred slowly but pervasively across the face of the earth precisely because the hunting-gathering populations were growing just enough to push the limit of the **carrying capacity** of their way of life (Boserup 1965; Cohen 1977; Harris and Ross 1987; Sanderson 1995). Carrying capacity refers to the number of people that can be supported in an area given the available physical resources and the way that people use those resources (Miller 2009). Since hunting and gathering use resources *extensively* rather than *intensively*, it was natural that over tens of thousands of years humans would move into the remote corners of the earth in search of sustenance. Eventually, people in most of those corners began to use the environment more intensively, leading to the more sedentary, agricultural way of life that has characterized most of human society for the past 10,000 years, starting first in what is now the Middle East, and then in what is now the eastern part of China.

The population began to grow more noticeably after the Agricultural Revolution, as Table 2.1 shows. Between 8000 B.C. and 5000 B.C., about 333 people on average were being added to the world's total population each year, but by 500 B.C., as major civilizations were being established in China, India, and Greece, the world was adding 100,000 people each year to the total. By the time of Christ (the Roman

Table 2.1 Population Growth Was Very Slow in the Earlier Years of Human Existence but Has Risen Dramatically in the Past 250 Years

Year	Population (in millions)	Average annual rate of growth (%)	Doubling time in years	Average annual increase in population
−8000	4	–	–	–
−5000	5	0.01	9,277	333
−3000	14	0.05	1,340	4,500
−2000	27	0.07	1,051	13,000
−1000	50	0.06	1,120	23,000
−500	100	0.14	498	100,000
1	242	0.18	392	282,768
500	198	−0.04	−1,728	−87,508
1000	276	0.07	1,035	156,667
1100	311	0.12	592	341,667
1200	380	0.20	342	695,000
1300	396	0.04	1,673	160,000
1400	362	−0.09	−769	−340,000
1500	458	0.24	292	963,333
1600	562	0.20	338	1,036,667
1700	645	0.14	504	825,000
1750	753	0.31	221	2,176,667
1800	927	0.41	166	3,473,333
1850	1,220	0.55	126	5,860,000
1900	1,646	0.60	115	8,520,000
1910	1,750	0.61	113	10,400,000
1920	1,860	0.61	113	11,000,000
1930	2,070	1.07	65	21,000,000
1940	2,300	1.05	65	23,000,000
1950	2,529	0.95	73	22,900,000
1955	2,763	1.77	39	46,800,000
1960	3,023	1.80	38	52,000,000
1965	3,332	1.95	35	61,800,000
1970	3,686	2.02	34	70,800,000
1975	4,061	1.94	36	75,000,000
1980	4,438	1.78	39	75,400,000
1985	4,846	1.76	39	81,600,000
1990	5,290	1.75	39	88,800,000
1995	5,713	1.54	45	84,600,000
2000	6,115	1.36	51	80,400,000
2005	6,512	1.26	55	79,400,000
2010	6,908	1.18	58	79,200,000
2015	7,302	1.11	62	78,800,000
2020	7,675	1.00	69	74,600,000

(continued)

Table 2.1 (conitnued)

Year	Population (in millions)	Average annual rate of growth (%)	Doubling time in years	Average annual increase in population
2025	8,012	0.86	80	67,400,000
2030	8,308	0.73	95	59,200,000
2035	8,570	0.62	111	52,400,000
2040	8,801	0.53	130	46,200,000
2045	8,996	0.44	157	39,000,000
2050	9,150	0.34	203	30,800,000

Note: Negative doubling times indicate the number of years for the population to reach half its current size.
Sources: The population data from −8000 through 1900 are drawn from the U.S. Census Bureau, International Programs Center "Historical Estimates of the World Population," (http://www.census.gov/ipc/www/worldhis.html), accessed 2010. The numbers reflect the average of the estimates made by Biraben (1979), Durand (1967), and McEvedy and Jones (1978). Numbers for 1910 through 1940 are from the United Nations Population Division (1999). Population figures for 1950 through 2050 are medium variant projections from the United Nations Population Division, 2009, World Population Prospects: The 2008 Revision (http://esa.un.org/unpp/index.asp/), accessed 2010.

Period, A.D. 1) there may well have been more than 200 million people on the planet, increasing by nearly 300,000 each year. There was some backsliding in the third through fifth centuries A.D., when increases in mortality, probably due to the plague, led to declining population size in the Mediterranean area as the Roman empire collapsed, and in China as the Han empire collapsed from a combination of flood, famine, and rebellion (McEvedy and Jones 1978). Population growth recovered its momentum only to be swatted down by yet another plague, the Black Death, that arrived in Europe in the middle of the fourteenth century and didn't leave until the middle of the seventeenth century (Cantor 2001). After that, during the period from about 1650 to 1850, Europe as a whole experienced rather dramatic population growth as a result of the disappearance of the plague, the introduction of the potato from the Americas, and evolutionary (although not revolutionary) changes in agricultural practice—probably a response to the receding of the Little Ice Age (Fagan 2000)—that preceded (and almost certainly stimulated) the Industrial Revolution (Cohen 1995). The rate of growth began clearly to increase after that, especially in Europe, and on the eve of the **Industrial Revolution** in the middle of the eighteenth century (about 1750), the population of the world was approaching one billion people and was increasing by more than two million every year.

It is quite likely that the Industrial Revolution occurred in part because of this population growth. It is theorized that the Europe of 300 or 400 years ago was reaching the carrying capacity of its agricultural society, so Europeans first spread out looking for more room and then began to invent more intensive uses of their resources to meet the needs of a growing population (Harrison 1993). The major resource was energy, which, with the discovery of fossil fuels (first coal, then oil, and more recently natural gas), helped to light the fire under industrialization.

Since the beginning of the Industrial Revolution approximately 250 years ago, the size of the world's population has increased even more dramatically, as you can visualize in Figure 2.2. For tens of thousands of years the population of the world

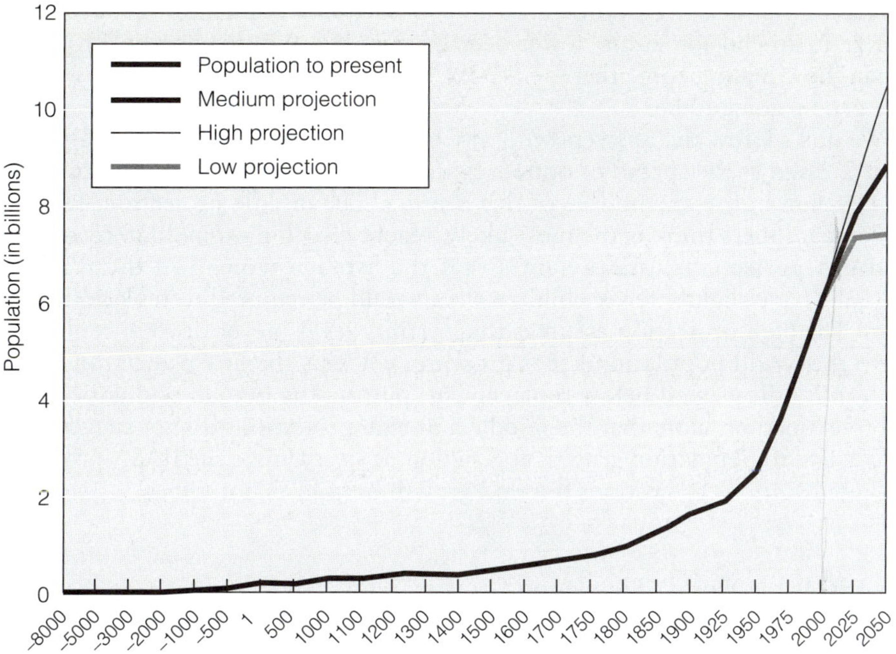

Figure 2.2 The World's Population Has Exploded in Size

Note: Time is not to scale.
Source: Table 2.1; projections are from United Nations Population Division (2009).

grew slowly, and then within less than 300 years, the number of people mushroomed to more than 6 billion. There can be little question why the term **population explosion** was coined to describe these historically recent demographic events. The world's population did not reach 1 billion until after the American Revolution—the United Nations fixes the year at 1804 (United Nations Population Division 1999)—but since then we have been adding each additional billion people at an accelerating pace. The 2 billion mark was hit in 1927, just before the Great Depression and 123 years after the first billion. In 1960, only 33 years later, came 3 billion; and 4 billion came along only 14 years after that, in 1974. We then hit 5 billion 13 years later, in 1987, we passed the 6 billion milestone 12 years later, in 1999 (officially on October 12th of that year), the seventh billion in 2011, and the United Nations expects that we will reach 8 billion in 2025, and then 9 billion in 2045 (based on projections by United Nations Population Division 2009).

Wolfgang Lutz and the researchers at the International Institute for Applied Systems Analysis (IIASA) in Vienna, Austria, have created a set of probabilistic population projections suggesting that the most likely future scenario is for the world's population to peak in about 2070 at approximately 9 billion people (Lutz, Sanderson, and Scherbov 2008). At the same time, there is about a 10 percent chance that the population in 2070 could be at least 9.9 billion and a similar chance that it could be as low as 7.8. It is obviously difficult to say what will happen a half century or more from now, because even small differences in the number of children born to women, or in the death rate, can create huge differences in long-range projections, but nearly everyone does agree that global population growth is likely to come to an end sometime in this century. The big questions are when will that happen, how many people there will be when it happens, and especially where are those people going to be?

We don't know the answers with any certainty, of course, but the right side of Figure 2.2 shows the spread of options as calculated by the United Nations Population Division out to the middle of this century. The middle projection, which the UN demographers think is the most likely, reaches 9.1 billion in 2050 (earlier than the IIASA projections) and assumes that the average woman in the world will eventually have slightly fewer children than would be required to replace the population. The high projection assumes that fertility levels never drop to replacement and so the world population keeps growing, whereas the low projection assumes that fertility drops well below replacement, putting the human population on the road to extinction. Note that the middle and high projections do not suggest an immediate end to population growth at 9 billion people. Unlike the IIASA projections, the United Nations projections portend growth beyond that number.

How Fast Is the World's Population Growing Now?

There is no question that the rate of growth over the past two hundred years has been explosive. The revolutionary consequence of that explosion is that the numbers of people are destined to stay vastly higher than they were two hundred years ago—creating huge problems that have to be dealt with. If we look back 250 years from the year 1800, just before we hit our first billion in the world, we find that the population was about half what it was in 1800 (see Table 2.1), and we were clearly in the early stages of the explosion. But if we look ahead 250 years from that point, we see there will be nine times as many people in 2050 as there were in 1800. Dealing with this dramatic rise in numbers has driven changes taking place everywhere in the world.

Regardless of the *rate* of growth (which is the explosive part), the *numbers* are what we actually cope with. In Figure 2.3, I have graphed the data from Table 2.1 showing that the rate of population growth for the world peaked around 1970 and has been declining since then. This ought to be good news, but you can see in Figure 2.3 that as we build on an ever larger base of human beings, the lower rates of growth are still producing very large absolute increases in the human population. When you build on a base of almost 7 billion (the population in 2010), the seemingly slow rate of growth of about 1.18 percent per year for the world still translates into the annual addition of more than 79 million people, whereas "only" 71 million were being added annually when the rate of growth peaked in 1970, and there were scarcely more than 20 million per year being added when the world was last growing at about one percent per year, back in the early 1950s. Put another way, during the next 12 months, approximately 136 million babies will be born in the world, while 57 million people of all ages will die, resulting in a net addition of more than 79 million people (see Table 2.2). In the two seconds that it took you to read that sentence, nine babies were born while four people died, and so the world's population increased by five.

Although it does not show up in Figure 2.3, you can see in Table 2.1 that the rate of growth in 1960 was not much different than it had been in 1955. This

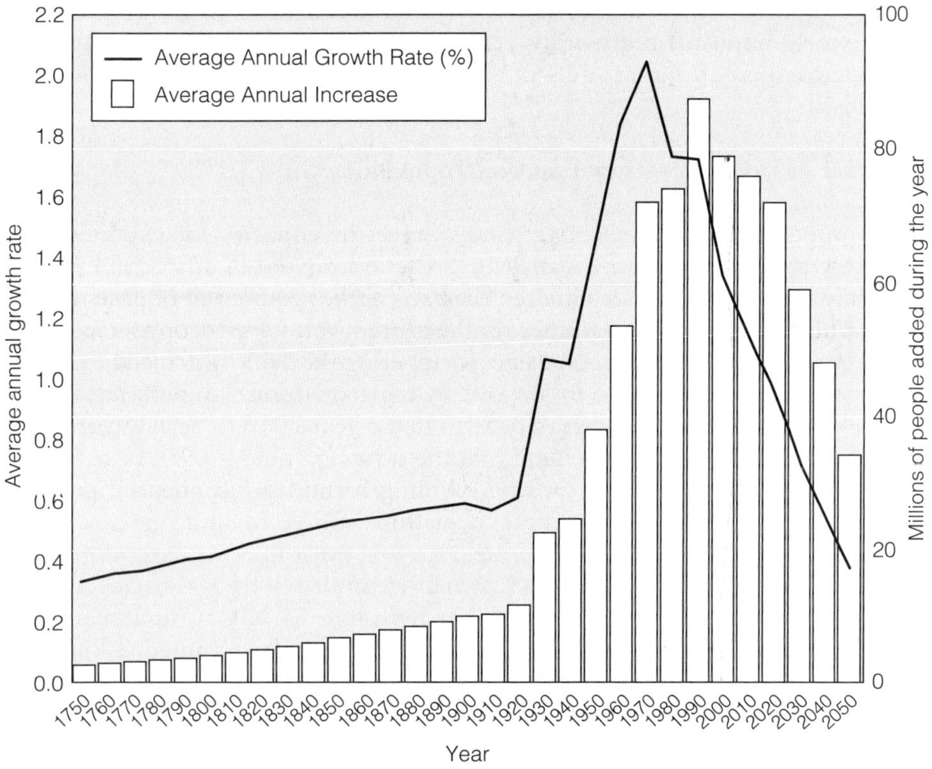

Figure 2.3 79 Million People Are Still Being Added to the World's Total Population Each Year, Despite the Drop in the Growth Rate

Source: Same as Table 2.1.

slowdown was due to a terrible famine in China in 1959–60, which was produced by Mao Zedong's Great Leap Forward program of 1958, in which the Chinese government "leapt forward" into industrialization by selling "surplus" grain to finance industrial growth. Unfortunately, the grain was not surplus, and the confiscation of food amounted to a self-imposed disaster that led to the deaths of 30 million Chinese in the following two years (1959 and 1960) (Becker 1997). Yet

Table 2.2 In One Day the World's Population Increases by More Than 200,000

Time Period	Births	Deaths	Natural Increase
Year	136,117,868	56,917,868	79,200,000
Day	372,926	155,939	216,986
Hour	15,539	6,497	9,041
Minute	259	108	151
Second	4.3	1.8	2.5

Source: Based on estimates from the United Nations Population Division (2009).

even though the Chinese famine may have been the largest single disaster in human history, world population growth quickly rebounded, and the growth rate hit its record high shortly after that.

The Power of Doubling—How Fast Can Populations Grow?

Human populations, like all living things, have the capacity for exponential increase. A common way of measuring the growth potential of any combination of birth and death rates is to calculate the **doubling time**, the number of years required for a population to double in number if the current rate of growth continues. You can calculate this easily for yourself by remembering the "rule of 69." The doubling time is approximately equal to 69 divided by the growth rate (in percent per year). So, if we estimate the world's rate of growth in the year 2010 to be 1.18 percent per year (see Table 2.1), we can calculate that the doubling time is 69/1.18 = 58 years. Where does the 69 come from in the doubling formula? Exponential growth is expressed mathematically by natural **logarithms.** Thus, to find out how long it would take a population to double in size, we first must find the natural logarithm (ln) of two. This turns out to be 0.69, which we multiply by 100 to get rid of the decimal point. Then dividing the rate of growth into 69 tells us how many years would be required for a population to double. Similarly, if we wanted to know how long it would take a declining population to be cut in half, we would first find the natural logarithm of 0.5, which is −0.69, or −69 when multiplied by 100. Dividing −69 by a negative rate of population growth then tells us how long it would take for the population to be only half as big as it currently is. As of 2009, Russia was estimated to be losing population at a rate of −0.3 percent per year (Population Reference Bureau 2009), at which pace it will halve its population in 230 years.

The incredible power of doubling can be illustrated by the tale of the Persian chessboard. The story is told that the clever inventor of the game of chess was called in by the King of Persia to be rewarded for this marvelous new game. When asked what he would like his reward to be, his answer was that he was a humble man and deserved only a humble reward. Gesturing to the board of 64 squares that he had devised for the game, he asked that he be given a single grain of wheat on the first square, twice that on the second square, twice *that* on the third square, and so on, until each square had its complement of wheat. The king protested that this was far too modest a prize, but the inventor persisted and the king finally relented. When the Overseer of the Royal Granary began counting out the wheat, it started out small enough: 1, 2, 4, 8, 16, 32 . . . but by the time the 64th square was reached, the number was staggering—nearly 18.5 quintillion grains of wheat (about 75 billion metric tons!) (Sagan 1989). This, of course, exceeded the "carrying capacity" of the royal granary in the same way that successive doublings of the human population threaten to exceed the carrying capacity of the planet.

Looking back at Table 2.1 you can see that early on in human history it took several thousand years for the population to double to a size eventually reaching 14 million. From there it took a thousand years to nearly double to 27 million and another thousand to nearly double to 50 million, but less than 500 years to double from 50 to 100 million (about 500 years B.C.). Another thousand years later, in

A.D. 500, it had doubled again, although it was then lower than in the Roman era. After another thousand years, in 1500, in the middle of the European Renaissance, the world's population had doubled again. About 400 years elapsed between the European renaissance and the Industrial Revolution, and the world's population doubled in size during that time. But from 1750, it took only a little more than 100 years to double again, and the next doubling occurred in less than 100 years. The most recent doubling (from 3 to 6 billion) took only about 40 years.

Will we double again in the future? Probably not, and indeed we should hope not because we don't really know at this point how we will feed, clothe, educate, and find jobs for the 7 billion alive now, much less the additional 2 billion or more who are expected between now and later in this century. Once you realize how rapidly a population can grow, it is reasonable to wonder why early growth of the human population was so slow.

Why Was Early Growth So Slow?

The reason the population grew so slowly during the first 99 percent of human history was that death rates were very high, and at the same time very few populations have ever tried to maximize the number of children born (Abernethy 1979; Livi-Bacci 2001). During the hunting-gathering phase of human history (hundreds of thousands of years), it is likely that life expectancy at birth averaged about 20 years (Petersen 1975; Livi-Bacci 2001). At this level of mortality, more than half of all children born will die before age five, and the average woman who survives through the reproductive years will have to bear nearly seven children in order to assure that two will survive to adulthood. This is still well below the biological limit of fertility, however, as I discuss in Chapter 6.

Research in the twentieth century among the last of the hunting-gathering populations in sub-Saharan Africa suggests that a premodern woman might have deliberately limited the number of children born by spacing them a few years apart to make it easier to nurse and carry her youngest child and to permit her to do her work (Dumond 1975). She may have accomplished this by abstinence, abortion, or possibly even **infanticide** (Howell 1979; Lee 1972). Similarly, sick and infirm members of society were at risk of abandonment once they were no longer able to fend for themselves. Other researchers, however, see little evidence of deliberate population control among early human populations and believe that high mortality was the norm and societies struggled to give birth to enough children to overcome the obstacle faced by the routine death among children (Caldwell and Caldwell 2003).

It was once believed that the Agricultural Revolution increased growth rates as a result of people settling down in stable farming communities, where death rates were lowered. Sedentary life was thought to have improved living conditions because of the more reliable supply of food. The theory went that birth rates remained high but death rates declined slightly, and thus the population grew. However, archaeological evidence combined with studies of extant hunter-gatherer groups has offered another explanation for growth during this period (Spooner 1972), which Bocquet-Appel (2008) has called **Neolithic Demographic Transition**. Fertility rates rose as new diets improved the ability of women to conceive and bear children (see Chapter 6). Also, it became easier to wean children from the breast earlier because of the greater availability of soft foods, which are easily eaten by babies. This would have shortened the birth intervals, and the birth rate could have risen on that account alone, and to a level higher than the death rate, thus promoting population growth. Meanwhile, the sedentary life and the higher-density living associated with farming actually raised death rates by creating sanitation problems and heightening exposure to communicable diseases, at the same time that the higher birth rate would have put pressure on what were surely limited resources. Nonetheless, growth rates probably went up even in the face of higher mortality as the constraints of hunter-gatherer life were reduced and fertility rates rose to a level slightly higher than the death rate.

It should be kept in mind, of course, that only a small difference between birth and death rates is required to account for the slow growth achieved after the Agricultural Revolution. Between 8000 B.C. and 1750, the world was adding an average of only 67,000 people each year to the population. At this moment in history, that many people are being added every seven and a half hours.

Why Are More Recent Increases So Rapid?

The acceleration in population growth after 1750 was due almost entirely to the declines in the death rate that accompanied the Industrial Revolution. First in Europe and North America and more recently in the rest of the world, death rates have decreased sooner and much more rapidly than have fertility rates. The result has been that many fewer people die than are born each year. In the more developed countries, declines in mortality at first were due to the effects of economic development and a rising standard of living—people were eating better, wearing warmer clothes, living in better houses, bathing more often, drinking cleaner water, and so on (McKeown 1976). These improvements in the human condition helped to lower exposure to disease and also to build up resistance to illness. Later, especially after 1900, much of the decline in mortality was due to improvements in public health and medical technology, especially vaccination against infectious diseases (Preston and Haines 1991).

Declines in the death rates first occurred in only those countries experiencing economic development. In each of these areas, primarily Europe and North America, fertility also began to decline within at least one or two generations after the death rate began its drop. However, since World War II, medical and public health technology has been available to virtually all countries of the world regardless of their level of economic development. In the less developed countries, although the risk of death has been lowered dramatically, birth rates have gone down less quickly, and the result is continuing population growth. As you can see in Table 2.3, virtually all of the growth of the world's population is originating in less developed nations. I say "originating" because some of that growth then spills into the more developed countries through migration, although the UN projections do not reflect the volume of migration that may well occur over the next few decades. For this reason, the middle variant projection for 2050 (considered by the United Nations to be the most likely projection of demographic events) assumes an actual decline in the size of the

Table 2.3 Less Developed Regions Are the Sites of Future Population Growth

		Area		
		More Developed Nations	Less Developed Nations	World
	Population in 2010 (in millions)	1,237	5,671	6,908
Medium fertility variant	Projection to year 2050 (in millions)	1,275	7,875	9,150
	Increase between 2010 and 2050 (in millions)	38	2,204	2,242
	Percent of world increase attributable to each area	1.7	98.3	100.0
High fertility variant	Projection to year 2050 (in millions)	1,439	9,022	10,461
	Increase between 2010 and 2050 (in millions)	202	3,351	3,553
	Percent of world increase attributable to each area	5.7	94.3	100.0
Low fertility variant	Projection to year 2050 (in millions)	1,126	6,832	7,958
	Increase between 2010 and 2050 (in millions)	−111	1,161	1,050
	Percent of world increase attributable to each area	0.0	100.0	100.0

Source: Adapted from United Nations Population Division, 2009. *World Population Prospects: The 2008 Revision* (New York: United Nations).

European population, where countries currently have very low fertility and also very restrictive immigration laws. As I discuss in the essay accompanying this chapter, the aging of the European population and the threat of depopulation may well result in a loosening of the immigration laws.

Are We Headed for a Population "Implosion"?

An implosion is something that collapses into itself—the opposite of an explosion. As the rate of population growth has slowed down over the past two decades, there has been talk of a **population implosion** (Eberstadt 2001; Wattenberg 2004), implying that "the world is in for some rapid downsizing" (Singer 1999:22). As you can see by looking at the data in Tables 2.1 through 2.3, this is either just rhetoric designed to gain attention or a misunderstanding of the actual demographic situation of the world.

Much of the discussion about an implosion at a global scale comes about in reaction to the changing population projections made by demographers at the Population Division of the United Nations. Every projection made for the year 2000 by the United Nations between 1958 and 1998 was higher than the 6.1 billion that was eventually estimated for that year. Although this "downsizing" has been highly publicized, none of the projections for 2000 was much over 6.1 billion—the highest being one made in 1968 that projected 6.5 billion by 2000 (Bongaarts and Bulatao 2000). Looking beyond 2000, the United Nations projected in 1992 that the world's population in 2025 could reach 8.5 billion (United Nations Population Division 1993), but in their projections made in 2009 show the lower figure of 8.0 billion that you can see in Table 2.1 (United Nations Population Division 2009). The differences are due partly to the devastating effects of HIV/AIDS mortality in sub-Saharan Africa, and partly to the fact that fertility in Europe and East Asia has dropped well below anyone's earlier expectations.

The demographics of the world are shifting, to be sure, and there are pockets of potential implosion, especially in Japan and in Eastern Europe, but there is no global implosion in sight. If you look at Figure 2.2 and Table 2.3, you will see that even under the United Nation's lowest projection scenario, there would still be more people in the world in 2050 than there are now. No matter what might happen at the end of this century and into the next one, the rest of *your* life will almost certainly take place in a world in which there will be more people tomorrow than there are today.

How Many People Have Ever Lived?

The fact that we have gone from 1 billion to 7 billion in scarcely more than 200 years has led some people to speculate that a majority of people ever born must surely still be alive. Let me burst that idea before it can take root in your mind. In fact, our current contribution to history's total represents only a relatively small fraction of all people who have ever lived. The most analytical of the estimates has been made by Nathan Keyfitz (Keyfitz 1966; Keyfitz and Caswell 2005), and I have used Keyfitz's formulas to estimate the number of people who have ever lived, assuming conservatively that we started with two people 200,000 years ago. The results of these calculations suggest that a total of 61.9 billion people have been born, of whom the 6.9 billion alive in 2010 constitute 11.2 percent. Livi-Bacci (2001) has a lower figure—7.3 percent—but that is based on a longer period of time than the 200,000 years I have used. Furthermore, since the population is now so much larger than ever before in history, this percentage keeps creeping up over time. Haub (2002) uses a different methodology to produce a lower percentage of 5.8, but from all of these estimates it is clear that a lot of people had been born into this world prior to the modern era.

Perhaps more significantly, Keyfitz and Caswell (2005) point out that the dramatic drop in infant and childhood mortality over the last two centuries means that babies are now far more likely than ever to grow up to be adults. Thus the adults alive today actually do represent a considerable fraction of all people who have ever lived to adulthood. Furthermore, if we look at specific categories of people, such as engineers or college professors, then it is probable that the vast majority of such individuals who have ever lived on earth are still alive today.

Sobering though this phenomenon is, however, the increase in size of the world's population is not the only important demographic change to occur in the past few hundred years. In addition, there has been a massive redistribution of population.

Redistribution of the World's Population through Migration

As populations have grown disproportionately in different areas of the world, the pressures or desires to migrate have also grown. This pattern is predictable enough that we label it the migration transition component of the overall demographic transition (which I will discuss in the next chapter). Migration streams generally flow from areas where there are too few jobs to areas where there is a greater availability of jobs. Thus we have migration from Latin America and Asia to the United States, from Asia to Canada, from Africa and Asia to Europe, and within Europe from the east to the west.

In earlier decades, the shortage of jobs generally occurred when the population grew dense in a particular region, and people then felt pressured to migrate to some other less populated area, much as high-pressure storm fronts move into low-pressure weather systems. This is precisely the pattern of migration that characterized the expansion of European populations into other parts of the world, as European farmers sought land in less densely settled areas. This phenomenon of European expansion is, of course, critically important because as Europeans moved around the world, they altered patterns of life, including their own, wherever they went.

European Expansion Beginning in the fourteenth century, migration out of Europe started gaining momentum, and this virtually revolutionized the entire human population. With their gun-laden sailboats, Europeans began to stake out the less-developed areas of the world in the fifteenth and sixteenth centuries—and this was only the beginning. Migration of Europeans to other parts of the world on a massive scale took hold in the nineteenth century, when the European nations began to industrialize and swell in numbers due to the decline in mortality. As Kingsley Davis has put it:

> Although the continent was already crowded, the death rate began to drop and the population began to expand rapidly. Simultaneous urbanization, new occupations, financial panics, and unrestrained competition gave rise to status instability on a scale never known before. Many a bruised or disappointed European was ready to seek his fortune abroad, particularly since the new lands, tamed by the pioneers, no longer seemed wild and remote but rather like paradises where one could own land and start a new life. The invention of the steamship (the first one crossed the Atlantic in 1827) made the decision less irrevocable (Davis 1974:98).

Before the great expansion of European people and culture, Europeans represented about 18 percent of the world's population, with almost 90 percent of them living in Europe itself. By the 1930s, at the peak of European dominance in the world, people of European origin in Europe, North America, and Oceania accounted for 35 percent of the world's population (Durand 1967). By the beginning of the twenty-first century, the percentage had declined to 16, and it is projected to drop to 13 percent by the middle of the century (United Nations Population Division 2009). However, even that may be a bit of an exaggeration, since the rate of growth in North American and European countries is increasingly influenced by immigrants and births to immigrants from developing nations.

"South" to "North" Migration Since the 1930s, the outward expansion of Europeans has ceased. Until then, European populations had been growing more rapidly than the populations in Africa, Asia, and Latin America, but since World War II that trend has been reversed. The less developed areas now have by far the most rapidly growing populations. It has been said that "population growth used to be a reward for doing well; now it's a scourge for doing badly" (Blake 1979). This change in the pattern of population has resulted in a shift in the direction of migration. For the past half-century there has been far more migration from less developed countries (the "South") to developed areas (the "North") than the reverse. Furthermore, since migrants from less developed areas generally have higher levels of fertility than natives of the developed regions, their migration makes a disproportionate contribution over time to the overall population increase in the developed area to which they have migrated. As a result, the proportion of the population whose origin is one of the modern world's less developed nations tends to be on the rise in nearly every developed country. Within the United States, for example, non-Hispanic whites (the European-origin population) are no longer the majority in the state of California, and it is likely that the Hispanic-origin population (largely of Mexican ancestry) will represent the majority of Californians by the middle of this century since the majority of all births in California (as in all southwestern states) are now to Hispanic mothers. Note that I use "Hispanic" rather than the often-used "Latino" only because the former term is most often found in government statistics.

When Europeans migrated, they were generally filling up territory that had very few people, because they tended to be moving in on land used by hunter-gatherers who, as noted above, use land extensively rather than intensively. Those seemingly empty lands or frontiers have essentially disappeared today, and as a consequence migration into a country now results in more noticeable increases in population density. And, just as the migration of Europeans was typically greeted with violence from the indigenous population upon whose land they were encroaching, migrants today routinely meet prejudice, discrimination, and violence in the places to which they have moved. The difference is that today's migrants tend to be showing up in cities, not the countryside, and this is part of a broader aspect of the entire urban transition—an important offshoot of the migration transition.

The Urban Revolution Until very recently in world history, almost everyone lived in basically rural areas. Large cities were few and far between. For example, Rome's population of 650,000 in A.D. 100 was probably the largest in the ancient world (Chandler and Fox 1974). It is estimated that as recently as 1800, less than one percent of the world's population lived in cities of 100,000 or more. Nearly half of all humans now live in cities of that size.

The redistribution of people from rural to urban areas occurred earliest and most markedly in the industrialized nations. For example, in 1800 about 10 percent of the English population lived in urban areas, primarily London. By the year 2000, 90 percent of the British lived in cities. Similar patterns of urbanization have been experienced in other European countries, the United States, Canada, and Japan as they have industrialized. In the less developed areas of the world, urbanization was initially associated with a commercial response to industrialization in Europe, America, and Japan. In other words, in many areas where industrialization was not occurring, Europeans had established colonies or trade relationships. The principal economic activities in these areas were not industrial but commercial in nature, associated with buying and selling. The wealth acquired by people engaged in these activities naturally attracted attention, and urban centers sprang up all over the world as Europeans sought populations to whom they could sell their goods.

During the second half of the twentieth century, when the world began to urbanize in earnest, the underlying cause was the rapid growth of the rural population (I discuss this in more detail in Chapter 9). The rural population in every less developed nation has outstripped the ability of the agricultural economy to absorb it. Paradoxically, in order to grow enough food for an increasing population, people have had to be replaced by machines in agriculture (as I will discuss in Chapter 11), and that has sent the redundant rural population off to the cities in search of work. Herein lie the roots of many of the problems confronting the world in the twenty-first century.

Geographic Distribution of the World's Population

The five largest countries in the world account for nearly half the world's population (48 percent as of the year 2010) but only 21 percent of the world's land surface. These countries include China, India, the United States, Indonesia, and Brazil, as you can see in Table 2.4. Rounding out the top 10 are Pakistan, Bangladesh, Nigeria, Russia, and Japan. Within these most populous 10 nations reside 59 percent of all people. You can see that you have to visit only the top twenty countries in order to shake hands with nearly three out of every four (71 percent) people in the world. In doing so, you would travel across 41 percent of the earth's land surface. The rest of the population is spread out among 175 or so other countries that account for the remaining 59 percent of the earth's terrain.

If you set a goal to be as efficient as possible in maximizing the number of people you visit while minimizing the distance you travel, your best bet would be to schedule a trip to China and the Indian subcontinent. Four out of every ten people live in those two contiguous regions of Asia, and you can see how these areas stand out in the map of the world drawn with country size proportionate to population (see Figure 2.1, at the beginning of this chapter). Population growth in Asia is not a new story. In Table 2.5 you can see that in 1500, as Europeans were venturing beyond their shores, China and India (or more technically the Indian subcontinent, including the modern nations of India, Pakistan, and Bangladesh) were already the most populous places on earth, and all of Asia accounted for 53 percent of the world's 461 million people. Five centuries later, the population in Asian countries accounts for 61 percent of all the people on earth, although it is projected to drop back to 58 percent by the year 2050.

Sub-Saharan Africa, on the other hand, had about as many people as did Europe in 1500. However, contact with Europeans tended to be deadly for Africans (as it was for the native peoples in North and South America) because of disease,

Table 2.4 The Twenty Most Populous Countries in the World, 1950, 2010, and 2050

	1950			2010			2050		
Rank	Country	Population (in millions)	Area (000 sq miles)	Country	Population (in millions)	Area (000 sq miles)	Country	Population (in millions)	Area (000 sq miles)
1	China	563	3,601	China	1,354	3,601	India	1,614	1,148
2	India	370	1,148	India	1,214	1,148	China	1,417	3,601
3	Soviet Union	180	8,650	United States	318	3,536	United States	404	3,536
4	United States	152	3,536	Indonesia	233	705	Pakistan	335	298
5	Japan	84	145	Brazil	195	3,265	Nigeria	289	352
6	Indonesia	83	705	Pakistan	185	298	Indonesia	288	705
7	Germany	68	135	Bangladesh	164	50	Bangladesh	222	50
8	Brazil	53	3,265	Nigeria	158	212	Brazil	219	3,265
9	United Kingdom	50	93	Russia	140	6,521	Ethiopia	174	386
10	Italy	47	114	Japan	127	705	Congo (Kinshasa)	148	905
11	Bangladesh	46	50	Mexico	111	737	Philippines	146	126
12	France	42	212	Philippines	94	115	Egypt	130	384
13	Pakistan	39	298	Vietnam	89	126	Mexico	129	737
14	Nigeria	32	352	Ethiopia	85	386	Russia	116	6,521
15	Mexico	28	737	Egypt	84	116	Vietnam	112	126
16	Spain	28	193	Germany	82	93	Japan	102	145
17	Vietnam	26	126	Turkey	76	297	Turkey	97	297
18	Poland	25	118	Iran	75	632	Iran	97	632
19	Egypt	21	384	Thailand	68	197	Uganda	91	93
20	Philippines	21	116	Congo (Kinshasa)	67	905	Sudan	76	967
Top 20		1,958	23,977		4,919	23,646		6,206	24,274
World		2,556	57,900		6,909	57,900		9,150	57,900
% top 5		53%	29%		48%	21%		44%	15%
% top 10		65%	37%		59%	35%		54%	23%
% top 20		77%	41%		71%	41%		68%	42%

Source: Adapted from Nations Population Division, 2009. *World Population Prospects: The 2008 Revision* (New York: United Nations).

Table 2.5 Geographic Distribution of the World's Population, from 400 B.C. to A.D. 2050

	Number of People (in millions) in the Region as of the Year:										
Region	−400	0	500	1000	1500	1750	1850	1900	1950	2000	2050
China	19	70	32	56	84	220	435	415	563	1,267	1,417
India/Pakistan/Bangladesh	30	46	33	40	95	165	216	290	455	1,332	2,151
Japan	1	2	5	4	10	26	30	45	84	127	102
Rest of Asia	45	52	49	52	56	89	109	153	296	972	1,561
Europe	32	43	41	43	84	146	288	422	547	727	691
North Africa	10	14	11	9	9	10	12	43	52	179	322
Sub-Saharan Africa	7	12	20	30	78	94	90	95	169	640	1,677
North America (U.S. and Canada)	1	2	2	2	3	3	25	90	172	319	448
Latin America	7	10	13	16	39	15	34	75	167	521	726
Oceania	1	1	1	1	3	3	2	6	13	31	51
	153	252	207	253	461	771	1,241	1,634	2,518	6,115	9,146
	Percentage										
China	12.4	27.8	15.5	22.1	18.2	28.5	35.1	25.4	22.4	20.7	15.5
India/Pakistan/Bangladesh	19.6	18.3	15.9	15.8	20.6	21.4	17.4	17.7	18.1	21.8	23.5
Japan	0.7	0.8	2.4	1.6	2.2	3.4	2.4	2.8	3.3	2.1	1.1
Rest of Asia	29.4	20.6	23.7	20.6	12.1	11.5	8.8	9.4	11.8	15.9	17.1
Europe	20.9	17.1	19.8	17.0	18.2	18.9	23.2	25.8	21.7	11.9	7.6
North Africa	6.5	5.6	5.3	3.6	2.0	1.3	1.0	2.6	2.1	2.9	3.5
Sub-Saharan Africa	4.6	4.8	9.7	11.9	16.9	12.2	7.3	5.8	6.7	10.5	18.3
North America (U.S. and Canada)	0.7	0.8	1.0	0.8	0.7	0.4	2.0	5.5	6.8	5.2	4.9
Latin America	4.6	4.0	6.3	6.3	8.5	1.9	2.7	4.6	6.6	8.5	7.9
Oceania	0.7	0.4	0.5	0.4	0.7	0.4	0.2	0.4	0.5	0.5	0.6
	100.0	100.0	100.0	100.0	100.0	100.0	100.0	100.0	100.0	100.0	100.0

Sources: Adapted from Biraben, Jean-Noël. 1979. "Essai Sur L'Évolution Du Nombre Des Hommes." *Population* 34 (1):13–24, Table 1, and updated by the author to 2000 and 2050 using data from United Nations Population Division, 2009. World Population Prospects: The 2008 Revision.

violence, and slavery. In the twentieth century, sub-Saharan Africa rebounded in population size, comprising 10 percent of the total world population in 2000. Of course, high mortality from HIV/AIDS is now slowing down the rate of growth in sub-Saharan Africa, but the United Nations projects that because of the continued high fertility levels in the region, sub-Saharan Africa could account for more than 18 percent of the world's population in 2050—even beyond where it had been in percentage terms in the year 1500, and with more than twice as many people as are projected to be in Europe in that year.

Global Variation in Population Size and Growth

World population is currently growing at a rate of 1.2 percent annually, implying a net addition of 79 million people per year (see Table 2.1), but there is a lot of variability underlying those global numbers. You can see in Table 2.5 that we expect Europe, as a region, and Japan, as a nation, to have fewer people in 2050 than they have now. All other areas of the world will continue to grow in size, including China, despite the one-child policy. In Figure 2.4, you can see that the most rapidly growing regions in the world tend to be in the mid-latitudes, and these are nations that are least developed economically, whereas the slowest growing are the richer nations, which tend to be more northerly and southerly. It has not always been that way, however.

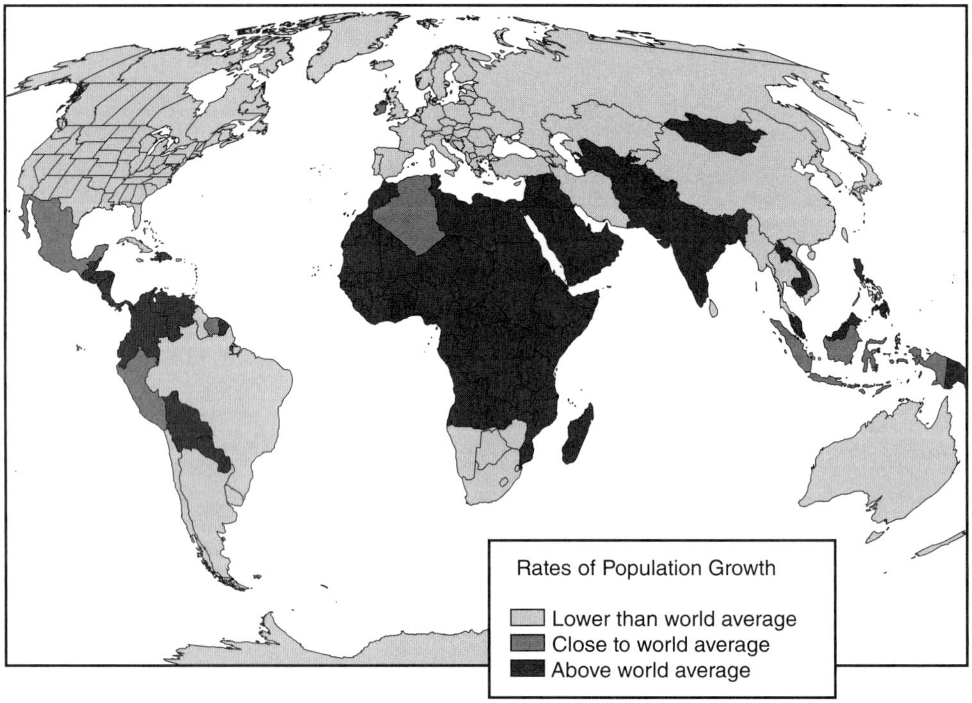

Figure 2.4 Rates of population growth are highest in the middle latitudes.

Before the Great Depression of the 1930s, the populations of Europe and, especially, North America were the most rapidly growing in the world. During the decade of the 1930s, growth rates declined in those two areas to match approximately those of most of the rest of the world, which was about 0.75 percent per year—a doubling time of 93 years. Since the end of World War II, the situation has changed again, and now Europe is on the verge of depopulation with rapid growth in the less developed countries of Africa, Asia, and to lesser extent Latin America, now responsible for almost all of the world's population increase.

Let's examine these trends in more detail, focusing particular attention on the 10 most populous nations, with a few other countries included to help illustrate the variability of demographic situations in which countries find themselves.

North America

Canada and the United States—North America—have a combined population of 344 million as of 2010, representing just under 5 percent of the world's total. Canada's nearly 34 million people account for 10 percent of North America's total, and the United States, with 310 million, has the remaining 90 percent. The demographic histories of the two countries are intertwined but are not identical.

United States It does not take a demographer to notice that the population of the United States has undergone a total transformation since John Cabot (an Italian hired by the British to search the new world) landed in Newfoundland in 1497 and claimed North America for the British. As was true throughout the western hemisphere, European guns and diseases rather quickly decimated the native American Indian population, making it easier to establish a new culture. Europeans had diseases and weapons that had never been seen by the indigenous populations, but the indigenous population had nothing that was new and dangerous to the Europeans, save perhaps for syphilis (Crosby 2004). It is estimated that the population of North America in 1650 consisted of about 50,000 European colonists and 2 to 3 million native American Indians the Europeans were outnumbered by as much as 60 to 1. By 1850, disease and warfare had reduced the native population to perhaps as few as 250,000, while the European population had increased to 25 million. Indeed, it was widely assumed that the American Indian population was on the verge of disappearing (Snipp 1989).

Although early America was a model of rapid population growth (at least for the European-origin population), it was also a land of substantial demographic contrasts. Among the colonies existing in the seventeenth century, for example, those in New England seem to have been characterized by very high birth rates (women had an average of seven to nine children) yet relatively low mortality rates (infant mortality rates in Plymouth Colony may have been as low or even lower than in some of today's less developed nations, apparently a result of the fairly good health of Americans even during that era) (Demos 1965; Wells 1971, 1982). Demos notes that "the popular impression today that colonial families were extremely large finds the strongest possible confirmation in the case of Plymouth. A sample of some ninety families, about whom there is fairly reliable information, suggests that there was an average of seven to eight children per family who actually grew to adulthood" (1965:270). In the southern colonies during the same time period, however, life was apparently much harsher, probably because the environment was more amenable to the spread of disease, including yellow fever and malaria. In the Chesapeake Bay colony of Charles Parish, higher mortality meant that few parents had more than two or three living children at the time of their death (Smith 1978).

Despite the regional diversity, the American population grew rather steadily during the seventeenth and eighteenth centuries, and though some of the increase in the number of Europeans in America was attributable to in-migration, the greater percentage actually was due to **natural increase** (the excess of births over deaths). The nation's first census, taken in 1790, shortly after the American Revolution, counted 3.9 million Americans, and although the population was increasing by nearly 120,000 a year, only about 3 percent of the increase was a result of immigration. With a crude birth rate of about 55 births per thousand population (comparable to the highest national birth rates in the world today) and a crude death rate of about 28 deaths per thousand, there were twice as many people being born each year as were dying. At this rate, the population was doubling in size every 25 years.

Americans may picture foreigners pouring in seeking freedom or fortune. Indeed, Benjamin Franklin lamented the "swarm" of German immigrants coming to the Pennsylvania of his day (Franklin 1751), but it was not until the last third of the nineteenth century that migration became a substantial factor in American population growth. In fact, during the first half of the nineteenth century, in-migrants accounted for less than 5 percent of the population increase in each decade, whereas in every decade from the 1850s through the 1920s in-migrants accounted for at least 20 percent of the growth of population.

Throughout the late nineteenth and early twentieth centuries, the birth rate in the United States was falling. There is evidence that fertility among American Quakers began to be limited at about the time of the American Revolution (Wells 1971; Leasure 1989), and the rest of the nation was only a few decades behind their pace. By the 1930s, fertility actually dropped below the level required to replace the next generation (as I discuss more thoroughly in Chapter 6). Furthermore, restrictions on immigration had all but halted the influx of foreigners, and Americans were facing the prospect of potential depopulation.

The early post–World War II era upset forecasts of population decline; they were replaced by the realities of a population explosion. The period from 1946 to 1964 is generally known as the "baby boom" era (and thus the people born during those years are the baby boomers). It was a time when the United States experienced a rapid rate of increase in population, accomplished almost entirely by increases in fertility. The baby boom, in turn, was followed in the late 1960s and early 1970s by a "baby bust" (now widely known as Generation X, as I noted in the previous chapter.). The birth rate bottomed out in the 1976 and has been higher ever since, although not by very much (Martin et al. 2009). An echo of the baby boom was experienced as the "baby boomlet" of the 1980s, but this was due largely to an increase in births from children of the baby boom, rather than an increase in the birth rate per women.

Since the 1980s, fertility in the United States has since remained at or just below the replacement level, although the average number of children being born per woman was higher in 2006 than it had been at any time since 1971. Despite this, population growth has continued to be the order of the day largely because in the 1960s and then again in the 1990s adjustments of the nation's immigration laws opened the nation's doors wider, and the result has been renewed high levels of migration into the United States. Indeed, the 1 million immigrants (legal and undocumented) being added each year account for more than one-third (36 percent) of the total annual population increase. More importantly, from a demographic perspective, immigrants are primarily people of reproductive age and they are having children at a rate that is above replacement level. The long-term implication of this continued immigration is that variations in fertility levels in the United States are increasingly determined by fertility differences among the various racial and ethnic groups.

By current world standards, the United States today is one of the slower-growing countries, but its rate of growth is still one of the highest among the more developed nations. With a total rate of growth of about 0.9 percent per year, the U.S. population is increasing at a rate that is higher than any European country except Ireland. Fertility in the United States is low (2.1 children per woman), but not as low as in virtually all European countries. On the other hand, mortality is also very low (female life expectancy in the United States is now 80 years), but not as low as in the countries of Western Europe and in Japan (where a life expectancy for women of 86 years is the highest in the world).

The only major demographic category in which the United States leads the world is in the number of immigrants received each year, and that has a lot to do with the demographic diversity that is so much a part of life in the United States. For example, the 38 million African Americans in the United States in 2010 represented the best-educated, wealthiest, and fourth-largest (after Nigeria, Ethiopia, and South Africa) population of African-origin persons in the world. At the same time, there is little wonder that Hispanics have caught the attention of America when you consider that the number of Hispanics more than doubled between 1990 and 2010. The 47 million Hispanics in 2010 represented more than 15 percent of the total U.S. population—surpassing the black population. And, of course, the Hispanic population is itself diverse, spanning different major groups, including those tracing ancestry to Mexico or one of the other Central American countries, as well as major Caribbean groups from Cuba and Puerto Rico. Asians represent a smaller, yet growing, population in the United States, and ethnically it is an even more diverse group than Hispanics. Asian immigrants have also been attracted to Canada in large numbers.

Canada The French were the first Europeans to settle the area that has become Canada, and by 1760 the population of New France included about 70,000 people of European (largely French) origin, along with a diminishing population of indigenous peoples. In 1763, the French government ceded control of the region to the British. The French-origin population was thus "cut off from intercourse with the French, and they received no further demographic reinforcements" (Overbeek 1980:10). Twenty years later, the establishment of American independence led about 30,000 "loyalists" to leave the United States and migrate to Canada, the forerunner of a much more massive migration from England to Canada during the nineteenth century (Kalbach and McVey 1979). The conflict between the British-origin and French-origin populations helped to stimulate the British North America Act of 1867, which united all of the provinces of Canada into the Dominion of Canada, and every census since then has asked about "origins" as a way of keeping track of the numerical balance between these historically rival groups (Boyd, Goldmann, and White 2000). In 1931, when Canada was granted independence from Great Britain, the Province of Québec, in which most French-speaking Canadians reside, accounted for 28 percent of the population of Canada. By 2010, that figure had dropped to 23 percent.

In the seventeenth and eighteenth centuries, the high fertility of women in New France was legendary, and French speakers in Canada maintained higher-than-average levels of fertility until the 1960s (Beaujot 1978), probably due to the strong influence of the Catholic Church in Québec (McQuillan 2004). In the rest of Canada, fertility began to drop in the nineteenth century and reached very low levels in the 1930s before rebounding after World War II in a baby boom that was similar in its impact on Canadian society to that experienced in the United States. This boom was similarly followed by a baby bust and then a small echo of the baby boom (Foot 1996). Canada now has a fertility level (1.6 children per woman) that is well below replacement, but women in Québec had lowered their fertility to only 1.3 children in the 1980s—making Francophone (French-speaking) Canada the lowest-fertility region in the western hemisphere. In response to this, the provincial government stepped in to offer subsidized day care for children, and that seems to have produced a "baby bump" bringing the birth rate up at least to the national average (*The Economist* 2009b).

Just as fertility is lower in Canada than in the United States, so is mortality, with life expectancy in Canada about three years longer than in the United States. In both of these respects the demographic profile of Canada is more like that of Europe than of the United States. However, when it comes to immigration, Canada reflects the Northern American history of being a receiving ground for people from other nations. Despite its lower fertility, Canada's overall rate of population growth exceeds that of the United States because it accepts more immigrants per person than the United States does. For example, in the first decade of this century, Canada was admitting about 250,000 immigrants per year (about eight per thousand population) and the foreign-born population represented about 18 percent of the Canadian population. In the same period 1 million immigrants annually entered the United States (about three per thousand population), and the foreign born accounted for about 12 percent of the U.S. population. Immigrants to Canada in recent years have come especially from Asia, but an increasing number are arriving from Latin America. Immigrants to the United States also come from Asia, but a larger fraction come from Latin America, especially Mexico.

Mexico and Central America

Mexico and the countries of Central America have been growing since the end of World War II as a result of rapidly dropping death rates and birth rates that have only more recently begun to drop. Mexico's population in 2010 was 110 million, and so Mexico accounts for about three-fourths of the population of the region, with the remaining population distributed among (in order of size) Guatemala, Honduras, El Salvador, Nicaragua, Costa Rica, Panama, and Belize. The combined regional population of 152 million as estimated for the year 2010 is a little more than 2 percent of the world's total.

Mexico and Central America had developed more advanced agricultural societies than had North America at the time of European contact. The Aztec civilization in central Mexico and the remnants of the Mayan civilization farther south centered near Guatemala encompassed many millions more people than lived on the northern side of what is now the United States–Mexico border. This fact, combined with the Spanish goal of extracting resources (a polite term for plundering) from the New World rather than colonizing it, produced a very different demographic legacy from what we find in Canada and the United States.

Mexico was the site of a series of agricultural civilizations as far back as 2,500 years before the invasion by the Spanish in 1519. Within a relatively short time after Europeans arrived, the population of several million was cut by as much as 80 percent due to disease and violence. This population collapse (a true implosion) was precipitated by contact with European diseases, but it reflects the fact that mortality was already very high before the arrival of the Europeans, and it did not take much to upset the demographic balance (Alchon 1997). By the beginning of the twentieth century, life expectancy was still very low in Mexico, less than 30 years (Morelos 1994), and fertility was very high in response to the high death rate. However, since the 1930s the death rate has dropped dramatically, and life expectancy in Mexico is now 78 years for women, seven years above the world average and only two years less than in the United States.

For several decades, this decline in mortality was not accompanied by a change in the birth rate, and the result was a massive explosion in the size of the Mexican population. In 1920, before the death rate began to drop, there were 14 million people in Mexico (Mier y Terán 1991). By 1950 that had nearly doubled to 26 million, and by 1970, it had nearly doubled again to 49 million. In the 1970s, the birth rate finally began to decline in Mexico. Mexican women had been bearing an average of six children each for many decades (if not centuries), but by 2010 this figure had dropped to 2.3 children per woman for the country, and in the capital of Mexico City fertility had dropped below replacement level to 1.7 children per woman (INEGI 2010). Nonetheless, the massive buildup of young people has strained every ounce of the Mexican economy, encouraging outmigration, especially to the United States.

The other countries of Central America have experienced similar patterns of rapidly declining mortality, leading to population growth and its attendant pressures for migration to other countries where the opportunities might be better. Not every country in the region has experienced the same fertility decline as Mexico, however. In particular, Guatemala, Nicaragua, and Honduras are countries in which a high proportion of the population is indigenous (rather than being of mixed native and European origin), and they have birth rates that are well above the world average of 2.7. Indeed, the average woman in Guatemala is having 4.4 children. However, Costa Rica has a more European pattern, with fertility that is below replacement, life expectancy that is higher than in the United States, and the need to import workers from its neighboring countries.

South America

The 393 million inhabitants of South America as of 2010 represent about 6 percent of the world's total population, with Brazil alone accounting for half of that. The modern history of Brazil began when Portuguese explorers found an indigenous hunter-gatherer population in that region and tried to enslave them to work on plantations. These attempts were unsuccessful, and the Portuguese wound up populating the colony largely with African slaves. The 4 million slaves taken to Brazil represent more than one-third of all slaves transported from Africa to the western hemisphere between the sixteenth and nineteenth centuries (Thomas 1997). The Napoleonic Wars in Europe in the early part of the nineteenth century allowed Brazil, like most Latin American countries, to gain independence from Europe, and the economic development that followed ultimately led to substantial migration into Brazil from Europe during the latter part of the nineteenth century. The result is a society that is now about half European-origin and half African-origin or mixed race. Brazil also attracted Japanese immigrants early in the twentieth century and again after World War II.

Brazil boasts a land area nearly equal in size to the United States, upon which an estimated 195 million people currently reside. Since 1965, Brazil has experienced a reduction in fertility that has been described as "nothing short of spectacular" (Martine 1996:47). In 1960, the average Brazilian woman was giving birth to six children, but it has since dropped to 1.9—just below replacement level. For many years, the influence of the Catholic Church was strong enough to cause the government to forbid the dissemination of contraceptive information or devices, but rapid economic development between 1960 and 2000 seems clearly to have encouraged a decline in fertility, even if that drop was spatially uneven—starting first in the south and southeast and then spreading north and northeast from there (Schmertmann, Potter, and Cavenaghi 2008). The infant mortality rate of 24 deaths per 1,000 live births in Brazil is half the world average, and female life expectancy of 77 years is also well above the world average. Birth and death rates in Brazil are very similar to those in Mexico.

The other countries of South America can be loosely divided into those three most southerly nations (including Argentina, Chile, and Uruguay) in which the populations are predominantly of European origin, and the remaining countries with higher proportions of indigenous and mixed (mestizo) populations. The former tend to have lower fertility and higher life expectancy—levels very similar to Brazil's. The other countries tend to have higher fertility, somewhat higher mortality, and higher rates of population growth.

Europe

The combined population of western, southern, northern (including Scandinavia), central, and eastern Europe (including Russia) is about 738 million, or about 11 percent of the world's total. Russia is the most populous, accounting for 19 percent of Europe's population, but as I discuss in the essay accompanying this chapter, that percentage will drop as Russia depopulates. The next most populous countries in Europe are, in order, Germany, France, the United Kingdom, and Italy and they, along with Russia, comprise more than half (56 percent) of all Europeans.

Europe as a region is on the verge of depopulating, as you can see in Table 2.5. This is largely because its two largest nations, Russia and Germany, currently have more deaths than births and neither country is taking in enough immigrants to compensate for that fact. Russia's situation is especially noteworthy because its death rate and birth rate have both been declining, signaling major societal stresses. Several researchers have argued that the breakup of the Soviet Union was foreshadowed by a rise in death rates (Feshbach and Friendly 1992; Shkolnikov, Meslé, and Vallin 1996), and it has not really recovered demographically from that collapse. The birth rate was already low in Russia before the breakup, and since then there has been a further baby bust, lowering the average number of children being born per woman to 1.5.

The trends in Russia mirror demographic events in East Germany just before and after the fall of the Berlin Wall, and in both cases the situation has been described as "a society convulsed by its stresses" (Eberstadt 1994:149). When East Germany was reunited with West Germany, the combined Germany inherited the East's dismal demographics and that largely explains why Germany teeters on depopulation. The rest of Europe has experienced very low birth rates without the drop in life expectancy that has plagued Russia. Where population growth is occurring, such as in France, the United Kingdom, and Ireland, it is largely attributable to the immigration of people from less developed nations (Sardon 2002; Castles and Miller 2003).

It should not be a surprise that fertility and mortality are both low in Europe, since that is the part of the world where mortality first began its worldwide decline approximately 250 years ago and where fertility began *its* worldwide decline about 150 years ago. What is surprising, however, is how low the birth rate has fallen. It is especially low in the Mediterranean countries of Italy and Spain, where fertility has dropped well below replacement level—in predominantly Catholic societies where fertility for most of history has been higher than in the rest of Europe. Sweden and the other Scandinavian countries have emerged with fertility rates that are now among the highest in Europe, although still below the replacement level, and Chesnais (1996) has offered the intriguing thesis that an improvement in the status of women may be required to push fertility levels in Europe back up to the replacement level. I return to this theme in Chapters 6 and 10.

I have already mentioned that a major consequence of the low birth rate is an aging of the population that has left Europe with too few young people to take jobs and pay taxes. Into this void have swept millions of immigrants, many of them illegal, and Europeans are very divided in their reaction to this phenomenon, as I note in the essay accompanying this chapter. Some see the immigrants as the necessary resource that will keep the economy running and pension checks flowing for aging Europeans. Others see the immigrants as a very real threat to the European way of life, coming as they mainly do from Africa and Asia.

Northern Africa and Western Asia

The area most often referred to as the Middle East includes Egypt and western Asia, whereas the remainder of northern Africa to the west of Egypt is usually referred to as the Maghreb. The entire region is characterized especially by the presence of Islam (with the obvious notable exception of Israel) and by the fact that it includes a globally disproportionate share of countries with high rates of population growth and youth bulges.

The total population in the region is 436 million, representing 6 percent of the world's total. Egypt is the most populous of the countries in northern Africa and western Asia, followed closely by Turkey, and together they account for more than one-third of the region's total population. There are 79 million Egyptians crowded into the narrow Nile Valley. With its rate of growth of 1.9 percent per year, Egypt's population could double in 36 years, and this rapid growth constantly hampers even the most ambitious strategies for economic growth and development. This explosion in numbers is due, of course, to the dramatic drop in mortality since the end of World War II. In 1937, the life expectancy at birth in Egypt was less than 40 years (Omran 1973; Omran and Roudi 1993), whereas by now it has risen to 74 for females. Even with such an improvement in mortality, however, death rates are only slightly above the world average, leaving room for improvement that will continue to exert demographic pressure.

As mortality declined, fertility remained almost intransigently high in Egypt until the 1980s, save for brief dips during World War II and again during the wars with Israel in the late 1960s and early 1970s. For as long as statistics had been kept, Egyptian women had been bearing an average of six children, until the late 1970s. Massive family planning efforts were initiated in the 1970s under President Sadat and then reinvigorated in the 1980s under President Mubarak. These programs, especially in combination with increasing levels of education among women (Fargues 1997, 2000), have had an effect, and the estimated fertility level is now an average of 3.0 children per woman, much lower than it used to be but still well above replacement level. Because of the high fertility, a very high proportion (33 percent) of the population is under age 15.

It is the size and rate of increase in the youthful population that has been especially explosive throughout northern Africa and western Asia, as I alluded to in the previous chapter. *The Economist* put it succinctly: "By far the biggest difficulty facing the Arabs—and the main item in the catalogue of socio-economic woes submitted as evidence of looming upheaval—is demography (*The Economist* 2009a:8). The rapid drop in mortality after World War II, followed by a long delay in the start of fertility decline, produced a very large population of young people in need of jobs. They have spread throughout the region looking for work, and many have gone to Europe and North and South America. The economies within the region have not been able to keep up with the demand for jobs, and this has produced a generation of young people who, paradoxically, are better educated than their parents but who face an uncertain future in an increasingly crowded world. The declining birth rates hold out hope that the situation will ease in a few decades (Fargues 2000), but in the meantime the demographic situation has fueled discontent and has almost certainly contributed to the rise of radical Islam and terrorism.

Sub-Saharan Africa

Sub-Saharan Africa is the place from which all human life originated, according to most evidence (Wilson and Cann 1992), and the 836 million people living there now comprise 12 percent of the world's total. Nigeria alone accounts for nearly 1 in 5 of those 836 million, followed by Ethiopia and Congo (Kinshasa). If you do a few quick calculations in Table 2.5, you will discover that between A.D. 1000 and A.D. 1500, before extensive European contact with sub-Saharan Africa, that part of the world was increasing in population at a higher rate than anywhere else. However, Europeans brought their diseases to Africa and, much more significantly, they commercialized slavery to an extent never previously known in human history. More than 11 million Africans were enslaved and sent off to the western hemisphere between the sixteenth and nineteenth centuries (Thomas 1997), contributing to a decline in population size in sub-Saharan Africa between 1600 and 1850.

Until only a few decades ago, death rates in Africa were frequently as high as 40 deaths per 1,000 population and were associated with life expectancy in the range of 30 to 40 years, which is lower than the United States has experienced at any time since the American Revolution. Currently, 15 countries in the world have a life expectancy for females of less than 50 years; all but one (Afghanistan) are in sub-Saharan Africa and one of them, Nigeria, is—incredibly enough—among the ten most populous nations in the world, with 153 million people and growing by 4 million per year because the birth rate remains well above the high death rate. Ever since Independence from Great Britain in 1960, Nigeria has been torn by ethnonationalist conflict (a concept I mentioned in Chapter 1). The main ethnic groups are the Hausa-Fulani in the largely rural north, who are predominantly Muslim and among whom the average woman is bearing more than seven children (Measure DHS 2010), the Igbo in the somewhat more urban southeast, who are predominantly Christian and whose fertility rate is five children each, and the Yoruba in the southwest, whose traditional religion has been overlaid with both Islam and Christianity, and among whom fertility levels are similar to the Igbo. This very high fertility even in the face of high mortality has led to a steady increase in ranking for Nigeria in terms of population size. As you can see in Table 2.4, Nigeria was the fourteenth most populous nation in 1950, moved up to number eight in 2010, and is projected to take over the number five slot in 2050.

The high birth rates throughout sub-Saharan Africa are almost certainly related to the relatively low status of women throughout the region (Ampofo and Boateng 2008). Dodoo and Frost (2008) argue that the more public empowerment of women through education and employment opportunities may not produce dramatic drops in fertility unless gender relations in the private realm are also addressed. Note, however, that the same dissonance between public and private statuses of women has been implicated in the very low fertility of Europe and East Asia, so we are talking about very complicated relationships. I will return to these themes in Chapters 6 and 10.

East Asia

East Asia has 1.6 billion people, with the region dominated demographically by China (accounting for 85 percent of the population in this part of the world) and Japan (with 8 percent of the region's population). East Asia includes nearly 25 percent of the world's total population, but its share is diminishing as China continues to brake its population growth and as Japan teeters on the edge of depopulation.

China The People's Republic of China has a population of 1.3 billion people, maintaining for the time being its long-standing place as the most populous country in the

IMPLOSION OR INVASION? THE CHOICES AHEAD FOR LOW-FERTILITY COUNTRIES

The world's population is in no danger of imploding anytime soon, but the same cannot be said for much of Europe and East Asia. Several countries in these areas are either already declining in population, or are on the verge of doing so. The populations in Europe and East Asia all have birth rates that are below replacement level and have been that way for some time now, leading to a declining number of people at the younger ages. It appears that the low fertility in countries like Russia is not just a temporary phenomenon. Rather, it appears that the motivation to have large families has disappeared and has been replaced by a propensity to try to improve the family's standard of living by limiting the number of children (Avdeev and Monnier 1995; Kholer, Billari, and Ortega 2006). Russia adds the complication of also having lost a few years of life expectancy over the past couple of decades, which has further accelerated its population implosion. Most of the other Eastern European nations add to low fertility the demographic complication that people are leaving to go elsewhere, primarily to Western Europe, but also to North America.

According to data from the United Nations Population Division, there were 16 countries in 2010 that had fewer people than in 2000. All 16 of these were in Eastern Europe, and they were led by Russia and several of its former members of the Soviet Union, including Ukraine, Belarus, Georgia, Kazakhstan, the Republic of Moldova, Lithuania, Latvia, and Estonia. It is probably safe to say that the former Soviet Union has imploded.

The more controversial issue has been the aging of all of Europe and East Asia as a consequence of the low birth rate. The accompanying map shows the countries that, according to United Nations projections, are expected to have at least 20 percent of the population aged 65 and older in 2025 while at the same time having less than 20 percent of the population under age 15. These are countries with some of the biggest and most dynamic economies in the world, yet the proportion of the population that is 65 and older is growing rapidly, whereas the younger population is shrinking. Note that Russia is not included in this group because its relatively low life expectancy keeps the older population smaller than it might otherwise be.

One reaction to this situation is to suggest that it is a good thing for the planet as a whole, if not necessarily for Europeans. Residents of these countries are among the highest per person consumers of the earth's resources, and if the populations eventually decline in size their impact on the environment will be lower and the chance of global collapse thereby lessened (Diamond 2005). Within most of these countries, however, there is a concern about the economic impact of what many people are calling a "silver tsunami." Who will earn the money that is to be paid to retirees as pensions? Who will pay for the health care and social needs of the elderly?

Countries with High Proportions of Older People and Low Proportions of Young People.

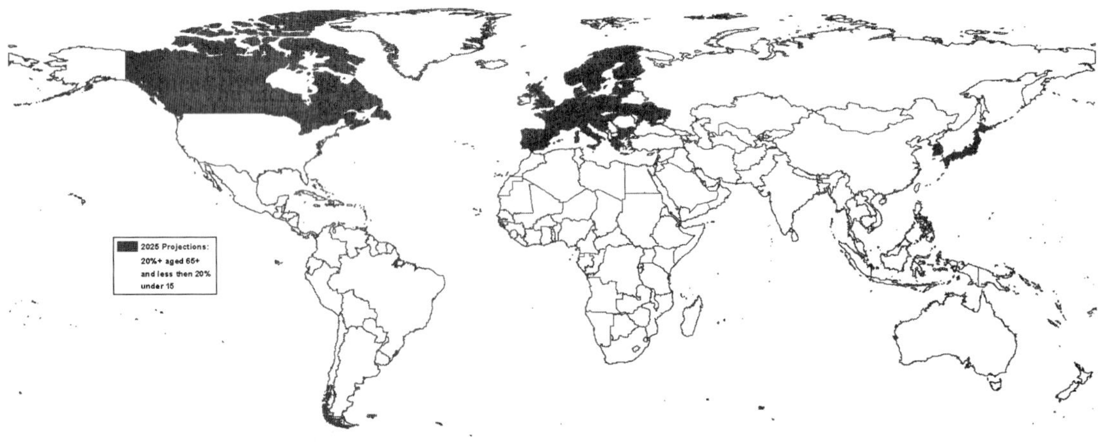

Source: Data from United Nations Population Division (2009).

Who will keep the economy going so that the standard of living does not drop even as the expenses associated with population aging go up?

Several solutions have been proposed, and they relate to (1) how to raise the birth rate; (2) how to increase labor force participation; and (3) how to replace the "missing" population with immigrants. In Chapter 6, I will discuss the fertility situation in some detail, but here we can note that countries with the lowest fertility rates are those in which the least accommodation has been made to permit women to simultaneously have a job and a family. The availability of daycare, programs for maternity leave and family leave, and societal pressure for men to help with child rearing and housework all increase the ability of women to participate in the labor force and still have children. Men have obviously always had that ability, but many countries, especially in Southern Europe and East Asia, have opened up the labor market to women without making it easy to combine a woman's participation in the labor force with a family, and that has depressed birth rates below what they might otherwise be. Researchers have also noted that the effect of a low birth rate would be a little less simply if women had children at a younger age, even if they had the same number as they are currently having (Lutz, O'Neill, and Scherbov 2003). This would shorten the time between generations and would actually increase the growth rate by a slight amount.

The impact of an aging population on a nation's economy is exacerbated by an early age at retirement. For most of human history people simply worked until they were physically no longer able to do so. Retirement has only been widely available for the past half-century, but ever since that option was offered, people have been grabbing it. Guess what? Most people prefer retirement to work. Thus, we have witnessed the situation in which even as life expectancy has increased, people have been choosing to retire earlier. This wouldn't be a problem if all of these people had actually saved up enough money to live comfortably during a protracted retirement, but this is largely not the case. For the most part, people have been promised a retirement pension that is based on the transfer of money from people currently in the labor force (through taxation) to people who are retired (the so-called "pay-as-you-go" scheme). As long as the population was growing and the economy was improving, these promises were easy to keep (almost like a Ponzi scheme), but when these very same people who now want to collect a pension have not had enough children to supply the needs of the labor force, there is a problem. One solution being promoted is to raise the age at retirement (Moffett 2005; Vaupel and Loichinger 2006), perhaps to as high as 75 (United Nations Population Division 2000). Encouraging older people to stay working longer means that they will continue to pay taxes to fund the pensions of those who are retired, while not burdening the system with their own pension demands. Vaupel and Loichinger (2006) have even suggested that if older people stayed in the work force longer, the number of hours worked by younger people could be reduced somewhat, which might in turn encourage a rise in the birth rate.

The short-term solution to labor shortages in the world has always been to import labor. This is the history of slavery in the Americas, and then the history of waves of immigrants to the United States from England, Germany, Italy, Mexico, and elsewhere. It is also the history of England, Germany, France, and several other European countries who needed labor to rebuild their economies after World War II. Between 1945 and the early 1970s, European nations allowed migration from former colonies, and they instituted guest worker programs, in which people contract to work for a few years and then go home again. The rub is that many workers choose not to go home. They stay, and build families, and become part of the fabric of their adopted society. If workers came for a while, worked, and then left as they got older and were replaced by younger people, immigration wouldn't be too much of an issue. The Gulf States in the Middle East have managed to accomplish this largely by prohibiting workers from having families with them, and by forcing the deportation of workers who overstay their contract (Castles and Miller 2003).

Europeans have rarely been willing to take those extreme measures, so guest workers are likely to stay past the end of their contract to become undocumented immigrants. The reality, then, is that replacement migration in Europe means the immigration of not just workers but also their families, and within a generation or two the children of immigrants can become a major force in the demographic makeup of the receiving countries, but in the meantime many of

(continued)

IMPLOSION OR INVASION? THE CHOICES AHEAD FOR LOW-FERTILITY COUNTRIES (CONTINUED)

these immigrants are not in the labor force, and thus they are not working and paying taxes, so they are not exactly "replacing" the older population (Bijak, Kupiszewska, and Kupiszewska 2008).

France and the United Kingdom have both taken in significant numbers of permanent immigrants from former colonies and as a result neither one is projected to decline in population over the next several decades. But the fact that an estimated 10 percent of France's population is now Muslim has created a variety of political and social dilemmas for that country. Studies conducted by the Pew Research Center have shown that immigration is strongly opposed throughout Europe, but paradoxically there is more support for it among the young than among the old (Pew Research Center 2004).

Japan, like other Asian countries, has an extremely restrictive immigration policy because of an

world. With one-fifth of all human beings, China dominates the map of the world drawn to scale according to population size (see Figure 2.1). If we add in the Chinese in Taiwan (which the government of mainland China still claims as its own), Singapore, and the overseas Chinese elsewhere in the world, closer to one out of every four people is of Chinese origin. Nonetheless, China's share of the world's total population actually peaked in the middle of the nineteenth century, as you can see in Table 2.5. In 1850, more than one in three people were living in China, and that fraction has steadily declined over time, even as China's population continued to grow in absolute numbers.

For years the Chinese tried to ignore their demographic bulk, perhaps fearful of criticism from the outside if reports of population size and growth rates did not take sufficient account of the fact that the Communist revolution had inherited a very large problem. However, in 1982, China took stock of the magnitude of its problem with its first national census since 1964 (which had been taken shortly after the terrible famine that I mentioned earlier). A total of just slightly more than one billion people were counted, and the results seemed to reinforce the government's belief that it was on the right track in vigorously pursuing a fairly coercive one-child policy to cut the birthrate. The general government attitude was summed up in the mid-1990s as follows:

> Despite the outstanding achievements made in population and development, China still confronts a series of basic problems including a large population base, insufficient cultivated land, under-development, inadequate resources on a per capita basis and an uneven social and economic development among regions. . . . Too many people has impeded seriously the speed of social and economic development of the country and the rise of the standard of living of the people. Many difficulties encountered in the course of social and economic development are directly attributable to population problems (Peng 1996:7).

Fertility decline actually began in China's cities in the 1960s and spread rapidly throughout the rest of the country in the 1970s, when the government introduced the family planning program known as *wan xi shao*, meaning "later" (marriage), "longer" (birth interval), "fewer" (children) (Banister 1987; Goldstein and Feng 1996). In 1979, this was transformed into the one-child policy, but fertility was already on its way down by that time (Riley 2004). Between 1963 and 1983, China experienced what Blayo (1992) called a "breathtaking drop in TFRs [total fertility rates, see Chapter 6] from 7.5 to 2.5 children" (p. 213), and what Riley and Gardner (1996) suggest was "the most rapid sustained fertility decline ever seen in a population of any size" (p. 1).

explicit desire to preserve the country's ethnic homogeneity. Although Japan does tolerate a small number of immigrants, it is unlikely that they will soon allow an invasion to prevent their impending implosion, despite concerns that declining population may significantly harm the nation's economy (Moffett 2006). Japan's low birth rate is slightly counterbalanced by the extreme longevity of the Japanese—they have the highest life expectancy in the world—but that translates into one in four Japanese being age 65 or older, giving the country the highest percentage of elderly per total population in the world.

Discussion Questions: (1) Do you think it is appropriate or even possible for Europeans to increase their birthrate in order to stave off depopulation? Why or Why Not? **(2)** Why do you think Europe is more worried about immigration than the United States, but at the same time less concerned than Japan?

China's fertility has continued to decline, although at a slower pace. China's birthrate has now dropped to 1.6 children per woman, which is below the replacement rate, although as I will discuss later in the book, that does not yet mean that the population has stopped growing. Furthermore, it is obviously well above the level of only one child per woman. Life expectancy at birth for females is 75 years, several years above the world average. Despite its low birth rate, the number of births each year in China is nearly twice the number of deaths just because China is paying for its previous high birth rate. There are so many young women of reproductive age (women born 25 to 45 years ago when birth rates were much higher) that their babies vastly outnumber the people who are dying each year. As a result, the rate of natural increase in China is essentially the same as in the United States, despite the lower fertility rate. Of course, since China has more than four times as many inhabitants as the United States, it is adding 7.7 million people each year to its territory, whereas the United States is accumulating "only" an additional 2.7 million (and that includes immigrants). Thus, population growth remains a serious concern in China, but the concern is now turning from the young population to the rapidly increasing number and proportion of older Chinese—the inevitable consequence of a rapid decline in fertility in a nation where mortality is also low. China may be unique, however, in getting old before it has gotten rich (Beck 2009).

Japan Let me also briefly mention Japan, which, for the moment, is the tenth most populous nation in the world. As noted, it has the lowest level of mortality in the world, with a female life expectancy at birth of 86 years. Japan's health (accompanied by its wealth) translates demographically into very high probabilities of survival to old age—indeed, more than half of all Japanese born in the year 2009 will likely still be alive at age 80. This very low mortality rate is accompanied by very low fertility. Japanese women are bearing an average of 1.4 children each, leading some pundits to suggest that Japan has its own "one-child policy." Japan is not yet losing population only because there are still enough women of reproductive age that, even at 1.4 each, they currently produce as many babies each year as there are people dying. This won't last for long, however. Japan's low mortality and low fertility have produced a population in which only 13 percent are under age 15, whereas 23 percent are 65 or older. The United Nations forecasts that by 2050 the percent under 15 will have dropped still further to 11 percent, while the percent 65 and older will have risen to 38. Not surprisingly, this is expected to be accompanied by a population decline from the current 128 million down to 102 million.

South and Southeast Asia

South and Southeast Asia are home to more than 2 billion people, one-third of the world's total. In contrast to Japan, this region of the world is dominated by youthful populations struggling with grinding poverty. The Indian subcontinent dominates this area demographically—India, Pakistan, and Bangladesh encompass two-thirds of the region's population. But Indonesia, the world's fourth most populous nation (and the one with the largest Muslim population in the world), is also part of southeast Asia, as are three other countries on the top 20 list—the Philippines, Vietnam, and Thailand.

India, Pakistan, and Bangladesh Second in population size in the world is India, with the current population estimated to be 1.1 billion, but projected to be 1.6 billion (more populous than China) by the middle of this century (see Table 2.4). Mortality is somewhat higher in India than in China, and the birth rate is quite a bit higher than in China. Indian females have a life expectancy at birth of 65 years—below the world average, but a substantial improvement over the life expectancy of less than 27 years that prevailed back in the 1920s (Adlahka and Banister 1995). The infant mortality rate of 55 per 1,000 is higher than the world average, but it is also far lower than it was just a few decades ago. Women are bearing children at a rate of 2.7 each, and most children in India now survive to adulthood. With an annual growth rate of 1.6 percent, the Indian population is increasing by 19 million people each year. Thus, nearly one in four of the 79 million people being added each year to the world's population is from India. The population of the Indian subcontinent is already more populous than mainland China (see Table 2.5), and that does not take into account the millions of people of Indian and Pakistani origin who are living elsewhere in the world.

India's population is culturally diverse, and this is reflected in rather dramatic geographic differences in fertility and rates of population growth within the country. In the southern states of Kerala and Tamil Nadu, fertility had dropped below the replacement level by the mid-1990s and has stayed there since. However, in the four most populous states in the north (Bihar, Madhya Pradesh, Rajasthan, and Uttar Pradesh), where 40 percent of the Indian population lives, the average woman was bearing more than three children, according to the most recent fertility survey (Measure DHS 2010).

At the end of World War II, when India was granted its independence from British rule, the country was divided into predominantly Hindu India and predominantly Muslim Pakistan, with the latter having territory divided between West Pakistan and East Pakistan. In 1971, a civil war erupted between the two disconnected Pakistans, and, with the help of India, East Pakistan won the war and became Bangladesh. Although Pakistan and Bangladesh are both Muslim, Bangladesh has a demographic profile that now looks more like India than Pakistan. The average woman in Bangladesh now gives birth to 2.5 children (slightly lower than India), whereas fertility in Pakistan has remained much higher (currently 4.0 children per woman). The overall rate of population growth in Bangladesh is 1.6 percent per year (exactly the same as India's), but it is 2.3 percent per year in Pakistan. Still, both Pakistan and Bangladesh have grown so much since independence in 1947 that, were they still one country, they would be the third most populous nation in the world, and would, of course, surpass Indonesia as the world's most populous Muslim nation.

Indonesia Indonesia is a string of islands in Southeast Asia and remains the world's most populous Muslim nation, with an estimated 243 million people. A former Dutch colony, it has experienced a substantial decline in fertility in recent years, and Indonesian women now bear an average of 2.5 children each—the same as Bangladesh, and one of the lower levels of fertility among Muslim nations outside of southern Europe (where predominantly Muslim Albania and Bosnia-Herzogovina have fertility levels that are below replacement level). Life expectancy for women in Indonesia at birth is 73 years (a bit above the world average). For several decades, Indonesia has dealt with population growth through a program of transmigration, in which people have been sent from the more populous to the less populous islands. These largely forested outer islands have suffered environmentally from the human encroachment, without necessarily dealing successfully with Indonesia's basic dilemma, which is how to raise its burgeoning young adult population out of poverty. This dilemma has contributed to increased political instability, as well as a rise in the level of Islamic fundamentalism and terrorism.

Oceania

Oceania is home to a wide range of indigenous populations, including Melanesian and Polynesian, but European influence has been very strong, and the region is generally thought of as being "overseas European." Its population of 36 million is about the same number as Canada's, less than one percent of the world's total. Australia accounts for two-thirds of the region's population, followed by Papua New Guinea and New Zealand. In a pattern repeated elsewhere in the world, the lowest birth rates and lowest death rates (and thus the lowest rates of population growth) are found in countries whose populations are largely European-origin (Australia and New Zealand, in this case), whereas the countries with a higher fraction of the population that is of indigenous origin have higher birth rates, higher mortality, and substantially higher rates of population growth (exemplified in Oceania by Papua New Guinea). Much of Australia's population growth is fueled by immigration, especially from Asia, and this is leading to a situation not unlike that in the United States, where an increasingly older European-origin population is supported by a younger generation of children of immigrants (Commonwealth of Australia 2010).

Global Demographic Contrasts

This whirlwind global tour should have put you in mind of the tremendous demographic contrasts that exist in the modern world. In the less developed nations, the population continues to grow quickly, especially in absolute terms. In sub-Saharan Africa this is happening even in the face of the HIV/AIDS pandemic. Yet, in the more developed countries population growth has slowed, stopped, or in some places even started to decline. As we look around the world, we see that the more rapidly growing countries tend to have high proportions of people who are young, poor, prone to disease, and susceptible to political instability. The countries that are growing slowly or not at all tend to have populations that are older, richer, and healthier, and these are the nations that are politically more stable and are calling the shots in the world right now. I do not want you to become a demographic determinist, because the world is more complicated than that, but keep in mind that there is almost certainly something to the idea that "demography is destiny"—a country cannot readily escape the demographic changes put into motion by the universally sought-after decline in mortality. Each country has to learn how to read its own demographic situation, and cope as well as it can with the inevitable changes that will take place as it evolves through all phases of the demographic transition.

Summary and Conclusion

High death rates kept the number of people in the world from growing rapidly until approximately the time of the Industrial Revolution. Then improved living conditions, public health measures, and, more recently, medical advances dramatically accelerated the pace of growth. As populations have grown, the pressure or desire to migrate has also increased. The vast European expansion into less developed areas of the world, which began in the fifteenth and sixteenth centuries, is a notable illustration of massive migration and population redistribution. Today migration patterns have shifted, and people are mainly moving from less developed to more developed nations. Closely associated with migration and population density is the urban revolution—that is, the movement from rural to urban areas.

The current world situation finds China and India as the most populous countries, followed by the United States, Indonesia, and Brazil. Everywhere population is growing we find that death rates have declined more rapidly than have birth rates, but there is considerable global and regional variability in both the birth and death rates and thus in the rate of population growth. Dealing with the pressure of an expanding young population is the task of developing countries, whereas more developed countries, along with China, have aging populations and are coping with the fact that the demand for labor in their economies may have to be met by immigrants from more rapidly growing countries.

Demographic dynamics represent the leading edge of social change in the modern world. It is a world of nearly 7 billion people, heading to 9 billion by the middle of this century and perhaps more beyond that, even assuming that there is no backsliding in the fertility declines currently under way in many less developed nations. In order to cope with the demographic underpinnings of our lives, we need to have a demographic perspective that allows us to sort out the causes and consequences of population change. We turn to that in the next chapter.

Main Points

1. During the first 90 percent of human existence, the population of the world had grown only to the size of today's New York City.
2. Between 1750 and 1950, the world's population mushroomed from 800 million to 2.5 billion, and since 1950 it has expanded to nearly 7 billion.
3. Doubling time is a convenient way to summarize the rate of population growth. It is calculated by dividing the average annual rate of population growth into 69.
4. Early population growth was slow not because birth rates were low but because death rates were high; on the other hand, continuing population

increases are due to dramatic declines in mortality without a matching decline in fertility.

5. World population growth has been accompanied by migration from rapidly growing areas into less rapidly growing regions. Initially, that meant an outward expansion of the European population, but more recently it has meant migration from less developed to more developed nations.
6. Migration has also involved the shift of people from rural to urban areas, and urban regions on average are currently growing more rapidly than ever before in history.
7. Although migration is crucial to the demographic history of the United States and Canada, both countries have grown largely as a result of natural increase—the excess of births over deaths—after the migrants arrived.
8. At the time of the American Revolution, fertility levels in North America were among the highest in the world. Now they are low, although not as low as in Europe.
9. The world's 10 most populous countries are the People's Republic of China, India, the United States, Indonesia, Brazil, Pakistan, Bangladesh, Nigeria, Russia, and Japan. Together they account for 59 percent of the world's population.
10. Almost all of the population growth in the world today is occurring in the less developed nations, leading to an increase in the global demographic contrasts among countries.

Questions for Review

1. Describe what you think might be the typical day in the life of a person living in a world where death rates and birth rates are both very high. How might those demographic imperatives influence everyday life?
2. The media in the United States and Europe regularly have stories about the impending decline of population in the world. If you were asked to be on a TV talk show commenting on such a story, how would you respond?
3. Migration of people into other countries is a major part of the demography of the modern world. How do you think the world of 2050 will look demographically as a consequence of the trends currently in place?
4. Even without migration, the world will look very different in 2050 than it did in 1950. Analyze Table 2.4 in terms of the idea that "the past is a foreign country."
5. How would you explain the regional patterns that are very observable with respect to global demography? European countries are more like each other than they are like Asian countries, which are more alike than they are like African countries. Are national boundaries therefore meaningless when it comes to population trends?

Suggested Readings

1. Massimo Livi-Bacci, 2001, *A Concise History of World Population*, Third Edition (Malden, MA: Blackwell Publishers).

   This is a very thoughtful and well-documented account of population growth from ancient to modern times.

2. Jared Diamond, 1997, *Guns, Germs, and Steel* (New York: W. W. Norton).

Diamond is a physiologist and geographer who has explored the ways in which disease and technology have aided the process by which the human population has evolved in the modern world.

3. K. Bruce Newbold, 2006, *Six Billion Plus: Population Issues in the Twenty-First Century*, Second Edition (Lanham, MD: Rowman & Littlefield).

As implied by the title, the focus of the book is on the consequences for the world of the momentum of population growth carried over into the twenty-first century.

4. *The Economist*, 2002, "Special Report: Demography and the West," *The Economist*, August 24th.

An impressively concise summary of the different demographic paths that the United States and Europe are taking. The U.S. has buffered its falling fertility rates with high levels of immigration, whereas Europe has not yet embraced that demographic solution.

5. George J. Demko, Grigory Ioffe, and Zhanna Zayonchkovskaya, eds., 1999, *Population Under Duress: The Geodemography of Post-Soviet Russia* (Boulder, CO: Westview Press).

The collapse of the Soviet Union had distinct demographic roots, as well as a fascinating set of consequences that provide important lessons about the linkage of demographic and social change. The authors of this volume explore these themes in depth.

Websites of Interest

Remember that websites are not as permanent as books and journals, so I cannot guarantee that each of the following websites still exists at the moment you are reading this. You may have to Google the name of the organization to find the current web address.

1. **http://www.pbs.org/wgbh/nova/worldbalance/**
   NOVA produced a television program (and DVD) in 2006 called "World in the Balance" that explored the relationship between population growth and environmental issues around the world. They also created a website with several interesting interactive features, including "Human Numbers Through Time," "Global Trends Quiz," and "Be a Demographer."
2. **http://www.censusindia.net**
   You don't have to take anybody else's word for what's happening demographically in India. This Indian census website is in English and has lots of data for the country and its regions.
3. **http://www.cpdrc.org.cn/en-cpdrc/en-home.htm**
   There is a great deal of useful and regularly updated information on China at this website hosted by the China Population and Development Research Center in Beijing. Other useful demographic information about China is available at the University of Michigan's China Data Center (**http://chinadatacenter.org**).
4. **http://sedac.ciesin.columbia.edu/plue/gpw**
   The Gridded Population of the World is a database created from censuses, surveys, satellite imagery, and other sources, producing a very realistic picture of population density and other characteristics at the global level. Regional maps and data are also available at this website.
5. **http://www.ornl.gov/sci/landscan/**
   LandScan is another globally gridded set of population data, designed at the Oak Ridge National Laboratory for the U.S. government as a way of evaluating the population anywhere in the world at risk of potential disasters.

CHAPTER 3
Demographic Perspectives

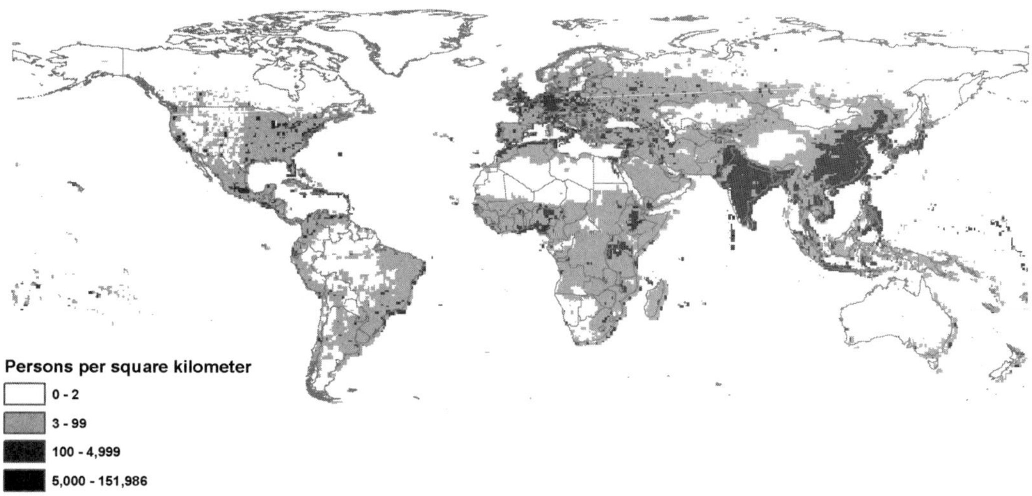

Figure 3.1 Population Density of the World
Source: Adapted by the author from the Gridded Population of the World, Columbia University, http//www.ciesin.columbia.edu, accessed 2006.

To get a handle on population problems and issues, you have to put the facts of population together with the "whys" and "wherefores." In other words, you need a **demographic perspective**—a way of relating basic information to theories about how the world operates demographically. A demographic perspective will guide you through the sometimes tangled relationships between population factors (such as size, distribution, age structure, and growth) and the rest of what is going on in society. As you develop your demographic perspective, you will acquire a new awareness about your own community, as well as about national and world political, economic, and social issues. You will be able to ask yourself about the influences that demographic changes have had (or might have had), and you will consider the demographic consequences of events, which historically have been huge and transformative.

In this chapter, I discuss several theories of how population processes are entwined with general social processes. There are actually two levels of population theory. At the core of demographic analysis is the technical side of the field—the mathematical and biomedical theories that predict the kinds of changes taking place in the more biological components of demography: fertility, mortality, and the distribution of a population by age and sex. Demography, for example, has played a central role in the development of the fields of probability, statistics, and sampling (Kreager 1993). This hard core is crucial to our understanding of human populations, but there is a "softer" (although no less important) outer wrapping of theory that relates demographic processes to the real events of the social world (Schofield and Coleman 1986). The linkage of the core with its outer wrapping is what produces a demographic perspective.

Two questions have to be answered before you will be able to develop your own perspective: (1) What are the causes of population growth (or, at least, population change)? and (2) What are the consequences of population growth or change? In this chapter, I discuss several perspectives that provide broad answers to these questions and that also introduce the major lines of demographic theory. The purpose of this review is to give you a start in developing your own demographic perspective by taking advantage of what others have learned and passed on to us.

I begin this chapter with a brief review of premodern thinking on the subject of population. Most of these ideas are what we call **doctrine**, as opposed to **theory**. Early thinkers were certain they had the answers and certain that their proclamations represented the truth about population growth and its implications for society. By contrast, the essence of modern scientific thought is to assume that you do not have the answer and to acknowledge that you are willing to consider evidence regardless of the conclusion to which it points. In the process of sorting out the evidence, we develop tentative explanations (hypotheses and then theories) that help guide our thinking and our search for understanding. In demography, as in all of the sciences, theories replace doctrine when new, systematically collected information (censuses and other sources discussed in the next chapter) becomes available, allowing people to question old ideas and formulate new ones (see, for example, Hirschman 1999). Table 3.1 summarizes the doctrines and theories discussed in the chapter.

Table 3.1 Demographic Perspectives over Time

	Date	Demographic Perspective
Examples of Premodern Doctrines	~1300 B.C.	Book of Genesis—"Be fruitful and multiply."
	~500 B.C.	Confucius—Population growth is good, but governments should maintain a balance between population and resources.
	360 B.C.	Plato—Population quality more important than quantity; emphasis on population stability.
	340 B.C.	Aristotle—Population size should be limited and the use of abortion might be appropriate.
	~50 B.C.	Cicero—Population growth necessary to maintain Roman influence
	A.D. 400	St. Augustine—Abstinence is the preferred way to deal with human sexuality; the second best is to marry and procreate.
	A.D. 1280	St. Thomas Aquinas—Celibacy is *not* better than marriage and procreation.
	A.D. 1380	Ibn Khaldun—Population growth is inherently good because it increases occupational specialization and raises incomes.
	1500–1800	Mercantilism—Increasing national wealth depends on a growing population that can stimulate export trade
	1700–1800	Physiocrats—Wealth of a nation is in land, not people, therefore population size depends on the wealth of the land, which is stimulated by free trade (laissez-faire).
Modern Theories	1798	Malthus—Population grows exponentially while food supply grows arithmetically, with misery (poverty) being the result in the absence of moral restraint
	~1800	Neo-Malthusian—Accepting the basic Malthusian premise that population growth tends to outstrip resources, but unlike Malthus believing that birth control measures are appropriate checks to population growth.

(continued)

Table 3.1 (continued)

Date	Demographic Perspective
~1844	Marxian—Each society at each point in history has its own law of population that determines the consequences of population growth; poverty is not the natural result of population growth.
1945	Demographic transition in its original formulation—The process whereby a country moves from high birth and death rates to low birth and death rates with an interstitial spurt in population growth. Explanations based originally on modernization theory.
1962	Earliest studies suggesting the need to reformulate the demographic transition theory.
1963	Theory of demographic change and response—Demographic response made by individuals to population pressures is determined by the means available to them to respond; causes and consequences of population change are intertwined.
1968	Easterlin relative cohort size hypothesis—Successively larger young cohorts put pressure on young men's relative wages, forcing them to make a tradeoff between family size and overall well-being.
1971–present	Decomposition of the demographic transition into its separate transitions—Health and mortality, fertility, age, migration, urbanization, and family and household.

Premodern Population Doctrines

Until about 2,500 years ago, human societies probably shared a common concern about population: They valued reproduction as a means of replacing people lost through universally high mortality. Ancient Judaism, for example, provided the prescription to "be fruitful and multiply" (Genesis 1:28). Indeed, reproductive power was often deified, as in ancient Greece, where it was the job of a variety of goddesses to help mortals successfully bring children into the world and raise those children to adulthood. In two of the more developed areas of the world 2,500 years ago, however, awareness of the potential for populations to grow beyond their resources prompted comment by well-known philosophers. In the fifth century B.C., the writings of the school of Confucius in China discussed the relationship between population and resources (Sauvy 1969), and it was suggested that the government should move people from overpopulated to underpopulated areas (an idea embraced in the twentieth century by the Indonesian government). Nonetheless, the idea of promoting population growth was clear in the doctrine of Confucius (Keyfitz 1973).

Plato, writing in *The Laws* in 360 B.C., emphasized the importance of population stability rather than growth. Specifically, Plato proposed keeping the ideal community of free citizens (as differentiated from indentured laborers or slaves who had few civil rights) at a constant 5,040. Charbit (2002:216) suggests that "what inspired Plato in his choice of 5,040 is above all the fact that it is divisible by twelve, a number with a decisive sacred dimension," a legacy carried on in the 12 months of the year, among dozens (pun intended) of other aspects of modern life. Nonetheless, the number of people desired by Plato was still moderately small, because Plato felt that too many people led to anonymity, which would undermine democracy, whereas too few people would prevent an adequate division of labor and would not allow a community to be properly defended. Population size would be controlled by late marriage, infanticide, and migration (in or out as the situation demanded) (Plato 360BC [1960]). Plato was an early proponent of the doctrine that quality in humans is more important than quantity.

Plato's most famous student, Aristotle, was especially concerned that the population of a city-state not grow beyond the means of families to support themselves. In *The Politics*, written in 340 B.C., he advocated that the number of children be limited by law, and that if a woman became pregnant after already having all the children that the law allowed, an abortion would be appropriate (Stangeland 1904). This is a reminder of how ubiquitous abortion has been in human society, and echoes of this idea are found today in the one-child policy in China (which I discuss in Chapter 6).

In the Roman empire, the reigns of Julius and Augustus Caesar were marked by clearly **pronatalist** doctrines—a necessity, given the very high mortality that characterized the Roman era (Frier 1999). In approximately 50 B.C., Cicero noted that population growth was seen by the leaders of Rome as a necessary means of replacing war casualties and of ensuring enough people to help colonize new lands. Several scholars have speculated, however, that by the second century A.D., as the old, pagan Roman empire was waning in power, the birth rate in Rome may have been declining (Stangeland 1904; Veyne 1987). In a thoroughly modern sentiment, Pliny ("the younger") complained that ". . . in our time most people hold that an only son is already a heavy burden and that it is advantageous not to be overburdened with posterity" (quoted in Veyne 1987:13).

The Middle Ages in Europe, which followed the decline of Rome and its transformation from a pagan to a Christian society, were characterized by a combination of both pronatalist and **antinatalist** Christian doctrines. Christianity condemned polygamy, divorce, abortion, and infanticide—practices that had kept earlier Roman growth rates lower than they otherwise might have been. But the writings of Paul in the New Testament led the influential Christian leader, mystic, and writer Augustine (A.D. 354–430) to argue that virgins were the highest form of human existence. Human sexuality was, in his view, a supernaturally good thing but also an important cause of sin (because most people are unable or unwilling to control their desires) (O'Donnell 2006). He believed that abstinence was the best way to deal with sexuality, but the second-best state was marriage, which existed for the purpose of procreation. His Christian philosophy held that the world has a beginning, a middle, and an end, the end being eternal life in the city (by which he meant "community") of God. Thus, his doctrine of otherworldliness held that if all men would abstain from intercourse, then "so much more speedily would the City of God be fulfilled and the end of the world hastened" (quoted in Keyfitz 1972:43). This was an economically stagnant, fatalistic period of European history, and for centuries Europeans were content with the idea that population was a matter best regulated by God.

Intellectual stagnation in Europe was countered by the flowering of Islamic scholarship in the Middle East and North Africa. By the fourteenth century, one of the great Arab historians and philosophers, Ibn Khaldun, was in Tunis writing about the benefits of a growing population. In particular, he argued that population growth creates the need for specialization of occupations, which in turn leads to higher incomes, concentrated especially in cities: "Thus, the inhabitants of a more populous city are more prosperous than their counterparts in a less populous one. . . . The fundamental cause of this is the difference in the nature of the occupations carried on in the different places. For each town is a market for different kinds of labour, and each market absorbs a total expenditure proportionate to its size" (quoted in Issawi 1987:93). Ibn Khaldun was not a utopian. His philosophy was that societies evolved and were transformed as part of natural and normal processes. One of these processes was that "procreation is stimulated by high hopes and resulting heightening of animal energies" (quoted in Issawi 1987:268).

While Europe muddled through the Middle Ages, Islam (which had emerged in the seventh century A.D.) was expanding throughout the Mediterranean. Muslims took control of southern Italy and the Iberian peninsula and, under the Ottoman empire, controlled the Balkans and the rest of southeastern Europe. Europe's reaction to this situation was the Crusades, a series of wars launched by Christians to wrestle control away from Muslims. These expeditions were largely unsuccessful from a military perspective, but they did put Europeans into contact with the Muslim world, which ultimately led to the Renaissance—the rebirth of Europe:

> The Islamic contribution to Europe is enormous, both of its own creations and of its borrowings—reworked and adapted—from the ancient civilizations of the eastern Mediterranean and from the remoter cultures of Asia. Greek science and philosophy, preserved and improved by the Muslims but forgotten in Europe; Indian numbers and Chinese paper; oranges and lemons, cotton and sugar, and a whole series of other plants along with the methods of cultivating them—all these are but a few of the many things that medieval Europe learned or acquired from the vastly more advanced and more sophisticated civilization of the Mediterranean Islamic world (Lewis 1995:274).

The cultural reawakening of Europe took place in the context of a growing population, as I noted in the previous chapter. Not surprisingly, then, new murmurings were heard about the place of population growth in the human scheme of things. The Renaissance began with the Venetians, who had established trade with Muslims and others as the eastern Mediterranean ceased to be a Crusade war zone in the thirteenth century. In that century, an influential Dominican monk, Thomas Aquinas, argued that marriage and family building were not inferior to celibacy, thus implicitly promoting the idea that population growth is an inherently good thing.

By the end of the fourteenth century, the plague had receded from Europe; by the sixteenth century, Muslims (and Jews) had been expelled from southern Spain, and Europeans had begun their discovery and exploitation of Africa, the Americas, and south Asia. Cities began to grow noticeably, and Giovanni Botero, a sixteenth-century Italian statesman, wrote that "the powers of generation are the same now as one thousand years ago, and, if they had no impediment, the propagation of man would grow without limit and the growth of cities would never stop" (quoted in Hutchinson 1967:111). The seventeenth and eighteenth centuries witnessed an historically unprecedented trade (the so-called **Columbian Exchange**) of food, manufactured goods, people, and disease between the Americas and most of the rest of the world (Crosby 1972), undertaken largely by European merchants, who had the best ships and the deadliest weapons in the world (Cipolla 1965).

This rise in trade, prompted at least in part by population growth, generated the doctrine of **mercantilism** among the new nation-states of Europe. Mercantilism maintained that a nation's wealth was determined by the amount of precious metals it had in its possession, which were acquired by exporting more goods than were imported, with the difference (the profit) being stored in precious metals. The catch here was that a nation had to have things to produce to sell to others, and the idea was that the more workers you had, the more you could produce. Furthermore, if you could populate the new colonies, you would have a ready-made market for your products. Thus population growth was seen as essential to an increase in national revenue, and mercantilist writers sought to encourage it by a number of means, including penalties for non-marriage, encouragements to get married, lessening penalties for illegitimate births, limiting out-migration (except to their own colonies), and promoting immigration of productive laborers. It is important to keep in mind that these doctrines were concerned with the wealth and welfare of a specific country, not all of human society. "The underlying doctrine was, either tacitly or explicitly, that the nation which became the strongest in material goods and in men would survive; the nations which lost in the economic struggle would have their populations reduced by want, or they would be forced to resort to war, in which their chances of success would be small" (Stangeland 1904:183).

Mercantilist doctrines were supported by the emerging demographic analyses of people like John Graunt, William Petty, and Edmund Halley (all English) in the seventeenth century and Johann Peter Süssmilch, an eighteenth-century chaplain in the army of Frederick the Great of Prussia (now Germany). In 1662, John Graunt, a Londoner who is sometimes called the father of demography, analyzed the series of Bills of Mortality in the first known statistical analysis of demographic data (Sutherland 1963). Although he was a haberdasher by trade, Graunt used his spare moments to conduct studies that were truly remarkable for his time. He discovered that for every 100 people born in London, only 16 were still alive at age 36 and only 3 at age 66 (Graunt 1662 [1939]; Dublin, Lotka, and Spiegleman 1949)—suggesting very high levels of mortality. With these data he uncovered the high incidence of infant mortality in London and found, somewhat to the amazement of people at the time, that there were regular patterns of death in different parts of London. Graunt "opened the way both for the later discovery of uniformities in many social or volitional phenomena like marriage, suicide, and crime, and for a study of these uniformities, their nature and their limits; thus he, more than any other man, was the founder of statistics" (Willcox 1936:xiii). Indeed, Harrison and Carroll (2005) note that Graunt's studies are thought by many people to mark the beginning of social science as we know it today.

One of Graunt's close friends (and probably the person who coaxed him into this work) was William Petty, a member of the Royal Society in London (Kreager 1988). Petty circulated Graunt's work to the Society (which would not have otherwise paid much attention to a "tradesman"), and this brought it to the attention of the scientific world of seventeenth-century Europe. Several years later, in 1693, Edmund Halley (of Halley's comet fame) became the first scientist to elaborate on the probabilities of death. Although Halley, like Graunt, was a Londoner, he came across a list of births and deaths kept for the city of Breslau in Silesia (now Poland). From these data, Halley used the life-table technique (discussed in Chapter 5) to determine that the expectation of life in Breslau between 1687 and 1691 was 33.5 years (Dublin et al. 1949).

Then, in the eighteenth century, Süssmilch built on the work of Graunt and others and added his own analyses to the observation of the regular patterns of marriage, birth, and death in Prussia and believed that he saw in these the divine hand of God ruling human society (Hecht 1987; Keyfitz 1973). His view, widely disseminated throughout Europe, was that a larger population was always better than a smaller one, and, in direct contradistinction to Plato, he valued quantity over quality. He believed that indefinite improvements in agriculture and industry would postpone overpopulation so far into the future that it wouldn't matter.

The issue of population growth was more than idle speculation, because we know with a fair amount of certainty that the population of England, for example, doubled during the eighteenth century (Petersen 1979), and as I discussed in the previous chapter, Europe as a whole was increasing in population. The increasing interest in population encouraged the publication of two important essays on population size, one by David Hume (Hume 1752 [1963]) and the other by Robert Wallace (Wallace 1761 [1969]), which were then to influence Malthus, whom I discuss later.

These essays sparked considerable debate and controversy, because there were big issues at stake: "Was a large and rapidly growing population a sure sign of a society's good health? On balance, were the growth of industry and cities, the movement of larger numbers from one social class to another—in short, all of what we now term 'modernization'—a boon to the people or the contrary? And in society's efforts to resolve such dilemmas, could it depend on the sum of individuals' self-interest or was considerable state control called for?" (Petersen 1979:139). These are questions we are still dealing with 250 years later.

The population had, in fact, increased during the Mercantilist era, although probably not as a result of any of the policies put forth by its adherents. However, it was less obvious that the population was better off. Rather, the Mercantilist period had become associated with a rising level of poverty (Keyfitz 1972). Mercantilism relied on a state-sponsored system of promoting foreign trade, while inhibiting imports and thus competition. This generated wealth for a small elite but not for most people. One of the more famous reactions against mercantilism was that mounted in the middle of the eighteenth century by François Quesnay, a physician in the court of King Louis XV of France (and an economist when not "on duty"). Whereas mercantilists argued that wealth depends on the number of people, Quesnay turned that around and argued that the number of people depends on the means of subsistence (a general term for level of living). The essence of this view, called **physiocratic** thought, was that land, not people, is the real source of wealth of a nation. In other words, population went from being an independent variable, causing change in society, to a dependent variable, being altered by societal change. As you will see throughout this book, both perspectives have their merits.

Physiocrats also believed that free trade (rather than the import restrictions demanded by mercantilists) was essential to economic prosperity. This concept of "laissez-faire" (let people do as they choose) was picked up by Adam Smith, one of the first modern economic theorists. Central to Smith's view of the world was the idea that, if left to their own devices, people acting in their own self-interest would produce what was best for the community as a whole. Smith differed slightly from the physiocrats, however, on the idea of what led to wealth in a society. Smith believed that wealth sprang from the labor applied to the land (we might now say the "value added" to the land by labor), rather than it being just in the land itself. From this idea sprang the belief that there is a natural harmony between economic growth and population growth, with the latter depending always on the former. Thus, Smith felt that population size is determined by the demand for labor, which is, in turn, determined by the productivity of the land. These ideas are important to us because Smith's work served as an inspiration for the Malthusian theory of population, as Malthus himself acknowledges (see the preface to the sixth edition of Malthus 1872) and as I discuss later.

The Prelude to Malthus

The eighteenth century was the Age of Enlightenment in Europe, a time when the goodness of the common person was championed. This perspective, that the rights of individuals superseded the demands of a monarchy, inspired the American and French Revolutions and was generally very optimistic and utopian, characterized by a great deal of enthusiasm for life and a belief in the perfectibility of humans. It ushered in an era of critically questioning traditional ideas and authority that is still reverberating around the world (Norris and Inglehart 2004). In France, these ideas were well-expressed by Marie Jean Antoine Nicolas de Caritat, marquis de Condorcet, a member of the French aristocracy who forsook a military career to pursue a life devoted to mathematics and philosophy. His ideas helped to shape the French Revolution, although despite his inspiration for and sympathy with that cause, he died in prison at the hands of revolutionaries. In hiding before his arrest, Condorcet wrote a *Sketch for an Historical Picture of the Progress of the Human Mind* (Condorcet 1795 [1955]). He was a visionary who "saw the outlines of liberal democracy more than a century in advance of his time: universal education; universal suffrage; equality before the law; freedom of thought and expression; the right to freedom and self-determination of colonial peoples; the redistribution of wealth; a system of national insurance and pensions; equal rights for women" (Hampshire 1955:x).

Condorcet's optimism was based on his belief that technological progress has no limits. "With all this progress in industry and welfare which establishes a happier proportion between men's talents and their needs, each successive generation will have larger possessions, either as a result of this progress or through the preservation of the products of industry, and so, *as a consequence of the physical constitution of the human race, the number of people will increase*" (Condorcet 1795 [1955]:188; emphasis added). He then asked whether it might not happen that eventually the happiness of the population would reach a limit. If that happens, Condorcet concluded, "we can assume that by then men will know that . . . their aim should be to promote the general welfare of the human race or of the society in which they live or of the family to which they belong, rather than foolishly to encumber the world with useless and wretched beings" (p. 189). Condorcet thus saw prosperity and population growth increasing hand in hand, and if the limits to growth were ever reached, the final solution would be birth control.

On the other side of the English Channel, similar ideas were being expressed by William Godwin (father of Mary Wollstonecraft Shelley, author of *Frankenstein*, and father-in-law of the poet Percy Bysshe Shelley). Godwin's *Enquiry Concerning Political Justice and Its Influences on Morals and Happiness* appeared in its first edition in 1793, revealing his ideas that scientific progress would enable the food supply to grow far beyond the levels of his day, and that such prosperity would not lead to overpopulation because people would deliberately limit their sexual expression and procreation. Furthermore, he believed that most of the problems of the poor were due not to overpopulation but to the inequities of the **social institutions**, especially greed and accumulation of property (Godwin 1793 [1946]).

Thomas Robert Malthus had recently graduated from Cambridge and was a country curate and a nonresident fellow of Cambridge as he read and contemplated the works of Godwin, Condorcet, and others who shared the utopian view of the perfectibility of human society. Although he wanted to be able to embrace such an openly optimistic philosophy of life, he felt that intellectually he had to reject it. In doing so, he unleashed a controversy about population growth and its consequences that rages to this very day.

The Malthusian Perspective

The **Malthusian** perspective derives from the writings of Thomas Robert Malthus, an English clergyman and college professor. His first *Essay on the Principle of Population as it affects the future improvement of society; with remarks on the speculations of Mr. Godwin, M. Condorcet, and other writers* was published anonymously in 1798. Malthus's original intention was not to carve out a career in demography, but only to show that the unbounded optimism of the physiocrats and philosophers was misplaced. He introduced his essay by commenting that "I have read some of the speculations on the perfectibility of man and society, with great pleasure. I have been warmed and delighted with the enchanting picture which they hold forth. I ardently wish for such happy improvements. But I see great, and, to my understanding, unconquerable difficulties in the way to them" (Malthus 1798 [1965]:7).

These "difficulties," of course, are the problems posed by his now famous **principle of population**. He derived his theory as follows:

> I think I may fairly make two postulata. First, that food is necessary to the existence of man. Secondly, that the passion between the sexes is necessary, and will remain nearly in its present state. . . . Assuming then, my postulata as granted, I say, that the power of population is indefinitely greater than the power in the earth to produce subsistence for man. Population, when unchecked, increases in a geometrical ratio. Subsistence increases only in an arithmetical ratio. . . . By the law of our nature which makes food necessary to the life of man, the effects of these two unequal powers must be kept equal. This implies a strong and constantly operating check on population from the difficulty of subsistence.
>
> This difficulty must fall somewhere; and must necessarily be severely felt by a large portion of mankind. . . . Consequently, if the premises are just, the argument is conclusive against the perfectibility of the mass of mankind. (Malthus 1798 [1965]:11)

Malthus believed that he had demolished the utopian optimism by suggesting that the laws of nature, operating through the principle of population, essentially prescribed poverty for a certain segment of humanity. Malthus was a shy person by nature (James 1979; Petersen 1979), and he seemed ill prepared for the notoriety created by his essay. Nonetheless, after owning up to its authorship, he proceeded to document his population principles and to respond to critics by publishing a substantially revised version in 1803, slightly but importantly retitled to read *An Essay on the Principle of Population; or a view of its past and present effects on human happiness; with an inquiry into our prospects respecting the future removal or mitigation of the evils which It occasions*. In all, seven editions of Malthus's essay on population were published, and as a whole they have undoubtedly been the single most influential work relating population growth to its social consequences. Although Malthus relied heavily on earlier writers such as Hume and Wallace, he was the first to draw a picture that links the consequences of growth to its causes in a systematic way.

Causes of Population Growth

Malthus believed that human beings, like plants and nonrational animals, are "impelled" to increase the population of the species by what he called a powerful "instinct," the urge to reproduce. Further, if there were no checks on population growth, human beings would multiply to an "incalculable" number, filling "millions of worlds in a few thousand years" (Malthus 1872 [1971]:6). We humans, though, have not accomplished anything nearly so impressive. Why not? Because of the **checks to growth** that Malthus pointed out—factors that have kept population growth from reaching its biological potential for covering the earth with human bodies.

According to Malthus, the ultimate check to growth is lack of food (the **"means of subsistence"**). In turn, the means of subsistence are limited by the amount of land available, the "arts" or technology that could be applied to the land, and "social

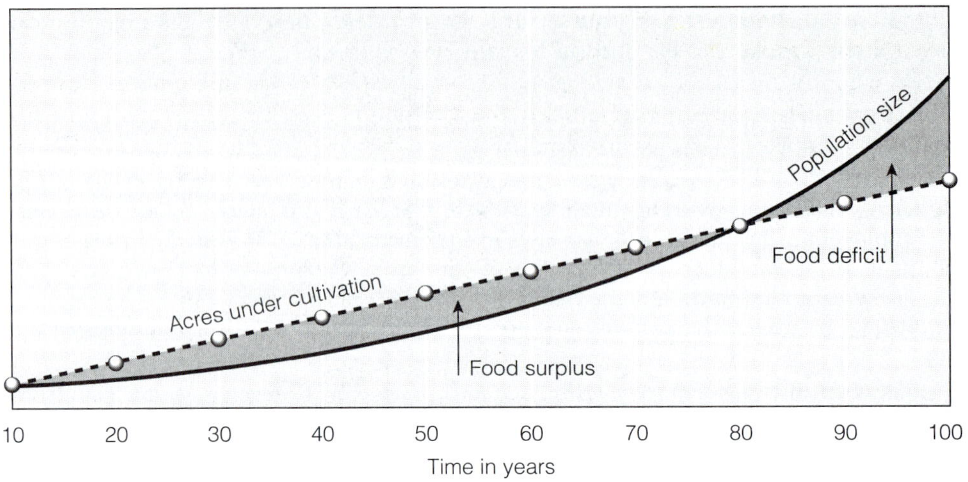

Figure 3.2 Over Time, Geometric Growth Overtakes Arithmetic Growth

Note: If we start with 100 acres supporting a population of 100 people and then add 100 acres of cultivated land per decade (arithmetic growth) while the population is increasing by 3 percent per year (geometric growth), the result is a few decades of food surplus before population growth overtakes the increase in the acres under cultivation, producing a food deficit, or "misery," as Malthus called it.

organization" or land ownership patterns. A cornerstone of his argument is that populations tend to grow more rapidly than the food supply does (a topic I return to in Chapter 11), since population has the potential for growing geometrically—two parents could have four children, sixteen grandchildren, and so on—while he believed (incorrectly, as Darwin later pointed out) that food production could be increased only arithmetically, by adding one acre at a time. He argued, then, that in the natural order, population growth will outstrip the food supply, and the lack of food will ultimately put a stop to the increase of people (see Figure 3.2).

Of course, Malthus was aware that starvation rarely operates directly to kill people, since something else usually intervenes to kill them before they actually die of starvation. This "something else" represents what Malthus calls **positive checks**, primarily those measures "whether of a moral or physical nature, which tend prematurely to weaken and destroy the human frame" (Malthus 1872 [1971]:12). Today we would call these the causes of death. There are also **preventive checks**—limits to birth. In theory, the preventive checks would include all possible means of birth control, including abstinence, contraception, and abortion. However, to Malthus the only acceptable means of preventing a birth was to exercise **moral restraint**; that is, to postpone marriage, remaining chaste in the meantime, until a man feels "secure that, should he have a large family, his utmost exertions can save them from rags and squalid poverty, and their consequent degradation in the community" (1872 [1971]:13). Any other means of birth control, including contraception (either before or after marriage), abortion, infanticide, or any "improper means," was viewed as a vice that would "lower, in a marked manner, the dignity of human nature." Moral restraint was a very important point with Malthus, because he believed that if people were allowed to prevent births by "improper means" (that is, prostitution, contraception, abortion, or sterilization), then they would expend their energies in ways that are, so to speak, not economically productive.

As a scientific theory, the Malthusian perspective leaves much to be desired, since he was wrong about how quickly the food supply could increase, as I note below, and because he constantly confuses moralistic and scientific thinking (Davis 1955). Despite its shortcomings, however, which were evident even in his time, Malthus's reasoning led him to draw some important conclusions about the consequences of population growth that are still relevant to us.

Consequences of Population Growth

Malthus believed that a natural consequence of population growth was poverty. This is the logical end result of his arguments that (1) people have a natural urge to reproduce, and (2) the increase in the food supply cannot keep up with population growth. In his analysis, Malthus turned the argument of Adam Smith upside down. Instead of population growth depending on the demand for labor, as Smith (and the physiocrats) argued, Malthus believed that the urge to reproduce always forces population pressure to precede the demand for labor. Thus, "overpopulation" (as measured by the level of unemployment) would force wages down to the point where people could not afford to marry and raise a family. At such low wages, with a surplus of labor and the need for each person to work harder just to earn a subsistence wage, cultivators could employ more labor, put more acres into production, and thus increase the means of subsistence. Malthus believed that this cycle of increased food resources, leading to population growth, leading to too many people for available resources, leading then back to poverty, was part of a natural law of population. Each increase in the food supply only meant that eventually more people could live in poverty.

As you can see, Malthus did not have an altogether high opinion of his fellow creatures. He figured that most of them were too "inert, sluggish, and averse from labor" (1798 [1965]:363) to try to harness the urge to reproduce and avoid the increase in numbers that would lead back to poverty whenever more resources were available. In this way, he essentially blamed poverty on the poor themselves. There remained only one improbable way to avoid this dreary situation.

Avoiding the Consequences

Borrowing from John Locke, Malthus argued that "the endeavor to avoid pain rather than the pursuit of pleasure is the great stimulus to action in life" (1798 [1965]:359). Pleasure will not stimulate activity until its absence is defined as being painful. Malthus suggested that the well-educated, rational person would perceive in advance the pain of having hungry children or being in debt and would postpone marriage and sexual intercourse until he was sure that he could avoid that pain. If that motivation existed and the preventive check was operating, then the miserable consequences of population growth could be avoided. You will recall that Condorcet had suggested the possibility of birth control as a preventive check, but Malthus objected to this solution: "To remove the difficulty in this way, will, surely

WHO ARE THE NEO-MALTHUSIANS?

"Picture a tropical island with luscious breadfruits [a Polynesian plant similar to a fig tree] hanging from every branch, toasting in the sun. It is a small island, but there are only 400 of us on it so there are more breadfruits than we know what to do with. We're rich. Now picture 4,000 people on the same island, reaching for the same breadfruits: Number one, there are fewer to go around; number two, you've got to build ladders to reach most of them; number three, the island is becoming littered with breadfruit crumbs. Things get worse and worse as the population gradually expands to 40,000. Welcome to a poor, littered tropical paradise" (Tobias 1979:49). This scenario would probably have drawn a nod of understanding from Malthus himself, and it is typical of the modern neo-Malthusian view of the world.

One of the most influential neo-Malthusians of the twentieth century was the biologist Garrett Hardin. In 1968, he published an article that raised the level of consciousness about population growth in the minds of professional scientists. Hardin's theme was simple and had been made by Kingsley Davis (1963) as he developed the theory of demographic change and response: Personal goals are not necessarily consistent with societal goals when it comes to population growth—Adam Smith was not completely correct to believe in laissez-faire. Hardin's metaphor is "the tragedy of the commons." He asks us to imagine an open field, available as a common ground for herdsmen to graze their cattle. "As a rational being, each herdsman seeks to maximize his gain. Explicitly or implicitly, more or less consciously, he asks, 'What is the utility to me of adding one more animal to my herd?'" (Hardin 1968:1244). The benefit, of course, is the net proceeds from the eventual sale of each additional animal, whereas the cost lies in the chance that an additional animal may result in overgrazing of the common ground. Since the ground is shared by many people, the cost is spread out over all, so for the individual herdsman, the benefit of another animal exceeds its cost. "But," notes Hardin, "this is the conclusion reached by each and every rational herdsman sharing a commons. Therein is the tragedy. Each man is locked into a system that compels him to increase his herd without limit—in a world that is limited" (1968:1244). The moral, as Hardin puts it, is that "ruin is the destination toward which all men rush, each pursuing his own best interest in a society that believes in the freedom of the commons. Freedom in a commons brings ruin to all" (1968:1244).

Hardin reminds us that most societies are committed to a social welfare ideal. Families are not completely on their own. We share numerous things in common: education, public health, and police protection, and in all of the richer nations of the world people are guaranteed a minimum amount of food and income at the public expense. This leads to a moral dilemma that is at the heart of Hardin's message: "To couple the concept of freedom to breed with the belief that everyone born has an equal right to the commons is to lock the world into a tragic course of action" (Hardin 1968:1246). He was referring, of course, to the ultimate Malthusian clash of population and resources, and Hardin was no more optimistic than Malthus about the likelihood of people voluntarily limiting their fertility before it is too late.

Meanwhile, in the 1960s the world was becoming keenly aware of the population crisis through the writings of the person who is arguably the most famous of all neo-Malthusians, Paul Ehrlich. Like Hardin, Ehrlich is a biologist (at Stanford University), not a professional demographer. His *Population Bomb* (Ehrlich 1968) was an immediate sensation when it came out in 1968 and to this day often sets the tone for public debate about population issues. In the second edition of his book, Ehrlich (1971) phrased the situation in three parts: "too many people," "too little food," and, adding a wrinkle not foreseen directly by Malthus, "environmental degradation" (Ehrlich called Earth "a dying planet").

In 1990, Ehrlich, in collaboration with his wife, Anne, followed with an update titled *The Population Explosion* (Ehrlich and Ehrlich 1990), reflecting their view that the bomb they worried about in 1968 had detonated in the meantime. The level of concern about the destruction of the environment has grown tremendously since 1968. Ehrlich's book had inspired the first Earth Day in the spring of 1970 (an annual event ever since in most communities across the United States and elsewhere in the world), yet in their 1990 book Ehrlich and Ehrlich rightly question why, in the face of the serious environmental degradation that had concerned them for so long, had people regularly failed to grasp its primary cause as being rapid population growth? "Arresting population growth should be second in importance only to avoiding nuclear war on humanity's agenda. Overpopulation and rapid population growth are intimately connected with most aspects of the current human predicament, including rapid depletion of nonrenewable resources, deterioration of the environment (including rapid climate change), and increasing international tensions" (Ehrlich and Ehrlich 1990:18).

Ehrlich thus argues that Malthus was right—dead right. But the death struggle is more complicated than that foreseen by Malthus. To Ehrlich, the poor are dying of hunger, while rich and poor alike are dying from the by-products of affluence—pollution and ecological disaster. Indeed, this is part of the "commons" problem. A few benefit, all suffer. What does the future hold? Ehrlich suggested that there are only two solutions to the population problem: the birth rate solution (lowering the birth rate) and the death rate solution (a rise in the death rate). He viewed the death rate solution as being the most likely to happen, because, like Malthus, he has had little faith in the ability of humankind to pull its act together. The only way to avoid that scenario, he argued, was to bring the birth rate under control, perhaps even by force. That idea generated death threats against him and his wife, but of course over time the world has responded with lower birth rates.

A major part of Ehrlich's contribution has been to encourage people to take some action themselves, to spread the word and practice what they preach. Ehrlich has long felt that population growth is outstripping resources and ruining the environment. If we sit back and wait for people to react to this situation, disaster will occur. Therefore, we need to act swiftly to push people to bring fertility down to replacement level by whatever means possible.

Neo-Malthusians thus differ from Malthus because they reject moral restraint as the only acceptable means of birth control and because they see population growth as leading not simply to poverty but also to widespread calamity. For neo-Malthusians, the "evil arising from the redundancy of population" (Malthus 1872 [1971]: preface to the fifth edition) has broadened in scope, and the remedies proposed are thus more dramatic.

Gloomy they certainly are, but the messages of Ehrlich and Hardin are important and impressive and have brought population issues to the attention of the entire globe. One of the ironies of neo-Malthusianism is that if the world's population does avoid future calamity, people will likely claim that the neo-Malthusians were wrong. In fact, however, much of the stimulus to bring down birth rates (including emphasis on the reproductive rights of women as the alternative to coercive means) and to find new ways to feed people and protect the environment has come as a reaction to the concerns they very publicly have raised.

Discussion Questions: (1) Discuss the tragedy of the commons in relation to global climate change and to the quality of water throughout the world, and relate that, as you think appropriate, to population growth; **(2)** If Malthus was wrong in his idea that the food supply could not grow as quickly as population, as Darwin seemed to suggest, do you think that the neo-Malthusians are also wrong in their analysis of how the world works? Why or why not?

in the opinion of most men, be to destroy that virtue, and purity of manners, which the advocates of equality, and of the perfectibility of man, profess to be the end and object of their views" (1798:154). So the only way to break the cycle is to change human nature. Malthus felt that if everyone shared middle-class values, the problem would solve itself. He saw that as impossible, though, since not everyone has the talent to be a virtuous, industrious, middle-class success story, but if most people at least tried, poverty would be reduced considerably.

To Malthus, material success is a consequence of the human ability to plan rationally—to be educated about future consequences of current behavior—and he was a man who practiced what he preached. He planned his family rationally, waiting to marry and have children until he was 39, shortly after getting a secure job in 1805 as a professor of history and political economy at East India College in Haileybury, England (north of London). Also, although Marx later thought that Malthus had taken the "monastic vows of celibacy" and other detractors attributed 11 children to him, he and his wife, 11 years his junior, had only three children (Nickerson 1975; Petersen 1979).

To summarize, the major consequence of population growth, according to Malthus, is poverty. Within that poverty, though, is the stimulus for action that can lift people out of misery. So, if people remain poor, it is their own fault for not trying to do something about it. For that reason, Malthus was opposed to the English Poor Laws (welfare benefits for the poor), because he felt they would actually serve to perpetuate misery. They permitted poor people to be supported by others and thus not feel that great pain, the avoidance of which might lead to birth prevention. Malthus argued that if every man had to provide for his own children, he would be more prudent about getting married and raising a family. In his own time, this particular conclusion of Malthus brought him the greatest notoriety, because the number of people on welfare had been increasing and English parliamentarians were trying to decide what to do about the problem. Although the Poor Laws were not abolished, they were reformed largely because Malthus had given legitimacy to public criticism of the entire concept of welfare payments (Himmelfarb 1984). The Malthusian perspective that blamed the poor for their own poverty endures, contrasted with the equally enduring view of Godwin and Condorcet that poverty is the creation of unjust human institutions. Two hundred additional years of debate have only sharpened the edges of the controversy.

Critique of Malthus

The single most obvious measure of Malthus's importance is the number of books and articles that have attacked him, beginning virtually the moment his first essay appeared in 1798 and continuing to the present (see, for example, Ross 1998; Lee and Wang 1999; Huzel 2006). Hodgson (2009) quotes from a letter written by Thomas Jefferson in 1804 discussing the fact that he had just read Malthus's book and that he (Jefferson) was sure the principle of population did not apply to the United States, where the amount of available land meant that population growth could readily be absorbed. But Hodgson also notes that later in the nineteenth century both sides in the debate over ending slavery in the United States called upon Malthusian arguments to bolster their case, even though Malthus himself was vociferously opposed to slavery.

The three most strongly criticized aspects of his theory have been (1) the assertion that food production could not keep up with population growth, (2) the conclusion that poverty was an inevitable result of population growth, and (3) the belief that moral restraint was the only acceptable preventive check. Malthus was not a firm believer in progress; rather, he accepted the notion that each society had a fixed set of institutions that established a stationary level of living. He was aware, of course, of the Industrial Revolution, but he was skeptical of its long-run value and agreed with the physiocrats that real wealth was in agricultural land. He was convinced that the increase in manufacturing wages that accompanied industrialization would promote population growth without increasing the agricultural production necessary to feed those additional mouths. Although it is clear that he was a voracious reader (Petersen 1979) and was a founder of the Statistical Society of London (Starr 1987), it is also clear that Malthus paid scant attention to the economic statistics that were available to him. "There is no sign that even at the end of his life he knew anything in detail about industrialization. His thesis was based on the life of an island agricultural nation, and so it remained long after the exports of manufacturers had begun to pay for the imports of large quantities of raw materials" (Eversley 1959:256). Thus, Malthus either failed to see or refused to acknowledge that technological progress was possible, and that its end result was a higher standard of living, not a lower one.

The crucial part of Malthus's ratio of population growth to food increase was that food (including both plants and nonhuman animals) would not grow exponentially. Yet when Charles Darwin acknowledged that his *Origin of the Species* was inspired by Malthus's essay, he implicitly rejected this central tenet of Malthus's argument. "Darwin described his own theory as 'the doctrine of Malthus applied with manifold force to the whole animal and vegetable kingdoms; for in this case there can be no artificial increase of food, and no prudential restraint from marriage.' Thus plants and animals, even more than men, would increase geometrically if unchecked" (Himmelfarb 1984:128).

Malthus's argument that poverty is an inevitable result of population growth is also open to scrutiny. For one thing, his writing reveals a certain circularity in logic. In Malthus's view, a laborer could achieve a higher standard of living only by being prudent and refraining from marriage until he could afford it, but Malthus also believed that you could not expect prudence from a laborer until he had attained a higher standard of living. Thus, our hypothetical laborer seems squarely enmeshed in a catch-22. Even if we were to ignore this logical inconsistency, there are problems with Malthus's belief that the Poor Laws contributed to the misery of the poor by discouraging them from exercising prudence. Historical evidence has revealed that between 1801 and 1835 those English parishes that administered Poor Law allowances did not have higher birth, marriage, or total population growth rates than those in which Poor Law assistance was not available (Huzel 1969, 1980, 1984). Clearly, problems with the logic of Malthus's argument seem to be compounded by his apparent inability to see the social world accurately. "The results of the 1831 Census were out before he died, yet he never came to interpret them. Statistics apart, the main charge against him must be that he was a bad observer of his fellow human beings" (Eversley 1959:256).

I noted in Chapter 1 that the term "demography" was first used by a French scientist, Achille Guillard, in the middle of the nineteenth century. Schweber (2006) has argued that one of Guillard's motivations in trying to develop a new discipline of demography was to pressure French academics to see that statistical analyses of births and deaths would show that Malthus was wrong about his claim that population growth inevitably led to poverty. Once again, the power of Malthusian thought lies partly in the strength of opposition that he aroused.

Neo-Malthusians

Those who criticize Malthus's insistence on the value of moral restraint, while accepting many of his other conclusions, are typically known as **neo-Malthusians**. Specifically, neo-Malthusians favor contraception rather than simple reliance on moral restraint. During his lifetime, Malthus was constantly defending moral restraint against critics (many of whom were his friends) who encouraged him to deal more favorably with other means of birth control. In the fifth edition of his *Essay*, he did discuss the concept of **prudential restraint**, which meant the delay of marriage until a family could be afforded without necessarily refraining from premarital sexual intercourse in the meantime. He never fully embraced the idea, however, nor did he ever bow to pressure to accept anything but moral restraint as a viable preventive check.

Ironically, the open controversy actually helped to spread knowledge of birth control among people in nineteenth-century England and America. This was aided materially by the trial and conviction (later overturned on a technicality) in 1877–78 of two neo-Malthusians, Charles Bradlaugh and Annie Besant, for publishing a birth control handbook (*Fruits of Philosophy: The Private Companion of Young Married People*, written by Charles Knowlton, a physician in Massachusetts, and originally published in 1832). The publicity surrounding the trial enabled the English public to become more widely knowledgeable about those techniques (Chandrasekhar 1979; Himes 1976). Eventually, the widespread adoption of birth control broke the connection between intercourse and fertility that had seemed so natural to Malthus: "In time fertility behavior came to be better epitomized by inverting the Malthusian assumption than by adhering to it. . . . The supplanting of the social control of fertility *within* marriage completely undermined the validity of the assumption that population growth rates would rise in step with prosperity" (Wrigley 1988:44, emphasis in original).

Criticisms of Malthus do not, however, diminish the importance of his work:

> There are good reasons for using Malthus as a point of departure in the discussion of population theory. These are the reasons that made his work influential in his day and make it influential now. But they have little to do with whether his views are right or wrong. . . . Malthus' theories are not now and never were empirically valid, but they nevertheless were theoretically significant (Davis 1955b:541).

As I noted earlier, part of Malthus's significance lies in the storm of controversy his theories stimulated. Particularly vigorous in their attacks on Malthus were Karl Marx and Friedrich Engels.

The Marxian Perspective

Karl Marx and Friedrich Engels were both teenagers in Germany when Malthus died in England in 1834, and by the time they had met and independently moved to England, Malthus's ideas already were politically influential in their native land, not just in England. Several German states and Austria had responded to what they believed was overly rapid growth in the number of poor people by legislating against marriages in which the applicant could not guarantee that his family would not wind up on welfare (Glass 1953). As it turned out, that scheme backfired on the German states, because people continued to have children, but out of wedlock. Thus, the welfare rolls grew as the illegitimate children had to be cared for by the state (Knodel 1970). The laws were eventually repealed, but they had an impact on Marx and Engels, who saw the Malthusian point of view as an outrage against humanity. Their demographic perspective thus arose in reaction to Malthus.

Causes of Population Growth

Neither Marx nor Engels ever directly addressed the issue of why and how populations grew. They seem to have had little quarrel with Malthus on this point, although they were in favor of equal rights for men and women and saw no harm in preventing birth. Nonetheless, they were skeptical of the eternal or natural laws of nature as stated by Malthus (that population tends to outstrip resources), preferring instead to view human activity as the product of a particular social and economic environment. The basic **Marxian** perspective is that each society at each point in history has its own law of population that determines the consequences of population growth. For **capitalism**, the consequences are overpopulation and poverty, whereas for **socialism**, population growth is readily absorbed by the economy with no side effects. This line of reasoning led to Marx's vehement rejection of Malthus, because if Malthus was right about his "pretended 'natural law of population'" (Marx 1890 [1906]:680), then Marx's theory would be wrong.

Consequences of Population Growth

Marx and Engels especially quarreled with the Malthusian idea that resources could not grow as rapidly as population, since they saw no reason to suspect that science and technology could not increase the availability of food and other goods at least as quickly as the population grew. Engels argued in 1865 that whatever population pressure existed in society was really pressure against the means of employment rather than against the means of subsistence (Meek 1971). Thus, they flatly rejected the notion that poverty can be blamed on the poor. Instead, they said, poverty is the result of a poorly organized society, especially a capitalist society. Implicit in the writings of Marx and Engels is the idea that the normal consequence of population growth should be a significant increase in production. After all, each worker obviously was producing more than he or she required—how else would all the dependents (including the wealthy manufacturers) survive? In a well-ordered society, if there were more people, there ought to be more wealth, not more poverty (Engels 1844 [1953]).

Not only did Marx and Engels feel that poverty, in general, was not the end result of population growth, they argued specifically that even in England at that time there was enough wealth to eliminate poverty. Engels had himself managed a textile plant owned by his father's firm in Manchester, and he believed that in

England more people had meant more wealth for the capitalists rather than for the workers because the capitalists were skimming off some of the workers' wages as profits for themselves. Marx argued that they did that by stripping the workers of their tools and then, in essence, charging the workers for being able to come to the factory to work. For example, if you do not have the tools to make a car but want a job making cars, you could get hired at the factory and work eight hours a day. But, according to Marx, you might get paid for only four hours, the capitalist (owner of the factory) keeping part of your wages as payment for the tools you were using. The more the capitalist keeps, of course, the lower your wages and the poorer you will be.

Furthermore, Marx argued that capitalism worked by using the labor of the working classes to earn profits to buy machines that would replace the laborers, which, in turn, would lead to unemployment and poverty. Thus, the poor were not poor because they overran the food supply, but only because capitalists had first taken away part of their wages and then taken away their very jobs and replaced them with machines. Thus, the consequences of population growth that Malthus discussed were really the consequences of capitalist society, not of population growth per se. Overpopulation in a capitalist society was thought to be a result of the capitalists' desire for an industrial reserve army that would keep wages low through competition for jobs and, at the same time, would force workers to be more productive in order to keep their jobs. To Marx, however, the logical extension of this was that the growing population would bear the seeds of destruction for capitalism, because unemployment would lead to disaffection and revolution. If society could be reorganized in a more equitable (that is, socialist) way, then population problems would disappear.

It is noteworthy that Marx, like Malthus, practiced what he preached. Marx was adamantly opposed to the notion of moral restraint, and his life repudiated that concept. He married at the relatively young age (compared with Malthus) of 25, proceeded to father eight children, including one illegitimate son, and was on intimate terms with poverty for much of his life.

In its original formulation, the Marxian (as well as the Malthusian) perspective was somewhat provincial, in the sense that its primary concern was England in the nineteenth century. Marx was an intense scholar who focused especially on the historical analysis of economics as applied to England, which he considered to be the classic example of capitalism. However, as his writings have found favor in other places and times, revisions have been forced upon the Marxian view of population.

Critique of Marx

Not all who have adopted a Marxian worldview fully share the original Marx–Engels demographic perspective. Socialist countries have had trouble because of the lack of political direction offered by the Marxian notion that different stages of social development produce different relationships between population growth and economic development. Indeed, much of what we call the Marxian thought on population is in fact attributable to Lenin, one of the most prolific interpreters of Marx. For Marx, the Malthusian principle operated under capitalism only, whereas under pure socialism there would be no population problem. Unfortunately, he offered no guidelines for the transition period. At best, Marx implied that the socialist law of population should be the antithesis of the capitalist law. If the birth rate were low under capitalism, then the assumption was that it should be high under socialism; if abortion seemed bad for a capitalist society, it must be good for a socialistic society.

Thus, it was difficult for Russian demographers to reconcile the fact that demographic trends in the former Soviet Union were remarkably similar to trends in other developed nations. Furthermore, Soviet socialism was unable to alleviate one of the worst evils that Marx attributed to capitalism, higher death rates among people in the working class than among those in the higher classes (Brackett 1967). Moreover, birth rates dropped to such low levels throughout pre-1990 Marxist Eastern Europe that it was no longer possible to claim (as Marx had done) that low birth rates were bourgeois.

In China, the empirical reality of having to deal with the world's largest national population led to a radical departure from Marxian ideology. As early as 1953, the Chinese government organized efforts to control population by relaxing regulations concerning contraception and abortion. Ironically, after the terrible demographic disaster that followed the "Great Leap Forward" in 1958 (see Chapter 2), a Chinese official quoted Chairman Mao as having said, "A large population in China is a good thing. With a population increase of several fold we still have an adequate solution. The solution lies in production" (Ta-k'un 1960:704). Yet by 1979 production no longer seemed to be a panacea, and with the introduction of the one-child policy, the interpretation of Marx took an about-face as another Chinese official wrote that under Marxism the law of production "demands not only a planned production of natural goods, but also the planned reproduction of human beings" (Muhua 1979:724).

Thus, despite Marx's denial of a population problem in a socialist society, the Marxist government in China dealt with one by rejecting its Marxist–Leninist roots and embracing instead one of the most aggressive and coercive government programs ever launched to reduce fertility through restraints on marriage (the Malthusian solution), the promotion of contraception (the neo-Malthusian solution), and the use of abortion (a remnant of the Leninist approach) (Teitelbaum and Winter 1988). In a formulation such as this, Marxism was revised in the light of new scientific evidence about how people behave, in the same way that Malthusian thought has been revised. Bear in mind that although the Marxian and Malthusian perspectives are often seen as antithetical, they both originated in the midst of a particular milieu of economic, social, and demographic change in nineteenth-century Europe.

The Prelude to the Demographic Transition Theory

The population-growth controversy, initiated by Malthus and fueled by Marx, emerged into a series of nineteenth-century and early-twentieth-century reformulations that have led directly to prevailing theories in demography. In this section, I briefly discuss three individuals who made important contributions to those reformulations: John Stuart Mill, Arsène Dumont, and Émile Durkheim.

Mill

The English philosopher and economist John Stuart Mill was an extremely influential writer of the nineteenth century. Mill was not as quarrelsome about Malthus as Marx and Engels had been; his scientific insights were greater than those of Malthus at the same time that his politics were less radical than those of Marx and Engels. Mill accepted the Malthusian calculations about the potential for population growth to outstrip food production as being axiomatic (a self-truth), but he was more optimistic about human nature than Malthus was. Mill believed that although your character is formed by circumstances, one's own desires can do much to shape circumstances and modify future habits (Mill 1873 [1924]).

Mill's basic thesis was that the standard of living is a major determinant of fertility levels. "In proportion as mankind rises above the condition of the beast, population is restrained by the fear of want, rather than by want itself. Even where there is no question of starvation, many are similarly acted upon by the apprehension of losing what have come to be regarded as the decencies of their situation in life" (Mill 1848 [1929]:Book I, Chap 10). The belief that people could be and should be free to pursue their own goals in life led him to reject the idea that poverty is inevitable (as Malthus implied) or that it is the creation of capitalist society (as Marx argued). One of Mill's most famous comments is that "the niggardliness of nature, not the injustice of society, is the cause of the penalty attached to overpopulation" (1848 [1929]:Book I, Chap. 13). This is a point of view conditioned by Mill's reading of Malthus, but Mill denies the Malthusian inevitability of a population growing beyond its available resources. Mill believed that people do not "propagate like swine, but are capable, though in very unequal degrees, of being withheld by prudence, or by the social affections, from giving existence to beings born only to misery and premature death" (1848 [1929]: Book I, Chap. 7). In the event that population ever did overrun the food supply, however, Mill felt that it would likely be a temporary situation with at least two possible solutions: import food or export people.

The ideal state from Mill's point of view is that in which all members of a society are economically comfortable. At that point he felt (as Plato had centuries earlier) that the population would stabilize and people would try to progress culturally, morally, and socially instead of attempting continually to get ahead economically. It does sound good, but how do we get to that point? It was Mill's belief that before reaching the point at which both population and production are stable, there is essentially a race between the two. What is required to settle the issue is a dramatic improvement in the living conditions of the poor. If social and economic development is to occur, there must be a sudden increase in income, which could give rise to a new standard of living for a whole generation, thus allowing productivity to outdistance population growth. According to Mill, this was the situation in France after the Revolution:

> During the generation which the Revolution raised from the extremes of hopeless wretchedness to sudden abundance, a great increase of population took place. But a generation has grown up, which, having been born in improved circumstances, has not learnt to be miserable; and upon them the spirit of thrift operates most conspicuously, in keeping the increase of population within the increase of national wealth (1848 [1929]: Book II, Chap. 7).

Mill was convinced that an important ingredient in the transformation to a non-growing population is that women do not want as many children as men do, and if they are allowed to voice their opinions, the birth rate will decline. Mill, like Marx, was a champion of equal rights for both sexes, and one of Mill's more notable essays, *On Liberty*, was co-authored with his wife. He reasoned further that a system of national education for poor children would provide them with the "common sense" (as Mill put it) to refrain from having too many children.

Overall, Mill's perspective on population growth was significant enough that we find his arguments surviving today in the writings of many of the twentieth- and twenty-first-century demographers whose names appear in the pages that follow. However, before getting to those people and their ideas, it is important to acknowledge at least two other nineteenth-century individuals whose thinking has an amazingly modern sound: Arsène Dumont and Émile Durkheim.

Dumont

Arsène Dumont was a late-nineteenth-century French demographer who felt he had discovered a new principle of population that he called "social capillarity" (Dumont 1890). **Social capillarity** refers to the desire of people to rise on the social scale, to increase their individuality as well as their personal wealth. The concept is drawn from an analogy to a liquid rising into the narrow neck of a laboratory flask. The flask is like the hierarchical structure of most societies, broad at the bottom and narrowing as you near the top. To ascend the social hierarchy often requires that sacrifices be made, and Dumont argued that having few or no children was the price many people paid to get ahead. Dumont recognized that such ambitions were not possible in every society. In a highly stratified aristocracy, few people outside of the aristocracy could aspire to a career beyond subsistence. However, in a democracy (such as late-nineteenth-century France), opportunities to succeed existed at all social levels. Spengler (1979) has succinctly summarized Dumont's thesis: "The bulk of the population, therefore, not only strove to ascend politically, economically, socially, and intellectually, but experienced an imperative urge to climb and a palsying fear of descent. Consequently, since children impeded individual and familial ascension, their number was limited" (p. 158).

Notice that Dumont added an important ingredient to Mill's recipe for fertility control. Mill argued that it was fear of social slippage that motivated people to limit fertility below the level that Malthus had expected. Dumont went beyond that to suggest that social aspiration was the root cause of a slowdown in population growth. Dumont was not happy with this situation, by the way. He was upset by the low level of French fertility and used the concept of social capillarity to propose policies to undermine it. He believed that socialism would undercut the desire for upward social mobility and would thus stimulate the birth rate.

Durkheim

While Dumont was concerned primarily with the causes of population growth, another late-nineteenth-century French sociologist, Émile Durkheim, based an entire social theory on the consequences of population growth. In discussing the increasing complexity of modern societies, characterized particularly by increasing divisions of labor, Durkheim proposed that "the division of labor varies in direct ratio with the volume and density of societies, and, if it progresses in a continuous manner in the course of social development, it is because societies become regularly denser and more voluminous" (Durkheim 1893 [1933]:262). Durkheim proceeded to explain that population growth leads to greater societal specialization, because the struggle for existence is more acute when there are more people.

If you compare a primitive society with an industrialized society, the primitive society is not very specialized. By contrast, in industrialized societies there is a lot of differentiation; that is, there is an increasingly long list of occupations and social classes. Why is this? The answer is in the volume and density of the population. Growth creates competition for society's resources, and in order to improve their advantage in the struggle, people specialize. Durkheim's thesis that population growth leads to specialization was derived (he himself acknowledged) from Darwin's theory of evolution. In turn, Darwin acknowledged his own debt to Malthus. You will notice that Durkheim also clearly echoes the words of Ibn Khaldun, although it is uncertain whether Durkheim knew of Ibn Khaldun's work.

The critical theorizing of the nineteenth and early twentieth centuries set the stage for a more systematic collection of data to test aspects of those theories and to examine more carefully those that might be valid and those that should be discarded. As population studies became more quantitative in the twentieth century, a phenomenon called the demographic transition took shape and took the attention of demographers.

The Theory of the Demographic Transition

Although it has dominated demographic thinking for the past half century, the **demographic transition** theory actually began as only a description of the demographic changes that had taken place in the advanced nations over time. In particular, it described the transition from high birth and death rates to low birth and death rates, with an interstitial spurt in growth rates leading to a larger population at the end of the transition than there had been at the start. The idea emerged as early as 1929, when Warren Thompson gathered data from "certain countries" for the period 1908–27 and showed that the countries fell into three main groups, according to their patterns of population growth:

> *Group A (northern and western Europe and the United States):* From the latter part of the nineteenth century to 1927, these countries had moved from having very high rates of natural increase to having very low rates of increase "and will shortly become stationary and start to decline in numbers" (Thompson 1929:968).

> *Group B (Italy, Spain, and the "Slavic" peoples of central Europe):* Thompson saw evidence of a decline in both birth rates and death rates but suggested that "it appears probable that the death rate will decline as rapidly or even more rapidly than the birth rate for some time yet. The condition in these Group B countries is much the same as existed in the Group A countries thirty to fifty years ago" (1929:968).

Group C (the rest of the world): In the rest of the world, Thompson saw little evidence of control over either births or deaths.

As a consequence of this relative lack of voluntary control over births and deaths (a concept we will question later), Thompson felt that the Group C countries (which included about 70–75 percent of the population of the world at the time) would continue to have their growth "determined largely by the opportunities they have to increase their means of subsistence. Malthus described their processes of growth quite accurately when he said 'that population does invariably increase, where there are means of subsistence. . . .'" (Thompson, 1929:971).

Thompson's work, however, came at a time when there was little concern about overpopulation. The "Group C" countries had relatively low rates of growth because of high mortality and, at the same time, by 1936, birth rates in the United States and Europe were so low that Enid Charles published a widely read book called *The Twilight of Parenthood*, which was introduced with the comment that "in place of the Malthusian menace of overpopulation there is now real danger of underpopulation" (Charles 1936:v). Furthermore, Thompson's labels for his categories had little charisma. It is difficult to build a compelling theory around categories called A, B, and C.

Sixteen years after Thompson's work, Frank Notestein (1945) picked up the threads of his thesis and provided labels for the three types of growth patterns that Thompson had simply called A, B, and C. Notestein called the Group A pattern **incipient decline**, the Group B pattern **transitional growth**, and the Group C pattern **high growth potential**. That same year, Kingsley Davis (1945) edited a volume of the *Annals of the American Academy of Political and Social Sciences* titled "World Population in Transition," and in the lead article (titled "The Demographic Transition") he noted that "viewed in the long-run, earth's population has been like a long, thin powder fuse that burns slowly and haltingly until it finally reaches the charge and explodes" (Davis 1945:1). The term **population explosion**, alluded to by Davis, refers to the phase that Notestein called transitional growth. Thus was born the term *demographic transition*. It is that process of moving from high birth and death rates to low birth and death rates, from high growth potential to incipient decline (see Figure 3.3).

At this point in the 1940s, however, the demographic transition was merely a picture of demographic change, not a theory. But each new country studied fit into the picture, and it seemed as though some new universal law of population growth—an evolutionary scheme—was being developed. The apparent historical uniqueness of the demographic transition (all known cases have occurred within the last 200 years) has spawned a host of alternative names, such as the "vital revolution" and the "demographic revolution." Between the mid-1940s and the late 1960s, rapid population growth became a worldwide concern, and demographers devoted a great deal of time to the demographic transition perspective. By 1964, George Stolnitz was able to report that "demographic transitions rank among the most sweeping and best-documented trends of modern times . . . based upon hundreds of investigations, covering a host of specific places, periods and events" (Stolnitz 1964:20). As the pattern of change took shape, explanations were developed for why and how countries pass through the transition. These explanations

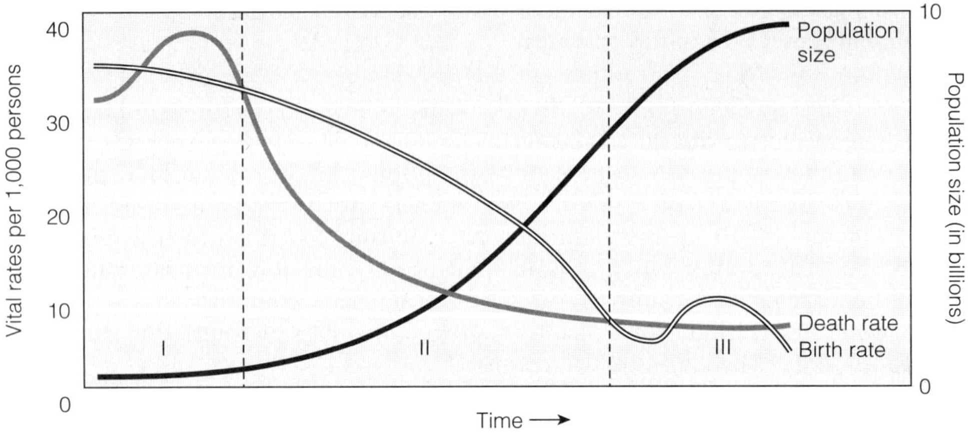

Figure 3.3 The Demographic Transition

Note: The original model of the demographic transition is divided roughly into three stages. In the first stage there is high growth potential because both birth and death rates are high. The second stage is the transition from high to low birth and death rates. During this stage the growth potential is realized as the death rate drops before the birth rate drops, resulting in rapid population growth. Finally, the last stage is a time when death rates are as low as they are likely to go, while fertility may continue to decline to the point that the population might eventually decline in numbers.

tended to be cobbled together in a somewhat piecemeal fashion from the nineteenth- and early-twentieth-century writers I discussed earlier in this chapter, but overall they were derived from the concept of **modernization.**

Modernization theory is based on the idea that in premodern times human society was generally governed by "tradition," and that the massive economic changes wrought by industrialization forced societies to alter traditional institutions: "In traditional societies fertility and mortality are high. In modern societies fertility and mortality are low. In between, there is demographic transition" (Demeny 1968:502). In the process, behavior has changed and the world has been permanently transformed. It is a macro-level theory that sees human actors as being buffeted by changing social institutions. Individuals did not deliberately lower their risk of death to precipitate the modern decline in mortality. Rather, society-wide increases in the standard of living and improved public health infrastructure brought about this change. Similarly, people did not just decide to move from the farm to town to take a job in a factory. Economic changes took place that created those higher-wage urban jobs while eliminating many agricultural jobs. These same economic forces improved transportation and communication and made it possible for individuals to migrate in previously unheard of numbers.

Modernization theory provided the vehicle that moved the demographic transition from a mere description of events to a demographic perspective. In its initial formulations, this perspective was perhaps best expressed by the sentiments "take care of the people and population will take care of itself" or "development is the best contraceptive" (Teitelbaum 1975). These were views that were derivable from Karl Marx, who was in fact one of the early exponents of the modernization theory (Inglehart and Baker 2000). The theory drew on the available data for most countries that had gone through the transition. Death rates declined as the standard of living improved, and birth rates almost always declined a few decades later, eventually dropping to low levels, although rarely as low as the death rate. It was argued that the decline in the birth rate typically lagged behind the decline in the death rate because it takes time for a population to adjust to the fact that mortality really is lower, and because the social and economic institutions that favored high fertility require time to adjust to new norms of lower fertility that are more consistent with the lower levels of mortality. Since most people value the prolongation of life, it is not hard to lower mortality, but the reduction of fertility is contrary to the established norms of societies that have required high birth rates to keep pace with high death rates. Such norms are not easily changed, even in the face of poverty.

Birth rates eventually declined, it was argued, as the importance of family life was diminished by industrial and urban life, thus weakening the pressure for large families. Large families are presumed to have been desired because they provided parents with a built-in labor pool, and because children provided old-age security for parents (Hohm 1975). The same economic development that lowered mortality is theorized to transform a society into an urban industrial state in which compulsory education lowers the value of children by removing them from the labor force, and people come to realize that lower infant mortality means that fewer children need to be born to achieve a certain number of surviving children (Easterlin 1978). Finally, as a consequence of the many alterations in social institutions, "the pressure from high fertility weakens and the idea of conscious control of fertility gradually gains strength" (Teitelbaum 1975:421).

Critique of the Demographic Transition Theory

It has been argued that the concept underlying the demographic transition is that population stability (sometimes called "homeostasis"—see, for example, Lee 1987) is the normal state of affairs in human societies and that change (the "transition") is what requires explanation (Kreager 1986). Not everyone agrees. Harbison and Robinson (2002) argue that transitions are the natural state of human affairs, and that each transition is followed by another one, a theme we will return to later in the chapter. In its original formulation, the demographic transition theory explained high fertility as a reaction to high mortality. As mortality declines, the need for high fertility lessens, and so birth rates go down. There is a spurt of growth in that transition period, but presumably the consequences will not be serious if the decline in mortality was produced by a rise in the standard of living, which, in its turn, produces a motivation for smaller families. But what will be the consequences if mortality declines and fertility does not? That situation presumably is precluded by the theory of demographic transition, but the demographic transition theory has not been capable of predicting levels of mortality or fertility or the timing of the fertility decline. This is because the initial explanation for the demographic behavior during the transition tended to be **ethnocentric**. It relied almost exclusively on the sentiment that "what is good for the goose is good for the gander." In other words, if this is what happened to the developed countries, why should it not also happen to other countries that are not so advanced? One reason might be that the preconditions for the demographic transition are considerably different now from what they were when the industrialized countries began their transition.

For example, prior to undergoing the demographic transition, few of the currently industrialized countries had birth rates as high as those of most currently less-developed countries, nor indeed were their levels of mortality so high. Yet when mortality did decline, it did so as a consequence of internal economic development, not as a result of a foreign country bringing in sophisticated techniques of disease prevention, as is the case today. A second reason might be that the factors leading to the demographic transition were actually different from what for years had been accepted as true. Perhaps it is not just change that requires explanation but also differences in the starting and ending points of the transition. Perhaps, then, the modernization theory, in and of itself, did not provide an appropriate picture of historical development. These problems with the original explanations of the demographic transition led to new research and a reformulation of the perspective.

Reformulation of the Demographic Transition Theory

One of the most important social scientific endeavors to cast doubt on the classic explanation was the European Fertility Project, directed by Ansley Coale at Princeton University. In the early 1960s, J. William Leasure, then a graduate student in economics at Princeton, was writing a doctoral dissertation on the fertility decline in Spain, using data for each of that nation's 49 provinces. Surprisingly, his thesis revealed that the history of fertility change in Spain was not explained by a simple version of the demographic transition theory. Fertility in Spain declined in contiguous areas that were culturally similar, even though the levels of urbanization and economic development might be different (Leasure 1962). At about the same time, other students began to uncover similarly puzzling historical patterns in European data (Coale 1986). A systematic review of the demographic histories of Europe was thus begun in order to establish exactly how and why the transition occurred. The focus was on the decline in fertility, because it is the most problematic aspect of the classic explanation. These new findings have been used to help revise the theory of the demographic transition.

With the discovery that the decline of fertility in Europe occurred in the context of widely differing social, economic, and demographic conditions, it became apparent that economic development is a sufficient cause of fertility decline, but not a necessary one (Coale 1973). For example, many provinces in Europe experienced a rapid drop in their birth rate even though they were not very urban, infant mortality rates were high, and a low percentage of the population was employed in industrial occupations. The data suggest that one of the more common similarities in those areas that have undergone fertility declines is the rapid spread of **secularization**. Secularization is an attitude of autonomy from otherworldly powers and a sense of responsibility for one's own well-being (Lesthaeghe 1977; Leasure 1982; Norris and Inglehart 2004). It is associated with an enlightened view of the world—a break from traditional ways of thinking and behaving.

It is difficult to know exactly why such attitudes arise when and where they do, but we do know that industrialization and economic development are virtually always accompanied by secularization. Secularization, however, can occur independently of industrialization. It might be thought of as a modernization of thought, distinct from a modernization of social institutions. Some theorists have suggested that secularization is part of the process of westernization (see, for example, Caldwell 1982). In all events, when it pops up, secularization often spreads quickly, being diffused through social networks as people imitate the behavior of others to whom they look for clues to proper and appropriate conduct.

Education has been identified as one potential stimulant to such altered attitudes, especially mass education, which tends to emphasize modernization and secular concepts (Caldwell 1980). Education facilitates the rapid spread of new ideas and information, which would perhaps help explain another of the important findings from the Princeton European Fertility Project, that the onset of long-term fertility decline tended to be concentrated in a relatively short period of time (van de Walle and Knodel 1980). The data from Europe suggest that once marital fertility had dropped by as little as 10 percent in a region, the decline spread rapidly. This "tipping point" occurred whether or not infant mortality had already declined (Watkins 1986). Some areas of Europe that were similar with respect to socioeconomic development did not experience a fertility decline at the same time, whereas other provinces that were less similar socioeconomically experienced nearly identical drops in fertility.

The data suggest that this riddle is solved by examining cultural factors, not just socioeconomic ones. Areas that share a similar culture (same language, common ethnic background, similar lifestyle) were more likely to share a decline in fertility than areas that were culturally less similar (Watkins 1991). The principal reason for this is that the idea of family planning seemed to spread quickly until it ran into a barrier to its communication. Language is one such barrier (Leasure 1962; Lesthaeghe 1977), and social and economic inequality in a region is another (Lengyel-Cook and Repetto 1982). Social distance between people turns out to effectively inhibit communication of new ideas and attitudes.

What kinds of ideas and attitudes might encourage people to rethink how many children they ought to have? To answer this kind of question we must shift our focus from the macro (societal) level to the micro (individual) level and ask how people actually respond to the social and economic changes taking place around them (see Kertzer and Hogan 1989 for an interesting Italian case study). A prevailing individual-level perspective is that of **rational choice theory** (sometimes referred to as RAT) (Coleman and Fararo 1992). The essence of rational choice theory is that human behavior is the result of individuals making calculated cost-benefit analyses about how to act and what to do. For example, Caldwell (1976, 1982) has suggested that "there is no ceiling in primitive and traditional societies to the number of children who would be economically beneficial" (1976:331). Children are a source of income and support for parents throughout life, and they produce far more than they cost in such societies. The **wealth flow**, as Caldwell calls it, is from children to parents.

The process of modernization eventually results in the tearing apart of large, extended family units into smaller, nuclear units that are economically and emotionally self-sufficient. As that happens, children begin to cost parents more (including the cost of educating them as demanded by a modernizing society), and the amount of support that parents get from children begins to decline (starting with the income lost because children are in school rather than working). As the wealth flow reverses and parents begin to spend their income on children, rather than deriving income from them, the economic value of children declines, and people no longer derive any economic advantage from children. Economic rationality would now seem to dictate having zero children, but in reality, of course, people continue having children for a variety of social reasons that I detail in Chapter 6. Keep this idea in mind if the conversation turns to how "irrational" the Europeans and Japanese are for having so few children.

Overall, then, the principal ingredient in the reformulation of the demographic transition perspective is to add "ideational" factors to "demand" factors as the likely causes of fertility decline (Cleland and Wilson 1987). The original version of the theory suggested that modernization reduces the demand for children and so fertility falls—if people are rational economic creatures, then this is what should happen. But the real world is more complex, and the diffusion of ideas can shape fertility behavior along with, or even in the absence of, the usual signs of modernization. People may generally be rational, but Massey (2002) has reminded us that much of human behavior is still powered by emotional responses that supersede rationality. We are animals, and though we may have vastly greater intellectual capacities than other species we are still influenced by a variety of nonrational forces, including our hormones (Udry 1994, 2000).

This does not necessarily mean that Wallerstein (1976) was correct when he declared that modernization theory was dead. On the contrary, there is evidence from around the world that "industrialization leads to occupational specialization, rising educational levels, rising income levels, and eventually brings unforeseen changes—changes in gender roles, attitudes toward authority and sexual norms; declining fertility rates; broader political participation; and less easily led publics" (Inglehart and Baker 2000:21). This is not a linear path, however. "Economic development tends to push societies in a common direction, but rather than converging, they seem to move on parallel trajectories shaped by their cultural heritages" (Inglehart and Baker 2000:49).

One strength of reformulating the demographic transition is that nearly all other perspectives can find a home here. Malthusians note with satisfaction that fertility first declined in Europe primarily as a result of a delay in marriage, much as Malthus would have preferred. Neo-Malthusians can take heart from the fact that rapid and sustained declines occurred simultaneously with the spread of knowledge about family planning practices. Marxists also find a place for themselves in the reformulated demographic transition perspective, because its basic tenet is that a change in the social structure (modernization) is necessary to bring about a decline in fertility. This is only a short step away from agreeing with Marx that there is no universal law of population, but rather that each stage of development and social organization has its own law, and that cultural patterns will influence the timing and tempo of the demographic transition—when it starts and how it progresses.

The Theory of Demographic Change and Response

The work of the European Fertility Project focused on explaining regional differences in fertility declines. This was a very important theoretical development, but not a comprehensive one because it only partially dealt with a central issue of the demographic transition theory: How (and under what conditions) can a mortality decline lead to a fertility decline? To answer that question, Kingsley Davis (1963) asked what happens to individuals when mortality declines. The answer is that more children survive through adulthood, putting greater pressure on family resources, and people have to reorganize their lives in an attempt to relieve that pressure; that is, people respond to the demographic change. But note that their response will be in terms of personal goals, not national goals. It rarely matters what a government wants. If individual members of a society do not stand to gain by behaving in a particular way, they probably will not behave that way. Indeed, that was a major argument made by the neo-Malthusians against moral restraint. Why advocate postponement of marriage and sexual gratification rather than contraception when you know that few people who postpone marriage are actually going to postpone sexual intercourse, too? In fact, Ludwig Brentano (1910) quite forthrightly suggested that Malthus was insane to think that abstinence was the cure for the poor.

Davis argued that the response that individuals make to the population pressure created by more members joining their ranks is determined by the means available to them. A first response, nondemographic in nature, is to try to increase resources by working harder—longer hours perhaps, a second job, and so on. If that is not sufficient or there are no such opportunities, then migration of some family members (typically unmarried sons or daughters) is the easiest demographic response. This is, of course, the option that people have been using forever (undoubtedly explaining in large part why human beings have spread out over the planet).

In the early eighteenth century, Richard Cantillon, an Irish–French economist, was pointing out what happened in Europe when families grew too large (and this was even before mortality began markedly to decline):

> If all the labourers in a village breed up several sons to the same work, there will be too many labourers to cultivate the lands belonging to the village, and the surplus adults must go to seek a livelihood elsewhere, which they generally do in cities. . . . If a tailor makes all the clothes there and breeds up three sons to the same, yet there is work enough for but one successor to him, the two others must go to seek their livelihood elsewhere; if they do not find enough employment in the neighboring town they must go further afield or change their occupation to get a living (Cantillon 1755 [1964]: 23).

But what will be the response of that second generation, the children who now have survived when previously they would not have, and who have thus put the pressure on resources? Davis argues that if there is in fact a chance for social or economic improvement, then people will try to take advantage of those opportunities by avoiding the large families that caused problems for their parents. Davis suggests that the most powerful motive for family limitation is not fear of poverty or avoidance of pain as Malthus argued; rather, it is the prospect of rising prosperity that will most often motivate people to find the means to limit the number of children they have (I discuss these means in Chapter 6). Davis here echoes the themes of Mill and Dumont, but adds that, at the very least, the desire to maintain one's relative status in society may lead to an active desire to prevent too many children from draining away one's resources. Of course, that assumes the individuals in question have already attained some status worth maintaining.

One of Davis's most important contributions to our demographic perspective is, as Cicourel put it, that he "seems to rely on an implicit model of the actor who makes everyday interpretations of perceived environmental changes" (Cicourel 1974:8). For example, people will respond to a decline in mortality only if they notice it, and then their response will be determined by the social situation in which they find themselves. Davis's analysis is important in reminding us of the crucial link between the everyday lives of individuals and the kinds of population changes that take place in society. Another demographer who extended the scope of the demographic transition with this kind of analysis is Richard Easterlin.

The Easterlin Relative Cohort Size Hypothesis

The **Easterlin relative cohort size hypothesis** (also sometimes known as the relative income hypothesis) is based on the idea that the birth rate does not necessarily respond to absolute levels of economic well-being but rather to levels that are relative to those to which one is accustomed (Easterlin 1968; 1978). Easterlin assumes that the standard of living you experience in late childhood is the base from which you evaluate your chances as an adult. If you can easily improve your income as an adult compared to your late childhood level, then you will be more likely to marry early and have several children. On the other hand, if you perceive that it is going to be rough sledding as an adult even to match the level of living you were accustomed to as a child, that fear may lead you to postpone marriage or at least postpone childbearing.

So far the theory of relative income is strikingly similar to Mill's writing more than 100 years earlier. But Easterlin goes on to ask what factors might cause you to be in a relatively advantageous or disadvantageous position as you begin adulthood. The answer lies in the relationship between economic conditions and the demographic responses to those conditions. The demographic response is a function of the age structure changes that occur in the context of declining mortality and fertility. Macunovich (2000) has summarized the scenario as follows:

> The increase in relative cohort size that occurs as a result of declining mortality during the demographic transition in part determines when the fertility portion of the transition begins. The increasing proportion of young adults generates a downward pressure on young men's relative wages; this in turn causes young adults to accept a tradeoff between family size and material wellbeing. This acceptance of a tradeoff could mark a turning point in a society's regulation of fertility, setting in motion a "cascade" or "snowball" effect in which total fertility rates tumble as social norms regarding individual control of fertility and acceptable family sizes begin to change. (p. 257)

If young people are relatively scarce in society and business is good, they will be in relatively high demand. In nearly classic Malthusian fashion, they will be able to command high wages and thus be more likely to feel comfortable about getting married and starting a family—the "lucky few" as Carlson (2008) has called them.

On the other hand, if young people are in relatively abundant supply, then even if business is good, the competition for jobs will be stiff and it will be difficult for people to maintain their accustomed level of living, much less marry and start a family.

Easterlin's thesis presents a model of society in which demographic change and economic change are closely interrelated. Economic changes produce demographic changes, which in turn produce economic changes, and so on. The model, however, has a certain middle-class bias. What about the people at the bottom end of the economic ladder, for whom relative deprivation does not necessarily apply because they already have so little? Are they caught in a constant Malthusian cycle of overpopulation and poverty? Mill suggested in 1848 that they were, unless one entire generation could be catapulted into the middle class. To be more broadly applicable, the theory may have to take into account the importance of social class as an independent factor influencing demographic behavior (Lesthaeghe and Surkyn 1988).

The importance of the Easterlin hypothesis can be judged by the large number of studies that have attempted to test it empirically. Several studies provide evidence that, in general, changes in cohort size and the birth rate tend to move in directions predicted by Easterlin (Lee 1976; Butz and Ward 1979; Pampel 1993; Crenshaw, Ameen, and Christenson 1997; Jeon and Shields 2005). On the other hand, tests of specific aspects of the Easterlin hypothesis have sometimes failed to support it (Kahn and Mason 1987; Behrman and Taubman 1989; Wright 1989) or have supported it only partially (Pampel 1996; Waldorf and Franklin 2002). Nonetheless, Macunovich (2000) makes the case that properly specified models demonstrate the usefulness of the theory, especially in predicting the timing of the fertility transition. The Easterlin hypothesis is intuitively appealing; the idea of a demographic feedback cycle, which is at the core of Easterlin's thinking, is compelling, and relative cohort size is certainly a factor that will influence various kinds of social change. This kind of interaction between population change and societal change is, in fact, at the heart of the realization among demographers that the demographic transition is really a whole suite of transitions, rather than one big transition.

The Second Demographic Transition

The dramatic changes taking place in family and household structure since World War II, especially in Europe, led van de Kaa (1987) to talk about the "second demographic transition." A demographic centerpiece of this change in the richer countries has been a fall in fertility to below-replacement levels, but van de Kaa suggested that the change was less about not having babies than it was about the personal freedom to do what one wanted, especially among women. So, rather than the pattern of grow up, marry, and have children, this transition is associated with a postponement of marriage, a rise in single living, cohabitation, and prolonged residence in the parental household (Lesthaeghe and Neels 2002; McLanahan 2004). In addition, an increasing lack of permanence in family relationships has led to "rising divorce rates and high separation rates of cohabitants. And the forms of family reconstitution are shifting away from remarriage in favor of postmarital cohabitation as well" (Lesthaeghe 1998:5–6).

Billari and Liefbroer (2004) have suggested that the Second Demographic Transition "constitutes 'the' mainstream concept among population scholars dealing with demographic change in European societies" (p. 1). For his part, van de Kaa (2004) has noted that, "in my view it is really impossible to understand the demographic changes that have occurred in Europe, and in many other industrialised countries as well, since the mid-1960s, without accepting the idea that the many and very varied changes we have observed in a whole series of demographic variables are interrelated and may in their totality be indicative of, and represent, the manifestation of a change in demographic regime" (p. 4). By this he means that instead of assuming that the end result of the demographic transition is homeostasis, or population stability, as I mentioned earlier in the chapter, this new demographic regime is one in which that assumption is thrown out the window and replaced by the idea that young people make decisions about having children on the basis of self-fulfillment, without regard to biological replacement, knowing as they do that, at least in the rich European countries in which this occurring, migrants can make up the difference if too few children are being born. We will return to this idea several times in the coming chapters.

The idea that change, not homeostasis, is the natural state of affairs is supported as well by the discussion in Chapter 2 about the Neolithic Demographic Transition (Bocquet-Appel 2008), which would actually represent the first demographic transition (an increase in both birth and death rates). That was followed by the more famous demographic transition of the past two hundred years or so (a decrease in both birth and death rates), followed by what we would then call not the second, but rather the third demographic transition (an unexpected further decline in birth rates), if you follow me. We humans may have experienced not one, but a sequence of transitions, and through it all the population has generally been increasing, as shown back in Table 2.1, rather than standing still.

The Demographic Transition Is Really a Set of Transitions

The reformulation driven by the European Fertility Project, the theory of demographic change and response, the Easterlin hypothesis, the Second Demographic Transition, and other research all have generated the insight that the demographic transition (by which I mean the one that started a couple of hundred years ago) is actually a set of interrelated transitions. Taken together, they help us understand not just the causes but the consequences of population change. Usually (but not always) the first transition to occur is the **health and mortality transition** (the shift from deaths at younger ages due to communicable disease to deaths at older ages due to degenerative diseases). This transition is followed by the **fertility transition**—the shift from natural (and high) to controlled (and low) fertility, typically in a delayed response to the health and mortality transition. The predictable changes in the age structure (the **age transition**) brought about by the mortality and fertility transitions produce social and economic reactions as societies adjust to constantly changing age distributions. The rapid growth of the population occasioned by the pattern of mortality declining sooner and more rapidly than fertility almost always leads to overpopulation of rural areas, producing the **migration transition**, especially toward urban areas, creating the **urban transition**. The **family and household transition** is occasioned by the massive structural changes that accompany longer life, lower fertility, an older age structure, and urban instead of rural residence—all of which are part and parcel of the demographic transition. The interrelationships among these transitions are shown in Figure 3.4.

The Health and Mortality Transition

The transition process almost always begins with a decline in mortality, which is brought about by changes in society that improve the health of people and thus their ability to resist disease, and by scientific advances that prevent premature death. However, death rates do not decline evenly by age; rather it is the very youngest and the very oldest—but especially the youngest—whose lives are most likely to be saved by improved life expectancy. Thus, the initial impact of the health and mortality transition is to increase the number of young people who are alive, ballooning the bottom end of the age structure in a manner that looks just like an increase in the birth rate. This sets all the other transitions in motion.

The Fertility Transition

The fertility transition can begin without a decline in mortality (as happened in France), but in most places it is the decline in mortality, leading to greater survival of children, that eventually motivates people to think about limiting the number of children they are having. Throughout most of human history, the average woman had two children who survived to adulthood. The decline in mortality, however, obviously increases that number and thereby threatens the very foundation of the household

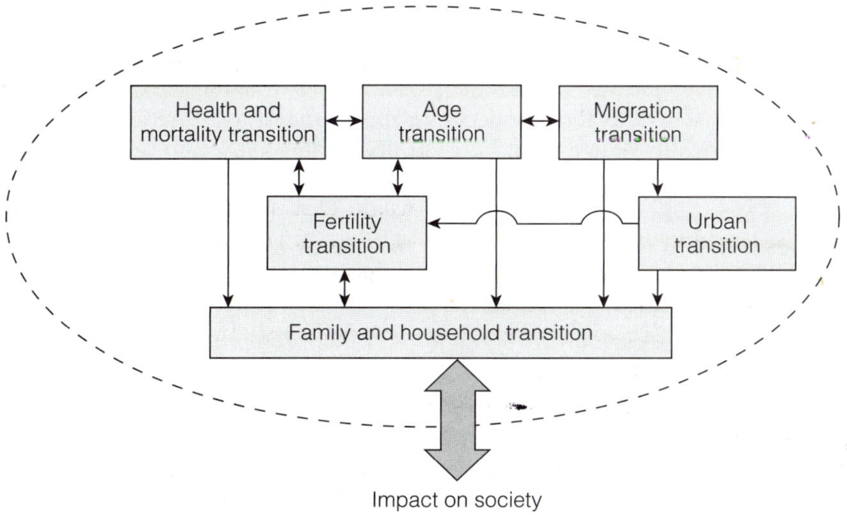

Figure 3.4 The Transitions That Comprise the Demographic Transition's Impact on Society

Note: Each box has its own set of theories that serve as explanations for the phenomenon under consideration.

economy. At the community or societal level, the increasing number of young people creates all sorts of pressures to change, often leading to peer pressure to conform to new standards of behavior, including the deliberate control of reproduction.

Another set of extremely important changes that occur in the context of the health and mortality transition is that the scope of life expands for women as they, too, live longer. They are increasingly empowered to delay childbearing and to have fewer children because they begin to realize that most of their children will survive to adulthood and they, themselves, will survive beyond the reproductive ages, beyond their children's arrival into adulthood. This new freedom gives them vastly more opportunities than ever before in human history to do something with their lives besides bearing and raising children. This realization may be a genuine tipping point in the fertility transition, leading to an almost irreversible decline.

As fertility declines, the health and mortality transition is itself pushed along, because the survival of children is enhanced when a woman has fewer children among whom to share resources. Also affected by the fertility decline is the age structure, which begins to cave in at the younger ages as fewer children are being born, and as most are now surviving through childhood. In its turn, that shift in the age transition to an increasingly older age structure has the potential to divert societal resources away from dealing primarily with the impact of children to dealing with broader social concerns, including raising the standard of living. A higher standard of living can then redound to the benefit of health levels throughout society, adding fuel to the fire of increasing life expectancy.

The Age Transition

In many respects, the age transition is the "master" transition in that the changing number of people at each age that occurs with the decline of mortality, and then the decline in fertility, presents the most obvious demographic pressure for social change. When both mortality and fertility are high, the age structure is quite young, but the decline in mortality makes it even younger by disproportionately increasing the number of young people. Then, as fertility declines, the youngest ages are again affected first, since births occur only at age zero, so a fertility decline shows up first as simply fewer young children than before. However, as the bulge of young people born prior to the fertility decline pushes into the older ages while fertility begins to decline, the age structure moves into a stage that can be very beneficial to economic development in a society—a large fraction of the population is composed of young adults of working age who are having fewer children as dependents at the same time that the older population has not yet increased in size enough to create problems of dependency in old age. As we will see, this phase in the age transition is often associated with a golden age of advancement in the standard of living—the leap forward that Mill was advocating.

That golden age can be transitory, however, if a society has not planned for the next phase of the age transition, when the older population begins to increase more rapidly than the younger population. The baby bulge created by the initial declines in mortality reaches old age at a time when fertility has likely declined, and so the age structure has a much greater number and a higher fraction of older people than ever before. We are only now learning how societies will respond to this challenge of an increasingly older population.

The Migration Transition

Meanwhile, back at the very young age structure put into motion by declining mortality, the theory of demographic change and response suggests that in rural areas, where most of the population lived for most of human history, the growth in the number of young people will lead to an oversupply of young people looking for jobs, which will encourage people to go elsewhere in search of economic opportunity. The Europeans who experienced the first wave of population growth, because they experienced the health and mortality transition first, still lived in a world where there was "empty" land. Of course, it wasn't really empty, as the Americas and the islands of the South Pacific (largely Australia and New Zealand) were populated mainly by hunter-gatherers who used the land extensively, rather than intensively, as I mentioned in Chapter 2.

As Europeans arrived in the Americas, they perceived land as being not used and so claimed it for themselves. We all know the consequences of this for the indigenous populations, as all of the land was eventually claimed for intensive human use. So, whereas the Europeans could initially spread out from rural Europe to rural areas in the Americas and the South Pacific, migrants from rural areas today no longer have that option.

Notice in Figure 3.4 that there is a double-arrow connecting the age and migration transitions. This is because migration takes people (mainly young adults) out of one area and puts them in another area, thus affecting the age structure in both places. As I have already mentioned, this difference in age structures between two places contributes to current migration patterns of people from younger societies filling in the "empty" places in the age structure of older societies.

The Urban Transition

With empty lands filling up, migrants from the countryside in the world today have no place to go but to cities, and cities have historically tended to flourish by absorbing labor from rural areas. A majority of people in the world now live in cities, and by the end of the twenty-first century, almost all of us will be there. The urban transition thus begins with migration from rural to urban areas but then morphs into the urban "evolution" as most humans wind up being born in, living in, and dying in cities. The complexity of human existence is played out in cities, leading us to expect a constant dynamism of urban places for most of the rest of human history. Because urban places are historically associated with lower levels of fertility than rural areas, as the world's population becomes increasingly urban we can anticipate that this will be a major factor in bringing and keeping fertility levels down all over the world.

The Family and Household Transition

It is reasonable to think that the transition in family and household structure, noted above with respect to the Second Demographic Transition, is not so much a second transition as it is another set of transitions within the broader framework of the demographic transition. As I show in Figure 3.4, the family and household transition is influenced by all the previously mentioned transitions. The health and mortality transition is pivotal because it gives women (and men, too, of course) a dramatically greater number of years to live in general, and more specifically a greater number of years that do not need to be devoted to children. Low mortality reduces the pressure for a woman to marry early and start bearing children while she is young enough for her body to handle that stress. Furthermore, when mortality was high, marriages had a high probability of ending in widowhood when one of the partners was still reasonably young, and families routinely were reconstituted as widows and widowers remarried. But low mortality leads to a much longer time that married couples will be alive together before one partner dies, and this alone is related to part of the increase in divorce rates. The age transition plays a role at the societal level, as well, because over time the increasingly similar number of people at all ages—as opposed to a majority of people being very young—means that any society is bound to be composed of a greater array of family and household arrangements. Diversity in families and households is also encouraged by migration (which breaks up and reconstitutes families) and by the urban transition, especially since urban places tend to be more tolerant of diversity than are smaller rural communities.

The rest of this book is devoted to more detailed examinations of each of these transitions, and you will discover that there are a variety of theoretical approaches that have developed over time to explain the causes and consequences of each set of transitions. Your own demographic perspective will be honed by looking for similarities and patterns in the transitions that link them together and, more importantly, link them to their potential impact on society.

Impact on Society

The modern field of population studies came about largely to encourage and inspire deeper insight into the causes of changes in fertility, mortality, migration, age and sex structure, and population characteristics and distribution. Demographers spent most of the twentieth century doing that, but always with an eye toward new things that could be learned about what demographic change meant for human society. Unlike in Malthus's day, population growth is no longer viewed as being caused by one set of factors nor as having a simple prescribed set of consequences.

Perhaps the closest we can come at present to "big" theories are those that try to place demographic events and behavior in the context of other global change, especially political change, economic development, and westernization. One of the more ambitious and influential of these theorists is Jack Goldstone (1986, 1991), whose work incorporates population growth as a precursor of change in the "early modern world" (defined by him as 1500 to 1800). He argues that population growth in the presence of rigid social structures produced dramatic political change in England and France, in the Ottoman empire, and in China. Population growth led to increased government expenditures, which led to inflation, which led to fiscal crisis. In these societies with no real opportunities for social mobility, population growth (which initially increases the number of younger persons) led to disaffection and popular unrest and created a new cohort of young people receptive to new ideas. The result in the four case studies he analyzes was rebellion and revolution. This hearkens back to the discussion in Chapter 1 about the role of the "youth bulge" in conflict in the Middle East, an issue that Goldstone has examined as well (Goldstone 2002).

Stephen Sanderson (1995) has promoted the idea that population growth has been an important stimulus to change throughout human history, but especially since the Agricultural Revolution. Thus, his scope is much broader than that of Goldstone. Sanderson largely synthesizes the work of others such as Boserup (1965), Cohen (1977), and Johnson and Earle (1987). "Had Paleolithic hunter-gatherers been able to keep their populations from growing, the whole world would likely still be surviving entirely by hunting and gathering" (Sanderson 1995:49). Instead, population growth generated the Agricultural Revolution (an idea discussed in Chapter 2) and then the Industrial Revolution. The sedentary life associated with the Agricultural Revolution increased social complexity (a very Durkheimian idea), which led to the rise of civilization (cities) and the state (city-states and then nation-states).

Regional and cultural differences in population growth and age structures have been implicated in the patterns of instability and conflict that characterize the world in the early twenty-first century. The consequences of population growth and change figure prominently in Huntington's *Clash of Civilizations and the Remaking of World Order* (Huntington 1996) as they do in Robert Kaplan's *The Coming Anarchy: Shattering the Dreams of the Post Cold War* (Kaplan 2000), Thomas Friedman's *Hot, Flat, and Crowded* (Friedman 2008), and Christopher Caldwell's *Reflections on the Revolution in Europe: Immigration, Islam, and the West* (Caldwell 2009). These and other writers have encouraged us to realize that because population change may seem largely imperceptible as it is occurring, it requires an analytic observer to tell us what is going on and what could happen if we fail to pay attention. Thus, if we can look back and see that there were momentous historical consequences of population growth and change in the past, can we look forward into the future and project similar kinds of influences? Many people (including me) would say yes, and the rest of this book will show you why.

Summary and Conclusion

A lot of thinking about population issues has taken place over a very long period of time, and in this chapter I have traced the progression of demographic thinking from ancient doctrines to contemporary systematic perspectives. Malthus was not the first, but he was certainly the most influential of the early modern writers. Malthus believed that a biological urge to reproduce was the cause of population growth and that its natural consequence was poverty. Marx, on the other hand, did not openly argue with the Malthusian causes of growth, but he vehemently disagreed with the idea that poverty is the natural consequence of population growth. Marx denied that population growth was a problem per se—it only appeared that way in capitalist society. It may have seemed peculiar that I discuss a person who denied the importance of a demographic perspective in a chapter dedicated to that very importance. However, the Marxian point of view is sufficiently prevalent today among political leaders and intellectuals in enough countries that this attitude becomes in itself a demographic perspective of some significance. Furthermore, his perspective on the world finds its way into many aspects of current mainstream thinking, including modernization theory, that underlay aspects of the demographic transition theory.

The perspective of Mill, who seems very contemporary in many of his ideas, was somewhere between that of Malthus and Marx. He believed that increased productivity could lead to a motivation for having smaller families, especially if the influence of women was allowed to be felt and if people were educated about the possible consequences of having a large family. Dumont took these kinds of individual motivations a step further and suggested in greater detail the reasons why prosperity and ambition, operating through the principle of social capillarity, generally lead to a decline in the birth rate. Durkheim's perspective emphasized the consequences more than the causes of population growth. He was convinced that the complexity of modern societies is due almost entirely to the social responses to population growth—more people lead to higher levels of innovation and specialization.

More recently developed demographic perspectives have implicitly assumed that the consequences of population growth are serious and problematic, and they move directly to explanations of the causes of population growth. The original theory of the demographic transition suggested that growth is an intermediate stage between the more stable conditions of high birth and death rates to a new balance of low birth and death rates. Reformulations of the demographic transition perspective have emphasized its evolutionary character and have shown that the demographic transition is not one monolithic change, but rather that it encompasses several interrelated transitions: A decline in mortality will almost necessarily be followed by a decline in fertility, and by subsequent transitions in migration, urbanization, the age structure, and the family and household structure in society.

As I explore with you the causes and consequences of population growth and the uses to which such knowledge can be applied, you will need to know about the sources of demographic data. What is the empirical base of our understanding of the relationship between population and society? We turn to that topic in the next chapter.

Main Points

1. A demographic perspective is a way of relating basic population information to theories about how the world operates demographically.
2. Population doctrines and theories prior to Malthus vacillated between pronatalist and antinatalist and were often utopian.
3. According to Malthus, population growth is generated by the urge to reproduce, although growth is checked ultimately by the means of subsistence.
4. The natural consequences of population growth according to Malthus are misery and poverty because of the tendency for populations to grow faster than the food supply. Nonetheless, he believed that misery could be avoided if people practiced moral restraint—a simple formula of chastity before marriage and a delay in marriage until one can afford all the children that God might provide.
5. Karl Marx and Friedrich Engels strenuously objected to the Malthusian population perspective because it blamed poverty on the poor rather than on the evils of social organization.
6. John Stuart Mill argued that the standard of living is a major determinant of fertility levels, but he also felt that people could influence their own demographic destinies.

7. Arsène Dumont argued that personal ambition generated a process of social capillarity that induced people to limit their number of children in order to get ahead socially and economically, while another French writer, Émile Durkheim, built an entire theory of social structure on his conception of the consequences of population growth.
8. The demographic transition theory is a perspective that emphasizes the importance of economic and social development, which leads first to a decline in mortality and then, after some time lag, to a commensurate decline in fertility. It is based on the experience of the developed nations, and is derived from the modernization theory.
9. The theory of demographic change and response emphasizes that people must perceive a personal need to change behavior before a decline in fertility will take place, and that the kind of response they make will depend on what means are available to them.
10. The demographic transition is really a set of transitions, including the health and mortality, fertility, age, migration, urban, and family/household transitions.

Questions for Review

1. What lessons exist within the ideas of pre-Malthusian thinkers on population that can be applied conceptually to the demographic situations we currently confront in the world?
2. It was obvious even in Malthus's lifetime that his theory had numerous defects. Why then, are we still talking about it?
3. Based on the information provided in this chapter, which writer—Malthus or Marx—would sound most modern and relevant to twenty-first-century demographers? Defend your answer.
4. Using the material in Chapter 2 and on the Internet as resources, reflect on the different demographic circumstances that gave rise to the Malthusian and Marxian views on population, compared to J. S. Mill, Dumont, and Durkheim. To what extent do demographic theories follow the times?
5. Review the basic premises of the theory of demographic change and response and discuss how it served to expand the concept of the demographic transition into the idea of a larger suite of transitions.

Suggested Readings

1. United Nations, 1973, *The Determinants and Consequences of Population Trends* (New York: United Nations).
   This volume was written by well-known and highly expert demographers and is the best single source for a comprehensive review of major demographic doctrines and early theories.
2. Thomas Robert Malthus, 1798, *An Essay on the Principles of Population*, 1st Ed. (available from a variety of publishers).
   Despite the fact that numerous good summaries of Malthus have been written, you owe it to yourself to sample the real thing.

3. Ansley Coale and Susan Cotts Watkins (eds.), 1986, *The Decline of Fertility in Europe: The Revised Proceedings of a Conference on the Princeton European Fertility Project* (Princeton: Princeton University Press).
The most comprehensive statement in the literature of ways in which the Princeton European Fertility Project caused a rethinking of the theory of the demographic transition.
4. Simon Szreter, 1993, "The Idea of Demographic Transition and the Study of Fertility Change: A Critical Intellectual History," *Population and Development Review* 19(4):659-702.
Szreter examines the intellectual roots of the demographic transition and suggests that demographers need to step back and reassess the adequacy of the theory for explaining fertility change in society.
5. Ron Lesthaeghe, 1998, "On Theory Development: Applications to the Study of Family Formation." *Population and Development Review* 24(1):1-14.
Lesthaeghe offers an insider's view into theorizing about demographic issues, using the "second demographic transition" as an example.

Websites of Interest

Remember that websites are not as permanent as books and journals, so I cannot guarantee that each of the following websites still exists at the moment you are reading this. You may have to Google the name of the organization to find the current web address.

1. **http://turnbull.mcs.st-and.ac.uk/~history/Biographies/Condorcet.html**
The Marquis de Condorcet, who helped to inspire Malthus's essay, is the subject of this website, located at the University of St. Andrews in Scotland. It includes biographical information and a list of his publications.
2. **http://www.efm.bris.ac.uk/het/malthus/popu.txt**
The beauty of this website, located in the Department of Economics at the University of Bristol in England, is that it contains the full text of Malthus's first (1798) *Essay on Population.*
3. **http://www.ined.fr/en/resources_documentation/doc_research/thesaurus**
French demographers have played key roles in developing population studies, and the National Institute of Demographic Studies (INED) in Paris carries on that tradition. At this part of the INED website, you can find a very useful thesaurus of demographic terms (in English), as well as data for most countries of the world.
4. **http://www.popcouncil.org**
The Population Council is a policy-oriented research center in New York City founded in 1952 by John D. Rockefeller III. It originated the journal *Population and Development Review* (now published by Blackwell), whose articles tend to focus on issues that directly or indirectly test demographic theories and perspectives. At this website you can, among other things, peruse abstracts of articles published in the journal to stay up to date on recent research.
5. **http://www.historyplace.com/worldhistory/famine/index.html**
The Irish Potato Famine occurred well after Malthus's death, but it has certain Malthusian elements that are worth considering, especially a population that was growing beyond the limits of the food supply. This is one of many websites that provides insight into this very important demographic event.

CHAPTER 4
Demographic Data

Figure 4.1 Population Center of the United States Based on Data from the Decennial Censuses
Source: U.S. Bureau of Census, Census Atlas of the United States (Washington, DC: U.S. Census Bureau), page 11.

I have offered you a variety of facts thus far as I described the history of population growth and provided you with an overview of the world's population situation. I do not just make up these numbers, of course, so in this chapter I discuss the various kinds of demographic data we draw on to know what is happening in the world. To analyze the demography of a particular society, we need to know how many people live there, how they are distributed geographically, how many are being born, how many are dying, how many are moving in, and how many are moving out. That, of course, is only the beginning. If we want to unravel the mysteries of why things are as they are and not just describe what they are, we have to know about the social, psychological, economic, and even physical characteristics of the people and places being studied. Furthermore, we need to know these things not just for the present but for the past as well. Let me begin the discussion, however, with sources of basic information about the numbers of living people, births, deaths, and migrants.

Sources of Demographic Data

The primary source of data on population size and distribution, as well as on demographic structure and characteristics, is the **census of population**. After an overview of the history of population censuses, I will take a closer look at census-taking in North America—the United States, Canada, and Mexico. The major source of information on the population processes of births and deaths is the registration of **vital statistics**, although in a few countries this task is accomplished by **population registers**, and in many developing nations vital events are estimated from **sample surveys**. **Administrative data** and **historical data** provide much of the information about population changes at the local level and about geographic mobility and migration.

Population Censuses

For centuries, governments have wanted to know how many people were under their rule. Rarely has their curiosity been piqued by scientific concern, but rather governments wanted to know who the taxpayers were, or they wanted to identify potential laborers and soldiers. The most direct way to find out how many people there are is to count them, and when you do that you are conducting a population census. The United Nations defines a census of population more specifically as "the total process of collecting, compiling, evaluating, analysing and publishing or otherwise disseminating demographic, economic and social data pertaining, at a specified time, to all persons in a country or in a well-delimited part of a country" (United Nations Statistics Division 2008:7). In practice, this does not mean that every person actually is seen and interviewed by a census taker. In most countries, it means that one adult in a household answers questions about all the people living in that household. These answers may be written responses to a questionnaire sent by mail or verbal responses to questions asked in person by the census taker.

The term *census* comes from the Latin for "assessing" or "taxing." For Romans, it meant a register of adult male citizens and their property for purposes of taxation, the distribution of military obligations, and the determination of political status

(Starr 1987). Thus, in A.D. 119 a person named Horos from the village of Bacchias left behind a letter on papyrus in which he states: "I register myself and those of my household for the house-by-house census of the past second year of Hadrian Caesar our Lord. I am Horos, the aforesaid, a cultivator of state land, forty-eight years old, with a scar on my left eyebrow, and I register my wife Tapekusis, daughter of Horos, forty-five years old. . . ." (Winter 1936:187).

As far as we know, the earliest governments to undertake censuses of their populations were those in the ancient civilizations of Egypt, Babylonia, China, Palestine, and Rome (Bryan 2004). For several hundreds of years, citizens of Rome were counted periodically for tax and military purposes, and this enumeration of Roman subjects was extended to the entire empire, including Roman Egypt, in 5 B.C. The Bible records this event as follows: "In those days a decree went out from Caesar Augustus that all the world should be enrolled. This was the first enrollment, when Quirinius was governor of Syria. And all went to be enrolled, each to his own city" (Luke 2:1–3). You can, of course, imagine the deficiencies of a census that required people to show up at their birthplaces rather than paying census takers to go out and do the counting. And, in fact, all that was actually required was that the head of each household provide government officials with a list of every household member (Horsley 1987).

In the seventh century A.D., the Prophet Mohammed led his followers to Medina (in Saudi Arabia), and after establishing a city-state there, one of his first activities was to conduct a written census of the entire Muslim population in the city (the returns showed a total of 1,500) (Nu'Man 1992). William of Normandy used a similar strategy in 1086, twenty years after having conquered England. William ordered an enumeration of all the landed wealth in the newly acquired territory in order to determine how much revenue the landowners owed the government. Data were recorded in the Domesday Book, *domesday* being the word in Middle English for *doomsday*, which is the day of final judgment. The census document was so named because it was the final proof of legal title to land. The Domesday Book was not really what we think of today as a census, because it was an enumeration of "hearths," or household heads and their wealth, rather than of people. In order to calculate the total population of England in 1086 from the Domesday Book, you would have to multiply the number of "hearths" by some estimate of household size. More than 300,000 households were included, so if they averaged five persons per household, the population of England at the time was approximately 1.5 million (Hinde 1995). The population actually was larger than that because, in fact, the Domesday Book does not cover London, Winchester, Northumberland, Durham, or much of northwest England, and the only parts of Wales included are certain border areas (U.K. National Archives 2009).

The European renaissance began in northern Italy in the fourteenth century, and the Venetians and then the Florentines were interested in counting the wealth of their region, as William had been after conquering England. They developed a *catasto* that combined a count of the hearth and individuals. Thus, unlike the Domesday Book, the Florentine catasto of 1427 recorded not only the wealth of households but also data about each member of the household. In fact, so much information was collected that most of it went unexamined until the modern advent of computers (Herlihy and Klapisch-Zuber 1985). The value of a census was well known to François de Salignac de La Mothe-Fénelon, who was a very influential

French political philosopher of the late seventeenth and early eighteenth centuries. He was the tutor to the Duke of Burgundy and much of his writing was intended as a primer of government for the young duke:

> Do you know the number of men who compose your nation? How many men, and how many women, how many farmers, how many artisans, how many lawyers, how many tradespeople, how many priests and monks, how many nobles and soldiers? What would you say of a shepherd who did not know the size of his flock? . . . A king not knowing all these things is only half a king (quoted in Jones 2002:110).

By that description, Louis XIV (the "Sun King") and his grandson Louis XV were only partial kings, because the demographic evidence now suggests that the French population was growing in the eighteenth century, rather than declining, as the royal advisors (including the physiocrat Quesnay) believed at the time. Fénelon's books and essays were widely read in the early eighteenth century, which ushered in the modern era of nation-states, in turn giving rise to a genuine quest for accurate population information (Hollingsworth 1969). Indeed the term *statistic* is derived from the German word meaning "facts about a state." Sweden was one of the first of the European nations to keep track of its population regularly with the establishment in 1749 of a combined population register and census administered in each diocese by the local clergy (Statistika Centralbyran [Sweden] 1983). Denmark and several Italian states (before the uniting of Italy in the late nineteenth century) also conducted censuses during the eighteenth century (Carr-Saunders 1936), as did the United States (where the first census was conducted in 1790). England launched its first modern census in 1801.

By the latter part of the nineteenth century, the statistical approach to understanding business and government affairs had started to take root in the Western world (Cassedy 1969). The population census began to be viewed as a potential tool for finding out more than just how many people there were and where they lived. Governments began to ask questions about age, marital status, whether and how people were employed, literacy, and so forth. Census data (in combination with other statistics) have become the "lenses through which we form images of our society." Frederick Jackson Turner announced this famous view on the significance of the closing of the frontier on the basis of data from the 1890 census. Our national self-image today is confirmed or challenged by numbers that tell of drastic changes in the family, the increase in ethnic diversity, and many other trends. Winston Churchill observed that "first we shape our buildings and then they shape us. The same may be said of our statistics" (Alonso and Starr 1982:30).

The potential power behind the numbers that censuses produce can be gauged by public reaction to a census. In Germany, the enumeration of 1983 was postponed to 1987 because of public concern that the census was prying unduly into private lives. Germany did not conduct another census until 2002, well after reunification, and even then it was a sample census, not a complete enumeration. In the past few decades, protests have occurred in England, Switzerland, and the Netherlands, as well. In the Netherlands case, the census scheduled for the 1980s was actually canceled after a survey indicating that the majority of the urban population would not cooperate (Robey 1983), and no census has been taken since. However, the Netherlands maintains a population register, which I discuss later, so it does have good demographic information even in the absence of a census.

Since the end of World War II, the United Nations has encouraged countries to enumerate their populations in censuses, often providing financial as well as technical aid. Between 1953 and 1964, 78 percent of the world's population (including that of mainland China) was enumerated by census. In the most recently completed census round (1995 through 2004), 89 percent of the world's population was enumerated, and in the current round (2005 through 2014), all but five countries in the world (Lebanon, Madagascar, Myanmar, Somalia, and Uzbekistan) have either completed a census or have one planned (although it may turn out that not all of those planned will actually be undertaken) (United Nations Statistics Division 2010). The world's two largest nations, China and India, each regularly conduct censuses, with the most recent being China in 2010 and India in 2011. India is, in fact, well into its second 100 years of census taking, the first census having been taken in 1881 under the supervision of the British.

In contrast to India's regular census–taking, another of England's former colonies, Nigeria (the world's eighth most populous nation), has had more trouble with these efforts. Nigeria's population is divided among three broad ethnic groups: the Hausa-Fulani in the north, who are predominately Muslim; the Yoruba in the southwest, who are of various religious faiths; and the largely Christian Igbo in the southeast. The 1952 census of Nigeria indicated that the Hausa-Fulani had the largest share of the population, and so they dominated the first postcolonial government set up after independence in 1960. The newly independent nation ordered a census to be taken in 1962, but the results showed that northerners accounted for only 30 percent of the population. A "recount" in 1963 led somewhat suspiciously to the north accounting for 67 percent of the population. This exacerbated underlying ethnic tensions, culminating in the Igbo declaring independence. The resulting Biafran war (1967–70) saw at least 3 million people lose their lives before the Igbo rejoined the rest of Nigeria. A census in 1973 was never accepted by the government, and it was not until 1991 that the nation felt stable enough to try its hand again at enumeration, after agreeing that there would be no questions about ethnic group, language, or religion, and that population numbers would not be used as a basis for government expenditures. The official census count was 88.5 million people, well below the 110 million that many population experts had been guessing in the absence of any real data (Okolo 1999).

In March 2006, Nigeria completed its first census since 1991, but not without protests, boycotts, rows over payments to officials, and at least 15 deaths (Lalasz 2006). The final count from the 2006 census was about 140 million and, given the history of census–taking in the country, there was a lot of skepticism surrounding the numbers. The census had steered clear of questions about religion, but the 2008 Nigeria Demographic and Health Survey (see later in this chapter for a discussion of these surveys) suggests that 54 percent of women and men aged 15–49 are Christian, while about 45 percent are Muslim, and one percent practice some other religion (National Population Commission [Nigeria] and ICF Macro 2009).

Lebanon has not been enumerated since 1932, when the country was under French colonial rule (Domschke and Goyer 1986). At the time, the country's population was divided nearly equally between Christians and Muslims, and that, combined with the political strife between those groups, made taking a census a very sensitive political issue. Before the nation was literally torn apart by civil war in the 1980s, the Christians had held a slight majority with respect to political representation. But Muslims almost certainly now hold a demographic majority, especially along Lebanon's southern border, next door to Israel. The Israelis knew something of the demographics of that area before they invaded it briefly in late 2006 because they had collected information about the population and infrastructure there during their military occupation of the region in the 1980s (Associated Press 1983).

I should note that censuses historically have been unpopular in that part of the world. The Old Testament of the Bible tells us that in ancient times King David ordered a census of Israel in which his enumerators counted "one million, one hundred thousand men who drew the sword. . . . But God was displeased with this thing [the census], and he smote Israel. . . . So the Lord sent a pestilence upon Israel; and there fell seventy thousand men of Israel" (1 Chronicles 21). Fortunately, in modern times, the advantages of census taking seem more clearly to outweigh the disadvantages. This has been especially true in the United States, where records indicate that no census has been followed directly by a pestilence.

The Census of the United States

Population censuses were part of colonial life prior to the creation of the United States. A census had been conducted in Virginia in the early 1600s, and most of the northern colonies had conducted a census prior to the Revolution (U.S. Census Bureau 1978). A population census has been taken every 10 years since 1790 in the United States as part of the constitutional mandate that seats in the House of Representatives be apportioned on the bases of population size and distribution. Article 1 of the U.S. Constitution directs that "representatives. . . . shall be apportioned among the several states which may be included within this union, according to their respective numbers. . . . The actual Enumeration shall be made within three years after the first meeting of the Congress of the United States, and within every subsequent term of ten years, in such manner as they shall by law direct." Even in 1790 the government used the census to find out more than just how many people there were. The census asked for the names of the following: head of family, free white males aged 16 years and older, free white females, slaves, and other persons. The census questions were reflections of the social importance of those categories.

For the first 100 years of census taking in the United States, the population was enumerated by U.S. marshals. In 1880, special census agents were hired for the first time, and finally in 1902 the Census Bureau became a permanent part of the government bureaucracy (Francese 1979; Hobbs and Stoops 2002). Beyond a core of inquiries designed to elicit demographic and housing information, the questions asked on the census have fluctuated according to the concerns of the time. Interest in international migration, for example, rose in 1920 just before the passage of a restrictive immigration law, and the census in that year added a battery of questions about the foreign-born population. In 2000, a question was added about grandparents as caregivers, replacing a question on fertility, and providing insight into the shift in focus from how many children women were having to the issue of who is taking care of those children. Questions are added and deleted by the Census Bureau through a process of consultation with Congress, other government officials, and census statistics users.

One of the more controversial items for the Census 2000 questionnaire was the question about race and ethnicity. The growing racial and ethnic diversity of the

United States has led to a larger number of interracial/interethnic marriages and relationships producing children of mixed origin (also called multiracial). Previous censuses had asked people to choose a single category of race to describe themselves, but there was a considerable public sentiment that people should be able to identify themselves as being of mixed or multiple origins if, in fact, they perceived themselves in that way (Harris and Sim 2002). Late in 1997, the government accepted the recommendation from a federally appointed committee that people of mixed racial heritage be able to choose more than one race category when filling out the Census 2000 (and the Census 2010) questionnaire. Thus, a person whose mother is white and whose father is African American was able to check both "White" and "Black or African American," whereas in the past the choice would have had to be made between the two. There was still a separate question on "Hispanic/Latino/Spanish Origin" identity, and that was retained for the 2010 census, as you can see in Figure 4.2.

An even deeper controversy concerns the question of whether "race" is even an appropriate category to ask about (Nobles 2000). Zuberi (2001) argues that because race is a social construct rather than a biological fact, it should be treated differently than it currently is in social statistics, and Hirschman, Alba, and Farley (2000) suggested replacing the racial category in the census with a question about "origins," which may be a more socially meaningful way of looking at the issue of minority status within a society.

The census is designed as a complete enumeration of the population, but in the United States only a few of the questions are actually asked of everyone. For reasons of economy, most items in the census questionnaire have been administered to a sample of households in the last several censuses. From 1790 through 1930, all questions were asked of all applicable persons, but as the American population grew and Congress kept adding new questions to the census, the savings involved in sampling grew, and in 1940 the Census Bureau began its practice of asking only a small number of items of all households, and using a sample of households to gather more detailed data. Fortunately, there has been no significant loss in accuracy. In 2000, there were 281 million people counted in more than 100 million households in the United States. Thus, the sampling of one out of every six households in 2000 who received a questionnaire with detailed questions still yielded data from nearly 50 million people.

A major change for the 2010 census in the United States was that it included only the short form, with the detailed data being collected through the ongoing **American Community Survey**, which I discuss later in the chapter. The items of information obtained from everyone (the so-called "short-form" items) include the basic demographic and housing characteristics—essentially the information required for congressional redistricting. The questionnaire for Census 2010 is reproduced as Figure 4.2. The first page asks that everyone in a household be listed by name, which allows the Census Bureau to check for duplicate listings of people (such as college students away from home). The first person listed is supposed to be someone in the household who owns, is buying, or rents this housing unit. This person used to be known as the "head of household" (and there is still a tax category in the United States for such a person), but the Census Bureau now refers to him or her on the census form simply as "Person 1." Information is then requested for each person in the household regarding his or her relationship to "Person 1," sex, age and year of birth, race, and whether the person is of Hispanic origin.

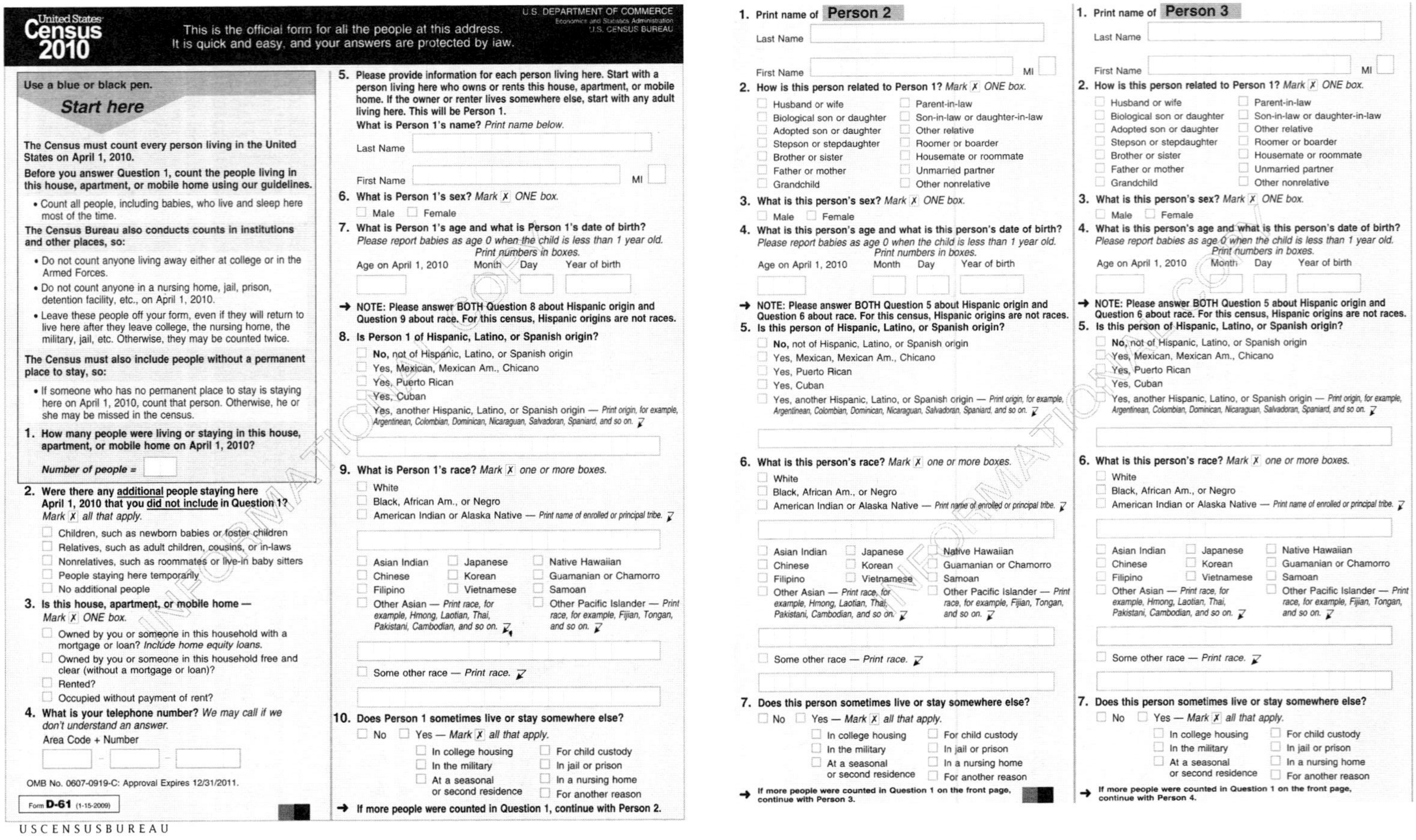

United States Census 2010

U.S. DEPARTMENT OF COMMERCE
Economics and Statistics Administration
U.S. CENSUS BUREAU

This is the official form for all the people at this address.
It is quick and easy, and your answers are protected by law.

Use a blue or black pen.

Start here

The Census must count every person living in the United States on April 1, 2010.

Before you answer Question 1, count the people living in this house, apartment, or mobile home using our guidelines.

- Count all people, including babies, who live and sleep here most of the time.

The Census Bureau also conducts counts in institutions and other places, so:

- Do not count anyone living away either at college or in the Armed Forces.
- Do not count anyone in a nursing home, jail, prison, detention facility, etc., on April 1, 2010.
- Leave these people off your form, even if they will return to live here after they leave college, the nursing home, the military, jail, etc. Otherwise, they may be counted twice.

The Census must also include people without a permanent place to stay, so:

- If someone who has no permanent place to stay is staying here on April 1, 2010, count that person. Otherwise, he or she may be missed in the census.

1. **How many people were living or staying in this house, apartment, or mobile home on April 1, 2010?**

   Number of people = ☐

2. **Were there any additional people staying here April 1, 2010 that you did not include in Question 1?**
   Mark ☒ all that apply.
   - ☐ Children, such as newborn babies or foster children
   - ☐ Relatives, such as adult children, cousins, or in-laws
   - ☐ Nonrelatives, such as roommates or live-in baby sitters
   - ☐ People staying here temporarily
   - ☐ No additional people

3. **Is this house, apartment, or mobile home —**
   Mark ☒ ONE box.
   - ☐ Owned by you or someone in this household with a mortgage or loan? *Include home equity loans.*
   - ☐ Owned by you or someone in this household free and clear (without a mortgage or loan)?
   - ☐ Rented?
   - ☐ Occupied without payment of rent?

4. **What is your telephone number?** *We may call if we don't understand an answer.*
   Area Code + Number

OMB No. 0607-0919-C: Approval Expires 12/31/2011.

Form **D-61** (1-15-2009)

5. **Please provide information for each person living here. Start with a person living here who owns or rents this house, apartment, or mobile home. If the owner or renter lives somewhere else, start with any adult living here. This will be Person 1.**
   What is Person 1's name? *Print name below.*
   Last Name
   First Name MI

6. **What is Person 1's sex?** *Mark ☒ ONE box.*
   ☐ Male ☐ Female

7. **What is Person 1's age and what is Person 1's date of birth?**
   Please report babies as age 0 when the child is less than 1 year old.
   Print numbers in boxes.
   Age on April 1, 2010 Month Day Year of birth

→ **NOTE: Please answer BOTH Question 8 about Hispanic origin and Question 9 about race. For this census, Hispanic origins are not races.**

8. **Is Person 1 of Hispanic, Latino, or Spanish origin?**
   - ☐ **No,** not of Hispanic, Latino, or Spanish origin
   - ☐ Yes, Mexican, Mexican Am., Chicano
   - ☐ Yes, Puerto Rican
   - ☐ Yes, Cuban
   - ☐ Yes, another Hispanic, Latino, or Spanish origin — *Print origin, for example, Argentinean, Colombian, Dominican, Nicaraguan, Salvadoran, Spaniard, and so on.*

9. **What is Person 1's race?** *Mark ☒ one or more boxes.*
   - ☐ White
   - ☐ Black, African Am., or Negro
   - ☐ American Indian or Alaska Native — *Print name of enrolled or principal tribe.*
   - ☐ Asian Indian ☐ Japanese ☐ Native Hawaiian
   - ☐ Chinese ☐ Korean ☐ Guamanian or Chamorro
   - ☐ Filipino ☐ Vietnamese ☐ Samoan
   - ☐ Other Asian — *Print race, for example, Hmong, Laotian, Thai, Pakistani, Cambodian, and so on.* ☐ Other Pacific Islander — *Print race, for example, Fijian, Tongan, and so on.*
   - ☐ Some other race — *Print race.*

10. **Does Person 1 sometimes live or stay somewhere else?**
    ☐ No ☐ Yes — *Mark ☒ all that apply.*
    - ☐ In college housing ☐ For child custody
    - ☐ In the military ☐ In jail or prison
    - ☐ At a seasonal or second residence ☐ In a nursing home
    - ☐ For another reason

→ **If more people were counted in Question 1, continue with Person 2.**

1. **Print name of Person 2**
   Last Name
   First Name MI

2. **How is this person related to Person 1?** *Mark ☒ ONE box.*
   - ☐ Husband or wife ☐ Parent-in-law
   - ☐ Biological son or daughter ☐ Son-in-law or daughter-in-law
   - ☐ Adopted son or daughter ☐ Other relative
   - ☐ Stepson or stepdaughter ☐ Roomer or boarder
   - ☐ Brother or sister ☐ Housemate or roommate
   - ☐ Father or mother ☐ Unmarried partner
   - ☐ Grandchild ☐ Other nonrelative

3. **What is this person's sex?** *Mark ☒ ONE box.*
   ☐ Male ☐ Female

4. **What is this person's age and what is this person's date of birth?**
   Please report babies as age 0 when the child is less than 1 year old.
   Print numbers in boxes.
   Age on April 1, 2010 Month Day Year of birth

→ **NOTE: Please answer BOTH Question 5 about Hispanic origin and Question 6 about race. For this census, Hispanic origins are not races.**

5. **Is this person of Hispanic, Latino, or Spanish origin?**
   - ☐ **No,** not of Hispanic, Latino, or Spanish origin
   - ☐ Yes, Mexican, Mexican Am., Chicano
   - ☐ Yes, Puerto Rican
   - ☐ Yes, Cuban
   - ☐ Yes, another Hispanic, Latino, or Spanish origin — *Print origin, for example, Argentinean, Colombian, Dominican, Nicaraguan, Salvadoran, Spaniard, and so on.*

6. **What is this person's race?** *Mark ☒ one or more boxes.*
   - ☐ White
   - ☐ Black, African Am., or Negro
   - ☐ American Indian or Alaska Native — *Print name of enrolled or principal tribe.*
   - ☐ Asian Indian ☐ Japanese ☐ Native Hawaiian
   - ☐ Chinese ☐ Korean ☐ Guamanian or Chamorro
   - ☐ Filipino ☐ Vietnamese ☐ Samoan
   - ☐ Other Asian — *Print race, for example, Hmong, Laotian, Thai, Pakistani, Cambodian, and so on.* ☐ Other Pacific Islander — *Print race, for example, Fijian, Tongan, and so on.*
   - ☐ Some other race — *Print race.*

7. **Does this person sometimes live or stay somewhere else?**
   ☐ No ☐ Yes — *Mark ☒ all that apply.*
   - ☐ In college housing ☐ For child custody
   - ☐ In the military ☐ In jail or prison
   - ☐ At a seasonal or second residence ☐ In a nursing home
   - ☐ For another reason

→ **If more people were counted in Question 1 on the front page, continue with Person 3.**

1. **Print name of Person 3**
   Last Name
   First Name MI

2. **How is this person related to Person 1?** *Mark ☒ ONE box.*
   - ☐ Husband or wife ☐ Parent-in-law
   - ☐ Biological son or daughter ☐ Son-in-law or daughter-in-law
   - ☐ Adopted son or daughter ☐ Other relative
   - ☐ Stepson or stepdaughter ☐ Roomer or boarder
   - ☐ Brother or sister ☐ Housemate or roommate
   - ☐ Father or mother ☐ Unmarried partner
   - ☐ Grandchild ☐ Other nonrelative

3. **What is this person's sex?** *Mark ☒ ONE box.*
   ☐ Male ☐ Female

4. **What is this person's age and what is this person's date of birth?**
   Please report babies as age 0 when the child is less than 1 year old.
   Print numbers in boxes.
   Age on April 1, 2010 Month Day Year of birth

→ **NOTE: Please answer BOTH Question 5 about Hispanic origin and Question 6 about race. For this census, Hispanic origins are not races.**

5. **Is this person of Hispanic, Latino, or Spanish origin?**
   - ☐ **No,** not of Hispanic, Latino, or Spanish origin
   - ☐ Yes, Mexican, Mexican Am., Chicano
   - ☐ Yes, Puerto Rican
   - ☐ Yes, Cuban
   - ☐ Yes, another Hispanic, Latino, or Spanish origin — *Print origin, for example, Argentinean, Colombian, Dominican, Nicaraguan, Salvadoran, Spaniard, and so on.*

6. **What is this person's race?** *Mark ☒ one or more boxes.*
   - ☐ White
   - ☐ Black, African Am., or Negro
   - ☐ American Indian or Alaska Native — *Print name of enrolled or principal tribe.*
   - ☐ Asian Indian ☐ Japanese ☐ Native Hawaiian
   - ☐ Chinese ☐ Korean ☐ Guamanian or Chamorro
   - ☐ Filipino ☐ Vietnamese ☐ Samoan
   - ☐ Other Asian — *Print race, for example, Hmong, Laotian, Thai, Pakistani, Cambodian, and so on.* ☐ Other Pacific Islander — *Print race, for example, Fijian, Tongan, and so on.*
   - ☐ Some other race — *Print race.*

7. **Does this person sometimes live or stay somewhere else?**
   ☐ No ☐ Yes — *Mark ☒ all that apply.*
   - ☐ In college housing ☐ For child custody
   - ☐ In the military ☐ In jail or prison
   - ☐ At a seasonal or second residence ☐ In a nursing home
   - ☐ For another reason

→ **If more people were counted in Question 1 on the front page, continue with Person 4.**

USCENSUSBUREAU

Figure 4.2 Questionnaire for United States Census 2010

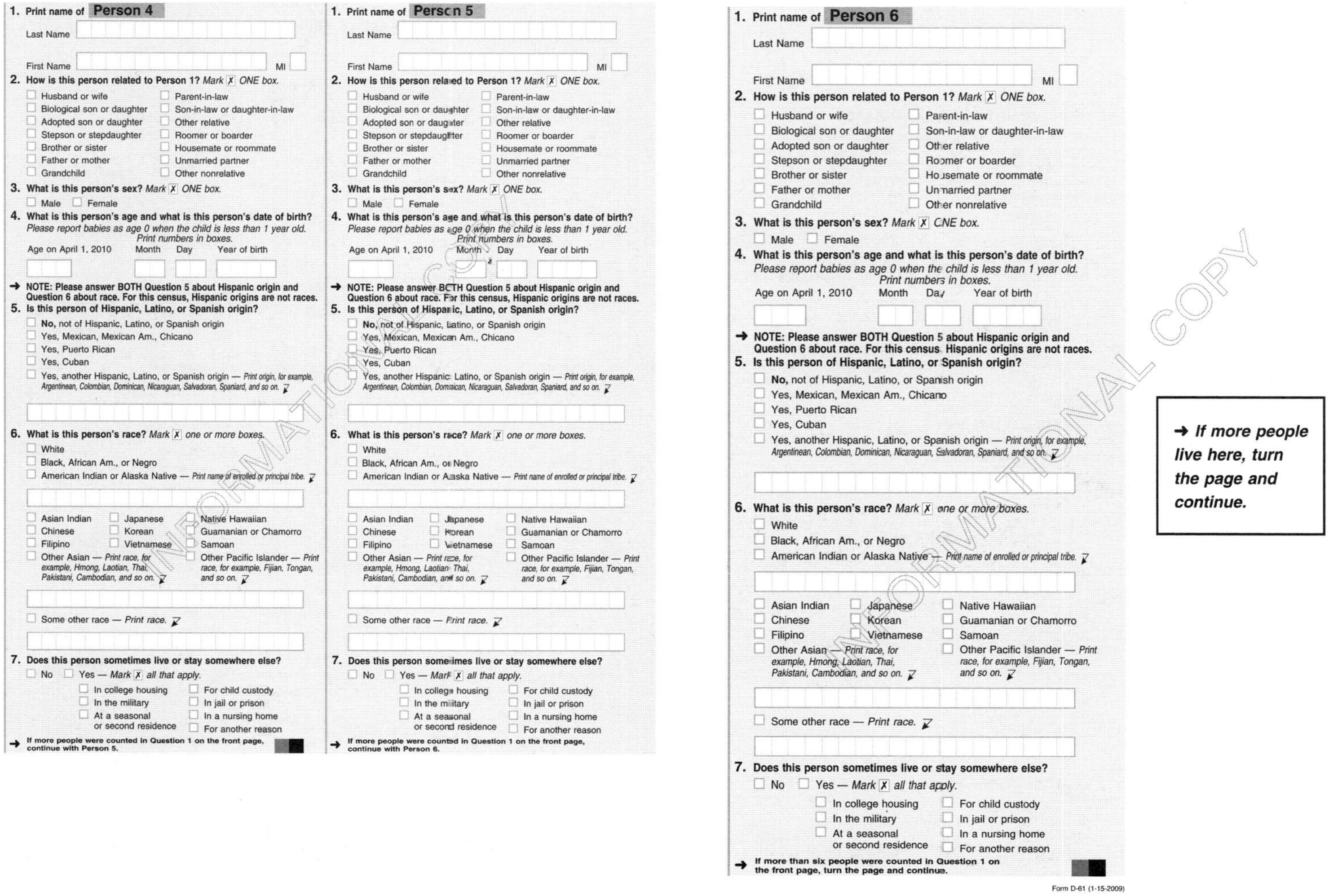

1. Print name of **Person 4**
Last Name
First Name MI
2. How is this person related to Person 1? *Mark* ☒ *ONE box.*
☐ Husband or wife ☐ Parent-in-law
☐ Biological son or daughter ☐ Son-in-law or daughter-in-law
☐ Adopted son or daughter ☐ Other relative
☐ Stepson or stepdaughter ☐ Roomer or boarder
☐ Brother or sister ☐ Housemate or roommate
☐ Father or mother ☐ Unmarried partner
☐ Grandchild ☐ Other nonrelative
3. What is this person's sex? *Mark* ☒ *ONE box.*
☐ Male ☐ Female
4. What is this person's age and what is this person's date of birth?
Please report babies as age 0 when the child is less than 1 year old. Print numbers in boxes.
Age on April 1, 2010 Month Day Year of birth
→ NOTE: Please answer BOTH Question 5 about Hispanic origin and Question 6 about race. For this census, Hispanic origins are not races.
5. Is this person of Hispanic, Latino, or Spanish origin?
☐ **No,** not of Hispanic, Latino, or Spanish origin
☐ Yes, Mexican, Mexican Am., Chicano
☐ Yes, Puerto Rican
☐ Yes, Cuban
☐ Yes, another Hispanic, Latino, or Spanish origin — *Print origin, for example, Argentinean, Colombian, Dominican, Nicaraguan, Salvadoran, Spaniard, and so on.*
6. What is this person's race? *Mark* ☒ *one or more boxes.*
☐ White
☐ Black, African Am., or Negro
☐ American Indian or Alaska Native — *Print name of enrolled or principal tribe.*
☐ Asian Indian ☐ Japanese ☐ Native Hawaiian
☐ Chinese ☐ Korean ☐ Guamanian or Chamorro
☐ Filipino ☐ Vietnamese ☐ Samoan
☐ Other Asian — *Print race, for example, Hmong, Laotian, Thai, Pakistani, Cambodian, and so on.* ☐ Other Pacific Islander — *Print race, for example, Fijian, Tongan, and so on.*
☐ Some other race — *Print race.*
7. Does this person sometimes live or stay somewhere else?
☐ No ☐ Yes — *Mark* ☒ *all that apply.*
☐ In college housing ☐ For child custody
☐ In the military ☐ In jail or prison
☐ At a seasonal or second residence ☐ In a nursing home
☐ For another reason
→ If more people were counted in Question 1 on the front page, continue with Person 5.

1. Print name of **Person 5**
Last Name
First Name MI
2. How is this person related to Person 1? *Mark* ☒ *ONE box.*
☐ Husband or wife ☐ Parent-in-law
☐ Biological son or daughter ☐ Son-in-law or daughter-in-law
☐ Adopted son or daughter ☐ Other relative
☐ Stepson or stepdaughter ☐ Roomer or boarder
☐ Brother or sister ☐ Housemate or roommate
☐ Father or mother ☐ Unmarried partner
☐ Grandchild ☐ Other nonrelative
3. What is this person's sex? *Mark* ☒ *ONE box.*
☐ Male ☐ Female
4. What is this person's age and what is this person's date of birth?
Please report babies as age 0 when the child is less than 1 year old. Print numbers in boxes.
Age on April 1, 2010 Month Day Year of birth
→ NOTE: Please answer BOTH Question 5 about Hispanic origin and Question 6 about race. For this census, Hispanic origins are not races.
5. Is this person of Hispanic, Latino, or Spanish origin?
☐ **No,** not of Hispanic, Latino, or Spanish origin
☐ Yes, Mexican, Mexican Am., Chicano
☐ Yes, Puerto Rican
☐ Yes, Cuban
☐ Yes, another Hispanic, Latino, or Spanish origin — *Print origin, for example, Argentinean, Colombian, Dominican, Nicaraguan, Salvadoran, Spaniard, and so on.*
6. What is this person's race? *Mark* ☒ *one or more boxes.*
☐ White
☐ Black, African Am., or Negro
☐ American Indian or Alaska Native — *Print name of enrolled or principal tribe.*
☐ Asian Indian ☐ Japanese ☐ Native Hawaiian
☐ Chinese ☐ Korean ☐ Guamanian or Chamorro
☐ Filipino ☐ Vietnamese ☐ Samoan
☐ Other Asian — *Print race, for example, Hmong, Laotian, Thai, Pakistani, Cambodian, and so on.* ☐ Other Pacific Islander — *Print race, for example, Fijian, Tongan, and so on.*
☐ Some other race — *Print race.*
7. Does this person sometimes live or stay somewhere else?
☐ No ☐ Yes — *Mark* ☒ *all that apply.*
☐ In college housing ☐ For child custody
☐ In the military ☐ In jail or prison
☐ At a seasonal or second residence ☐ In a nursing home
☐ For another reason
→ If more people were counted in Question 1 on the front page, continue with Person 6.

1. Print name of **Person 6**
Last Name
First Name MI
2. How is this person related to Person 1? *Mark* ☒ *ONE box.*
☐ Husband or wife ☐ Parent-in-law
☐ Biological son or daughter ☐ Son-in-law or daughter-in-law
☐ Adopted son or daughter ☐ Other relative
☐ Stepson or stepdaughter ☐ Roomer or boarder
☐ Brother or sister ☐ Housemate or roommate
☐ Father or mother ☐ Unmarried partner
☐ Grandchild ☐ Other nonrelative
3. What is this person's sex? *Mark* ☒ *ONE box.*
☐ Male ☐ Female
4. What is this person's age and what is this person's date of birth?
Please report babies as age 0 when the child is less than 1 year old. Print numbers in boxes.
Age on April 1, 2010 Month Day Year of birth
→ NOTE: Please answer BOTH Question 5 about Hispanic origin and Question 6 about race. For this census, Hispanic origins are not races.
5. Is this person of Hispanic, Latino, or Spanish origin?
☐ **No,** not of Hispanic, Latino, or Spanish origin
☐ Yes, Mexican, Mexican Am., Chicano
☐ Yes, Puerto Rican
☐ Yes, Cuban
☐ Yes, another Hispanic, Latino, or Spanish origin — *Print origin, for example, Argentinean, Colombian, Dominican, Nicaraguan, Salvadoran, Spaniard, and so on.*
6. What is this person's race? *Mark* ☒ *one or more boxes.*
☐ White
☐ Black, African Am., or Negro
☐ American Indian or Alaska Native — *Print name of enrolled or principal tribe.*
☐ Asian Indian ☐ Japanese ☐ Native Hawaiian
☐ Chinese ☐ Korean ☐ Guamanian or Chamorro
☐ Filipino ☐ Vietnamese ☐ Samoan
☐ Other Asian — *Print race, for example, Hmong, Laotian, Thai, Pakistani, Cambodian, and so on.* ☐ Other Pacific Islander — *Print race, for example, Fijian, Tongan, and so on.*
☐ Some other race — *Print race.*
7. Does this person sometimes live or stay somewhere else?
☐ No ☐ Yes — *Mark* ☒ *all that apply.*
☐ In college housing ☐ For child custody
☐ In the military ☐ In jail or prison
☐ At a seasonal or second residence ☐ In a nursing home
☐ For another reason
→ If more than six people were counted in Question 1 on the front page, turn the page and continue.

→ *If more people live here, turn the page and continue.*

Form D-61 (1-15-2009)

Figure 4.2 *(continued)*

Use this section to complete information for the rest of the people you counted in Question 1 on the front page. *We may call for additional information about them.*

Person 7 **Last Name** **First Name** **MI**

Sex ☐ Male ☐ Female **Age on April 1, 2010** **Date of Birth** Month Day Year **Related to Person 1?** ☐ Yes ☐ No

Person 8 **Last Name** **First Name** **MI**

Sex ☐ Male ☐ Female **Age on April 1, 2010** **Date of Birth** Month Day Year **Related to Person 1?** ☐ Yes ☐ No

Person 9 **Last Name** **First Name** **MI**

Sex ☐ Male ☐ Female **Age on April 1, 2010** **Date of Birth** Month Day Year **Related to Person 1?** ☐ Yes ☐ No

Person 10 **Last Name** **First Name** **MI**

Sex ☐ Male ☐ Female **Age on April 1, 2010** **Date of Birth** Month Day Year **Related to Person 1?** ☐ Yes ☐ No

Person 11 **Last Name** **First Name** **MI**

Sex ☐ Male ☐ Female **Age on April 1, 2010** **Date of Birth** Month Day Year **Related to Person 1?** ☐ Yes ☐ No

Person 12 **Last Name** **First Name** **MI**

Sex ☐ Male ☐ Female **Age on April 1, 2010** **Date of Birth** Month Day Year **Related to Person 1?** ☐ Yes ☐ No

Thank you for completing your official 2010 Census form.

FOR OFFICIAL USE ONLY
JIC1 **JIC2**

If your enclosed postage-paid envelope is missing, *please mail your completed form to:*
U.S. Census Bureau
National Processing Center
1201 East 10th Street
Jeffersonville, IN 47132

If you need help completing this form, *call 1-866-872-6868 between 8:00 a.m. and 9:00 p.m., 7 days a week. The telephone call is free.*

TDD — *Telephone display device for the hearing impaired. Call 1-866-783-2010 between 8:00 a.m. and 9:00 p.m., 7 days a week. The telephone call is free.*

¿NECESITA AYUDA? *Si usted necesita ayuda para completar este cuestionario, llame al 1-866-928-2010 entre las 8:00 a.m. y 9:00 p.m., 7 días a la semana. La llamada telefónica es gratis.*

The U.S. Census Bureau estimates that, for the average household, this form will take about 10 minutes to complete, including the time for reviewing the instructions and answers. Send comments regarding this burden estimate or any other aspect of this burden to: Paperwork Reduction Project 0607-0919-C, U.S. Census Bureau, AMSD-3K138, 4600 Silver Hill Road, Washington, DC 20233. You may e-mail comments to <Paperwork@census.gov>; use "Paperwork Project 0607-0919-C" as the subject.

Respondents are not required to respond to any information collection unless it displays a valid approval number from the Office of Management and Budget.

Figure 4.2 *(continued)*

Table 4.1 lists the items included on the U.S. Census 2010 questionnaire (the short form), the American Community Survey (from which "long form" data are collected), compared with a list of information obtained by the 2006 and 2011 censuses of Canada and the 2010 census of Mexico, both of which countries are discussed later in this chapter. The table indicates which items are asked of every household and which are asked of a sample of households.

Table 4.1 Comparison of Items Included in the U.S. Census 2010 Questionnaire and the American Community Survey, the 2006 and 2011 Censuses of Canada, and the 2010 Census of Mexico

Census Item	U.S. Census 2010 and ACS	Canada 2006 and 2011	Mexico 2010
Population Characteristics:			
Age	XX	XX	XX
Sex	XX	XX	XX
Relationship to householder (family structure)	XX	XX	XX
Race	XX	X	
Ethnicity	XX	X	
Marital status	X	XX	XX
Fertility			XX
Child mortality			XX
Income	X	X	XX
Sources of income	X	X	X
Health insurance			XX
Job benefits			X
Unpaid household activities		X	
Labor force status	X	X	XX
Industry, occupation, and class of worker	X	X	XX
Work status last year	X		
Veteran status	X		
Grandparents as caregivers	X		
Place of work and journey to work	X	X	XX
Journey to work	X	X	
Vehicles available	X		
Ancestry	X	X	
Place of birth	X	X	XX
Birthplace of parents		X	
Citizenship	X	X	
Year of entry if not born in this country	X	X	
Language spoken at home	X	XX	XX
Language spoken at work		X	
Religion		X	XX
Educational attainment	X	X	XX
School enrollment	X	X	XX

(continued)

Table 4.1 (continued)

Residence one year ago (migration)		X	
Residence five years ago (migration)	X	X	XX
International migration of family members			X
Disability (activities of daily living)	X	X	XX
Housing Characteristics:			
Tenure (rent or own)	XX	XX	XX
Type of housing	XX	XX	XX
Agricultural use of property	X	XX	
Acreage of property	X		
Business use of property	X		
Material used for construction of walls			XX
Material used for construction of roof			XX
Material used for construction of floors			XX
Repairs needed on structure		X	
Year structure built	X	X	X
Units in structure	X		
Rooms in unit	X	X	XX
Bedrooms	X	X	XX
Kitchen facilities	X		XX
Electricity in house			XX
Water source			XX
Toilet facilities	X		XX
Sewerage			XX
Material possessions (TV, radio, etc.)			XX
House heating fuel	X		XX
Year moved into unit	X		
Value of property	X	X	
Selected housing costs	X	X	
Rent or mortgage payment	X	X	

Note: XX = Included and asked of every household; X = Included but asked of only a sample of households. Questions asked on each census may be different; similar categories of questions asked do not necessarily mean strict comparability of data.

In theory, a census obtains accurate information from everyone. But the first question that census workers have to ask is: Who is supposed to be included in the census? Are visitors to the country to be included? Are people who are absent from the country on census day to be excluded?

Who Is Included in the Census? There are several ways to answer that question, and each produces a potentially different total number of people. At one extreme is the concept of the **de facto population**, which counts people who are in a given territory on the census day. At the other extreme is the **de jure population**, which represents people who legally "belong" to a given area in some way or another, regardless of whether they were there on the day of the census. For countries with few foreign workers and where working in another area is rare, the distinction makes little difference. But many countries, including nearly all of the Gulf states in the Middle East, have large numbers of guest workers from other countries, and thus have a larger de facto than de jure population. On the other hand, a country such as Mexico, from which migrants regularly leave temporarily to go to the United States, has a de jure population that is larger than the de facto.

Most countries (including the United States, Canada, and Mexico) have now adopted a concept that lies somewhere between the extremes of de facto and de jure, and they include people in the census on the basis of **usual residence**, which is roughly defined as the place where a person usually sleeps. College students who live away from home, for example, are included at their college address rather than being counted in their parents' household. People with no usual residence (the homeless, including migratory workers, vagrants, and "street people") are counted where they are found. On the other hand, visitors and tourists from other countries who "belong" somewhere else are not included, even though they may be in the country when the census is being conducted. At the same time, the concept of usual residence means that undocumented immigrants (who legally do not "belong" where they are found) will be included in the census along with everyone else.

Where you belong became a court issue following Census 2000 in the United States. The Census Bureau includes in the census members of the military and the federal government who are stationed abroad. They are counted as belonging to the state in the United States that was their normal domicile, and in 2000 this turned out especially to benefit North Carolina. However, Utah filed suit in federal court, objecting that Mormon missionaries from Utah who were serving abroad should also be counted as residents of Utah, rather than being excluded because they were living outside the United States. In 2001, the U.S. District Court ruled against that idea, and so North Carolina gained a seat in Congress on the basis of its "overseas residents" while Utah did not. Utah pushed the idea again for the 2010 census, but again the plan was rejected by the Census Bureau, which pointed out that an estimated 6 million Americans live abroad who are not on the U.S. government payroll and there is no reliable way to count them (Associated Press 2009).

Knowing who should be included in the census does not, however, guarantee that they will all be found and accurately counted. There are several possible errors that can creep into the enumeration process. We can divide these into the two broad categories of **nonsampling error** (which includes **coverage error** and **content error**) and **sampling error**.

Coverage Error The two most common sources of error in a census are coverage error and content error. A census is designed to count everyone, but there are always people who are missed, as well as a few who are counted more than once. The combination of the undercount and the overcount is called coverage error, or **net census undercount** (the difference between the undercount and the overcount). As I discuss below and in the essay that accompanies this chapter, there are several ways to measure and adjust for undercount, but it becomes more complicated (and political) when there is a **differential undercount**, when some groups are more likely to be underenumerated than other groups.

In the United States, the differential undercount has meant that racial/ethnic minority groups (especially African Americans) have been less likely to be included in the census count than whites. Table 4.2 shows estimates of the net undercount in the last several censuses, along with the differential undercount of the black population. The overall undercount in the 1940 census was 5.6 percent, and you can see that it has been steadily declining since then as the Census Bureau institutes ever more sophisticated procedures. But you can also see that in 1940 more than 10 percent of African Americans in the country were missed by the census. This was the year that the differential undercount was discovered as a result of a "somewhat serendipitous natural experiment" (Anderson and Fienberg 1999:29). Because of World War II, men were registering for the draft when that census was taken, providing demographers with a chance to compare census returns with counts of men registering for the draft. It turned out that 229,000 more black men signed up for the draft than would have been expected based on census data (Price 1947), signaling some real problems with the completeness of the census coverage in 1940. Since then, a great deal of time, effort, and controversy have gone into attempts to reduce both the overall undercount and the differential undercount. The numbers in Table 4.2 show that Census 2000 appears to have been more successful than any previous census in this regard, and I discuss this issue in more detail in the essay that accompanies this chapter. Note that undercount results from the 2010 census were not yet available as this chapter was being written, but as they become available you can find them at www.census.gov.

Coverage is improved in the census by a variety of measures, such as having better address identification so that every household receives a questionnaire and having a high-profile advertising campaign designed to encourage a high response

Table 4.2 Net Undercount and Differential Undercount in U.S. Censuses

Year	Net undercount for total population (%)	Undercount of black population (%)	Undercount of white population (%)(*)	Differential undercount (percentage point difference between black and white undercount)
1940	5.6	10.3	5.1	5.2
1950	4.4	9.6	3.8	5.8
1960	3.3	8.3	2.7	5.6
1970	2.9	8.0	2.2	5.8
1980	1.4	5.9	0.7	5.2
1990	1.8	5.7	1.3	4.4
2000	1.1	2.1	1.0	1.1

Sources: Data for 1940 through 1980 are from Anderson and Fienberg (1999: Table 4.1); and data for 1990 and 2000 are from Robinson, West, and Adlakha (2002: Table 6). The undercount for 1940 through 1990 is based on demographic analysis, and the undercount for 2000 is based on the Accuracy Coverage and Evaluation Survey.

(*) The data for 1990 and 2000 represent the nonblack population rather than specifically the white population.

to the mail-out questionnaire. Nearly three-fourths (72 percent) of households responded to the mailed questionnaire in 2010, and the rest were contacted by the Census Bureau in the Non-Response Follow-Up (NRFU) phase of data collection. The Census Bureau sends staff members into the field to interview people who do not complete the forms, and, in some cases, to find out about people whom they were unable to contact. When you combine this with the fact that one member of a household may have filled in the information for all household members, it is easy to see why so many people routinely think they have not been counted in the census—someone else answered for them.

In China, coverage error has focused not on racial/ethnic groups but on children. Goodkind (2004) estimated that there were nearly 37 million children under the age of ten who were not counted in the 2000 census in China. The reason for this was not that the census-takers could not find them, but rather that they were being hidden. Acknowledging them would have provided evidence that the government-mandated birth quotas had been exceeded. Since local officials, not just parents, were held responsible for failure to keep the birth rate down, everybody at the local level had an interest in suppressing information about these children.

Measuring Coverage Error Right now you are probably asking yourself how the Census Bureau could ever begin to estimate the number of people missed in a census. This is not an easy task, and statisticians in the United States and other countries have experimented with a number of methods over the years. The two principal methods used are (1) **demographic analysis (DA)**, and (2) **dual-system estimation (DSE)**. The demographic analysis approach uses the **demographic balancing equation** to estimate what the population at the latest census should have been, and then compares that number to the actual count. The demographic balancing equation says that the population at time 2 is equal to the population at time 1 plus the births between time 1 and 2, minus the deaths between time 1 and 2, plus the in-migrants between time 1 and 2, minus the out-migrants between time 1 and 2. Thus, if we know the number of people from the previous census, we can add the number of births since then, subtract the number of deaths since then, add the number of in-migrants since then, and subtract the number of out-migrants since then to estimate what the total population count should have been. A comparison of this number with the actual census count provides a clue as to the accuracy of the census. Using these methods, the Census Bureau is able to piece together a composite rendering of what the population "should" look like. Differences from that picture and the one painted by the census can be used as estimates of under- or over-enumeration. By making these calculations for all age, sex, and racial/ethnic groups, we can arrive at an estimate of the possible undercount among various groups in the population. This, for example, was the basis for deciding that China's 2000 census had missed 37 million children.

Of course, if we do not have an accurate count of births, deaths, and migrants, then our demographic-analysis estimate may itself be wrong, so this method requires careful attention to the quality of the non-census data. And, you say, why should we even take a census if we think we can estimate the number of people more accurately without it? The answer is that the demographic-analysis approach usually only produces an estimate of the total number of people in any age, sex, racial/ethnic

TO ADJUST OR NOT TO ADJUST—THAT IS THE QUESTION; OR IS IT MUCH ADO ABOUT NOTHING?

The differential undercount, which I discuss in this chapter, matters for many reasons that explain why census agencies in every country go to great lengths to encourage people to respond. The motto of the 2010 census in Mexico, for example, was "En México todos contamos" ("in Mexico we all count"—a nice play on words). In the United States, those communities that are less well counted will receive less legislative representation as a result of census-based apportionment and redistricting. They will also stand to lose out in the distribution of population-based funding from federal or state governments. Also important is the fact that those who are typically missed in the U.S. censuses, including especially African Americans and Hispanics, are historically more likely to vote for Democratic candidates than for Republican candidates. That puts the issue of the differential undercount very much in the political spotlight as each census rolls around. Census 2000 was as politically charged as any census ever, and the controversy spilled over into the 2010 census.

After the 1990 census, the Census Bureau had produced a set of very detailed adjusted numbers, reflecting the Bureau's estimates of undercount by age and race/ethnicity for each county in the United States. However, the U.S. Department of Commerce (the bureaucracy within which the Census Bureau is housed—and at that time headed by a Republican in the George H. W. Bush administration) had refused to make the adjusted numbers "official." So the adjusted numbers were there, but were not used for apportionment, redistricting, or the distribution of governmental resources. Had the adjustments been made in 1990, the states of Wisconsin and Pennsylvania would each have lost a seat in Congress and California and Arizona would each have gained a seat. The decision not to adjust sparked a flurry of lawsuits, of course, and in 1996 the U.S. Supreme Court finally ruled unanimously that the Census Bureau was under no legal obligation to adjust the final figures, despite the acknowledged undercount of urban minority group members (Barrett 1996).

You might well think that a unanimous Supreme Court decision would settle an issue, but you would be wrong in this case, because in the meantime the Census Bureau had decided to take the advice offered by the National Academy of Sciences (National Research Council 1993; Edmonston and Schultze 1995; White and Rust 1997) and announced that for Census 2000 it intended to use statistical sampling techniques to estimate and include those people who were otherwise missed by the census enumeration. This is a process known as sampling for nonresponse follow-up (SNRFU for you lovers of acronyms). The basic idea was that rather than having a post-enumeration survey to estimate how many people were missed by the census, the survey process would become part of the census and thus those who were estimated to have been missed would be included in the final count instead of being lamented and fought over later. The traditional methods of enumeration would be used to obtain the first 90 percent of responses, but the last 10 percent (the really hard-to-find people) would be estimated from a large (750,000 households) sample survey. This idea sparked a new flurry of congressional mandates and lawsuits.

On one side of the debate were those members of Congress who wanted no sampling (i.e., no adjustment) whatsoever and who introduced bills in Congress to forbid the Census Bureau from spending any money even on planning for sampling (Duff 1997). Some of these members of Congress were, in fact, proposing that the decennial census be reduced to a few questions that could fit on a postcard (an idea that, of course, did take root with the 2010 census). On the other side of the debate was the Census Bureau, arguing that its congressional mandate to make Census 2000 more accurate and yet less costly than the 1990 census could only be met by the judicious use of sampling (Riche 1997).

Was the uproar over sampling genuinely an issue about how best to conduct a census? No, the real issue was politics: because of historical voting trends, those people missed by the census in the United States are perceived to be more sympathetic to the Democratic political party. It had been estimated that including all those people in 2000 who have typically been missed by the census would cause Democrats to gain two dozen seats in the House of Representatives, at the expense, of course, of the Republican party (Spar 1998). Members of Congress took the issue to the Supreme Court, and in January 1999 the Court ruled that any population counts that had been "statistically adjusted" to compensate for overcounts and undercounts could not be used for congressional apportionment; only the "raw" numbers could be used for that purpose. However, that left open the question of whether adjustments should be made to the numbers for purposes other than apportionment.

The Census Bureau responded by establishing an Executive Steering Committee for Accuracy and Coverage Evaluation (A.C.E.) Policy (ESCAP) charged with deciding whether or not statistical adjustments should be made to the Census 2000 numbers. The Clinton administration delegated the responsibility for making that decision to the director of the Census Bureau, but when the Bush administration came into power just before the decision was to be made in 2001, the decision was put in the hands of the politically appointed Secretary of Commerce. The nation was poised for a battle over whether to adjust or not to adjust.

The drama deflated, however, when the ESCAP concluded in March 2001 that its review of the demographic-analysis approach and the dual-system estimation approach (the A.C.E. survey) showed that they were sufficiently inconsistent in their results that the Census Bureau could not recommend making an adjustment to the numbers (Census 2000 Initiative 2001). The Census 2000 numbers considerably exceeded the estimates based on the demographic-analysis approach, whereas the A.C.E. indicated that the Census 2000 data were of very high quality. The Secretary of Commerce thus made the announcement that no adjustments were going to be made. The city of Los Angeles and several other cities and counties immediately filed suit to force an adjustment, but the U.S. District Court wasted little time in dismissing that suit.

That did not end the story, however. A lawsuit was filed to force the Census Bureau to release the adjusted census figures—the numbers derived from the A.C.E. survey—even if the official numbers were not going to be adjusted. In 2003, the U.S. Court of Appeals for the Ninth Circuit ordered the data released, and they are now available from a website at the University of California, Los Angeles (http://www.sscnet.ucla.edu/issr/da/Adjusted/adjust_web.html). The 1999 Supreme Court decision that adjusted numbers could not be used for congressional apportionment meant that there was no attempt to use sampling for that purpose in relation to the 2010 census, but post-enumeration sampling is still an important part of census activities in terms of evaluating the overall quality of the census, as discussed elsewhere in this chapter.

In late 2006 the director of the Census Bureau and his top deputy both resigned, reportedly as a result of disagreement with Department of Commerce officials in the Bush administration over sampling issues (Krunholz 2006), and the position went unfilled for almost three years. When the Obama administration proposed a new director early in 2009, the nomination was held up in Congress for several months, threatening the success of the 2010 census. Finally, in July 2009, Robert Groves was sworn in as the new director, just in time to battle an effort by several members of Congress to require a question in the 2010 census regarding citizenship status. Had this legislation passed, it would have prevented funding from being used to collect census data that did not include a question regarding United States citizenship and immigration status, and it would have prevented states from counting illegal aliens when determining population levels.

And there is no rest for the Census Bureau. Suggestions for the 2020 census have already been offered by a National Research Council committee (Brown et al. 2010).

Discussion Questions: (1) Do you think that the United States and Mexico should follow the example of Canada and allow people to respond to the census over the Internet? Why or why not? **(2)** Why do you think some groups are undercounted relative to other groups? Would this situation be improved or made worse if the census dropped the question on race/ethnicity?

group, without providing a way of knowing the details of the population—which is what we obtain from the census questionnaire.

The dual-system estimation method involves comparing the census results with some other source of information about the people counted. After Census 2010 in the United States, the Census Bureau implemented its Accuracy and Coverage Evaluation (A.C.E.) Survey, which was similar to, albeit somewhat more complex than, the post-enumeration A.C.E survey conducted after the 2000 census, because it incorporated a variety of innovations suggestions made by a committee of the National Research Council (Bell and Cohen 2008). The process involves taking a carefully constructed sample survey right after the census is finished and then matching people in the sample survey with their responses in the census. This process can determine whether households and individuals within the households were counted in both the census and the survey (the ideal situation); in the census but not in the survey (possible but not likely); or in the survey but not in the census (the usual measure of underenumeration), or counted in the wrong place. Obviously, some people may be missed by both the census and the survey, but the logic underlying the method is analogous to the capture-recapture method used by biologists tracking wildlife (Choldin 1994). That strategy is to capture a sample of animals, mark them, and release them. Later, another sample is captured, and some of the marked animals will wind up being recaptured. The ratio of recaptured animals to all animals caught in the second sample is assumed to represent the ratio of the first group captured to the whole population, and on this basis the wildlife population can be estimated. Although some humans are certainly "wild," a few adjustments are required to apply the method to human populations.

Content Error Although coverage error is a concern in any census, there can also be problems with the accuracy of the data obtained in the census (content error). Content error includes nonresponses to particular questions on the census or inaccurate responses if people do not understand the question. Errors can also occur if information is inaccurately recorded on the form or if there is some glitch in the processing (coding, data entry, or editing) of the census return. By and large, content error seems not to be a problem in the U.S. census, although the data are certainly not 100 percent accurate. There is always the potential for misunderstanding the meaning of a question, and these problems appear to be greater for people with lower literacy skills (Iversen, Furstenberg, and Belzer 1999). In general, data from the United Nations suggest that the more highly developed a country is, the more accurate the content of its census data will be, and this is probably accounted for largely by higher levels of education.

In less developed countries, content error may be more problematic because interviewers may not be sufficiently motivated to press respondents for accurate information. Over the years, a seemingly simple question such as age has been prone to error because of "age-heaping" in which people round their age to the nearest zero or five instead of giving a precise answer.

Sampling Error If any of the data in a census are collected on a sample basis (as is done in the United States, Canada, and Mexico), then sampling error is introduced into the results. With any sample, scientifically selected or not, differences are likely to exist between the characteristics of the sampled population and the larger group from which the sample was chosen. However, in a scientific sample, such as that used in most census operations, sampling error is readily measured based on the mathematics of probability. To a certain extent, sampling error can be controlled—samples can be designed to ensure comparable levels of error across groups or across geographic areas. Furthermore, if the sample is very large, then sampling error will be relatively small. Nonsampling error and the biases it introduces throughout the census process probably reduce the quality of results more than sampling error (Schneider 2003).

Continuous Measurement—American Community Survey Almost all the detailed data about population characteristics obtained from the decennial censuses in the United States come from the "long form," which for several decades was administered to about one in six households. The success of survey sampling in obtaining reliable demographic data led the U.S. Census Bureau in 1996 to initiate a process of "continuous measurement" designed to replace the long form in subsequent decennial censuses, beginning with the 2010 census (Torrieri and Jennifer 2000; Torrieri 2007; Mather, Rivers, and Jacobsen 2005). The vehicle for this is the monthly American Community Survey (ACS), which is a "rolling survey" of approximately 3 million American households each year, designed to collect enough data over a 10-year period to provide detailed information down to the census block level, and in the process provide updated information on an annual basis, rather than having to wait for data at ten-year intervals. Just as with the census, questionnaires are mailed out to the households selected for the sample, and if they are not returned, the data are collected by phone, or by a personal visit from the Census Bureau (Griffin and Waite 2006).

The first data from the American Community Survey were made available on the Internet for the 2005 round of data, and data for the nation, states, and large populations within states are now available on an annually updated basis (subject, of course, to issues of sampling error, as noted above) at factfinder.census.gov. By 2010 enough surveys had been collected to produce five-year estimates for areas with populations less than 20,000. There are about 115 million households in the United States, and 3 million of those are surveyed each year, so over the course of its ten years between the 2000 and 2010 censuses, the ACS encompassed about 30 million households, representing slightly more than one in four households that wound up providing the detailed data no longer collected in the decennial census. The five-year estimates from the ACS produce data similar to that generated by Canada's five-year census cycle.

The Census of Canada

The first census in Canada was taken in 1666 when the French colony of New France was counted on the order of King Louis XIV (perhaps under Fénelon's influence, as I mentioned earlier). This turned out to be a door-to-door enumeration of all 3,215 settlers in Canada at that time. A series of wars between England and France ended with France ceding Canada to England in 1763, and the British undertook censuses on an irregular but fairly consistent basis (Statistics Canada 1995). The several regions of Canada were united under the British North America Act of 1867, which specified that censuses were to be taken regularly to establish the number of representatives that each province would send to the House of Commons. The first of these was taken in 1871, although similar censuses had been taken in 1851 and 1861. In 1905, the census bureau became a permanent government agency, now known as Statistics Canada.

Canada began using sampling in 1941, the year after the United States experimented with it. In 1956, Canada conducted its first quinquennial census (every five years, as opposed to every 10 years—the decennial census), and in 1971 Canada mandated that the census be conducted every five years. The U.S. Congress passed similar legislation in the 1970s but never funded those efforts, so the United States stayed with the decennial census until the recent implementation of continuous measurement provided by the American Community Survey.

Two census forms are used in Canada—a short form with just a few key items (see Table 4.1) and a more detailed long form. The long form goes to a sample of 20 percent of Canadian households, while 80 percent complete the long form. An innovation first implemented in the 2006 census was that households in Canada are now able to complete their census forms over the Internet. The U.S. Census Bureau has thus far chosen not to provide that option.

Public opinion influences census activities in Canada, as it does in the United States, and so the 1996 Census of Canada included a set of questions on unpaid household activities because of a Saskatoon housewife's protest. She refused to fill out the 1991 census form (and risked going to jail as a result) because the census form's definition of work did not include household work or child care. This helped to galvanize public opinion to include a set of questions on this type of activity in the 1996 census (De Santis 1996), and those questions have been repeated in subsequent censuses. On the other hand, the Canadian government decided that the number of children born to a woman might be too private a question to be asked any longer (it had been asked on every decennial census since 1941), and it is no longer included in the census. Canada's population is even more diverse than that of the United States and so the census asks several questions about language—indeed, the split between English and French speakers nearly tore the country apart in the 1990s. Detailed questions are also asked about race/ethnicity, place of birth, citizenship, and ancestry.

Statistics Canada estimates coverage error by comparing census results with population estimates (the demographic analysis approach) and by conducting a Reverse Record Check study to measure the undercoverage errors and also an Overcoverage Study designed to investigate overcoverage errors. The Reverse Record Check is the most important part of this, and involves taking a sample of records from other sources such as birth records and immigration records and then looking for those people in the census returns. An analysis of people not found who should have been there is a key component of estimating coverage error. The results of the Reverse Record Check and the Overcoverage Study are then combined to provide an estimate of net undercoverage, which was 2.99 percent in the 2001 census (Ministry of Management Services [Canada] 2003), and almost exactly the same in 2006 (Statistics Canada 2008).

The Census of Mexico

Like Canada and the United States, Mexico has a long history of census taking. There are records of a census in the Valley of Mexico taken in the year 1116, and the subsequent Aztec empire also kept count of the population for tax purposes. Spain conducted several censuses in Mexico during the colonial years, including a general census of New Spain (Nueva España, as they knew it) in 1790. Mexico gained independence from Spain in 1821, but it was not until 1895 that the first of the modern series of national censuses was undertaken. A second enumeration was done in 1900, but since then censuses have been taken every 10 years (with the exception of the one in 1921, which was one year out of sequence). From 1895 through the 1970s, the census activities were carried out by the General Directorate of Statistics (Dirección General de Estadística), and there were no permanent census employees. However, the bureaucracy was reorganized for the 1980 census, and in 1983 the Instituto Nacional de Estadística, Geografía e Informática (INEGI) became the permanent government agency in charge of the census and other government data collection.

A somewhat different set of questions are asked in Mexican censuses than in those of the United States and Canada, as you can see in Table 4.1. The 2000 census was the first in Mexico to use a combination of a basic questionnaire administered to most households, plus a lengthier questionnaire administered to a sample of households, and this was replicated in the 2010 census. Furthermore, the sampling strategy was a bit different than in the United States and Canada. Most of the questions are asked of all households, and the sample involves asking 10 percent of households to respond to a set of more detailed questions about topics included in the basic questionnaire. Especially noteworthy is a set of questions seeking information about family members who had been international migrants at any time during the previous five years. In 1995 and again in 2005, Mexico conducted a mid-decade census, which it calls a "Conteo," to distinguish it from the decennial censuses. The Conteo uses only the basic questionnaire, and does not include a sample to receive the extended questionnaire. In Mexico, all census forms are administered in person by census-takers hired by INEGI. Neither mail-back nor Internet forms are yet available.

Less income detail is obtained in Mexico than in Canada or the United States, and socioeconomic categories are more often derived from outward manifestations of income, such as housing quality, and material possessions owned by members of the household, about which there are several detailed questions. Because most Mexicans are mestizos (Spanish for mixed race, in this case mainly European and indigenous), no questions are asked about race or ethnicity. The only allusion to diversity within Mexico on the basic questionnaire is found in the question about language, in which people are asked if they speak an Indian language. If so, they are also asked if they speak Spanish. On the long form administered to a sample of households, a question is also asked specifically about whether or not they belong to an indigenous group.

In Mexico, the evaluation of coverage error in the census has generally been made using the method of demographic analysis. On this basis, Corona Vásquez (1991) estimated that underenumeration in the 1990 Mexican census was somewhere between 2.3 and 7.3 percent. No analysis has been published of the accuracy of subsequent censuses, which, in all events, would be difficult to establish because of the large number of Mexican nationals living outside of the country, especially in the United States. Perhaps more important is the fact that post-enumeration surveys and other types of coverage error analyses are expensive and, as it was, budget cuts forced INEGI to trim several questions from the extended questionnaire administered in the 2010 census.

IPUMS—Warehouse of Global Census Data

It is taken for granted in North America that census data can be downloaded for free from the Internet. The United States, Canada, and Mexico all provide such access, as do an increasing number of countries around the world. In all cases, however, the data are already tabulated for you by the statistical agencies. For researchers interested in uncovering trends and patterns in the data, it is vastly preferable to have access to data from the individual census records so that detailed statistical analysis can be undertaken. Census agencies provide these kinds of data by creating what are known in the United States as **Public Use Microdata Samples (PUMS)**, or as they are more generally known, anonymized census samples. A small sample of all census records, typically 5 to 10 percent, is randomly selected. These records are stripped of all personally identifying information, but with a geographic code left in place so that a person's general location can be determined, and then this data set is made available to researchers for analysis.

Over the past two decades, the Minnesota Population Center at the University of Minnesota has been creating a genuinely amazing resource of public use microdata samples from the censuses and American Community Survey of the United States (1790 to the present), the Current Population Survey of the United States (discussed later in the chapter) from 1962 to the present, and an ever-growing library of data from censuses all over the globe. The files are harmonized so that variable definitions are similar from one census to another, and they are provided in standard statistical software formats, along with links to digital maps for those countries. These are the kinds of data that truly move us forward in our understanding of what's going on in the world, and I encourage you to investigate the resource at www.ipums.org.

Registration of Vital Events

When you were born, a birth certificate was filled out for you, probably by a clerk or volunteer staff person in the hospital where you were born. When you die, someone (again, typically a hospital clerk) will fill out a death certificate on your behalf. Standard birth and death certificates used in the United States are shown in Figure 4.3. Births and deaths, as well as marriages, divorces, and abortions, are known as vital events, and when they are recorded by the government and compiled for use they become vital statistics. These statistics are the major source of data on births and deaths in most countries, and they are most useful when combined with census data.

Registration of vital events in Europe actually began as a chore of the church. Priests often recorded baptisms, marriages, and deaths, and historical demographers have used the surviving records to reconstruct the demographic history of

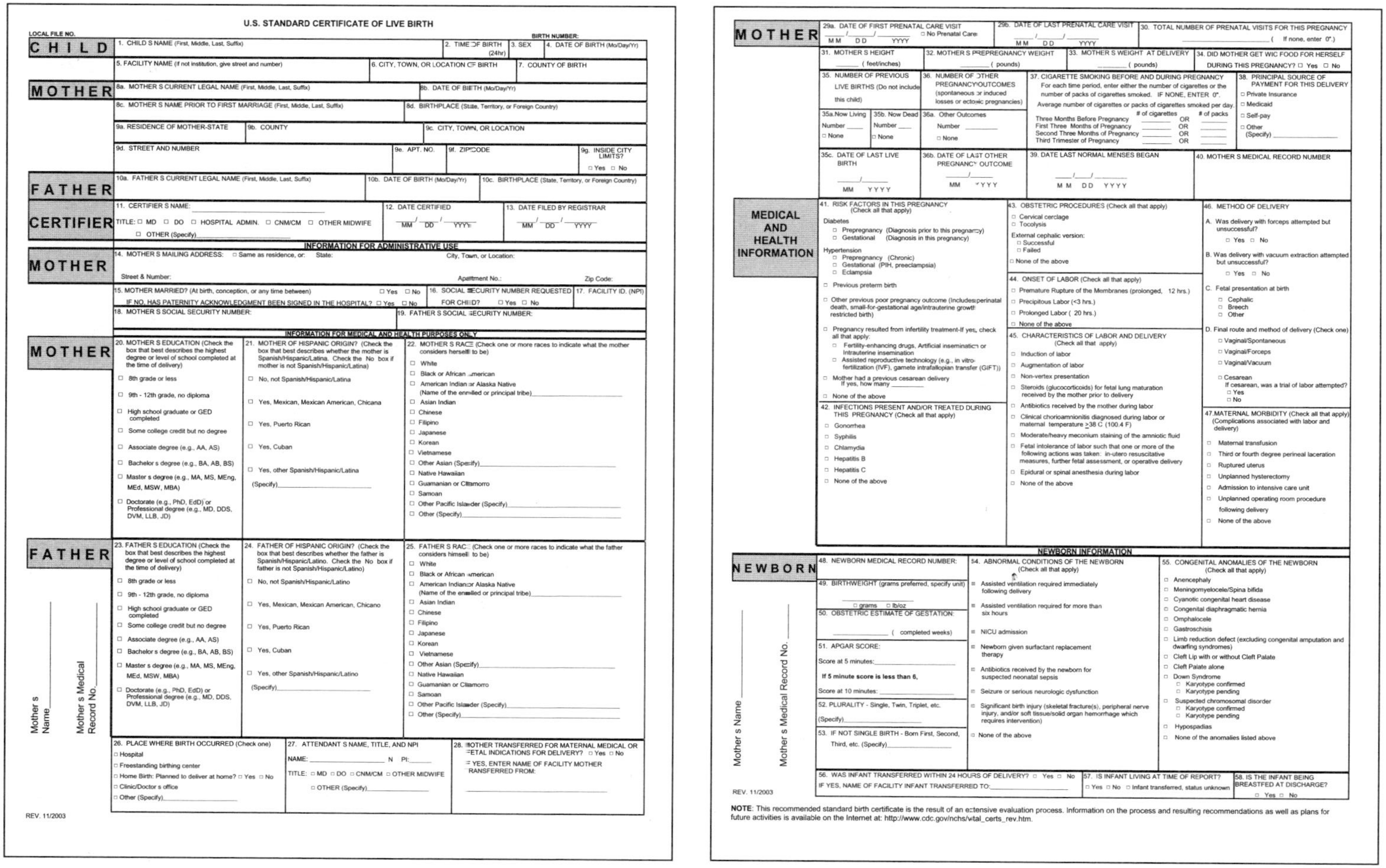

U.S. STANDARD CERTIFICATE OF LIVE BIRTH

LOCAL FILE NO. BIRTH NUMBER:

CHILD
1. CHILD S NAME (First, Middle, Last, Suffix)
2. TIME OF BIRTH (24hr)
3. SEX
4. DATE OF BIRTH (Mo/Day/Yr)
5. FACILITY NAME (If not institution, give street and number)
6. CITY, TOWN, OR LOCATION OF BIRTH
7. COUNTY OF BIRTH

MOTHER
8a. MOTHER S CURRENT LEGAL NAME (First, Middle, Last, Suffix)
8b. DATE OF BIRTH (Mo/Day/Yr)
8c. MOTHER S NAME PRIOR TO FIRST MARRIAGE (First, Middle, Last, Suffix)
8d. BIRTHPLACE (State, Territory, or Foreign Country)
9a. RESIDENCE OF MOTHER-STATE
9b. COUNTY
9c. CITY, TOWN, OR LOCATION
9d. STREET AND NUMBER
9e. APT. NO.
9f. ZIP CODE
9g. INSIDE CITY LIMITS? □ Yes □ No

FATHER
10a. FATHER S CURRENT LEGAL NAME (First, Middle, Last, Suffix)
10b. DATE OF BIRTH (Mo/Day/Yr)
10c. BIRTHPLACE (State, Territory, or Foreign Country)

CERTIFIER
11. CERTIFIER S NAME: ________
TITLE: □ MD □ DO □ HOSPITAL ADMIN. □ CNM/CM □ OTHER MIDWIFE
□ OTHER (Specify) ________
12. DATE CERTIFIED __/__/__ MM DD YYYY
13. DATE FILED BY REGISTRAR __/__/__ MM DD YYYY

INFORMATION FOR ADMINISTRATIVE USE

MOTHER
14. MOTHER S MAILING ADDRESS: □ Same as residence, or: State: City, Town, or Location:
Street & Number: Apartment No.: Zip Code:
15. MOTHER MARRIED? (At birth, conception, or any time between) □ Yes □ No
IF NO, HAS PATERNITY ACKNOWLEDGEMENT BEEN SIGNED IN THE HOSPITAL? □ Yes □ No
16. SOCIAL SECURITY NUMBER REQUESTED FOR CHILD? □ Yes □ No
17. FACILITY ID. (NPI)
18. MOTHER S SOCIAL SECURITY NUMBER:
19. FATHER S SOCIAL SECURITY NUMBER:

INFORMATION FOR MEDICAL AND HEALTH PURPOSES ONLY

MOTHER
20. MOTHER S EDUCATION (Check the box that best describes the highest degree or level of school completed at the time of delivery)
□ 8th grade or less
□ 9th - 12th grade, no diploma
□ High school graduate or GED completed
□ Some college credit but no degree
□ Associate degree (e.g., AA, AS)
□ Bachelor s degree (e.g., BA, AB, BS)
□ Master s degree (e.g., MA, MS, MEng, MEd, MSW, MBA)
□ Doctorate (e.g., PhD, EdD) or Professional degree (e.g., MD, DDS, DVM, LLB, JD)

21. MOTHER OF HISPANIC ORIGIN? (Check the box that best describes whether the mother is Spanish/Hispanic/Latina. Check the No box if mother is not Spanish/Hispanic/Latina)
□ No, not Spanish/Hispanic/Latina
□ Yes, Mexican, Mexican American, Chicana
□ Yes, Puerto Rican
□ Yes, Cuban
□ Yes, other Spanish/Hispanic/Latina (Specify) ________

22. MOTHER S RACE (Check one or more races to indicate what the mother considers herself to be)
□ White
□ Black or African American
□ American Indian or Alaska Native (Name of the enrolled or principal tribe) ________
□ Asian Indian
□ Chinese
□ Filipino
□ Japanese
□ Korean
□ Vietnamese
□ Other Asian (Specify) ________
□ Native Hawaiian
□ Guamanian or Chamorro
□ Samoan
□ Other Pacific Islander (Specify) ________
□ Other (Specify) ________

FATHER
23. FATHER S EDUCATION (Check the box that best describes the highest degree or level of school completed at the time of delivery)
□ 8th grade or less
□ 9th - 12th grade, no diploma
□ High school graduate or GED completed
□ Some college credit but no degree
□ Associate degree (e.g., AA, AS)
□ Bachelor s degree (e.g., BA, AB, BS)
□ Master s degree (e.g., MA, MS, MEng, MEd, MSW, MBA)
□ Doctorate (e.g., PhD, EdD) or Professional degree (e.g., MD, DDS, DVM, LLB, JD)

24. FATHER OF HISPANIC ORIGIN? (Check the box that best describes whether the father is Spanish/Hispanic/Latino. Check the No box if father is not Spanish/Hispanic/Latino)
□ No, not Spanish/Hispanic/Latino
□ Yes, Mexican, Mexican American, Chicano
□ Yes, Puerto Rican
□ Yes, Cuban
□ Yes, other Spanish/Hispanic/Latino (Specify) ________

25. FATHER S RACE (Check one or more races to indicate what the father considers himself to be)
□ White
□ Black or African American
□ American Indian or Alaska Native (Name of the enrolled or principal tribe) ________
□ Asian Indian
□ Chinese
□ Filipino
□ Japanese
□ Korean
□ Vietnamese
□ Other Asian (Specify) ________
□ Native Hawaiian
□ Guamanian or Chamorro
□ Samoan
□ Other Pacific Islander (Specify) ________
□ Other (Specify) ________

26. PLACE WHERE BIRTH OCCURRED (Check one)
□ Hospital
□ Freestanding birthing center
□ Home Birth: Planned to deliver at home? □ Yes □ No
□ Clinic/Doctor s office
□ Other (Specify) ________

27. ATTENDANT S NAME, TITLE, AND NPI
NAME: ________ NPI: ____
TITLE: □ MD □ DO □ CNM/CM □ OTHER MIDWIFE
□ OTHER (Specify) ________

28. MOTHER TRANSFERRED FOR MATERNAL MEDICAL OR FETAL INDICATIONS FOR DELIVERY? □ Yes □ No
IF YES, ENTER NAME OF FACILITY MOTHER TRANSFERRED FROM:

Mother s Name ________
Mother s Medical Record No. ________

REV. 11/2003

MOTHER
29a. DATE OF FIRST PRENATAL CARE VISIT __/__/__ MM DD YYYY □ No Prenatal Care
29b. DATE OF LAST PRENATAL CARE VISIT __/__/__ MM DD YYYY
30. TOTAL NUMBER OF PRENATAL VISITS FOR THIS PREGNANCY ________ (If none, enter 0 .)
31. MOTHER S HEIGHT ____ (feet/inches)
32. MOTHER S PREPREGNANCY WEIGHT ____ (pounds)
33. MOTHER S WEIGHT AT DELIVERY ____ (pounds)
34. DID MOTHER GET WIC FOOD FOR HERSELF DURING THIS PREGNANCY? □ Yes □ No
35. NUMBER OF PREVIOUS LIVE BIRTHS (Do not include this child)
35a. Now Living Number ___ □ None
35b. Now Dead Number ___ □ None
36. NUMBER OF OTHER PREGNANCY OUTCOMES (spontaneous or induced losses or ectopic pregnancies)
36a. Other Outcomes Number ___ □ None
37. CIGARETTE SMOKING BEFORE AND DURING PREGNANCY
For each time period, enter either the number of cigarettes or the number of packs of cigarettes smoked. IF NONE, ENTER 0 .
Average number of cigarettes or packs of cigarettes smoked per day.
# of cigarettes OR # of packs
Three Months Before Pregnancy ___ OR ___
First Three Months of Pregnancy ___ OR ___
Second Three Months of Pregnancy ___ OR ___
Third Trimester of Pregnancy ___ OR ___
38. PRINCIPAL SOURCE OF PAYMENT FOR THIS DELIVERY
□ Private Insurance
□ Medicaid
□ Self-pay
□ Other (Specify) ________
35c. DATE OF LAST LIVE BIRTH __/__ MM YYYY
36b. DATE OF LAST OTHER PREGNANCY OUTCOME __/__ MM YYYY
39. DATE LAST NORMAL MENSES BEGAN __/__/__ MM DD YYYY
40. MOTHER S MEDICAL RECORD NUMBER

MEDICAL AND HEALTH INFORMATION
41. RISK FACTORS IN THIS PREGNANCY (Check all that apply)
Diabetes
□ Prepregnancy (Diagnosis prior to this pregnancy)
□ Gestational (Diagnosis in this pregnancy)
Hypertension
□ Prepregnancy (Chronic)
□ Gestational (PIH, preeclampsia)
□ Eclampsia
□ Previous preterm birth
□ Other previous poor pregnancy outcome (Includes perinatal death, small-for-gestational age/intrauterine growth restricted birth)
□ Pregnancy resulted from infertility treatment-If yes, check all that apply:
□ Fertility-enhancing drugs, Artificial insemination or Intrauterine insemination
□ Assisted reproductive technology (e.g., in vitro fertilization (IVF), gamete intrafallopian transfer (GIFT))
□ Mother had a previous cesarean delivery If yes, how many ____
□ None of the above

42. INFECTIONS PRESENT AND/OR TREATED DURING THIS PREGNANCY (Check all that apply)
□ Gonorrhea
□ Syphilis
□ Chlamydia
□ Hepatitis B
□ Hepatitis C
□ None of the above

43. OBSTETRIC PROCEDURES (Check all that apply)
□ Cervical cerclage
□ Tocolysis
External cephalic version:
□ Successful
□ Failed
□ None of the above

44. ONSET OF LABOR (Check all that apply)
□ Premature Rupture of the Membranes (prolonged, 12 hrs.)
□ Precipitous Labor (<3 hrs.)
□ Prolonged Labor (20 hrs.)
□ None of the above

45. CHARACTERISTICS OF LABOR AND DELIVERY (Check all that apply)
□ Induction of labor
□ Augmentation of labor
□ Non-vertex presentation
□ Steroids (glucocorticoids) for fetal lung maturation received by the mother prior to delivery
□ Antibiotics received by the mother during labor
□ Clinical chorioamnionitis diagnosed during labor or maternal temperature ≥38 C (100.4 F)
□ Moderate/heavy meconium staining of the amniotic fluid
□ Fetal intolerance of labor such that one or more of the following actions was taken: in-utero resuscitative measures, further fetal assessment, or operative delivery
□ Epidural or spinal anesthesia during labor
□ None of the above

46. METHOD OF DELIVERY
A. Was delivery with forceps attempted but unsuccessful? □ Yes □ No
B. Was delivery with vacuum extraction attempted but unsuccessful? □ Yes □ No
C. Fetal presentation at birth
□ Cephalic
□ Breech
□ Other
D. Final route and method of delivery (Check one)
□ Vaginal/Spontaneous
□ Vaginal/Forceps
□ Vaginal/Vacuum
□ Cesarean
If cesarean, was a trial of labor attempted?
□ Yes
□ No

47. MATERNAL MORBIDITY (Check all that apply) (Complications associated with labor and delivery)
□ Maternal transfusion
□ Third or fourth degree perineal laceration
□ Ruptured uterus
□ Unplanned hysterectomy
□ Admission to intensive care unit
□ Unplanned operating room procedure following delivery
□ None of the above

NEWBORN INFORMATION

NEWBORN
48. NEWBORN MEDICAL RECORD NUMBER:
49. BIRTHWEIGHT (grams preferred, specify unit) ____ □ grams □ lb/oz
50. OBSTETRIC ESTIMATE OF GESTATION: ____ (completed weeks)
51. APGAR SCORE:
Score at 5 minutes: ____
If 5 minute score is less than 6,
Score at 10 minutes: ____
52. PLURALITY - Single, Twin, Triplet, etc. (Specify) ____
53. IF NOT SINGLE BIRTH - Born First, Second, Third, etc. (Specify) ____

54. ABNORMAL CONDITIONS OF THE NEWBORN (Check all that apply)
□ Assisted ventilation required immediately following delivery
□ Assisted ventilation required for more than six hours
□ NICU admission
□ Newborn given surfactant replacement therapy
□ Antibiotics received by the newborn for suspected neonatal sepsis
□ Seizure or serious neurologic dysfunction
□ Significant birth injury (skeletal fracture(s), peripheral nerve injury, and/or soft tissue/solid organ hemorrhage which requires intervention)
□ None of the above

55. CONGENITAL ANOMALIES OF THE NEWBORN (Check all that apply)
□ Anencephaly
□ Meningomyelocele/Spina bifida
□ Cyanotic congenital heart disease
□ Congenital diaphragmatic hernia
□ Omphalocele
□ Gastroschisis
□ Limb reduction defect (excluding congenital amputation and dwarfing syndromes)
□ Cleft Lip with or without Cleft Palate
□ Cleft Palate alone
□ Down Syndrome
□ Karyotype confirmed
□ Karyotype pending
□ Suspected chromosomal disorder
□ Karyotype confirmed
□ Karyotype pending
□ Hypospadias
□ None of the anomalies listed above

56. WAS INFANT TRANSFERRED WITHIN 24 HOURS OF DELIVERY? □ Yes □ No
IF YES, NAME OF FACILITY INFANT TRANSFERRED TO: ________
57. IS INFANT LIVING AT TIME OF REPORT? □ Yes □ No □ Infant transferred, status unknown
58. IS THE INFANT BEING BREASTFED AT DISCHARGE? □ Yes □ No

Mother s Name ________
Mother s Medical Record No. ________

REV. 11/2003

NOTE: This recommended standard birth certificate is the result of an extensive evaluation process. Information on the process and resulting recommendations as well as plans for future activities is available on the Internet at: http://www.cdc.gov/nchs/vital_certs_rev.htm.

Figure 4.3 Standard Birth and Death Certificates Used in the United States

NAME OF DECEDENT________
For use by physician or institution

U.S. STANDARD CERTIFICATE OF DEATH

LOCAL FILE NO. STATE FILE NO.

To Be Completed/Verified By: FUNERAL DIRECTOR

1. DECEDENT S LEGAL NAME (Include AKA s if any) (First, Middle, Last)
2. SEX
3. SOCIAL SECURITY NUMBER

4a. AGE-Last Birthday (Years)
4b. UNDER 1 YEAR — Months / Days
4c. UNDER 1 DAY — Hours / Minutes
5. DATE OF BIRTH (Mo/Day/Yr)
6. BIRTHPLACE (City and State or Foreign Country)

7a. RESIDENCE-STATE
7b. COUNTY
7c. CITY OR TOWN

7d. STREET AND NUMBER
7e. APT. NO.
7f. ZIP CODE
7g. INSIDE CITY LIMITS? □ Yes □ No

8. EVER IN US ARMED FORCES? □ Yes □ No
9. MARITAL STATUS AT TIME OF DEATH □ Married □ Married, but separated □ Widowed □ Divorced □ Never Married □ Unknown
10. SURVIVING SPOUSE S NAME (If wife, give name prior to first marriage)

11. FATHER S NAME (First, Middle, Last)
12. MOTHER S NAME PRIOR TO FIRST MARRIAGE (First, Middle, Last)

13a. INFORMANT S NAME
13b. RELATIONSHIP TO DECEDENT
13c. MAILING ADDRESS (Street and Number, City, State, Zip Code)

14. PLACE OF DEATH (Check only one: see instructions)
IF DEATH OCCURRED IN A HOSPITAL: □ Inpatient □ Emergency Room/Outpatient □ Dead on Arrival
IF DEATH OCCURRED SOMEWHERE OTHER THAN A HOSPITAL: □ Hospice facility □ Nursing home/Long term care facility □ Decedent s home □ Other (Specify):

15. FACILITY NAME (If not institution, give street & number)
16. CITY OR TOWN, STATE, AND ZIP CODE
17. COUNTY OF DEATH

18. METHOD OF DISPOSITION: □ Burial □ Cremation □ Donation □ Entombment □ Removal from State □ Other (Specify):________
19. PLACE OF DISPOSITION (Name of cemetery, crematory, other place)

20. LOCATION-CITY, TOWN, AND STATE
21. NAME AND COMPLETE ADDRESS OF FUNERAL FACILITY

22. SIGNATURE OF FUNERAL SERVICE LICENSEE OR OTHER AGENT
23. LICENSE NUMBER (Of Licensee)

To Be Completed By: MEDICAL CERTIFIER

ITEMS 24-28 MUST BE COMPLETED BY PERSON WHO PRONOUNCES OR CERTIFIES DEATH
24. DATE PRONOUNCED DEAD (Mo/Day/Yr)
25. TIME PRONOUNCED DEAD

26. SIGNATURE OF PERSON PRONOUNCING DEATH (Only when applicable)
27. LICENSE NUMBER
28. DATE SIGNED (Mo/Day/Yr)

29. ACTUAL OR PRESUMED DATE OF DEATH (Mo/Day/Yr) (Spell Month)
30. ACTUAL OR PRESUMED TIME OF DEATH
31. WAS MEDICAL EXAMINER OR CORONER CONTACTED? □ Yes □ No

CAUSE OF DEATH (See instructions and examples)

Approximate interval: Onset to death

32. **PART I.** Enter the chain of events--diseases, injuries, or complications--that directly caused the death. DO NOT enter terminal events such as cardiac arrest, respiratory arrest, or ventricular fibrillation without showing the etiology. DO NOT ABBREVIATE. Enter only one cause on a line. Add additional lines if necessary.

IMMEDIATE CAUSE (Final disease or condition ---------> resulting in death) a.________
Due to (or as a consequence of):
Sequentially list conditions, if any, leading to the cause listed on line a. Enter the **UNDERLYING CAUSE** (disease or injury that initiated the events resulting in death) **LAST**
b.________
Due to (or as a consequence of):
c.________
Due to (or as a consequence of):
d.________

PART II. Enter other significant conditions contributing to death but not resulting in the underlying cause given in PART I.
33. WAS AN AUTOPSY PERFORMED? □ Yes □ No
34. WERE AUTOPSY FINDINGS AVAILABLE TO COMPLETE THE CAUSE OF DEATH? □ Yes □ No

35. DID TOBACCO USE CONTRIBUTE TO DEATH? □ Yes □ Probably □ No □ Unknown
36. IF FEMALE: □ Not pregnant within past year □ Pregnant at time of death □ Not pregnant, but pregnant within 42 days of death □ Not pregnant, but pregnant 43 days to 1 year before death □ Unknown if pregnant within the past year
37. MANNER OF DEATH □ Natural □ Homicide □ Accident □ Pending Investigation □ Suicide □ Could not be determined

38. DATE OF INJURY (Mo/Day/Yr) (Spell Month)
39. TIME OF INJURY
40. PLACE OF INJURY (e.g., Decedent s home; construction site; restaurant; wooded area)
41. INJURY AT WORK? □ Yes □ No

42. LOCATION OF INJURY: State: City or Town:
Street & Number: Apartment No.: Zip Code:

43. DESCRIBE HOW INJURY OCCURRED:
44. IF TRANSPORTATION INJURY, SPECIFY: □ Driver/Operator □ Passenger □ Pedestrian □ Other (Specify)

45. CERTIFIER (Check only one):
□ Certifying physician-To the best of my knowledge, death occurred due to the cause(s) and manner stated.
□ Pronouncing & Certifying physician-To the best of my knowledge, death occurred at the time, date, and place, and due to the cause(s) and manner stated.
□ Medical Examiner/Coroner-On the basis of examination, and/or investigation, in my opinion, death occurred at the time, date, and place, and due to the cause(s) and manner stated.
Signature of certifier:________

46. NAME, ADDRESS, AND ZIP CODE OF PERSON COMPLETING CAUSE OF DEATH (Item 32)

47. TITLE OF CERTIFIER
48. LICENSE NUMBER
49. DATE CERTIFIED (Mo/Day/Yr)
50. **FOR REGISTRAR ONLY**- DATE FILED (Mo/Day/Yr)

To Be Completed By: FUNERAL DIRECTOR

51. DECEDENT S EDUCATION-Check the box that best describes the highest degree or level of school completed at the time of death.
□ 8th grade or less
□ 9th - 12th grade; no diploma
□ High school graduate or GED completed
□ Some college credit, but no degree
□ Associate degree (e.g., AA, AS)
□ Bachelor s degree (e.g., BA, AB, BS)
□ Master s degree (e.g., MA, MS, MEng, MEd, MSW, MBA)
□ Doctorate (e.g., PhD, EdD) or Professional degree (e.g., MD, DDS, DVM, LLB, JD)

52. DECEDENT OF HISPANIC ORIGIN? Check the box that best describes whether the decedent is Spanish/Hispanic/Latino. Check the No box if decedent is not Spanish/Hispanic/Latino.
□ No, not Spanish/Hispanic/Latino
□ Yes, Mexican, Mexican American, Chicano
□ Yes, Puerto Rican
□ Yes, Cuban
□ Yes, other Spanish/Hispanic/Latino (Specify) ________

53. DECEDENT S RACE (Check one or more races to indicate what the decedent considered himself or herself to be)
□ White
□ Black or African American
□ American Indian or Alaska Native (Name of the enrolled or principal tribe) ________
□ Asian Indian
□ Chinese
□ Filipino
□ Japanese
□ Korean
□ Vietnamese
□ Other Asian (Specify)________
□ Native Hawaiian
□ Guamanian or Chamorro
□ Samoan
□ Other Pacific Islander (Specify)________
□ Other (Specify)________

54. DECEDENT S USUAL OCCUPATION (Indicate type of work done during most of working life. DO NOT USE RETIRED).

55. KIND OF BUSINESS/INDUSTRY

REV. 11/2003

Figure 4.3 *(continued)*

parts of Europe (Wrigley 1974; Wrigley and Schofield 1981; Wall, Robin, and Laslett 1983; Landers 1993). Among the more demographically important tasks that befell the clergy was that of recording burials that occurred in England during the many years of the plague. In the early sixteenth century, the city of London ordered that the number of people dying be recorded in each parish, along with the number of christenings. Beginning in 1592, these records (or "bills") were printed and circulated on a weekly basis during particularly rough years, and so they were called the London Bills of Mortality (Lorimer 1959; Laxton 1987). Between 1603 and 1849, these records were published weekly (on Thursdays, with an annual summary on the Thursday before Christmas) in what amounts to one of the most important sets of vital statistics prior to the nineteenth-century establishment of official government bureaucracies to collect and analyze such data.

Initially, the information collected about deaths indicated only the cause (since one goal was to keep track of the deadly plague), but starting in the eighteenth century the age of those dying was also noted. Yet despite the interest in these data created by the analyses of Graunt, Petty, Halley, and others mentioned in Chapter 3, people remained skeptical about the quality of the data and unsure of what could be done with them (Starr 1987). So it was not until the middle of the nineteenth century that civil registration of births and deaths became compulsory and an office of vital statistics was officially established by the English government, mirroring events in much of Europe and North America (Linder 1959). It was not until 1900 that birth and death certificates were standardized in the United States.

Today, we find the most complete vital registration systems in the most highly developed countries and the least complete (often nonexistent) systems in the least developed countries. Such systems seem to be tied to literacy (there must be someone in each area to record events), adequate communication, and the cost of the bureaucracy required for such record keeping, all of which is associated with economic development. Among countries where systems of vital registration do exist, there is wide variation in the completeness with which events are recorded. Even in the United States, the registration of births is not 100 percent complete, yet the public so takes for granted the existence of vital statistics that the National Research Council was asked to convene a panel in 2009 to lay out the case for why continued funding is so vital (no pun intended) to our knowledge about the health of the nation (Siri and Cork 2009).

Although most nations have a system of birth and death registration that is separate from census activities, dozens of countries, mostly in Europe, maintain **population registers**, which are lists of all people in the country, and which can be used as a substitute for a census, as I mentioned earlier. Alongside each name are recorded the vital events for that individual, typically birth, death, marriage, divorce, and change of residence. Such registers are kept primarily for administrative (that is, social control) purposes, such as legal identification of people, election rolls, and calls for military service, but they are also extremely valuable for demographic purposes, since they provide a demographic life history for each individual. Registers are expensive to maintain, but many countries that could afford them, such as the United States, tend to avoid them because of the perceived threat to personal freedom that can be inherent in a system that compiles and centralizes personally identifying information.

Combining the Census and Vital Statistics

Although recording vital events provides information about the number of births and deaths (along with other events) according to such characteristics as age and sex, we also need to know how many people are at risk of these events. Thus, vital statistics data are typically teamed up with census data, which do include that information. For example, you may know from the vital statistics that there were 4.2 million births in the United States in 2009 (the most recent year for which data are available at this writing), but that number tells you nothing about whether the birth rate was high or low. In order to draw any conclusion, you must relate those births to the 307 million people residing in the United States as of mid-2009, and only then do you discover a relatively low birth rate of 13.7 births per 1,000 population, down from 16.7 in 1990.

Since in 2009 no census had been taken since 2000, you may wonder how an estimate of the population could have been produced for an **intercensal** year such as 2009. The answer is that once again census data are combined with vital statistics data (and migration estimates) using the demographic balancing equation that I discussed earlier in the chapter: the population in 2009 is equal to the population as of the 2000 census, plus the births, minus the deaths, plus the in-migrants, minus the out-migrants between 2000 and 2009. Naturally, deficiencies in any of these data sources will lead to inaccuracies in the estimate of the number of people alive at any time, and this is exactly what happened in the United States in 2000. The census counted 281,421,906 people as of April 1, 2000, but the demographic balancing equation had produced an estimate for that day of only 274,520,000. The difference was probably accounted for largely by undocumented immigration between 1990 and 2000.

Administrative Data

Knowing that censuses and the collection of vital statistics were not originally designed to provide data for demographic analysis has alerted demographers everywhere to keep their collective eyes open for any data source that might yield useful information. For example, an important source of information about immigration to the United States is the compilation of **administrative records** filled out for each person entering the country from abroad. These forms are collected and tabulated by the U.S. Citizenship and Immigration Service (USCIS) within the U.S. Department of Homeland Security. Of course, we need other means to estimate the number of people who enter without documents and avoid detection by the government, and I discuss that more in Chapter 7.

Data are not routinely gathered on people who permanently leave the United States, but the administrative records of the U.S. Social Security Administration provide some clues about the number and destination of such individuals because many people who leave the country have their Social Security checks follow them. An administrative source of information on migration within the United States used by the Census Bureau is a set of data provided to them by the Internal Revenue Service (IRS). Although no personal information is ever divulged, the IRS can match Social Security numbers of taxpayers each year and see if their address has changed, thus providing a clue about geographic mobility, at least among those people who file income tax returns. At the local level, a variety of administrative data can be tapped to determine demographic patterns. School enrollment data provide clues to patterns of population growth and migration. Utility data on connections and disconnections can also be used to discern local population trends, as can the number of people signing up for government-sponsored health programs (Medicaid and Medicare) and income assistance (various forms of welfare).

Sample Surveys

There are two major difficulties with using data collected in the census, by the vital statistics registration system, or derived from administrative records: (1) They are usually collected for purposes other than demographic analysis and thus do not necessarily reflect the theoretical concerns of demography, and (2) They are collected by many different people using many different methods and may be prone to numerous kinds of error. For these two reasons, in addition to the cost of big data-collection schemes, sample surveys are frequently used to gather demographic data. Sample surveys may provide the social, psychological, economic, and even physical data I referred to earlier as being necessary to an understanding of why things are as they are. Their principal limitation is that they provide less extensive geographic coverage than a census or system of vital registration.

By using a carefully selected sample of even a few thousand people, demographers have been able to ask questions about births, deaths, migration, and other subjects that reveal aspects of the "why" of demographic events rather than just the "what." In some poor or remote areas of the world, sample surveys can also provide good estimates of the levels of fertility, mortality, and migration in the absence of census or vital registration data.

Demographic Surveys in the United States

I have already mentioned the American Community Survey (ACS), which is now a critically important part of the census itself. It is modeled after the Current Population Survey (CPS) conducted monthly by the U.S. Census Bureau in collaboration with the Bureau of Labor Statistics, and which for many decades has been one of the country's most important sample surveys. Since 1943, thousands of households (currently more than 50,000) have been queried each month about a variety of things, although a major thrust of the survey is to gather information on the labor force. Each March, detailed demographic questions are also asked about fertility and migration and such characteristics as education, income, marital status, and living arrangements. These data have been an important source of demographic information about the U.S. population, filling in the gap between censuses, and providing the Census Bureau with the experience necessary to launch the more ambitious ACS.

Since 1983, the Census Bureau has also been conducting the Survey on Income and Program Participation (SIPP), which is a companion to the Current Population Survey. Using a rotating panel of more than 40,000 households that are queried several times over a two- to four-year period, the SIPP gathers detailed data on sources of income and wealth, disability, and the extent to which household members participate in government assistance programs. The Census Bureau also regularly conducts the American Housing Survey for the U.S. Department of Housing and Urban Development, and this survey generates important data on mobility and migration patterns in the United States. The National Center for Health Statistics (NCHS) within the U.S. Centers for Disease Control and Prevention generates data about fertility and reproductive health in the National Survey of Family Growth (NSFG), which it conducts every five years or so, and also obtains data on health and disability from the regular National Health Interview Survey (NHIS).

Canadian Surveys

Canada has a monthly Labor Force Survey (LFS), initiated in 1945 to track employment trends after the end of World War II. Similar to the CPS in the United States, it is a rotating panel of more than 50,000 households, and although its major purpose is to produce data on the labor force (hence the name), it gathers data on most of the core sociodemographic characteristics of people in each sampled household, so it provides a continuous measure of population trends in Canada. Since 1985, Statistics Canada has also conducted a regular (currently every five years) General Social Survey, a sample of about 25,000 respondents designed to elicit detailed data about various aspects of life in Canada, such as health and social support, families, time use, and related topics.

Mexican Surveys

Mexico conducts a regular national survey that is comparable to the CPS and the LFS. The National Survey of Occupation and Employment (Encuesta Nacional de Ocupación y Empleo [ENOE]) is a large (120,000 household) monthly sample of households undertaken by INEGI that is designed to be representative of the entire country. As with the CPS, the goal is to provide a way of regularly measuring and monitoring the social and economic characteristics of the population. Some of the population questions asked in the census (see Table 4.1) are also asked in the ENOE, along with a detailed set of questions about the labor force activity of everyone in the household who is 12 years of age or older.

Demographic and Health Surveys

One of the largest social scientific projects ever undertaken was the World Fertility Survey, conducted under the auspices of the International Statistical Institute in the Netherlands. Between 1972 and 1982, a total of nearly 350,000 women of childbearing age from 42 developing nations and 20 developed countries were interviewed (Lightbourne, Singh, and Green 1982). These data contributed substantially to our knowledge of how and why people in different parts of the world were (or were not) controlling their fertility at that time. Concurrent with the World Fertility Survey was a series of Contraceptive Prevalence Surveys, conducted in Latin America, Asia, and Africa with funding from the U.S. Agency for International Development (USAID).

In 1984, the work of the World Fertility Survey and the Contraceptive Prevalence Surveys was combined into one large project called the Demographic and Health Surveys (DHS), which are now carried out by a private company, ICF Macro, with funding from USAID. The focus is on fertility, reproductive health, and child health and nutrition, but the data provide national estimates of basic demographic processes, structure, and characteristics, since a few questions are asked about all members of each household in the sample. More than 215 surveys have been conducted in more than 85 developing countries in Africa, Asia, and Latin America. This is a rich source of information, as you will see in subsequent chapters, and for several poorer nations, especially in sub-Saharan Africa, where vital statistics may not be routinely available, the DHS serves as an unofficial substitute set of information.

A complementary set of surveys has been conducted in poorer countries that, for a variety of reasons, have not had a Demographic and Health Survey. Known as the Multiple Indicators Cluster Surveys (MICS), they were developed by the United Nations Children's Fund (UNICEF) and are funded by a variety of international agencies. These surveys collect data that are very similar to those in the DHS.

Demographic Surveillance Systems

In Africa, many people are born, live, and die without a single written record of their existence because of the poor coverage of censuses and vital registration systems (de Savigny 2003; Korenromp et al. 2003). To provide a way of tracking the lives of people in specific "sentinel" areas of sub-Saharan Africa (and to a lesser extent south Asia), an INDEPTH network has been created that works with individual countries to select one or two defined geographic regions that are representative of a larger population. A census is conducted in that region and then subsequent demographic changes are continuously measured by keeping track of all births, deaths, migration, and related characteristics of the population. As of 2010, this method permitted the estimation of fertility and death rates and their changes over time for 37 sites in 18 different countries of Africa and Asia.

European Surveys

Declining fertility in Europe has generated a renewed interest in the continent's demography, and there are now several surveys in Europe that capture useful demographic information. In particular, the Population Activities Unit of the United Nations Economic Commission for Europe funded the Family and Fertility Surveys (FFS) in most European nations during the 1990s. Since 2000, they have funded a new round of surveys called "Generations and Gender: Research into their Behaviour and Quality of Life," which has a slightly different focus, but incorporates many of the questions asked in the FFS.

Historical Sources

Our understanding of population processes is shaped not only by our perception of current trends but also by our understanding of historical events. Historical demography requires that we almost literally dig up information about the patterns of mortality, fertility, and migration in past generations—to reconstruct "the world we have lost," as Peter Laslett (1971) once called it. You may prefer to whistle past the graveyard, but researchers at the Cambridge Group for the History of Population and Social Structure in the Department of Geography at Cambridge University (U.K.) have spent the past several decades developing ways to recreate history by reading dates on tombstones and organizing information contained in parish church registers and other local documents (Reher and Schofield 1993; Wrigley and Schofield 1981), extending methods developed especially by the great French historical demographer Louis Henry (Rosental 2003).

Historical sources of demographic information include censuses and vital statistics, but the general lack of good historical vital statistics is what typically necessitates special detective work to locate birth records in church registers and death records in graveyards. Even in the absence of a census, a complete set of good local records for a small village may allow a researcher to reconstruct the demographic profile of families by matching entries of births, marriages, and deaths in the community over a period of several years. Yet another source of such information is family genealogies, the compilation of which has become increasingly common in recent years throughout the world. Detailed genealogies in China, for example, have allowed researchers at Cambridge University to develop simulation models of what the demographic structure of China must have been like in the past (Zhao 2001).

The results of these labors can be of considerable importance in testing our notions about how the world used to work. For example, through historical demographic research we now know that the conjugal family (parents and their children) is not a product of industrialization and urbanization, as was once thought (Wrigley 1974). In fact, such small family units were quite common throughout Europe for several centuries before the Industrial Revolution and may actually have contributed to the process of industrialization by allowing the family more flexibility to meet the needs of the changing economy. In the United States, conversely, extended families may have been more common prior to the nineteenth century than has generally been thought (Ruggles 1994). In subsequent chapters, we will have numerous occasions to draw on the results of the Princeton European Fertility Project, which gathered and analyzed data on marriage and reproduction throughout nineteenth- and early-twentieth-century Europe.

By quantifying (and thereby clarifying) our knowledge of past patterns of demographic events, we are also better able to interpret historical events in a meaningful fashion. Wells (1982) has reminded us that the history of the struggle of American colonists to survive, marry, and bear children may tell us more about the determination to forge a union of states than a detailed recounting of the actions of British officials.

Geodemographics and Spatial Demography

Demographers have been using maps as a tool for analysis for a long time, and some of the earliest analyses of disease and death relied heavily on maps that showed, for example, where people were dying from particular causes (Cliff and Haggett 1996). In the middle of the nineteenth century, London physician John Snow used maps to trace a local cholera epidemic. He was able to show that cholera occurred much more frequently among customers of a water company that drew its water from the lower Thames River (downstream from the city), where it had become contaminated with London sewage, whereas another company was associated with far fewer cases of cholera because it obtained water from the upper Thames—prior to its passing through London, where sewage was dumped in the river (Snow 1936). Today a far more sophisticated version of this same idea is available to demographers through **geographic information systems** (GIS), which form the major part of the field of geographic information science (GISc). The advent of powerful desktop computers created a "GIS revolution" (Longley and Batty 1996) that encourages demographers (and others, of course) to bring maps together with data in innovative ways (Ricketts et al. 1997; Rindfuss and Stern 1998; Weeks 2004).

A GIS is a computer-based system that allows us to combine maps with data that refer to particular places on those maps and then to analyze those data using spatial statistics (part of GISc) and display the results as thematic maps or some other graphic format. The computer allows us to transform a map into a set of areas (such as a country, state, or census tract), lines (such as streets, highways, or rivers), and points (such as a house, school, or a health clinic). Our demographic data must then be **geo-referenced** (associated with some geographic identification such as precise latitude-longitude coordinates, a street address, ZIP code, census tract, county, state, or country) so the computer will link them to the correct area, line, or point. Demographic data are virtually always referenced to a geographic area, and in the United States the Geography Division of the U.S. Census Bureau works closely with the Population Division to make sure that data are identified for appropriate levels of "census geography," as shown in Table 4.3.

The "revolutionary" aspect of GIS is that geo-referencing data to places on the map means we can combine different types of data (such as census and survey data) for the same place, and we can do it for more than one time (such as data for 2000 and 2010). When geographic information systems incorporate demographic data, the resulting combination is called **geodemographics** (demographic data analyzed for specific geographic regions) or more generally **spatial demography** (as I mentioned in Chapter 1). As you can see in Figure 4.4, this may incorporate other geospatial techniques, including remotely sensed satellite imagery (that can help us understand aspects of population size and distribution) and spatial statistical methods. Spatial demography improves our ability to visualize and analyze the kinds of demographic changes taking place over time and space. Since 1997, for example, most of the Demographic and Health Surveys in less-developed countries have used global positioning system (GPS) devices (another geospatial technique) to record the location of (geo-reference) each household in the sample in order to allow for more sophisticated spatial demographic analysis of the survey data.

Table 4.3 The U.S. Census Provides Geographically Referenced Data for a Wide Range of Geographic Areas

Basic Geographic Hierarchy of Census Data:
United States
Region (4)
Division (9)
State (50, plus the outlying areas of American Samoa, Guam, northern Mariana Islands, Palau, Puerto Rico, and the Virgin Islands)
County (the basic administrative and legal subdivision of states)
County Subdivision (also known as minor civil divisions, including towns and townships)
Place (incorporated cities and unincorporated census-designated places)
Census Tract/ Block Numbering Area (tracts are small, relatively permanent subdivisions of a county, delineated for all metropolitan areas and other densely settled areas; block numbering areas are similar to census tracts except that they are set up for nonmetropolitan areas that have not been tracted)
Block Group (a cluster of blocks within census tracts, usually containing about housing units)
Census Block (the smallest geographic unit, usually bounded on all sides by readily identifiable features such as streets, railroad tracks, or bodies of water)

Source: U.S. Census Bureau, 2008.

GIS and the U.S. Census Bureau

It is a gross understatement that the computer—the revolutionary element that has created GIS (maps and demographic data have been around for a long time)—has vastly expanded our capacity to process and analyze data. It is no coincidence that census data are so readily amenable to being "crunched" by the computer; the histories of the computer and the U.S. Census Bureau go back a long way together. Prior to the 1890 census, the U.S. government held a contest to see who could come up

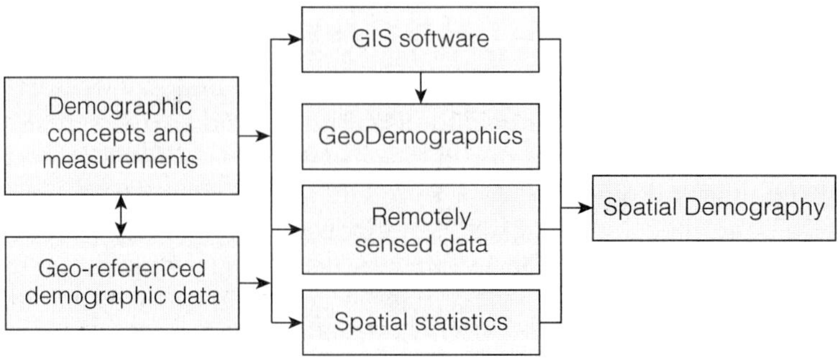

Figure 4.4 The Elements of Spatial Demography

with the best machine for counting the data from that census. The winner was Herman Hollerith, who had worked on the 1880 census right after graduating from Columbia University. His method of feeding a punched card through a tabulating machine proved to be very successful, and in 1886 he organized the Tabulating Machine Company, which in 1911 was merged with two other companies and became the International Business Machines (IBM) Corporation (Kaplan and Van Valey 1980). Then, after World War II, the Census Bureau sponsored the development of the first computer designed for mass data processing—the UNIVAC-I—which was used to help with the 1950 census and led the world into the computer age. Photo-optical scanning, which we now heavily rely on for entering data from printed documents into the computer, was also a by-product of the Census Bureau's need for a device to tabulate data from census forms. FOSIDC (film optical sensing device for input to computers) was first used for the 1960 census (U.S. Census Bureau 1999).

Another useful innovation was the creation for the 1980 U.S. census of the DIME (Dual Independent Map Encoding) files. This was the first step toward computer mapping, in which each piece of data was coded in a way that could be matched electronically to a place on a map. In the 1980s, several private firms latched onto this technology, improved it, and made it available to other companies for their own business uses.

By the early 1990s, the pieces of the puzzle had come together. The data from the 1990 U.S. census were made available for the first time on CD-ROM and at prices affordable to a wide range of users. Furthermore, the Census Bureau reconfigured its geographic coding of data, creating what it calls TIGER (Topologically Integrated Geographic Encoding and Referencing), described as "the name for the system and digital database developed at the U.S. Census Bureau to support its mapping needs for the Decennial Census and other Bureau programs" (U.S. Census Bureau 2005:1). At the same time, and certainly in response to increased demand, personal computers came along that were powerful enough and had enough memory to store and manipulate huge census files, including both the geographic database and the actual population and housing data. Not far behind was the software to run those computers, and several firms now make software for desktop computers that allow interactive spatial analysis of census and other kinds of data and then the production of high-quality color maps of the analysis results. Two of these firms—Environmental Systems Research Institute (ESRI) and Geographic Data Technology (GDT—now Tele Atlas)—were awarded contracts in 1997 to help the U.S. Census Bureau update its computerized Master Address File (the information used to continuously update the TIGER files) in order to improve accuracy in Census 2000. In a very real sense, the census and the TIGER files more specifically helped to spawn the now-booming GIS industry. By the time the 2010 census rolled around, it had become possible to map census data online through the Census Bureau's website and to download digital boundary files for use on your own computer.

Knowledge and understanding are based on information, and our information base grows by being able to tap more deeply into rich data sources such as censuses and surveys. GIS is an effective tool for doing this, and you will see numerous examples of GIS at work in the remaining chapters. You can also see it at work on the Internet. Virtually all of the data from recent censuses and the American Community Survey are available on the U.S. Census Bureau's website (http://factfinder.census.gov), where you can create thematic maps on the fly.

Summary and Conclusion

The working bases of any science are facts and theory. In this chapter, I have discussed the major sources of demographic information, the wells from which population data are drawn. Censuses are the most widely known and used sources of data on populations, and humans have been counting themselves in this way for a long time. However, the modern series of more scientific censuses dates only from the late eighteenth and early nineteenth centuries. The high cost of censuses, combined with the increasing knowledge we have about the value of surveys, has meant that even so-called complete enumerations often include some kind of sampling. That is certainly true in North America, as the United States, Canada, and Mexico all use sampling techniques in their censuses. Even vital statistics can be estimated using sample surveys, especially in developing countries, although the usual pattern is for births and deaths (and often marriages, divorces, and abortions) to be registered with the civil authorities. Some countries take this a step further and maintain a complete register of life events for everybody.

Knowledge can also be gleaned from administrative data gathered for nondemographic purposes. These are particularly important in helping us measure migration. It is not just the present that we attempt to measure; historical sources of information can add much to our understanding of current trends in population growth and change. Our ability to know how the world works is increasingly enhanced by incorporating our demographic data into a geographic information system, permitting us to ask questions that were not really answerable before the advent of the computer.

In this and the preceding three chapters, I have laid out for you the basic elements of a demographic perspective. With this in hand (and hopefully in your head as well), we are now ready to probe more deeply into the analysis of population processes, to come to an appreciation of how important the decline in the death rate is, yet why it is still so much higher in some places than in others, why birth rates are still high in some places yet very low in others, and why some people move and others do not.

Main Points

1. In order to study population processes and change, you need to know how many people are alive, how many are being born, how many are dying, how many are moving in and out, and why these things are happening.
2. A basic source of demographic information is the population census, in which information is obtained about all people in a given area at a specific time.
3. Not all countries regularly conduct censuses, but most of the population of the world has been enumerated since 2000.
4. Errors in the census typically come about as a result of nonsampling errors (the most important source of error, including coverage error and content error) or sampling errors.
5. It has been said that censuses are important because if you aren't counted, you don't count.
6. Information about births and deaths usually comes from vital registration records—data recorded and compiled by government agencies. The most complete

vital registration systems are found in the most highly developed nations, while they are often nonexistent in less-developed areas.

7. Most of the estimates of the magnitude of population growth and change are derived by combining census data with vital registration data (as well as administrative data), using the demographic balancing equation.
8. Sample surveys are sources of information for places in which census or vital registration data do not exist or where reliable information can be obtained less expensively by sampling than by conducting a census.
9. Parish records and old census data are important sources of historical information about population changes in the past.
10. Geographic information systems combine maps and demographic data into a computer system for innovative types of spatial demographic analysis.

Questions for Review:

1. In the United States, data are already collected from nearly everyone for Social Security cards and drivers' licenses. Why then does the country not have a population register that would eliminate the need for the census?
2. Survey data are never available at the same geographic detail as are census data. What are the disadvantages associated with demographic data that are not provided at a fine geographic scale?
3. Virtually all of the demographic surveys and surveillance systems administered in developing countries are paid for by governments in richer countries. What is the advantage to richer countries of helping less-rich countries to collect demographic data?
4. What is the value to us in the twenty-first century of having an accurate demographic picture of earlier centuries?
5. Do you agree with the statement that "demographic data are inherently spatial"? Why or why not?

Suggested Readings

1. David A. Swanson and Jacob S. Siegel, 2003, *Methods and Materials of Demography*, Second Edition (San Diego: Academic Press).
   The first edition of this book, by Henry Shryock and Jacob Siegel, was published in 1976 and immediately became a classic in the field of population studies. It has now been revised and updated to reflect the important changes occurring over the past 25 years in the sources of data and techniques for analyzing them.
2. National Research Council, 2007, *Tools and Methods for Estimating Populations at Risk From Natural Disasters and Complex Humanitarian Crises* (Washington, DC: National Academies Press). This report summarizes the state of the art in using geodemographic techniques to estimate the number and characteristics of people living in areas at risk of various kinds of disasters, who may thus be in need of humanitarian relief.

3. Dominique Arel, 2002, "Demography and Politics in the First Post-Soviet Censuses: Mistrusted State, Contested Identities," *Population* (English Edition) 57(6):801-828.
The breaking up of the Soviet Union meant the restructuring of the census in the new Russian Federation, and this process has offered important insights into the social and political issues that lie behind censuses everywhere in the world.
4. Monica Boyd, Gustave Goldmann, and Pamela White, 2000, "Race in the Canadian Census," in Leo Driedger and Shiva S. Halli, eds., *Race and Racism: Canada's Challenge* (Montreal: McGill/Queen's University Press).
Canada has been a country marked by demographic diversity from its earliest national roots, and these authors trace the way in which the census has reflected the country's angst over how best to measure the ethnic and cultural diversity of the population.
5. Christine E. Bose, 2001, *Women in 1900: Gateway to the Political Economy of the 20th Century* (Philadelphia: Temple University Press).
This is a fascinating example of the social scientist as detective using historical census data to allow women to "speak" to us from the past.

Websites of Interest

Remember that websites are not as permanent as books and journals, so I cannot guarantee that each of the following websites still exists at the moment you are reading this. You may have to Google the name of the organization to find the current web address.

1. **http://www.census.gov**
The home page of the U.S. Census Bureau. From here you can locate an amazing variety of information, including the latest releases of census data, the American Community Survey, and all of the surveys conducted by the Census Bureau. This is one of the most accessed websites in the world.
2. **http://www.statcan.gc.ca**
The home page of Statistics Canada, which conducts the censuses in Canada. From here you can obtain census data and track other demographically related information about Canada, including vital statistics and survey data, and you can do so in either English or French.
3. **http://www.inegi.gob.mx**
The home page of INEGI (Instituto Nacional de Estadística, Geografía, y Informática), which is the government agency in Mexico that conducts the censuses and related demographic surveys, as well as compiling the vital statistics for Mexico. You can obtain all of the latest census and survey information from this site, although you will need to be able to read Spanish to do so.
4. **http://www.cdc.gov/nchs/**
In many countries (including Canada and Mexico), a central statistical agency conducts censuses and also collects vital statistics. Not so in the United States, where these functions were divided up in the 1940s. The vital statistics data are collected from each state, tabulated, analyzed, and disseminated by the National Center for Health Statistics (NCHS), which is part of the U.S. Centers for Disease Control and Prevention (CDC).
5. **http://mumford.albany.edu/2000plus/**
The Center for Social and Demographic Analysis and the Lewis Mumford Center at the University at Albany (SUNY) provides the user with the ability to create online maps of sociodemographic variables for areas down to the county level in the United States, using data from Census 2000 and the more recent American Community Survey.

CHAPTER 5
The Health and Mortality Transition

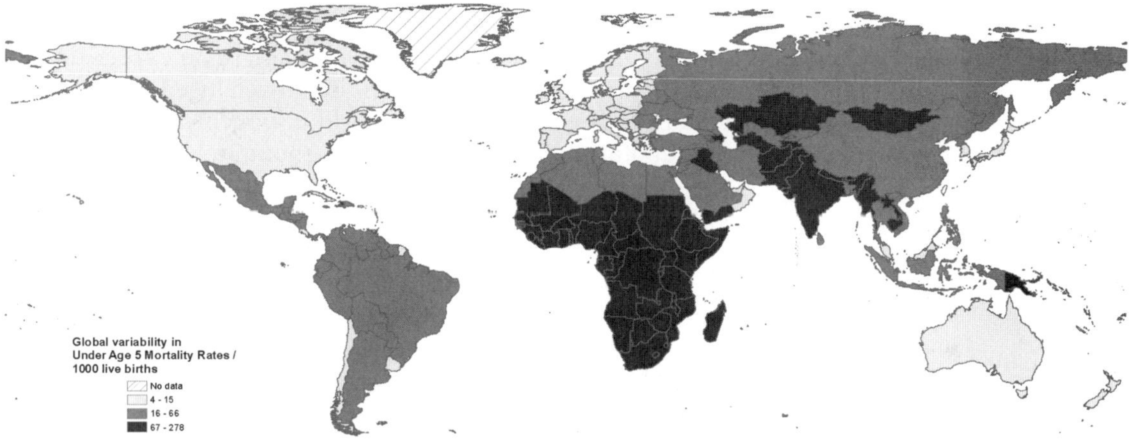

Figure 5.1 Global Variability in Under Age 5 Female Mortality Rates

Source: Adapted by the author from data in United Nations Population Division, 2005, World Population Prospects, The 2004 Revision.

It isn't that people now breed like rabbits; it's that we no longer die like flies—declining mortality, not rising fertility, is the root cause of the revolutionary increase in the world's population size and growth over the past two centuries. Only within that time has mortality been brought under control to the point that most of us are now able to take a long life pretty much for granted. Human triumph over disease and early death represents one of, if not the single, most significant improvements ever made in the condition of human life, and it is tightly bound up in all other aspects of the vastly higher standard of living that we now enjoy. Nevertheless, an important unintended by-product of declining mortality is the mushrooming of the human population from just 1 billion two hundred years ago to an expected 9 billion by the middle of this century. This increase has literally changed everything in the world, and you cannot fully understand the world in which you live without knowing how the health and mortality transition came about and what this means for the future.

I begin the chapter with a brief description of the health and mortality transition and then illustrate its impact by reviewing the changes in health and mortality over time, up to the present. The transition is by no means over, however, so I next consider how far it can go, given what we know about human life span and longevity, and about the things that can and do kill us and what we are doing about them. We will measure the progress of the transition using a variety of indices that I review in the chapter, and I employ some of those tools in the last part of the chapter to examine important inequalities that exist in the world with respect to health and mortality.

Defining the Health and Mortality Transition

Health and death are really two sides of the same coin—morbidity and mortality, respectively—with morbidity referring to the prevalence of disease in a population and mortality the pattern of death. The link is a familiar one to most people—the healthier you are, the longer you are likely to live. At the societal level, this means that populations with high mortality are those with high morbidity; therefore, as health levels improve, so does life expectancy. Most of us in the richer countries take our long life expectancy for granted. Yet scarcely a century ago, and for virtually all of human history before that, death rates were very high and early death was commonplace. Within the past 200 years, and especially during the twentieth century, country after country has experienced a transition to better health and lower death rates—a long-term shift in health and disease patterns that has brought death rates down from very high levels in which people die young, primarily from communicable diseases, to low levels, with deaths concentrated among the elderly, who die from degenerative diseases. This phenomenon was originally defined by Omran (1971, 1977) as the "epidemiological transition," but since the term "epidemiology" technically refers only to disease and not to death, I have chosen to broaden the term to the health and mortality transition.

As a result of this transition, the variability by age in mortality is reduced or *compressed,* leading to an increased rectangularization of mortality. This means that most people survive to advanced ages and then die pretty quickly (as I will discuss in more detail later in the chapter). The vast changes in society brought about as more people survive to ever older ages represent important contributions to the overall demographic transition. We can begin to understand this most readily by examining how health and mortality have changed dramatically during the course of human history, especially European history, for which we tend to have better data than for the rest of the world.

Health and Mortality Changes Over Time

In much of the world and for most of human history, life expectancy probably fluctuated between 20 and 30 years (United Nations 1973; Weiss 1973; Riley 2005). At this level of mortality, only about two-thirds of babies survived to their first birthday, and only about one-half were still alive at age five, as seen in Table 5.1. This means that one-half of all deaths occurred before age five. At the other end of the age continuum, around 10 percent of people made it to age 65 in a premodern society. Thus, in the premodern world, about one-half the deaths were to children under age five and only about one in 10 were to a person aged 65 or older.

In hunter-gatherer societies, it is likely that the principal cause of death was poor nutrition—people literally starving to death—combined perhaps with selective infanticide and geronticide (the killing of older people) (McKeown 1988), although there is too little evidence to do more than speculate about this (Livi Bacci 1991; Bocquet-Appel 2008). As humans gained more control over the environment by domesticating plants and animals (the Agricultural Revolution), both birth and death rates probably went up, as I mentioned in Chapter 2. It was perhaps in the sedentary, more densely settled villages common after the Agricultural Revolution that infectious diseases became a more prevalent cause of death. People were almost certainly better fed, but closer contact with one another, with animals, and with human and animal waste encouraged the spread of disease with especially disastrous results for infants, a situation that prevailed for thousands of years.

The Roman Era to the Industrial Revolution

Life expectancy in the Roman era is estimated to have been 22 years (Petersen 1975). Keep in mind that this does not mean that everybody dropped dead at age 22. Looking at Table 5.1 you can see that it means that the majority of children born did not survive to adulthood. People who reached adulthood were not too likely to reach a very advanced age, but of course some did. The major characteristic of high mortality societies was that there was a lot more variability in the ages at which people died than is true today, but in general people died at a younger, rather than an older, age.

The Roman empire began to break up by the third century, and the period from about the fifth to the fifteenth centuries represents the Middle Ages. Nutrition in Europe during this period probably improved enough to raise life expectancy to more than 30 years. The plague, or Black Death, hit Europe in the fourteenth century, having spread west from Asia (Cantor 2001; Christakos et al. 2005). It is estimated that one-third of the population of Europe may have perished from the

Table 5.1 The Meaning of Improvements in Life Expectancy

Period	Life Expectancy (females)	**Percentage Surviving to Age:** 1	5	25	65	**Percentage of Deaths:** <5	65+	Number of Births Required for ZPG
Premodern	20	63	47	34	8	53	18	6.1
	30	74	61	50	17	39	17	4.2
Some sub-Saharan African countries (comparable to Europe/US in 19th century)	40	82	73	63	29	27	29	3.3
World average circa 2010	71	97	97	96	75	9	74	2.1
Mexico	77	97	97	96	83	2	83	2.1
United States	80	99	99	99	87	<1	87	2.1
Canada	83	99	99	99	91	<1	90	2.1
Japan (highest in world)	86	99	99	99	93	<1	93	2.1

Sources: Life expectancies less than 69 are based on stable population models in Ansley Coale and Paul Demeny, 1966, Regional Model Life Tables and Stable Populations (Princeton, NJ: Princeton University Press); other life table are from World Health Organization, Life Tables for WHO Member States, http://www3.who.int/whosis/life/life_tables/life_tables.cfm, accessed 2010.

disease between 1346 and 1350. The plague then made a home for itself in Europe and, as Cipolla says, "For more than three centuries epidemics of plague kept flaring up in one area after another. The recurrent outbreaks of the disease deeply affected European life at all levels—the demographic as well as the economic, the social as well as the political, the artistic as well as the religious" (Cipolla 1981:3). The constant uncertainty about life could crush you, but it could also encourage you to take risks, as some Europeans did, spreading out around the world.

I mentioned in Chapter 2 that Europe's increasing dominance in oceanic shipping and weapons gave it an unrivaled ability not only to trade goods with the rest of the world but to trade diseases as well. The most famous of these disease transfers was the so-called **Columbian Exchange**, involving the diseases that Columbus and other European explorers took to the Americas (and a few that they took back to Europe). Their relative immunity to the diseases they brought with them, at least in comparison with the devastation those diseases wrought on the indigenous populations, is one explanation for the relative ease with which Spain was able to dominate much of Latin America after arriving there around 1500. The populations in Middle America at the time of European conquest were already living under conditions of "severe nutritional stress and extremely high mortality" (McCaa 1994:7), but contact with the Spaniards turned a bad situation into what McCaa (1994) has called a "demographic hell," with high rates of orphanhood and with life expectancy probably dipping below 20. Spain itself was hit by at least three major plague outbreaks between 1596 and 1685, and McNeill (1976) suggests that this may have been a significant factor in Spain's decline as an economic and political power.

Industrial Revolution to the Twentieth Century

The plague had been more prevalent in the Mediterranean area (where it is too warm for the fleas to die during the winter) than farther north or east, and the last major sighting of the plague in Europe was in the south of France, in Marseilles, in 1720. It is no coincidence that this was the eve of the Industrial Revolution. The plague retreated (rather than disappeared) probably as a result of "changes in housing, shipping, sanitary practices, and similar factors affecting the way rats, fleas, and humans encountered one another" (McNeill 1976:174), and other causes of poor health were diminished by the receding of the little ice age in Europe (Fagan 2000).

At the end of eighteenth century, after the plague had receded and as increasing income improved nutrition, housing, and sanitation, life expectancy in Europe and the United States was approximately 40 years (Vallin and Meslé 2009). As Table 5.1 shows, this was a transitional stage at which there were just about as many deaths to children under age five as there were deaths at age 65 and over. Infectious diseases (including influenza, acute respiratory infections, pneumonia, enteric fever, malaria, cholera, and smallpox) were still the dominant reasons for death, but their ability to kill was diminishing. Analyses of recently created sets of mortality data have shown, however, that the highest life expectancy recorded anywhere in the world began to go up almost without interruption beginning in about 1800 (Oeppen and Vaupel 2002; Vallin and Meslé 2009). This was led almost exclusively by Scandinavian countries until the 1980s when Japan took over the lead.

Although death rates began to decline in the nineteenth century, improvements were at first fairly slow to develop for various reasons. Famines were frequent in Europe as late as the middle of the nineteenth century—the Irish potato famine of the late 1840s and Swedish harvest failures of the early 1860s are prominent examples. These crop failures were widespread, and it was common for local regions to suffer greatly from the effects of a poor harvest because poor transportation made relief very difficult. Epidemics and pandemics of infectious diseases, including the 1918 influenza pandemic, helped to keep death rates high even into the twentieth century. In August 1918, as World War I was ending, a particularly virulent form of the flu apparently mutated almost spontaneously in West Africa (Sierra Leone), al though it was later called "Spanish Influenza." For the next year, it spread quickly around the world, killing more than 20 million people in its path, including more than 500,000 in the United States and Canada (Crosby 1989).

Until recently, then, increases in longevity were primarily due to environmental changes that improved health levels, especially better nutrition and increasing standards of living, not to better medical care:

> Soap production seems to have increased considerably in England, and the availability of cheap cotton goods brought more frequent change of clothing within the economic feasibility of ordinary people. Better communication within and between European countries promoted dissemination of knowledge, including knowledge of disease and the ways to avoid it, and may help to explain the decline of mortality in areas which had neither an industrial nor an agricultural revolution at the time (Boserup 1981:124–25).

McKeown and Record (1962), who did the pioneering research in this area, and more recently Fogel (2004), argue that the factors most responsible for nineteenth-century mortality declines were improved diet and hygienic changes, with medical improvements largely restricted to smallpox vaccinations. Preston and Haines (1991), while noting the importance of nutrition, have also highlighted the role that knowledge about public health plays in controlling infectious disease:

> In 1900, the United States was, as it is now, the richest country in the world (Cole and Deane 1965:Table IV). Its population was also highly literate and exceptionally well-fed. On the scale of per capita income, literacy, and food consumption, it would rank in the top quarter of countries were it somehow transplanted to the present. Yet 18 percent of its children were dying before age 5, a figure that would rank in the bottom quarter of the contemporary countries. Why couldn't the United States translate its economic and social advantages into better levels of child survival? Our explanation is that infectious disease processes . . . were still poorly understood . . . (Preston and Haines 1991:208).

Clean water, toilets, bathing facilities, systems of sewerage, and buildings secure from rodents and other disease-carrying animals are all public ingredients for better health. We now accept the importance of washing our hands as common sense, but the important work of Semmelweis in Vienna, Lister in Glasgow, and Pasteur in Paris in validating the germ theory all took place in the mid-nineteenth century—just a heartbeat away from us in the overall timeline of human history. Public health is largely a matter of preventing the spread of disease, and these kinds of measures have been critical in the worldwide decline in mortality. The medical model of curing disease gets much more attention in the modern world, but its usefulness is predicated on the underlying foundation of good public health (Meade and Earickson 2000). Cutler and Miller (2005) point to the particularly important role played by the introduction of clean water technology (chlorination and filtration) in cities of the United States in the late nineteenth and early twentieth centuries, the time period when life expectancy made its single biggest jump in U.S. history. This was, of course, a direct application of the germ theory.

Public health improvements, as implied by their name, are viewed as public goods that are paid for societally, rather than individually. Medical care, on the other hand, is still viewed in many parts of the world as an individual responsibility, not a public one. It was not until the early twentieth century in the United States that the health of children came to be seen as a responsibility of the community, rather than just a private family matter (Preston and Haines 1991). Working especially with the school system, this created an atmosphere in which, for example, vaccinations for childhood diseases became widespread. Later on, especially in Europe and Canada, the idea emerged strongly that all aspects of health care, including medical care, should be treated as a public good rather than as an individual affair.

Life expectancy has increased enormously since the mid-nineteenth century. In 1851 in England, the life expectancy for males was only 40 years, and it was 44 for women. At the beginning of the twentieth century it had increased to 45 for men and 49 for women. But, at the beginning of the twenty-first century, life expectancy in the United Kingdom is 77 for men and 82 for women. As you can see in Figure 5.2, this pattern has been closely followed in the United States. In 1850, the numbers in the United States were 38.3 years for males and 40.5 years for females. Referring to Table 5.1, this meant that about 72 babies out of 100 would survive to age five and

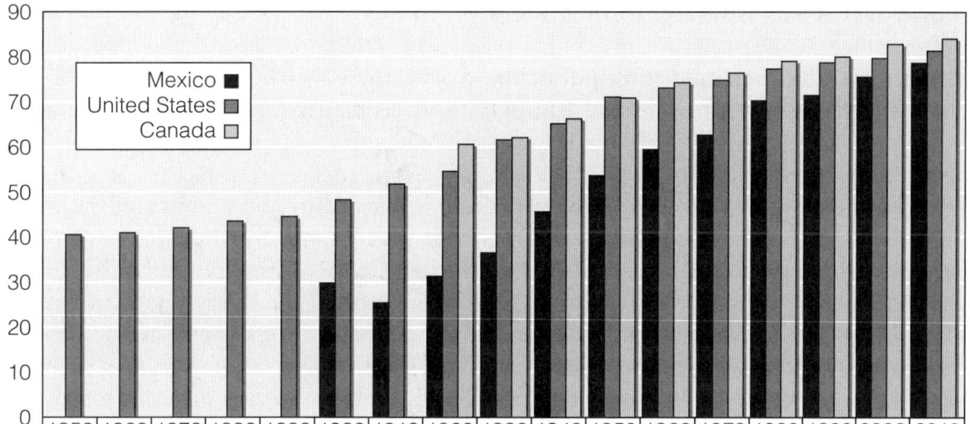

	1850	1860	1870	1880	1890	1900	1910	1920	1930	1940	1950	1960	1970	1980	1990	2000	2010
■ (Mexico)						29.8	25.4	31.5	36.7	45.7	53.7	59.5	62.7	70.3	71.5	75.6	78.7
■ (United States)	40.5	40.9	42.0	43.5	44.5	48.3	51.8	54.6	61.6	65.2	71.1	73.1	74.8	77.4	78.8	79.8	81.4
□ (Canada)								60.6	62.1	66.3	70.9	74.3	76.5	79.1	80.1	82.9	84.1

Figure 5.2 Life Expectancy Has Improved Substantially in the United States, Canada, and Mexico

Sources: Data for the United States 1850 through 1970 are from the U.S. Census Bureau, 1975, *Historical Statistics of the United States, Colonial Times to the 1970 Bicentennial Edition, Part I* (Washington, DC: Government Printing Office); Tables B107-115 and B126-135 (data for 1850 through 1880 refer only to Massachusetts); data for Mexico 1900 to 1950 are from Martha Mier y Terán, 1991, "El Gran Cambio Demográfico," *Demos* 5:4-5; Data for Canada 1920 to 1970 are from Statistics Canada, Catalogue no. 82-221-XDE; all other data are from the United Nations Population Division 2009, World Population Prospects, the 2008 Revision http://esa.un.org/unpp/ (accessed 2010).

about 30 percent of people born would still be alive at age 65. Figure 5.2 also shows that life expectancy began to increase more rapidly as we moved into the twentieth century and public health measures, in particular, started to have a positive impact. Data for Canada are available only since 1920, but you can see that Canada has always had a slightly higher life expectancy than has the United States.

Looking at Latin America, we can see that prior to the Spanish invasion in the sixteenth century, the area was dotted with primitive civilizations in which medicine was practiced as a magic, religious, and healing art. In an interesting reconstruction of history, Ortiz de Montellano (1975) conducted chemical tests on herbs used and claimed to have particular healing powers by the Aztecs in Mexico. He found that a majority of the remedies he was able to replicate were, in fact, effective. Most of the remedies were for problems very similar to those for which Americans spend millions of dollars a year on over-the-counter drugs: coughs, sores, nausea, and diarrhea. Unfortunately, these remedies were not sufficient to combat most diseases and mortality remained very high (life expectancy less than 30 years) in Mexico until the 1920s, when it started to decline at an accelerating rate. Since the 1920s, death rates have been declining so rapidly that Mexico has reduced mortality to the level that the United States achieved in the early 1980s. Thus, in 1920, life expectancy for females in Mexico was 23 years less than in the United States, whereas by 2010 that difference had been cut to less than 3 years.

World War II as a Modern Turning Point

As mortality has declined throughout the world, the control of communicable diseases has been the major reason, although improved control of degenerative disease has played an increasingly important part (Meade and Earickson 2000). This is true for the less developed nations of the world today, just as it was for Europe and North America before them. However, there is a big difference between the more developed and less developed countries in what precipitated the drop in death rates. Whereas socioeconomic development was a precursor to improving health in the developed societies, the less developed nations have been the lucky recipients of the transfer of public health knowledge and medical technology from the developed world. Much of this has taken place since World War II.

World War II conjures up images of German bombing raids on London, desert battles in Egypt, D-Day, and the nuclear explosion in Hiroshima. It was a devastating war costing more lives than any previous combat in history. Yet it was also the staging ground for the most amazing resurgence in human numbers ever witnessed. To keep their own soldiers alive, each side in that war spent huge sums of money figuring out how to prevent the spread of disease among troops, including ways to clean up water supplies and deal with human waste, and at the same to work on new ways to cure disease and heal sick and wounded soldiers. Very importantly, for example, World War II brought us penicillin, the world's first "miracle drug" (Hager 2006).

All of this knowledge and technology was transferred to the rest of the world at the war's end, leading immediately to significant declines in the death rate. Thus, it took only half a century in Latin America for mortality to fall to a point that had taken at least five centuries in European countries, as I noted above with respect to Mexico. Countries no longer have to develop economically to improve their health levels if public health facilities can be emulated and medical care imported from richer countries. As Arriaga (1970) noted during the time that this phenomenon was first becoming obvious, "Because public health programs in backward countries depend largely on other countries, we can expect that the later in historical time a massive public health program is applied in an underdeveloped country previously lacking public health programs, the higher the rate of mortality decline will be." As you can see in Figure 5.3 this applies especially to Latin America and Asia, where improvements in life expectancy have been nothing short of remarkable since the end of World War II.

Progress is not, however, automatic. Sub-Saharan Africa was generally experiencing a rise in life expectancy until being devastated by HIV/AIDS over the past decades, as you can see in Figure 5.3 and as I will discuss later in the chapter. Eastern Europe in the post-Soviet era has also experienced a mortality backslide (Carlson and Watson 1990), which pushed life expectancy for Europe as a region below that of North America, as can be seen in Figure 5.3. Data for Russia reveal that life expectancy for males in 2005 was lower than it had been in 1955. Life expectancy had been falling behind other Western nations since at least the 1970s (Vishnevsky and Shkolnikov 1999), and it has been suggested that Russia's health system was unable to move beyond the control of communicable disease to the control of the degenerative diseases that kill people in the later stages of the epidemiological transition. With the collapse of the Soviet Union in 1989, the health of Russians undoubtedly was further threatened by "political instability and human turmoil"

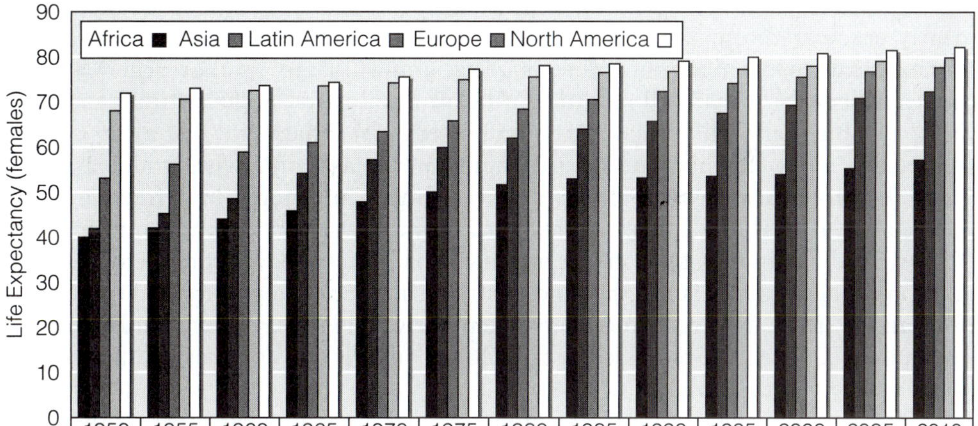

	1950	1955	1960	1965	1970	1975	1980	1985	1990	1995	2000	2005	2010
■	40.0	42.0	44.0	45.9	47.9	50.1	51.7	53.0	53.2	53.6	54.0	55.3	57.2
■	41.9	45.2	48.6	54.2	57.2	59.9	62.0	64.0	65.7	67.5	69.3	70.8	72.3
■	53.1	56.2	58.9	61.0	63.4	65.8	68.4	70.5	72.3	74.1	75.5	76.7	77.7
■	68.0	70.6	72.5	73.5	74.2	74.9	75.5	76.5	76.8	77.3	78.0	79.1	79.9
□	71.9	73.0	73.6	74.3	75.5	77.3	78.1	78.5	79.1	80.0	80.8	81.5	82.2

Figure 5.3 Regional Changes in Life Expectancy since the End of World War II
Source: Adapted from data in United Nations Population Division 2009, World Population Prospects, the 2008 Revision http://esa.un.org/unpp/ (accessed 2010).

(Chen, Wittgenstein, and McKeon 1996:526). Life expectancy seems now to have stopped its decline in Russia, but it is not yet clear how quickly (or even, if) it will begin to climb to the levels of western Europe.

Postponing Death by Preventing and Curing Disease

Improvements in health and medical care can only postpone death to increasingly older ages; we are obviously not yet able to prevent death altogether. There are two basic ways to accomplish the goal of postponing death to the oldest possible ages: (1) preventing diseases from occurring or from spreading when they do occur; and (2) curing people of disease when they are sick. Not getting sick in the first place is clearly the ideal route to travel, a route with both communal (public) and individual elements. Prevention of disease is aided by improved nutrition, both in terms of calories and in terms of vitamin and mineral content; clean water to prevent the spread of water-borne disease and to encourage good personal hygiene; piped sewers to eliminate contact with human waste; treatment of sewage so that it does not come back around to "bite" you; adequate clothing and shoes to prevent parasites from invading the body; adequate shelter to keep people dry and warm; eradication of or at least protection against disease-carrying rodents and insects; vaccinations against childhood diseases; use of disinfectants to clean living and eating areas; sterilization of dishes, bed linen, and clothes of sick people; and the use of gloves and masks to prevent the spread of disease from one person to another. Smallpox has been eliminated as a disease from the world (although there are reportedly still vials in laboratories) as a result of massive vaccination campaigns, and polio is very nearly eradicated after a two-decade campaign of worldwide vaccination by the World Health Organization. India, Nigeria, and Pakistan (in that order) are the places in the world that still record significant numbers of polio victims each year. It is probable that if all 7 billion of us wore sterile face masks for just a few days in succession, we could eliminate several important diseases on a worldwide basis.

Cures for disease range from relatively simple but incredibly effective treatments such as oral rehydration therapy for infants (widely available only since the 1970s), and antibiotics used in the treatment of bacterial infections (widely available only since the 1940s), to the more complex and technology-oriented treatments for cancer, heart disease, and other degenerative diseases, even including organ transplants. These high-tech measures include combinations of drug therapy, radiation therapy, and surgery.

This wide range of options available for pushing back death reveals the complexity of mortality decline in any particular population. As Schofield and Reher (1991) noted in a review of the European mortality decline, "There is no simple or unilateral road to low mortality, but rather a combination of many different elements ranging from improved nutrition to improved education" (p. 17). Nonetheless, Caldwell (1986) pointed out that although a high level of national income is nearly always associated with higher life expectancies, the bigger question is whether it is possible for poorer countries to lower their mortality levels. The answer is at least a qualified yes, and there are several ways to do it. China offers an example of a country that was very poor and had a low life expectancy no higher than 40 years at the time of the communist revolution after the end of World War II. A combination of public health measures and the implementation of a very basic health care system (the "barefoot doctors") increased life expectancy to more than 60 years by the mid-1970s. Increasing incomes in China since then have helped life expectancy rise to 75 for females by now. Geography also makes some difference. Caldwell (1986) notes that islands and other countries with very limited territories seem to be able to lower their mortality more readily than territorially larger nations. Being "in the path" of European expansion has also been fortuitously beneficial to some countries (such as Costa Rica and Sri Lanka) because it increases the opportunities for the transfer of death control technology.

The Nutrition Transition and Its Link to Obesity

It used to be axiomatic that the poor were skinny and only the rich could afford to be fat. That's no longer true even in poorer countries where obesity is rapidly becoming a health problem. This is bound up in a phenomenon that Barry Popkin (1993; 2002; Popkin and Gordon-Larsen 2004; Popkin 2009) calls the **nutrition transition**—a marked worldwide shift toward a diet high in fat and processed foods and low in fiber, accompanied by lower levels of physical exercise, leading to corresponding increases in degenerative diseases.

Hunting and gathering populations had a pattern of collecting food; early agriculturalists had a pattern related to avoiding famine; then as time progressed and the economy improved, the pattern evolved to what Popkin and his associates call "receding famine." More recently, especially in Western nations, the diet associated with industrialization has shifted to one high in fat, cholesterol, and sugar (and often accompanied by a sedentary lifestyle) that they call the "degenerative disease pattern." There is ample evidence that people living in the wealthier societies of the world are larger in size than ever before in history. More importantly, modern society, even in poorer nations, is increasingly associated with obesity and with less active lifestyles than ever before, and these factors threaten to limit our ability to push life expectancy to higher levels. We have bodies that are built to live on the edge of famine in a physically active world (the human condition until recently), but the majority of humans now have a relatively secure food supply and the ability to avoid at least some of the manual labor of the past. The proliferation of motorized transportation also means that we are walking far less than ever before. All of these things add up to the finding reported in 2010 that more than 25 percent of children (ages 2 through 14) in the United States have at least one chronic health condition, especially obesity and/or asthma (Van Cleave, Gortmaker, and Perrin 2010). The evidence seems clear that obesity is likely to shorten a person's life expectancy in rich and not-so-rich countries alike (Monteverde et al. 2010).

Over the course of history, our body's ability to store fat is what saved us when the food ran out for a while. Especially in the richer nations, we no longer face such periodic shortages and so that fat isn't used up unless we consciously limit its intake and/or engage in regular physical exercise. If we are going to reduce the burden of degenerative disease and prolong our health, we are almost certainly going to have to restructure our everyday life to reduce the consumption of fat and sugar while increasing our level of exercise.

Life Span and Longevity

Could you live forever if you were able to avoid fatal accidents and fatal communicable diseases, and if you were scrupulous about lifestyle choices? The answer is almost certainly no (Olshansky, Hayflick, and Carnes 2002). Biologists suggest that as we move past the reproductive years (past our biological "usefulness"), we undergo a set of concurrent processes know as **senescence**: a decline in physical viability accompanied by a rise in vulnerability to disease. Several theories are in vogue as to why people become susceptible to disease and death as age increases. These can be roughly divided into theories of "**wear and tear**" and "**planned obsolescence.**" Wear and tear is one of the most popularly appealing theories of aging and likens humans to machines that eventually wear out due to the stresses and strains of constant use. But which biological mechanisms might actually account for the wearing out? One possibility is that errors occur in the synthesis of new proteins within the body. Protein synthesis involves a long and complex series of events, beginning with the DNA in the nucleus and ending with the production of new proteins. At several steps in this delicate process, it seems possible that molecular errors can occur that lead to irreversible damage (and thus aging) of a cell. Of special concern is the possibility that errors may occur in the body's immune system so that the body begins to attack its own normal cells rather than just foreign invaders. This process is called autoimmunity. Alternatively, the immune system may lose its ability to attack the outside invaders, leading to a situation in which the body no longer can fight off disease. The planned obsolescence theories revolve around the idea that each of us has a built-in biological time clock that ticks for a predetermined length of time and then is still. It essentially proposes that you will die "when your number is up," because each cell in your body will regenerate only a certain number of times and no more.

Which of these theories makes the most sense? Good question. If you had a solid answer, you could bottle it and retire, although given the emerging advances in human genome analysis, we may approach some answers to these questions in your lifetime (Olshansky 2008). Until that time comes, let me remind you that current evidence points to two basic conclusions: (1) aging is much more complex than we have previously assumed, and different theories fill in only part of the puzzle; and (2) we have not yet discovered the basic, underlying mechanism of aging that (if it exists) would explain everything. The planned obsolescence theory could explain why animal species each have a different life span, whereas the various aspects of wear and tear seem better able to explain why members of the same species show so much variability in the actual aging process. Olshansky and Carnes (1997) have offered their opinion that "although there is probably not a genetic program for death, the basic biology of our species, shaped by the forces of evolution acting on us since our inception, places inherent limits on human longevity" (p. 76).

Life Span

The previous paragraph uses the terms "life span" and "longevity" as though they were interchangeable. There is, however, a subtle difference. Demographers define **life span** as referring to the oldest age to which human beings can survive; whereas **longevity** refers to the ability to remain alive from one year to the next—the ability to resist death. We do not yet have a good theory about aging to help us to predict how long humans *could* live, so we must be content to assume that the oldest age to which a human actually *has* lived (a figure that may change from day to day) is the oldest age to which it is possible to live. Claims of long human life span are widespread, but confirmation of those claims is more difficult to find. As of this writing, the oldest authenticated age to which a human has ever lived is 122 years and 164 days, an age achieved by a French woman, Jeanne Louise Calment, who died in August 1997. Her authenticated birth date was February 21, 1875, and on her 120th birthday in 1995, she was asked what kind of future she expected. "A very short one," she replied (Wallis 1995:85). You can stay up-to-date by visiting the following website: http://www.recordholders.org/en/list/oldest.html.

So, humans can live to at least age 122, yet very few people come close to achieving that age. Most, in fact, can expect to live scarcely more than half that long (life expectancy at birth for the world as a whole is estimated to be about 69 years). It is this latter concept, the age to which people *actually* survive, their demonstrated ability to stay alive, as opposed to the theoretical maximum, that we refer to as longevity.

Longevity

Longevity is usually measured by **life expectancy**, the statistically average length of life (or average expected age at death, which I will discuss in greater detail later in the chapter). This is greatly influenced by the society in which we live because of the variability in public health and medical care systems, as I discussed above. The very same person born into a poorer country such as Nigeria will have a lower life expectancy than if she had been born in the United States. Your own longevity is also influenced by the genetic characteristics with which you are born. The strength of vital organs, predisposition to particular diseases, metabolism rate, and so on are biological factors over which we presently have little control. Studies of identical twins separated at birth and raised in different environments show that their average age at death is more similar than non-identical twins, and that both groups of twins have life expectancies that are more similar than you would expect by chance (see, for example, Herskind et al. 1996). Nonetheless, the available evidence suggests that no more than 35 percent of the variability in longevity is due to inherited characteristics (Carey and Judge 2001). The remaining differences in mortality are due to social, economic, and even political factors that influence when and why death occurs.

The social world influences the risk of death in a variety of ways that can be reasonably reduced to two broad categories: (1) the social, economic, and political infrastructure (how much control we exercise over nature) and (2) lifestyle (how much control we exercise over ourselves). The infrastructure of society refers to the way in which wealth is generated and distributed, reflecting the extent to which water and milk are purified, diseases are vaccinated against, rodents and other pests are controlled, waste is eliminated, and food, shelter, clothing, and acute medical care and long-term assistance are made available to members of society. Within any particular social setting, however, death rates may also be influenced by lifestyle. An increasing body of evidence has implicated smoking, drug use, excessive alcohol use, fatty food, and too little exercise as lifestyle factors that may shorten longevity.

Although one key to a long life may be your "choice" of long-lived parents, prescriptions for a long life are most often a brew of lifestyle choices. A typical list of ways to maximize longevity includes regular exercise, daily breakfast, normal weight, no smoking, only moderate drinking, seven to eight hours of sleep daily, regular meal-taking, and an optimistic outlook on life. Note that the latter idea of "don't worry, be happy, you'll live longer" has the backing of medical research (Davidson, Mostofsky, and Whang 2010). These suggestions, by the way, are not unique to the Western world, nor are they particularly modern. A group of medical workers studying older people in southern China concluded that the important factors for long life are fresh air, moderate drinking and eating, regular exercise, and an optimistic attitude (Associated Press 1980). Similarly, note the words of a Dr. Weber, who was 83 in 1904 when he published an article in the *British Medical Journal* outlining his prescriptions for a long life:

> Be moderate in food and drink and in all physical pleasures; take exercise daily, regardless of the weather; go to bed early, rise early, sleep for no more than 6–7 hours; bathe daily; work and occupy yourself mentally on a regular basis—stimulate the enjoyment

> of life so that the mind may be tranquil and full of hope; control the passions; be resolute about preserving health; and avoid alcohol, narcotics, and soothing drugs (quoted in Metchnikoff 1908).

Other fascinating examples of the way in which social and psychological processes can apparently influence death have been given by David Phillips. In the first of a series of studies, Phillips (1974) found that mortality from suicide tends to increase right after a famous person commits a well-publicized suicide (see also Wasserman 1984; Stack 1987). Thus, some people seem to "follow the leader" when it comes to dying. Further, people do so in more invidious ways than just simple suicide. In follow-up studies, Phillips found that the number of fatal automobile crashes (especially single-car, single-person crashes) goes up after publicized suicides (Phillips 1977) and (incredibly enough) that private airplane accident fatalities also increase just after newspaper stories about a murder-suicide. It appears "that murder-suicide stories trigger subsequent murder-suicides, some of which are disguised as airplane accidents" (Phillips 1978:748). In another study, Phillips demonstrated that mass-media violence can also trigger homicides. He discovered that in the United States between 1973 and 1978, homicides regularly increased right after championship prizefights. Furthermore, the more heavily publicized the fight, the greater the rise in homicides (Phillips 1983).

The mind is a wondrous thing, illustrated by the intriguing finding that Chinese-Americans who are born in a year that Chinese astrology considers ill-fated and who have a disease that Chinese medicine considers to be ill-fated, have significantly lower life expectancy than normal (Phillips 1993). It may be, of course, that Chinese astrology and medicine are correct about the fates, but Phillips thinks it is more likely that people succumb to an earlier death because of psychosomatic processes—their *belief* that they are fated to die. Even your name might affect your longevity. Christenfeld, Phillips, and Glynn (1999) examined 27 years of death certificates in California and concluded that males with "positive" initials such as A.C.E. or W.I.N. or G.O.D. lived 4.5 years longer on average than a control group with neutral or ambiguous initials (such as J.R.W. or D.J.H.). Conversely, men with "negative" initials just as P.I.G. or D.U.D. or B.U.M. died an average of 2.8 years earlier than the control group. Effects were less strong for females, though still present, and the findings could not be explained by race, socioeconomic status, or any other variables available on the death certificate. There is no clear explanation for this except that somehow the impact of your initials on health must be psychosocial in nature, although as one critic put it, we have to remember that this is only an "initial" study.

It is easier, of course, to die than to resist death, adding interest to another angle of Phillips's research. He has found that there is a tendency for people who are near death to postpone dying until after a special event, especially a birthday. The story is often told that Thomas Jefferson lingered on his deathbed late on the evening of July 3, 1826, until his physician assured him that it was past midnight and was now the fourth of July, whereupon Jefferson died. Phillips and Smith (1990) found in two large samples of nearly 3 million people that women, especially, are indeed more likely to die in the week right after their birthday than in any other week of the year, suggesting the deliberate prolongation of life. Men, on the other hand, show a peak mortality just before their birthday, suggesting a "deadline" for death.

Disease and Death over the Life Cycle

Age Differentials in Mortality

Disease and death are not randomly distributed across the life cycle. Humans are like most other animals with respect to the general pattern of death by age—the very young and the old are most vulnerable, whereas young adults are least likely to die. In Figure 5.4, you can see that the pattern of death by age is similar whether the actual death rates are high or low. After the initial year of life, there is a period of time, usually lasting at least until middle age, when risks of death are relatively low. Beyond middle age, mortality increases, although at a decelerating rate (Manton, Stallard, and Corder 1997; Manton and Land 2000).

The genetic or biological aspects of longevity have led many theorists over time to believe that the age patterns of longevity shown in Figure 5.4 could be explained by a simple mathematical formula similar perhaps to the law of gravity and other laws of nature. The most famous of these was put forward in 1825 by Benjamin Gompertz and describes a simple geometric relationship between age and death rates from the point of sexual maturity to the extreme old ages (Olshansky and Carnes 1997). These mathematical models are interesting, but they have so far not been able to capture the actual variability in the human experience with death. Part of the problem, as we are reminded by Carey and Judge (2001), is that we may

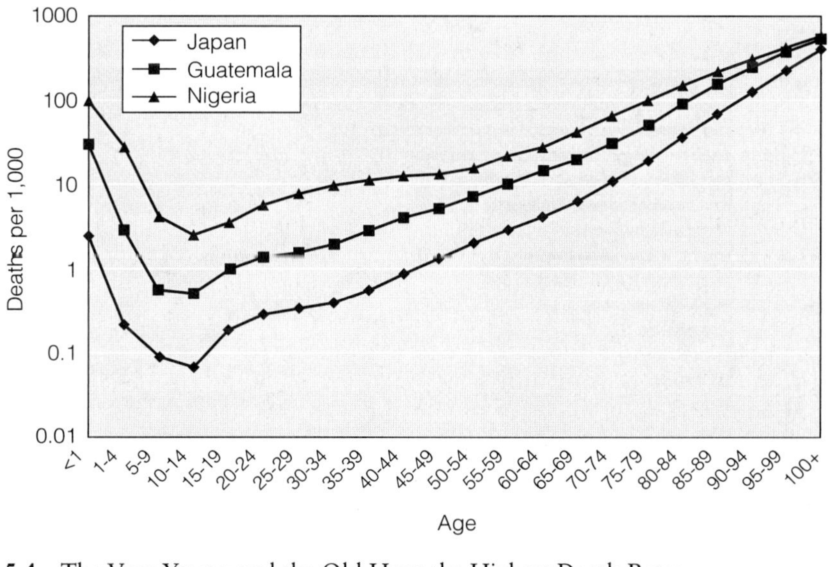

Figure 5.4 The Very Young and the Old Have the Highest Death Rates

Note: Nigeria has among the highest death rates in the world, Japan is among the lowest, and Guatemala is near the world average. Yet all three countries exhibit the virtually universal age pattern of mortality—high at both ends and lowest in the middle. Data are for females, but the pattern is the same for males. Data refer to 2006.

Source: Adapted from data in World Health Organization, Life Tables for WHO Member States, http://www3.who.int/whosis/life/life_tables/life_tables.cfm (accessed 2010).

know what *kills* us, but we are less certain about what it is that allows us to *survive*. This is why, even if we were able to rid ourselves of all diseases, we do not know how long we might live. We do know, however, that since our susceptibility to disease and death varies over the life cycle, it is important to look at those differences in more detail.

Infant Mortality There are few things in the world more frightening and awesome than the responsibility for a newborn child, fragile and completely dependent on others for survival. In many societies, the fragility and dependency are translated into high **infant mortality rates** (the number of deaths during the first year of life per 1,000 live births). Infant death rates are closely correlated with life expectancy, and Figure 5.5 shows the infant mortality rates for a sample of countries around the world. Japan and Sweden have had the world's lowest rates of infant mortality among the more populous countries for a number of years, and both have rates that are now below three deaths per 1,000 live births. All western European countries have rates that are below four per 1,000. Canada's rate is five per 1,000, whereas the United States has a slightly higher rate of just under seven per 1,000. Mexico's level of 19 per 1,000 is obviously higher, but it is still well below the world average of 46 per 1,000. By contrast, in some of the less-developed nations, especially in equatorial Africa, infant death rates are above 100 deaths per 1,000 live births. This is a region of the world that has some of the highest mortality rates ever recorded for a human population (McDaniel 1992).

Why are babies so vulnerable? One of the most important causes of death among infants is dehydration, which can be caused by almost any disease or dietary

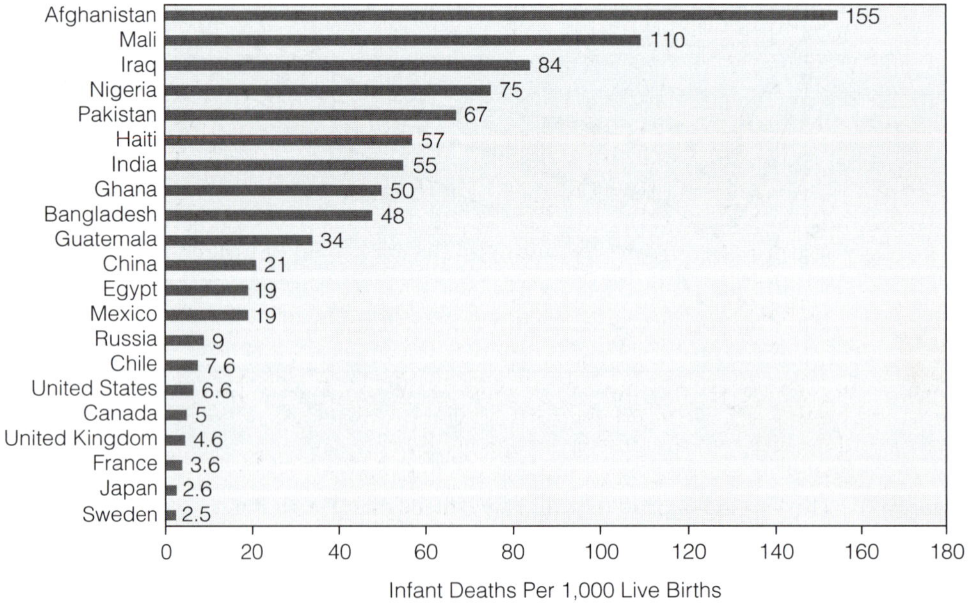

Figure 5.5 Variations in Infant Mortality around the World

Source: Adapted from data in Population Reference Bureau, *2009 World Population Data Sheet.*

imbalance, with polluted water being a common source of trouble for babies. How can dehydration and other causes of death among infants be avoided? In the broadest sense, the answer can be summed up by two characteristics common to people in places where infant death rates are low—high levels of education and income. These are key ingredients at both the societal level and the individual level. In general, those countries with the highest levels of income and education are those with enough money to provide the population with clean water, adequate sanitation, food and shelter, and, very importantly, access to health care services.

At the individual level, education here can refer simply to knowledge of a few basic rules that would avoid unnecessary infant death. Afghanistan has one of the highest infant death rates and the highest maternal mortality rate in the world. An important reason is that the lack of medical facilities in that country means that most births are attended by a traditional midwife who may be "dangerously ignorant. Some refuse to tie umbilical cords, so that 'dirty' blood can flow from the baby. Others seek to cure infections by placing dead mice—and other treats—in the vagina. Many insist babies be born in a bowl of dirt. Tetanus contracted by newborns from the dirt is dismissed as demonic possession" (*The Economist* 2003:42).

Higher incomes increase the chance that babies will have a nutritious, sanitary diet that prevents diarrhea. Nursing mothers can best provide this service if their diet is adequate in amount and quality. Income is also frequently associated with the ability of a nation to provide, or an individual to buy, adequate medical protection from disease. In places where infant death rates are high, communicable diseases are a major cause of death, and most of those deaths could be prevented with medical assistance. We know, for example, that between 1861 and 1960 the infant death rate in England and Wales dropped from 160 to 20 and more than two-thirds of that decline was due to the control of communicable diseases.

Throughout the world, infant health has been aided especially by the fact that the World Health Organization of the United Nations has promoted the use of **oral rehydration therapy (ORT)**, which involves administering an inexpensive glucose and electrolyte solution to replenish bodily fluids. Oral rehydration therapy was first shown to be effective in clinical trials in Bangladesh in 1968 (Nalin, Cash, and Islam 1968), and it has proven to be very effective in controlling diarrhea among infants (and adults as well) all over the world, as I mentioned earlier.

When infant mortality drops to low levels, such as in advanced nations like the United States and Canada, prematurity becomes the single most important reason for deaths among infants, and in many cases prematurity results from lack of proper care of the mother during pregnancy. Pregnant women who do not maintain an adequate diet, who smoke, take drugs, or in general do not care for themselves have an elevated chance of giving birth prematurely, thus putting their baby at a distinct disadvantage in terms of survival after birth.

Throughout the world, the infant mortality rate is a fairly sensitive indicator of societal development because as the standard of living goes up, so does the average level of health in a population, and the health of babies typically improves earlier and faster than of people at other ages. This greater ability to resist death past infancy generally holds up throughout the reproductive years (with the exception of maternal mortality, which I discuss below), but beyond that time of life, death rates start to increase.

Mortality at Older Ages It has been said that in the past parents buried their children; now, children bury their parents. This describes the health and mortality transition in a nutshell. The postponement of death until the older ages means that the number of deaths among friends and relatives in your own age group is small in the early years and then accumulates more rapidly in the later decades of life. But even at the older ages, there are revolutionary changes taking place in death rates. In the more developed countries of the world, the risk of death has been steadily going down even at the very oldest ages. We have not yet unlocked the key to living beyond age 122, but we are pushing toward the day when a large fraction of people will approach that age before they die.

As life expectancy has increased and people survive in greater proportions to older ages, societies experience less variability in the ages at which their members die. Instead of people being likely to die at almost any age (even if most at risk when young or old), death gets compressed into a narrow range of ages. Wilmoth and Horiuchi (1999) calculated, for example, that the variability in ages at death in Sweden in the 1950s was only about one-fourth of what it had been 100 years before that. The result of this compression of death into a narrow range at the older ages is called **rectangularization**. This means that the curve of the proportion of people surviving to any given age begins to square off, rather than dropping off smoothly. Figure 5.6 gives you an example of this using data for females in the United States.

Going back to 1901–10, when life expectancy in the United States was 52 years, Figure 5.6 shows that the proportion surviving drops off fairly quickly at the younger ages because of high infant and child mortality, and then it drops off fairly smoothly after that until everybody has died off at around 100. By the middle of the twentieth century, in 1951–60, when life expectancy had increased rather dramatically to 72 years, the proportions alive at each successive age are noticeably larger than they were at the beginning of that century, and the trend continued on to the end of the century when, in the year 2000, life expectancy had reached 79. An almost totally rectangular situation is shown as the extreme case in Figure 5.6. If everyone survived to age 100, and then died quickly after that, mortality would be compressed into a very short time period, with an estimated life expectancy of 108 years, and the survival curve would be squared off at the oldest ages, as you can see. In general, the limited data available seem to support the idea that compression and rectangularization are occurring (Wilmoth and Horiuchi 1999; Kannisto 2001), although not everybody agrees (Lynch and Brown 2001). The principal argument against it is that it assumes a fixed human life span of around 120 years. If we are somehow able to crack that barrier, then people could live to increasingly older ages, which might "decompress" mortality and smooth out the mortality curve at the older ages (Caselli and Vallin 2001).

Even if we are never able to crack the 120-year barrier, one of the most dramatic changes in mortality in richer countries over the past few decades has been the drop in death rates at the older ages. It is not simply that deaths are being compressed into a relatively short period in old age; that age has been getting progressively older. Consider that in 1900 a woman who reached age 65 in the United States could expect to live another 12 years. At the time of World War II that had increased a bit to 14 years, but by 2006 (the latest data available at this writing) it

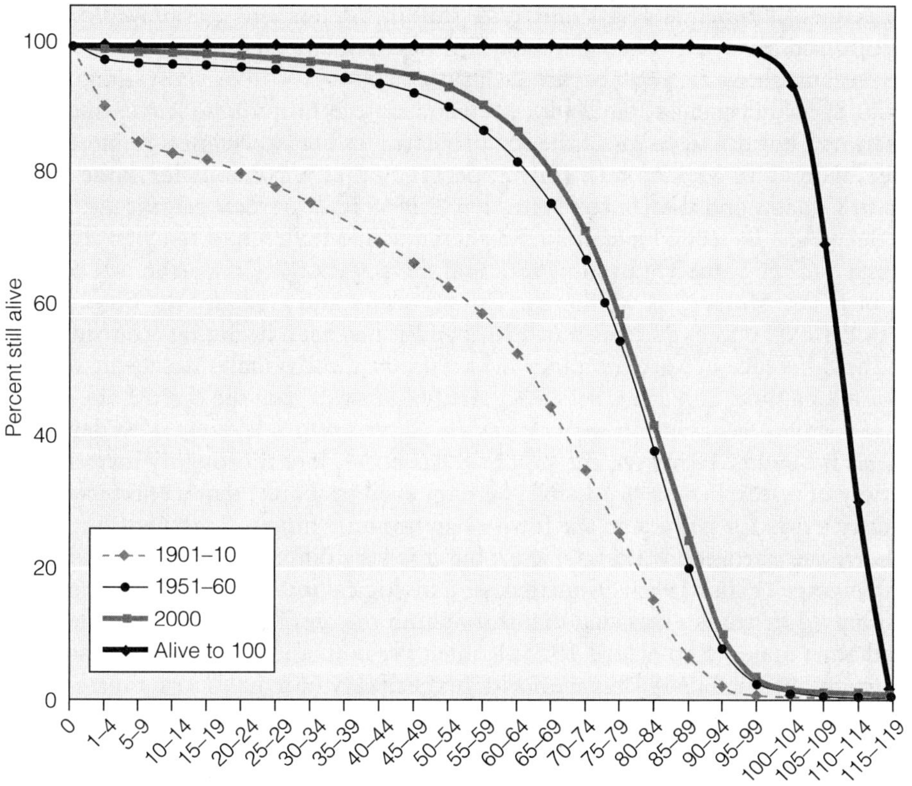

Figure 5.6 The Rectangularization of Mortality in the United States

Sources: Data for 1901-10 and 1951-60 are from the Berkeley Mortality Database (http://demog.berkeley.edu/wilmoth/mortality), based on life tables prepared by the Office of the Chief Actuary of the Social Security Administration. Data for 2000 are based on death data from the U.S. National Center for Health Statistics, and the "Alive to 100" data were generated by the author.

was up to 20 years (Heron et al. 2009). These things may not matter much to you now, but as you approach old age, you'll start to give them more thought.

Sex and Gender Differentials in Mortality

Although the age pattern of death is the most obvious way in which biology affects our lives, it is also true that at every age there are differences between males and females in the likelihood of death. Some of these differentials seem to be strictly biological in origin (the "sex" differences) whereas others are induced by society (the "gender" differences), although it is not always easy to tell the difference between the biological and social influences.

The most basic health difference between males and females is that women generally live longer than men do, and the gap had been widening until recently. In 1900, women could expect to live an average of two years longer than men in the United States, and by 1975, the difference had peaked at 7.8 years. Since then, the difference has dropped to 5.1 years as of 2006 (Heron et al. 2009), but the survival advantage of women is nearly universal among the nations of the world. Canada has followed a similar pattern, with a 1.8-year advantage in 1920 expanding to a 7.2-year advantage in 1980 before dropping back to a 4.6-year advantage in 2006 (World Health Organization 2009). Mexico is in catch-up mode with respect to life expectancy, but not in terms of the sex difference in life expectancy. In 1960, for example, women in Mexico had a life expectancy that was about the same as it had been in Canada and the United States back in 1920, and their advantage over men was 3.2 years. By 2006, female life expectancy in Mexico had reached the level of Canada and the United States in 1980, and the advantage for women was 5.0 years. However, for Mexico, as well as the United States and Canada, the biggest gender gap (6.8 years) was experienced in 1980, and it has been declining a bit since then.

The difference in life expectancy between males and females has attracted curiosity for a long time, and it has been suggested facetiously that the early death of men is nature's way of repaying those women who have spent a lifetime with demanding, difficult husbands. However, the situation has been more thoroughly investigated by a variety of researchers. It is possible, perhaps even probable, that a real biological superiority exists for women in the form of an immune function, perhaps imparted by the hormone estrogen (Waldron 1986); but it is very difficult to measure this biological advantage (Vallin 1999). Nonetheless, a biological interpretation of the difference is supported by studies showing that throughout the animal kingdom females survive longer than males (Retherford 1975; Kohler, Preston, and Lackey 2006), suggesting some kind of basic biological superiority in the ability of females to survive relative to males (biologists refer to this as an aspect of *sexual dimorphism*).

In human populations, the survival advantage of women is widespread, but it is not quite universal. There are still a handful of countries—Afghanistan and a few nations in sub-Saharan Africa—where life expectancy for females is the same as or lower than that for males. This implies that there are social factors at work, especially related to the status of women. It is in those countries where women are most dominated by men that women have been least likely to outlive men (Cardenas and Obermeyer 1997). In sub-Saharan Africa this shows up in the victimization of women by men who have HIV but force women to have unprotected sex with them. In south Asia, it is noticeable at the younger ages, when girls may be fed less well than boys, and parents may be less likely to seek health care for sick girls than for sick boys (Muhuri and Preston 1991; Yount 2003; Oster 2009).

The social aspect of mortality also shows up in what is certainly an important part of the explanation for the widening and then narrowing of the gap in mortality between men and women over the course of the twentieth century—smoking. Since 1900, males have smoked cigarettes much more than have females, and this has helped to elevate male risks of death from cancer, degenerative lung diseases (such as chronic bronchitis and emphysema), and cardiovascular diseases (Preston 1970). However, cigarette smoking by women increased after World War II, and by now women are nearly as likely as men to be smokers (the smoking version of gender equality). Deaths associated with smoking tend to occur many years after smoking begins, so the result of women's post–World War II smoking habits has been a predictable recent rise in death rates from lung cancer, which has helped to narrow the gap in male-female mortality (Preston and Wang 2006). Rogers and Powell-Griner (1991) calculated that males and females who smoke heavily have similar (and lower-than-average) life expectancies, but nonsmoking males still have lower life expectancies than nonsmoking females (although still higher than smokers). Overall, Rogers and his colleagues (Rogers, Hummer, and Nam 2000) estimate that smoking accounts for 25 percent of the gender gap.

Causes of Poor Health and Death

The things that make us sick and can kill us have been wrapped into virtually every paragraph up to this point, but it is useful to discuss them in a more systematic fashion, keeping in mind that this is only a brief review of an incredibly complex field of study. The World Health Organization puts deaths into one of three major categories: (1) communicable, maternal, perinatal, and nutritional conditions; (2) noncommunicable diseases; and (3) injuries. Within each of these categories are subgroups, as shown in Table 5.2, and as discussed below.

Communicable Diseases

For most of human history, infectious diseases have been the major cause of death, killing people before they had a chance to die of something else. Infectious diseases include bacterial (such as tuberculosis, pneumonia, and the plague), viral (such as influenza and measles), and protozoan (such as malaria and diarrhea). They are spread in different ways (by different vectors), and have varying degrees of severity. You can see in Table 5.2 that they account for one-third (32.1 percent) of all deaths in the world, but the higher the life expectancy, the less important these diseases are as causes of death.

Tuberculosis is an example of a bacterial infection that still kills 1.5 million people each year, despite the known treatments for it, and it is estimated that ten times that number of people are infected with the disease worldwide but do not show symptoms. The World Health Organization has a "Stop TB Strategy" and the U.S. Centers for Disease Control has a "Division of TB Elimination," but the disease remains untreated in many parts of the world. In Table 5.2 you can see, for example, that it accounts for more than 4 percent of all deaths in a very poor country such as Afghanistan. Somalia is actually the country that has the highest death rate from TB, and eight of the top ten countries with respect to TB are in sub-Saharan Africa. Some drug-resistant strains of TB have emerged, and preventing the spread of these forms of the disease is clearly an important issue in the world. China, for example, has discovered that many migrants from the countryside to cities are infected with tuberculosis and have stopped taking the months-long treatment course. The surviving germs from these uncompleted treatments are the ones that are strongest and most resistant to drugs and it is their spread that is particularly worrisome (Zamiska 2006).

Measles is an example of an acute viral disease that is severe in infancy and adulthood but less so in childhood. It is usually spread by droplets passed through the air when an infected person coughs or sneezes. If left untreated in an infant or adult, the chance of death is 5–10 percent. Vaccinations now protect most people in

Table 5.2 Major Causes of Death in the World and Selected Countries

	World		United States	Japan	Guatemala	Afghanistan	Botswana
Cause of Death	Number of deaths (000)	Percent of Deaths	Percent of Deaths	Percent of Deaths	Percent of Deaths	Percent of Deaths	Percent of Deaths
1. Communicable diseases, maternal and perinatal conditions, and nutritional deficiencies	18324	32.1	6.1	11.9	49.8	65.5	87.4
Tuberculosis	1566	2.7	0.0	0.5	1.8	4.4	1.5
STIs, excluding HIV	180	0.3	0.0	0.0	0.1	0.1	0.0
HIV/AIDS	2777	4.9	0.5	0.0	7.2	0.0	80.1
Diarrheal diseases	1798	3.2	0.1	0.1	4.2	8.5	1.0
Measles	611	1.1	0.0	0.0	0.0	0.5	0.0
Other childhood diseases	513	0.9	0.0	0.0	0.5	2.7	0.0
Malaria	1272	2.2	0.0	0.0	0.1	0.2	0.5
Other infectious and parasitic diseases	2187	3.8	2.0	1.6	20.0	18.6	1.2
Respiratory infections	3963	6.9	2.5	9.5	7.2	11.7	1.2
Maternal conditions	510	0.9	0.0	0.0	1.1	3.9	0.2
Perinatal conditions	2462	4.3	0.7	0.0	5.1	12.8	1.9
Nutritional deficiencies	485	0.9	0.3	0.2	2.4	2.1	0.2
2. Noncommunicable conditions	33537	58.8	87.6	80.5	39.8	29.0	10.2
Malignant neoplasms	7121	12.5	23.1	31.7	6.5	3.9	2.2
Other neoplasms	149	0.3	0.6	1.0	0.0	0.4	0.0
Diabetes mellitus	988	1.7	3.2	1.3	2.1	0.6	0.2
Endocrine disorders	243	0.4	1.3	0.7	1.2	0.7	0.0

(continued)

Table 5.2 (continued)

	World		United States	Japan	Guatemala	Afghanistan	Botswana
Cause of Death	Number of deaths (000)	Percent of Deaths	Percent of Deaths	Percent of Deaths	Percent of Deaths	Percent of Deaths	Percent of Deaths
Neuropsychiatric disorders	1112	1.9	6.4	1.5	2.4	0.2	0.2
Cardiovascular diseases	16733	29.3	38.1	32.0	11.7	13.9	4.8
Respiratory diseases	3702	6.5	7.5	5.0	9.2	1.8	1.0
Digestive diseases	1968	3.5	3.6	4.0	4.6	2.6	0.7
Genitourinary Diseases	848	1.5	2.5	2.5	1.1	1.4	0.5
Other conditions	673	1.2	1.3	0.9	1.0	3.5	0.5
3. Injuries	5168	9.1	6.3	7.6	10.4	5.5	2.4
Unintentional	3551	6.2	4.4	4.3	4.6	3.8	1.9
Suicide	873	1.5	1.2	3.2	3.7	0.3	0.2
Homicide	559	1.0	0.6	0.1	5.5	0.2	0.2
War	172	0.3	0.0	0.0	0.0	1.2	0.0
TOTAL	57029	100.0	100.0	100.0	100.0	100.0	100.0
LIFE EXPECTANCY FOR FEMALES		67.0	80	8	71	42	40
HEALTHY LIFE EXPECTANCY (HALE) FOR FEMALES			71	78	60	35	35
EXPECTATION OF LOST HEALTHY YEARS AT BIRTH FOR FEMALES			9	8	9	7	5

Source: Adapted from data in World Health Organization, http://www.who.int/research/en/, accessed 2010. Data refer to 2002.

the developed world from measles, and the United Nations has been working to increase immunization elsewhere. The countries with the highest death rates from measles are Guinea-Bissau, Niger, and Somalia. All of the top ten countries in terms of measles death rates are in sub-Saharan Africa.

Malaria is an example of a complex protozoan disease typically spread by female mosquitoes first biting an infected person. Then the blood from the malarial person spends a week or more in the mosquito's stomach, where the malarial spores develop and enter the mosquito's salivary gland. The disease is passed along with the mosquito's next bite to a human. There are two major types of malaria: (1) *Plasmodium falciparum* is the most deadly, and it is prevalent in sub-Saharan Africa, but it is less commonly found elsewhere, probably because it requires consistently high temperatures; and (2) *Plasmodium vivax*, which is the most common form of malaria and is found especially in Latin America and south Asia. It is less deadly (albeit still serious) than *p. falciparum*, but is less sensitive to low temperature and was once endemic in southern Europe, as well as the southern United States (until the 1940s).

Children and pregnant women are most at risk of dying from malaria, and in areas where the disease is endemic (constantly present), such as sub-Saharan Africa, people who survive to adulthood may have built up an immunity as a result of repeated infections—a variation on the theme of "that which doesn't kill you makes you stronger." Malaria has been around for thousands of years, and it is likely that Egyptian King Tut died of malaria 33 centuries ago (Hawass et al. 2010). However, it was not until the late nineteenth century that it was proven that mosquito bites were the way in which the disease was transmitted. The first effective treatments, dating from the nineteenth century, were quinine, followed by chloroquine, and more recently artemisinin. Because of the complexity of the disease, no vaccines have been perfected as of this writing, although a great deal of work is under way.

HIV/AIDS Five percent of all deaths in the world are related to HIV/AIDS, but you can see in Table 5.2 that in Botswana, as in a few other sub-Saharan African countries, an astounding 80 percent of all deaths are HIV/AIDS-related, dropping life expectancy to only 40 years in 2002—a level that Europeans haven't seen since the Middle Ages. HIV/AIDS literally exploded on the scene in the early 1980s to become a worldwide pandemic. UNAIDS (the Joint United Nations Programme on HIV/AIDS) estimates that as of 2009 there were 33 million people in the world who have HIV/AIDS. That number is rising, but largely because new treatment options are keeping people alive longer once the disease is contracted. In 2009 there were almost 3 million new infections and about 2 million deaths (UNAIDS 2009), but those numbers are down from previous years, and it now appears that new infections peaked in 1996 and have been dropping slowly since then, while the annual number of deaths peaked in 2004 and has been going down ever since.

The disease appears to have the potential to kill virtually everyone who develops its symptoms, unless an infected person is treated with antiretroviral drugs that slow down the progression of HIV to AIDS. However, it has been estimated that the lifetime cost of caring for someone with HIV in the United States is at least $300,000 (Schackman et al. 2006), underlining the importance of prevention, rather than taking a chance that if you get the disease you can be effectively treated.

The spread of HIV can be prevented, as you undoubtedly know, especially by using condoms during intercourse and by not sharing needles to inject drugs. These relatively simple control measures have been very effective in North America and Europe, but they have been slow to catch on in sub-Saharan Africa, where prevalence rates and new infection rates are by far the highest in the world. Although HIV prevalence rates are still fairly low in Asia and North Africa, they are nonetheless rising in those areas of the world because governments have been slow to recognize and respond to local risks of transmission among injection-drug users, prostitutes, and men having sex with men.

In sub-Saharan Africa, women are as likely as men to be infected, since the disease is spread largely through heterosexual intercourse. The difference between sub-Saharan Africa and much of the rest of the world appears to be related to the fundamentally different pattern of sexual networking prevalent throughout the region. Premarital and extramarital sexual intercourse have long been fairly common in sub-Saharan Africa. Factors that seem to encourage these sexual patterns include long periods of postpartum abstinence on the part of women, which may encourage males to seek sexual encounters elsewhere; polygyny, which institutionalizes male sexual adventurousness; and the low status of women, which forces them to be sexually submissive, all compounded by high rates of male migration for employment, which separates husbands and wives for long periods of time and encourages men, in particular, to have intercourse with other partners (Caldwell 2000). In such an environment, any sexually related disease has increased opportunities for transmission through heterosexual channels. Other sexually transmitted diseases, such as gonorrhea and chlamydia, are already much more prevalent in sub-Saharan Africa than elsewhere in the world, and the open sores associated with those diseases increase the risk of HIV transmission.

Probably the most disturbing aspect of AIDS in Africa has been the widespread denial of the disease's existence, and the general lack of political support for putting prevention programs into place. In particular, condom use in Africa has been slowed down by suspicions that condoms themselves carried the disease, and by cultural norms that associate the use of condoms with prostitution, thus limiting their use within marriage, even though one or both partners in a marriage may have been at risk for HIV due to their own extramarital sexual activity (Messersmith et al. 2000). Added to this was the belief of the previous president of South Africa, Thabo Mbeki, that AIDS was not caused by HIV, and whose health minister had proposed garlic, lemon juice, and beetroot as AIDS remedies (Chigwedere et al. 2008). This slowed down the government response in that country until 2003, when a report by former president Nelson Mandela finally forced Mbeki to change his position and respond to the serious problem of HIV/AIDS.

In the meantime, however, the impact of AIDS on sub-Saharan Africa has been devastating. In three southern African nations (Botswana, Lesotho, and Swaziland), one in four adults aged 15–49 is infected with HIV/AIDS. In four other sub-Saharan African nations (Malawi, South Africa, Zambia, and Zimbabwe) at least one in ten adults is infected (UNAIDS 2009). Since people of reproductive age are the principal victims, the disease has created millions of orphans in Africa (see, for example, Evans and Miguel 2007). When the disease first hit Africa, it was called the "slim" disease, because sufferers lost so much weight as a result of the infection. Over time, it has been transformed into the "grandmother's disease" because it falls upon the older women to care for the orphans, as well for the sick and dying. In the Americas, the highest prevalence of HIV/AIDS is found in Haiti, where the sexual networking patterns (and HIV prevalence rates) are similar to those in sub-Saharan Africa.

Emerging Infectious Diseases Just as malaria may have emerged when humans cleared forests and settled into Neolithic agricultural villages thousands of years ago (Pennisi 2001), so it is that the desire of humans to add more animal protein to their diet may be creating opportunities for coronaviruses (animal viruses) to be spread to humans. It is generally believed that HIV crossed to humans from monkeys and/or chimpanzees (Gao et al. 1999; de Groot et al. 2002), and the evidence suggests that SARS (severe acute respiratory syndrome) may have come from animals captured for food in China (Lingappa et al. 2004).

Birds can also be sources of disease. Although West Nile virus has existed in Africa and the Middle East for decades, it was brought to New York City in 1999, apparently by an imported infected bird that was bitten by a mosquito, which then bit a human who became sick and died. It has since spread to other communities all over the country. In 2003, a new H5N1 avian influenza (popularly called "bird flu") was reported in Asia and has to date killed several hundred people worldwide (World Health Organization 2010). This is a disease that originated in Asian poultry farms, especially in Indonesia and Vietnam, and has now crossed over to humans and keeps cropping up in different places around the world, spread especially by migratory birds. In 2009 yet another new strain of influenza, H1N1 (popularly known as "swine" flu), emerged as a worldwide pandemic. As of this writing, its exact origins are unknown, but the disease shares some of the characteristics of viruses that are endemic in pigs as well as in birds (U.S. Centers for Disease Control 2010).

Maternal Mortality A very special category of infectious diseases is that associated with pregnancy and childbirth. Birth can be a traumatic and dangerous time not only for the infant, as discussed above, but for the mother as well. More than half a million women die each year from maternal causes—the equivalent of three jumbo jets crashing each day and killing all passengers. These deaths leave a trail of tragedy throughout the world, but disproportionately so in less-developed nations, where pregnancies are more frequent among women and health care systems are less adequate. There are three factors, in particular, that increase a woman's risk of death when she becomes pregnant: (1) lack of prenatal care that might otherwise identify problems with the pregnancy before the problems become too risky; (2) delivering the baby somewhere besides a hospital, where problems can be dealt with immediately; and (3) seeking an unsafe abortion because the pregnancy is not wanted (Reed, Koblinsky, and Mosley 2000; World Health Organization 2007).

Women are obviously only at risk of a maternal death if they become pregnant, and maternal death rates attempt to take that risk into account. We do not have good data on the number of pregnancies worldwide, however, so we must use the number of live births as an estimate of how many pregnancies have occurred within a group of women. Thus, the **maternal mortality ratio** measures the number of maternal deaths per 100,000 live births. Estimates by the World Health Organization (2007) indicate that the world average is 400 deaths to women per 100,000 live births. In the United States, however, the figure is 11 per 100,000 and it is even lower (7) in Canada, though it is higher in Mexico (60). The lowest levels are in Europe, while the highest levels of maternal mortality are found in sub-Saharan Africa, led (if that is the right word) by Sierra Leone, with a ratio of 2,100 maternal deaths per 100,000 live births. Outside of Africa, the highest rate, by far, is in Afghanistan.

Another way of measuring maternal mortality that takes into account the number of pregnancies a woman will have is to estimate a woman's lifetime risk of maternal death. As a woman begins her reproductive career by engaging in intercourse, the question asked is: What is the probability that she will die from complications of pregnancy and childbirth? This risk represents a combination of how many times she will get pregnant and the health risks she faces with each pregnancy, which are influenced largely by where she lives. For the average woman in the world, that probability is .011, or one chance in 92, but for women in sub-Saharan Africa, the risk is one in 22 (World Health Organization 2007). Looked at another way, if you line up 22 young African women, statistically one of them will wind up dying of maternal-related causes. In Sierra Leone (as in Niger and Afghanistan), the risk is 1 in 8. By contrast, the risk is only 1 in 11,000 in Canada; 1 in 4,800 in the United States; and 1 in 670 in Mexico.

Noncommunicable Conditions

In American medicine, "Chronic diseases have been referred to as chronic illnesses, noncommunicable diseases, and degenerative diseases. They are generally characterized by uncertain etiology, multiple risk factors, a long latency period, a prolonged course of illness, noncontagious origin, functional impairment or disability, and incurability" (Taylor et al. 1993). As you already know, as we move through the health and mortality transition, these diseases take precedence over communicable diseases as the important causes of death. As you can see looking back at Table 5.2, noncommunicable diseases account for 59 percent of all deaths in the world, and in the United States they are responsible for nearly 9 out of every 10 (87.6 percent) deaths.

It is also apparent in Table 5.2 that cardiovascular diseases and malignant neoplasms (cancer) are the major killers among the degenerative diseases. Cardiovascular diseases include especially the conditions that lead to heart attack or stroke. Deaths from coronary heart disease occur as a result of a reduced blood supply to the heart muscle, most often caused by a narrowing of the coronary arteries, which can be a consequence of atherosclerosis, "a slowly progressing condition in which the inner layer of the artery walls become thick and irregular because of plaque—deposits of fat, cholesterol, and other substances. As the plaque builds up, the arteries narrow, the blood flow is decreased, and the likelihood of a blood clot increases" (Smith and Pratt 1993). Stroke is part of the family of **cardiovascular diseases**, but whereas heart disease produces death by the failure to get enough blood to the heart muscle, stroke is the result of the rupture or clogging of an artery in the brain. This causes a loss of blood supply to nerve cells in the affected part of the brain, and these cells die within minutes.

Malignant neoplasms represent a group of diseases that kill by generating uncontrolled growth and spread of abnormal cells. These cells, if untreated, may then metastasize (invade neighboring tissue and organs) and cause dysfunction and death by replacing the normal tissue in your vital organs. In the United States, lung cancer is responsible for more cancer deaths than any other type, almost certainly reflecting the fact that as recently as 40 years ago more than 50 percent of men and nearly one-third of women were regular cigarette smokers. If a person is going to smoke, they will probably start as a teenager, a time when they are healthy enough not to be negatively affected by smoking. The ill effects of smoking take time to catch up with you, so lung cancer rates are high in the United States despite the rapid decline in smoking over the past few decades. China is currently confronting the fact that its smoking-related diseases and deaths are on the rise and there are now more smokers in China than there are people in the United States (Fairclough 2007).

The other important cancers in the United States are colon and rectal cancer, breast cancer, and prostate cancer. According to the National Cancer Institute, skin cancer is one of the more rapidly growing malignancies in the United States, encouraged by long exposure to the sun, but because treatment is available it has not become an important cause of death, despite its increased incidence. Another treatable form of cancer that nonetheless continues to kill women is cervical cancer. This disease reminds us of the complexity of trying to categorize illness and cause of death, because cervical cancer is caused by an infection of the human papillomavirus (HPV), which is a sexually transmitted infection (STI), a category that includes gonorrhea, syphilis, and, of course, HIV/AIDS. Not surprisingly, then, AIDS is also associated with certain malignancies such as Kaposi's sarcoma.

Another noncommunicable condition that is an important cause of death is respiratory disease (not including TB). This is a family of problems, including bronchitis, emphysema, and asthma. The underlying functional problem is difficulty breathing, symptomatic of inadequate oxygen delivery. Also on the list is diabetes mellitus, a disease that inhibits the body's production of insulin, a hormone needed to convert glucose into energy. Like most of the other degenerative diseases, diabetes is part of a group of related diseases, all of which can lead to further health complications such as heart disease, blindness, and renal failure. Finally, let me note that the relatively large fraction (6.4 percent) of deaths in the United States due to "neuropsychiatric disorders" does not mean that Americans are going crazy and then dying. Rather, it reflects the diagnosis of death from **Alzheimer's Disease**, which involves a change in the brain's neurons, producing memory loss and behavioral shifts in its victims. This is a major cause of organic brain disorder among older people, and the aging of the American population has put more people in its path. You will notice that Japan has an even older population than does the United States, yet Alzheimer's is less important as a cause of death, whereas respiratory diseases are more important in Japan than in the United States. This comparison cautions us to remember, as I pointed out earlier, that there are many routes to low mortality.

Injuries

Despite the widespread desire of humans to live as long as possible, we have devised myriad ways to put ourselves at risk of **accidental or unintentional death** as a result of the way in which we organize our lives and deal with products of our technology.

Furthermore, we are the only known species of animal that routinely kills other members of the same species (homicide) for reasons beyond pure survival, and we seem to be alone in deliberately killing ourselves intentionally (suicide). These uniquely human causes of death are included among the top killers in North America.

Though about half of all accidental deaths in the United States are attributable to motor vehicles, compared with one-third in Canada and less than one-fifth in Mexico, in all three countries they are among the top five causes of death. Each year tens of thousands of lives are lost in traffic accidents in Canada, the United States, and Mexico; tens of thousands more are injured and face permanent disability. These victims are disproportionately young males, and alcohol is involved in a high, although declining, fraction of cases.

Violence (including suicide, homicide, and war) is an important cause of death throughout the world, taking the lives of 1.6 million people annually as you can see in Table 5.2. It is associated with personal and societal instability and conflict, and it has a strong spatial, cultural component (Tyner 2009). You can see in Table 5.2 that the World Health Organization estimates that about a million people commit suicide each year, and it may be that as many as 20 times that number attempt to kill themselves (World Health Organization 2002a). Suicide rates are highest by far in eastern Europe, especially in Russia and several of the countries that were part of the former Soviet Union. At least some of this is due to alcoholism, which also contributes to the fact that a Russian man is ten times more likely to die accidentally or from violence than is a man in the United Kingdom.

Throughout the world, suicide rates rise through the teen years (a phenomenon that has always received considerable publicity), peak in the young adult ages, plateau in the middle years, and then rise in the older ages. Almost universally among human societies, the suicide rate is considerably higher for males than for females (World Health Organization 2002), and so around the world it is older men who are most prone to suicide. Beyond these general patterns, however, the actual difference from one country to another in the suicide rate seems to be a cultural phenomenon (Pampel 1996; Cutright and Fernquist 2000).

Men are not only more successful at killing themselves, they are also more likely to be killed by someone else. Homicide rates are highest for young adult males in virtually every country for which data are available (World Health Organization 2002b). In the United States in 2004, males were nearly four times more likely than females to be homicide victims, with the homicide rate peaking in the young adult ages. Note that for white males the homicide rate in 2004 was highest at ages 15–24 at 10 per 100,000. Among African American males the rate peaked at 25–34 at an astounding 82 homicides per 100,000 people. Hispanic males peaked at 15–24 with a rate of 30 per 100,000 (U.S. Centers for Disease Control 2007). Homicide death rates in the United States are higher than for any other industrialized nation except Russia (World Health Organization 2002b), possibly reflecting the cultural acceptance of violence as a response to conflict (Straus 1983) combined with the ready availability of guns (which are used in two-thirds of homicides in the United States). The remarkable contrast between African American and white homicide rates within the United States has existed for decades and appears to be most readily explained by the proposition that "economic stress resulting from the inadequate or unequal distribution of resources is a major contribution to high rates of interpersonal violence" (Gartner 1990:95). Put another way, a "subculture of exasperation" (Harvey 1986) promotes a "masculine way of violence" (Staples 1986).

War is the World Health Organization's final category of cause of death, as you can see from Table 5.2. The number killed in war does not take into account the injuries and disruption that war causes, going well beyond what is likely to be associated with any other cause of death. The numbers in Table 5.2 are estimates from just before the United States invaded Iraq in 2003, so deaths from that conflict are not included. Estimating war deaths, especially among civilians, is not easy to do, since many people flee a war zone and may die elsewhere, or they may die not from violence but rather from disease as the water, sewerage, health, and food supply infrastructures implode due to the conflict. As of 2010, the U.S. Department of Defense had identified 4,400 U.S. military casualties in Iraq and an additional 1,000 military deaths in Afghanistan (U.S. Department of Defense 2010), but estimates of civilian deaths in Iraq related to the war beginning in 2003 range from 85,000, based on a study from the Iraq Human Rights Ministry (Santana 2009), to 100,000, based on media reports of civilian deaths (Iraq Body Count 2010), to a much higher number from a group of researchers at Johns Hopkins University who used a cluster probability sample approach to interview nearly 2,000 households in Iraq about births and deaths prior to the U.S. invasion and subsequent to the invasion. Their estimates indicate that somewhere between 400,000 and 800,000 Iraqis died as a result of the war there (Burnham et al. 2006). Most conflict in the world gets less publicity than the war in Iraq has, and information from the Uppsala Conflict Database suggests that in 2008, for example, there were 35 armed conflicts in 23 different countries in the world (Uppsala Conflict Data Program 2010).

The "Real" Causes of Death

The causes of death discussed above reflect those items listed on a person's death certificate. The World Health Organization has worked diligently over the years to try to standardize those causes under a set of guidelines called the International Classification of Diseases (ICD), so that the pathological conditions leading to death will be identified consistently from one person to the next and from one country to the next. This enhances comparability, but it ignores the actual things going on that contribute to that death. Thus, when public concern first arose over the role of alcohol in traffic fatalities, there were no data available to suggest whether a person who died in an accident was a victim of his or her own alcohol use or the alcohol use of someone else. Similarly, a person who dies of lung cancer or heart disease may really be dying of smoking, no matter what the actual pathological condition that led immediately to death.

There is a vast amount of literature in the health sciences tracing the etiology (origins) of the diseases listed on death certificates, and McGinnis and Foege (1993) culled those studies in order to estimate the "real" or "actual" causes of death in the United States in 1990, in comparison with the 10 leading causes of death as shown in vital statistics data. This study was so widely cited, and so important to our understanding of health risks, that it was later updated to reflect deaths as of 2000 (Mokdad et al. 2004). The actual causes of death, as traced by both studies, offer a different picture than is shown in a summary such as Table 5.2. The winner in the actual-cause-of-death sweepstakes was—tobacco. Of the 2,403,351 people who died in the United States in 2000, 435,000 (18 percent) died as a result of tobacco use. Tobacco has been traced to cancer deaths (especially cancers of the lung, esophagus, oral cavity, pancreas, kidney, and bladder), cardiovascular deaths (coronary heart disease, stroke, and high blood pressure), chronic lung disease, low birth weight, and other problems of infancy as a result of mothers who smoke, and to accidental deaths from burning cigarettes. Smoking has emerged as an increasingly important real cause of death throughout the world, and with a slowdown in tobacco use in developed countries, the burden of smoking has shifted to developing, countries, where more than half of the world's smoking-related deaths now occur (Ezzati and Lopez 2003).

The second most important "real" cause of death in the United States relates to the diet and activity patterns of the U.S. population, accounting for 365,000 deaths or 15 percent of the total in 2000, a noticeable increase from the results for 1990. Most of these deaths are due to obesity, according to Mokdad and associates (2004). Being overweight is associated with, among other things, major dietary abuses including high consumption of cholesterol, sodium, and animal fat. The principal activity pattern of concern is the lack thereof—a couch potato lifestyle. Poor diet and inactivity can lead to obesity, which then contributes to heart disease and stroke, cancers (especially colon, breast, and prostate), and diabetes mellitus.

Alcohol misuse was found to be the third (albeit a distant third) real cause of death in the United States, although the consequences of alcohol misuse extend well beyond death and include the ruination of lives due to alcohol dependency. Alcohol contributes to death from cirrhosis, vehicle accidents, injuries in the home, drowning, fire fatalities, job injuries, murder, mayhem, and some cancers. A great deal of publicity has been given over the years to the beneficial effects of red wine in keeping heart disease rates lower in France than in the United States, but closer inspection of death rates suggests that red wine has not protected the French against other causes of death, and the French have death rates that are almost identical to those in the United States. Klatsky and Friedman (1995) noted "a J-shaped alcohol-mortality curve, with the lowest risk among drinkers who take less than three drinks daily" (p. 16). Recently, health care practitioners have been more cautious in their assessment of the positive effects of limited alcohol consumption.

Number four on the list is death by microbial agents—infectious diseases (beyond HIV or infections associated with tobacco, alcohol, or drug use). In theory, at least, these 75,000 deaths could have been largely preventable through appropriate vaccination and sanitation. Next on the list are toxic agents, which are responsible for an estimated 55,000 deaths annually in the United States. These agents include occupational hazards, environmental pollutants, contaminants of food and water supplies, and components of commercial products. Toxins are known to contribute to cancer and to diseases of the heart, lungs, liver, kidneys, bladder, and the neurological system.

Motor vehicles were the direct cause of death of 43,000 people in 2000, which was a decline from 1990. This is probably attributable to the improved safety of vehicles, greater attention to making sure that children and adults are properly belted in, and high publicity campaigns to reduce drunk driving.

Firearms contributed to an estimated 29,000 deaths as of 2000, which was also a smaller number (and percentage) than in 1990. The United States is unique in the world in the number of deaths from firearms, and the most pressing problem is that of guns in the hands of teenagers and young adults, who disproportionately use the weapons to kill—including themselves. Guns are meant to be lethal, of course, but sex can kill you, as well. In 2000, there were another 20,000 deaths calculated as being the result of sexual behavior, including 15,000 from sexually acquired HIV infection. Illicit use of drugs rounded out the top ten real killers in 2000. It is estimated to have caused 17,000 deaths in 2000 by contributing to infant deaths (through the mother's use of drugs), as well as to drug overdose, suicide, homicide, motor vehicle deaths, HIV infection, pneumonia, hepatitis, and heart disease.

Researchers have explored the real causes of death in other countries as well. For example, Nizard and Muñoz-Pérez (1994) found that 16 percent of deaths in France in 1986 were attributable to tobacco use (a little lower than in the United States), and that 10 percent of deaths in France are traceable to alcohol consumption (higher than in the United States).

Thus far I have discussed life expectancy and death rates in some detail, but I have not actually defined those rates for you, because I didn't want to scare you away from a topic that is vitally important to our understanding of what's happening in the world. Nonetheless, in order to evaluate data on health and mortality, it is important to have a background on the rates and measures that are being used.

Measuring Mortality

In measuring mortality, we are attempting to estimate the **force of mortality**, the extent to which people are unable to live to their biological maximum age. The ability to measure accurately varies according to the amount of information available, and as a consequence, the measures of mortality differ considerably in their level of sophistication. The least sophisticated and most often quoted measure of mortality is the crude death rate.

Crude Death Rate

The **crude death rate (CDR)** is the total number of deaths in a year divided by the average total population. In general form:

$$CDR = \frac{d}{p} \times 1{,}000,$$

where d represents the total number of deaths occurring in a population during any given year, and p is the total average (midyear) population in that year. It is called crude because it does not take into account the differences by age and sex in the likelihood of death. Nonetheless, it is frequently used because it requires only two pieces of information, total deaths and total population, which often can be estimated with reasonable accuracy even in developing countries where the cost of censuses and vital registration systems may limit the availability of more detailed data.

Differences in the CDR between two countries could be due entirely to differences in the distribution of the population by age, even though the force of mortality is actually the same. Thus, if one population has a high proportion of old people, its crude death rate will be higher than that of a population with a high proportion of young adults, even if at each age the probabilities of death are identical. For example, in 2009, Mexico had a crude death rate of 5 per 1,000, or half of the 10 per 1,000 in Slovakia in that year. Nonetheless, the two countries actually had an identical life expectancy at birth of 75 years. The difference in crude death rates was accounted for by the fact that only 6 percent of Mexico's population was aged 65 and older, whereas the elderly accounted for 12 percent of Slovakia's population. Mexico's crude death rate was also lower than the level in the United States (8 per 1,000 in 2009). Yet in Mexico a baby at birth could expect to live three years less than a baby in the United States. The somewhat younger age structure in Mexico puts a smaller fraction of the population at risk of dying each year, even though the actual probability of death at each age is higher in Mexico than in the United States (although the gap has been steadily closing over the years). In order to account for the differences in dying by age (and sex), we can calculate age/sex-specific death rates.

Age/Sex-Specific Death Rates

To measure mortality at each age and for each sex we must have a vital registration system (or a large survey) in which deaths by age and sex are reported, along with census or other data that provide estimates of the number of people in each age and sex category. The age/sex-specific death rate (${}_nM_x$ or ASDR) is measured as follows:

$${}_nM_x = \frac{{}_nd_x}{{}_np_x} \times 100{,}000,$$

where ${}_nd_x$ is the number of deaths in a year of people of a particular age group in the interval x to $x + n$ (typically a five-year age group, where x will be lower limit of the age interval and n represents the width of the interval in years of age) divided by the average number of people of that age, ${}_np_x$, in the population (again, usually defined as the midyear population). It is typically multiplied by 100,000 to get rid of the decimal point.

In the United States in 2006, the ASDR for males aged 65 to 69 was 2,040 per 100,000, while for females it was 1,321 (Heron et al. 2009). In 1900, the ASDR for males aged 65 to 69 was 5,000 per 100,000, and for females 5,500. Thus, we can see that over the course of the twentieth century, the death rate for males aged 65 to 69 dropped by 59 percent, while for females the decline was 76 percent. To be sure, in 1900, the death rate for females was actually a bit higher than for males, whereas by 1990 it was well below that for males.

Age-Adjusted Death Rates

It is possible to compare crude death rates for different years or different regions, but it is analytically more informative if the data are adjusted for differences in the age structure of the populations prior to making those comparisons. The usual method is to calculate age-specific death rates for two different populations and then apply those rates to a standard population. For this reason, this method is also known as **standardization**. The formula for the age-adjusted death rate (AADR) is as follows:

$$AADR = \sum {}_n ws_x \times {}_n M_x,$$

where ${}_n ws_x$ is the standard weight representing this age group's proportion in the total population and ${}_n M_x$ is the age-specific death rate as calculated in the previous section. We can apply this methodology to compare the crude death rate in Egypt in 2006 (6 deaths per 1,000 population) with that in the United States in that same year (8 deaths per 1,000 population). Could it be that mortality was really higher in the United States than in Egypt? We use the U.S. population as the standard weights and apply the age-specific death rates for Egypt (as estimated by the World Health Organization) to the United States age/sex structure in 2006 (as estimated by the U.S. Census Bureau) to see what the crude death rate would be in Egypt if its age-sex structure were identical to that of the United States. The result is that the age-adjusted death rate for Egypt in 2006 was 13 deaths per 1,000 population—63 percent higher than that of the United States.

Life Tables

Although the age-adjusted death rate takes the age differences in mortality into account, it does not provide an intuitively appealing measure of the overall mortality experience of a population. We would like to have a single index that sums that up, and so we turn to a frequently used index called **expectation of life at birth**, or more generally **life expectancy**. This measure is derived from a **life table**, which is part of a whole statistical family of "survival analysis," and even though it is complicated it is used so widely that I have included a brief discussion of it here for you. You will recall from Chapter 3 that the life table has a long history, having been first used in 1662 by John Graunt to uncover the patterns of mortality in London.

Life expectancy can be summarized as the average age at death for a hypothetical group of people born in a particular year and being subjected to the risks of death experienced by people of all ages in that year. The expectation of life at birth for U.S. females in 2006 of 80.5 years (see Table 5.3) does not mean that the average age at death in that year for females was 80.5. What it does mean is that if all the females born in the United States in the year 2006 had the same risks of dying throughout their lives as those indicated by the age-specific death rates in 2006, then their average age at death would be 80.5. Of course, some of them would have died in infancy while others might live to be 120, but the age-specific death rates for females in 2006 *implied* an average of 80.5.

Note that life expectancy is based on a hypothetical population, so the *actual* longevity of a population would be measured by the average age at death. Since it is undesirable to have to wait decades to find out how long people are actually going to live, the hypothetical situation set up by life expectancy provides a useful, quick comparison between populations.

One of the limitations of basing the life table on rates for a given year, however, is that in most instances the death rates of older people in that year will almost certainly be higher than will be experienced by today's babies when they reach that age. This will especially be true for a country that is in the midst of a rapid decline in mortality, but even in the United States in the twenty-first century, current life tables are assumed to underestimate the actual life expectancy of people at all ages (Bongaarts and Feeney 2003; Schoen and Canudas-Romo 2005).

Life Table Calculations Life table calculations, as shown in Table 5.3 for U.S. females for 2006 and in Table 5.4 for U.S. males in 2006, begin with a set of age/sex-specific death rates, and the first step is to find the probabilities of dying during any given age interval. Table 5.3 is called an abridged life table because it groups ages into five-year categories, rather than using single years of age. The probability of dying ($_nq_x$) between ages x and $x + n$ is obtained by converting age/sex-specific death rates ($_nM_x$) to probabilities. A probability of death relates the number of deaths during any given number of years (that is, between any given exact ages) to the number of people who started out being alive and at risk of dying. For most age groups, except the very youngest (less than five) and oldest (100 and older), for which special adjustments are made, death rates ($_nM_x$) for a given sex for ages x to $x + n$ may be converted to probabilities of dying according to the following formula:

$$_nq_x = \frac{(n)(_nM_x)}{1+(a)(n)(_nM_x)}$$

This formula is only an estimate of the actual probability of death, because the researcher rarely has the data that would permit an exact calculation, but the difference between the estimation and the "true" number will seldom be significant. The principal difference between reality and estimation is the fraction *a*, where *a* is usually 0.5. This fraction implies that deaths are distributed evenly over an age interval, and thus the average death occurs halfway through that interval. This is a reasonable estimate for every age from 5 through 100, regardless of race or sex (Arias, Rostron, and Tejada-Vera 2010). At the very youngest ages, however, death tends to occur earlier in the age interval, whereas at the oldest ages the rate of increase in the probability of death actually slows down and so deaths occur slightly later in the age interval. The more appropriate fraction for ages zero to one is 0.85 and for ages one to four is 0.60. Note that since the interval 100+ is open-ended, going to the highest age at which people might die, the probability of death in this interval is 1.0000—death is certain.

In Table 5.3, the age-specific death rates for females in 2006 in the United States are given in column (4). In column (5), they have been converted to probabilities of death from exact age x to exact age $x + n$. Once the probabilities of death have been calculated, the number of deaths that would occur to the hypothetical life table population is calculated. The life table assumes an initial population of 100,000 live births, which is then subjected to the specific mortality schedule. These

Table 5.3 Life Table for Females in the United States, 2006

(1)	(2)	(3)	(4)	(5)	(6)	(7)	(8)	(9)	(10)
					Of 100,000 hypothetical people born alive:		**Number of years lived**		**Expectation of life**
Age interval	Number of females in the population	Number of deaths in the population	Age-specific death rates in the interval	Probabilities of death (proportion of persons alive at beginning who die during interval)	Number alive at beginning of interal	Number dying during age interval	In the age interval	In this and all subsequent age intervals	Average number of years of live remaining at beginning of age interval
x to *x* + *n*	*nPx*	*nDx*	*nMx*	*nqx*	*lx*	*ndx*	*nLx*	*Tx*	*ex*
Under 1	2,017,203	12,547	0.00622	0.006187	100,000	619	99,474	8,046,872	80.5
1–4	7,946,768	2,090	0.00026	0.001051	99,381	104	397,274	7,947,398	80.0
5–9	9,605,660	1,184	0.00013	0.000650	99,277	65	496,223	7,550,123	76.1
10–14	10,033,251	1,340	0.00014	0.000700	99,212	69	495,888	7,053,901	71.1
15–19	10,354,505	3,821	0.00036	0.001798	99,143	178	495,269	6,558,013	66.1
20–24	10,127,043	4,996	0.00047	0.002347	98,965	232	494,242	6,062,744	61.3
25–29	10,028,353	5,716	0.00053	0.002646	98,732	261	493,008	5,568,502	56.4
30–34	9,645,535	7,048	0.00072	0.003594	98,471	354	491,470	5,075,494	51.5
35–39	10,482,842	11,368	0.00107	0.005336	98,117	524	489,277	4,584,024	46.7
40–44	11,246,362	19,525	0.00172	0.008563	97,594	836	485,879	4,094,747	42.0
45–49	11,514,848	30,250	0.00262	0.013015	96,758	1,259	480,641	3,608,868	37.3
50–54	10,440,169	39,609	0.00378	0.018723	95,499	1,788	473,023	3,128,227	32.8
55–60	9,370,670	51,680	0.00550	0.027127	93,711	2,542	462,198	2,655,204	28.3
60–64	6,977,461	60,734	0.00881	0.043101	91,168	3,929	446,019	2,193,007	24.1
65–69	5,532,900	73,162	0.01352	0.065390	87,239	5,705	421,934	1,746,988	20.0
70–74	4,711,030	98,766	0.02139	0.101521	81,535	8,277	386,979	1,325,054	16.3

(*continued*)

Table 5.3 (continued)

(1)	(2)	(3)	(4)	(5)	(6)	(7)	(8)	(9)	(10)
					Of 100,000 hypothetical people born alive:		**Number of years lived**		**Expectation of life**
Age interval	Number of females in the population	Number of deaths in the population	Age-specific death rates in the interval	Probabilities of death (proportion of persons alive at beginning who die during interval)	Number alive at beginning of interal	Number dying during age interval	In the age interval	In this and all subsequent age intervals	Average number of years of live remaining at beginning of age interval
75–79	4,268,013	143,483	0.03417	0.157404	73,257	11,531	337,458	938,075	12.8
80–84	3,492,167	196,540	0.05745	0.251175	61,726	15,504	269,870	600,617	9.7
85–89	2,191,242	210,140	0.09590	0.386772	46,222	17,877	186,417	330,747	7.2
90–94	1,032,579	164,159	0.15898	0.568822	28,345	16,123	101,416	144,330	5.1
95–99	321,163	84,042	0.26168	0.790956	12,222	9,667	36,941	42,914	3.5
100+	57,963	24,791	0.42771	1.000000	2,555	2,555	5,973	5,973	2.3

Sources: Calculated by the author: death rates are from World Health Organization, 2008, Life Tables for WHO Member States; population data are from U.S. Census Bureau, American Community Survey 2006.

Table 5.4 Life Table for Males in the United States, 2006

(1)	(2)	(3)	(4)	(5)	(6)	(7)	(8)	(9)	(10)
					Of 100,000 hypothetical people born alive:		**Number of years lived**		**Expectation of life**
Age interval	Number of males in the population	Number of deaths in the population	Age-specific death rates in the interval	Probabilities of death (proportion of persons alive at beginning who die during interval)	Number alive at beginning of interal	Number dying during age interval	In the age interval	In this and all subsequent age intervals	Average number of years of live remaining at beginning of age interval
x to *x* + *n*	*nPx*	*nDx*	*nMx*	*nqx*	*lx*	*ndx*	*nLx*	*Tx*	*ex*
Under 1	2,195,055	15,980	0.00728	0.007235	100,000	724	99,385	7,548,004	75.5
1–4	7,940,625	2,541	0.00032	0.001279	99,276	127	396,801	7,448,619	75.0
5–9	10,049,281	1,507	0.00015	0.000750	99,150	74	495,562	7,051,818	71.1
10–14	10,529,025	2,211	0.00021	0.001049	99,075	104	495,116	6,556,257	66.2
15–19	10,891,624	9,585	0.00088	0.004390	98,971	435	493,770	6,061,141	61.2
20–24	10,803,745	15,017	0.00139	0.006926	98,537	682	490,977	5,567,371	56.5
25–29	10,459,178	14,015	0.00134	0.006678	97,854	653	487,637	5,076,394	51.9
30–34	9,886,954	14,138	0.00143	0.007125	97,201	693	484,273	4,588,756	47.2
35–39	10,588,993	19,272	0.00182	0.009059	96,508	874	480,356	4,104,484	42.5
40–44	11,162,393	31,478	0.00282	0.014001	95,634	1,339	474,823	3,624,128	37.9
45–49	11,240,279	48,221	0.00429	0.021222	94,295	2,001	466,472	3,149,305	33.4
50–54	10,014,972	64,597	0.00645	0.031738	92,294	2,929	454,146	2,682,833	29.1
55–60	8,836,165	79,437	0.00899	0.043962	89,365	3,929	437,001	2,228,687	24.9
60–64	6,373,734	87,511	0.01373	0.066372	85,436	5,671	413,004	1,791,685	21.0
65–69	4,837,027	98,337	0.02033	0.096734	79,765	7,716	379,537	1,378,682	17.3
70–74	3,834,210	122,273	0.03189	0.147676	72,049	10,640	333,647	999,145	13.9

(continued)

Table 5.4 (continued)

(1)	(2)	(3)	(4)	(5)	(6)	(7)	(8)	(9)	(10)
					Of 100,000 hypothetical people born alive:		**Number of years lived**		**Expectation of life**
Age interval	Number of males in the population	Number of deaths in the population	Age-specific death rates in the interval	Probabilities of death (proportion of persons alive at beginning who die during interval)	Number alive at beginning of interal	Number dying during age interval	In the age interval	In this and all subsequent age intervals	Average number of years of live remaining at beginning of age interval
75–79	3,124,901	155,964	0.04991	0.221867	61,409	13,625	272,985	665,497	10.8
80–84	2,182,964	174,681	0.08002	0.333403	47,785	15,932	199,095	392,512	8.2
85–89	1,144,693	145,136	0.12679	0.481368	31,853	15,333	120,933	193,417	6.1
90–94	420,679	83,513	0.19852	0.663370	16,520	10,959	55,203	72,484	4.4
95–99	98,614	30,293	0.30719	0.868762	5,561	4,831	15,727	17,281	3.1
100+	14,071	6,610	0.46975	1.000000	730	730	1,554	1,554	2.1

Sources: Calculated by the author: death rates are from World Health Organization, 2008, Life Tables for WHO Member States; population data are from U.S. Census Bureau, American Community Survey 2006.

100,000 babies represent what is called the **radix** (l_0). During the first year, the number of babies dying is equal to the radix (100,000) times the probability of death. Subtracting the babies who died ($_1d_0$) gives the number of people still alive at the beginning of the next age interval (l_1). These calculations are shown in columns (7) and (6) of Table 5.3. In general:

$$_nd_x = (_nq_x)(l_x)$$

and

$$l_{x+n} = l_x - {_nd_x}.$$

The next two columns that lead to the calculation of life expectancy are related to the concept of number of years lived. During the five-year period, for example, between the fifth and the tenth birthdays, each person lives five years. If there were 99,248 girls sharing their tenth birthdays, then they all would have lived a total of 5 × 99,248 = 496,240 years between their fifth and tenth birthdays. Of course, if a person died after the fifth but before the tenth birthday, then only those years that were lived prior to dying would be added in. The lower the death rates, the more people there are who will survive through an entire age interval and thus the greater the number of years lived will be. The number of years lived ($_nL_x$) can be estimated as follows:

$$_nL_x = n(l_x - a\ {_nd_x}).$$

The fraction a is 0.50 for all age groups except zero to one (for which 0.85 is often used) and one to five (for which 0.60 is often used). Furthermore, this formula will not work for the oldest, open-age interval (100+ in Table 5.3), since there are no survivors at the end of that age interval and the table provides no information about how many years each person will live before finally dying. The number of years lived in this group is estimated by dividing the number of survivors to that oldest age (l_{100}) by the death rate at the oldest age (M_{100}):

$$L_{100+} = l_{100} / M_{100}.$$

The results of these calculations are shown in column (8) of Table 5.3. The years lived are then added up, cumulating from the oldest to the youngest ages. These calculations are shown in column (9) and represent T_x, the total number of years lived in a given age interval and all older age intervals. At the oldest age (100+), T_x is just equal to $_nL_x$. But at each successively younger age (e.g., 95 to 99), T_x is equal to T_x at all older ages (e.g., 100+, which is T_{100}), plus the number of person-years lived between ages x and $x + n$ (e.g., between ages 95 and 99, which is $_5L_{95}$). Thus at any given age:

$$T_x = T_{x+n} + {_nL_x}.$$

The final calculation is the expectation of life (e_x), or average remaining lifetime. It is the total years remaining to be lived at exact age x and is found by dividing T_x by the number of people alive at that exact age (l_x):

$$e_x = T_x / l_x.$$

Thus, for U.S. females in 2006, the expectation of life at birth (e_0) was 8,046,872 / 100,000 = 80.5, while at age 55 a female could expect to live an additional 28.3 years. For males (Table 5.4), the comparable numbers are a life expectancy at birth of 75.5 and at age 55 of an additional 24.9 years.

Although it has required some work, we now have a sophisticated single index that summarizes the level of mortality prevailing in a given population at a particular time. I should warn you that the formulas I have provided to generate the data in Tables 5.3 and 5.4 are very close, but not identical, to those produced by the U.S. National Center for Health Statistics (NCHS) (see Arias, Rostron, and Tejada-Vera 2010), because the NCHS uses single year of age data and slightly more complex formulas for its calculations at the youngest and oldest ages. The resulting differences in life table values are, however, very small.

Disability-Adjusted Life Years If increasing life expectancy meant simply that we spent more years at the end of our life being bedridden and/or mentally incompetent, few people would be interested in pursuing that goal. Fortunately, the close connection between health and mortality is, as I have emphasized, that the increased life expectancy comes about precisely because we are healthier for longer than ever before. In the early 1990s the World Bank initiated a joint project between the World Health Organization and the Harvard School of Public Health (with recent funding from the Bill and Melinda Gates Foundation and now led by a consortium including Harvard University, the Institute for Health Metrics and Evaluation at the University of Washington, Johns Hopkins University, the University of Queensland, and the World Health Organization) designed to measure this aspect of health and mortality. The result has been the very influential Global Burden of Disease project that is designed to actually look at the economic downside of poor health by asking how many years of productivity in a society are lost to its members because of poor health (Murray and Lopez 1996; Lopez et al. 2006a). This is a powerful argument that has been made strongly by labor unions and other groups that have argued for many years that if governments and/or employers will pay for health care, they will more than get their money back in increased productivity—healthy workers do more work than sick ones. It is the flip side of the idea that a high standard of living promotes good health; it suggests that good health promotes a high standard of living. It is likely that both sides of the argument are correct.

The important statistical index derived from the Global Burden of Disease project is the **disability-adjusted life year (DALY).** "The DALY is a health gap measure that extends the concept of potential years of life lost due to premature death to include equivalent years of healthy life lost by virtue of individuals being in states of poor health or disability. One DALY can be thought of as one lost year of healthy life and the burden of disease as a measure of the gap between current health status and an ideal situation where everyone lives into old age free from disease and disability" (Lopez et al. 2006b:1). This can then be calculated from the more "positive" side of things to show what the healthy life expectancy (HALE) is in each country. The two bottom lines of Table 5.2 show these numbers for females, and you can compare the healthy life expectancy with the overall life expectancy, also shown in that table. In the United States, for example, a woman can expect to live 80 years, of which 71 will be disability-free.

MORTALITY CONTROL AND THE ENVIRONMENT

"Live long and prosper." Every newborn child should have such a toast offered on her or his behalf, but it is not easy to accomplish. For most of human history, children could look forward neither to a long life nor a prosperous one, and the achievement of both has required that we bring the environment under our control. We do this, for example, by growing a greater abundance of nutritious food than nature would otherwise provide, by killing the bacteria in our water supply, by protecting ourselves from disease-carrying insects and rodents, by using herbs and chemicals to create medications that kill the parasites that attack our bodies, and other devices and concoctions that help to repair or replace failing body parts. We control nature by draining swamps, clearing forests, plowing land, building roads and bridges, constructing water and sewerage systems, building dams and levies, and so forth. Then we protect ourselves from nature by building houses that keep predators at bay, keep the rain and snow outside, and adjusting the indoor atmosphere so we don't get too hot or too cold, using large amounts of generated energy in the process.

Controlling nature and protecting ourselves from its ravages is not done without a cost, of course. In the process we rearrange our relationship to nature and risk degrading the environment to the point of unsustainability. This is all because of the natural linkage between living long and prospering—the two go together, as you can see in the accompanying diagram. The obvious impact of a declining death rate on the environment is that more people mean more resources used. This is the classical Malthusian view—population growth means that more people are trying to live at the same standard of living. That model simply says that we live long, but don't prosper. The prosperity comes from our greater per-person productivity as we become more clever and efficient in using environmental resources for our personal and collective improvement. Two important components of this are linked to the decline in mortality. The lower death rate is a result of our being healthier, and healthy people work harder and longer and thus are more productive. But there is also a psychosocial aspect, which I have labeled an increase in the "scope" of life. The prospect of a long life, unburdened by the threat of imminent death, means that we can think about life in the long term, making plans and implementing changes and improvements that would have been unthinkable and unimaginable in the days when life was so uncertain.

This greater scope means that each of us has the potential to be more creative and productive in each year that we live. So, on the one hand, declining mortality increases the size of the population and increases the demand for resources. But, at the same time, the demand for resources is increasing more quickly than the growth of population, because a healthier, longer-living population has the potential to prosper—to improve per person productivity, which also increases per person use of resources. One of the most elemental of these impacts is on the food supply. As we have become healthier, we have become bigger people, causing the demand for food to increase at a faster pace even than the population is growing (Fogel and Helmchen 2002). Consider this—in 1969, each of the 3.6 billion people then alive consumed an average of 2,386 calories of food per day; but in 2003 (the most recent estimates currently available from the United Nations Food and Agriculture Organization), the 6.5 billion people alive were consuming food at the rate of 2,798 calories per day. Population had increased by 45 percent, but the total amount of food demanded (population times daily calories) had increased by 111 percent!

Can we go on this way? I will consider that question in more detail in Chapter 11, but let me give you an example from Brazil, which in that same period from 1969 to 2003 increased from 93 million to 181 million people. This was a result of a death rate that was declining much more quickly than the birth rate—Brazilians added more than 13 years to their life expectancy during that 34-year period. Brazilians, like many others in the world, were healthier at least partly because they were eating better, increasing their per-day calorie consumption from 2,440 in 1969 to 3,060 in 2003. Thus, Brazil experienced a 95 percent increase in population, and a 144 percent increase in food consumed. How did the country manage this? As I noted in Chapter 2, this was a period of rapid economic development in Brazil, which allowed people better nutrition and better health—these things all go together.

Our greater productivity—that which makes us prosper—depends heavily on the use of energy, and the by-products of energy use include the emission of greenhouse gases, which have contributed to global warming. Mosquitoes and other disease-carrying insects flourish in warmer weather, and there is a real concern that the reemergence of infectious diseases will be among the many undesirable consequences of global warming (Epstein 2000). If that happens, of course, we run the risk that by living longer and prospering, we have created a heap of other troubles with which we will have to cope.

Discussion Questions: (1) How do you think your life would be different if you were not pretty certain that you would survive to an old age? **(2)** The more rapid increase of the food supply than of population is contrary to what Malthus thought would happen—how might Malthus try to explain this?

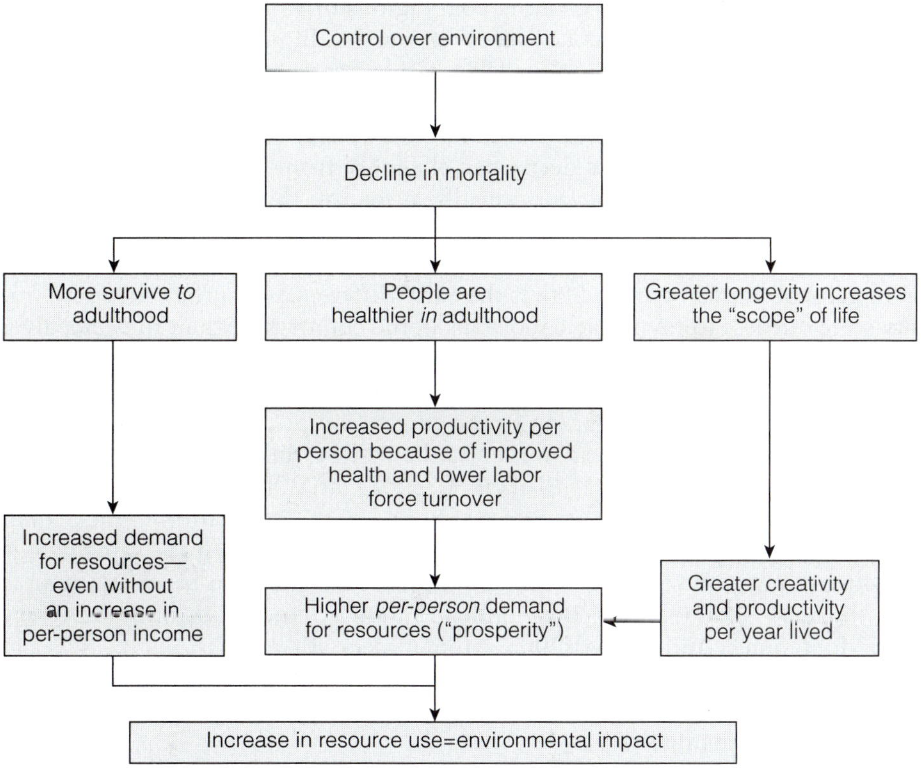

Health and Mortality Inequalities

The regional differences in mortality that have emerged repeatedly in the chapter are clear reminders that similar cultural and economic features of societies can have a major impact on human well-being. Our health is very dependent on massive infrastructure developments such as piped clean water, piped sewerage, transportation and communications systems that deliver food and other goods, and a health care system that is affordable and available. Regions in the world vary considerably in their access to these resources, and within the same regions and countries some people are more advantaged than others in these respects.

Urban and Rural Differentials

Until the twentieth century, cities were deadly places to live. Mortality levels were invariably higher there than in surrounding areas, since the crowding of people into small spaces, along with poor sanitation and contact with travelers who might be carrying disease, helped maintain fairly high levels of communicable diseases. For example, life expectancy in 1841 was 40 years for native English males and 42 years for females, but in London it was five years less than that (Landers 1993). In Liverpool, the port city for the burgeoning coal regions of Manchester, life expectancy was only 25 years for males and 27 years for females. In probability terms, a female child born in the city of Liverpool in 1841 had less than a 25 percent chance of living to her fifty–fifth birthday, while a rural female had nearly a 50 percent chance of surviving to age 55. Sanitation in Liverpool at that time was atrociously bad. Pumphrey notes that "pits and deep open channels, from which solid material (human wastes) had to be cleared periodically, often ran the whole length of streets. From June to October, cesspools were never emptied, for it was found that any disturbance was inevitably followed by an outbreak of disease" (Pumphrey 1940:141).

In general, we can conclude that the early differences in urban and rural mortality were due less to favorable conditions in the countryside than to decidedly unfavorable conditions in the cities (Alter and Oris 2005). Over time, however, medical advances and environmental improvements have benefited the urban population more than the rural, leading to the current situation of the worst mortality conditions existing in poor rural areas and the best mortality conditions existing in the richest urban areas (Murray, Kulkarni, and Ezzati 2006). As the world continues to urbanize (see Chapter 9), a greater fraction of the population in each country will be in closer contact with systems of prevention and cure. At the same time, the sprawling slums of many third world cities blur the distinction between urban and rural and may produce their own unhealthy environments (Montgomery et al. 2003; Montgomery and Hewett 2005; Montgomery 2009).

Neighborhood Inequalities

Research on urban and rural differences in mortality has tended to obscure the differences that can exist at the neighborhood level within a city. "Interest in the effects of the local environment on human health is not new. It has been manifest for some 2,500 years and reached its peak during the public health movements of the mid to late nineteenth century in Europe and America. *Interest waned with improvement in basic living conditions (the provision of clean water and air, better housing, sanitation, etc.) and the epidemiologic transition that rendered infectious diseases apparently less important than chronic diseases*" (MacIntyre and Ellaway 2003: 38 [emphasis added]).

In Europe and the United States it was clearly the poorer neighborhoods where death rates were the highest (Gordon 2003). Over time the general rise in wealth in cities and the public health improvements that benefitted all residents of a city diminished those differences. There have been renewed concerns, however, about the disproportionate risks (often referred to as environmental injustice or inequality) that poorer residents of cities face from the location of hazardous materials near their neighborhoods (see, for example, Pastor, Sadd, and Hipp 2001; Crowder and Downey 2010), and from the health issues, especially obesity and diabetes, that follow from reliance on packaged and fast foods, rather than from fresh foods, because of the general lack of availability of good grocery stores in less well-off neighborhoods—the so-called "food desert" phenomenon (Whitacre and Tsai 2009).

Cities in less developed countries have gotten a later start on the health and mortality transition and we are now beginning to realize that there may be important neighborhood differences in health in these cities in which virtually all of the future population growth of the world will show up. Child mortality, for example, is still a major issue throughout the developing world, and although child mortality rates in a city like Accra, the capital of Ghana, are lower than in rural areas, there are still important differences from one part of the city to another (Weeks et al. 2006). But even among adults, the nutrition transition that is associated with urban life has led to noticeable increases in hypertension and obesity (Hill et al. 2007)—the same health issues that are arising in poorer neighborhoods in richer countries.

Education Differentials in Mortality

One of the strongest predictors of all demographic phenomena is education. It influences the number of children you will likely have, if and where you will migrate, and when and from what you might die. Indeed, your educational level may well influence the health levels of other family members, not just your own (Zimmer et al. 2007). Death data for the United States in 2006 show that age-adjusted death rates for people with at least some college were almost one-third the level of people with less than a high school education (Heron et al. 2009). This is consistent with Kitagawa and Hauser's earlier study, in which they found that a white male in 1960 with an eighth grade education had a 6 percent chance of dying between the ages of 25 and 45, whereas for a college graduate the probability was only half as high (Kitagawa and Hauser 1973). For women, education makes an even bigger difference, especially at the extremes. A white female with a college education could expect, at age 25, to live 10 years longer than a woman who had only four or fewer years of schooling.

For virtually every major cause of death, white males with at least one year of college had lower risks of death than those with less education. The differences appear to be least for the degenerative chronic diseases and greatest for accidental deaths. This is consistent with the way you might theorize that education would affect mortality, since it should enhance an individual's ability to avoid dangerous, high-risk situations. Kitagawa and Hauser's work was partially replicated by Duleep (1989) using 1973 Current Population Survey data matched to 1973–78 Social

Security records. This study showed a persistence of the pattern of mortality differentials by education. Overall, death rates were 45 percent higher for white males aged 25 to 64 who had less than a high school education than for those who had at least some college education. Pappas and his associates used the 1986 National Mortality Followback Survey and the 1986 National Health Interview Survey to further replicate Kitagawa and Hauser's analysis. They found that "despite an overall decline in death rates in the United States since 1960, poor and poorly educated people still die at higher rates than those with higher incomes and better education, and the disparity increased between 1960 and 1986" (Pappas et al. 1993:103). Data from Canada (Choiniére 1993), as well as from the Netherlands (Doornbus and Kromhout 1991), confirm that these patterns are not unique to the United States.

Social Status Differentials in Mortality

Differences in mortality by social status are among the most pervasive inequalities in modern society, and they are especially apt to show up in cities. The connection between income and health has been obvious for a long time. Marx attributed the higher death rate in the working classes to the evils of capitalism and argued that mortality differentials would disappear in a socialist society. That may have been overly optimistic, but data do clearly suggest that by nearly every index of status, the higher your position in society, the longer you are likely to live.

I should note here that good data on social status are not always easy to come by, since death certificates virtually never contain information on income and rarely on occupation, and when they do have occupation data, many indicate "retired" or "housewife," giving no further clues to social status. Thus, more circumlocutory means must be devised to obtain data on the likelihood of death among members of different social strata. An important method used is record linkage, such as used in the classic study by Kitagawa and Hauser (1973) for the United States, that I mentioned above, in which death certificates for individuals in a census year were linked with census information obtained for that individual prior to death. Age and cause of death were ascertained from the death certificate, while the census data provided information on occupation, education, income, marital status, and race.

Among white American men aged 25 to 64 when they died in 1960, mortality rates for laborers were 19 percent above the average, while those for professional men were 20 percent below the average (Kitagawa and Hauser 1973). Similar kinds of results have been reported more recently for all Americans (not just males) followed in the National Longitudinal Mortality Study, in which the risk of death was clearly lowest for the highest occupational positions and highest for those in the lowest occupational strata (Gregorio, Walsh, and Paturzo 1997). A study at the census tract level in Ohio found that even though infant mortality rates dropped significantly over the 40-year span from 1960 to 2000, rates remained persistently higher in the lowest status neighborhoods (Stockwell, Goza, and Balistreri 2005).

In England, researchers followed a group of 12,000 civil servants in London who were first interviewed in 1967–69, when they were aged 40 to 64. They were tracked for the next 10 years, and it was clear that even after adjusting for age and sex, the higher the pay grade, the lower the death rate. Furthermore, within each pay grade, those who owned a car (a more significant index of status in England than in the United States) had lower death rates than those without a car (Smith, Shipley, and Rose 1990). An update of this study revealed that even as life expectancy has improved in the United Kingdom, the social class differences have remained very stable (Hattersly 2005). The importance of this latter set of studies is that it relates to a country that has a highly egalitarian national health service. Even so, equal access to health services does not necessarily lead to equal health outcomes. The most important aspects of occupation and social class that relate to mortality are undoubtedly income and education (Johnson, Sorlie, and Backlund 1999)—income to buy protection against and cures for diseases, and education to know the means whereby disease and occupational risks can be minimized.

Race and Ethnicity

In most societies in which more than one racial or ethnic group exists, one group tends to dominate the others. This generally leads to social and economic disadvantages for the subordinate groups, and such disadvantages frequently result in lower life expectancies for the racial or ethnic minority group members. Some of the disadvantages are the obvious ones in which prejudice and discrimination lead to lower levels of education, occupation, and income and thus to higher death rates. But a large body of evidence suggests that there is a psychosocial component to health and mortality, causing marginalized peoples in societies to have lower life expectancies than you might otherwise expect (Kunitz 1994; Ross and Wu 1995; Barr 2008).

In the United States, African Americans and Native Americans have been particularly marginalized and have historically experienced higher-than-average death rates. In Canada and Mexico, the indigenous populations are similarly disadvantaged with respect to the rest of society. U.S. data for 2006 from the National Center for Health Statistics show that at every age up to 85, African American mortality rates are significantly higher than for the white population (Heron et al. 2009). In 1900, African Americans in the United States had a life expectancy that was 15.6 years less than for whites, and that differential had been reduced to 4.5 years by 2006. Yet that is a larger gap than exists, for example, between the United States as a whole and the population of Mexico.

African Americans have higher risks of death from almost every major cause of death than do whites (Rogers, Hummer, and Nam 2000). However, there are three causes of death, in particular, that help to account for the overall difference—cardiovascular disease, malignant neoplasms, and cerebrovascular disease. Most important is the higher rate of heart disease for African Americans of both sexes (Heron et al. 2009), which may be explained partly by the stress associated with higher rates of unemployment among African Americans (Guest, Almgren, and Hussey 1998). There is also a spatial component, since African Americans tend to have the highest levels of residential segregation of any group in the United States (which I discuss more in Chapter 9) and this has been shown to negatively affect health levels (Williams, Neighbors, and Jackson 2003; Pearlman et al. 2006).

Age-adjusted death rates from homicides are an astonishing six times higher for blacks than for whites in the United States. Also disturbing is the fact that life expectancy for African Americans actually declined between 1984 and 1988 and again between 1990 and 1991, and by 1995 it was only back to where it had been in 1984. This was particularly noticeable for males and was apparently caused by an increase in deaths from HIV/AIDS and by a rise in the already high homicide rates. For example, in 1990 the life expectancy for white males in the United States was 72.7 years. In that same year, in the Central Harlem section of New York City, an African American male had a life expectancy of 53.8 years (about the same as a male in Bangladesh at the time) (Findley and Ford 1993). This was due especially to the effect of AIDS, compounded by homicide, suicide, and the spread of infectious diseases in a poverty- and crime-ridden area.

In general, the data suggest that socioeconomic status is more important than lifestyle factors in explaining the racial difference in mortality (Hayward et al. 2000). An important part of socioeconomic status is wealth, not just income. Low income increases your risk of health problems, but a low level of wealth lowers your resilience—your ability to recover from illness and its social and economic ramifications—even if you have a reasonable income. Thus, Huie and associates (Huie et al. 2003) found that the much lower level of assets among blacks, compared to whites, negatively affects their health, even when controlling for education and income.

This is generally consistent with the pattern for other racial/ethnic groups. For example, over time, the income and social status gap has narrowed between "Anglos" (non-Hispanic whites) and the Mexican-origin population in the United States. As this happened, differences in death rates between the groups disappeared and more recently have crossed over, so that age-adjusted death rates among both males and females are lower for Hispanics in the United States than for non-Hispanic whites (Heron et al. 2009). Some of this difference may be due to differences in the way Hispanic identity is coded in the vital statistics data (the numerator of the death rate) and how it is coded in the census (the denominator of the rate). Smith and Bradshaw (2005) think that similar coding would eliminate the "Hispanic Paradox," but other research using data sets that were not affected by the coding of Hispanic identity do consistently show this lower mortality for Hispanics, so it cannot yet be dismissed (Peak and Weeks 2002; Hummer et al. 2007). In all events, even if Hispanic mortality were simply the same as that for non-Hispanic whites, it still highlights the tremendous disparity between blacks and others in the United States.

As immigrants have once again become more numerous in the United States, where you were born has reemerged as a characteristic of importance. Hummer and his associates (1999) used data from the National Health Interview Survey to calculate the probabilities of survival for different groups. They found that U.S.-born young adult blacks had the highest odds of dying after controlling for socioeconomic status, whereas older foreign-born blacks and Asians had the lowest likelihood of dying in comparison to other groups—Americanization isn't necessarily good for your health!

The United States is, of course, not the only country with racial or ethnic groups that may experience inequalities in mortality. For example, in the 1940s, before Palestine was partitioned to create the state of Israel, the death rate among Muslims was two to three times that of the Jewish population, probably due to the higher economic status of the Jews (United Nations 1953). The mortality gap between Jews and Muslims within the modern state of Israel has narrowed considerably, but Jews continue to have a slightly higher life expectancy (Israel Central Bureau of Statistics 2010).

Marital Status

It has long been observed that married people tend to live longer than unmarried people. This is true not only in the United States but in other countries as well (Hu and Goldman 1990; Kaplan and Kronick 2006). A long-standing explanation for this phenomenon is that marriage is selective of healthy people; that is, people who are physically handicapped or in ill health may have both a lower chance of marrying and a higher risk of death. At least some of the difference in mortality by marital status certainly is due to this (Kisker and Goldman 1987).

Another explanation is that marriage is good for your health: protective, not just selective. Marriage may be associated with social and psychological support that keeps men, in particular, from committing suicide or from abusing themselves with alcohol and cigarettes, and which also provides a more nurturing environment when a person is ill (Gove 1973). It is probably also protective in economic terms. Married women are healthier than unmarried women partly because they have higher incomes (Hahn 1993), and unmarried men are especially more likely to die than married men if they are living below the poverty line (Smith and Waitzman 1994).

Does this mean that if you are currently single you should jump into a marriage just because you think it might prolong your life? Not necessarily, but Lillard and Panis (1996) found evidence in the Panel Study of Income Dynamics in the United States that relatively unhealthy men tend to marry early and to remain married longer, presumably using marriage as a protective mechanism. The flip side of that is to suggest that it is the ending of a marriage that especially elevates the risk of death. Divorced people, especially males, have a noticeably higher death rate than people in any other marital category (Johnson 2000; Heron et al. 2009).

Summary and Conclusion

The control of disease and mortality has vastly improved the human condition and has, in the process, revolutionized life. Yet there are still wide variations between nations with respect to both the probabilities of dying and the causes of those deaths. The differences between nations exist because countries are at different stages of the health and mortality transition, the shift from high mortality (largely from infectious diseases, with most deaths occurring at young ages) to low mortality (with most deaths occurring at older ages and largely caused by degenerative diseases). The different timing is due to a complex combination of political, economic, and cultural factors. There are many routes to low mortality, including genuine bumps in the road such as the HIV/AIDS pandemic that has been gripping sub-Saharan Africa. That disease is so perverse that it has upset the usual pattern in which the very young and the very old are more vulnerable to death than are young adults, and the pattern is even emerging that women are more at risk than are men. In general, females have a survival advantage over males at every age in most of the world, and a gender gap in mortality that favors women seems to be a feature of the health and mortality transition, at least in the absence of a disease like HIV/AIDS.

We have been most successful at controlling communicable diseases, which are largely dealt with through public health measures, but medical technology has become increasingly good at limiting disability and postponing death from noncommunicable diseases, as well. This has helped to slow down the death rates at the older ages. It is ironic, however, that our very success at creating a life that is relatively free of communicable disease and that is built on a secure food supply has produced in its wake a transition in our pattern of nutrition that threatens to increase our risk of noncommunicable disease.

Differences in mortality within a society tend to be due to social status inequalities. As status and prestige (indexed especially by education, occupation, income, and wealth) go up, death rates go down. The social and economic disadvantages felt by minority groups, such as among blacks in the United States, often lead to lower life expectancies. Marital status is also an important variable, with married people tending to live longer than unmarried people.

Although mortality rates are low in the more developed nations and are declining in most less developed nations, diseases that can kill us still exist if we relax our vigilance. The explosion of HIV/AIDS onto the world stage was a reminder of that, as was the emergence of SARS and recent new strains of influenza. Worldwide efforts have been put into malaria and tuberculosis control because those deadly diseases have also been making a resurgence in many regions of the world, reminding us that death control cannot be achieved and then taken for granted, for as Zinsser (1935:13) so aptly put it:

> However secure and well-regulated civilized life may become, bacteria, protozoa, viruses, infected fleas, lice, ticks, mosquitoes, and bedbugs will always lurk in the shadows ready to pounce when neglect, poverty, famine, or war lets down the defenses. And even in normal times they prey on the weak, the very young, and the very old, living along with us, in mysterious obscurity waiting their opportunities.

If the thought of those lurking diseases scares you to death, then I suppose that too is part of the health and mortality transition. Also lurking around the corner is Chapter 6, in which we examine fertility concepts, measurements, and trends.

Main Points

1. The changes over time in death rates and life expectancy are captured by the perspective of the health and mortality transition.
2. Significant widespread improvements in the probability of survival date back only to the nineteenth century and have been especially impressive since the end of World War II. The drop in mortality, of course, precipitated the massive growth in the size of the human population.
3. The role played by public health preventive measures in bringing down death rates is exemplified by the saying a century ago that the amount of soap used could be taken as an index of the degree of civilization of a people.
4. World War II was a turning point in the transition because it led to new medicines and to a transfer of public health and medical technology all over the world, creating rapid declines in the death rate.
5. The things that can kill us are broadly categorized as communicable diseases, noncommunicable conditions, and injuries, whereas the most important "real"

cause of death in the United States (and increasingly in the world as a whole) is the use of tobacco.

6. Life span refers to the oldest age to which members of a species can survive, whereas longevity is the ability to resist death from year to year.
7. Although biological factors affect each individual's chance of survival, social factors are also important overall determinants of longevity.
8. Among the important biological determinants of death are age and sex, with the very young and the very old being at greatest risk, and with males generally having higher death rates than females.
9. Mortality is measured with tools such as the crude death rate, the age-specific death rate, and life expectancy.
10. Living in a city used to verge on being a form of latent suicide, but now cities tend to have lower death rates than rural areas, and rich people live longer than poor people on average.

Questions for Review

1. Discuss how different the world of the twenty-first century would be if (a) death rates had not declined as they did in the first part of the twentieth century; and (b) if World War II had not happened.
2. What are the ways in which society is going to have to change in order to ward off the potentially fatal side effects of the nutrition transition?
3. What are the possible explanations for the apparent biological regularity that women live longer than men? How is the social world affected by this difference?
4. Although causes of death are neatly categorized, we know that there are complex reasons for many deaths. Discuss some of those complexities and what they reveal about the many different routes to low mortality for a population as a whole.
5. What changes do you think would have to be made in American society to eliminate the racial differences in disease and mortality that we currently observe? Would universal health coverage make a difference? Why or why not?

Suggested Readings

1. Abdel Omran, 1977, "Epidemiological Transition in the United States," *Population Bulletin* 32(2).
   The concept of the health and mortality transition was first developed by Omran, who called it the epidemiological transition, and it is well summarized in this report.
2. Alan Lopez, Colin Mathers, Majid Ezzati, Dean Jamison, and Christopher Murray, 2006, *Global Burden of Disease and Risk Factors* (New York: Oxford University Press).
   This volume is part of a massive project undertaken by the Harvard School of Public Health in collaboration with the World Health Organization and the World Bank to assess the societal impact of disease and death on human societies. It can be downloaded chapter by chapter from the World Health Organization (http://www.who.int/en/).

3. Norman F. Cantor, 2001, *In the Wake of the Plague: The Black Death and the World it Made* (New York: Free Press).
   Europe, and by historical extension the rest of the world, was remade as a result of having to cope with the huge population losses brought about periodically by the plague. This book, which was a *New York Times* bestseller, lays out the role of mortality in our lives.
4. Richard G. Rogers, Robert A. Hummer, and Charles B. Nam, 2000, *Living and Dying in the USA: Behavioral, Health, and Social Differentials of Adult Mortality* (San Diego: Academic Press).
   This book provides a comprehensive review of the literature on mortality differences in the United States and then offers important new insights into those relationships through a careful analysis of survey data.
5. Benjamin Caballero and Barry M. Popkin, Editors, 2002, *The Nutrition Transition: Diet and Disease in the Developing World* (San Diego: Academic Press).
   Barry Popkin and his associates have pioneered the concept that a nutrition transition accompanies the epidemiological transition, posing a new set of challenges to human health even as we bring some of the bigger causes of mortality under control.

Websites of Interest

Remember that websites are not as permanent as books and journals, so I cannot guarantee that each of the following websites still exists at the moment you are reading this. You may have to Google the name of the organization to find the current web address.

1. **http://www.who.int/en**
   The World Health Organization of the United Nations, located in Geneva, Switzerland, is the first place to go for updates on disease outbreaks, as well as for global statistics of mortality and morbidity.
2. **http://www.yourdiseaserisk.wustl.edu/**
   This site allows you to evaluate your risk of several important noncommunicable diseases; then you can augment that with respect to heart attack risk by going to **www.american-heart.org** and searching for "heart attack risk assessment." If you are a woman, you may wish to visit **www.cancer.gov/bcrisktool** to calculate your risk of breast cancer.
3. **http://www.northwesternmutual.com/learning-center/the-longevity-game.aspx**
   How long can you expect to live? Play the Longevity Game and calculate your life expectancy. This innovative "game" from Northwestern Mutual Life Insurance Company lets you calculate your own expected age at death, given the data that you enter about yourself, your health, and your lifestyle characteristics. When you are finished with that, you can go to **http://www.realage.com** and take the "Real Age Test" and record your real age; then go to **http://www.livingto100.com/** for another opinion about your life expectancy—consider why each site gives you a different life expectancy.
4. Diseases are often spread by contact with "bodily fluids," especially fecal matter—which is why washing up is so important. Visit the following two websites and consider your reaction to these findings: **http://www.globalhandwashingday.org/** and **http://www.biochemist.org/news/page.htm?item=8607**
5. **http://www.map.ox.ac.uk/**
   The Malaria Atlas Project (MAP) project is based at Oxford University, organized by a group of scholars who represent the most knowledgeable researchers in the world with respect to malaria.

CHAPTER 6
The Fertility Transition

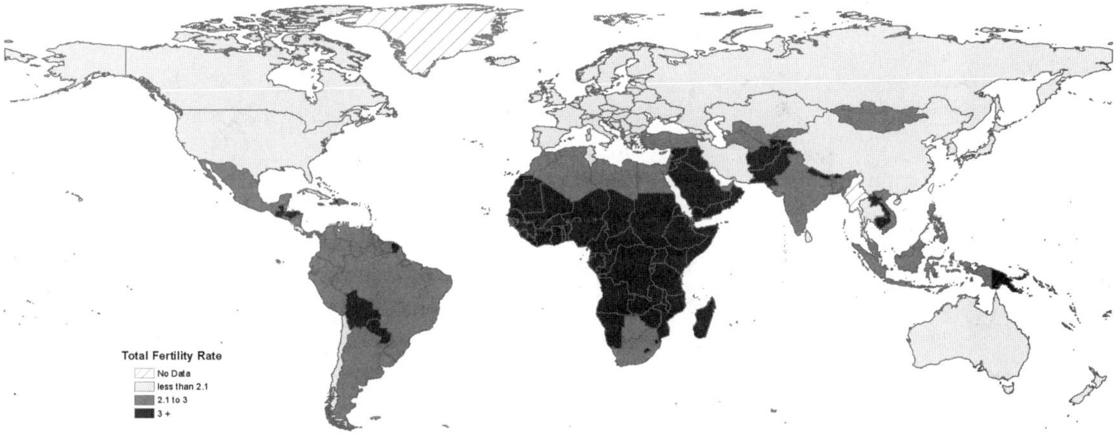

Figure 6.1 Total Fertility Rates by Country

> I am inclined to think that the most important of Western values is the habit of a low birth-rate. If this can be spread throughout the world, the rest of what is good in Western life can also be spread. There can be not only prosperity, but peace. But if the West continues to monopolize the benefits of low birth-rate(s), war, pestilence, and famine must continue, and our brief emergence from those ancient evils must be swallowed in a new flood of ignorance, destitution and war.

When Bertrand Russell, the great British philosopher and historian whose words these are (Russell 1951:49), died in 1970 at age 97, he had witnessed almost the entire demographic transition in the Western nations; birth rates in many less developed areas, however, seemed stubbornly high and few people predicted much of a drop. Yet drop they did, and here in the twenty-first century we are witnessing a fertility transition that represents a truly incredible revolution in the control of human reproduction, comparable in many ways to the amazing progress in postponing death, which I discussed in the previous chapter.

What Is the Fertility Transition?

The **fertility transition** is the shift from high fertility, characterized by only minimal individual deliberate control, to low—perhaps very low—fertility, which is entirely under a woman's (or more generally a couple's) control. The phenomenon has been summarized by Lloyd and Ivanov (1988) as the shift from "family building by fate" to "family building by design." The transition almost always involves a delay in childbearing to older ages (at least beyond the teen years) and also an earlier end to childbearing. This process helps to free women and men alike from the bondage of unwanted parenthood and helps to time and space those children who are desired, which has the desirable side effect of improving the health of mothers and their children.

To control fertility does not necessarily mean to limit it, yet almost everywhere you go in the world, the two concepts are nearly synonymous. This suggests, of course, that as mortality declines and the survival of children and their parents is assured, people generally want smaller families, and the wider the range of means available to accomplish that goal, the greater the chance of success.

The central questions of the fertility transition are why, when, and how does fertility decline from high to low levels? This means that we have to start with an understanding of why fertility has been high for all of the previous millennia of human history, and then proceed to explanations for its decline. In that process, we will also need to define some concepts related to human reproduction, and review the ways in which we measure it, so that we can talk more intelligently about trends in fertility over time and across the globe.

How High Could Fertility Levels Be?

When demographers speak of **fertility**, we are referring to the number of children born to women. This can be confusing, because physicians and agriculturalists routinely use the term to refer to reproductive *potential*—how fertile a woman is, or how fertile the soil might be. This measures the capacity to grow things (humans in the first instance, crops in the second). But in population studies fertility means the actual reproductive performance of women or men—how many children have they parented? Note that although our concern lies primarily with the total impact of childbearing on a society, we must recognize that the birth rate is the accumulation of millions of individual decisions to have or not have children. Thus, when we refer to a "high-fertility society," we are referring to a population in which most women have several children, whereas a "low-fertility society" is one in which most women have few children. Naturally, some women in high-fertility societies have few children, and vice versa.

Fertility, like mortality, is composed of two parts, one biological and one social. The biological component refers to the capacity to reproduce, and though obviously a necessary condition for parenthood, it is not sufficient alone. Whether children will actually be born and, if so, how many, given the capacity to reproduce, is largely a result of the social environment in which people live.

The Biological Component

The physical ability to reproduce is usually called **fecundity** by demographers. A fecund person can produce children; an infecund (sterile) person cannot. However, since people are rarely tested in the laboratory to determine their level of fecundity, most estimates of fecundity are actually based on levels of fertility (by which we mean the number of children a person has had). Couples who have tried unsuccessfully for at least 12 months to conceive a child are usually called "infertile" by physicians (demographers would say "infecund"). The 2002 National Survey of Family Growth (NSFG) showed that 7 percent of American couples (where the wife was aged 15 to 44) are infecund/infertile by that criterion (Chandra et al. 2005)—about the same level as in 1995 (Abma et al. 1997). A more general concept is the idea of **impaired fecundity** (also known as *subfecundity*), measured by a woman's response to survey questions about her fecundity status. A woman is classified as having impaired fecundity if she believes it is impossible for her to have a baby, if a physician has told her not to become pregnant because the pregnancy would pose a health risk for her or her baby, or if she has been continuously married for at least

36 months, has not used contraception, and yet has not gotten pregnant. In 2002, 12 percent of American women fell into that category—an increase from 8 percent in 1982 (Chandra and Stephen 1998; Chandra et al. 2005).

For most people, fecundity is not an all-or-none proposition and varies according to age. Among women it usually increases from **menarche** (the onset of menstruation, which usually occurs in the early teens), peaks in the twenties, and then declines to **menopause** (the end of menstruation) (Wood and Weinstein 1988; Kline, Stein, and Susser 1989). Male fecundity increases from puberty to young adulthood, and then gradually declines, though men are generally fecund to a much older age than are women.

At the individual level, very young girls occasionally become mothers. In 2006, there were more than 6,000 babies born to mothers under 15 years of age in the United States, whereas at the other end of the age continuum, there were more than 400 mothers in that year whose age was listed as 50–54 (Martin et al. 2009). Until the mid-1990s, the oldest verified mother in the world had been an American named Ruth Kistler, who gave birth to a child in Los Angeles, California, in 1956 at the age of 57 years, 129 days (McFarlan et al. 1991). Now, however, hormone treatment of postmenopausal women suggests that a woman of virtually any age might be able to bear a child by implantation of an embryo created from a donated egg impregnated with sperm, and this has been done successfully for several women over the age of 50, including a 67-year-old unmarried Spanish woman, who was successfully impregnated in 2006 at a clinic in Los Angeles (what is it with Los Angeles?), and gave birth to twins (Associated Press 2007).

Guinness World Records claims that the world's verified most prolific mother was a Russian woman in the eighteenth century who gave birth to 69 children. She actually had "only" 27 pregnancies, but experienced several multiple births (Guinness World Records 2008). But putting the extremes of individual variation aside and assuming that most couples are normally fecund, how many babies could be born to women in a population that uses no method of fertility control? If we assume that an average woman can bear a child during a 35-year span between the ages of 15 and 49, that each pregnancy lasts a little less than nine months (accounting for some pregnancy losses such as miscarriages), and that, in the absence of fertility limitation, there would be an average of about 18 months between the end of one pregnancy and the beginning of the next, then the average woman could bear a child every 2.2 years for a potential total of 16 children per woman (see Bongaarts 1978). This can be thought of as the maximum level of reproduction for an entire group of people.

No known society has ever averaged as many as 16 births per woman, however, and there are biological reasons why such high fertility is unlikely. For one thing, pregnancy is dangerous (in the previous chapter, I noted the high rates of maternal mortality in many parts of the world), and many women in the real world would die before (if not while) delivering their sixteenth child, assuming they had not died from other disease in a high-mortality society. Another problem with the calculation is the assumption that all couples are "normally" fecund. The principal control a woman has over her fecundity is to provide herself with a good diet and physical care. Without such good care, of course, the result will probably be lower fertility. In some sub-Saharan African countries nearly one in four women of reproductive age may be subfecund (Larsen 2000). Studies of fertility rates of U.S. blacks also suggest that the drop in fertility between the late 1880s and early 1930s was due in part to the deteriorating health conditions of black women, and that part of the post–World War II baby boom among blacks was due to improved health conditions, especially the eradication of venereal disease and tuberculosis (Farley 1970; McFalls and McFall 1984; Tolnay 1989).

Naturally, disease is not the only factor that can lower the level of fecundity in a population. Nutrition also plays a role, and Rose Frisch (1978; 2002) was among the first to suggest that a certain amount of fat must be stored as energy before menstruation and ovulation can occur on a regular basis. Thus, if a woman's level of nutrition is too low to permit fat accumulation, she may experience **amenorrhea** (a temporary absence or suppression of menstruation) and/or **anovulatory** cycles, in which no egg is released. For younger women, the onset of puberty may be delayed until an undernourished girl reaches a certain critical weight (Komlos 1989). Conversely, improved nutrition has been linked to girls beginning menstruation at earlier ages than their less well-fed counterparts. Such findings have been reported for Bangladesh (Haq 1984), as well as for the United States (Kaplowitz and Oberfield 1999). Increased levels of fat among girls in the United States appear to have stimulated hormonal change and induced puberty in an increasing proportion of preteens.

Frisch (2002) reports that in 1800 the average age at menarche in the United States was 16.0, dropping to 14.7 by 1880, and to 12.7 in the post–World War II era. The nutrition transition, discussed in the previous chapter, thus has the effect of making it easier for younger women to conceive, even though it is paradoxically associated with the lower mortality that would reduce the need for women to bear children at a young age.

Since the maximum level of fertility described above would require modern levels of health and nutrition, it is not the level that we would expect to find in premodern societies. A slightly different concept, **natural fertility**, has historically been defined as the level of reproduction that exists in the absence of deliberate (or at least modern) fertility control (Coale and Trussell 1974; Henry 1961). This seems to be closer to an average of six or seven live births per woman. This is clearly lower than the maximum possible level of fertility, and it may be that the secret of human success lies in the very fact that as a species we have not actually been content to let nature take its course (Potts and Short 1999); that rather than there being some "natural" level of fertility, humans have always tried to exercise some control over reproduction. "The genius of the species has not been to rely on a birth rate so high that it can overcome almost any death rate, no matter how high. The genius of the species is rather to have few offspring and to invest heavily in their care and training" (Davis 1986:52). The clear implication of this idea is that the social component of human reproductive behavior is more important than the biological capacity to reproduce. Rodgers and his associates (2001) used data from Denmark on twins to conclude that "slightly more than one-quarter of the variance in completed fertility is attributable to genetic influence" (p. 39). Perhaps it is only a coincidence that this is very nearly the same proportion that has been assigned to the biological component of mortality (as I discussed in Chapter 5).

The Social Component

Opportunities and motivations for childbearing vary considerably from one social environment to another, and the result is great variability in the average number of children born to women. As I mentioned in Chapter 2, hunter-gatherer societies may have been motivated to space children several years apart, thus keeping fertility lower than it might otherwise have been. It would be difficult to be pregnant and have other small children and be on the move. It may also have been, of course, that women in hunter-gatherer societies had sufficiently little body fat that their risk of conception was low enough to provide adequate spacing between children. Agricultural societies provide an environment in which more children may be advantageous, and where improved nutrition might well have improved a woman's chances of becoming pregnant more often. On the other hand, the low mortality and high standard of living of urban industrial and postindustrial societies reduce the demand for children well below anything previously imagined in human existence, yet paradoxically the biological capacity to reproduce is probably the highest it has ever been because people are healthier than they have ever been in human history.

It was the combination of modern medical science and a prosperous agricultural community that produced the world's most famous high-fertility group. The Hutterites are an Anabaptist (Christians who believe in adult baptism) religious group who live in agrarian communes in the northern plains states of the United States and the western provinces of Canada. In the late nineteenth century, about 400 Hutterites migrated to the United States from Russia, having originally fled there from eastern Europe (Kephart 1982), and in the span of about 100 years they have doubled their population more than seven times to a current total of more than 40,000. In the 1930s, the average Hutterite woman who survived her reproductive years could expect to give birth to at least 11 children (Eaton and Mayer 1954).

The secret to high Hutterite fertility has been a fairly early age at marriage, a good diet, good medical care, and a passion to follow the biblical prescription to "be fruitful and multiply." Also, of course, they engage regularly in sexual intercourse without using contraception or abortion, believing as they do that any form of birth control is a sin. In the past few decades, however, population growth has slowed among the Hutterites. Each Hutterite farming colony typically grows to a size of about 130 people. Then, in a manner reminiscent of Plato's Republic, the division of labor becomes unwieldy and part of the colony branches off to form a new group.

Branching requires that additional land be purchased to establish the new colony, and the gobbling up of vacant land by Hutterites has caused considerable alarm, especially in Canada, where the majority of Hutterites now live. Laws were passed in Canada—although subsequently repealed—restricting the Hutterites' ability to buy land and, at the same time, new technological changes in farming methods (which the Hutterites tend to keep up with) have changed the pattern of work in the colonies. These social dynamics have apparently had the effect of raising Hutterite women's average age at marriage by as many as four or five years. Furthermore, access to modern health care has led women at the other end of their reproductive years to agree to sterilization for "health reasons" (Peter 1987; White 2002). Overall fertility levels among Hutterites in 1980 were only half what they had been in 1930 (Nonaka, Miura, and Peter 1994), and this downward trend has continued into the twenty-first century as Hutterites confront the scarcity of new land for the expansion of their colonies (White 2002).

In Figure 6.2, you can see the fertility rates by age that produced the Hutterites' 11 children per woman only a few decades ago (from Robinson 1986). For comparison, the figure also offers you the age pattern of fertility for women as estimated

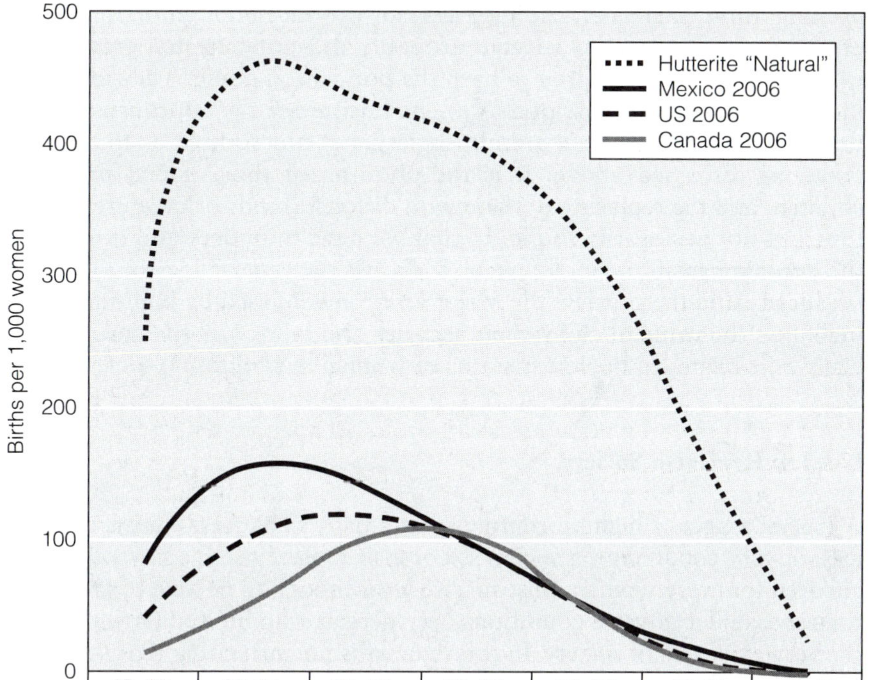

	15–19	20–24	25–29	30–34	35–39	40–44	45–49
Hutterite "Natural"	250	460	431	396	321	167	24
Mexico 2006	82	157	138	94	50	16	2
US 2006	41	103	118	94	48	9	1
Canada 2006	14	52	100	101	46	7	0

Figure 6.2 Hutterite Fertility Compared with Fertility Levels in Contemporary Mexico, the United States, and Canada

Sources: Hutterite data are from Robinson (1986), Table 6, and the data for Canada, Mexico and the United States are from United Nations Population Division (2009b).

by the United Nations Population Division (2009b) for Mexico (2.7 children per woman), the United States (2.1 children per woman), and Canada (1.6 children per woman). Notice that Hutterite fertility levels were dramatically higher at every age than contemporary North American levels, but especially at ages 20–24. Mexico, on the other hand, has a pattern that is higher than the United States at ages up to 30, but then is nearly identical at the older ages. Similarly, the major difference between the fertility patterns in the United States and Canada is that Canadian women wait longer than U.S. women to begin childbearing, but after that their pattern is very similar to that of U.S women.

Why Was Fertility High for Most of Human History?

You will recall that for the first 99 percent of human history, mortality was very high. Only those societies with sufficiently high fertility managed to survive over the years. There may have been lower-fertility societies in the past, but we know nothing about them because they did not produce enough offspring to make the grade. Societies that did survive probably did not take for granted that people would have enough children to keep the population going. They instituted multiple inducements—pronatalist pressures—to encourage the appropriate level of reproduction: high enough to maintain society, but not so high as to threaten its existence, as discussed above. It is the undoing of those social pressures to have children, and the replacing of them with different kinds of pressures to keep fertility low (but not necessarily too low), that we have to understand if we are to explain the fertility transition. So, let me now discuss the general idea of the need to replenish society and then review the major inducements used by high-mortality societies, including the value of children as security and labor and the desire for sons, especially as it relates to the lower status of women in traditional societies.

Need to Replenish Society

A crucial aspect of high mortality is that a baby's chances of surviving to adulthood are not very good. Yet if a society is going to replace itself, an average of at least two children for every woman must survive long enough to be able to produce more children. So, under adverse conditions, any person who limited fertility might threaten the very existence of society. In this light, it is not surprising that societies have generally been unwilling to leave it strictly up to the individual or to chance to have the required number of children. Societies everywhere have developed social institutions to encourage childbearing and reward parenthood in various ways. For example, among the Kgatla people of South Africa, mortality was very high during the 1930s when they were being studied by Schapera. He discovered that "to them it is inconceivable that a married couple should for economic or personal reasons deliberately seek to restrict the number of its offspring" (Schapera 1941:213). Several social factors encouraged the Kgatla to desire children, as noted by Nag (1962:29):

> A woman with many children is honored. Married couples acquire new dignity after the birth of their first child. Since the Kgatla have a patrilineal descent system (inheritance passes through the sons), the birth of a son makes the father the founder of a line that will perpetuate his name and memory . . . [and the mother's] kin are pleased because the birth saves them from shame.

In a 1973 study of another African society, the Yoruba of western Nigeria, families with fewer than four children were (and still are) looked upon with horror. Ware reports that "even if it could be guaranteed that two children would survive to adulthood, Yoruban parents would find such a family very lonely, for many of the features of the large family which have come to be negatively valued in the West, such as noise and bustle, are positively valued by them" (Ware 1975:284). The 1989 Kenya Demographic and Health Survey (DHS) discovered that in the coastal province of that eastern African nation, the average ideal family size of 5.6 children was higher than the actual level of reproduction. Women wanted larger families than they were having, but they were slowed down by involuntary infecundity (Cross, Obungu, and Kizito 1991). The 2008–9 Kenya DHS showed that the average ideal family size had dropped to below the number of children that women were having—but fertility was still very high. The average woman in Kenya wants four children, but is having between four and five.

Social encouragements to fertility have been discussed in a more general form by Kingsley Davis (1949:561):

> We often find for example that the permissive enjoyment of sexual intercourse, the ownership of land, the admission to certain offices, the claim to respect, and the attainment of blessedness are made contingent upon marriage. Marriage accomplished, the more specific encouragements to fertility apply. In familistic societies where kinship forms the chief basis of social organization, reproduction is a necessary means to nearly every major goal in life. The salvation of the soul, the security of old age, the production of goods, the protection of the hearth, and the assurance of affection may depend upon the presence, help, and comfort of progeny. . . . This articulation of the parental status with the rest of one's statuses is the supreme encouragement to fertility.

You may notice from these examples that social pressures are not actually defined in terms of the need to replace society, and an individual would likely not recognize them for what they are. By and large, the social institutions and norms that encourage high fertility are so taken for granted by the members of a premodern, high-mortality society that anyone who consciously said, "I am having a baby in order to continue the existence of my society" would be viewed as a bit weird. Further, if people really acted solely on the basis that they had to replace society, then higher-fertility societies would now actually have much lower levels of fertility, since in all such countries the birth rates exceed the death rates by a substantial margin, whereas the very low fertility societies would have higher fertility, since in many of those countries the birth rate is now lower than the death rate, as I mentioned in Chapters 1 and 2.

The *societal* disconnection between infant and child mortality and reproductive behavior probably explains why at the *individual* level there is not much evidence of a relationship between infant deaths in a family and the number of children born to those parents (Montgomery and Cohen 1998; Preston 1978). Thus, the more culturally oriented perspectives on fertility begin with the assumption that fertility is maintained at a high level in the premodern setting by institutional arrangements that bear no logical relationship to mortality. Premodern groups accepted high mortality, especially among children, as a given, and so they devised various ways to ensure that fertility would be high enough to ensure group survival. Pronatalist pressures encourage family members to bring power and prestige to themselves and to their group by having children, and this may have no particular relationship to the level of mortality within a family.

This is not to say, however, that there is not a long-term relationship between mortality and fertility. It is just that the generation of parents who experience the improvement in their children's chances of survival is unlikely to be the generation that responds to that change with a decline in fertility. It will be their children or even grandchildren who become aware that lower mortality is changing the way society works, and thus they respond by lowering the number of children they have relative to their parents or grandparents.

Children as Security and Labor

In a premodern society, human beings were the principal economic resource. Even youngsters were helpful in many tasks, and as people matured into young adulthood they provided the bulk of the labor force that supported those, such as the aged, who were no longer able to support themselves. More broadly speaking, children can be viewed as a form of insurance that rural parents, in particular, have against a variety of risks, such as a drought or a poor harvest (Cain 1981). Though at first blush it may seem as though children would be a burden under such adverse conditions, many parents view a large family as providing a safety net—at least one or two of the adult children may be able to bail them out of a bad situation. One important way in which this may happen in the modern world is that one or more children may migrate elsewhere and send money home. Although children may clearly provide a source of income for parents until they themselves become adults (and parents), it is less certain that children will actually provide for parents in their old age. Despite an almost worldwide norm that children should care for parents in old age, there is very little empirical evidence to suggest a positive relationship between fertility and the perceived need for old-age security (Dharmalingam 1994; Vlassoff 1990). In a high mortality society, parents were probably aware of two things: (1) each child born has only a limited chance of surviving to adulthood; and (2) the chances are very good that they (the parents) will themselves die before needing assistance in old age. For now, it is most noteworthy that in a premodern setting, the *quantity* of children may matter more than the *quality*, and the nature of parenting is more to *bear* children than to *rear* them (Gillis, Tilly, and Levine 1992). Still, the noneconomic, nonrational part of society (the sexist part) intrudes by often suggesting that male children are more desirable than female children.

Lower Status of Women in Traditional Societies

Although it is obvious that in many less-developed countries the status of women is steadily improving, it is nonetheless still true that in many societies around the world desired social goals can be achieved only by the birth and survival of a son—indeed, most known societies throughout human history have been dominated by men. Since in most societies males have been valued more highly than females, it is easy to understand why many families would continue to have children until they have at least one son. Furthermore, if babies are likely to die, a family may have at least two sons in order to increase the likelihood that one of them will survive to adulthood (an "heir and a spare"). For example, given the level of mortality in Pakistan, the total fertility rate of 4.1 children per woman in 2007 was just about the level of fertility required to ensure an average of two surviving sons per woman. In Angola, where mortality is much higher, the total fertility rate of 5.8 in 2007 was also very close to the level at which the average woman would have two sons surviving to adulthood.

India is a country where the desire for a surviving son is strong, since the Hindu religion requires that parents be buried by their son (Mandelbaum 1974). Malthus was very aware of this stimulus to fertility in India and, in his *Essay on Population*, quoted an Indian legislator who wrote that under Hindu law a male heir is "an object of the first importance. 'By a son a man obtains victory over all people; by a son's son he enjoys immortality; and afterwards by the son of that grandson he reaches the solar abode'" (Malthus 1872 [1971]:116). Such beliefs, of course, also serve to ensure that society will be replaced in the face of high mortality. Yet, as Fred Arnold and associates (Arnold 1988; Arnold, Choe, and Roy 1998) remind us, the desire for sons cannot alone account for high birth rates. In Korea and China, two Asian societies with very strong male preferences (Park and Cho 1995), the drop in fertility has been rapid, and Vietnam, another nation with a marked preference for sons (Goodkind 1995), has also experienced a rapid fertility decline.

The major impact of son preference in the midst of a fertility decline is to increase the chance that a female fetus may be aborted, leading to the phenomenon of the "missing females" in China (Coale and Banister 1994)—fewer girls enumerated in censuses at younger ages than you would expect, given the number of boys enumerated. In the 1980s, there was a great deal of speculation and concern that the missing females were victims of female infanticide. Since female infanticide had been fairly common during the pre-Communist era, the probability seemed great that the one-child policy in China would lead a couple to kill or abandon a newborn female infant, reserving their one-child quota for the birth of a boy (Mosher 1983). But further analyses of data in both China and Korea (where a similar pattern of fertility decline has occurred without a coercive one-child policy) suggest that sex-selective abortion, combined with the nonregistration of some female births, accounts for almost all of the "missing" females, and that the role of infanticide probably was exaggerated (Banister 2004). An important reason for a rural Chinese couple to want a son is the belief that a son is their most viable form of old-age support, since daughters marry and move in with (and wind up caring for) their husband's family. Indeed, Ebenstein and Leung (2010) found that in rural Chinese counties where government pension plans were put in place in the 1990s, the sex ratio at birth has become less skewed toward boys because parents no longer have to worry about having a son to care for them in old age.

Male preference was also an indelible part of European patterns of primogeniture, which were designed to maintain a family's wealth by passing it on only to the oldest son. Over time, however, the preference for sons in North America and Europe has abated as a consequence of increasing gender equity, and data from 17 European countries suggest a strong tendency for a mixed-sex composition, with some countries exhibiting a slight preference for males and others a slight preference for females (Hank and Kohler 2000). Furthermore, unlike Asian societies, Europeans (and overseas Europeans such as Americans, Canadians, Australians, and New Zealanders) have been more inclined to assume that daughters, rather than sons, would be the caregivers in their old age.

Encouragements to high fertility often persist even after mortality declines. Childbearing is rarely an end in itself, but rather a means to achieve other goals, so if the attainment of the other goals is perceived as being more important than limiting fertility, a woman may continue to risk pregnancy because she is **ambivalent** about having a child—caught between competing pressures and thus unsure of how she feels. Smelser (1997) suggests that ambivalence can be thought of as a rational-choice situation in which a person is rational, but has no choice. A woman may rationally prefer a smaller family, yet not be in a position to exercise that choice in her life. Some of the factors that may enhance feelings of ambivalence at various points in a woman's life include a woman's role being exclusively associated with reproduction (that is, where males do not help with child rearing), lack of opportunities for women to participate in work outside of the immediate family, low levels of education, lack of communication between husband and wife, lack of potential for social mobility, and an extended family system in which couples need not be economically independent to afford children (Davis 1955). Most of these factors are related to the domination of women by men and go to the heart of women's empowerment (Dixon-Mueller 2001; Inglehart and Norris 2003).

Remember that for most women in most of human history it was easier to have several children than to limit the number to one or two, regardless of the level of motivation. For the average person, a high level of desire and access to the means of fertility control are required to keep families small. Thus, the fertility transition was by no means automatically assured just because mortality declined. Certain preconditions need to be in place before birth rates will drop.

The Preconditions for a Decline in Fertility

In 1973, in response to the findings emerging from the Princeton European Fertility Project (which I discussed in Chapter 3), Ansley Coale tried to deduce how an individual would have to perceive the world on a daily basis if fertility were to be consciously limited. In this revised approach to the demographic transition, he argued that there are three **preconditions for a substantial fertility decline**: (1) the acceptance of calculated choice as a valid element in marital fertility, (2) the perception of advantages from reduced fertility, and (3) knowledge and mastery of effective techniques of control (Coale 1973). Although the societal changes that produced mortality declines may also induce fertility change, they will do so, Coale argued, only if the three preconditions exist.

Coale's first precondition goes to the very philosophical foundation of individual and group life: Who is in control? If a supernatural power is believed to control reproduction, then it is unlikely that people will run the risk of offending that deity by impudently trying to limit fertility. On the other hand, the more secular people are (even if still religious), the more likely it is that they will believe that they and other humans have the right to control important aspects of life, including reproduction. Control need not be in the hands of a god for a person not to be empowered. If a woman's life is controlled by her husband or other family members, then she is not going to run the risk of insult or injury by doing things that she knows are disapproved of by those who dominate her (Bledsoe and Hill 1998). The status of women, not just secularization, is an important part of this first, basic precondition for a decline in fertility.

The second precondition recognizes that more is required than just the belief that you can control your reproduction. You must have some reason to want to limit fertility. Otherwise, the natural attraction between males and females will lead to unprotected intercourse and, eventually, to numerous children. What kinds of changes in society might motivate people to want fewer children? Davis (1963,

1967) suggested that people will be motivated to delay marriage and limit births within marriage if economic and social opportunities make it advantageous for them to do so. Since having children is generally a means to some other end, if the important goals change, then the desire to have children may change.

Coale's third precondition involves the knowledge and mastery of effective means of fertility control. Specific methods of fertility control may be thought of as technological innovations, the spread of which is an example of diffusion. Women in the United States and Canada now typically use the pill to space children and then use surgical contraception to end reproduction after the desired number of children are born. This is a different set of techniques than prevailed 30 years ago, and 30 years from now the mix will doubtless be different still. At the same time that knowledge of methods is being diffused, part of the decision about what method of fertility regulation to use is based on the individual's cost-benefit calculation about the "costs of fertility regulation." The economic and psychosocial costs of various methods may well change over time and cause people to change their fertility behavior accordingly, keeping in mind that not all possible avenues of fertility control are open to all people. Abortion is a good example. Although it is a legal method of birth control in the United States, it is not "available" to people who object to it for religious or personal reasons.

The remainder of the chapter uses these three preconditions for a fertility decline as an organizing framework to understand the fertility transition. First, I briefly review the changes in social structure that may be associated with the way in which humans view their role in reproduction (the first precondition) and that also influence the motivations to limit childbearing (the second precondition), which lead people to seek the means whereby they can do so (the third precondition). During this discussion you should keep in mind that the three preconditions do not necessarily operate in a strictly linear fashion; in particular, it is possible that the availability of a particular type of contraceptive method (e.g., sterilization becoming available to Hutterite women) can encourage people to think in different ways about their control over reproduction and to reassess the number of children they want or intend to have.

Ideational Changes That Must Take Place

Tradition is, by definition, the enemy of change, so it is not surprising that so-called traditional societies are those that are most resistant to the idea that women, or couples working as a team, should be in charge of their bodies when it comes to reproduction. Among the earliest nations to undergo a change in this regard were those that first experienced the Enlightenment, as I discussed in Chapter 3. The Enlightenment allowed people to break free from traditional ideas about the role of humans in the universe and, as I pointed out in the previous chapter, this was the opening door to science, which has provided us with the long lives that we now very nearly take for granted. The acceptance of secular ideas, associated especially with nonreligious education, occurred first in Europe and among overseas European countries such as the United States and Canada. Thus, it is not surprising that it was these countries that first experienced the fertility transition and now have among the lowest levels of fertility in the world.

An essential element in this process is a rise in the status of women, as I detail in the essay that accompanies this chapter, but historically this has been a slow and sometimes painful set of changes. Most people view the acceptance of ways to stay healthier and alive longer as much less controversial than how women are treated, and death control has been the Trojan horse, so to speak, for major ideational changes in societies that weren't otherwise interested in breaking away from tradition. As I pointed out in the previous chapter, the decline in mortality that has spread around the globe leads to an incredible increase in child survival that forces people to think differently about the world than they did before. Having more living children than ever imagined demands attention from everyone in a group. It is a wonderful prospect in the abstract, but it forces a new balance to be struck between people and resources. This is, of course, the basic point that Malthus—an early product of the Enlightenment—was making more than 200 years ago. But Malthus was pessimistic that people would or could change their ways and work out ways to limit the number of children born in order to prevent resources from being overrun and pushing everyone into perpetual poverty. History has, fortunately, generally proven him wrong on that point. Most people, though not all, do recognize that one way to cope with declining mortality is to limit fertility as well.

Motivations for Lower Fertility Levels

The motivational and ideational aspects of the fertility transition are most often explained as some combination of rational factors embodied in the supply-demand framework, and sociocultural influences captured by the innovation/diffusion perspective. Let me discuss each of these complementary perspectives in turn.

The Supply-Demand Framework

The original formulation of the demographic transition envisioned a world in which the normal state of affairs is a balance between births and deaths (homeostasis). Mortality is assumed to decline for reasons that are often beyond the control of the average person (**exogenous factors**), but a person's reproductive behavior is dominated by a rational calculation of the costs and benefits to himself or herself (**endogenous factors**) of maintaining high fertility in the face of declining mortality. The idea is that people will eventually perceive that lower mortality has produced a situation in which more children are going to survive than can be afforded and, at that point, fertility will decline.

The economist Richard Easterlin (mentioned earlier in Chapter 3) is especially notable for his work in this regard, and the resulting perspective is somewhat clumsily called "the theory of supply, demand, and the costs of regulation," or, in shorthand, "the supply-demand framework." It is also known as "the new household economics" because the household, rather than the individual or the couple, is often taken as the unit of analysis. High fertility, for example, may help households avoid risk in the context of low economic development and weak institutional stability, especially when children generate a positive net flow of income to the parents. Under those conditions, it is rational to want to produce a large number of children.

The supply-demand framework draws its concepts largely from the field of neoclassical economics, which assumes that people make rational choices about what they want and how to go about getting it. The essence of the theory is that the level of fertility in a society is determined by the choices made by individual couples within their cultural (and household) context (Easterlin 1978; Bulatao and Lee 1983; Easterlin and Crimmins 1985; Bongaarts 1993; McDonald 1993; Robinson 1997; McDonald 2000).

Couples strive to maintain a balance between the potential supply of children (which is essentially a biological phenomenon determined especially by fecundity) and the demand for children (which refers to a couple's ideal number of surviving children). If mortality is high, the number of surviving children may be small, and the supply may approximate the demand. In such a situation, there is no need for fertility regulation. However, if the supply begins to exceed the demand, either because infant and child survival has increased, or because the **opportunity costs** of children are rising, then couples may adjust the situation by using some method of fertility regulation. The decision to regulate fertility will be based on the couple's perception of the costs of doing so, which include the financial costs of the method and the social costs (such as stigmas attached to the use of methods of fertility control).

What are the opportunity costs of children? Let us assume that people are rational and that they make choices based on what they perceive to be in their best self-interest. The idea that children might be thought of as "commodities" was introduced in 1960 by University of Chicago economist Gary Becker, whose work on the economic analysis of households and fertility earned him a Nobel Prize in 1992. Becker's theory treated children as though they were consumer goods that require both time and money for parents to acquire. Then he drew on classic microeconomic theory to argue that for each individual a utility function could be found that would express the relationship between a couple's desire for children and all other goods or activities that compete with children for time and money (Becker 1960). It is important to note that time as well as money is being considered, for if money were the only criterion, then one would expect (in a society where there are social pressures to have children) that the more money a person had, the more children he or she would want to have. Yet we know that in virtually every richer nation, those who are less well-off financially tend to have more children than do those who are more well-off.

With the introduction of time into the calculations, along with an implicit recognition that social class determines a person's tastes and lifestyle, Becker's economic theory turns into a trade-off between quantity and quality of children. For the less well-off, the expectations that exist for children are presumed to be low and thus the cost is at its minimum. In the higher economic strata, the expectations for children are presumed to be greater, both in terms of money and especially in terms of time spent on each child. The theory asserts that parents in the higher strata are also exposed to a greater number of opportunities to buy goods and engage in time-consuming activities. Thus, to produce the kind of child desired, the number must be limited.

REPRODUCTIVE RIGHTS, REPRODUCTIVE HEALTH, AND THE FERTILITY TRANSITION

The ability of women to control their own reproduction, and the overall level of their reproductive health, are closely related to the changes that occur in the context of the fertility transition. By now you are familiar with the fact that pronatalist pressures have always been strong in societies characterized by high mortality and high fertility, especially agricultural societies. In those areas, several children must be born just to ensure that enough will survive to replace the adult membership. Thus, one component of the social status of women is that with a regime of high mortality, women are busy with pregnancy, nursing, and child care, and men, who are biologically removed from the first two of these activities, are able to manipulate and exploit women by tying the status of women to their performance in reproduction and the rearing of children. Furthermore, high mortality means that childbearing must begin at an early age, because the risk of death even as an adult may be high enough that those younger, prime reproductive years cannot afford to be "wasted" on activities other than family building. In a premodern society with a life expectancy of about 30 years, fully one-third of women age 20 died before reaching age 45, making it imperative that childbearing begin as soon as possible. Of course, the catch in all of this, as you will recall from the previous chapter, is that pregnancy and childbirth are major causes of death for women between the ages of 20 and 45. This means that reducing fertility is a major cause of the improvement in women's reproductive health (Velkoff and Adlakha 1998), an idea captured by the phrase "family planning saves lives" (Smith et al. 2009).

Women who marry young and begin having children may be "twice cursed"—having more years to be burdened with children and also being in a more vulnerable position to be dominated by a husband. Men need not marry as young as women, since they are not the child-bearers, and they also remain fecund longer. The older and more socially experienced a husband is compared to his wife, the easier it may be for him to dominate her. It is no coincidence that in Africa, western Asia, and southern Asia, where women are probably less free than anywhere in the world (and where fertility is higher than anywhere else), men are consistently several years older than their wives. In the Gambia, husbands are nine years older than their wives, in Afghanistan they are eight years older, and in Egypt they are almost six years older (United Nations Population Division 2009c). In India and Afghanistan, among other countries, a large percentage of young women are forced into marriage before the legal minimum age of 18 and 16 respectively, and there has been a growing international backlash against these practices (Arnoldy 2009; *The Economist* 2009). By contrast, in most European countries the difference in age of husband and wife averages only two to three years, and in the United States from 1970 through 1995, the age gap at first marriage was about two years (Clarke 1995). Detailed data on marriage and divorce, however, have not been kept by the United States since 1996.

Among the uglier aspects of traditional approaches to reproductive "health" is the practice of **female genital mutilation** (FGM), sometimes known as female circumcision, which involves practices that are technically clitoridectomy and infibulation. Clitoridectomy accounts for about 80 percent of such mutilation practices (Chelala 1998) and involves the total removal of the clitoris, whereas infibulation involves cutting the clitoris, the labia minora, and adjacent parts of the labia majora and then stitching up the two sides of the vulva. These are useless and dangerous practices to which an estimated 2 million girls and women in at least 28 countries in northern and sub-Saharan Africa and parts of Asia are subjected annually. The effect is to dramatically lower a woman's enjoyment of sexual intercourse, but as was true for foot binding in an earlier era in China, the real purpose is to "control access to females and ensure female chastity and fidelity" (Mackie 1996).

The migration of refugees from African countries such as Somalia, where the practice is common, to North America and Europe helped to ignite worldwide knowledge of and outrage about FGM, and there are now international movements in place bringing pressure on governments to make it illegal. A significant event occurred in 1997 when the highest court in Egypt upheld the government's ban on FGM. There is evidence as well that better-educated women are less willing to submit to FGM, so the trend in Africa toward increasing female education bodes well for the eventual elimination of this form of male domination (Islam and Uddin 2001). Female genital mutilation appears not to adversely affect a woman's ability to bear children (Larsen and Yan 2000), but the same cannot be said for violence against women, which is also common in many less-developed nations. Women in India seem especially likely to be beaten by their husbands, and there is evidence that this kind of brutality is associated with elevated levels of pregnancy loss and infant mortality (Jejeebhoy 1998).

Three demographic processes—a decline in mortality, a drop in fertility, and increasing urbanization—have importantly influenced the ability of women to expand their social roles and improve their life chances. A major factor influencing the rise in the status of women has been the more general liberation of people from early death. The decline in mortality does not mean that pressures to have children have evaporated. That is far from the case, but there is a greater chance that the pressures will be less; indeed, remaining single and/or childless is more acceptable for a woman now than at any time in history.

In North America, Europe, and much of Latin America and Asia, most of a woman's adult life is now spent doing something besides bearing and raising children, because she is having fewer children than in previous generations and she is also living longer. An average American woman, for example, bearing two children in her late 20s and early 30s would, at most, spend about 20 years bearing and rearing them. Of course, she will actually have far more than 20 years of relative (indeed increasing) independence from child-rearing

(continued)

The Demographic Linkage between the Fertility Transition and Reproductive Health

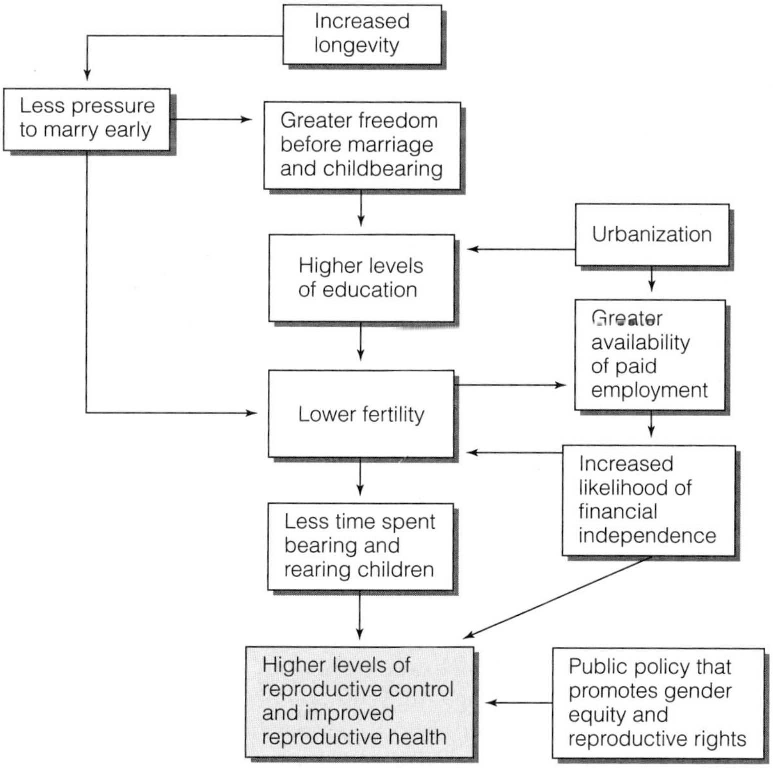

REPRODUCTIVE RIGHTS, REPRODUCTIVE HEALTH, AND THE FERTILITY TRANSITION (CONTINUED)

obligations, since if her two children are spaced two years apart and the first child is born when she is 30, by age 38 her youngest child will be in school all day, and she will still have 44 more years of expected life, as you can see by looking back at Table 5.3. Is it any wonder, then, that women have searched for alternatives to family building and have been recruited for their labor by the formal economic sector? In a sociocultural setting in which the reproduction of children consumes a great deal of societal energy, the domestic labor of women is integral to the functioning of the economy. With a slackening in demand for that type of activity, it is only natural that a woman's time and energy would be employed elsewhere, and elsewhere is increasingly likely to be in a city.

Cities are more likely than rural areas to provide occupational pursuits for both women and men that encourage a delay in marriage (thus potentially lowering fertility) and lead to a smaller desired number of children within marriage. Furthermore, since urbanization involves migration from rural to urban areas, this has meant that women, as they migrate, are distanced a bit from the pressures to marry and have children that may have existed for them while living in their parents' homes. Thus migration may lead to a greater ability to respond independently to the social environment of urban areas, which tend to value children less than rural areas. Young adults are especially prone to migration and every adult who moves may well be leaving a mother behind. This means the migrant will have more time on her hands to look for alternatives and question the social norms that prescribe greater submissiveness, a lower status, and fewer out-of-the-home opportunities for women than for men.

Of course, it isn't quite that simple. For one thing, the process of urbanization in the Western world initially led to an increase in the dependency of women before promoting increased gender equity (Nielsen 1978). Urbanization is typically associated with a transfer of the workplace from the home to an outside location—a severing of the household economy and the establishment of what Kingsley Davis (1984) called the "breadwinner system," in which a member of the family (traditionally the male) leaves home each day to earn income to be shared with other family members. In premodern societies, women generally made a substantial contribution to the family economy through agricultural work and the marketing of produce (Boserup

When an advanced education, a prestigious career, and a good income were not generally available to women, the lack of such things was not perceived as a cost of having children. But when those advantages are available, reducing or foregoing them for the sake of raising a family may be perceived as a sacrifice. Again, the reflexive nature of the connection between fertility and women's status is apparent. As fertility has gone down, more time has become available for women to pursue alternate lifestyles; and as the alternatives grow in number and attractiveness, the costs of having children have gone up. The benefits of having children are less tangible, though no less important, than the costs. They include psychological satisfaction and proof of adulthood, not to mention being more integrated into the family and community.

The latter reasons reflect a broad category of reward that society offers for parenthood—social approval. In addition, most people are most comfortable in families with children, since by definition everyone was raised in a situation involving at least one child. Thus, having children may allow you vicariously to relive (and perhaps revamp) your own childhood, helping to recreate the past and take the sting out of any failures you may experience as an adult. In a more instrumental way, children tend to provide a means for establishing a network of social relationships

1970), but the city changed all that. Men were expected to be breadwinners (a task that women had previously shared), while women were charged with domestic responsibility (tasks that men had previously shared). From our vantage point in history, the breadwinner system seems "traditional," but from a longer historical view, it is really an anomaly. Thus, the idea of men and women sharing economic responsibility for the family is a return to the way in which most human societies have been organized for most of human history.

As the life expectancy of the urban woman increased and as her childbearing activity declined, the lack of alternative activities was bound to create pressures for change, and over time the urban opportunities for women have multiplied. In the figure accompanying this essay, I have diagrammed the major paths by which mortality, fertility, and urbanization influence the status of women and lead to more egalitarian gender roles and improved reproductive health. Increased longevity eventually lessens the pressure for high fertility and lessens the pressure to marry early. These changes permit a woman greater freedom for alternative activities before marrying and having children, as well as providing more years of life beyond childbearing. Women are left to search for the alternatives, which are importantly wrapped up in higher levels of education. Society is then offered a "new" resource—nondomestic female labor. This creates new opportunities for a woman's economic independence, which is key to controlling her life, including her reproduction.

Having greater control over her own life, enhanced by lower fertility, also improves a woman's health in the process, even without government programs designed to increase reproductive health. Keep in mind, however, that public policy supporting gender equity, reproductive rights, and reproductive health can go a long way toward accelerating these changes in society. For its part, the fertility transition can be viewed as a key element in the broader pattern of changes involved in the demographic transition associated with women being able to take control of their lives and their bodies.

Discussion Questions: (1) Discuss the different kinds of decisions that couples are likely to make about having children if an older man marries a teenage girl, compared to a man in his late 20s marrying a woman in her late 20s; **(2)** Why is the status of women in society so intimately bound up with the number of children women have?

in a community through school, organized sports, and activity groups. The rewards of childbearing thus are greatest in terms of the personal and social satisfaction derived from them, since in richer nations there is certainly little, if any, economic advantage derived from having children.

The fertility transition is not something that occurs in a vacuum—it occurs because other changes are taking place in society to which individual couples or people within households are responding. The health and mortality transition actually increases the potential supply of children because healthier women are better able to successfully conceive and bear a child. But the changes in society that are generating that improved health are assumed by the supply-demand framework to be largely economic in nature, and it is the changing economic circumstances, not the decline in mortality per se, that couples are believed to respond to as they choose to lower their demand for children. An improved economy generates other things in life that compete with children. Other sources of income are more productive than what children can produce, and there are other ways to spend one's time and money besides just on children. Thus, if the means for fertility regulation are sufficiently effective, the lowered demand for children will lower fertility. In 1938, an Englishman put it rather succinctly: "In our existing economic system, apart from luck, there are two ways of rising in the economic system; one is by ability, and the other by infertility. It is clear that of two equally able men—the one with a single child, and the other with eight children—the one with a single child will be more likely to rise in the social scale" (quoted in Daly 1971:33).

In 1942, Joseph Schumpeter discussed the emerging attitudes of middle-class families toward childbearing and rearing. Heralding yuppie ideas, but 40 years ahead of his time, he posed the question "that is so clearly in many potential parents' minds: 'why should we stunt our ambitions and impoverish our lives in order to be insulted and looked down upon in our old age?'" (Schumpeter 1942:157). This is a very different view of the world from that in which family members work primarily for the mutual survival of all other family members or the view from the bottom of the social heap in which the only thing that matters is day-to-day survival. Increasing income and acquiring wealth may require that a family be kept small, whereas already having wealth may permit, and even encourage, the growth of families.

Although wealth and prestige are characteristics of premodern as well as contemporary societies, mass education is a new dimension that has been added to the mix by the combination of the Renaissance and the Industrial Revolution. As I have already mentioned, education (and its closely related cousin, secularization) is the single best clue to a person's attitude toward reproduction, and thus a clue to how responsive a person will be to changes that could lead to a lower demand for children (see, for example, Axinn and Barber 2001). An increase in education is strongly associated with the kind of rational decision making implied in the supply-demand framework. Furthermore, the better-educated members of society are most likely to be the agents of change who will encourage the diffusion of an innovation such as fertility limitation.

Until very recently I had never seen a set of data from anywhere in the world that did not show that better-educated women had lower fertility than less-educated women in a given society. It is nearly axiomatic, and it is the identification of this kind of **fertility differential** that helps to build our understanding of reproductive dynamics in human societies, because it causes us to ask what it is about education that makes reproduction so sensitive to it. In general terms, the answer is that education offers to people (men and women) a view of the world that expands their horizon beyond the boundaries of traditional society and causes them to reassess the value of children and reevaluate the role of women in society. Education also increases the opportunity for social mobility, which, in turn, sharpens the likelihood that people will be in the path of innovative behavior, such as fertility limitation, that they may try themselves.

In Figure 6.3, I have summarized data from Demographic Health Surveys in less developed nations, along with data from the United States, showing the relationship between fertility and education. The data are for women aged 40–49, so the number of children ever born approximates the completed fertility rate—the total number of children these women will ever have. The countries are arranged by the fertility level of women with no education (except in the United States, where it refers to women with less than a high school education), representing the situation in virtually all human societies prior to the fertility transition. Below that is the bar showing the completed fertility rate for women with secondary education (the equivalent of high school) or higher—representing the kind of structural change in

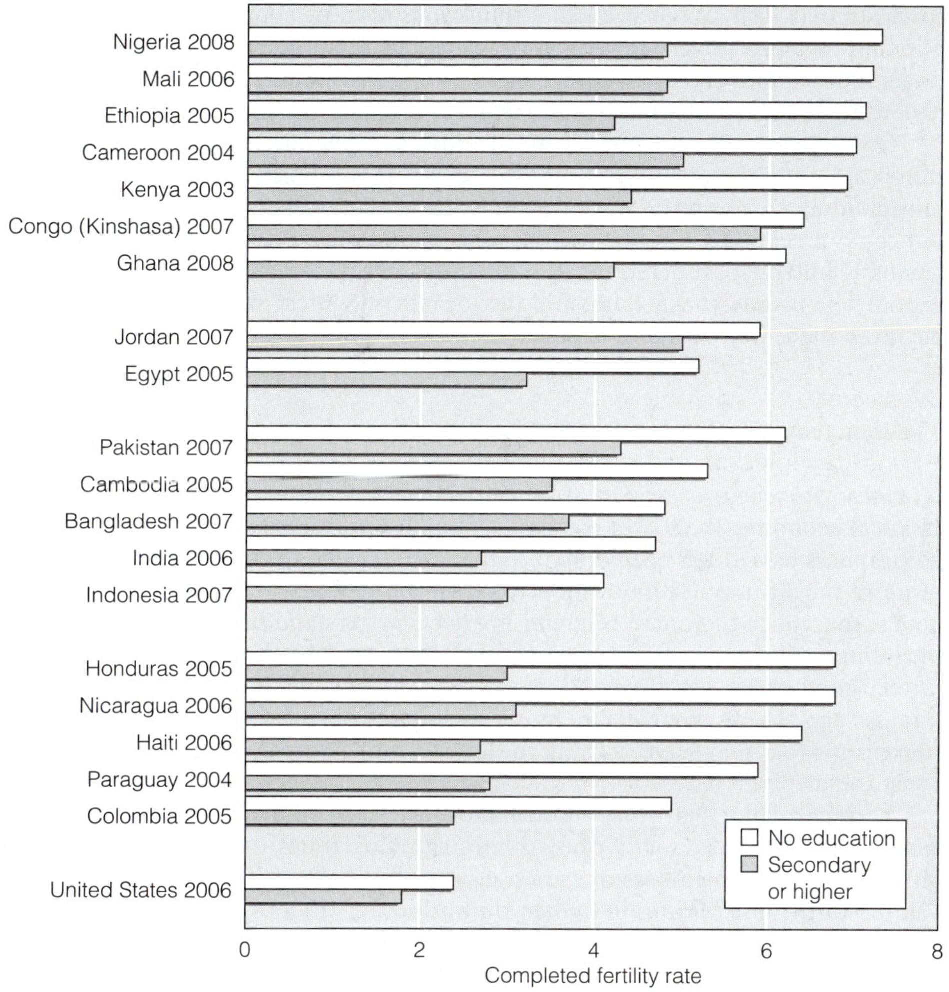

Figure 6.3 The Education of Women Is an Important Part of the Fertility Transition

Source: Data for all countries except the United States are from Measure DHS, ICF Macro, STATcompiler, http://www.statcompiler.com (accessed 2010); U.S. data are from Jane Lawler Dye, 2008, "Fertility of American Women: 2006," *Current Population Reports,* P20–558.

a society that is likely to change the relationship between the supply and demand for children.

You can see in Figure 6.3 that education leads to fertility differentials within each of these populations, but similar levels of education do not always lead to similar levels of fertility in different populations. Part of the reason for this difference may be economic: Education will buy you more in some societies than in others, and the more it will buy you, the higher the opportunity costs of children may be. Another reason may be cultural—education is not necessarily comparable from one country to another. On the other hand, education is such a critical determinant of fertility that Bongaarts (2003) has suggested that low levels of schooling in developing countries may well cause the fertility transitions in those countries to stall. Once fertility has dropped to very low levels, however, its relationship to education appears to get more complicated, as we are now learning from case studies in Europe (see, for example, Kravdal and Rindfuss 2008).

One must also recognize that motivations for low fertility do not appear magically just because one aspires to wealth, or has received a college education, or is an only child and also prefers a small family. Motivations for low fertility arise out of our communication with other people and other ideas. Fertility behavior, like all behavior, is in large part determined by the information we receive, process, and then act on. The people with whom, and the ideas with which, we interact in our everyday lives shape our existence as social creatures.

The Innovation/Diffusion and "Cultural" Perspective

Not all social scientists agree that human behavior is fully described by rational neoclassical economic theory. In particular, sociologists, anthropologists, and cultural geographers have often been drawn to the idea that many changes in society are the result of the diffusion of innovations (Brown 1981; Rogers 1995). We know, for example, that much of human behavior is driven by fads and fashions. Last year's style of clothing will go unworn by some people this year, even though the clothes may be in very good repair, just because that is not what "people" are wearing—it is so five minutes ago. These "people" are important agents of change in society—those who, for reasons that may have nothing to do with money or economic factors, are able to set trends.

You may call it charisma, or karma, or just plain influence, but some people set trends and others do not. We see it happen many times in our lives. Often these change agents are members of the upper strata of society. They may not be the inventors of the innovation, but when they adopt it, others follow suit. Notice, too, that the innovation may be technological, such as the cell phone, or it may be attitudinal and behavioral, such as deciding that two children is the ideal family size and then using the most popular means to achieve that number of children.

In Chapter 3, I mentioned that the fertility history of Europe suggests a pattern of geographic diffusion of the innovation of fertility limitation within marriage. The practice seemed to spread quickly across regions that shared a common language and ethnic origin, despite varying levels of mortality and economic development (Watkins 1991). This finding led to speculation that fertility decline could be induced in a society, even in the absence of major structural changes such as economic development, if the innovation could be properly packaged and adopted by the appropriately influential change agents. However, this is where the concept of "culture" comes into play, because some societies are more prone to accept innovations than are others (Pollack and Watkins 1993).

To accept an innovation and change your behavior accordingly, you must be "empowered" (to use an overworked term) to believe that it is within your control to alter your behavior. Not all members of all societies necessarily feel this way. In many premodern and "traditional" societies, people accept the idea that their behavior is governed by God, or multiple gods, or more generally by "fate," or more concretely by their older family members (dead or alive). In such a society, an innovation is likely to be seen as an evil intrusion and is not apt to be tolerated, which gets us back to the first precondition for a fertility decline—the ideational shift.

You can perhaps appreciate, then, that the diffusion of an innovation requires that people believe that they have some control over their life, which is the essence of the rational-choice model that underlies the economic approach to the fertility transition. In other words, the supply-demand model and the innovation-diffusion model tend to be complementary to one another, not opposed to one another. Both approaches can be helpful in explaining why fertility declines. In any social situation in which influential couples are able to improve their own or their children's economic and social success by concentrating resources on a relatively smaller number of children, other parents may feel called upon to follow suit if they and their offspring are to be socially competitive (Caldwell 1982; Handwerker 1986; Turke 1989).

The importance of "influential couples" is sometimes ignored by North Americans who prefer the ideal of a classless society. European demographers offer the reminder that two enduring theories of social stratification have strong implications for fertility behavior: (1) Cultural innovation typically takes place in higher social strata as a result of privilege, education, and concentration of resources, whereas lower social strata adopt new preferences through imitation, and (2) Rigid social stratification or closure of class or caste inhibits such downward cultural mobility (Lesthaeghe and Surkyn 1988). Thus, the innovative behavior of influential people will be diffused downward through the social structure, as long as there are effective means of communication among and between social strata. From our perspective, the innovation of importance is the preference for smaller families, implemented through the innovations of delayed marriage/sexual partnership and/or fertility limitation.

The Role of Public Policy

It is in the modern world of nation-states that the fertility transition has taken place, and so we cannot ignore the role that public policy may play in making it relatively more or less attractive to have children, and relatively easier or harder to control fertility. In Chapter 3, I alluded to the laws that existed in England and the United States well into the twentieth century that limited a couple's access to birth control information, so that only the most highly motivated couples were able to effectively limit their fertility. But since the 1970s the availability of contraception and abortion, not to mention the ease of divorce and women's access to the labor force, have all contributed to the birth rate dropping to and below the replacement level.

You will also recall that Marx was adamantly opposed to government intervention in the reproductive lives of people. So, in 1920s Russia, after the Communist revolution, Lenin repealed antiabortion laws and abolished the restrictions on divorce in order to free women; the result was a fairly rapid decline in the birth rate (although it turned out to be too rapid for the government's taste and in the 1930s abortions were again made illegal under Stalin's rule). On the other hand, the Cuban response to a Marxist government was exactly the opposite. Shortly after the Cuban revolution in 1959, the crude birth rate soared from 27 births per 1,000 population in 1958 to 37 per 1,000 in 1962. A Cuban demographer, Juan Perez de la Riva, explained that after the revolution, rural unemployment disappeared, new opportunities arose in towns, and an exuberant optimism led to a lowering of the age at marriage and an abandonment of family planning (Stycos 1971)—an ironically "Malthusian" response to a Marxist reorganization of society. The birth rate in Cuba did later reestablish its prerevolutionary decline, facilitated by eased restrictions on abortion and increasing availability of contraceptives (Hollerbach 1980; Diaz-Briquets and Perez 1981). However, low fertility has been maintained over time by improved female education and increased participation of women in the labor force (Catasús Cervera and Fraga 1996).

In Egypt, there has been long and sustained governmental support for family planning programs, but Fargues (1997) has argued that fluctuations in the birth rate over the years have been much more responsive to state policies affecting the economy than they have been to family planning programs. In particular, the government's policy of liberalizing the economy through market reforms has probably increased the motivation of couples to limit fertility because it has created opportunities to increase levels of income and wealth, which in turn compete with children for parents' attention. Conversely, Fargues (2000) suggests that decades of conflict between Israelis and Arabs have kept fertility rates in both Israel and Palestine higher than they would otherwise be, in particular preventing a fertility transition from occurring within the Palestinian population, especially among those living in the Gaza Strip (Khawaja 2000).

How Can Fertility Be Controlled?

Assuming that people feel that they can control their fertility, and they have a desire to do so, how can they accomplish this? What means are available to them? The answers have varied across both time and space. Earlier in the chapter, I mentioned that "natural" fertility is rarely as high as the maximum level that would be possible. In most societies, families are trying (or at least hoping) to have the number of surviving children that will be most beneficial to them. But people for most of human history have lived close to the subsistence level and have lived in the shadow of high death rates. Thus, it is not surprising that in such circumstances, couples are unlikely to have a preference for a specific number of children (van de Walle 1992). The vagaries of both child mortality and the food supply were apt to cause people to "play things by ear" rather than plan in advance the number of children desired. With high mortality, how many children are born is less important than how many survive.

When we realize that it is net reproduction (surviving children, not just children ever born) that is of importance, we can see that human beings have been very clever at dealing with family size by controlling the *family*, rather than by controlling *fertility*. These societal interconnections are diagrammed in Figure 6.4. For example, higher-than-desired fertility in terms of live births can be responded to after a child is born by what Skinner (1997) has called "**child control**," or by what Mason (1997) has labeled "postnatal control." There are at least three ways of dealing

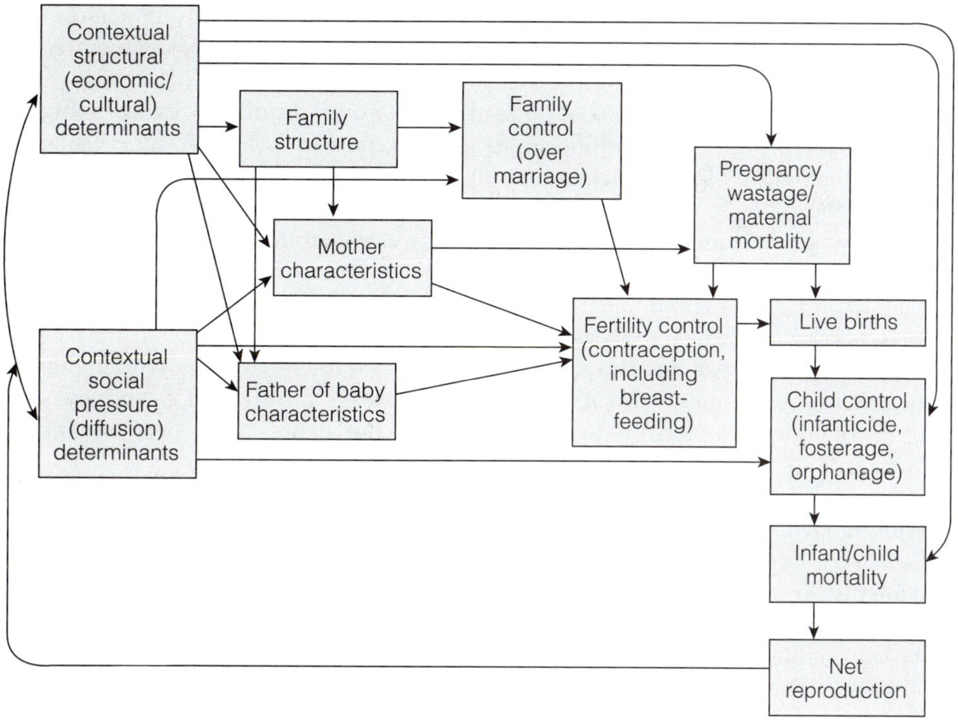

Figure 6.4 The Interconnecting Influences on the Fertility Transition

with a child who is not wanted or cannot be cared for by his or her parents after birth: (1) **infanticide** (known to have been practiced in much of Asia), or a less dramatic general neglect of or selective inattention to an unwanted child that leads to early death because she is not properly nourished or cared for (Scrimshaw 1978; Cherfas 1980; Simmons et al. 1982); (2) **fosterage** (sending, or even selling, an "excess" child to another family that needs or can afford it—a relatively common practice in sub-Saharan Africa and parts of Asia, and not uncommon in pre-transition Europe); and (3) **orphanage,** which involves abandoning a child in such a way that she or he is likely to be found and cared for by strangers. This was a pre-transition practice in much of Europe, where children were abandoned on the steps of a church (Kertzer 1993).

Family control does not end at that point, of course. As more children survive through childhood, the child-control options become more difficult because the number of children who can no longer be afforded may stretch the limits of what families can get away with in terms of infanticide, fosterage, and orphanage. This hearkens back to the theory of demographic change and response, which I discussed in Chapter 3. As declining infant and child mortality impinges on familial resources, the family's reaction may be to work harder, especially if "child control" is not available to them. Then, as children become teenagers (sometimes even before that), they may be sent elsewhere in search of work, either to reduce the current burden on the family or more specifically to earn wages to send back to the parents. These decisions are typically made by the family, not by the individual young person, and they are made in direct, albeit belated, response to the drop in the death rate that permitted these "excess" children to survive to adulthood.

Families have also exercised important control over fertility by determining the age at which their daughters will be allowed to marry, and by heavily supervising the premarital activities of young female family members to ensure that they are not exposed to the risk of pregnancy prior to marriage. The practice of chaperoning teenagers and other unmarried young adults was very common in much of the world until fairly recently, but it requires that there be a substantial system of surveillance in place within a household, and that is generally inconsistent with a world in which both parents work and where the older generation (the grandparents) may reside separately from the parents and their children. These family and household changes have gone hand in hand with major advances in the variety and effectiveness of methods of controlling fertility by directly influencing its proximate determinants.

Proximate Determinants of Fertility

The means for regulating fertility have been popularly labeled (popular, at least, in population studies) the **intermediate variables** (Davis and Blake 1955). These represent 11 variables through which any social factor influencing the level of fertility will operate. Davis and Blake point out that there are actually three phases to fertility: *intercourse*, *conception*, and *gestation*. Intercourse is required if conception is to occur; if conception occurs, successful gestation is required if a baby is to be born alive. Table 6.1 lists the 11 intermediate variables according to whether they influence the likelihood of intercourse, conception, or gestation. Although each of the 11 intermediate variables plays a role in determining the overall level of fertility in a society, the relative importance of each varies considerably.

Bongaarts (1978, 1982) has been instrumental in refining our understanding of fertility control first by calling these variables the **proximate determinants of fertility** instead of intermediate variables, and secondly by suggesting that differences in fertility from one population to the next are largely accounted for by only four of those variables: proportion married, use of contraceptives, incidence of abortion, and involuntary infecundity (especially **postpartum** infecundity as affected by breastfeeding practices). These variables are noted with a checkmark in Table 6.1. Bongaarts does not mean to imply, however, that the other intermediate or proximate determinants are irrelevant to our understanding of fertility among humans, only that they are relatively less important, and for this reason I will focus attention on the most important determinants—those checked in Table 6.1. As we review these determinants, you will discover, by the way, that there is heavier emphasis on the behavior of women than of men. That is simply because if a woman never has intercourse, she will never have a child (aside from the still relatively rare cases of *in vitro* fertilization in a woman who is not otherwise having intercourse with a man), whereas a man will never have a child no matter what he does. Of course, avoiding preventing conception by sterilization or contraceptives can be done by either sex, but if conception occurs, it is only the woman who bears the burden and the risk of either pregnancy or abortion.

Table 6.1 The Proximate Determinants of Fertility—Intermediate Variables through Fertility

Most Important of the Proximate Determinants	Proximate Determinants or Intermediate Variables
	I. Factors affecting exposure to intercourse ("intercourse variables").
	A. Those governing the formation and dissolution of unions in the reproductive period.
✔	1. Age of entry into sexual unions (legitimate and illegitimate).
	2. Permanent celibacy: proportion of women never entering sexual unions.
	3. Amount of reproductive period spent after or between unions.
	a. When unions are broken by divorce, separation, or desertion.
	b. When unions are broken by death of husband.
	B. Those governing the exposure to intercourse within unions.
	4. Voluntary abstinence.
	5. Involuntary abstinence (from impotence, illness, unavoidable but temporary separations).
	6. Coital frequency (excluding periods of abstinence).
	II. Factors affecting exposure to conception ("conception variables")
✔	7. Fecundity or infecundity, as affected by involuntary causes, but including breastfeeding.
✔	8. Use or nonuse of contraception.
	a. By mechanical and chemical means.
	b. By other means.
	9. Fecundity or infecundity, as affected by voluntary causes (sterilization, medical treatment, and so on).
	III. Factors affecting gestation and successful parturition ("gestation variables").
	10. Fetal mortality from involuntary causes (miscarriage).
✔	11. Fetal mortality from voluntary causes (induced abortion).

Sources: Kingsley Davis and Judith Blake, 1955, "Social Structure and Fertility: An Analytic Framework," Economic Development and Cultural Change 4 (3). Used by permission; modified using information from John Bongaarts, 1982, "The Fertility-Inhibiting Effects of the Intermediate Fertility Variables," *Studies in Family Planning* 13:179–89.

Proportion Married—Limiting Exposure to Intercourse

Permanent virginity is obviously very rare, but the longer past puberty a woman waits to begin engaging in sexual unions, the fewer children she will probably have because of the shorter time she will be at risk of bearing children (Variable 1 in Table 6.1). Perhaps due to lower surveillance by the family, compounded by earlier ages at menarche, 50 percent of teenage girls aged 15–17 in the United States had engaged in sexual intercourse at least once as of the early 2000s (Mosher, Chandra, and Jones 2005). At the same time, however, the average age at first marriage has been rising in the United States, suggesting that women are sexually active for an increasingly longer time prior to marriage (helping to account for the increase in out-of-wedlock births, as I will discuss in Chapter 10). The percentage of teenage boys who have ever had intercourse seems to be on the decline (Santelli et al. 2000), and in 2002 the percentage (just less than 50) was lower than for girls (Mosher, Chandra, and Jones 2005).

Modern contraception has altered the relationship between intercourse and having a baby, but it remains true that an effective way to postpone childbearing is to postpone engaging in sexual activity, particularly on the regular basis implied in marriage. Historically, those societies with a later age at marriage have been the ones in which fertility was lower, and it is still true that more traditional populations in sub-Saharan Africa and south Asia are characterized by early marriage for women and consequent higher-than-average levels of fertility. At the other extreme, the very low fertility in Europe is accomplished by a substantial delay in marriage for both men and women, and then a severe limitation of childbearing within marriage.

Use of Contraceptives

It is probable that at least some people in most societies throughout human history have pondered ways to prevent conception (Himes 1976). Abstinence, withdrawal, and the douche are the most ancient of such premodern means, but there is some historical evidence that various plants were used in earlier centuries to produce "oral contraceptives" and early-stage abortifacients (Riddle 1992). We do not know much about the actual effectiveness of such methods, but they were almost certainly far less effective in preventing conception or birth and far riskier for a woman's health than are modern methods. The lack of effectiveness of the premodern methods meant that a badly unwanted pregnancy was more likely to end in an attempted abortion or the woman trying to conceal her pregnancy and then abandoning the baby (probably leading to the infant's death) after a secret delivery (van de Walle 2000).

There have been references to douching throughout recorded history, stretching back to ancient Egypt (Baird et al. 1996; Himes 1976), and it is one of the principal means of contraception mentioned by Charles Knowlton in his famous *Fruits of Philosophy* early in the nineteenth century (which I mentioned in Chapter 3). Over time, it has been recommended as a means of treating specific gynecological conditions and also as a contraceptive, on the theory that washing sperm out of the vagina right after intercourse (the "dash for the douche") might prevent conception. Unfortunately, for the one doing the douching, the sperm take only about 15 seconds to travel through the vagina into the cervical canal, so the effectiveness of douching is very limited.

Withdrawal is an essentially (although not exclusively) male method of birth control. It has a long history (it is, in fact, referenced in the Bible). It is actually a form of incomplete intercourse (thus its formal name "coitus interruptus") because it requires removal of the erect penis from the vagina just before male ejaculation. The method leaves little room for error, especially since there may be an emission of semen just before ejaculation, but it is one of the more popular methods historically for trying to control fertility. Indeed, even today in the United States it is used fairly often, as you can see in Table 6.2, which lists the major forms of contraception by the proportion of women at each age who use them, and by their effectiveness, based on the most recent data available at this writing.

The importance of any kind of contraception can be gauged by the likelihood of getting pregnant if no method is used. The right-hand column of Table 6.2 illustrates the number of pregnancies per 100 women during the first year of use of any given method. This is a rate of use-effectiveness that approximates the chances of getting pregnant when using any method. Thus, a sexually active woman who is using no method at all has an 85 percent chance of getting pregnant over the course of a year. Even though withdrawal is the least reliable method on the list, you can see that its use reduces the chance of pregnancy to 27 percent. This is not very good by modern standards, but it is a large improvement on doing nothing. Data from a variety of surveys also have shown clearly that the more highly motivated couples (that is, those who do not want any more pregnancies, as opposed to those merely spacing their children) have higher use-effectiveness rates than less motivated couples, regardless of the method chosen.

It can be seen in Table 6.2 that the methods are listed in an order that closely approximates their use-effectiveness. Thus **surgical contraception** tends to be the most effective and from ages 25 up it is the most common method of contraception in the United States. It is, for all intents and purposes, a method of permanent contraception. For females, these procedures largely involve **tubal ligation**, although there are other, more extreme surgical techniques such as a hysterectomy (the removal of the uterus) that are normally done for health reasons, rather than contraceptive reasons (although the result is the same). For males there are also drastic as well as simple means of sterilization for males. The drastic means is castration, which is removal or destruction of the testes. This generally eliminates sexual responsiveness in the male, causing him to be impotent (incapable of having an erection). Eunuchs (males who have been castrated) have an interesting place in history, but castration is practiced now mainly in the case of life-threatening disease. **Vasectomy** is the male surgical contraceptive, and like a tubal ligation, it does not alter a person's sexual response. A vasectomy involves cutting and tying off the vas deferens, which are the tubes leading from each testicle to the penis. The male continues to generate sperm, but they are unable to leave the testicle and are absorbed into the body. Vasectomy is quite popular in the United States, as you can see in Table 6.2. In fact, it is the second most common method of fertility control among older American couples, trailing only female sterilization.

A close inspection of Table 6.2 will show you that there are only four methods that account for at least 80 percent of contraception at every age group: female sterilization, male sterilization, the pill, and the male condom. At the younger ages, the pill and condom are most important, but at ages 35 and older—when most women have had all the children they are likely to want—surgical methods take over as most popular.

The **oral contraceptive**, or "the pill" as it is popularly known, has revolutionized birth prevention for millions of women all over the world. The pill is a compound of synthetic hormones that suppress ovulation by keeping the *estrogen* level high in a female. This prevents the pituitary gland from sending a signal to the ovaries to release an egg. In addition, the *progestin* content of the pill makes the cervical mucus hostile to implantation of the egg if it is indeed released and may block the passage of sperm as well. In the 1960s and 1970s, the pill was the method of

Table 6.2 Contraceptive Methods—Use by Age among U.S. Women, 2002, and Use-Effectiveness

	Age Group							Number of pregnancies per 100 women during first year of use
	15–44	15–19	20–24	25–29	30–34	35–39	40–44	
Not currently using contraception	38.1	68.5	39.4	32.1	30.8	29.1	31.0	85.0
Among those using contraception:								
Female sterilization	27.0	0.0	3.6	15.2	27.5	41.2	50.3	0.5
Male sterilization	9.2	0.0	0.8	4.1	9.2	14.1	18.4	0.2
Pill	30.7	53.0	52.5	37.7	31.5	18.6	11.0	8.0
Implant, Lunelle, or contraceptive patch	1.3	1.3	1.5	2.5	1.3	0.7	0.3	0.1
3-month injectable (Depo-Provera)	5.3	14.0	10.1	6.5	4.2	2.1	1.6	3.0
Intrauterine device (IUD)	2.1	0.3	1.8	3.7	3.2	1.4	1.2	0.8
Diaphragm	0.3	0.0	0.2	0.4	0.1	0.0	0.6	16.0
Male condom	17.9	27.0	23.1	20.6	17.1	15.7	11.6	15.0
Periodic abstinence calendar rhythm	1.1	0.0	1.3	0.4	1.3	1.6	1.7	25.0
Periodic abstinence natural family planning	0.3	0.0	0.0	0.6	0.3	0.4	0.6	15.0
Withdrawal	4.0	2.5	5.1	7.8	3.8	3.4	1.4	27.0
Other methods	1.0	1.9	0.3	0.6	0.6	0.7	1.6	

Sources: Contraceptive use data are from A. Chandra, G. M. Martinez, W. D. Mosher, J. C. Abma, and J. Jones, *Fertility, Family Planning, and Reproductive Health of U.S. Women: Data from the 2002 National Survey of Family Growth.* National Center for Health Statistics. Vital Health Statistics 23 (25), 2005: Table 56; use-effectiveness data are from Hatcher, Robert A., James Trussell, Felicia Stewart, Anita Nelson, Willard Cates, Felicia Guest, and Deborah Kowal. 2004. *Contraceptive Technology, 18th Edition.* New York: Ardent Media.

choice for women of all ages in the United States, and it continues to be the most popular nonsurgical method of birth control in the United States. You can see in Table 6.2 that more than half of women under age 25 who are using a contraceptive are using the pill, but that fraction declines at ages 25 and older as more women (and men) employ sterilization as a method of surgical contraception.

All things considered, the pill would be just about the perfect solution except for the concern about side effects, which has put the pill in a storm of controversy ever since its introduction. It is the most widely studied drug ever invented, and much of the early scare about increased risk of cancer has subsided as researchers have been able to lower the dosages of chemicals in the pills and as they have learned that oral contraceptives do not, in fact, increase the risk of breast cancer, even after prolonged use (Hatcher et al. 2004). More encouraging are the studies suggesting that using the pill may actually reduce a woman's risk of anemia and certain cancers (Blackburn, Cunkelman, and Zlidar 2000).

The **male condom** is a rubber or latex sheath inserted over the erect penis just prior to intercourse. During ejaculation, the sperm are trapped inside the condom, which is then removed immediately after intercourse while the penis is still erect, to avoid spillage. The condom is very effective, and when used properly in conjunction with a spermicidal foam, it is virtually 100-percent effective. The condom is of course also useful in preventing the spread of sexually transmitted diseases, including venereal disease and HIV/AIDS. Although use of the condom dropped off considerably during the 1960s and 1970s, by 2002 (the most recent year for which data are available), it had regained its place just after the pill in popularity among younger Americans, as you can see in Table 6.2. The condom is a method that is associated with the decline in the birth rate in the United States and Europe, having been around in Europe since at least the seventeenth century, originally made of animal intestines. The modern type, made of rubber, dates to the mid-nineteenth century—the time that fertility was clearly beginning to drop in Europe and North America.

The **diaphragm** is another method that helped to lower the birth rate in the richer countries. It was invented in the late nineteenth century, just as fertility in Europe and the United States was clearly beginning to fall. It is a rubber disk that is inserted deep into the vagina and over the mouth of the uterus sometime before sexual intercourse. It thus provides a barrier to the passage of the sperm. To increase its effectiveness, it is normally used in conjunction with a **spermicide** that is spread in and around the diaphragm before insertion into the vagina. The spermicide acts to kill the sperm, and the diaphragm operates to keep the spermicide in place, preventing the sperm from entering the uterus and the fallopian tubes, where fertilization occurs. Since sperm can live in the vagina for several hours, a woman must leave the diaphragm in place for a while after intercourse. Until the 1960s, when oral contraceptives were placed on the market, the diaphragm was a fairly common method of birth control for married women.

The **intrauterine device** (IUD) was first designed in 1909, but it was not widely manufactured and distributed until the 1960s. At that time, it was the contraceptive technique that many family planners believed would bring an end to the world's population explosion. Its success, however, has been much less spectacular than was hoped, although it may be the most widely used nonsurgical contraceptive method used by women outside of the United States, due mainly to its popularity in China. Although different IUDs may work in slightly different ways, the IUD appears to operate largely as a barrier method, preventing the sperm from reaching the egg.

The principal method of contraception that requires couple cooperation is the calendar rhythm method, more formally known as periodic abstinence. Though users of this technique are jokingly referred to as parents, you can see that the use-effectiveness is still an improvement over using no method at all. Periodic abstinence may seem old-fashioned, but it is actually a reasonably new technique because the timing of ovulation in the menstrual cycle (which is central to the method) was unknown until the 1930s when Kyusako Ogino and Herman Knaus independently discovered the fact that peak fecundity in women occurs at the approximate midpoint between menses and that, despite the variability in the amount of time between the onset of menses and ovulation, the interval between ovulation and the next menses is fairly constant at about 14 days" (Population Information Program 1985).

Other methods of couple-oriented contraception represent non-vaginal sexual activity, such as mutual masturbation and oral-genital sex. In Davis and Blake's 1955 article, these forms of incomplete intercourse were listed as "perversions," but in more recent decades, with a significant change in openness about sex, they have become more openly acceptable techniques for engaging in sexual activity with limited risk of pregnancy.

If unprotected intercourse has taken place, it may still be possible for a woman to prevent conception, if she acts immediately—and I don't mean by douching. **Emergency contraception** (or *postcoital contraception*) is meant to avert pregnancy within a few days after intercourse. There are two principal means to do this: (1) emergency contraceptive pills—"the morning after pill"—and (2) the Copper-T Intrauterine device (IUD) (Princeton University Office of Population Research 2010). The IUD method tends to be more effective than the pill method.

Induced Abortion

Assuming that conception has occurred, a live birth may still be prevented. This could happen as a result of involuntary fetal mortality (Variable 10 among the intermediate variables shown in Table 6.1), which is either a spontaneous abortion (miscarriage) or a stillbirth. More important for our discussion, though, is voluntary fetal mortality, or induced **abortion** (Variable 11). Induced abortions became legal in Canada in 1969 and in the United States in 1973, and they are legal in all three of the world's most populous nations (China, India, and the United States), as well as in Japan and virtually all of Europe, except Ireland (although Irish women may travel to England for an abortion).

Back in the 1970s, abortion in many countries "changed from a largely disreputable practice into an accepted medical one, from a subject of gossip into an openly debated public issue" (Tietze and Lewit 1977:21). Worldwide, the demand for abortion has been dropping, but it is still high, even in places where it is not legal, and it has been estimated that one of five pregnancies in the world may end in abortion (Sedgh et al. 2007), with east Asia and eastern Europe leading the list in total numbers of abortions per year. There is increasing concern that women in developing countries, where the greatest restrictions on abortion tend to be in place, and yet where the greatest number of abortions are occurring, are seeking unsafe abortion. It has been estimated that as many as half of all abortions in the world are illegal (and thus have a high probability of being unsafe), which means that we have only indirect evidence about their existence (Yin 2005).

Abortion is probably the single most often used form of birth control in the world and is resorted to especially as a result of an unintended pregnancy due to lack of use or availability of contraceptive methods or when contraception failed. Abortions have played a major role in fertility declines around the world, and they are an important reason for the continued low birth rate in many countries, including the United States and Canada. The number of legally induced abortions reported in the United States increased steadily from 1974 to 1990, but the number has been declining since then (Henshaw and Kost 2008). Abortions have played a role in Mexico's fertility decline as well, despite the fact that elective abortion is not legally available to women in that country. A law was passed in Mexico City in 2007 (and subsequently upheld by the Mexican Supreme Court) legalizing abortion in that city, and this may lead eventually to a country-wide change.

There are at least two different ways to measure abortion: (1) the abortion rate, which is the number of abortions per 1,000 women aged 15–44, and (2) the abortion ratio, which is the number of abortions per 100 known pregnancies. The latter is the best measure, but also the most difficult to estimate. In the United States, abortion ratios are higher for unmarried women than for married, higher for African Americans than for other racial/ethnic groups, and higher for teenagers than for older women (Henshaw and Kost 2008). This profile has not changed much over time. The abortion ratio has remained fairly constant in Canada since abortion laws were liberalized. Canadian women are less likely than women in the United States to use abortion, and since the fertility rate in Canada is slightly lower than in the United States, the implication is that Canadian women are also more efficient users of other methods of contraception. Indeed, a glance back at Table 6.2 reminds you that at each age between 15 and 44 more than one-third of women in the United States are not using any contraceptive method.

There are now two major different types of abortions: (1) medical and (2) surgical. A medical abortion refers to the use of a pharmaceutical agent such as mifepristone (RU 486), methotrexate, or misoprostol to terminate a pregnancy after conception has occurred. This drug was developed in France and approved for use in the United States in 2000. This approach to abortion can occur from the time a women knows she is pregnant up to 49 days after the beginning of her last menstrual period. Surgical abortion is the "standard" method of induced abortion. In the United States, nearly all (97 percent) surgical abortions are done during the first trimester (the first three months) of a pregnancy with a procedure called *vacuum aspiration*, in which a tube the size of a pencil is placed into the uterine cavity and then suction is applied to remove the fetus (Koonin et al. 2000).

Involuntary Infecundity from Breastfeeding

Breastfeeding prolongs the period of postpartum amenorrhea and suppresses ovulation, thus producing in most women the effect of temporarily impaired fecundity. In fact, nature provides the average new mother with a brief respite from the risk of conception after the birth of a baby whether she breast-feeds or not; however, the period of infecundity is typically only about two months among women who do not nurse their babies, compared with 10–18 months among lactating mothers (Konner and Worthman 1980). Research suggests that stimulation of the nipple during nursing sets up a neuroendocrine reflex that reduces the secretion of the luteinizing hormone (LH) and thus suppresses ovulation. A study in Indonesia found that women whose babies nurse intensively (several nursing bouts per day of fairly long duration) delay the return of menses by an average of 21 months, nearly twice the delay of those women who breast-feed with low intensity (Jones 1988). On the other hand, the cessation of lactation signals a prompt return of menstruation and the concomitant risk of conception in most women (Guz and Hobcraft 1991).

Although breastfeeding is a natural contraceptive and keeps fertility lower than it would otherwise be, the percentage of women who breastfeed their babies has tended to decline with modernization, and so we find the seemingly contradictory fact that breastfeeding declines as fertility declines. In the earlier decades of modernization, bottle-feeding was seen as preferable to breastfeeding because it gave the mother more flexibility to work and have someone else care for her child, and there was a certain cachet attached to being able to bottle-feed rather than engaging in the more "peasant" activity of breastfeeding. In Paris in the nineteenth century, for example, there was an increase in the percentage of women working outside the home (especially among middle-class artisans and shopkeepers). Before bottle-feeding, a woman with a baby who wished to continue working had to hire a wet nurse. Most wet nurses were peasant women who lived in the countryside, and a mother would have to give up the child for several months if she wished to keep working. Infant mortality was as high as 250 deaths per 1,000 infants among those placed with wet nurses (Sussman 1977), yet in the early 1800s nearly one-fourth of all babies born in Paris were placed with wet nurses. Infants were a bother, and the risk was worth taking.

Over the past few decades, there has been concern that women in less developed nations were abandoning breastfeeding in favor of bottle-feeding. In the absence of some method of contraception, a decline in breastfeeding would, of course, increase fertility by spacing children closer to one another. Closer spacing poses a threat to the health of both mother and child, and bottle-feeding is also likely to raise the infant death rate, since in less developed nations bottle-feeding may be accompanied by watered-down formulas that are less nutritious than a mother's milk, and/or the water used may be unsafe. Bacteria growing in unsterilized bottles and reused plastic liners can also lead to disease, especially diarrhea, which is often fatal to infants. In response to these concerns, UNICEF and the World Health Organization approved a voluntary code in 1981 to regulate the advertising and marketing of infant formula. However, it was not until ten years later that that the giant Swiss firm Nestlé finally decided to limit its supply of free baby formula to third world hospitals (Freedman 1991), and other baby formula suppliers quickly followed suit. The women most likely to lead the movement back to breastfeeding in any given country are, somewhat ironically, the better educated (Akin et al. 1981; Hirschman and Butler 1981), the very same women whose fertility is apt to be kept low by deliberate use of other means of contraception rather than by the influence of lactation. In the United States in 2006, 86 percent of women with a college degree had breastfed at least one of their babies, compared with 66 percent among those with only a high school education or less (U.S. Centers for Disease Control 2010).

The Relative Importance of the Proximate Determinants

Bongaarts (1978) helped us to narrow down the original list of intermediate variables to the most important group of four proximate determinants. But even these four are not equally important, and their importance varies across time and space. In the now developed countries, delayed marriage (without much premarital intercourse) and then the use within marriage of whatever contraceptive methods were available at the time were almost certainly the paths to low fertility. Although from eastern Europe to China and Japan induced abortion has been a major factor in bringing fertility to low levels, it is reasonable to say that of all the proximate determinants of fertility, modern contraception has been by far the most important, at least since the 1960s. Without modern contraception, fertility can be maintained at levels below the biological maximum, perhaps even as low as three children per woman (especially through abstinence once the desired number of children has been born), but it is very difficult to achieve low levels of fertility without a substantial fraction of reproductive-age couples using some form of modern fertility control.

The exact nature of the relationship between fertility and contraception has been measured with increasing accuracy and frequency over the past few decades, beginning with the Knowledge, Attitude, and Practice (KAP) surveys of the 1960s and 1970s, followed by the World Fertility Surveys and Contraceptive Prevalence Surveys of the 1970s and 1980s and then by the Demographic and Health Surveys of the 1980s to the present. In North America, these kinds of data have come to us through the National Surveys of Family Growth in the United States, the General Social Survey in Canada, and the National Fertility Studies in Mexico. In Europe, such data have been derived from the Fertility and Family Dynamics Surveys.

Contraceptive use is usually measured by calculating the rate of **contraceptive prevalence**, which is the percentage of "at risk" women who are using a method of contraception. Being at risk of a pregnancy means that a woman is in a sexual union and is fecund, but is not currently pregnant. That is very difficult to estimate, and so the number of at-risk women is usually estimated by referring more simply to the number of women of reproductive age (15–49). There are approximately 1.8 billion women in the world right now who are of reproductive age and thus presumably at risk of pregnancy, and about 63 percent of them are using some contraceptive method (United Nations Population Division 2009a). Contraceptive methods tend to be lumped into two broad categories: modern and traditional. The modern methods include the methods listed in Table 6.2, whereas traditional methods include things such as douching or taking herbal teas. Estimates suggest that about 55 percent of "at-risk" women in the world are using a modern contraceptive.

As of the year 2009, data on contraceptive prevalence were available for 180 countries, as summarized by the United Nations Population Division (2009a). In Figure 6.5, I have charted the percentage of married women using modern contraception against the total fertility rate (TFR, an index similar to the total number of children born to women, as I discuss below). Each point on the graph represents one of those 180 countries in terms of its total fertility rate and contraceptive prevalence. Thus Niger, in the upper left of the graph, has a very high fertility rate (more than seven children per woman) and a very low 5 percent of married women using any method of contraception. In the middle of the graph is India, with a TFR of 2.8 and 49 percent of women using contraception. Mexico is farther down the line with a TFR of 2.7 and a fairly high 67 percent of women using contraception. Toward the lower right-hand side of the graph are the United States (TFR of 2.1 and 68 percent using contraception) and Canada (TFR of 1.6 and 72 percent using contraception).

You do not need a degree in statistics to see that there is a close relationship between these two variables, and the correlation coefficient (r) of .71 confirms that fact for those of you familiar with statistics. This is not a perfect relationship, however, and you can see in the graph that not every country is exactly on the line (which would represent a perfect relationship between fertility and contraceptive prevalence). Some countries have very high fertility, even though they appear to have

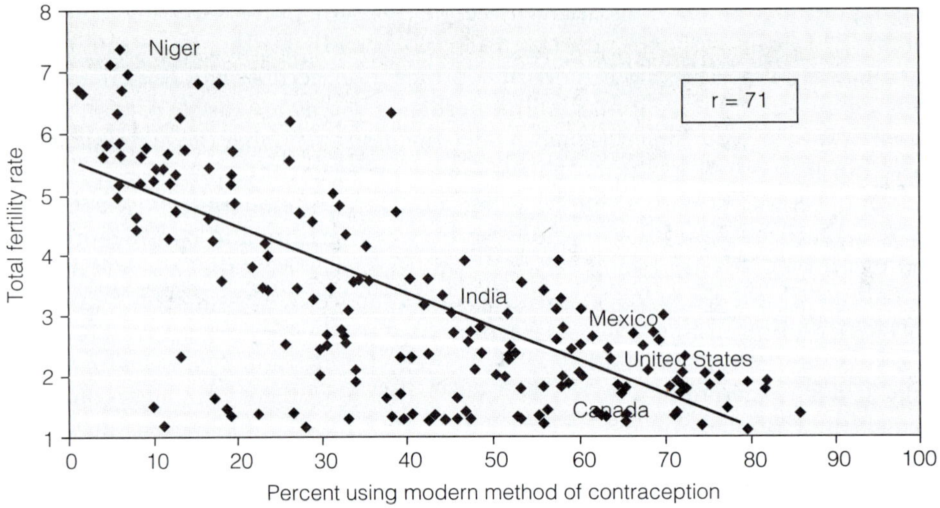

Figure 6.5 Higher Levels of Contraceptive Use Lead to Lower Levels of Fertility

Source: Data are from United Nations Population Division (2010) and Population Reference Bureau (2009).

reasonably high levels of contraceptive prevalence. In general, the explanation is that in these countries couples are using relatively less effective methods of contraception, although in some cases it is also true that couples have not been using contraception long enough for it to yet have a significant impact on the birth rate. Figure 6.6 maps countries according to contraceptive utilization, so that you can compare this spatial distribution with the pattern of fertility in the world shown in Figure 6.1.

Some of the countries shown in Figure 6.5 have quite low levels of fertility, even though the rate of contraceptive prevalence seems quite modest. In these cases, induced abortion (whether legal or not) rather than contraception is the probable cause of the low fertility rate. Most central and eastern European nations fall into this category with respect to legal abortions, as do several east Asian nations. In a few African and Latin American countries, the evidence suggests that illegal induced abortions also play an important auxiliary role in limiting fertility (World Health Organization 2004). If contraceptive effectiveness were increased generally, and in particular if effective contraceptive use replaced abortion, the fit between fertility and contraceptive prevalence would likely approach a perfect relationship (Bongaarts and Westoff 2000).

How Do We Measure Changes in Fertility?

How do we know that fertility has changed over time? The measures of fertility used by demographers attempt generally to gauge the rate at which women of reproductive age are bearing live children. As I have noted before, this is partly a function of how healthy a woman is. Since poor health can lead to lower levels of conception and higher rates of pregnancy "wastage" (spontaneous abortions and stillbirths), improved health associated with declining mortality can actually increase fertility rates by increasing the likelihood that a woman who has intercourse

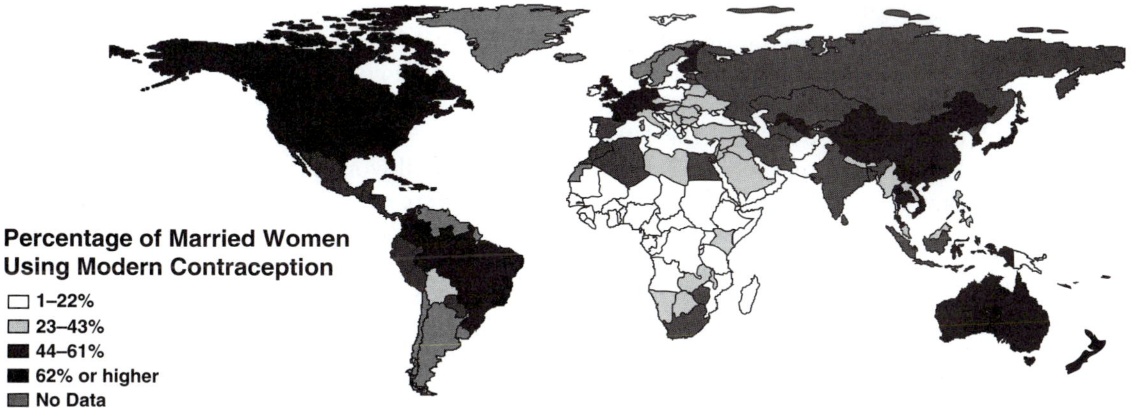

Figure 6.6 Global Variability in Contraceptive Utilization

will eventually have a live birth. Most rates are based on **period** data, which refer to a particular calendar year and represent a cross section of the population at one specific time. **Cohort** measures of fertility, on the other hand, follow the reproductive behavior of specific birth-year groups (cohorts) of women as they proceed through the childbearing years. Some calculations are based on a **synthetic cohort** that treats period data as though they referred to a cohort. Thus, data for women aged 20–24 and 25–29 in the year 2005 represent the period data for two different cohorts. If it is assumed that the women who are now 20–24 will have just the same experience five years from now as the women who are currently 25–29, then a synthetic cohort has been constructed from the period data.

Period Measures of Fertility

A number of period measures of fertility are commonly used in population studies, including the crude birth rate, the general fertility rate, the child woman ratio, the age-specific fertility rate, the total fertility rate, the gross reproduction rate, and the net reproduction rate. Each one tells a little different story because each is based on a slightly different set of data. I will discuss the one that requires the least data first. Then each successive measure requires a bit more information (or at least harder-to-get information) for its calculation.

The **crude birth rate** (CBR) is the number of live births (b) in a year divided by the total midyear population (p). It is usually multiplied by 1,000 to reduce the number of decimals:

$$CBR = \frac{b}{p} \times 1{,}000.$$

The CBR is "crude" because (1) it does not take into account which people in the population were actually at risk of having the births, and (2) it ignores the age structure of the population, which can greatly affect how many live births can be expected in a given year. Thus, the CBR (which is sometimes called simply "the birth rate") can mask significant differences in actual reproductive behavior between two populations and, on the other hand, can imply differences that do not really exist.

For example, if a population of 1,000 people contained 300 women who were of childbearing age and 10 percent of them (30) had a baby in a particular year, the CBR would be (30 births/1,000 total people) = 30 births per 1,000 population. However, in another population, 10 percent of all women may also have had a child that year. Yet, if out of 1,000 people there were only 150 women of childbearing age, then only 15 babies would be born, and the CBR would be 15 per 1,000. Crude birth rates in the world in 2009, for example, ranged from a low of eight per 1,000 (in Germany and Taiwan—all of the lowest rates are in Europe and East Asia) to a high of 53 per 1,000 in Niger (all of the highest rates are in sub-Saharan Africa). The CBR in Canada was 11, compared with 14 in the United States, and 20 in Mexico (Population Reference Bureau 2009).

Despite its shortcomings, the CBR is often used because it requires only two pieces of information: the number of births in a year and the total population size. If, in addition, a distribution of the population by age and sex is available, usually obtained from a census (but also obtainable from a large survey, especially in less developed nations), then more sophisticated rates can be calculated.

The **general fertility rate** (GFR) uses information about the age and sex structure of a population to be more specific about who actually has been at risk of having the births recorded in a given year. As you can see in Table 6.3, the GFR (which is sometimes simply called "the fertility rate") is the total number of births in a year (b) divided by the number of women in the childbearing ages (${}_{30}F_{15}$—denoting females starting at age 15 with an interval width of 30, i.e., women aged 15–44):

$$GFR = \frac{b}{{}_{30}F_{15}} \times 1{,}000.$$

Smith (1992) has noted that the GFR tends to be equal to about 4.5 times the CBR. Thus, in 2006, the GFR in the United States of 68.5 was just slightly more than 4.5 times the CBR of 14.2 that year (Martin et al. 2009).

If vital statistics data are not available, it is still possible to estimate fertility levels from the age and sex data in a census or large survey. The **child–woman ratio** (CWR) provides an index of fertility that is conceptually similar to the GFR but relies solely on census data. The CWR is measured by the ratio of young children (aged zero to four) enumerated in the census to the number of women of childbearing ages (15 to 49):

$$CWR = \frac{{}_{4}p_{0}}{{}_{35}F_{15}} \times 1{,}000.$$

Notice that an older upper limit on the age of women is typically used with the CWR than with the GFR, because some of the children aged 0 to 4 will have been born up to five years prior to the census date. In the United States in 2010 there were 21,965,000 children aged 0 to 4 and 75,894,000 women aged 15 to 49; thus, the CWR was 289 children aged 0 to 4 per 1,000 women of childbearing age. By contrast, in Mexico in 2010 there were 10,042,000 children aged 0 to 4 and 30,593,000 women aged 15–49, for a CWR of 328.

Table 6.3 Calculation of Fertility Rates, United States 2006

(1)	(2)	(3) F	(4) b	(5) ASFR	(6) $ASFR_f$	(7)	(8)	(9)	(10)
Age group	Midpoint of interval	Number of women in age group	Number of births to women in age group	Age-specific birth rate (per 1,000)	Number of female births to women in age group	Female births per 1,000 women	Proportion of female babies surviving to midpoint of age interval	Surviving daughters per woman during 5-year interval	Column (2) × Column (9)
10–14	12.5	10,660,000	6,396	0.6	3,124	0.3	0.9918	0.00145	0.01817
15–19	17.5	10,392,267	435,436	41.9	212,710	20.5	0.9905	0.10137	1.77402
20–24	22.5	10,202,427	1,080,437	105.9	527,793	51.7	0.9885	0.25568	5.75285
25–29	27.5	10,127,669	1,181,899	116.7	577,358	57.0	0.9860	0.28105	7.72898
30–34	32.5	9,726,285	950,258	97.7	464,201	47.7	0.9829	0.23456	7.62324
35–39	37.5	10,541,564	498,616	47.3	243,574	23.1	0.9786	0.11305	4.23947
40–44	42.5	11,227,553	105,539	9.4	51,556	4.6	0.9718	0.02231	0.94822
45–49	47.5	10,800,000	5,480	0.6	3,165	0.3	0.9718	0.00142	0.06765
TOTALS		83,677,766	4,265,061	420.1		205.2		1.01091	28.15259
			× sum of ages 15–44 in column (3) × 1000 = GFR: 68.5	× 5 = TFR: 2,100.5 (or 2.1 per woman)		× 5 and divided by 1,000 = GRR: 1.03		= NRR	divided by NRR = 27.85 = mean length of generation

Source: Birth data are from (Martin et al. 2009); death data are from Table 5.3.

The CWR can be affected by the underenumeration of infants, by infant and childhood mortality (some of the children born will have died before being counted), and by the age distribution of women within the childbearing years, and researchers have devised various ways to adjust for each of these potential deficiencies (Smith 1992; Weeks et al. 2004). Furthermore, just as the GFR is roughly 4.5 times the CBR, the CWR is approximately 4.5 times the GFR. The CWR for the United States in 2010, as noted above, was 289, which was slightly less than 4.5 times the GFR in 2006 (the most recent GFR as of this writing) of 68.5.

As part of the Princeton European Fertility Project, a fertility index was produced that has been useful in making historical comparisons of fertility levels. The overall index of fertility (I_f) is the product of the proportion of the female population that is married (I_m) and the index of marital fertility (I_g). Thus:

$$I_f = I_m \times I_g.$$

Marital fertility (I_g) is calculated as the ratio of marital fertility (live births per 1,000 married women) in a particular population to the marital fertility rates of the Hutterites in the 1930s. Since they were presumed to have had the highest overall level of "natural" fertility, any other group might come close to, but not likely exceed, that level. Thus, the Hutterites represent a good benchmark for the upper limit of fertility. An I_g of 1.0 would mean that a population's marital fertility was equal to that of the Hutterites, whereas an I_g of 0.5 would represent a level of childbearing only half that. Calculating marital fertility as a proportion, rather than as a rate, allows the researcher to readily estimate how much of a change in fertility over time is due to the proportion of women who are married and how much is due to a shift in reproduction within marriage.

One of the more precise ways of measuring fertility is the **age-specific fertility rate** (ASFR). This requires a rather complete set of data: births according to the age of the mother and a distribution of the total population by age and sex. The ASFR is the number of births (b) occurring in a year to mothers aged x to $x + n$ (${}_nb_x$) per 1,000 women (p_f or F) of that age (usually given in five-year age groups):

$$ASFR = \frac{{}_nb_x}{{}_nF_x} \times 1{,}000.$$

As you can see in Table 6.3, in 2006 in the United States there were 106 births per 1,000 women aged 20 to 24. However, in 1955 in the United States childbearing activity for women aged 20 to 24 had been more than twice that, reflected in an ASFR of 242. In 2006, the ASFR for women aged 25 to 29 was 117, compared with 191 in 1955. Thus, we can conclude that between 1955 and 2006 fertility dropped more for women aged 20 to 24 (a 56 percent decline) than for women aged 25 to 29 (a 39 percent drop).

ASFRs require that comparisons of fertility be done on an age-by-age basis. Demographers have also devised a method for combining ASFRs into a single fertility index covering all ages. This is called the **total fertility rate** (TFR). The TFR uses the synthetic cohort approach and approximates knowing how many children women have had when they are all through with childbearing by using the age-specific fertility rates at a particular date to project what could happen in the future if all women went through their lives bearing children at the same rate as women at that given date. For example, as noted above (and in Table 6.3), in 2006 American women aged 25 to 29 were bearing children at a rate of 117 births per 1,000 women per year. Thus, over a five-year span (from ages 25 through 29), for every 1,000 women we could expect 585 (= 5 × 117) births for every thousand women if everything else remained the same. By applying that logic to all ages, we can calculate the TFR as the sum of the ASFRs over all ages:

$$TFR = \Sigma ASFR \times 5.$$

As shown in Table 6.3, the ASFR for each age group is multiplied by five only if the ages are grouped into five-year intervals. If data by single year of age are available, that adjustment is not required. The TFR can be readily compared from one population to another because it takes into account the differences in age structure, and its interpretation is simple and straightforward. The TFR is an estimate of the average number of children born to each woman, assuming that current birth rates remain constant and that none of the women dies before reaching the end of the childbearing years. In 2006, the TFR in the United States was 2,100 children per 1,000 woman, or 2.10 children per woman, which was well below the 1955 figure of 3.60 children per woman. A rough estimate of the TFR (measured per 1,000 women) can be obtained by multiplying the GFR by 30 or, or by multiplying the CBR by 4.5 and then again by 30. Thus, in the United States in 2006, the TFR of 2,100 per 1,000 women was slightly less than, but still close to, 30 times the GFR of 68.5.

A further refinement of the TFR is to look at female births only (since it is only the female babies who eventually bear children), producing a measure called the **gross reproduction rate** (GRR). The most precise way to do this is to calculate age-specific birth rates using only female babies, and then the calculation of the TFR for females represents the GRR, as shown in Table 6.3:

$$GRR = (\Sigma\, ASBR_f \times 5)/1{,}000.$$

The GRR is interpreted as the number of female children that a female just born may expect to have during her lifetime, assuming that birth rates stay the same and ignoring her chances of survival through her reproductive years. A value of one indicates that women will just replace themselves, whereas a number less than one indicates that women will not quite replace themselves, and a value greater than one indicates that the next generation of women will be more numerous than the present one, such as the 1.03 for the United States in 2006, suggesting that the next generation of women could be 3 percent greater than in 2006.

The GRR is called "gross" because it assumes that a woman will survive through all her reproductive years. Actually, some women will die before reaching the oldest age at which they might bear children. The risk of dying is taken into account by the **net reproduction rate** (NRR). The NRR represents the number of female children that a female child just born can expect to bear, taking into account her risk of dying before the end of her reproductive years. It is calculated as follows:

$$NRR = \sum \left(\frac{{}_nb^f{}_x}{{}_np^f{}_x} \times \frac{{}_nL_x}{500{,}000} \right)$$

where ${}_nbf_x$ represents the number of female children born to women between the ages of x and $x + n$, which is divided by the total number of women between the ages of x and $x + n$ (${}_npf_x$). This is the age-sex-specific birth rate, which, in this example assumes a five-year age grouping of women. Each age-sex-specific birth rate is then multiplied by the probability that a woman will survive to the midpoint of the age interval, which is found from the life table by dividing ${}_nL_x$ (the number of women surviving to the age interval x to $x + n$) by 500,000 (which is the radix multiplied by 500,000). Note that if single-year-of-age data were used, the denominator would be 100,000 rather than 500,000.

The NRR is always less than the GRR, since some women always die before the end of the reproductive period. How much before, of course, depends on death rates. In a low-mortality society such as the United States, the NRR is only slightly less than the GRR—the GRR of 1.03 is associated with a NRR of 1.01, whereas in a high-mortality society, the GRR may be considerably higher than the NRR. As an index of **generational replacement**, an NRR of one indicates that each generation of females has the potential to just replace itself. This indicates a population that will eventually stop growing if fertility and mortality do not change. A value less than one indicates a potential decline in numbers, and a value greater than one indicates the potential for growth, unless fertility and mortality change. It must be emphasized that the NRR is not equivalent to the rate of population growth in most societies. For example, in the United States, the NRR in 2006 was scarcely above one, yet the population was still increasing by more than 2.6 million people each year. The NRR represents the future potential for growth inherent in a population's fertility and mortality regimes. However, peculiarities in the age structure (such as large numbers of women of childbearing age), as well as migration, affect the actual rate of growth at any point in time.

By adding one more column to Table 6.3, we are able to provide another useful index called the **mean length of generation**, or the average age at childbearing (typically labeled *T*) (Palmore and Gardner 1983). Column 10 illustrates the calculation. You multiply the midpoint of each age interval (column 2) by the surviving daughters per woman for that age interval (column 9), and then you divide the sum of those calculations by the net reproduction rate (the sum of column 9), yielding a figure for 2006 in the United States of 27.85 years.

Cohort Measures of Fertility

Cohort data follow people through time as they age, rather than taking snapshots of different people at regular intervals, which is what period data do. Thus, the basic measure of cohort fertility is births to date, measured as the **cumulated cohort fertility rate** (CCFR), or the total number of **children ever born** (CEB) to women.

For example, women born in 1915 began their childbearing during the Depression. By the time those women had reached age 25 in 1940, they had given birth to 890 babies per 1,000 women (Heuser 1976). By age 44 (in 1959), those women had finished their childbearing in the baby boom years with a completed fertility rate of 2,429 births per 1,000 women. We can compare those women with another cohort of women who were raised during the Depression and began their childbearing right after World War II. The cohort born in 1930 had borne a total of 1,415 children per 1,000 women by the time they were age 25 in 1955. This level is 60 percent greater than the 1915 cohort. By age 44 (in 1974), the 1930 cohort had borne 3,153 children per 1,000 women, 30 percent higher than the 1915 cohort. Indeed, examining cohort data for the United States, it turns out that the women born in 1933 were the most fertile of any group of American women since the cohort born in 1881.

Frejka and Kingkade (2001) have tracked more recent trends in U.S. fertility with cohort data by calculating the average number of children born to women by exact age 27 (the average age at childbearing, which we just calculated in Table 6.3) among successive birth cohorts of women. Women born in 1950–51 had given birth to an average of 1.201 children by age 27 (which for them was 1977–78), whereas women born in 1960–61 had given birth to an average of 1.057 children by age 27 (which was 1987–88), but the cohort of women born in 1970–71 had given birth to 1.072 children by age 27 (1998–99). This is indicative of a rise in fertility in the United States over the past two decades, which is partly a consequence of increasing immigration to the nation, as I will discuss in more detail later. Cohort information is very illuminating, but since we cannot always wait for women to go through their childbearing years to estimate their level of fertility, we typically use the synthetic cohort approach to calculate the TFR.

Fertility Intentions

Our understanding of the fertility transition in the world has been quietly, but importantly, influenced by research on fertility intentions. These are data on what the women who are presently of childbearing age say they intend do in the future in terms of having children. The idea for collecting this kind of information was inspired by demographers who had failed to forecast the baby boom that occurred after World War II. They realized after the fact that many couples had been postponing having babies before the war (because of the Depression) and during the war (because of the uncertainty and disruptions caused by the war), but they still intended to have more babies. The eventual fulfillment of these intentions helped to fuel the baby boom, as I will discuss later.

Period rates are prone to this problem of being influenced by the *timing* or *tempo* of births, which may distort the underlying *quantum* of births (Bongaarts and Feeney 1998; Rodriguez 2006), but data on lifetime births expected by women can provide a clue to the number of births that will eventually be produced, even if the timing cannot be well predicted. For example, between 1976 and 1998, the TFR increased from 1.7 to 2.1 births per woman in the United States, seeming to show that fertility was on the rise during that 22-year period of time. However, data on lifetime births expected by women who were ages 30 to 34 actually went down from 2.4 in 1976 to 2.1 in 1998, while the number of lifetime births expected by women ages 18 to 24 and 25 to 29 remained virtually the same, at 2.1 and 2.0 respectively. This tells us that the TFR in 1976 was lower than it should have been because, as mentioned above, women were just postponing births to a later date. Although the timing had changed, young women in 1998 had exactly the same family size in mind (an average of 2.1 children) as did young women back in 1976.

Westoff (1990) used data from 134 different fertility surveys conducted in 84 different countries to conclude that "the proportion of women reporting that they want no more children has high predictive validity and is therefore a useful tool for short-term fertility forecasting" (p. 84). An exhaustive review of the literature a decade later led Morgan (2001:160) to conclude that "the evidence is clear: intentions strongly predict subsequent behavior."

You can see that measures of fertility are no less complex than the fertility transition itself. With this set of measuring tools in hand, we can now return to the question that I raised earlier in the chapter: What is it that eventually convinces people that they should want to have a small family, given that people seemed to want large families until very recently in human history?

How Is the Fertility Transition Accomplished?

There is no single straight path that a population is likely to take to get from high fertility to low fertility, but there are some patterns that show up more regularly than others. Keep in mind that Coale's three preconditions for a fertility decline suggest that nothing will happen as long as women do not feel that they are in control of their own reproduction, so the first part of the transition is ideational in nature. Even assuming such an ideational change in society, fertility will only decline if people are motivated to break the old rules of life's game that funneled women into a world of having children early and often. Finally, women or couples must decide how they are going try to limit the children born.

One of the first signs of a fertility decline in a population is an increase in the age at which a woman has her first birth. You might call this the transition from children having children to women having children, and it is part and parcel of the rising status of women in society. This may be accomplished more through abstinence than anything else, but in societies where girls are sexually active prior to marriage this will obviously require either an effective contraceptive or the availability of abortion. At older ages, women who already have children may decide not to have an additional one, and completed family size becomes five children born instead of six, or four instead of five. Thus, during the fertility transition birth rates are apt to drop noticeably at the two age extremes of a woman's reproductive career.

Research suggests that even when couples have an ideal family size in mind, they make decisions about children one at a time. This information is captured by what demographers call **parity progression ratios**, which represent the proportion of women with a given number of children (parity refers to how many children have already been born) who "progress" to having another child. Thus, as fertility declines, parity progression ratios will decline at the higher parities. The consequence is a "compression" of reproduction (to borrow the term I used in Chapter 5 in discussing mortality) into a shorter number of years. Instead of women routinely having babies between the ages of 15 and 44, most women will have all of their children in their 20s and early 30s. The decline in parity progression ratios at the older ages may be accomplished especially with surgical contraception, although as I have suggested, the time-honored method was abstinence. In between the younger and older ages, the use of effective temporary contraception or the availability of abortion or emergency contraception provides couples with the opportunity to space children as they see most appropriate. In that process, they may decide, for example, not to have a third child now that they have two—making their own personal contribution to the fertility transition.

In Figure 6.7, I provide some examples of how age-specific fertility rates change over time in the context of the fertility transition, using illustrations from Latin America (Mexico), south Asia (India), west Asia (Jordan), and Africa (Kenya). You can see that each of these four countries had a variation on the same theme—the percentage decline in the age-specific fertility rates since the 1970s tends to be most extreme at the older and younger ages, and less dramatic in the young adult years. Keep in mind, however, that the majority of babies are born to those women in the 20–34 age group, so it is their absolute decline in fertility that makes the big difference in the long run.

All of the perspectives on the fertility transition discussed above assume that fertility will not decline until people see limiting fertility as being in their interest. The supply-demand framework assumes that people are making rational economic choices between the quantity and quality of children, whereas the innovation-diffusion

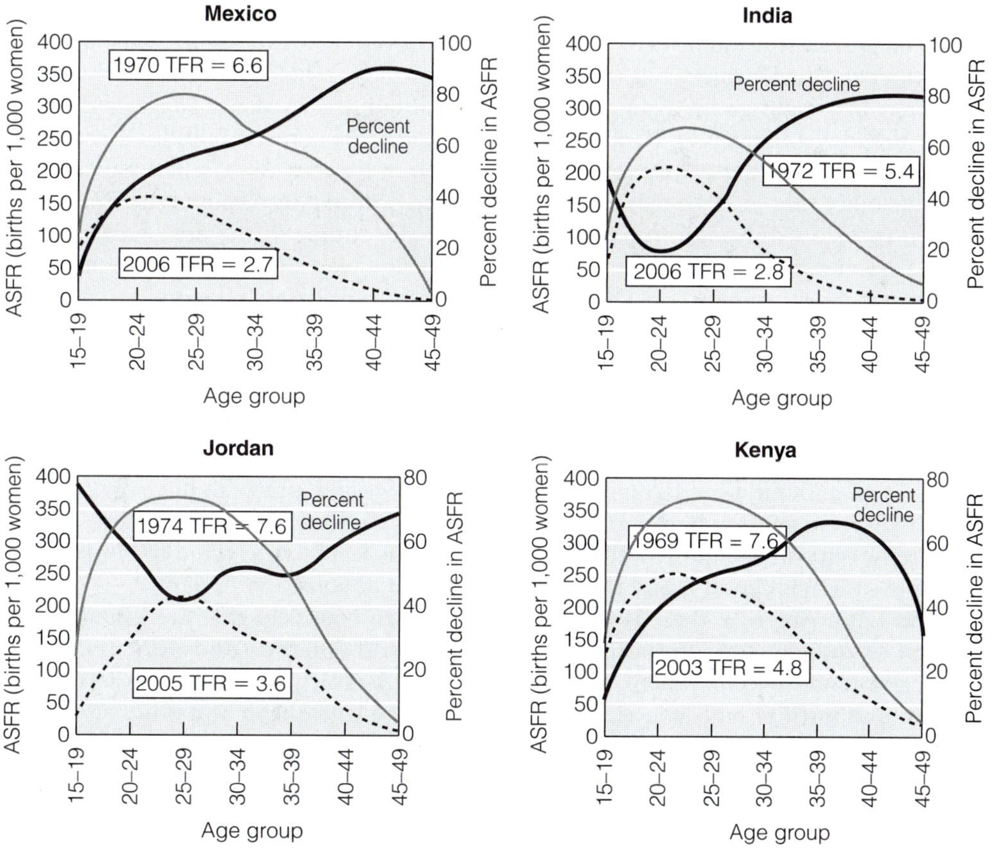

Figure 6.7 Changes in ASFRs in the Context of the Fertility Transition

Source: Data for the graphs are from United Nations Population Division (2010) and MeasureDHS (2010).

perspective argues that social pressure is the motivation, regardless of the underlying economic circumstances. Coale's three preconditions do not specify what the motivating factors might be, leaving open the possibility of some mix of economic and social motivations, sometimes stimulated or retarded by public policy decisions that make it easier or harder for people interested in controlling their reproduction actually to do so. In the real world, a combination of forces seems to produce the observed fertility transitions and we can see these combinations at work in the following illustrations drawn from different countries of the world.

Geographic Variability in the Fertility Transition

It is fair to say that by the early part of the twenty-first century there is no region of the world that has not experienced at least the early stages of the fertility transition, although it is still true in the world that a woman gives birth to more than four children every second (we've got to find this woman and stop her!). In 1950, Europe had the lowest fertility levels in the world, and it has now dropped to below replacement throughout that region. The major question being asked is whether or not it will ever rise, or indeed if it might even drop to a lower level. You can see in Table 6.4 that the UN's medium projections (typically the ones they think are most likely) suggest that fertility might go up again in Europe and, in fact, the evidence suggests that this may already be happening (Goldstein, Sobotka, and Jasilioniene 2009).

The most dramatic drop in fertility has been in Eastern Asia, where the average total fertility rate in 1950 was 5.42 but has since dropped by almost four children—down to 1.75—although it may rise a bit over the course of the next half century. The remainder of Asia continues to have fertility well above replacement level, although the United Nations thinks that all areas will drop to below replacement by the middle of this century.

Sub-Saharan Africa had very high fertility in 1950 and has experienced the slowest decline. The United Nations expects that at the middle of this century, sub-Saharan Africa will still have by far the highest fertility levels in the world, though significantly lower than current levels. Desired family size remains very high in western and middle sub-Saharan Africa, where women prefer to have six children and men have an even higher preference (Westoff 2010). However, northern Africa, where fertility still remains well above replacement level, is expected to continue its decline over this century, and the same is expected of southern Africa.

In Latin America, there is a distinction between countries that are heavily composed of indigenous populations (much of Central America and northern South America) and the remainder of the region. Latin America had very high fertility in 1950, and fertility has dropped most rapidly in the Caribbean and South America. Nonetheless, the United Nations thinks that the entire region could be below replacement level by the middle of this century. In order for this to happen, the proportion of births in the region that are unwanted—currently the highest rate in the world (Westoff 2010)—will have to decline substantially. In North America, there is a divergence between the United States, where fertility is just at replacement level, and Canada, where it has dropped to below replacement. Australia and New Zealand, like Canada, have taken a path more similar to Europe than to the U.S.

Table 6.4 Regional Differences in the Fertility Transition, 1950–2050

	Total Fertility Rates		
	1950–55	2010–15	2045–50
WORLD	4.92	2.49	2.02
More-developed regions	2.82	**1.65**	**1.80**
Less-developed regions	6.00	2.62	2.05
Least-developed countries	6.62	4.08	2.41
AFRICA	6.63	3.89	2.40
Eastern Africa	7.03	4.85	2.44
Middle Africa	6.03	5.18	2.48
Northern Africa	6.84	2.70	**1.97**
Southern Africa	6.22	2.49	**1.88**
Western Africa	6.42	4.82	2.58
ASIA	5.73	2.26	**1.90**
Eastern Asia	5.42	**1.75**	**1.83**
South-central Asia	6.04	2.60	**1.94**
South-eastern Asia	5.98	2.18	**1.89**
Western Asia	6.33	2.76	**1.98**
EUROPE	2.65	**1.53**	**1.80**
Eastern Europe	2.82	**1.43**	**1.79**
Northern Europe	2.38	**1.83**	**1.85**
Southern Europe	2.62	**1.50**	**1.80**
Western Europe	2.41	**1.59**	**1.79**
LATIN AMERICA AND THE CARIBBEAN	5.85	2.09	**1.82**
Caribbean	5.21	2.29	**1.90**
Central America	6.73	2.27	**1.85**
South America	5.66	2.00	**1.80**
NORTHERN AMERICA	3.33	**1.98**	**1.85**
Canada	3.65	**1.62**	**1.85**
United States of America	3.45	2.02	**1.85**
OCEANIA	3.83	2.39	**1.98**
Australia/New Zealand	3.25	**1.88**	**1.85**
Melanesia	6.29	3.58	2.18
Micronesia	6.20	2.36	**1.76**
Polynesia	6.74	2.73	**1.93**

Source: Data are from United Nations Population Division (2009; numbers in boldface type are total fertility rates that are below replacement level; data for 2010–15 and 2045–50 are based on the medium projections.

These regional trends give us a feel for what is happening, but not necessarily for why it's happening. It helps to take a look at a few countries in more detail to better understand the fertility transition.

Case Studies in the Fertility Transition

There are as many interesting stories of the fertility transition as there are countries and even subregions within countries, but for illustrative purposes I am going to choose first a country that has had low fertility for a long time and is now well below replacement level—the United Kingdom (while also commenting on some other European nations). Then I will review the situation in two of the world's most populous nations—China and the United States—each of which has taken a different path through the fertility transition.

United Kingdom and Other European Nations

Historical Background In England and other parts of Europe, the beginnings of a potential fertility decline may well have existed even before the Industrial Revolution touched off the dramatic rise in the standard of living. In English parishes, there is evidence that withdrawal (coitus interruptus) was used to reduce marital fertility during the late seventeenth and early eighteenth centuries, and it was apparently also a major reason for a steady decline in marital fertility in France during the late eighteenth and early nineteenth centuries. Indeed, it has been suggested that the root cause of France's fertility decline was that after the French Revolution the government, in 1793, introduced a change in inheritance from everything going only to the oldest son (*primogeniture*) to a system where property was to be divided among all sons (or daughters, if there were no sons)—a system known as *partible inheritance*. The French responded by deliberately limiting family size in order to restrict the number of heirs among whom the property would have to be divided (Jones 2002). The birth rate fell and has never recovered. The higher preindustrial birth rates in the European colonies of America rather than in Europe also point to the fact that fertility limitation in Europe was widely accepted and practiced, especially through the mechanism of deliberately delayed marriage (meaning abstinence, not cohabitation), as well as the other, more direct means, including abortion (Wrigley 1974).

The evidence for the use of some means of fertility control as far back as the eighteenth century in Europe is circumstantial, to be sure, but powerful nonetheless. Consider the comment by the great Scottish economist Adam Smith, writing in 1776, that "barrenness, so frequent among women of fashion, is very rare among those of inferior station. Luxury in the fair sex, while it enflames perhaps the passion for enjoyment, seems always to weaken, and frequently to destroy altogether, the powers of generation" (Smith 1776:I.viii.37).

The enormous economic and social upheaval of industrialization took place earlier in England than anywhere else, and by the first part of the nineteenth century, England was well into the Machine Age. For the average worker, however, it was not until the latter half of the nineteenth century that sustained increases in real wages actually occurred. During the first part of that century, the Napoleonic Wars were tripling the national debt in England, increasing prices by as much as 90 percent without an increase in production. Thus, during most of Malthus's professional life, his country was experiencing substantial inflation and job insecurity. These relatively adverse conditions undoubtedly contributed to a general decline in the birth rate during the first half of the nineteenth century, brought about largely by delayed marriage (Wrigley 1987). After about 1850, economic conditions improved considerably, and the first response was a rise in the birth rate (as the marriage rate increased), followed by a long-run decline. This was a period in which all of Ansley Coale's preconditions for a fertility decline existed: (1) People had apparently accepted calculated choice as a valid element, (2) people perceived advantages from lowered fertility, and (3) people were aware of at least reasonably effective means of birth control. As I already mentioned, the British were accustomed to thinking in terms of family limitation, and delayed marriage, abstinence, and coitus interruptus within marriage were known to be effective means to reduce fertility. In the second half of the nineteenth century, then, motivation to limit family size came in the form of larger numbers of surviving children combined with aspiration for higher standards of living.

It is important to remember that the restriction of fertility was in many ways a return to preindustrial family patterns, in which an average of about two children survived to adulthood in each generation (remember the concept of the net reproduction rate). Thus, as I mentioned earlier, mortality declines produced changes in the lives of people to which they had to respond. The English reacted in ways consistent with the theory of demographic change and response. They responded to population growth by migrating (to America, especially) and by delaying marriage, and then, only when those options were played out, did marital fertility clearly decline (Friedlander 1983). In a world now characterized by very open sexuality, it is sometimes hard to believe that large numbers of people were willing to suppress their sexuality in order to achieve some measure of economic success, but Szreter and Garrett (2000) remind us that "the available historical evidence suggests that the late marriage regime of early modern Britain entailed systematic sexual restraint among young adults up to their mid-20s, the point at which marriage could be realistically anticipated. A sexual culture of this sort might lend itself to restraint *after* marriage, as well, if and when the need arose" (p. 70).

The best-known explanation of the fertility decline in England in the latter half of the nineteenth century is that offered by J. A. Banks (1954) in *Prosperity and Parenthood* and its sequel, *Feminism and Family Planning in Victorian England* (Banks and Banks 1964). Banks's thesis is by now a familiar one: The rising standard of living in England, especially among the middle classes, gave rise to a decline in fertility by (1) raising expectations of upward social mobility, (2) creating fears of social slippage (you had to "keep up with the Joneses"), and (3) redefining the roles of women from housewife to a fragile luxury of a middle-class man.

Though it is true that birth rates dropped more quickly in the upper social strata of English society than in the lower social strata, by 1880 all segments of English society were experiencing fertility declines. From about 1880 to 1910, England shared with much of continental Europe in what Knodel and van de Walle (1979) called "the momentous revolution of family limitation." Fertility has continued on a slow downward trend since then, interrupted by a postwar baby boom, which peaked in the mid-1960s. Since about 1964, however, birth rates have resumed their downward trend—England's baby bust (Hobcraft 1996)—and England has settled into a consistent pattern of below-replacement-level fertility, with a TFR of only 1.8 children per woman, accomplished by widespread use of contraceptives (especially the pill), delayed marriage, delayed childbearing, and the use of surgical contraception when the desired family size has been achieved.

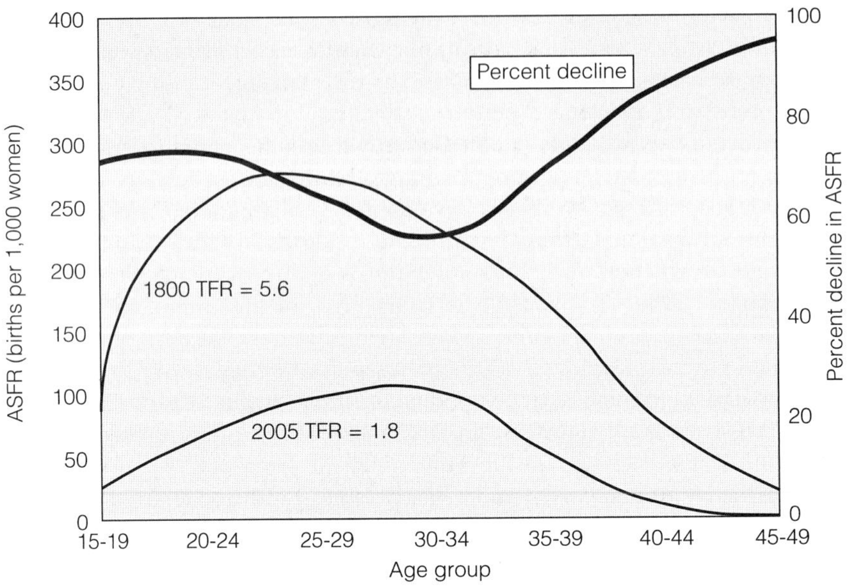

Figure 6.8 The Fertility Transition in England

Figure 6.8 shows the change in fertility that has taken place in England over the course of the past 200 years. As dramatic as the change has been, you can see that it follows the same pattern as the more recent declines in less-developed countries, as shown in Figure 6.7. In 1800, the TFR in England is estimated to have been 5.6 children per woman (Livi Bacci 2000). The transition down to a TFR of 1.8 means that contraception is used by 84 percent of sexually active couples (Population Reference Bureau 2009) and that, along with abortion, means that women do not have to delay sexual activity even though they delay marriage and/or having children. And surgical contraception means that when they decide to stop having children, it is a permanent decision.

Below-Replacement Fertility England mirrors other European nations, all of which currently have below-replacement-level fertility. There has been a good deal of hand-wringing over this in Europe because the low fertility, especially when combined with increasing life expectancy, is producing an increasingly older population with a shrinking base in the younger ages. As I mentioned in Chapter 2, governments are worried about how old-age pensions will be funded and how economic growth will be maintained if there are too few young people to carry the load. However, this low fertility should not be too surprising because it can be explained in terms of both the supply-demand framework and the diffusion of innovations.

Europeans grow up knowing that they and any children they have will almost certainly survive to a rather old age. They also know that highly effective contraceptives make it possible to engage in sexual activity without fear of pregnancy (and of course the use of condoms will protect them as well from sexually transmitted diseases, including HIV). Should the contraceptive fail, either emergency contraception or abortion is available. Thus, European women are in almost total control over the supply of children. The important question is how large is the demand for children? Surveys throughout Europe suggest that Europeans would prefer two children, but at the same time women are investing heavily in their own education and are seeking jobs and careers comparable to those of men. Though gender equity may be approachable on those two fronts, it is has been less obvious within marriage. Women are still expected to be the principal providers of care to children and to their husbands, and this extra burden placed on women has created a climate of caution about getting married and having those two children. Women know that they most likely will bear a disproportionate share of the burden of child rearing and household labor, while suffering substantial opportunity costs from delayed careers and lost wages.

The movement toward gender equity in education and in the labor force has thus not been matched by gender equity in domestic relationships (McDonald 2000), and so the demand for children has dropped to what we might think of as female replacement—a woman having a child (whether male or female) that allows her to experience reproduction and replacement, but not much more than that. This mismatch seems to be greatest in southern Europe, most notably Italy and Spain, where attitudes about the woman's role in the family are more traditional than in the rest of Europe (de Sandre 2000; Dalla Zuanna 2001; Kertzer et al. 2009). Chesnais (1996) and McDonald (2000) have offered the suggestion that in highly developed countries, a *rise* in the status of women within family-oriented institutions may be necessary to bring fertility back up to replacement level. Consistent with this view, a study in Spain has shown that fertility is higher in that country in those regions where child care is more readily available (Baizan 2009).

China

At the time of the Communist revolution in 1949, the average woman in China was bearing 6.2 children and the population, which was already more than half a billion, was growing rapidly. The government of the People's Republic of China realized decades ago that the population problem was enormous, and it implemented the largest, most ambitious, most significant, and certainly the most controversial policy to slow population growth ever undertaken in the world. The 1978 constitution of the People's Republic of China declared that "the state advocates and encourages birth planning" and the reasons for this were that (1) too rapid an increase in population is detrimental to the acceleration of capital accumulation, (2) rapid population increase hinders the efforts to raise the scientific and cultural level of the whole nation quickly, and (3) rapid population growth is detrimental to the improvement of the standard of living (Muhua 1979).

The goal of the Chinese government at that time was, incredibly enough, to achieve zero population growth (ZPG) by the year 2000, with the population stabilizing at 1.2 billion people. To accomplish this meant that at least one generation of Chinese parents had to limit their fertility to only one child, because the youthful age structure in China in the 1970s meant a high proportion of people were in their childbearing years. If all of those women had two children, the population would still be growing too fast. How did they go about trying to achieve this goal? The first step was to suggest that people should delay marriage and childbearing, while also trying to convince women not to have a third child (third or higher-order births accounted for 30 percent of all births in 1979). The second step was to promote the one-child family. These goals have been accomplished partly by increased social pressure (propaganda, party worker activism, and almost certainly coercion as well) and partly by the increased manufacture and distribution of contraceptives.

The heart of the policy as originally formulated, though, was a carefully drawn system of economic incentives (rewards) for one-child families and disincentives (punishments) for larger families. However, the one-child policy is directed by the central government, but implemented at the local level in ways that vary from place in place (Gu Baochang et al. 2007), with the Han majority finding themselves under greater pressure to conform (and thus having lower fertility) than minority group members, who comprise about 10 percent of the Chinese population (Poston, Chang, and Dan 2006).

In general, the policy has been that in cities couples with only one child who pledge that they will have no more children can apply for a one-child certificate. The certificate entitles the couple to a monthly allowance to help with the cost of child rearing until the child reaches age 14. Furthermore, one-child couples receive preference over others in obtaining housing and are allotted the same amount of space as a two-child family; their child is given preference in school admissions and job applications; and the parents with a one-child certificate are promised a larger-than-average pension when they retire. Some local areas do allow a second child if the first is a girl (the so-called 1.5 rule) and some allow a second child only if the couple agrees to space the children by five or six years (Gu Baochang et al. 2007).

In the countryside, the incentives were designed to be a bit different. Depending upon the local area, one-child rural families might receive additional monthly work points (which determine the rural payments in cash and in kind) until the child reaches age 14. These one-child families also get the same grain ration as a two-child family. In addition, all rural families receive the same-sized plot for private cultivation, regardless of family size, thus indirectly rewarding the small family. Although each province and prefecture in China has been encouraged by the central government to tailor specific policies to meet the particular needs of its residents, some of the more widely implemented policies have included an increasingly heavy tax on each child after the second and the expectation that for each child after the second, parents will pay full maternity costs as well as full medical and educational costs.

Figure 6.9 reveals that the total fertility rate was already declining in China at the time the government implemented the one-child policy, and it may well be argued that the government policy merely reinforced changes in reproduction that were already well under way. Furthermore, fertility fell not only in urban areas where the motivation for small families might be greatest, but in rural areas as well (Attané 2001). In 1971, the government had instituted the *wan xi shao* (later, longer, fewer) campaign and that helped to accelerate fertility decline in China prior to the implementation of the one-child policy.

The one-child policy in China was never intended to be anything more than an interim measure that would finally put the brake on population growth in that country (Greenhalgh 1986). From the beginning, the plan had been to ease back to a two-child family after hitting the 1.2 billion level of population size. Nonetheless, in 2007 the Chinese government completed a three-year review of the one-child policy and concluded that it needed to remain in place for the time being to ensure that the population did not go much beyond the current level of 1.3 billion (Batson 2007).

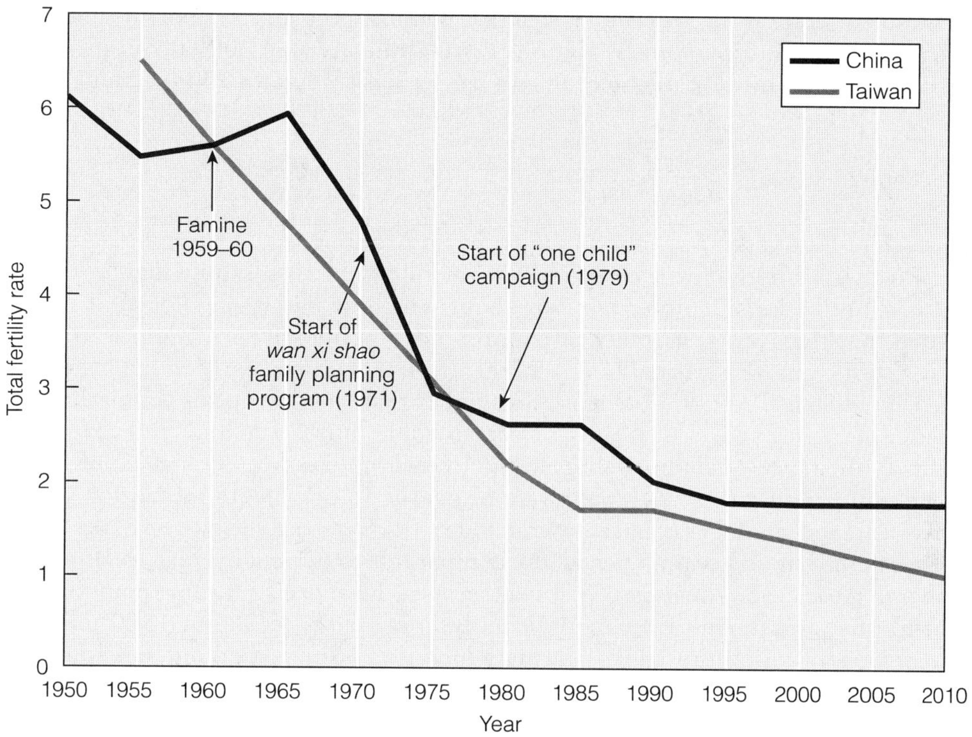

Figure 6.9 The Fertility Transition in China and Taiwan

Source: Data for China are from United Nations Population Division (2009); data for Taiwan from 1955 to 1990 are from Freedman, Change and Sun (1994) and for more recent dates from the Population Reference Bureau (2009).

Several researchers have concluded that socioeconomic development in China has been at least as important a factor as government policy in motivating couples to want fewer children (Poston and Gu 1987; Tu 2000; Attané 2001; Gu Baochang et al. 2007), although the government's attitude certainly facilitated and enhanced those motivations (Greenhalgh, Chuzhu, and Nan 1994). It is also intriguing to note the cultural similarities between mainland China and Taiwan (which, as you know, is actually claimed by China as part of its territory) and the coincidence of rapid fertility declines in the two countries—one with a clearly defined set of incentives and disincentives, and the other with a more normal voluntary family planning program, but both with rapidly expanding economies during the latter part of the twentieth century (Freedman, Chang, and Sun 1994). The overall comparisons are shown in Figure 6.9, where you can see that Taiwan now has a self-imposed one-child level of fertility—the lowest fertility level in the world.

I should note that there is universal agreement that fertility in China is well below replacement level, but there is not agreement on precisely what the level is, because of concerns over data quality as well as the belief that some children may be hidden from official counts (Morgan, Guo Zhigang, and Hayford 2009). Furthermore, despite the intense publicity given to forced abortions, the United Nations estimates that 90 percent of married women of reproductive age are using a modern contraceptive in China, with the IUD being the most popular "temporary" method, backed up by abortion (United Nations Population Division 2009a). Surgical contraception is the method of choice once a couple has completed childbearing.

The United States

Historical Background Around 1800, when Malthus was writing his *Essay on Population*, he found the growth rate in America to be remarkably high and commented on the large frontier families about which he had read. Indeed, it is estimated that the average number of children born per woman in colonial America was about eight. It is probably no exaggeration to say that early in the history of the United States, American fertility was higher than any European population had ever experienced. Early data are not very reliable, but Coale and Zelnick (1963) made estimates of crude birth rates in the United States going back as far as 1800; these indicate that the crude birth rate of nearly 55 per 1,000 population would have matched the highest in the world today (in Niger). Even in 1855, the crude birth rate in America was 43 per 1,000, comparable to current average levels in sub-Saharan Africa. The American Civil War seems to have been a turning point in marital fertility, and fertility declined virtually unabated from about 1870 until the Great Depression of the 1930s, during which time it bottomed out at a low level only recently reapproached (Hacker 2003). Why the precipitous drop?

As I discussed in Chapter 2, almost all voluntary migrants to the North American continent up to the late nineteenth century were western Europeans. The people who made up much of the population of the early United States came from a social environment in which fertility limitation was known and practiced. Despite the frontier movement westward, America in the century after the Revolution was urbanizing and commercializing rapidly. Furthermore, the United States was experiencing the process of secularization, and people's lives were increasingly loosened from the control of church and state. Malthus had commented that, with respect to all aspects of life, including reproduction, "despotism, ignorance, and oppression produced irresponsibility; civil and political liberty and an informed public gave grounds for expecting prudence and restraint" (quoted by Wrigley 1988:39). Bolton and Leasure (1979) have shown that throughout Europe, the early decline in fertility occurred near the time of revolution, democratic reform, or the growth of a nationalist movement. Analogously, Leasure (1989) found that the decline in fertility in the United States in the nineteenth century was closely associated with a rise in what he calls the "spirit of autonomy," measured early in the century by the proportion of the population in an area belonging to the more tolerant Protestant denominations (Congregational, Presbyterian, Quaker, Unitarian, and Universalist) and measured later in the century by educational level.

Lower fertility was accomplished by a rise in the average age at marriage and by various means of birth control within marriage, including coitus interruptus, abortion (even though it was illegal), and extended breastfeeding (Sanderson 1995). Nineteenth-century America also witnessed the secret spread of knowledge about douching and periodic abstinence, neither of which is necessarily very effective on the face of it, but the fact that women were searching for ways to prevent pregnancy is clear evidence of the motivation that women had to limit fertility (Brodie 1994).

New immigrants arriving in the United States in the late nineteenth and early twentieth centuries came especially from southern and eastern Europe, where ideas of contraception were less well known than in western Europe. As a nurse in New York City working among immigrants in the first decade of the twentieth century, Margaret Sanger witnessed firsthand the tragic health consequences for mothers and their babies of having too many children. Sanger herself decided to have only three children after watching her own Irish Catholic mother die prematurely as a result of having 11 children. Her patients kept asking her about the secrets that middle-class women must know that allowed them to keep their families small. But the secrets she did have at that time, including coitus interruptus and abstinence, were dismissed by women as being impossible without a husband's cooperation, which they knew they would never get. In 1912, after helplessly watching a young mother with several children die from a botched self-inflicted abortion, she "resolved to seek out the root of evil, to do something to change the destiny of mothers whose miseries were vast as the sky" (Sanger 1938:92).

Sanger immersed herself in finding out all she could about contraception and began to write on the subject, landing herself in continuing legal difficulty for publishing "pornographic" material. In 1915, she was introduced to a newly designed diaphragm developed in the Netherlands. It required a health professional to fit a woman for the right size, but it was far more effective than anything else that existed at that time and it was probably the most effective contraceptive in the world until the pill came along in the 1960s (Douglas 1970). The next year, in 1916, Sanger opened her notorious birth control clinic in Brooklyn. She spent the remainder of her life trying to legalize the publication of information about family planning, and to legalize the distribution and use of contraceptives themselves.

Sanger, then, played a very critical role in the contraceptive revolution; she was the founder in 1939 of the Planned Parenthood Federation of America and in 1952 helped to create the International Planned Parenthood Federation. Astoundingly, until 1965, it was technically illegal in the United States for even a married couple to use any method of birth control. In that year the U.S. Supreme Court ruled in *Griswold v. Connecticut* that married couples had a right to privacy that extended to the use of contraceptives. The Court granted that same right to unmarried couples in 1972, and the following year extended the same argument to the legalization of abortion.

After World War I, the use of condoms became widespread in the United States (and in Europe as well) and, along with withdrawal and abstinence (and the clandestine use of the diaphragm), contributed to very low levels of fertility during the Depression (Himes 1976). The condom was available for sale not because it was a contraceptive (that use was illegal) but rather because it was a "prophylactic" that prevented the spread of sexually transmitted disease. During the Depression, fertility fell to levels below generational replacement. Though the United States was not unique in this respect, that bottoming out in the United States did cap the most sustained drop in fertility the world had seen up to that time. It was undoubtedly a response to the economic insecurity of the period, especially since that insecurity had come about as a quick reversal of increasing prosperity. Fear of social slippage was thus a very likely motive for keeping families small. The American demographic response for many couples was to defer marriage and to postpone having children, hoping to marry later on and have a larger family. Gallup polls starting in 1936 indicate that the average ideal family size was three children, and that most people felt that somewhere between two and four was what they would like. Thus, people were apparently having fewer children than they would have liked to have under ideal circumstances.

In 1933, the birth rate hit rock bottom because women of all ages, regardless of how many children they already had, lowered their level of reproduction. This was, however, mainly a matter of timing. From 1934 on, the birth rates for first and second children rose steadily (reflecting people getting married and having small families), while birth rates for third and later children continued to decline (reflecting the postponement of larger families) until about 1940 (Grabill, Kiser, and Whelpton 1958). Just as the United States was entering World War II in late 1941 and 1942, there was a momentary rise in the birth rate as husbands went off to war, followed by a lull during the war. However, the end of World War II signaled one of the most dramatic demographic phenomena in North American history—the **baby boom**.

The Baby Boom Most of you can probably appreciate that immediately after the end of a war, families and lovers are reunited and the birth rate goes up temporarily as people make up for lost time. This occurred in the United States as well as in England and Canada and several of the other countries actively involved in World War II. Surprisingly, these baby booms lasted not for one or two years, but for several years after the war. Birth rates in the United States continued to rise through the 1950s, as the total fertility rate went from 2.19 in 1940 to 3.58 in 1957, an increase of nearly 1.5 children per woman. Note that in the United States the term "baby boomers" is usually applied to people born between 1946 and 1964, but the "boom" peaked in 1957—12 years after the war ended.

An important contribution to the baby boom was the fact that after the war women started marrying earlier and having their children sooner after marriage. For example, in 1940, the average first child was born when the mother was 23.2 years old, whereas by 1960, the average age had dropped to 21.8. This had the effect of bunching up the births of babies, which in earlier times would have been more spread out. Further, not only were young women having children at younger ages, but older women were having babies at older-than-usual ages, due at least in part to their having postponed births during the Depression and the war. After the war, many women stopped postponing and added to the crop of babies each year. These somewhat mechanical aspects of a "catching up" process explain only the early part of the baby boom. What accounts for its prolongation?

We do not have a definitive answer to this question (and remember that it occurred in other countries besides just the United States), but a widely discussed explanation is offered by Easterlin (1978; 1968), which I mentioned in Chapter 3 as the relative cohort size hypothesis—a spin-off of the supply-demand perspective. Easterlin begins his analysis by noting that the long-term decline in the birth rate in the United States was uneven, sometimes happening more rapidly than at other times. In particular, the birth rate declined less rapidly during times of greater economic growth. If a young man could easily find a well-paying job, he could get married and have children; if job hunting was more difficult, marriage (and children within marriage) would be postponed.

Thus, it was natural that the postwar baby boom occurred, because the economy was growing rapidly during that time. What was unusual was that economic growth was more rapid than in previous decades, and the resultant demand for labor was less easily met by large numbers of immigrants, because in the 1920s the United States had passed very restrictive immigration laws. Furthermore, the number of young people looking for work was rather small because of the low birth rates in the 1920s and 1930s. Finally, the demand for labor was not easily met by females, since there was a distinct bias against married women working in the United States, particularly a woman who had any children. Some states passed legislation that actually restricted married women from working in certain occupations. To be sure, women did work, especially single women, but their opportunities were limited. Thus, economic expansion, restricted immigration, a small labor force, and discrimination against women in the labor force meant that young men looking for jobs could find relatively well-paying positions, marry early, and have children. Indeed, income was rising so rapidly after the war and on into the 1950s that it was relatively easy for couples to achieve the lifestyle to which they were accustomed, or even to which they might modestly aspire, and still have enough money left over to have several children.

In 1958, the crude birth rate and the general fertility rate in the United States registered clear declines—a downward change that carried into the late 1970s—as you can see in Figure 6.10. In the early 1960s there was still no discernible trend toward smaller families. The ideal family size among Americans had remained quite stable between 1952 and 1966, ranging only between 3.3 and 3.6 children. But in 1967, Blake discovered in a national sample taken the year before that "young women (those under age 30) gave 'two' children as their ideal more frequently than

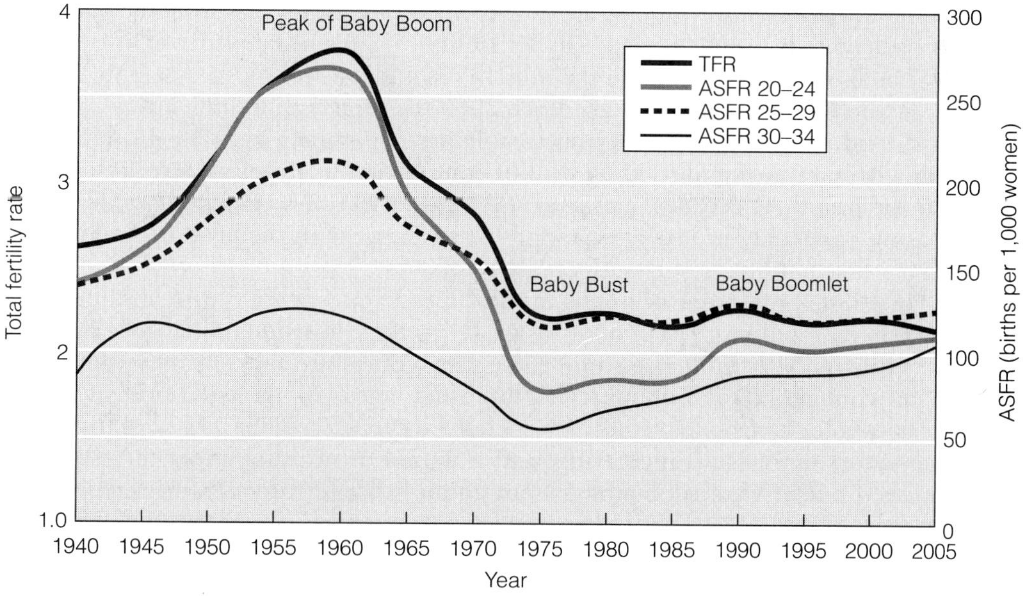

Figure 6.10 The U.S. Baby Boom, Baby Bust, Baby Boomlet, and Beyond

Source: Data are from National Center for Health Statistics (1990), Table 1–6; and Martin et al. (2009), Table 8.

they had in any surveys since the early nineteen-fifties" (Blake 1967:20). This was the first solid evidence that the desired family size might be on the way down—that the baby bust period had arrived.

The Baby Bust, Baby Boomlet, and Beyond Social and economic factors in the late 1960s suggested that fertility might continue to decline for a while. The rate of economic growth had slackened off, and there was no longer a labor shortage. As Norman Ryder (1965:845) very presciently noted:

> In the United States today the cohorts entering adulthood are much larger than their predecessors. In consequence they were raised in crowded housing, crammed together in schools, and are now threatening to be a glut on the labor market. Perhaps they will have to delay marriage, because of too few jobs or houses, and have fewer children. It is not entirely coincidental that the American cohorts whose fertility levels appear to be the highest in this century were those with the smallest number.

This was, of course, the kernel of Easterlin's relative cohort hypothesis, and younger couples did indeed alter their fertility behavior. Almost all of the fertility decline was due to a drop in marital fertility (Gibson 1976), mainly as a result of more efficient use of contraception, and to a rise in the use of abortion. As fertility dropped, family size ideals dropped as well. Gallup surveys showed that the proportion of white women under age 30 saying that two children was an ideal number rose dramatically from a low of 16 percent in 1957 to 57 percent in 1971 (Blake 1974). The decline in fertility following the baby boom peak thus seemed to signal a major shift in the norms surrounding parenthood in American society. "Motherhood is becoming a legitimate question of *preferences*. Women are now entitled to seek rewards from the pursuit of activities other than childrearing" (Ryder 1990:477, emphasis added).

The baby bust troughed in the mid-1970s and was followed by a baby boomlet, as you can see in Figure 6.10. Since 2000 the total fertility rate has pushed upward, and the rise is especially noticeable among women ages 30–34. However, these general trends hide a great deal of complexity in American fertility patterns over the past three decades, including: (1) a rise in out-of-wedlock births; (2) an increasing variability in family size; and (3) an increase in the proportion births to racial/ethnic minority groups, especially Hispanics.

In 1980, 18 percent of births in the United States were out-of-wedlock, but by 2006 that had more than doubled to 39 percent (Martin et al. 2009). The general explanation for this rise seems to be that women are engaging in sexual activity at younger ages, but marrying at older ages, in an environment where out-of-wedlock births have become socially acceptable. Thus, the sexually active time before marriage is increasing, and it would be unusual under these circumstances if out-of-wedlock births did not go up, since fertility control is rarely perfect. In 1980 the birth rate for married women was five times higher than for unmarried women, and it was especially teenagers who were having the babies without being married. In 2006, the birth rate for married women was not even twice that of unmarried women, and it was women in their twenties who had the highest rates of out-of-wedlock births. Indeed, teenage birth rates have been declining since the early 1990s.

At the same time that teenage birth rates are going down, the rates for women 30 and older have been going up, shifting the average age at motherhood (the mean length of generation, as I discussed earlier) into the late 20s. Although most women do eventually have a child, the percentage of voluntarily childless women is higher than it used to be, yet there is also an increase in the number of women having their third or fourth child.

One of the important underlying causes of this increasing variability in birth patterns is, as you might suspect, the increasing diversity of the American population. Figure 6.11 shows the levels and trends in the total fertility rate for major racial/ethnic groups in the United States. Although the overall TFR for the country was virtually the same in 2006 as it had been 16 years earlier, there were clear differences among groups in the patterns. Non-Hispanic whites remained unchanged at a level well below replacement, very similar in fact to the TFRs in France and the United Kingdom. Non-Hispanic blacks experienced a drop from 2.5 children per woman to 2.2 per woman. Asians and Pacific Islanders experienced almost no change, with a level just below replacement. The Native American population showed a drop from just above replacement to well below replacement. The Hispanic population had the same TFR in 2006 as in 1990, although over that time it dropped a bit and then rose again. Most importantly, however, the birth rate was nearly one child higher on average than any other group, with a TFR of 3.0, led by Hispanics of Mexican origin.

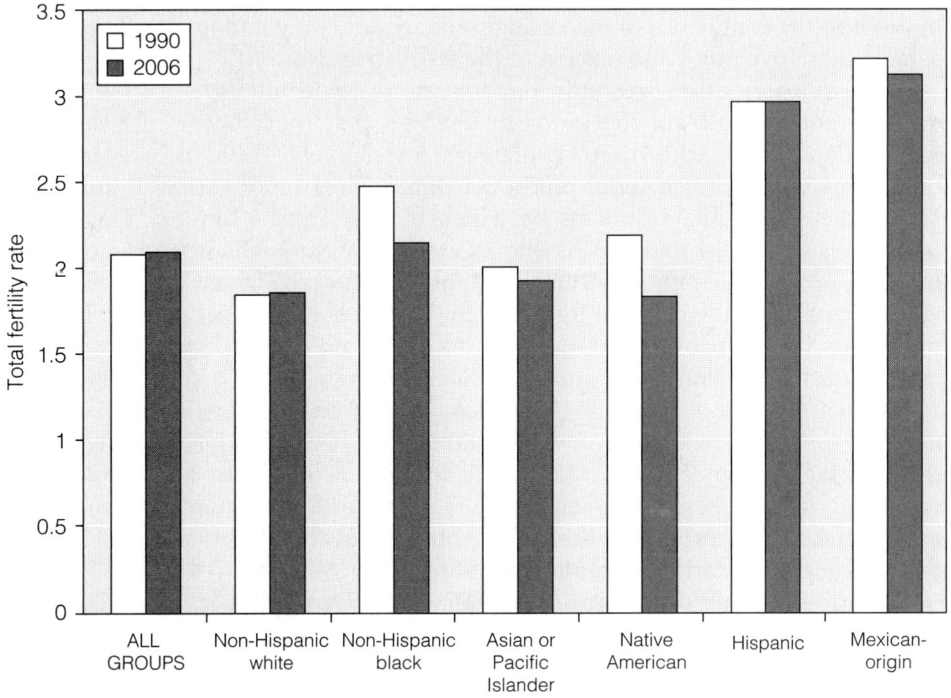

Figure 6.11 Changes over Time in Fertility by Ethnic Group, United States
Source: Data are from Martin et al. (2009), Tables 4 and 8.

The high Hispanic fertility seems to be due especially to the influx of immigrants from Mexico since the 1980s who have brought with them views of the world that place a higher value on the number of children in a family than is generally true of the native-born non-Hispanic population (Bean, Swicegood, and Berg 2000). Fertility has been declining steadily in Mexico since the 1970s, but it is still higher than in the United States, so immigrants continue to come from a culture with expectations for a larger family size. However, current estimates of fertility in Mexico indicate a TFR of 2.7, as noted in Figure 6.7, and that is actually lower than the TFR for the Mexican-origin population in the United States. No one is yet sure whether or when Hispanics in the United States will lower their fertility to replacement level, but that will be a decisive factor in future fertility levels because it is already the case that in populous southwestern states such as California and Texas, a majority of births are to women of Mexican origin, and Hispanics are contributing disproportionately to births throughout the United States (Johnson and Lichter 2008).

Summary and Conclusion

Fertility has both a biological and a social component. The capacity to reproduce is biological (although it can certainly be influenced by the environment), but we have to look to the social environment to find out why women are having a particular number of children. For most of human history, fertility was high and "natural" because every group had to overcome high mortality if it was to survive and not disappear. But, the confluence of increasing standards of living and lower mortality has changed those dynamics and has led to the fertility transition.

Ansley Coale's three preconditions for a fertility decline offer a useful framework for conceptualizing the kinds of changes that must occur in a society if reproduction is going to drop to significantly lower levels. These include the acceptance of calculated choice about reproductive behavior, a motivation to limit fertility, and the availability of means by which fertility can be limited. The fertility transition is viewed by many as having an essentially economic interpretation, emphasizing the relationship between the supply of children (which is driven by biological factors) and the demand for children (based on a couple's calculations about the costs and benefits of children), given the costs (monetary and psychosocial) of fertility regulation. This is the supply-demand framework. It is complemented by those who argue that fertility limitation is an innovation that is diffused through societies across social strata and over distances in ways that may be independent of economic factors. Once motivated to limit fertility, people must have some means available to do so. These are generally referred to as the proximate determinants of fertility, and include especially the age at which regular intercourse begins, the use of contraception, breastfeeding, and abortion.

Theories of the fertility transition emphasize the role of wealth and economic development in lowering levels of fertility, although it is clear that these are sufficient but not necessary reasons for fertility to decline. You must also assess the overall social environment in which change is occurring. When there are desired and scarce resources, wealth, prestige, status, education, and other related factors often help to lower fertility because they change the way people perceive and think about the social world and their place in it. Human beings are amazingly adaptable when they want to be. When people believe that having no children or only a few children is in their best interest, they behave accordingly. Sophisticated contraceptive techniques make it easier, but they are not necessary, as the histories of fertility decline in places like the United Kingdom and the United States illustrate.

One of the most important ways in which societies change in the modern world is through migration. Migrants bring not only their bodies but also their ideas with them when they move, and as communication and transportation get increasingly easier, they are more apt to diffuse ideas and innovations back to their place of origin. In the following chapter, we turn our attention, then, to this next aspect of the demographic transition: the migration transition.

Main Points

1. The fertility transition represents the shift from "natural fertility" to more deliberate fertility limitation, and is associated with a drop in fertility at all ages, but especially at the older ages (beyond the 30s) and younger ages (under 20).
2. Fertility refers to the number of children born to women (or fathered by men), whereas fecundity refers to the biological capacity to produce children.
3. For most of human history, high mortality meant that societies were more concerned with maintaining reasonably high fertility levels, rather than contemplating a decline in fertility—surviving children, not children ever born, was the goal.
4. Ansley Coale's three preconditions for a fertility decline include: (1) acceptance of calculated choice in reproductive decision making; (2) motivations to limit fertility; and (3) the availability of means by which fertility can be regulated.
5. The supply-demand perspective on the fertility transition suggests that couples strive to maintain a balance between the potential supply of children and the demand (desired number of surviving children), given the cost of fertility regulation.
6. The innovation-diffusion model of fertility draws on sociological and anthropological evidence that much of human behavior is driven by the diffusion of new innovations—both technological and attitudinal—that may have little to do with a rational calculus of costs and benefits.
7. Government public policy may influence the course of the fertility transition by stimulating or retarding the motivations for limiting fertility and/or the availability of means of fertility control.
8. The fertility transition is typically accomplished through a later age at marriage, through older women deciding not to have that additional child, and through women in their prime reproductive years using effective means of fertility control, including especially contraception and abortion.
9. Virtually all wealthy societies now have below-replacement fertility levels, and in almost all less developed nations in the world today there are genuine stirrings of a fertility decline, as high-fertility norms and behavior give way to low-fertility preferences.

10. Some women wonder if they should have a baby after 35, but the answer is: No, 35 is probably enough. On the other hand, if your parents never had children, the chances are that you won't either.

Questions for Review

1. How have the three preconditions for a fertility decline played out thus far in your own life?
2. Do you agree that the supply-demand framework and the innovation/diffusion theories seem like complementary perspectives on the fertility transition, rather than competing with each other? Defend your answer.
3. How do think your perspective on the number of children you want to have in your lifetime would differ if you lived in western Europe as compared to living in sub-Saharan Africa?
4. What are the arguments for and against the idea that fertility control is a moral dilemma rather than preventive medicine?
5. Why is it that different racial/ethnic groups in the United States have such different levels and trends in fertility? How do the perspectives on the fertility transition help us to understand these differences?

Suggested Readings

1. Rodolfo A. Bulatao and John B. Casterline, Editors, 2001, *Global Fertility Transition, A Supplement to Volume 27 of Population and Development Review* (New York: Population Council).
   This collection of research papers and commentaries reviews the rather dramatic changes that emerged in world fertility levels at the end of the twentieth century, and which are setting the stage for demographic change in the twenty-first century.
2. John B. Casterline, Editor, 2001, *Diffusion Processes and Fertility Transition* (Washington, DC: National Academy Press).
   The decline of fertility even in relatively low-income countries has spurred research into the processes of diffusion that can help us understand why and when the fertility transition occurs, and this book looks at these issues from a variety of angles.
3. C. Y. Cyrus Chu and Ronald Lee, Editors, 2000, *Population and Economic Change in East Asia (A Supplement to Volume 26 of Population and Development Review)* (New York: Population Council).
   This book offers detailed insight into the fertility transitions that have taken place rather suddenly in East Asia over the past few decades. Much of the economic miracle of Asia is related to its rapidly changing demographic structure, fueled in part by a rapid decline in fertility, and this book discusses these issues in depth.
4. V. M. Zlidar, R. Gardner, S. O. Rutsetin, L. Morris, H. Goldberg, and K. Johnson, 2003, "New Survey Findings: The Reproductive Revolution Continues." *Population Reports*, Series M, No. 17. (Baltimore: Johns Hopkins Bloomberg School of Public Health, the INFO Project), http://www.populationreports.org/m17.

This report is packed with data and analyses summarizing recent research on fertility trends, contraceptive use, fertility preferences, and the relationship between the fertility transition and other aspects of reproductive health.

5. Fred R. Harris, Editor, *The Baby Bust: Who Will Do the Work? Who Will Pay the Taxes?* (New York: Rowman & Littlefield Publishers, Inc), 2006.
   This is a policy-oriented book, including chapters by prominent demographers, addressing the societal impact in the richer nations of the long-term trend toward below replacement fertility.

Websites of Interest

Remember that websites are not as permanent as books and journals, so I cannot guarantee that each of the following websites still exists at the moment you are reading this. You may have to Google the name of the organization to find the current web address.

1. **http://info.k4health.org/RHGateway/index.shtml**
   This website at the Johns Hopkins University is actually a portal or gateway to other sites on its server and on the Internet covering a wide range of topics related to reproductive health, including contraceptive methods and many of the issues covered in this chapter. It provides a good set of navigation and search tools so you can find the information you are looking for.
2. **http://www.measuredhs.com**
   Most of the information that we have about fertility and reproductive health in developing countries comes from the Demographic and Health Surveys (DHS), conducted by ICF Macro as part of the Measure project. At their website you can produce your own summary of results by using the *DHS STATcompiler.*
3. **http://www.un.org/esa/population/publications/WCU2009/Main.html**
   The United Nations Population Division has put together an Excel spreadsheet summarizing information about contraceptive utilization for most developing countries in the world. Of course, much of this information is drawn from Demographic and Health Surveys.
4. **http://www.unfpa.org/**
   The UNFPA is the United Nations Population Fund—the population "outreach" arm of the UN. They publish an informative annual report that is available at this website and recent volumes have all focused on issues of reproductive rights and gender equity and their relationship (implied or explicit) to the fertility transition.
5. **http://www.smith.edu/libraries/libs/ssc/prh/prh-intro.html**
   The Population and Reproductive Health Oral History Project at Smith College includes interviews with key people throughout the world who have been instrumental in implementing the dramatic fertility transition that occurred in the twentieth century.

CHAPTER 7
The Migration Transition

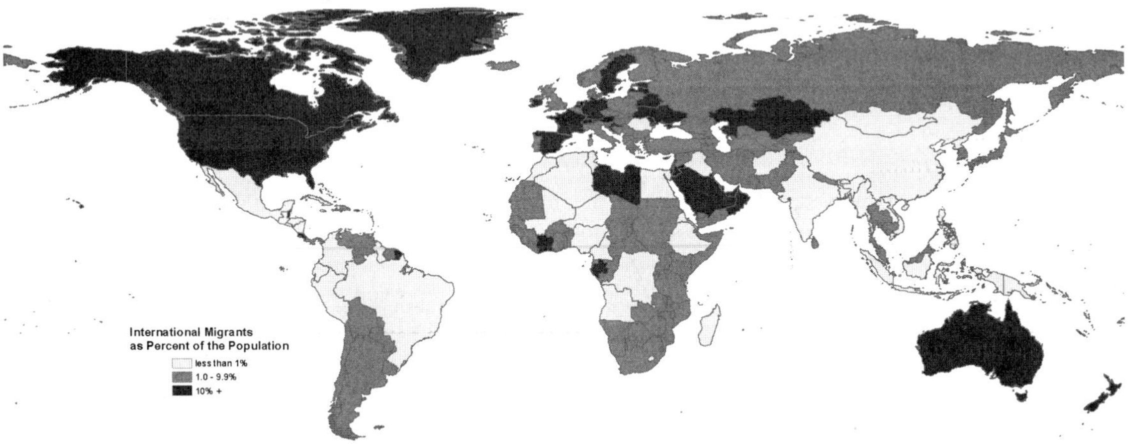

Figure 7.1 Map of the World According to the Percent That Is Foreign Stock

"The sole cause of man's unhappiness," quipped Pascal in the seventeenth century, "is that he does not know to stay quietly in his room." If this is so, unhappiness is enjoying unprecedented popularity as people are choosing to leave their rooms, so to speak, in record numbers. Sometimes they are fleeing from unhappiness; sometimes they are producing it. Always they are responding to and, in their turn, creating change. Because migration brings together people who have probably grown up with quite different views of the world, ways of approaching life, attitudes, and behavior patterns, it contributes to many of the tensions that confront the world, leading Kingsley Davis many years ago to comment that "so dubious are the advantages of immigration that one wonders why the governments of industrial nations favor it" (1974:105).

Even if a country tried to slam its doors to immigrants, however, would it stop people from migrating? More than 75 million people are being added to the world's population each year, and there is still a youth bulge in many less developed countries that strains local economic resources because there just aren't enough jobs to go around. What are these people to do? As it becomes ever more complex to find a niche in the world economy, a would-be worker is often compelled to move. An old Mexican saying goes, "Don't ask God to give it to you, ask Him to put you where it is." "Where it is" for many in Mexico is the United States. Today's pilgrims are from places such as Jalisco, Sinaloa, and Michoacán. They look to their northern neighbor for economic advancement in life and, although entrants from Mexico often cross the border with every intention of returning home, many never do. Similar tales are told of Algerians migrating to France, Moroccans to Spain, and Turks to Germany.

What Is the Migration Transition?

This vast transnational migration is part of the **migration transition** that is a component of the broader demographic transition, as I discussed earlier. Population growth changes the ratio of people to resources, and this forces various kinds of local adjustment. One such adjustment is to move somewhere else—to "get out of town" or to "head west, young person." Humans have been migrating throughout history (or else we would not be found in every nook and cranny of the globe), but the advent of relatively inexpensive and quick ground, water, and air transportation has given migration a new dimension at the very same time (and for many of the same reasons) that rapidly declining mortality has accelerated population growth. Migration may occur within the same country (**internal migration**) or between countries (**international migration**). In either case, migration within the context of the demographic transition often involves people moving from rural to urban areas—an important enough topic on its own that I have devoted the entirety of Chapter 9 to the *urban transition.*

Migration has no biological components in the way that mortality and fertility do. As far as we know, humans as a species are by nature neither sedentary (prone to staying in one place) nor inherently mobile (prone to moving from place to place). At the same time, the fact that we study migration rather than immobility means we assume that people prefer not to move and that it is the moving that requires explanation. We accept the idea that humans have an innate sense of and attachment to place that may transcend rational decision making about the desirability of staying in one place or moving to another.

The relationship of migration to the demographic transition arises from the fact that control of mortality and fertility has historically occurred within the context of urban places and then been diffused to rural areas. The population growth resulting from the decline in mortality in rural areas creates the paradoxical situation in which many of the people working in agriculture need to be replaced by machines so that enough food can be grown for a burgeoning population. Thus, people become less useful in agriculture as the population grows. Fortunately, the same forces creating this situation typically are creating employment opportunities in cities, and together these changes in both rural and urban economies help to spur the movement of the population from rural to urban places.

However, even if there were no demographic transition—and even when all demographic transitions are completed—migration still has the potential to profoundly alter a community or an entire country within a short time. In-migration and out-migration can increase or decrease population size, respectively, far more quickly than either mortality or fertility. And even if the number of in-migrants just equals the number of out-migrants, the flow of people in and out will affect the social and economic structure of a community.

Migration, then, is a huge topic of tremendous importance for all human societies, regardless of levels of fertility and mortality. At the same time, however, migration is influenced by relative levels of mortality and fertility, and migration has its own influence on mortality and fertility, not just in the places to which migrants go, but also in the places from which they came. The topic of migration is far too huge for one chapter in a book, and so my relatively limited purpose in this chapter is to provide you with an overview of the ways in which we define, measure, and conceptualize the migration process and understand the migration transition, looking separately at the situation within and between countries. I also examine migration that occurs forcibly, including slavery and refugee movements.

Defining Migration

Migration is defined as any permanent change in residence. It involves the "detachment from the organization of activities at one place and the movement of the total round of activities to another" (Goldscheider 1971:64). Thus the most important aspect of migration is that it is spatial by definition. You cannot be a migrant unless you "leave your room." However, just because you leave your room, you are not necessarily a migrant. You may be a traveler or perhaps a daily commuter from your home to work. These activities represent **mobility**, but not *migration*. You might be a temporary resident elsewhere (such as a construction worker on a job away from home for a few weeks or even months), or a seasonal worker (returning regularly to a permanent home), or a **sojourner** (typically an international migrant seeking temporary paid employment in another country). Again, such people are mobile, but they are not migrants because they have not changed their residence permanently.

Of course, even when you change your permanent residence, if your new home is only a short distance away and you do not have to alter your round of activities (you still go to the same school, have the same job, shop at the same stores), then you are a **mover** (and maybe even a shaker), but not a migrant. All migrants are movers, but not all movers are migrants. Less clear conceptually are *transients* and *nomads*. Technically, you could say that because they are constantly changing their residence and round of activities, they should be thought of as migrants. However, the lack of a permanent residence creates a problem in defining them as migrants. Most demographers deal with this by simply ignoring transients and nomads, and I do much the same, since they represent a very small part of most contemporary human populations.

Internal and International Migrants

Internal migration, that which occurs within a country, has traditionally been thought of as "free" or voluntary in the sense that people are choosing to migrate or not, often basing that decision on economic factors. This is not to say that, within a country, people are never forced to move. As I discuss later in the chapter, **internally displaced persons** (IDPs) account for very large proportion of the world's refugee population. Especially in developing nations whose boundaries may have been created without due regard to ethnic and religious differences among inhabitants, civil strife can force people out of their homes to seek safety and refuge somewhere else in their own country, as happened in Darfur, Sudan. Environmental disasters can have the same effect, as we saw in the United States in the aftermath of Hurricane Katrina, because of which tens of thousands were forced to flee the flooding in New Orleans, with many of them relocating permanently. We witnessed people heading back to the countryside in Haiti after the massive earthquake hit Port-au-Prince, and many of them may never return to the city.

People have also been forcibly moved within a country by government-led efforts in response to political and ideological factors. Witness the migration of hundreds of thousands of Chinese who were forced to relocate so that the Three Gorges Dam could be built, or the massive transmigration that Indonesia periodically attempts—moving people from the crowded island of Java to other, less populous islands. This kind of internal migration, although forced, is usually planned. People's needs are anticipated in advance and, presumably, the migration is expected (or, at least, advertised) to improve the lives of the people involved, although the associated trauma often has the opposite effect.

Migration across international boundaries is usually voluntary, but it typically means that a person has met fairly stringent entrance requirements, or is entering without documents (which carries a load of stress with it), or is being granted refugee status, fleeing from a political, social, or military conflict. You can easily imagine that most kinds of international migration are apt to be more stressful than internal migration. On top of the move itself is heaped the burden of accommodating to a new culture and often a new language, being dominated perhaps by a different religion, being provided different types and levels of government services, and adjusting to different sets of social expectations and obligations.

With reference to your area of origin (the place you left behind), you are an **out-migrant**, whereas you become an **in-migrant** with respect to your destination. If you move from one country to another, you become an international migrant—an **emigrant** in terms of the area of origin and an **immigrant** in terms of the area of destination. Because commuters and sojourners also may cross international boundaries, the United Nations has tried to tighten the definition of an international migrant by developing the concept of a **long-term immigrant**, which includes all persons who arrive in a country during a year and whose length of stay in the country of arrival is more than one year (Kraly and Warren 1992).

International migration can be differentiated further between **legal immigrants**, **illegal (or undocumented) immigrants**, **refugees**, and **asylees**. Legal immigrants are those who have governmental permission to live in the place to which they are migrating, whereas illegal or undocumented migrants do not. A refugee is defined by the United Nations (and by most countries of the world) as a person who "owing to a well-founded fear of being persecuted for reasons of race, religion, nationality, membership of a particular social group, or political opinion, is outside the country of his nationality, and is unable to or, owing to such fear, is unwilling to avail himself of the protection of that country" (UNHCR 2010). Asylees are refugees—with a geographic twist: they are already in the country to which they are applying for admission, whereas refugees are outside the country at the time of application.

You can see that the definition of migration is confounded by the fact that migration is an activity (changing residence) carried out by people (the migrants) under varying legal and sociopolitical circumstances. If we have this much trouble defining migration, you can be sure that it is hard to measure.

Measuring Migration

Defining migration as a permanent change of residence still leaves several important questions open that have to be answered before we can measure the phenomenon and know who is a migrant and who is not. For example, how far does a person have to move to be considered a migrant instead of just a mover? That is fairly straightforward in the case of international migrants, but not so easily determined for internal migrants. As a rule of thumb, people moving within a country are classified as migrants if they move across administrative boundaries. For example, the U.S. Census Bureau usually defines a migrant as a person who has moved to a different county within the United States. Note, however, that from the standpoint of a city within a county, a migrant would be anyone moving into or out of the city limits. From the standpoint of a local school district, a migrant would be anyone moving into or out of the school district's boundaries. This issue of geographic scale is one that must be dealt with in all migration research. A birth is a birth, and a death is a death, but whether or not you are considered a migrant when you move varies according to who is asking the question.

Another question that has to be asked is: What do we mean by permanent? Most people who move tend to move more than once in their life, so we have to decide how long you must stay at the new place before your move is considered permanent. As noted above, the United Nations has somewhat arbitrarily decided that anyone who spends at least one year in the new locale is a migrant. It is sometimes the case that the data you are dealing with will determine what your definition of permanent will be. The decennial census in the United States up through Census 2000 routinely asked people a question about where they lived five years prior to the census. So, a migrant is defined from these census data as someone who lived in a different county (or a different state or a different country) five years prior to the census, regardless of how many times they may have moved in between. Of course, such a definition fails to capture the migration of someone who moved out and then back to the point of origin within that five-year time period. The Current Population Survey, by contrast, has asked a question in each year's March demographic supplement about where a respondent lived a year prior to the survey. This one-year time frame has also been incorporated into the American Community Survey, which as you know replaced the census long form in the 2010 Census.

To tangle the situation further, migration may involve more than a single individual—a family or even an entire village may migrate together. A ghost town, it has been suggested, does not necessarily signal the end of a community, only its relocation.

Stocks versus Flows

One of the more important things to keep in mind as we discuss the migration transition is that it involves both a process and a transformation. The process is that people move from one place to another, and this represents the **migration flow**. The transformation is that the **migrant stock**—those people living in a different place than where they were born—changes as people move into and out of a given place. The fact that an average of one million legal immigrants per year were admitted to the United States between 2000 and 2010 represents a measure of the flow of people from other places into the country. Those people were added to the stock of immigrants (the foreign-born population) already residing in the United States at the time. The total stock of foreign-born persons in 2010 was 40 million, accounting for nearly 13 percent of the population. The contrasts between stocks and the flows are illustrated by the idea that if a million previous migrants had left the country just as a million new migrants were entering, the in- and out-flows would have been pretty large, but the stock itself would not have changed numerically. On the other hand, the demographic composition of the stock of migrants (e.g, their places of origin) could have been changed by the flows, even if the stock did not change numerically.

Information about the migrant stock comes largely from censuses and surveys where everybody is asked a question about whether or not they used to live in a different place. If they did (and they meet the criteria for being a migrant rather than just a mover), then they are part of the stock of migrants. If one additional question is asked about where they came from, then we can infer something about migration flows, as well, since we can then measure the number of people in the stock who flowed from point A to point B. Migration flow data can come from a variety of other sources, such as the Department of Homeland Security, which keeps track of people entering the United States. Figure 7.2 combines a map produced by the Department

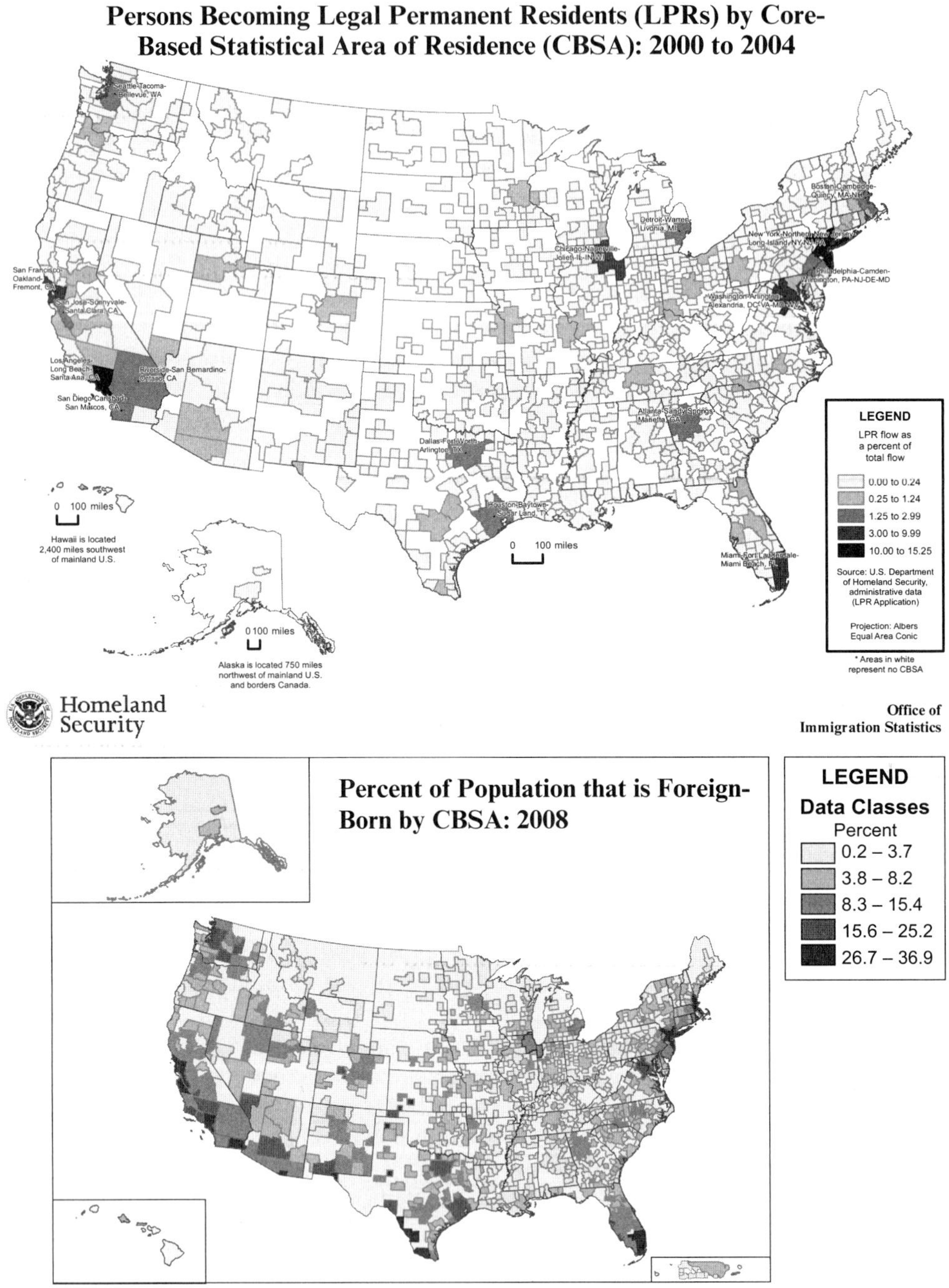

Figure 7.2 Flows and Stocks of Immigrants to Metropolitan Areas in the United States

Flow data refer to the proportion of all migrants entering during the years 2000–2004 who are living in a given metropolitan area; stock data represent the proportion of the population in each of those metro areas that is foreign-born as of 2008.

Sources: U.S. Department of Homeland Security: http://www.dhs.gov/files/statistics/data/lprmaps.shtm (accessed 2010); and U.S. Census Bureau: http://factfinder.census.gov/jsp/saff/SAFFInfo.jsp?_pageId=thematicmaps&_submenuId=maps_1 (accessed 2010).

of Homeland Security showing the flow of legal migrants into the country's metropolitan areas during the years 2000–2004, with a map from the Census Bureau's American Community Survey for 2008 showing the percent of the population in each of those metropolitan areas that is foreign-born. As you would expect, there is considerable overlap between the two. Note that the flows of undocumented immigrants have to be estimated from arrests by the Border Patrol and by various surveys that attempt to assess the legal status of immigrants through indirect means, and so they are not shown in the flow data in Figure 7.2. Nonetheless, undocumented immigrants will be reflected in the stock data because they are routinely included along with everybody else in census and survey counts.

We also do not have a good source of data on migration flows out of the United States and so must rely on outside estimates, such as the number of Social Security checks sent to people living outside the country. The same can be said for Canada, where Citizenship and Immigration Canada (CIC) records the arrival of immigrants but has no data on people who leave the country. This stands in contrast to at least a few European nations that, as I mentioned in Chapter 4, maintain population registers and thus have a pretty accurate fix on the extent of both internal and international migration. Most countries, however, have little available information, and we either do not know what is happening or have to rely on sample surveys or other indirect evidence (such as the stock of foreign-born people counted in a census) to infer patterns of migration flow.

With respect to internal migration, data are obtained from the Current Population Survey and the American Community Survey, as noted above. The U.S. Census Bureau also conducts the American Housing Survey every other year, which tracks changes in the nation's housing stock and thereby generates data on **residential mobility** (changing residence regardless of how long or short the distance) within the country. Furthermore, the Census Bureau has an arrangement with the Internal Revenue Service that allows the Bureau to periodically examine the address changes reported by people on tax returns, and that drill provides yet another way of tracking migration flows within the country. Confused? Don't worry, you're in good company, but do remember the definitions and distinctions we have just discussed as we sort through the major ways by which we index migration.

Migration Indices

When data are available, migration is measured with rates similar to those constructed for fertility and mortality. These rates can be used to measure internal or international migration, depending on the focus of your analysis and the data you have at your disposal.

Gross or total out-migration represents the flow of all people who leave a particular region during a given time period (usually a year), and the **crude or gross rate of out-migration** (*OMigR*) relates those people to the total midyear population (*p*) in the region (and then we multiply by 1,000):

$$OMigR = \frac{OM}{p} \times 1{,}000.$$

Similarly, the **crude or gross rate of in-migration** ($IMigR$) is the ratio of all people who moved into the region (the flow) during a given year relative to the total midyear population in that region:

$$IMigR = \frac{IM}{p} \times 1{,}000.$$

The gross rate of in-migration is a little misleading because the midyear population refers to the people living in the area of destination, which is not the group of people at risk of moving in (indeed, they are precisely the people who are *not* at risk of moving in because they are already there). Nonetheless, the in-migration rate does provide a sense of the impact that in-migration has on the region in question, so it is useful for that reason alone.

The numerical difference between those who move in and those who move out is called net migration. If these numbers are the same, then net migration is zero, even if there has been a lot of migration activity. If there are more in-migrants than out-migrants, net migration is positive; and if the out-migrants exceed the in-migrants, net migration is negative. The **crude net migration rate** ($CNMigR$) is thus the net number of migrants in a year per 1,000 people in a population, and it is the difference between the net in- and out-migration rates, calculated as follows:

$$CNMigR = IMigR - OMigR.$$

The total volume (flow) of migration also may be of interest to people because it can have a substantial impact on a community even if the net rate is low. This is measured as **the total or gross migration rate** ($TMigR$)—also sometimes called the **migration turnover rate**—which is the sum of in-migrants and out-migrants divided by the midyear population, or more simply the in-migration rate plus the out-migration rate:

$$TMigR = IMigR + OMigR.$$

Another way of viewing migration is through the concept of **migration effectiveness** (E), which measures how "effective" the total volume of migration is in redistributing the population (Plane and Rogerson 1994; Manson and Groop 2000). For example, if there were a total of 10 migrants in a region in a year and all 10 were in-migrants, the "effectiveness" of migration would be 10/10, or 100 percent; whereas if four were in-migrants and six were out-migrants, the effectiveness would be much lower: $(4 - 6)/10$, or -20 percent. In general, the rate of effectiveness is as follows:

$$E = \frac{CNMigR}{TMigR} \times 100.$$

There is no universally agreed-upon measure of migration that summarizes the overall levels in the same way that the total fertility rate summarizes fertility and life expectancy summarizes mortality. However, one way of measuring the contribution that migration makes to population growth is to calculate the ratio of net migration to natural increase (the difference between births and deaths); this is called the **migration ratio** ($MigRatio$):

$$MigRatio = \frac{IM - OM}{b - d}.$$

For example, between July 1, 2007, and July 1, 2008, the U.S. Census Bureau estimates that there was a net migration of 888,825 people into the country (U.S. Census Bureau 2009). During that same one-year period there were 4,328,543 births in the United States and 2,447,976 deaths, so the natural increase was 1,880,567. The ratio of the net migrants to natural increase was thus 888,825 to 1,880,567 or .47, indicating that migration was only about half as important as natural increase in its contribution to that year's population growth in the United States. If we rearrange that equation a little, we can calculate the percentage of growth attributable to migration, which in this case is 32 percent:

$$\text{Percent of total growth due to migration} = \frac{IM - OM}{(IM - OM) + (b - d)} \times 100.$$

Because we often do not have complete sets of data on the number of in- and out-migrants, we can "back into" the migration rate by solving the demographic balancing equation (which I discussed in Chapter 4) for migration. This is known as the **components of change (or residual) method of estimating migration**. The demographic balancing equation states that population growth between two dates is a result of the addition of births, the subtraction of deaths, and the net effect of migration (the number of in-migrants minus the number of out-migrants). If we know the amount of population growth between two dates, and we also know the number of births and deaths, then by subtraction we can estimate the amount of net migration. Let me give you an example. Based on the 1990 census of the United States, we know that on April 1, 1990, there were 248,709,873 residents counted in the country. Between that date and April 1, 2000, there were 39,865,670 births and 22,715,464 deaths in the country. Thus on April 1, 2000, we should have expected the census to find 265,860,079 residents if no migration had occurred. However, the 2000 census counted 281,421,906 people. That difference of 15,561,827 people was estimated to be the result of migration (note that a small fraction of the difference could also be the result of differences in coverage error between the two censuses, as discussed in Chapter 4).

In an analogous way, we can also calculate intercensal net migration rates for specific age groups by gender. If we know the number of people at ages 15–24 in 1990, for example, and if we can estimate how many of them died between 1990 and 2000, then we know how many people aged 25–34 there should have been in 2000 in the absence of migration. Any difference between the observed and the expected number in 2000 can be attributed to migration. Typically, we use a life table (see Chapter 5) to calculate the proportion of people who will die between two different ages, and we call this whole procedure the **forward survival (or residual) method of migration estimation**. For example, in 1990 in the United States, there were 17,996,033 females aged 15–24. Life table values suggest that 99.5 percent of those women (or 17,906,052) should still have been alive at ages 25–34 in 2000 (the forward survival). In fact, Census 2000 counted 20,083,131 women in that age group, or 2,177,079 more than expected. We assume, then, that those "extra" women (the residual) were immigrants, so this is a measure of net migration.

Once again, we note that this assumption ignores any part of that difference that may have been due to differences in the coverage error in the two censuses. If one census undercounted the population more or less than the next census, this could account for at least part of the residual that is otherwise being attributed to migration. Conversely, if we knew the number of migrants, then the difference between the actual and expected number of migrants would tell us something about the accuracy of the census (and that *is* one of the ways of evaluating the census, as I discussed in Chapter 4).

The residual method is also the key to estimating the undocumented immigrant population in the United States. The Current Population Survey and the American Community Survey ask people in large random samples of households questions about their place of birth, and these survey results provide estimates for the entire country. The assumption is made that everyone who entered the country prior to 1980 is now a legal resident, given the opportunities afforded to them (Hoefer, Rytina, and Baker 2010). We know how many people have been granted legal permanent residence in the United States since 1980 and can create estimates of how many of them may have subsequently left the country. The difference between the total number of foreign-born people estimated to be in the country and our estimate of how many of them are legal residents leaves us with an estimate of how many of the foreign-born are in the country without documentation. In 2009, the estimate was that there were 10.8 million such persons, down from the peak of 11.8 million in 2007, just before the economic downturn (Hoefer, Rytina, and Baker 2010; Passel and Cohn 2008).

Now, having worn you out trying to measure the nearly unmeasurable, let us move on to yet another difficult (but inherently more interesting) task: explaining the migration transition. We will do this first in the context of migration within countries, and then we will turn our attention to international migration.

The Migration Transition within Countries

In the premodern world, rates of migration typically were fairly low, just as birth and death rates were generally high. The decline in mortality, in particular, helped to unleash migration, and a migration transition has occurred virtually everywhere in concert with the fertility and mortality transitions discussed in earlier chapters (Zelinsky 1971). The theory of demographic change and response (see Chapter 3) suggested that migration is a ready adaptation that humans (or other animals, for that matter) can make to the pressure on local resources generated by population increase. However, people do not generally move at random—they tend to go where they believe opportunity exists. Because the demographic transition occurred historically in the context of economic development, which involves the centralization of economic functions in cities, migrants have been drawn to cities, and the urban transition is a central part of the migration transition, as will be discussed more fully in Chapter 9. Yet the mere existence of a migration transition does not explain why people move, who moves, and where they go. We need to dig deeper for those explanations.

Why Do People Migrate?

Over time, the most frequently heard explanation for migration has been the so-called **push-pull theory**, which echoes common sense by saying that some people move because they are pushed out of their former location, whereas others move because they have been pulled or attracted to someplace else. This idea was first put forward by Ravenstein (1889), who analyzed migration in England using data from the 1881 census of England and Wales. He concluded that pull factors were more important than push factors: "Bad or oppressive laws, heavy taxation, an unattractive climate, uncongenial social surroundings, and even compulsion (slave trade, transportation), all have produced and are still producing currents of migration, but none of these currents can compare in volume with that which arises from the desire inherent in most men to 'better' themselves in material respects" (p. 286). Thus Ravenstein is saying that it is the desire to get ahead more than the desire to escape an unpleasant situation that is most responsible for the voluntary migration of people, at least in late-nineteenth-century England. This theme should sound familiar to you. Is it not the same point made by Davis (1963) in discussing personal motivation for having small families (see Chapter 6)? Remember, Davis argued that it is the pursuit of pleasure or the fear of social slippage, not the desire to escape from poverty, that motivates people to limit their fertility.

In everyday language, we could label the factors that might push a person to migrate as stress or strain. However, it is probably rare for people to respond to stress by voluntarily migrating unless they feel there is some reasonably attractive alternative, which we could call a pull factor. The social science model conjures up an image of the rational decision maker computing a cost-benefit analysis of the situation. The potential migrant weighs the push and pull factors and moves if the benefits of doing so exceed the costs. For example, if you lost your job, it could benefit you to move if there are no other jobs available where you live now, unemployment compensation and welfare benefits have expired, and there is a possibility of a job at another location. Or, to be more sanguine about your employability, the process may start, for example, when you are offered an excellent executive spot in a large firm in another city. Will the added income and prestige exceed the costs of uprooting the family and leaving the familiar house, community, and friends behind?

In truth, whether or not you migrate will likely depend on a more complicated set of circumstances than this simple example might suggest. The decision to move usually develops over a fairly long period of time, proceeding from a desire to move, to the expectation of moving, to the actual fact of migrating (Rossi 1955). In Rossi's longitudinal sample of families in the 1950s, half of those interviewed expressed a desire to move, but only about 20 percent of them actually did so. Sell and De Jong (1983) produced a set of longitudinal data for the 1970s that reinforced Rossi's findings—migration rates reflect a whole spectrum of attitudes, ranging from people who are "entrenched nonmovers" (who have no desire to move and no expectation of moving and who do not migrate) to "consistent decision-maker movers" (who desire to, expect to, and do migrate).

Between the desire to move and the actual decision to do so there also may be **intervening obstacles** (Lee 1966). The distance of the expected destination, the cost of getting there, poor health, and other such factors may inhibit migration. These obstacles are hard to predict on any wide scale, however, and so we tend to lump them together with the overall "costs" of moving and concentrate our attention on explaining the desire to move. Economic variables dominate most explanations of why people migrate, although housing variables have become increasingly important in the United States. Beginning in 1998, a question was added to the Current Population Survey in the United States asking people who had moved during the previous year why they had moved. The results show that, as expected, people mentioned a work-related reason more often than any other for migrating (defined as moving between counties), whereas shorter-distance moves (within the same county) are most likely to be housing related (Schachter 2001).

Migration associated with career advancement, as happens so often in the military, academics, and large companies, illustrates the hypothesis that migration decisions "arise from a system of strategies adopted by the individual in the course of passing through the life cycle" (Stone 1975:97). If it is assumed that people spend much of their life pursuing various goals, then migration may be seen as a possible means—an **implementing strategy**—whereby a goal (such as more education, a better job, a nicer house, a more pleasant environment, and so on) might be attained.

Although this is not a startling new hypothesis (it is little more than a modern restatement of Ravenstein's nineteenth-century conclusions), it is nonetheless a very reasonable one. Indeed, Lee (1966) has observed that two of the more enduring generalizations that can be made about migration are:

1. Migration is selective (that is, not everyone migrates, only a selected portion of the population).
2. The heightened propensity to migrate at certain stages of the life cycle is important in the selection of migrants.

One particular stage of life disproportionately associated with migration is that of reaching maturity. This is the age at which the demand or desire for obtaining more education tends to peak, along with the process of finding a job or a career, and getting married. Furthermore, as you know from the discussion about the health and mortality transition, it is also the time of life when people are most healthy and thus capable of moving.

Agreement is nearly universal on the general ideas about migration I have outlined above, but the devil, as they say, is in the details. There are so many different aspects to the process of migration that no one has yet produced an all-encompassing theory of migration. Figure 7.3 provides an overview of the major aspects of the migration process that require explanation, adapted from a conceptual model devised by De Jong and Fawcett (1981) and revised by De Jong (2000). These are analogous in certain respects to the three preconditions for a fertility decline. The migration process can be thought of as having three major stages including: (1) the propensity to migrate in general, (2) the motivation to migrate to a specific location, and (3) the actual decision to migrate.

The migration process begins with individuals and household members in the context of a given culture and society, represented by the community in which they live. The decision about who will migrate and when and to where may often be part of a household strategy for improving the group's quality of life—consistent with the perspective of demographic change and response, as you will recall from Chapter 3. Furthermore, the household decision is not made in a vacuum; it is influenced by the sociocultural environment in which the household members live. Individual and household characteristics are important because of the selectivity of migrants—households with no young adults are less likely to contemplate migration. Social and cultural norms are important because they provide the context in which people might think

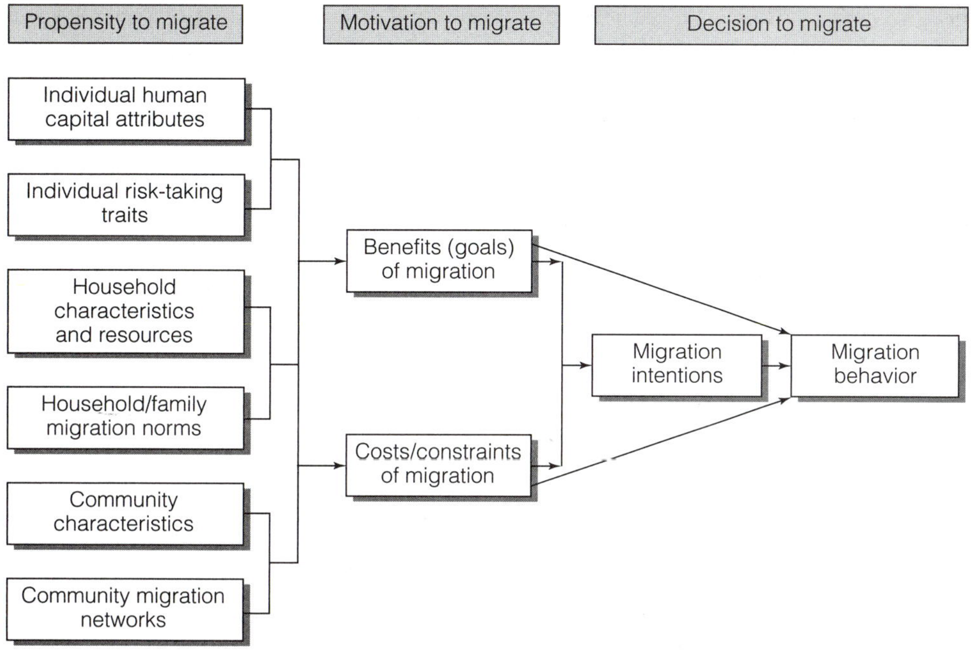

Figure 7.3 A Conceptual Model of Migration Decision Making

Source: Adapted by the author from Gordon De Jong and James Fawcett, 1981, "Motivations for Migration: An Assessment and a Value-Expectancy Research Model," in G. De Jong and R. Gardner (eds.), *Migration Decision Making* (New York: Pergamon Press), Figure 2.2; and Gordon De Jong, 2000, "Expectations, Gender, and Norms in Migration Decision-Making," *Population Studies* 54:307–319, Figure 1.

consciously of migration as a necessary or desirable thing to do. Social norms can play a role in discouraging migration by emphasizing the importance of place and community or, on the other hand, political and economic instability may cause people to rethink their commitment to an area.

Personal traits are important because some people are greater risk takers than others. In the United States, the "average" person can expect to move 11.7 times in his or her lifetime (Hansen 1994; U.S. Census Bureau 2010). Nonetheless, an average like that hides a lot of variability. Some people account for a disproportionate amount of migration by migrating frequently, while others rarely or never move. This may be an application of the famous "80-20 rule." In criminology, it refers to the idea that 80 percent of crime may be committed by 20 percent of the criminals. In the case of migration, it may be that 80 percent of all migration is undertaken by 20 percent of the movers (although be forewarned that I have not yet found a study that puts this idea to the test).

Part of the explanation for the propensity to move may be cultural, of course. Long (1991) examined rates of residential mobility (which are highly correlated to migration rates) for a number of developed nations and found that the "overseas European" nations, including the United States, Canada, Australia, and New Zealand—populated by descendents of migrants who supplanted the indigenous population—are the countries with the highest rates of mobility.

Demographic characteristics combine with societal and cultural norms about migration to shape the values people hold with respect to migration—the benefits they hope to gain by migrating. Such benefits represent clusters of motivations to move, including the desires for wealth, status, comfort (better living or working conditions), stimulation (including entertainment and recreation), autonomy (personal freedom), affiliation (joining family or friends), and morality (especially religious beliefs). At the same time, personal traits (such as being a risk-taking person) combine with the opportunity structure within the household and within the community to affect the costs and constraints that might keep a person from migrating. All of these personal and social environmental factors combine to affect a person's expectation of actually achieving the goals they have in mind that might be facilitated by migration.

The amount of information a person has about the comparative advantages of moving also contributes to the expectation of attaining migration values or goals—that balancing of the likelihood of obtaining the benefits with the perceived costs involved in migrating. If the benefits appear to outweigh the costs, then the person may decide to migrate. Given the intention to move, a person may discover that, by making adjustments in his or her current situation, personal or family goals can be achieved without having to move. "Such adjustments might include a change in occupation, alterations to the physical structure of the house, a change in daily and friendship patterns, or lifestyle changes" (De Jong and Fawcett 1981:56). Finally, the intention to move (or to stay) leads ultimately to the act of moving (or staying) itself, although unanticipated events may still affect that decision. Indeed, events may overtake a person in something akin to the diffusion model, so that even though there was no original intention to migrate, the person migrates anyway. We have all been swept up in situations and done things that we wouldn't necessarily have done had we given them more thought.

Who Migrates?

Selectivity by Age In virtually every human society, young adults are far more likely to migrate than people at any other age. This is about as close as we are likely to get to a "law" of migration (Tobler 1995). The data in Figure 7.4 show the age pattern of intercounty migrants in the United States between 2005 and 2006, using data from the Current Population Survey. As you can see, young adults were much more mobile than people of other ages, and this same pattern has existed in the United States in the past and holds true in other countries as well (Long 1988). The young adult ages, 20–29, are clearly those at which migration predominates.

One in eight American females aged 20–24 is an intercounty migrant, but from there the percentage of people who migrate drops off steeply, with a few little bumps around the time of retirement. At ages younger than 20, children typically are just following their parents around, so it is not surprising that younger children (who have the youngest parents) move more than older children. We can see, then, that age is an important determinant of migration because it is related to life-cycle changes that affect most humans in most societies.

Selectivity by Gender In the United States, women have virtually the same rates of migration as do men (see Figure 7.4), reflecting the rise in gender equity. Women are increasingly apt to migrate on their own, rather than to move only because they are trailing a husband. In so-called traditional societies, the role of women is to be

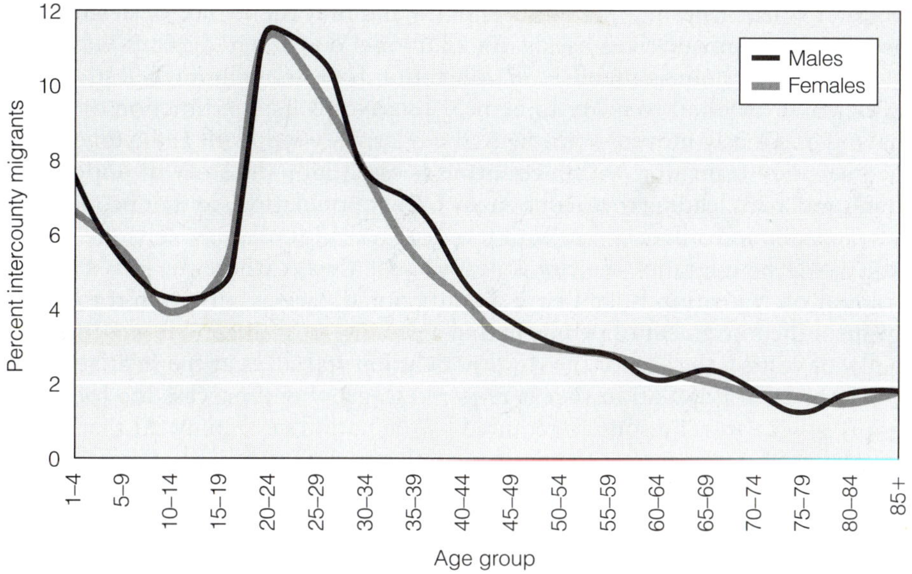

Figure 7.4 Young Adults Are Most Likely to be Migrants
Source: Adapted from data in U.S. Census Bureau, Current Population Survey 2008 (www.census.gov, accessed 2010).

at home caring for children and other family members, and under such circumstances migration is dominated more by males than by females. In fact, many models of household decision making about migration take for granted that it is the male of the household who will be making the migration decision (Cerrutti and Massey 2001). Therefore, it should not surprise you that men are more likely to outnumber women among migrants in those areas of the world where the status of women is lowest—Africa and Asia—whereas women are as likely or even more likely to be migrants in Europe, North America, Latin America, and the Caribbean (United Nations Population Division 2009).

Any generalization about gender and migration is likely to be misleading, however, because, like all aspects of migration, this one is complicated by varying regional patterns. Women represent a slight majority of migrants throughout Latin America, but this pattern may be only loosely connected to the rising status of women, since many are following their husband or other family members (Findley 1999). Women are still less likely than men to have made the decision to move, even when they are involved in the move, and their own situation may actually suffer as a result of being a trailing spouse. Data consistently show that when families move, employment opportunities for women are apt to be less favorable than they were prior to the move (Boyle et al. 2001).

Migration within the United States

The decision about whether you are going to move cannot be divorced from where you might be going. Data from the American Housing Surveys and the more recent Current Population Surveys suggest that about one in five internal migrants in the

United States is involved in a job transfer, implying that the choice of destination may have been in someone else's hands. An additional one in ten migrants was moving closer to relatives, and obviously their location fixes the migrant's destination, but the fact that they had to move to be near relatives is itself a function of somebody having previously moved—otherwise the relatives would still all be together.

The migration transition within countries is essentially the story of population growth in rural areas leading to a redundancy of that population, so that people look elsewhere for jobs and a livelihood. With few new agricultural areas left in the world to be taken over by migrants, the city is now almost always where the jobs are, and so the migration transition is, as I have already noted, largely an urban transition. Initially, then, the movement of people within a country is from rural to urban areas. Eventually, of course, the size of the rural population stabilizes at the relatively low fraction of the total population that is required to grow and process the food and harvest any other natural resources required by the nation's economy. At that point, it may no longer be appropriate to speak of a migration transition, but rather to refer to a **migration evolution**, which implies that the population is largely urban-based, and people are moving between and within urban places (Pumain 2004).

We know that every country in the world has experienced a migration transition as part of the overall demographic transition, but some countries experience a larger migration evolution than others. The United States, for example, is quite literally a nation on the move, and it always has been. Data from the American Community Survey show that 47 million Americans (16 percent of the population) aged one and older in 2008 were living in a different house than in the year before. Some of these people had undoubtedly moved more than once during that period, so that represents a probable minimum level of mobility. Of those movers, 19 million crossed county lines and would thus be considered migrants. An additional 1.9 million persons moved in from outside the United States during the previous year, including U.S. citizens returning from abroad (about one-third of that total) and immigrants. At the same time, we can note that the number of migrants has kept pace with the population growth in the United States, and the actual rate of migration (measured as the *percentage* of people moving each year) has remained remarkably steady since the end of World War II and, if anything, may have declined, not risen (Gober 1993; Schachter 2004).

As I will discuss in more detail in Chapter 9, though the migration transition in the United States is essentially complete, population movements are part and parcel of American life, and so the country continues to evolve demographically as a consequence of emerging patterns of migration in and between urban areas. There were several decades when migration was in the direction of the industrializing centers in the northeastern and north central states and to the rich farmland and industry in the Midwest. The strongest of these movements was the one westward (Shryock 1964). At first this meant that the mountain valley areas west of the Atlantic seacoast were migration destinations; then the plains states were settled; and, especially since the end of World War II, the Pacific Coast states have been popular destinations.

From World War I through the 1960s, white and black migrants had also been heading out of the southern states and into the northeastern and north central states, a phenomenon that has been called the Great Migration (Tolnay et al. 2005; Eichenlaub, Tolnay, and Alexander 2010). This generally represented rural-to-urban migration out of the economically depressed South into the industrialized cities of the

Table 7.1 Americans at the Beginning of the Twenty-first Century Were Heading South

	Origin in 2000				
Destination in 2005:	Northeast	Midwest	South	West	Totals
Northeast	**–1,024**	228	710	352	1,290
Midwest	288	**–420**	930	691	1,909
South	1,512	1,382	**1,422**	1,230	4,124
West	514	719	1,062	**22**	2,295
Totals	2,314	2,329	2,702	2,273	9,618

Note: Between 2000 and 2005, 9,618,000 Americans migrated between the four major geographic regions of the country. This table shows the number of migrants (in thousands) according to their origin (where they lived in 2000) and their destination (where they lived in 2005). The diagonal (highlighted) shows the net number of migrants for that region. Thus, there were 2,702,000 people who moved out the South between 2000 and 2005, but they were replaced by 4,124,000 in-migrants, for the largest regional net gain of 1,422,000 migrants.

Source: Adapted from U.S. Census Bureau, Current Population Survey, March 2005, Geographical Mobility: March 2000 to March 2005, http://www.census.gov/population/www/socdemo/migrate/cps2005–5yr.html, accessed 2010.

North. In the 1970s, this pattern of net out-migration from the South reversed itself and the northeastern and north central states found themselves increasingly to be migration origins rather than destinations, as migrants headed not only west, but also back to the South, the "New Great Migration," as Frey (2004) has called it. This pattern has continued into the twenty-first century. Table 7.1 shows that the northeastern states (the "Rust Belt" or "Snow Belt") have had more out-migrants than in-migrants, and people have been moving west and especially south to the Sun Belt.

Table 7.1 shows you, however, only the first half of what Frey (2009) has called a "rollercoaster decade" for migration within the United States. In 2005, Hurricane Katrina led to a substantial forced outmigration from the New Orleans area. At the same time, the housing bubble was encouraging migration to more inland areas of the West and Southeast, in particular, where new homes were being built that were affordable largely because of the now infamous sub-prime lending practices of major banks. The ensuing bursting of that housing bubble and the deep recession that followed in its wake rather dramatically slowed migration throughout the country (as well as into the country, as I discuss later). But even as migration slowed, Texas and North Carolina, where housing is relatively less expensive, were taking in more people than other states, while New York and California (with high housing costs) were the country's biggest losers.

Migration between Countries

Immigration may be the sincerest form of flattery, but few countries encourage it. Migration between countries is fraught with the potential for conflict among people of different cultural backgrounds and, as technology has made transportation and thus migration easier, the issues surrounding international migration have come into sharper focus. Nowhere is this more true than in the United States, where international immigration has been a way of life for more than two centuries and toward which a large fraction of the annual volume of the world's international migrants still heads.

Referring back to Figure 7.3, we can make the general statement that internal migration is more strongly influenced by individual characteristics of people, whereas international migrants are more apt to be influenced by the social and political climate and by the opportunity structure (especially the lack of barriers to migration that influence the costs and constraints of migration). The kinds of migration goals that internal migrants have are also likely to differ somewhat from those of international migrants. Massey and his associates (Massey et al. 1993; Massey and Espinosa 1997; Massey, Durand, and Malone 2002; Massey 2008) have reviewed and evaluated various theories that try to explain contemporary patterns of international migration, as I discuss below.

Although the migration transition originally referred to the mobility of people *within* a nation, it has expanded its scope to become an international global phenomenon of movement *between* countries as well. Of the factors laid out in Figure 7.3, the most important elements in explaining migration in the modern world appear to be: (1) the creation of new opportunity structures for migration, which raise the benefit of migrating (pull factors) partly by undermining existing local relationships between people and resources (push factors); while (2) cheaper and quicker transportation and communication can (a) increase the information that people have about a potential new location (lowering the risk of migration by closing the gap between the anticipated benefits and the perceived likelihood of attaining those goals) and (b) make it easier to migrate and to return home if things do not work out.

Step migration and **chain migration**, two migration strategies that have stood out over time, help determine where migrants go. Step migration is a process whereby migrants attempt to reduce the risk of their decision by sort of inching away from home. The rural resident may go to a nearby city, and from there to a larger city, and perhaps eventually to a huge megalopolis. Chain migration reduces risk because it involves migrants in an established flow from a common origin to a predetermined destination where earlier migrants have already scoped out the situation and laid the groundwork for the new arrivals.

Chain migration also has a built-in multiplier effect that is the underlying source of the dramatic way in which immigration is changing the face of North America and Europe. The "pioneer" or "principle" immigrant arrives in the new country and becomes established and then sends for other family members—family reunification. Once the family is in place, the second generation is born and one immigrant has become many (Bin Yu 2008). This is a pattern that especially characterizes migration from Mexico and the Philippines to the United States, and it reminds us that the choice of *where* to move is a large component of *why* people decide to migrate internationally.

Why Do People Migrate Internationally?

The major theories that exist to help explain various aspects of international migration, as originally outlined by Massey and his associates (1993, 1994), include first those that focus on the initiation of migration patterns: (1) neoclassical economics; (2) the new household economics of migration; (3) dual labor market theory; and (4) world systems theory. Then there are three perspectives that help to explain the perpetuation of migration, once started: (1) network theory; (2) institutional theory; and (3) cumulative causation. All of these perspectives are aimed at explaining the *flow* of migrants *between* countries, although of course they may also be applicable in some instances to internal migration, especially in developing nations.

The Neoclassical Economics Approach By applying the classic supply-and-demand paradigm to migration, this theory argues that migration is a process of labor adjustment caused by geographic differences in the supply of and demand for labor. Countries with a growing economy and a scarce labor force have higher wages than a region with a less developed economy and a larger labor force. The differential in wages causes people to move from the lower-wage to the higher-wage region. This continues until the gap in wages is reduced merely to the costs of migration (both monetary and psychosocial). At the individual level, migration is viewed as an investment in **human capital** (investments in individuals that can improve their economic productivity and thus their overall standard of living) (Borjas 1999). People choose to migrate to places where the greatest opportunities exist. This may not be where the average wages are currently the highest, but rather where the individual migrant believes that, in the long run, his or her own skills will earn the greatest income. These skills include education, experience, training, and language capabilities. This approach has been used to explain internal as well as international migration. It is also the principle that underlies Ravenstein's conceptualization of push factors (especially low wages in the region of origin) and pull factors (especially high wages in the destination region).

The New Household Economics of Migration The neoclassical approach assumes that the individual is the appropriate unit of analysis, but the new household economics of migration approach argues that decisions about migration are often made in the context of what is best for an entire family or household. This approach accepts the idea that people act collectively not only to maximize their expected income, but also to minimize risk. Thus migration is not just a way to get rid of people; it is also a way to diversify the family's sources of income. Migrating members of the household have their journey subsidized and then remit portions of their earnings back home. This cushions households against the risk inherent in societies with weak institutions. If there is no unemployment insurance, no welfare, no bank from which to borrow money or even in which to invest money safely, then the remittances from migrant family members can be cornerstones of a household's economic well-being. This has become a huge part of the international migration story and I will return to it at the end of the chapter.

Dual Labor Market Theory This theory offers a reason for the creation of opportunities for migration. It suggests that in developed regions of the world there are essentially two kinds of job markets: the primary sector, which employs well-educated people, pays them well, and offers them security and benefits; and the secondary labor market, characterized by low wages, unstable working conditions, and lack of reasonable prospects for advancement. It is easy enough to recruit people into the primary sector, but the secondary sector is not so attractive. Historically, women, teenagers, and racial and ethnic minorities in the richer countries were recruited into these jobs, but in the past few decades women and racial and ethnic minority groups have succeeded in moving increasingly into the primary sector, at the same time that the low birth rate has diminished the supply of teenagers available to work. Yet the lower echelon of jobs still needs to be filled, and so immigrants from developing countries are recruited—either actively (as in the case of agricultural workers) or passively (the diffusion of information that such jobs are available).

World Systems Theory This theory offers a different perspective on the emerging opportunity structure for migration in the contemporary world. The argument is that, since the sixteenth century (and as part of the Industrial Revolution in Europe), the world market has been developing and expanding into a set of core nations (those with capital and other forms of material wealth) and a set of peripheral countries (in essence, the rest of the world) that have become dependent on the core, as the core countries have entered the peripheral countries in search of land, raw materials, labor, and new consumer markets.

According to world systems theory, migration is a natural outgrowth of disruptions and dislocations that inevitably occur in the process of capitalist development. As capitalism has expanded outward from its core in western Europe, North America, Oceania, and Japan, ever-larger portions of the globe and growing shares of the human population have been incorporated into the world market economy. As land, raw material, and labor within peripheral regions come under the influence and control of markets, migration flows are inevitably generated. Migration flows do not tend to be random, however. In particular, peripheral countries are most likely to send migrants (including refugees and asylees) to those core nations with which they have had the greatest contact, whether economic, political, or military.

Network Theory Once migration has begun, it may well take on a life of its own, quite separate from the forces that got it going in the first place, in a process that is part of the chain migration concept that I mentioned above. Network theory argues that migrants establish interpersonal ties that "connect migrants, former migrants, and non-migrants in origin and destination areas through ties of kinship, friendship, and shared community origin. They increase the likelihood of international movement because they lower the costs and risks of movement and increase the expected net returns to migration" (Massey et al. 1993:449). Once started, migration sustains itself through the process of diffusion until everyone who wishes to migrate can do so. In developing countries, such migration eventually may become a rite of passage into adulthood for community members, having little to do with economic supply and demand.

Institutional Theory Once started, migration also may be perpetuated by institutions that develop precisely to facilitate (and profit from) the continued flow of immigrants (Agunias 2009). These organizations may provide a range of services, from humanitarian protection of exploited persons to more illicit operations such as smuggling people across borders and providing counterfeit documents, and might include more benign services such as arranging for lodging or credit in the receiving country. These organizations help perpetuate migration in the face of government attempts to limit the flow of migrants.

Cumulative Causation This perspective recognizes that each act of migration changes the likelihood of subsequent decisions about migration because migration has an impact on the social environments in both the sending and receiving regions. The sending back of remittances increases the income levels of migrants' families relative to others in the community of origin, and in this way may contribute to an increase in the motivation of other households to send migrants. Migrants themselves may become part of a culture of migration and be more likely to move again, increasing the overall volume of migration. In the receiving country, the entry of immigrants into certain occupational sectors may label them as "immigrant" jobs, which reinforces the demand for immigrants to fill those jobs continually.

Data from Massey's *Mexican Migration Project* suggest that migration streams are much easier to start than to stop, because migration cumulatively begets more migration as community members in the sending area derive a real benefit (**human capital**) from migration and as expanded networks (**social capital**) make it increasingly easier to migrate (Massey and Espinosa 1997). In this context, human capital refers to the benefits derived by the migrants who have been to the United States, whereas social capital refers to the links with friends and relatives already abroad.

Which Theories Are Best? Massey and his associates (1994) attempted to evaluate the adequacy of each of the just-discussed theories in explaining contemporary patterns of international migration. Their conclusion was that each of the theories is supported in some way or another by the available evidence and, in particular, none of the theories is specifically refuted. Most of the research on migration since the mid-1990s has specifically tested one or another of these theories, with the same conclusion that each of them helps explain an important part of this complex phenomenon. No single theory seems able to capture all of its nuances, but all of the previous perspectives add something to our understanding of migration. Recognizing now that the reasons for migrating are numerous and complex, we also must bear in mind that when people migrate, the impact is felt deeply at both individual and societal levels.

Who Migrates Internationally?

You can appreciate from the theories of international migration that it is dominated by a combination of economic and familial incentives. People migrate for job-related reasons and then, very often, their family members follow them in a pattern of chain migration that involves family reunification. The flow of labor ought to be explained by a simple supply-and-demand model, with people moving from places where there aren't enough jobs to places where there are jobs. And, to a certain extent, that model does shape the "big picture" in the world right now. Improved communication and transportation technology have greatly facilitated a time-honored way of solving short-term labor shortages—the importation of workers from elsewhere. Population growth in less developed nations has put incredible pressure on resources in those nations, while the declining rate of population growth in the more developed nations has, in many instances, heightened the demand for lower-cost workers from less developed nations.

Labor shortages in northern and western Europe, in the United States and Canada, and in Japan and Australia—the more developed societies with aging populations—have created opportunities for workers from Africa, western and southern Asia, Latin America and, within Europe, from eastern Europe. At the same time, the regional ebb and flow of economies stimulates movements of large numbers of people among the less developed nations themselves.

The problem for the receiving societies is that it is not a simple process to import labor. If you call the plumber in your neighborhood to come work on your house, he or she will come over and do the work, get paid, and go back home. But if you call a plumber from another country, they are apt to bring not just themselves, but also family members, and they are likely to have children, and the arrival of these people will create both a new supply of labor and a rising demand for goods and services, both public and private. This is not necessarily a bad thing, but it raises a bigger and broader set of issues with which not just you, but the entire community, must deal.

Guest labor programs helped to spark the migration from Mexico to the United States, as I discuss in the essay accompanying this chapter. They also flourished in post–World War II Europe, and they have been very popular in the Middle East and Africa (Gould and Findlay 1994; Castles and Miller 2009). The Arab oil-producing nations became centers of rapid immigration in the late 1970s and early 1980s as they benefited economically from the rise in oil prices. Libya and Saudi Arabia, in particular, became attractive destinations for Egyptian and Jordanian migrants, along with substantial numbers of Indians and Pakistanis. But the idea behind guest labor programs has been that people would come to the host country, work under contract for a certain period of time, and then go back to their country of origin. However, like the proverbial brother-in-law sleeping on your living room couch, they do not necessarily leave willingly when their time is up.

A common way to deal with guest laborers who become permanent residents is a variation on the segmented assimilation model, which I will discuss below. Many countries (including virtually all of the oil-producing Gulf states, for example) deny citizenship to those people who were not born in the country, and then deny it to their children because the children were not born to citizens. Thus, the workers and their offspring may have the legal right to live and work in their adopted country, but they will never be fully participating citizens. This has also been accomplished informally in several European countries, as immigrant communities evolve into ethnic minority groups who then suffer discrimination as a result of that labeling. This kind of discrimination probably has the unintended consequence of encouraging the immigrants and their children to maintain close ties with relatives in the country of origin, in which case they may be less likely to become fully integrated and assimilated into the country in which they are living.

Migration Origins and Destinations

Global Patterns of Migration

There are currently an estimated 214 million people who are living in a country different from where they were born (United Nations Population Division 2009)—the current global stock of migrants. That number, while large, is only 3 percent of the world's total population, but as I have noted, migrants have social, economic, political, and demographic impacts that are far larger than these numbers suggest.

How did we get to this point? The massive waves of international migration that characterized the nineteenth and early twentieth centuries have already been described in Chapter 2. They primarily represented the voluntary movement of people out of Europe into the "new" worlds of North and South America and Oceania. Restrictive immigration laws throughout the world (not just in the United States) and the worldwide economic depression between World Wars I and II severely limited international migration in the 1920s and 1930s. However, World War II unleashed a new cycle of European and Asian migration—this time a forced push of people out of war-torn countries as boundaries were realigned and ethnic groups were transferred between countries (United Nations 1979). Shortly after the end of the war, the 1947 partition of the Indian subcontinent into India and Pakistan led to the transfer of more than 15 million people—Muslims into East and West Pakistan and Hindus into India. Meanwhile, in the Middle East, the partitioning of Palestine to create the new state of Israel produced 700,000 Palestinian out-migrants and an influx of a large proportion of the north African and Middle Eastern Jewish population into that area. Substantial migration into Israel from Europe, the Soviet Union, and other areas continued well into the 1960s (Wolffsohn 1987). In the 1980s, the flow of migrants into Israel began to dry up, replaced by a small but steady stream of out-migrants, but this trend was quickly turned around in the early 1990s following the Soviet Union's decision to allow Soviet Jews to emigrate. Those choosing to leave headed primarily for Israel and the United States.

Another unexpected political event in Eastern Europe in the late 1980s and early 1990s was the collapse of the Berlin Wall and the amazingly rapid reunification of Germany. Stimulated by Gorbachev's policy of openness in the Soviet Union (and by the former USSR's economic inability to continue subsidizing other Communist nations), the reunification of Germany was both the cause and the effect of migration from East Germany into West Germany (Heilig, Büttner, and Lutz 1990). Between 1950 and 1988, more than 3 million East Germans had fled to the West, but most of those had done so before the Berlin Wall went up in 1961. Then, in 1989, East Germany relaxed its visa policies, allowing East Germans to visit West Germany, and Hungary relaxed the patrol of its border with Austria, allowing vacationing East Germans to escape to the West. Within weeks, migration from east to west was transformed from a trickle into a flash flood.

This east-west migration in Europe is in many respects a continuation of a pattern that has evolved over centuries. Between 1850 and 1913 (the start of World War I), more than 40 million Europeans moved from east to west to populate North America (Hatton and Williamson 1994), but as that was occurring Polish, Slavic, and Ukrainian workers were also migrating west to Germany and France, and

IS MIGRATION A CRIME? ILLEGAL IMMIGRATION IN GLOBAL CONTEXT

Migration should be the most easily controlled of the three population processes, at least in theory. You cannot legislate against death (except for laws prohibiting homicide or suicide), and few countries outside China have dared try to legislate directly against babies. But you can set up legal and even physical barriers to migration—keeping people in (as in the former Soviet Union) or out (as practiced by most countries in the world). In reality, of course, controlling migration can be very difficult if people are highly motivated to move. Undocumented migration from Mexico to the United States is a leading example, although illegal or undocumented immigration is not a problem peculiar to the United States.

All over the globe, people without papers are moving in the millions. Is that a crime? Actually, that question could get us into a huge philosophical discussion, since different cultures define crime in different ways, but in general if a government passes a law and you violate that law, you have committed a crime. If a government says that only people with official permission may enter a country and reside permanently with full legal rights, and you enter that country without permission, then you have violated the law and, in that sense, you may have committed a crime. On the other hand, we could as easily call this a semantic problem—it's a matter of words. If you show up without documents, then you are simply undocumented (and that term is increasingly preferred to the word "illegal"), not a criminal. After all, the usual penalty for being caught as an undocumented immigrant is to be returned to your country of origin, rather than serving time in jail (though, of course, you might temporarily be detained in a jail of some sort).

In fact, being undocumented (in legal terms, having a "lack of legal status") in the United States is a civil, not a criminal offense, which entails a completely different (and less severe) set of consequences (Seghetti, Viña, and Ester 2005). On the other hand, the penalty for being an illegal immigrant if you are not caught is that you may be exploited because unscrupulous employers know they can turn you in to authorities for deportation if you dare to complain. This can lead to people being forced to work in sweatshops, under near-slavery conditions, with little dignity and few legal rights (Appleyard and Taran 2000).

The reason for the rise in undocumented immigration throughout the world is straightforward—there are more people who want to get into the more developed countries than the governments of more developed countries are willing to let in; so people sneak in. Some people want to get a better job; some want to join family members who are already there (with or without documents); some are fleeing for their lives from an awful situation and are seeking asylum. In the United States this amounted to an estimated 10.8 million undocumented immigrants (the U.S. government uses "undocumented," "unauthorized," and "illegal" to describe this population) as of 2009, although the recession has pushed that number down from its peak of 11.8 million in 2007 (Hoefer, Rytina, and Baker 2010).

Migration from Mexico to the United States began in earnest early in the twentieth century as a reaction to the Mexican Revolution, which started in 1910 and ended in the creation of the modern United Mexican States (the official name of the Republic of Mexico). The migration northward from Mexico began to increase in the 1920s and 1930s. That flow was then halted by a combination of the Great Depression, which raised unemployment levels in the United States, and the concomitant discrimination against immigrants that surfaced during this period, leading to massive deportations of many immigrants (legal and otherwise), including many from Mexico.

Labor shortages in agriculture during World War II, however, led to a renewed invitation for Mexican workers to migrate to the United States. In 1942, the United States signed a treaty with the government of Mexico to create a system of contract labor whereby Mexican laborers ("braceros"—literally those who work with their arms, which are *brazos* in Spanish) would enter the United States for a specified period of time to work. After the war ended, the bracero program remained in place, but it was not until the early 1950s that the number of Mexican contract workers began to increase noticeably (Garcia y Griego, Weeks, and Ham-Chande 1990). By the mid-1950s, the contract workers had been joined by many undocumented immigrants from Mexico, and the United States reacted in 1954 by deporting more than a million Mexicans (some later found to be U.S. citizens) in what was called "Operation Wetback."

The bracero program was ended formally in 1964, and in 1965 the new immigration act, which ended the national origins quota system, also put a numerical limit on the number of legal immigrants to the United States from countries in the Western Hemisphere. Neither action noticeably slowed the migration from Mexico, which was by then well entrenched because there was and still is a demand for immigrant labor. However, both of these government actions did jointly conspire to increase the number of immigrants classified as illegal or undocumented (U.S. Immigration and Naturalization Service 1991). This is a critical point with respect to undocumented immigration from Mexico: The flow from Mexico to the United States began because workers were needed and the government agreed to provide them with temporary work visas. More recently, however, the labor supply is still needed, albeit less so in an economic recession, but the government has been less willing to provide documentation for the immigrants, so they "enter without inspection" (EWI—another way of describing people in this category). In other words, the same flow has continued, but now much of it is defined as illegal.

Each year more than one million people are apprehended trying to enter the United States from Mexico, although about 40 percent of those are people who are apprehended more than once, so the absolute number of people is closer to "only" 600,000 per year (Weeks, Jankowski, and Stoler 2010). When the U.S. Border Patrol apprehends "UDAs" (undocumented aliens), most are returned to Mexico and of course most of them will keep trying to cross until they are successful, as most eventually are (Cornelius et al. 2008). People are motivated not only by the lure of a better job, but also because they may already have a job and without papers the only way they can go between their home in Mexico and their job in the United States is by crossing the border someplace other than a legal checkpoint. Border Patrol statistics on apprehensions, for example, always show a seasonal pattern that drops off throughout the year to a low point just before Christmas, and then spikes to a high after Christmas. The clear implication is that people working illegally in the United States have gone home to celebrate the holidays in Mexico, but then attempt to return after the holidays are over.

I should point out that there are two primary ways by which a person becomes an undocumented immigrant. A person may enter the country with a tourist or other visa and then overstay the visa. For example, you may arrive with a student visa, attend college in the United States, but then decide not to return home, at which point you become an illegal immigrant. The more usual and dramatic way is to cross the border without papers. People may try to do this on their own, but especially after 9/11 and the ensuing increase in border security efforts, people are likely to pay a smuggler to assist them. Most of the crossings into the United States are by land, and by building massive fences along the border at the two historically most popular entry places—San Diego and El Paso—the United States has made it increasingly more challenging for people to cross illegally. Unfortunately, the fences have largely served just to divert migrants to cross the border in other areas that are either rugged mountains or barren deserts, and in both cases the risk of death from dehydration, frost, or injury is not inconsequential (Nevins 2002). In 2001, the U.S. Border Patrol responded to an increase in the number of injuries and deaths of people crossing the border by launching a publicity campaign in Mexico aimed at describing the potential dangers of trying to cross into the United States.

In the wake of 9/11 the number of agents patrolling the border has increased significantly and new technologies have been employed, such as land sensors, cameras, and even drone aircraft with cameras, to alert agents to the presence of people crossing the border so that they can be apprehended. In line with Massey's "perverse laws of international migration" that I mention in this chapter, it is likely that the greater restrictions on entering the United States have encouraged people to stay, rather than leave even temporarily to go back home, because once in they realize that it will be hard to re-enter the country should they leave. Thus, the stricter border controls have had the

(continued)

IS MIGRATION A CRIME? ILLEGAL IMMIGRATION IN GLOBAL CONTEXT (CONTINUED)

"perverse" effect of increasing, rather than decreasing, the population of unauthorized persons living in the United States.

People trying to enter the European Union (EU) without papers will often use the Mediterranean or the Adriatic Seas to do so. Only eight miles separate Africa from Europe at the Strait of Gibraltar—the western end of the Mediterranean where it meets the Atlantic—and Africans are willing to pay considerable sums of money for a seat in a small boat for a rough nighttime journey from Morocco to Spain, across what is sometimes called the "Sea of Death" (Simons 2000). Or, they may choose the longer and more dangerous passage from Libya to Italy (Fergany and Santana 2009). If they make it past Frontex (the EU's border control agency), the payoff for these largely unskilled workers has been, at least until the global recession, a job in agriculture or construction in Spain, Portugal, or Italy, where below-replacement fertility has created vacancies in the labor market. Furthermore, the European Union provides a labor market that transcends individual EU members, allowing EU citizens to move within the EU to find the best job. This big economy is, of course, attractive to workers outside of the EU, and since legal migration into EU countries is very limited, undocumented immigration has increased over time.

Undocumented immigration represents a true conundrum because it is a problem with no easy solution that everyone can agree to. There are those in the United States and Europe who argue that the solution is simple—fortify the borders and do not let anyone in who has not been preapproved, immediately deport anyone who is found inside the country without papers, and do a better job of punishing those who knowingly hire undocumented immigrants (Simcox 2006). The latter issue was supposed to have been taken care of in the United States by the 1986 Immigration Reform and Control Act, but over time the continued demand for labor in the United States has not been met by legal immigrants, and in seeming recognition of this, the U.S. government has devoted very few resources to tracking down and fining these employers. This changing emphasis was reflected in the 1996 passage of the Illegal Immigration Reform and Immigrant Responsibility Act (IIRIRA), the main thrust of which was to focus Border Patrol attention on deterring, finding, and deporting illegal immigrants, rather than on penalizing employers of those immigrants.

Consensus in the United States is so difficult to achieve on this issue that, despite a variety of bills having been introduced in Congress to deal with immigration issues, nothing has been passed, at least not as of this writing. Inaction at the federal level has led many states and local governments to pass their own legislation aimed at punishing employers, arresting undocumented immigrants, or even penalizing landlords who rent to them. Since immigration policy has historically been the sole responsibility of the federal government, these initiatives are always challenged in federal courts.

So, the reality is that people continue to enter without valid papers—once again, a civil offense—and this "crime" begets other genuinely serious

Italians were migrating west to France to find work. The Cold War, which cut off much of that flow, was simply a temporary aberration in a long-term trend.

To this trend has been added a mixture of other patterns: (1) south-north migration (particularly of migrant laborers from developing countries of the "south" to developed countries of the "north"); (2) a flow of migrant laborers from some of the poorer developing countries to some of the "emerging" economies, especially in south and southeast Asia; (3) a flow of workers into the Persian Gulf region from the non–oil-producing to the oil-producing nations; and (4) a flow of refugees in Africa and western Asia (especially Iraq and Afghanistan). We have moved into what Castles and Miller (2009) have called "the age of migration." "The hallmark of the age of migration is the global character of international migration: the way it affects more and more countries and regions, and its linkages with complex processes crimes related to exploitation of the immigrants. The Mexican government employs troops to patrol its northern border with the United States, not to prevent people from crossing, but to keep them from being robbed by their countrymen who know that these people have money to pay a smuggler. The smugglers then take advantage of the immigrants by failing to warn them of the dangers of crossing the desert without water, or of going into the mountains in winter without a jacket, and of course the smugglers will leave the immigrants to fend for themselves at the first sign of trouble, sometimes simply leaving them to die. Once in the United States, the immigrants are, as I mentioned earlier, susceptible to many kinds of abuses from employers and others who know that the immigrants have few resources, legal or otherwise, to fight back. This set of circumstances leads many people to believe that illegal immigrants need to have some type of amnesty or "regularization" granted as soon as possible in order to provide a status that will protect their human rights (Bacon 2008). Immigrants understand this idea, of course, and the most common route to amnesty is to become legal by marrying a U.S. citizen (Jasso et al. 2000).

In 2008 the European Council (the governing body of the European Union) approved the "European Immigration and Asylum Pact," designed to provide guidance to member nations, who ultimately retain the power to decide for themselves how they wish to deal with immigrants. The pact was agreed to by the heads of state of all 27 members, so there is some high-level consensus, and the key element with respect to undocumented immigration is what might be called a zero-tolerance policy. The pact calls for all undocumented immigrants to be forced out of Europe, and it explicitly rejects the idea of a general amnesty for undocumented immigrants currently living in Europe.

At the opposite end of the spectrum from the idea of completely shutting down the border and throwing out all undocumented immigrants is that of an open border, which would allow people to come and go in quick response to changes in demand for their services. This idea generally appeals more to prospective employers, who would like to hire cheaper labor, while it has relatively little appeal to the currently employed, who do not relish the thought of increased competition for their jobs. This idea is not likely to be implemented in the near future because there is still a fair amount of anti-immigrant sentiment in the United States and in Europe. In the post-9/11 era, the idea of open borders has become even less popular, given the perception that terrorists could mingle with legitimate workers.

Discussion Questions: (1) If you lived in a developing country and thought you could have a better life by migrating to the United States even though you did not have U.S. government permission to do so, would you do it? Why or why not? **(2)** Do you think that richer countries should be less restrictive about legal immigration, more restrictive, or do you think the current situation does not require any change in policy? Explain your answer.

affecting the entire world" (Castles and Miller 2009:278). Sassen (2001) has argued that the globalization of migration is, in part at least, a consequence of economic globalization—economic connections lead inevitably to flows of people. Income differences between regions attract migrants from lower- to higher-income places, and globalization has helped both to increase the income differences and increase the chance that people will migrate in hopes of improving their economic situation.

Figure 7.5 shows United Nations estimates of the annual net migration (including refugees) for the countries of the world that sent or received the greatest absolute number of net international migrants during the period from 2005 to 2010. You can see that the United States is the top receiving country (a nation of *immigrants*), mirrored of course by the fact that Mexico is the top sending nation (a nation of *emigrants*—Fitzgerald 2008). Low fertility in Europe is fueling immigration

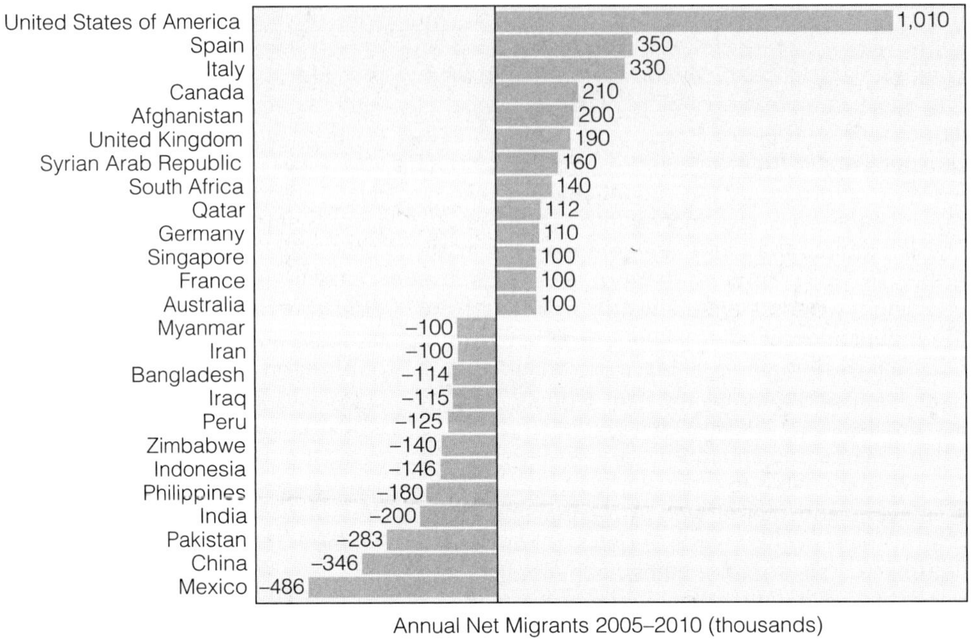

Figure 7.5 The United States Takes in More Immigrants (Net) Than Any Other Country, and Mexico Sends More Emigrants Than Any Other Country

Source: Adapted from data in United Nations Population Division (2009).

especially to Spain, Italy, the United Kingdom, Germany, and France. These immigrants come from developing countries, but also from the less economically developed regions of central and eastern Europe—part of the western drift of the human population. Canada and Australia also have good economies and low birth rates that attract immigrants, especially from Asia.

The estimates in Figure 7.5 reflect refugees returning to Afghanistan. Some fled the country when the Russians invaded in the 1970s, and then more refugees left under the Taliban regime that was set up after the Russians withdrew in 1989, and then yet more left after the United States went in after 9/11. Thus, there is a large pool of people wanting to return to Afghanistan. Note, however, that these estimates were made prior to the Obama administration's decision to shift troops from Iraq back to Afghanistan, so the estimates for Afghanistan may be too high. Syria, by the same token, has accepted a large number of refugees from Iraq, who began fleeing there after the U.S.-led invasion in 2003. South Africa has immigrants from all over sub-Saharan Africa, but especially from Zimbabwe, its troubled neighbor, attracted there by the fact that South Africa's economy dominates that region of the world. The estimates for both Qatar and Singapore are probably a bit too high, since they were made prior to the world-wide recession that hit in 2008 and which heavily impacted both of those small city-states.

At the other end of the migration extremes, we know that Mexico each year sends hundreds of thousands of mainly undocumented immigrants to the United

States (and to other countries as well). China and India, as the world's two most populous nations—but not the richest ones—also contribute a large number of emigrants each year, in what amounts to the Chinese and Indian Diasporas (see, for example, Ma and Cartier 2003; Naujoks 2009). The youth bulge in Peru has sent many of its citizens in search of better opportunities in the United States, Spain, Italy, some of Peru's wealthier neighbors in Latin America, and also Japan, in a type of return migration of children or grandchildren of earlier immigrants to Peru from Japan (Salgado Mendoza 2004). The other countries on the top sending list are in west, south, and southeast Asia, and each has a substantial youth bulge that cannot be absorbed by the national economies. Thus, these countries are sending young people to Europe, the Americas, and the oil-producing Gulf States in search of jobs and a better life.

The global picture in terms of the stock of immigrants, expressed as the percentage of the population that is foreign-born, is shown in Figure 7.1 at the beginning of the chapter. The United States, Canada, and Australia have always had among the highest fractions of foreign-born in the world, but European nations are now included. The Gulf states have many guest workers, as I have mentioned. The other less-rich countries with high percentages of foreign-born are largely sheltering refugees from their neighbors.

Many countries have accepted guest workers on the naive assumption that they can be sent home when the need arises. This is never easy, regardless of whether the host country is in the "north" or the "south." Germany is dealing with immigrants from eastern Europe and Turkey (and other less developed nations); the United Kingdom accepts nearly 200,000 immigrants a year, especially from Africa, Eastern Europe, and Asia, although it began to tighten rules of entry as the economy slowed down in 2008 (MacDonald 2008). Even Italy—long a source of migrants itself—was forced in 1986 to enact its first law controlling immigration into the country. About 15,000 immigrants enter Denmark each year for family unification, but after Denmark discovered that 90 percent of Danish Turks (mainly men) find their spouses in Turkey, legislation was enacted in 2000 to deter any immigrant younger than 25 from bringing a foreign spouse to Denmark.

To remind you that this is not just an issue with more developed nations, the government of Thailand imposed a deadline in 2010 for an estimated 1.5 million undocumented immigrants from Myanmar, Cambodia, Laos, and other nearby nations to register and prove their nationality or be deported (Barta 2010). In another remarkable migration story, it turns out that even as Mexico sends hundreds of thousands of migrants to the United States each year, tens of thousands of Guatemalans go north each year to work as undocumented immigrants in Mexico, especially in the southern state of Chiapas (Smith 2006; *The Economist* 2009).

To date, the success of attempts to limit immigration has been highly variable at best, consistent with what Massey (1996) has called his "perverse laws of international migration":

1. Immigration is a lot easier to start than it is to stop.
2. Actions taken to restrict immigration often have the opposite effect.
3. The fundamental causes of immigration may be outside the control of policy makers.

4. Immigrants understand immigration better than politicians and academicians.
5. Because they understand immigration better than policy makers, immigrants are often able to circumvent policies aimed at stopping them.

In the final analysis, most attempts to limit immigration are motivated less by a desire to limit population growth in general, and more by a desire to limit the entry of certain kinds of people into the country (no matter what country we are talking about). The greater the social and cultural differences between receiving and sending societies, the more likely it is that attempts will be made to slow down the pace of immigration (Castles and Miller 2009). This is certainly what has happened over time in the United States.

Migration into the United States

Prior to World War I, there were few restrictions on migration into the United States and Canada, so the number of immigrants was determined more by the desire of people to move than anything else. Particularly important as a stimulus to migration, of course, was the drop in the death rate in Europe during the nineteenth century, which launched a long period of population growth, with its attendant pressure on Europe's economic resources. Economic opportunities in America looked very attractive to young Europeans who were competing with increasing numbers of young people for jobs. Voluntary migration from Europe to the temperate zones of the world—especially the United States—represents one of the significant movements of people across international boundaries in history. The social, cultural, economic, and demographic impacts of this migration have been truly enormous (Davis 1988).

Immigration to the United States in most of the nineteenth century was dominated by people arriving from northern and western Europe (beginning with England, Ireland, Scotland, and Sweden, then stretching to the south and east to draw immigrants from Germany, especially), as seen in Table 7.2. There was a lull during the American Civil War, but after the war the pace of immigration resumed. The opening up of new land in the United States in the middle of the nineteenth century coincided with a variety of political and economic problems in Europe, and that helped to generate a great deal of labor migration to the United States, particularly after the end of the Civil War. The United States responded in the spring of 1882 with its first immigration restrictions. The first of these was the Chinese Exclusion Act of 1882. The discovery of gold in California had prompted a demand for labor—for railroad building and farming—that had been met in part by the migration of indentured Chinese laborers. However, in 1869, after the completion of the transcontinental railroad, American workers moved west more readily and the Chinese showed up in the East on several occasions as strikebreakers. Resentment against the Chinese built to the point that in 1882 Congress was willing to break a recently signed treaty with China and suspend Chinese immigration for 10 years (Stephenson 1964). But Congress was not through for the year. The 1882 Immigration Act levied a head tax of 50 cents on each immigrant and blocked the entry of idiots, lunatics, convicts, and persons likely to become public charges (U.S. Immigration and Naturalization Service 1991).

The Chinese Exclusion Act was challenged unsuccessfully in the courts and, over time, restrictions on the Chinese, even those residing in the United States, were tightened (indeed, the Chinese Exclusion Acts passed in 1882 were not repealed until 1943). The exclusion of the Chinese led to an increase in Japanese immigration in the 1880s and 1890s, but by the turn of the century hostility was building against them, too (the Japanese Exclusion Act was passed in 1924), and against several other immigrant groups.

By the late nineteenth and early twentieth centuries, the immigrants from northern and western Europe were being augmented by people from southern and eastern Europe (Spain and Italy, then stretching farther east to Poland and Russia). In 1890, 86 percent of all foreign-born persons in the United States were of European origin, but only 2 percent were from southern Europe—almost exclusively Italy. Only 30 years later, in 1920, it was still true that 86 percent of the foreign-born were Europeans, but 14 percent were southern Europeans—a sevenfold increase.

The immigrant processing center in New York City was moved to Ellis Island in 1892 to help screen people entering the United States from foreign countries, since the changing mix of ethnicity had led to public demands for greater control over who could enter the country. In 1891, Congress legislated that aliens were not to be allowed into the country if they suffered from "a loathsome or dangerous contagious disease" (Auerbach 1961:5) or if they were criminals. Tuberculosis was added to the unacceptable list in 1907, and then in 1917, a highly controversial provision was passed that established a literacy requirement, thus excluding aliens over age 16 who were unable to read.

Despite the new set of requirements, immigration to the United States (and Canada) reached a peak in the first decade of the twentieth century, when 1.6 million entered Canada and nearly 9 million entered the United States, accounting for more than one in ten of all Americans at that time. "They came thinking the streets were paved with gold, but found that the streets weren't paved at all and that they were expected to do the paving" (Leroux 1984).

This represents one of the most massive population shifts in history, and virtually all of the theories of international migration discussed earlier have something to offer by way of explanation (Hatton and Williamson 1994; Massey et al. 1994; Moch 1992). Compared to the United States, European wages were low and unemployment rates high. Capital markets were beginning to have a disruptive effect in some of the less developed areas of southern and eastern Europe. Eastern Europe was also undergoing tremendous social and political instability, and the Russian pogrom against Jews caused many people to flee the region.

Nor was all this emigration from Europe aimed at North America. Millions of Italians and Spaniards, as well as Austrians, Germans, and other Europeans, settled throughout Latin America during this period. Most notable among the destinations were Brazil and Argentina (Sanchez-Albornoz 1988). The migration peaked at about the time of World War I, and Europe has never since experienced emigration of this magnitude, partly because wages rose in Europe, helping to keep people there (and encouraging some return migration from the Americas), compounded by the Great Depression of the 1930s (which also encouraged return migration to one's "roots"). In the latter part of the nineteenth century, the percentage of the population enumerated in the U.S. Census as foreign–born hovered near 14 percent, as seen in Table 7.2.

Table 7.2 The Geographic Origin of Immigrants to the United States Has Changed Dramatically over the Decades

Time Period	Total	N/W Europe	S/E Europe	Latin America	Asia	Africa	Elsewhere	% Foreign-born
1820 to 1829	128,502	95,945	3,327	4,297	34	15	24,884	
1830 to 1839	538,381	416,981	5,790	8,238	55	50	107,267	
1840 to 1849	1,427,337	1,364,950	4,309	4,428	121	61	53,468	9.7
1850 to 1859	2,814,554	2,599,397	20,283	7,527	36,080	84	151,183	13.1
1860 to 1869	2,081,261	1,851,833	25,893	3,563	54,408	407	145,157	14
1870 to 1879	2,742,137	2,078,952	172,926	6,415	134,128	371	349,345	13.3
1880 to 1889	5,248,568	3,802,722	835,955	4,638	71,151	763	533,339	14.7
1890 to 1899	3,694,294	1,825,897	1,750,514	2,772	61,285	432	53,394	13.6
1900 to 1909	8,202,388	1,811,556	5,761,013	53,782	299,836	6,326	269,875	14.7
1910 to 1919	6,347,380	1,112,638	3,872,773	240,964	269,736	8,867	842,402	13.2
1920 to 1929	4,295,510	1,273,297	1,287,043	558,481	126,740	6,362	1,043,587	11.6
1930 to 1939	699,375	257,592	186,807	49,539	19,231	2,120	184,086	8.8
1940 to 1949	856,608	362,084	110,440	95,955	34,532	6,720	246,877	6.9
1950 to 1959	2,499,268	1,008,223	396,750	392,466	135,844	13,016	552,969	5.5
1960 to 1969	3,213,749	627,297	506,146	791,138	358,605	23,780	906,783	4.7
1970 to 1979	4,248,203	287,127	538,463	1,015,200	1,406,544	71,408	929,461	6.2
1980 to 1989	6,244,379	339,038	329,828	1,748,824	2,391,356	141,990	1,293,343	7.9
1990 to 1999	9,775,398	405,922	942,690	3,938,231	2,859,899	346,416	1,282,240	11.1
2000 to 2008	9,168,612	379,613	935,924	2,839,450	2,994,336	636,938	1,382,351	13.5

Sources: Immigration data are from U.S. Department of Homeland Security (2009); Table 1, and refer to legal permanent residents; data on foreign-born are from Lollock (2001), and the 2008 American Community Survey.

Never since has it reached that level, although it was getting close (13 percent) by 2010. I mention this as a reminder that the rapid increase in the foreign-born population at the end of the twentieth century in the United States and Canada, which I will discuss below, is something that both countries have seen before.

Recognition of the problems created by still relatively free migration led to a new era of restrictions right after World War I, fueled by the belief that "millions of war-torn Europeans were about to descend on the United States—a veritable flood which would completely subvert the traditional American way of life" (Divine 1957:6). The United States and Canada both passed restrictive legislation in step with the eugenics movement that had gained popularity throughout Europe and North America in the 1920s (Boyd 1976). As it was applied to migration, the ideology was ethnic purity, and the sentiment of the time about migrants is perhaps best expressed as "not too tired, not too poor, and not too many."

In 1921, Congress passed the first act in American history to put a numeric limit on immigrants. The Quota Law of 1921 "limited the number of aliens of any nationality to three percent of foreign-born persons of that nationality who lived in the U.S. in 1910" (Auerbach 1961:9). For example, in 1910, 11,498 people in the United States had been born in Bulgaria (U.S. Census Bureau 1975), so 3 percent of that number, or 345, would be permitted to enter each year from Bulgaria. Under the law, about 350,000 people could enter the United States each year as quota immigrants, although close relatives of American citizens and people in certain professions (for example, artists, nurses, professors, and domestic servants) were not affected by the quotas. The law of 1921 remained in effect only until 1924, when it was replaced by the Immigration Quota Act.

The 1924 law was even more restrictive than that of 1921, because public debate over immigration had unfortunately led to a popularization of racist theories claiming that "Nordics [people from northwestern Europe] were genetically superior to others" (Divine 1957:14). To avoid the charge that the immigration law was deliberately discriminatory, though, a new quota system—the National Origins Quota—was adopted in 1929 (Auerbach 1961). This was a complex scheme in which a special Quota Board took the percentage of each nationality group in the United States in 1790 (the first U.S. Census) and then traced "the additions to that number of subsequent immigration" (Divine 1957:28). The task was not an easy one, since by and large the necessary data did not exist, so a lot of arbitrary assumptions and questionable estimates were made in the process. Once the national origins restriction had been established, the actual number of immigrants allowed from each country each year was calculated as a proportion of 150,000, which was established as the maximum number of all immigrants. Thus if 60 percent of the population was of English origin, then 60 percent of the 150,000 immigrants, or 90,000, could be from England. The number turned out to be slightly more than 150,000, because every country was allowed a minimum of 100 visas. Furthermore, close relatives of American citizens continued to be exempt from the quotas, under the philosophy of family unification.

In Canada, a similar immigration act was passed in 1927 (Boyd 1976). Congress, of course, retained the ability to override those quotas if the need arose, as it did during and after World War II, when refugees from Europe were accommodated. In 1952, in the middle of the anti-Communist McCarthy era, another attempt was made in the United States to control immigration by increasing the "compatibility" of migrants with established U.S. society. The McCarran-Walter Act (the Immigration and Naturalization Act of 1952) retained the system of national origin quotas and added to it a system of preferences based largely on occupation (Keely 1971). The McCarran-Walter Act permitted up to 50 percent of the visas from each country to be taken by highly skilled persons whose services were urgently needed. Relatives of American citizens were ranked next, followed by people with no salable skills and no relatives who were citizens of the United States. Thus, the freedom of migration into the United States was severely restricted, even from those countries with an advantage according to the national origins quota system. The same was true in Canada, which passed similar legislation in the same year. Canada, I should note, had at least two reasons for echoing the immigration policies of the United States. In the first place, it shares much of the sociocultural heritage of the United States, and, second, of course, it shares a border with the United States. This cultural similarity and close proximity would have left Canada inundated with migrants excluded from the United States had Canada not passed its own restrictive laws.

These restrictive laws, coupled with the Great Depression and then World War II, effectively slowed migration to the United States and Canada to a trickle during the 1930s and 1940s. In the 1950s, there was a brief post–World War II upsurge in migration from northern and western Europe, but the 1950s represented a transition time to a new set of "origins and destinies" for immigrants to North America (Rumbaut 1994).

In the 1960s, the ethnically discriminatory aspects of North America's immigration policy ended, but its restrictive aspects were maintained. The Immigration Act of 1965 ended the nearly half-century of national origins as the principal determinant of who could enter this country from non–Western Hemisphere nations. Again, related changes had occurred in Canada in 1962. Although the criterion of national origins is gone, restrictions on the numbers of immigrants remain, including a limit on immigrants from Western Hemisphere as well as non–Western Hemisphere nations. A system of preference was retained, but modified to give first crack at immigration to relatives of American citizens. Parents of U.S. citizens could migrate regardless of the quota. In addition, a certification by the U.S. Labor Department is now required for occupational preference applicants to establish that their skills are required in the United States. In 1976, the law was amended so that parents of U.S. citizens had highest priority only if their child was at least 21 years old. The intent of that change was to eliminate what many people believed to be a fairly frequent ploy of a pregnant woman entering the country illegally, bearing her child in the United States (the child then being a U.S. citizen), and then applying for citizenship on the basis of being a parent of a U.S. citizen. Although there is little evidence to suggest that pregnant women now routinely cross the border illegally to have babies, there are many undocumented immigrant women in the United States who get pregnant and have a baby. These children are sometimes referred to as "anchor babies" because they provide an "anchor" for the family in the United States.

Since the change in immigration legislation in the 1960s, European immigrants to the United States have been replaced almost totally by those from Latin America (especially Mexico, but also Nicaragua and El Salvador), Asia (especially the

Philippines, China, and India), and increasingly from Africa, as well (see Table 7.2). The annual number of legal permanent immigrants peaked in 2006, at 1.2 million, not coincidentally at the same time that the housing bubble was peaking. With the deep recession that followed the burst in that bubble, the annual number of immigrants dropped back to about 1 million per year.

Although only one person is recorded as having migrated from Mexico to the United States in 1820, the number of Mexican and other Latin American immigrants has increased so tremendously since then that census data now show that immigrants from Mexico account for nearly one in three of all foreigners now living the United States. Between 1820 and 2008, more than 7 million Mexicans migrated legally into the United States, with more than half of them arriving just since 1990 (U.S. Department of Homeland Security 2009). A nearly equal number of undocumented immigrants have entered the country, probably permanently, and almost all of them have arrived since 1980 (Hoefer, Rytina, and Baker 2008). Migration between Mexico and the United States is the largest sustained flow of migrant workers in the contemporary world, although it also took a hit with the global recession starting in 2007.

A large portion of Mexican immigrants to the United States expect eventually to return to Mexico (even if they eventually do not). This has dampened their enthusiasm for becoming U.S. citizens, even if they are legal permanent residents. The United States, unlike many other countries, technically does not allow dual citizenship, although in reality you cannot be punished for holding another citizenship and many people do. Still, this is at least one reason why Mexican immigrants have been somewhat politically underrepresented in the United States, even when they are eligible for citizenship. The Mexican government has worried about this over time, and in 1998 the Mexican Nationality Act went into effect, allowing Mexicans to retain their Mexican nationality even if they become a citizen of another country such as the United States. The dual-nationality status means that Mexican nationals who become U.S. citizens will have the right to buy and sell land in Mexico free of the restrictions imposed on foreigners, to receive better treatment under investment and inheritance laws in Mexico, to attend public schools and universities as Mexicans, and to access other Mexican government services and jobs. As I noted in Chapter 1, they are also allowed to vote in Mexican national elections, as long as they have returned to Mexico to sign up for that privilege.

The second most sustained flow of immigrants to the United States has come from the Philippines. In 1898, the United States gained control of the Philippines from Spain as a result of the Spanish-American War. From that date until 1936, immigrants from the Philippines were routinely excluded from the United States, as the Chinese and Japanese had been (Tyner 1999; 2009). Since Filipinos were technically U.S. nationals, they were not subject to the usual immigration laws, but their entry was generally restricted, and by 1930 only 45,000 Filipinos lived in the United States, almost all of them male. The majority of these men came without families, and either returned home or stayed and married non-Filipino women.

The United States granted the Philippines its independence in 1936 and that immediately brought Filipinos under federal immigration law, which effectively excluded them altogether from entering the country until after the end of World War II. At the time, there was an influx of Filipino veterans who had served in the U.S. military during the war. However, the biggest boon to Filipino immigration was the change in the law in the 1960s that gave highest immigration preference to family members. Americans of Filipino origin began to sponsor the immigration of their relatives (especially parents and siblings). Thus, since 1980, about three-fourths of the 40,000 to 60,000 immigrants each year from the Philippines have been relatives of U.S. citizens (U.S. Department of Homeland Security 2009).

Migration out of the United States

The U.S. government does not keep track of people who emigrate from the country, but that doesn't mean that people are not leaving. Using data from the Current Population Surveys and other sources, Woodrow-Lafield (1996) estimated that there were approximately 220,000 emigrants from the United States each year as of the mid-1990s, of whom a majority were foreign-born persons (probably returning to their country of origin). The rest were native-born U.S. citizens leaving the country for a variety of personal reasons. Since most emigrants are people who had immigrated at an earlier time, you can see that the overall level of emigration is heavily dependent on the size of the foreign-born population, which has been steadily increasing, as shown in Table 7.2.

The U.S. Census Bureau estimates that about 1.2 percent of the foreign-born population emigrates annually, which drives their projection of a steady increase in out-migration during the first half of the twentieth century, with an expected average of more than 300,000 emigrants per year (Hollman, Mulder, and Kallan 2000). However, by matching persons in households that respond to the Current Population Survey, Van Hook and her associates (2006) have estimated that 2.9 percent of foreign-born persons are leaving the United States and that the rate is more than twice as high (4.3 percent) for people who arrived within the prior 10 years than for those who have been in the United States for 10 years or longer (2.0 percent).

The evidence suggests that there are two main patterns of return migration, accounting for most emigration from the United States (Rumbaut 1997; Reagan and Olsen 2000). The first pattern is for some people who migrate into the country to quickly become discouraged or disenchanted, or perhaps to reach a short-term goal, and then to return home, having stayed in the United States for only a short while. The other pattern is for people to migrate to the United States when young, and then retire back to their country of origin. We know, for example, that each month the Social Security Administration sends more than half million checks to foreign addresses (U.S. Social Security Administration 2010), and it is likely that most of these are being sent to people who migrated to the United States to work, and then when they reached retirement age went back from whence they came—where their retirement check in dollars is likely to go farther than in the United States.

Migration into and out of Canada

Canada's immigration experience has been similar, but not identical, to the pattern in the United States, as I have already highlighted. Although Canada has historically had a high level of immigration, it also experienced considerable emigration

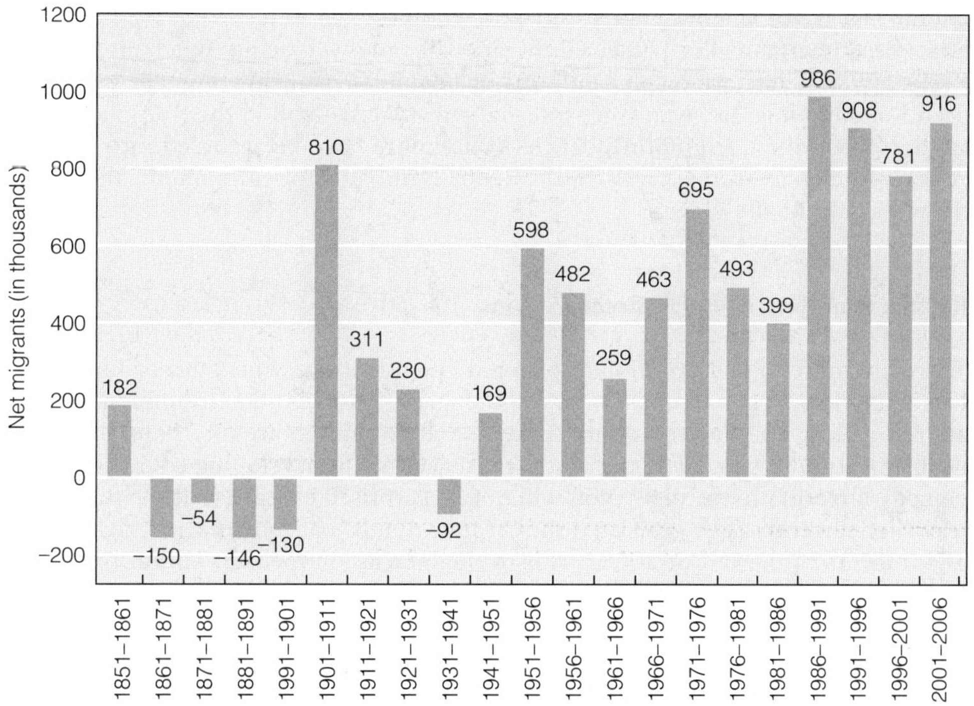

Figure 7.6 Immigration into Canada

Sources: Data for 1851 to 2001 from Statistics Canada (2005); 2001–2006 data are estimates by the author.

(people leaving to return home, or entering the United States from Canada) until after World War II, as you can see in Figure 7.6. Net migration jumped in the late 1980s and early 1990s as a result of immigration policy changes, but has slackened some since then. However, it is still at historically high levels.

The 2006 census data for Canada show that one in nine Canadians speaks a language other than English or French at home, and the number of people reporting a mother tongue other than English or French totals more than 6 million of Canada's 31 million residents (Statistics Canada 2009). Chinese is the most common language spoken at home other than English or French, followed by Punjabi, Spanish, and German. This is a clear transition from the 1971 census when German, Italian, and Ukrainian were the leading nonofficial languages (Migration News 1998). As in the United States, recent immigrants to Canada are far less likely to have come from Europe than was true in the past. Since at least the mid-1990s, more than half of all immigrants have been from Asia and the Pacific Islands (Statistics Canada 2009).

Forced Migration

Sitting on the sidelines of the migration transition are people who may not have originally intended to move but wound up being forced to do so anyway. A **forced**

migrant is, as you might expect, someone who has been forced to leave his or her home because of a real or perceived threat to life and well-being (Reed, Haaga, and Keely 1998). There are tens of millions of people alive at this moment who have been forced to migrate. Many are internally displaced—still in their original country but not in their original residence. Many more have been forced into another country and so are refugees. A third category, and a historically important one, is the worst one of all—slavery.

Refugees and Internally Displaced Persons

There are more than 42 million "uprooted" people in the world, according to the United Nations High Commissioner for Refugees (2009). About 15 million of these are refugees, 1 million are asylum seekers, and 26 million are internally displaced people. About 80 percent of the world's refugees are in developing countries and if you pay attention to the news, you will not be surprised to learn that the two countries that currently have generated the greatest number of refugees are Afghanistan and Iraq. As of the end of 2008, prior to the increase in the U.S. military presence in Afghanistan, there were already 2.8 million Afghan refugees and 1.9 million Iraqi refugees (United Nations High Commissioner for Refugees 2009). It falls disproportionately on neighbors to shelter refugees, and so Pakistan, Syria, Iran, and Jordan are hosting more refugees than any other countries in the world. Among the rich countries, Germany hosts the greatest number of refugees (about half a million), followed by the United Kingdom and the United States.

Refugees from Palestine actually represent the majority of the long-term "warehoused" group, although the majority of these individuals have been born into refugee status and so the United Nations does not always include them in their statistics. Jordan is the only one of the Middle Eastern countries that has typically allowed a Palestinian to become a citizen of the country of asylum, and so Palestinians have remained as refugees for nearly a half century in other countries.

There are essentially three solutions to the problem of refugee populations, including: (1) repatriation to the country of origin; (2) resettlement in the country to which they have fled; and (3) resettlement in a third country. None of these is easy to accomplish, and the situation is complicated by the fact that birth rates tend to be high among refugee groups, and therefore many of these refugees are children who have been born outside their parents' country of origin. The problem therefore compounds itself and there are no easy solutions.

Slavery

There can be no doubt that the most hideous of migratory movements are those endured by slaves. Slavery has existed within various human societies for millennia, and McDaniel (1995:11) has summarized the early historical situation as follows:

> The international slave trade in Africans began with the Arab conquests in northern and eastern Africa and the Mediterranean coast in the seventh century. From the seventh to

> the eleventh century, Arabs and Africans brought large numbers of European slaves into the North African ports of Tangier, Algiers, Tunis, Tripoli, and Fez. In fact, most of the slaves traded throughout the Mediterranean before the fall of Constantinople were European.

Between the thirteenth and fifteenth centuries Africans, along with Turks, Russians, Bulgarians, and Greeks, were slaves on the plantations of Cyprus. However, the most massive migration of slaves was that of the Atlantic slave trade, which transported an estimated 11 million African slaves to the western hemisphere between the end of the fifteenth century and the middle of the nineteenth century (Thomas 1997). The slaves came largely from the west coast of sub-Saharan Africa, from countries that now comprise Senegal, Sierra Leone, the Ivory Coast, Dahomey, Benin, Cameroon, Gabon, Ghana, the Congo, and Nigeria, the northern part of which has been described as one of the largest slave societies in modern times (Lovejoy and Hogendorn 1993). "The preponderance of Africans who were sold into slavery were taken by force. Some were taken directly by Arab or European slave traders, but most were sold into slavery by the elite Africans who had captured them in warfare or who were holding them either for their own use as slaves or to be traded as slaves later" (McDaniel 1995:14).

The destinations were largely the sugar and coffee plantations of the Caribbean and Brazil, but hundreds of thousands were also sold in the United States to serve as laborers on cotton and tobacco plantations. The slave traders themselves were initially Portuguese and Spanish, but the French, Dutch, and especially the British were active later on. It was eventually the British, however, who pushed for a worldwide abolition of slavery. Slavery was abolished throughout the British empire, including Canada, in 1833, although Canada had never tolerated slavery, and the impact of slavery on Canada was primarily that it was a place of refuge for those seeking to escape slavery. Similarly there is little history of slavery in Mexico, which in 1827 declared that no person could be born a slave in Mexico. In the United States, it was not until 1865 (in the context of the Civil War) that the Thirteenth Amendment to the Constitution finally abolished slavery.

Actually, though, slavery has not been abolished. It is still found in countries like Niger, Cameroon, Chad, Mali, Mauritania, and Sudan, where it is illegal, but where offenders often go unpunished (*The Economist* 2005; Polgreen 2008), and from where it has spilled over into other countries, including the United States (Bales 2007). Furthermore, one of slavery's latest incarnations is politely called "human trafficking." This involves the forcible migration of hundreds, if not thousands, of women and children each year for purposes of sexual exploitation and forced labor (see, for example, International Labour Organization 2008).

Consequences of Migration

Why does migration matter? It has the potential to significantly affect the lives of the people who move, whether forced or not, the people they leave behind, and the new people with whom they interact after making the move. And, depending on the size of the migration flow over time, migration has the potential to dramatically alter the demographic structure of a community within a very short period of time, as well as to subtly, but importantly, alter the social structure over the long term as the immigrant stock adds its children to the societal recipe, and the stock changes its flavor, so to speak.

Consequences for Migrants

Although migrants typically move in order to improve their lives, we must recognize that, for the individual migrant, relocation may nonetheless produce anxiety and stress as a new social environment has to be negotiated. Part of that negotiation process may be to deal with discrimination (possibly including violence) that is often the result of **xenophobia**, fear and mistrust of strangers on the part of people already residing in the place to which the migrant has moved. One of the ways in which migrants cope with a new environment is to seek out others who share their cultural and geographic backgrounds (sometimes called **co-ethnics**). This is often aided or even forced by the existence of an **enclave** (a place in a larger community within which members of a particular subgroup tend to concentrate) of recent and former migrants from the same or similar areas. In fact, the development of an enclave may facilitate migration, since a potential migrant need not be too fearful of the unknown, as discussed above in the network theory of migration. The enclave in the host area has guides to the new environment—former migrants who have made the adaptation and stand ready to aid in the social adjustment and integration of new migrants. Ethnic ties may also provide entrepreneurial newcomers with access to working capital, protected markets, and a pool of labor to help get a business started (Portes and Rumbaut 2006).

Although finding people of similar background may ease the coping burden for a new migrant, there is some evidence to suggest that the long-run social consequences of "flocking together" (especially among relatives) in a closed society of other immigrants will retard the migrant's adjustment to and assimilation into the new setting. John F. Kennedy's comment that "the way out of the ghetto lies not with muscle, but with the mastery of English" is more than a facile phrase. It points to a key to educational success and labor force entry (Portes and Rumbaut 2001), especially for the children of immigrants (Kasinitz et al. 2008).

On arrival in the host area, an immigrant may go through a brief period of euphoria and hopefulness—a sort of honeymoon. However, that may be followed by a period of shock and depression, especially for refugees. Rumbaut (1995:260) quotes a Cambodian refugee to the United States he interviewed:

> I was feeling great the first few months. But then, after that, I started to face all kinds of worries and sadness. I started to see the real thing of the United States, and I missed home more and more. I missed everything about our country: people, family, relatives and friends, way of life, everything. Then, my spirit started to go down; I lost sleep; my physical health weakened; and there started the stressful and depressing times. By now [almost 3 years after arrival] I feel kind of better, a lot better! Knowing my sons are in school as their father would have wanted [she was widowed], and doing well, makes me feel more secure.

Immigrants undergo a process of **adaptation** or adjustment to the new environment, in which they adjust to the new physical and social environment and learn how best to negotiate everyday life. Some immigrants never go beyond this, but most proceed to some level of **acculturation**, in which they adopt the host language, bring their diet more in line with the host culture, listen to the music and read the newspapers, magazines, and books of the host culture, and make friends outside of their immigrant group. This may be more likely to happen if the immigrant has children, because children often are exposed to the new culture more intensively than are adults. Language use is frequently employed as an indicator of acculturation, and the United States has been called a "graveyard" for languages because an immigrant's native language is unlikely to last much beyond his or her own generation (Rumbaut, Massey, and Bean 2006). Many migrants never go beyond linguistic acculturation, but some migrants (and especially their children raised in the host culture) **assimilate**, in which they take on not just the outer trappings of the host culture, but also assume the behaviors and attitudes of members of the host culture (Alba and Nee 1997; Rumbaut 1997). Intermarriage with a member of the host society is often used as an index of assimilation.

These individual adjustments to a receiving society assume an open society and assume that immigrants are considered on an individual basis. In fact, nations rarely are open with regard to immigrants, and because immigration occurs regularly in clumps (with groups of refugees, or new guest workers arriving nearly *en masse*), immigrants often are treated categorically. Although assimilation is one model by which a society might incorporate immigrants into its midst, there are at least three other types of incorporation: **integration** (mutual accommodation); **exclusion** (in which immigrants are kept separate from most members of the host society and are maintained in separate enclaves or ghettos); and **multiculturalism** or *pluralism* (in which immigrants retain their ethnic communities but share the same legal rights as other members of the host society) (Zlotnick 1994).

Multiculturalism, in particular, is enhanced by the **transnational migrant**, who sets roots in the host society while still maintaining strong linkages to the donor society (Schiller, Basch, and Blanc 1995). Such individuals have also been called "skilled transients" (Findlay 1995)—relatively skilled workers moving internationally on assignment and, in the process, having an impact on the area of destination while always intending to return to the area of origin. In parts of sub-Saharan Africa, a type of transnationalism has been institutionalized into the social structure among migratory laborers (Guilmoto 1998), and there is evidence that elsewhere in the world less-skilled workers are adopting this strategy of living dual lives—working in one environment but maintaining familial ties in another (Levitt, DeWind, and Vertovec 2003).

Children of Immigrants

Most of the explanations about how immigrants deal with their new society focus on adult immigrants who were raised in one country and are now adapting and adjusting to another. The children born to them in the new country (the second generation) will have the task of growing up mainly (or only) knowing the new country, but having to deal with immigrant parents. Note, however, that the youngest immigrants (those who are prepubescent, approximately 12 or younger) are actually in that same situation—too young for the country of origin to have had a strong impact on their own development, and growing up in the new country almost as though they had been born there. This is sometimes known as the 1.5 generation—halfway between the first generation (the immigrants), and the second generation (the children of immigrants) (Rumbaut 1997; Perlmann 2005).

The path that receiving societies often have in mind for the children of immigrants is a straight-line process of assimilation from the country of their parents' origin into the country of their own birth. You are already primed for the idea, however, that when it comes to migration, life is never going to be so simple. In Europe, and increasingly in the Americas, the second generation may fall into one of two possible patterns of **segmented assimilation**, in which the children of immigrants (1) adopt the host language and behavior, but find themselves identified with a racial/ethnic minority group that effectively limits their full participation in society, or (2) assimilate economically into the new society, but retain strong attachments to the ethnic group of origin (Portes 1995). These variations in the path of assimilation are occasioned especially by the fact that immigrants to Europe and to North America are likely to come from different ethnic and cultural backgrounds than prevail in the host country. In Canada, these are known as *visible minorities*, and children of immigrants who are visible minorities are more likely to experience some form of segmented assimilation rather than assimilating directly into the mainstream of Canadian society (Boyd and Grieco 1998).

Societal Consequences

Although the consequences of migration for the individual are of considerable interest (especially to the one uprooted), a more pervasive aspect of the social consequences of migration is the impact on the demographic composition and social structure of both the donor and host areas. The demographic composition is influenced by the selective nature of migration, particularly selectivity by age. The **donor area** typically loses people from its young adult population, as those people are then added to the **host area**. Many small towns in Latin America, for example, are left with older adults and children whose parents are abroad, a situation that carries with it a host of economic and psychological challenges. Further, because it is at those ages that the bulk of reproduction occurs, the host area has its level of natural increase augmented at the expense of the donor area. This natural-increase effect of migration is further enhanced by the relatively low probability of death of young adults compared with the higher probability in the older portion of a population.

The selective nature of migration, when combined with its high volume, such as in the United States and Canada, helps to alter the patterns of social relationships and social organization in both the host and donor communities. Extended kinship relations are weakened, although not destroyed, and local economic, political, and educational institutions have to adjust to shifts in the number of people serviced by each.

Remittances

Nearly hidden from view is the tremendous economic benefit that less developed sending countries receive when their citizens go off to work in the more developed nations. Oded Stark and his associates (see, for example, Stark and Lucas 1988) were among the first researchers to investigate the fact that many, if not most, immigrant workers send part of their pay back home, thereby raising the standard of living of the family members who stayed behind, and encouraging a certain dependence on the income being earned by the migrating family members. To be sure, the promise of remittances is part of the household strategy for sending a family member abroad. Since foreign travel is expensive, including for many the cost of a smuggler, families "invest" in young people who will send back "migradollars," as they are sometimes called (Kanaiaupuni and Donato 1999). This money can finance the purchase of homes and consumer durables in the country of origin, provide startup money for new businesses, and even provide enough resources in poor communities of Mexico, for example, to lower the infant death rate. Although we know that males are generally more likely to migrate than females, some households prefer to send their daughters in the belief that they are more likely than sons to actually send money back home (Castles and Miller 2009).

So important have remittances become that the World Bank monitors the flow between countries in order to better understand the impact on both sending and receiving economies. The World Bank estimates that in 2009 (the most recent year available at this writing) 430 billion dollars in remittances was sent around the world, most of it from richer to poorer countries (but some of it between less developed nations) (Ratha, Mohapatra, and Silwal 2009). It probably won't surprise you to learn that in terms of total dollars, Mexico receives more than any other country, and more remittances are sent from the United States than from any other nation.

In terms of the impact on economies, remittances account for less than one percent of the world's estimated gross domestic product, but they are extremely important for some developing countries. World Bank data suggest that in 2008 there were 24 countries in which remittances from migrants accounted for 10 percent or more of national income, including 25 percent of Lebanon's economy, 19 percent of Jordan's, 19 percent of Haiti's (and that was before the big earthquake in 2010), and more than 10 percent in El Salvador, Honduras, and Guatemala. The 23 billion dollars going to Mexico that year accounted for only 2 percent of Mexico's national economy, but remittances have had a huge impact on those communities that have participated most heavily in the migration to the United States (Weeks and Weeks 2010).

Remittances may be one way out of poverty, but they are not received without a cost. There is the real possibility that family members in the sending countries will become dependent on the remittances as a source of income, and will be vulnerable to economic changes not just in their own country, but also in the country to which their remitting relatives have moved. This is not something that people are going to think about in their initial cost-benefit analysis, but it is something they may have to deal with later on, especially in the wake of the global recession that started in 2007. It is clear that the flow of remittances slowed down measurably after 2008, especially to Latin America, thus contributing to harder times throughout the regions from which migrants had come (Ratha, Mohapatra, and Silwal 2009).

Overall, then, migration has the greatest short-run impact on society of any of the three demographic processes. It is a selective process that always requires changes and adjustments on the part of the individual migrant. More importantly, when migration occurs with any appreciable volume, it may have significant consequences for the social, cultural, and economic structure of both donor and host regions. Because of these potential consequences, patterns of migration are harbingers of social change in a society.

Summary and Conlusion

Migration is any permanent change of residence. It is the most complex of the three population processes because we have to account for the wide variety in the number of times people may move, the vast array of places migrants may go, and the incredible diversity of reasons there may be for who goes where, and when. Of importance to demographers is the fact that the migration transition is an inevitable consequence of the mortality transition, which lowers the death rate prior to the initiation of the fertility transition. This unleashes population growth in rural areas that cannot be accommodated by agricultural economies, pushing people (usually young adults) to migrate to where the jobs are—usually cities within their own country, but sometimes to other countries.

For decades, migration theory advanced little beyond the basic idea of push and pull factors operating in the context of migration selectivity. More recently, conceptual models have developed that are very reminiscent of the explanations of the fertility transition. To begin with, we need a model of how the migration decision is arrived at (not unlike the first precondition for a fertility decline—the acceptance of the idea that you are empowered to act). Then, most importantly for the study of migration, we need to understand what might motivate a person to migrate. A variety of theoretical perspectives has been offered, including the neoclassical approach, the new household economics of migration approach, the theory of the dual labor market, and world systems theory. Finally, the means available to migrate represent those things that "grease the skids," making it easy to migrate once a person is motivated to do so. These include not only improved transportation and communication but also the development of social networks and institutions that facilitate the migration process.

Voluntary migration on a massive global scale did not begin in earnest until the mid-nineteenth century, and it was primarily a movement of Europeans to the Americas. As the volume increased and the cultural mix changed, the United States began to put up hurdles to slow things down. This led in the 1920s to a set of very restrictive immigration policies that effectively choked off immigration for more than a generation. In the 1960s the immigration laws were liberalized, and when President Lyndon Johnson signed the new bill into law he argued that it was largely symbolic and would not really have an impact on immigration levels. He could not have been more wrong, and the United States has been adjusting to a new reality of immigration ever since.

Throughout the world, population growth has induced an increase in the volume of migration, both legal and undocumented. "Temporary" labor migration has also increased throughout the world as jobs have become more available in the aging, more developed societies for the burgeoning number of younger workers from less developed countries. Understandably, guest workers are often reluctant to leave higher-income countries, even when the economies in those places slow down and pressure builds for foreigners to go home. Such people are only a few steps away from the unhappily large fraction of the world's migrants who are refugees, seeking residence in other countries after being forced out of their own.

Migration has dynamic consequences for the migrants themselves, for the areas from which they came, and for the places to which they go. Some of these consequences are fairly predictable if we know the characteristics of the migrants. If immigrants are well-educated young adults, for example, they will be looking for well-paying jobs, they may add to the economic prosperity of an area, and they will probably be establishing families, which will further add to the area's population and increase the demand for services.

Although it is not always apparent, the quality of our everyday life is greatly affected by the process of migration, for even if we ourselves never move, we will spend a good part of our lifetime adjusting to people who have migrated into our lives and to the loss of people who have moved away. Each new person coming into our life greatly expands our social capital by increasing the potential size of our social network, especially since many people who move away do so physically but not symbolically; that is, we remain in communication.

In the next chapter, I put the dynamics of migration together with those of mortality and fertility to show you how they collectively influence the age/sex structure. That may not sound very interesting, but in fact it is through the changing age structure that population growth makes itself felt, making the age structure one of the most important drivers of social change in the world. For that reason, it is like a stealth bomber—without a really good radar system (in this case, the tools of demography), you may not see it until it's too late to do anything about it.

Main Points

1. Migration is the process of changing residence and moving your whole round of social activities from one place to another.
2. The migration transition initially referred to internal migration occurring as a result of population growth, which created a redundant rural population.
3. Migration can be assessed in terms of flows (the movement of people) or stocks (the characteristics of people according to their migration status).
4. Explanations of why people move typically begin with the push-pull theory, first formulated in the late nineteenth century.
5. Migration is selective and is associated especially with age and gender, giving rise to the idea that migration is an implementing strategy—a means to a desired end.
6. Migration within countries tends to be for economic reasons, but housing-related moves are especially common in the United States.
7. Major theories offered to explain international migration include neoclassical economics, the new household economics of migration, the dual labor market theory, world systems theory, network theory, institutional theory, and cumulative causation.

8. The United States accepts more migrants (legal and undocumented) than any other country in the world, and for more than a century the U.S. government has implemented numerous complex efforts to control the number and characteristics of people entering the country.
9. Migration of all kinds, whether forced or voluntary, demands adjustment to a new environment on the part of the migrant, and sets in motion a societal response to the immigrant on the part of the receiving society.
10. Ross Baker once suggested that the "First Law of Demographic Directionality" is that a body that has headed west remains at west, and while that is still generally an accurate statement for the world, it is no longer as true in the United States as it once was.

Questions for Review

1. Discuss the way in which the theory of demographic change and response (introduced in Chapter 3) provides a conceptual framework for understanding the migration transition. How does that framework help us to understand future demographic changes in the developing nations?
2. Discuss the differences between migration stocks and flows, and then show how the two are interrelated in terms of their impact on both receiving and sending societies.
3. Describe your own lifetime experiences with migration, and relate them to the decision-making model shown in Figure 7.3.
4. What do you think the migration policy of the United States should be? Defend your answer and explain the connection between U.S. and Canadian policies.
5. Evaluate the way in which the timing of demographic transitions in other parts of the world has helped to explain the patterns of migration to the United States over the past two hundred years.

Suggested Readings

1. Charles Hirschman, Philip Kasinitz, and Josh De Wind, Editors, 1999, *The Handbook of International Migration: The American Experience* (New York: Russell Sage Foundation).

   The chapters in this important volume are written by the top researchers in the field of international migration as it relates to the United States. Although the focus is only on the U.S., the concepts and theories are applicable on a global scale.
2. Douglas Massey, Joaquín Arango, Graeme Hugo, Ali Kouaouci, Adela Pellegrino, and J. Edward Taylor, 1993, "Theories of International Migration: A Review and Appraisal," *Population and Development Review* 19(3):431–466; and 1994, "An Evaluation of International Migration Theory: The North American Case," *Population and Development Review* 20(4):699–752.

   These two articles, representing a matched set, will have a long-lasting influence on the field of international migration analysis because they bring together a long-needed review of theoretical perspectives.

3. Stephen Castles and Mark J. Miller, 2003, *The Age of Migration*, Third Edition (New York: Guilford Press).

   There is no better source than this book for a good global perspective on the volume and direction of international migration.

4. Philip Martin and Jonas Widgren, 2002, "International Migration: Facing the Challenge," Population Bulletin 57(1); and Philip Martin and Elizabeth Midgley, 2003, "Immigration: Shaping and Reshaping America," *Population Bulletin* 58(2).

   The first of these two reports from the Population Reference Bureau provides an excellent summary of the global migration situation, with discussions of regional patterns as well. The second report focuses on the impact of immigration on the United States.

5. Alejandro Portes and Rubén G. Rumbaut, 2006, *Immigrant America: A Portrait,* Third Edition. (Berkeley and Los Angeles: University of California Press).

   Portes and Rumbaut have been studying immigrant communities in America for several decades and are the foremost authorities on the topic, as you will see in this volume.

Websites of Interest

Remember that websites are not as permanent as books and journals, so I cannot guarantee that each of the following websites still exists at the moment you are reading this. You may have to Google the name of the organization to find the current web address.

1. **http://www.dhs.gov/files/statistics/immigration.shtm**
   This is the immigration statistics page of the website for the U.S. Department of Homeland Security. The site provides access to immigration and border enforcement statistics. In Canada, the immigration agency is known as Citizenship and Immigration Canada (CIC), and its website includes information on government policy, as well as links to research on immigration: **http://www.cic.gc.ca/english/index.asp**

2. **http://www.migrationinformation.org**
   The Migration Information Source is a project of the Migration Policy Institute in Washington, DC, and offers an extensive, and constantly growing, range of articles and resources useful to policy makers and people in academia.

3. **http://migration.ucdavis.edu**
   Migration Dialogue was developed by Philip Martin at the University of California–Davis, and is a tremendous resource, especially because it includes full issues of the newsletter *Migration News,* in which newspaper, magazine, and journal articles and books about migration are summarized and commented on.

4. **http://borderbattles.ssrc.org**
   The Social Science Research Council has a series of topical papers that deal with social science and public-policy issues. This set of papers, authored by experts in the field of migration studies, looks at immigration policy in the United States.

5. **http://www.refugees.org**
   The United States Committee for Refugees (USCR) is a private, nonprofit organization working to help refugees throughout the world. This site includes information about refugees, asylees, and internally displaced persons for almost every country of the world. Because the estimation of refugees is as much an art as it is a science, you should also visit the site of the United Nations High Commissioner for Refugees (UNHCR) at **http://www.unhcr.org** for comparisons.

CHAPTER 8
The Age Transition

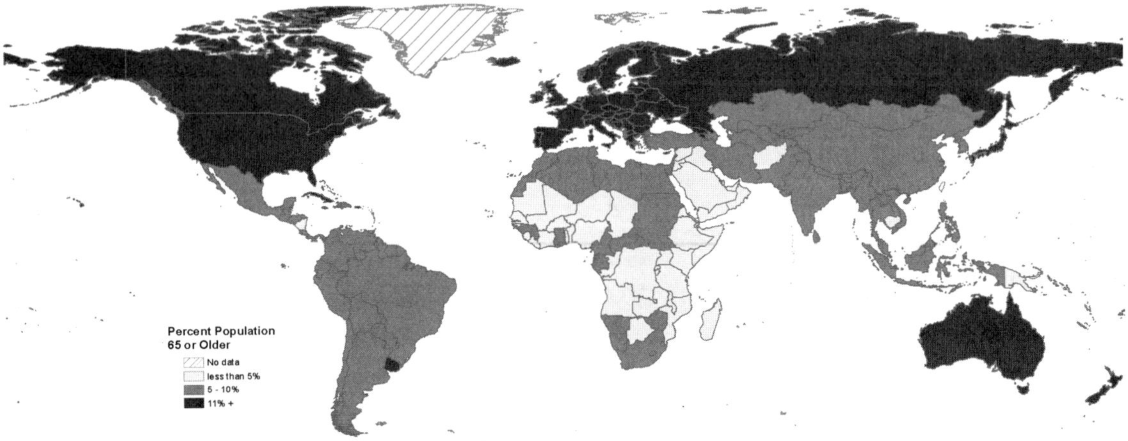

Figure 8.1 Percent of the Population That Is 65 or Older

Discussions of population growth often make it seem (to those less well-informed than you now are) as though population increases the same way your bathtub fills up with water—evenly all over. You, however, know from previous chapters that the issues of age and sex rear their heads over and over again. Mortality differs by age and sex; fertility differs by age and sex; migration differs by age and sex. It is time, then, to deal more explicitly with the concepts of age and sex, because population growth takes place age by age and somewhat differently for males than for females. It matters not just how fast the population is growing, but which age and sex groups are growing and which ones are growing faster or slower than others. In particular, predictable changes occur in the distribution of a population by age and sex as a society goes through the demographic transition.

What Is the Age Transition?

This **age transition** represents a shift from a very young population in which there are slightly more males than females to an older population in which there are more females than males. In between, bumps and dents in the age and sex structure represent powerful forces for social, economic, and political change. In general, it is the interaction of fertility, mortality, and migration that produces the **age and sex structure**, which can be viewed as a key to the life of a social group—a record of past history and a portent of the future. Population processes not only produce the age and sex structure but are, in turn, affected by it—yet another example of the complexity of the world when seen through your demographic "eye." It would not, in fact, be exaggerating too much to say that changes in the age and sex structure affect virtually all social institutions. In this chapter, I escort you through that complexity by first defining the concepts of age and sex as they relate to population dynamics, and then by examining the dynamics of the age transition.

The Concepts of Age and Sex

Age and sex influence the working of society in important ways because society assigns social roles and frequently organizes people into groups on the basis of their age and gender (the social component of sex). Age is a biological characteristic, but it is constantly changing, whereas sex is biological in nature, but does not change (except by human intervention in rare cases). Gender roles can and do change, however, so the social side of sex (you know what I mean here!) is clearly dynamic. The changing nature of age imposes itself on society because younger people are treated differently from older people, and different kinds of behavior are expected of people as they move through different ages. At the same time, biological changes inherent in the aging process influence what societies expect of people which, in turn, influences how people behave.

Age Stratification

The idea that societies have separate sets of expected roles and obligations for people of different ages is captured by the concept of **age stratification**. Kingsley Davis noted in 1949 that "all societies recognize age as a basis of status, but some of them emphasize it more than others" (Davis 1949:104). The age stratification theory begins with the proposition that age is a basis of social differentiation in a manner analogous to stratification by social class (Foner 1975; Riley 1976). The term *stratification* implies a set of inequalities, and in this case it refers to the fact that societies distribute resources unequally by age. These resources include not only economic goods but also such crucial intangibles as social approval, acceptance, and respect. This theory is not a mere description of status, however; it introduces a dynamic element by recognizing that aging is a process of social mobility. Foner (1975) notes that "as the individual ages, he too moves within a social hierarchy. He goes from one set of age-related social roles to another and at each level receives greater or lesser rewards than before" (p. 156). Contrasted to other forms of social mobility, however, which may rely on merit, luck, or accident of birth, social mobility in the age hierarchy is "inevitable, universal and unidirectional in that the individual can never grow younger" (p. 156).

What aspects of life are influenced by age (and in some instances by sex or gender as well)? In Table 8.1 I have listed just a few of the important things that vary by age in most human societies. As the number and percentage of people at each age and sex change, the distribution of these characteristics will therefore also change, and this is the force for social, economic, and political change. For example, a very young population will have a relatively small fraction of its population in the labor

Table 8.1 Aspects of Human Society That Vary by Age and Sex (or Gender)

Category	Characteristic or Activity
Demographic	Being sick and having restricted activities of daily living
	Dying
	Being sexually active
	Having a baby
	Moving or migrating
Social	Getting married/divorced
	Being involved in religious organizations and activity
	Being involved in political organizations and activity
	School enrollment
	Level of educational attainment
	Being involved in criminal or other socially disapproved behavior
Economic	Being in the labor force
	Occupation within the labor force
	Current income
	Level of accumulated wealth

force unless, as happens in poorer countries, children are put to work at a young age. However, in such a society, those younger people in the labor force will have lower-status occupations. It typically takes time and experience (including education and other training) to reach the higher occupational strata. Since income is closely related to occupation, it is the older adults who tend to have the highest incomes, and it is the maintenance of higher incomes for several years that increases the chance that people will accumulate wealth. Thus, all other things being equal, we would expect that a population with a high proportion of middle-aged adults would have more people in the labor force with higher incomes and more wealth than a population with a high proportion of children.

Age strata, though identifiable, are not viewed as fixed and unchanging. The assumption is that the number of age strata, and the prestige and power associated with each, are influenced by the needs of society and by characteristics of people at each age (their numbers and sociodemographic characteristics). European society of a few hundred years ago seems to have been characterized by three age strata—infancy, adulthood, and old age (Aries 1962); and power (highest status) seems to have been concentrated in the hands of older people (Simmons 1960). Modern Western societies appear to have at least seven strata—infancy, childhood, adolescence, young adulthood, middle age, young-old, and old-old, with power typically concentrated in the hands of the middle-aged and the young-old.

As we age from birth to death, we are allocated to **social statuses** (your relative position or standing in society) and **social roles** (the set of obligations and expectations that characterize your particular position in society) considered appropriate to our age. Thus, children and adolescents are typically allocated to appropriate educational statuses, adults to appropriate positions of power and prestige, and the older population to positions of retirement and waning influence. We all learn the roles that society deems appropriate to our age, and we reward each other for fulfilling those roles and tend to cast disapproval on those who do not fulfill the societal expectation. But neither the allocation process nor the overall **socialization** process (learning the behavior appropriate to particular social roles) is static. They are in constant flux as changing cohorts alter social conditions and as social conditions, in turn, alter the characteristics of cohorts. This leads us to the concept of cohort flow.

Age Cohorts

In population studies, a cohort refers to a group of people born during the same time period, and **cohort flow** captures the notion that at each age we are influenced by the historical circumstances that similarly affect other people who are the same age. As Riley (1976:194–195) points out:

> Each cohort starts out with a given size which, save for additions from immigration, is the maximum size it can ever attain. Over the life course of the cohort, some portion of its members survive, while others move away or die until the entire cohort is destroyed.
>
> Each cohort starts out also with a given composition; it consists of members born with certain characteristics and dispositions. Over the life course of the individual, some of these characteristics are relatively stable (a person's sex, color, genetic makeup, country

> of birth, or—at entry into adulthood in our society—the level of educational attainment are unlikely to change). . . . When successive cohorts are compared, they resemble each other in certain respects, but differ markedly in other respects: in initial size and composition, in age-specific patterns of survival (or longevity), and in the period of history covered by their respective life span.

At any given moment, a cross section of all cohorts defines the current age strata in a society. Figure 8.2 displays a Lexis diagram, a tool often used in population studies to help us discern the difference between period data (the cross-sectional snapshot of all ages at one time) and cohorts (of which there are many at any point in time). The diagram is named for a German demographer, Wilhelm Lexis (1875), who helped develop it in the nineteenth century as an aid for analyzing life table data (Vandeschrick 2001). Age is shown on the vertical axis, and time (the moment of birth in units of years) is shown along the horizontal axis. The cohort of people born in 2006 (starting at 2006 and ending just at 2007) "advance through life along a 45° line" (Preston, Heuveline, and Guillot 2001:31), which is represented by the area (*C*) in Figure 8.2.

The period data, crosscutting many cohorts, are illustrated by the shaded area (*P*), whereas comparing people at the same age across many cohorts over time

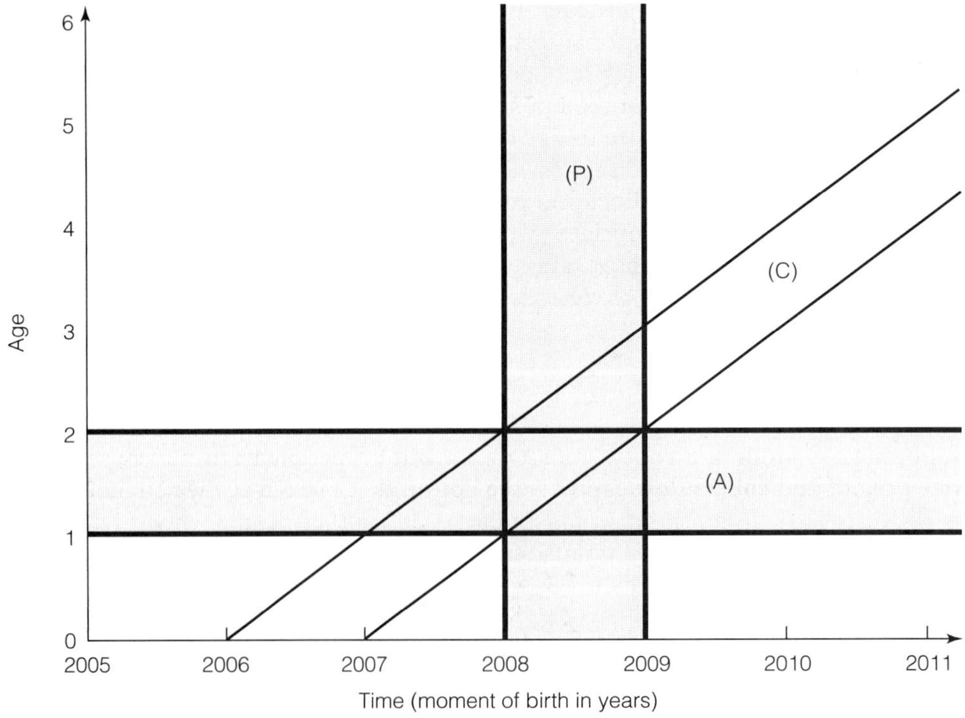

Figure 8.2 A Lexis Diagram Visualizes the Relationship Between Cohorts and Period Data

would be done with data shaded as (*A*) in Figure 8.2. Researchers use the Lexis diagram to calculate age-period-cohort (*APC*) rates that disentangle the combined influences of things specific to a particular age (the age effect), things unique to a time in history (the period effect), and things unique to specific birth cohorts (the cohort flow effect) (Knorr-Held and Rainer 2001; O'Brien 2000; Robinson and Jackson 2001). Lung cancer, for example, is most likely to kill people at older ages (the age effect), but death rates from it will depend partly on when a person was diagnosed (the period effect influenced by the timing of new treatments for the disease), and partly on cohort effects (cohorts born from the 1920s through the 1940s were more heavily into cigarette smoking than earlier or later cohorts).

As cohorts flow through time, their respective sizes and characteristics may alter the allocation of status and thus their socialization into various age-related roles because members of each cohort are moving through history together, whereas each separate cohort moves through moments in history at a different age (and thus with a different potential effect) than every other cohort. As cohorts move through time, their characteristics may change in response to changing social and economic conditions (such as wars, famines, and economic prosperity), and those changing conditions will influence the formation of new cohorts. This continual feedback between the dynamics of successive cohorts and the dynamics of other changes in society produces a constant shifting in the status and meaning attached to each age stratum, providing an evolutionary link between the **age structure** and the social structure (Gordon and Longino 2000).

An excellent example of the way in which we can better understand society by knowing about cohort flow is the analysis of the "Lucky Few" by Carlson (2008). He builds on Easterlin's relative cohort size hypothesis (discussed in Chapter 3) to show how the fortunes of people born in the United States between 1929 and 1945 were influenced by being sandwiched historically between the "Greatest Generation"—that cohort that fought and won World War II (Brokaw 1998), and the baby boomers. Drawing on microdata samples from past censuses (using data from IPUMS, as discussed in Chapter 4), Carlson shows that the Lucky Few were too young to fight in World War II, but were then ideally situated in the age structure to be propelled forward by the demand for labor that followed the war. Indeed, they have spent their lives being pushed along by the younger baby boomers, the generation to which they as parents gave birth. Furthermore, as Easterlin (2008) has noted, the Lucky Few cohort grew up in the Great Depression, at a time of dramatically lowered expectations in life. Thus, they were more readily able to achieve their own goals in life, both in terms of family size and economic well-being, than either the prior or subsequent cohorts. They have also managed to move into the retirement years just ahead of the fiscal crisis that looms as the baby boomers retire, as I discuss in the essay accompanying this chapter.

Gender and Sex Ratios

One of the important trends in the modern world has been increasing gender equity, first in the richer nations, and now progressing, albeit unevenly, on a global scale. Note that I use the term *sex* when referring to the biological differences between males and females, reserving the term *gender* for the social aspects of behavior. There is enough overlap between biology and the social world, however, that this distinction is often pretty fuzzy. Sorting out which is which is still important, though, because while we may not be able to do very much about biological differences, we can do something about the fact that women are still treated differently from men in most societies and different kinds of behavior are often expected from each. Women have been what Simone de Beauvoir (1953) called "The Second Sex" in a book that helped to spark feminism in the twentieth century (quoted by Clarke 2000:v):

> One is not born, but rather becomes a woman. No biological, psychological, or economic fate determines the figure that the human female presents in society; it is civilization as a whole that determines this creature.

In the more than half century since de Beauvoir made these comments, there has been a considerable amount of research that somewhat tempers her claim that civilization is the sole cause of gendered behavior. I mentioned sex dimorphism in Chapter 5 in connection with the apparent superiority of females with respect to longevity. The same concept has been applied to various aspects of human and other primate behavior in which hormones do seem to underlie certain kinds of behavior (for a review, see Udry 2000). The social environment is clearly the strongest influence on gendered behavior, but the biological differences between males and females cannot be ignored, partly because they have a direct effect on both fertility and mortality, and because of that they affect the age structure as well.

It is a common assumption, for example, that there are the same numbers of males and females at each age—actually, this is rarely the case. Migration, mortality, and fertility operate differently to create inequalities in the ratio of males to females (known as the sex ratio).

$$\text{Sex ratio} = \frac{\text{Number of males}}{\text{Number of females}} \times 100.$$

A sex ratio greater than 100 thus means that there are more males than females, while a value of less than 100 indicates there are more females than males. The ratio can obviously be calculated for the entire population or for specific age groups.

Fertility has the most predictable impact on the sex ratio because in virtually every known human society more boys are born than girls. Sex ratios at birth are typically between 104 and 110. The United States tends to be on the low end of that range and Asian societies tend to be on the high end. India and China, in particular, have high sex ratios that appear to be increasing, not decreasing. It is generally believed that the high sex ratio is indicative of discrimination against girls, both before and after birth. Oster (2009) has estimated that sex differences in vaccinations, malnutrition, and treatment when sick can account for about half of the sex ratio imbalance in India, but the recent increases in the sex ratio around the world are due especially to selective abortion, which is now possible because of ultrasound technology that can identify the sex of a fetus (Attané and Guilmoto 2007). Many years ago, Westoff and Rindfuss (1974) argued that if these methods ever enjoyed widespread acceptance, there would be a short-run rise in the sex ratio at birth, since a preference for sons as first children (and for more total sons than daughters) is fairly common throughout the world, as discussed in Chapter 6. Indeed, it appears that the highest sex ratios in Asia are among third children (Attané and Guilmoto 2007; Guilmoto 2009), suggesting that the motivation to have a boy at this stage of family-building is very strong.

Westoff and Rindfuss also concluded that after an initial transition period, the sex ratio at birth would probably revert to the natural level of about 105 males per 100 females, because the disadvantage of too many or too few of either sex would be controlled by a shift to the other sex. China, however, seems to be pushing the envelope on this concept, because it has been wrapped into the one-child policy, which creates an extreme situation when people are having only one child and they prefer that child to be a male. Thus, China's sex ratio at birth is one of, if not the, highest in the world, and there has been a concern raised that too many young men relative to women could lead to increased risks of violence and conflict. "The masculinization of Asia's sex ratios in one of the overlooked 'megatrends' of our time, a phenomenon that may very likely influence the course of national and perhaps even international politics in the twenty-first century" (Hudson and den Boer 2004:4).

Despite the concern about the high and even increasing sex ratio in some countries, there is still the underlying question of why the "normal" sex ratio is not simply 100. The answer is that no one really knows (Clarke 2000). This is perhaps a biological adaptation to compensate partially for higher male death rates (or vice versa, since we also are not sure why death rates are higher for males, as I mentioned in Chapter 5). In fact, data on miscarriages and fetal deaths suggest that more males are conceived than females, and that death rates are higher for males from the very moment of conception. Thus, some of the variability in the sex ratio at birth could be due to differences in fetal mortality. But we aren't sure why those differences exist, either. Research being done as part of the human genome project suggests a role played by the X chromosome, but that is still just a guess (Gunter 2005).

Despite these societal differences in the sex ratio at birth, there is still a fairly predictable pattern in the sex ratio by age as a population moves through the demographic transition. These patterns are observable in Figure 8.3, where I have plotted the sex ratios at each age group for three countries representing different cultural patterns with respect to the sex ratio: Ghana, the United States, and China. All three countries show the general pattern that the sex ratio declines with increasing age, but in Ghana the sex ratio is lower at birth and the younger ages and then declines a little more slowly than in the other countries because women are dying at a higher rate relative to men than in the other countries. China has the highest sex ratio at birth among these three countries (as among virtually all countries), but then after about age 60 it drops much more quickly than in either Ghana or the United States. The United States is in the middle in terms of sex ratio at birth and in terms of the steepness with which the sex ratio drops in the older ages.

The Feminization of Old Age

Women live longer than men in almost every human society, which means they disproportionately populate the older ages, as you can see from the three examples in Figure 8.3. As recently as 1930 in the United States, there were equal numbers of males and females at age 65 and older (partly a result of the earlier influx of immigrant males)

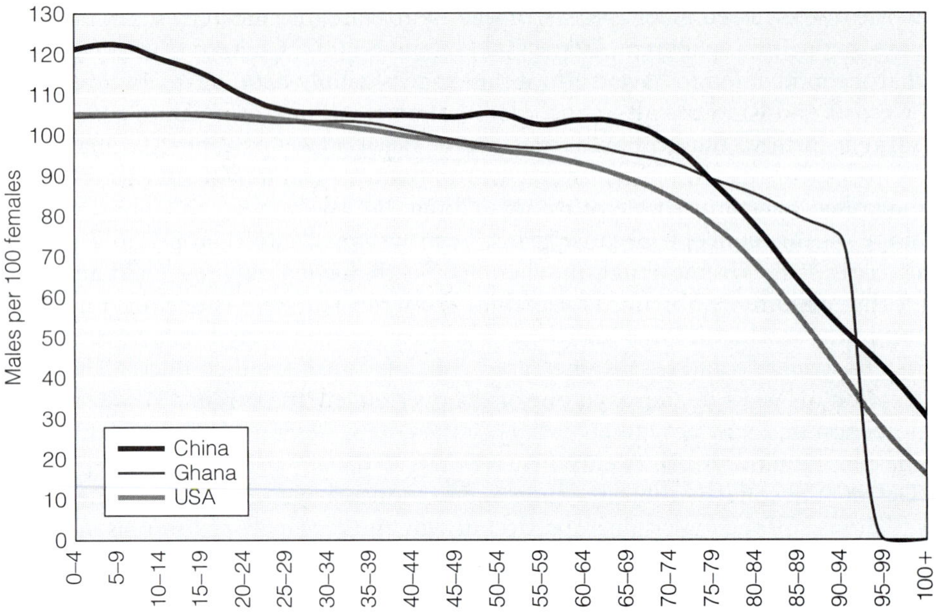

Figure 8.3 Comparing Sex Ratios by Age

Source: Adapted from United Nations Population Division, 2009, World Population Prospects: the 2008 Revision, Population Database, http://esa.un.org/unpp (accessed 2010). Data are estimates for 2010.

(Siegel 1993), but by 2010 there were only 73 males for every 100 females at the older ages. In the United States, the ratio of males to females aged 65–74 declined steeply between 1950 and 1970, leveled off, and has risen a bit since 1980 as men have begun to close the gender gap in life expectancy. Both United Nations and U.S. Census Bureau projections assume that life expectancy gains will be greater for males than females (a reversal of historical trends, probably due to the effects of smoking catching up with women, rather than a lot of positive things happening to men), and that will help push up the ratio of men to women as time goes by.

At age 75 and older, the higher mortality of males really has taken its toll: In 1950, there were 83 males per 100 females at that age in the United States, but this declined to only 54 males per 100 females by the 1990 census, with a rise since then to 62 in 2010. That means that at age 75 and older, nearly two-thirds of the people alive in the United States are women. The general pattern in the sex ratio at older ages has been similar in Canada and the United States, but the actual level of the sex ratio is consistently higher (albeit not by much) in Canada. This is probably due to the joint effects of immigration (immigrants account for a higher fraction of the Canadian than of the U.S. population), and the fact that the gender difference in life expectancy has been slightly less in Canada than in the United States. In Mexico, the feminization of old age is clearly under way, especially in urban areas where death rates are lowest. Projections for Mexico suggest that by the year 2025, the ratio of males to females from ages 65–74 in Mexico will actually be lower than in the United States, as Mexico moves through that part of the demographic transition where these differences seem to widen for a while, in this instance compounded by the disproportionate loss of males to migration out of Mexico and into the United States.

The data for Pakistan tell a different story. Pakistan is one of several countries in the world where there are still more men than women at oldest ages (indeed, at every age). This is a result of the lower status of women, which increases their mortality rates compared to men over the entire life course. In 1950 in Pakistan, there were 142 men aged 65–74 for every 100 women that age, but by 2010 the ratio had dropped to 103, so there has been considerable improvement. Progress has been made on a cohort-by-cohort basis to improve the status of women, and each new group of people moving into the older ages in Pakistan is increasingly feminine.

Demographic Drivers of the Age Transition

For most of human history, populations were very young. They had a high proportion of people in the younger ages, a modest fraction in the middle adult ages, and very few older people. Reaching an advanced age was truly an exceptional circumstance, and it is easy to see why the elderly would be revered and maybe even feared. The demographic transitions have changed all that in complex, but still decipherable ways. The end of the demographic transition, if such a thing really occurs, is assumed in the ideal to be a population with essentially the same number of people at each age until the very older ages when people die off fairly quickly, as I discussed in Chapter 5 in the context of the compression of mortality.

In between the historical pattern and this expected future pattern is where it gets messy, and that's where we are in the world. Figure 8.4 illustrates this with examples from four different countries—Nigeria, Mexico, the United States, and Italy, as of 2010. The graphs themselves are called **population pyramids**. They are called pyramids because the "classic" picture is of a high-fertility, high-mortality society with a broad base built of numerous births, rapidly tapering to the top (the older ages) because of high death rates in combination with the high birth rate. Nigeria's age and sex structure still reflects the classic look of the population pyramids, as you can see in Figure 8.4. Until very recently, Mexico also looked like that, but the decline in fertility in Mexico since the 1970s has narrowed the base of the pyramid rather noticeably. A country such as the United States where fertility is still at replacement level has an age and sex distribution that tends toward being rectangular, whereas Italy is somewhat barrel-shaped because of its very low fertility. No matter the shape, we still call the graph a population pyramid.

The population pyramids shown in Figure 8.4 do not happen by chance. Each of the three population processes has predictable impacts on the age structure. I have alluded to them before, but let me be more systematic now, looking at the impact of each population process in the order I introduced them to you in the previous chapters.

The Impact of Declining Mortality

Mortality declines affect every age and both sexes, but in virtually all societies the very youngest and the very oldest ages are most susceptible to death, and in modern

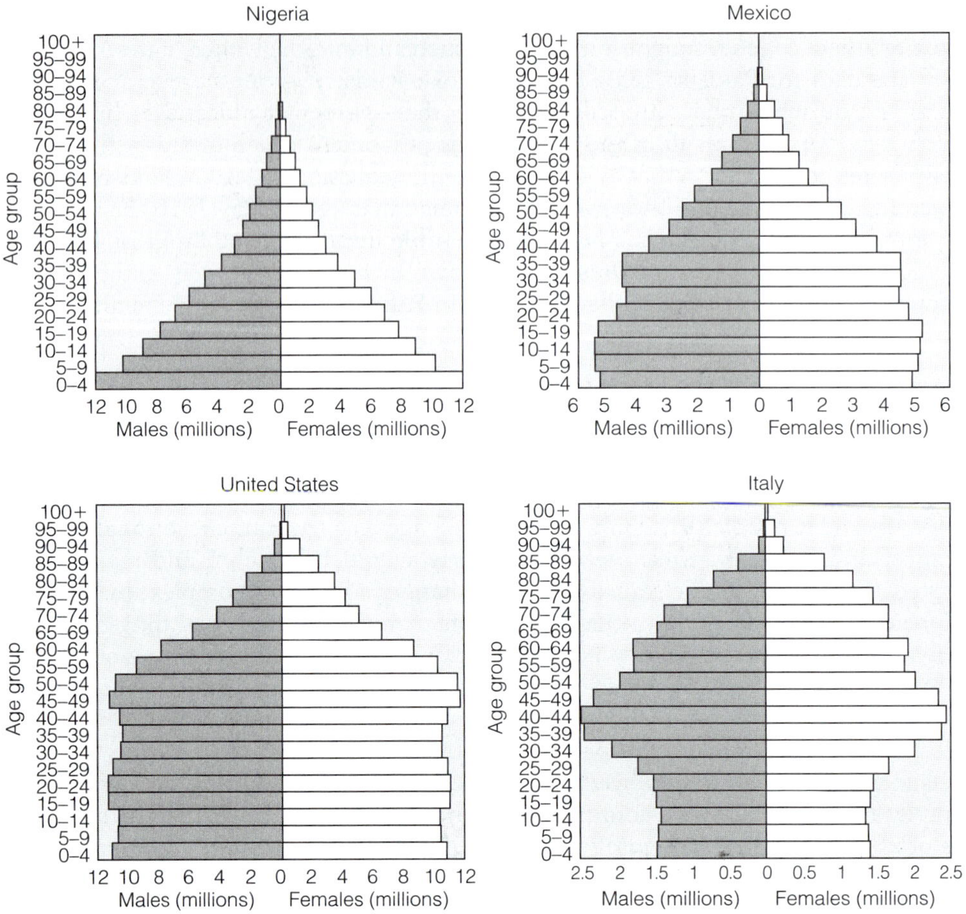

Figure 8.4 Illustrative Population Pyramids

Source: Adapted from United Nations Population Division, 2009, World Population Prospects: the 2008 Revision, Population Database, http://esa.un.org/unpp (accessed 2010). Data are estimates for 2010.

societies (where maternal mortality is fairly low), males are more likely than females to die at any given age. As I discussed in Chapter 5, however, the early stages of the health and mortality transition are characterized by bringing communicable diseases under control. This tends to affect infants and children more than any other age. As a result, the early drop in mortality increases the proportion of children who survive and thus serves to increase the fraction of the population at the younger ages. Furthermore, as I discussed above, the decline in mortality is also apt to affect male children slightly more than females, thus slightly increasing the sex ratio at the younger ages.

We can use data from **stable population models** to demonstrate the impact on an age structure as life expectancy increases. A stable population is a formal demographic model in which neither the age-specific birth rates nor the age-specific death rates have changed for a long time. Thus, a stable population is stable in the sense that the percentages of people at each age and sex do not change over time. A stable population could be growing at a constant rate (that is, the birth rate is higher than the death rate), it could be declining at a constant rate (the birth rate is lower than the death rate), or it could be unchanging (the birth rate equals the death rate). The latter is the case of **zero population growth** (ZPG), and if this prevails, we call it a stationary population. Thus, a stationary population is a special case of a stable population—all stationary populations are stable, but not all stable populations are stationary. The life table (discussed in Chapter 5) is one type of stationary population model. For analytical purposes, a stable population is usually assumed to be closed to migration. Since 1760, when Leonhard Euler first devised the idea of a stable population, demographers have used the concept to explore the exact influence of differing levels of mortality and fertility on the age/sex structure. Such analyses are possible using a stable population model because it smoothes out those dents and bumps in the age structure created by migration and by shifts in the death rate or the birth rate. Thus, if demographers were forced to study only real populations, we would be unable to ferret out all of the kinds of relationships we are interested in.

In this example, we want to see what would happen to a population's age-sex structure as life expectancy increased from 20 years for females (the premodern era) to 50 years for females (near the lower levels in the world today). Note that the life expectancy for males is just a bit lower than for females in each case. In order to see the impact only of mortality, we assume that fertility does not change (remaining at the TFR of 6.2 required for replacement with a life expectancy of 20 years) and that there is no migration. The results are shown in Figure 8.5, which has pyramids drawn as line graphs rather than bar graphs to better visualize the overlap of the age patterns.

As mortality declines without any change in fertility, you can see in Figure 8.5-A (the top panel) that the age structure actually becomes more pyramidal than it was before, as a result of the greater survivability of children, which means that the younger population is growing faster than the population at the older ages. In fact, as mortality declines, the average age of females in this population drops from 25.5 to 21.8.

While the average age is one way to summarize an age structure, another index commonly used to measure the social and economic impact of different age structures is the dependency ratio—the ratio of the dependent-age population (the young and the old) to the working-age population. The higher this ratio is, the more people each potential worker has to support; conversely, the lower it is, the fewer the people dependent on each worker:

$$\text{Dependency ratio} = \frac{(\text{population } 0\text{–}14) + (\text{population } 65+)}{\text{population } 15\text{–}64}.$$

In the age structure shown in the top panel of Figure 8.5, the dependency ratio increases from 0.71 to 0.99 as life expectancy increases from 20 to 50. The percentage of the population under age 15 increases from 36 to 45, whereas the percentage aged 65 and older increases from just under 3 percent to just over 3 percent. And, of course, because of the decline in mortality, this population is now growing much faster than it was before. Indeed, in this example, the control of mortality, unmatched by a drop in fertility, causes the rate of population growth to jump from

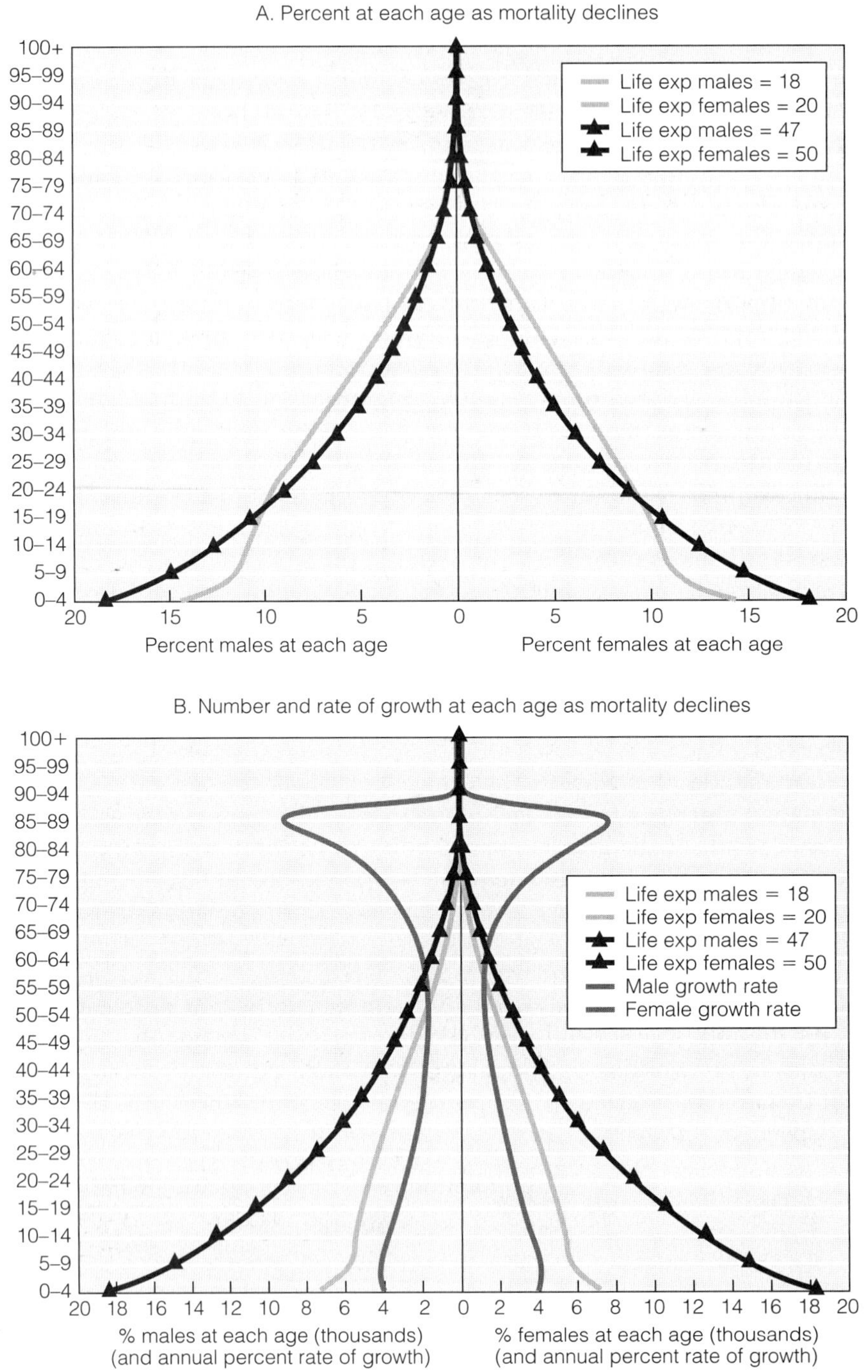

Figure 8.5 The Impact of a Decline in Mortality on the Age Structure Early in the Health and Mortality Transition

Source: Calculations by the author.

0 to 3 percent per year (which by the "rule of 69" implies a population doubling every 23 years).

The age pyramids in Figure 8.5-A do not fully capture the impact of the decline in mortality, because careful study of that picture shows that the change in the percentage of the population at each age is not very dramatic, despite the tremendous difference that it makes to have a life expectancy of 50, compared to 20. This is because when mortality levels change, all ages tend to be affected in some way or another, even though some, especially the very young, are affected more than others. It is not so much the change in the percentage at each age that makes the drop in mortality important; rather, it is the differing numbers and rates of growth by age caused by the absolute increase in population. Thus, the bottom panel (B) of Figure 8.5 shows the age structure in terms of the absolute number of people rather than the percent at each age. I have assumed that the population began with 100,000 people and then doubled to 200,000, as implied by the rate of growth, as mortality declined. In this view, it is more obvious that there is a huge increase at the younger ages. This is what families and communities have to deal with as mortality declines—a huge increase in the number of young people. It looks like a baby boom, but in reality it's a survival boom.

The broader gray lines show you the average annual rate of increase for each age group, based on the overall growth rate of 3 percent per year. Even though the population as a whole may be increasing at a rate of 3 percent, there is considerable variability age-by-age, as you can see in Figure 8.5-B. The rate is highest at the youngest and oldest ages and lowest in the adult ages. It is no coincidence, of course, that the pattern of growth rates by age looks exactly like the pattern of age-specific death rates. In this example, the drop in death rates is the only thing influencing population change, so you can see graphically what that means from one age to the next. The high growth rates at the very oldest ages are, of course, building on a very small base of older people.

In the short run, then, a decrease in mortality levels in all but already low-mortality societies will substantially increase the number of young people, and one of the best studies of this effect is by Arriaga (1970) in his analysis of Latin American countries. Arriaga examined data from 11 countries for which information was available on the mortality decline from 1930 to the 1960s. He discovered that "of the 27 million people alive in all the eleven countries in the 1960s who would not have been alive if there had not been a mortality decline since the 1930s, 16 million—59 percent—were under 15" (1970:103). In relative terms, a lowering of mortality in Latin America noticeably raised the proportion of people at young ages, slightly elevated the proportion at old ages, and lowered the proportion at the middle ages (14–64). However, in absolute terms, the number of people at all ages increased.

Declining mortality had an impact similar to that of a rise in fertility, while also making a contribution to higher fertility. The appearance of higher fertility is, of course, produced by the greater proportion of children surviving through each age of childhood. It is as though women were bearing more children, thereby broadening the base of the age structure. The actual contribution to higher fertility is generated by the higher probabilities of women (and their spouses) surviving through the reproductive ages, since under conditions of high mortality, a certain percentage of women will die before giving birth to as many children as they might have. When death rates go down, a higher percentage of women live to give birth to more children, assuming that social changes are not producing motivations for limiting fertility.

Note that the only time a change in mortality generates a change in the percentage of the population at each age is when the mortality shifts are different at different ages. If there is a change in the probability of survival from one age to the next that is exactly equal for all ages and for both sexes, then the age and sex structure will remain unchanged in percentage terms. On the other hand, in a low-mortality society such as the United States, where the vast majority of all deaths occur at ages 65 or older, a drop in mortality will age the population largely because the death rates are now so low at the younger ages that it is very hard to improve on them. So, at the later stages of the health and mortality transition, continued declines in mortality will age the population, assuming there is no change in fertility or migration. Figure 8.6 illustrates this point. Let us assume that a country had reached replacement-level fertility at a female life expectancy of 65 (just slightly lower than the current world average), and that fertility does not change as life expectancy rises to 80 for females (very close to the current U.S. level). You can see that the proportion of the population that is older increases, while the population that is younger decreases. In other words, the rate of growth is positive at ages over 55 and negative at every younger age. At a life expectancy of 65 with replacement-level fertility,

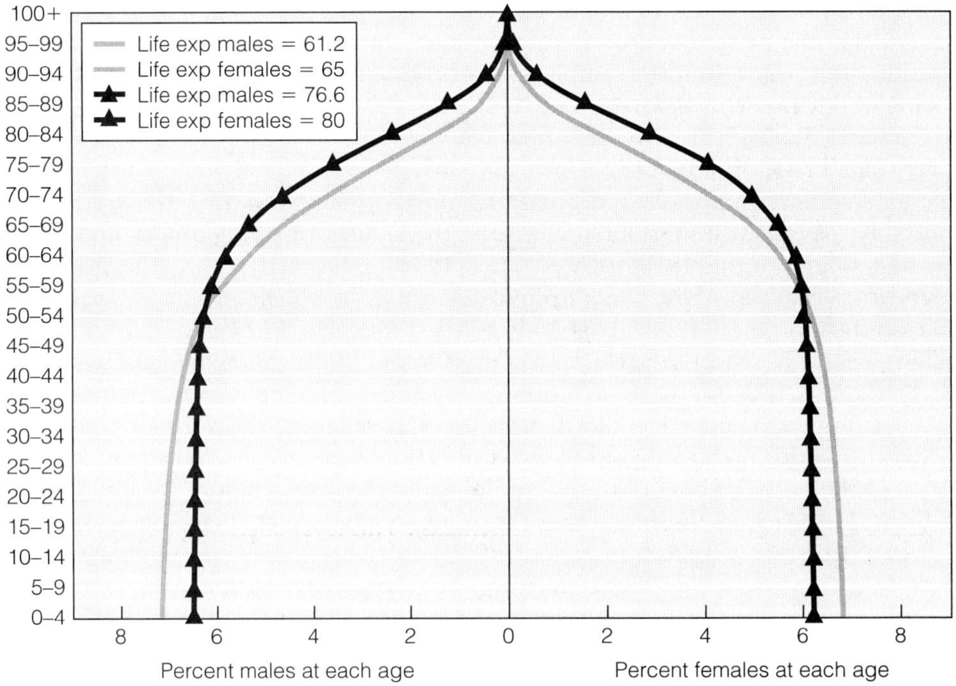

Figure 8.6 The Impact of a Decline in Mortality on the Age Structure Later in the Health and Mortality Transition

Source: Calculations by the author.

the average age is 38; the average age rises to 41 as life expectancy improves to 80. The percentage of the population aged 65 and older increases from 15 percent to 24 percent, while the percentage under 15 drops from 21 percent to 19 percent. Once again, however, you can appreciate from Figure 8.6 that a drop in life expectancy does not have a spectacular impact on the proportion at each age. Fertility has a much more dramatic impact.

The Impact of Declining Fertility

Both migration and mortality can affect all ages and differentially affect each sex. However, the impact of fertility is not quite the same as that of mortality or migration, and it is for this reason that changes in fertility tend to have the most dramatic long-term impact on the age structure (migration has the biggest short-term impact, as I discuss below). Fertility obviously adds people only at age zero to begin with, but that effect stays with the population age after age. Thus if the birth rate were to drop suddenly in one year, then as those people get older, there will always be fewer of them than there are people of surrounding ages. For example, in Japan in 1966 the birth rate made a sudden one-year dip—this was the Year of "Hinoeuma," the Fiery Horse. According to a widely held Japanese superstition, girls born in the Year of the Fiery Horse (which occurs every 60 years) will have troublesome characters, such as a propensity to murder their husbands. Thus, girls born in that year are hard to marry off, and many couples avoided having children in 1966, creating a permanent dent in the Japanese age structure.

If fertility goes up, then there will be more people in each successive birth cohort. Both of these situations—rising and declining fertility—have had strong influences on the age/sex structure of the United States, as I will discuss in a moment. In Figure 8.7, I have used stable population models to show how different fertility levels can affect the shape of the age structure if everything else is held constant. The top panel (A) of Figure 8.7 assumes that no migration is occurring. Then it assumes that mortality is constant, with a female life expectancy of 40 years, representing a typical population in the world until about 100 years ago, on the verge of the demographic transition. The high fertility level is equivalent to a total fertility rate of 7.1 (only slightly higher than that of present-day Nigeria). All other things being equal, a high-fertility, high-mortality society will have a very youthful age distribution, as you saw with Nigeria in Figure 8.4. Indeed, the average age in this hypothetical population is 22 years, with 44 percent of the population under age 15, and 2 percent 65 or older; the dependency ratio is 0.95. The middle fertility level is equivalent to a total fertility rate of 4.3 children per woman (about the same as Guatemala). This level of fertility still produces a youthful age structure, although less so than was associated with the higher fertility level. This population has an average age of 30 years, and with 31 percent of the population under age 15 and 6 percent 65 or older, the dependency ratio is 0.68. At the low fertility level, we are talking about a total fertility rate of 2.1, which is exact replacement when mortality is low, but at this high mortality level it means that women are not reproducing themselves and the population will soon implode. This population has an average age of 36 years, and only 21 percent of the population is under age 15, while 12 percent is 65 or older; the dependency ratio is 0.61. You can see then

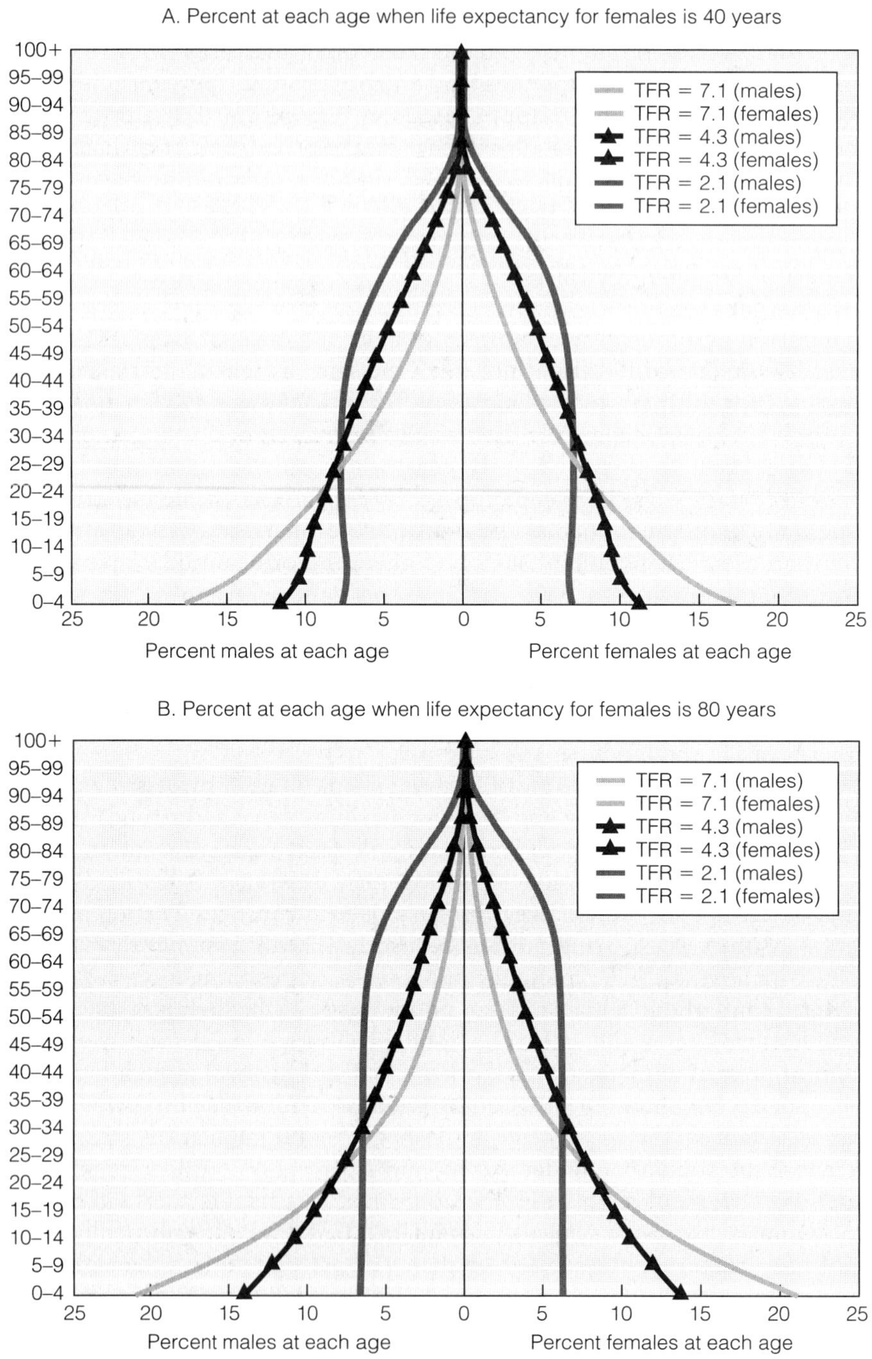

Figure 8.7 Using Stable Population Models Shows That Different Levels of Fertility Have Dramatically Different Effects on the Age Structure

Source: Calculations by the author.

that at high fertility levels, the age pyramid is a pyramid; at middle levels, it is still a pyramid, but not so dramatically; and at low fertility levels, the age structure takes on a barrel shape.

Now examine the lower panel (B) of Figure 8.7, in which the age pyramids represent the same three levels of fertility, but this time they are paired up with a high life expectancy of 80 years for females, representing a population nearing the end of the demographic transition. You can see that despite a doubling of female life expectancy, the age structures at each of the three fertility levels are very nearly identical to those in the upper panel of Figure 8.7, regardless of mortality level. The only real difference is that at the higher life expectancy, the extremes are more noticeable. At the fertility level of 7.1 children, the average age is 20 and 51 percent of the population is under age 15, while only 3 percent is 65 or older; the dependency ratio is a whopping 1.20. This is the kind of age structure that is bound to cause problems for a country, and helps to account for the previous high levels of out-migration of young people from parts of Asia and the Middle East, as I discussed in the previous chapter. At the lower level of 4.3 children, the average age is 28 with 36 percent under 15 and 7 percent 65 or older, and a dependency ratio of 0.87. Finally, replacement-level fertility produces an average age of 41 with 19 percent of the population under 15 and 20 percent aged 65 or older; the dependency ratio is 0.80.

In general, the impact of fertility levels is so important that with exactly the same level of mortality, just altering the level of fertility can produce age structures that run the gamut from those that might characterize primitive to highly developed populations. The data I have shown you come from stable population models rather than the real world, but they help us know what to look for. For example, let us suppose we are looking at two countries with high female life expectancies of 77 years (such as Saudi Arabia and Latvia). However, one country (Saudi Arabia) still has high fertility—a total fertility rate (TFR) of 3.9 in 2010—whereas the other has very low fertility (a TFR of only 1.4 in 2010). The respective age distributions of these two nations are already very different, because Saudi Arabia has had high fertility for a long time, whereas Latvia, part of the former Soviet Union, has had low fertility for some time now. In Saudi Arabia, 38 percent of the population was under age 15 in 2010, compared with only 14 percent of the Latvian population. By contrast, in Saudi Arabia, only 2 percent of the population was 65 or older, compared to 17 percent in Latvia. What you now know, however, is that when fertility drops in Saudi Arabia to below replacement level, such as it currently is in Latvia, the age structure will automatically assume the barrel shape that currently characterizes Latvia, its average age will rise, and the young will decline as a fraction of the total, while the old increase as a fraction. This is the age transition at work in conjunction with the fertility transition component of the demographic transition.

Where Does Migration Fit In?

A population experiencing net in- or out-migration (and virtually all populations except the world as a whole experience one or the other) will almost certainly have its age and sex structure altered as a consequence. Since immigration has been especially important in the United States, it provides a good beginning for our

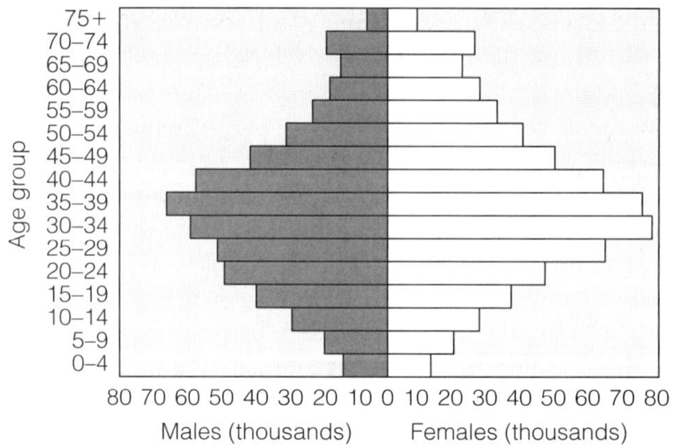

Figure 8.8 The Age Structure of Legal Immigrants to the United States

Source: Adapted from data in U.S. Department of Homeland Security, 2010, Yearbook of Immgration Statistics 2009, Table 8.

analysis. We can assess the potential impact of international migrants into the United States by looking at the age and sex distribution of legal permanent immigrants into the country in 2009 as compiled by the U.S. Department of Homeland Security (2010). You can see in Figure 8.8 that men outnumber women only at the youngest ages, and then, by about age 20, there are more female than male legal immigrants in the older ages. However, the most significant part of the picture is that both males and females exhibit the pattern of migration by age which, as I discussed in Chapter 7, is that though there are migrants at virtually every age, migrants are far more likely to be young adults than they are to be people of any other age.

Estimates of the undocumented immigrants entering the United States suggest that there are fewer younger and older people who enter without inspection than is true among legal immigrants, and that males are a much higher fraction of undocumented than of legal immigrants (Passel and Cohn 2009; Weeks, Jankowski, and Stoler 2010). Remember, too, that in the United States there are many more in-migrants than out-migrants, but out-migrants are generally older than in-migrants, so that could have at least a small impact on the age structure.

In the short run, immigration adds people mainly into the young adult ages in the host area, and of course those people have been taken out of the age structure in the donor area. In the long run, however, the impact of migration is felt indirectly through its influence on reproduction, because these young adult immigrants are of prime reproductive ages. For example, it is estimated that there were 230,000 legal immigrants to the state of California during 2005 (California Department of Finance 2007), but these people represented less than one percent of the total population of California (37 million) in that year. So, the arrival of immigrants in any given year is nearly undetectable in California's overall demographic structure. On the other hand, the American Community Survey data show that 27 percent of California's population was foreign-born in 2005 and three-fourths of these people had entered the United States since 1980. Because most of these immigrants are still young adults, it is therefore not too surprising to see that among births in California in 2005, 48 percent were to women born outside the United States.

Despite the age structure of migrants you saw in Figure 8.8, in the long term the impact of immigration is largely to increase the population at each age. The migrants have babies, who grow up through each age, and of course the immigrants themselves proceed through each successive age. Conversely, emigration has the effect of dramatically slowing population growth because those young adults are taking not only themselves out of the community, but also their potential future children. Nor will they be around to contribute even to the aging process within the community they left behind.

Having discussed the way in which the age and sex structure is built on the foundation of mortality, fertility, and migration rates, it is time now to see how the changing age structure influences life in human societies.

Age Transitions at Work

The dynamics of the age and sex structure translate all demographic changes into a force to be reckoned with. A high birth rate does not simply mean more people: It means that a few years from now there will be more kids entering school than before; that 18 years from now there will be more new job hopefuls and college freshmen than before. An influx of young adult immigrants this year means a larger-than-average number of older people 30 to 40 years from now (and it may mean an immediate sudden rise in the number of births, with all the attendant consequences). The very low birth rates in Europe and East Asia do not imply just that there will be fewer people in the future: They mean that schools will be closing, jobs will go begging, businesses will close, houses will be vacant, and life will be very different than it once was.

The Progression from a Young to an Old Age Structure

At the beginning of the demographic transition, every population had a young age structure with a characteristic pyramidal shape, as shown earlier in Panel A of Figure 8.6, or as exemplified even now by Nigeria, as shown in Figure 8.1. If the end of the demographic transition is associated with homeostasis (a stationary population), every population will have an old age structure, with a characteristic barrel shape, as shown in Panel B of Figure 8.7. In between those extremes, the age structure will undergo a period of time when it caves in at the younger ages as fertility declines, and there will be a bulge in the younger adult ages. Indeed, as I noted in Chapter 3, it may be that there will be no real end to the demographic transition—it will continue to evolve in new cycles of change, especially of fertility and migration, to which society must constantly adapt.

Youth Bulge—Dead End or Dividend?

I mentioned youth bulges in Chapter 1 as a potentially incendiary demographic phenomenon, especially today in the Middle East. Way back in the 1960s, Moller (1968) picked up on Ryder's (1965) concept of an age cohort that I mentioned earlier in the chapter, and paired it with the huge swelling of young people in the world—the result of the post–World War II decline in infant mortality—and wondered what it would portend:

> Social change is not engineered by youth, but it is most manifest in youth. . . . The presence of a large contingent of young people in a population may make for a cumulative process of innovation and social and cultural growth; it may lead to elemental, directionless acting-out behavior; it may destroy old institutions and elevate new elites to power; and the unemployed energies of the young may be organized and directed by totalitarian regimes (Moller 1968:260).

The size and timing of such bulges—of which there are many in the world today, along with society's response to them, will help tell the tale of how dramatic the changes are in the context of the age transition and whether those changes will be used for good or evil. The "good" reaction relates especially to the use of the young population to spur economic development and lift people out of poverty. The "evil" reaction relates to the use of young people to promote violence and terrorism.

A quick drop in fertility that occurs early in the mortality transition has the most dramatic and potentially positive impact on a society, increasing the economic productivity of the adult population, with few children to deal with and also few older people to worry about. A slower transition to an older age will be socially and economically less disruptive than a very sudden change. However, it may not be as conducive to the kind of positive evolutionary change a struggling economy needs in the face of the population growth that ensues as mortality declines and the demographic transition takes hold.

Crenshaw and his associates (1997) examined the pattern of age-specific growth rates and economic development for the period 1965–90 and concluded that an increase in the child population (the impact of declining mortality in a high-fertility society) does indeed hinder economic progress in less developed nations. On the other hand, an increase in the adult population relative to other ages (the delayed effect of a decline in fertility) fosters economic development, producing what they call a "demographic windfall effect whereby the demographic transition allows a massive, one-time boost in economic development as rapid labor force growth occurs in the absence of burgeoning youth dependency" (p. 974). The demographic "windfall" has also been called the "demographic dividend" (Bloom, Canning, and Sevilla 2003), the "demographic bonus" and the "window of opportunity" (Adioetomo et al. 2005), and China has been the poster child.

China's Demographic Dividend

In 1960, China had a population of 650 million, plagued by high mortality (a life expectancy around 45 years) and high fertility (a total fertility rate of more than five children per woman), although fertility was starting to decline, as you know from Chapter 6. Its age structure exhibited the classic pyramidal shape, reflecting a high proportion of the population in the very young ages, as you can see in Figure 8.9. By 2000, China had transformed itself. Its population had doubled to 1.3 billion, due especially to declining mortality, but fertility had declined dramatically (see Figure 8.9). Most noteworthy about the age structure in 2000 was the big bulge in

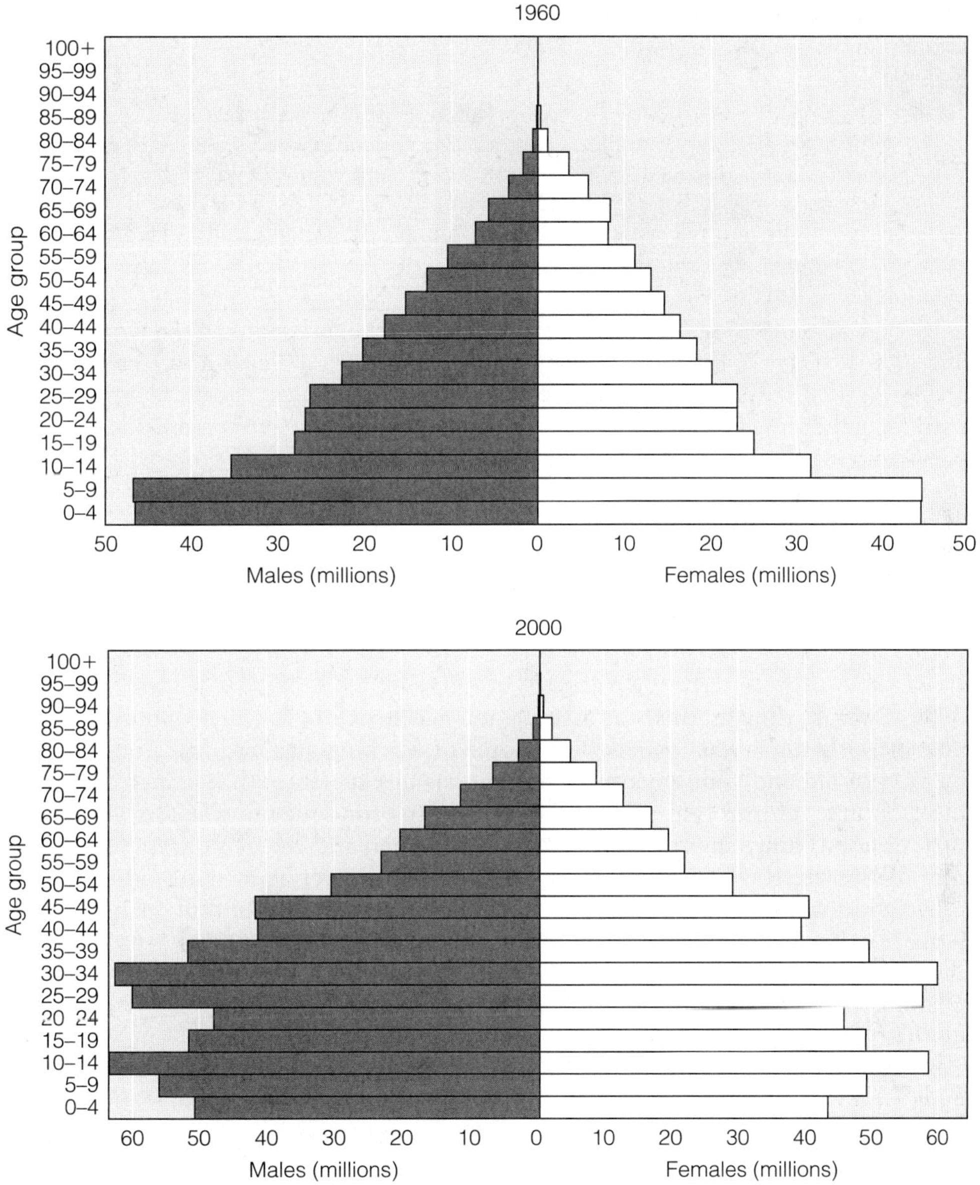

Figure 8.9 China's Demographic Dividend

Source: Adapted from United Nations Population Division, 2009, World Population Prospects: the 2008 Revision, Population Database, http://esa.un.org/unpp (accessed 2010). Data are estimates for 2010.

the young adult ages, combined with the still small number of older people and the small number of young children.

The bulge at ages 10–14 in 2000 is due to the births to the huge cohort of women born just before the big fertility decline in China—the births that prompted the One-Child Policy in 1979, and who were in their prime reproductive ages in

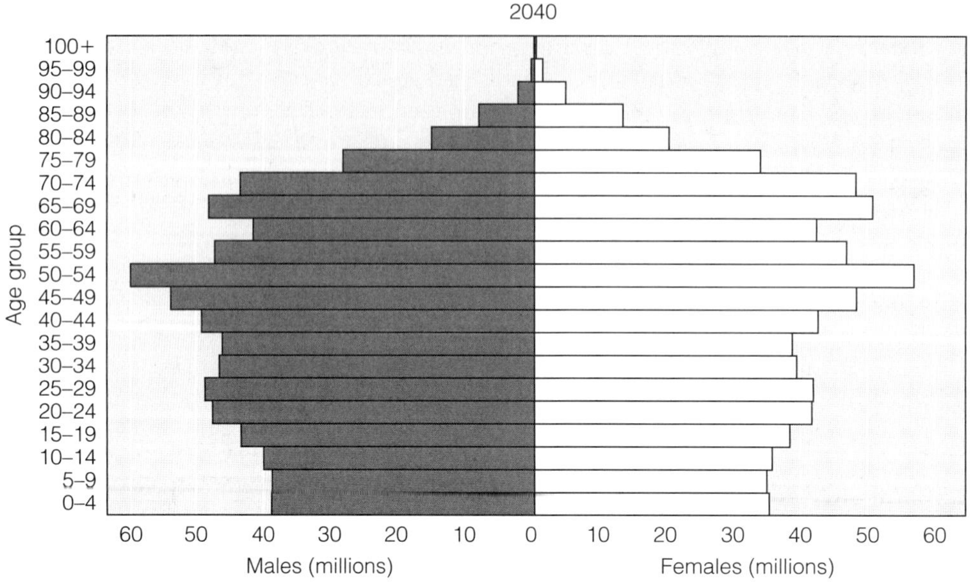

Figure 8.9 (continued)

2000. Overall, though, this was a very good age structure for an economy trying to take off, because it was loaded with people of working age, and was not burdened by a lot of old and young people. This was the age structure that helped accelerate the economic reforms that created the East Asian economic miracle.

All good things must come to an end, however, and the demographic momentum of the age transition in China will increasingly act as a brake on economic growth in that country. The Chinese government knows this and understands that it needs to maximize its advantage from this window of opportunity provided by the age transition, and this helps to explain the aggressiveness with which China is pursuing its current global economic expansion.

The United Nations projects that by 2040 the population of China will have grown to about 1.5 billion. By this time, the bulge in the age structure will have moved into the middle adult ages, where productivity gains may be less than at the younger ages, but where consumption patterns tend to peak (see Figure 8.9). Overall, by 2040 the population of China will be heavily weighted toward the older ages and the country will face important policy issues arising from a rapidly aging population (Adamchak 2001; Qiao 2001). China is already facing internal pressures to increase the birth rate in order to create a pool of new workers whose infusion of resources into the population at younger ages will keep the economy growing and will help to support the older population.

What Happened to India's Demographic Dividend?

In 1960 India had a population of 448 million, and by 2040 the United Nations projects that it will have more people than China. In between, however, it has not experienced the same kind of demographic windfall that has helped catapult China to economic power. An important difference, of course, is that India's fertility decline has been much more gradual than China's, and so its age structure has not delivered that "tipping point" into rapid economic change. A convenient way to compare the age transitions in India and China is by examining the differing rates of growth at each age. In Table 8.2, I provide an illustration of these kinds of comparisons, contrasting the changes in age structure in China and India during the critical period between 1980 and 2000 when China was taking off and India was not.

During that 20-year interval, the average income in China went from $168 per year to $727 per year—a 333 percent increase; whereas in India it went from $311 to $440—a 41percent increase (World Bank 2000). Income changes such as this are normally an indicator of increases in per-person productivity in the labor force (Lindh and Malmberg 1999), and this is enhanced by favorable changes in the age

Table 8.2 A Comparison of the "Windows of Opportunity" in India and China, 1980 to 2000

	China		India	
Age Group	Absolute change 1980–2000 (thousands)	Growth rate 1980–2000 (percentage change per year)	Absolute change 1980–2000 (thousands)	Growth rate 1980–2000 (percentage change per year)
0–4	−2,670	−0.14	23,660	1.14
5–9	−15,562	−0.64	34,128	1.92
10–14	−4,226	−0.17	35,354	2.22
15–19	−4,157	−0.20	34,385	2.39
20–24	9,757	0.57	31,642	2.46
25–29	31,380	1.79	27,514	2.42
30–34	59,273	4.56	32,155	3.75
35–39	51,925	5.11	30,109	4.08
40–44	33,804	3.52	25,586	3.79
45–49	38,120	4.21	22,244	3.79
50–54	21,542	2.77	13,030	2.65
55–59	12,804	1.95	10,698	2.69
60–64	14,482	2.79	10,067	3.27
65–69	14,481	3.66	8,020	3.64
70–74	10,367	3.65	5,435	3.73
75–79	7,267	4.35	3,469	4.48
80–84	5,270	10.12	1,573	4.05
85–89	1,615	6.36	685	5.61
90–94	474	8.37	166	4.46
95–99	75	9.38	33	5.69
100+	5	12.50	4	4.00
Total	286026	1.46	349957	2.53

Source: Calculated from data in United Nations Population Division (2009).

structure. In Table 8.2, you can see that between 1980 and 2000, the numbers of people at all ages under 20 actually declined in China, whereas the rate of growth and the absolute increase of people was high in the ages 30–39—prime ages for economic productivity. In India, by contrast, the rates of growth were positive at all ages, and despite the fact that the overall rate of growth in India (1.93 percent per year) was higher during this 20-year period than in China (1.23 percent per year), no age group in India, except the very oldest, had as high a rate of growth as the adult population in China. It was true in India that the rate of growth was lower at the younger ages than at the older ages, reflecting the slow decline in fertility, but there was no demographic windfall as there was in China from the delayed effect of that country's rapid drop in fertility during the 1960s and 1970s.

In both countries, you can see that the highest rates of growth are occurring at ages 80 and above. This is the result of the improved survival in increasingly larger younger cohorts (so that the ratio between a younger cohort and its next older cohort is very high) and is the signal that increased old-age dependency will be an issue for both countries over the next few decades. China, with its improving income and declining number of children, will be in the better position to deal with that.

Demographic Dividends in the United States and Mexico

The United States also had a youth bulge in the 1960s, as you well know. The U.S. population was 181 million people in 1960, and the age structure for that year is noticeable for the effect of the baby boom generation at the younger ages, as seen in Figure 8.10, where I have graphed the age distribution for the total population, rather than as an age pyramid (simply to make the comparisons more obvious). Of course,

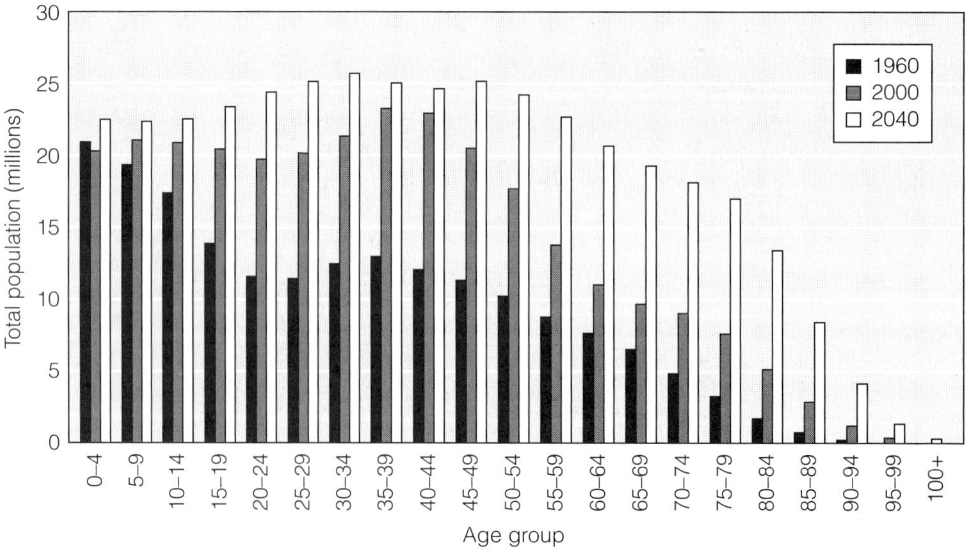

Figure 8.10 The Age Transition in the United States

Source: Adapted from United Nations Population Division, 2009, World Population Prospects: the 2008 Revision, Population Database, http://esa.un.org/unpp (accessed 2010). Data are estimates for 2010.

another way of viewing the age distribution in 1960 is to see the baby boom as the continuation of trends that existed prior to the Depression, and to view the low fertility of the Depression as an aberration, rather than thinking of the baby boom as the aberration. Seen in this way, the United States in 1960 had a clear pyramidal age structure with a heavy burden coming from the young population. Between 1960 and 2000, the population grew from 186 million to 288 million, but fertility levels declined significantly (even if not as dramatically as in China)—the total fertility rate dropping from 3.6 children per woman in 1960 down to 2.0 children per woman in 2000.

Just as I noted above for China, the rapid drop in fertility produced a demographic windfall in the age structure that coincided nicely with the economic expansion of the 1990s and the first half decade of the twenty-first century. The U.S. age structure in 2000 bulged at the young adult ages, without the burden of huge numbers of either older or younger people. The picture for 2040 in the United States, however, is not quite like that for China. China's age structure begins to cave in at the young ages from the continuation of very low fertility, but the U.S. population begins to straighten out a bit. Even though the U.S. population is expected to increase to 389 million and the big bulge in the age structure will be transitioning toward the older, higher-consuming years, the number of younger people will be leveling off, rather than declining as in China. This is due both to continued immigration into the United States and, as noted above, to the children of those immigrants.

Many of those current and future immigrants to the United States will be from Mexico. In 1960, Mexico had 39 million people and a classic pyramidal age structure, and fertility in Mexico was higher that year than in either the United States or China (see Figure 8.11). Mortality has been steadily declining over time in Mexico, and since the mid-1970s so has fertility, as I discussed in Chapter 6. You can see in

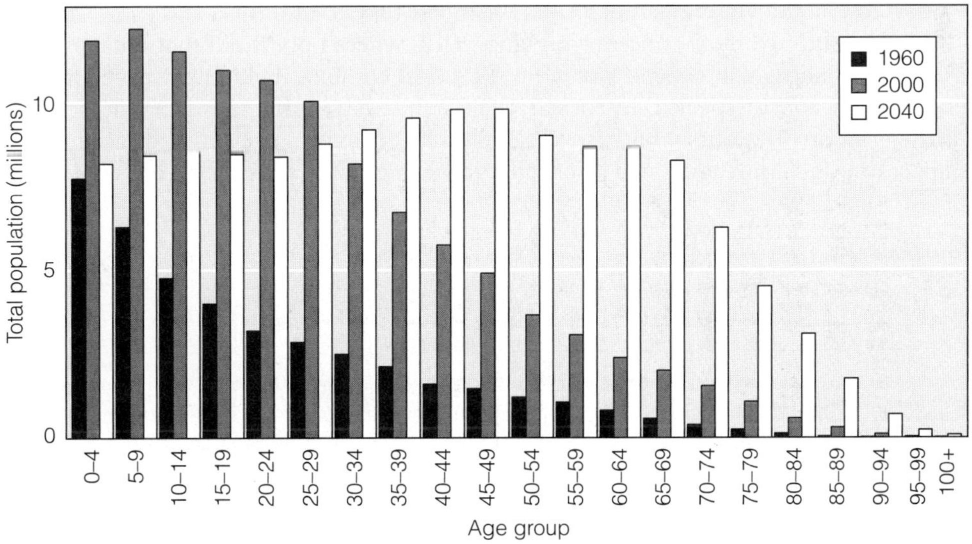

Figure 8.11 The Age Transition in Mexico

Source: Adapted from United Nations Population Division, 2009, World Population Prospects: the 2008 Revision, Population Database, http://esa.un.org/unpp (accessed 2010). Data are estimates for 2010.

the graph for Mexico that by 2000, the younger ages had been truncated by the fertility decline. But you can also see that the slowness of the fertility decline and its more recent start in Mexico than in either China or the United States meant that there was no bulge of population in the young adult ages—no demographic windfall to spur on an economy that was trying hard to grow but was being weighed down by the demographic burden of its youth bulge.

United Nations projections for the year 2040 in Mexico suggest that fertility will continue its slow drop, and Mexico will transition gradually to an older, barrel-shaped age structure, never having experienced the windfall that comes with a rapid drop in fertility. Thus, Mexico's economy will likely never receive the boost that the age structure provided at the end of the twentieth century for both China and the United States. Mexico's muddling toward low fertility has deprived it of a golden chance to use the age dividend to leap ahead economically.

Population Aging as Part of the Age Transition

The natural consequence of the demographic transition is for the population to age—for there to be both higher numbers of older people (due to a decline in mortality) and a greater fraction of the population that is older (due to a decline in fertility). This *population* aging produces changes in the organization of society that are partly the result of the process of *individual* aging—people change biologically with age and societies react differently to older than to younger people—the age stratification I discussed earlier—generating the social changes that we see accompanying population aging. These individual changes occur in the context of each birth cohort, however, because improvements in health are brought about largely by technological and environmental changes in life over which we have very little personal control (no matter how many vitamin supplements we might take each day).

I have outlined these concepts in Figure 8.12, where I point out that the nature of the social changes will depend partly on the social context, including aspects of society such as cohort-specific historical events that have affected different cohorts throughout the life course, but also societal levels of sexism, ageism, and racism. The impact of population aging will also differ according to the proportion of people who

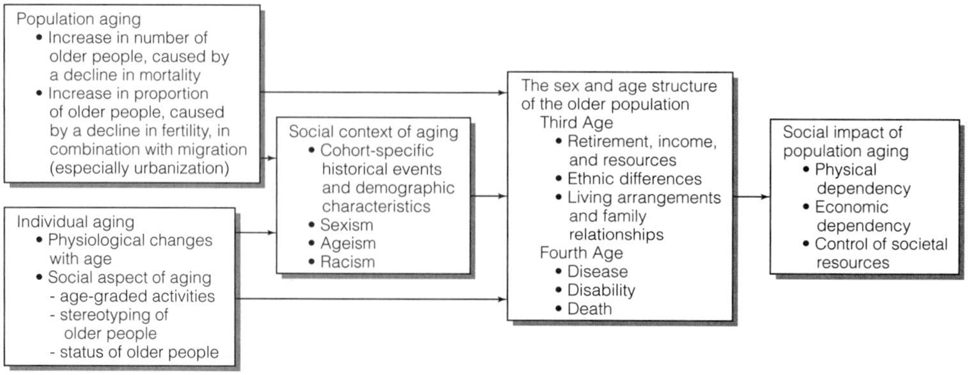

Figure 8.12 Population Aging and Individual Aging Combine to Produce Change in Society

are young-old (the "third" age of life—in which the impact of aging on society is more social), compared with the proportion who are old-old (the "fourth" age of life—in which society must cope more with the individual biological aspects of aging).

What Is Old?

Population aging doesn't mean that everyone is old. It really only means that on average people are getting older. But the end game here is a population that includes a lot more older people than ever before in human history, and it is this fact that attracts our attention. Old age as we usually think of it is a social construct—something we talk about, define, and redefine on the basis of social categories, not purely biological ones. A good way to visualize this concept is to contemplate Satchel Paige's famous question: "How old would you be, if you didn't know how old you was?," which illustrates the point that age takes on its meaning from our interaction with other people in the social world. If we are defined by others as being old, we may be treated like an old person regardless of our own feelings about whether or not we are, in fact, old.

We humans depend heavily on visual clues to assess the age of other people, and we learn quickly that there are certain kinds of outward physical changes typically associated with aging—the graying hair, the wrinkling skin, the muscle tone decline, and the changing shape caused by the redistribution of fat. These are taken as signs of physical decline, and it is fair to say that most of us are, at best, ambivalent about the aging process—an attitude that is itself probably as old as human society (Warren 1998). In what might be thought of as a form of denial, research has shown that Americans are more prone than Germans, for example, to think of themselves as being younger than their biological age and that the discrepancy increases with age, especially among healthier older people (Westerhof, Barrett, and Steverink 2003).

Among women, the physical symptoms of aging may be associated with the end of reproduction. Indeed, humans are among the few species that have a substantial post-reproductive existence (Albert and Cattell 1994). Still, these changes do not follow a rigid time schedule, and some can be successfully hidden or disguised (think of dyed hair, hair implants, Botox injections, face lifts, and liposuction).

In general, then, there is no inherent chronological threshold to old age; however, in the United States and much of the world, old age has come to be defined as beginning at age 65. The number 65 assumes its almost mystical quality in the United States because that is the age at which important government-funded benefits such as Social Security (at least until recently) and Medicare become fully available. In 1935, when the present Social Security benefits were designed in the United States, the eligibility age was set at 65, "more because of custom than deliberate design. That age had become the normal retirement age under the few American pension plans then in existence and under the social insurance system in Germany" (Viscusi 1979:96). Keep in mind, however, that Congress has increased the flexibility of the Social Security system over time. For example, every person not yet 65 at the time you read this will have to be older than 65 to get "full" Social Security benefits. If you were born in 1960 or more recently, you cannot start collecting full Social Security until age 67. Everybody can start collecting as young as age 62, but your benefit will be permanently reduced. On the other hand, if you wait until after your "full" retirement age, your benefit will be permanently higher. Despite this tweaking of the system, we still think of 65 as somehow magical with respect to old age. Remember, though, that the number is arbitrary, and people obviously will not fit neatly into any senior citizen mold on reaching their sixty–fifth birthday. In fact, most people in low-mortality societies do not think of themselves as being old until well beyond that age, whereas most people in high-mortality societies would probably think of themselves as old well before age 65.

How Many Older People Are There?

There are currently more than 500 million people in the world aged 65 and older, according to United Nations estimates (United Nations Population Division 2009). If they all lived together under one flag, they would represent the third largest nation in the world. As a fraction of the total world population, the older population accounts for a little more than 7 percent, but this percentage varies considerably from one part of the world to another, as is illustrated in Figure 8.1 at the beginning of the chapter. For example, only about 20 percent of the total population of the world lives in the more developed nations, yet more than 40 percent of the world's population aged 65 or older is there, accounting for 16 percent of the total population of these wealthier countries. Still, that leaves the other 60 percent of people in the world aged 65 and older living in developing countries, even though the older generation represents only 6 percent of those populations.

Since the end of World War II the fraction of the world population aged 65 and older has increased uninterruptedly. However, in the less developed nations, the percentage aged 65 and older actually went down between 1950 and 1970 before starting a sustained rise in 1980. In the period right after World War II, the death rate was declining, but the birth rate was not, and, as I have mentioned before, the earlier declines in the death rate tend to favor the young, so that had the early effect of increasing the youthful population at the proportionate expense of the elderly. In 1950, only 5 percent of the world's population was aged 65 and older, and by 2000 that had climbed a bit to 7 percent. However, that was the lull before the storm, since the huge batch of babies born all over the world after World War II are now moving into the older ages. By 2025 the percentage aged 65 and over is projected to rise to 10 percent, and then by 2050 it will be 16 percent. By that time, the United Nations projects that world population growth overall will have slowed to less than 1 percent per year, but the older population will still be growing by more than 2 percent per year. By 2050, it is anticipated that there will be 1.5 billion older people in the world—more than the entire current population of China.

Where Are the Older Populations?

You can perhaps appreciate the fact that there are different answers to two seemingly similar questions, one dealing with the percentage of the population that is old, and the other dealing with the absolute number of older people. If the question is: "Where are the nations that have the highest percentage of older people?" then we point to the richer countries, especially those in Europe, for the answer. As of the year 2010, 16 percent of Europe's population was 65 and older, and it is projected that by 2050 the percentage will rise to 27 percent. North America and Oceania were both in the double digits by 2010, and by 2050 we can expect that at least 10 percent of the population in every region of the world except sub-Saharan Africa will be aged 65 and older.

I noted earlier in the chapter that declining mortality will always lead, eventually, to an increase in the number of older people, but the percentage age 65 and older will only increase noticeably if fertility declines. In Table 8.3, I have calculated the percentage of the population that would be aged 65 and older if a population maintained over time the various combinations of mortality and fertility that I have shown in the table. For example, a country whose life expectancy was only 30 years would have 3.9 percent of the population aged 65 and older if the total fertility rate (TFR) were five children per woman, and it would drop to 2.8 percent if the TFR went up to six (note that at a TFR of four or below, the country would be depopulating, so the percentage aged 65 and older would be temporarily high until everybody died off).

Let us stay focused for the moment on the total fertility rate of five children. You can see that as life expectancy increases from 30 to 60 years, the percentage aged 65 and older actually goes down slightly. This happened in Mexico, where mortality was declining between 1950 and 1970, but fertility had not begun to decline, so the older population was declining as a percentage of the total population. However, you can also see in Table 8.3 that, as mortality continues to decline, eventually it gets low enough that the percentage representing the elderly begins to increase even if fertility does not change. Of course, a population with a life expectancy of 75 years and a total fertility rate of five children would be doubling in size every 20 years, and the number of older people eventually would be very large, even if they represented only 4 percent of the total.

If you look at any given level of life expectancy in Table 8.3, you can see clearly that at each lower level of fertility, the percentage of the population aged 65 and older is higher. Now, finally, if you go down the diagonal of this table from the top right (low life expectancy and high fertility) to the bottom left (high life expectancy and low fertility), you can trace the typical path of the percentage aged 65 and older as a country passes through the demographic transition.

Table 8.3 The Percentage of the Population 65 and Older Is Determined More by Fertility Than by Mortality

	Total Fertility Rate (TFR)				
Life Expectancy at Birth	2	3	4	5	6
30	a	a	a	3.9	2.8
40	a	a	5.6	3.8	2.7
50	a	8.8	5.5	3.7	2.6
60	15.0	8.8	5.4	3.6	2.5
70	16.5	9.2	5.7	3.7	2.6
75	18.0	9.9	6.1	4.0	2.8

Source: Data are based on Coale–Demeny "West" Stable Population Models.

[a]No calculation made because this represents a situation of depopulation.

A high proportion of the population in the older ages thus means that we are talking about a low-fertility society, most of which are the richer ones in the world today. If, however, the question is, "Where are the people who are 65 and older?" we point to the less developed countries. This is a result of where the world is with respect to the age transition. Even though Europe currently has more than 100 million older people, Eastern Asia (especially China, Japan, and South Korea) had a combined total that is considerably higher than Europe's. By 2040, when Europe's older population will likely number 180 million, there are projected to be 377 million in Eastern Asia, and 243 million in South Central Asia (which includes India).

If we look at the older population in individual countries instead of regions, you can see in Table 8.4 the estimates for the year 2010 of the population (both percentage and absolute number) aged 65 and older. Using the percentage of the

Table 8.4 The Top 10 Countries in Terms of Percentage Aged 65 and Older and in Terms of Number of People Aged 65 and Older as of 2010

Rank	Country	Number 65+ (thousands)	Percent 65+
Top 10 Countries in Terms of Percentage Aged 65 and Older			
1	Japan	28,667	23
2	Germany	16,799	21
3	Italy	12,285	20
4	Greece	2,049	18
5	Sweden	1,702	18
6	Portugal	1,916	18
7	Bulgaria	1,319	18
8	France	10,626	17
9	Spain	7,777	17
10	Belgium	1,862	17
Top 10 Countries in Terms of Number of People Aged 65 and Older			
Rank	Country	Number 65+ (thousands)	Percent 65+
1	China	111,432	8
2	India	59,734	5
3	United States of America	41,155	13
4	Japan	28,667	23
5	Russian Federation	18,120	13
6	Germany	16,799	21
7	Indonesia	14,133	6
8	Brazil	13,481	7
9	Italy	12,285	20
10	France	10,626	17

Source: Adapted from United Nations, 2009, World Population Prospects: The 2008 Revision (New York: United Nations).

population aged 65 and older as the index to an older population, nine of the top 10 countries were in Europe and the other one was Japan. You can see that the list is led by Japan (23 percent), followed by Germany (21 percent), and Italy (20 percent). The United States, by the way, is way down on this list, with "only" 13 percent of its population aged 65 and older. For the total number of people aged 65 and older, the top 10 list looks more like the list you have seen earlier in terms of total population size: China had the largest number of older people as of 2010, followed by India and the United States. Only four countries show up on both of the top 10 lists: Japan, Germany, Italy, and France.

If we zoom in on data for individual countries, we typically find spatial concentrations of the elderly in different parts of a country. Within the United States, for example, the state of Florida exceeds all others in its percentage of the population that is 65 or older (17 percent), according to the 2008 American Community Survey, followed by West Virginia (16 percent) and Pennsylvania, Maine, Hawaii, and Iowa (all at 15 percent). At the other extreme, the youngest states are, in order, Alaska, Utah, Georgia, Texas, and California. Canada's provinces are much less variable than the states in the U.S., but Saskatchewan and Nova Scotia lead with 15 percent of the population aged 65 or older, according to the 2006 census. Canada's territories, which are populated especially by indigenous groups, have much lower fractions of older people, with Nunavut having the lowest at 3 percent.

The comparison of U.S. states with Canadian provinces is interesting because Florida has the highest percentage aged 65 and older largely as a result of the in-migration of retirees. By contrast, Saskatchewan and Nova Scotia have the highest percentage 65 and older largely as a result of the out-migration of young adults to other parts of Canada. Mexico's states all have much lower percentages of older people than in the United States or Canada, a reflection of the much more recent fertility decline in Mexico. The highest is Zacatecas with 8 percent, according to the 2005 census, followed by Oaxaca, Distrito Federal (Mexico City), and Michoacán at 7 percent, while Quintana Roo has the lowest at 3 percent.

The Third Age (Young-Old) and Fourth Age (Old-Old)

Throughout most of human history, and still today in many less developed societies, old age was implicitly that age at which a person could no longer make a full economic contribution to the household economy due to one or more disabilities that would eventually (and sooner rather than later, in most cases) lead to death. The same wealth in the modern world that has lowered death rates has also made it possible to separate the decline in economic productivity from a decline in physical functioning.

Since you are reading this book, you are probably one of the lucky humans living in a place and time (e.g., twenty-first-century America) when you can take for granted both a long life and a comfortable income. You have grown up expecting, and almost certainly looking forward to, a time interval between the end of your work career and death—a time of leisurely retirement. This is a very recent invention. Less than one hundred years ago, the older population in the United States was concentrated in the ages 65–74. High mortality meant that people at that age were pretty close to death, and most worked for as long as they were physically able. As health has improved and mortality has declined, a greater fraction of people have survived into older ages, thus creating a new period between the traditional entrance into old age (approximately age 65, as I discussed above) and the time when death begins to stalk us. We have taken advantage of this in society and have been able to act on the old adage that "youth is wasted on the young" by giving ourselves a youth-like carefree period toward the end of life. This is the so-called Third Age (Laslett 1991), a time when we are still healthy enough to engage in all of the normal activities of daily life, but are able to be free of regular economic activity.

Being in the Third Age is related to the concept of disability-free life expectancy, which I mentioned in Chapter 5. If life expectancy refers to when we die, the concept of disability-free life expectancy refers essentially to when we arrive at the transition from the Third Age to the "Fourth Age"—when the rest of our life will be increasingly consumed by coping with the health effects of old age. The distinguishing characteristic of this stage of life is an increasing susceptibility to senescence—increases in the incidence of chronic disease and associated disabilities, and, of course, death.

There is no clear age that defines the entrance to the Fourth Age, although 80 or even 85 are probably the ages in most demographers' mind when they think about this concept. Fortunately, this age keeps being pushed back to later in life (Cambois, Robine, and Hayward 2001). Each group of people moving into old age is healthier than the previous one (Manton and Land 2000), so if you have a few decades to go before you reach your 80s, the health of the oldest may by then be markedly better. We might even have redefined what it means to be old.

Centenarians and Rectangularization—Is This the End of the Age Transition?

At the beginning of the twenty-first century, it has to be recognized that most people do not survive to be 100 years old. Nonetheless, this is one of the fastest-growing ages in the population, reminding us that the life course in the future is going to be very different from what it was just a few decades ago. In 1911 there were only 100 centenarians (people who are least 100 years old) in England and Wales, and that had increased to only a few hundred by the end of World War II; now there are ten thousand, almost all of whom are women (Thatcher 2001; U.K. Office for National Statistics 2009).

As the most populous low mortality country in the world, the United States has led the world in the probable number of centenarians. There were an estimated 2,300 centenarians in 1950, after adjusting for likely age exaggeration (Krach and Velkoff 1999). There were more than 50,000 counted in Census 2000, most of whom were women. That number is not adjusted for age exaggeration (Kinsella and Wan He 2009), but it was nonetheless used in the U.S. Census Bureau's national population projections (U.S. Census Bureau 2008). Those projections suggest that in 2010 there were 79,000 in the United States, with 600,000 expected by 2050. Projections from the United Nations Population Division suggest that by 2050 China's population of centenarians will catch up with that of the United States, although at present there are only about half as many centenarians in China as in the United States.

The numbers for the present are still pretty small, but you can see the trend: It looks like the end of the age transition is associated with increasing numbers of people at the highest ages. Thus far, then, we have not seen a clear pattern of rectangularization, which, as I discussed in Chapter 5, would mean that people essentially live to an advanced age and then quickly die off. The emerging pattern is that we are continuing to push the envelope, so to speak, of old age. This is, in reality, one way in which population growth can be maintained even in the face of below-replacement fertility. Or, put more accurately, if people live to ever older ages, we will have to redefine what below-replacement-level fertility really is, because additional years lived at old age essentially compensate for some of the babies who are not being born—at least in terms of the total population size.

Reading the Future from the Age Structure

In a very real sense, the age and sex structure of a population is like a concise picture of its demographic history. Knowing what you do about the way in which mortality, fertility, and migration impact the age and sex structure, you should be able to look at a population pyramid and know what the past was like, and what the future portends. We are, in fact, able to put all of the pieces together—mortality, fertility, migration, and the age-sex structure—to model the future course of a population. We do this with a very useful set of tools called population projections.

Population Projections

A population projection is the calculation of the number of persons we can expect to be alive at a future date given the number now alive and given reasonable assumptions about age-specific mortality, fertility, and migration rates (Keyfitz 1968). By enabling us to see what the future size and composition of the population might be under varying assumptions about demographic trends, we can intelligently evaluate what the likely course of events will be many years from now. Also, by projecting the population forward through time from some point in history, we are able to determine the sources of change in the population over time. A word of caution, however, is in order. Population projections are always based on a conditional future—this is what will happen if a certain set of conditions are met.

Demographic theory is not now, nor is it likely ever to be, sophisticated enough to be able to predict future shifts in demographic processes, especially fertility and migration, over which we as individuals exercise considerable control. Thus we must distinguish projections from forecasts. A **population forecast** is a statement about what you *expect* the future population to be. This is different from a projection, which is a statement about what the future population *could be under a given set of assumptions*. As Keyfitz (1982:746) has observed, "Forecasts of weather and earthquakes, where the next few hours are the subject of interest, and of unemployment, where the next year or two is what counts, are difficult enough. Population forecasts, where one peers a generation or two ahead, are even more difficult." Population projections are rarely right on the money, but in comparing past projections with subsequent censuses, the Panel on Population Projections of the National Research Council concluded that our ability to correctly guess the future is better over the short term than the long term, better for larger than for smaller countries, and better for more developed than for less developed nations (Bongaarts and Bulatao

WHO WILL PAY FOR BABY BOOMERS TO RETIRE IN THE RICHER COUNTRIES?

In industrialized societies, old age is now stereotypically a time of retirement from labor force activity. Indeed, when the Social Security Act was passed in the United States in the middle of the Great Depression in the 1930s, it was designed quite literally to encourage people to leave the labor force. At the time, the idea was to remove older workers from the workforce in order to replace them with younger workers and thus lower the rate of unemployment among younger people. Most companies and government entities alike then turned age 65 into a mandatory age of retirement, forcing people out of the labor force whether or not they wanted to retire. People became increasingly interested in retiring before reaching age 65 if they could afford to do so, and the U.S. Congress facilitated this in the 1950s and 1960s by allowing reduced Social Security benefits to be available at age 62, which has been a popular option ever since. In the 1950s the average man in the United States was almost 69 years old when he retired. By 2000, that had dropped down close to 62 (Gendell 2001), and it has stayed there since, but with a new wrinkle. In 1983, amendments to the Social Security law raised the age at which full retirement was available, beginning with the baby boomers, and at the same time it reduced the percentage of the full retirement check that early retirees could receive. Thus far, however, it appears that some people are gaming the system by applying for disability, rather than retirement, because the disability benefits were not cut (Duggan, Singleton, and Song 2007). People are retiring earlier than they used to, but living longer. Can we afford that?

Back in 1935, when President Roosevelt's Committee on Economic Security was putting the finishing touches on the Social Security legislation in the United States, two committee members met to discuss the projections that had been made for Social Security expenditures for 1935 through 1980. Treasury Secretary Henry Morgenthau, Jr., and Harry Hopkins, head of the Federal Emergency Relief Administration, were aware of possible problems ahead, as is evidenced by their comments at the meeting (quoted in Graebner 1980:256):

> *Hopkins*: Well, there are going to be twice as many old people thirty years from now, Henry, than there are now.
>
> *Morgenthau*: Well, I've gotten a very good analysis of this thing . . . and I want to show them [other members of the committee] the bad curves.
>
> *Hopkins*: That old age thing is a bad curve.

That "bad curve" referred to the ratio of workers to retirees, which, although quite favorable in the early years of Social Security, could be foreseen to worsen over the years as the small birth cohorts of the early 1930s tried to support the numerically larger older cohorts. Despite the fact that reference is often made to the term "trust fund," you are probably aware that old age Social Security systems in most countries, including the United States, were never designed to have the government actually deposit money in an account with your name on it and have the money accrue principal and interest until you retire and start withdrawing your pension. Rather, almost every system is "pay as you go"—current benefits are paid from current revenue. The age curve looked bad in 1935, but in truth it has turned out to be even worse than expected in all of the wealthier countries of the world: Life expectancy has increased, and then the unexpected baby boom in Europe and North America has injected large cohorts that will soon have to be dealt with in retirement (but that, in the meantime, have helped delay the funding crisis because of their members' payroll tax contributions). On top of all that, the U.S. Congress considerably expanded Social Security coverage and raised benefits after the legislation was passed in 1935.

The demographic impact on the U.S. Social Security system was felt keenly through the 1980s as the older population grew more rapidly than the number of younger workers. In 1990, for example, there were 10 percent more people aged 60 to 69 (people moving into retirement) in the United States than in 1980, yet there were 3 percent fewer people aged 20 to 29 (people moving into the labor force). These changes, of course, had been projected for some time, and in the mid-1970s (and again in the 1980s), Congress made adjustments to increase payroll taxes and cut back on the annual allowable increase in Social Security payments. These measures (along with a little borrowing from the disability and Medicare trust funds) allowed the system to survive the 1980s and early 1990s. The late 1990s saw a hiatus in the Social Security crisis because of the slowdown in the increase of new retirees as the Depression-era cohorts (the "lucky few") reached old age. For example, between 1990 and 2000, the number of people aged 60 to 69 in the United States declined by 6 percent. This eased the pressure of expenditures while revenues rose—the calm before a storm that promises to bring rain for the foreseeable future.

The baby boomers are starting to retire in large numbers, and as you know, they represent a far larger older population than ever before in American history. The confluence of this demographic phenomenon and a bad economy meant that in 2010 Social Security paid out more than it brought in (Walsh 2010). You can see clearly here the dilemma of a pay-as-you-go (so-called PAYGO) program. People were losing their jobs, so they decided to retire earlier than might otherwise have been the case (thus more pay-out), but when people lose their jobs there are fewer people to pay into the system.

As we look at the huge influx of baby boom retirees, we need to keep in mind that when the baby boomers were younger, Congress felt generous about retirement benefits because the baby boom cohort was supplying an influx of new workers to pay taxes, and inflation was showering Social Security with unexpected revenue. In 1972, Congress boosted retirement benefits by 20 percent and built in an automatic adjustment to keep benefits increasing each year along with inflation. Back in the early 1980s, Robert Myers, former chief actuary of the Social Security Administration, worried that Congress would use the growing surplus of the 1990s to increase benefits, lower taxes, or pay off the national debt. Such a course of action could be disastrous, he felt, because around 2010, the baby boom generation will really crunch the pension system. In fact, in 2001, the surplus was used to lower taxes. Will that result in disaster? Quite possibly. Between the years 2000 and 2010, there was nearly a 50 percent increase in the population aged 60 to 69—an unprecedented rise in the number of people who might be retiring—and this increase will continue until 2030.

In the 1960s, there were nearly four workers for every Social Security retiree, but by 2030 that will have dropped to only two. The burden on the younger generation will obviously be intense. As a result, there may be considerable pressure on the elderly to be more self-sufficient—not only to work longer (retire later) but also to become involved in mutual self-help organizations that could relieve some of the burden on public agencies. It is ironic indeed that the Social Security system, which was designed in large part to encourage older people to leave the workforce, may in the future be bailed out because people can stay in the labor force longer. Congress has already thought of this, of course, and, as I mention in this chapter, people born after 1959 in the United States will have to wait until age 67 before receiving full Social Security benefits. (They will still be able to retire as early as age 62, but only at a lower benefit level than currently prevails.) Another hedge—less predictable, of course, especially given the severe recession that hit in 2007—is for the economy to grow fairly rapidly in the decade that the baby boom generation reaches retirement age. The kind of structural mobility (when everyone's economic situation is improving) that has typically accompanied rapid economic growth in the United States would make the transfer of money from the younger to the older generation a little less painful.

The experience of countries such as the United States has pushed less developed countries to think of different ways of attempting to finance retirement for their own aging populations. The model popularized in the 1990s was the "Chile" model, crafted for that country by economists trained at the University of Chicago. The concept is that people must save for their own retirement, but they must be forced to do so by the government (or else the temptation is to spend the money on other things), while at the same time having a reasonably low level of risk of losing their money. In Chile (and now in many other countries as well), workers are required to put a certain fraction of their earnings into a governmentally regulated (but privately managed) set of mutual funds. The savings provide a pool of investment funds that is supposed to help the national economy develop, thus ensuring that the workers will have a nice pension benefit when

(continued)

WHO WILL PAY FOR BABY BOOMERS TO RETIRE IN THE RICHER COUNTRIES? (CONTINUED)

they retire. The program in Chile has fallen somewhat short of covering everyone that was intended to be covered, forcing the government in 2010 to increase its subsidy of the program (James, Cox Edwards, and Iglesias 2010). And, of course, the global recession that hit in 2007 has served as a cautionary tale about relying too heavily on private investment instead of the largesse of taxpayers.

Part of the problem in the United States and in most European nations, of course, is that people are already paying Social Security taxes, so if they are allowed to lower their tax payment to invest in the stock market (on the assumption that in the long term it will rebound), the Social Security system will be even worse off in the future. The only real way to implement a system of this kind is to force one generation of workers to pay double, to keep paying taxes to finance Social Security payments to the currently retired population while at the same time saving more money than ever before for their own retirement. Very few politicians are willing to propose this to voters, yet something will have to give. Bear in mind that, as critical as the situation is in the United States, it is even worse in most European nations. Throughout Europe, the benefit levels for retirees are higher than in the United States, while the retirement age is younger, and the more rapid drop in fertility has created an even greater imbalance between workers and retirees. It is indeed a bad curve.

Europeans are now facing up to the fact that the bad curve can be dealt with only by making some fundamental changes in society. As I have discussed

2000). The U.S. Census Bureau has concluded that its projections are limited mainly by demographers' (and almost everybody else's) inability to predict turning points—those events, such as the baby boom, or the massive increase in immigration—that are nearly impossible to foresee but which have long term impacts on population growth and change (Mulder 2001). This is a reminder that we will do well to keep in mind the old Chinese proverb: "Prediction is very difficult—especially with regard to the future."

There are several ways in which a demographer might project the population. These include: (1) extrapolation methods, (2) the components-of-growth method, and (3) the cohort component method. In addition, some of these methods can be used to project backward, not just into the future. As you will see, given the importance of the age structure, the best method is the cohort component approach, which follows age cohorts through time, but it is important to have a quick overview of all the usual methods of projection in order to see why we usually prefer to use a method that incorporates information about the age distribution.

Extrapolation The easiest way to project a population is to extrapolate past trends into the future. This can be done using either a linear (straight-line) extrapolation or a logarithmic (curved-line) method. Both methods assume that we have total population counts or estimates at two different dates. If we know the rate of growth between two past dates, and if we assume that rate will continue into the future, then we can project what the population size will be at a future date. For example, in 1990, 248,709,873 people were enumerated in the U.S. Census, and in 2000 the census counted 281,421,906. The average annual linear rate of growth between those two dates was 0.013153 or approximately 13.2 per thousand per year, which we can calculate using the following formula:

earlier in the book, the proposals for "replacement migration," which would bring in younger people from other countries to fill in the gaps created by the European baby bust, would not really solve the problem in the long run, and in the short term the immigrants have created political issues for societies trying to cope with the inevitable cultural differences between older Europeans and younger immigrants who, by and large, are not from Europe. The fundamental changes now being discussed in Europe include especially the ideas that (1) workers are going to have to stay in the labor force longer, although this wouldn't necessarily imply a shorter retirement if, for example, retirement age increased in tandem with increases in life expectancy; (2) an even larger fraction of women in the labor force would help to increase the number of people paying into the system; (3) reducing unemployment among young people will get them into the labor force and paying into the system; (4) increasing productivity per person could raise wages and thus the payments into the system; and (5) pension plans will have to be restructured (Nyce and Schreiber 2005). And why do we have to think about all of these societal changes? The answer is simple: The age transition has forced us into it.

Discussion Questions: (1) Explain how a PAYGO system is affected both positively and negatively by the changing age structure; **(2)** One solution to the problem of dependency in old age would be to give up on the concept of retirement—would you be in favor or that or oppose it? Explain your answer.

$$r_{lin} = \left[\frac{\text{population at Time 2} - \text{population at Time 1}}{\text{population at Time 1}}\right]/n.$$

In this example, the population at Time 1 is the census count in 1990, which we call the **base year**; the population at Time 2 is the census count in 2000, and n is the number of years (10) between the two censuses. You can plug in the above numbers to see that the average annual linear rate of growth turns out to be 0.013153. Now, we use that rate of growth to extrapolate the population forward, for example, from our **launch year** (the beginning year of a population projection) of 2000 to a **target year** (the year to which we project a population forward in time) of 2050, using the following formula:

$$\text{population in target year} = \text{population in base year} \times [1 + (r_{\text{lin}} \times n)].$$

In this formula, r_{lin} is the average annual linear rate of growth just calculated (0.013153) and n is the number of years (in this case) between the base year (1990) and the target year (2050). So, plugging in the numbers from above, the projected population in the year 2050 is

$$248{,}709{,}873 \times [1 + (.013153 \times 60)] = 444{,}986{,}731.$$

You may recall from Chapter 2 that populations are typically thought to grow exponentially, not in a straight-line fashion, and this hearkens back to the formula that we used in that chapter to derive an estimate of the doubling time of the population. In that problem, our concern was estimating the likely time it would take a population to double in size when we knew the rate of population growth. By algebraically rearranging that equation, we can produce a formula that expresses the logarithmic growth of a population, assuming a constant rate of growth. This formula is as follows:

$$\text{population at Time 2} = \text{population at Time 1} \times e^{rn}.$$

In this case, r represents the geometric or exponential rate of increase (r_{exp}) and is calculated with the following formula:

$$r_{exp} = [ln(\text{population at Time 2/population at Time 1})]/n.$$

The term *ln* represents the natural logarithm of the ratio of the population at Time 2 (the launch year) to the population at Time 1 (the base year). It is one of the function buttons on most handheld calculators (including the one that comes with the iPhone). Once again, n is the time between censuses. So, to calculate the exponential average annual rate of population growth between 1990 and 2000, first find that the ratio of the population at those two dates (281,421,906/248,709,873) is 1.13153 (which is what we found when calculating the linear rate of growth), then find that the natural logarithm of that number is 0.12357, which is then divided by 10 to find that the rate of increase is 0.012357 (or 12.4 per thousand per year). Next, plug this rate of growth (0.012357) back into the formula for exponential or logarithmic growth (above) in order to project the population forward from the launch year of 2000 to the target year of 2050. The answer is

$$281{,}421{,}916 \times e^{(.012357 \times 50)} = 522{,}014{,}164.$$

This is of course a higher number than we found with the linear method of extrapolation, reminding us of the power of geometric growth (the power of doubling as discussed in Chapter 2). But is this really what the future holds for the United States? Is the United States really expecting a huge increase in population between 2000 and 2050? Notice that these extrapolation methods of projection refer simply to total population size without taking into consideration the combination of births, deaths, or migration that would produce the projected population. If we have a way of projecting those details, then we can project the population to a target year using the **components-of-growth** method.

Components-of-Growth This is an adaptation of the demographic balancing equation mentioned earlier in the book. The population of the United States in the year 2050 will be equal to the population in 2000 plus all the births between 2000 and 2050, less the deaths, plus the net migration between those two dates. But how will we figure out the number of births, deaths, and migrants that we might expect over those 50 years? We know that all of these population processes differ by age and sex, and we also know that as the population grows we cannot expect that the number of births and deaths will remain constant over time. A simple components-of-growth approach will work reasonably well for a short time period, but it is not very useful for a long time period such as that from 2000 to 2050. What is needed is a more sophisticated approach to figuring out what those components of growth are likely to be, since they are apt to change over time, especially as the age structure changes. This means a method that takes the age structure into account, and we call this the cohort component method.

Cohort Component Method To make a population projection using the **cohort component method**, we begin with a distribution of the population by age and sex (in absolute frequencies, not percentages) for a specific base year, which in this projection method will usually be the same as the launch year. Usually a base year is a year for which we have the most complete and accurate data—typically a census year. Besides the age and sex distributions, you need to have base-year age-specific mortality rates (that is, a base-year life table), base-year age-specific fertility rates, and, if possible, age-specific rates of in- and out-migration. Cohorts are usually arranged in five-year groups, such as ages 0 to 4, 5 to 9, 10 to 14, and so on, which facilitates projecting a population forward in time in five-year intervals.

For example, if we are making projections from a base year of 2000 to a target year of 2050, we would make intermediate projections for 2005, 2010, 2015, and so forth. With the base-year data in hand and a target year in mind, we must next make some assumptions about the future course of each component of population growth between the base year and the target year. Will mortality continue to drop? If so, which ages will be more or less affected and how big will the changes be? Will fertility decline, remain stable, or possibly rise at some ages while dropping at others? If there is an expected change, how big will it be? Can we expect rates of in- and out-migration to change? Note that if our population is an entire country, our concern will be with international migration only, whereas if we are projecting the population of an area such as a state, county, or city, we will have to consider both internal and international migration.

The actual process of projecting a population involves several steps and is carried out for each five-year cohort between the base and target years. First, the age-specific mortality data are applied to each five-year age group in the base-year population to estimate the number of survivors in each cohort five years into the future. Since there were 9,303,809 females aged 20–24 in the United States in 2000 and the probability of a female surviving from age 20–24 to age 25–29 (derived from the life table, as discussed in Chapter 5) is 0.9977, then in 2005 we would have expected there to be 9,282,410 women surviving to age 25–29, before we make any adjustment for migration. This process of "surviving" a population forward through time is carried out for all age groups in the base-year population. The probabilities of migration (assuming that such data are available) are applied in the same way as are mortality data.

Fertility estimation is complicated by the fact that only women are at risk of having children, and of course those children are added into the population only at age zero. The tasks include (1) calculating the number of children likely to be born during the five-year intervals, and (2) calculating how many of those born will also die during those intervals. The number to be born is estimated by multiplying the appropriate age-specific fertility rate by the number of women in each of the child-bearing ages. Then we add up the total number of children and apply to that number the probability of survival from birth to the end of the five-year interval. Experience suggests that fertility behavior often changes more rapidly (both up and down) than demographers may expect, so population projectionists hedge their bets by producing a range of estimates from high to low, with a middle or medium projection that incorporates what the demographer thinks is the most likely scenario. The highest estimate reflects the demographer's estimate of the highest fertility trend possible in the future, along with the highest decline likely in mortality, and the maximum net immigration likely. Conversely, the lowest projection incorporates the most rapid decline in fertility, the least rapid drop in mortality, and the lowest level of net immigration probable. More sophisticated projection methods use statistical modeling to assign probabilities to the likelihood of one or another future course of demographic events (Lutz, Sanderson, and Scherbov 2004).

Differences in fertility often account for the biggest chunk of variation between high and low projections. For example, in the projection of the population of Mexico made by the U.S. Census Bureau in the late 1970s (U.S. Census Bureau 1979), the high projection for 1990 was 102,349,000, whereas the low projection was 88,103,000. Virtually all the difference was found in the ages zero to 14. The 1990 census in Mexico, however, counted "only" 86 million people. Part of the difference was almost certainly due to an acknowledged undercount in the Mexican census, but most of the difference was a result of the unanticipated success of Mexico's campaign to lower the birth rate.

Calculating a cohort component projection is somewhat complicated, and other sources contain more details (Murdock and Ellis 1991; Smith, Tayman, and Swanson 2001; Lutz, Sanderson, and Scherbov 2004). The U.S. Census Bureau uses these methods in preparing its series of population projections for the United States (U.S. Census Bureau 2008). Notice that the folks at the Bureau keep revising their projections because new information comes along that alters some of the previous assumptions. They use single year of age cohorts, rather than five-year age groups, in order to produce as much detailed information as possible. They also do their projections separately by race/ethnicity since different groups have somewhat different patterns of fertility, mortality, and migration. For example, the Census Bureau's projections made in 2008 (the latest available at this writing), assume that the total fertility rates for Hispanics and Blacks will decline between now and 2050, while all other groups combined will rise slightly, and overall this leads to the expectation that the total fertility rate at the middle of the twenty-first century in the United States will be nearly identical to what it was at the beginning of the century. The projection for the United States also assumes that life expectancy will rise by a few years between now and the middle of the century, and that net international migration will increase over time from its current level of just over a million persons per year to slightly more than 2 million persons per year by 2050.

The projection begins with the age and sex structure as enumerated in the census, with separate projections for each race and ethnic group, which are then combined for the total population. To this age structure are applied the age-specific birth rates among women, the age-sex-specific death rates for everyone, and the age-sex specific rates of net international migration. The process is repeated for each year up to 2050. The total population projected for 2050 is 439 million, which is slightly lower than the figure obtained by the straight-line extrapolation method but 83 million fewer people than the exponential extrapolation would have had us believe are going to be around by the middle of the century.

Backward or Inverse Projection Population data are projected into the future in order to estimate what could happen down the road. Similar methods can be used to work backward to try to understand what happened in the past. The basic idea is to begin with census data that provide a reasonably accurate age and sex distribution for a given base year. Then, making various assumptions about the historical trends in fertility, mortality, and migration, you work back through time to "project" what earlier populations must have been like in terms of the number of people by age and sex. Wrigley and Schofield (1981) used this method to work backward from the 1871 census of England and Wales to reconstruct that region's population history. Whitmore (1992) used a complex backward projection model to show how it was possible for European contact to have led to a 90 percent depopulation of the indigenous peoples living in the Basin of Mexico at the time that Cortés arrived. Details of these methods are contained in other sources (Smith 1992; Oeppen 1993).

Population Momentum

One of the important lessons that we take away from population projections is that age structures carry with them the potential for substantial **momentum of population growth**. This is a concept not unlike the idea that a heavy freight train takes longer to stop than does a light commuter train, or that a Boeing 747 requires a longer runway for landing than does a 737. The amount of momentum built into an age structure is determined by answering the following question: How much larger would the population eventually be, compared to now, if replacement fertility were instituted in the population right now? Put another way, how much larger would the stable population be based on replacement-level fertility compared to the current population? (Keyfitz 1971; Kim and Schoen 1997). Of course, we can turn this around, as Europeans are increasingly having to do, and ask about the momentum toward depopulation built into an older age structure.

You can probably see intuitively that if a population has a large fraction of women in their reproductive years, before the population stops growing, these women will contribute many additional babies to the future population even at replacement level; whereas an older population, with fewer women in their reproductive ages contributing fewer babies, will stop growing. Most populations that now have above-replacement-level fertility will not immediately drop to replacement level. You know from Chapter 6 that the fertility transition does not normally work like that. So, researchers have devised formulas to calculate the momentum built into more gradual declines in fertility (Schoen and Kim 1998; Li and Tuljapurkar 1999). For example, a population that was growing at a rate of 3 percent per year (similar to Guatemala) would be 1.7 times larger when it stopped growing if replacement-level fertility were achieved immediately. That would require the TFR to drop instantaneously from 4.4 to 2.1, which is very unlikely. More probable would be a decline over several decades. If the drop from 4.4 to 2.1 took 28 years, then the population would be 3.9 times larger when it stopped growing, and if it took as long as 56 years, the population would be 7.7 times larger when replacement level was finally reached (Schoen and Kim 1998).

Understanding population momentum allows you to appreciate that slowing down the rate of population growth requires both forethought and patience. The payoff, which is the "window of opportunity" that I discussed earlier in the chapter, is apt to be at least two decades down the road from the time that fertility begins to decline in earnest. The flip side of that is that if you are worried about the depopulating influence of an aging population, you cannot wait until it is happening to start doing something about it, because it also takes a while to rebuild momentum once you lose it.

Summary and Conclusion

The age and sex structure of a society is a subtle, commonly overlooked aspect of the social structure, yet it is one of the most influential drivers of social change in human society. The number of people at each age and of each sex is a very important factor in how a society is organized and how it operates, and for this reason the age transition that accompanies the mortality and fertility transitions is a critical force for change. Age composition is determined completely by the interaction of the three demographic processes. Mortality has the smallest short-run impact on the age distribution, but when mortality declines suddenly (as in the less developed nations), it makes the population more youthful. At the same time, a decline in mortality influences the sex structure at the older ages by producing increasingly greater numbers of females than males. Changes in fertility generally produce the biggest changes in a society's age structure, regardless of the level of mortality. Falling fertility, for example, is the single biggest driver of the increase in the proportion of the population that is in the older ages. Migration can have a sizable impact, because migrants tend to be concentrated among young adults, and are thus likely to contribute not only themselves, but also their children to a shifting age structure.

In all of the more developed societies in the world today, the fertility rate has been low for long enough that we may be approaching the end of the age transition, and population aging has become a major societal concern—not because we are afraid of old people, but rather because the demands on societal resources are very different for an older than for a younger population. "Life in an era of declining and ageing populations will be totally different from life in an era of rising and youthful populations. A new age calls for a new mind-set" (Wallace 2001:220).

Creating that mind-set is aided by the use of population projections, which allow us to chart the course of change implied by different age structures. There are some fairly predictable changes that occur to a population in the context of the age transition from a younger population at the beginning of the demographic transition to an older population at the end of the demographic transition. The critical question is how quickly that transition occurs, because the distortions in the age structure that are part of the age transition can lead to changes in economic organization, political dominance, and social stability that must be dealt with by society—and they have the potential to be either positive or negative in their impact, depending on how society responds. Another important change in human society that is taking place simultaneously—and intimately bound up with the age transition—is the broad scale transfer of human existence into urban places. The next chapter looks at this transition.

Main Points

1. The age transition is a predictable shift from a predominantly younger population when fertility is high (usually when mortality is high) to a predominantly older population when fertility is low (usually when mortality is also low).
2. The age composition of a society is a powerful stimulant to social change.
3. More male babies than females are generally born, but the age structure is further influenced by the fact that at almost every age more males than females die, and the sex ratio drops dramatically in the older ages.

4. Mortality has very little long-run impact on the age structure, but in the short run a decline in mortality typically makes the population younger in medium- to high-mortality societies and a little older in lower-mortality societies; declining mortality mainly operates to increase population size, rather than dramatically affecting the age and sex structure.
5. Fertility is the most important determinant of the shape of the age/sex structure—high fertility produces a young age structure, whereas low fertility produces an older age structure.
6. Migration can have a very dramatic short-run impact on the age and sex structure of a society, especially in local areas.
7. Age transitions can provide a demographic dividend for countries experiencing a rapid fertility decline.
8. The end result of the age transition is to produce a population with a higher fraction of people in the older ages.
9. The percentage of the population that is 65 and older is greatest in more developed countries because its increase largely depends on a decline in the birth rate, but the majority of the world's older population lives in developing countries.
10. Population projections provide a way of using the age structure to read the future and are developed from applying the age and sex distribution for a base year to sets of age-specific mortality, fertility, and migration rates for the interval between the base year and the target year.

Questions for Review

1. It seems backward that fertility levels affect the age structure more than mortality levels, especially given the importance of declining mortality to all of the transitions. Discuss this seeming paradox and show why it makes sense after all.
2. The U.S. baby boom generation has sometimes been called "a pig in a python." Describe how that metaphor might help us to understand the age transitions associated with cohort flows.
3. The demographic dividend has been heralded as one of the more positive aspects of the age transition. Discuss exactly what that means, and what a society has to do in order to cash in on this dividend.
4. Discuss the way in which the health and mortality transition has helped to differentiate the older population into the third and fourth ages. What changes do you foresee in the older population by the time you get there, compared to the current situation?
5. Discuss how the changing age structure of the United States as shown in Figure 8.10 has altered American society. What changes in American society do you foresee if the age structure changes in the way suggested by the projection to 2040 in that graph? What might cause the actual age structure in 2040 to be different than projected?

Suggested Readings

1. John I. Clarke, 2000, *The Human Dichotomy: The Changing Numbers of Males and Females* (Amsterdam: Pergamon).

   A scholarly but very readable analysis of the way in which the sex ratio has been changing in tandem with the demographic transition and related global changes.

2. Paul Wallace, 2001, *Agequake: Riding the Demographic Rollercoaster Shaking Business, Finance, and Our World* (London: Nicholas Brealey).

   A popular and very readable (and also well-researched) examination of the impact of changing age structures on the modern world.

3. Peter G. Peterson, 1999, *Gray Dawn: How the Coming Age Wave Will Transform America—and the World* (New York: Times Books).

   Although the author of this book is a former chairman of Lehmans, not an academic, the book contains a great deal of interesting information about the impact of aging on society. The book received considerable publicity when it was published.

4. Linda J. Waite, Editor, 2005, *Aging, Health and Public Policy: Demographic and Economic Perspectives* (A Supplement to Volume 30 of Population and Development Review) (New York: The Population Council).

   An older population requires a whole new way of thinking about health and the public's response to these changing needs. Contributors to this volume explore these issues with the goal of producing as realistic an assessment as possible about the economic consequences of aging in the U.S. and how they can be successfully coped with.

5. Steven A. Nyce and Sylvester J. Schreiber, 2005, *The Economic Implications of Aging Societies: The Costs of Living Happily Ever After* (New York: Cambridge University Press).

   This is a very accessible discussion of the complex demographic causes of aging, and the social consequences of an expanding older population.

Websites of Interest

Remember that websites are not as permanent as books and journals, so I cannot guarantee that each of the following websites still exists at the moment you are reading this. You may have to Google the name of the organization to find the current web address.

1. **http://www.census.gov/ipc/www/idb/informationGateway.php**
   At this website, the U.S. Bureau of the Census allows you to produce tables of age data for every country of the world, based on their projections out to the year 2050.

2. **http://www12.statcan.ca/english/census01/products/analytic/companion/age/pyramid.cfm**
   Statistics Canada has an age pyramid that changes over time for the past century, nicely illustrating the age transition discussed in this chapter.

3. **http://www.statistics.gov.uk/populationestimates/svg_pyramid/default.htm**
   Watch the age structure of England and Wales change over time in this interactive age pyramid.

4. **http://esa.un.org/unpp/index.asp**
   This online resource lets you create your own summary tables of data from the United Nations Population Division's latest revisions of world population projections, including population data by age and sex. Compare their projections with those of the U.S. Census Bureau.

5. **http://www.rand.org/pubs/monograph_reports/MR1274/index.html**
   This detailed report from RAND's Population Matters program, authored by David Bloom, David Canning, and Jaypee Sevilla, details the "demographic dividend" inherent in the age transition.

CHAPTER 9
The Urban Transition

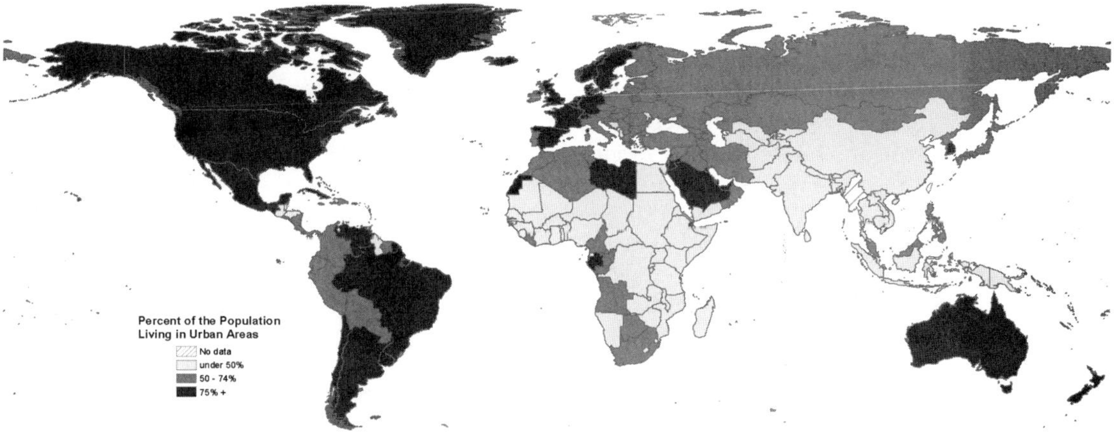

Figure 9.1 Map of the World According to Percentage of Urban Population

The world is rapidly becoming urban. Consider that as recently as 1850 only 2 percent of the entire population of the world lived in cities of 100,000 or more people. By 1900, that figure had edged up to 6 percent, and it had risen to 16 percent by 1950 (Davis 1972). So for most of human history almost no one had lived in a city—cities were small islands in a sea of rurality. But within just one century, from 1850 to 1950, cities had pulled in one of every six human beings, and a short 60 years after that, in the year 2010, just over half the population was living in an urban place (United Nations Population Division 2010). By the middle of this century, that fraction is projected to increase to more than two-thirds of all people living in urban areas.

The present historical epoch, then, is marked by population redistribution as well as by population increase. This redistribution is represented generally by the migration transition, as I mentioned in Chapter 7. At that time I also mentioned that the migration transition has increasingly morphed into the urban transition, although as you will see in this chapter the urban transition is not solely a product of migration.

What Is the Urban Transition?

The urban transition represents the reorganization of human society from being predominantly rural and agricultural to being predominantly urban and nonagricultural (Firebaugh 1979). It is no exaggeration to suggest that this is a genuinely revolutionary shift in society. Reissman (1964:154) described it this way:

> Urbanization is social change on a vast scale. It means deep and irrevocable changes that alter all sectors of a society. In our own history [the United States] the shift from an agricultural to an industrial society has altered every aspect of social life . . . the whole institutional structure was affected as a consequence of our urban development. Apparently, the process is irreversible once begun. The impetus of urbanization upon society is such that society gives way to urban institutions, urban values, and urban demands.

The vast majority of Americans live in—indeed were born in—cities, and almost everyone in the richer countries of the world shares that urban experience. Most of us take the city for granted, some curse it, some find its attractions irresistible, but no one denies that urban life is the center of modern civilization. Cities, of course, are nothing new, and their influence on society is not a uniquely modern feature of life; however, the widespread emergence of urban life—the explosive growth of the urban population—is very much a recent feature of human existence. This urban transition is one of the most significant demographic movements in world history partly because it is intimately tied to population growth and all aspects of the demographic transition. We can reasonably say that in the world today, population growth is originating in the countryside but showing up in the cities.

Cities are implicated in a wide range of problems, issues, and triumphs in all societies, but my intention here is not to review what life is like in a city. That is increasingly the story of human life in general and it is well beyond the scope of this book. Rather, I want to provide you with a demographic perspective on the urban transition. First I examine the drivers of the urban transition—the reasons why urban places have become so popular. From there we will examine the more proximate determinants of the urban transition—the demographic mechanisms by which the transition is accomplished. Then we look at some of the more important ways in which the urban transition becomes an evolutionary process, as people constantly readjust to life in urban places. Finally, I examine the extent to which cities are sustainable. What is it that allows most humans to effectively disassociate themselves from living on the land, growing food, and being close to nature?

Defining Urban Places

What exactly is an urban place, you might well ask. We tend to know it when we see it, but how do we define it? An urban place can be thought of as a *spatial concentration* of people whose lives are organized around *nonagricultural activities*. The essential characteristic here is that urban means high density and nonagricultural, whereas rural means any place that is not urban. A farming village of 5,000 people should not be called urban, whereas a tourist spa or an artist colony of 2,500 people may well be correctly designated as an urban place. You can appreciate, then, that "urban" is a fairly complex concept. It is a function of (1) population size, (2) space (land area), (3) the ratio of population to space (density or concentration), and (4) economic and social organization.

As the number and fraction of people living in urban places has increased, the importance of urban life obviously becomes more important. The study of human society is increasingly the study of urban society, and the variability across space and time in the urban environment is a crucial part of the changes occurring in every society. The urban environment, however, is a combination of social and built environments. The concept of *urban* is, at root, a place-based idea (Weeks 2004). The definitions of *urban* used in most demographic research, unfortunately, rarely encompass the more complex ingredients. Due to limitations in available data and sometimes simply for expediency, researchers (and government bureaucrats as well) typically define urban places on the basis of population size alone, implying that density is the major criterion. Thus, all places with a population of 2,000, 5,000, 10,000, or more (the lower limit varies) might be considered urban for research purposes.

A variation on that theme is to designate cities and towns as being, by definition, urban and everything else as rural: "Of the 228 countries for which the United Nations (UN) compiles data, roughly half use administrative considerations—such as residing in the capital of the country or of a province—to designate people as urban dwellers. Among the other countries, 51 distinguish urban and rural populations based on the size or density of locales, 39 rely on functional characteristics such as the main economic activity of an area, 22 have no definition of 'urban,' and eight countries define all (Singapore, for example) or none (several countries in Polynesia) of their populations as living in urban areas" (Brockerhoff 2000:Box 1).

Such an arbitrary cutoff, of course, disguises a lot of variation in human behavior. Although the difference between rural and urban areas may at first appear to be a dichotomy, it is really a continuum in which we might find an aboriginal hunter-gatherer near one end and an apartment dweller in Manhattan near the other.

In between will be varying shades of difference. The next time you drive from the city to the country (or the other way around), you might ask yourself where you would arbitrarily make a dividing line between the two. In the United States in the nineteenth and early twentieth centuries rural turned into urban when you reached streets laid out in a grid. Today, such clearly defined transitions are rare, and besides, even living in a rural area in richer countries does not preclude your participation in urban life. The flexibility of the automobile combined with the power of telecommunications puts most people in touch with as much of urban life (and what is left of rural life) as they might want. Even in the most remote areas of developing countries, radio and satellite-relayed television broadcasts and mobile phones can make rural villagers knowledgeable about urban life, even if they have never seen it in person.

Beginning with Census 2000, the U.S. Census Bureau has used the power of geographic information systems (GIS) to create a more flexible definition than ever before of what is urban. To be called urban in the United States, a place must be part of an **urban area** (UA) or an **urban cluster** (UC). A UA consists of contiguous, densely settled census block groups (BGs) and census blocks that meet minimum population density requirements, typically 1,000 persons per square mile, along with adjacent densely settled census blocks, typically with at least 500 persons per square mile, that together encompass a population of at least 50,000 people. A UC consists of contiguous, densely settled census BGs and census blocks that meet those minimum population density requirements, along with adjacent densely settled census blocks that together encompass a population of at least 2,500 people, but fewer than 50,000 people (U.S. Census Bureau 2002).

Thus, to be urban, you start with a core census block or block group (an area that is part of a census tract) that has a population density of at least 1,000 persons per square mile, and then add any contiguous areas that have at least 500 persons per square mile. As long as the total population of this combined area is at least 2,500 people, the area is defined as urban, and any smaller place within that urban area is called urban. Any place that is not within an urban area or urban cluster is defined as rural.

Canada defines an urban place in a similar but not identical fashion. An *urban place* or *urban area*, as defined by Statistics Canada, has a population of at least 1,000 concentrated within a continuously built-up area, at a density of at least 400 per square kilometer (equivalent to about 1,000 persons per square mile) (Statistics Canada 2007). Mexico has traditionally defined *urban* as being any locality that has at least 2,500 inhabitants (Villalvazo Peña, Corona Medina, and García Mora 2002), although Mexico, like Canada, typically defines a *city* as a place that has at least 100,000 inhabitants.

You can see that the United States and Canada use a combination of population size and density to define urban, whereas Mexico relies largely on population size. None of the three give consideration to the economic and social characteristics of a place. Yet an essential ingredient of being urban is economic and social life organized around nonagricultural activities. There is an explicit recognition that urban people order their lives differently than rural people do; they perceive the world differently and behave differently, and this is why being in an urban place is important. You should thus keep in mind that there is a discontinuity between the *concept* of urban and the *definition* of urban as I turn now to a discussion of the demographic aspects of the process whereby a society is transformed from rural to urban—the urban transition, or the process of urbanization.

What Are the Drivers of the Urban Transition?

In its most basic form, the urban transition is the same concept as urbanization and refers to the change in the proportion of a population living in urban places; it is a relative measure ranging from 0 percent, if a population is entirely rural or agricultural, to 100 percent, if a population is entirely urban. The earliest cities were not very large because most of them were not demographically self-sustaining. The ancient city of Babylon (about 50 miles south of modern Baghdad, Iraq) might have had 50,000 people, Athens possibly 80,000, and Rome as many as 500,000; but they represented a tiny fragment of the total population of the region in which they were located. They were symbols of civilization, visible centers that were written about, discussed by travelers, and densely enough settled to be dug up later by archaeologists. Our view of ancient history is colored by the fact that our knowledge of societal detail is limited primarily to the cities, although we can be sure that most people actually lived in the countryside.

Precursors

Early cities had to be constantly replenished by migrants from the hinterlands, because they had higher death rates and lower birth rates than the countryside did, which usually resulted in an annual excess of deaths over births. The economically self-sustaining character of modern urban areas began with the transformation of economies based on agriculture (produced in the countryside) to those based on manufactured goods (produced in the city) and has expanded to those based on servicing the rest of the economy (and often located in the suburbs). Control of the economy made it far easier for cities to dominate rural areas politically and thus ensure their own continued existence in economic terms.

A crucial transition in this process came between about 1500 and 1800 with the European discovery of "new" lands, the rise of mercantilistic states (that is, based on goods rather than landholdings, as I discussed in Chapter 3), and the inception of the Industrial Revolution. These events were inextricably intertwined, and they added up to a diversity of trade that gave a powerful stimulus to the European economy. This was a period of building a base for subsequent industrialization, but it was still a preindustrial and largely pre-urban era. During this time, for example, cities in England were growing at only a slightly higher rate than the total population, and thus the urban population was rising only very slowly as a proportion of the total. Between 1600 and 1800, London grew from about 200,000 people to slightly less than a million (Wrigley 1987)—an average rate of growth considerably less than 1 percent per year; also during this span of 200 years, London's population increased from 2 percent of the total population of England to 10 percent—significant, but not necessarily remarkable, especially considering that in 1800 London was the largest city in Europe. In 1801, only 18 percent of the population in England lived in cities of

30,000 people or more, and nearly two-thirds of those urban residents were concentrated in London. Thus, on the eve of the Industrial Revolution, Europe (like the rest of the world) was predominantly agrarian.

Neither England nor any other country was urbanizing with any speed at that time because industry had not yet grown sufficiently to demand a sizable urban population, and because cities could not yet sustain their populations through natural increase. Early competitive, laissez-faire capitalism characterized the economies of Europe and North America from the late eighteenth through the mid-nineteenth centuries, and cities were still largely commercial in nature, with many of the newly emerging manufacturing businesses located in the countryside close to the source of materials and the labor supply. In the nineteenth century, urbanization began in earnest, its timing closely tied to industrialization and the decline in mortality that triggered population growth.

Urban factory jobs were the classic magnets sucking young people out of the countryside in the nineteenth century (Davis 1965). This happened earliest in England, and in Figure 9.2 you can see the rapid rise in urbanization in the United Kingdom in response to early industrialization. Japan and Russia entered the industrial world later than the United Kingdom or the United States, and you can see in Figure 9.2 that their pattern of urbanization was therefore delayed. Once started, however, urbanization proceeded quickly in these countries, and the countries will essentially merge at about 80 percent urban by 2025.

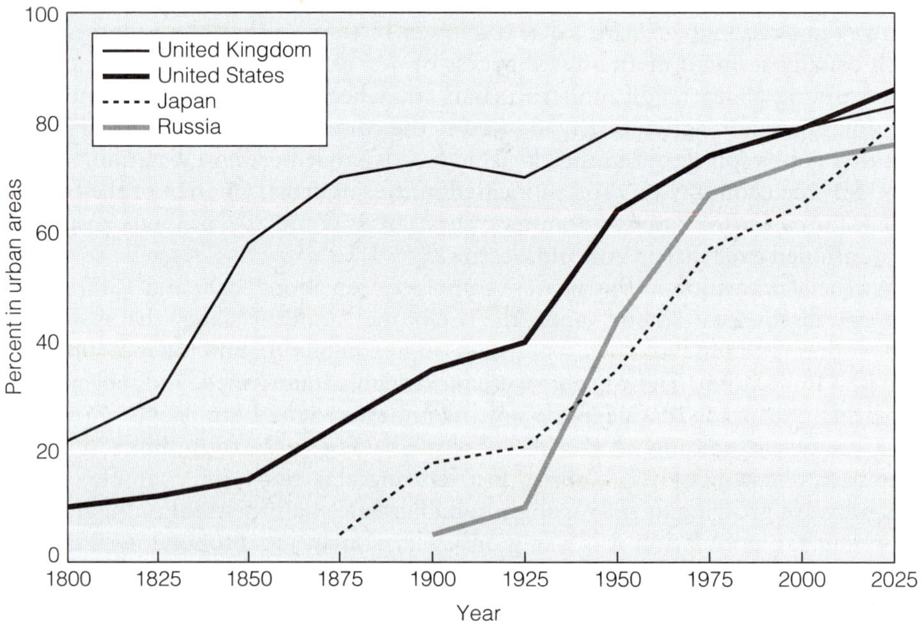

Figure 9.2 Industrialized Nations Have Passed Through Most of the Urban Transition

Sources: Prepared by the author using data for 1800 through 1925 from Kingsley Davis, 1965, "The Urbanization of the Human Population," Scientific American 213(3):40-54; and data for 1950-2025 from United Nations Population Division, 2010, "World Urbanization Prospects: The 2009 Revision," (New York: United Nations).

Current Patterns

In the contemporary post-industrial world characterized by what is often called advanced capitalism, the function of cities is changing again. In the developed, already urbanized part of the world, cities are losing their industrial base and are increasingly service centers to economic activities occurring in the hinterlands of the same country, or in another country altogether, essentially reversing the trends of the mid-nineteenth to mid-twentieth centuries. In less developed countries, especially the so-called emerging nations, commercial and industrial activities combine with historically unprecedented rates of city growth to generate patterns of urbanization somewhat different from those that occurred in the now-developed nations. But even in the poorest countries of the world, city growth is occurring at a rapid pace.

Figure 9.1 at the beginning of the chapter maps the countries of the world according to the percentage of the population living in urban places at the beginning of the twenty-first century. These data are based on each individual country's own definition of "urban," but typically it refers to places with 2,000 people or more. A little less than one-fourth of the countries of the world (24 percent) have less than 50 percent of the population living in urban places. As you can see from the map, these include the two most populous nations, China and India, as well as the rest of the Indian subcontinent, most of Southeast Asia, and nearly half of the sub-Saharan nations. More than four in 10 of the world's nations (43 percent) have between 50 and 74 percent of the population living in urban places. In the Americas, these include countries in Central and South America with large indigenous populations. Sub-Saharan Africa is sprinkled with countries in this range, and most of the former Soviet republics in central Asia are in this category. Some European countries are also in this range, as you can see from the map, including Portugal, Italy, Greece, and most of central Europe northward through the Balkan states up into Finland. The remaining one-third of the world's nations have 75 percent or more of their population residing in urban places. This includes most countries in North and South America, as well as most European nations, Japan and Korea in Asia, and Australia and New Zealand in Oceania. In essence, the highest percentage of the urban population tends to be found among European and "overseas" European nations.

The pace of urbanization at the global level can be seen graphically in Figure 9.3. In 1950, more than half of the population (52 percent) in more developed regions of the world already lived in urban places, but less than one in five people (18 percent) in the less developed nations were urban. By 2000, nearly three-fourths (73 percent) of the population in more developed regions was urban, compared to 40 percent in the less developed regions. By 2025, the United Nations projects that 79 percent of the population in more developed regions will be urban, and that 52 percent in less developed regions will be urban, producing a world total of 57 percent urban (United Nations Population Division 2010).

Impressive as they are, the data in Figure 9.3 nonetheless understate the real growth in the urban population. Most of the world's population growth since 1950 has occurred in less developed nations, so the increase in the percentage that is urban hides a staggering rise in the *number* of people living in urban places of those countries. Table 9.1 summarizes the United Nations' estimates of the size of the

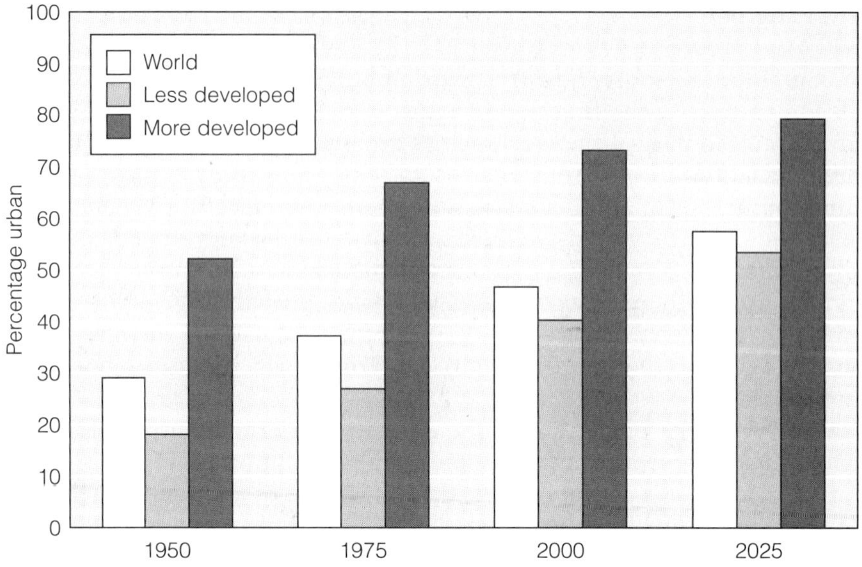

Figure 9.3 The World Has Urbanized at a Rapid Pace since 1950

Sources: Adapted from data in United Nations Population, 2010. *World Urbanization Prospects: The 2009 Revision* (New York: United Nations).

urban and rural populations by major geographic region of the world. Especially noteworthy is Asia, which in 1950 had 229 million people in urban areas, but by 2000 had nearly 1.4 billion people in urban places, with an expected near-doubling of that number by 2025. In Africa, the urban population in 2000 was almost 10 times the size it was in 1950. In Latin America and the Caribbean, the urban population in 2000 was nearly six times what it had been in 1950. The United Nations expects that the world's rural population in 2025 will be about the same number as in 2000 (3.3–3.5 billion people), and that it will represent about twice as many people as there were in 1950 (1.8 billion) (United Nations Population Division 2010). However, the urban population of the world in 2025 (4.5 billion) will be 60 percent larger than it was in 2000 (2.8 billion), and that will be a sixfold increase over the world's urban population of 1950 (which was 729 million).

As economic development occurred, cities grew because they were economically efficient places. Commercial centers bring together in one place the buyers and sellers of goods and services. Likewise, industrial centers bring together raw materials, laborers, and the financial capital necessary for the profitable production of goods. They are efficient politically because they centralize power and thus make the administrative activities of the power base that supports them more efficient. In sum, cities perform most functions of society more efficiently than is possible when people are spatially spread out. Mumford said it well: "There is indeed no single urban activity that has not been performed successfully in isolated units in the open country. But there is one function that the city alone can perform, namely the synthesis and synergy of the many separate parts by continually bringing them together in a common meeting place where direct fact-to-face intercourse is possible. The office of

Table 9.1 Asian, African, and Latin American Urban Populations Have Increased at a Staggering Rate since 1950

	1950	1975	2000	2025
Urban population (thousands)				
World	729,317	1,511,414	2,837,431	4,535,925
Northern America	109,667	178,973	252,154	340,490
Europe	280,685	441,226	514,422	560,560
Oceania	7,940	15,227	21,932	30,107
Latin America and the Caribbean	69,227	196,394	393,420	560,911
Asia	229,080	571,848	1,360,900	2,383,268
Africa	32,719	107,745	294,602	660,589
Rural population (thousands)				
World	1,800,028	2,549,903	3,277,937	3,475,608
Northern America	61,948	63,387	66,500	57,032
Europe	266,775	234,982	212,146	168,704
Oceania	4,867	6,060	9,227	12,400
Latin America and the Caribbean	98,080	126,929	127,807	108,622
Asia	1,173,808	1,807,526	2,337,395	2,389,255
Africa	194,551	311,020	524,861	739,595
Percent Urban				
World	29	37	46	57
Northern America	64	74	79	86
Europe	51	65	71	77
Oceania	62	72	70	71
Latin America and the Caribbean	41	61	75	84
Asia	16	24	37	50
Africa	14	26	36	47

Source: Adapted from data in United Nations Population, 2010. World Urbanization Prospects: The 2009 Revision (New York: United Nations).

the city, then, is to increase the variety, the velocity, the extent, and the continuity of human intercourse" (Mumford 1968:447).

Cities are efficient partly because they reduce costs by congregating together both producers and consumers of a variety of goods and services. By reducing costs, urban places increase the benefits accruing to business—meaning, naturally, higher profits. Those profits translate into higher standards of living, and that is why cities have flourished in the modern world. They are part and parcel of the modern rise of capitalism.

The theory of the demographic transition was derived originally from the modernization theory, which focused on the role played by cities. The basic thesis of modernization theory was that economic development is built on the efficiencies of cities. Cities are the engines of growth because of the concentration of capital (to build industry), labor (to perform the industrial tasks), and the financial, governmental, and administrative services necessary to manufacture, distribute, sell, and regulate the goods that comprise the essence of economic development. Once economic growth begins, the principle of cumulative causation (discussed in Chapter 7 with reference to migration) kicks in to promote further local development, often at the expense of other regions.

Modernization theory focused attention on individual nations, examining the role that cities played in the development process in that particular country. The fact that cities are crucial to modernization led many developing nations such as Chile, Kenya, Malaysia, and Mexico to establish industrial cities precisely to mimic the process of modernization that occurred in the more developed nations (Potter 1992). The results of those experiments have been mixed at best.

Modernization theory offers a generally good explanation of what happened in the now-developed countries, especially in the period up to World War II, as individual nation building was taking place but transportation and communication still limited the amount of direct interaction between countries. Most of the still-quoted theories of modernization were developed in the 1950s (such as those of Myrdal 1957; and Hirschman 1958), when urbanization in developing countries was still in its early stages. Patterns of urbanization in different parts of the world may reflect when a country entered the modern economic system, which adds globalization to the process of urbanization (Douglass 2000), creating new types of city systems and urban hierarchies.

The Urban Hierarchy and City Systems

In virtually every nation of the world there is one city that stands out as the leading urban center and is noticeably more populous than other cities in the region. Such a place is called a primate city—a disproportionately large leading city holding a central place in the economy of the country. Other cities are less important, but may have their own pecking order, so to speak. In the 1930s, Christaller (1966) developed the concept of central place theory to describe why and how some cities were territorially central and thus in a position to control markets and the regional economy.

Early empirical studies of city systems within countries suggested that a common pattern of cities by size could be expressed by the **rank-size rule**. As set out by Zipf (1949), this says that the population size of a given city (P_i) within a country will be approximately equal to the population of the largest city (P_1) divided by the rank of city *i* by population size (R_i). Thus, the rank-size rule is:

$$P_i = P_1/R_i.$$

So, if the largest city in a country has a population of five million, then the second largest city should have a population size of approximately 5/2 or 2.5 million, whereas the third largest city should have a population of 5/3 or 1.7 million people.

Many countries follow a pattern that is basically similar to the rank-size rule, but there are important exceptions. For example, in Mexico, the largest city (Mexico City) has a population of 19.3 million people, so the rank-size rule would predict a population of 19.3/2, or 9.6 million, for the second largest city (Guadalajara) and a population of 19.3/3, or 6.4 million, for the third largest city (Monterrey). However, the estimated actual sizes of Guadalajara and Monterrey in 2010 were only 4.4 million and 3.9 million, respectively. Clearly, the urban hierarchy in Mexico follows a different pattern than that expressed by the rank-size rule. Nonetheless, so compelling is the idea of the rank-size rule that people keep working to improve upon it by adding greater complexity (see, for example, Zengwang Xu and Harriss 2010).

Even though an empirical generalization such as the rank-size rule does not fit all countries, the importance of such ideas is that they led to the realization among scholars that most countries had a somewhat predictable system of cities that might be amenable to a consistent theoretical interpretation. An important set of such theoretical perspectives was the **core-periphery model** put forth by Friedmann in 1966 (Potter 1992). Prior to economic development, a series of independent cities may exist in a region, but development tends to begin in, and will be concentrated in, one major site (the primate city). This is especially apt to happen in less developed countries that have a history of colonial domination, in which colonial functions were centralized in one city. Over time, the development process diffuses to other cities, but this happens unequally because the primate city (the core) controls the resources, and the smaller cities (the periphery) are dependent on the larger city. It was only a small step to apply these ideas of the core and periphery to a world system of countries and cities.

The **world systems theory** (which I discussed in Chapter 7 in relation to drivers of international migration) is based on the notion that inequality is part of the global economic structure and has been since at least the rise of capitalism 500 years ago (Wallerstein 1974). "Core" countries are defined as the highly developed nations that dominate the world economy and that were the former colonizers of much of the rest of the world. The "periphery" is composed of those countries that, in order to become a part of the global economic system (the alternative to which is to remain isolated and undeveloped), have been forced to be dependent on the core nations, which control the basic resources required for development and a higher standard of living. Because countries tend to be dominated by cities, the world systems theory predicts that cities of core countries ("core cities") will control global resources, operating especially through multinational corporations headquartered in core cities (Chase-Dunn and Hall 1997; Chase-Dunn 1998), and cities in peripheral countries will be dependent on the core cities for their own growth and development (and, of course, that will filter down from the primate city to the other cities in a nation's own city system). These models suggest that the core cities are networked globally and emphasize services over manufacturing, whereas peripheral cities tend to be linked to more local markets and emphasize manufacturing over services (Maume 1983).

As is so often the case, no single model seems capable of explaining all of the complexity in the process of the urban transition. Several tests of modernization and world systems theories have suggested that variations of both contribute to our understanding of the real-world experience of urbanization (see, for example, London 1987; Bradshaw 1987; Firebaugh and Beck 1994; Firebaugh 2003). Part of the complexity is created by the fact that the sheer size of a city does not guarantee its importance in the system of world cities. To be a global city means to have economic power, which is often characterized by the presence of headquarters or major subsidiary locations of multinational corporations (Godfrey and Zhou 1999; Sassen 2001). Sheer size will be more important at the national or regional level. The larger the city, the greater the economic opportunity is likely to be for its residents and the greater the attraction will be to potential migrants from rural areas. Empirical data show that cities in the United States are indeed rank-ordered with respect to the income of workers. In general, the more global a city is, the higher the income, and the lower down in the ranking a city is, the higher the likelihood that its residents will be involved in low-income work (Elliott 1999). Keep these complexities in mind as I illustrate the urban transition with examples from Mexico and China.

An Illustration from Mexico

The impact of population processes on the urban transition is illustrated from the perspective of rural areas by what has happened to people in one village in Mexico—Tzintzuntzan (which in the indigenous language means "the place of hummingbirds"), situated midway between Guadalajara and Mexico City in the state of Michoacán. Historically, the site was the capital of the Tarascan empire (Brandes 1990), but today it is a village of artisans, farmers, merchants, and teachers. For nearly 400 years, the population of Tzintzuntzan stayed right at about 1,000 people (Foster 1967). In the mid-1940s, as Foster began studying the village, the population size was starting to climb slowly because death rates had started to decline in the late 1930s at about the time a government project gave the village electricity, running water, and a hard-surfaced highway connecting it to the outside world (Kemper and Foster 1975).

In 1940, the population was 1,077 and the death rate was about 30 per 1,000, while the birth rate of 47 per 1,000 was leading to a rate of natural increase of 17 per 1,000. For some time, there had been small-scale, local out-migration from the village to keep its population in balance with the limited local resources, but by 1950 the death rate was down to 17 per 1,000 and the birth rate had risen. Better medical care had reduced the incidence of miscarriage and stillbirth, and in 1950 the village had 1,336 people (Foster 1967). By 1970 the population had reached about 2,200 (twice the 1940 size); however, were it not for out-migration draining away virtually all of the natural increase of Tzintzuntzan, the population would again have doubled in about 20 years (Kemper and Foster 1975).

What, you ask, does growth in a small Mexican village have to do with the urban transition? The answer, of course, is that population growth meant that the local population was larger than the local economy could handle, and so some of these villagers were forced to migrate out in search of work. The migrants headed for the cities, and therein lies the tale of the urban transition. Poverty is extensive in rural Mexico, and almost all of those people who leave Tzintzuntzan go to urban places where better opportunities exist—with Mexico City (230 miles away) having been the most popular destination (Kemper and Foster 1975). One of the easiest demographic responses that people can make to population pressure is migration, and in Mexico, as in most countries of the world, the city has been the receiving ground. Furthermore, the demographic characteristics of those who go to the city are what you would expect; they tend to be younger, slightly better educated, of higher occupational status, and more innovative than nonmigrants (Kemper 1977).

For Tzintzuntzeños, migration to Mexico City raised the standard of living of migrant families, altered the world view of both adults and their children toward greater independence and achievement, and, indirectly, "urbanized" the village they left behind. This last effect is due to the fact that having friends and relatives in Mexico City was one factor that led the villagers to be aware of their participation in a wider world. This has made it easier for each successive generation to make the move to Mexico City, because they know what to expect when they arrive and they know people who can help them.

Tzintzuntzeños have also been attracted to the United States, initially recruited through the bracero program (which I mentioned in Chapter 7), and the same patterns of mutual assistance have encouraged the flow of money and ideas from cities in the United States to this small village in the interior of Mexico (Kemper 1991, 1996). International migration can be an extremely important source of income in rural Mexico (Massey, Durand, and Malone 2002; Cornelius, Fitzgerald, and Fischer 2008), and over time migrants have sent or brought back to the village many of the accoutrements of urban life, from new stoves and sewing machines to stereos, television sets, and mobile phones, in effect urbanizing what was once a remote village.

From a theoretical perspective, we can see that modernization is the key to the transformation of the lives of Tzintzuntzeños. However, the process of modernization was not endogenous—it sought the villagers out, rather than the other way around. In a very literal sense, the modernization of the village and its inhabitants depended on what was happening elsewhere. Government leaders in Mexico City (the core) made the decision to provide rural areas (the periphery) with health care, electricity, and paved highways. The rest, as they say, is history, because few villagers, when given the choice, turn down the opportunity for a higher standard of living (Critchfield 1994).

An Illustration from China

China is a very interesting case of urbanization because it is one of the few countries in the world where the government fairly successfully "kept them down on the farm." The Chinese Communist Party officially adopted an anti-urban policy when it came to power in 1949, believing that cities were a negative "Western" influence, and Chinese government policies in the 1960s and 1970s were designed to counteract the urban transition occurring in most of the rest of the world. These policies attempted to "promote wider income distribution, reduce regional inequalities, and create a more balanced urban hierarchy, which would lead to a greater decentralization of economic activities. In doing so, the intention was to slow population growth in the largest cities, while allowing continued increases in medium-sized and smaller urban centers" (Goldstein 1988, as quoted in Bradshaw and Fraser 1989:989). As wonderful as that may sound, the basic policy was actually reinforced (or enforced) by a rigid system of household registration called *hukou*, which created a type of occupational apartheid in China. "Anyone in a rural county is automatically registered as a farmer, anyone in a city as a non-farmer; and the distinction is near rigid. A city-dwelling woman (though not a man) who marries a farmer loses the right to urban life" (*The Economist* 1998:42). Various reforms since the 1980s have diminished the importance of the *hukou* system, although it is still officially in place (Hutzler and Lawrence 2003; Zhu 2004), creating a situation whereby millions of Chinese are "illegal immigrants" in cities within their own country.

Government policies in China thus prevented (or at least delayed) the high rate of natural increase in the rural areas from spilling over disproportionately into migration to urban areas, and the government located heavy industry in rural areas to help soak up the rural labor force (Hsu 1994). Of course, that does not mean that the urban population was not growing. Quite the contrary. Between 1953 and 1990, 326 new cities were created in China (Hsu 1994), and urban growth occurred primarily in small to medium-sized places (Han and Wong 1994), just as the government had planned. Also according to plan, urbanization is low by world standards. At the time of the Communist revolution, China was just 13 percent urban, and by 2010 it had climbed to 47 percent, but most of that increase came in the 1990s as the age structure and the economy were in rapid transition (Friedmann 2005), as I discussed in Chapter 8.

China has thus been able administratively to create a much flatter urban hierarchy than exists in most modern nations (Fan 2000, 2008). The obvious examples are that Beijing is the politically most important city, Shanghai the most populous city, and Hong Kong the richest city (although it was already that way when China annexed it in 1997). This flatness means that China is at the opposite extreme of the rank-size rule from Mexico. Shanghai had an estimated 16.6 million people in 2010, while Beijing had 12.2 million, and an additional six cities, including Hong Kong, had at least 7 million residents. But more important has been the creation of new cities and the growth of existing small to mid-sized cities, rather than huge increases in the larger urban agglomerations. Of particular importance to China's recent urbanization has been the government's emphasis on creating nonagricultural jobs in rural areas, which leads to a reclassification of areas from rural to urban (Zhu 2004).

The Proximate Determinants of the Urban Transition

As you watch the number and percentage of the population that is urban climb over time, you may assume that the explanation is very easy—people move out of rural areas into urban areas. That is a major part of the story, of course, but not the whole story. The urban transition occurs not only as a result of internal rural-to-urban migration, but also through natural increase, international urban migration, reclassification of places from rural to urban, and combinations of these processes. Another important thing to keep in mind is that the urban transition, in the simple sense of urbanization or the percentage of people living in an urban place, may end when nearly everybody is living in an urban area, but the urban *evolution*—changes taking place within urban areas—may continue forever, as I discuss later in the chapter.

Internal Rural-to-Urban Migration

The migration of people within a country from rural to urban places represents the classic definition of the urban transition because it is intuitively the most obvious way by which a population can be shifted from countryside to curbside. There is no question that in the developed countries, rural-to-urban migration was a major force in the process of urbanization. Over time, the agricultural population of these countries has tended to decline in absolute numbers, as well as in relative terms, even in the face of overall population growth. In less developed countries, though, rural-to-urban migration has been occurring in large absolute terms, but without a consequent depopulation of rural areas—although such a depopulation is projected for later in this century in the more developed countries, as you can see by looking back at Table 9.1. The reason, of course, is the difference in the rates of natural increase in less developed countries compared with rates in developed nations.

Had it not been for migration, cities of the nineteenth century and before could not have grown in population size. In fact, in the absence of migration, the excess of deaths over births would actually have produced deurbanization. Of course, migration did occur, because economic development created a demand for an urban population that was largely met by migrants from rural areas. Industrial cities drew the largest crowds, but commercial cities, even in nonindustrial countries, also generated a demand for jobs and created opportunities for people to move from agrarian to urban areas. The cities of most previously colonized countries bear witness to this fact. For example, migration accounted for 75–100 percent of the total growth of nineteenth-century cities in Latin America (Weller, Macisco, and Martine 1971).

The growth of cities in southern Asia and western Africa was also stimulated by the commercial contacts of an expanding European economy. Naturally, in the richer, highly urbanized countries, the agricultural population is now so small that cities (also nations) depend on the natural increase of urban areas, or immigrants from other countries, rather than migration from their own rural areas, for population growth. This helps to explain why Europe—one of the world's most urban regions—is facing depopulation: The low birth rate can no longer be compensated for by migrants coming in from the countryside, because the countryside is emptied out of young people.

Natural Increase

The underlying source of urbanization throughout the world is the rate of natural increase of the rural population. The decline in death rates in rural places, without a commensurate drop in the birth rate, has led to overpopulation in rural areas (too many people for the available number of jobs) and causes people to seek employment elsewhere (the now-familiar tale of demographic change and response). If there were no opportunities for rural-to-urban migration, then the result might simply be that the death rate would eventually rise again in rural areas to achieve a balance between population and resources (the "Malthusian" solution). However, opportunities typically have existed elsewhere in urban places precisely because the innovations that led to a drop in the rural death rate have originated in the cities—the site of technological and material progress and the source of economic development.

The speed of the urban transition—the number of years it takes to go from low-percentage urban to high-percentage urban—depends partly on the difference in the rates of natural increase between urban and rural areas. The rapid urban transition in China, for example, was made possible partly by the rapidly declining birth rate in cities, which meant that migrants from the countryside were making a larger proportionate contribution to the shift in the percent urban. In turn, the rate of natural increase depends on trends in both mortality and fertility, and these patterns have changed dramatically over time, as I have already discussed at length in general terms, but let me now put them into the context of urban places.

Mortality Kingsley Davis (1973) estimated that in the city of Stockholm, Sweden, in 1861–70, the average life expectancy at birth was only 28 years, whereas for the country as a whole at that time, life expectancy was 45 years. I discussed in Chapter 5 that the ability to resist death has been passed to the rest of the world by the industrialized nations, and the diffusion of death control has usually started in the cities and spread from there to the countryside. This phenomenon, though, actually required a crucial reversal in the original urban-rural difference in mortality. When the now-industrialized nations were urbanizing, death rates were higher in the city than in the countryside (see, for example, Williams and Galley 1995), and this helped keep the rate of natural increase in the city lower than in rural areas. In turn, that meant that rural-to-urban migration was a more important factor influencing the urban percentage in a country.

For the past several decades, however, death rates have been lower in the city than in the countryside in virtually every part of the world. We can see this clearly from the calculation of child mortality rates derived from the Demographic and Health Surveys taken in developing countries around the world. Table 9.2 shows the death rate to children under the age of five per 1,000 births for urban and rural places, according to all DHS surveys taken from 2004 through 2009. You can see, for example, that in Benin in 2006, the death rate was 145 for rural children (i.e., 14.5 percent of children born alive died before their fifth birthday) compared to 116 for urban children. These are very high death rates, to be sure, but the risk of dying is still lower in urban than in rural areas. The only exceptions to this rule were in Swaziland, where the urban rate is slightly higher than the rural rate, and in the Dominican Republic, where the rates were identical.

As a consequence of lower urban mortality, the process of urbanization in less developed countries is taking place in the context of historically high rates of urban natural increase. Furthermore, when mortality declines as a response to economic development, structural changes also take place that tend to reduce fertility; but when death control is introduced independently of economic development, mortality and fertility declines lose their common source, and mortality decreases whereas fertility takes quite a while to respond. This results in fertility levels being higher today in less developed countries (urban and rural places alike) than they were at a comparable stage of mortality decline in the currently advanced countries.

Fertility We can usually anticipate that people residing in urban areas will have fairly distinctive ways of behaving compared with rural dwellers. So important and obvious are these differences demographically that urban and rural differentials in fertility are among the most well documented in the literature of demographic research. John Graunt, the seventeenth-century English demographer whom I first mentioned in Chapter 3, concluded that London marriages were less fruitful than those in the country because of "the intemperance in feeding, and especially the Adulteries and Fornications, supposed more frequent in London than elsewhere . . . and . . . the minds of men in London are more thoughtful and full of business than in the Country" (quoted by Eversley 1959:38). In rural areas, large families may be useful (for the labor power), but even if they are not, a family can "take care of" too many members by encouraging migration to the city. Once in the city, people have to cope more immediately with the problems that large families might create for them. At the same time, the importance of the large family is challenged by the many alternatives to family life that cities offer compared to rural areas.

It is nearly axiomatic that urban fertility levels are lower than rural levels; it is also true, of course, that fertility is higher in less developed than in developed nations. Putting these two generalizations together, you can conclude that urban fertility in less developed nations will be lower than rural fertility but still higher than the urban fertility of cities in the industrialized nations. Cities in developing countries, especially in Africa and western Asia, have fertility levels that are probably higher than those ever experienced in European cities. Data from Demographic and Health Surveys in Table 9.2 show total fertility rates (TFRs) in urban areas in 14 countries that are at or above 4.0 children per woman and an additional eight countries in which urban areas have TFRs between 3.0 and 3.9.

You can see in Table 9.2 that sub-Saharan Africa is especially noteworthy for high urban fertility rates—which are nonetheless lower than the very high rural rates. In Mali in 2006, the total fertility rate (TFR) among urban women was 5.4 children each, although that was lower than the 7.2 children per woman in rural areas. Significantly, those rates were virtually identical to the survey done ten years prior to that. At the lower end of fertility within sub-Saharan Africa was Ghana in 2008, with an urban TFR of 3.1 children, compared to the rural rate of 4.9 children. However, once again, these rates did not show any decline from the previous survey. At the other end of the extreme, you can see that even in the very low fertility nations of the former Soviet Union (Georgia, Moldova, and Ukraine), the fertility is very low in rural areas, yet lower still in urban areas.

The emphasis in Table 9.2 is on developing countries because they are the places in the world where both mortality and fertility are still high—in some cases still very high. Furthermore, the richer countries have very few people still residing in rural areas. By the early 1990s, fewer than 2 percent of women in the United States of reproductive age were living on farms, and their fertility was only slightly higher than the other 98 percent of the population (Bachu 1993). By the late 1990s, farm residence and urban-rural residence more generally were no longer even reported in the data for the United States, although women who worked in occupations listed as "farming, forestry, and fishing" did have higher fertility levels than any other group of employed women (Bachu and O'Connell 2000).

Urban fertility levels are also related to migration, since migrants tend to be young adults of reproductive ages. Furthermore, migrants from rural areas typically wind up having levels of fertility lower than people in the rural areas they left, but they still have higher fertility levels than those in the urban areas to which they have

Table 9.2 Urban-Rural Mortality and Fertility Differences Are Still Pronounced in Most Developing Countries

	TFR		Child mortality	
	Urban	Rural	Urban	Rural
Sub-Saharan Africa				
Benin 2006	4.9	6.3	116	145
Cameroon 2004	4.0	6.1	119	169
Chad 2004	5.7	6.5	179	208
Congo (Brazzaville) 2005	3.8	6.1	108	136
Congo Democratic Republic 2007	5.4	7.0	122	177
Ethiopia 2005	2.4	6.0	98	135
Ghana 2008	3.1	4.9	75	91
Guinea 2005	4.4	6.3	133	204
Lesotho 2004	1.9	4.1	86	105
Liberia 2009	4.2	7.5	138	170
Liberia 2007	3.8	6.2	132	146
Madagascar 2003–4	3.7	5.7	73	120
Malawi 2004	4.2	6.4	116	164
Mali 2006	5.4	7.2	158	234
Namibia 2006–7	2.8	4.3	60	76
Niger 2006	6.1	7.3	139	231
Nigeria 2008	4.7	6.3	121	191
Rwanda 2005	4.9	6.3	123	192
Senegal 2008–9	4.0	5.8	67	117
Sierra Leone 2008	3.8	5.8	167	168
Swaziland 2006–7	3.0	4.2	107	105
Tanzania 2004–5	3.6	6.5	108	138
Uganda 2006	4.4	7.1	115	147
Zambia 2007	4.3	7.5	132	139
Zimbabwe 2005–6	2.6	4.6	64	72
North Africa/West Asia/Europe				
Armenia 2005	1.6	1.8	26	42
Azerbaijan 2006	1.8	2.3	52	64
Egypt 2005	2.7	3.4	39	56
Georgia 2005	1.5	1.7	27	38
Moldova 2005	1.5	1.8	20	30
Ukraine 2007	1.0	1.5	19	20
South & Southeast Asia				
Bangladesh 2007	2.4	2.8	63	77
Cambodia 2005	2.8	3.5	76	111
India 2005–6	2.1	3.0	61	94
Indonesia 2007	2.3	2.8	38	60

(continued)

Table 9.2 (continued)

	TFR		Child mortality	
	Urban	Rural	Urban	Rural
Nepal 2006	2.1	3.3	47	84
Pakistan 2006–7	3.3	4.5	78	100
Philippines 2008	2.8	3.8	28	46
Latin America & Caribbean				
Colombia 2005	2.1	3.4	23	33
Dominican Republic 2007	2.3	2.8	37	37
Ecuador 2004	2.8	3.8	35	39
Haiti 2005–6	2.7	5.0	78	114
Honduras 2005–6	2.6	4.1	29	43
Nicaragua 2006	2.2	3.5	35	47

Source: Macro International Inc, 2010. MEASURE DHS STATcompiler. http://www.measuredhs.com, accessed 2010.

moved (Goldstein and Goldstein 1981; Kulu 2005). Migration rarely involves a simple move of people out of a rural area into the city and, as a result, lower fertility in urban areas may diffuse back to the countryside. The new urban dwellers are likely to go back for visits, bringing money and other things that aren't widely available in the countryside. They also bring back new ideas, new ambitions, and new motivations that can produce behavioral changes in the rural areas, including new ways of thinking about family size.

International Urbanward Migration

International migration also operates to increase the level of urbanization, because most international migrants move to cities in the host area regardless of where they lived in the donor area. From the standpoint of the host area, then, the impact of international migration is to naturally add to the urban population without adding significantly to the rural population, thereby shifting a greater proportion of the total to urban places. More than 90 percent of immigrants to the United States wind up as urban residents in big cities or their suburbs (Gober 2000), a fact driven home by data from the U.S. Census Bureau showing that several cities in the United States would have lost population between 2000 and 2009 had it not been for the influx of international migrants (U.S. Census Bureau 2010). Indeed, of the 19 cities in the world that have at least a million immigrants as of 2010, eight are in the United States (Migration Policy Institute 2010). Yet despite the massive increase in international migration in the past few decades and the fact that most international migrants live in urban areas, the actual impact on the global process of urbanization has been less dramatic than it might seem. The reason for this is that many international migrants have headed toward cities in countries that are already highly urbanized (Berry 1993).

Reclassification

It is also possible for the urban transition to occur "in-place." This happens when the absolute size of a place grows so large, whether by migration, natural increase, or both, that it reaches or exceeds the minimum size criterion used to distinguish urban from rural places. Note that reclassification is more of an administrative phenomenon than anything else and is based on a unidimensional (size-only) definition of urban places, rather than also incorporating any concept of economic and social activity. Of course, it is quite probable that as a place grows in absolute size it will at the same time diversify economically and socially, probably away from agricultural activities into more urban enterprises. This tends to be part of the social change that occurs everywhere in response to an increase in population size; an agricultural population can quickly become redundant and the lure of urban activities (such as industry, commerce, and services) may be strong under those conditions.

Another administrative trick that can lead to rapid city growth is annexation, either formally or simply through the spread of a city outward from its center. City boundaries are almost constantly changing, and the effect is often to bring people into the city limits who might otherwise be classified as rural. Urban growth rates can thus be misleading. For example, "The city of Houston grew 29 percent during the 1970s—one of the most rapidly growing large cities in the country. But the city also annexed a quarter of a million people. Without the annexation, the city would have grown only modestly" (Miller 2004:31). Throughout the world, this kind of phenomenon is associated with urban sprawl, which I discuss in the essay that accompanies this chapter. In developing countries, reclassification is apt to be less formal but no less important. The greater metropolitan area of Cairo, for example, has been swallowing up rural villages in its hinterland for several decades. As people move to Cairo they seek affordable housing, and existing villages near Cairo represent one set of opportunities. In the process, these villages become unintentionally, but inextricably, connected to Cairo (Rodenbeck 1999; Weeks, Larson, and Fugate 2005).

Metropolitanization and Agglomeration

Anywhere you go in the world you will find cities that have grown so large and their influence extended so far that a distinction is often made between metropolitan and nonmetropolitan areas, definitions developed to refine the more traditional terms of urban and rural. This happened first in the richer countries such as the United States, and back in 1949 the U.S. Census Bureau developed the concept of a standard metropolitan area (SMA), consisting of a county with a core city of at least 50,000 people and a population density of at least 1,000 people per square mile. The concept proved useful in conjunction with the 1950 census and was subsequently revised to be called the **standard metropolitan statistical area** (SMSA), which was later shortened to be just an MSA (metropolitan statistical area). The basic idea of a metropolitan statistical area "is that of an area containing a recognized population nucleus and adjacent communities that have a high degree of integration with that nucleus" (U.S. Office of Management and Budget 2000:82228). Over time, modifications have been made to the calculation of the SMSA, ordered always by the U.S. Office of Management and Budget (OMB), which uses these classifications for a variety of government purposes.

Many people were unhappy with the various ways of classifying metropolitan areas that were used up to the 1990s because they seemed inadequate to the task of defining the newly emerging patterns of urban growth in the United States (Adams, VanDrasek, and Phillips 1999). Among the problems identified were that they used counties as the basic building block and thus wound up defining as "metropolitan" a lot of areas that would not normally be thought of as urban, and they also failed to take into account the way in which contiguous counties were or were not integrated with one another (Morrill, Cromartie, and Hart 1999).

So, in the 1990s, the OMB ordered that the MSA definitions be revised yet again, for use with the Census 2000 data. The Metropolitan Area Standards Review Project completed its work in December 2000 and decided that counties should continue to be the building blocks of a redefined **Core-Based Statistical Area** (CBSA) classification scheme (Fitzsimmons and Ratcliffe 2004), which includes both **metropolitan areas** and a new category of **micropolitan areas.** To be a metropolitan area, a CBSA must have a core urban area (as described earlier in the chapter) of at least 50,000 people, whereas a micropolitan area is a Census Bureau–defined urban cluster of at least 10,000 people, but less than 50,000. Contiguous counties are then added to the CBSA if they meet specific criteria of connectivity: Either 25 percent or more of the employed residents of the county work in the central county of the CBSA or at least 25 percent of employment in the county is accounted for by workers who reside in the central county of the CBSA (I'm not making this up).

In Canada, the definition of metropolitan is similar, although not identical, to that in the United States. The Canadian **census metropolitan area** (CMA) has a core urban area of at least 100,000 and includes those adjacent urban and rural areas that have a high degree of economic and social integration with the urban core. Government agencies in Mexico have not defined metropolitan areas quite as precisely as have those in Canada and the United States (Garza 2004).

Another level of aggregation is the **urban agglomeration**, a term used largely by the United Nations, and defined as "the de facto population contained within the contours of a contiguous territory inhabited at urban density levels without regard to administrative boundaries. It usually incorporates the population in a city or town plus that in the suburban areas lying outside of but being adjacent to the city boundaries" (United Nations Population Division 2009:glossary). The concept accepts a country's own definition of what is urban, and then puts together (agglomerates) all of the contiguous urban areas. If the total population is at least 750,000, then it is an urban agglomeration. It has the advantage of providing international comparisons. In 2009, the United Nations counted nearly 606 such urban agglomerations in the world, and I'll bet that you can't name most of them. However, the larger ones that you haven't heard of actually have the highest rates of population growth in the world, leading Short (2004) to call them "black holes"—cities that are not part of a global network but are absorbing large numbers of people.

In general, the United Nations' definitions of urban agglomerations are slightly more limited geographically than the metropolitan areas defined for the U.S. by the Census Bureau, but are nearly identical to those of the Canadian definitions. By UN

NIMBY AND BNANA—THE POLITICS OF URBAN SPRAWL IN AMERICA

Where will suburbanization end? How far away from a city's center are people willing to live? Does the concept of a city center even mean much anymore? These are the kinds of questions that are inspired by **urban sprawl**—"the straggling expansion of an urban area into the adjoining countryside" (Brown 1993:3002). Urban lives are increasingly complicated by multiple-earner households and by greater movement of people from job to job within the same area, often leading to longer commutes (Reschovsky 2004). But the underlying cause of urban sprawl is almost certainly the desire of people to live in a low-density area yet be part of the urban scene. Trying to have it both ways has produced the phenomena of NIMBY and BNANA.

NIMBY, which stands for Not In My Back Yard, refers to the idea that whatever is proposed to be built should be built somewhere else besides your neighborhood. You do not mind that it (whatever it is) is built (you understand that urban places need these things), you just don't want it near you. BNANA, which stands for Build Nothing Anywhere Near Anyone, is more extreme. This represents a generalized antigrowth attitude expressed by people who essentially want to close the urban door behind them and let nothing and no one else in. The problem with both attitudes is that there is worldwide pressure for an increase in urban areas—the urban transition is an inevitable consequence of population growth everywhere in the world. So, if new homes and businesses are not built near you, they will nonetheless be built somewhere else near the urban area, in a rural area that will soon become part of the urban area (no matter how hard the BNANAs may protest) and that will contribute to urban sprawl, which contributes to the demise of the countryside, widespread traffic gridlock, and a lowering of the perceived quality of life.

Since sprawl occurs especially in the absence of regional planning, even in the presence of protests, planning movements have arisen in metropolitan areas around the world to create "smart growth," defined as follows by the Smart Growth Network (2010):

> The features that distinguish smart growth in a community vary from place to place. In general, smart growth invests time, attention, and resources in restoring community and vitality to center cities and older suburbs. New smart growth is more town-centered, is transit and pedestrian oriented, and has a greater mix of housing, commercial and retail uses. It also preserves open space and many other environmental amenities.

Smart growth is thus about containing growth spatially. This implies higher population densities, but within a context in which communities are rethought and well thought-out. Higher, but smarter, densities might mean improved public transportation, more small but well-planned urban open spaces, and the creation of urban villages that attempt to recreate the (largely mythical) atmosphere of small towns in the past.

Two important aspects of American public policy have contributed to urban sprawl and are addressed by smart growth policies: (1) massive public spending on highways, and (2) local government authority over land use and taxation. If the government is willing to help subsidize the building

definitions, Mexico City, with 19.5 million people, is just slightly more populous than the New York–Newark metropolitan area (19.4 million). Toronto is Canada's most populous metropolitan area with 5.4 million people, and its size would make it the sixth largest metro area in the United States and the second largest in Mexico.

As a further "refinement," the United Nations refers to any urban agglomeration with more than 10 million people as a **mega-city**. By this definition, there were 21 mega-cities in the world in 2010, and that number is projected to increase to 29 by 2025, as you can see in Table 9.3. In 1950 there were only two mega-cities in the world—New York and Tokyo. Mexico City had joined that list by 1975, but after of highways, then people can keep living farther from the central city without a huge jump in commute time. Of course, they can only do that if there are places to live farther out. The building of homes in the exurbs is aided by the ability and willingness of local governments to zone land for urban-residential uses, often as a way of increasing local tax revenue—which may then be used to improve local infrastructure (water, sewage, electricity, communications, etc.), which of course stimulates even more urban development. However, if a state or other regional authority is able to draw an urban boundary line, beyond which urban uses are not permitted no matter what local governments might otherwise be willing to tolerate, then smart growth might have a chance—although the issues are extremely complex (Handy 2005; Fillion and McSpurren 2007; Barnett 2007).

A prevailing view of sprawl is that it was induced by public policies that inadvertently encouraged it, so new kinds of public policies are necessary to successfully cope with it (Wolch, Pastor, and Dreier 2004). One state that has passed a smart growth initiative is Maryland, which did so in 2000 under a Democratic governor. The essence of the program is that certain areas are designated for growth and only within those areas will the state of Maryland provide any funding for infrastructure for water, sewers, highways, schools, and economic development projects (Bouvier and Stein 2000). In 2004, the Maryland Office of Smart Growth was transferred to the Department of Planning by the new governor (a Republican), but it continues to be a part of state planning efforts helping, for example, to push through the Smart and Sustainable Growth Act of 2009. Voters in the states of Arizona and Colorado have rejected similar kinds of smart growth plans, so the concept has not gotten the traction that its supporters had hoped for at the state level, but many communities have embraced the ideas for themselves, and the United States Environmental Protection Agency devotes space on its website to smart growth concepts (U.S. Environmental Protection Agency 2010).

As is true with any movement, there is apt to be a counter movement. In the case of urban sprawl, the argument has been made that sprawl is part of the long history of people wanting to be part of the city without having to endure its crowds, crime, and crud. Thus, rather than being a policy failure, sprawl is an inevitable part of urban life, at least in some places, and not necessarily a bad part. Bruegmann (2005) argues that sprawl provides opportunity, mobility, and new choices for people who might not otherwise be able to take advantage of the better life that cities offer. Smart growth for some areas may refer to the creation of densely settled, amenity-rich, and very walkable urban neighborhoods, but many people have been voting with their automobiles, so to speak, in the opposite direction, and the exurbs are currently the fastest-growing places in the large metropolitan areas of the United States (Berube et al. 2006).

Discussion Questions: (1) Do you think that urban sprawl is a threat to the quality of life or an opportunity for a better life? Defend your answer; **(2)** Provide one example each of a NIMBY and a BNANA situation that has arisen or could possibly arise where you live.

1975 there was literally an explosion of mega-cities (a result of the global population explosion), almost all of them emerging in developing nations. Note that in 2010, only four of the 21 mega-cities—New York, Tokyo, Los Angeles, and Paris—were in the world's richer countries.

The rapid growth of cities in the context of continuing population growth in developing countries deserves considerable scrutiny on your part because it represents a potent source of social change with which each of these nations must cope. How they cope will almost certainly affect the rest of the world. On the positive side, successful coping will mean an increase in the standard of living of people in

Table 9.3 The World's Largest Urban Agglomerations (Mega-Cities) Have Changed Dramatically over Time

1950		1975		2010		2025	
City	Population (millions)	City	Population (millions)	City	Population (millions)	City	Population (millions)
New York-Newark	12.3	Tokyo	26.6	Tokyo	36.7	Tokyo	37.1
Tokyo	11.3	New York-Newark	15.9	Delhi	22.2	Delhi	28.6
		Mexico City	10.7	São Paulo	20.3	Mumbai	25.8
				Mumbai	20.0	São Paulo	21.7
				Mexico City	19.5	Dhaka	20.9
				New York- Newark	19.4	Mexico City	20.7
				Shanghai	16.6	New York- Newark	20.6
				Calcutta	15.6	Calcutta	20.1
				Dhaka	14.6	Shanghai	20.0
				Karachi	13.1	Karachi	18.7
				Buenos Aires	13.1	Lagos	15.8
				Los Angeles–Long Beach–Santa Ana	12.8	Kinshasa	15.0
						Beijing	15.0
				Beijing	12.4	Manila	14.9
				Rio de Janeiro	11.9	Buenos Aires	13.7
				Manila	11.6	Los Angeles–Long Beach–Santa Ana	13.7
				Osaka-Kobe	11.3		
				Cairo	11.0	Cairo	13.5
				Lagos	10.6	Rio de Janeiro	12.7
				Moskva (Moscow)	10.5	Istanbul	12.1
				Istanbul	10.5	Osaka-Kobe	11.4
				Paris	10.5	Shenzhen	11.1
						Chongqing	11.1
						Guangzhou, Guangdong	11.0
						Paris	10.9
						Jakarta	10.8
						Moscow	10.7
						Bogotá	10.5
						Lima	10.5
						Lahore	10.3

Source: Adapted from data in United Nations Population Division, 2010. *World Urbanization Prospects: The 2009 Revision*; http://esa.un.org/unpd/wup/doc_highlights.htm (accessed 2010).

cities of developing nations, which would indirectly benefit the whole world through the increased potential for profitable interactions. The negative impacts have to do with the potential for the implosion of urban infrastructure under the weight of more people than can be sustained in these cities, leading perhaps to the need for humanitarian relief measures, possibly even in the context of urban violence. In between these extremes lies an almost unlimited range of possibilities for cities, and neighborhoods within cities.

The Urban Evolution that Accompanies the Urban Transition

As the richer countries approach a situation where almost everybody lives in urban places, it is important to remember that the end of the urban transition does not necessarily signal the end of the process of urban *evolution* (Pumain 2002). The mere fact that people are increasingly likely to live in places defined as urban does not mean that the urban environment itself stops changing and evolving across time and space. Indeed, there is probably more variability among urban places, and within the populations in urban places, than ever before in human history (Batty 2008). This is, of course, precisely why the definition of metropolitan areas keeps changing in the United States—it has to keep up with the evolution of those places.

Within cities, people do not just live anywhere—they sort themselves into neighborhoods in such a way that people who are more similar to one another socially and economically are more likely to live closer to one another than are people who are not so alike (a fact that underlies the concept of geodemographics, as you will recall from Chapter 1). Neighborhoods differ also with respect to the **built environment**—the physical transformation of the physical and natural environment that humans undertake in order to create a place where they can and want to live. It includes the infrastructure for piped water and sewerage, electricity and other types of energy, roads, buildings, parks, and everything else that physically represents what we think of as a city. These neighborhoods represent the context in which much of life will be played out for its residents, and this is an interactive process in which the people help to shape the social and physical fabric of a neighborhood and, at the same time, the nature of the neighborhood promotes or constrains the options that people have in life. This is an organic process—sometimes improving neighborhoods and the lives of its residents, and sometimes not. It is why you can't "go home again." Home is constantly evolving.

The benefits of cities, of course, are what make them attractive, and they at least partially explain the massive transformation of countries like the United States and Canada from predominantly rural to primarily urban nations within a few generations. But there are also costs involved in living in cities, and the evolution of cities is partly a result of people trying to mitigate the downside of city life. Indeed, most of the demographically oriented changes that I discuss below—slums, suburbs and exurbs, and residential segregation—deal in one way or another with the impact of crowding, which most humans find distasteful in some way or another. We are a social species, but we also like our space.

Urban Crowding

For centuries, the **crowding** of people into cities was doubtless harmful to existence. Packing people together in unsanitary houses in dirty cities raised death rates. Furthermore, as is so often the case, as cities grew to unprecedented sizes in nineteenth-century Europe, death struck unevenly within the population. Mortality went down faster for the better off, leaving the slums as the places where lower-income people were crowded into areas "with their sickening odor of disease, vice and crime" (Weber 1899:414).

When early students of the effects of urbanization such as Weber and Bertillon discussed crowding and overcrowding, they had in mind a relatively simple concept of density—the number of people per room, per block, or per square mile. Thus Weber quotes the 1891 census of England, "regarding as overcrowded all the 'ordinary tenements that had more than two occupants to a room, bedrooms and sitting rooms included'" (1899:416). The prescription for the ill effects (literally) of overcrowding was fairly straightforward as far as Weber was concerned: "The requirement of a definite amount of air space to each occupant of a room will prevent some of the worst evils of overcrowding; plenty of water, good paving, drainage, etc. will render the sanitary conditions good." Crime and vice are also often believed to be linked to urban life and, as a matter of fact, crime rates are almost always higher in cities than in the countryside. But what is it about crowding that might lead to differences in social behavior between urban and rural people? To examine that question, you have to ask more specifically what crowding is.

The simplest definition of crowding is essentially demographic and refers to **density**—the ratio of people to physical space. As more and more people occupy a given area, the density increases and it therefore becomes relatively more crowded. Under these conditions, what changes in behavior can you expect? In a 1905 essay, Georg Simmel suggested that the result of crowding was an "intensification of nervous stimulation" (Simmel 1905:48), which produced stress and, in turn, was adapted to by people reacting with their heads rather than their hearts. "This means that urban dwellers tend to become intellectual, rational, calculating, and emotionally distant from one another" (Fischer 1976:30). Here were the early murmurs of the **urbanism** concept—that the crowding of people into cities changes behavior—a concept often expressed with negative overtones.

Perhaps the most famous expression of the negative consequences of the city is Louis Wirth's paper "Urbanism as a Way of Life" (1938), in which he argued that urbanism will result in isolation and the disorganization of social life. Density, Wirth argued, encourages impersonality and leads to people exploiting each other. For two decades, there was little questioning of Wirth's thesis and, as Hawley put it, "In one short paper, Wirth determined the interpretation of density for an entire generation of social scientists" (Hawley 1972:524). The idea that increased population density had harmful side effects lay idle for a while, but it was revived with considerable enthusiasm in the 1960s following a report by Calhoun on the behavior of rats under crowded conditions.

Although he initiated his studies of crowding among rats in 1947, it was not until 1958 that Calhoun (1962) began his most famous experiments (which later helped inspire the popular stories and a movie about the rats of NIMH). In a barn in

Rockville, Maryland, he designed a series of experiments in which rat populations could build up freely under conditions that would permit detailed observations without humans influencing the behavior of the rats relating to each other. Calhoun built four pens, each with all the accoutrements for normal rat life and divided by electrified partitions. Initially, eight infant rats were placed in each pen, and when they reached maturity, Calhoun installed ramps between each pen. At that point, the experiment took its own course in terms of the effects of population growth in a limited area.

Normally, rats have a fairly simple form of social organization, characterized by groups of 10 to 12 hierarchically ranked rats defending their common territory. There is usually one male dominating the group, and status is indicated by the amount of territory open to an individual. As Calhoun's rat population grew from the original 32 to 60, one dominant male took over each of the two end pens and established harems of eight to 10 females. The remaining rats were congregated in the two middle pens, where problems developed over congestion at the feeding hoppers. As the population grew from 60 to 80, behavior patterns developed into what Calhoun called a "behavioral sink"—gross distortions of behavior resulting from animal crowding. Behavior remained fairly normal in the two end pens, where each dominant male defended his territory by sleeping at the end of the ramp, but in the two middle pens there were severe changes in sexual, nesting, and territorial behavior. Some of the males became sexually passive; others became sexually hyperactive, chasing females mercilessly; and still another group of males was observed mounting other males, as well as females. Females became disorganized in their nesting habits, building very poor nests, getting litters mixed up, and losing track of their young. Infant mortality rose significantly. Finally, males appeared to alter their concept of territoriality. With no space to defend, the males in the two middle pens substituted time for territory, and three times a day, the males fought at the eating bin.

Calhoun's study can be summarized by noting that, among his rats, crowding (an increase in the number of rats within a fixed amount of space) led to the disruption of important social functions and to social disorganization. Related to these changes in social behavior were signs of physiological stress, such as changes in their hormonal systems that made it difficult for females to bring pregnancies to term and care for their young. Other studies have shown that not only rats but also monkeys, hares, shrews, fish, elephants, and house mice tend to respond to higher density by reducing their fertility (Galle, Gove, and McPherson 1972).

Although the severe distortions of behavior that Calhoun witnessed among rats have never been replicated among humans, research has suggested that at the macro (group) level, there may be some fairly predictable consequences of increasing population density (mainly as a result of increases in population size). For example, Mayhew and Levinger have argued that violent interaction can be expected to increase as population size increases: "The opportunity structure for murder, robbery, and aggravated assault increases at an increasing rate with aggregate size" (Mayhew and Levinger 1976:98). There are more people with whom to have conflict, and an increasingly small proportion of people over whom we exercise direct social control (which would lessen the likelihood of conflict leading to violence). Increasing size leads to greater superficiality and to more transitory human interaction—that is, greater anonymity. Mayhew and Levinger point out that "since humans are by nature finite organisms with a finite amount of time to devote to the total stream of incoming signals, it is necessarily the case that the average amount of time they can devote to the increasing volume of contacts . . . is a decreasing function of aggregate size. This will occur by chance alone" (1976:100).

Because no person has the time to develop deeply personal relationships (primary relations) with more than a few people, the more people there are entering a person's life, the smaller the proportion one can deal with in depth. This leads to the appearance that people in cities are more estranged from each other than in rural settings, but Fischer (1981) offers evidence that in all settings, people are distrustful of strangers—we just encounter more of them in the city. This may lead to personal stress as people try to sort out the vast array of human contacts, since the more people there are, the greater the variety of both expectations others have of you and obligations you have toward others. The problems of not enough time to go around and of contradictory expectations lead to "role strain"—a perceived difficulty in fulfilling role obligations. On a more positive note, data from the General Social Survey of the National Opinion Research Center have been used to suggest that moving to a big city increases your tolerance for other human beings, rather than the other way around (Wilson 1991).

It might be fair to say that the most reasonable reaction to the negative aspects of city life is to figure out how best to cope with them and minimize them. The most common response has been to get as far away from high-density city life as possible, while also staying close enough to it so that you can participate in its benefits. This is probably the underlying reason for the evolution in urban places I have been discussing in this chapter. Most people do not really prefer to be packed together with others, and the increasing sophistication of transportation and information technologies has made it increasingly easy to spread out, at least in the richer countries. In cities in poorer countries, however, people are more likely just struggling to get by, and many of them are living in densely settled slums.

Slums

European and American cities dealt with slums in the late nineteenth and early twentieth centuries, as cities bulged with migrants who overran the local infrastructure. That process of rapid growth is now taking place in the cities of developing countries, so it is not surprising that the world's slums tend to be concentrated there. The United Nations Human Settlements Programme known as UN-Habitat defines slums as places that lack one or more of the following: (1) access to potable water, (2) access to piped sewerage, (3) housing of adequate space, (4) housing of adequate durability, and (5) security of tenure (UN-Habitat 2006)—a definition that is not very different from Weber's ideas about London slums in the nineteenth century. Nearly one in six human beings is estimated by the UN to be living in a slum, and nearly one in three urban residents lives in one. Figure 9.4 shows that in sub-Saharan Africa nearly three in four urban dwellers live in a slum. Davis (2006) describes the area in West Africa between Lagos, Nigeria, and Accra, Ghana, as a conurbation that may have "the single biggest footprint of poverty in the world" (p. 6).

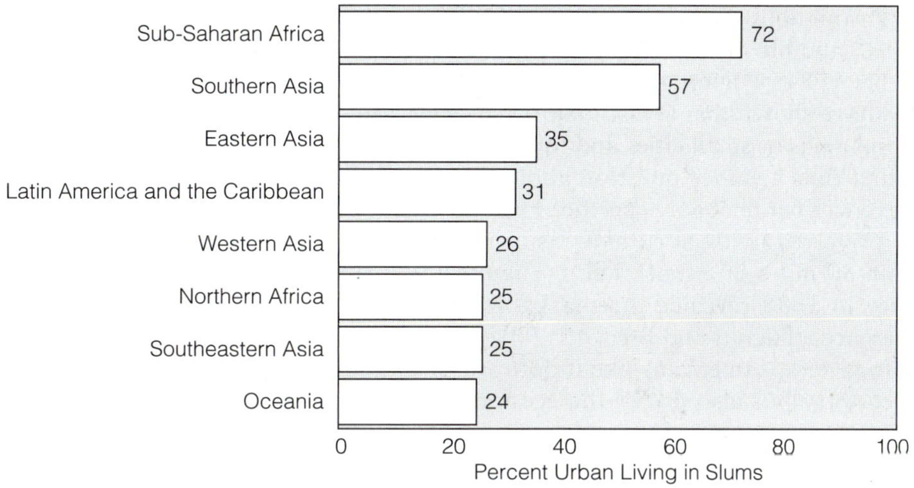

Figure 9.4 Percent of the Urban Population Living in Slums, by Region of the World

In South Asia (including Bangladesh, India, and Pakistan), more than half (57 percent) are in slums. In Eastern Asia (including China), nearly one in three (31 percent) are in slums. As you can see, then, it is not inconsequential to understand what exactly a slum is and how it might affect the health and life of urban residents.

The existence of slums signals that the urban population is growing more quickly than the local government can afford to build urban infrastructure. If people are poor, and governments themselves have little money, then urban residents are forced to deal with life informally. These informal settlements are not necessarily squalid slums, but neither are they likely to be the healthiest environments in which to live (Hardoy, Mitlin, and Satterthwaite 2001; Roy and Alsayyad 2004; Montgomery 2009).

Suburbanization and Exurbanization

Being crowded into a slum probably represents the worst aspect of city life. This and other negative impacts of the urban transition on the human condition represent the set of unintended consequences that may prevent the city from being as attractive as it might otherwise be. The efficiencies of the city have generally been translated into higher incomes for city dwellers than for farmers and, as I mentioned earlier, the larger the city, the higher the wages tend to be. Wage differentials undoubtedly have been and continue to be prime motivation for individuals to move to cities and stay there. But so-called "urban amenities" are also important, especially for the young adults who represent the majority of rural-to-urban migrants in cities of developing nations. Cities offer not only opportunity, but also entertainment and excitement that are rarely present in the countryside.

Throughout American history, the sins and foibles of urban life have been decried, and life in the city is often compared unfavorably with a pastoral existence (Fischer 1984). Fuguitt and Zuiches have pointed out that public opinion polls since 1948 have shown that a vast majority of Americans indicate a preference for living in rural areas or small cities and towns. However, in the 1970s, when they asked for the first time a survey question about the desire to be near a large city, those rural preferences became more specific. Their data showed that of all the people who said they preferred living in rural areas or in small cities, 61 percent also wanted to be within 30 miles of a central city (Fuguitt and Zuiches 1975). A replication of the survey in 1988 revealed a remarkable consistency over time in those residential preferences (Fuguitt and Brown 1990).

In general, Americans like it both ways. They aspire to the freedom of space in the country but also prefer the economic and social advantages of the city. The compromise, of course, is the suburb. More than a century has passed since Adna Weber (1899) noted that American cities were beginning to **suburbanize**—to grow in the outlying rings of the city. It was not until the 1920s, however, that suburbanization really took off. Hawley (1972) calculated that between 1900 and 1920 people were still concentrating in the centers of cities, but after 1920 the suburbs began to regularly grow in population at a faster pace than the central cities. Two factors related to suburbanization are people's desire to live in the less-crowded environment of the outlying areas and their ability to do so—a result of increasing wealth and the availability of transportation, especially automobiles. Such transportation has added an element of geographic flexibility not possible when the early suburbanites depended on fixed-rail trolleys to transport them between home in the suburbs and work in the central city.

From the 1920s through the 1960s, the process of suburbanization continued almost unabated in the United States (as indeed in most cities of the world). Admittedly, the process was hurried along by automobile manufacturers and tire companies that bought local trolley lines in order to dismantle them and force people to rely on gasoline-powered buses (Kunstler 1993). Nonetheless, the advantages of the automobile are numerous and it was inevitable that cars would influence the shape of urban areas. According to the 2008 American Community Survey, 76 percent of all workers get to work by driving alone in their automobile (car, truck, or van)—a higher fraction than in 1990—and an additional 11 percent carpooled to work in an automobile, meaning that altogether 87 percent of American workers get to work by driving. Only a small fraction of Americans (less than 5 percent) use public transportation, and the remaining 8 percent walk or bike to work or work at home.

Furthermore, the commute may not be the classic suburb-to-city drive, but rather from one suburb to another because it turns out that "America is in the suburbs. The suburbs are America" (Frey 1995:314), and this has led even to a fading of the original distinction between urban and suburban (Frey 2004). The rest of the world is generally headed in the same direction. Tourists to Paris, London, or Tokyo may spend most of their time near the older "cultural" center of the city, but most of the people in these global cities now live and work out in the suburbs.

The fact that North America has become predominantly suburban adds new complexity to the metropolitan structure. Several trends are worth commenting on: (1) A decided westward tilt to urbanization in the United States has facilitated suburbanization through the creation of new places; (2) Many of those new places are **edge cities** within the suburbs, replacing the functions of the old central city; and (3) Older parts of cities have been gentrified. Let us examine each of these in a bit more detail, remembering that, although my comments are directed primarily at the United States, many of these same trends are being seen in other developed nations as well. Suburbanization has, in fact, become an integral part of the urban transition and is now fully under way even in China (Zhou and Ma 2000).

The western United States, the land of open spaces, had become the most highly metropolitanized area of the country by the 1980s (Abbott 1993). A higher fraction of residents lives in metropolitan areas in the West than in any other part of the country. This has happened because the flow of migration in the United States has been consistently westward, especially since the end of World War II, as you will recall from Chapter 7, and migration in the modern world is almost always toward or between urban places. People and jobs have been moving west, and increasingly south as well—definitely toward the warmer climates (although obviously climate is not necessarily the most important factor). Kasarda (1995) noted that in 1960, 25 percent of all Fortune 500 firms were headquartered in New York City, but by 1990 that had declined to 8 percent. Companies shifted their operations to Sunbelt cities, but not necessarily to the central parts of those cities. The suburbs have become the new sites of company headquarters, congregating near major highways and regional airports. It is perhaps a sign of the times that the richest person in the United States (Bill Gates) founded a company (Microsoft) located in the suburbs (Redmond, Washington) of a western city (Seattle).

Increasing suburbanization has meant greater metropolitan complexity, as new areas spring up on the edges of cities, competing with each other for jobs and amenities (Frey 2004). Garreau (1991) coined the term "edge city" to describe the suburban entities that have emerged in the rings and beltways of metropolitan areas and are replicating, if not replacing, the functions of older central cities. Some of the edge cities are actually within the same city limits as the central city, but are distinct from it. Furthermore, larger metropolitan areas may have several edge cities, each with its own pattern of dominance over specific economic functions (such as high technology or financial services) in conjunction with a full range of retail shops and dining and entertainment establishments. Muller (1997) argues, in fact, that it is precisely in these edge cities that the globalization of American cities has taken place.

The growth of edge cities and the increasing economic and social complexity of the suburbs help to explain the shift in commuting patterns in the United States. In essence, the flexibility of the automobile allows people to live and work almost anywhere within the same general area. The number of commuters going from one suburban area to another far exceeds the number of commuters going from the suburbs to the central city. As noted above, those cars on the freeway in the morning are not all headed downtown—they are headed every which way.

These trends in metropolitan complexity and diversity have tended to leave the central cities with a daytime population of "suits" who commute downtown to work at various service companies (especially government administration and financial services industries) that have remained in the central city. At the same time, shopping centers, corporate headquarters, many new high-technology industries, and traffic gridlock have all relocated to the suburbs.

The baby boom generation in the United States grew up in the suburbs to a greater extent than any previous cohort, but as they reached an age to buy homes, baby boomers found themselves caught in the midst of spiraling housing costs amid increasing density in the suburbs. One alternative was to head even farther out of town, to what sometimes are called the **exurbs**—the suburbs of the suburbs. Another term for this is the **peri-urban region**—the periphery of the urban zone that looks rural to the naked eye but houses people who are essentially urban. "The peri-urban region is a distinctive zone that spans the landscape between contiguous urban development and the rural countryside" (Ford 1999:298).

As the urban population sprawls deeper into the countryside, some people have reversed that trend and moved back into the central city, where gentrification of buildings and of whole neighborhoods has been taking place in some, although not all, older cities of developed nations. This process has the potential to remove the lower-income population that had settled into the areas previously abandoned by higher-income households, and may dramatically alter the social structure of the surrounding area, although this is not an inevitable result of gentrification (McKinnish, Walsh, and White 2010). Because these innovative renovators tend to be white and upwardly mobile (and often without children), they have been likened to the gentry moving back into the city, and thus the term **gentrification** is applied, referring to the restoration and habitation of older homes in central city areas by urban or suburban elites.

The popularity of downtown living has expanded the scope of renovation in an increasing number of cities to include tearing down entire blocks of older buildings and erecting new high-rise, high-priced condominiums (Ford 2003), in what has been called "new-build gentrification" (Rérat, Söderström, and Piguet 2009). Some of this development immediately preceded the burst in the housing bubble and so progress has slowed since 2007. Furthermore, gentrification has not yet involved enough people to counter the continuing movement of people out of the central cities and into the suburbs and the peri-urban region. Those who are unable to leave the older sections of urban, and even suburban, places find themselves residentially segregated and left out of the mainstream.

Residential Segregation

Although suburbia has become a legendary part of American society and seems to be a major force of urban evolution, suburbanization can be viewed as an innovation that started with some people and then diffused to others. In particular, it is a residential transformation that disproportionately involved whites in the United States until the 1970s. For example, in 1970 in 15 large metropolitan areas studied by Farley (1976), 58 percent of whites lived in the suburbs compared with 17 percent of nonwhites. Beginning in the 1930s, the proportion of whites living in central cities declined steadily and the proportion of African Americans rose steeply (Schnore, Andre, and Sharp 1976); the African American population was undergoing a very rapid urbanization (the Great Migration that I mentioned in Chapter 7) at the same time that whites were suburbanizing.

During the period 1910–30, there was a substantial movement of African Americans out of the South headed for the cities of the North and the West. The urban population of blacks grew by more than 3 percent per year during that 20-year period, whereas the rural population declined not only relatively but in absolute terms as well. The reasons for migration out of rural areas were primarily economic, with the decline in the world demand for southern agricultural products providing the push out of the South. But there were concurrent pull factors as well in the form of demands in northern and western cities for labor, which could be met cheaply by blacks moving from the South (Farley 1970; Tolnay et al. 2005). The Depression brought a slowdown in the urbanization of African Americans, but by the beginning of World War II half of the nation's blacks lived in cities, reaching that level 30 years later than whites had.

After World War II, the urban transition of blacks resumed at an even higher level than after World War I, and by 1960 the African American population was 58 percent urban in the South and 95 percent urban in the North and West. Urbanization was associated not only with the economic recovery after the war but also with severely restricted international migration, which, until the law was changed in 1965, meant that foreigners no longer were entering the labor force to take newly created jobs, thus providing a market for African American labor. An important consequence of the urban transition of blacks, accompanied by suburbanization of whites, has been the segregation of black and white populations within metropolitan areas (Massey and Denton 1993; Massey 1996).

The segregation of people into different neighborhoods on the basis of different social characteristics (such as ethnicity, occupation, or income) is a fairly common feature of human society (Bobo et al. 2000). However, in the United States residential segregation by race is much more intense than segregation by any other measurable category. Residential segregation of blacks in the United States has been called an "American apartheid system" (Massey and Denton 1993), and the maintenance of this pattern until fairly recently has been due especially to the following factors: (1) Mortgage lending policies were discriminatory; (2) Suburbs developed strategies for keeping African Americans out; and (3) Federally sponsored public housing encouraged segregation in many cities (Farley and Frey 1994; Iceland and Nelson 2008).

Specific action has been taken over time to try to mitigate the most egregious causes of residential segregation while, at the same time, patterns of residential segregation have been impacted by the 1965 changes in the Immigration Act. Immigrants have diversified the ethnic structure of the country, and data suggest that Asians and Hispanics have a greater propensity or ability to suburbanize than do blacks, who remain residentially more segregated than other groups (Danziger and Gottschalk 1993; Farley, Danziger, and Holzer 2000; Logan, Alba, and Zhang 2002; Iceland and Nelson 2008). The slower rate of suburbanization of African Americans continues to be the result of discrimination on the part of whites (Emerson, Yancy, and Chai 2001). "Thus, decades after the passage of the Civil Rights Act of 1964, the Voting Rights Act of 1965, the Immigration Act Amendments (Hart-Celler) of 1965, and the Fair Housing Act of 1968, our society continues to be driven by a historical legacy of deep racism, spasms of nativism, and the current condition of persistent racial and ethnic inequality in life chances" (Bobo et al. 2000:32).

From the standpoint of demographic characteristics, the suburbs are composed especially of higher-education, higher-income, married-couple families (Berube and Thacher 2004)—a pattern that disproportionately works against blacks who have lower levels of education, lower incomes, and lower marriage rates than whites. But demographic components of suburbanization do not explain residential segregation; they merely point to its existence. The explanations are essentially social in nature, and one of the prevailing ones is based on the idea that "status rankings are operationalized in society through the imposition of social distance" (Berry et al.

1976:249). In race relations, the social status of blacks has been historically lower than that of whites. That status ranking used to be maintained symbolically by such devices as uniforms, separate facilities, and so forth, which were obvious enough to allow social distance even though blacks and whites lived in close proximity to each other. However, as African Americans left the South and moved into industrial urban settings, many of those negative status symbols were also left behind. As a result, spatial segregation has served as a means of maintaining social distance "where 'etiquette'—the recognition of social distance symbols—breaks down" (Berry et al. 1976:249). Thus as blacks have improved in education, income, and occupational status, whites have maintained social distance by means of residential segregation facilitated by suburbanization.

Differential suburbanization by race has done more than just keep whites separate from blacks. It has also separated blacks from job opportunities. Jobs have followed the population to the suburbs, making it increasingly difficult for people living in the central city—who may have inadequate access to transportation—to find employment. This "spatial mismatch" has been shown to be associated with higher unemployment rates for blacks living in Detroit and Chicago (Mouw 2000), as well as in other American cities (Wagmiller 2007). Massey (1996) has suggested that the spatial isolation of poverty and especially of low-income blacks portends future community instability and violence in America.

However, there is some evidence that a trend toward desegregation does exist. As you know, immigration to the United States has increasingly involved people from Latin America and Asia, and almost all immigrants are in cities, as I discussed above. This increasing diversity of the U.S. population has combined with increasing suburbanization to create a more variegated and integrated suburban population, and blacks have been incorporated into these trends (Fasenfest, Booza, and Metzger 2004). This process has been encouraged by the spreading out of Asians from the Pacific Coast, Hispanics out of the Southwest, and by the flow of many blacks to a "new" South whose economy is based on growth in higher-income service industries rather than agriculture (Frey 2006). Nonetheless, census data suggest that blacks are still segregated more from whites than are either Asians or Hispanics (Iceland and Nelson 2008; Iceland, Weinberg, and Steinmetz 2002).

European cities are also characterized by a certain amount of residential segregation, largely with respect to the ethnic minority groups that have comprised the guest-worker populations. The immigrant suburbs of Paris boiled over in riots in 2005, but in many parts of Europe a large segment of the housing market for working-class families is subsidized and controlled by the government, and this has limited the scope of residential segregation compared to the United States (Bulpett 2002; Maloutas 2004; Agnew 2010).

Cities as Sustainable Environments

For better or worse, human existence is increasingly tied to the city, which raises the key question of whether cities are sustainable places for humans to live. The answer seems to be that we have to make them so, because we do not really have another acceptable choice (Low et al. 2005). "Poor countries' cities are bursting at the seams, yet rural migrants are coming in faster than ever; a social and environmental meltdown is waiting to happen" (*The Economist* 1996:44). That is how one writer described the rationale for the United Nations Conference on Human Settlements (Habitat II) held in Istanbul in 1996 (Habitat I had been held in 1976 in Vancouver, British Columbia). These UN-sponsored events are now on a two-year schedule, underlining the increasing global emphasis on how to sustain life in cities (Copetake 2006).

The opportunities that cities offer to rural peasants in less developed nations may seem meager to those of us raised in a wealthier society. Most third-world cities have long since outgrown their infrastructure and, as a result, drinkable water may be scarce (or available only in plastic sleeves sold by street vendors), sewage is probably not properly disposed of, housing is hard to find, transportation is inadequate, and electricity may be only sporadically available (Montgomery et al. 2003). This is not a pretty picture, but it is still an improvement on the average rural village. Thus, "despite these problems, the flood of migrants to the cities continues apace. Why? The answer lies in the natural population increase in rural areas, limited rural economic development, and the decision-making calculus of urban migrants. . . . What this all means, of course, is that the primary cause of what some have termed 'overurbanization' (more urban residents than the economies of cities can sustain) is increasingly severe 'overruralization' (more rural residents than the economies of rural areas can sustain)" (Dogan and Kasarda 1988:19).

In the 1980s, Mexico City was the third most populous city in the world (see Table 9.3) and many people projected it to continue growing almost forever. However, the serious environmental problems in the Valley of Mexico created by population growth convinced the Mexican government to undertake a concerted effort to move industry out of the area and divert migrants to other metropolitan areas. The effort clearly paid off, because the 1990 census counted fewer people than anticipated and, on that basis, the United Nations demographers revised their projections of population growth in Mexico City downward. Still, the 19.5 million people living in Mexico City in 2010 was a huge increase from the 3.1 million in 1950, and the United Nations projects that the population of Mexico City will be approaching 21 million by the year 2025, as it sprawls well beyond the older central city. Terrible smog, a dwindling water supply, and an increase in crime rates are all features of modern Mexico City—yet it offers more opportunity for the average rural peasant of Mexico than does the countryside, so people continue to move there.

Evaluations of the quality of life in the largest cities of the world reveal, not surprisingly, that the metropolitan areas of the richer countries are the preferred places to live. In 2010, the Economist Intelligence Unit, based in London, ranked Vancouver as the world's "most livable city," followed by Vienna, Melbourne, Toronto, and Calgary (The Economist Intelligence Unit 2010). Seven of the top ten most livable cities were in either Canada or Australia (none was in the United States). At the other end of the scale, among the ten least livable cities, eight were in either sub-Saharan Africa (Harare, Zimbabwe, was the worst) or South Asia. Indeed, the Second African Population Conference in 1984 concluded that African cities are "plagued by the adverse effects of rapid growth—urban sprawl, unemployment, delinquency, inadequate social services, traffic congestion, and poor housing" (Goliber 1985:17)—a statement that is as true today as it was in 1984. A major reason for this situation is that urban areas in Africa have consistently been growing at more rapid rates than urban areas anywhere else in the world, as I've noted and as you can see by referring back to Table 9.1.

I keep coming back to the same theme, however, that, as dismal as urban life is in developing countries, it is typically (although of course not always) a step up from life in rural areas. Cities are where economic development is occurring in the world, and it is where infrastructure and housing will continue to be built. The demand for housing itself is a function of the relationship between the population of young adults wanting to form their own family household and the number of people who are dying and thus presumably freeing up existing housing. The high rates of growth and attendant youthful age structures of the developing countries tell us that the worldwide demand for housing will be predominantly in the cities of less developed nations.

Along with that housing will be needed infrastructure improvements—water, sewers, electricity, roads, and public transportation, all of which make urban life possible (UN Habitat 2005, 2010). This is a daunting task, considering that the volume of housing needed is unprecedented in world history and, of course, we have not come even close to adequately sheltering the current generation of people. Furthermore, as I will discuss in more detail in Chapter 11, if the world is going to grow enough food for the 9 or more billion people that we expect by the middle of this century, we need machines to largely replace people on the world's farms. Large volumes of food need more "horsepower" than humans (or horses) can generate, so people are increasingly incidental to the main activities taking place in agriculture. The only other place for them is in the city, although of course, improving life for billions of people living in cities will use a tremendous amount of resources. It is contrary to the usual perspective, but let me suggest that the benefit of these people moving into the city is that they bring their poverty with them to a place where it is exposed to public view and, as a consequence, is more likely to be acted upon by governments and NGOs (non-governmental organizations).

A related and very important cost of the urban transition is that, as we gather ourselves into cities, we lose perspective of where our resources come from, and where our waste goes. It seems like magic on both ends, but of course it is not. It is dangerous to forget our link to nature, because there is a very real possibility that we have already overshot our capacity to sustain life for everybody in the world at a level even approaching that of the average urban resident of the United States or Canada. We must learn how to deal successfully with the earth's limited resources, because there are, in fact, no viable alternatives to the urban transition.

Summary and Conclusion

The urban transition describes the process whereby a society shifts from being largely bound to the country to being bound by the city. It is a process that historically has been the close companion of economic development, which, of itself, suggests the close theoretical connection of the urban transition with the other facets of the demographic transition. The urban transition is associated with increasing differentiation among cities, leading to identifiable urban hierarchies throughout the world. Every country has its own rank-ordering of cities, but there is also a world ranking, leading to the designation of some cities as being world or global cities. These are generally thought of as being core cities;

the other peripheral cities depend on the core for their place in the global economic scheme of things.

More than half of the human population now resides in urban places, and that percentage is climbing steadily. Although rural-to-urban migration is a major contributor to the urban transition, mortality and fertility are importantly associated as well, as both cause and consequence. Population pressures created by declining mortality in rural areas, combined with the economic opportunities offered by cities, have been historically linked to urbanization. On the other hand, mortality is now almost always lower in cities than in rural areas, which permits higher rates of urban natural increase than in the past.

The development of industrialized countries is replete with examples of how urban life helps generate or ignite the first two of Ansley Coale's three preconditions for a fertility decline—the acceptance of calculated choice as an element in personal family size decisions and the perception of advantages to small families (see Chapter 6). Nonetheless, in the cities of less developed nations, urban fertility, even though lower than rural fertility, is still typically much higher than in cities of the developed world. As a result, cities in less developed nations are the most rapidly growing places on earth.

As richer countries reach the point where the vast majority of people are already residing in urban places (which we might define as the end of the urban transition), a new set of urban evolution processes takes place. Most of these changes are attempts to deal somehow or another with the effects of crowding in urban places—the worst example of which is found in slums. Solutions to this problem include especially suburbanization, which is now a worldwide phenomenon, but other trends such as exurbanization and gentrification are all part of the process as well. Other aspects of the urban evolution relate to the city's ability to support diversity among humans. The complexity of life in urban places is part and parcel of the overall demographic complexity of life in the modern world. Urban places are where mortality is lowest, fertility is lowest, the age structure is the most variable, and people of all different kinds of backgrounds can mingle together with deliberate anonymity or closeness. This combination of transitions has been especially noticeable in its effects on the family and household structure of humans, and we turn to that transition in the next chapter.

Main Points

1. The world is at the point at which one of every two people lives in an urban area; by the middle of this century, nearly two out of three will be there.
2. The urban transition reflects the process whereby human society moves (quite literally) from being predominantly rural to being largely urban.
3. One of the most striking features of urbanization is its recency in world history, because it depends heavily on all of the other changes that comprise the demographic transition: Highly urban nations like England and the United States were almost entirely agricultural at the beginning of the nineteenth century.
4. Cities are centerpieces of the development process associated with demographic transitions because they are centers of economic efficiency.

5. Cities throughout the world are arranged in urban hierarchies that are often described in terms of the core and periphery model.
6. Until the twentieth century, death rates in cities were so high and fertility was low enough that cities could not have grown had it not been for migration of people from the countryside.
7. In virtually every society, fertility levels are lower in cities than in rural areas, yet cities in less developed nations almost always have higher fertility levels than cities in developed nations.
8. The urban transition is morphing into the urban evolution, as urban places become increasingly spread out and complex.
9. Urbanization in the United States has now turned into suburbanization, with most Americans living in suburbs—a trend that is spreading to the rest of the world.
10. Population growth in cities has given rise to fears about the potential harmful effects of crowding, and especially to concerns about the environmental sustainability of cities.

Questions for Review

1. Compare the positive and negative qualities of urban places with the positive and negative qualities of rural places. Which do you prefer and why?
2. What are the characteristics of a city that would make it a global city, rather than just a city?
3. Discuss the ways in which the different levels of mortality and fertility between urban and rural places wind up making an important contribution to the urban transition.
4. How does the long-time concern with the ill-effects of urban crowding square with the movement for smart growth that aims to increase urban density?
5. Are slums an inevitable part of the urban transition? Why or why not?

Suggested Readings

1. Martin Brockerhoff, 2000, "An Urbanizing World," *Population Bulletin* 55(3).

   An excellent overview of the urban transition, focusing on the world as a whole, with discussion of regional variability in urban processes.
2. Mark R. Montgomery, Richard Stren, Barney Cohen, and Holly Reed, eds., 2003, *Cities Transformed: Demographic Change and Its Implication in the Developing World* (Washington, DC: National Academy Press).

   Developed by the Committee on Urban Population Dynamics of the National Research Council, this book provides an excellent overview of virtually all topics covered in this chapter, with an emphasis on cities in developing countries.

3. Tony Champion and Graeme Hugo, eds., 2004, *New Forms of Urbanization: Beyond the Urban-Rural Dichotomy* (London: Ashgate Publishing).

The chapters in this book are based on papers prepared for a conference in Bellagio, Italy, organized by the International Union for the Scientific Study of Population (IUSSP) and represent state-of-the-art developments in the study of the urban transition.

4. Robert Neuwirth, 2005, *Shadow Cities: A Billion Squatters, A New Urban World* (New York: Routledge).

The author lived in slums and squatter settlements in different parts of the world, and brings a very personal perspective to life in these areas of cities in developing nations.

5. William Frey, Jill H. Wilson, Alan Berube, and Audrey Singer, 2004, *Tracking Metropolitan America into the 21st Century: A Field Guide to the New Metropolitan and Micropolitan Definitions* (Washington, DC: The Brookings Institution).

The United States has a whole new set of measurements of urban areas and the authors walk you through the definitions and provide a wide range of data on metropolitan and micropolitan areas in the country.

Websites of Interest

Remember that websites are not as permanent as books and journals, so I cannot guarantee that each of the following websites still exists at the moment you are reading this. You may have to Google the name of the organization to find the current web address.

1. **http://www.unhabitat.org**
   UN-Habitat, more formally the United Nations Human Settlements Programme, monitors the cities of the world, with a focus on those in developing countries.
2. **http://www.un.org/esa/population/unpop.htm**
   This website has information on the United Nations Population Division's latest estimates and projections of the world's urban and rural populations.
3. **http://www.populstat.info/**
   Jan Lahmeyer of the University of Utrecht in the Netherlands has compiled census and other population statistics from all over the world, and this website provides data on the "growth of the population per country in a historical perspective, including the administrative divisions and principal towns." It is a very useful research resource.
4. **http://www.iied.org/human-settlements/home**
   The International Institute for Environment and Development, based in London, has a Human Settlements program that has been very influential in the area of environment and health in cities.
5. **http://www.smartgrowth.org**
   Do you want to help slow down urban sprawl? Learn more about smart growth at this website.

CHAPTER 10
The Family and Household Transition

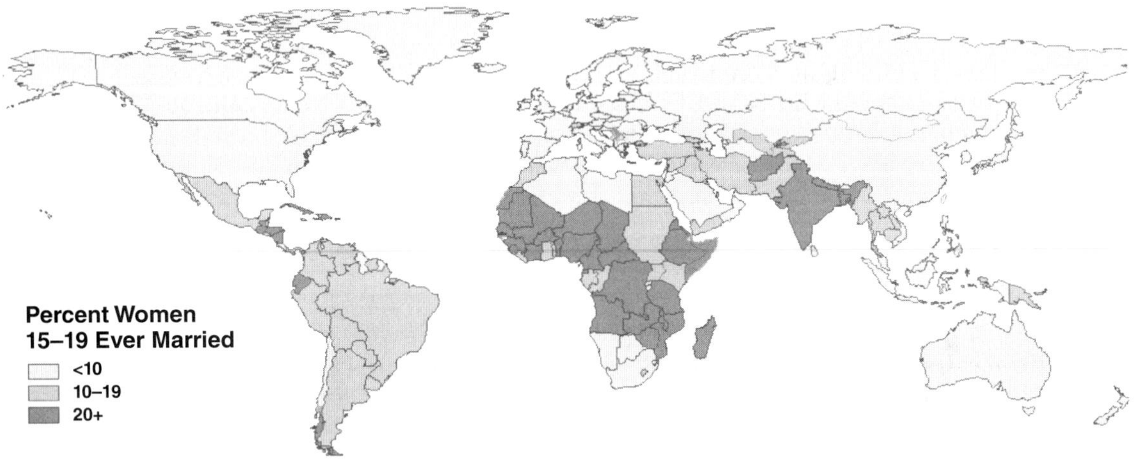

Figure 10.1 Percent of Women 15–19 Who Are Married

Source: Adapted by the author from data in United Nations Population Division, 2009, *World Marriage*, Data 2008 (POP/DB/Marr/Rev2008).

Households used to be created by marriage and dissolved by death—in between there were children. Throughout the world this pattern has been transformed by what some have called the "second demographic transition," which I will discuss as the "family and household transition" in the context of the broader demographic transition. "The demographic transition is in essence a transition in family strategies: the reactive, largely biological family-building decision rules appropriate to highly uncertain environments come eventually to be supplanted by more deliberate and forward-looking strategies that require longer time horizons" (Cohen and Montgomery 1998:6). Put another way, the transition is from "family building by fate" to "family building by design" (Lloyd and Ivanov 1988:141). I mentioned this in Chapter 6 as being key to the fertility transition and, as I have often repeated, all of the previously discussed transitions conspire to create the family and household transition.

What Is the Family and Household Transition?

In general terms, we can describe the family and household transition as the increasing diversity in family and household structure occasioned by people living longer, with fewer children born, increasingly in urban settings, and subject to higher standards of living, all as part of the demographic transition. Households no longer depend on marriage for their creation, nor do they depend on death to dissolve them, and children are encountered in a wide array of household and living arrangements. "The family is in crisis, as witnessed by increasing instability of unions, fluidity of the 'marital' home and the economic stress experienced by women and children of disrupted marriages" (Makinwa-Adebusoye 1994:48). Although that certainly sounds like the subject matter of books and talk shows in the United States over the past two or three decades, the author of that quote was referring to sub-Saharan Africa. "Marriage is becoming rarer and the age at first marriage is increasing; the number of couples who cohabit before and without marrying is rapidly increasing; and so as a consequence, are births out of wedlock" (Blossfeld and de Rose 1992:73). That, too, could be a description of the United States, but in this instance the authors were talking about Italy.

All over the world changes in household formation and living arrangements are being discussed and discoursed, and in the United States it has been suggested that "one of the most widely debated issues in contemporary sociology has been how to interpret patterns of family change . . ." (Brooks 2002:191). Curiously, however, these debates rarely include a review of the underlying demographic changes that helped spawn this massive social shift, and so my purpose in this chapter is to rectify that deficiency for you. The changes we see occurring all over the world are the inevitable result of powerful social forces unleashed by the demographic transition. I am not going to go so far as to suggest that we can predict exactly which changes will take place at a given time in a given society, but I will suggest to you that no social system could remain unchanged in the face of massive declines in mortality, followed by massive declines in fertility, and accompanied by massive migration, especially to urban areas, and a dramatic change in the age structure—all of the changes we have discussed in the previous chapters.

The demographic transition promotes a diversity of family types and household types because (1) people are living longer, which means that they are more likely to be widowed, more likely to tire of the current spouse and seek a divorce, and less likely to feel pressure to marry early and begin childbearing; (2) the latter pressure is relieved by the decline in both mortality and fertility, which means that women, in particular, do not need to begin childbearing at such a young age, and both men and women have many years of life after the children are grown; and (3) an increasingly urban population is presented with many acceptable lifestyle options besides marriage and family-building. I will discuss these drivers of diversity in more detail later in the chapter.

I begin the chapter with a discussion of exactly how the structure of households and living arrangements have, in fact, changed over time—how big is this transition in the United States and elsewhere? Particularly noteworthy is the change in the status of women. I have referred to that repeatedly in previous chapters, but we need to keep reminding ourselves that gender equity is central to the well-being of any society. Next I turn to the specific demographic changes that have contributed to the increasing diversity in household structure. A critical element is the changing set of **life chances** that people are experiencing in the United States and all over the world—changes in the population (or demographic) characteristics that influence how your life will turn out. These include especially education, labor force participation, occupation, and income, which in turn affect **gender roles** (the social roles considered appropriate for males or females) and marital status. All of these things have influenced the changing family and household structure, although differently for some cultural groups than others. Indeed, race and ethnicity, along with religion, mediate the impact of life chances in every human society. The intersection of your population characteristics and family and household structure is a crucial determinant of what life will be like for you. Similarly, at the societal level, the distribution of the population by different characteristics and by family and household structure will be influenced by where a society is in the demographic transition: thus, we are in a position to say something about the future by fitting all of these pieces together.

Defining Family Demography and Life Chances

In virtually every human society ever studied, people have organized their lives around a family unit. In a general sense, a **family** is any group of people who are related to one another by marriage, birth, or adoption. The nature of the family, then, is that it is a *kinship* unit (Ryder 1987). But it is also a mini-society, a micropopulation that experiences births, deaths, and migration, as well as changing age structures as it goes through its own life course. The changes that occur in the broader population—the subject of this book in general—mainly occur within the context of the family unit, so the study of population necessitates that we study the family.

Implicit in the definition of a family is the fact that its members share a sense of social bonding: the mutual acceptance of reciprocal rights and obligations, and of responsibility for each other's well-being. We usually make a distinction between the **nuclear family** (at least one parent and their/his/her children) and the **extended family**, which can extend to other generations (add in grandparents and maybe even great-grandparents) and can also extend laterally to other people within each generation (aunts and uncles, cousins, and so forth).

The next question of interest to us is, Where do these people live? People live in a **housing unit**, which is the physical space used as separate living quarters for people. It may be a house, an apartment, a mobile home or trailer, or even a single room or group of rooms. People who share a housing unit are said to have formed a **household**. The household is thus a *residential unit*, and a **family household** is a housing or residential unit occupied by people who are all related to one another. More specifically, we can say that a family household is a household in which the **householder** (defined by the U.S. Census Bureau as the person in whose name the house is owned or rented) is living with one or more persons related to him or her by birth, marriage, or adoption. On the other hand, a **nonfamily household** is considered by the Census Bureau to be a housing unit that includes only a person who lives alone, or consists of people living with nonfamily co-residents, such as friends living together, a single householder who rents out rooms, or cohabiting couples. Note that many people would consider cohabiting couples to be a family, and I adopt that approach in this chapter to the extent that data permit.

Especially important to the concept of the family household is that the family part of it makes it a kinship unit, as noted above, while the household part of it makes it a *consumption unit* (Wall, Robin, and Laslett 1983). Part of the responsibility that family members have when they live in the same household is to produce goods and services that are shared by, and for the mutual benefit of, the family members who live together. So, family members do not necessarily share a household, and household members are not necessarily family members. But when family members are sharing a housing unit, we have the most powerful kinship and consumer unit that we are likely to find in any society.

Family demography is concerned largely with the study and analysis of family households: their formation, their change over time, and their dissolution. Families represent the *fusion* of people who were born into other families, and long before a family household dissolves, it is likely to have *fissured* into yet other families, as children born into the family grow up and leave the family household of their parents to create (fuse) their own households. All humans grow up in, and typically live for all of their lives, in social groups that represent some sort of family, and our lives are shaped and bounded by our membership in the group. Clearly, we cannot understand the changes taking place elsewhere in society unless we connect those changes to what is happening to the family.

We can describe a family in terms of its *geographic location* because where you are in the world will influence the kinds of social, cultural, economic, and physical resources that will be available to the family. We can also describe a family in terms of its *social location* (where it is positioned in the local social system) because that standing will influence the family's access to whatever local resources exist on which the family can draw. And we can describe the family in terms of its own *social structure*, which refers to the number of people within the family, their age and gender, and their relationship to each other. Each of these characteristics of the family will influence the life chances of family members. Your own life chances refer, for example, to your probability of having a particular set of demographic characteristics, such as having a high-prestige job, lots of money, a stable marriage or not marrying at all, and a small family or no family at all. These differences in life chances, of course, are not necessarily a reflection of your worth as an individual, but they are reflections of the social and economic makeup of society—indicators of the demographic characteristics that help to define what a society and its members are like.

We are born with certain **ascribed characteristics**, such as sex or gender and race and ethnicity, over which we have essentially no control (except in extreme cases). These characteristics affect life chances in very important ways because virtually every society uses such identifiable human attributes to the advantage of some people and the disadvantage of others. Religion is not exactly an ascribed characteristic, but worldwide it is typically a function of race or ethnicity and, as with ascribed characteristics, it is often a focal point for prejudice and discrimination, which influence life chances.

Life chances are also directly related to **achieved characteristics** or your personal human capital, those sociodemographic characteristics, such as education, occupation, labor force participation, income, and marital status, over which you do exercise some degree of control. For example, the better educated you are, the higher your occupational status is apt to be, and thus the higher your level of income will likely be. Indeed, income is a crass, but widely accepted, index of how your life is turning out. Ascribed characteristics affect your life chances primarily by affecting your access to achieved characteristics, which then become major ingredients of social status—education, occupation, and income. Population characteristics affect your own demographic behavior, especially family formation and fertility, although they also influence mortality and migration, as I have already discussed in Chapters 5 and 7, respectively.

The demographics of your family, in turn, affect life chances through the possession or acquisition of social capital—the ability to facilitate or retard your access to opportunities for higher education, a higher status occupation, or a better-paying job. All of these aspects of population characteristics and their influence on life chances converge to affect the kind of family we choose to create and the type of household we form.

The Growing Diversity in Household Composition and Family Structure

The "traditional" family household of a married couple and their children is no longer the statistical norm in North America and in many other parts of the world, even if it remains the ideal type of household in the minds of many people. Families headed by females, especially with no husband present, are common, as are "non-traditional" households inhabited by unmarried people (including never-married, divorced, widowed, and cohabiting couples, who may represent opposite sex or same sex couples), by older adults raising their grandchildren, or by married couples with no children. You are almost certainly aware of these societal shifts through personal experience or the mass media. What may be less obvious is that these changes are closely linked to demographic trends.

The total number of households in the United States increased from 63 million in 1970 to 113 million in 2008, but within that increase was a dramatic change in the composition of the American household, as Figure 10.2 illustrates. In 1970, the classic "married with children" households accounted for 40 percent of all households in

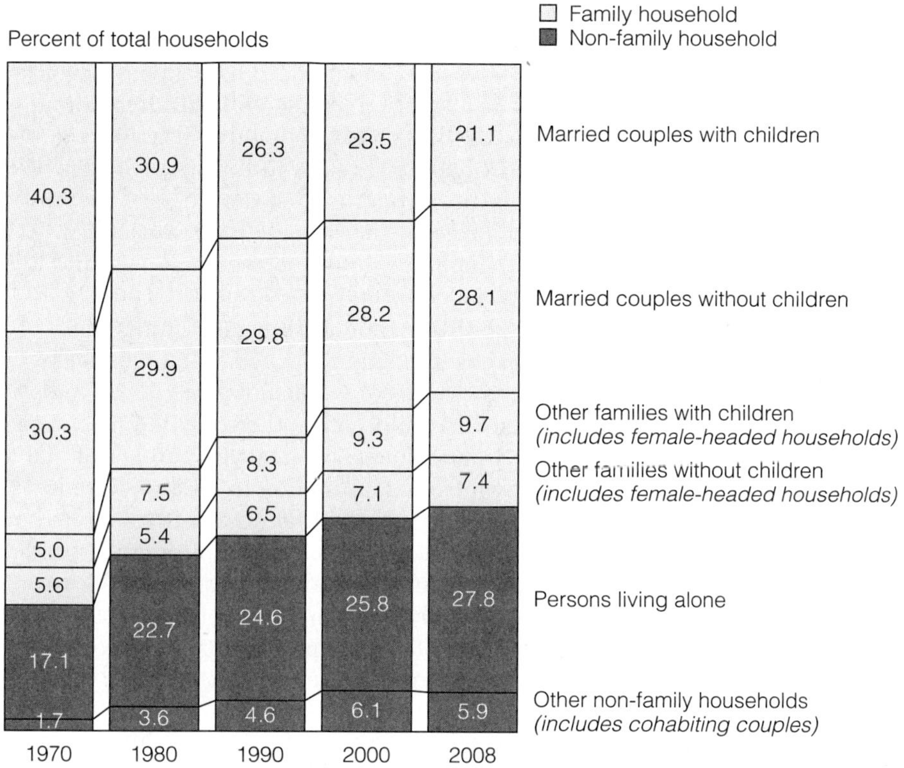

Figure 10.2 Households Have Become Increasingly Diverse in the United States

Sources: Data for 1970 through 1990 are from Jason Fields, 2001, "America's Families and Living Arrangements," Current Population Reports, P20-537, Figure 1; data for 2000 are from U.S. Census Bureau, 2001, Census 2000: Table DP-1, Profile of General Demographic Characteristics: 2000; data for 2008 are from U.S. Census Bureau, American Community Survey 2008 (factfinder.census.gov; accessed 2010).

the United States. Married couples without children (either before building a family or after the kids were grown) accounted for another 30 percent. The "other" families included male- and, disproportionately, female-headed households in which other family members (usually children) were living with the householder. In Figure 10.2, you can see that the light shading represents all family households (a household in which the householder is living with one or more persons related to her or him by birth, adoption, or marriage). In 1970, they comprised 81 percent of all households—a drop from 90 percent in 1940, when the Census Bureau first began to compile these data (Fields 2001). By 2008, it had dropped even further to 66 percent, and by then scarcely one in five households included a married couple with children.

As married couples with children have become less common, they have been replaced most often by female-headed, mother-only families, and by nonfamily households, including people who live alone and nonfamily co-residents (friends living together, a single householder who rents out rooms, cohabiting couples, etc.). The phrase that best describes the changes in household composition as shown in

Figure 10.2 is increased diversity or "pluralization" (meaning that no single category captures a majority of households). Although I focus here on the United States, Canada and most European nations have also experienced a decline in the relative importance of households composed of a married couple with children, along with an increase in female-headed households with children present, although the rise in the latter is more pronounced in the United States than in Europe (Kuijsten 1999). Indeed, in Italy almost all children are born to a married mother and there is very little divorce among parents with children in the home (Anderson 2002). At the same time, Italy has one of the world's highest rates of delayed marriage and lowest rates of fertility, so there is undoubtedly a connection here.

The rise in female-headed households is not a necessary component of the changes that occur during the demographic transition, but as I will discuss below, it is tied at least transitionally to the rise in the status of women. Between 1970 and 2008, the number of female-headed families with children (mother-only families) went up from 2.8 million to 8.3 million in the United States, whereas the number of married-couple-with-children families went down from 25.5 million to 23.8 million. In 1970, female-headed households accounted for 10 percent of families with children, but by 2008 that had jumped to 24 percent (see Figure 10.3). Even those numbers hide the true scope of the transformation, because a married-couple family in 2008 was more likely than in 1970 to be a recombined family, involving previously married spouses and children from other unions. At the end of this chapter, I discuss the social impact of these transformations, but my goal at present is to describe the changes themselves.

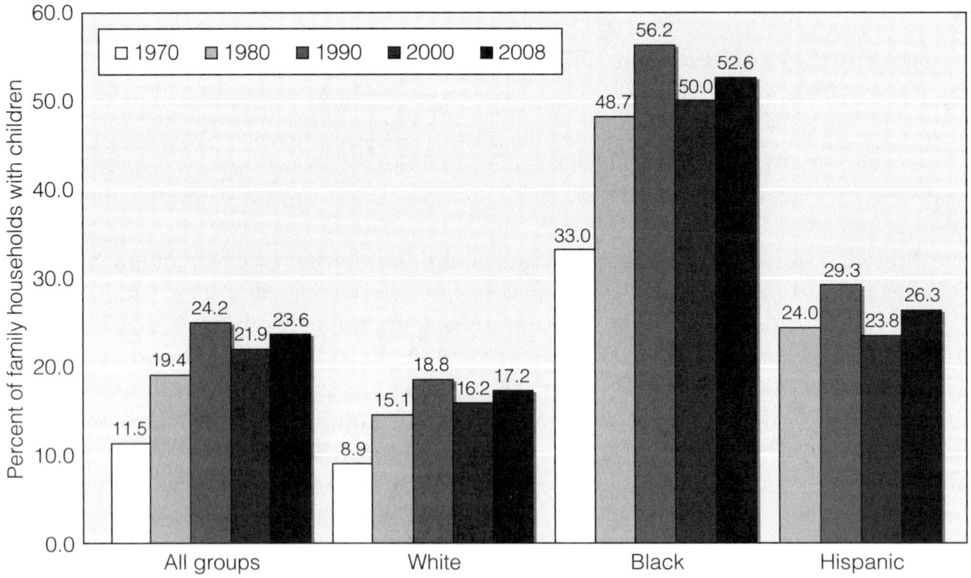

Figure 10.3 Racial/Ethnic Differences in the Percentage of Family Households with Children that Are Mother-Only Families, United States

Sources: Data for 1970 through 1990 are from S. Rawlings, 1994, "Household and family characteristics: March 1993," *Current Population Reports,* P20-477, Table F; data for 2000 are from Jason Fields, 2001, "America's Families and Living Arrangements," *Current Population Reports,* P20-537, Table F; 2008 data are from the U.S. Census Bureau, 2009 Current Population Survey, Table F (www.census.gov, accessed 2010).

Widely discussed in public debate is the fact that substantial racial/ethnic differences exist with respect to female-headed households, especially among families with children, as shown in Figure 10.3. Although the rise in mother-only families has been experienced by all groups in American society, in 1970, African American families were already more apt to be headed by a female than were white or Hispanic households at any time between 1970 and 2000. Ruggles (1994) has found that, since at least 1880, African American children have been far more likely to reside with only their mothers (or with neither parent) than white children. Nonetheless, the data in Figure 10.3 show that the percentage of African American mother-only families has increased considerably just in the past few decades, although it too declined a bit between 1990 and 2000 before bouncing back in 2008. Since 1990 more than half of all black households with children in the United States have been headed by a female.

In 2008, one in three households in the United States was a nonfamily household, as you can see looking back at Figure 10.2. This is part of the trend away from what is often thought of as the traditional family, enshrined by old TV sitcoms—a family in which a married couple live together with their children and the husband works full-time while the wife cares for the children and attends to domestic chores. In fact, this type of *Leave It to Beaver* family (after the 1950s and 1960s TV show of that name) is a relatively new phenomenon historically—itself a product of the demographic transition. High mortality alone (but especially when combined with high fertility and an agrarian economic environment) prevented this type of household from being the norm for most of human history. Let me explain.

Human beings are by nature social animals. We prefer to live with others, and nearly all human economic activities are based on cooperation and collaboration with other humans. Our identity as individuals paradoxically depends on our interaction with other people. We only know who we are by measuring the reaction of other people to us, and we depend on others to teach us how to behave and how to negotiate the physical and social worlds. Furthermore, humans are completely dependent creatures at birth, and every known society has organized itself into social units (households/families) to ensure the survival of children and the reproduction of society. In high-mortality societies, the rules about who can and should be part of that social unit must be a bit flexible because death can take a mother, father, or other important household members at almost any time.

I referred in Chapter 5 to the Nuatl-speaking Mexican families in Morelos in the sixteenth century, who lived in a "demographic hell" where high mortality produced high rates of orphan- and widowhood. In response to these "vagaries of severe mortality," they developed a complex household structure that was "extremely fluid and in constant flux. Headship and household composition shifted rapidly because marriages and death occurred at what must have been a dizzying pace" (McCaa 1994:10). Zhao (1994) used genealogies from China from the thirteenth through the nineteenth centuries to show that high mortality kept most Chinese from actually living in a multigenerational family at any particular time, although, as in Mexico, the high death rate produced a complex form of the family because of shifting membership.

The bottom line here is that what we think of as the "traditional" family depends on low mortality, which is a historically recent phenomenon, in combination with a fairly young age structure, characterized by young adults with their children.

This combination of demographic processes is found largely in the middle phase of the demographic transition, when mortality has dropped but fertility is still above replacement level. Over time, as mortality remains low and fertility drops to low levels, the population ages (as I discussed in Chapter 8), older married couples are left without children any longer in the household, and then women are left without husbands in the household. But, at younger ages, people are still marrying and having children, marrying and not having children, not marrying but having children, and neither marrying nor having children. All of those things are possible in a low-mortality, low-fertility society with a barrel-shaped age structure.

Given the fact that societies have historically changed in response to demographic conditions, it should be no surprise to you that since the end of World War II, with demographic conditions undergoing tremendous change all over the globe, the status of women has been one of the facets of social organization undergoing a significant transition.

Gender Equity and the Empowerment of Women

The demographic transition does not inherently produce gender equity and the empowerment of women, but it creates the conditions under which they are much more likely to happen. The combination of longer life and lower fertility, even if achieved in an environment in which women are still oppressed, opens the eyes of society—including women themselves—to the fact that women are in a position to contribute in the same way that men do when not burdened by full-time parenting responsibility. And, as I have already mentioned (see especially the essay in Chapter 6), the fact that this combination of low mortality and low fertility typically occurs in an urban setting means that women have many more opportunities than would exist in rural areas to achieve the same kind of economic and social independence that has been largely the province of men for much of human history.

Let me suggest to you that at no time in human history has there been a good justification for the domination of women by men, but the demographic conditions that prevailed for most of human history did at least facilitate that domination. Demographic conditions no longer provide that prop, and in most of the world the impediment to full social, economic, and political empowerment of women is simply the attitude of men, often aided by women who have grown up as "codependents" in the system of male domination. Thus, an important part of the demographic divide in the world is the gender divide or, as Inglehart and Norris (2003) have called it—"the true clash of civilizations."

At the beginning of the twentieth century, it would have been unthinkable for a woman in America to go out to dinner without being accompanied by a man, and equally unthinkable for her to drive one of the cars that were making their first appearance at that time. At the beginning of the twenty-first century, those things are still unthinkable to most women in Saudi Arabia (one of the world's most gender-segregated societies), but just as demographic changes were occurring in the United States 100 years ago, so they are occurring in Saudi Arabia today (Yamani 2000; *The Economist 2010*), where the principal battlefield has been described as the battle of the sexes (Lacey 2009).

The changes under way in much of the world mean that the life chances for women are beginning to equal those of men, and thus women are in a position to voluntarily head their own household if they want to, or to do so successfully even if forced into that position. It is certainly no coincidence that those countries still in the early to mid stages of the demographic transition are also those where the rights of women are most trampled. In much of sub-Saharan Africa and South Asia, women's access to economic resources is restricted by severe limitations on their ability to inherit property and own land (World Bank 1999). In India, women's access to the formal labor market is restricted, so women wind up in the informal sector, where they are far more likely to be economically exploited (Dunlop and Velkoff 1999). In Accra, the capital of Ghana, in West Africa, women are just as likely as men to be in the labor force, but nearly three-fourths of those women are in the informal sector, compared to about half of men (Weeks 2010).

Countries at the later stages of the demographic transition have generally discovered the benefits of unleashing the resources of the half of the population that had previously been excluded from full societal participation. Since 1979, the United Nations has been encouraging all countries to sign on to the Convention on the Elimination of All Forms of Discrimination against Women (CEDAW) and as of 2010, 186 countries had approved it (90 percent of all UN member states), although the United States was not one of them at the time of this writing. The empowerment of women contributes to further change in society by expanding women's life chances, which, in turn, expand economic opportunity and enrich society and households. All of these transformations contribute to the diversity of family and household structure. Let us now examine some of the direct proximate causes of the household structure transformation societies have been experiencing.

Proximate Determinants of Family and Household Changes

The increasing diversity in household structure is a result of several interdependent trends taking place in society, including especially delays in marriage, accompanied by young people leaving their parents' home (which in most more developed nations has increased the incidence of cohabitation), and an increase in divorce (which also contributes to cohabitation); whereas at the older ages, the greater survivability of women over men has increased the incidence of widowhood, which has an obvious impact on family and household structure. In between the younger and older ages, the smaller number of children in each family means that a much shorter period of time in each parent's life is devoted to activities directly related to childbearing. The life course of the family has thus been revolutionized.

Delayed Marriage Accompanied by Leaving the Parental Nest

One of the most important mechanisms preventing women from achieving equality with men is early marriage. When a girl is encouraged or even forced to marry at a young age, she is likely to be immediately drawn into a life of childbearing and family-building that makes it very difficult, if not impossible, for her to contemplate other options in life. This is one of the principal reasons why high fertility is so closely associated with low status for women. The map in Figure 10.1 at the beginning of this chapter shows the world pattern in the percentage of women who are already married by the time they reach their twentieth birthday. You will not be surprised to notice that the highest percentage married at young ages occurs in those countries where fertility is highest and where the status of women is known to be low. By contrast, it is no coincidence that in the low-fertility regions of North America, Europe, Oceania, and East Asia, the percentage of women who marry at young ages is very low and the status of women is higher than in other places in the world.

Even though women typically marry at young ages in high-fertility societies, men tend to be under less constraint on that score. This means that in those places where women are young when they marry, the chance is good that their husband is several years older. This further contributes to the ability of a man to dominate his spouse. "A girl with minimal education, raised to be submissive and subservient, married to an older man, has little ability to negotiate sexual activity, the number of children she will bear or how she spends her time" (Gupta 1998:22). The flip side of this is that a rising age at marriage in sub-Saharan Africa since the 1970s has had the beneficial side effect of reducing the rate of polygynous marriages, which normally involve a young woman marrying an older man as his second or third wife—a situation that typically will diminish a woman's life chances (Chojnacka 2000).

Table 10.1 shows that as the percentage of women who are married at ages 15–19 goes up, the difference in age between husband and wife also increases. Thus, in those countries where less than 10 percent of women are married at ages 15–19, a man is on average 2.8 years older than the woman he marries. At the other end of the continuum, in those countries where 40 percent or more of women are married at ages 15–19, the average difference between bride and groom is 6.8 years. Although husbands tend to be older than their wives in the United States, data for the year 2000 show that 32 percent of married couples are within one year of each other, and in 12 percent of couples, the wife is older than the husband by at least two years (Fields 2001). An increasing body of evidence from Demographic

Table 10.1 The Average Difference in Age of Brides and Grooms Declines as The Percent of Women Married at Ages 15–19 Goes Down

% of women married at ages 15–19	Average difference in age between bride and groom	Number of countries
40 or higher	6.8	6
30–39	5.9	11
20–29	4.7	19
10–19	3.7	53
Less than 10	2.8	123
Total	3.5	212

Source: Calculated from data in United Nations Population Division, 2009, *World Marriage Patterns, 2008* (POP/DB/Marr/Rev2008).

and Health Surveys indicates that the age at marriage is on the rise in many developing countries, signaling a potential change in fertility, female empowerment, and family change in those parts of the world (Westoff 2003).

In the United States, as in many northern and western European countries, the early decline in fertility more than 100 years ago was accomplished especially by a delay in marriage. It is thus easy to understand that it was in these countries that some of the early feminist movements were able to take root. At a time when very few effective contraceptives were available, and when it was extremely difficult to get a divorce, postponement of marriage was the principal route by which women were able to increase their options in life. In 1890 in the United States, more than one-third of all women aged 14 and older (34 percent) and close to one-half of all men (44 percent) were single. Between 1890 and 1960, being single became progressively less common as women and, especially men, married at earlier ages.

Since the 1960s has there been a resurgence of delayed marriage, initiated by females born after the Lucky Few Generation of the Great Depression. The trends over time are shown in Figure 10.4, which graphs the percentage of males and females of each birth cohort that were married by age 20 (the lower two lines on the graph) and by age 25 (the two upper lines). Among women born in 1935 to 1939,

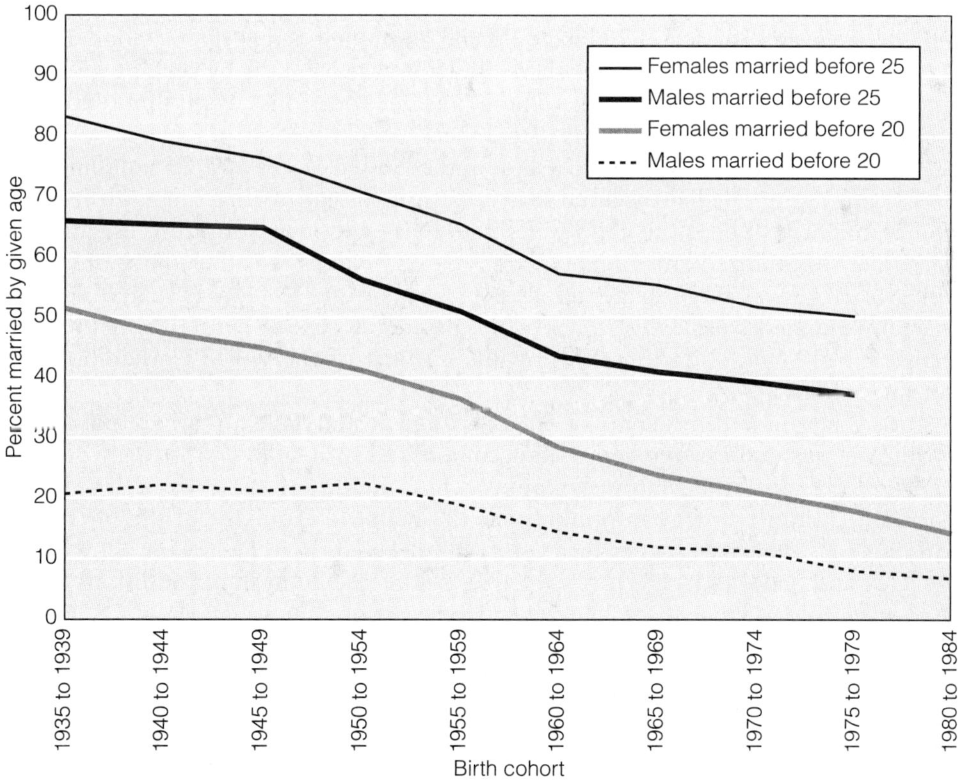

Figure 10.4 Percent of U.S. Women and Men Married by Given Ages, by Birth Cohort

Source: Adapted from data in U.S. Census Bureau, Survey of Income and Program Participation (SIPP), 2004 Panel, Wave 2 Topical Module.

half were already married by age 20 (which they reached in 1955 through 1959) and more than 80 percent were married by the time they reached 25 in 1960 through 1964. From that point on, you can see the steady decline over time in the proportion of American women married at these younger ages. Among those born since 1975, less than 10 percent were married by age 20 and only about 50 percent by age 25. The downward trend started later for males, launched by the baby boomers born in 1950–54. In interpreting these data, however, we must keep in mind that the rise in popularity of cohabitation in the United States (as in Europe) has created some fuzziness around the concept of age at marriage, and the U.S. Census Bureau has not published data on age at marriage since 2004, while at the same increasing its collection of data on cohabitation, as I discuss below.

Since the 1960s, the contraceptive revolution, especially the birth control pill, has allowed people to disconnect marriage from sexual intercourse, and it is not a coincidence that the declines in the percent of women married at younger ages shown in Figure 10.4 are especially noticeable among women who reached maturity just as the pill was coming onto the market. Of course, people have known about and used birth control methods for a long time (refer to Chapter 6 if you need a review), but the failure rate of all of those pre-pill methods was significantly higher than that of the pill, and a couple engaging in intercourse ran a clear risk of an unintended pregnancy. Prior to 1973 and the legalization of abortion in the United States, an American woman could end an unintended pregnancy only by flying to a country such as Sweden, where abortion was legal, or by seeking an illegal (and often dangerous) abortion. These unsafe abortions were often done in Mexico, even though abortion was illegal there.

In more traditional societies (including the United States and Canada until the 1960s), an unintended pregnancy was most apt to lead to marriage, although a woman might also bear the child quietly and give it up for adoption. Illegitimacy was widely stigmatized and having a child out of wedlock was the course of last resort. Marriage was the only genuinely acceptable route to regular sexual activity, and only married couples were routinely granted access to available methods of birth control. That situation still prevails in most of the world's predominantly Muslim nations.

In the late nineteenth century, the older age at marriage already alluded to in North America and Europe had been accomplished by a delay in the onset of regular sexual activity—the Malthusian approach to life. Intercourse was delayed until marriage, and in this way nuptiality was the main determinant of the birth rate: Early marriage meant a higher birth rate, and delayed marriage meant a lower one (Wrigley and Schofield 1981). A variety of social and economic conditions might discourage an early marriage. The societal expectation that a man should be able to provide economic support for his wife and children tended to delay marriage for men until those expectations could be met. Under conditions of rising material expectations, as was the case in the late nineteenth century, marriage had to be delayed even a bit longer than in previous generations because the economic bar had been raised higher than before.

Delayed marriage typically meant that young people stayed with their parents in order to save enough money to get ahead financially and thus be able to afford marriage. Staying with parents also minimized the opportunities for younger people to be able to engage in premarital sexual intercourse, which might lead to an unintended pregnancy and destroy plans for the future. Thus, prior to the latter half of the twentieth century, delayed marriage did not typically lead younger people to leave home and set up their own independent household prior to marriage.

In the early post–World War II period, economic robustness allowed a young person to leave the parental home at an earlier age without an economic penalty and, since the risk of pregnancy meant that intercourse was still tied closely to marriage, the age at marriage reached historic lows in the United States and Europe. In discussing the situation in Germany, Blossfeld and de Rose (1992) have argued that "until the late 1960s, the opportunity for children to leave their parental home had increased remarkably because of the improvement of economic conditions. But the social norm requiring that they be married if they wanted to live together with a partner of the opposite sex was still valid, so that age at entry into marriage was decreasing until the end of the 1960s" (p. 75). Similar arguments could be made for the United States and for other European countries, even for a country like Spain, where out-of-wedlock births accounted for only 2 percent of births in 1975, but had jumped to 30 percent by 2007 (Castro-Martín 2010). Several things have facilitated this change in Spain, including a law passed in 1981 that gave equal rights to children born in or outside of marriage, the legalization of contraception, and a loosening of restrictions on abortion. Still, these changes are taking place in a low-low fertility environment. Throughout southern Europe women seem reluctant to marry and have children because employment opportunities are more fragile than in other parts of Europe, and once they leave the labor force to have a child they find it difficult to return (Adsera 2004).

Modern contraception has allowed sex to be disconnected from marriage and this has been accompanied by a dramatic rise in the fraction of young people who leave their parental home before marriage, even while delaying marriage. In 1940, 82 percent of unmarried males and females aged 18–24 lived with their parents (Goldscheider and Goldscheider 1993; 1999); by 2000, that had declined to only 42 percent for women and 56 percent for men (Fields 2001). "By the 1980s, leaving home before marriage had evidently become institutionalized in the United States" (Goldscheider and Goldscheider 1993:34). Goldscheider and Goldscheider (1994) analyzed data from the National Survey of Families and Households to show that until the early 1960s, the majority of women who left home after age 18 were doing so to get married. That pattern changed in the 1960s, and by the late 1980s, only one-third of women were leaving home to marry. Men, however, have been leaving home for reasons other than marriage for a long time. So the recent delay in marriage and nest-leaving behavior has been a more significant force of change for women than for men.

You may have asked yourself how the data on increasing independence of young people can square with the wide array of stories about these same people returning home to live with their parents. The answer is that as the fraction of young people who leave home to live independently increases, the absolute volume of people available to move back in with parents increases. Children graduating from college and those returning from the military are especially likely to return home for a short while, whereas those who left home to marry are the least likely to return home (Goldscheider and Goldscheider 1999). Nonetheless, because children do not necessarily return for very long, a snapshot photo of society (such as the census or a survey) does not capture many young people who have returned home, even though a fairly high percentage may do so at some time or another. Data from Canada show that from 1981 to 1996 the percentage of young people remaining in their parents' home increased (Boyd and Norris 2000), but even this is consistent with the fact that delayed marriage increases the options available to young people and allows both an increase in leaving home for reasons other than marriage and an increase in staying in or returning to the parental home.

Cohabitation

The delay in marriage has not necessarily meant that young people have been avoiding a family-like situation, nor that they have necessarily avoided having children out of wedlock, as I have already mentioned. When leaving the parental home, young people may set up an independent household either by living alone or sharing a household with nonfamily members, or they may move into nonhousehold group quarters such as a college dormitory. From these vantage points, many then proceed to **cohabitation**, which can be defined as the sharing of a household by unmarried persons who have a sexual relationship (Cherlin 2005). As this trend was unfolding in the 1970s, the Census Bureau created estimates of its extent in the United States from data on household composition. The resulting measure was "partners of the opposite sex sharing living quarters," which became widely known as POSSLQ (pronounced "PAH-sul-cue"). Over time the measure has been refined based on more direct questions about unmarried partners, and the Census Bureau now uses the more mundane term "opposite sex unmarried couples." Researchers have found that POSSLQ was, in fact, a pretty good measure, although it probably underestimated cohabiting couples with children (Casper and Cohen 2000).

In 1970, when a large percentage of women in the United States were already married by age 20, there were about 500,000 cohabiting couples in the United States, and the ratio of cohabiting to married couples was 1 to 100. By 2009, when only a very small percentage of women had ever been married by age 20, the number of cohabiting couples had increased to 6.7 million and the ratio of cohabiting to married couples also had jumped to 12 per 100 (U.S. Census Bureau 2010a). A snapshot number like that almost certainly underestimates the importance of cohabitation, however, because it has become a widely accepted part of the life course in many low-fertility societies. Rather than being an alternative to marriage (a "poor person's marriage"), it has become a stepping-stone to marriage for many, as well as a step back from marriage after a divorce for others. Although a relatively small, albeit growing, fraction of couples are cohabiting at any one time, the data for the United States suggest that more than half of women between the ages of 19 and 44 have cohabited at least once, and that about 40 percent of children have experienced time in a cohabiting family by the time they are 12 years old (Kennedy and Bumpass 2008). Similar rapid increases have been observed elsewhere. For example, survey data from France suggest that in 1965 only 8 percent of couples cohabited before marriage, but by 1995 that figure had jumped to 90 percent (Toulemon 1997).

Nonmarital Childbearing

The delay in marriage accompanied by high rates of premarital sexual activity (aided by the fact that young people have been getting out of the parental home before marriage) means that the United States and some of the other low-fertility nations have been experiencing an increase in the proportion of nonmarital births. This is an event, of course, that immediately transforms a woman living alone, or an unmarried couple, from a nonfamily to a family household. In France, the percentage of births outside marriage increased from 6 percent in 1965 to 40 percent in 1998 (Muñoz-Peréz and Prioux 2000). Between 1970 and 2006, the proportion of babies in the United States who were born outside of marriage increased from 11 percent to 39 percent (Martin et al. 2009).

Data from the American Community Survey provide a broader portrait of the women who are bearing a child outside of marriage. There are two ways to look at these data. The first perspective is to ask about the percentage of births in a given demographic category (e.g., age or educational level) that are taking place outside of marriage, whereas the second perspective asks which groups of women are having the greatest number of nonmarital births (even if the risk is lower than for some groups). With respect to the first perspective, certain groups have stood out for many years: (1) nearly 90 percent of births to girls under age 20 are nonmarital, and more than half of births to women aged 20–24 are nonmarital; and (2) nearly two-thirds of births to African American women are outside of marriage.

Among younger women, the nonuse of contraception and lack of local access to abortion may push up the likelihood of young women getting pregnant and bearing a child. The United States is more restrictive than most low-fertility societies in providing teenagers with easy and inexpensive access to methods of fertility limitation. Prior to the 1970s, most young women conceiving out-of-wedlock would have married prior to the baby's birth (Bachu 1999), so the ratio of nonmarital births to all births would have been much lower, even with the same level of premarital conceptions. Of course, the odds were also very high that the marriage would have ended in divorce after only a few years, so neither scenario—marriage or nonmarriage—is particularly rosy for a teenage mother and her baby.

A disproportionate share of younger women bearing children outside of marriage are African American. Since birth rates overall are nearly as low for blacks as they are for whites in the United States, the proportion of nonmarital births represents a different pattern of parenting, not a different overall level of childbearing. The pattern is to have children at a younger age than the rest of the population does, and then to stop having them at a younger age as well. Thus, in 2006, the age-specific birth rates for black women were quite a bit higher than for whites at ages younger than 25, but then lower than for whites at ages 25 and higher (Martin et al. 2009). It is not clear why this pattern exists, but even in the 1930s, when only 6 percent of white women in the United States were having a baby out-of-wedlock, the percentage among blacks was 31 (Bachu 1999).

Regardless of the reasons, the data suggest that only 15 percent of black mothers raise their children in an intact two-parent family, compared with 60 percent of non-Hispanic white mothers (Rendall 2000). Furthermore, it is not just that the children are born outside of marriage; the fact that 22 percent of black children are born to teenage mothers (compared to 11 percent of whites) negatively affects their life chances, as I noted previously.

These data have fueled enormous public debate about the social cost of nonmarital births (measured monetarily by welfare benefits and socioculturally by the deprivations suffered by fatherless children) and they have been interpreted as signs of imminent cultural decay. But, as McLanahan and Casper (1995) have pointed out, the situation is not quite what it seems, and this gets us to the second perspective on nonmarital childbearing—which groups of women account for such births. Of 1.6 million U.S. nonmarital births in 2006, 37 percent were to non-Hispanic white women, 32 percent to Hispanics, and 27 percent to blacks. Thus, blacks accounted for scarcely one in four nonmarital births, despite the much higher fraction of black babies born outside of marriage than is true for the other groups. Furthermore, 60 percent of nonmarital births were to women aged 20–29, while only 22 percent were to teenagers, despite the much higher percentage of teenage births that are outside of marriage. Finally, we can note that in 2006, less than 15 percent of nonmarital births were born to cohabiting couples (Dye 2008), despite the considerable attention that researchers and the media have paid to such couples.

Childlessness

About 10 percent of couples in the United States may remain childless because of impaired fecundity. In the 1970s, data from the Current Population Survey suggested that, in fact, this percentage of women (10 percent) was reaching ages 40–44 without having had a child. However, the percentage slowly but steadily increased to 20 percent by 2006 (Dye 2008). Many of these women probably "drifted" toward childlessness by continually postponing the first child, since we know that most reproductive decisions, in both high- and low-fertility societies, are made sequentially from one birth to the next (Morgan 1996). An important consequence of gender equality is that there is less pressure on a woman to have children, even if she is married, particularly if she has a rewarding career that she doesn't want to interrupt or, as certainly happens in some cases, she and her husband simply prefer a life without children. Childlessness increases household diversity by increasing the percentage of households represented either by someone living alone, or a married couple with no children of their own, or a cohabiting couple with no children, or a multiple-person nonfamily household.

Divorce

Not only has marriage been increasingly pushed to a later age, but once accomplished, marriages are also more likely to end in divorce than at any previous time in history. This trend reflects many things. An obvious reason is that changes in divorce laws since the 1970s have made it easier for either partner to end the marriage at any time for any reason (Waite 2000). Friedberg (1998) concluded that divorce laws alone might explain about 17 percent of divorces in the United States. For the other 83 percent of the explanation, we can start by asking ourselves why legislators were motivated to make those changes. For answers, we can look to the loosening hold of men over women and the longer lives we are leading, both of which may produce greater conflict within marriage. In 1857 in the United States, there was only a 27 percent chance that a husband aged 25 and a wife aged 22 would both still be alive when the wife reached 65, but for couples marrying in the early twenty-first century, the chances have rocketed to 60 percent. Conversely, only about 5 percent of marriages contracted in 1867 ended in divorce (Ruggles 1997), whereas it has been estimated that about half of the marriages contracted since the 1970s will end in divorce (Kreider and Fields 2002; Raley and Bumpass 2003). That probability seems to have stabilized since the 1990s, suggesting that we may have passed the period of rising divorce rates (Schoen and Standish 2001).

The United States is certainly not unique in having experienced an increase in divorce probabilities. Goode (1993) compiled data showing that throughout Europe the percentage of marriages ending in divorce virtually doubled between 1970 and the mid-1980s. For example, in Germany in 1970, it was estimated that 16 percent of marriages would end in divorce, increasing to 30 percent in 1985. In France, the increase went from 12 percent to 31 percent during that same time period. After that rapid rise, the divorce rate appears more recently to have plateaued in Europe (UN Economic Commission for Europe 2003), just as has happened in the United States.

Cherlin (2005) summarizes the major risk factors for divorce as including low income for the couple (which causes stresses and tension), early age at marriage (which often means a poorer job of choosing a spouse), spouse's lack of similarity (this kind of similarity is known as *homogamy*, referring to the fact that people who are more similar to one another are more likely to get along with each other or, conversely, those who are less similar will be more likely to divorce), parental divorce (the copycat phenomenon, in which people whose parents divorced are more likely themselves to divorce), and cohabitation.

Given the previous discussion of cohabitation, it is of some interest to note that, contrary to popular belief in the value of "trial" marriage, cohabitation before marriage appears to be one of the factors that increases the odds of a marriage ending in divorce, at least in North America. Several studies have suggested that cohabitation is selective of people who are mistrustful of marriage, probably because of their own "social inheritance of divorce" (Diekmann and Englehardt 1999). If cohabitation leads to marriage among these people, they may thus be more prone to end that marriage by divorce.

Many marriages that in earlier days would have been dissolved by death are now dissolved by divorce. This seems apparent from the fact that the annual combined rate of marital dissolution from both the death of one spouse and divorce remained remarkably constant for more than a century—essentially unchanged between 1860 and 1970 (Davis 1972). As widowhood declined, divorce rose proportionately. Only with the rapid increase in divorce during the 1970s did that pattern begin to diverge. So dramatic was the rise in divorce in the 1970s that in the mid-1960s the elimination of divorce would have added an additional 6.7 years to the average marriage, whereas by the mid-1970s its elimination would have added 17.2 years (Goldman 1984).

Widowhood

As death has receded to older ages, the incidence of widowhood has steadily been pushed to the older years as well. Divorce is a more important cause of not being married than is widowhood up to age 65, beyond which widowhood increases geometrically because of the higher death rate of men, undoubtedly compounded by the tendency of divorced women to change their status to widow upon the death of a former husband. As is true with so many social facts in the United States, African American women are disadvantaged compared to whites in terms of marital status. At every age, blacks are more likely to be either divorced or widowed than are other racial/ethnic groups.

The Combination of These Determinants

As the demographic transition unfolds, then, we are finding that people are waiting longer to marry, although often cohabiting in the meantime, and when they do marry, their marriage is more likely to end in divorce than in widowhood. Schoen and Standish (2001) used life table methodology to try to quantify the relative importance of these changes in family demography. Their results showed that between 1970 and 1995, for example, the proportion of women who could expect ever to marry declined from 96 percent to 89 percent. At the same time, the average age at marriage was increasing, the percentage of marriages ending in divorce was increasing, and the percentage of marriages ending in widowhood was declining. Furthermore, as life expectancy increases while the average duration of a marriage shortens, and the percentage of divorced people remarrying goes down, the percentage of a person's life spent being married declines, thus adding to the individual diversity of household types in which a person might live during an entire lifetime.

Cherlin (2009) argues that family life in the United States, even more than in other nations, is characterized by frequent transitions. I argue, of course, that these transitions—whether you like them or not—have come about only because of the other transitions that make up the overall demographic transition, including the drop in the death rate and birth rate, the resulting changing age structure, and the migration and urban transitions.

Having described the principal features of the transformation of families and households, let us see how they have been influenced by changing life chances and how, in turn, life chances interact with family formation and household structure.

Changing Life Chances

The leading explanations for the shift in household structure in Western nations combine elements of the demographic transition perspective with the life course perspective. The demographic transition perspective relates changing demographic conditions (especially declining mortality, declining fertility, and urbanization) to the rise in women's status. This is aided especially by delayed marriage, which encourages higher levels of educational attainment. In turn, this has increased a woman's ability to enter the labor force and earn sufficient income to have the economic and social freedom to choose her own pattern of living. As these changes have unfolded, women's differing life chances have contributed to the transformation of families and households. Again, I emphasize that these demographic conditions are probably necessary, but not sufficient, to initiate the current rise in the status of women in industrialized societies. What is also required is some change in circumstance to act as a catalyst for the underlying demographic factors. This is where the life course perspective comes in, because women who have grown up in a different demographic and social milieu, and thus see the world differently than did earlier generations of women, have the potential to generate change in society. It is easy to know where to begin the discussion of changes in life chances, because nothing is more important than education.

Education

Becoming educated is probably the most dramatic and significant change you can introduce into your life. It is the locomotive that drives much of the world's economic development, and it is a vehicle for personal success used by generation after generation of people in the highly developed nations of the world. Still, the relative recency with which advanced education has taken root in American society can be seen in Table 10.2. In 1940, less than one in four Americans aged 25 or older had graduated from high school, although women were more likely than men to have done so. Slightly more than 5 percent of men and less than 4 percent of women

Table 10.2 U.S. Educational Attainment Has Increased Significantly Over Time

	Male			Female		
Year	% high school graduate or more	% college graduate	median years of education	% high school graduate or more	% college graduate	median years of education
2008	84.3	28.4	13.1	85.6	27.0	13.2
2000	84.2	27.8	13.0	84.0	23.6	12.9
1990	77.7	24.4	12.8	77.5	18.4	12.7
1980	69.2	20.9	12.6	68.1	13.6	12.4
1970	55.0	14.1	12.2	55.4	8.2	12.1
1960	39.4	9.6	10.3	42.5	5.8	10.9
1950	31.5	7.1	9.0	35.1	5.0	9.6
1940	22.3	5.4	8.6	25.9	3.7	8.7

Sources: Data for 1940 to 1990 are from U.S. Census Bureau, 2000, Educational Attainment Historical Table A-1 (http://www.census.gov, accessed 2001); data for 2000 are from U.S. Census Bureau, 2000, *Educational Attainment of the Population 15 Years and Over, by Marital Status, Age, Sex, Race, and Hispanic Origin;* March 2000, Table 3; data for 2008 are from American Community Survey 2008 (http://factfinder.census.gov, accessed 2010). Median year calculations for 2000 and 2008 are by the author.

were college graduates. You can see that the median number of years of education was 8.6 for men and 8.7 for women. A historically short six decades later, in 2000, 84 percent of both men and women were high school graduates and about one in four Americans had graduated from college—with men still being more likely than women to have accomplished that milestone. By 2008, women had surpassed men both in terms of high school graduation and with respect to college education, as the younger generations move through the life course. For example, back in 2000 among people aged 25–34, 89 percent of women were high school graduates compared to 87 percent of men, and 30 percent of women were college graduates, compared to 29 percent of men.

In Canada in 2006, among people aged 25–34, 89 percent were high school graduates, while 33 percent were college graduates. As is true in the United States, women are now slightly better educated on average than men, with the crossover occurring among people under age 35 in 2006 (OEDC 2009). From the 2005 census in Mexico, we have data on the median number of years of school completed among people aged 15 and older, and the data show an average of 8.4 for men and 7.9 for women—levels below those that prevailed in the United States in 1940, but still higher than they used to be in Mexico, and each successive generation in Mexico now has a higher average level of educational attainment than the previous one.

The world as a whole has been experiencing an increasing equalization of education among males and females—an important component in raising the global status of women. The ratio of females per males attending secondary school has been steadily increasing worldwide since at least the 1970s, according to World Bank estimates. In some areas of the world, such as North America and Europe, women have already achieved parity with men, or are even more likely than men to be enrolled in secondary school.

In sub-Saharan Africa and southern Asia, as well as in northern Africa and western Asia, in all of which areas the status of women has been notably low and where education for girls continues to lag behind that of boys, there have nonetheless been notable improvements in the ratio of girls to boys attending school. Fargues (1995) has noted that in the middle of the twentieth century most of the countries of northern Africa and western Asia had gender equity with respect to education in the sense that most people—males and females alike—were illiterate. Education was extended first to young men, creating for a while both a gender and a generation gap in education. Now, as more generations of children have been educated, and as education has been offered to girls as well as boys, both of those gaps are closing, and this will certainly help accelerate the process of social and economic development (Grant and Behrman 2010).

The comments about closing the gap should not be taken to mean that we are galloping toward gender equity in education everywhere on the planet. Table 10.3 lists the 20 countries in the world (representing 25 percent of the world's population) as of 2008 in which illiteracy among young women (aged 15–24) was at least 10 percentage points higher than that for males in the same age range. A good example of this situation was found in Iraq at the time of American invasion, where 40 percent of young men were unable to read or write, but a whopping 70 percent of young women were in that boat. Note that Yemen, a western Asian country just to the south of Saudi Arabia, gets the "honor" of having the lowest level of gender equity

Table 10.3 World Educational "Hot Spots": Countries Where the Illiteracy Rate Among Young (Aged 15–24) Women Is at Least 10 Percentage Points Higher Than for Young Men, circa 2008

Country	Region	Female illiteracy	Male illiteracy	Excess of female over male illiteracy
Yemen	Western Asia	30	5	25
Benin	Sub-Saharan Africa	58	36	22
Sierra Leone	Sub-Saharan Africa	54	34	20
Pakistan	South Central Asia	41	21	20
Mali	Sub-Saharan Africa	69	53	17
Morocco	North Africa	32	15	16
Chad	Sub-Saharan Africa	63	47	16
Guinea-Bissau	Sub-Saharan Africa	38	22	16
Central African Republic	Sub-Saharan Africa	44	28	16
Mozambique	Sub-Saharan Africa	38	22	16
Angola	Sub-Saharan Africa	35	19	16
Zambia	Sub-Saharan Africa	33	18	15
India	South Central Asia	26	12	14
Nigeria	Sub-Saharan Africa	35	22	14
Burkina Faso	Sub-Saharan Africa	67	53	14
Senegal	Sub-Saharan Africa	55	42	14
Gambia	Sub-Saharan Africa	42	30	12
Cote d'Ivoire	Sub-Saharan Africa	40	28	12
Nepal	South Central Asia	25	14	11

Source: Adapted from data in World Bank, *World Development Indicators*, 2010 (Washington, DC: World Bank Group).

with respect to literacy. Fifteen of the 20 countries are on the African continent, and the other four are in Asia. As bad as the gender inequality shown in Table 10.3 is, the situation is at least better than ten years prior, when there were 30 countries in this group, accounting for nearly 30 percent of the world's population.

Our interest in education lies especially in the fact that by altering your worldview, education tends to influence nearly every aspect of your demographic behavior, as I have discussed to varying degrees in the previous chapters. Data from censuses and from sources such as the Demographic and Health Surveys show that nearly anywhere you go in the world, the more educated a woman is, the fewer children she will have. Not that education is inherently antinatalist; rather, it opens up new vistas—new opportunities and alternative approaches to life, other than simply building a family—and in so doing it delays the onset of childbearing, which is a crucial factor in setting the tone for subsequent fertility. So, education tends to lower fertility, or to keep it lower than it might otherwise be, and this contributes to the variety of household and family structures we will see.

The fact that education alters the way you view the world also has implications for the marriage market in the United States. For much of American history, a major concern in choosing a marriage partner was to pick someone who shared your religious background (social scientists call this "religious homogamy"). Over time, however, the salience of religion has given way to "educational homogamy"—people want to marry someone with similar amounts of education, thus education has been replacing religion as an especially important factor in spouse selection (Schwartz and Mare 2005). This trend is almost certainly related to gender equity. When men were generally more educated than women—a difference arising from the more traditional kind of society that also places a higher emphasis on religion—well-educated men, in particular, were less likely to find women with a level of education similar to their own. But as women caught up with men in terms of education—due to the modernization of society—men and women began to sort themselves into marriage with a similarly educated mate.

Gender equity, combined with the greater proportion of people going to college, has altered the lifestyles of many young Americans. It has been accompanied by delayed marriage, delayed and diminished childbearing, and consequently, higher per-person income among young adult householders. Young people today have more personal disposable income than any previous generation. In 2008, women consistently earned less than men, but for both men and women the data in Table 10.4 show that those with a graduate or professional degree were earning more than twice as much per year as those who were only high school graduates. This has become known as the "college premium," and its existence has almost certainly contributed to increased education (investment in human capital) and increased economic productivity.

Although the college premium is the same for males and females in relative terms, you can also see that at each educational level women are earning only about two-thirds of what men earn. Part of this is because women are less likely than men to be full-time workers, but if adjusted for that, women would still be earning only about three-fourths of what men make. We may be headed toward gender equity, but we are not there quite yet.

For the investment in education to pay off for people, households, and society more generally, it must lead to higher levels of labor force participation and more productive occupations. Let us examine these aspects of your life chances.

Table 10.4 Better-Educated Workers Have Higher Median Incomes

People Aged 25 and Over with Earnings	Males	Females	Ratio of female income to male income
Total	$41,108	$28,512	0.69
Not high school graduate	$23,675	$14,944	0.63
High School Graduate	$33,109	$21,856	0.66
Some college or associate's degree	$41,325	$27,555	0.67
Bachelor's degree	$58,062	$39,346	0.68
Graduate or professional degree	$79,342	$51,824	0.65

Source: Adapted from U.S. Census Bureau, 2008 American Community Survey (factfinder.census.gov, accessed 2010).

Labor Force Participation

As education increases, so does the chance of being in the labor force. Among both males and females in the United States in 2008, the higher the level of education attainment among people aged 25 to 64, the higher the percentage of people who were currently in the labor force. Women are less likely than men to be in the labor force at any given level of education, but it is nonetheless true that the pattern over time has been for women to be working more and men to be working less. Prior to the 1970s, for example, women who worked typically did so only before they married or became pregnant. Thus, the labor force participation rates by age peaked in the early 20s and declined after that. That is still a common pattern in many less developed countries, but it no longer characterizes women in the richer nations, where labor force participation rates by age are now very similar for males and females.

Keep in mind as we talk about labor force participation rates that most countries include unemployed persons as being in the labor force. Thus, if you are looking for work, even though you are not actually working or even if you have never before held a job, you are considered to be in the labor force. Unemployment rates are strongly related to age—the older the age, the lower the rate. At younger ages, considerable numbers of people are looking for work even if they haven't found it yet, whereas at older ages, people are more likely to give up on employment and seek a retirement pension as soon as it is available if they experience difficulty finding a job. Women also tend to have lower unemployment rates than men do.

By far the biggest gain in employment over the past few decades has been the movement of baby boom women, especially married women, into the labor market. They literally burst their way into the workforce in the 1970s, and by 2008, 69 percent of women aged 40–64 (the baby boomers) had a job, although this was down from 78 percent a decade earlier, before the boomers started to retire. In 1960, just before the baby boomers came of age, labor force participation rates among married women in the United States were well below those for single women at every age from 20 through 64. By 1970, as the first wave of baby boomers had reached adulthood, the rates for married women were clearly on the rise, by 2000 they had nearly reached those of single women, and by 2010 the distinction did not matter much anymore.

Working, as I have mentioned before, cuts down on fertility under normal circumstances, and this is one of the ways in which working has an effect on the family and household structure. It is certainly no coincidence that the birth rate in the United States began to drop at about the same time that labor force participation rates for married women began to rise. Overall, the highest levels of fertility in the United States are found among poor women who do not work, whereas the lowest levels of fertility are among those who do work and are well paid.

The ability of married women to work helps bring fertility down and maintain it at low levels, but, as I mentioned in Chapter 6, it can also help keep fertility from dropping to below-replacement levels. When women are able to combine having a family, even if small, with a career, they are more likely to choose both. In European countries such as Italy and Spain, where family values discourage that combination, women seem to choose in favor of career over family, contributing to very low levels of fertility. The pattern that has emerged in the richer countries is that a high proportion of women work before marriage, remain working after marriage, and adjust their fertility downward to accommodate their working. How far down they adjust may depend on how much familial and societal support they receive in making that accommodation. If child care is readily available and if husbands share domestic chores, we may well expect that fertility will be higher.

We have already discussed the new household economics as an approach to explaining why fertility is kept low in developed societies and why households might encourage family members to migrate. Now, we can call on it again to explain why the rise in the status of women and increased female labor force participation might generate the household transformations we have been reviewing in this chapter. The basic idea is that "the rises in women's employment opportunities and earning power have reduced the benefits of marriage and made divorce and single life more attractive. Though marriage still offers women the benefits associated with sharing income and household costs with spouses, for some women these benefits do not outweigh other costs, whatever these may be" (McLanahan and Casper 1995:33).

In most social systems, people who can take care of themselves and have enough money to be self-reliant have higher status and greater freedom than those who depend economically on others. Further, a pecking order tends to exist among those who are economically independent, with higher incomes being associated with higher status than are low incomes. Being independent, though, is definitely the starting point, and an increasing number of women in the world are arriving at that point. However much you might take for granted the fact that in a rich nation women are as readily employable in the paid labor force as men, it is actually a rather recent phenomenon.

Although mortality and fertility have been declining since the nineteenth century in the United States and urbanization has been occurring throughout that time, it was during World War II that the particular combination of demographic and economic circumstances arose to provide the leading edge of a shift toward labor force equality of males and females. The demand for armaments and other goods of war in the early 1940s came at the same time that men were moving out of civilian jobs into the military, and there was an increasing demand for civilian labor of almost every type.

Earlier in American history, the demand for labor would have been met by foreign workers migrating into the country, but the Immigration Act passed in the 1920s (see Chapter 7) had set up national quotas that severely limited immigration. The only quotas large enough to have made a difference were those for immigrants from countries also involved in the war and thus not a potential source of labor. With neither males nor immigrants to meet the labor demand, women were called into the labor force. Indeed, not just women per se, but more significantly married women, and even more specifically married women with children. Single women had been consistently employable and employed since at least the beginning of the century, as each year 45–50 percent of them had been economically active, as I pointed out earlier. But in the early 1940s there were not enough young single women to meet labor needs, partly because the improved economy was also making it easier for young couples to get married and start a family. It was older women, past their childbearing years, who were particularly responsive to making up the deficit in the labor force (Oppenheimer 1967, 1994).

These were the women who broke new ground in female employment in America, with the biggest increase in labor force participation between 1940 and 1950 coming from women aged 45 to 54, and because more than 92 percent of those women were married, this obviously represented a break with the past. Who were these women? They were the mothers of the Depression, mothers who had sacrificed the larger families they wanted (as I noted in Chapter 6) to scrape by during one of America's worst economic crises. They were women who had smaller families than their mothers and thus were more easily able to participate in the labor force. However, the ideal family size remained more than three children, and the improved economy permitted the low fertility of the 1930s to give way to higher levels in the 1940s and 1950s. Women with small families from the Depression actually opened the door to employment for married women, but younger women were not ready to respond to those opportunities in the 1940s and 1950s. Indeed, after the end of World War II the labor force activity rates of women aged 25 to 34 actually declined.

Things changed, as you know, and between 1950 and 2000 the number and proportion of American women who were in the labor force and earning independent incomes increased substantially. In 1950, for example, there were 29 female, year-round, full-time workers for every 100 males in that category; by 2000, there were 70 females working full-time, year-round per 100 male workers. This increase in labor force activity was accomplished initially by younger women; especially those aged 25 to 34, whose children tended to be in school.

Getting a job is one thing, of course, but the kind of job you get—your occupation—depends heavily on education and is also influenced by factors such as gender and race/ethnicity.

Occupation

Occupation is without question one of the most defining aspects of a person's social identity in an industrialized society. It is a clue to education, income, and residence—in general, a clue to lifestyle and an indicator of social status, pointing to a person's position in the social hierarchy. From a social point of view, occupation is so important that it is often the first (and occasionally the only) question a stranger may ask about you. It provides information about what kind of behavior can be expected from you, as well as how others will be expected to behave toward you. Although such a comment may offend you if you believe that "people are people," it is nonetheless true that there is no society in which all people are actually treated equally.

Since there are literally thousands of different occupations in every country, we need a way of fitting occupations into a few slots. Organizations like the U.S. Census Bureau and the International Labour Organization (ILO, a specialized agency within the United Nations) have devised classification schemes to divide occupations into several mutually exclusive categories. In Table 10.5, I have listed the occupational distribution of employed males and females in the United States as measured in the American Community Survey in 2008. These categories form a rough status ranking, with the higher status occupations at the top of the table, and the lower status occupations on the bottom. You can see that women are more

Table 10.5 U.S. Occupational Distributions Are Different for Males and Females

	Percentage Distribution by Occupational Category—2008	
Employed civilians 16 and older	Males	Females
TOTAL	100	100
Management, business, and financial occupations	15	13
Professional and related occupations	17	25
Service occupations	14	21
Sales and office occupations	18	34
Farming, fishing, and forestry occupations	1	0
Construction, extraction, maintenance, and repair occupations	17	1
Production, transportation, and material moving occupations	18	6

Sources: Adapted from data in U.S. Census Bureau, 2008 American Community Survey (factfinder.census.gov, accessed 2010).

likely than men to be in the top two categories of management and professional occupations, with a clearly higher percentage in the professions. Women are also more likely to be in service and sales occupations. Almost no one any longer works in farming, but those who do are men. Similarly, men are much more likely than women to be in the "blue-collar" occupations of construction, repair, production, and transportation.

As different as these occupational distributions look for men and women, they are less different than they used to be. The index of dissimilarity (sometimes also known as the Gini coefficient) for the data in Table 10.5 is 32, but it was 43 in 1970. We would interpret that to mean that, in 2008, you would had to have moved 32 percent of women into other occupational categories to achieve exactly the same distribution as for men, compared to having to move 43 percent of women back in 1970.

There is a global tendency for women not to be in the best jobs, and there are three important issues that the International Labour Organization sees as still needing considerable improvement in order to achieve gender equality in the workplace: (1) the "global glass ceiling" (women being less likely than men to make it to top management) (Coleman 2010); (2) the gender pay gap (worldwide, women earn an average of about two-thirds what men earn); and (3) the "sticky floor" (women tend to get stuck in the lowest-paid jobs) (International Labour Organization 2003).

People holding the higher status occupations are more likely to think of themselves as having a career as opposed to just a job, and they are apt to derive more intrinsic satisfaction from their work. They are also less likely to be working in what Kalleberg and his associates (2000) have labeled as "bad jobs"—those with low pay and no health or pension benefits. Nearly one in seven jobs in the United States are in this category, and they are the types of jobs more likely to be held by women than by men, especially if the woman is not a college graduate (McCall 2000). The kind of job you have, and the income you earn from it, will be your key to economic and social independence.

Income

Even after the disastrous economic crisis of 2007–8, the average CEO (chief executive officer) at the 500 biggest companies in the United States made $8 million in 2009, including salary, bonuses, and stock gains (DeCarlo 2010). This works out to about $30,000 per workday, so if we assume a normal workday, this average CEO has already made $7,000 by the time the bagels and cream cheese arrive for his (yes, "his") morning coffee break (only 3 percent of those CEOs are women). The CEO's average daily salary, by the way, was equivalent to more than half the entire annual income for the average American household ($52,029 in 2008). There is a good deal of controversy about whether the average CEO is worth that kind of money, but there is no doubt that income is at least partially a consequence of the way in which we have parlayed a good education into a good job. Occupation may be the primary clue that people have about our social standing, yet our well-being is thought by most people to be a product of our income level.

People are too polite to ask you how much you make, but by knowing your occupation, they will have important clues about your income level. Little has changed since the late 1970s, when Coleman and Rainwater concluded that "money, far more than anything else, is what Americans associate with the idea of social class" (Coleman and Rainwater 1978:29). It is not just having the money; rather it is how you spend it that signals to others where you stand in society. The principal indicators of having money include the kind of house you live in, the way your home is furnished, the car or cars you drive, the clothes you wear, the vacations and recreations (the "toys") you can afford, and even the charities you support.

It is no mystery that there is an uneven distribution of income in virtually every human society, including the United States. Data from the 2008 American Community Survey show that in the United States, the richest 20 percent of families earned 50 percent of the nation's total income (in fact, the top 5 percent brought in 23 percent of the nation's total income), while the poorest 20 percent earned 3 percent. Although this was similar to the pattern several years earlier in 2002 (DeNavas-Walt, Cleveland, and Webster 2003), there has been a deterioration of the income distribution that had prevailed in the late 1960s, when the top 20 percent commanded "only" 43 percent, while the bottom 20 percent shared more than 4 percent of the nation's income.

These changes have produced the "hourglass" economy, which bulges with households at the high and low ends of incomes and is squeezed in the middle. Three broad explanations have been offered for the increasing inequality: (1) public policy changes, such as tax "reforms" that benefit some groups more than others; (2) labor market changes (occurring throughout the world, not just in the United States), such as an increasing mismatch between the demands of jobs and the skills of the labor force, or a polarization of jobs into those that require high skills and those that require few skills, with little in between; and (3) changes in demographic structure, such as the increasing fraction of households headed by females.

In 2008, the average female wage earner, working year-round, full-time, earned only 75 percent of the income garnered by males, as noted above. This was an improvement from 1977, however, when pay for women was 58 percent of that for men. Some of this difference is due to the fact that women are likely to have been in the labor force less time than men and in their current job for a shorter period of time, and that women are more likely than men to delay the completion of their education (which delays their reaching better-paid occupational levels). Yet, these "compositional" differences between males and females are unable to fully account for the gender gap.

Why is there a differential in income by gender? The obvious answer is that there has been a history of discriminating against women in the labor market in terms of what kinds of jobs they are hired for and what pay they receive (Marini and Fan 1997). This is true almost everywhere you go in the world. It has been quipped that "Japan is the land of the rising sun, but only the son rises." In the German Democratic Republic right up to the period before the Berlin Wall collapsed, communism was supposed to guarantee gender equality. Yet women with the same education as men, working at the same jobs as men, were receiving less pay than men (Sörenson and Trappe 1995).

The good news is that in the United States the data clearly seem to suggest that the gap in status between men and women is narrowing, especially for younger people (Bianchi, Robinson, and Milkie 2006), as younger women's wages have been rising more quickly than those for younger men. The U.S. economy, for example, had to swallow a "Big Gulp" to find employment for the baby boomers, since not only were there a lot of boomers, but a larger proportion of females than ever before were looking for jobs. Although the economy did eventually absorb these people, it did so without offering much improvement in earnings over previous generations. This is partly because male wages were bound to suffer somewhat from the competition with women for spots in the labor force (Waite 2000). Economic improvement for households has required that two-earner households become the norm, and this has certainly contributed to the delay in marriage and the rise in divorce.

Family income rose steadily for American families during the 1950s and 1960s, leveled off a bit in the 1970s and early 1980s, and then rose, albeit unevenly, between the mid-1980s and the early 2000s. These patterns can be seen in Figure 10.5. In 1947 (the first year for which such data are available from the Current Population Survey), a white family in the United States had an income equivalent to $25,372 at 2008 prices; that had nearly tripled to $70,070 by 2008. African American families have experienced not just a tripling, but nearly a quadrupling of income since the end of World War II, from the equivalent of $11,724 in 1947 to $39,879 in 2008.

In relative terms, income for black families has grown slightly faster than that for white families. Thus "the ratio" in Figure 10.5 shows that in 1947, African American family income was less than half that of whites (a ratio of 0.46). By 2000, that ratio had gone up to nearly two-thirds (0.64), although there has been some backsliding since then. Yet, despite the rise in family income and a general narrowing of the income gap with whites in relative terms, blacks were actually losing ground to white families in absolute terms. In 1947, the "dollar gap" between black and white families (the difference between the two shaded areas in Figure 10.5) had been $13,648, but by 2008 it had grown to $30,191.

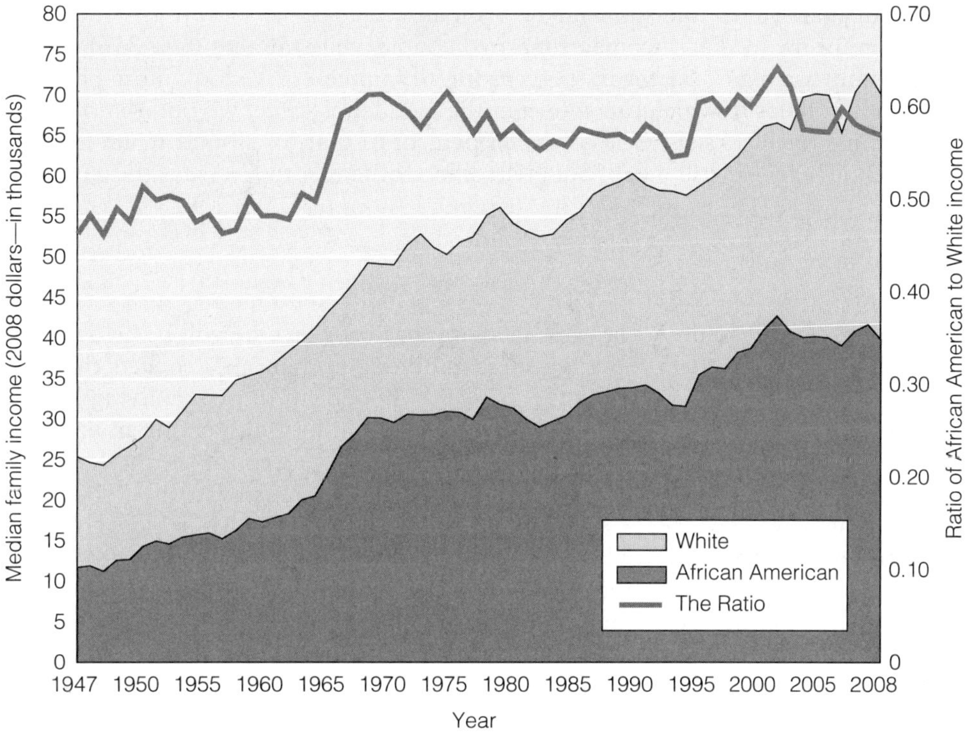

Figure 10.5 The Gap in Family Income of Whites and African Americans Has Widened over Time

Sources: Adapted from data in U.S. Census Bureau, 1992, Current Population Reports P60-180, Table B-7; 2003, P60-221, Table 6; and 2010, "Income" (www.census.gov/hhes/www/income/dinctabs.html, accessed 2010). Data are for family households and are expressed in constant 2008 dollars.

Blacks have thus been in the peculiar position of having their incomes rise faster in percentage terms than whites, but in dollar terms (the actual money available to spend on family members) they are falling further behind. This is one of the paradoxes that results from **structural mobility**—that situation in which an entire society is improving its situation economically, even though some groups may be gaining at a faster rate than others. That is the only time in which one group can improve itself socially or economically without forcing an absolute sacrifice from another group. Indeed, you can see in Figure 10.5 that most of the gains made by blacks relative to whites came during the 1960s and 1970s after the passage of major civil rights legislation during the Johnson administration. Progress has been slow since then.

In comparing family incomes of whites and blacks in the United States, we need to be aware of the differences in family structure that I have already noted. Blacks have slightly fewer earners per family than do whites, which will reduce family income, all other things being equal. Furthermore, a much larger proportion of black families are headed by a female than is true for whites, and since females in the United States tend to earn on average about two-thirds of what men make (see Table 10.4), that too lowers black family income compared to whites. We can control for these factors by looking at specific family groups. For example, in 2008, an African

American married couple family had a median income of $61,509, which was 80 percent of the median income of married couple white families ($77,356), a substantial improvement over the 57 percent for all families. If we look more precisely at married couples in which the wife is in the paid labor force, we find that the median income for blacks ($75,154) was 83 percent of that for similar white families ($90,632). There was still a gap, but controlling for family type lessens the gap.

Poverty

If you have several children, the odds increase that your income will be below average, and if, on top of that, you are a single mother, the chance skyrockets that you will be living below the poverty level. In 2008, 39 percent of people living in U.S. families headed by a woman with no husband present but with children under 18 were living below the poverty level, compared to the 13 percent of the total population that was living below the poverty line (U.S. Census Bureau 2010b).

To imagine the struggle it is to manage successfully in the United States on so little money, it is necessary only to review the definition of the poverty level. The **poverty index** was devised initially in 1964 by Mollie Orshansky of the U.S. Social Security Administration. It was a measure of need based on the finding of a 1955 Department of Agriculture study showing that approximately one-third of a poor family's income was spent on food, and on a 1961 Department of Agriculture estimate of the cost of an "economy food plan"—a plan defined as a minimally nutritious diet for emergency or temporary use (Orshansky 1969). By calculating the cost of an economy food plan and multiplying it by three, the poverty level was born. It has been revised along the way, but the idea has remained the same, and since 1964 it has been raised at the same rate as the consumer price index.

The poverty threshold for a single person under the age of 65 was $11,161 in 2009. This was the equivalent of earning $5.05 an hour if you were a year-round, full-time worker, but keep in mind that the federal minimum wage in that year was $7.25. A single parent with two children under the age of 18 could be earning $17,285 (the equivalent of $7.82 per hour for a year-round, full-time worker) and still be right at the poverty-level threshold. Between 1960 and 1973, the percentage of Americans living below the poverty level was cut in half, from 22 percent to 11 percent, and it remained that low as recently as 2000. Since that time, the poverty level has climbed a bit to 13 percent in 2009, as I noted in the previous paragraph.

Canada has adopted a strategy similar to that of the United States for measuring the lower end of the income scale, but the Canadian government has tried to avoid controversy by not officially defining a poverty threshold. Rather, Statistics Canada produces what are labeled "low income before tax cut-offs." As of 2007, 14 percent of Canadians lived below that cut-off, but 40 percent of people in families headed by a female lone parent of children under the age of 18 were living with low income (Statistics Canada 2009).

On the basis of global comparisons, it might be argued that very few people in North America are poor in absolute terms—it is the relative deprivation that is socially and morally degrading. Organizations such as the International Labour

Table 10.6 A Huge Percentage of People in Developing Countries Live on Less than $2 Per Day

Region	Selected Countries within the Region	Poverty Rate (% below)	
		$1.25/day	$2.00/day
East Asia & the Pacific		17	39
	China	16	36
	Indonesia	29	60
East Europe & Central Asia		4	9
	Russia	2	2
	Georgia	13	30
Latin America & Caribbean		8	17
	Mexico	4	8
	Colombia	16	28
Middle East & North Africa		4	17
	Egypt	5	18
	Yemen	18	47
South Asia		40	74
	India	42	76
	Pakistan	23	60
Sub-Saharan Africa		51	73
	Ghana	30	54
	Congo (Kinshasa)	59	80
Total		20	37

Source: Adapted from data in World Bank, 2010, "Poverty" (http://data.worldbank.org/topic/poverty, accessed 2010). Data are circa 2005.

Organization and the World Bank have adopted an international standard that defines poverty as an income of less than $1.25 per day—an astonishingly small amount of money on which to try to survive. If $1.25 seems like an odd number, it is only because the index started a few years ago at $1 per day and has since been adjusted upward for inflation. Using this definition, data from World Bank produce the estimate that about one in five humans lives in poverty, as shown in Table 10.6. If we stretch the poverty line to $2.00 a day, we find that nearly two in five humans are living at this level of income. The numbers are especially striking for South Asia and sub-Saharan Africa, as you can see in Table 10.6. "We live not as we wish, but as we can" is how a southern Indian peasant described life in a country where 76 percent of the population lives on less than $2.00 per day (quoted by Hockings 1999:213). To put that number in perspective, the poverty line in the United States in 2009 for a single person under the age of 65 was $11,161, which works out to be more than $30 per day—a fortune for a huge percentage of the world's population.

Wealth

Poverty implies not only the lack of adequate income from any and all sources, but also the lack of any other assets from which a person might draw sustenance. As people obtain and build assets, they create wealth. An asset is something that retains value or has the potential to increase in value over time. Every generation produces its share of self-made people like Bill Gates of Microsoft, but his three children will inherit that wealth, rather than have to produce it for themselves. Wealth and its attendant high income are essentially ascribed characteristics for those born into families that own huge homes, large amounts of real estate, and tremendous interests in stocks and bonds or other business assets. For most people, a home is the most important asset they will acquire in a lifetime, but assets can also include personal property such as jewelry or other collectibles, stock in companies or mutual funds, savings accounts in banks, rental property, or ownership in a business venture.

Typically, wealth is measured as net worth—the difference between the value of assets and the money owed on those assets. If your only asset is the house you just bought for $271,000 (the average sale price of a home in the United States in 2009), you are in the process of building wealth, but your net worth may be close to zero because you still may owe as much on the mortgage as the house is worth. There are three basic ways to generate wealth: (1) inherit assets from your parents or other relatives (the easiest way), (2) save part of your income to purchase assets (the hardest way), and (3) borrow money to purchase assets (the riskiest way).

Since most of us do not have fabulously wealthy parents, our ability to inherit enough from our parents (assuming that they have been able to accumulate some wealth) to build on to create our own wealth will, in fact, be determined importantly by two basic demographic characteristics: (1) how many siblings we have; and (2) how long our parents can expect to live. The fewer people with whom we have to share our parents' inheritance, the more there is for us to use ourselves, so those groups with the lowest fertility are likely to have a higher proportion of people who are able to accumulate wealth. The age of our parents, especially relative to our own age, will influence the likelihood that they will die and leave us something while we are still young enough to do something with it. In fact, as life expectancy continues to increase, the older generation has been hanging on to its money, as I discuss in the essay that accompanies this chapter.

The principal sources of data on the wealth of Americans are household surveys, although of course any survey relies on the truthfulness of the responses. One of our best sources of information is the Survey of Income and Program Participation (SIPP) conducted by the U.S. Census Bureau. At this writing the most recent data are those from 2002. These data show that net worth among Americans averages $59,000 per household, but almost one in five households has zero or negative net worth (U.S. Census Bureau 2008).

Marriage is an important ingredient in accumulating wealth (as long as the couple stays married) and thus we find that the highest level of net worth occurs among older (65 and older) married-couple households, whose net worth in 2002 of $202,000 was more than twice the net worth of unmarried male householders ($92,000) or unmarried female householders ($91,000) of that age. Figure 10.6

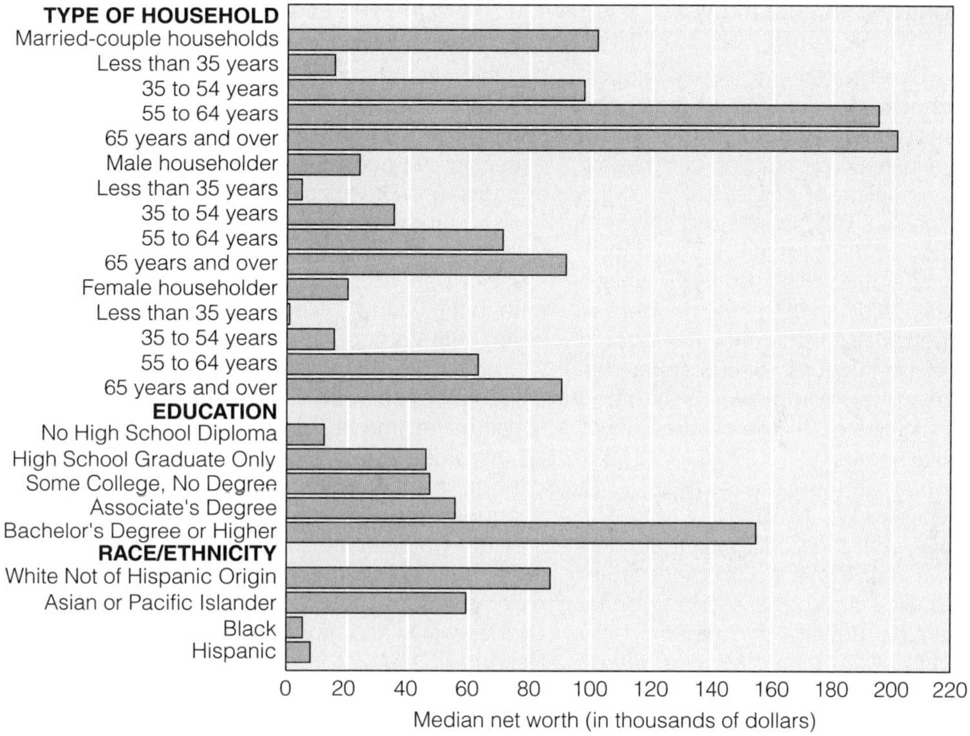

Figure 10.6 Median Net Worth Is Highest for Older Married Couples in the United States
Source: Adapted from data in U.S. Census Bureau, 2008, "Wealth and Asset Ownership, Detailed Tables: 2002." Table 1 (http://www.census.gov/hhes/www/wealth/2002_tables.html).

shows additional detail that should remind you of the value of a college education. Householders with at least a bachelor's degree had assets with a net worth $155,000, which was more than three times the level of householders who had not gone beyond high school.

However, there can be little question that one of the most striking comparisons is by race and ethnicity. Figure 10.6 shows that the average non-Hispanic white household has a net worth of $87,000, compared to $8,000 for Hispanics and only $5,400 for blacks. Some of this difference is due to differences in the age structure, especially among Hispanics who are relatively young, and some is due to differences in marital status, especially among blacks; but much of it is due to the greater difficulty that racial and ethnic minority household members have in generating enough income for long enough to be able to acquire higher levels of wealth.

Race and Ethnicity

The assimilation model of immigration, which I discussed in Chapter 7, assumes that a nation is a melting pot where everyone eventually shares cultural values and norms, and ultimately every person becomes pretty much like everyone else. This is

SHOW ME THE MONEY: HOUSEHOLD DIVERSITY AND WEALTH AMONG THE ELDERLY

In the past, and still today in many less developed countries, the higher status of the elderly has been tied partly to the fact that as old age approached, they were situated in their own housing unit. Even if they lived with their children, it was likely that the children (typically a son with his wife and children) were actually living in the parental home, rather than the other way around (Kertzer 1995; United Nations Population Division 2005). The concept of filial piety, of respect for one's parents, has been a traditional value in most cultures, encouraging children to take care of their parents when the need arises, and this is facilitated by the children never leaving the parental home.

Of course, in high-mortality societies, the probability that parents would survive to old age (and the probability that their children would survive to help them) was low enough so that relatively few people ever had to make good on that concept. For example, under a constant mortality regime of 40 years of life expectancy, a person aged 30 has less than one chance in four of having both parents still alive, and there is about one chance in two that one parent will be still alive. A high level of mortality increases the odds that a younger person will be able to inherit the family farm or business, or will be able to move into some other position in society being vacated by the relatively early deaths of other people. However, at a life expectancy of 70 years, nearly two out of every three adults aged 30 can expect to have both parents still alive, and nearly eight in 10 people aged 30 can expect to have at least one parent still alive.

In the modern world, society after society has bemoaned the fact that the multigenerational family has been a victim of "the movement toward smaller families, the expansion of the female labor market, the geographic mobility of villagers, and the tendency of the young toward more individualistic life styles" (Sung 1995:240). That particular description was applied to South Korea, but it is echoed in many other places. Older people are no longer assured that they will live out their days nestled in the bosom of their family. To be sure, not all older people necessarily want to live with their children, especially if they are forced to be dependent on the children. A worldwide phenomenon has been emerging of older people wanting "intimacy at a distance." In Malaysia, for example, survey results have shown that the more economically advantaged older people are, the less likely they are to live with adult children. Those who co-reside with children do so out of necessity, not necessarily because they prefer that arrangement (DaVanzo and Chan 1994).

In Europe and North America it is reasonable to say that diversity in living arrangements is as much a part of the lives of older people as it is among the young. Living arrangements among the elderly are compounded by patterns of marriage, widowhood, divorce, cohabitation, and remarriage in combination with differences in mortality between males and females. The unbalanced sex ratio at older ages in most societies signals a change in marital status, which in turn means a change in living arrangements for many people as they grow older. Males, of course, are less likely to experience a change in marital status as they grow older, because they are more likely to be outlived by their wives and more likely than older women to remarry if they are the surviving spouse. The United Nations Population Division has assembled data from all over the globe to summarize the living arrangements of the older population (defined by them as people 60 and older), so we are able to compare different regions of the world in this regard. In Asia and Africa, older people are most likely to be living with a spouse or other family member, whereas those in Latin America are in between the Asian and North American extremes (United Nations Population Division 2005). Culture and demography almost certainly interact to create these regional patterns.

The cultural part is obvious in that some societies place a greater emphasis on respect for the elderly than do others. The demographic part of this is that the forces driving the living arrangements for the older population are the same ones that have put all of the elements of the demographic transition into motion—people living longer with fewer children, located in urban areas, with higher incomes than at any previous time in history. This latter element is a key one, because throughout human history it was economically most advantageous for family members to live together as protection against demographic and economic uncertainty. As incomes have risen throughout the world, but especially in the richer nations, the economic and demographic necessity of co-residence drops away and we are left only with the cultural preferences.

Remember that for men, in particular, being old and living with your children was likely to mean that you were the one who owned the home and economic necessity encouraged your children to be with you. The longer a person lives, the greater the chance to acquire whatever resources might exist to help the family economy. So, an older person was likely to be relatively rare but also relatively rich (with an emphasis on "relatively," rather than on "rich"). For women the situation has tended to be different because they historically have not had automatic rights of inheritance of their husband's property, and so when their spouse dies they may become dependent on their children. They may live in exactly the same house with the same children, but now the eldest son in the house will be householder, not his mother.

The decline in mortality tends to throw a monkey wrench into these kinds of arrangements. Increasing survivability of people to old age increases the likelihood that a young or middle-aged adult will have surviving parents, and that these parents will be heading up the family household (Ruggles and Heggeness 2008). This pattern essentially clogs up familial and societal mobility, because it means that family assets are not turned over as rapidly as would otherwise be the case. It also means, of course, that enough people are living long enough to accumulate a substantial portion of any society's resources.

The upshot of all this is that the older households in the United States are those in which net worth now tends to be the greatest. More specifically, we can find out who controls the United States by looking at the Forbes Magazine list of the 400 richest Americans to see what their ages are. The accompanying figure shows the data for the year 2009; it is very clear that the elderly are far more likely to be very wealthy than are younger people. Of the wealthiest 400, you can see that 222, or 56 percent, were age 65 or older, and they commanded 56 percent of the wealth among the

(continued)

The 400 Wealthiest People in the United States Are Disproportionately Older

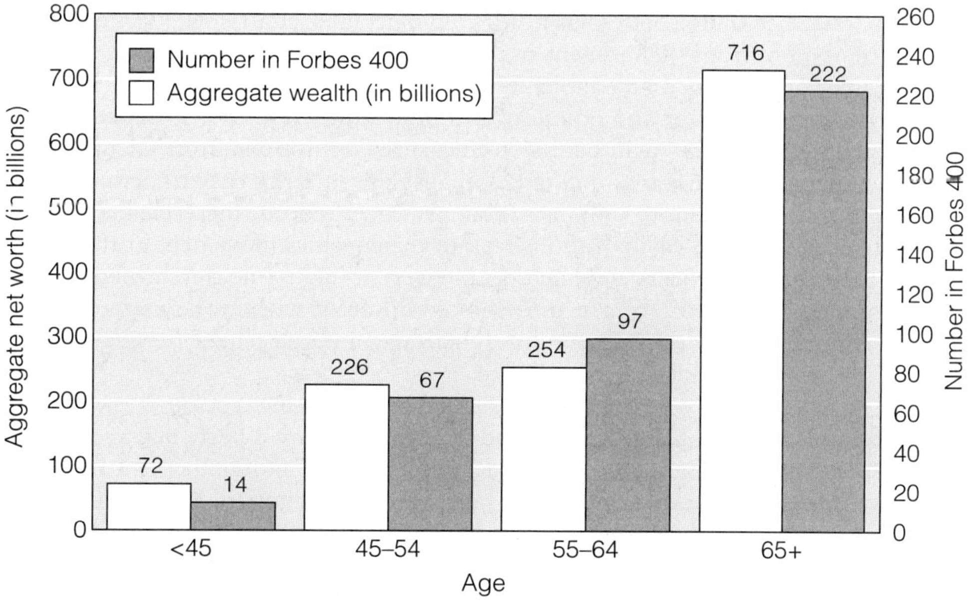

Source: Adapted from data in Forbes.com, "The 400 Richest Americans 2009," (http://www.forbes.com/lists/2009/54/rich-list-09_The-400-Richest-Americans_Rank.html, accessed 2010)

SHOW ME THE MONEY: HOUSEHOLD DIVERSITY AND WEALTH AMONG THE ELDERLY (CONTINUED)

400 richest Americans, despite the fact that the elderly comprise only 13 percent of the population, as I discussed in Chapter 8.

The wealthy are disproportionately old, and among the wealthy, it is the oldest members who tend to have the greatest wealth. This would be more clear in the accompanying figure were it not for Bill Gates, who is the world's richest person, but was only 53 in 2009. His net worth is $50 billion, and the only American close to him is his good friend Warren Buffet (net worth of $40 billion), who was 79 in that year. The average net worth among this wealthiest 65-and-older group is $3.2 billion. If we focus on the ten wealthiest persons in 2009, six of the ten are 65 or older, and besides Bill Gates the other three people who are under 65 are all members of the Walton family, which founded Wal-Mart. The cohort of people now aged 65 and older in the United States is better off than any that came before, and as they die, there will be a huge intergenerational transfer of wealth, probably the largest that the world has ever seen (Herman 1999). However, because people are living longer, the children who inherit that wealth will probably be fairly old themselves when they come into their money, so the wealth will stay among the elderly,

sometimes referred to as the "North American Model" of race and ethnic relations, which is aimed at combating racial discrimination and ethnic inequality (Haug 2000). The multicultural model, on the other hand, assumes a salad bowl where everybody stays different but gets along just fine. European nations, with the notable exception of France, have tended to prefer this approach, and it has actually been adopted as the main U.S. model in the past two decades, encouraged by a positive governmental emphasis on diversity. The assimilation model assumes that distinctions of race and ethnicity will eventually be wiped out by intermarriage, whereas the multicultural model assumes not only that things won't work like that, but that people prefer to remain separate. The United States has historically fluctuated somewhere between those two extremes, but from the moment of the country's creation more than 200 years ago, the issue of race was on the table. It has been there ever since.

Recognizing that race and ethnicity are important issues in a society does not necessarily mean that they will be easy to measure (see, for example, Glenn 2009). They are not easy to measure, of course, because they are not easy to define and so measurement becomes more of an art than a science. Indeed, the "science" part is scary because it can too easily lead us back to the eugenics movement at the beginning of the twentieth century in which people were trying to measure genetic differences among people who, in fact, only looked different without having any other distinguishing characteristics. Our cultural heritage, not our genetic heritage, distinguishes us, and that is not easy to measure.

Race and ethnicity represent human differences with some type of physical manifestation that allows people to identify and be identified with a particular group. The characteristics may be physical in nature such as skin pigmentation, hair texture, shape of the eyes or nose (these would normally fall under the category of **race**), or they may be more behavioral, such as language, or identification with a particular ancestry and geographic place (these would normally fall under the category of **ethnicity**).

The history of racism in the world suggests that anything that distinguishes you can, and probably will, be used against you. Therefore, to be a member of a subordinate (not in political control) racial, ethnic, or religious group in any society is to be at jeopardy of impaired life chances. African Americans, Hispanics, Asians, and complicating life along the way as people decide when and how to share the wealth (Angel 2007).

Rising life expectancy in the absence of substantial wealth can be a different story, of course, because the younger generation may build up some resentment to older people. An anecdotal, but perhaps significant, bit of evidence about the status of the elderly in developing countries emerged in the People's Republic of China in 1997 when the government passed a law protecting the rights and interests of the elderly. In a nation that made famous the concept of filial piety, a law now exists that forbids discrimination against the aged by "insulting, mistreating, or forsaking them," and the law calls for appropriate measures to be taken against anyone committing such abuse (Global Aging Report 1997). The result was an explosion of lawsuits by parents against their children (Chang 2000).

Discussion Questions: (1) Do you think that respect for older people has eroded in last several decades, despite the clear fact that much of the wealth is held by older people? Defend your answer; **(2)** What are the underlying demographic reasons for the fact that 56 percent of the wealthiest people in America are 65 and older even though only 13 percent of the population is 65 and older?

American Indians in the United States are well aware of this, as are indigenous people in Mexico, Tamils in Sri Lanka, Muslims in Israel or India, Indians in Malaysia, and virtually any foreigner in Japan or China.

Race and Ethnicity in the United States In the 2008 American Community Survey, 98 percent of the population indicated that they belonged to only one racial category. Those who chose white, and indicated furthermore that they were not Hispanic, account for 66 percent of the population. This was, of course, a rather dramatic change from fifty years prior to that, when 89 percent of the population was white—when white was not yet thought of as an ethnic category (Perry 2001). By the twenty-first century, the racial and ethnic changes have been so substantial that Perez and Hirschman (2009) refer to the phenomenon of "emerging American identities."

I mentioned in Chapter 4 that Census 2000 permitted people for the first time ever to choose more than one racial category. The underlying purpose was to be able to capture more accurate information about multiracial individuals. If you accept the assimilation theory, then you would expect an increasing fraction of the population to identify with more than one racial/ethnic group, whereas the multicultural perspective would not expect this to be happening. In the United States, the major racial categories are defined as "white," "Black or African American," "Native American or Alaska Native," "Asian," and "Native Hawaiian and other Pacific Islander." You will also see tables from the census that include a number of people in the "some other race" category, but almost all of them turn out to be Hispanic, which represents the principal ethnic (as opposed to race) category asked about in the census. A person of "Hispanic or Latino" origin is defined as one who is "of Cuban, Mexican, Puerto Rican, South or Central American, or other Spanish culture or origin regardless of race." The relatively "indeterminate" concept of Hispanic (Idler 2007) is often confusing to those arriving in the United States from those origin countries, because it is not used anywhere outside of the United States. Immigrants from Nicaragua, for example, will find themselves identified officially as Hispanic, while having a high probability of being thought of unofficially as Mexican.

The majority of Hispanics in the United States are indeed from Mexico, and despite the discrimination that they have faced over time, they are less discriminated against than blacks. "Mexican Americans intermarry much more than do blacks, live in less segregated areas, and face less labor market discrimination. . . . In this sense, racial boundaries for Mexican Americans are clearly less rigid than for African Americans, despite even more schooling" (Telles and Ortiz 2008:264).

In the United States, blacks were the largest minority group for all of the nation's history—until recently. By 2005 the Hispanic or Latino population (15 percent of the population) had passed the black population (13 percent of the population) in size, as I mentioned in Chapter 2. No longer being the numerically largest minority group in the country does not necessarily make life easier. Being of African origin in the United States is associated with higher probabilities of death, lower levels of education, lower levels of occupational status, lower incomes, and higher levels of marital disruption than for the non-Hispanic white population. Zuberi (2001) has argued that the different life chances of whites and blacks in American society are due to **racial stratification**, which he defines as a socially constructed system that characterizes one or more groups as being distinctly different. Your membership in a group defined as different from the others then creates, in essence, a different social world for you than for those who are in other groups, and this affects your behavior and your life chances in society, because there is no genuine societal expectation that you will be assimilated into the rest of the society. "The ability of a group to be assimilated depends on whether it is considered an ethnic or racial group. . . . For example, immigrants from Nigeria and Ghana assimilate into the African American race, and immigrants from Sweden and Ireland assimilate into the European American race" (McDaniel 1996:139).

For better or worse, official statistics in the United States make extensive use of the racial and ethnic categories I have just discussed, but on an everyday basis, people are also conscious of ethnicity in a broader context, as measured by the question about ancestry that has appeared in the last several U.S. censuses and is incorporated into the American Community Survey. Overall, the most-often-recorded ancestry in the 2008 American Community Survey was German (17 percent of the U.S. population—51 million people). Next most often listed was Irish (12 percent, or 36 million people), which is pretty remarkable when you consider that there are fewer than 5 million people living in Ireland, and not even all of them are Irish! English, American, and Italian round out the top five ancestries.

Ethnicity in Canada and Mexico The United States does not have a corner on the racial and ethnic minority market, nor are demographic differences by race and ethnicity peculiar to the United States (see, for example, Reitz 2005). As befits a multiracial, multiethnic, officially bilingual society, Canada has several ways to measure diversity. What would be called "race" in the United States is labeled "visible minority" in Canada. The visible minority accounted for 16 percent of Canada's population in the 2006 census, up from 11 percent in 1996. The most populous group was South Asians (largely from India), followed closely by Chinese and then African-origin blacks (albeit coming largely from the Caribbean). Ethnicity is essentially a geographic concept, based on a place with which you identify, similar to the concept of "ancestry" as measured by the U.S. Census. The single biggest ethnic group in Canada is, guess what—Canadian. However, the largest non-Canadian origin identified was the British Isles. Another identifier in Canada is whether or not you are a member of the aboriginal population, which accounts for just less than 4 percent of the country's total population and coincides with the ethnic identification of North American Indian. Language is the other major identifier in Canadian society, with English being listed most often as the language spoken at home (66 percent of the population), followed by French (21 percent, with 91 percent of French-speakers living in the province of Québec).

Language is a divisive-enough issue in Canada that in the 1990s it led the francophone (French-speaking) population in the eastern edge of the country (Québec) to attempt to secede from the anglophone (English-speaking) remainder of the country. Demographics played a role in defeating the referendum on separation held in 1995, however, because the traditionally Catholic francophone population now has very low levels of fertility—probably the lowest anywhere in North America. French Canadians are not replacing themselves, and non-francophones (especially recent immigrants) generally did not support separation, leading Canadian demographers correctly to predict that separation would not be approved by the voters (Kaplan 1994; Samuel 1994). Still, the controversy over language in Canada underscores the power of society to turn any population characteristic into a sign of difference, from which prejudice and discrimination often follow.

Language is also an issue in Mexico, where the lowest stratum of society tends to be occupied by those who speak an indigenous language (linguistically related to Aztec and Mayan languages), rather than Spanish. According to the 2005 census, 7 percent of Mexicans speak an indigenous language, but in the Yucatán, the percentage is 38 percent; in Oaxaca it is 37 percent; and in Chiapas, where native-speaking people have been challenging the authority of the central government since the 1990s, it is 27 percent. These are also the Mexican states where people are poorest and fertility is highest. Language minorities thus represent both the geographic and demographic extremes in North America, from francophone Québec in the northeast, with very low fertility, to Mayan-language Chiapas in the south, with very high fertility.

Ethnicity in Other Countries Ethnicity in sub-Saharan countries refers largely to membership in groups that have different geographic, and sometimes religious, histories in a region. The worst consequence of ethnic differences is violence among groups, such as between the Tutsi and Hutu in Rwanda and Burundi. More commonly, different groups reside peacefully within the same city, such as in Accra, the capital of Ghana, where no ethnic group has a majority citywide, but where members of the same ethnic groups have a tendency to cluster geographically near each other in neighborhoods (Weeks et al. 2006). The Akan (whose main subgroup is the Ashanti) represent the single largest group and are generally the politically and economically dominant group in the city. The Ga, who were the original settlers of the city in the late seventeenth century, occupy the older parts of the city, where child mortality rates tend to be the highest:

> . . . there is an overall modest level of residential segregation by ethnic group in Accra, but most notable are the spatial concentrations of the Ga along the coastal area, and the Akan in the western part of the city. This pattern seems not coincidentally to be associated with child mortality because the areas with the lowest child mortality are

> neighborhoods dominated by the Akan, whereas areas with the highest child mortality are contiguous to, if not exactly the same as, neighborhoods dominated demographically by the Ga. A further nuance on the analysis was the finding that the one area with a majority Muslim population is also part of the cluster of high child mortality neighborhoods. This is consistent with the findings that being Ga and/or being non-Christian put women at increased risk of losing a child (Weeks et al. 2006:544).

Goldscheider (1996, 1999) has examined the demographics of ethnic pluralism in Israel and found that the Muslim Arab population in that country has been growing at twice the rate of the Jewish population. In 1950, Muslims represented 8 percent of the total population, but that percentage has grown consistently, and in 2005, 16 percent of Israel's population was Muslim and nearly one in four residents of Israel was non-Jewish (Israel Central Bureau of Statistics 2010). Like minority group members in the United States, the Muslim minority in Israel is less educated, holds lower status jobs on average, and has a lower life expectancy and higher fertility levels than does the Jewish majority. Fertility has declined significantly among Arabs in Israel since 1969, when the Muslim population recorded a total fertility rate in excess of nine children, but since Jewish fertility has also declined, the gap in fertility levels remains. In 2004, the total fertility rate for the Jewish population was 2.7 children per woman, compared with 4.0 for the Muslim population. However, high fertility in Israel is not simply a function of being Arab, because the Christian minority, which is predominantly Arab, has the lowest total fertility rate (2.1) of any group in Israel. The contrasts among Muslims, Jews, and Christians take us next into the realm of religion.

Religion

Virtually everyone is born into some kind of religious context, which is why I have likened religion to an ascribed characteristic, closely affiliated with ethnicity. Yet people can willingly change their religious preference during their lifetime, so it is akin to an achieved status. Despite the appearance of choice, however, most people do not alter religious affiliation, so it is a nearly permanent feature of their social world. People may become more or less religious within their particular group, but they are unlikely to change the major affiliation. Like race and ethnicity, religion sets people apart from one another and has historically been a common source of intergroup conflict throughout the world. Because it is an often-discussed sociodemographic characteristic, religion has regularly come under the demographer's microscope, with particular attention being paid to its potential influence on fertility, which is bound up with factors including gender equity and family and household structure.

America's history of **religious pluralism**, in which a wide variety of religious preferences have existed side-by-side, perhaps sensitized American demographers to the role of religion in influencing people's lives. A good deal of attention was focused over the years on the comparison between Protestants and Catholics. Until the late twentieth century, Catholics routinely had more children than Protestants in the United States, and internationally it has been true that predominantly Protestant areas (such as the United States and northern Europe) experienced low fertility sooner than did predominantly Catholic areas (such as southern and eastern

Europe). However, analyses of data from the U.S. National Survey of Family Growth revealed that in the mid-1960s, as the baby boom was ending, it was particularly noticeable that Catholics were increasing their use of modern contraception, even as the papal encyclical was trying to push them in the opposite direction (Westoff and Westoff 1971). This turned into a genuine revolution in birth control practices of U.S. Roman Catholics (Westoff and Bumpass 1973), which shortly thereafter led to the end of 'Catholic' fertility in the United States (Westoff and Jones 1979).

In the middle of the twentieth century, no one could have imagined that Catholic fertility would ever drop to the level of non-Catholics in the United States, much less dip below those levels. Indeed, fertility is now lowest in Europe precisely in the most Catholic countries of Spain and Italy, as I have already discussed, and it is even below replacement level in predominantly Catholic Mexico City (INEGI 2010), as I have noted. Data from the 2002 National Survey of Family Growth suggest that the differences in fertility rates among women of different religious background in the United States are now minuscule, although those who say they grew up as fundamentalist Protestants have slightly larger families than other groups (Chandra et al. 2005).

Does this mean that religion is less important demographically than it used to be? Obviously, the relationship between religion and demographic behavior is not a simple one, but there are two major themes that run through the literature: (1) religion plays its most important role in the middle stage of the demographic transition; and (2) religiosity (how intensely you practice your religion) may be more important than religious belief.

Looking first at differences in religion, we find a classic study by Joseph Chamie (1981) of differentials in Lebanese fertility, in which he concluded that a major effect of religion may be to retard the adoption of more modern, lower-fertility attitudes during the transitional phase of the demographic revolution. Adherents to religious beliefs that have been traditionally associated with high fertility will be slower to give ground than will people whose religious beliefs are more flexible with respect to fertility. In the United States, Jews have generally had lower fertility levels than the rest of the population. Trends in Jewish fertility have followed the American pattern (a decline in the Depression, a rise with the baby boom, a drop with the baby bust), but at a consistently lower level. "Widespread secularization processes, upward social mobility, a value system emphasizing individual achievement, and awareness of minority status have all been indicated as factors that are both typical of American Jews and conducive to low fertility" (DellaPergola 1980:261). Indeed, it is not just Jews in America whose fertility has been low for a long time. DellaPergola (1980) points out that Jewish communities in central and western Europe have also been characterized by low fertility since as early as the second half of the nineteenth century, largely because contraception is readily accepted in the Jewish normative system (at least among non-Orthodox Jews). Leasure (1982) also found that, in the United States, fertility declined earliest in those areas dominated by more secularized religious groups. People who are more traditional in their religious beliefs tend to be less educated and have less income, and are thus more prone to higher fertility.

In the twenty-first century, Islam has emerged as the religion that is characterized by above-average levels of fertility. There are now an estimated 1.6 billion Muslims in the world, representing nearly one in four people globally, and nations that are growing in population at rates above the world average are disproportionately those in which a majority of the population is Muslim: the average rate of growth among Muslim-majority countries is 2 percent per year, double that of the non-Muslim-majority countries (1 percent per year). However, there is considerable variability in fertility among the Muslim-majority countries, ranging from Iran at below replacement level (1.7 based on the 2006 census) to Niger at nearly 7 children per woman, according to the 2006 Demographic and Health Survey.

Will Muslims follow the pattern of Catholics and quickly lower fertility levels to replacement level or below? If secularization is a key to low fertility, then it is not religion *per se* that matters, but how strongly one holds any given set of religious beliefs, which we call **religiosity**. Regardless of the religion to which one adheres, research has consistently shown that higher levels of religiosity are associated with higher fertility, either directly by intention or indirectly through the non-use of methods to prevent pregnancy (Bertrand and Bogue 1977; Philipov and Berghammer 2007; Westoff and Frejka 2007; Zhang 2008).

In terms of doctrine, Islam may not be any more **pronatalist** (expressing an attitude that favors high fertility) than other religions (McQuillan 2004), but the way in which Islam structures societies may promote a type of religiosity that lowers status for women relative to men in ways that will indirectly promote pronatalism. At the same time, the extent to which communities are structured in this way may well be regionally variable, reflecting underlying cultural attributes shared by all populations in a region, whether Muslim or not. Thus, Muslims in South Asia and sub-Saharan Africa tend to have higher fertility than Muslims in North Africa or Europe, at least partly because fertility levels are higher for everyone in South Asia and sub-Saharan Africa (Westoff and Weeks 2010).

Westoff and Frejka (2007) have shown that even in Europe fertility is positively associated with religiosity; yet among the most religious, Muslim fertility is still higher, suggesting that there might be an interaction between religion and religiosity. Their analysis leads to the conclusion that in general the strength of one's religious beliefs is predictive of fertility because the greater the level of religiousness, the more traditional are family values and the more oppressed are women, and it is these factors that are especially influential in determining family size (Inglehart and Norris 2003; Norris and Inglehart 2004). This may be particularly important among Muslims because "Islam is not merely a religion of worship, but is also a pervasive social system" (Rashad and Eltigani 2005: 186). Similarly, Goldscheider (2006), in discussing high fertility among Muslims in Israel, argues that "values that emphasize the subordinate role of women within households and gender hierarchies appear to be critical in sustaining high fertility levels" (46).

The Intersection of Changing Life Chances and the Family and Household Transition

At the beginning of this chapter, I noted that the family is usually thought of as both a kinship and an economic unit. The kinship part provides its members with social capital (the connection to networks of people who may be in a position to help you out in life), and the economic part provides its members with human capital (access to resources such as education). These familial resources play a role in each person's life and throughout each person's life, but they are especially crucial when you are a child. Thus, societies tend to pay particular attention to the type of household in which children are growing up, no matter how diverse the household structure may be in society as a whole. Are children being raised in a household environment that maximizes their opportunities to acquire human and social capital, and thus to increase the odds of success in the next generation? This is how family and household structures intersect with life chances.

Westoff (1978) has suggested that the institutions of marriage and the family were showing signs of change back in the 1970s because "the economic transformation of society has been accomplished by a decline in traditional and religious authority, the diffusion of an ethos of rationality and individualism, the universal education of both sexes, the increasing equality of women, the increasing survival of children and the emergence of a consumer-oriented culture that is increasingly aimed at maximizing personal gratification" (p. 53). It has been argued that many of these cultural changes have followed, rather than preceded, the changes in household structure. They may not have initiated the trends, but they have reinforced the transformations and ensured their spread within each country and from one country to another.

Global changes are, however, occurring unevenly. In predominantly Muslim nations, as well as in South Asia, the gender gap between men and women remains especially wide (Westley 2002; Inglehart and Norris 2003). Worldwide economic changes have emphasized the value of nondomestic labor, and this has marginalized the economic contribution that women make to the family economy. It has also aggravated the problems associated with cultural practices such as the dowry that Indian families are expected to pay to their new in-laws on the marriage of each daughter. Because in India girls traditionally do not receive an inheritance on the death of their parents, the dowry is in essence an up-front payment of a potential inheritance. However, from a practical point of view, it means that any investment in a girl will accrue to her husband's family, so parents are not necessarily motivated to do much for daughters. Indeed, it has been suggested that child labor is used in India as a way for girls to defray the costs of the dowry. These kinds of "cultural entrapments embroidered by female submissiveness" (Mhloyi 1994) can only be resolved by political changes such as the law already in place in the Indian state of Maharashtra that grants women the same rights of inheritance as men, and also reserves up to 30 percent of government jobs for women.

The cultural model prevalent for the past few decades in the richer nations has been that self-fulfillment and individual autonomy are the most important values in life and serve to justify scrapping a marriage. If women are approaching the level of economic independence previously reserved for men, perhaps the value of marriage has been permanently eroded, and marriage will (or has) become only one option among many from which people may reasonably choose. One of the complaints about marriage often registered by women is that the move toward gender equality in the division of labor in the formal marketplace has not necessarily been translated into equity in the division of labor within the household. Women in the Western world are able to operate in society independently of a husband or other male patriarch or protector, but they may not have the same ability to have an equal relationship at home with a husband (Fuwa 2004). Data from the National Survey of Families and Households show that married couples are the least egalitarian of all households with respect to the division of domestic chores. Marriage is the household setting in which women do the greatest amount of domestic work (regardless of their own labor force status), while men do the least (Shelton 2000).

So, does marriage matter? A substantial body of evidence suggests that marriage matters very much even in a rich modern society—it enhances household income and wealth and promotes the well-being of spouses and children, while adding to sexual gratification in the bargain. Waite and Gallagher (2000) have reviewed the literature and analyzed numerous data sets in order to draw the following conclusions about the benefits of marriage: (1) married couples have higher household income than the unmarried; (2) married couples save more of their income than the unmarried; and therefore (3) married couples have more wealth than the unmarried; (4) married men and women live longer than the unmarried, and engage in fewer high-risk behaviors; (5) children in a married-couple family are better off financially than those in a one-parent family; (6) children in a married-couple family are less likely to drop out of school, less likely to have a teenage pregnancy, and less likely to be "idle" (out of both school and work) as a young adult than children in a one-parent family; and (7) married couples have sex more often and derive greater satisfaction from it than the unmarried do.

The social impact of marriage derives from these personal benefits. Perhaps most compelling is the fact that the family remains the primary social unit in which society is reproduced—in which children are taught the rights and reciprocal obligations of membership in human society. The evidence seems to suggest that this is accomplished most efficiently in a household/family unit that includes both parents of the children in question. The evidence is persuasive that children derive few, if any, positive benefits from growing up without a father and, indeed, tend to suffer both short- and long-term ill effects if fatherless (Furstenberg and Cherlin 1991; McLanahan and Sandefur 1994; Cherlin 2005; Wagmiller et al. 2006). The same is probably true for motherless families, although we have fewer studies of such family settings. "The data clearly indicate that a healthy two-parent family optimizes both the economic well-being and the physical and mental health of children" (Angel and Angel 1993:199).

It appears that the diversification of households in the richer countries has leveled off, at the same time that family and household change is well under way in developing nations (Bongaarts 2001). Smaller families and longer lives lived out in predominantly urban areas seem inevitably to lead to diversification in the household and family structure of a society. There is little controversy in that proposition. The controversy arises largely when children are involved, because some family situations and household structures seem more likely to offer children the social and human capital resources most societies believe to be important for children as they grow up. These were some of the uncharted waters that more developed countries wandered into in the course of the demographic transition, and family demographers have been working hard to map the territory for you.

Summary and Conclusion

The past few decades have witnessed a fundamental shift in household structure in the United States and other richer nations, and these changes are beginning to evolve all over the world as the family and household transition accompanies the health and mortality, fertility, migration, urban, and age transitions. Married-couple households with children have become less common, being replaced by a combination of married couples without children, cohabiting couples with and without children, lone parents with children, people living alone, people living with nonfamily members, and just about anything else that you can think of. This greater diversity in household structure is a direct result of the trends in marriage and divorce, which are themselves influenced by trends in mortality and fertility and urban living. Marriage has been increasingly delayed (although most people do eventually marry), but people are leaving the parental nest to live independently by themselves, with friends, or in a cohabiting relationship prior to marriage, a pattern greatly facilitated by access to effective methods of contraception. Once married, there is an increased tendency to dissolve the marriage. Some of this is due to the fact that spouses are far less likely to die than in earlier times, and some is due to the fact that divorce laws have accommodated the changing relationships between men and women. Accompanying these trends has been an increase in the proportion of children born outside of marriage, contributing to the increased percentage of children who are living with only one parent.

Less directly, but no less importantly, the transformation of family and household structure has been a result of changing population characteristics, especially the improvement in women's life chances. Women have become less dependent on men as they have begun to live longer and spend more of their lives without children in an urban environment, where there are alternatives to childbearing and family life. Throughout the world, women are closing the education gap between themselves and men, entering the paid labor force, and moving up the occupational ladder.

These new opportunities to be more fully engaged in all aspects of social, economic, and political life have been simultaneously the cause and consequence of declining fertility and improved life expectancy. They have enabled women to delay marriage while becoming educated and establishing a career, choose marriage or not (most do), choose children or not (most choose at least one), and, if married, to choose to stay married (only about half do). Therein lie the principal explanations for the increased diversity of families and households.

Not all people have equal access to societal resources such as advanced education, a well-paying job, and other assets with which to build wealth. In the United States, blacks, Hispanics, and American Indians are less likely than others to be highly educated, and this without doubt contributes to their relative social and economic disadvantage in American society, although racial prejudice and discrimination continue to play a role. On the other hand, Asians tend to have higher levels of education than other groups, which helps account for their higher levels of income (and higher life expectancies, as well). In most countries of the world we find one or more groups who, for reasons of discrimination beyond their control, are disadvantaged compared to the dominant group.

The impact of the trends toward greater family and household diversity falls disproportionately on children. Growing up in a household that is not a two-parent family means lower household income, increased odds of health and social problems in childhood and young adulthood, and it generally increases the risk that your their life chances may be limited. However, another group also bears the brunt of dissolved marriages. Today's divorced or otherwise not married women could become the biggest group of elderly poor in the future. This is a trend we will have to watch over time, but it will be easier to track than in previous generations because most households with older people in industrialized nations are now in urban areas, where they may be more visible than the elderly poor in rural areas of less developed nations.

Another trend that we are watching with great trepidation is the overall degradation of our environment. As we try to improve the lives of a larger and increasingly diverse population in the world, our efforts have created numerous negative side effects and we take a look at these issues in the next chapter.

Main Points

1. Married-couple households with children are declining as a fraction of all households, being replaced by a variety of other family and nonfamily household types.
2. The direct causes of these changes in household composition are a delay in marriage, an increase in cohabitation and nonmarital births, a rise in the propensity to divorce, and, to a lesser extent, widowhood in the older population.
3. The underlying indirect causes of these changes are the several other transitions associated with the overall demographic transition, including declining mortality, declining fertility, migration to urban areas, and the underlying age structure changes brought about over time by demographic change.
4. The transformation of families and households has accompanied improved life chances for women, including higher levels of education, labor force participation, occupation, and income.
5. Average educational attainment has increased substantially over time in most countries, and, especially in industrialized nations, women appear now to have closed the gender gap in education.
6. In the United States during World War II, a combination of demand for labor and too few traditional labor force entrants created an opening for married women to move into jobs previously denied them, and since 1940, the rates of labor force participation have risen for women, especially married women, while declining for men.
7. Over time in the United States, poverty has declined while at the same time Americans of almost all statuses have become wealthier in real absolute terms, but there have been only minor changes in the relative status of most groups.

8. Race may be just "a pigment of your imagination," but blacks, in particular, tend to be disadvantaged compared to whites in American society.
9. The diversity of households seems to have plateaued in richer nations but is on the rise in most of the rest of the world.
10. Family demographers can prove that the average person in Miami, Florida, is born Cuban and dies Jewish.

Questions for Review

1. What is the difference between a kinship unit and a consumption unit, and why is the difference important to an understanding of the family and household transition?
2. Discuss the ways in which each of the other components of the demographic transition lead up to and help explain the family and household transition.
3. How do the differences in or changes in life chances for an individual affect the proximate determinants of his or her own family and household living arrangement? Pick one demographic characteristic such as education and discuss how different levels of that characteristic could affect the living arrangement choices that a person might make.
4. Why do you think that race and ethnicity affect life chances in so many different societies?
5. What is/are the most important reason(s) why we should care about the increasing diversity in family and household structure?

Suggested Readings

1. Martha Shirk, Neil G. Bennett, and J. Lawrence Aber, 1999, *Lives on the Line: American Families and the Struggle to Make Ends Meet* (Boulder, CO: Westview Press).

   The diversification of American families has created new dilemmas in how to deal with the emotional and financial costs of raising children. This book offers data and case studies to illustrate the complexities of the problem.
2. Daniel T. Lichter and Martha L. Crowley, 2002, "Poverty in America: Beyond Welfare Reform," *Population Bulletin* 57(2).

   Although poverty levels have dropped in the United States over the past few decades, a disproportionate number of children are growing up in poverty. This bulletin examines this and other family-related issues in the context of welfare reform legislation.
3. Harriet B. Presser and Gita Sen, 2000, *Women's Empowerment and Demographic Processes: Moving Beyond Cairo* (Oxford: Oxford University Press).

   The papers in this volume are aimed at helping put the issue of the empowerment of women squarely in the middle of demographic theory and research.
4. Linda J. Waite and Maggie Gallagher, 2000, *The Case for Marriage* (New York: Doubleday).

Experimentation with diverse models of family-building since the 1970s has led social scientists to reexamine the place that marriage has in a modern developed society. This book does that by building on academic research, although it is intended for a general audience.

5. Jane Lewis, 2001, *The End of Marriage? Individualism and Intimate Relations* (Northampton, MA: Edward Elgar).

   The United Kingdom is wrestling with the same issues of the "decline of marriage" as is the United States and this book puts the changes into historical perspective.

Websites of Interest

Remember that websites are not as permanent as books and journals, so I cannot guarantee that each of the following websites still exists at the moment you are reading this. You may have to Google the name of the organization to find the current web address.

1. **http://psidonline.isr.umich.edu/**
   The Panel Study of Income Dynamics (PSID), which began in 1968 at the University of Michigan, is a longitudinal study emphasizing the dynamic (changing) aspects of demographic and economic behavior in American society.
2. **http://crcw.princeton.edu/**
   The Center for Research on Child Wellbeing at Princeton University is associated with Princeton's Office of Population Research and it aims to combine research with advocacy to promote the well-being of children.
3. **http://www.iser.essex.ac.uk/**
   The Economic and Social Research Council (ESRC) Research Centre on Micro-Social Change is the home of the British Household Panel Study, a longitudinal study begun in 1989.
4. **http://www.unfpa.org/support/friends/34million.htm**
   The United Nations Population Fund (UNFPA) has been active for a long time in promoting the well-being and empowerment of women all over the world. When the U.S. government in 2002 withdrew its pledge of $34 million in support of the work of the UNFPA, a group of volunteers set about collecting the money from private sources instead.
5. **http://www.unicef.org/statistics/index.html**
   The United Nations Children's Fund (UNICEF) maintains a database for all countries in which you can obtain a profile of the basic indicators of the life chances of the average child. Combine that with a visit to the World Bank's website (**http://www.worldbank.org/poverty/**), where you can obtain poverty level data for each country.

CHAPTER 11
Population and the Environment

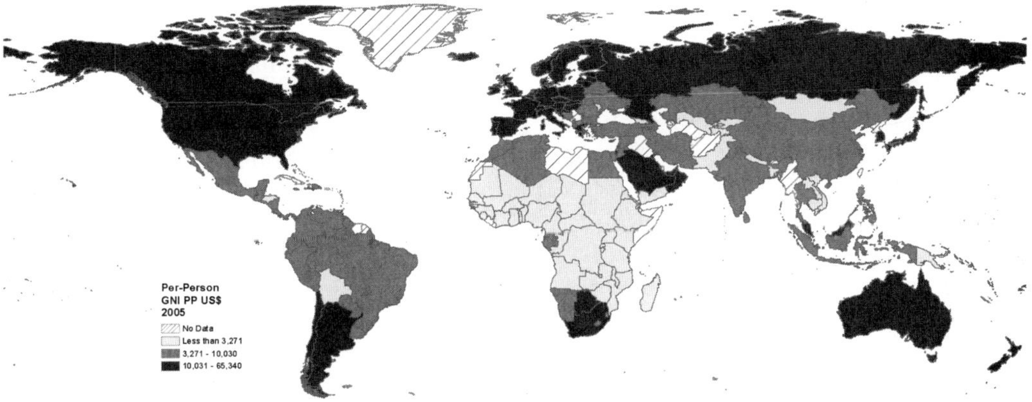

Figure 11.1 The Highest Per Capita Incomes Are Found in the "North"

It is elementary, my dear Watsons: Humans cannot survive without food and water. Those favored few of us in the world who can rely on water from the tap and groceries from the supermarket deal with this principle pretty much on a theoretical level. We know intellectually that some areas of the world have regularly been faced with the prospect of famine and drought. We also know that more than 200 years ago Malthus was already stewing about population growth outstripping the food supply. Although it is certainly a shame that all people cannot find a seat on the gravy train, the fact is that Malthus was wrong. Right? After all, food production has actually outpaced population growth over the past 200 years. It is a fact, and there are **boomsters** who believe that population growth stimulates economic development and that the food record speaks for itself—we can grow it as we need it (in this context the boomsters are known as **cornucopians**). The logical extension of this perspective is the idea that somehow we will be able to find the magical formula whereby everybody is better off in the future and we can all live happily ever after—that is the promise of the obviously popular concept of **sustainable development.**

However, look a little closer—the picture is less rosy, even for people fortunate enough to live in wealthier nations. The clues increasingly point to the grim reality that we will all be paying a very heavy price for coaxing ever-higher yields from our increasingly overburdened planet. In trying not only to feed but also to improve the lives of an ever-larger population, we are polluting the land, affecting our global climate, and using up our supply of fresh water. The plot of our mystery has taken a turn. Maybe Malthus and the **doomsters** are right. Although the formula for ultimate disaster was more complicated than he knew, critical resources such as land and water are finite. At some point, we may exhaust the earth's capacity to produce—then, everybody loses.

These issues juxtapose the views of the doomsters with those of the boomsters. Doomsters are the neo-Malthusians, exemplified most famously by Paul Ehrlich, who, as I discussed in Chapter 3, has argued for decades that continued population growth will lead to certain economic and environmental collapse in a worldwide tragedy of the commons (Ehrlich 1968, 1971; Ehrlich and Ehrlich 1972, 1990; Ehrlich, Ehrlich, and Daily 1997; Ehrlich and Ehrlich 2004). For Ehrlich, the policy choices have always been clear—population limitation must be a part of any development or sustainability strategy, or that strategy will fail.

The boomsters have been most famously influenced by the late Julian Simon, who argued for decades that population growth stimulates development, rather than slowing it down (Simon 1981; 1992). For Simon, the policy choices were also clear—development strategies should not deliberately slow down population growth because such growth is both a cause and a symptom of economic development. The boomster view recognizes that population cannot grow indefinitely, but argues that people will lower their fertility when they see an advantage from doing so, which means lifting them out of poverty through free trade and globalization (World Bank 2000). These have been the central ingredients in the idea of sustainable development, which I will discuss in greater detail later in the chapter.

A related perspective that is often put forth is a neo-Marxian view that population growth has nothing to do with economic development at all. Economic development, where it lags, is held back by the injustice of the world system that creates dependency by the periphery on the dominant core countries. Like the boomster view, this perspective recognizes that population cannot grow indefinitely, and similarly argues that people will lower their fertility when they see an advantage from doing so, which means lifting them out of poverty. The difference (and it is a huge one) is that the neo-Marxian policy perspective is that this should be accomplished by dismantling multinational corporations and putting the money into the hands of local populations, where it can be distributed equitably to relieve poverty and improve the human condition.

Each of these perspectives—boomster, doomster, neo-Marxian—carries with it a very different set of policy prescriptions and a different range of environmental consequences, so it matters which one is right. I will not leave you in suspense on this—each of these perspectives has some merit. To understand this, though, we need some definitions.

Economic Development—The Use and Abuse of Resources

Economic development represents a growth in average income, usually defined as **per capita (per person) income**. A closely related idea is that economic development occurs when the output per worker is increasing; since more output should lead to higher incomes, you can appreciate that they are really two sides of the same coin. Of course, if you are holding down two jobs this year just to keep afloat financially, you know that producing more will not necessarily improve your economic situation. Rather, it may only keep it from getting worse. Thus, a more meaningful definition of economic development refers to a rise in real income—an increase in the amount of goods and services you can actually buy.

An important aspect of development is that it is concerned with improving the welfare of human beings. It includes more than just increased productivity; it includes the resulting rise in the ability of people to consume (either buy or have available to them) the things they need to improve their level of living. Included in the list of improvements might be higher income, stable employment, more education, better health, consumption of more and healthier food, better housing, and increased public services such as water, sewerage, power, transportation, entertainment, and police and fire protection. Naturally, these improvements in human welfare, in turn, help increase economic productivity because the relationship is synergistic.

The starting point of economic development is the investment of financial capital. Capital represents a stock of goods used for the production of other things rather than for immediate enjoyment. Although capital may be money spent on heavy machinery or on an assembly line or on infrastructure such as highways and telecommunication, it can better be thought of as anything we invest today to yield income tomorrow (Spengler 1974). This means not only equipment and construction, but also investments in human capital—education, health, and, in general, the accumulation and application of knowledge. For an economy to grow, the level of capital investment must grow. Clearly, the higher the rate of population growth, the higher the rate of investment must be; this is what Leibenstein (1957) called the "population hurdle." If a population is growing so fast that it overreaches the rate of investment, then it will be stuck in a vicious Malthusian cycle of poverty; the economic growth will have been enough to feed more mouths, but not enough to escape from poverty.

Crucial to our understanding of economic development is the fact that this increase in well-being typically requires that we use more of the earth's resources—especially more energy and more water, not to mention more minerals and timber. How efficiently we are able to use these resources influences how widely they can be spread out among the entire (and growing) population. The use of every resource leads to waste products, and our efficiency in reducing waste and dealing with it effectively influences the extent to which we can minimize damage to the environment and thus sustain a larger population, or sustain a smaller population at a higher level of living.

Economic Development Compared to Economic Growth

Economic growth refers to an increase in the total amount of productivity or income in a nation (or whatever your geographic unit of analysis might be) without regard to the total number of people, whereas economic development relates that amount of income to the number of people. But how do we measure that income? The most commonly used index of a nation's income is the gross national income, or GNI (the term now preferred by the World Bank), which is also more famously known as gross national product, or GNP. The World Bank somewhat obscurely defines this as "the sum of value added by all resident producers plus any product taxes (less subsidies) not included in the valuation of output plus net receipts of primary income (compensation of employees and property income) from abroad" (World Bank 2007). Basically, if you add up the value of all of the paid work that goes on in a country, and then add in the money received from other countries, you have the measure of gross national product. If you exclude the money from abroad and just include the income generated within a country's own geographic boundaries, you have **gross domestic product** (GDP).

Measuring GNI and Purchasing Power Parity

Gross national income is the most widely used measure of economic well-being in the world, but it is important to keep in mind the things that GNI does not measure: (1) it does not take into account the depletion and degradation of natural resources; (2) it does not make any deduction for depreciation of manufactured assets such as infrastructure; (3) it does not measure the value of unpaid domestic labor such as that generated especially by women in developing nations; and (4) it does not account adequately for regional or national differences in purchasing power. This latter limitation is one in which the World Bank has been particularly interested. Although GNI figures are usually expressed in terms of U.S. dollars, a dollar may go farther in Ghana than it will in England, even when exchange rates have been taken into account. The United Nations and the World Bank have sponsored a number of household expenditure surveys in developing countries to try to estimate actual differences in the standard of living, in order to produce more meaningful income comparisons. The wealthier nations have also been encouraged to conduct such surveys, along the lines of the U.S. Bureau of Labor Statistics' Consumer Expenditure Survey.

The product of these efforts is a measure called **purchasing power parity** (PPP), defined as "a price which measures the number of units of country B's currency that are needed in country B to purchase the same quantity of an individual good or service as 1 unit of country A's currency will purchase in A" (World Bank 2007). One way of expressing this concept is through the use of what *The Economist* calls its "Big Mac Index." McDonald's sells its hamburgers in nearly 120 countries, and in each country, the sandwich must conform to essentially the same standards of ingredients and preparation. If the Big Mac costs $3.15 in the United States, then it should cost the same in real terms anywhere else in the world. So, if you go to Switzerland and discover that you're paying 4.93 Swiss Francs for a Big Mac, that should tell you that there are 4.93 / 3.15 = 1.57 Swiss Francs per U.S. dollar, in terms of the "real" cost of living (*The Economist* 2006).

By expressing gross national income in terms of purchasing power parity (rather than official exchange rates), the result is the **gross national income in PPP** (GNI PPP). In 2005, the gross national income in the United States was $12.4 trillion, as you can see in Figure 11.2, which shows the GNI PPP for the world's 20 largest economies. The U.S. economy is so big that it accounts for 22 percent of

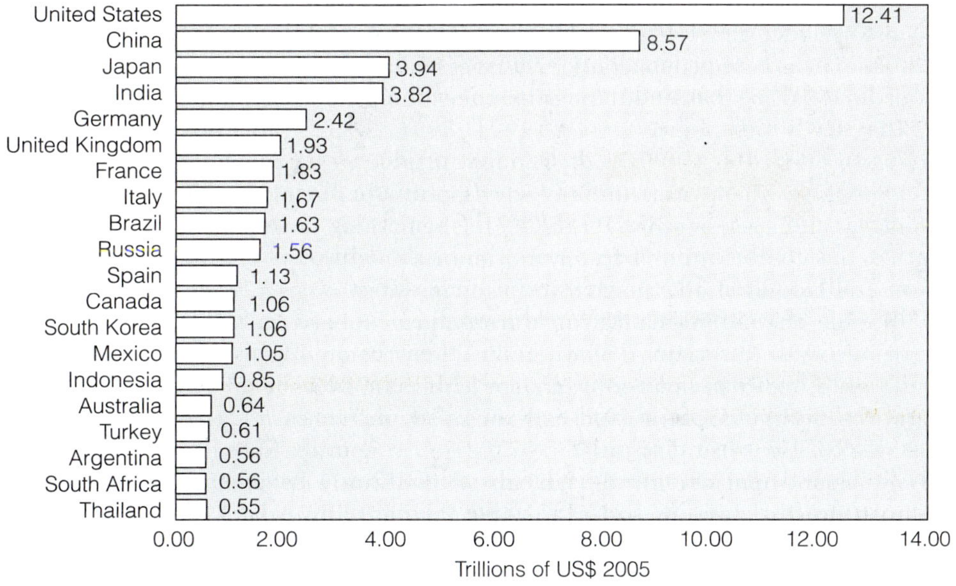

Figure 11.2 The 20 Largest Economies of the World, Based on Gross National Income Measured in Purchasing Power Parity

Source: Adapted by the author from World Bank, 2006, World Bank Indicators Database 2006, http://web.worldbank.org, accessed 2007.

the world's entire income, despite the fact that the U.S. population is less than 5 percent of the world total. The other two most populous countries of the world, China and India, are also in the top five of economies, and those top five (which also include Japan and Germany) represent more than 50 percent of the entire economic product of the world. The 20 countries shown in Figure 11.2 account for 82 percent of the world's economic output, but only 64 percent of the world's total population. However, if we take the United States off the list, the remaining 19 countries account for 60 percent of the world's economy and 59 percent of the world's population.

If we divide total national income by the number of people, we obtain a measure of per capita income, which gives a sense of the relative well-being of people in one country compared to another. In Table 11.1, I have listed the per person income for selected countries according to gross national income based on purchasing power parity. China may have one of the largest economies in the world, but its huge population means that its per person income is only a fraction of that in the United States. On a per capita basis, the Chinese have only 16 percent of the average American's income—or, put another way, the average American is about six times better off than the average person in China, and 12 times better off than the average person in India. All but one of the countries at the bottom of the income ladder are in sub-Saharan Africa, and you can see that the average person in those countries has only about 2 percent of the average American's income.

What are the sources of income that go into these measures? Much of it comes from the transformation of natural resources into things that are more useful to us—converting a tree into a house and furniture; converting the "fruit" of cotton plants into shirts and dresses; converting minerals found in rocks into the steel body of an automobile; transforming a hidden pool of underground oil into fuel used by machines. Then these products must be packaged, delivered, and sold; people have to coordinate all of that and make sure that the infrastructure exists to do everything that needs to be done.

We can divide the resources that go into producing income into two broad categories—**natural resources** (what is given to us on the planet), and **human resources** (how clever and successful we are in making something of those natural resources). Together, this combination of resources can be thought of as the **wealth of a nation** (Dixon and Hamilton 1996). Measuring these things is not easy, as you can imagine, although researchers at the World Bank have worked on it (applying their human resources to this issue, as it were) and their results suggest, for example, that Canada has a higher per person level of wealth than the United States, based on the natural resources in Canada, and that the value of human resources in the United States exceeds the natural resources wealth of the country. More importantly, their analysis suggests that natural capital is distributed fairly evenly around the inhabitable portions of the globe, so the variable factors in global economic well-being tend to be the level of human resources in one area compared with another, and the number of humans in one area compared with another, among whom these resources are shared (Bravo-Ortega and De Gregoria 2005). Either way, demography seems to be playing a role.

Table 11.1 The Top 10 and Bottom 10 Countries and Other Selected Countries in Terms of Per Person Gross National Income at Purchasing Power Parity (GNI PPP)

Top 10 Countries	Per Person GNI PPP ($US) 2005	Ratio to United States
United States	41,950	1.00
Norway	40,420	0.96
Switzerland	37,080	0.88
Ireland	34,720	0.83
Denmark	33,570	0.80
Austria	33,140	0.79
United Kingdom	32,690	0.78
Belgium	32,640	0.78
Netherlands	32,480	0.77
Canada	32,220	0.77
Other Selected Countries		
Japan	31,410	0.75
France	30,540	0.73
Chile	11,470	0.27
Russia	10,640	0.25
Mexico	10,030	0.24
China	6,600	0.16
Indonesia	3,720	0.09
India	3,460	0.08
Bottom 10 Countries		
Yemen	920	0.02
Madagascar	880	0.02
Congo, Rep.	810	0.02
Niger	800	0.02
Sierra Leone	780	0.02
Tanzania	730	0.02
Congo, DRC	720	0.02
Guinea-Bissau	700	0.02
Malawi	650	0.02
Burundi	640	0.02

Source: Adapted by the author from World Bank, 2006, World Bank Indicators Database 2006, http://web.worldbank.org, accessed 2007.

How Is Population Related to Economic Development?

There is a nearly indisputable, albeit somewhat complex, statistical association between economic development and population growth; that is, when one changes, the other also tends to change. As you no doubt already know, though, two things may be related to each other without one causing the other. Furthermore, the patterns of cause and effect can conceivably change over time. Does population growth promote economic development? Are population growth and economic development only coincidentally associated with each other? Or is population growth a hindrance to economic development?

The problem is that the data presently available lend themselves to a variety of interpretations. If we look at the global pattern of per person income (measured with per capita GNI based on PPP) you can see in Figure 11.1 at the beginning of this chapter, and from Table 11.1, that the poorest countries are in sub-Saharan Africa and South Asia, whereas the richest countries are the European and "overseas" European countries (the United States, Canada, Australia, and New Zealand), as well as Japan. The rest of the world generally falls in between, and includes most of Latin American, northern Africa, western and eastern Asia, and eastern Europe.

There is a high correlation between being a high-income country by World Bank standards and being a "core" country as defined by **world systems** analysts. "Core nations are linked to other core countries and to semiperipheral and peripheral nations; peripheral nations are linked to core nations but not to each other, and semiperipheral nations are linked to core countries and other semiperipheral nations, but are only weakly linked to peripheral nations" (Bollen and Appold 1993:286–87).

The upper-middle-income countries tend to be the "semiperipheral" nations and the lower-middle- and low-income nations tend to be the "peripheral" countries. The geographic pattern shown in Figure 11.1 is similar to maps showing the components of the demographic transition. Those places in the world where incomes are highest also tend to have the lowest levels of fertility, the lowest mortality levels, the lowest overall rates of population growth, the oldest age structures, the highest rates of immigration, the highest levels of urbanization, and the greatest diversity in family and household structure. The picture is fairly compelling, buttressed by the data in Figure 11.3. In that graph, I have compiled data for the 140 countries with at least a million people in 2005 for which the World Bank has generated estimates of the per person income measured in terms of GNI PPP—the same data that were used for Table 11.1. The income data refer to 2005, while the population growth data represent the average annual rate of growth during the previous 20-year period. You can see that, in general, countries in which average income levels are low tend to be clustered around the high end of population growth rates. I have partitioned the graph into four parts. The horizontal break represents the average per person income for all countries ($10,282 in U.S. dollars as of 2005), and the vertical break represents the average annual rate of population growth between 1985 and 2005 (1.61 percent). Thus, Jordan is a nation that is below the world average in terms of income but well above the world average with respect to population growth. Indeed, Jordan has the highest rate of population growth of any of the countries for which the World Bank has per person income. Only two other

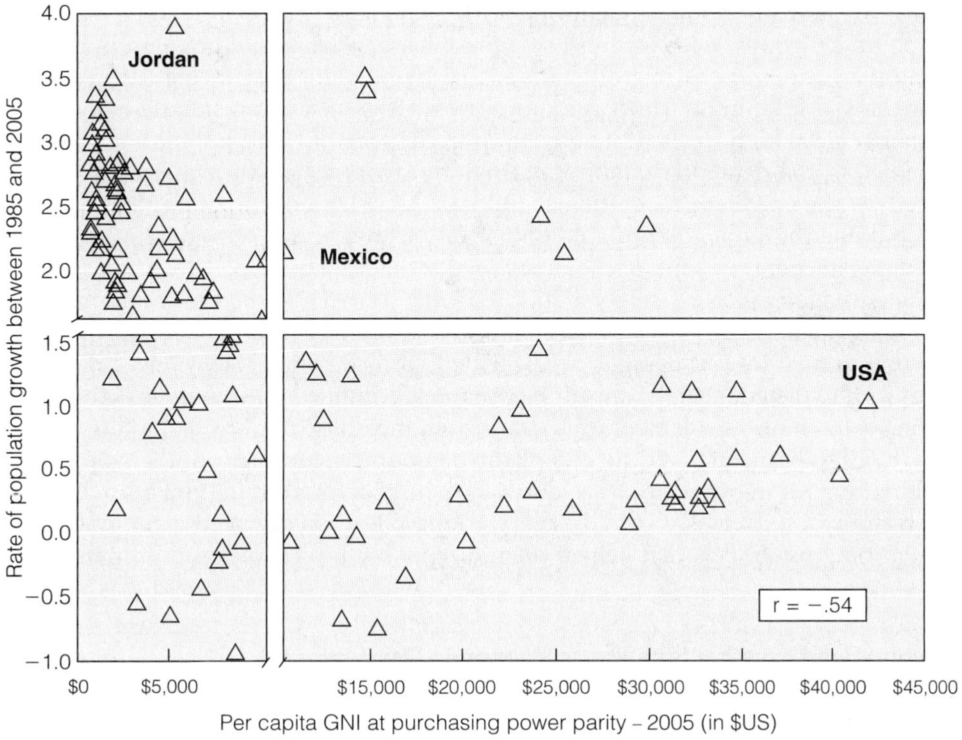

Figure 11.3 Countries with High Per Capita Income Tend to Have Low Rates of Population Growth

countries have higher rates of population growth during this period and they are both in this same region—the West Bank (growth rate of 4.13 percent per year) and Qatar (growth rate of 4.58 percent per year). Joining Jordan in that quadrant are countries like India and most of the non-oil-producing nations of Africa, Asia, and Latin America.

At the other extreme are the wealthier countries with low rates of population growth, exemplified by the United States, Japan, Switzerland, and the other countries of western and northern Europe. The countries that do not fit the expected pattern include the wealthy oil-producing Middle Eastern nations such as Saudi Arabia and the United Arab Emirates, where fertility rates have only recently begun to decline, and also Israel, which, as I've noted, has a low rate of population growth in comparison to countries in the region (e.g., its neighbors include Jordan and the West Bank), but the rate of growth is high in comparison to European nations.

Also off the track are those countries that have not been able to translate low rates of population growth into higher standards of living. Some of them are former members of the Soviet Union, and others, like Bulgaria, are just emerging from decades of their own state socialism. China fits into that category, but like Brazil, which is also in that group, the lower rate of growth is associated with rising per person incomes, even if the levels have not reached or exceeded the world average.

Clearly, a low rate of population growth is no assurance of a high income, but that point is obvious, since for most of human history the rate of population growth was low and so was the overall standard of living. The data in Figure 11.3 also show that, at least in the short run, countries with sufficient resources (especially oil) can achieve high levels of income even in the face of rapid population growth. Nonetheless, the data also exhibit a reasonably strong negative relationship as evidenced by the correlation coefficient (*r*) of −.54. Mexico, for example, has been sliding down the slope toward a combination of lower rates of population growth and higher incomes in spite of the occasional setbacks experienced by the Mexican economy (which are increasingly associated with setbacks in the U.S. economy).

Figure 11.3 does not suggest to us that the relationship between population growth and human well-being is necessarily described by a straight line. Like most things in life, the connection appears to be more complicated. Think of it this way. At the beginning of the demographic transition, most populations had a low rate of growth and low income. At the end of the demographic transition, the goal of the world is that all nations will have a low rate of growth and high income. But between the two extremes, virtually every country has experienced a time of rapid population growth. Has that helped them, been a hindrance, or hasn't it mattered?

Is Population Growth a Stimulus to Economic Development?

An early proponent of the idea that population growth could be the trigger of economic development was the Danish economist Ester Boserup. In a set of extremely influential writings (see, especially, Boserup 1965, 1981), she advanced the idea that, in the long run, a growing population is more likely than either a non-growing or a declining population to lead to economic development. The history of Europe shows that the Industrial Revolution and the increase in agricultural production were accompanied almost universally by population growth. Boserup's argument (also advanced by Clark 1967) is based on the thesis that population growth is the motivating force that brings about the clearing of uncultivated land, the draining of swamps, and the development of new crops, fertilizers, and irrigation techniques, all of which are linked to revolutions in agriculture. The kernel of the argument has been well stated by British agricultural economist Colin Clark (1967: Preface):

> [Population growth] is the only force powerful enough to make such communities change their methods, and in the long run transforms them into much more advanced and productive societies. The world has immense physical resources for agriculture and mineral production still unused. In industrial communities, the beneficial economic effects of large and expanding markets are abundantly clear. The principal problems created by population growth are not those of poverty, but of exceptionally rapid increase of wealth in certain favoured regions of growing population, their attraction of further population by migration, and the unmanageable spread of their cities.

This same line of reasoning was part of an influential strategy of development forwarded by Hirschman (1958), who argued as follows: (1) an increase in population size will lower a population's standard of living unless people reorganize their lives to increase production; (2) it is "a fundamental psychological postulate" that people will resist a lowering in their standard of living; and (3) ". . . the activity undertaken by the community in resisting a decline in its standard of living causes an increase in its ability to control its environment and to organize itself for development. As a result, the community will now be able to exploit the opportunities for economic growth that existed previously but were left unutilized" (1958:177).

The thesis that population growth is beneficial to economic development does have some foundation in fact. In Europe and the United States, development may well have been stimulated by population increase. Indeed, some historians regard preindustrial declines in death rates in Europe, associated partly with the disappearance of the plague (perhaps also with the introduction of the potato), as the spark that set off the Industrial Revolution. The reasoning goes that the lowered death rates created a rise in the rate of population growth, which then created a demand for more resources (see Clark 1967 for a review). An analogous example of population growth influencing development is the case of the American railroad, which opened up the frontier and hastened resource development in the United States. Fishlow (1965) demonstrated that the railroad (which helped accelerate the economic development of the western states) was actually following people westward rather than the other way around.

Although history may show that population growth was good for development in the now highly industrialized nations, statistics also reveal very important differences between the European/American experience and that of modern, less developed nations. The less developed countries today are not, in general, retracing the steps of the currently developed nations. In particular, less developed nations are building from a base of much lower levels of living than those that prevailed in either Europe or the United States in the early phases of economic development. Furthermore, although the rate of economic growth in many underdeveloped countries has recently been higher than at comparable periods in the history of developed nations, population growth is also significantly higher. Underdeveloped countries have experienced higher rates of population growth than European or American countries ever did, with the possible exception of America during the colonial period. In fact, over the past half century, the rates of population growth in the underdeveloped world have been virtually unparalleled in human history.

It appears that population growth may have helped stimulate economic growth in developed countries "by forcing men out of their natural torpor and inducing innovation and technical change, or by speeding up the replacement of the labour force with better educated labour" (Ohlin 1976:9). The less developed nations of today, however, do not seem to require any kind of internal stimulation to be innovative. They can see in the world around them the fruits of economic development, and quite naturally they want to share in as many of those goodies as possible—a situation often referred to as "the revolution of rising expectations." People in less developed nations today know what economic development is, and by studying the history of the highly industrialized nations, they can see at least how it used to be achievable.

If it was ever true that more people meant a greater chance of producing the genius who would solve the world's problems, it is a difficult argument to sustain today. As Nathan Keyfitz has pointed out, "the England that produced Shakespeare and shortly after that Newton held in all 5 million people, and probably not more than one million of these could read or write. . . . The thought that with more people there will be more talent for politics, for administration, for enterprise, for technological advance, is best dismissed. . . . For the most part, innovation comes from those who are comfortably located and have plenty of resources at their disposal" (quoted in United Nations Population Fund 1987:16).

It seems unlikely that a spark such as population growth is necessary any longer to stimulate economic development, but nonetheless in the 1980s, Julian Simon popularized his still widely cited thesis that a growing human population is the "ultimate resource" in the search for economic improvement. Eschewing the Malthusian idea that resources are finite, Simon suggested that resources are limited only by our ability to invent them and that, in essence, such inventiveness increases in proportion to the number of brains trying to solve problems. Coal replaced wood as a source of energy only to be replaced by oil, which may ultimately be replaced by solar and other renewable sources of energy—if we can figure out how to do it properly. From Simon's vantage point, innovation goes hand in hand with population growth, although he was quick to point out that moderate, rather than fast (or very slow) population growth is most conducive to an improvement in human welfare (Simon 1981). Simon made another crucial assumption: To be beneficial, population growth must occur in an environment in which people are free to be expressive and creative. To him, that meant a free market or capitalist system. Ironically, the idea that the important element in economic development is the prevailing type of economic system draws him into the same perspective on population growth and economic development as that shared by Marxists and **neo-Marxists.**

Is Population Growth Unrelated to Economic Development?

In his later writings, Simon moved toward the position that population growth is far less important an issue in economic development than is the marketplace itself. He suggested that "the key factor in a country's economic development is its economic and political system. . . . Misplaced attention to population growth has resulted in disastrously unsound economic advice being given to developing nations" (Simon 1992:xiii). With respect to the relationship between population growth and economic development, this is not far from the usual Marxist view that population problems will disappear when other problems are solved, and that economic development can occur readily in a socialist society. Marx (and Engels) believed that each country at each historical period has its own law of population, and that economic development is related to the political-economic structure of society, not at all to population growth. Indeed, Marx seemed to be arguing that whether population grew as a nation advanced economically was due to the nature of social organization. In an exploitive capitalist society, the government would encourage population increase to keep wages low, whereas in a socialist state there would be no such encouragement. Socialists argue that every member of society is born with the means to provide his or her own subsistence; thus economic development should proportionately benefit every person. The only reason why it might not is if society is organized to exploit workers by letting capitalists take large profits, thereby depriving laborers of a full share of their earnings.

It is increasingly difficult to find economists who believe that socialism is a more successful route to economic development than capitalism is, but neo-Marxists share many ideas in common with the world systems approach to understanding the global economic situation. The world system, it is argued, works much as Marx described capitalism—except that the scope is global, not country-specific. The developed nations of the West "are charged with buying raw materials cheap from developing countries and selling manufactured goods dear, thus putting developing countries permanently in the role of debtors and dependents" (Walsh 1974:1144).

That assessment, published in the very prestigious journal *Science*, was made, of course, long before China's communist-yet-capitalist manufacturing success rearranged some of the economic relationships between developed and developing nations. The idea is that if the economic power of developed nations could be reduced and that of developing nations enhanced, the boost to developing nations would dissipate problems such as hunger and poverty that are believed to be a result of too many people. At such time, the population problem will disappear because, it is argued, it is not really a problem after all. When all other social problems (primarily economic in origin) are taken care of, people will deal easily with any population problem if, indeed, one occurs. This was obviously the attitude of Friedrich Engels, who wrote in a letter in 1881, "If at some stage communist society finds itself obligated to regulate the production of human beings . . . it will be precisely this and this society alone, which can carry this out without difficulty" (Hansen 1970:47).

The evidence from countries such as Russia, Cuba, and, indeed, China suggests that a revolution may alter the demographic picture of a nation, but the relationship to economic development is somewhat cloudy. In the previously Marxist, centrally planned economies of eastern Europe and Russia, low rates of population growth did not translate into commensurately high levels of living. On the contrary, there is widespread speculation that low birth rates in those countries were a response to the economic limits placed on the family—especially scarce housing and limited consumer goods—although female education and labor force participation were being promoted at the same time, and they always lead to lower fertility.

The idea that population growth and economic development may be only tenuously related to each other is also reflected in empirical work that seems to support a non-Marxist, but still "neutral," view of the relationship between population growth and per capita income. Using data for developing societies for the period 1965–84, Bloom and Freeman (1986) concluded that despite rapid population growth, the labor markets in most developing countries were able to absorb large population increases at the same time that per-worker incomes were rising and productivity was increasing. In other words, just as Davis (1963) had pointed out in the theory of demographic change and response, a society's initial response to rapid population growth is to work harder to support its new members. But can that be sustained? Preston (1986) argued that it could be in those areas that have sufficient natural resources and, more importantly, are making increasingly efficient use of their major societal resource—human capital. This means not simply more people (as Simon seemed to infer) but a better-educated and better-managed labor force, combined with improved methods of communication and transportation (the economic infrastructure).

Is Population Growth Detrimental to Economic Development?

The neo-Malthusian position that economic development is hindered by rapid population growth is a simple proposition in its basic form. Regardless of the reason for an economy starting to grow, that growth will not be translated into development unless the population is growing slower than the economy. An analogy can be made to business. A storekeeper will make a profit only if expenses (overhead) add up to less than gross sales. For an economy, the addition of people involves expenses (**demographic overhead**) in terms of feeding, clothing, sheltering, and providing education and other goods and services for those people, and if demographic overhead equals or exceeds national income, there will be no improvement (profit) in the overall standard of living. If overhead exceeds income, then a business (or a country) can avert disaster for a while by borrowing money, but eventually that money has to be repaid and if the loan is used simply to pay the overhead, rather than being invested in human capital, it is unlikely that there will be money available to pay the loan when it comes due. So the loan is extended or refinanced, and disaster is averted for just a little while longer . . .

Let me illustrate the point further with a few numbers. Between 1980 and 2000, the population of Nigeria increased from 71 million to 123 million people, representing an average annual rate of population growth of 2.7 percent per year. The economy was also growing, thanks to substantial oil resources. In fact, at a rate of 2.3 percent per year, Nigeria's economy was growing at almost exactly the same clip as that of most European nations during that same time period. However, that was not fast enough to keep up with population growth in Nigeria and, as a consequence, the per capita gross national product (in constant dollars) in Nigeria in 2000 was less than it had been in 1980. Despite a growing economy, the average person was worse off. In fact, not just worse off, but doing very badly, since in 2005 the average Nigerian lived on less than $3 per day, compared to an American's average of more than $100 per day.

It is easy to ignore the impact of population growth when you are dealing with a country such as Nigeria, where an oppressive and corrupt government has skimmed off much of the country's wealth for the benefit of a small elite group. This is a blatant example of what Leibenstein (1957) politely called "organizational inefficiencies"—the existence of corruption and bribery in an environment without a stable banking or insurance system. In such a context, it is easy to see why people would pay little attention to population growth, but we can be sure that population growth has been compounding an already bad situation.

The more positive side of this equation is that lower mortality and fertility can lead to higher incomes, in turn encouraging still lower mortality and fertility, which in turn foster higher levels of income (Birdsall and Sinding 2001). This reciprocal relationship is at least partially a result of the several transitions put in place by the overall demographic transition. As I noted in Chapter 8, the age transition can provide a demographic windfall or bonus for countries by creating a period of time when an increasingly larger fraction of the population is in the economically productive ages. Since this is a function largely of declining fertility, it is also usually accompanied by a delay in marriage and childbearing among women (part of the family and household transition) that, as I discussed in Chapter 10, can lead to increased levels of education and labor force participation for women. The movement of women into the paid labor force may then have the effect of noticeably increasing the overall level of productivity, which contributes to economic development.

Overall, then, the most important part of the discussion about population growth and the improvements in societal well-being is that the rate of total population growth is less important than is the rate of growth of different age groups (Headey and Hodge 2009). As I discussed in Chapter 8 in comparing the economic trajectories of China and India, China has benefited economically from rapid growth in the young to middle adult ages at the same time that it was experiencing declining rates at the younger ages. However, as countries move through the health and mortality transition, and then the fertility transition, the age structure inevitably becomes older and, as Mason (1988) has pointed out, an older age structure may also be conducive to lower levels of saving, since in retirement people may be taking money out rather than putting it in. In between the young and the old age structure—in between the start and the end of the age transition—is the period in which the age structure helps promote economic development. All of this suggests that there is a curvilinear, rather than a straight-line, relationship between the demographic transition and its relationship to economic development. This implies that the end of the age transition (if there is such a thing—after all, fertility could rise again) may be associated with lower levels of economic productivity than the middle stages of the transition.

We turn now, however, to an aspect of human well-being that is less reliant on the age structure and more dependent on the sheer numerical size of the population—feeding the people.

The Bottom Line for the Future: Can Billions More People Be Fed?

It seems intuitively obvious to neo-Malthusians (and a lot of other people who do not think of themselves as neo-Malthusians) that population growth can make a difference in how many resources are consumed in the world. This discussion typically starts with the bottom-line question: Can we feed the population of the world? Despite our concern with the overall standard of living, the issue of just having enough food to sustain a large and growing population is still a huge problem for the world, and we cannot simply assume that there will always be enough food to go around.

The Food and Agriculture Organization (FAO) of the United Nations estimates that more than 1 billion people in the world do not have access to an adequate amount of food (Food and Agriculture Organization 2009b)—almost the same number of all people alive when Malthus first wrote his *Essay on Population* in 1798. During the next minute, as you read this page, 11 children under the age of five will die of diseases related to malnutrition, although their places will be more than taken by the 264 babies who will be born during that same minute. The good news is that the number of undernourished humans in the early 2000s is less than it was in the 1970s, although not by much; the bad news is that the number has been going up, not down, since the early 1990s.

The question is: Can we increase the food supply enough to feed the 75 million additional people on the planet every year while also improving everyone's diet in the process? We do not really know (Diouf 2009). Do we have enough fresh water to support all those people? We do not know that either. How did we get to this point and what can we learn from the past that might help us in the future?

The Relationship between Economic Development and Food

Roughly 10,000 years ago, humans began to seriously domesticate plants and animals, thereby making it possible to grow food and settle down in permanent villages. The domestication of plants, of course, hinged on the use of tools to work the ground near the settlement site, and the invention of those tools and their application to farming can be traced to many different areas of the world. Some of the earliest known sites are in the Dead Sea region of the Middle East (Cipolla 1965; Diamond 1997), where the Agricultural Revolution apparently took place around 8000 B.C. From the eastern end of the Mediterranean, agricultural innovations spread slowly westward through Europe (being picked up in the British Isles around 3000 B.C.) and east through Asia.

Plants and animals were also domesticated in the western hemisphere several thousand years ago (Harlan 1976), resulting in an increase in the amount of food that could be produced per person. As you know by now, increased food production was associated with population growth (possibly as a cause, possibly as a consequence).

Overall, the Agricultural Revolution "created an economy which, by . . . giving men a more reliable supply of food, permitted them to multiply to a hitherto unknown degree" (Sanchez-Albornoz 1974:24). The classic Malthusian view, of course, is that cultivating land caused population increase by lowering mortality and possibly raising fertility. However, the Boserupian view is that independent increases in population size among hunter-gatherers, perhaps through a long-run excess of births over deaths, led to a need for more innovative ways of obtaining food, and so, of necessity, the revolution in agriculture gradually occurred. Seen from this perspective, the Agricultural Revolution was the result of a "resource crisis," in which population growth, slow though it may have been 10,000 years ago, generated more people than could be fed just by hunting and gathering. The crisis led to a revolution in human control over the environment—humans began to deliberately produce food, rather than just take what nature provided. In turn, this had the cumulative effect of sustaining slow but fairly steady population growth in most areas of the world for several thousand years preceding the Industrial Revolution.

Industrialization and economic development in general require a massive increase in energy use. If everyone is consuming more, it is because production per person has increased, and that comes about by applying nonhuman energy to tasks previously done less efficiently by people, or not done at all because people could not do them. Wood has served as the major energy source for most of human history, but in Europe a few hundred years ago, population growth and the beginnings of industrialization led inexorably to deforestation, producing an "energy crisis" (Harrison 1993). That crisis forced a new way of thinking about energy sources—a new way of controlling the environment—and the result was the Industrial Revolution.

Keep in mind that the Agricultural and Industrial Revolutions are linked together. The Industrial Revolution of the nineteenth century was preceded, and indeed made possible, by important changes in agriculture that significantly improved output (Clough 1968). Through most of human history, including in Malthus's day, increases in the food supply depended largely on **extensification of agriculture**—putting more land under production. However, since we have essentially run out of new land that can be farmed without great difficulty, the modern rise in agricultural output has come about through **intensification of agriculture**—getting more out of the land than we used to. In Europe and North America, the factors helping to increase agricultural productivity in a relatively short time included the mechanization of cultivating and harvesting processes, increased use of fertilizers and irrigation, and the reorganization of land holdings so that farming could be more efficient.

The Industrial Revolution generated a host of mechanical devices, especially mechanical reapers, to greatly speed up harvesting. Drawn first by horses or oxen, reapers were pulled later by an even more efficient energy converter—the tractor. Like most early engines of industrialization, tractors were driven by steam. Their thirst for fuel was quenched by wood as long as it lasted, but the use of coal became necessary as a result of deforestation. The idea behind the steam engine, by the way, has been around for a long time, just waiting for the right moment to be adapted to something dramatically useful. In the ancient world, "Greek mechanics invented amusing steam-operated automata but never developed the steam engine; the crankshaft and connecting rod were not invented until the middle ages, and without a crankshaft it is impossible to transform longitudinal into circular motion" (Veyne 1987:137). Overall, the mechanization of agriculture vastly increased the number of acres that one or a few people could farm, and also increased the amount of land that could be devoted to more than one crop per growing season, since land could be cultivated and harvested so much more easily.

Although mechanization was certainly a prime mover of increased productivity in agriculture, especially in North America, where land was plentiful in relation to people, it is not an absolute requirement. In North America, where population density was low and labor was scarce, the increase in energy needed to intensify agriculture came from mechanical devices. In Japan, on the other hand, where labor was at a surplus even at the beginning of industrialization and land is scarce, the initial increase in energy came from people—people working harder and more efficiently on the land (Gordon 1975). Still, there is a limit to human power, which is why as Japan's population grew to its current size, the country has been forced to import a significant fraction of its food except rice, which is protected by high import taxes (Nagata 2008).

Many agricultural innovations have also been made possible by reorganizing agricultural land and developing better policies for land use (Dyson 1996). Collecting farms into large units and using meadows and pastures for cultivation rather than extensive grazing have increased production, particularly in the United States and Europe, since large farms introduce economies of scale that permit investment in expensive tractors, harvesters, fertilizers, irrigation systems, and the like. In the United States, this process has a long history and is still continuing; for example, between 1950 and 2002, the number of small farms (less than 180 acres) in the United States decreased from 4.1 million to 1.4 million, a 66 percent decline (U.S. Census Bureau 2007). In the 1990s, the total number of farms in the United States dropped below 2 million for the first time since 1850, after reaching a peak of 6.8 million in 1935. This does not mean that the number of acres under cultivation has declined much (it has changed very little), but rather that there is a trend toward large commercial farms and away from small family farms.

Although it may be intuitively obvious, it bears repeating that industrial expansion cannot occur unless agricultural production increases proportionately. Industrialization is typically associated with people migrating out of rural and into urban areas, naturally resulting in a shift of workers out of agriculture and into industry. Therefore, those workers left behind must be able to produce more—enough for themselves and also for the nonagricultural sector of the population. The flip side of that scenario is that as both the population and demand for food grow, the need to mechanize agriculture to increase production leads to a declining demand for agricultural workers. Thus you can see that the Industrial Revolution would have been impossible if agricultural production had not increased—and vice versa. Adam Smith, the classical economist, once remarked that "when by the improvement and cultivation of land . . . the labor of half the society becomes sufficient to provide food for the whole, the other half . . . can be employed . . . in satisfying the other wants and fancies of mankind" (quoted in Nicholls 1970:296).

So let us ask ourselves, how can food production be increased? There are two aspects to feeding the world's growing population. The first is the technical problem of growing enough food, and the second is the organizational problem of getting it to the people who need it. As I have already mentioned, food production can be increased through either extensification or intensification of agriculture. Let us examine each approach.

Extensification—Increasing Farmland

Water covers about 71 percent of the earth's surface, leaving the remaining 29 percent for us to scratch out our respective livings. Only 12 percent of the world's land surface is readily suitable for crop production, and an additional 26 percent is devoted to permanent pasture. Forests and woodlands cover about 32 percent of the land surface, and the remaining 31 percent is too hot or too cold for any of those things, or is used for other purposes (such as cities and highways). Most of the land that could be fairly readily cultivated is already cultivated; the rest is covered by ice, or is too dry, too wet, too hot, too cold, or too steep, or has soil unsuitable for growing crops (Bruinsma 2003). Of course, as Lester Brown, founder and board chairman of Worldwatch Institute, once commented, "If you are willing to pay the price, you can farm the slope of Mt. Everest" (*Newsweek* 1974:62).

In 1860, there were an estimated 572 million hectares (1.4 billion acres) of land in the world that had been cleared for agricultural use (Revelle 1984). As the populations of Europe and North America expanded in the late nineteenth century, the amount of farmland in these regions virtually doubled. More recently, the population pressure in developing countries has been accompanied by an expansion of farmland in those parts of the world, often generated by slash-and-burn techniques in relatively fragile ecosystems such as the forests of the Amazon. All of this adds up to a total of 1.5 billion hectares (3.7 billion acres) of farmland in the world today—more than two and a half times that of 1860. This seems to be the real limit of decent-quality farmland. Table 11.2 traces the data on population and agriculture for the world between 1961 and 2007. You can see that the amount of agricultural land in use in the world increased slightly from 1.4 billion hectares in 1961 to 1.5 billion in 1991 and has stayed there since. However, the population increased from 3.1 billion in 1961 to 6.7 billion in 2007, so the amount of farmland per person has been steadily declining.

The amount of irrigated agricultural land has also been increasing over time, but it too has failed to keep pace with population growth. The same is true for fertilizer, although no data are available since 2001 on total fertilizer consumption in the world. The number of tractors per 1,000 people increased from 1961 to 1981, but it has dropped since then, as tractor use has not kept pace with population. Finally, we can note that fish consumption (fresh and saltwater), as a proxy for fish

Table 11.2 Inputs to Agriculture Are Not All Keeping Pace with Population Growth

Year	Total population (1,000)	Arable and permanent cropland (1,000ha)	Irrigated agric area (1,000ha)	Fertilizer consumption (metric tons)	Tractors in use	Fish consumption (metric tons)
1961	3,072,759	1,356,722	139,134	31,182,244	11,318,243	7,884,969
1971	3,751,254	1,405,053	171,807	73,310,242	16,524,147	11,634,475
1981	4,506,550	1,442,386	213,532	115,147,224	22,311,077	14,974,575
1991	5,367,098	1,504,117	248,724	134,606,391	26,248,089	22,863,674
2001	6,194,891	1,532,090	273,052	137,729,730	26,854,002	36,767,113
2007	6,670,799	1,553,689	286,793	n/a	29,320,418	40,233,830
		Per 1,000 Persons				
1961		442	45	10	3.7	2.6
1971		375	46	20	4.4	3.1
1981		320	47	26	5.0	3.3
1991		280	46	25	4.9	4.3
2001		247	44	22	4.3	5.9
2007		233	43		4.4	6.0

Source: Adapted from Food and Agricultural Organization of the United Nations, FAOSTATS database, http://faostats.fao.org, accessed 2010.

production, has steadily increased over time, but in the past few years it has just barely kept pace with population increase.

In reaching the limits of readily cultivable land, we have been encroaching on land that supports plant and animal habitats that we really cannot do without. We are only now beginning to discover how much we depend on biological diversity (Miller 2009), and we threaten our environment as we search for more land on which to grow food. If that list of problems is not dismal enough, consider that the amount of good farmland is actually shrinking. In some parts of the world, this is a result of soil erosion or desertification, whereas in many other places it is a consequence of urban sprawl. Most major cities are in abundant agricultural regions that can provide fresh food daily to the city populations; only recently have transportation and refrigeration lessened (but not eliminated) that need. As cities have grown in size, nearby agricultural land has been increasingly graded and paved for higher-profit residential or business uses. About 4 percent of the earth's land surface is devoted to urban and other built-up uses (Mock 2000), which may sound like a small amount, but it looms large next to the 12 percent that is devoted to crops, because of the fact that so much cropland is in the vicinity of cities.

The allure of farmland to the developer is clear: It is generally flat and well-drained, thus good for building. It is probably outside town limits and therefore taxed at cheaper county rates. And the land may be family owned, with the potential that nonfarming family members will pressure their other family members to sell it as a means of converting the property to other assets. Such conversion is extremely difficult to reverse: "When farmland goes, food goes. Asphalt is the land's last crop" (The Environmental Fund 1981:1). The government of the Philippines recognized in 2008 that population growth was encroaching on valuable farmland and imposed a temporary ban on building on farmland, in an effort to become self-sufficient with respect to rice (*The Economist* 2008).

Soil erosion is a major problem throughout the world, as more topsoil is washed or blown away each year, a result of overplowing, overgrazing, and deforestation, all of which leave the ground unprotected from rain and wind. In the world as a whole, it appears that we are losing soil to erosion faster than nature can rebuild the supply. Thus we are losing ground (quite literally) at the same time that few places in the world still await the plow. It has also been suggested that a viable source of "land" is the sea—**mariculture**, or the "blue revolution," as some have called it. Farming the sea includes both fishing and harvesting kelp and algae for human consumption, although the expense of growing kelp and other plants is so great that it does not appear to be an economically viable alternative to cultivating land. Farming fish (including shellfish), or **aquaculture**, has been steadily increasing as a source of fish for food. It appears that we have reached the level of the ocean's sustainable fish catch, so any increase in fish production will of necessity be through aquaculture. Just in the years between 1994 and 2004, aquaculture increased as a percentage of fish production for human consumption from less than 19 percent to more than 40 percent (Food and Agriculture Organization 2007). It seems very doubtful that either extending agricultural land or farming the ocean will produce the amount of food needed by the world in the next century, given current world population projections. The output per acre of land under production must continue to increase if we are to feed billions more.

Intensification—Increasing Per-Acre Yield

There are several different ways to increase output from the land, and often methods must be combined if substantial success is to be realized. Those methods include plant breeding, increased irrigation, and increased use of pesticides and fertilizers. In combination, they add up to the **Green Revolution**. The Green Revolution is a term coined by the U.S. Agency for International Development back in the 1960s, but it began quietly in the 1940s in Mexico at the Rockefeller Foundation's International Maize and Wheat Improvement Center. The goal was to provide a means to increase grain production, and under the direction of Norman Borlaug (who received a Nobel Peace Prize for his work), new **high-yield varieties** (HYV) of wheat were developed. Known as dwarf types, they have shorter stems that produce more stalks than do most traditional varieties.

In the mid-1960s, these varieties of wheat were introduced into a number of countries, notably India and Pakistan, with spectacular early success—a result that had been anticipated after what the researchers had seen in Mexico (Chandler 1971). In 1954, the best wheat yields in Mexico had been about three metric tons per hectare, but the introduction of the HYV wheat (now used in almost all of Mexico's wheat land) raised yields to six or even eight tons per hectare if crops were carefully managed. A major difference was that more traditional varieties were too tall and tended to lodge (fall over) prior to harvest, thus raising the loss per acre, whereas the dwarf varieties (being shorter) prevented lodging. This is critical, because lodging can be devastating; it destroys some ears of grain and damages others. Furthermore, resistance to lodging makes it easier to apply the heavy fertilization and irrigation that are necessary for high yields.

The Green Revolution was not restricted to high-yield wheat and maize. In 1962, the Ford Foundation began a research program of rice breeding at the International Rice Research Institute in the Philippines. In a few short years, a high-yield variety of dwarf rice had been developed that, like HYV wheat, dramatically raised per-acre yields. Rice production increased in India and Pakistan, as well as in the Philippines, Indonesia, South Vietnam, and several other less developed countries. China and India both have embraced the Green Revolution as a means for ensuring the food security of their people. **Food security**, by the way, is a United Nations term meaning that people have physical and economic access to the basic food they need in order to work and function normally; that is, the food is there, and they can afford to buy it.

There is, as it turns out, a huge set of costs attached to the Green Revolution—success requires more than simply planting a new type of seed. These plants require fertilizers, pesticides, and irrigation in rather large amounts, a problem compounded by the fact that fertilizer and pesticides are normally petroleum-based and the irrigation systems require fuel for pumping. These are expensive items and usually demand that large amounts of adjacent land be devoted to the same crops and the same methods of farming, which in turn often means using tractors and other farm machinery in place of less-efficient human labor. This is the true meaning of the revolution.

The plants involved in the Green Revolution have principally been wheat, maize, and rice, but considerable research has also gone into the development of HYV soybeans, peanuts, and other high-protein plants. Related research includes breeding synthetic species such as triticale, a very hardy and high-yield cross of wheat and rye that has mainly been used as forage for feed animals in developed countries (especially Europe) rather than for people in less developed nations. Another candidate for continued development is the winged bean (or goa bean), sometimes known as "a supermarket on a stalk" because the plant combines the desirable nutritional characteristics of the green bean, garden pea, spinach, mushroom, soybean, bean sprout, and potato—all in one plant that is almost entirely edible, save the stalk. It is becoming a staple in poorer regions of Africa and South Asia because it grows quickly in tropical areas, is disease resistant, and is high in protein.

At least as important as the nutritional aspect of plant breeding is the development of disease- and pest-resistance. The rapid change in pest populations requires constant surveillance and alteration of seed strains. Insects are very much our competitors for the world food supply, and are a problem both before and after crops are harvested. Efforts to control pest damage have focused on designing seed varieties that are resistant to pests, or that are hardy enough to tolerate pesticides and herbicides, so that these chemicals can be used on plants without destroying the plant itself. However, in the United States and Europe there has been a consumer backlash against these kinds of genetically modified seeds, so food manufacturers have become cautious about using them, and instead have chosen to charge premium prices for organic foods that have not had chemicals applied to them, but which, as a consequence, will have lower average yields per acre.

High-yield seeds generally require substantial amounts of water to be successful, and irrigation is the only way to ensure that they get it (nature is a bit too fickle). This is because they, like all crops, grow best with a controlled supply of water, and also because irrigation can increase the opportunities for multiple cropping. In 2007, only 18 percent of the world's cropland was irrigated, as you can calculate from the data in Table 11.2, but irrigated land has been estimated to account for 40 percent of all the world's food (Food and Agriculture Organization 2009a), so this is a very important input to agriculture. Irrigation, of course, requires a water source (typically a reservoir created by damming a river), an initial capital investment to dig canals and install pipes, and energy to drive the pumps. Each of these elements represents an expensive resource. "There is widespread agreement that the future supply of water for agriculture represents a much more significant constraint to raising food production than do any likely foreseeable difficulties relating to soil or land" (Dyson 1996:149).

Remember that we humans need clean water for our own health, and yet we compete with agriculture for that limited supply. This is such an important issue that targets for improving the availability of safe water for human consumption are built into the Millennium Development Goals (which I discuss below), and in 2003 the United Nations created an initiative called UN-Water, coordinated by FAO, which focuses on this specific topic. To give you some sense of the magnitude of the water issue, it takes about half a million gallons of water to grow an acre of rice, and irrigated agriculture accounts for about 70 percent of the water consumed worldwide (Food and Agriculture Organization 2009a). The tremendous expense of providing irrigation imposes serious limits to any sizable future increase in the amount of land being irrigated in developing nations.

As I mentioned above, only 18 percent of the world's cropland is irrigated (the remainder is fed by rain), but that was a major increase from 10 percent in 1961, and there is also considerable variability in the world. As a country, Egypt leads the world in having virtually all of its cropland irrigated, but regionally the highest overall levels of irrigation (34 percent of cropland in 2001) are in Asia. Japan, for example, irrigates 63 percent of its cropland, and 52 percent of China's cropland is under irrigation. Europe can get by with very little irrigation because the growing season is associated with considerable rainfall. That is not the case in much of sub-Saharan Africa, however, where nonetheless only a small fraction of cropland is irrigated.

In order to maximize yields, plants must be fed (fertilized) and farm machinery used. These are key ingredients in the success of the Green Revolution. Table 11.2 shows that both of these inputs increased substantially between 1961 and 2001. The increases were especially rapid in Asia—representing major investments in agriculture in both China and India. At the beginning of the twenty-first century, Asia led the major regions of the world in terms of fertilizer use per 1,000 hectares, and it had surpassed Latin America in mechanization per hectare. Europe continues to be the most mechanized agricultural region of the world.

Pesticides represent another important input to the Green Revolution, but their use is decidedly a two-edged sword. Although heavy use of pesticides initially kills insects and increases per-acre yield, pesticides can also kill beneficial predators of insects and diseases that feed off the crops. Pesticide production has increased steadily worldwide, but its use has become more judicious—too much pesticide in the short term actually lowers crop productivity in the long term.

The Green Revolution, to be effective in all parts of the world, would require major changes in the way social life is organized in rural areas, not just a change in the plants grown or the fertilizers used. This is because the Green Revolution is based on Western (especially American and Canadian) methods of farming, in which the emphasis is on using expensive supplies and equipment and on the high-risk, high-profit principle of economies of scale—plant one crop in high volume and do it well.

As already noted, the data in Table 11.2 show that little global progress has been made in agricultural inputs per person since the mid 1990s. Does this mean that the Green Revolution simply ran its course? Not necessarily, and this gets us back to the issue of genetically modified foods. In its 2001 Human Development Report, the United Nations argued strongly that the world's richest nations must get over the fear of genetically modified foods if poverty and food insecurity are to be eradicated in poorer nations, because producing these kinds of foods is the only known way to keep increasing yield per acre in a world that has essentially run out of agricultural acreage (United Nations 2001). The Green Revolution's "founder," Norman Borlaug, put it this way:

> I've spent the past 20 years trying to bring the Green Revolution to Africa—where the farmers use traditional seeds and the organic farming systems that some call "sustainable." But low-yield farming is only sustainable for people with high death rates, and thanks to better medical care, more babies are surviving. . . . Africa desperately needs the simple, effective high-yield farming systems that have made the First World's food supply safe and secure (Borlaug 2002:A16).

Africa almost certainly needs a major investment in agriculture to overcome its food insecurity problem, but elsewhere in the world a subtle, yet effective, way of getting more out of each acre of food production is to waste less. Governments that help farmers use water and fertilizer more efficiently will clearly have more of those resources to spread around. A great deal of waste occurs once food is grown, both in its storage (where it may become spoiled or eaten by other creatures) and in the hands of consumers. One way of wasting less food is to use some form of preservative. Especially in developed nations, chemical substances are added to food to protect its nutritional value, to lengthen its shelf life (preservatives), and to change or enhance flavors and colors. Additives can greatly aid the process of feeding people by keeping food from spoiling and helping preserve its value. This has aided in the mass distribution of food and has made it possible for people to live considerable distances from food sources. Of course, since food is coming from strangers, it's important to remember to practice safe eating—always use condiments.

The use of preservatives is one means of deterring food spoilage by microorganisms, and more widespread use of preservatives could at least partially alleviate worldwide food shortages. For example, the World Health Organization estimates that about 20 percent of the world's food supply is lost to microorganism spoilage. Nonetheless, preservatives have increasingly been attacked as potential cancer agents. Sodium nitrate, used for centuries in curing meat to prevent botulism, is now suspected of being a carcinogen, at least in some dietary combinations. In 1984, the U.S. Food and Drug Administration approved the use of low doses of irradiation as a form of food preservation, and data suggest that it is about as safe as food prepared in a microwave oven. Currently, spices, vegetables, fruit, poultry, eggs, and meat can be irradiated. The World Health Organization and the American Medical Association endorse the practice. Nonetheless, U.S. consumers have been far more suspicious of so-called nuked food than have people in most of the rest of the world, so its use is somewhat limited in the United States.

With respect to consumption, it is certainly true that Americans, for example, could eat less meat and still be well nourished, and there is increasing pressure in that direction. It takes several pounds of grain to produce one pound of red meat, and there are other, more efficient ways to get protein (such as soybeans, peanuts, peas, and beans). Cutting back on animal protein could then free up the production of grain for human rather than animal consumption. Of course, most Americans do not welcome the suggestion that they should eat less meat, since eating beef, especially, is as much a part of American culture as not eating meat is in India. Thus, in the United States there is resistance to the idea of meatless meals, just as in India many people resist killing cows, monkeys, and even rats, in the belief that all living things are sacred. But, then, who would have guessed 50 years ago that Catholics would today have among the lowest levels of fertility in North America?

The Demand for Food Is Growing Faster Than the Population

The seemingly not-so-good news about the slow growth of agricultural inputs is countered by the fact that over the past several decades we have, in fact, been able to improve the diet of the average human being, which is one of the elements of the improvement in life expectancy in developing countries. Unfortunately, this has gotten us into a vicious circle from which it will not be easy to disentangle ourselves (Brown 2003). Declining mortality means more than people surviving longer; it is associated with healthier people who consume more food, after becoming healthier at least in part by consuming more food.

Improved nutrition brings with it not only healthier people, but also an increase in the size of the average human, and in the number of daily calories used per person (Fogel and Helmchen 2002; Fogel 2004). Table 11.3 shows the change in daily caloric intake in the world in the years between 1961 and 2005. You can see that there was a 23 percent increase in the world as a whole, with a higher increase in calories from animal products (mainly meat) than from vegetable products. So, the food capacity of the world was obviously outpacing population growth during this time period, because the average person was consuming more in 2005 than in 1961.

You can also see in Table 11.3 that there is considerable regional variability in the overall intake of food per day, and in the change over time. Europe and North

Table 11.3 Differences in Per Person Daily Caloric Intake over Time

	Calories per day per person		
	1961	2005	Percent increase
World—all food products	2,255	2,781	23%
From vegetable products	1,916	2,306	20%
From animals products	338	475	41%
North America—all food products	2,877	3,825	33%
From vegetable products	1,861	2,790	50%
From animals products	1,017	1,036	2%
Europe—all food products	3,046	3,360	10%
From vegetable products	2,274	2,242	−1%
From animals products	772	1,118	45%
Central America—all food products	2,226	3,029	36%
From vegetable products	1,951	2,471	27%
From animals products	275	558	103%
Asia—all food products	1,803	2,649	47%
From vegetable products	1,694	2,254	33%
From animals products	109	395	262%
Africa—all food products	2,061	2,407	17%
From vegetable products	1,909	2,232	17%
From animals products	152	175	15%
Least developed countries—all food products	1,930	2,110	9%
From vegetable products	1,806	1,964	9%
From animals products	124	146	18%

Source: Adapted from Food and Agricultural Organization of the United Nations, FAOSTATS, "Food Balance Sheets," (http://www.fao.org, accessed 2010).

America are the best-fed places on earth, but Europeans were increasing their meat intake while North Americans were increasing the non-meat portion of their diet. Most noteworthy in the table is the increase in Asia. In 1961, Asia as a region had the poorest diet on the planet, but that had increased substantially by 2005 at which point Asia exceeded Africa in terms of its diet. But that did not mean that the African diet was not improving in terms of caloric intake, because it was, as you can see. Even among the least developed nations, encompassing a bit more than 10 percent of the global population, people were getting more calories on average in 2005 than they were in 1961.

More food, especially when young, means bigger people. The increase in body mass, at least up to a point, is a good thing for economic productivity—bigger, healthier people work better than smaller, sicklier people—but we have already seen that there was a slowdown in the last part of the twentieth century in inputs to agriculture. That raises the obvious question of whether or not it will be possible to grow enough food for a population that is increasing both in number and in body mass.

How Many People Can Be Fed?

We are approaching the limits of exploitable land and water, but per-acre yield can still be increased, and we can reduce waste. Could this combination produce enough food to meet the needs of the 9 billion or more people who we anticipate will inhabit the planet by the middle of this century? We know how dangerous it is to try to predict the future, but the value of trying to do so is that we may be able to invent a future that is more to our liking. In 1968, Paul Ehrlich wrote in *The Population Bomb* that the world population situation "boils down to a few elementary facts. There is not enough food today. How much there will be tomorrow is open to debate. If the optimists are correct, today's level of misery will be perpetuated for perhaps two decades into the future. If the pessimists are correct, massive famines will occur soon, possibly in the early 1970's, certainly by the early 1980's" (Ehrlich 1968:44). Over the years, many people have derided Ehrlich for being so wrong, but of course he noted in the final chapter of his book that this is a situation in which the "penalty" for being wrong is that fewer people will be starving than expected, and that perhaps the dire warnings about the problems of population growth and food will have helped to spur action to avoid that consequence.

Bearing these things in mind, others step forward periodically to assess the world's potential for feeding itself. Vaclav Smil, a Canadian geographer, did so a few years ago (Smil 1994, 2000). He began by reviewing estimates made during the past 100 years that range from Ehrlich's low estimate of 2 billion people being sustainable from the world's food supply (Ehrlich 1968) to Simon's conclusion that the food supply has no upper limit (Simon 1981). Most other estimates are between 6 billion and 40 billion (see also Cohen 1995). Smil then reminded us that no reasonable calculation of the earth's capacity for growing food generates an estimate even close to the idea that the 7 billion alive today would have a diet similar to that of the average American. We have, for all intents and purposes, exceeded the carrying capacity with respect to the average American diet. Smil goes on to say that this is not as big a problem as it might seem, because Americans are overfed and very wasteful (Smil 2000).

The world should not aim for the average American diet, but rather all people should aim for a better diet, in line with the discussion about the nutrition transition that I reviewed in Chapter 5. Throughout the world there is tremendous slack ("recoverable inefficiencies") in the way food is produced and eaten. Smil calculated that by improving agricultural practices, reducing waste, and promoting a healthier diet (limiting fat intake to 30 percent of total energy, especially by reducing meat intake), the world in 1990 could have had a 60 percent gain in the efficiency of food production without putting a single additional acre under production. This would have fed an additional 3.1 billion in 1990, raising the supportable total in 1990 to 8.4 billion rather than the actual 5.3 billion in that year.

Supportability back in 1990, however, does not necessarily imply sustainability down the road. Smil introduced a series of conservative assumptions to suggest how a population of 10–11 billion could be supported during the next century, even without assuming some kind of magical technological fix. Applying the same logic of reducing inefficiencies, he calculated that the biggest gains (47 percent) could come from increasing the per-acre yield, followed by a continued extension of cultivated land, cultivating idle land, using high-efficiency irrigation, reducing beef production, irrigating some crops with salt water, and farming the sea. Underlying these estimates are assumptions that all populations will have a healthier (not necessarily a higher-calorie) diet, and that the food will be grown where it can be and distributed to where the demand is. These are huge assumptions and they tell us only that in the best of circumstances it might be possible to feed a much larger population than we currently have.

The assumptions of changing diets and food distribution take us from the realm of technology to social organization and culture. People are remarkably adaptable if they want to be, but "culture" often intervenes to prevent the "rational" response to situations. For example, the idea that nations need to be self-sufficient with respect to food (which underlies the idea of food security) may wind up wasting a nation's resources that could be used to produce something else that can be sold in order to buy food. Most of us living in developed nations are not personally self-sufficient with respect to either food or water. We rely on the good faith of strangers to provide us with what we need because we are willing to pay for it. The billions of people who will be sharing the planet with us later in this century will be properly fed only if the entire world adopts that same trading principle. Trade and a surplus for aid are necessary antidotes to the maldistribution of the physical and social resources required for growing food. At the same time, we must remember that trade implies trust, and the world is not always a trustworthy place, so countries that depend on others for food resources are naturally going to be anxious about the producers of food "blackmailing" them by withholding food in exchange for some other kind of concession.

Keep in mind that since much of the world depends on rain-fed agriculture, the weather is still an important issue in our food supply. In a review of evidence linking weather to population changes in the preindustrial world, Galloway concluded that "an important driving force behind long term fluctuations in populations may very well be long term variations in climate and its effects on agricultural yields and vital rates" (Galloway 1984:27). Historical data for China and Europe suggest that, much as you would expect, bad weather contributes to poor harvests, higher mortality, and slower population growth, whereas good weather has the opposite effect. In the African Sahel south of the Sahara, **drought** (a prolonged period of less-than-average rainfall) occurs with devastating predictability, and for the thousands of years that people have lived there, they have learned to combat drought and high mortality by having large families.

Drought is only one of several adverse weather conditions that can lead to a **famine**—defined as "food shortage accompanied by a significant increase in deaths" (Dyson 1991:5). Famine periodically hits South Asia either as a result of a drought caused by the lack of monsoon rains or by flooding caused by over-heavy rains. Either extreme can devastate crops and lead to an increase in the death rate. As in Africa, the high death rates are typically compensated for by high birth rates, and the famine-struck regions of the world continue to increase in population size. That maintains the pressure on the agricultural sector to improve productivity all it can. Still, we always have to come back to the fact that in the long run, the only solution is to halt population growth; at some point, the finite limit to resources will close the gate on population growth.

Worldwide dependence on the weather is all the more troubling given the mounting empirical evidence of global warming that will alter food production throughout the world. The United Nations Working Group of the Intergovernmental Panel on Climate Change (IPCC) issued a report in 2007 suggesting that global warming may lead to the melting of glaciers in Latin America and Asia, thus negatively affecting runoff and the water supply for millions of people (IPCC 2007). At the same time, glacier melting in areas closer to the poles could at least partially compensate for that, but only at considerable cost—economic, social, and political.

A key finding of the IPCC is that the current pattern of global warming is not due just to random weather variations. Rather, it is anthropogenic (human-induced). Our success at improving agricultural and industrial productivity has come at a cost. Some of the techniques that have seemed to offer the greatest hope for increasing the food supply and improving standards of living may be changing the very ecosystem upon which food production depends. This raises the question: If we stay on our current course of environmental degradation, will we permanently lower the sustainable level of living on the planet? We are in the midst of what Paul Harrison (1993) called "the pollution crisis," and we will either work our way through this on a global scale or be faced with a major ecocatastrophe that could greatly diminish the quality of life for all of us.

By-products of Development—Degradation of the Environment

The environmental issues that confront the world today deal largely with the side effects of trying to feed and otherwise raise the standard of living of an immense number of human beings. In coping with an ever-increasing number of humans, we are, as noted, damaging the lithosphere, the hydrosphere, and the atmosphere. This is because the reality of the environment is that everything is connected:

> The web of life is seamless, and the consequences of disruption to one part of the ecosystem ripple throughout the whole; soil erosion in the Himalayas contributes to massive flooding in Bangladesh; the deforestation of the Amazon may alter the atmospheric balance over the whole globe; and chemicals and gases produced in the richer industrialized countries are destroying the ozone layer that protects everyone, rich and poor alike (Seager 1990:Preface).

In order to examine these interconnections as they relate to the environmental byproducts of development in the context of a still-growing population, we need to remind ourselves of a few basic concepts and definitions.

Environmental Concepts and Definitions

The world inhabited by humans is known to scientists as the biosphere—the zone of Earth in which life is found (Miller 2009). As mentioned in Chapter 1, the **biosphere** consists of three major parts: (1) the lower part of the **atmosphere** (known as the **troposphere**—the first 11 miles or so of the atmosphere above the surface of the earth); (2) the **hydrosphere** (most surface water and groundwater); and (3) the **lithosphere** (the upper part of the earth's crust containing the soils, minerals, and fuels that plants and animals require for life). Within the biosphere are **ecosystems** representing communities of species interacting with each other and with the inanimate world. All of the world's ecosystems then represent the **ecosphere**, which is the living portion of the biosphere.

All living organisms in the biosphere require three basic things: (1) resources (food, water, and energy); (2) space to live; and (3) space to "dump waste." The carrying capacity of the biosphere, or of any ecosystem within the ecosphere, is the number of organisms that can be sustained indefinitely—the number for whom there are renewable resources, sufficient space to live, and sufficient space to get rid of waste products (all forms of life generate waste products). If the population exceeds an ecosystem's carrying capacity in any one of these categories, we have a situation of **overshoot** or **overpopulation**.

Damage to the Lithosphere—Polluting the Ground

We survive on the thin crust of the earth's surface. Actually, as you know, we live on only 29 percent of the surface. The rest is covered with water, especially the oceans, which we tend to treat as open sewers, but we also exploit resources that are in the ground under that water. The land surface of the earth is where most things we humans are interested in grow, and the damage we do to this part of the environment has the potential to lower the ability of plants and animals to survive. We have been busy doing damage such as: (1) soil erosion; (2) soil degradation from excess salts and water; (3) desertification; (4) deforestation; (5) loss of biodiversity; (6) strip mining for energy resources; and (7) dumping hazardous waste.

Almost every step of improving agricultural productivity has its environmental costs—from irrigation to the use of fertilizers and pesticides to the creation of energy sources and the production of machinery. "In spite of the increasing pace of world industrialization and urbanization, it is ploughing and pastoralism which are responsible for many of our most serious environmental problems and which are still causing some of our most widespread changes in the landscape" (Goudie 2006:296). If not carefully managed, farming can lead to an actual destruction of the land (think of the Dust Bowl in the United States in the 1930s). For example, improper irrigation is one of several causes of soil erosion to which valuable farmland is lost every year. In the United States alone it is estimated that during the past 200 years, at least one-third of the topsoil on croplands has been lost, ruining as much as 100 million acres of cultivated land (Brown and Mitchell 1998). Even if cropland is not ruined, its productivity is lowered by erosion, because few good chemical additives exist that can adequately replace the nutrition of natural topsoil. Unfortunately, the push for greater yield per acre may lead a farmer to achieve short-term gains in productivity without concern for the longer-term ability of the land to remain productive.

In many human cultures, agriculture is practiced as an extractive industry, in which the nutrition in the soil is sucked out by the repeated growing of crops, and soils are routinely degraded throughout the world. Continuation of the observed rate of soil degradation from 1945 to 1990 suggests an effective half-life of the vegetated soils of the earth of about 182 years. The conversion of land to agricultural purposes alters the entire ecosystem, and the resulting impact on soil structure and fertility, quality and quantity of both surface and groundwater and the biodiversity of both terrestrial and aquatic communities diminishes present and future productivity (Vanderpool 1995). Crop rotation and the application of livestock manure help to reduce soil erosion, but in some parts of the world the land is robbed of even cow dung by the need of growing populations for something to burn as fuel for cooking and staying warm.

The eroded soil has to go somewhere, of course, and its usual destinations are riverbeds and lake bottoms, where it often causes secondary problems by choking reservoirs. Desertification and deforestation are ecological crises associated with the pressure of population growth on the environment. The southern portion of the Sahara desert has been growing in size as overgrazing (complicated by drought) has denuded wide swaths of land. At the dawn of human civilization, forests covered about half of the earth's land surface (excepting Greenland and Antarctica). Only about half of that forest is left (Abramovitz 1998). Most, if not all, of that deforestation can be attributed to the impact of population growth, either directly through people moving into areas and clearing forests for their own use, or indirectly through the economic demands for more resources made by growing populations elsewhere in the world (Marcoux 2000). One of the most discussed areas of the world is the huge Amazon forest in Brazil. Over the past several decades, population pressure has led the government to encourage people to head for the Amazon Basin in search of land. The land they find is covered with a rain forest, which they have been cutting down at a prodigious rate, despite concerted efforts at reforestation (Rudel et al. 2005; Lu et al. 2007).

Forests are also susceptible to the effects of air pollution, which can damage the vegetation and lessen plants' resistance to disease. In their turn, fewer trees and less-healthy trees may alter the climate because the forests play a key role in the **hydrologic cycle** as well as in the **carbon cycle**. In the hydrologic cycle, water is being continuously converted from one status to another as it rotates from the ocean, the air, the land, through living organisms, and then back to the ocean. Solar energy causes evaporation of water from the oceans and from land, and it condenses into liquid as clouds, from whence comes rain, sleet, and snow to return water to the ground. Trees are important in this cycle both directly, because water transpires through the plants and is evaporated into the air, and indirectly, because the trees slow down the runoff and heighten the local land's absorption of the water. More than half of the moisture in the air above a forest comes from the forest itself (Miller 2009), so when the forest is gone, the local climate will become drier. These changes can mean that an area once covered by lush and biologically diverse tropical forest can be converted into a sparse grassland or even a desert.

The carbon cycle is that process through which carbons, central to life on the planet, are exchanged between living organisms and inanimate matter. Plants play an important role in this cycle through photosynthesis, and forests are sometimes called the earth's "lungs." Deforestation thus has the effect of reducing the planet's lung capacity, so to speak, and that contributes to global warming because it increases the amount of greenhouse gases that, in the right number, otherwise keep us at just the right temperature for normal existence.

Damage to the Atmosphere—Polluting the Air

The atmosphere is the mixture of gases surrounding the planet, and it is a layered affair (each layer being a "sphere"). We spend our life in the troposphere, that part of the atmosphere near the surface, where all the weather takes place. But other layers are of importance as well, such as the ozone in the stratosphere that protects us from the ultraviolet radiation from the sun. Most famous of the gases are the **greenhouse gases** (mainly carbon dioxide and water, but also ozone, methane, nitrous oxide, and chlorofluorocarbons), which allow light and infrared radiation from the sun to pass through the troposphere and warm the earth's surface, from which it then rises back into the troposphere. Some of this heat just escapes back into space, but some of it is trapped by the greenhouse gases, and this has the effect of warming the air, which radiates the heat back to the earth (Drake 2000). In general, the greenhouse effect is a good thing, because without it the average temperature on the planet would be 0°F (–18°C) and life would not exist in its present form, but too many greenhouse gases have the effect of **global warming**—an increase in the global temperature.

As I already mentioned, and you probably know anyway, global warming has the potential to change climatic zones, warm up and expand the oceans, and melt ice caps. The result would (will?) be a rise in average sea level—inundating coastal areas (where a disproportionate share of humans live), and a shift in the zones of the world where agriculture is most productive. The evidence is virtually overwhelming that we have been adding to greenhouse gases and that human activity is contributing to a rise in global temperature (IPCC 2007). This has happened as a polluting side effect of trying to support more humans, and to do so at a higher standard of living.

Population growth, the intensification of agriculture, and the overall increase in people's standard of living have been made possible by substantial increases in the amount of energy we use. Holdren (1990) has estimated that in 1890, when the world's population was 1.5 billion, the annual world energy use was 1.0 terawatts. (A terawatt is equal to five billion barrels of oil.) One hundred years later, in 1990, when the world's population was at 5.3 billion, total world energy use had rocketed to 13.7 terawatts. This is an important number because "*energy supply accounts for a major share of human impact on the global environment*" (Holdren 1990:159, emphasis added). By 2006 energy use had gone up still more to 15.8 terawatts (U.S. Energy Information Administration 2010), while the population had increased to 6.6 billion, which would mean (assuming these energy estimates are correct) that less energy was used per person in 2006 than in 1990. This would be good news if it meant that we were moving to higher levels of conservation and beginning to use renewable sources, as well. However, there is no clear evidence that either of these is happening. Rather, we are getting more desperate to find additional sources of fossil fuels because we can't keep up with the demand. Indeed, the vast majority of energy used in the world is based on fossil fuels, which is why BP was drilling for oil in deep water in the Gulf of Mexico in 2010. You know how well that worked out . . .

The by-products of our energy use (especially carbon dioxide and methane) wind up disproportionately in the atmosphere and contribute to global warming. As you can see from Table 11.4, we have met the enemy who is pumping carbon dioxide (CO_2) into the atmosphere, and the enemy is us. Well, the United States is second to China as of 2006 on the list of CO_2 producers in absolute terms only because China now manufactures many of the products sold in the United States (and elsewhere). We have off-loaded that portion of our **ecological footprint** (see the essay accompanying this chapter) onto China. The right-hand side of Table 11.4 lists the top 20 countries in terms of per person CO_2 emissions. You can see that the top four are all small oil-producing and exporting countries in the Middle East. Their emissions also represent the effect of the richer nations' demand for oil. Of the larger industrialized countries, the United States, Australia, and Canada are very high on the list with respect to per person carbon emissions. Mexico is twelfth in terms of total output of carbon dioxide emissions, but its volume is less than 10 percent of the U.S. volume and its per capita use is seventy-fourth on the world list.

The list of countries ranked by CO_2 emissions is very similar to the list of the largest economies of the world, which I showed you earlier in Figure 11.1 and Table 11.1. This is no coincidence, of course, since emissions are directly related to energy use, which is directly related to levels of income. Indeed, the United States has 22 percent of the total income in the world and produces 19 percent of the world's CO_2 emissions. The top five countries on the list in Table 11.4 of total emissions (China, United States, Russia, India, and Japan) account for 46 percent of the world's population (see Table 2.4) and 54 percent of all the world's carbon dioxide emissions. It is fair to say that the biggest countries make the biggest mess.

Other gases that we send into the environment—especially chlorofluorocarbons—have the potential to thin the **ozone layer**, which protects us from deadly ultraviolet light. These "holes" in the ozone layer, which have been documented especially in the southern hemisphere, can damage crops and livestock and, of

Table 11.4 Emissions of Carbon Dioxide by Country

Top 20 countries by total emissions	Total CO^2 emissions in metric tons	Top 20 countries by per person emissions	Per capita CO^2 emissions (metric tons per person)
China	6,099,054	Qatar	46.1
United States	5,748,105	Kuwait	33.3
Russia	1,563,531	United Arab Emirates	32.9
India	1,509,253	Bahrain	28.6
Japan	1,292,469	Luxembourg	23.9
Germany	804,504	United States	19.3
United Kingdom	568,107	Australia	18.0
Canada	544,284	Canada	16.7
Korea, Rep.	474,902	Saudi Arabia	16.1
Italy	473,803	Brunei	15.6
Iran, Islamic Rep.	466,636	Oman	15.5
Mexico	435,833	Estonia	13.0
South Africa	414,347	Singapore	12.8
France	382,870	Finland	12.7
Saudi Arabia	381,287	Kazakhstan	12.6
Australia	371,742	Czech Republic	11.2
Brazil	352,268	Russia	11.0
Spain	351,978	Netherlands	10.3
Indonesia	333,241	Ireland	10.3
Ukraine	318,926	Belgium	10.2

Source: Adapted from data in World Bank, 2010, *World Development Indicators Database 2010* (Washington, DC: World Bank) (http://data.worldbank.org/data-catalog/world-development-indicators, accessed 2010). Data are for 2006.

course, humans as well. Although the switch from wood to coal for creating steam may have helped save forests, the by-product of burning coal is "acid rain"—sulfur particles trapped in the air, which then cause damage by killing plants, undermining animal habitat, and eroding human-built structures, especially those made of marble and limestone. Photochemical smog produced by automobile and industrial emissions creates a wide band of air pollution known to be harmful to humans, other animals, and plants as well. In a variation on the theme "what goes up, must come down," the gases and particles that we pump into the atmosphere come back to haunt us in myriad ways, none of them beneficial.

Damage to the Hydrosphere—Water Supply and Water Quality

Water is an amazing liquid. It covers 71 percent of the earth's surface, including almost all of the southern hemisphere and nearly half of the northern hemisphere.

HOW BIG IS YOUR ECOLOGICAL FOOTPRINT?

Demographers are sometimes at a loss to explain why the relationship between population growth and economic change does not show up more clearly in the statistics of world development. It is intuitively obvious that more people consuming resources and leaving behind the detritus of the industrial world are detrimental to the long-term health of the planet. But it is maddeningly difficult to show that population growth in Mexico, for example, is more or less damaging to the earth than population growth in Indonesia. One of the problems is that those of us in the highly industrialized countries don't always make the biggest mess where we live—we are able to get someone else somewhere else to make our mess for us, which means that they (usually in less developed nations) in turn have an environmental impact that really should not be directly attributed to them. The best way to visualize this is with the concept of the ecological footprint.

An ecological footprint has been defined as the land and water area required to support indefinitely the material standard of living of a given human population, using prevailing technology (Wackernagel and Rees 1996; Rees 1996; WWF 2008). For most of human history, this was easy to figure out. If you farmed two hectares (about five acres) and all of your needs were met from the resources within those two hectares and all of your waste products were deposited within that acreage, then you did not influence life outside that zone in any demonstrable way. Your ecological footprint was 2.0 hectares. But urbanization changed all that because, as I noted in Chapter 9, an urban population requires that someone else in the countryside grow their food, cut their wood, gather their sources of energy, get their water for them, and stow their trash and other waste. Thus, it is not easy to determine how big an impact an urban resident has on the resources of the earth, since the resources are drawn from multiple sources and the waste is spread out in multiple directions.

Urban areas are not sustainable on their own, as I discussed in Chapter 9; they must borrow their carrying capacity from elsewhere, and this is why it has been so important historically for cities to establish political and economic dominance over the countryside. Who are city residents borrowing from, and how much are they borrowing? Those are questions that William Rees of the University of British Columbia sought to answer, in collaboration with Mathis Wackernagel, then one of his graduate students. They devised a set of calculations to estimate the total land and water required to generate the materials used by humans (including materials for food, shelter, consumer goods, energy, and so forth) and the land and water needed by each human to deposit the waste products generated by

Ecological Footprints of Country

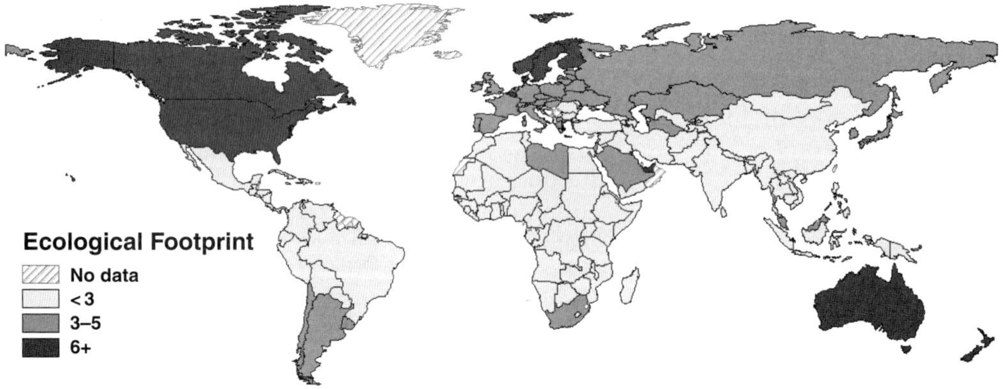

consumption of those materials. The estimate for 2005 was that 2.1 hectares of biocapacity were available to each human being for their use (see the accompanying table).

The wealth of cities virtually ensures that they will exceed the average footprint. Rees calculated that the 472,000 residents of his home city of Vancouver, British Columbia, generated an average ecological footprint of more than four hectares per person, which meant that the city had a footprint of more than 2 million hectares. Vancouver itself comprises only 11,400 hectares, so Rees points out that "the ecological locations of cities no longer coincide with their locations on the map" (Rees 1996:2). A city like Tokyo, for example, has an ecological footprint that would cover a large section of Southeast Asia if it were aggregated all in one place. The same analysis can be applied to countries.

Many wealthy countries exceed their own carrying capacity by borrowing ecological resources from other parts of the globe. In the long run, sustainability means that those countries that are running an ecological deficit (we might call them the "exploiters") must be offset by those who have an ecological surplus. The numbers in the accompanying table summarize data for several countries of the world, and the accompanying map gives you a global perspective. It probably will not surprise you to learn that the average resident of the United States has the second largest ecological footprint in the world, at 9.4 hectares per person, which is equivalent to about 24 football fields per person used up to sustain the lifestyle of the average American. Only the small United Arab Emirates exceeds the U.S. average. The vastness of the country's size and resources offers the average

(continued)

Ecological Footprints of Selected Nations

Country	Ecological footprint in hectares per person	Available biocapacity per person within the nation	Ecological reserve or deficit (if negative) in hectares per capita
United States	9.4	5.0	−4.4
Australia	7.8	15.4	7.6
New Zealand	7.7	14.1	6.4
Canada	7.1	20.0	12.9
United Kingdom	5.3	1.6	−3.7
Switzerland	5.0	1.3	−3.7
France	4.9	3.0	−1.9
Russia	3.7	8.1	4.4
Mexico	3.4	1.7	−1.7
China	2.1	0.9	−1.2
Nigeria	1.3	1.0	−0.3
Indonesia	0.9	1.4	0.5
India	0.9	0.4	−0.5
Burundi	0.8	0.7	−0.1
WORLD	**2.7**	**2.1**	**−0.6**

Note: A hectare is 10,000m^2, or approximately 2.5 acres as measured in the U.S.; one acre is approximately the size of an American football field.

Source: Adapted from data in WWF, 2008, *Living Planet Report 2008* (Gland, Switzerland: WWF International), Table 1. Data refer to 2005.

HOW BIG IS YOUR ECOLOGICAL FOOTPRINT? (CONTINUED)

American an ecological capacity of 5.0 hectares per person—well above the world average of 2.1. Yet, Americans still exceed that capacity by 4.4 hectares per person. Canada, on the other hand, has an estimated available ecological capacity of 20.0 hectares per person, and Canadians use 7.1 hectares each, leaving surplus ecological capacity for the moment, but of course that surplus is essentially being "used" by others, especially by residents of the United States.

The wealth of most European countries causes them to exceed their capacity, but even Mexico was estimated to be exceeding its ecological capacity as of 2005, and so were China and India, even though the latter two countries have national ecological footprints that are well below the world average. The last country in the table is Burundi, which is the poorest nation in the world, as you will recall from Table 11.1. Burundi has the biocapacity for 0.7 hectares per person, but it is estimated to be using 0.8 per person, so it is already running a deficit, and its rate of population growth is nearly twice the world average.

The bottom line of the table shows that, by these calculations, the average person in the world in 2005 required the constant production of 2.7 hectares in order to maintain his or her standard of living,

You are full of it—about 65 percent of your weight is water. Despite all of that water, only a small fraction—3 percent—of it is the fresh water that humans, other animals, and plants need. Furthermore, most of that 3 percent is water that is locked up as ice in the poles and glaciers or in extremely deep groundwater. Only about 0.003 percent of the total volume of water on the planet is fresh water readily available to us in lakes, soil moisture, exploitable groundwater, atmospheric water vapor, and streams (Falkenmark and Widstrand 1992). Although fixed in amount, the water supply is constantly renewed in the hydrologic cycle of evaporation, condensation, and precipitation. The principal issues with respect to water have to do with its management (distributing it where it is needed), purity from disease (in order to be drinkable), and pollution.

It has been estimated that in 1850 the freshwater resources in the world were equivalent to 33,000 cubic meters per person per year (United Nations Population Fund 1991), but by 2000 that had shrunk to scarcely more than 7,000 (World Resources Institute 2000), and the World Resources Institute estimates that only 15 percent of people in the world live in relative water abundance (Damassa 2006). Within the ecosphere, salt water is converted to fresh water through the hydrologic cycle, but it is very expensive to mimic nature. In fact, it has been joked that the two most difficult things to get out of water are politics and salt.

Most desalination plants are based on a process of distillation that imitates the water cycle by heating water to produce vapor that is then condensed to produce fresh, potable (drinkable) water. The problem is that it is very costly to heat the water and, as a result, desalinated water is typically several times more expensive than drinkable local water, and the resulting salt brine waste is environmentally damaging, as well. For this reason, the major producer of desalted water is Saudi Arabia, which is, for all intents and purposes, turning oil into water. Reverse osmosis as a desalination process may hold some promise, but it seems unlikely that anything but naturally generated fresh water will be able to supply human needs for the foreseeable future, and we will have to survive by using that resource more efficiently than in the past.

whereas only 2.1 hectares were estimated to be available on a sustainable basis. If these data represent the real impact of humans on the environment, then we have already overshot our carrying capacity, like people who continue to charge things on their credit card without knowing if or how they will pay back that indebtedness.

York, Rosa, and Dietz (2003) examined cross-national comparisons of ecological footprints (using data such as those provided in the accompanying table) and concluded that "basic material conditions, such as population, economic production, urbanization, and geographical factors all affect the environment and explain the vast majority of cross-national variation in environmental impact. . . . Taken together, these findings suggest societies cannot be sanguine about achieving sustainability via a continuation of current trends in economic growth and institutional change" (p. 279).

Discussion Questions: (1) How could you personally lower your personal ecological footprint, in order to increase the chances of sustainability? **(2)** Given the large populations of both China and India, discuss the global consequences of those countries lowering the percentage of their population that lives on less than $2 per day.

All over the globe more people are competing for water even as water consumption per person has been on the rise, and, all the while, we have been sending pollutants into the water, degrading the already limited supply. Some of the pollution goes directly into the water, and some goes into the ground, where it seeps into the water supply or into the air where it then falls on us as acid rain. We know as well that polluted water can alter marine life, killing fish and other sources of marine food. Ironically, among the main sources of water pollution are the chemicals we add to the soil to improve agricultural productivity, and this is aggravated by using irrigation, which increases the amount of water exposed to the chemicals.

Irrigation requires dams, of course, and there has been a worldwide movement to stop the construction of dams as we learn more about the ecological damage caused upstream, downstream, and on the cropland itself by dams and the irrigation water, not to mention the displacement of millions of people around the world because their home was going to be underwater in the reservoir behind the dam. Most of the choice dam sites have already been taken, but not all. Asia has a higher percentage of its land under irrigation than any other area of the world, and China, in particular, is adding to the total. China built three major dams in the early 2000s, the largest and most famous of which is the Three Gorges Dam on the Yangtze River, which is designed to supply irrigation water and generate hydroelectric power (estimated at more than 10 percent of China's total), and has forced the migration/relocation of an estimated 1.3 million people.

The World Bank has very succinctly summarized the world's water resources situation as follows:

> During the past century, while the world's population tripled, the aggregate use of water increased sixfold, with irrigation consuming over 70 percent of available water. These increases have come at high environmental costs: half of the world's wetlands disappeared over the last century, with some rivers now no longer reaching the sea, and 20 percent of freshwater fish now endangered or extinct. If current trends continue, 4 billion people will live under conditions of severe water stress by 2025, particularly in Africa, the Middle East, and South Asia (Shafik and Johnson 2003:2).

Assessing the Damage Attributable to Population Growth

The role of population in environmental degradation differs from place to place, from time to time, and depends on what type of degradation we are discussing. In general terms, however, environmental degradation can be seen as the combined result of population growth, the growth in production (transformation of products of the natural environment for human use) that we call economic development, and the technology applied to that transformation process. Ehrlich and Ehrlich (1990) summarized this relationship in their now-famous **impact (IPAT) equation**:

$$\text{Impact } (I) = \text{Population } (P) \times \text{Affluence } (A) \times \text{Technology } (T).$$

Impact refers to the amount of a particular kind of environmental degradation; population refers to the absolute size of the population; affluence refers to per person income; and technology refers to the environmentally damaging properties of the particular techniques by which goods are produced (measured per unit of a good produced). "Technology is double-edged. An increase in the technical armoury sometimes increases environmental impact, sometimes decreases it. When throwaway cans replaced reusable bottles, technology change increased environmental impact. When fuel efficiency in cars was increased, impact was reduced" (Harrison 1993:237).

A major limitation of the IPAT formula is that it treats population size as a simple driver of environmental change. As you now know, some age groups have a different impact than others, so the age structure matters. Furthermore, urban populations use resources disproportionately, because they are the wealthier people and have different household structures that influence energy use, in particular (O'Neill and Chen 2002). Everything is more complicated than it appears at first glance, but we can say that, although those of us living in developed nations still consume a vastly disproportionate share of the earth's resources and thus contribute disproportionately to the pollution crisis, the rates of population growth and economic development in developing countries mean that the global impact is shifting increasingly in that direction. For example, the data in Table 11.4 show that China and India are among the five biggest CO_2 polluters in the world, despite very low per person rates in those two relatively poor countries. Second, notice that technological improvements are already operating to dampen the environmentally degrading impact of consumption, but population growth has been exerting continual upward pressure on degradation.

You can see the dilemma here: Just to maintain the current impact on the environment, technology must completely counteract the impact of population growth and increasing affluence. Much of the affluence in developed nations has come at the expense of the rest of the world—we have used resources without paying for them because the price of goods we purchased did not typically include the environmental costs associated with their production and consumption. We cannot continue to draw down the "capital" of nature indefinitely to supplement our income. The price of goods will have to increasingly include some measure of the cost of dealing with the environmental impact of making that product (the pollution from the manufacturing process) and the cost of getting rid of the product when it is used up (the pollution from waste). Measuring the cost of goods in this way may slow down the rate of economic development, measured in a purely economic way, but it should increase overall human well-being by balancing economic growth with its environmental impact. Nowhere in this set of equations can it be concluded, however, that increased population is beneficial. Population growth is something that must be coped with at the same time that we continue to try to slow it down, because "rational people do not pursue collective doom; they organize to avoid it" (Stephen Sandford, quoted by Harrison 1993:264). In the world as a whole we expect there to be more than 9 billion people by the middle of this century—all of whom will likely be hoping for a good diet and a reasonably high standard of living. Is it possible not only to provide that kind of development, but to sustain it?

Sustainable Development—Possibility or Oxymoron?

In 1987, the United Nations World Commission on Environment and Development issued its extremely influential report "Our Common Future" (World Commission on Environment and Development 1987). This is usually called the report of the Brundtland Commission, named for its chair, Gro Harlem Brundtland, who was then Prime Minister of Norway and later became Director of the World Health Organization. The Commission defined the now-popular term **sustainable development** as "development that meets the needs of the present without compromising the ability of future generations to meet their own needs" (p. 43). At the same time, and for the first time in the world arena, the issue of environment and equity was laid on the table. It was made clear that part of the environmental problem is that some (rich) nations are consuming too much, while at the other end of the continuum, environmental problems are caused by people living in poverty who use the environment unsustainably because their own survival is otherwise at stake. Within the concept of sustainable development, the Commission recommended that "overriding priority" should be given to the essential needs of the world's poor.

The Brundtland Commission defined sustainable development in a deliberately vague way. That has had the advantage of building a worldwide constituency for the concept, with the attendant disadvantage that everybody defines it the way they want to. One of the most popular ways to define sustainable development is to translate it to mean "let's sustain development," implying that economic growth is the best solution to all of the world's problems (Chambers, Simmons, and Wackernagel 2002; Daly 2008). In particular, economic growth is viewed as the way to salvation for the world's poor. The World Bank and the United Nations have taken up the theme of eliminating poverty as one of the world's important missions. The World Bank's Development Report for 2000/2001 was subtitled *Attacking Poverty* (World Bank 2000), and the World Bank and the United Nations collaborated to design a set of subsequently very influential Millennium Development Goals (MDGs), which are listed for you in Table 11.5.

The goal of reducing poverty in developing nations is without question an important one, but it sidesteps the issue that continues to drive poverty in developing nations—population growth and its aftermath (which is the impact of the age transition). Indeed, four of the eight MDGs shown in the table (1, 4, 5, and 6) are aimed directly at improving health. To the extent that they succeed, the death rate will drop and the rate of population growth will be pushed up. At the same time, two of the MDGs (2 and 3) should indirectly help to push the birth rate down, but there is no assurance that those forces will counteract the anticipated drop in the death rate.

The Brundtland Commission report led directly to the first Earth Summit—the United Nations Conference on Environment and Development in Rio de Janeiro in 1992, with a series of follow-up meetings, especially the one in Kyoto in 1997 at which a framework was established for a worldwide treaty to limit long-term carbon emissions (a treaty the Bush administration refused to sign when it came into power in the United States in 2001, and as of this writing the Obama administration has not signed it, either). Another follow-up meeting of the United Nations Framework Convention on Climate Change was held in 2000 in The Hague, but ended with no firm agreements being reached beyond those agreed to in Kyoto. A follow-up Earth Summit was held in 2002 in Johannesburg, South Africa, to which the United States chose not to send a delegation. The World Bank's Development Report for 2003 was about sustainability (World Bank 2003) and was written in response to Earth Summit 2002. The report did address the need to monitor the age and urban transitions, but population was not the central focus. The concern among demographers that population issues might be buried in the Earth Summit discussions was expressed very well at the time by the Global Science Panel on Population & Environment: "If we do not put the human population at the core of the sustainable development agenda, our efforts to improve human well-being and preserve the quality of the environment will fail" (Lutz and Shah 2002:1).

The UN meetings regarding sustainability, discussed above, have focused especially on climate change, continuing the concern over the polluting aspect of resource consumption, and on poverty, continuing the concern about the North-South divide. Still, these meetings have generally sidestepped the connection between growing populations aspiring to a higher standard of living and the environmental degradation that we trying to bring under control (O'Neill, Landis, and Lutz 2004). Will the combination of population growth for another several decades and our continuing quest for higher standards of living push us beyond the point of sustainability?

Table 11.5 Millennium Development Goals for the World Community

1. Eradicate extreme poverty and hunger
2. Achieve universal primary education
3. Promote gender equality and empower women
4. Reduce child mortality
5. Improve maternal health
6. Combat HIV/AIDS, malaria, and other diseases
7. Ensure environmental sustainability
8. Develop a global partnership for development

Source: United Nations, 2010, "We can end poverty 2015: Millennium Development Goals" (http://www.un.org/millenniumgoals/global.shtml, accessed 2010).

Are We Overshooting Our Carrying Capacity?

In animal populations, overshoot occurs with a certain regularity in some ecosystems, and the consequence is a die-back of animals to a level consistent with resources, or at the extreme, a complete die-off in that area. A good rain one winter may produce an abundance of food for one species, creating an abundance of food for its predators, and so on. In classic Malthusian fashion, each well-fed species breeds beyond the region's carrying capacity, and when normal rainfall returns the following season there is not enough food to go around, and the death rate goes up from one end of the food chain to the other. Biologists have been documenting such stories for a long time.

Premodern humans were susceptible to the same phenomena. The apocryphal story is told of the goat that destroyed a civilization. A civilization existed that depended heavily on goats for meat and milk. "The goat population thrived, vegetation disappeared, erosion destroyed the arable land, sedimentation clogged what once had been a highly efficient irrigation system. The final result was no water to drink or food to eat. It did not happen overnight, but gradually the people had to leave to survive and the civilization perished" (Freeman 1992:3). In general form, this is apparently what happened to the great Mesopotamian civilizations of Sumeria and Babylon that flourished in western Asia nearly 9,000 years ago. The region at the time was covered with productive forests and grasslands, but each generation over time made greater and greater modifications to the environment—deforesting the area and building great irrigation canals. Around 1900 B.C., it appears that the population peaked at a level that greatly exceeded the ecosystem's carrying capacity (Simmons 1993). A combination of environmental degradation, climate change, drought, and a series of invading armies led to a long-term decline in population in the region (Miller 2009), and the area became the barren desert that today makes up parts of Iran and Iraq. In more recent history, the Mayan civilization in Central America reached a peak of population size about the year A.D. 800, and the civilization then collapsed as the population overshot the region's agricultural capacities, perhaps aggravated by a severe drought (Hodell, Curtis, and Brenner 1995).

These are only a few stories among many of premodern humans exceeding the carrying capacity of a region. Human life has survived these catastrophes, but human civilizations have not. Carrying capacity is, to be sure, a moving target. We know that the carrying capacity of the earth is greater than Malthus thought because we have discovered that certain kinds of technological and organizational improvements can improve the productivity of the land. Cornucopians (the boomsters in farmer attire) assume that human ingenuity will permit a continued expansion of carrying capacity up to the point at which the world's population stops growing of its own accord, which we expect to happen sometime this century, with a population somewhere in excess of 9 billion. However, the stories of Mesopotamia and of the Mayans remind us that factors generally beyond our control, such as the weather, can also reduce the carrying capacity of a region—and perhaps of the entire planet. Furthermore, as you know, we as humans have been in the process of trashing our environment to the point that we might ourselves be lowering the carrying capacity of the earth, rather than increasing it. This phenomenon is less visible at the local level than it used to be because, especially in the highly industrialized nations, we use up resources that are very distant from where we live, and we try to dump our pollution as far away as we can.

Let us assume that for all of human history up to the beginning of the nineteenth century, the carrying capacity of the globe was essentially fixed (even if it fluctuated over time from region to region) and was greater than the existing global population, but that the gap between population and sustainable resources had been narrowing—the perception of which spurred Malthus to write his *Essay on Population*. The Industrial Revolution was associated with increasing population growth, of course, but also with innovations in agriculture that allowed food production to stay ahead of that population growth, as I discussed earlier, and at least some of these innovations in growing food are certainly sustainable, so it is reasonable to assume (even if it cannot be proven) that the carrying capacity is greater today than it has ever been in history. Thus, the assumption is that since the dawn of the Industrial Revolution, both population size and the global carrying capacity have increased.

The problem is that we don't know whether or not we have now already exceeded that carrying capacity. This is partly because the global carrying capacity is a somewhat elusive concept (Sayre 2008). It is easy to know if a ship has exceeded its carrying capacity because it sinks. But we don't know for sure how big a load the earth can carry. If we have exceeded carrying capacity, then we are in a period of global **overshoot** and will face a catastrophe down the road.

There is strong evidence that we have, indeed, exceeded the global carrying capacity for sustaining more than about 2 billion people at the current North American standard of living (Cohen 1995; Pimentel et al. 1997; Chambers, Simmons, and Wackernagel 2002). If you and everyone else in the world were content to live at the level of the typical South Asian peasant, then the number of humans the world could carry would be considerably larger than if everyone were trying to live like the CEO of Goldman Sachs. Indeed, it is improbable that the world has enough resources for 7 billion people (much less 9 billion) to ever approach the standard of living of a successful business executive (much less the CEO). That implies that we are doomed to global inequality with respect to the consumption of resources, unless we in the highly developed world are willing (or are forced) to lower our standard of living dramatically. Chase-Dunn (1998) put it this way: "If the Chinese try to eat as much meat and eggs and drive as many cars (per capita) as the Americans the biosphere will fry" (p. xxi). A headline in the *Wall Street Journal* in late 2003 noted ominously that "China's Growing Thirst for Oil Remakes the Global Market" (Wonacott, Whalen, and Bahree 2003:A1), and that followed a story from earlier in 2003 about "The Great Leap Forward: Demand for Cars in China Is Accelerating at a Remarkable Rate" (*The Economist* 2003). Sure enough, in 2009 there were more cars sold in China than in either the United States or Europe (Deveau 2010).

But even if we assume that we have not yet exceeded the global carrying capacity, how much additional room do we have before we do? Are we headed in the same direction as Mesopotamia and the Mayan civilization? One of the most elaborate and best-known empirical investigations to examine this question was the "Club of Rome study," *Limits to Growth* (Meadows et al. 1972; Meadows 1974), which addressed the population size that would enable the earth to maximize the socioeconomic well-being of its citizens. After building a computer model simulating various paths of population growth and capital investment in resource development, this team of social scientists came to the conclusion that the world's population was already so large in the 1970s and was consuming resources at such a prodigious rate that by the year 2100 resources will be exhausted, the world economy will collapse, and the world's population size will plummet. After introducing their most optimistic assumptions into the model, the Meadows team described the potential result in the following way:

> Resources are fully exploited, and 75 percent of those used are recycled. Pollution generation is reduced to one-fourth of its 1970 value. Land yields are doubled, and effective methods of birth control are made available to the world population. The result is a temporary achievement of a constant population with a world average income per capita that reaches nearly the present U.S. level. Finally, though, industrial growth is halted, and the death rate rises as resources are depleted, pollution accumulates, and food production declines. (1972:147)

The authors freely acknowledged that their models did not replicate the complexities of the real world, nor were they attempting to predict the future. Nonetheless, the study demonstrated the possibility that, for the world as a whole, the optimum population was perhaps no larger than the level of the 1970s (much less the level of the early 2000s).

Meadows and associates discussed the need for "dynamic equilibrium" in which population and capital remain constant, while other "desirable and satisfying activities of man—education, art, music, religion, basic scientific research, athletics, and social institutions . . ." also flourish (1972:180). These same ideas (which in fact hearken back to the nineteenth-century writings of John Stuart Mill—see Chapter 3) have been put forth by Herman Daly (1996), who argues that when we think of sustainable development, we must think of development in qualitative, not quantitative terms. We need to think about improving the quality of our life in ways that put less burden on the earth's resources, rather than in ways that just use and abuse the earth.

In 1977, in response to the *Limits to Growth* study, President Carter directed that a study be conducted "of the probable changes in the world's population, natural resources, and environment through the end of the century" (Council on Environmental Quality 1980). The result was the *Global 2000* report, released in 1980 and containing the following dreary conclusions:

> If present trends continue, the world in 2000 will be more crowded, more polluted, less stable ecologically, and more vulnerable to disruption than the world we live in now. . . . Barring revolutionary advances in technology, life for most people on earth will be more precarious in 2000 than it is now. (Council on Environmental Quality 1980:1–3)

You tell me. Was the world in 2000 "more crowded, more polluted, less stable ecologically, and more vulnerable to disruption" than the world in 1980? The answer has to be yes, although warnings such as these have helped shape policies designed to mitigate the worst effects of population growth and environmental degradation. Still, there is little comfort here for countries not yet fully developed, since for them, the implication is that they need to follow the dual policies of stopping population growth as soon as possible and then hoping for a redistribution of income from wealthier nations.

The Malthusian specter of sheer numbers of people potentially exhausting available resources is rather overwhelming, and, as a result, it disguises other, more subtle consequences that population growth has for economic development and degradation. The consequences to which I refer are those associated with each of the transitions that not just nations, but local areas, pass through during the course of the overall demographic transition.

Population and Environment at the Micro-Level

It is important to have the macro-level view of the world, which is what I have tried to provide for you thus far in this chapter. That helps us to set the parameters for what is possible and problematic at the global scale. But demography, like politics, tends to be local. You may be generally concerned about global trends, but you are directly influenced by what is happening in your region or even neighborhood. Of course, you need to have the macro-level picture in mind because the drivers of what is happening locally often originate a long way away from you. At the same time, what happens at the local level may in turn influence the macro-level changes, as suggested by the vicious circle feedback model that I mentioned earlier.

Environmental Disasters Lead to Death and Dispersion

History is replete with examples of how humans have had to respond to natural catastrophes of one kind or another. I have already mentioned in this chapter the Mesopotamians and Mayans, whose civilizations were dispersed by environmental degradation, probably self-inflicted, compounded by drought. Earlier in the book I reminded you of the Irish potato famine, in which the Irish put themselves at risk by developing a dietary dependency on one type of potato, which then was wiped out by a rogue imported fungus in the middle of the nineteenth century. The result was a permanent change in Irish society, and a concomitant change in the ethnic makeup of the United States. Many of the Irish died during the famine, but the long-term consequence was a dispersal of the Irish population, mainly to America. Within the United States there have been multiple natural disasters to which the population has responded largely by dispersing to other parts of the country, including famously the Dust Bowl of the 1930s and the Katrina Hurricane disaster that hit New Orleans and the Gulf Coast in 2005, killing 1,800 people and displacing hundreds of thousands (for a review, see Gutmann and Field 2010).

Earthquakes represent another type of natural disaster that affects the population directly through mortality and migration and then indirectly through the adjustments that have to be made in the aftermath of the disaster. Furthermore, the size of the impact is directly related to how well protected the population is, since earthquake damage is largely driven by how well people are able to get out of harm's way, and on the resources that they have (their resilience) to bounce back after the disaster (Cutter, Mitchell, and Scott 2000; Rashed and Weeks 2003; Rashed et al. 2007). In 2004 an under-ocean earthquake triggered a tsunami tidal wave that killed 130,000 people in Aceh, Indonesia, who, unable to reach high ground, were thus drowned or crushed by the water. In 2010 a 7.0 magnitude earthquake hit Port-au-Prince, Haiti, and killed an estimated 230,000 people—nearly 10 percent of the city's population—many of whom were crushed by falling buildings (Over and McCarthy 2010). Yet a few months later an even stronger 7.2 magnitude earthquake hit Mexicali, Mexico, but killed only two of its one million residents. The difference in the death toll between Port-au-Prince and Mexicali lay largely in how buildings were constructed in the two places.

In Chapter 2 I discussed the terrible governmentally imposed famine in China in 1959–60 that led to the deaths of 30 million Chinese peasants. In that chapter I also mentioned the enormous consequences for Europe of the plague ("Black Death") over a several-century period. The major consequence was a rise in the death rate that essentially restructured European society. Earlier in European history, in A.D. 79, Italy had experienced the eruption of Mt. Vesuvius, which wiped out the city of Pompeii and, in the process, buried alive a large fraction of its population. Note, by the way, that Mt. Vesuvius is still an active volcano and there are today an estimated 2 to 3 million people living in its vicinity.

I mention all of these examples mainly to remind you of the two major direct human responses to specific environmental and other natural disasters—an increase in mortality, and a high out-migration rate (Hunter 2005; Lutz 2009). The threat of death or at least poor health from environmental degradation is a common concern in the literature, and that is consistent with the importance of the health and mortality transition to our entire existence. Having gained better health and a longer life expectancy than ever previously imagined in human society, we are loath to give those things up. Yet there is widespread worry that crowding people into cities, as we are doing, is still potentially harmful to health, and that this could erase some of the gains made over the past century in the health of urban residents. Air pollution in cities is generally worse than elsewhere and it is especially bad in cities of less developed nations. At the macro-level we worry about the effect on climate change of the emissions into the atmosphere from cities (a clear example of the human dimension of global environmental change), and then we worry about the vicious circle of that climate change coming back to affect the cities (Krellenberg, Heinrichs, and Barton 2010), but at the local level we are mainly concerned about the negative health effects of that air pollution on residents in cities (National Research Council 2008). For example, in cities of developing countries, households often cook with wood or charcoal and thus are subjected to intense local air pollution from that cooking source (Ezzati and Kammen 2001; Ezzati and Lopez 2003).

The migration of people vulnerable to ecological disasters may tell the entire story of why the earth is now covered with humans. We have spent millennia trying to find better and/or safer places to live, and the most widely anticipated reaction that demographers foresee from climate change is the need for people to move out of affected areas into other places where they are less exposed to the risks of loss of livelihood or even death. But the political side of the world now enters into that equation because we have spent the last 200 years fencing the planet off into nation-states. This limits the range of options readily open for people to respond to changes in the local environment. To deal with global climate change will mean reckoning as well with global social change (Chase-Dunn and

Babones 2006), as people from different cultural groups reorganize themselves spatially. This is unlikely to go smoothly.

Human Dimensions of Local Environmental Change

One of the more important ways that population growth influences the environment is through the change in land use. The most obvious of these is deforestation. Forests are cleared in order to grow crops and pasture animals and to provide space for buildings and other human uses, and the wood is then used for materials and fuels. Since forests are very unlikely to disappear on their own, at least in the short term, the path of humans through the environment can be readily traced by these land cover and land use changes (LCLUC) (de Sherbinin et al. 2007). The biggest impact of this type comes when people initially migrate into an area and transform the environment. Population growth that occurs after that initial surge is apt to be associated with incremental, less dramatic LCLUC. For this reason, emerging evidence suggests that an increase in the number of households in a local area is a more important determinant of environmental impact than the number of people itself (An and Liu 2010). More households create more damage, no matter how many people are in the household. For this reason, it seems that the family and household transition plays a role that can be thought of as generally detrimental to the environment. Diversity of living arrangements may encourage the kind of independence that promotes innovation and higher productivity, but it may also lead to a less-than-efficient use of resources (O'Neill, MacKellar, and Lutz 2004). As the number of households in an area increases because the number of people per household is declining, people are less likely to share the use of basic resources such as water and energy. Heating a house, for example, uses about the same amount of energy whether the house is occupied by one or five people. A car uses about the same amount of energy whether it is occupied by one or five people. Washing dishes or clothes for one person may use just about the same amount of water as for two people. You get the idea.

The availability and quality of local water represents, in fact, a major connection between population and the environment. Earlier in the chapter we discussed this in global terms, but human life and water need to exist side-by-side. If a place has no water, then it won't support life. But, even if there is water, if it is polluted and cannot safely be drunk by people, then life is threatened, because water-borne diseases can cause diarrhea, which can lead to dehydration and death, particularly among children, as I noted in Chapter 5.

Nearly half of all people in the world do not have water piped into their homes, which means that people may have to travel considerable distances from their homes to get water and carry it home. This work is typically done by women, in cities and in rural areas, and you can imagine the loss of local economic productivity that is wrapped up in the time spent dealing with water every day (Ray 2007; Rosenberg 2010). Nearly half of the world's population also lacks access to sanitation systems (Nelson and Murray 2008) and this also creates problems directly for the environment and for the health of those people.

Finally on this theme, you almost certainly know that one of the expected consequences of the melting of the glaciers throughout the world—which is already documented as being under way—is a rise in sea level. This will obviously affect vulnerable coastal populations and researchers have been working to understand how to mitigate the impact of the loss of homes and livelihood that will inevitably result from this sea change (pun intended) (Mustelin et al. 2010).

Demographic Components of Environmental Justice

In the run-up to the United Nations Climate Change Conference held in Copenhagen in 2009, the *Wall Street Journal* headlined the question: "If It Warms Up, Who's Going to Pay?" (Fankhouser 2009). At the global level this frames the problem of environmental justice: Those who degrade the environment are not necessarily the ones, or at least are not the only ones, who pay the price. Populations that are economically and politically weaker (the "periphery" in world systems terminology) bear a disproportionate burden (World Bank 2009).

The same principle operates at the local level in rich and less-rich societies alike: The poor and politically weak members of the population are (a) more likely to have waste dumped near where they live; and (b) because places near waste sites are cheaper than other places, the poor will also "choose" such places to live on their own (Pastor, Sadd, and Hipp 2001; Mennis and Jordan 2005; Mohai and Saha 2006). This is an example of the way in which the life chances that I discussed in Chapter 10 come back to make a difference in people's lives. Low levels of human capital increase the risk of living in environmentally dangerous places. But the effects go beyond just one generation. Since in virtually every society the poor are apt to have more children than average, a disproportionate share of children are likely to be growing up in those neighborhoods that are at elevated environmental risk. It is not yet clear how important this might be in the long run.

Summary and Conclusion

If people did not think that population growth was related in some way to economic development, there would be far less interest in population issues than exists today in the world. Although most people seem to share the view that too much population growth is not good, it has been frustratingly difficult to prove a cause-and-effect relationship. Into this void of conclusions have leapt several competing perspectives. The doomsters are neo-Malthusians who argue that population growth must slow down or the economic well-being of the planet will deteriorate over time. Boomsters are those who believe that population growth is a good thing—it stimulates development and is a sign of, rather than a threat to, well-being. A third perspective is shared by Marxists, neo-Marxists, and adherents (whether Marxist or not) to the world systems perspective. This position argues that population growth is irrelevant to economic development. It is the relationships among national economies, and a nation's place in the global economic system, that determine the pace and pattern of economic development.

There can be little question that population growth creates long-term pressures on societal resources that must be dealt with. In the final analysis, each of the several perspectives of the relationship between population growth and economic development has some merit—it is just that each is describing a different part of a complicated process, one that is unfolding differently for today's developing or emerging nations than it did historically for the already richer countries. A major difference is the experience with much more rapid rates of population growth among developing countries over the past few decades than were ever encountered in the history of wealthier nations. This creates more opportunities for commerce than might otherwise exist (more feet to be shod, more food to be processed, more people to buy iPhones and laptops), but it also means that we have been consuming resources at a historically unprecedented rate. Early capitalists were accustomed to saving to build up capital (hence the name), which was crucial as the building block for future success. However, rapid population growth has meant that we have been dipping into our capital—not just the financial capital, but the resource base of the planet. We have been using up our environmental resources and changing the very nature of human life in the process, and that raises some very legitimate concerns about how long we can sustain both development and increasing population size.

Overall, it seems reasonable to conclude that in order to reach a high level of economic development a country must bring its rate of population growth down to a very low level, and that must happen much more quickly for peripheral nations than it did in the history of the core nations, because the less developed nations have experienced economic development in the context of much more rapid rates of population growth than the now-developed countries did.

The world's still increasing population naturally requires an increase in food production, unless we dramatically alter what we eat, and how we waste food once produced. Since the world is almost out of land that can be readily cultivated, increases in yield per acre, combined with reducing wasted food, seem to offer the principal hope for the future. Indeed, that is what the Green Revolution has been all about—combining plant genetics with pesticides, fertilizer, irrigation, crop rotation, land reorganization, and multiple cropping to get more food out of each acre. At current levels of technology, it may be reasonable to suppose that the world's population could be fed for many years to come if food can be properly distributed, if farmers in less developed nations are able to reach their potential for production, and if environmental degradation (especially global warming) does not intervene to limit productivity. Whether that happens is more a political, social, and economic question than anything else. What does seem clear is that it is almost inconceivable that all of the world's people will ever be able to eat or even more generally to live as Americans currently do. We have almost certainly exceeded the carrying capacity for that level of living.

A major constraint in providing food and a better life for the growing billions of newcomers to the planet is that, in the process of providing for our sustenance, we are degrading the environment—perhaps irreparably. In the early 1990s, Paul Harrison (1993:270) offered a summary that is still accurate:

> We are in the embrace of an environmental crisis that is coiling around more and more regions and ecosystems. Accelerating deforestation in the South, forest death in the North, red tides, the ozone hole, the threat of global warming: all have arrived over the

> space of a mere fifteen years. Underlying them is the long attrition of biological diversity, and the progressive degradation of land. These problems arose when perhaps no more than 1.4 billion people were consuming at levels of at least moderate material affluence. Yet ahead lie four decades of the fastest growth in human numbers in history.

Demographers, of course, cannot provide direct solutions to the problems of feeding the population or of halting environmental degradation, but they have wrestled mightily with what lies ahead for us as a consequence of population change. I continue the discussion of these issues in the next, and final, chapter.

Main Points

1. Economic development represents a growth in average income—a rise in the material well-being of people in a society.
2. Data for the world indicate that higher levels of average income typically are associated with lower rates of population growth, whereas higher rates of population growth generally are accompanied by lower levels of average income.
3. Ester Boserup and Julian Simon led the "boomster" argument that population growth serves as a stimulus for technological development and economic advancement, whereas neo-Malthusians express the "doomster" view that population growth is detrimental to economic development.
4. Those concerned about international economic relationships (such as proponents of the world systems theory) argue that population growth is irrelevant to the process of economic development, and that no meaningful relationship exists.
5. Food production can be increased by increasing farmland or per-acre yield. The latter can be accomplished by continued plant breeding and increased use of irrigation, fertilizers, and pesticides, along with new patterns of land tenure.
6. It is often said that if you give a man a fish, he will eat for a day, but if you teach him how to fish, he will sit in a boat and drink beer all day.
7. It is estimated that the world could not grow enough food for the entire population to eat an average American diet, yet it is perhaps within the realm of possibility that 11 to 12 billion people could be sustained at current levels of agricultural technology if food production and distribution worked far more efficiently and if environmental degradation did not intervene to lower agricultural productivity.
8. In trying to feed ever more people and attempting to elevate world standards of living, we have managed to do a great deal of damage to the environment, the immediate or proximate causes of which are population growth, economic development, and technology. The relative contribution of each varies from place to place, from time to time, and according to the specific type of degradation.
9. There is a very real possibility that we have overshot the carrying capacity for life at the average American level; achieving sustainable development will require a

different definition of a desirable standard of living and/or acceptance of permanent inequalities in levels of living around the world.

10. At the local level, we can see the relationship between population and environmental change reflected in land cover and land use change, as well as in issues that arise over environmental justice.

Questions for Review

1. How would you describe economic development as it applies to your own life? Do you aspire to more material goods? Do you aspire to more cultural goods that use human rather than natural resources?
2. Thinking about the community in which you grew up, would you say that population growth was positively or negatively related to the local economy, or not related at all? Defend your answer.
3. How would you reconcile the concern in rich countries for organic foods and the banning of genetically modified foods with the demand in the rest of the world for more food for more people? Can we have it both ways?
4. Given the strong evidence that human-induced global climate change is occurring, what do you think might be the long-term consequences for the choices (voluntary or forced) that people will make about where to live in response to climate changes, especially in places where the population is continuing to increase? How will these choices impact the world community?
5. What is your perception of the strengths and weaknesses of the ecological footprint concept? How useful is the concept to you in helping you to understand your own impact on the earth?

Suggested Readings

1. Ansley Coale and Edgar Hoover, 1958, *Population Growth and Economic Development in Low-Income Countries* (Princeton, NJ: Princeton University Press).

   This book is such a classic in the area of the demography of economic development that it is the basis of comparison for evaluating virtually all theories and research findings.
2. Nancy Birdsall, Allen C. Kelley, and Steven W. Sinding, Editors, 2001, *Population Matters: Demographic Change, Economic Growth, and Poverty in the Developed World* (New York: Oxford University Press).

   At the behest of the United Nations Population Fund, a workshop was convened in Bellagio, Italy, in 1998 to reassess the relationship between population growth and economic development. The results of that very important workshop are the chapters in this book, accompanied by an excellent overview chapter by the editors.
3. Glenn Firebaugh, 2003, *The New Geography of Global Income Inequality* (Cambridge, MA: Harvard University Press).

Firebaugh reviews data on national income levels over time and concludes that the world has been experiencing a transition in global income inequality in which inequalities between countries are decreasing while inequality within countries is increasing. He discusses this in the context of population changes.

4. Herman E. Daly, 1996, Beyond Growth: The Economics of Sustainable Development (Boston: Beacon Press).

   Daly was one of the first economists to suggest the possible inconsistencies in the global push for sustainable development—especially the general lack of consideration given to population growth in most discussions of sustainable development.

5. Jared Diamond, 2004, Collapse: How Societies Choose to Fail or Succeed (New York: Viking).

   Societies have indeed collapsed in the past and we are not necessarily immune from that threat. The interaction of population growth and environmental degradation is a central theme in this important book.

Websites of Interest

Remember that websites are not as permanent as books and journals, so I cannot guarantee that each of the following websites still exists at the moment you are reading this. You may have to Google the name of the organization to find the current web address.

1. **http://www.myfootprint.org/**
   Calculate your own ecological footprint at this website, and estimate your impact on the earth's resources.

2. **http://www.wri.org/**
   The World Resources Institute provides a valuable set of resources for examining the relationships among development, poverty, and a host of environmental issues.

3. **http://www.worldbank.org**
   Over the years, the World Bank has devoted considerable resources to compiling in one place a set of comparative world data that relate to topics such as population growth and economic development. This website summarizes the most recent World Development Indicators (WDI), and contains several tables of data that can be viewed online or downloaded and analyzed on your own computer.

4. **http://www.fao.org**
   The Food and Agriculture Organization (FAO) of the United Nations is the principal source of data on land use and agricultural production. Its FAOSTATS online database at this website lets you choose the information you want and the format you want it in. Search the site carefully because there are a lot of other things there.

5. **http://www.cgdev.org/section/initiatives/_active/demographicsanddevelopment**
   The Center for Global Development in Washington, DC, has launched an initiative to analyze the relationship between demography and development, and has invited well-known demographers to participate in a lecture series that is available at this site.

CHAPTER 12
Coping With Demographic Change

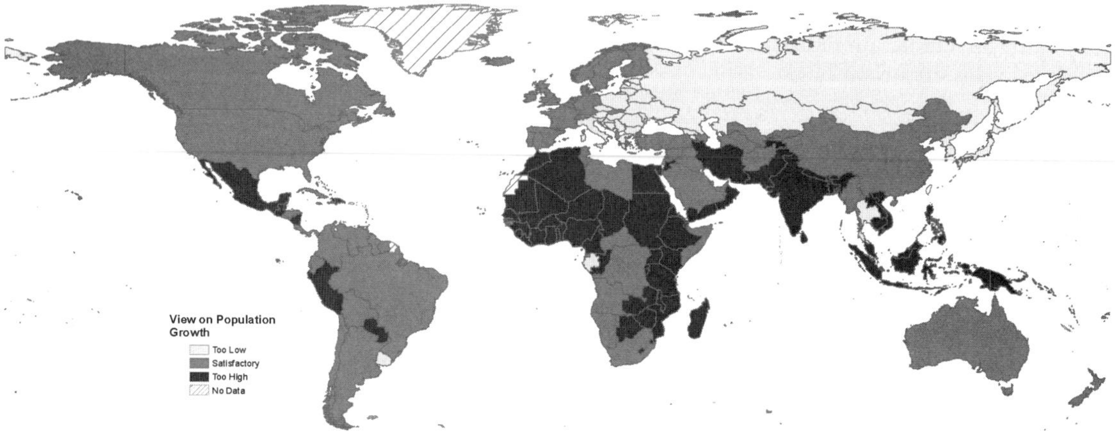

Figure 12.1 Countries According to the Government View on the Overall Rate of Population Growth

Is the population "problem" over?

Trick question—I'm checking to see if you have been paying attention.

Are we on the rapid road to the end of the worldwide demographic transition?

Well, nobody knows for sure.

I never promised that coping with demographic change would be easy—we don't have all the answers. But, in the preceding chapters you have learned that there is much we *do* know, and it is important to keep adding to our stock of knowledge, for with knowledge comes the power to help shape the future. In this chapter, I will review the global policy making that has been brought to bear to slow the rate of population growth so far. Then I review where we think we might be heading, demographically speaking, between now and the middle of this century. Hang on—dealing with our demographic future may not be a smooth cruise.

Global Action: From Demographic Revolution to Evolution

It's predictable—policy intervention does make a difference, and I'm going to take you on a short walk down memory lane to show you how this has mattered when it comes to population issues. As WWII was coming to an end, it became clear that a new demographic era was dawning in Europe, and researchers at Princeton's Office of Population Research began laying out a plan of research to study the phenomenon. At about the same time, the League of Nations (the precursor to the modern United Nations) economic group moved from Geneva to Princeton, and they commissioned a series of studies designed to enhance the quality of postwar planning. These studies, funded by the Carnegie Foundation and the Milbank Memorial Fund, included *The Future Population of Europe and the Soviet Union* (Notestein *et al.* 1944), *Economic Demography of Eastern and Southern Europe* (Moore 1945), *Europe's Population in the Interwar Years* (Kirk 1946), and *The Population of the Soviet Union: History and Prospects* (Lorimer 1946). As these projects were unfolding, the US Department of State asked that the studies be extended to Asia. This produced two important volumes, *The Population of India and Pakistan* (Davis 1951), and *The Population of Japan* (Taeuber 1958).

The basic findings of all of these studies were summarized in 1945 in a special issue of the *Annals of the American Academy of Political and Social Science* titled "World Population in Transition." The issue was edited by Kingsley Davis, who began his introductory article with this well-known blockbuster sentence: "Viewed in the long-run perspective, the growth of the earth's population has been like a long, thin powder fuse that burns slowly and haltingly until it finally reaches the charge and then explodes." Sound familiar? With these studies, the League of Nations set a precedent for seeking expert advice on policy matters related to world population issues. The United Nations subsequently did the same, and there is no doubt we would be living in a very different world had these instruments of global policy not been put into play.

Instruments of Global Policy

In 1954, the United Nations and the IUSSP organized a World Population Conference in Rome—the conference generally credited with alerting the world community to the very high rates of growth in less-developed nations (Harkavy 1995). The idea of having a world conference to discuss population policy is essentially a variation on the diffusion-of-innovations model. If you gather together experts on the demographic situation and on how human behavior can be transformed to achieve differing demographic goals, best practices will emerge; they can be agreed on; and then copied by everyone. Indeed, following that conference, the Ford Foundation began its deep involvement in the field.

In 1965, the United Nations again joined forces with the IUSSP for a follow-up World Population Conference in Belgrade. Up to this point, the United Nations had been reluctant to get involved in policy making per se, because policy would certainly involve the touchy subject of birth control which was opposed by a seemingly unlikely combination of the Vatican, the French government, and the Soviet Union and other communist countries (Harkavy 1995). The Vatican and the French government (which was officially pronatalist) were opposed to birth control on moral grounds, whereas the communist countries were still swayed by the Marxist idea that overpopulation was impossible in a socialist society, as you will recall from Chapter 3.

The papers from the 1965 conference made very plain, however, that population growth was potentially out of control and that concerted world policy action was advisable. The United Nations responded in 1969 with the creation of the United Nations Fund for Population Activities (UNFPA), which is now known more simply as the United Nations Population Fund. The UNFPA coordinates a wide range of population-related activities around the world, primarily in developing countries.

Unlike earlier world population conferences, which had been organized for professional demographers (don't worry, those kinds of meetings still take place), the UNFPA decided to organize World Population Conferences that brought together policy makers from government and from nongovernmental organizations, with the explicit goal of developing world population policy. This format had the advantage of bringing to the table the representatives of agencies that could actually implement policies, but with the disadvantage that underlying population concerns could be lost in the midst of political battles that had nothing to do with demographic change (Finkle and McIntosh 2002). The first of these policy-oriented conferences was held in Bucharest in 1974.

After nearly two weeks of "often acrimonious debate" (Demeny 1994:5), the delegates to the conference (government representatives from all over the world) agreed to a World Population Plan of Action. The plan was important for several reasons: (1) This was the first time that an international body had established anything approximating a world population policy; (2) The subsequent 1984 and 1994 Population Conferences were designed in advance to evaluate and alter this plan as necessary; and (3) The "Plan" incorporated elements from both sides of the "acrimonious debate," which, in essence, represented the U.S. perspective on the one hand (with the general support of other industrialized nations) and the perspective of developing countries on the other (Finkle and Crane 1975).

Key U.S. government representatives went to the Bucharest meeting with a very clear perspective: Developing countries should establish population growth rate targets, and those targets should be met by the provision of family planning (Donaldson and Tsui 1990; Donaldson 1990). Highlights of the conference included a statement that countries are "invited to set quantitative goals," and another statement that countries should "encourage appropriate education concerning responsible parenthood."

In contrast to the U.S. position, leaders of developing countries arrived in Bucharest with the growing conviction that they were the less-advantaged participants in a world economic system organized by and for the benefit of the industrialized nations. The UN itself had tacitly endorsed that view just before the 1974 World Population Conference with a General Assembly resolution calling for a "New International Economic Order." Developing nations were thus interested in seeing a world plan that integrated population policy with economic development programs. Indeed, it was at this conference that a delegate from India coined the phrase "development is the best contraceptive" (Visaria and Chari 1998).

In the decade between the meeting in Bucharest and the next one in Mexico City, most developing countries came to the conclusion that rapid population growth did, indeed, hinder their efforts to develop economically, and many of those countries implemented family planning programs to help slow down population growth, regardless of how they might have felt about this in 1974. Thus, the stage was set for the 1984 Mexico City conference to be a better meeting of the minds. However, the United States threw cold water on that prospect by proposing, instead, that "population growth is, by itself, a neutral phenomenon." This was a "choice piece of nonsense," as Demeny (1994:10) has remarked, and it was inspired by Julian Simon's influence within the Reagan administration (and abetted by a coalition of groups opposed to abortion). Simon's basic premise, as you remember from Chapter 11, is that population growth can help stimulate development, which, in fact, is what the developing countries have in mind as their ultimate goal. The implication is that if you are focusing your energies on population control rather than economic development (especially establishing free markets and democratic institutions), you may never achieve your goal of improving the well-being of your citizens.

It has been said that "in Bucharest, the Chinese had declared that overpopulation was no problem under socialism. In 1984, the Americans declared that overpopulation could be solved by capitalist development" (Donaldson 1990:130). Neither of those views is actually supportable by evidence from the real world, but the turnabout of attitudes among delegates meant that the 1984 conference did not move the world population policy agenda along in any important way. Demeny (1994) has succinctly characterized the outcome of the Mexico City conference as follows:

> The "Recommendations for the Further Implementation of the World Population Plan of Action" adopted at Mexico City amplified the language of Bucharest but added no qualitatively novel elements. The 88 Recommendations placed added emphasis and urgency on concerns with the environment, the role and status of women, meeting "unmet needs" for family planning, and education (1994:12).

At the conclusion of the conference, the delegates agreed to a Declaration on Population and Development, summarizing the major accomplishments of the conference. The consensus was that the World Population Plan of Action adopted at Bucharest was still valid, even if countries had not yet done very much to implement their national population policies.

One of the most significant events at the Mexico City conference was the announcement by the United States that any organization in the world that received money from the U.S. government was prohibited from providing abortion, abortion counseling, or abortion-related services. This was called the "Mexico City Policy" and later dubbed the "Global Gag Rule." The Reagan administration, which had devised this policy, later decided that the UNFPA was in violation (despite repeated denials by the United Nations) and the Reagan and then the Bush administrations withheld all U.S. funding from the UNFPA during the years 1987–92. U.S. funding was reinstated by the Clinton administration in 1993, withheld again when George W. Bush took office in 2001, and then reinstated after Barack Obama was inaugurated in 2009.

The 1994 International Conference on Population and Development (ICPD) In the early 1990s, as people began to anticipate UN plans for a 1994 population conference to be held in Cairo, the discussion split off into the three sides of the debate about the relationship between population growth and economic development outlined in Chapter 11.

Representing the view that the world has a tremendous population problem that we must collectively continue to try to resolve were experts in the social and environmental sciences who study the issues, as well as people in the public and medical health service fields who deal regularly with the repercussions of rapid population growth (see, for example, Westoff 1994).

Representing the view that population growth was not the issue—that building free markets and capitalism were the important tasks—was, once again, Julian Simon and other "boomsters" (see, for example, Eberstadt 1994). From this group's perspective, there was no particular reason to have a population conference, and that view was shared by the Vatican, which has been opposed to all of the world population conferences, because of their emphasis on the provision of family planning.

The newest and loudest voices added to the debate over world population policy were those of feminists, whose arguments centered on the idea that abstract population targets represent additional ways in which men try to exploit women for their own purposes. In particular, the idea that "population control is a euphemism for the control of women" (Seager 1993:216) drew evidence from the coercive policies put into place in China. Although in agreement on this point, the feminist movement splintered into two differing views on the importance of population issues and thus on the relevance of a population conference. One view was an essentially neo-Marxist position that the problems in the world are caused not by population growth but by inequities in the distribution of power and resources (Hartmann 1995). The other feminist perspective did not deny the importance of population growth as a constraint to human well-being, but argued that the most important issue for the world is to improve the levels of women's rights and reproductive health on a global basis (Dixon-Mueller 1993; Chesler 1994). If that were done, it was argued, the "solution" to the high birth rate would be effected.

Although differing views of birth control and women's rights were on the table at the IPCD, the goal was to achieve some kind of consensus that could provide genuine policy guidance to governments. The world's experience over the past several decades suggests that when governments are committed to a program of reducing population growth, the goal is likely to be accomplished (United Nations Population Division 2009a).

Governments do not work in a vacuum, however. They can be assisted and prodded by a variety of **non-governmental organizations** (NGOs). Jain (1998) has suggested that NGOs are "among the most influential actors in the policymaking process" (p. 11). NGOs that have been involved in population issues include private donor agencies, such as the Rockefeller Foundation, the Ford Foundation, the Andrew J. Mellon Foundation, the Packard Foundation, the Hewlett Foundation, the Bill and Melinda Gates Foundation, and the Wellcome Trust. Other NGOs work with their own money and/or that of donor agencies (both private and public) to provide direct reproductive health services in developing countries. These include organizations such as the International Planned Parenthood Federation (IPPF), Pathfinder International, John Snow, Inc., and Management Sciences for Health. Another group of NGOs is largely devoted to providing information and education materials and resources that can be used to promote population policy messages wherever they might be useful. Organizations in this category include Futures Group International, Population Action International, Population Connection (formerly Zero Population Growth), the Population Institute, the Population Reference Bureau, the Population Resource Center, the World Population Foundation, and the World Resources Institute. This is not an exhaustive list, but it gives you an idea of which organizations are NGOs in the field of population.

The value of NGOs is that they are not burdened by a government bureaucracy, and they have well-developed policy initiatives that can help set the agenda for a nation's population program. They also provide technical assistance that government personnel might otherwise lack, and they can also fund demonstration projects to convince government leaders of the value of population programs (Jain 1998). For example, in the 1950s and 1960s, the Ford Foundation was especially instrumental in organizing population policy in India, and its activities helped draw the U.S. government into the population movement (Harkavy 1995). The work of NGOs in the population field tends to focus on reducing both infant and maternal mortality while at the same time promoting the empowerment of women, reproductive health, and family planning. These programs are thus not always devoted exclusively and explicitly to retarding population growth, though that is typically an underlying motivation. NGOs emerged as important policy drivers at the 1994 Population Conference.

The International Conference on Population and Development was preceded by several preparatory meetings (PrepComs) sponsored by the United Nations Population Division and the United Nations Population Fund, as well as meetings sponsored by NGOs, and by a plethora of books, professional journal and magazine articles, newspaper columns and editorials, talk radio and TV shows, and any other imaginable medium of human communication. In the process, the World Population Plan of Action from the 1974 Bucharest meeting was essentially scrapped, and in its place a new Programme of Action was drafted and circulated in printed form to the delegates and made available to the rest of us on the Internet. Most of the content of the Programme of Action had been agreed to ahead of time at the PrepComs, but controversial material was bracketed [literally—the text had brackets around it] for discussion by the delegates in Cairo. No surprise: The most controversial issue was abortion, and the Vatican created worldwide public attention with its opinion of the matter. After five days of debate and special committee meetings, the Vatican was successful in altering some of the language regarding safe abortions.

As approved at the conclusion of the Cairo conference, the Programme of Action covers an extremely wide range of topics, in recognition of the fact that the causes and consequences of population growth reach into almost every aspect of human existence. Some critics have complained that many of the action items are too vague to be effective—drafted that way to avoid controversy. Indeed, the conference report stayed away from China's controversial population policies by simply never mentioning China at all! Still, the conference regalvanized world interest in and concern about population growth. Nafis Sadik, then the executive director of the United Nations Population Fund, served as secretary-general of the conference, and she summarized the work of the conference as follows:

> The delegates have crafted a Programme of Action for the next 20 years which starts from the reality of the world we live in, and shows us the path to a better reality. The Programme contains highly specific goals and recommendations in the mutually reinforcing areas of infant and maternal mortality, education, and reproductive health and family planning, but its effect will be more wide-ranging than that. This Programme of Action has the potential to change the world. Implementing the Programme of Action recognizes that healthy families are created by choice, not chance.
>
> The Programme of Action recognizes that poverty is the most formidable enemy of choice. One of its most important effects will be to draw women into the mainstream of development. Better health and education, and freedom to plan their family's future, will widen women's economic choices; but it will also liberate their minds and spirits. As the leader of the Zimbabwe delegation put it, it will empower women, not with the power to fight, but with the power to decide. That power of decision alone will ensure many changes in the post-Cairo world (Sadik 1994:4–5).

Delegates agreed to the set of 15 principles that are listed in Table 12.1. You will recognize many of the same themes here that were integrated into the Millennium Development Goals that I discussed in Chapter 11. Each of these principles was associated with a specific set of actions for dealing with the demographic issues addressed by the principle. Together, they comprised the Programme of Action, which is still in the process of being monitored globally by UNFPA.

Some of the action items that were addressed included numeric target goals (despite the disdain for targets), and the major target agreed to was to try to limit world population to no more than 9.8 billion as of 2050. This was the UN's medium variant projection at the time of the conference, which as you know from Chapter 2 has been revised down partly because of the expected impact of HIV/AIDS on mortality (that's a bad thing) and because fertility is now expected to decline a bit more quickly than was expected in the early 1990s (that's a good thing).

Perhaps most importantly, the "Cairo Consensus" meant that concerns held by feminists about the role of women in society were addressed very specifically in a variety of places within the Programme of Action and many were specifically endorsed for funding by organizations such as the U.S. Agency for International Development and the World Bank. It is in this context of reproductive decision making that the language of the 1994 International Conference on Population and Development differs most from its predecessors, "moving away from a focus on numbers to a focus on human rights and dignity" (Obaid 2009:1). The World Bank called it a paradigm shift, while Halfon (2006) has labeled it a "regime change."

Table 12.1 The 15 Principles Underlying Population Policy as Established at the Cairo Population Conference

The implementation of the recommendations contained in the Programme of Action is the sovereign right of each country, consistent with national laws and development priorities, with full respect for the various religious and ethical values and cultural backgrounds of its people, and in conformity with universally recognized international human rights.

International cooperation and universal solidarity, guided by the principles of the Charter of the United Nations, and in a spirit of partnership, are crucial in order to improve the quality of life of the peoples of the world.

In addressing the mandate of the International Conference on Population and Development and its overall theme, the interrelationships between population, sustained economic growth and sustainable development, and in their deliberations, the participants were and will continue to be guided by the following set of principles:

Principle 1

All human beings are born free and equal in dignity and rights. Everyone is entitled to all the rights and freedoms set forth in the Universal Declaration of Human Rights, without distinction of any kind, such as race, colour, sex, language, religion, political or other opinion, national or social origin, property, birth or other status. Everyone has the right to life, liberty and security of person.

Principle 2

Human beings are at the centre of concerns for sustainable development. They are entitled to a healthy and productive life in harmony with nature. People are the most important and valuable resource of any nation. Countries should ensure that all individuals are given the opportunity to make the most of their potential. They have the right to an adequate standard of living for themselves and their families, including adequate food, clothing, housing, water and sanitation.

Principle 3

The right to development is a universal and inalienable right and an integral part of fundamental human rights, and the human person is the central subject of development. While development facilitates the enjoyment of all human rights, the lack of development may not be invoked to justify the abridgement of internationally recognized human rights. The right to development must be fulfilled so as to equitably meet the population, development and environment needs of present and future generations.

Principle 4

Advancing gender equality and equity and the empowerment of women, and the elimination of all kinds of violence against women, and ensuring women's ability to control their own fertility, are cornerstones of population and development-related programmes. The human rights of women and the girl child are an inalienable, integral and indivisible part of universal human rights. The full and equal participation of women in civil, cultural, economic, political and social life, at the national, regional and international levels, and the eradication of all forms of discrimination on grounds of sex, are priority objectives of the international community.

Principle 5

Population-related goals and policies are integral parts of cultural, economic and social development, the principal aim of which is to improve the quality of life of all people.

Principle 6

Sustainable development as a means to ensure human well-being, equitably shared by all people today and in the future, requires that the interrelationships between population, resources, the environment and development should be fully recognized, properly managed and brought into harmonious, dynamic balance. To achieve sustainable development and a higher quality of life for all people, States should reduce and eliminate unsustainable patterns of production and consumption and promote appropriate policies, including population-related policies, in order to meet the needs of current generations without compromising the ability of future generations to meet their own needs.

(continued)

Table 12.1 (continued)

Principle 7

All States and all people shall cooperate in the essential task of eradicating poverty as an indispensable requirement for sustainable development, in order to decrease the disparities in standards of living and better meet the needs of the majority of the people of the world. The special situation and needs of developing countries, particularly the least developed, shall be given special priority. Countries with economies in transition, as well as all other countries, need to be fully integrated into the world economy.

Principle 8

Everyone has the right to the enjoyment of the highest attainable standard of physical and mental health. States should take all appropriate measures to ensure, on a basis of equality of men and women, universal access to health-care services, including those related to reproductive health care, which includes family planning and sexual health. Reproductive health-care programmes should provide the widest range of services without any form of coercion. All couples and individuals have the basic right to decide freely and responsibly the number and spacing of their children and to have the information, education and means to do so.

Principle 9

The family is the basic unit of society and as such should be strengthened. It is entitled to receive comprehensive protection and support. In different cultural, political and social systems, various forms of the family exist. Marriage must be entered into with the free consent of the intending spouses, and husband and wife should be equal partners.

Principle 10

Everyone has the right to education, which shall be directed to the full development of human resources, and human dignity and potential, with particular attention to women and the girl child. Education should be designed to strengthen respect for human rights and fundamental freedoms, including those relating to population and development. The best interests of the child shall be the guiding principle of those responsible for his or her education and guidance; that responsibility lies in the first place with the parents.

Principle 11

All States and families should give the highest possible priority to children. The child has the right to standards of living adequate for its well-being and the right to the highest attainable standards of health, and the right to education. The child has the right to be cared for, guided and supported by parents, families and society and to be protected by appropriate legislative, administrative, social and educational measures from all forms of physical or mental violence, injury or abuse, neglect or negligent treatment, maltreatment or exploitation, including sale, trafficking, sexual abuse, and trafficking in its organs.

Principle 12

Countries receiving documented migrants should provide proper treatment and adequate social welfare services for them and their families, and should ensure their physical safety and security, bearing in mind the special circumstances and needs of countries, in particular developing countries, attempting to meet these objectives or requirements with regard to undocumented migrants, in conformity with the provisions of relevant conventions and international instruments and documents. Countries should guarantee to all migrants all basic human rights as included in the Universal Declaration of Human Rights.

Principle 13

Everyone has the right to seek and to enjoy in other countries asylum from persecution. States have responsibilities with respect to refugees as set forth in the Geneva Convention on the Status of Refugees and its 1967 Protocol.

Principle 14

In considering the population and development needs of indigenous people, States should recognize and support their identity, culture and interests, and enable them to participate fully in the economic, political and social life of the country, particularly where their health, education and well-being are affected.

(continued)

Table 12.1 (continued)

Principle 15

Sustained economic growth, in the context of sustainable development, and social progress require that growth be broadly based, offering equal opportunities to all people. All countries should recognize their common but differentiated responsibilities. The developed countries acknowledge the responsibility that they bear in the international pursuit of sustainable development, and should continue to improve their efforts to promote sustained economic growth and to narrow imbalances in a manner that can benefit all countries, particularly the developing countries.

Source: United Nations Population Fund, Master Plans for Development, http://www.unfpa.org/public/icpd/International-Conference-on-Population-and-Development/pid/5066#ch2, accessed 2010.

In 1999, the United Nations convened an international forum in The Hague, Netherlands, to review country-by-country accomplishments in achieving the Programme of Action laid out at the 1994 ICPD. This session laid the groundwork for a Special Session of the United Nations General Assembly held in July 1999 to consider these accomplishments. That session was kicked off with an important address by Kofi Annan, the UN Secretary-General at the time, in which he noted that the ICPD "was part of a process, going back twenty-five years or more, during which we have all learned that every society's hopes of social and economic development are intimately linked to its demography." He added that "the world does understand . . . that we have to stabilize the population of this planet. Quite simply, there is a limit to the pressures our global environment can stand" (Annan 1999:632–633). You will recognize these as concepts I have spent this entire book exploring with you.

The General Assembly then went on to accept a proposal by Brazil that public health systems should train and equip health service providers and should take other measures to ensure that abortion is safe and accessible in countries where abortion is legal. The Vatican objected to this, of course, but Brazil—the proposer of this policy—is a predominantly Catholic country, so there was little other dissent. The General Assembly also approved a new set of benchmarks for the Programme of Action to be monitored by the UNFPA.

Despite the wording regarding safe abortions, the Programme of Action has consistently avoided a realistic assessment of the role of abortion in the fertility transition. Hodgson (2009:508) has summarized the situation as follows:

> Program of Action population documents since 1984 have urged countries with high fertility to lower it by implementing effective family planning programs while simultaneously maintaining that "in no case should abortion be promoted as a method of family planning," and that governments "should reduce the recourse to abortion through expanded and improved family-planning services." Yet it has been known since the 1960s, and particularly widely known since the 1970s, that countries undergoing the fertility transition can expect, almost without exception, to experience increases in both contraceptive use and induced abortion. . . . These inconvenient facts have never been addressed at international population conferences.

The 1994 conference had established goals for the world that extended 20 years out from that date, but it was still expected that a 2004 conference would be held, as a way of reinforcing the importance of those goals. However, for a variety of reasons, including the fact that the Bush administration withdrew all U.S. funding for the UNFPA, the decision was made not to have a 2004 World Population Conference, but rather to maintain a focus on the Programme of Action, especially since many of those action items had been incorporated into the Millennium Goals, which I discussed in Chapter 11. The UNFPA received money from the Swiss government to help its regional offices coordinate regional and country-by-country reviews of progress toward the ICPD goals, and it has continued to do that as of this writing (UNFPA 2010).

Global Policy in the Context of Demographic Theory

All three World Population Conferences (excluding follow-ups to the 1994 ICPD, which have essentially been extensions of that meeting) were built on the basic premise that population growth is a potential hindrance to a country's ability to develop economically, and that a plan for the improved well-being of a population needs to include a strategy for limiting population growth (even if some delegates did not necessarily agree with that premise). All three conferences further accepted the idea that mortality reduction should always be a high priority, despite the fact that reductions in mortality put added pressure on population growth. All three conferences accepted the idea that migration should be controlled, although none of the conferences was very specific about how to do that. The biggest problem that each conference dealt with was how to cope with high fertility, even if the issue of abortion was consistently sidestepped. If we follow the U.S. perspective over time, we see that each of Coale's three preconditions for a fertility decline (see Chapter 6) has been presented as the predominant U.S. policy prescription, except that they have been presented in reverse order.

In 1974, the United States thought that family planning (Coale's third precondition) was the most important aspect of fertility on which to concentrate policy initiatives. In 1984, the emphasis on development implicitly recognized that the motivation to reduce fertility (Coale's second precondition) must accompany (indeed, precede) the demand for family planning services. Only by 1994 did the United States position get to the first precondition—that couples (especially women) must be empowered to take control of their own reproductive decisions. Only when that happens will the other preconditions become relevant for policy. To be sure, each of these elements was listed in the Action Plans of all three conferences, but with respect to fertility, in particular, the emphasis is important because it influences what will likely be funded by international donors and put into place by countries facing rapid population growth.

Finally, then, by 1994 it seemed as if the world community may have gotten it right in terms of a global perspective on population policy. Of course, setting a course is a lot easier than taking the trip, and policy making and policy implementation are both extremely difficult tasks. As Rumbaut (1995) reminds us, policy makers are always faced with a difficult task: "Condemned to try to control a future they cannot predict by reacting to a past that will not be repeated, policy makers are nonetheless faced with an imperative need to act that cannot be ignored as a practical or political matter" (p. 311).

Different Nations; Different Solutions

The global policies discussed thus far assume a country or a group of people oriented toward the future and anticipating change. If a population or its government leadership is "traditional" and hopes or expects tomorrow to be just like today, policies aimed at altering behavior are not likely to be adopted. If demographic policies exist at all in such a country, they may have as a goal the maintenance of the status quo and are probably inherently **pronatalist**; that is, they might forbid divorce or abortion, impede the progress of women, and so forth. In general, they would probably discourage the kind of innovative behavior that might lead to positive demographic change.

Randall (1996) provides an interesting example of a traditionally nomadic population in Mali in sub-Saharan Africa. Their fertility levels had been lower than those of sedentary farmers in the area, and demographic analysis revealed that this was due to the influence of monogamous marriages in a society in which husbands are substantially older than wives, and where high adult mortality produces a marriage squeeze that reduces the exposure of women to reproduction. However, the local perception is that women have a very high rate of sub-fecundity and that this is a problem that needs to be solved. Any policy implemented on the basis of that flawed perception would likely have very different consequences than a policy based on demographic reality.

The biggest obstacle to population policy in the world is probably gender inequality. In societies where the legal, social, and economic status of women is inferior to that of men, there is apt to be greater resistance to implementation of policies that lead indirectly to lower fertility by empowering women to have greater control over their own health and well-being (Campbell, Sahin-Hodoglugil, and Potts 2006). Thus, in the twenty-first century, global policy planners have focused their sights less on achieving specific demographic targets and more on achieving gender equality.

It is also easy to misperceive the important role that demography plays in the modern world. It is, as Westoff (1997) has noted, a large problem with low visibility. As you can appreciate from having read this book, there are few corners of the earth and few aspects of human existence that are not influenced by demography, but the demographic roots of social and technological change are not always recognized for what they are, with the result being that their influence may be denigrated or ignored (Smail 1997).

How Governments View Their Own Situation

No country in the world today can completely ignore the issue of population policy. This is partly because population growth is a world-renowned issue, even if its visibility may be lower than it should be, and partly because the United Nations Population Division regularly queries each country of the world about its policy position on population growth. The first survey was conducted in 1974, and it has been repeated every few years since.

Over the years there has been a steady increase in the number of governments saying that their policy is to slow down the rate of population growth. Government attitudes toward the overall rate of growth as of 2005 are shown in Figure 12.1, at the beginning of the chapter. The figure shows the worldwide distribution of countries according to whether their government thinks the overall rate of population growth is too high, too low, or satisfactory. Those governments that think the rate of population growth is too high are likely to have a policy to try to lower it. These countries are located in Latin America, Africa, and Asia. The countries thinking their rate of growth is too low are mainly in Europe, though very few of these countries are really trying to do much to increase it. Outside Europe, the countries that think their rates of growth are too low include Israel (for the obvious reason that the Palestinian population is one of the fastest-growing populations in the world), Uruguay, and Gabon. This last country, situated on the west coast of Africa, has a very high birth rate, life expectancy that is well below the world average, and oil reserves that may give the government some confidence that a larger population can be afforded, at least for a while.

The group of nations in which the government is satisfied with the growth rate, and more specifically with the birth rate, is divided into those that are satisfied with a low birth rate (North America, the southern nations of South America, northern Europe, China, and Australia) and those that are satisfied with a high rate (including countries in the northern part of South America, Africa, and Asia). The government of Somalia, for example, says that it is satisfied with the country's current birth rate—one that translates into an average of seven children per woman, and Saudi Arabia's government is similarly satisfied with its birth rate, which produces an average of four children per woman.

If a government is so inclined, several different basic policy orientations can be adopted either to close the gap or maintain the fit between goals and projections, based on combinations of managing the mortality, fertility, and migration transitions. Each policy orientation offers a wide variety of specific means that can be implemented to achieve the desired kind of demographic future. These different paths to population growth may seem fairly obvious to us now, but we have only very recently in human history arrived at the point where we have reasonable control over demographic phenomena.

What Is the Population Policy of the United States?

In response to the UN surveys on population policies, the United States has consistently indicated that the government is satisfied with current growth and fertility rates and has no plans for intervention. The closest the country has come to an explicit population policy was under President Nixon, who in 1969 proposed a commission (that Congress thereafter legislated into existence) to examine population growth in the United States, assess that growth's impact on the U.S. future, and "make recommendations on how the nation can best cope with that impact" (Commission on Population Growth and the American Future 1972:Preface). The commission, directed by a well-known Princeton demographer, Charles Westoff, spent three years gathering information, listening to the public and experts, and deliberating before producing its findings in 1972. Its essential conclusion was that "no substantial benefits would result from continued growth of the nation's population" (Commission, 1972:1), and its principal recommendation was that the United States pursue a policy of population stabilization.

The report's recommendations were not implemented in any direct way and the U.S. population continues to grow—from a little more than 200 million at the time of the commission's report to more than 300 million at present, and pushing toward 400 million by the middle of this century. From these facts might flow the facile conclusion that there is no population policy at all in the United States. Though there is no *explicit* policy aimed at limiting the U.S. population, the United States does have a set of *implicit* domestic population policies that influence the course of demographic events. Though the U.S. government has never supported a target number of people either for the country or the world, it does support improved health and longer life domestically and internationally; it supports fertility regulation domestically and, to a lesser extent, internationally. It also encourages low fertility and family diversity by enforcing laws against youthful marriages and by having liberal laws regarding divorce. The U.S. government places no limits on internal migration, while placing considerable restrictions on immigration from other countries, even though, as you know, the United States accepts more immigrants than any other country in the world.

Congress has provided federal funding for family planning programs in the United States since 1967, although the Family Planning Services and Population Research Act of 1970 specifically forbade funds to any organization that provided abortion services, even though several states already had liberalized abortion laws at that time. In 1973, the Supreme Court struck down restrictive abortion laws in the United States and one of the last obstacles to free choice in birth prevention was hurdled. Of course attempts to reverse that decision and once again restrict the access of American women to legal abortion are ongoing.

We know that government policy is not a necessary precursor to change, but it can help to both solidify and accelerate changes that are under way. In the United States, as in other parts of the world, a decline in fertility did not wait for the legal restrictions to be removed from contraception and abortion. Nor did it await government programs to develop new contraceptive technologies such as the IUD and the pill (both were privately financed), or for the government to provide free or subsidized birth control measures. Fertility declined dramatically from the nineteenth century to World War II, went up briefly, and then declined dramatically again. The first decline in the United States, as in England, was probably due as much to the "culture of abstinence"—reflecting a strong motivation to limit fertility—as to specific birth control methods (Szreter 1996). Only during the second decline did a wide range of birth prevention methods become readily available to women; in essence, the methods were part of the overall rise in the standard of living.

At the beginning of the twentieth century, it was unusual for women in the United States to go out in public alone, and they were not eligible to vote—they gained the right to vote only in 1920 when the Nineteenth Amendment was passed. More recently, attempts have been made to add a constitutional amendment that would further establish gender equity in the United States. The proposed Equal Rights Amendment (ERA) to the Constitution would have guaranteed that women have the same legal rights as males, thereby potentially expanding their ability to be financially and socially independent. The ERA was initially passed by Congress in 1972 and required approval by 38 states before it could become part of the U.S. Constitution. After 10 years without ratification, the ERA expired in 1982, only to be reintroduced in the House and then defeated there in 1983. President Reagan argued that a constitutional amendment was not needed to fight sexual bias, and a majority of congressional members apparently agreed. The issue has not been raised since.

The United States has played a key role in explicitly encouraging governments of developing nations to slow down their rate of population growth, and it has provided a great deal of money to establish and maintain family planning programs all over the world. Donaldson (1990) has chronicled the growing American consciousness from the 1940s through the 1960s that rapid population growth in less-developed nations might not be good either for those nations specifically or for the United States more generally. President Kennedy's establishment of the Agency for International Development (USAID) within the Department of State in 1961 was an early recognition that population was an important factor in development. By 1967, that idea bore fruit when Congress earmarked USAID funds for the purpose of providing population assistance along with economic assistance. For the next 18 years, the United States played a crucial part in helping to slow down the rate of population growth in the world—an effort that may have reduced the world population by nearly half a billion people compared to the growth that would have occurred in the absence of organized family planning efforts in developing countries (Bongaarts, Mauldin, and Phillips 1990).

Things changed in 1985, however, as a result of Reagan administration policies (the "Mexico City Policy" I mentioned earlier with respect to the 1984 World Population Conference) that were carried over into the subsequent Bush administrations, with an interstitial eight-year reprieve during the Clinton administration, and a new reprieve under the Obama administration. The opposition to abortion created controversy in both the implicit domestic policy, because of the push to reverse *Roe v. Wade*, and in the international policy, because in 1985, U.S. opposition to abortions in China was used as a pretext for cutting off all U.S. government funding for the United Nations Population Fund, as I discussed above. The halt in U.S. funding for the UNFPA did not mean the end of population assistance, however. Even during the 1989–93 Bush administration USAID remained the single largest source of international support for family planning programs, although there were plenty of strings attached to this money. Most of the funding is provided to NGOs working in various parts of the world. USAID also supports important programs in training and research activities. Furthermore, other countries, especially Germany, Japan, and Norway, have picked up some of the slack left by the United States.

Surveys have consistently shown that a majority of Americans are in favor of providing aid to help slow the growth of population in developing nations (Adamson et al. 2000; Grammich, DaVanzo, and Stewart 2004). At the same time, Americans tend to be fairly ignorant of the actual size of the world's population—only 14 percent of respondents to a 1998 RAND survey knew that the world population at that time was about 6 billion, and 40 percent simply did not know what to guess. Nonetheless, a majority believe that the world is overpopulated and that this contributes to environmental problems, civil strife, and economic problems in developing countries. The vast majority support the fundamental right of individuals to choose the number of children they want, and a majority are in favor of offering family planning assistance to developing countries. In this way, then, the majority of Americans seem to support the basic thrust of the U.S. international population policy, which was explicitly stated by Secretary of State Hillary Clinton (2010) as being supportive of universal access to reproductive health worldwide. She made those comments at an event marking the fifteenth anniversary of the ICPD in Cairo.

The most explicit population-related policy of the United States relates, of course, to immigration, and I refer you back to Chapter 7 for details. It is worth reminding you here, however, that the U.S. immigration policy itself has both explicit and implicit elements. The explicit part represents the rules and regulations that govern the ability of a person to become a legal permanent resident and eventually, if desired, a citizen of the United States. The implicit part represents the lack of agreement among and between the U.S. Congress and presidential administrations over how to deal with undocumented immigration. That lack of agreement has meant that the "policy" is to attempt to prevent people from entering the country without documentation, but being largely ineffective in doing so. Still, as I discussed in Chapter 7, the increased efforts have raised the cost of entering the country and led to the unanticipated consequence that, once here, undocumented immigrants are less likely than in the past to return home. This, of course, increases the chance that they will begin family-building and contribute in the long-term to even more growth of the U.S. population.

The dilemma for U.S. policy makers is that it is difficult to do anything about undocumented immigration without taking a critical look at the policies regarding legal immigration, because the two are closely connected. The family preference philosophy of U.S. immigration laws has always favored family members of current citizens instead of workers. It is difficult for a would-be immigrant to respond legally to the need for labor in the United States. The easiest way to become a legal immigrant to the United States is to be a close relative of someone who is already here and has become a citizen, although there is a long backlog even of these applications, especially for family members from Mexico and the Philippines (Hayes and Hill 2008). One of the hardest ways to enter legally is to be a relatively low-skilled worker trying to meet the structural needs created by the demographic fit between the United States and Latin America (Weeks and Weeks 2010). However, much of the concern about undocumented immigration is less an issue of migration itself, and more an issue of the migrants themselves, who tend to be seen as "different" (see, for example, Newton 2008). These nativist or xenophobic responses to immigration are not new, but they show up all over the world as part of the global migration transition/evolution, as I discuss later in the chapter.

What Demographic Destinies Lie Ahead?

In Chapter 2, I took you on a brief world tour of the current demographic situation, with an overview of the projected population out to 2050. However, because that discussion preceded our analysis of the various components of the demographic transition, now I want to take you on a return tour of the projected demographic future, this time from the perspective of how those transitions are unfolding and evolving. You already know that the more than 2 billion people projected to be added to the world's population by 2050 will show up in some places more than others. What I want to emphasize is the tremendous influence these national and regional differences in population increase, health and mortality, birth rates, migration and urbanization, the age structure, and in the diversity of families and households will have on what the future looks like for everyone.

Figure 12.2 maps the countries of the world by the projected increase in total population *size* between 2010 and 2050, according to the U.S. Census Bureau, whereas Figure 12.3 maps the world according to the *rate* of population increase between those two dates. You can see clearly in Figure 12.2 that India is projected to be the single most important source of population increase between now and the middle of the century. It takes the prize of being on a trajectory to add nearly half a billion people to its current population. Recalling from Table 10.6 that three out of four residents of India currently live on less than $2 per day, you can appreciate the struggle that will be part of India's future. It will share that struggle with its subcontinental neighbors of Pakistan and Bangladesh, who will together grow by about 175 million people. The southeast Asian nations of Indonesia and the Philippines are both expected to add tens of millions more people. Sub-Saharan Africa is projected to contribute another half billion people in just four countries alone, led by Ethiopia, Congo (Kinshasa), Nigeria, and Uganda. The countries in western Asia—regionally between sub-Saharan Africa and South Asia—are also projected to grow by tens of millions of people.

The United States is in the top ten list of countries in terms of expected growth between now and 2050, with the U.S. Census Bureau projecting that the country will grow from 310 million to almost 400 million by 2050. In 2009, the Census Bureau made projections assuming zero net international migration and that showed a very different scenario with an increase to only 322 million by 2050, if

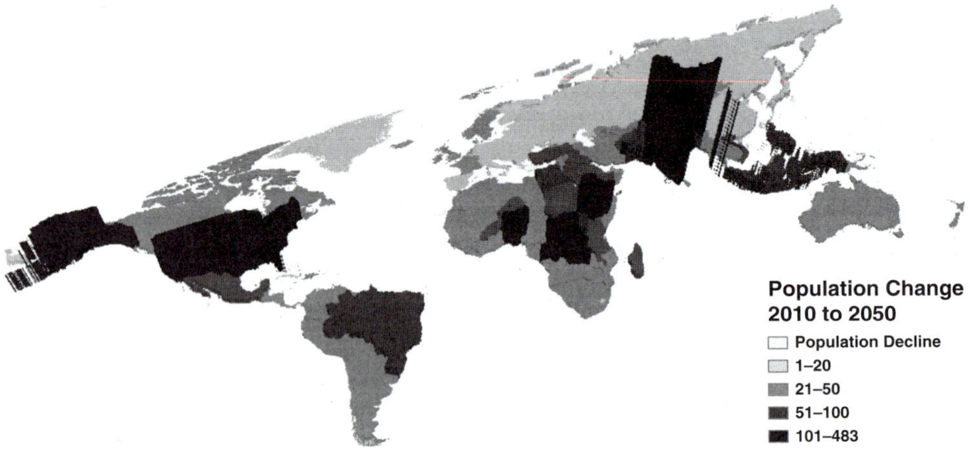

Figure 12.2 Projected Population Increase Between 2010 and 2050

Note: The height of each country represents the actual projected population increase in millions of people; the shadings correspond to the broad categories shown in the legend.

Source: Adapted by the author from data in U.S. Census Bureau, International Data Base (updated 2009) (http://www.census.gov/ipc/www/idb/, accessed 2010).

there were no more immigrants after 2010. We can see that if we really do approach 400 million by 2050, that growth will be fueled almost entirely by immigrants and their children. On these grounds alone, it is understandable that immigration is both a hot topic (witness the highly controversial law passed in Arizona in 2010 giving state law enforcement officers the authority to arrest suspected undocumented immigrants) and an issue that cannot easily be resolved. Brazil and Mexico are expected to be other major contributors of people in the Americas, some of whom will likely show up in the United States.

Conspicuously absent from future growth is China, which experienced its huge increase (three-quarters of a billion people) since the end of WWII, but which is expected soon to have reached its goal of halting population growth. As you can appreciate from the discussion in Chapter 11, this should help the country to deal economically with its increasingly older population and simultaneously raise a larger fraction of its population out of poverty. The growth hot-spots of the world are shown in Figure 12.3, which maps the percentage increase in projected population between 2010 and 2050, regardless of the total size of the population. Africa and the Middle East jump out as the places that are anticipated to be growing most quickly in the world—places where local communities will certainly be under the greatest stress to cope. But it is inconceivable that rapid growth in these places will not forcefully impact the richer, slower (or non-) growing nations as well.

The Health and Mortality Evolution

Despite the angst that you are bound to feel as you contemplate the expansion of the world population between now and 2050, remember that virtually everyone in the world is happy to be able to live a longer, healthier life than ever before imagined.

Figure 12.3 Projected Percentage Increase in Population Size Between 2010 and 2050

Note: The height of each country represents the actual percentage increase in the projected population; the shadings correspond to the broad categories shown in the legend.

Source: Adapted by the author from data in U.S. Census Bureau, International Data Base (updated 2009) (http://www.census.gov/ipc/www/idb/, accessed 2010).

The health and mortality transition is, of course, both the root cause of population growth and the single most revolutionary transformation in human existence. Everywhere in the world where populations are increasing rapidly, the single most important reason is that mortality has been declining more quickly than fertility. Even so, nearly all of the most rapidly growing countries in the world will still have higher mortality at midcentury than countries in Europe, North America, and East Asia.

The infant mortality rate is, as you know, a key indicator of overall health and well-being. In Figure 12.4 you can see that sub-Saharan Africa, western Asia (especially Afghanistan), and south Asia are the regions of the world in which infant death rates are expected to remain the highest in the world in 2050. These are the same places that show up as growing most quickly between 2010 and 2050. They are countries where the status of women and children is lower than elsewhere, and where death rates have always been among the highest in the world.

As death rates are gradually brought under control, everything else in life is changed in the process, as I have repeatedly emphasized in this book. That very different view of life puts into focus both the increasing certainty of child survival and the consequences of having too many children survive. As that context changes, the rational link between infant mortality and fertility is apt to take hold, because with greater certainty comes an ability to create a forward-looking strategy, rather than spending life reacting to one crisis after another (Lloyd and Ivanov 1988). In the end, then, programs that link the survival of children with family planning strategies are apt to be most successful in promoting maternal and child health (Montgomery and Cohen 1998).

One of the still evolving health issues in those parts of the world with high infant mortality rates is HIV/AIDS, as I discussed in Chapter 5. It has already altered the social fabric of sub-Saharan Africa, still threatens much of Southeast Asia, and

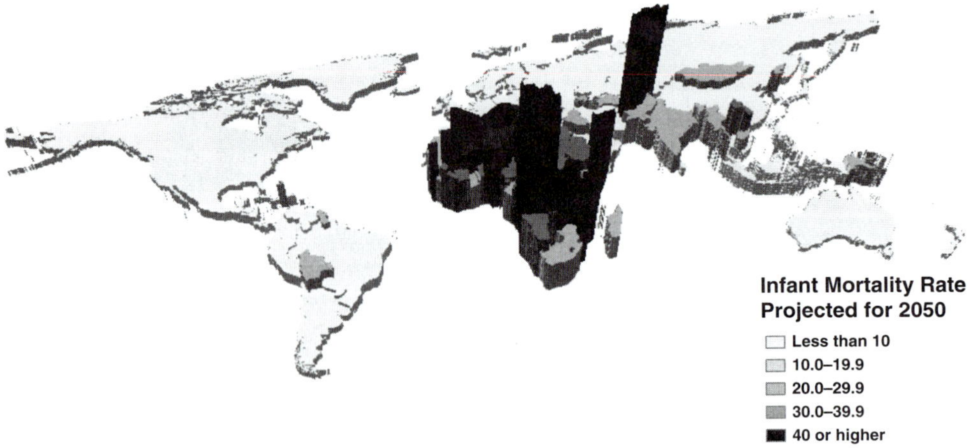

Figure 12.4 Projected Infant Mortality Rates in 2050

Note: The height of each country represents the actual projected infant mortality rate in 2050; the shadings correspond to the broad categories shown in the legend.

Source: Adapted by the author from data in U.S. Census Bureau, International Data Base (updated 2009) (http://www.census.gov/ipc/www/idb/, accessed 2010).

is an emerging issue in China, India, and Russia, where governments have been slow to acknowledge the potential for a major spread of HIV.

Projections from the United Nations Population Division suggest that between 2010 and 2050 AIDS may be responsible for the deaths of more than 150 million people (United Nations Population Division 2009b). Most of the people affected will be in sub-Saharan Africa, especially southern Africa, and you can see in Figures 12.2 and 12.3 that southern Africa is, in fact, projected to grow less quickly than the rest of Africa.

Yet another concern is the changing diets of people around the globe that may lead to greater obesity, hypertension, heart disease, and other risks of death in adulthood that may at least partially counteract efforts to lower death rates from malaria and other parasitic and infectious diseases, especially in sub-Saharan Africa (Hill et al. 2007). In the richer countries, the medical and pharmaceutical resources exist to keep people alive longer despite these degenerative risks, but there are no assurances that this will diffuse to any but the elite segments of developing countries.

The Fertility Evolution

As you know, the trend around the globe has been for birth rates to be on their way down; transitioning not simply to replacement level, but evolving to even lower levels in many parts of the world. They are already below replacement level in most of Europe, and in much of the rest of the world outside of Africa they are projected to reach replacement level by 2050, as you can see in Figure 12.5, which maps the projected total fertility rates as of that year. Keep in mind, though, that these projections assume that we will keep the pedal to the metal in terms of providing women everywhere with

Figure 12.5 Projected Total Fertility Rates in 2050

Note: The height of each country represents the projected total fertility rate in 2050; the shadings correspond to the broad categories shown in the legend.

Source: Adapted by the author from data in U.S. Census Bureau, International Data Base (updated 2009) (http://www.census.gov/ipc/www/idb/, accessed 2010).

the means to achieve their desired family size, and that desired family size will continue to decline in those places where it is still well above replacement.

The projected fertility rates for 2050 show that we have once again rounded up the usual suspects. Fertility will likely still be highest in sub-Saharan Africa, western Asia, and South Asia, while lowest in Europe and East Asia. Interestingly, the United States is projected by the Census Bureau to have fertility levels even slightly higher than Mexico's by the middle of this century.

As I discussed in Chapters 6 and 10, the status of women is a key ingredient both in lowering fertility and in explaining why fertility remains well above replacement level in so many countries. Lifting the penalties for antinatalist behavior is notably dependent upon redefining gender roles, including a more positive evaluation of single or childless persons, as well as believing that a small family is a good thing. Historically, the socialist centrally planned societies taught us that fertility can be indirectly influenced to decline through a combination of the following factors: (1) educating women; (2) providing women with access to the paid labor force; (3) legalizing the equality in status of males and females; (4) legalizing abortion and/or making contraceptives freely available; and (5) raising the standard of living, while at the same time making housing and major consumer items difficult to obtain, forcing a couple to ask themselves: "Kicsi or kosci?" (as they say in Hungarian—"A child or a car?").

A common element of those socialist countries was a strong central government that was able to implement policies that both directly and indirectly led to lower levels of fertility. Government policies that encourage access to family planning programs are not necessary to a decline in fertility, as I have noted before, but they certainly help because they provide an environment in which such services are more likely to be available. A perhaps surprising example of this is that governments in predominantly Catholic countries all over the world have evolved their policies to encourage lower fertility. The Philippines, however, has been a genuine outlier among predominantly Catholic countries, probably because "the Roman Catholic Church has exerted its influence on the Philippines like it has in few other countries" (Hookway 2008:A9). It is for this reason that the projected TFR of the Philippines for 2050 is clearly above replacement level. Furthermore, even if the influence of the church wanes and fertility drops more than expected, the Philippines has a sufficiently large young population that its momentum will carry it along for several decades.

An important breakthrough in encouraging governments to sponsor family programs was the recognition that family planning programs are implicitly designed to close the gap of **unmet needs** in a population, rather than explicitly designed to change reproductive behavior. A sexually active women who would prefer not to get pregnant but is nevertheless not using any method of contraception has an unmet need for family planning (Westoff and Bankole 1996; Westoff 2001, 2010). Seen from this perspective, the goal of family planning programs is to respond to this health need and provide contraceptive methods to these women, which may be more socially acceptable, especially in more traditional societies, than a program aimed at trying to limit family size.

Diffusion of the unmet needs concept has encouraged the diffusion of contraception. Only 21 countries in the world in 1965 admitted to actively supporting family planning programs (Isaacs and Cook 1984), but by 1976 the United Nations had counted 95 governments that provided direct support for family planning. By 2009 the number was up to 146, covering approximately half of the world's population (United Nations Population Division 2010).

Although the basic goal of family planning programs is to make sure that people have access to methods of birth control, some family planning programs do this better than others. Researchers at the Carolina Population Center at the University of North Carolina, Chapel Hill, spent several years trying to understand how family planning programs work. Several ingredients emerged that might be thought of as the seven secrets of successful family programs, including:

1. Easy accessibility of services is very important.
2. A community-based approach (as opposed to only having clinics to which people must go) increases continuation rates.
3. High-quality services increase the prevalence rate.
4. A greater variety of methods increases the prevalence rate.
5. Mass-media messages increase the prevalence rate.
6. Informal discussions by users with nonusers increases the prevalence rate.
7. Women tend to prefer contraception to abortion (Samara, Bucker, and Tsui 1996).

In Chapter 6, I discussed the situation in China, which has brought its level of fertility down to below replacement level through a coercive policy that was layered over an underlying fertility transition that was already under way. Indeed, the population has seemingly bought into the idea of very low fertility, and there is evidence that Chinese couples who would be legally allowed to have more than one child typically do not exercise that option (Cai Yong et al. 2010). If you compare the data in Figure 12.2 with those in Figure 12.5, you will see that, unlike China, India is expected to add a lot of people to the planet over the next few decades, despite the fact that by 2050, the TFR in India is expected to come down to the level of the United States—slightly above replacement level. Will fertility really decline that much?

Is India on the Road to Replacement Level Fertility? In 1952, long before China started thinking of fertility limitation, India began experimenting with family planning programs to keep the population "at a level consistent with requirements of the economy" (Samuel 1966:54). Although initial progress was pretty slow—the Indian government was moving cautiously—by 1961, there were about 1,500 clinics in operation, providing condoms, diaphragms, jellies, foam tablets, and other services, largely free (Demerath 1976). By 1963, the birth rate was still not responding and the government, now with the advice of the Ford Foundation, reorganized its family planning effort, mainly with an outreach effort to spread the birth control message to more people.

Still, the birth rate did not go down, so in 1966 there was another reorganization, and in 1967 Dr. S. Sripati Chandrasekhar, a demographer, was named Minister of State for Health and Family Planning. Chandrasekhar boosted the use of the mass media, offered transistor radios to men undergoing vasectomy, pushed through a legalization of abortion, and generally brought about more family planning action than had occurred in all the previous years of family planning. Male sterilization, being both permanent and the cheapest method of birth control, has been pushed especially hard by the Indian government, and between 1967 and 1973 (when Chandrasekhar left his position) 13 million men were sterilized in India. The birth rate in India declined ever so slightly between 1961 and 1971, but the death rate sank even more, so by the mid-1970s, the Indian population was growing faster than ever before. Why had the family planning efforts failed? Because family planners had not taken into account the broader social context within which reproduction occurs. It was naive to think that family planners could, of their own accord, generate the kind of social and cultural revolution required to make small-family norms an everyday practice throughout India (Demerath 1976).

By 1976, Indira Gandhi's government in India was beginning to show signs of desperation at being unable to slow the rate of population growth, and it became the first government in the world to lean toward compulsory measures (remember that China's one-child policy was not implemented until 1979). Dr. D. N. Pai, director of family planning in Bombay (now Mumbai), reportedly said, "Ninety percent of the people have no stake in life. How do you motivate them? They have nothing to lose. The only way out of the situation is compulsion" (Rosenhause 1976). The government implemented a now-famous, if not infamous, program of enforced sterilization. "Officially, there was no coercion, but the elaborate system of 'disincentives' amounted to the same thing. Government employees had to produce two or more candidates for sterilization. However, for such civil servants, or for anybody who was being pressured into submitting to sterilization himself, it was usually possible to hire a stand-in for about 200 rupees ($22). For those not in government service all sorts of privileges—such as licenses for guns, shops, ration cards—were denied unless the applicant could produce a sterilization certificate" (Guihati 1977:1301).

As a result of the policy of enforced sterilization, the number of people (largely male) who were sterilized in India jumped from 13 million in 1976 to 22 million in 1977. As it turned out, however, the average male who was sterilized was in his 30s and already had several children (Guihati 1977), so the program was less effective in reducing fertility than those numbers might imply.

Although her campaign effectively raised the level of sterilization, Indira Gandhi's policies generated violent hostility, and in 1977 she was defeated in her bid for reelection. Her successor, 82-year-old Morarji Desai, professed support for family planning, but only half-facetiously suggested that self-control (that is, abstinence), rather than birth control, was the solution to India's high rate of population growth (Bhatia 1978). Gandhi was elected once again in 1979, but she kept a relatively low profile with respect to her support for family planning, right up to the time of her assassination in 1984. Interestingly enough, the period up to her assassination was a time during which the birth rate did appear to be dropping, although survey results have shown that no change in *desired* family size took place between 1970 and 1980 (Khan and Prasad 1985).

In 1984, Indira Gandhi's son, Rajiv, was elected prime minister of India. He had been actively involved in the family planning movement during his mother's administration and in 1985 he declared that the nation was on "war footing" to reduce its rate of population growth to a two-child family norm by 2000 (Population Action Council 1985). A five-year, $3.6 billion program was unveiled that included monetary rewards to women who limited their family size and a broadening of the scope and quality of the nation's family planning services. He was voted out of office in 1989 and later assassinated, although neither event seemed to be related specifically to his views on population limitation.

One of the distinguishing characteristics of population policy in India until recently was its emphasis on family planning targets:

> Annual fixed targets for all methods, imposed from the top down, are set for family planning workers at all levels, and their performance is judged in terms of the fulfillment of the target. The pressure to achieve the targets starts at the top and works its way down to the field worker, who ultimately bears the brunt of the challenge. No excuses are accepted when targets are not achieved, and punitive action is taken in the form of salary freezes. This approach was most severe during the emergency period [in the 1970s] (Visaria and Chari 1998:90).

These were, in fact, precisely the kinds of targets that had come under sharp attack at the 1994 ICPD, and it was probably no coincidence that within two years after that conference the government of India moved its family planning approach away from method-specific targets. The National Population Policy, implemented in 2000, laid the framework for a broad program of reproductive health aimed at improving the lives of women and children, rather than aiming for specific targets.

Family planning in India still depends on sterilization, although the emphasis is now on tubal ligation for women rather than male vasectomies. Other contraceptive methods represent only a small fraction of family planning efforts in India (Santhya 2003; Sullivan et al. 2006). Mathews and colleagues (2009) have argued that relying on sterilization and not focusing on delayed marriage and contraception shortens the generations in India and may add 50 million more to the population by 2050 compared to a "later, longer, and fewer" approach (like China's policy in the 1970s). The lack of method mix and the checkered history of family planning in India are certainly obstacles to long-term success, but success is important because India and the world will be very different places according to the rate at which fertility declines in India (Dyson, Cassen, and Visaria 2004).

Will Fertility Go Up in Europe? Europe has the lowest fertility rates in the twenty-first century, just as it did in the nineteenth (and perhaps even the eighteenth) century, and the U.S. Census Bureau projects that in 2050 every single European nation will have below replacement level fertility, as you can see in Figure 12.5. You may recall from Chapter 3 that Arséne Dumont developed his theory of social capillarity as a way of explaining France's low fertility. France has experienced a low birth rate for longer than almost any other existing society, and it has also maintained its long-standing policy of providing monthly allowances to couples who have a second or higher-order child, despite the lack of evidence that such allowances have had any measurable impact on the birth rate. What does seem to work is the child care support that the government provides to mothers with children. All mothers in France have access to nursery school placement for their children by age three, so they can return to work, and the law guarantees that there will be a job to which they can return. Although these measures have not been enough to raise the birth rate in France to a level clearly above replacement, they almost certainly contribute to the fact that, at 1.9 children per woman, France's fertility has not dropped too far below replacement and is now the highest fertility rate in all of Europe (Rendall et al. 2009).

Another European country, Romania, has the distinction of having done the most in recent decades to try to raise the birth rate. In 1966, the Romanian government decided to halt the downward trend in the birth rate (which was being accomplished primarily by abortion) by establishing a policy that made abortions illegal except under extreme circumstances. The government also discouraged the use of other contraceptives by stopping their importation and making them available only for medical reasons. The result was that the birth rate skyrocketed from 14 per 1,000 population in 1966 to 27 per 1,000 in 1967. Although it did begin to fall again after 1967, as women resorted to illegal abortions and found other means of birth control (primarily rhythm and withdrawal), by 1989, the total fertility rate of 2.3 was still higher than the 1.9 level of 1966. But 1989 brought a significant event—a change in government. In December 1989, Nicolae Ceausescu, longtime dictator of Romania, was overthrown and executed. One of the first legislative acts of the new government was to legalize abortion in order to reduce the high maternal mortality rate that had resulted from botched illegal abortions during the prior two decades (Serbanescu et al. 1995). By 2010, the total fertility rate had dropped to 1.3, among the world's lowest, but in line with its eastern European neighbors.

In 2006 the European Commission published a report titled *The Demographic Future of Europe—From Challenge to Opportunity* (Commission of the European Communities 2006). The report emphasized that Europe's demographic situation of population aging was the result of good things—higher life expectancy and an increasing ability to choose whether and when to have children (Špidla 2007). The report further emphasized the point that I made above with respect to France—support for women to combine jobs with a family generally seems to encourage a higher birth rate, and if more European countries followed that model, then fertility might rise. Demographers responding to the commission's report added that fertility might rebound a bit in Europe if scientific advances are made that permit women to conceive at progressively later ages (Grant and Hoorens 2007). While discussing low fertility, the report also recognized the need for immigrants to fill both skilled and unskilled jobs in the future, although Coleman (2007) argues that workers are needed less in Europe than is social welfare reform, because labor productivity is very low.

I would be remiss if I didn't point out that fertility is not quite as low in Europe as it seems. The TFR we normally use to measure fertility is, as you recall from Chapter 6, a period measure that does not readily capture the difference in the tempo of childbearing. European women have spent the past two decades postponing children, which has lowered the TFR below its "real" level, but more recently they have stopped postponing, and have been doing some catch-up (Lutz 2007; Prioux 2007). It is also true that low fertility in Europe is bemoaned by many people on the basis of societal "need," but there is little research to show that couples themselves are complaining about their small families (Kravdal 2010).

Though we have shone some light on the question, the real answer about the future course of fertility in Europe is that we really don't know. Nonetheless, the answer does matter, not only for Europe but also for developing nations: If fertility were to rise among native Europeans, and if labor market reforms kept people in the labor force longer, the demand for immigrants might drop. In the potential sending countries, that fact could result in a pileup of people whose leaving might have served as a demographic safety valve, and it would diminish the flow of remittances back to the potential sending countries, thus lowering their citizens' standard of living.

The Migration Evolution

As you know from Chapter 7, migration is the most volatile of the demographic processes, so our projections about migration patterns in 2050 depend on educated guesswork, based almost entirely on what is happening now. As you can see from Figure 12.6, the receiving countries are expected to be the richer countries, especially western Europe, North America, and Australia. There are a couple of developing country outliers in the mix—Bostwana in southern Africa, and Costa Rica in Central America. Both of them are small countries that currently have the lowest fertility in their respective neighborhoods. The projected sending countries in 2050 are the usual suspects—China, Mexico, the Philippines, India, most countries of Africa, and western and southern Asia.

The United States, Canada, and Australia have quite literally been created by successive waves of immigrants (see, for example, Hirschman 2005). So, as difficult as it may be for any country to absorb new people today, those countries have more experience in doing it. Europe, on the other hand, was the quintessential source of migrants to the United States, Canada, and Australia, and had very little experience with in-migration until the end of World War II. This helps explain why many European

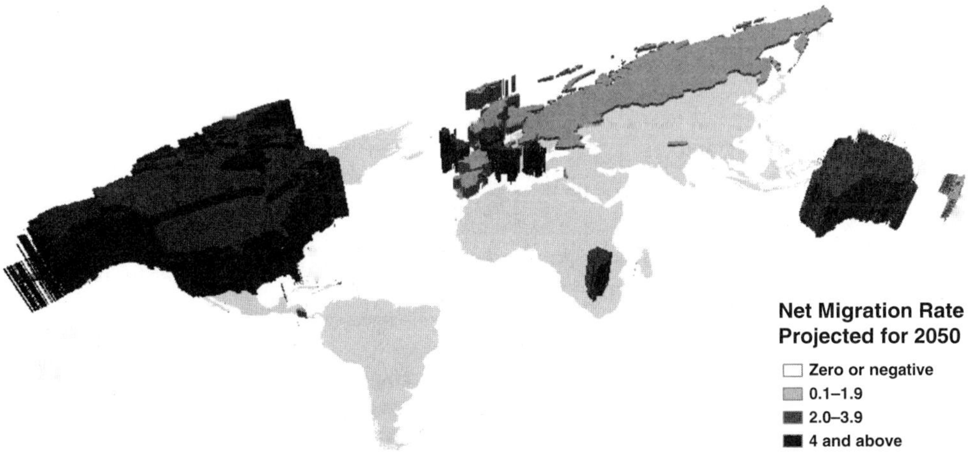

Figure 12.6 Projected Net Migration Rates in 2050

Note: The height of each country represents the projected net migration rate in 2050; the shadings correspond to the broad categories shown in the legend.

Source: Adapted by the author from data in U.S. Census Bureau, International Data Base (updated 2009) (http://www.census.gov/ipc/www/idb/, accessed 2010).

A CALIFORNIA COMMUNITY COPES WITH THE MIGRATION EVOLUTION

In early 2008 the United States Congress passed the Refugee Crisis in Iraq Act and the face of El Cajon, California was changed forever. For it is at the local level that the migration evolution has its most dramatic effect, and in this essay I offer a ground-level example of this phenomenon featuring Iraqi immigrants crowding into a small suburban community in San Diego County.

By way of background, the ethnic mix of California neighborhoods has been evolving continuously since the mid-1960s due especially to the influx of Latin Americans (mainly from Mexico) and southeast Asians (especially from the Philippines, Cambodia, Laos, and Vietnam), creating what William A.V. Clark (1998) has called the "California Cauldron." Many other groups have gone into that ethnic melting pot, of course, including an Iranian population in Los Angeles large enough to create the image of "Irangeles" (Kelley, Friedlander, and Colby 1993; Waldinger and Bozorgmehr 1997).

In 2008, 10 percent of the total population of San Diego County had been born in Mexico, 3 percent had been born in the Philippines, and many other countries of origin represented a larger share of the population than those from Iraq. Nevertheless, when more than 10,000 people of the same immigrant group congregate in a small area within the county and, when new waves of refugees are adding people quickly, the local impact is a force to be reckoned with.

Data from the American Community Survey show that there were about 100,000 residents in the United States in 2008 who had been born in Iraq. Zooming in for a closer look reveals that 55 percent of these residents lived either in Michigan (29 percent) or California (26 percent). Coming in even closer, we see that the Iraqi-origin population is spatially concentrated in or near just a few communities—Southfield, Michigan (in metropolitan Detroit), and El Cajon, California (in metropolitan San Diego). So, even if El Cajon is no stranger to diversity, the rather abrupt arrival of large numbers of refugees from Iraq has added new spice to the mix and stirred the cauldron.

The population of Iraq is predominantly Muslim with only about 2 percent estimated to be Christian, but a disproportionate share of the Iraqi-origin population living in the United States is non-Muslim. More specifically, they are Chaldean Christian Catholics, with ethnic roots tracing back to early Mesopotamian empires, long before the rise of Islam (Bazzi 2009).

Although no definitive numbers exist to tell us exactly how many Chaldeans there are among the Iraqis in the United States, we can use the 2008 American Community Survey Public Use Microdata Sample (PUMS) data, available from the Minnesota Population Center (Ruggles et al. 2010), to create estimates based on questions asked about birthplace and ancestry. The ACS (census long-form) questionnaire includes ancestry codes for Chaldean and Assyrian, the latter being one of the names for the neo-Aramaic language spoken by Chaldeans, especially in religious services. From these data we can estimate that in 2008, 32 percent of all Iraqi-born residents of the United States were Chaldean, a number 14 times what we would expect if immigrants from Iraq were a random sample from that country.

Altogether, an estimated 90,000 Chaldeans were in the United States in 2008, of whom about 40 percent had been born in Iraq, with most of the remainder having been born in the United States, although some had been born in one of the countries neighboring Iraq (Iran, Syria, and Lebanon) after their families had fled the violence and persecution of Christians at home. Of those Chaldeans living in the United States in 2008, approximately one in ten resided in or near El Cajon, California, radiating around the Chaldean church, and the number has been growing rapidly. Let's take a closer look at the causes and consequences of this local phenomenon.

According to local historians in El Cajon, the first Chaldean immigrant arrived in 1951 (Bazzi, 2009). Every year or so after that a few new families arrived, usually originating in Baghdad but arriving in California by way of Detroit, where they had gone because Detroit has been home to one of the larger Arab-speaking communities in the United States for a long time. By 1973 there were an estimated 70 Chaldean families living prosperously in San Diego County, a large enough critical mass to motivate them to pool their money, buy land, and build a Chaldean church in El Cajon. Ten years later that church had become the St. Peter Chaldean Catholic Cathedral, one of only two Chaldean churches in America that is headed by a bishop. The other one, of course, is in Detroit.

In the accompanying graph, I have traced the growth of the Iraqi-origin population in San Diego County since 1960, based on the PUMS data for each census (Ruggles et al. 2010). Although these numbers include all persons from Iraq, the 2008 ACS data show that a majority of Iraqi-origin persons in San Diego County are Chaldean. There were about 100 people in 1960 and about 300 in 1970—the latter number consistent with the estimated 70 families who sparked the building of the church. That number increased a bit as Saddam Hussein took over in Iraq and then launched a lengthy war with Iran.

There was a noticeable increase in numbers after the first Gulf War, as the area received about 200 Iraqi refugees per year. The local Iraqi-origin population approached 10,000 by the time of the Iraq War following 9/11. Although the invasion of Iraq in 2003 led to a flood of refugees out of Iraq, most were initially settled in neighboring Jordan, Iran, Lebanon, and Syria (Tavernise 2006). The perspective of the U.S. government at the time was that the toppling of the Saddam Hussein regime would lead to a democratically elected government that would improve personal safety for all Iraqis. For Chaldeans, however, the result was exactly the opposite, as the Muslim population began to persecute local Christians. In response, the Refugee Crisis in Iraq Act was introduced into Congress in 2007 (although it was not signed into

(continued)

Growth of the Iraqi Population in San Diego County 1960 to 2012

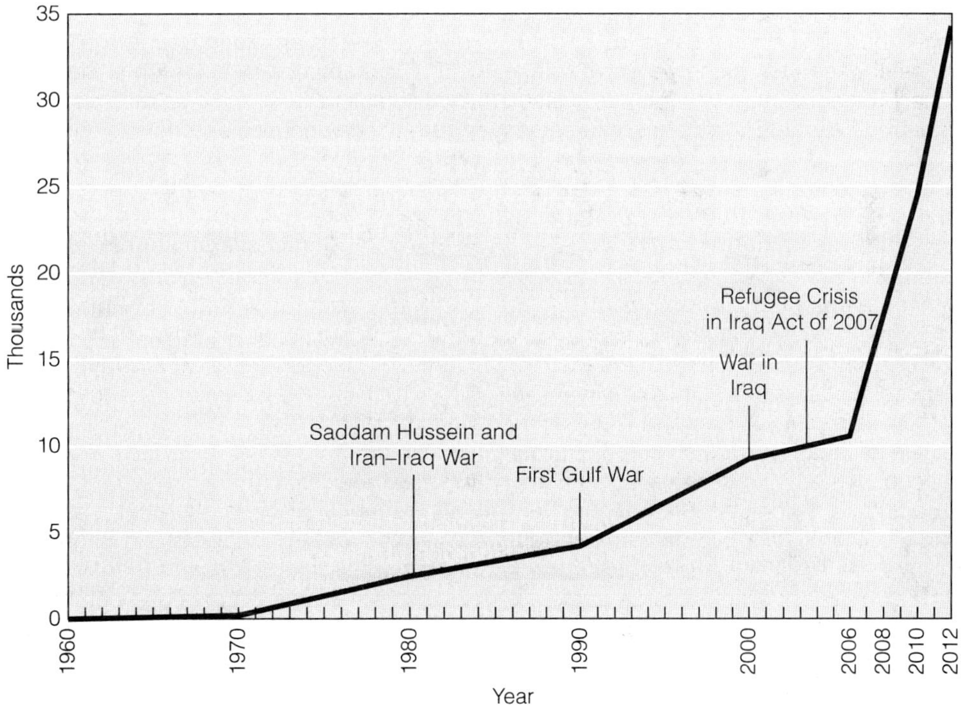

Source: see text for sources.

A CALIFORNIA COMMUNITY COPES WITH THE MIGRATION EVOLUTION (CONTINUED)

law until January 2008), and the State Department immediately began processing Iraqi applications for refugee status (King and Dreazen 2007). Since then the number of Iraqi refugees admitted to the United States has literally exploded, from 202 in 2006, to 1,608 in 2007, to 13,822 in 2008, and 18,838 in 2009 (U.S. Department of State 2010).

According to estimates from the Refugee Center of Catholic Charities of San Diego, approximately 400 Iraqi refugees arrived each month in San Diego County during 2009 (compared to about 60 per *year* between 2003 and 2006), and that number was expected to continue for at least two to three more years. These numbers imply that one in four Iraqi refugees admitted to the United States has settled in San Diego County, especially in or near the City of El Cajon, as noted above. By combining the census and ACS data with estimates of incoming refugees, we estimate that there were 17,016 individuals who were born in Iraq, or have Iraqi or Chaldean ancestry (i.e., the U.S.-born children of Iraqi immigrants) living in San Diego County as of mid-2008. When we add the approximately 400 refugees per month arriving in the county since October 2008, the estimate rises to 23,416 Iraqi-origin (largely Chaldean) residents in San Diego County as of early 2010, of whom more than one is four is a recently arrived refugee. What will be very important in the long run is the fact that 63 percent of the arriving refugees are younger, single persons. As you know, this is the age at which people marry and have children and, eventually, given the family preference system of the United States immigration laws, these young people will be eligible to apply for admission for their close relatives. Thus, each refugee has a potential multiplier effect in the local community.

The accompanying map depicts the location quotient of Chaldeans in San Diego County's census tracts using data taken from Census 2000, which is the most recent neighborhood-level data available for all persons of Iraqi-origin as of this writing. The location quotient measures the spatial clustering of Chaldeans compared to the general population. For example, the value of 39 in the census tract that includes the church indicates that there were 39 times as many Chaldeans in that area as you would have expected based on the distribution of San Diego County's population.

The map is visual evidence of the impact to the local area. In fact, refugee records indicate that nearly 75 percent of Iraqi-origin refugees arriving in

The Spatial Concentration of the Iraqi-Origin Population in San Diego County

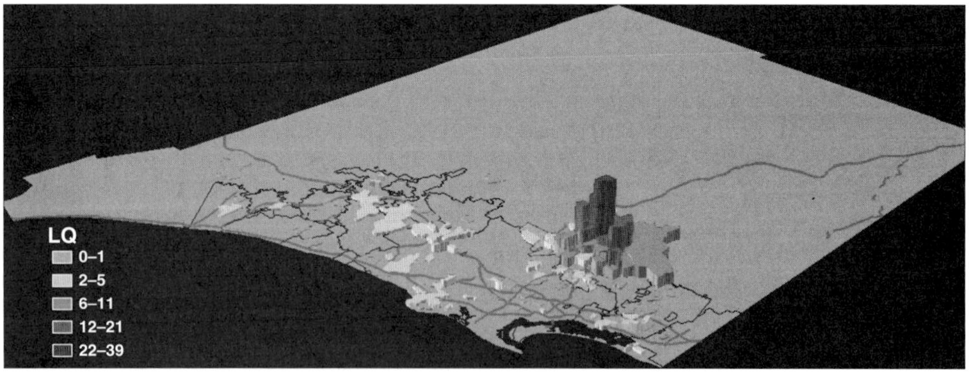

Source: Created by the author from data in U.S. Census Bureau, 2000 Census of Housing and Population.

nations are having such a struggle with the new experience of adapting themselves to the cultural changes that are involved as immigrant communities alter the pattern of business as usual (Coleman 2009). The Spanish are absorbing families from the Gambia (Bledsoe, Houle, and Sow 2007), Italians are coping with Senegalese and

San Diego County since October 2008 have settled in the Grossmont-Cuyamaca Community College District (GCCCD) and the Grossmont Union High School District (GUHSD) service areas. One of the first signals that this was creating a problem was when the community college district discovered that it could not afford to offer as many English as a Second Language (ESL) classes as were all of a sudden being demanded by the refugees. In order to receive their monthly stipends from the U.S. Office of Refugee Resettlement, each adult refugee had to show that they were attending ESL classes, but the local resources did not exist to meet that need.

The refugees arrived in the United States during the middle of the recent economic crisis, when local jobs were already very scarce. Data from the American Community Survey show that recent arrivals have limited proficiency in English, and have very high unemployment rates (although many may be employed in the informal economy). Furthermore, they have brought with them some of the gender inequities that have prevailed over time in Iraq, especially in terms of large differences in educational attainment between men and women. For example, among adults, 14 percent of males have less than a high school education, but 47 percent of women are in that category. At the other extreme, 11 percent of adult men have a college degree, compared to only 2 percent of women. Even among those who speak English well (about half the adult population), the unemployment rate among women is much higher than among men.

Anecdotal evidence suggests that the local residents who may be most affected by the influx of new refugees are, in fact, the longer-term Iraqi-origin residents. This group has achieved economic success, is politically active in the community, and tends to live very close to the Chaldean church, which is located in a neighborhood where housing values are above average for the region. The new immigrants have, in essence, raised the profile of the Chaldean community in ways that are not viewed by longer-term immigrants as entirely beneficial, especially at a time when they perceive that there is discrimination against people of "Middle Eastern" origin. There is also concern that because the new immigrants are living in close proximity to one another, and to the longer-term residents, a closed community of non-English-speaking households may develop. This is perceived locally as having potentially negative consequences for those families and for their neighbors. On that score, we will have to wait and see.

More immediately, the exhaustion of local resources led the community college district to organize a "summit" of elected officials, educators, and social service agencies to assess the situation and figure out how to proceed (Krueger 2009). Local schools and libraries are now providing information in Arabic, along with English and Spanish, but refugee assistance programs are underfunded and overloaded. Furthermore, half of the children entering kindergarten programs at some neighborhood schools are from refugee families, and the schools are quickly having to adapt to this change. For the time being, the community and its new members are muddling along together, hoping that the economy will get better and lives will improve for everyone.

One glimpse of the future comes from the story of the Class of 2010 Valedictorian of Cuyamaca College—located scarcely a mile away from the Chaldean church. This young woman left Iraq with her family after the first Gulf War in 1991. After marrying and having three children, she decided to get an education so that she could help them with their homework. She started with ESL classes and moved from there into a major in business administration, in which she obviously excelled. Anything is possible.

Discussion Questions: (1) Describe two possible future scenarios for the way in which the immigrants discussed in the essay might adapt and/or assimilate to the local community; **(2)** How do you think the issue of gender inequality among immigrants is likely to evolve over time?

other West Africans (Riccio 2008), and throughout Europe there is stress over the integration of Muslim immigrants (Caldwell 2009), even though the youth bulge in the predominantly Muslim Middle East and North Africa (MENA) region represents a nearly perfect demographic fit for Europe's aging population (Fargues 2008).

The Age Evolution

The demographic fit between Europe and MENA is tied to a theme that will be resonating around the world for the rest of your life—the evolution of very different age structures from one group and region to another. We are coping with a world in which the haves and have-nots—the developed and developing countries—are divided not only by income and rates of population growth, but by distinctly different population structures. The legacy of several decades of low fertility and low mortality in the developed countries is an increasingly older population, whereas a much later start to the fertility decline, combined with ever lower mortality, produces populations in developing areas (countries "in transition," as they are sometimes called) with significantly younger population age structures.

In Figure 12.7, you can see that the map of the world by projected median age in 2050 is nearly the flip side of Figure 12.5 which showed the pattern of fertility rates. Higher fertility rates produce younger populations, while lower rates produce older populations. Since fertility has been lower in Europe than anywhere else, Europe is naturally projected to have the oldest populations in 2050, especially southern and eastern Europe. Japan and Korea are also projected to have very old populations. By contrast, the youngest populations will still be in sub-Saharan Africa, western Asia, and South Asia, just as is true today. The large and youthful populations in these areas in 2050 will be both "challenges and opportunities," to borrow the phrase from the European Commission's report on the future of Europe.

In the western hemisphere, the United States, in particular, is not facing depopulation in the way that Europe is, largely as a result of several decades of strong immigration, which has produced higher fertility than in Europe and has meant a slower slide to an older population. On the other hand, you can readily imagine that the

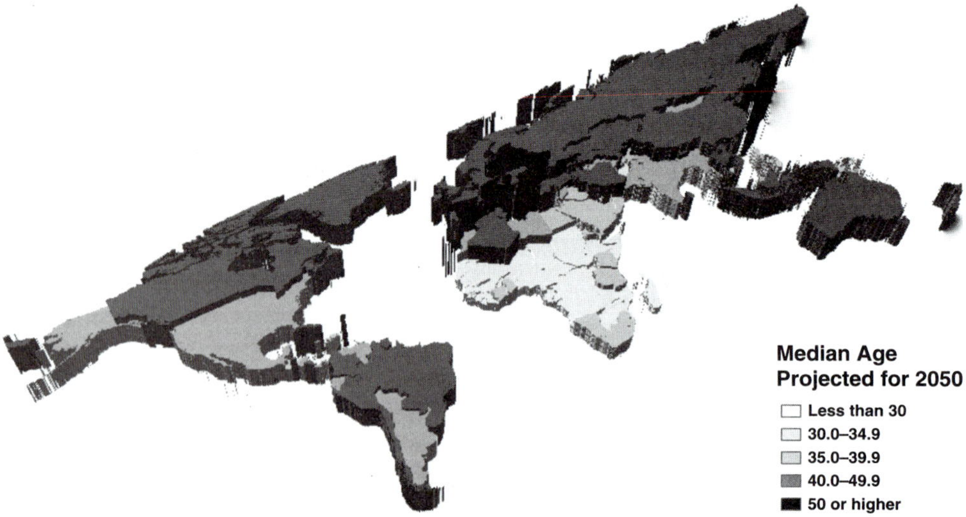

Figure 12.7 Projected Median Age in 2050

Note: The height of each country represents the projected median age of the population in 2050; the shadings correspond to the broad categories shown in the legend.

Source: Adapted by the author from data in U.S. Census Bureau, International Data Base (updated 2009) (http://www.census.gov/ipc/www/idb/, accessed 2010).

less-developed nations will still be struggling to meet the payroll, so to speak, in 2050—wondering how to find jobs for the numerous young people in their midst. If migration is not an option as a demographic safety valve, young age structures can present societies with real problems. Hagan and Foster (2001:874) remind us that "adolescence is a time of expanding vulnerabilities and exposures to violence that can be self-destructive as well as destructive of others." You might have that in mind as you read that Central American countries, for example, have faced a wave of gang activity exacerbated by a very young age structure in an environment where there are not enough jobs to go around. These age structure strains have also helped to produce the spread of terrorism in the Middle East, western Asia and South Asia, as young people grow up in an increasingly crowded urban setting where there are too many of them for the available economic and social resources (Slackman 2008; Tavernise 2009; Goldstone 2010).

The Urban Evolution

By the middle of this century, there are projected to be only a handful of countries—all of them in sub-Saharan Africa—in which less than a majority of people live in urban areas. You can see the expected pattern in Figure 12.8. Europe and North America are projected to have the highest percentages of the population living in urban areas, along with the desert nations of western Asia (such as Saudi Arabia, Jordan, Syria, Iraq, and Iran).

Despite the increase in urbanization, few rural areas in the world are projected to decline in population; rather, they are projected to send their excess population to the cities. Furthermore, as I discussed in the previous chapter, if we are going to feed more than 9 billion people, the global community is going to have to make significant infrastructure investments in agriculture. However, like most changes that are forced upon us by population growth, this will be a painful process for

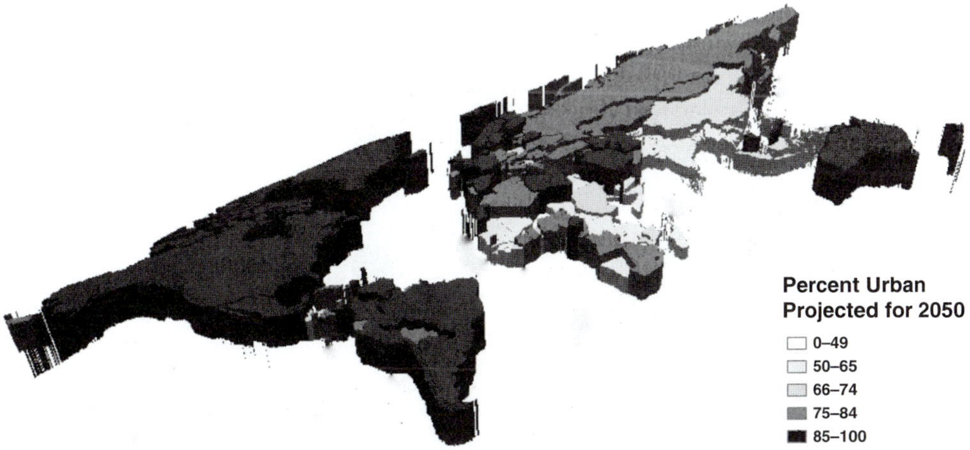

Figure 12.8 Projected Percent Urban in 2050

Note: The height of each country represents the projected percent of the population living in urban places in 2050; the shadings correspond to the broad categories shown in the legend.

Source: Adapted by the author from data in United Nations Population Division, 2009, World Population Prospects: The 2008 Revision, data online (http://www.un.org/esa/population/unpop.htm, accessed 2010).

less-developed nations will still be struggling to meet the payroll, so to speak, in 2050—wondering how to find jobs for the numerous young people in their midst. If migration is not an option as a demographic safety valve, young age structures can present societies with real problems. Hagan and Foster (2001:874) remind us that "adolescence is a time of expanding vulnerabilities and exposures to violence that can be self-destructive as well as destructive of others." You might have that in mind as you read that Central American countries, for example, have faced a wave of gang activity exacerbated by a very young age structure in an environment where there are not enough jobs to go around. These age structure strains have also helped to produce the spread of terrorism in the Middle East, western Asia and South Asia, as young people grow up in an increasingly crowded urban setting where there are too many of them for the available economic and social resources (Slackman 2008; Tavernise 2009; Goldstone 2010).

The Urban Evolution

By the middle of this century, there are projected to be only a handful of countries—all of them in sub-Saharan Africa—in which less than a majority of people live in urban areas. You can see the expected pattern in Figure 12.8. Europe and North America are projected to have the highest percentages of the population living in urban areas, along with the desert nations of western Asia (such as Saudi Arabia, Jordan, Syria, Iraq, and Iran).

Despite the increase in urbanization, few rural areas in the world are projected to decline in population; rather, they are projected to send their excess population to the cities. Furthermore, as I discussed in the previous chapter, if we are going to feed more than 9 billion people, the global community is going to have to make significant infrastructure investments in agriculture. However, like most changes that are forced upon us by population growth, this will be a painful process for

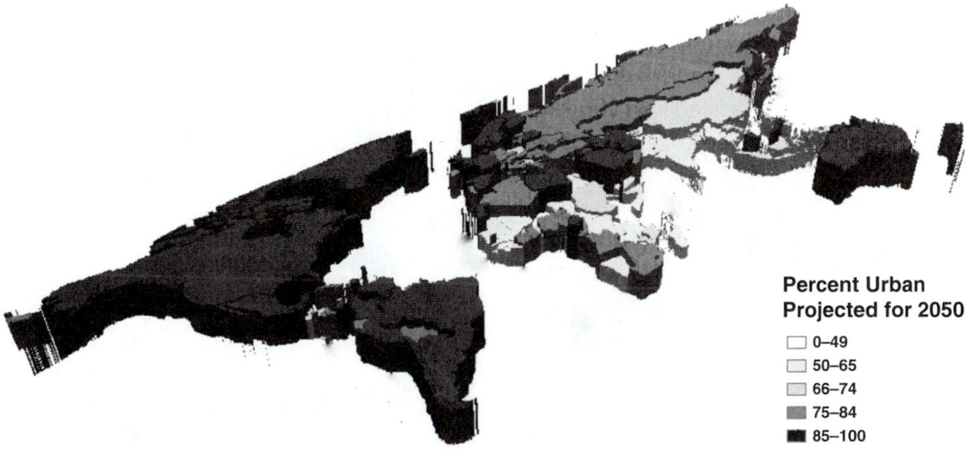

Figure 12.8 Projected Percent Urban in 2050

Note: The height of each country represents the projected percent of the population living in urban places in 2050; the shadings correspond to the broad categories shown in the legend.

Source: Adapted by the author from data in United Nations Population Division, 2009, World Population Prospects: The 2008 Revision, data online (http://www.un.org/esa/population/unpop.htm, accessed 2010).

many rural people whose livelihoods will be turned upside down as ancient patterns of subsistence agriculture are converted to more modern methods of growing food and cash crops to meet the ever-increasing global demand.

The Family and Household Evolution

The evolutions in the age structure and urban population will, in turn, likely drive the evolution of families and households as we move toward the middle of this century. There are no projections of these characteristics out to 2050, but in Figure 12.9 I have mapped the current average age at marriage for females in each country. This is a very good index of the status of women, of the number of children they will likely have, and of the overall level of modernity in their country. We can anticipate that the lower the age at marriage, the more traditional the society, and the less diverse the family and household structures. The picture is a familiar one, as you can see.

The ICPD Programme of Action, discussed earlier, gives voice to the idea that family transformations are part and parcel of the other demographic changes taking place in society, as it emphasizes issues of gender equity and protecting the rights of women in families and households. Of particular importance is the idea that women should have access to education and the paid labor force, with governments assisting women by providing access to child care.

In the richer, aging nations, the very changes in family size and household structure that produced such a high fraction of older people has led also to the near disappearance of the traditional family structure that in earlier generations might have taken care of the elderly (Ogawa and Retherford 1997; Waite 2004). Let me explain. The elderly in more developed nations will have fewer children to call upon for support. Furthermore, the trend toward equality in labor force participation among men and women means that there will be fewer daughters available to care for their aging

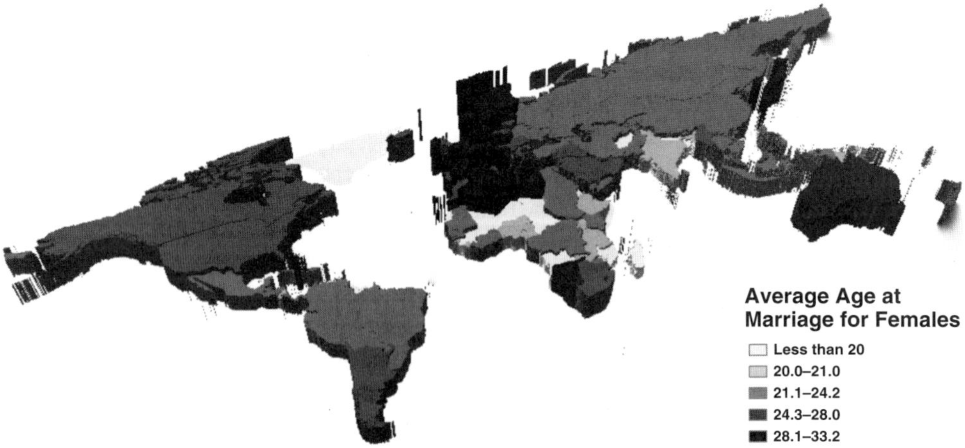

Figure 12.9 Average Age at Marriage For Females

Note: The height of each country represents the singulate mean age at marriage for females; the shadings correspond to the broad categories shown in the legend.

Source: Adapted by the author from data in United Nations Population Division, 2009, World Marriage Data 2008 (POP/DB/Marr?Rev2008), (http://www.un.org/esa/population/publications/WMD2008/Main.html, accessed 2010).

parents, or their aged in-laws. The same women who have hoped for governmental assistance with child care are unlikely to be ready to provide elder care.

The increasing life expectancy among older people also means that by the time they get to the "Fourth Age," when they may be in genuine need of assistance, their own children may already be moving into the "Third Age" and be less inclined to help because they too are growing old. Younger service providers will be the answer for many older people, probably paid for partly by government subsidies and partly by the older persons themselves, who are growing older with unprecedentedly high levels of living (Gaymu, Ekamper, and Beets 2007).

The world in 2050 will be more urban and populated by people with a longer life expectancy and a smaller expected number of children than prevail today. Recall from Chapter 10 that we can surmise from this likely combination of trends that families and households will continue to evolve toward greater diversity everywhere in the world. Keep in mind, though, that in many parts of the world this will create intergenerational tension, as it did earlier in the richer countries, and so will probably not happen without a struggle.

A key ingredient in all demographic processes and in the overall improvement of human health and well-being is education, as I have repeated throughout this book. Demographers at the International Institute for Applied Systems Analysis (IIASA) and the Vienna Institute for Demography, in Austria, have produced an innovative set of population projections for each country of the world that take into account different scenarios of educational attainment over time (Samir et al. 2010). As you know, education indirectly but importantly influences mortality (the better educated live longer), fertility (the better educated have fewer children), and migration (especially urbanization, because the better educated head to the cities), and it directly influences the ability of an economy to develop. Everywhere in the world, school enrollment rates are on the rise for both girls and boys, as I discussed in Chapter 10, but there is considerable global variability in the speed of these transitions (Samir et al. 2010:424):

> By 2050 nearly 40% of the working population in the case of Ethiopia [one of the fastest growing countries in the world—see Figure 12.3], and 35% in the case of Burkina Faso, may be educated to less than primary level. It is noteworthy that, by 2050, the average proportion of the "less than primary" category exceeds 10% only in ten countries, all but one of them in Africa. This means that, if the above situation arises, these countries will have fallen hopelessly behind compared to the rest of the world. It should be noted, however, that some of the countries not included in the study due to non-availability of data are also likely to suffer equally bad or even worse prospects (such as Afghanistan or Sierra Leone, among others). Nevertheless, there is a genuine threat that sub-Saharan Africa may remain the most problematic development region for another hundred years, if not longer.

Summary and Conclusion

"Demographic transition theory might seem to imply that, after a period of exceptional population growth resulting from the time lag between mortality and fertility declines, every population, and then the whole world population will stabilize and, consequently, no more acute population problems will appear. Does the claim, recently gaining credibility, that the end of the transition is at hand actually imply a stage without major population problems? Nothing is less sure" (Vallin 2002:105).

On the contrary, we can be pretty sure that we are in for some rough times between now and whenever, or if ever, we might reach the end of the demographic transition. As I have tried to emphasize, the major reason for the rough times is that different countries are in different stages of their various transitions, making it almost impossible to generalize about the global population situation.

One of the major uses of demographic science is as a tool for shaping the future, for trying to improve the conditions, both social and material, of human existence. To do that requires a demographic perspective—an understanding of how the causes of population change are related to the consequences. Throughout the previous 11 chapters, I have explored the ins and outs of those causes and consequences: how and why mortality, fertility, and migration change; how they affect the age and sex structure of society and the urban environment; how households and families change as a consequence of demographic shifts; and how population growth affects economic development, food resources, and environmental degradation. Implicit in all those discussions is the idea that an understanding of what has happened in the past and what is happening now will provide you with insights about the future, which is, of course, your first step toward advocating or promoting a local, regional, or global population policy, and toward managing your own personal demographic transitions and evolutions.

In the first chapter of this book I emphasized that the past is a "foreign country" because of all the changes that have taken place over time that have been related in one way or another to population growth and change. On the basis of what you now know about population change, you should be able to make some reckoning of what the future may be, and recognize that the future will also be a foreign country. If what you see concerns you, then I have tried to provide you with ideas about what can be done to cope with the population changes put into play by demographic transitions all over the world. If what you see does not worry you, then perhaps you should reread the book.

Main Points

1. As the demographic transition became a demographic revolution after World War II, the global community moved into action to try to develop policies to slow down the rate of population growth, especially in developing countries.
2. The 1974 World Population Conference produced a World Population Plan of Action that was aimed at promoting family planning in developing nations, although delegates from those countries argued that development is the best contraceptive.
3. The 1984 World Population Conference is notable because of the imposition by the United States of a "global gag rule" with respect to the use of funds for anything having to do with abortion.
4. The 1994 International Conference on Population and Development produced a new Programme of Action emphasizing the importance of women's social and reproductive rights, and that plan is still in place, being reviewed periodically by the United Nations.
5. Although the United States does not have an explicit population policy, it has strong implicit domestic policies regarding fertility and immigration, and a strong explicit international policy that is largely focused on the fertility transition, although assistance is also offered to other countries with respect to health issues in general.

6. Projections of the population out to 2050 suggest that India will be the single biggest contributor to population growth, followed by the African nations of Ethiopia, Congo, and Nigeria; with sub-Saharan nations growing at the fastest rate of any region in the world.
7. In the middle of this century, all countries are expected to have lower fertility and higher life expectancies, but Europe and East Asia are projected still to have the lowest fertility and highest life expectancy, while sub-Saharan Africa will still have the highest fertility and lowest life expectancy.
8. We can anticipate that North America and Europe will absorb immigrants at the highest rates over the next few decades, and that the sending countries will continue to be the rapidly growing developing nations, where the cities will be bulging with internal migrants.
9. The evolving demographic changes all portend a continuation of the demographically divided world—richer older nations in the "North" and less-rich younger nations in the "South."
10. The next time someone says that the population problem is "solved," remind them that if you read this book continuously at the pace of one chapter every two hours, more than 200,000 people were added to the world's population between the time you started reading Chapter 1 and now. That is the equivalent of nearly 700 full flights on a Boeing 777, or 60 flight loads of people per chapter. Even if they are not landing near you, you will know about them soon enough.

Questions for Review

1. Discuss the outcomes of the 1974, 1984, and 1994 World Population Conferences in terms of the three preconditions for a fertility decline. Do you think it would have mattered to the world if the conferences had been in reverse order?
2. Is it likely that policies aimed at raising birth rates would work in Europe (or Japan)? Why or why not?
3. Do you think that India should do more to try to bring down its birth rate quickly? Why or why not?
4. Do you believe that the United States should have an explicit population policy? If not, why not? If so, what should it be?
5. What do you believe will be the single most important demographic issue with which the world must cope over the next half century, and how do you think this issue should be dealt with?

Suggested Readings

1. Louise Lassonde, 1997, *Coping with Population Challenges* (translated by Graham Grayston) (London: Earthscan Publications Ltd).

   This book was written after the 1994 population conference in Cairo as a way of addressing the many issues left unresolved by the conference. It is also interesting because it is written by a French demographer with a European perspective on how to cope with population change.

2. Nicholas Polunin, Editor, 1998, *Population and Global Security* (Cambridge: Cambridge University Press).

   This book is another "post-Cairo" assessment of where the world is in terms of population growth and the relationship between population and the environment.

3. East-West Center, 2002, *The Future of Population in Asia* (Honolulu: East-West Center).

   Asia has been the world's most populous region for all of recorded history and its future is obviously of considerable importance to the global population picture. This volume provides a thorough review of where Asia is headed demographically.

4. Oscar Harkavy, 1995, *Curbing Population Growth: An Insider's Perspective on the Population Movement* (New York: Plenum Press).

   Oscar Harkavy was an official with the Ford Foundation who helped to map the path of world population policy in the 1950s and 1960s—helping to get us to where we are today.

5. National Research Council, 2001, *Preparing for an Aging World: The Case for Cross-National Research* (Washington, DC: National Academy Press).

   The aging of populations is really less of a "crisis" than it is simply a reality—the inevitable consequence of the demographic transition. This volume is devoted to examining the ways in which societies need to think about the future, which will be occupied by an older population than we have today.

Websites of Interest

Remember that websites are not as permanent as books and journals, so I cannot guarantee that each of the following websites still exists at the moment you are reading this. You may have to Google the name of the organization to find the current web address.

1. **http://www.un.org/esa/population/publications/wpp2009/WPP2009%20web/Countries/WPP2009%20Frame.htm**
   The United Nations Population Division has placed the results of its regular survey of government population policies online so that you can see the trends in specific countries.

2. **http://www.unfpa.org/icpd/index.htm**
   The United Nations Population Fund (UNFPA) was the organizer of the 1994 ICPD and the ICPD+5. This site includes the full text of the 20-year Programme of Action, as well as the documents from the ICPD+5, and has links as well to the Millennium Goals.

3. **http://www.prcdc.org/**
   The Population Resource Center, based in Princeton, NJ, and Washington, DC, is an NGO whose goal is to disseminate information about population issues in order better to inform public policy.

4. **http://www.npg.org/**
   Negative Population Growth is an organization devoted to slowing down the rate of population growth (leading eventually to fewer people), with an emphasis on the United States, but with a global focus as well, especially in terms of the impact of population on the environment.

5. **http://www.pop.org**
   Not all the voices on the Internet are in favor of implementing population policies, and this website seeks to "dispel the myth of overpopulation."

APPENDIX

Population Data for the World 2010, Keyed to Figure 2.1

Rank (ID in Figure 2.1)	Country	Population in 2010	Crude birth rate per 1,000	Crude death rate per 1,000	Net migration rate per 1,000	Rate of natural increase per 1,000	Average annual rate of growth per 1,000	Total fertility rate	Infant mortality rate (both sexes)	Male life expectancy	Female life expectancy	Percent under 15	Percent 65+
1	China	1,330,141,295	12.2	6.9	−0.3	5.30	4.90	1.5	16.5	72.5	76.8	17.9	8.6
2	India	1,173,108,018	21.3	7.5	−0.1	13.80	13.80	2.7	49.1	65.5	67.6	30.1	5.3
3	United States	310,232,863	13.8	8.4	4.3	5.50	9.70	2.1	6.1	75.8	80.8	20.1	13.0
4	Indonesia	242,968,342	18.5	6.3	−1.2	12.20	11.00	2.3	28.9	68.5	73.7	27.7	6.1
5	Brazil	201,103,330	18.1	6.4	−0.1	11.80	11.70	2.2	21.9	68.7	76.0	26.5	6.6
6	Pakistan	177,276,594	25.1	7.1	−2.9	18.00	15.10	3.3	65.3	63.8	67.5	36.0	4.2
7	Bangladesh	158,065,841	23.8	9.1	−2.0	14.70	12.70	2.7	57.8	57.9	63.4	34.1	4.1
8	Nigeria	152,217,341	36.1	16.3	−0.1	19.80	19.70	4.8	93.0	46.5	48.1	41.2	3.1
9	Russia	139,390,205	11.1	16.0	0.3	−4.90	−4.70	1.4	10.3	59.5	73.2	15.0	13.3
10	Japan	126,804,433	7.4	9.8	0.0	−2.40	−2.40	1.2	2.8	78.9	85.7	13.3	22.6
11	Mexico	112,468,855	19.4	4.8	−3.4	14.60	11.20	2.3	17.8	73.5	79.2	28.7	6.4
12	Philippines	99,900,177	25.7	5.1	−1.3	20.60	19.30	3.2	19.9	68.5	74.5	34.9	4.2
13	Vietnam	89,571,130	17.3	6.0	−0.4	11.30	11.00	1.9	21.6	69.5	74.7	25.6	5.5
14	Ethiopia	88,013,491	43.3	11.3	0.0	32.10	32.00	6.1	79.0	53.3	58.4	46.2	2.7
15	Germany	82,282,988	8.2	11.0	2.2	−2.80	−0.60	1.4	4.0	76.4	82.6	13.5	20.4
16	Egypt	80,471,869	25.0	4.9	−0.2	20.20	20.00	3.0	26.2	69.8	75.1	32.8	4.4
17	Turkey	77,804,122	18.3	6.1	0.5	12.20	12.70	2.2	24.8	70.4	74.2	26.9	6.2
18	Congo (Kinshasa)	70,916,439	42.3	11.4	0.8	30.90	31.70	6.1	79.4	52.9	56.6	46.7	2.5
19	Iran	67,037,517	17.3	5.8	−2.2	11.60	9.40	1.7	34.7	69.9	73.0	21.3	5.4
20	Thailand	66,404,688	13.2	7.2	0.0	6.00	6.00	1.7	16.9	71.0	75.8	20.3	9.0
21	France	64,768,389	12.4	8.7	1.5	3.80	5.30	2.0	3.3	77.9	84.4	18.6	16.5
22	United Kingdom	61,284,806	10.7	10.0	2.2	0.70	2.80	1.7	4.8	76.7	81.8	16.5	16.4
23	Italy	58,090,681	8.0	10.8	2.1	−2.80	−0.80	1.3	5.4	77.4	83.5	13.4	20.3
24	Burma	53,414,374	19.5	8.2	−0.3	11.30	11.00	2.3	50.8	62.2	66.9	27.9	5.0
25	South Africa	49,109,107	19.6	17.0	−3.1	2.60	−0.50	2.3	43.8	50.1	48.3	28.6	5.5
26	Korea, South	48,636,068	8.7	6.2	0.0	2.60	2.60	1.2	4.2	75.6	82.3	16.2	11.1
27	Ukraine	45,415,596	9.6	15.7	−0.1	−6.10	−6.20	1.3	8.7	62.6	74.7	13.7	15.5
28	Colombia	44,205,293	17.8	5.2	−0.7	12.50	11.80	2.2	16.9	71.0	77.8	27.2	6.0
29	Sudan	41,980,182	33.3	12.3	0.6	21.00	21.50	4.4	78.1	51.6	53.5	40.2	2.5
30	Tanzania	41,892,895	33.4	12.3	−0.8	21.10	20.30	4.3	68.1	51.0	54.0	42.5	2.9

31	Argentina	41,343,201	17.8	7.4	0.0	10.40	10.40	2.3	11.1	73.5	80.2	25.5	10.9
32	Spain	40,548,753	9.5	10.1	1.0	−0.50	0.50	1.3	4.2	76.9	83.7	14.5	18.4
33	Kenya	40,046,566	35.1	9.3	0.0	25.90	25.90	4.4	53.5	58.3	59.3	42.3	2.7
34	Poland	38,463,689	10.0	10.1	−0.5	−0.10	−0.50	1.3	6.7	71.9	80.1	14.8	13.5
35	Algeria	34,586,184	16.7	4.7	−0.3	12.10	11.80	1.8	26.8	72.6	76.0	24.7	5.1
36	Canada	33,759,742	10.3	7.9	5.6	2.40	8.00	1.6	5.0	78.7	84.0	15.9	15.5
37	Uganda	33,398,682	47.6	11.9	0.0	35.70	35.60	6.7	63.7	51.9	54.1	50.0	2.1
38	Morocco	31,627,428	19.4	4.7	−3.9	14.70	10.80	2.2	28.6	72.6	78.9	28.2	6.0
39	Peru	29,907,003	19.0	6.1	−0.9	12.90	11.90	2.3	27.7	69.1	73.0	28.5	5.8
40	Iraq	29,671,605	29.4	4.9	0.0	24.50	24.50	3.8	43.2	68.9	71.7	38.4	3.1
41	Saudi Arabia	29,207,277	28.2	2.5	−8.3	25.80	17.50	3.8	11.2	74.4	78.7	38.0	2.5
42	Afghanistan	29,121,286	38.1	17.7	4.2	20.50	24.70	5.5	151.5	44.5	44.9	42.9	2.4
43	Nepal	28,951,852	22.4	6.9	−1.4	15.50	14.20	2.5	46.0	64.6	67.1	35.6	4.3
44	Uzbekistan	27,865,738	17.5	5.3	−2.8	12.20	9.40	1.9	22.7	69.2	75.4	27.3	4.7
45	Venezuela	27,223,228	20.3	5.1	0.0	15.20	15.20	2.5	21.1	70.7	77.0	30.0	5.3
46	Malaysia	26,160,256	22.1	5.0	0.0	17.00	17.00	2.9	15.4	70.8	76.5	31.0	5.1
47	Ghana	24,339,838	28.1	8.9	−0.6	19.20	18.60	3.6	49.9	59.4	61.8	36.8	3.6
48	Yemen	23,495,361	34.4	7.2	0.0	27.10	27.10	4.8	56.8	61.4	65.5	43.5	2.6
49	Taiwan	23,024,956	9.0	6.9	0.0	2.10	2.10	1.2	5.3	75.3	81.2	16.2	10.8
50	Korea, North	22,757,275	14.6	10.6	−0.1	4.00	3.90	1.9	50.2	61.5	66.9	20.9	9.6
51	Syria	22,198,110	24.4	3.7	−1.2	20.70	19.50	3.0	16.1	72.1	77.0	35.8	3.7
52	Romania	22,181,287	10.4	11.9	−0.1	−1.50	−1.60	1.4	22.1	69.2	76.4	15.5	14.7
53	Mozambique	22,061,451	37.8	19.8	0.0	18.00	18.00	5.1	103.8	42.1	40.7	44.1	2.9
54	Australia	21,515,754	12.4	6.8	6.1	5.60	11.70	1.8	4.7	79.3	84.3	18.4	13.7
55	Sri Lanka	21,513,990	15.9	6.2	−1.1	9.70	8.60	2.0	18.1	73.2	77.5	23.6	8.3
56	Madagascar	21,281,844	37.9	8.0	0.0	29.90	29.90	5.1	52.8	61.3	65.3	43.3	3.0
57	Cote d'Ivoire	21,058,798	31.5	10.4	0.0	21.10	21.10	4.0	66.4	55.3	57.1	40.2	2.9
58	Cameroon	19,294,149	33.6	12.0	0.0	21.60	21.60	4.3	62.2	53.2	54.9	40.7	3.3
59	Netherlands	16,783,092	10.3	3.8	2.4	1.50	3.90	1.7	4.7	76.9	82.3	17.2	15.2
60	Chile	16,746,491	14.5	5.9	0.0	8.60	8.60	1.9	7.5	74.3	81.0	22.7	9.3
61	Burkina Faso	16,241,811	44.0	13.0	0.0	31.00	31.00	6.2	83.0	51.4	55.3	46.0	2.5
62	Niger	15,878,271	51.1	14.5	0.0	36.60	36.60	7.7	114.5	51.8	54.3	49.7	2.3
63	Kazakhstan	15,460,484	16.7	9.4	−3.3	7.30	4.00	1.9	24.9	62.9	73.8	21.6	7.6
64	Malawi	15,447,500	41.3	13.7	0.0	27.60	27.60	5.5	83.5	50.2	51.6	45.3	2.7
65	Ecuador	14,790,608	20.3	5.0	−0.7	15.30	14.70	2.5	20.3	72.6	78.6	30.6	6.3

Rank (ID in Figure 2.1)	Country	Population in 2010	Crude birth rate per 1,000	Crude death rate per 1,000	Net migration rate per 1,000	Rate of natural increase per 1,000	Average annual rate of growth per 1,000	Total fertility rate	Infant mortality rate (both sexes)	Male life expectancy	Female life expectancy	Percent under 15	Percent 65+
66	Cambodia	14,753,320	25.8	8.0	0.0	17.80	17.80	3.0	53.0	60.4	64.7	32.2	3.7
67	Senegal	14,086,103	36.4	9.6	0.0	26.80	26.80	4.9	57.7	57.5	61.3	42.0	3.0
68	Mali	13,796,354	46.1	14.6	−5.4	31.50	26.10	6.5	113.7	50.6	53.8	47.5	3.0
69	Guatemala	13,550,440	27.4	5.0	−2.2	22.40	20.20	3.4	26.9	68.8	72.5	38.7	3.8
70	Angola	13,068,161	43.3	23.7	1.1	19.60	20.60	6.1	178.1	37.5	39.5	43.4	2.7
71	Zambia	12,056,923	39.9	21.2	−2.6	18.80	16.20	5.1	99.9	38.8	39.0	44.8	2.3
72	Zimbabwe	11,651,858	31.6	14.9	12.9	16.70	29.50	3.7	30.9	48.0	47.1	43.1	3.9
73	Cuba	11,477,459	11.0	7.3	−1.6	3.70	2.20	1.6	5.7	75.4	80.1	18.1	11.6
74	Rwanda	11,055,976	37.3	10.2	1.1	27.10	28.20	5.0	65.6	56.1	58.9	43.0	2.4
75	Greece	10,749,943	9.3	10.6	2.3	−1.30	1.10	1.4	5.1	77.2	82.5	14.2	19.4
76	Portugal	10,735,765	10.1	10.7	3.1	−0.60	2.40	1.5	4.7	75.1	81.9	16.3	17.8
77	Tunisia	10,589,025	15.3	5.2	−0.4	10.10	9.70	1.7	21.8	74.2	77.9	22.2	7.3
78	Chad	10,543,464	40.1	15.8	−4.0	24.30	20.40	5.2	97.1	47.0	49.1	46.4	2.9
79	Belgium	10,423,493	10.1	10.5	1.2	−0.40	0.80	1.7	4.4	76.2	82.7	16.0	17.8
80	Guinea	10,324,025	37.2	10.7	0.0	26.50	26.50	5.2	63.1	56.1	59.1	42.7	3.5
81	Czech Republic	10,201,707	8.8	10.8	1.0	−2.00	−1.10	1.3	3.8	73.7	80.5	13.5	15.9
82	Somalia	10,112,453	43.3	15.2	0.0	28.10	28.10	6.4	107.4	48.1	51.9	45.0	2.5
83	Bolivia	9,947,418	25.2	7.0	−1.0	18.20	17.20	3.1	43.4	64.5	70.1	35.1	4.5
84	Hungary	9,880,059	9.4	12.9	0.9	−3.50	−2.60	1.4	7.7	69.5	78.1	14.8	16.0
85	Burundi	9,863,117	41.4	9.9	4.1	31.60	35.60	6.3	63.4	56.7	60.0	46.1	2.5
86	Dominican Republic	9,794,487	22.1	5.3	−2.0	16.90	14.80	2.7	25.0	72.1	75.9	31.1	6.0
87	Belarus	9,612,632	9.8	13.8	0.4	−4.10	−3.70	1.3	6.3	65.3	76.9	14.2	14.2
88	Haiti	9,203,083	28.7	8.4	−1.9	20.30	18.40	3.7	58.1	59.7	63.1	37.5	3.4
89	Sweden	9,074,055	10.1	10.2	1.7	−0.10	1.60	1.7	2.7	78.7	83.4	15.5	19.3
90	Benin	9,056,010	38.7	9.2	0.0	29.40	29.40	5.4	63.1	58.2	60.7	45.0	2.7
91	Azerbaijan	8,303,512	17.8	8.3	−1.4	9.50	8.10	2.0	52.8	62.9	71.7	23.4	6.6
92	Austria	8,214,160	8.7	10.1	1.8	−1.40	0.40	1.4	4.4	76.7	82.7	14.3	18.1
93	Honduras	7,989,415	25.6	5.0	−1.3	20.60	19.40	3.2	21.0	68.8	72.3	37.4	3.7
94	Switzerland	7,623,438	9.6	8.7	1.3	0.90	2.20	1.5	4.1	78.1	84.0	15.4	16.6
95	Tajikistan	7,487,489	26.5	6.7	−1.3	19.80	18.50	2.9	39.8	62.6	68.9	34.1	3.5

96	Israel	7,353,985	19.5	5.5	2.2	14.10	16.30	2.7	4.2	78.7	83.1	27.8	10.0
97	Serbia	7,344,847	9.2	13.9	0.0	−4.70	−4.70	1.4	6.7	71.3	77.1	15.2	16.6
98	Bulgaria	7,148,785	9.4	14.3	−2.8	−4.90	−7.70	1.4	17.3	69.7	77.2	13.8	17.9
99	Hong Kong	7,089,705	7.5	6.9	4.2	0.50	4.80	1.0	2.9	79.2	84.9	11.9	13.3
100	Laos	6,993,767	33.4	10.5	0.0	22.90	22.90	4.3	76.0	54.8	59.2	40.5	3.1
101	Libya	6,461,454	24.6	3.4	0.0	21.20	21.20	3.0	20.9	75.2	79.9	32.9	4.5
102	Jordan	6,407,085	27.1	2.7	−2.8	24.40	21.60	3.4	17.0	78.6	81.3	35.6	4.7
103	Paraguay	6,375,830	17.7	4.6	−0.1	13.20	13.10	2.2	23.8	73.4	78.7	29.5	6.0
104	Togo	6,199,841	36.2	8.8	0.0	27.40	27.40	4.7	55.5	57.7	62.3	41.2	2.8
105	Papua New Guinea	6,064,515	27.0	6.6	0.0	20.30	20.30	3.5	44.6	63.8	68.3	36.9	3.5
106	El Salvador	6,052,064	18.1	5.6	−9.1	12.50	3.30	2.1	21.0	69.9	76.6	31.5	6.3
107	Nicaragua	5,995,928	22.8	4.3	−1.1	18.50	17.40	2.5	24.2	69.6	74.1	33.1	3.4
108	Eritrea	5,792,984	33.5	8.3	0.0	25.20	25.20	4.6	42.3	60.1	64.3	42.5	3.6
109	Denmark	5,515,575	10.4	10.2	2.5	0.20	2.70	1.7	4.3	76.1	81.0	17.9	16.6
110	Kyrgyzstan	5,508,626	23.6	6.9	−2.6	16.70	14.10	2.6	30.3	65.7	73.9	29.4	5.5
111	Slovakia	5,470,306	10.6	9.6	0.3	1.00	1.30	1.4	6.7	71.7	79.7	15.7	12.6
112	Finland	5,255,068	10.4	10.2	0.6	0.20	0.80	1.7	3.5	75.6	82.8	16.2	17.2
113	Sierra Leone	5,245,695	38.8	12.0	−4.7	26.80	22.20	5.0	80.2	53.3	58.2	41.8	3.6
114	United Arab Emirates	4,975,593	16.0	2.1	21.7	13.90	35.60	2.4	12.3	73.8	79.0	20.4	0.9
115	Turkmenistan	4,940,916	19.6	6.3	−2.0	13.40	11.40	2.2	43.8	65.3	71.3	28.2	4.1
116	Central African Republic	4,844,927	36.8	15.3	0.0	21.50	21.50	4.7	101.6	48.5	51.0	41.1	3.8
117	Singapore	4,701,069	8.7	4.8	4.8	3.90	8.60	1.1	2.3	79.5	84.9	14.1	9.0
118	Norway	4,676,305	10.9	9.3	1.7	1.60	3.30	1.8	3.6	77.4	82.9	18.3	15.6
119	Bosnia and Herzegovina	4,621,598	8.9	8.7	0.0	0.20	0.20	1.3	8.9	75.1	82.5	14.2	14.9
120	Georgia	4,600,825	10.7	9.8	−4.2	0.90	−3.30	1.4	15.7	73.6	80.6	15.8	16.2
121	Costa Rica	4,516,220	16.7	4.3	1.1	12.40	13.50	1.9	9.7	74.9	80.3	25.0	6.2
122	Croatia	4,486,881	9.6	11.8	1.6	−2.20	−0.60	1.4	6.3	72.0	79.4	15.3	16.9
123	Moldova	4,317,483	11.2	10.8	−1.1	0.40	−0.70	1.3	12.8	67.4	75.0	15.7	10.6
124	New Zealand	4,252,277	13.8	7.1	2.3	6.70	9.00	2.1	4.9	78.5	82.5	20.5	13.0
125	Ireland	4,250,163	14.1	7.7	4.7	6.40	11.00	1.9	5.0	75.8	81.2	20.9	12.2
126	Congo (Brazzaville)	4,125,916	41.0	11.8	−1.2	29.30	28.10	5.8	77.9	53.3	55.8	45.8	2.8
127	Lebanon	4,125,247	15.1	6.5	−2.4	8.60	6.20	1.8	16.4	73.3	76.4	23.4	8.8
128	Puerto Rico	3,977,663	11.7	8.0	−0.9	3.70	2.80	1.7	8.2	74.9	82.4	19.4	14.5

Rank (ID in Figure 2.1)	Country	Population in 2010	Crude birth rate per 1,000	Crude death rate per 1,000	Net migration rate per 1,000	Rate of natural increase per 1,000	Average annual rate of growth per 1,000	Total fertility rate	Infant mortality rate (both sexes)	Male life expectancy	Female life expectancy	Percent under 15	Percent 65+
129	Liberia	3,685,076	38.1	10.9	0.6	27.30	27.80	5.2	76.4	55.1	58.1	44.3	2.9
130	Albania	3,659,616	15.4	5.7	−4.2	9.70	5.60	2.0	18.0	75.5	81.1	22.6	10.0
131	Lithuania	3,545,319	9.2	11.3	−0.7	−2.00	−2.80	1.2	6.4	70.2	80.3	13.9	16.3
132	Uruguay	3,510,386	13.7	9.1	−0.1	4.60	4.50	1.9	11.0	73.3	79.9	22.1	13.4
133	Panama	3,410,676	19.7	4.6	−0.5	15.10	14.60	2.5	12.0	74.9	80.5	28.9	7.0
134	Mauritania	3,205,060	33.7	9.0	−0.9	24.70	23.70	4.4	61.9	58.6	63.0	40.7	3.4
135	Mongolia	3,086,918	21.0	6.1	0.0	15.00	15.00	2.2	38.6	65.5	70.5	27.7	4.0
136	Oman	2,967,717	23.9	3.5	−0.5	20.40	20.00	2.9	16.0	72.2	75.9	31.6	3.0
137	Armenia	2,966,802	12.7	8.4	−4.2	4.30	0.20	1.4	19.5	69.3	77.1	17.9	10.3
138	Jamaica	2,847,232	19.5	6.5	−5.5	13.00	7.50	2.2	14.9	71.8	75.3	30.7	7.5
139	Kuwait	2,789,132	21.6	2.3	15.7	19.40	35.00	2.7	8.8	76.6	79.2	26.2	3.0
140	West Bank	2,514,845	24.9	3.6	0.0	21.30	21.30	3.1	15.4	72.8	76.9	36.5	3.7
141	Latvia	2,217,969	9.9	13.6	−2.3	−3.70	−6.00	1.3	8.6	67.3	77.8	13.4	17.0
142	Namibia	2,128,471	21.8	13.0	0.3	8.90	9.10	2.6	45.5	52.3	51.6	35.1	4.0
143	Macedonia	2,072,086	11.9	8.9	−0.5	3.10	2.60	1.6	8.8	72.4	77.6	18.8	11.5
144	Botswana	2,029,307	22.5	9.0	4.9	13.50	18.40	2.5	11.8	61.1	60.8	34.3	3.9
145	Slovenia	2,003,136	8.9	10.7	0.4	−1.80	−1.40	1.3	4.2	73.5	81.0	13.5	16.6
146	Lesotho	1,919,552	27.2	15.7	−8.7	11.50	2.80	3.0	56.4	50.6	50.8	33.7	5.4
147	Gambia, The	1,824,158	37.3	12.0	0.0	25.30	25.30	5.0	67.5	52.3	55.9	43.4	2.9
148	Kosovo	1,815,048	18.5	7.1	−5.8	11.50	5.70	2.3	43.9	67.9	72.0	27.5	6.6
149	Gaza Strip	1,604,238	36.3	3.4	0.0	32.90	32.90	4.9	17.7	72.1	75.4	44.1	2.6
150	Guinea-Bissau	1,565,126	35.6	15.5	0.0	20.00	20.00	4.6	98.1	46.4	50.2	40.6	3.1
151	Gabon	1,545,255	35.4	12.9	−2.2	22.50	20.30	4.6	50.9	52.0	53.6	42.2	3.9
152	Swaziland	1,354,051	27.1	15.0	0.0	12.10	12.10	3.2	66.7	48.1	47.8	38.2	3.6
153	Mauritius	1,294,104	14.2	6.6	0.0	7.50	7.50	1.8	11.9	70.8	77.9	22.2	7.2
154	Estonia	1,291,170	10.4	13.5	−3.3	−3.10	−6.40	1.4	7.2	67.7	78.8	15.0	17.6
155	Trinidad and Tobago	1,228,691	14.4	8.2	−7.1	6.20	−0.90	1.7	28.9	68.2	74.0	19.5	8.1
156	Timor-Leste	1,154,625	25.9	5.9	0.0	20.00	20.00	3.2	39.3	65.2	70.1	34.2	3.5

Source: U.S. Census Bureau, International Programs Center, Online Database, Accessed 2010.

GLOSSARY

This glossary contains words or terms that appeared in boldface type in the text. I have tried to include terms that are central to an understanding of the study of population. The chapter notation in parentheses refers to the chapter(s) in which the term is discussed in detail, not necessarily the first time it is used in the text.

abortion the induced or spontaneous premature expulsion of a fetus (Chapter 6).

abridged life table a life table (see definition) in which ages are grouped into categories (usually five-year age groupings) (Chapter 5).

accidental or unintentional death loss of life unrelated to disease but attributable to the physical, social, or economic environment (Chapter 5).

acculturation a process undergone by immigrants in which they adopt the host language, bring their diet more into line with the host culture's diet, and participate in cultural activities of the host society (Chapter 7).

achieved characteristics those sociodemographic characteristics such as education, occupation, income, marital status, and labor force participation over which we have some degree of control (Chapter 10).

adaptation a process undergone by immigrants in which they adjust to the new physical and social environment of the host society (Chapter 7).

administrative data demographic information derived from administrative records, including tax returns, utility records, school enrollment, and participation in government programs (Chapter 4).

administrative records with respect to migration, this refers to forms filled out for each person entering the U.S. from abroad that are then collected and tabulated by the U.S. Citizenship and Immigration Service (Chapter 4).

age and sex structure the number (or percentage) of people in a population distributed by age and sex (Chapter 8).

age pyramid graph of the number (or percentage) of people in a population distributed by age and sex (Chapter 8).

age-sex-specific death rate (ASDR) the number of people of a given age and sex who died in a given year divided by the total (average midyear) number of people of that age and sex (Chapter 5).

age-specific fertility rate (ASFR) the number of children born to women of a given age divided by the total number of women that age (Chapter 6).

age stratification the assignment of social roles and social status on the basis of age (Chapter 8).

age structure the distribution of people in a population by age (Chapter 8).

age transition the shift from a predominantly younger to a predominantly older population as a society moves through the demographic transition (Chapters 3 and 8).

Agricultural Revolution change that took place roughly 10,000 years ago when humans first began to domesticate plants and animals, thereby making it easier to live in permanent settlements (Chapter 2).

Alzheimer's disease a disease involving a change in the brain's neurons, producing behavioral shifts; a major cause of organic brain disorder among older persons (Chapter 5).

ambivalent an attitude of being caught between competing pressures and thus being uncertain about how to behave properly (Chapter 6).

amenorrhea temporary absence or suppression of menstruation (Chapter 6).

American Community Survey an ongoing "continuous measurement" survey conducted by the U.S. Census Bureau to track the detailed population characteristics of every American community; designed to allow the long form to be dropped from the decennial census in 2010 (Chapter 4).

anovulatory pertaining to a menstrual cycle in which no ovum (egg) is released (Chapter 6).

antinatalist based on an ideological position that discourages childbearing (Chapters 3 and 12).

applied demography see *demographics* (Chapter 1).

apportionment the use of census data to determine the number of seats in the U.S. Congress that will be allocated to each state (Chapter 1).

aquaculture farming fish (including shellfish); a steadily increasing source of fish for food (Chapter 11).

arable land that is suitable for agricultural purposes (Chapter 11).

ascribed characteristics sociodemographic characteristics such as sex or gender, race, and ethnicity that we are born with and over which we have essentially no control (Chapter 10).

assimilate what immigrants do as they not only accept the outer trappings of the host culture, but also assume the behaviors and attitudes of the host culture (Chapter 7).

asylee a person who has been forced out of his or her country of nationality and who is seeking legal refuge (permanent residency) in the country to which he or she has moved (Chapter 7).

atmosphere the whole mass of air surrounding the earth (Chapters 1 and 11).

average age of a population one measure of the age distribution of a population—may be calculated as either the mean or the median (Chapter 8).

baby boom the dramatic rise in the birth rate following World War II. In the United States it refers to people born between 1946 and 1964; in Canada it refers to people born between 1947 and 1966 (Chapters 2 and 6).

base year the beginning year of data on which a population projection is based (Chapter 8).

biosphere the zone of Earth where life is found, including the atmosphere, hydrosphere, and lithosphere (Chapter 11).

birth control regulation of the number of children you have through the deliberate prevention of conception; note that birth control does not necessarily include abortion, although it is often used in the same sense as the terms contraception, family planning, and fertility control (Chapter 6).

birth rate see *crude birth rate* (Chapter 6).

boomsters a nickname given to people who believe that population growth stimulates economic development (Chapter 11).

breastfeeding its role as a contraceptive is to temporarily impair fecundity by prolonging postpartum amenorrhea and suppressing ovulation (Chapter 6).

capital a stock of goods used for the production of other goods rather than for immediate enjoyment; anything invested to yield income in the future (Chapter 11).

capitalism an economic system in which the means of production, distribution, and exchange of wealth are maintained chiefly by private individuals or corporations, as contrasted to government ownership (Chapter 3).

carbon cycle that process through which carbons, central to life on the planet, are exchanged between living organisms and inanimate matter (Chapter 11).

cardiovascular disease a disease of the heart or blood vessels (Chapter 5).

carrying capacity the size of population that could theoretically be maintained indefinitely at a given level of living with a given type of economic system (Chapters 2 and 11).

celibacy permanent nonmarriage, implying as well that a celibate is a person who never enters a sexual union (Chapter 6).

census metropolitan area (CMA) metropolitan areas as defined in Canada, including a core urban area of at least 100,000 and adjacent urban and rural areas that have a high degree of economic and social integration with that core urban area (Chapter 9).

census of population an official enumeration of an entire population, usually with details as to age, sex, occupation, and other population characteristics; defined by the United Nations as "the total process of collecting, compiling and publishing demographic, economic and social data pertaining, at a specified time or times, to all persons in a country or delimited territory" (Chapter 4).

chain migration the process whereby migrants are part of an established flow from a common origin to a prepared destination where others have previously migrated (Chapter 7).

checks to growth factors that, according to Malthus, keep population from growing in size, including positive checks and preventive checks (Chapter 3).

child control the practice of controlling family size after the birth of children (postnatally), through the mechanisms of infanticide, fosterage, and orphanage (Chapter 6).

child–woman ratio a census-based measure of fertility, calculated as the ratio of children aged 0–4 to the number of women aged 15–49 (Chapter 6).

children ever born births to date for a particular cohort of women at a particular point in time (Chapter 6).

cluster marketing identifying neighborhoods on the basis of a whole set of shared sociodemographic characteristics and using that information to market goods and services to people in the identified geographic areas (Chapter 1).

co-ethnic a person who shares your ethnic heritage (Chapter 7).

cohabitation the sharing of a household by unmarried people who have a sexual relationship (Chapter 10).

cohort people who share something in common; in demography, this is most often the year (or grouped years) of birth (Chapter 6).

cohort component method of population projection a population projection made by applying age-specific survival rates, age-specific fertility rates, and age-specific measures of migration to the base year population in order to project the population to the target year (Chapter 8).

cohort flow the movement through time of a group of people born in the same year (Chapter 8).

cohort measures of fertility following the fertility of groups of women as they proceed through their childbearing years (Chapter 6).

Columbian Exchange the exchange of food, products, people, and diseases between Europe and the Americas as a result of explorations by Columbus and others (Chapters 3 and 5).

communicable disease (also called infectious disease) a disease capable of being communicated or transmitted from person to person (Chapter 5).

completed fertility rate (CFR) the cohort measure of fertility, calculated as the number of children ever born to women who have reached the end of their reproductive career (Chapter 6).

components of change or residual method of migration estimation a method of measuring net migration between two dates by comparing the estimate of total population with that which would have resulted solely from the components of birth and death, with the residual attributable to migration (Chapter 7).

components of growth a method of estimating and/or projecting population size by adding births, subtracting deaths, and adding net migration occurring in an interval of time, then adding the result to the population at the beginning of the interval (Chapter 8).

condom a thin sheath, usually of rubber, worn over the penis during sexual intercourse to prevent conception or venereal disease (Chapter 6).

consolidated metropolitan statistical areas (CMSAs) groupings of the very largest Metropolitan Statistical Areas in the United States (Chapter 9).

content error an inaccuracy in the data obtained in a census; possibly an error in reporting, editing, or tabulating (Chapter 4).

contraception the prevention of conception or impregnation by any of various techniques or devices (Chapter 6).

contraceptive device mechanical or chemical means of preventing conception (Chapter 6).

contraceptive prevalence the percentage of "at risk" women of reproductive age (15 to 44 or 15 to 49) who are using a method of contraception (Chapter 6).

Core-Based Statistical Area (CBSA) a method for identifying metropolitan areas adopted by the U.S. Office of Management and Budget in 2000 and implemented by the U.S. Census Bureau in connection with Census 2000 data (Chapter 9).

core-periphery model a model of city systems in which the primate city (the core) controls the resources, and the smaller cities (the periphery) depend on the larger city (Chapter 9).

cornucopians "boomsters" who believe that we can always grow enough food to feed whatever size population we have (Chapter 11).

coverage error the combination of undercount (the percentage of a particular group or total population that is inadvertently not counted in a census) and overcount (people who are counted more than once in the census) (Chapter 4).

crowding the gathering of a large number of people closely together; the number of people per space per unit of time (Chapter 9).

crude birth rate (CBR) the number of births in a given year divided by the total midyear population in that year (Chapter 6).

crude death rate (CDR) the number of deaths in a given year divided by the total midyear population in that year (Chapter 5).

crude net migration rate (CNMR) a measure of migration calculated as the number of in-migrants minus the number of out-migrants divided by the total midyear population (Chapter 7).

cumulated cohort fertility rate see *children ever born* (Chapter 6).

de facto population the people actually in a given territory on the census day (Chapter 4).

de jure population the people who legally "belong" in a given area whether or not they are there on census day (Chapter 4).

degeneration the biological deterioration of a body (Chapter 5).

demographic analysis (DA) a method of evaluating the accuracy of a census by estimating the demographic components of change since the previous census and comparing it with the new census count (Chapter 4).

demographic balancing equation the formula that shows that the population at time 2 is equal to the population at time 1, plus the births between time 1 and 2, minus the deaths between time 1 and 2, plus the in-migrants between time 1 and 2, minus the out-migrants between time 1 and 2 (Chapter 4).

demographic change and response the theory that the response made by individuals to population pressures is determined by the means available to them (Chapter 3).

demographic characteristics see *population characteristics* (Chapter 10).

demographic overhead the general cost of adding people to a population caused by the necessity of providing goods and services (Chapter 11).

demographic perspective a way of relating basic information to theories about how the world operates demographically (Chapter 3).

demographic processes see *population processes* (Chapter 1).

demographic transition the process whereby a country moves from high birth and high death rates to low birth and low death rates with an interstitial spurt in population growth, accompanied by a set of other transitions, including the migration transition, age transition, urban transition, and family and household transition (Chapter 3).

demographics the application of demographic science to practical problems; any applied use of population statistics (Chapter 1).

demographics of human resource management using demographic information to help manage an organization's labor force (Chapter 1).

demography the scientific study of human populations (Chapter 1).

density the ratio of people to physical space (Chapter 9).

dependency ratio the ratio of people of dependent age (usually considered to be 0–14 and 65+) to people of economically active ages (15–64) (Chapter 8).

diaphragm a barrier method of fertility control—a thin, dome-shaped device, usually of rubber, inserted in the vagina and worn over the uterine cervix to prevent conception during sexual intercourse (Chapter 6).

differential undercount the situation that occurs in a census when some groups of people are more likely to be underenumerated than other groups (Chapter 4).

direct population policy a population policy that is aimed specifically at altering demographic behavior (Chapter 12).

disability-adjusted life year (DALY) a summary measure of the burden of disease that incorporates the number of years of life lost to a premature death plus the number of unhealthy years lived because of a specific cause of death (Chapter 5).

disability-free life expectancy the period of time up until a person's arrival at the "Fourth Age," when the rest of his or her life is increasingly consumed by coping with the health effects of old age (Chapter 5).

doctrine a principle laid down as true and beyond dispute (Chapter 3).

donor area the area from which migrants come (Chapter 7).

doomster a nickname given to people who believe that population growth retards economic development (Chapter 12).

doubling time the number of years required for a population to double in number if the current rate of growth continues (Chapter 2).

douche (as a contraceptive) washing of the vaginal area after intercourse to prevent conception (Chapter 6).

drought a prolonged period of less-than-average rainfall (Chapter 11).

dual-system estimation (DSE) a method of evaluating a census by comparing respondents in the census with respondents in a carefully selected postenumeration survey or through a matching with other records (Chapter 4).

Easterlin relative cohort size hypothesis the perspective that fertility is influenced less by absolute levels of income than by relative levels of well-being produced by generational changes in cohort size (Chapter 3).

ecological footprint the total area of productive land and water required to produce the resources for and assimilate the waste from a given population (Chapter 11).

economic development a rise in the average standard of living associated with economic growth; a rise in per capita income (Chapter 11).

economic growth an increase in the total amount of income produced by a nation or region without regard to the total number of people (Chapter 11).

ecosphere all of the earth's ecosystems; the living portion of the biosphere (Chapter 11).

ecosystem communities of species interacting with one another and with the inanimate world (Chapter 11).

edge cities cities that have been created in suburban, often unincorporated, areas and that replicate most of the functions of the older central city (Chapter 9).

emergency contraceptive pills methods designed to avert pregnancy within 72 hours after intercourse, usually by taking a large dosage of the same hormones contained in the contraceptive pill (Chapter 6).

emigrant a person who leaves one country to settle permanently in another; an international out-migrant (Chapter 7).

enclave a place within a larger community within which members of a particular subgroup tend to concentrate (Chapter 7).

endogenous factors those things that are within the scope of (internal to) one's own control (Chapter 6).

epidemiologic transition the pattern of long-term shifts in health and disease patterns as mortality moves from high levels (dominated by death at young ages from communicable diseases) to low levels (dominated by death at older ages from degenerative diseases)—part of the health and mortality transition (Chapter 5).

ethnic group a group of people of the same race or nationality who share a common and distinctive culture while living within a larger society (Chapter 10).

ethnicity the ancestral origins of a particular group, typically manifested in certain kinds of attitudes and behaviors (Chapter 10).

ethnocentric characterized by a belief in the inherent superiority of one's own group and culture accompanied by a feeling of contempt for other groups and cultures (Chapter 3).

exclusion dealing with immigrants to an area by keeping them separate from most members of the host society, forcing them into separate enclaves or ghettos (Chapter 7).

exogenous factors those things that are beyond the control of (external to) the average person (Chapter 6).

expectation of life at birth see *life expectancy* (Chapter 5).

extended family family members beyond the nuclear family (Chapter 10).

extensification of agriculture increasing agricultural output by putting more land into production (Chapter 11).

exurbs nonrural population beyond the suburbs (Chapter 9).

family a group of people who are related to each other by birth, marriage, or adoption (Chapter 10).

family control ways of limiting family size after the birth of children (Chapter 6).

family demography the study and analysis of family households: their formation, their change over time, and their dissolution (Chapter 10).

family household a household in which the householder is living with one or more persons related to her or him by birth, marriage, or adoption (Chapter 10).

family and household transition the shift in family and household structure occasioned in societies by people living longer, with fewer children born, increasingly in urban settings, and subject to higher standards of living, all as part of the demographic transition (Chapters 3 and 10).

famine food shortage accompanied by a significant increase in deaths (Chapter 11).

fecundity the physical capacity to reproduce (Chapter 6).

female genital mutilation (FGM) sometimes known as female circumcision, which typically involves removing a woman's clitoris, thus lessening her enjoyment of sexual intercourse (Chapter 6).

fertility reproductive performance rather than the mere capacity to reproduce; one of the three basic demographic processes (Chapter 6).

fertility awareness methods of birth control methods of natural family planning that are combined with a barrier method to protect against conception during the fertile period (Chapter 6).

fertility differential a variable in which people show clear differences in fertility according to their categorization by that variable (Chapter 6).

fertility rate see *general fertility rate* (Chapter 6).

fertility transition the shift from "natural" fertility (high levels of fertility) to fertility limitation (low levels of fertility) (Chapters 3 and 6).

food security a term meaning that people have physical and economic access to the basic food they need in order to work and function normally (Chapter 11).

force of mortality the factors that prevent people from living to their biological maximum age (Chapter 5).

forced migrant someone who has been forced to leave his or her home because of a real or perceived threat to life and well-being (Chapter 7).

forward survival (or residual) method of migration estimation a method of estimating migration between two censuses by combining census data with life table probabilities of survival between the two censuses (Chapter 7).

fosterage the practice of placing an "excess" child in someone else's home (Chapter 6).

gender role a social role considered appropriate for males or females (Chapter 10).

general fertility rate the total number of births in a year divided by the total midyear number of women of childbearing age (Chapter 6).

generational replacement a net reproduction rate of one, which indicates that each generation of females has the potential to just replace itself (Chapter 6).

gentrification restoration and habitation of older homes in central city areas by urban or suburban elites (Chapter 9).

geodemographics analysis of demographic data that have been georeferenced to specific locations (Chapters 1 and 4).

geographic information system (GIS) computer-based system that allows the user to combine maps with data that refer to particular places on those maps and then to analyze those data and display the results as thematic maps or some other graphic format (Chapter 4).

georeferenced a piece of information that includes some form of geographic identification such as precise latitude-longitude coordinates, a street address, ZIP code, census tract, county, state, or country (Chapter 4).

global warming an increase in the global temperature caused by a buildup of greenhouse gases (Chapter 11).

Graunt, John Seventeenth-century London haberdasher who has become known as the "father of demography" for his pioneering studies of the regular patterns of death in London (Chapters 3 and 5).

Green Revolution an improvement in agricultural production begun in the 1940s based on high-yield-variety strains of grain and increased use of fertilizers, pesticides, and irrigation (Chapter 11).

greenhouse gases those atmospheric gases (especially carbon dioxide and water) that trap radiated heat from the sun and warm the surface of the earth (Chapter 11).

gross domestic product the total value of goods and services produced within the geographic boundaries of a nation in a given year, without reference to international trade (Chapter 11).

gross national income in PPP (GNI PPP) gross national product expressed in terms of Purchasing Power Parity (rather than the official exchange rates) (Chapter 11).

gross national product (GNP) the total output of goods and services produced by a country, including income earned from abroad (Chapter 11).

gross (or crude) rate of in-migration the total number of in-migrants divided by the total midyear population in the area of destination (Chapter 7).

gross (or crude) rate of out-migration the total number of out-migrants divided by the total midyear population in the area of origin (Chapter 7).

gross reproduction rate the total fertility rate multiplied by the proportion of all births that are girls. It is generally interpreted as the number of female children that a female just born may expect to have in her lifetime, assuming that birth rates stay the same and ignoring her chances of survival through her reproductive years (Chapter 6).

growth rates by age a way of measuring population growth by calculating age-specific rates of growth (Chapter 8).

high growth potential the first stage in the demographic transition, in which a population has a pattern of high birth and death rates (Chapter 3).

high-yield varieties (HYV) dwarf types of grains that have shorter stems and produce more stalks than most traditional varieties (Chapter 11).

historical sources data derived from sources such as early censuses, genealogies, family reconstitution, grave sites, and archaeological findings (Chapter 4).

host area the destination area of migrants; the area into which they migrate (Chapter 7).

household all of the people who occupy a housing unit (Chapter 10).

householder the person in whose name the house is owned or rented (sometimes called the head of household) (Chapter 10).

housing unit a house, apartment, mobile home or trailer, group of rooms (or even a single room if occupied as a separate living quarters) intended for occupancy as a separate living quarters (Chapter 10).

human capital investments in individuals that can improve their economic productivity and thus their overall standard of living; including things such as education and job-training, and often enhanced by migration (Chapters 7 and 10).

human resource management see *demographics of human resource management* (Chapter 1).

human resources the application of human ingenuity to convert natural resources to uses not originally intended by nature (Chapter 11).

hydrologic cycle the water cycle by which ocean and land water evaporates into the air, is condensed, and then returns to the ground as precipitation (Chapter 11).

hydrosphere the earth's water resources, including water in oceans, lakes, rivers, groundwater, and water in glaciers and ice caps (Chapters 1 and 11).

illegal (undocumented) immigrants immigrants who lack government permission to reside in the country to which they have moved (Chapter 7).

immigrant a person who moves into a country of which he or she is not a native for the purpose of taking up permanent residence—an international inmigrant (Chapter 7).

impact (IPAT) equation a formula developed by Paul Ehrlich and associates to express the relationship between population growth, affluence, and technology and their impact on the environment: Impact (I) = Population (P) × Affluence (A) × Technology (T) (Chapter 11).

impaired fecundity a reduced ability to reproduce, defined as a woman who believes that it is impossible for her to have a baby; or a physician has told her not to become pregnant because the pregnancy would pose a health risk for her or her baby; or she has been continuously married for at least 36 months, has not used contraception, and yet has not gotten pregnant (Chapter 6).

implementing strategy a possible means (such as migration) whereby a goal (such as an improvement in income) might be attained (Chapter 7).

incipient decline the third (final) stage in the demographic transition when a country has moved from having a very high rate of natural increase to having a very low (possibly negative) rate of increase (Chapter 3).

index of fertility product of the proportion of the female population that is married times the index of marital fertility (Chapter 6).

indirect population policy a population policy that is not necessarily designed just to influence population changes but instead does so by changing other aspects of life (Chapter 12).

Industrial Revolution the totality of the changes in economic and social organization that began about 1750 in England and later in other countries; characterized chiefly by the replacement of hand tools with power-driven machines and by the concentration of industry in large establishments (Chapter 2).

infant mortality death during the first year of life (Chapter 5).

infant mortality rate the number of deaths to infants under one year of age divided by the number of live births in that year (and usually multiplied by 1,000) (Chapter 5).

infanticide the deliberate killing or abandonment of an infant; a method of "family control" in many premodern and some modern societies (Chapter 2).

infecundity the inability to produce offspring, synonymous with sterility (Chapter 6).

in-migrant a person who migrates permanently into an area from somewhere else. This term usually refers to an internal migrant; an international inmigrant is an *immigrant* (Chapter 7).

integration incorporating immigrants into the receiving society through the mechanism of mutual accommodation (Chapter 7).

intensification of agriculture the process of increasing crop yield by any means—mechanical, chemical, or otherwise (Chapter 11).

intercensal the period between the taking of censuses (Chapter 4).

intermediate variables means for regulating fertility; the variables through which any social factors influencing the level of fertility must operate (Chapter 6).

internal migration permanent change in residence within national boundaries (Chapter 7).

internally displaced person (IDP) a person who is forced to flee from home but seeks refuge elsewhere in the country of origin (Chapter 7).

international migration permanent change of residence involving movement from one country to another (Chapter 7).

intervening obstacles factors that may inhibit migration even if a person is motivated to migrate (Chapter 7).

intrauterine device (IUD) any small, mechanical device for semipermanent insertion in the uterus as a contraceptive (Chapter 6).

investment demographics basing investment decisions at least partly on the analysis of projected population changes (Chapter 1).

launch year the beginning year of a population projection (Chapter 8).

legal immigrants immigrants who have legal permission to be permanent residents of the country to which they have moved (Chapter 7).

life chances the probability of having a particular set of demographic characteristics, such as having a high-prestige job, lots of money, a stable marriage or not marrying at all, a small family or no family at all (Chapter 10).

life course perspective the idea that people's live are embedded in specific times and places and that people are influenced throughout their life by events shared by other members of their age cohort (Chapter 10).

life expectancy the average duration of life beyond a specific age, of people who have attained that age, calculated from a life table (Chapter 5).

life span the oldest age to which an organism or species may live (Chapter 5).

life table an actuarial table showing the number of people who die at any given age, from which life expectancy is calculated (Chapter 5).

lifeboat ethic the population policy perspective that suggests that health assistance should only be offered to countries that have a reasonable chance of success in limiting population growth (Chapter 12).

lithosphere the upper part of the earth's crust, which contains the soils, minerals, and fuels that plants and animals require for life (Chapter 1 and 12).

logarithm the exponent indicating the power to which a fixed number, the base, must be raised to produce a given number; related to the concept that human populations have the capacity to grow in a logarithmic fashion, increasing geometrically in size from one generation to the next (Chapter 2).

long-term immigrant an international migrant whose stay in the place of destination is more than one year (Chapter 7).

longevity the ability to resist death, measured as the average age at death (Chapter 5).

Malthusian pertaining to the theories of Malthus, which state that population tends to increase at a geometric rate, while the means of subsistence increase at an arithmetic rate, resulting in an inadequate supply of the goods supporting life, unless a catastrophe occurs to reduce (check) the population or the increase of population is checked by sexual restraint (Chapter 3).

mariculture farming the sea, including both fishing and harvesting kelp and algae for human consumption (Chapter 11).

marital status the state of being single, married, separated, divorced, widowed, or living in a consensual union (cohabiting) (Chapter 10).

marketing demographics the use of demographic information to improve the marketing of a product or service (Chapter 1).

marriage squeeze an imbalance between the numbers of males and females in the prime marriage ages (Chapter 10).

Marxian pertaining to the theories of Karl Marx, which reject Malthusian theory and argue instead that each society at each point in history has its own law of population that determines the consequences of population growth (Chapter 3).

maternal mortality the death of a woman as a result of pregnancy or childbearing (Chapter 5).

maternal mortality ratio the number of deaths to women due to pregnancy and childbirth divided by the number of live births in a given year (and usually multiplied by 100,000) (Chapter 5).

mean length of generation the average age at childbearing (Chapter 6).

means of subsistence the amount of resources (especially food) available to a population (Chapter 3).

mega-city a term used by the United Nations to denote any urban agglomeration with more than 10 million people (Chapter 9).

megalopolis see *urban agglomeration* (Chapter 9).

menarche the onset of menstruation, usually occurring when a woman is in her teens (Chapter 6).

menopause the time when menstruation ceases permanently, usually between the ages of 45 and 50 (Chapter 6).

mercantilism the view that a nation's wealth depended on its store of precious metals and that generating this kind of wealth was facilitated by population growth (Chapter 3).

metropolitan area an urban place extending beyond a core city; in the United States this refers to a core-based statistical area with at least 50,000 people (Chapter 9).

micropolitan area in the United States this is a core-based statistical area with at least 10,000 people, but less than 50,000 (Chapter 9).

migrant a person who makes a permanent change of residence substantial enough in distance to involve a shift in that individual's round of social activities (Chapter 7).

migrant stock the number of people in a region who have migrated there from somewhere else (Chapter 7).

migration the process of permanently changing residence from one geographic location to another; one of the three basic demographic processes (Chapter 7).

migration effectiveness the crude net migration rate divided by the total migration rate (Chapter 7).

migration evolution the current state of migration, with the population largely urban-based and people moving between and within urban places (Chapter 7).

migration flow the movement of people between regions (Chapter 7).

migration ratio the ratio of the net number of migrants (in-migrants minus out-migrants) to the difference between the number of births and deaths—measuring the contribution that migration makes to overall population growth (Chapter 7).

migration transition the shift of people from rural to urban places (see urban transition), and the shift to higher levels of international migration (Chapters 3 and 7).

migration turnover rate the total migration rate divided by the crude net migration rate (Chapter 7).

mobility geographic movement that is either not permanent, or is of sufficiently short distance that it is not considered to be migration (Chapter 7).

model stable population a population whose age and sex structure is implied by a given set of mortality rates and a particular rate of population growth (Chapter 8).

modernization the process of societal development involving urbanization, industrialization, rising standards of living, better education, and improved health that is typically associated with a "Western" lifestyle and worldview and was the basis for early explanations of the demographic transition (Chapter 3).

momentum of population growth the potential for a future increase in population size that is inherent in any present age and sex structure even if fertility levels were to drop to replacement level (Chapter 8).

moral restraint according to Malthus, the avoidance of sexual intercourse prior to marriage and the delay of marriage until a man can afford all the children his wife might bear; a desirable preventive check on population growth (Chapter 3).

morbidity the prevalence of disease in a population (Chapter 5).

mortality deaths in a population; one of the three basic demographic processes (Chapter 5).

mortality transition the shift from deaths at younger ages due to communicable diseases to deaths at older ages due to degenerative diseases (Chapter 5).

mover a person who moves within the same county and thus, according to the U.S. Census Bureau definitions, has not moved far enough to become a migrant (Chapter 7).

multiculturalism incorporating immigrants into a host society in a manner that allows the immigrants to retain their ethnic communities but share the same legal rights as other members of the host society (Chapter 7).

natural fertility fertility levels that exist in the absence of deliberate, or at least modern, fertility control (Chapter 6).

natural increase the excess of births over deaths; the difference between the crude birth rate and the crude death rate is the rate of natural increase (Chapter 2).

natural resources those resources available to us on the planet (Chapter 11).

Neolithic Agrarian Revolution see Agricultural Revolution (Chapter 2).

Neolithic Demographic Transition the increase in fertility, not quite matched by an increase in mortality, that occurred as societies settled into agriculture and which led to an increase in population growth as a result of the Agricultural Revolution (Chapter 3).

neo-Malthusian a person who accepts the basic Malthusian premise that population growth tends to outstrip resources, but (unlike Malthus) believes that birth control measures are appropriate checks to population growth (Chapter 3).

neo-Marxist a person who accepts the basic principle of Marx that societal problems are created by an unjust and inequitable distribution of resources of any and all kinds, without necessarily believing that communism is the answer to those problems (Chapter 11).

net census undercount the difference between the undercount and the overcount (Chapter 4).

net migration the difference between those who move in and those who move out of a particular region in a given period of time (Chapter 7).

net reproduction rate (NRR) a measure of generational replacement; specifically, the average number of female children that will be born to the female babies who were themselves born in a given year, assuming no change in the age-specific fertility and mortality rates and ignoring the effect of migration (Chapter 6).

noncommunicable disease disease that continues for a long time or recurs frequently (as opposed to acute)—often associated with degeneration (Chapter 5).

nonfamily household one that includes people who live alone, or with nonfamily coresidents (friends living together, a single householder who rents out rooms, etc.) (Chapter 10).

non-governmental organizations (NGOs) private social service agencies that work to implement specific social policies (Chapter 12).

nonsampling error an error that occurs in the enumeration process as a result of missing people who should be counted, counting people more than once, respondents providing inaccurate information, or recording or processing information inaccurately (Chapter 4).

nuclear family at least one parent and his/her/their children (Chapter 10).

nutrition transition a predictable shift in diet that accompanies the stages of the health and mortality transition (Chapters 5 and 11).

opportunity costs with respect to fertility, the things foregone in order to have children (Chapter 6).

optimum population size the number of people that would provide the best balance of people and resources for a desired standard of living (Chapter 11).

oral rehydration therapy an inexpensive glucose and electrolyte solution that is very effective in controlling diarrhea, especially among young children (Chapter 5).

orphanage the practice of abandoning children in such a way that they are likely to be cared for by strangers (Chapter 6).

out-migrant a person who permanently leaves an area and migrates someplace else. This term usually refers to internal migration, whereas *emigrant* refers to an international migrant (Chapter 7).

overpopulation a situation in which the population has overshot a region's carrying capacity (Chapter 11).

overshoot exceeding a region's carrying capacity (Chapter 11).

ozone layer the region of the earth's upper atmosphere that protects the earth from the sun's ultraviolet rays (Chapter 11).

parity progression ratio the proportion of women with a given number of children (parity refers to how many children have already been born) who "progress" to having another child (Chapter 6).

per-capita (per-person) income a common measure of average income, calculated by dividing the total value of goods and services produced (GNP or GDP or PPP) by the total population size (Chapter 11).

period data population data that refer to a particular year and represent a cross section of population at one specific time (Chapter 6).

period rates rates referring to a specific, limited period of time, usually one year (Chapter 6).

peri-urban region the periphery of the urban zone that looks rural to the naked eye but houses people who are essentially urban (Chapter 9).

physiocratic the philosophy that the real wealth of a nation is in the land, not in the number of people (Chapter 3).

planned obsolescence theories of aging based on the idea that each person has a built-in programmed biological time clock; barring death from accidents or disease, cells still die because each is programmed to reproduce itself only a fixed number of times (Chapter 5).

population (or demographic) characteristics those demographic traits or qualities that differentiate one individual or group from another, including age, sex, race, ethnicity, marital status, occupation, education, income, wealth, and urban-rural residence (Chapters 1 and 8 through 10).

population distribution where people are located and why (Chapter 1).

population explosion a popular term referring to a rapid increase in the size of the world's population, especially the increase since World War II (Chapters 2 and 3).

population forecast a statement about what you expect the future population to be; distinguished from a projection, which is a statement about what the future population could be under a given set of assumptions (Chapter 8).

population growth or decline how the number of people in a particular place is changing over time (Chapter 1).

population implosion a popular term referring (somewhat misleadingly) to the end of the population explosion, but more generally meaning a decline in population size (Chapter 2).

population momentum see *momentum of population growth* (Chapter 8).

population policy a formalized set of procedures designed to achieve a particular pattern of population change (Chapter 12).

population processes fertility, mortality, and migration; the dynamic elements of demographic analysis (Chapter 1).

population projection the calculation of the number of people we can expect to be alive at a future date, given the number now alive and given reasonable assumptions about age-specific mortality and fertility rates and migration (Chapter 8).

population pyramid see *age pyramid* (Chapter 8).

population register a list of all people in a country on which are recorded all vital events for each individual, typically birth, death, marriage, divorce, and change of residence (Chapter 4).

population size how many people are in a given place (Chapter 1).

population structure how many males and females there are of each age (Chapter 1).

positive checks a term used by Malthus to refer to factors (essentially mortality) that limit the size of human populations by "weakening" or "destroying the human frame" (Chapter 3).

postpartum following childbirth (Chapter 6).

poverty index a measure of need that in the United States is based on the premise that one third of a poor family's income is spent on food; then calculated as the cost of an economy food plan multiplied by three. Since 1964, it has increased at the same rate as the consumer price index (Chapter 10).

preconditions for a substantial fertility decline Ansley Coale's theory as to how an individual would have to perceive the world on a daily basis if fertility were to be consciously limited (Chapter 6).

preventive checks in Malthus's writings, any limits to birth, among which Malthus himself preferred moral restraint (Chapter 3).

primary metropolitan statistical area (PMSA) MSA within a CMSA (Chapter 9).

primate city a disproportionately large leading city (Chapter 9).

principle of population the Malthusian theory that human population increases geometrically whereas the available food supply increases only arithmetically, leading constantly to "misery" (Chapter 3).

pronatalist an attitude, doctrine, or policy that favors a high birth rate; also known as "populationist" (Chapter 10).

proximate determinants of fertility a renaming of the intermediate variables (defined previously) with an emphasis on age at entry into marriage and proportions married, use of contraception, use of abortion, and prevalence of breast-feeding (Chapter 6).

prudential restraint a Malthusian concept referring to delaying marriage without necessarily avoiding premarital intercourse (Chapter 3).

Public Use Microdata Sample (PUMS) data a random sample of individual census records that have been stripped of personally identifying information (Chapter 4).

purchasing power parity (PPP) a refinement of GDP that is defined as the number of units of a country's currency required to buy the same amounts of goods and services in the domestic market as one dollar would buy in the United States (Chapter 11).

push–pull theory a theory of migration that says some people move because they are pushed out of their former location, whereas others move because they have been pulled, or attracted, to another location (Chapter 7).

race a group of people characterized by a more or less distinctive combination of inheritable physical traits (Chapter 10).

racial stratification a socially constructed system that characterizes one or more groups as being distinctly different (Chapter 10).

radix the initial hypothetical group of 100,000 babies that is used as a starting point for life table calculations (Chapter 5).

rank–size rule a hypothesis derived from studies of city–systems that says that the population size of a given city in a country will be approximately equal to the population of the largest city divided by the city's rank in the city-system (Chapter 9).

rational choice theory any theory based on the idea that human behavior is the result of individuals making calculated cost–benefit analyses about how to act (Chapter 3).

rectangularization refers to the process whereby the continuing decline in death rates at older ages means that the proportion of people surviving to any given age begins to square off at the oldest ages, rather than dropping off smoothly over all ages (Chapter 5).

redistricting spatially redefining U.S. congressional districts (geographic areas) represented by each seat in Congress (Chapter 1).

refugee a person who has been forced out of his or her country of nationality (Chapter 7).

religious pluralism the existence of two or more religious groups side by side in society without one group dominating the other (Chapter 10).

religiosity the strength with which one adheres to religious beliefs (Chapter 10).

remittances money sent by migrants back to family members in their country of origin (Chapter 7).

residential mobility the process of changing residence over a short or a long distance (Chapter 7).

rural of, or pertaining to, the countryside. Rural populations are generally defined as those that are nonurban in character (Chapter 9).

sample surveys a method of collecting data by obtaining information from a sample of the total population, rather than by a complete census (Chapter 4).

sampling error error that occurs in sampling due to the fact that a sample is rarely identical in every way to the population from which it was drawn (Chapter 4).

secularization a spirit of autonomy from other worldly powers; a sense of responsibility for one's own well-being (Chapter 3).

segmentation manufacturing and packaging products or providing services that appeal to specific sociodemographically identifiable groups within the population (Chapter 1).

segmented assimilation a situation in which the children of immigrants either adopt the host language and behavior, but are prevented from fully participating in society by their identification with a racial/ethnic minority group, or assimilate economically in the new society, but retain strong attachments to their own ethnic/racial group (Chapter 7).

senescence a decline in physical viability accompanied by a rise in vulnerability to disease (Chapter 5).

sex ratio the number of males per the number of females in a population (usually multiplied by 100 to get rid of the decimal point) (Chapter 8).

sex structure see *age and sex structure* (Chapter 8).

site selection demographics using demographic information to help decide where to locate a business (Chapter 1).

social capillarity Arsène Dumont's term for the desire of a person to rise on the social scale to increase one's individuality as well as one's personal wealth (Chapter 3).

social capital the network of family, friends, and acquaintances that increases a person's chances of success in life (Chapters 7 and 10).

social institutions sets of procedures (norms, laws, etc.) that organize behavior in society in fairly predictable and ongoing ways (Chapter 3).

social roles the set of obligations and expectations that characterize a particular position within society (Chapter 8).

social status relative position or standing in society (Chapter 8).

socialism an economic system whereby the community as a whole (i.e., the government) owns the means of production; a social system that minimizes social stratification (Chapter 3).

socialization the process of learning the behavior appropriate to particular social roles (Chapter 8).

sojourner an international mover seeking paid employment in another country but never really setting up a permanent residence in the new location (Chapter 7).

spatial demography any analysis of population data that takes location into account by using georeferenced information (Chapter 1).

spermicide a chemical agent that kills sperm (Chapter 6).

stable population a population in which the percentage of people at each age and sex eventually stabilizes (no longer changes) because age-specific rates of fertility, mortality, and migration remain constant over a long period of time (Chapter 8).

standard metropolitan statistical area (SMSA) a term used by the U.S. Census Bureau to define a county or group of contiguous counties that contain at least one city of 50,000 inhabitants or more and any contiguous counties that are socially and economically integrated with the central city or cities (Chapter 9).

stationary population a type of stable population in which the birth rate equals the death rate, so that the number of people remains the same, as does the age/sex distribution (Chapter 8).

step migration the process whereby a migrant moves in stages progressively farther away from his or her place of origin (Chapter 7).

sterilization the process (either voluntarily—surgically—or involuntarily) of rendering a person permanently incapable of reproducing (Chapter 6).

structural mobility the situation in which most, if not all, people in an entire society experience an improvement in living levels, even though some people may be improving faster than others (Chapter 10).

subfecundity see *impaired fecundity* (Chapter 6).

suburban pertaining to populations in low-density areas close to and integrated with central cities (Chapter 9).

suburbanize to become suburban—a city suburbanizes by growing in its outer rings (Chapter 9).

supply-demand framework a version of neoclassical economics in which it is assumed that couples attempt to maintain a balance between the potential supply of and demand for children, taking into account the costs of fertility regulation (Chapter 6).

surgical contraception permanent methods of contraception, including tubal ligation for women and vasectomy for men (Chapter 6).

sustainable development defined by the Brundtland Commission as "development that meets the needs of the present without compromising the ability of future generations to meet their own needs" (Chapter 11).

synthetic cohort a measurement obtained by treating period data as though they represented a cohort (Chapter 6).

target year the future year to which a population projection is made (Chapter 8).

targeting a marketing technique of picking out particular sociodemographic characteristics and appealing to differences in consumer tastes and behavior reflected in those particular characteristics (Chapter 1).

theoretical effectiveness with respect to birth control methods, the probability of preventing a pregnancy if a method is used exactly as it should be (Chapter 6).

theory a system of assumptions, accepted principles, and rules of procedure devised to analyze, predict, or otherwise explain a set of phenomena (Chapter 3).

total fertility rate (TFR) a synthetic cohort estimate of the average number of children who would be born to each woman if the current age-specific birth rates remained constant (Chapter 6).

total or gross migration rate the sum of in-migrants plus out-migrants, divided by the total midyear population (Chapter 7).

transitional growth the second (middle) stage of the demographic transition when death rates have dropped but birth rates are still high. During this time, population size increases steadily—this is the essence of the "population explosion" (Chapter 3).

transnational migrant an international migrant who maintains close ties in both his or her country of origin and his or her country of destination (Chapter 7).

troposphere that portion of the atmosphere which is closest to (within about 11 miles of) the earth's surface (Chapter 11).

tubal ligation method of female sterilization (surgical contraception) in which the fallopian tubes are "tied" off with rings or by some other method (Chapter 6).

unmet need as applied to family planning, the number of sexually active women who would prefer not to get pregnant but are nevertheless not using any method of contraception (Chapter 12).

urban describes a spatial concentration of people whose lives are organized around nonagricultural activities (Chapter 9).

urban agglomeration according to the United Nations, the population contained within the contours of contiguous territory inhabited at urban levels of residential density without regard to administrative boundaries (Chapter 9).

urban cluster part of the U.S. Census Bureau's definition of a place considered to be "urban"; an urban cluster has 2,500–50,000 people (Chapter 9).

urban sprawl the straggling expansion of an urban area into the adjoining countryside (Chapter 9).

urban transition the shift over time from a largely rural population to a largely urban population (see *urbanization*) (Chapters 3, 7, and 9).

urbanism the changes that occur in lifestyle and social interaction as a result of living in urban places (Chapter 9).

urbanization the process whereby the proportion of people in a population who live in urban places increases (Chapter 9).

urbanized area part of the U.S. Census Bureau's definition of a place considered to be "urban"; an urbanized area has at least 50,000 people (Chapter 9).

use-effectiveness the actual pregnancy prevention performance associated with using a particular fertility control measure (Chapter 6).

usual residence the concept of including people in the census on the basis of where they usually reside (Chapter 4).

vasectomy a technique of male sterilization (surgical contraception) in which each vas deferens is cut and tied, thus preventing sperm from being ejaculated during intercourse (Chapter 6).

vital statistics data referring to the so-called vital events of life, especially birth and death, but usually also including marriage, divorce, and sometimes abortion (Chapter 4).

wealth flow a term coined by Caldwell to refer to the intergenerational transfer of income (Chapter 3).

wealth of a nation the sum of known natural resources and our human capacity to transform those resources into something useful (Chapter 11).

wear-and-tear theory the theory of aging that argues that humans are like machines that eventually wear out due to the stresses and strains of constant use (Chapter 5).

withdrawal a form of fertility control that requires the male to withdraw his penis from his partner's vagina prior to ejaculation; also called *coitus interruptus* (Chapter 6).

world–systems theory the theory that since the sixteenth century the world market has developed into a set of core nations and a set of peripheral countries dependent on the core (Chapters 9 and 11).

xenophobia fear of strangers, which often leads to discrimination against migrants (Chapter 7).

zero population growth (ZPG) a situation in which a population is not changing in size from year to year, as a result of the combination of births, deaths, and migration (Chapter 8).

BIBLIOGRAPHY

Abbott, C. 1993. *The Metropolitan Frontier: Cities in the Modern American West*. Tucson: The University of Arizona Press.

Abernethy, V. 1979. *Population Pressure and Cultural Adjustment*. New York: Human Sciences Press.

Abma, J., A. Chandra, W. Mosher, L. Peterson, and L. Piccinino. 1997. Fertility, Family Planning, and Women's Health: New Data From the 1995 National Survey of Family Growth. *National Center for Health Statistics Vital Health Statistics* 23 (19).

Abramovitz, J. N. 1998. Sustaining the World's Forests. In *State of the World 1998*, eds. L. Brown, C. Flavin and H. French. New York: W. W. Norton & Company.

Adamchak, D. J. 2001. The Effects of Age Structure on the Labor Force and Retirement in China. *The Social Science Journal* 38 (1): 1–11.

Adams, J. S., B. J. VanDrasek, and E. G. Phillips. 1999. Metropolitan Area Definition in the United States. *Urban Geography* 20 (8): 695–726.

Adamson, D. M., N. Belden, J. DaVanzo, and S. Patterson. 2000. *How Americans View World Population Issues: A Survey of Public Opinion*. Santa Monica: Rand Corporation.

Adioetomo, S. M., G. Beningisse, S. Guitiano, Y. Hao, K. Nacro, and I. Pool. 2005. *Policy Implications of Age-Structural Changes*. Paris: CICRED.

Adlahka, A., and J. Banister. 1995. Demographic Perspectives on China and India. *Journal of Biosocial Science* 27:163–78.

Adsera, A. 2004. Changing Fertility Rates in Developed Countries: The Impact of Labor Market Insitutions. *Journal of Population Economics* 17 (1): 17–43.

Agnew, J. A. 2010 Slums, Ghettos, and Urban Marginality. *Urban Geography* 31 (2): 144–47.

Agunias, D. R. 2009. *Guiding the Invisible Hand: Making Migration Intermediaries Work for Development (Human Development Research Paper 2009/22)*. United Nations Development Programme 2009 [cited 2010]. Available from http://www.migrationpolicy.org/pubs/agunias_HDRP_2009.pdf.

Akin, J., R. Bilsbarrow, D. Guilkey, B. Popkin, D. Benoit, P. Cantrelle, M. Garenne, and P. Levi. 1981. The Determinants of Breast-Feeding in Sri Lanka. *Demography* 18 (3): 287–308.

Alba, R., and V. Nee. 1997. Rethinking Assimilation Theory for a New Era of Immigration. *International Migration Review* 31 (4): 826–74.

Albert, S. 1998. Site Selection's Essential Ingredients. *Business Geographics* (May):44.

Albert, S. M., and M. G. Cattell. 1994. *Old Age in Global Perspective*. New York: G.K. Hall & Co.

Alchon, S. A. 1997. The Great Killers in Precolumbian America: A Hemispheric Perspective. *Latin American Population History Bulletin* (27): 2–11.

Alonso, W., and P. Starr. 1982. The Political Economy of National Statistics. *Social Science Research Council Items* 36 (3): 29–35.

Alter, G., and M. Oris. 2005. Childhood Conditions, Migration, and Mortality: Migrants and Natives in 19th-Century Cities. *Social Biology* 52 (3–4): 178–91.

Ampofo, A. A., and J. Boateng. 2008. Understanding Masculinities: Empowering Women: What Have Boys in Ghana Got to Do with It? In *Global Empowerment of Women: Responses to Globalization and Politicized Religions*, ed. C. M. Elliott. New York: Routledge.

An, L., and J. Liu. 2010. Long-term Effects of Family Planning and Other Determinants of Fertility on Population and Environment: Agent-Based Modeling Evidence From Wolong Nature Reserve, China. *Population and Environment* Published online 19 May.

Anderson, G. 2002. *Children's Experience of Family Disruption and Family Formation: Evidence From 16 FFS Countries* 2002 [cited 2004]. Available from http://www.demographic-research.org/

Anderson, M. J., and S. E. Fienberg. 1999. *Who Counts? The Politics of Census-Taking in Contemporary America*. New York: Russell Sage Foundation.

Angel, J. L. 2007. *Inheritance in Contemporary America: The Social Dimensions of Giving Across Generations*. Baltimore, MD: The Johns Hopkins University Press.

Angel, R. J., and J. L. Angel. 1993. *Painful Inheritance: Health and the New Generation of Fatherless Families*. Madison: The University of Wisconsin Press.

Annan, K. 1999. Address of Kofi Annan, UN Secretary-General, to the Special Session of the UN General Assembly on the Follow-Up to the International Conference on Population and Development. *Population and Development Review* 25 (3): 632–34.

Appleman, P. 1965. *The Silent Explosion: With a Foreward by Julian Huxley*. Boston: Beacon Press.

Appleyard, R., and P. Taran. 2000. Introduction to Special Issue on Human Rights. *International Migration* 38 (6): 3–6.

Arias, E., B. L. Rostron, and B. Tejada-Vera. 2010. United States Life Tables, 2005. *National Vital Statistics Reports* 58 (10).

Aries, P. 1962. *Centuries of Childhood*. New York: Vintage Books.

Arnold, F. 1988. The Effect of Sex Preferences on Fertility and Family Planning: Empirical Evidence. *Population Bulletin of the United Nations* 23/24:44–56.

Arnold, F., M. K. Choe, and T. K. Roy. 1998. Son Preference, the Family-Building Process and Child Mortality in India. *Population Studies* 52:301–15.

Arnoldy, B. 2009. India listens after a child bride says 'I won't'. *The Christian Science Monitor*, 24 April.

Arriaga, E. 1970. *Mortality Decline and Its Demographic Effects in Latin America*. Berkeley, CA: University of California Institute of International Studies.

Associated Press. 1980. Study on Old Age Released in China. *San Diego Union*, 10 November:A3.

———. 1983. Israel Collects Detailed Information on Population of South Lebanon. *San Diego Union-Tribune*, 14 March.

———. 2007. *Report: World's oldest mom lied about age* 2007 [cited 2010]. Available from http://www.msnbc.msn.com/id/16850751/.

———. 2009. Census won't count missionaries abroad. *The San Diego Union-Tribune*, 17 August.

Attané, I. 2001. Chinese Fertility on the Eve of the 21st Century: Fact and Uncertainty. *Population: An English Selection* 13 (2): 71–100.

Attané, I., and C. Z. Guilmoto. 2007. Introduction. In *Watering the Neighbor's Garden: The Growing Demographic Female Deficit in Asia*, eds. I. Attané and C. Z. Guilmoto. Paris: CICRED.

Auerbach, F. 1961. *Immigration Laws of the United States, 2nd Edition*. New York: Bobbs-Merrill.

Avdeev, A., and A. Monnier. 1995. A Survey of Modern Russian Fertility. *Population: An English Selection* 7:1–38.

Axinn, W. G., and J. S. Barber. 2001. Mass Education and Fertility Transition. *American Sociological Review* 66: 481–505.

Bachu, A. 1993. Fertility of American Women: June 1992. *Current Population Reports* Series P20 (No. 470).

———. 1999. Trends in Premarital Childbearing: 1930 to 1994. *Current Population Reports* (P23–197).

Bachu, A., and M. O'Connell. 2000. Fertility of American Women: June 1998. *Current Population Reports* P20–526.

Bacon, D. 2008. *Illegal People: How Globalization Creates Migration and Criminalizes Immigrants*. Boston: Beacon Press.

Baird, D. D., C. R. Weinberg, L. F. Voigt, and J. R. Daling. 1996. Vaginal Douching and Reduced Fertility. *American Journal of Public Health* 86 (6): 844–50.

Baizan, P. 2009. Regional Child Care Availablity and Fertility Decisions in Spain. *Demographic Research* 21 (27): 803–42.

Bales, K. 2007. *Ending Slavery: How We Free Today's Slaves*. Berkeley: University of California Press.

Banister, J. 1987. *China's Changing Population*. Stanford, CA: Stanford University Press.

———. 2004. Shortage of Girls in China Today. *Journal of Population Research* 21 (1): 20–45.

Banks, J. A. 1954. *Prosperity and Parenthood: A Study of Family Planning Among the Victorian Middle Classes*. London: Routledge & Kegan Paul.

Banks, J. A., and O. Banks. 1964. *Feminism and Family Planning in Victorian England*. Liverpool: Liverpool University Press.

Barnett, J. ed. 2007. *Smart Growth in a Changing World*. Chicago, IL/Washington, DC: American Planning Association.

Barr, D. A. 2008. *Health Disparities in the United States: Social Class, Race, Ethnicity, and Health*. Baltimore, MD: Johns Hopkins University Press.

Barrett, P. M. 1996. High-Court Ruling on Census Sets Back Some Cities That Disputed '90 Numbers. *Wall Street Journal*, 21 March:B6.

Barta, P. 2010. New Thai Immigration Rules Come Under Fire. *Wall Street Journal*, 2 March:A15.

Batson, A. 2007. China to Continue Birth Rate Control. *Wall Street Journal*, 13 January:A5.

Batty, M. 2008. The Size, Scale, and Shape of Cities. *Science* 319 (5864): 769–71.

Bean, F. D., C. G. Swicegood, and R. Berg. 2000. Mexican-Origin Fertility: New Patterns and Interpretations. *Social Science Quarterly* 81 (1): 404–20.

Beaujot, R. 1978. Canada's Population: Growth and Dualism. *Population Bulletin* 33.

Beck, B. 2009. Peak Labour. *The Economist's The World in 2010*, 13 November, 60.

Becker, G. 1960. An Economic Analysis of Fertility. In *Demographic Change and Economic Change in Developed Countries*, ed. National Bureau of Economic Research. Princeton, NJ: Princeton University Press.

Becker, J. 1997. *Hungry Ghosts: Mao's Secret Famine*. New York: Free Press.

Beckett, M. K., and P. A. Morrison. 2010. Assessing the Need for a New Medical School: A Case Study in Applied Demography. *Population Research and Policy Review* 29:19–32.

Behrman, J., and P. Taubman. 1989. A Test of the Easterlin Fertility Model Using Income For Two Generations and a Comparison with the Becker Model. *Demography* 26:117–23.

Bell, M. 2006. *Child Alert: Democratic Republic of Congo*. New York: UNICEF.

Bell, R., and M. L. Cohen eds. 2008. *Coverage Measurement in the 2010 Census*. Washington, DC: The National Academies Press.

Bellman, E. 2010. Novelty of Mexican food in India is a Hit for Yum. *Wall Street Journal*, 30 March:B8.

Bellman, E., and K. Hudson. 2006. Wal-Mart Stakes India Claim. *Wall Street Journal* 18 January:B1.

Berry, B., C. Goodwin, R. Lake, and K. Smith. 1976. Attitudes Toward Integration: The Role of Status. In *The Changing Face of the Suburbs*, ed. B. Schwartz. Chicago: University of Chicago Press.

Berry, B. J. L. 1993. Transnational Urbanward Migration, 1830–1980. *Annals of the Association of American Geographers* 83 (3): 389–405.

Bertrand, J., and D. Bogue. 1977. A Research-Based System for Improving Family Planning Adoption: The Guatemala Study. *Intercom* 5:8–9.

Berube, A., A. Singer, J. H. Wilson, and W. H. Frey. 2006. *Finding Exurbia: America's Fast-Growing Communities at the Metropolitan Fringe*. Washington, DC: The Brookings Institution.

Berube, A., and T. Thacher. 2004. *The Shape of the Curve: Household Income Distributions in U.S. Cities, 1979–1999*. Washington, DC: The Brookings Institution Living Cities Census Series.

Bhatia, P. 1978. Abstinence—Desai Solution for Baby Boom. *San Francisco Chronicle* 11 June.

Bianchi, S., J. P. Robinson, and M. A. Milkie. 2006. *Changing Rhythms of American Family Life*. New York: Russell Sage Foundation.

Bijak, J., D. Kupiszewska, and M. Kupiszewska. 2008. Replacement Migration Revisited: Simulatons of the Effects of Selected Population and Labor Market Strategies for the Aging Europe, 2002–2052. *Population Research and Policy Review* 27:321–42.

Billari, F. C., and A. C. Liefbroer. 2004. Is the Second Demographic Transition a useful concept for demography? Introduction to a a debate. *Vienna Yearbook of Population Research 2004*:1–3.

Bin Yu. 2008. *Chain Migration Explained: The Power of the Immigration Multiplier*. New York: LFB Scholarly Publishing.

Biraben, J.-N. 1979. Essai Sur L'Évolution Du Nombre Des Hommes. *Population* 34 (1): 13–24.

Birdsall, N., and S. W. Sinding. 2001. How and Why Population Matters: New Findings, New Issues. In *Population Matters: Demographic Change, Economic Growth, and Poverty in the Developing World*, eds. N. Birdsall, A. C. Kelley and S. W. Sinding. New York: Oxford University Press.

Blackburn, R. D., J. A. Cunkelman, and V. M. Zlidar. 2000. Oral Contraceptives—An Update. *Population Reports* Series A (9).

Blake, J. 1967. Family Size in the 1960s—A Baffling Fad. *Eugenics Quarterly* 14:60–74.

———. 1974. Can We Believe Recent Data in the United States. *Demography* 11 (1): 25–44.

Blayo, Y. 1992. Political Events and Fertility in China Since 1950. *Population: An English Selection* 4:209–32.

Bledsoe, C., and A. G. Hill. 1998. Social Norms, Natural Fertility, and the Resumption of Post-partum "Contact" in The Gambia. In *The Methods and Uses of Anthropological Demography*, eds. A. M. Basu and P. Aaby, Ch 12. Oxford: Clarendon Press.

Bledsoe, C., R. Houle, and P. Sow. 2007. High Fertility Gambians in Low Fertility Spain: The Dynamics of Child Accumulation Across Transnational Space. *Demographic Research* 16:375–412.

Bloom, D., and R. Freeman. 1986. The Effects of Rapid Population Growth on Labor Supply and Employment in Developing Countries. *Population and Development Review* 12 (3): 381–414.

Bloom, D. E., D. Canning, and J. Sevilla. 2003. *The Demographic Dividend: A New Perspective on the Economic Consequences of Population Change*. Santa Monica, CA: RAND.

Blossfeld, H., and A. de Rose. 1992. Educational Expansion and Changes in Entry Into Marriage and Motherhood, the Experience of Italian Women. *Genus* XLVIII (3–4): 73–91.

Bobo, L. D., M. L. Oliver, J. H. Johnson, Jr., and A. Valenzuela, Jr. 2000. Analyzing Inequality in Los Angeles, eds. L. D. Bobo, M. L. Oliver, J. H. Johnson, Jr. and A. Valenzuela, Jr. New York: Russell Sage Foundation.

Bocquet-Appel, J.-P. 2008. Explaining the Neolithic Demographic Transition. In *The Neolithic Demographic Transition and its Consequences*, eds. J.-P. Bocquet-Appel and O. Bar-Yosef. New York: Springer.

Bollen, K. A., and S. J. Appold. 1993. National Industrial Structure and the Global System. *American Sociological Review* 58:283–301.

Bolton, C., and J. W. Leasure. 1979. Evolution Politique et Baisse de la Fecondite en Occident. *Population* 34: 825–44.

Bongaarts, J. 1978. A Framework for Analyzing the Proximate Determinants of Fertility. *Population and Development Review* 4 (1): 105–32.

———. 1982. The Fertility-Inhibiting Effects of the Intermediate Fertility Variables. *Studies in Family Planning* 13:179–89.

———. 1993. The Supply-Demand Framework for the Determinants of Fertility: An Alternative Implementation. *Population Studies* 47:437–56.

———. 2001. Household Size and Composition in the Developing World in the 1990s. *Population Studies* 55: 263–79.

———. 2003. Completing the Fertility Transition in the Developing World: The Role of Educational Differences and Fertility Preferences. *Population Studies* 57 (3): 321–36.

Bongaarts, J., and R. A. Bulatao eds. 2000. *Beyond Six Billion: Forecasting the World's Population*. Washington, DC: National Academy Press.

Bongaarts, J., and G. Feeney. 1998. On the Quantum and Tempo of Fertility. *Population and Development Review* 24 (2): 271–292.

———. 2003. Estimating Mean Lifetime, Population Council Working Paper No. 179. New York: Population Council.

Bongaarts, J., W. P. Mauldin, and J. Phillips. 1990. The Demographic Impact of Family Planning Programs. *Studies in Family Planning* 21:299–310.

Bongaarts, J., and C. F. Westoff. 2000. The Potential Role of Contraception in Reducing Abortion. *Studies in Family Planning* 31 (3): 193–202.

Borjas, G. J. 1999. *Heaven's Door: Immigration Policy and the American Economy*. Princeton, NJ: Princeton University Press.

Borlaug, N. 2002. We Can Feed the World. Here's How. *Wall Street Journal*, 13 May:A16.

Boserup, E. 1965. *The Conditions of Agricultural Growth*. Chicago: Aldine.

———. 1970. *Woman's Role in Economic Development*. New York: St. Martin's Press.

———. 1981. *Population and Technological Change: A Study of Long-Term Trends*. Chicago: University of Chicago Press.

Bouvier, L. F., and S. M. Stein. 2000. *Is Smart Growth Enough? Maryland's Population in 2050*. Washington, DC: Negative Population Growth.

Boyd, M. 1976. Immigration Policies and Trends: A Comparison of Canada and the United States. *Demography* 13:83–104.

Boyd, M., G. Goldmann, and P. White. 2000. Race in the Canadian Census. In *Race and Racism: Canada's Challenge*, eds. L. Driedger and S. S. Halli. Montreal: McGill/Queen's University Press.

Boyd, M., and E. M. Grieco. 1998. Triumphant Transitions: Socioeconomic Achievements of the Second Generation in Canada. *International Migration Review* 32 (4): 853–76.

Boyd, M., and D. Norris. 2000. Demographic Change and Young Adults Living with Parents, 1981–1996. *Canadian Studies in Population* 27 (2): 267–81.

Boyle, P., T. J. Cooke, K. Halfacree, and D. Smith. 2001. A Cross-National Comparison of the Impact of Family Migration on Women's Employment Status. *Demography* 38 (2): 201–13.

Brackett, J. 1967. The Evolution of Marxist Theories of Population: Marxism Recognizes the Population Problem. Paper read at Annual Meeting of the Population Association of America, at Cincinnati, Ohio.

Bradshaw, Y. 1987. Urbanization and Underdevelopment: A Global Study of Modernization, Urban Bias, and Economic Dependency. *American Sociological Review* 52 (2): 224–39.

Bradshaw, Y., and E. Fraser. 1989. City Size, Economic Development, and Quality of Life in China: New Empirical Evidence. *American Sociological Review* 54:986–1003.

Brandes, S. 1990. Ritual Eating and Drinking in Tzintzuntzan: A Contribution to the Study of Mexican Foodways. *Western Folklore* 49:163–75.

Brat, I., and P. Kiernan. 2009. Heinz Seeks to Tap Mexico's Taste for Ketchup. *Wall Street Journal*, 24 November:B1.

Bravo-Ortega, C., and J. De Gregoria. 2005. The Relative Richness of the Poor? Natural Resources, Human Capital, and Economic Growth. *World Bank Policy Research Working Paper No.3484*.

Brentano, L. 1910. The Doctrine of Malthus and the Increase of Population During the Last Decade. *Economic Journal* 20:371–393.

Brockerhoff, M. 2000. An Urbanizing World. *Population Bulletin* 55 (3).

Brodie, J. F. 1994. *Contraception and Abortion in Nineteenth-Century America*. Ithaca, NY: Cornell University Press.

Brokaw, T. 1998. *The Greatest Generation*. New York: Random House.

Brooks, C. 2002. Religious Influence and the Politics of Family Decline Concern: Trends, Sources, and U.S. Political Behavior. *American Sociological Review* 67: 191–211.

Brown, A. D. 2003. *Feed or Feedback: Agriculture, Population Dynamics and the State of the Planet*. Tuross Head, Australia: International Books.

Brown, L. ed. 1993. *The New Shorter Oxford English Dictionary on Historical Principles*. Oxford: Clarendon Press.

Brown, L., and J. Mitchell. 1998. Building a New Economy. In *State of the World 1998*, eds. L. Borwn, C. Flavin and H. French. New York: W.W. Norton & Company.

Brown, L. A. 1981. *Innovation Diffusion: A New Perspective*. London and New York: Methuen.

Brown, L. D., M. L. Cohen, D. L. Cork, and C. F. Citro eds. 2010. *Envisioning the 2020 Census*. Washington, DC: National Academies Press.

Bruegmann, R. 2005. *Sprawl: A Compact History*. Chicago: University of Chicago Press.

Bruinsma, J. 2003. *World Agriculture: Towards 2015/2030, An FAO Perspective*. London: Earthscan.

Bryan, T. 2004. Basic Sources of Statistics. In *The Methods and Materials of Demography, Second Edition*, eds. J. S. Siegel and D. A. Swanson. San Diego: Elsevier Academic Press.

Bulatao, R., and R. Lee. 1983. *Determinants of Fertility in Developing Countries, Volume 1, Supply and Demand for Children*. New York: Academic Press.

Bulpett, C. 2002. Regimes of Exclusion. *European Urban and Regional Studies* 9 (2): 137–49.

Burnham, G., R. Lafta, S. Doocy, and L. Roberts. 2006. Mortality After the 2003 Invasion of Iraq: A Cross-Sectional Cluster Sample Survey. *Lancet* 368:1421–28.

Butz, W., and M. Ward. 1979. Will U.S. Fertility Remain Low? A New Economic Interpretation. *Population and Development Review* 5:663–88.

Cai Yong, Wang Feng, Gu Baochang, and Zheng Zhenshen. 2010. Fertility Intention and Fertility Behavior: Why Stop at One? The Socioeconomic Factors Behind China's Below Replacement Fertility. Paper read at Annual Meeting of the Population Association of America, at Dallas, TX.

Cain, M. 1981. Risk and Fertility in India and Bangladesh. *Population and Development Review* 7:435–74.

Caldwell, C. 2009. *Reflections on the Revolution in Europe: Immigration, Islam, and the West*. New York: Doubleday.

Caldwell, J. 1976. Toward a Restatement of Demographic Transition Theory. *Population and Development Review* 2 (3–4): 321–66.

———. 1980. Mass Education as a Determinant of the timing of Fertility Decline. *Population and Development Review* 6 (2): 225–56.

———. 1982. *Theory of Fertility Decline*. New York: Academic Press.

———. 1986. Routes to Low Mortality in Poor Countries. *Population and Development Review* 12 (2): 171–220.

Caldwell, J. C. 2000. Rethinking the African AIDS Epidemic. *Population and Development Review* 26 (1): 117–35.

Caldwell, J. C., and B. K. Caldwell. 2003. Pretransitional Population Control and Equilibrium. *Population Studies* 57 (2): 199–215.

Calhoun, J. 1962. Poplation Density and Social Pathology. *Scientific American* (May): 118–25.

California Department of Finance. 2006. California Public Postsecondary Enrollment Projections, 2005 Series. Sacramento, CA: State of California, Department of Finance, Demographic Research Unit.

Cambois, E., J.-M. Robine, and M. D. Hayward. 2001. Social Inequalities in Disability-Free Life Expectancy in the French Male Populaiton, 1980–1991. *Demography* 38 (4): 513–24.

Campbell, M., N. N. Sahin-Hodoglugil, and M. Potts. 2006. Barriers to Fertility Regulation: A Review of the Literature. *Studies in Family Planning* 37 (2): 87–98.

Cann, R. L., and A. C. Wilson. 2003. The Recent African Genesis of Humans. *Scientific American Special Edition* 13 (2): 54–61.

Cantillon, R. 1755 [1964]. *Essai sur la Nature du Commerce en General, Edited with an English Translation by Henry Higgs*. New York: A. M. Kelley.

Cantor, N. F. 2001. *In the Wake of the Plague: The Black Death & the World it Made*. New York: Free Press.

Caramés, A. P. 2004. Los Residentes Latinoamericanos en España: de la Presencia Diluida a la Mayoritaria. *Papeles de Poblacion* 10:259–95.

Cardenas, R., and C. M. Obermeyer. 1997. Son Preference and Differential in Morocco and Tunisia. *Studies in Family Planning* 28 (3): 235–44.

Carey, J. R., and D. S. Judge. 2001. Principles of Biodemography with Special Reference to Longevity. *Population: An English Selection* 13 (1): 9–40.

Carlson, E. 2008. *The Lucky Few: Between the Greatest Generation and the Baby Boom*. New York: Springer.

Carlson, E., and M. Watson. 1990. The Family and the State: Rising Hungarian Death Rates. In *Aiding and Aging: The Coming Crisis in Support for the Elderly by Kin and State*, ed. J. Mogey. Westport, CT: Greenwood Press.

Carr-Saunders, A. M. 1936. *World Population: Past Growth and Present Trends*. Oxford: Clarendon Press.

Caselli, G., and J. Vallin. 2001. Demographic Trends: Beyond the Limits? *Population: An English Selection* 13 (1): 41–72.

Casper, L. M., and P. N. Cohen. 2000. How Does POSSLQ Measure Up? Historical Estimates of Cohabitation. *Demography* 37 (2): 237–45.

Cassedy, J. 1969. *Demography in Early America: Beginnings of the Statistical Mind, 1600–1800*. Cambridge, MA: Harvard University Press.

Castles, S., and M. J. Miller. 2003. *The Age of Migration, Third Edition*. New York: The Guilford Press.

———. 2009. *The Age of Migration, Fourth Edition*. New York: The Guilford Press.

Castro-Martín, T. 2010. Single Motherhood and Low Birthweight in Spain: Narrowing Social Inequalities in Health? *Demographic Research* 22:863–90.

Catasús Cervera, S., and J. C. A. Fraga. 1996. The Fertility Transition in Cuba. In *The Fertility Transition in Latin America*, eds. J. M. Guzmán, S. Singh, G. Rodríguez and E. Pantiledes. Oxford: Clarendon Press.

Census 2000 Initiative. 2001. *Commerce Secretary Chooses Unadjusted Census Data After Census Bureau Recommends Against Statistical Correction* 2001 [cited 2001]. Available from http://www.census2000.org

Cerrutti, M., and D. S. Massey. 2001. On the Auspices of Female Migration From Mexico to the United States. *Demography* 38 (2): 187–200.

Chambers, N., C. Simmons, and M. Wackernagel. 2002. *Sharing Nature's Interest*. London: Earthscan Publications.

Chandler, R. F. 1971. The Scientific Basis for the Increased Yield Potential of Rice and Wheat. In *Food, Population and Employments: The Impact of the Green Revolution*, eds. T. Poleman and D. Freebain. New York: Praeger.

Chandler, T., and G. Fox. 1974. *3000 Years of Urban Growth*. New York: Academic Press.

Chandra, A., G. M. Martinez, W. D. Mosher, C. Abma, and J. Jones. 2005. Fertility, Family Planning, and Reproductive Health of U.S. Women: Data From the 2002 National Survey of Family Growth. *National Center for Health Statistics, Vital Health Reports* 23 (25).

Chandra, A., and E. H. Stephen. 1998. Impaired Fecundity in the United States: 1982–95. *Family Planning Perspectives* 30 (1): 34–42.

Chandrasekhar, S. 1979. *"A Dirty, Filthy Book"—The Writings of Charles Knowlton and Annie Besant on Reproductive Physiology and Birth Control and an Account of the Bradlaugh-Besant Trial*. Berkeley: University of California Press.

Chang, L. 2000. Confucius Said: Sons, Care for Your Elders; Elders Say: We Sue. *Wall Street Journal*, 3 April: A1.

Charbit, Y. 2002. The Platonic City: History and Utopia. *Population-E* 57 (2): 207–236.

Charles, E. 1936. *The Twilight of Parenthood*. London: Watt's and Co.

Chase-Dunn, C. 1998. *Global Formation: Structures of the World Economy, Updated Edition*. Lanham, MD: Rowman and Littlefield.

Chase-Dunn, C., and S. Babones eds. 2006. *Global Social Change: Historical and Comparative Perspectives*. Baltimore, MD: Johns Hopkins University Press.

Chase-Dunn, C. K., and T. D. Hall. 1997. *Rise and Demise: Comparing World Systems*. Boulder, CO: Westview Press.

Chelala, C. 1998. A Critical Move Against Female Genital Mutilation. *Populi25* 1 (13–15).

Chen, L. C., F. Wittgenstein, and E. McKeon. 1996. The Upsurge or Mortality in Russia: Causes and Policy Implications. *Population and Development Review* 22 (3): 457–82.

Cherfas, J. 1980. The World Fertility Survey Conference: Population Bomb Revisited. *Science 80* 1 (November): 11–14.

Cherlin, A. 2009. *The Marriage-go-round: The State of Marriage and the Family in America Today*. New York: Alfred A. Knopf.

Cherlin, A. J. 2005. *Public and Private Families: An Introduction, Fourth Edition*. New York: McGraw-Hill Higher Education.

Chesler, E. 1994. No, the First Priority Is: Stop Coercing Women. *New York Times Magazine* 6 February.

Chesnais, J.-C. 1996. Fertility, Family, and Social Policy in Contemporary Western Europe. *Population and Development Review* 22 (4): 729–40.

Chigwedere, P., G. R. Seage, S. Gruskin, T.-H. Lee, and M. Essex. 2008. Estimating the Lost Benefits of Antiretroviral Drug Use in South Africa. *Journal of Acquired Immune Deficiency Syndrome* 49:410–15.

Choiniére, R. 1993. Les Inégalités Socio-Économiques et Culturelles de la Mortalité à Montréal à la Fin des Années 1980. *Cahiers Québécois de Démographie* 22 (2): 339–62.

Chojnacka, H. 2000. Early Marriage and Polygyny: Feature Characteristics of Nuptiality in Africa. *Genus* LVI (3–4): 179–208.

Choldin, H. 1994. *Looking For the Last Percent: The Controversy Over the Census Undercounts*. New Brunswick, NJ: Rutgers University Press.

Choucri, N. 1984. Perspectives on Population and Conflict. In *Multidisciplinary Perspectives on Population and Conflict*, ed. N. Choucri. Syracuse: Syracuse University Press.

Christakos, G., R. A. Olea, M. L. Serre, H.-L. Yu, and L.-L. Wang. 2005. *Interdisciplinary Public Health Reasoning and Epidemic Modelling: The Case of the Black Death*. New York: Springer.

Christaller, W. 1966. *Central Places in Southern Germany: Translated from from Die zentralen Orte in Süddeutschland by Carlisle W. Baskin*. Englewood Cliffs, NJ: Prentice-Hall.

Christenfeld, N., D. P. Phillips, and L. M. Glynn. 1999. What's in a Name: Mortality and the Power of Symbols. *Journal of Psychosomatic Research* 47 (3): 241–54.

Cicourel, A. 1974. *Theory and Method in a Study of Argentina*. New York: Wiley.

Cincotta, R. P., R. Engelman, and P. Anastasion. 2003. *The Security Demographic: Population and Civil Conflict After the Cold War*. Washington, DC: Population Action International.

Cipolla, C. 1965. *The Economic History of World Population*. London: Penguin.

———. 1981. *Fighting the Plague in Seventeenth-Century Italy*. Madison: University of Wisconsin Press.

Clark, C. 1967. *Population Growth and Land Use*. New York: St. Martin's Press.

Clark, R. L., and L. S. Ghent. 2010. Strategic HR Management with an Aging Workforce: Using Demographic Models to Determine Optimal Employment Policies. *Population Research and Policy Review* 29:65–80.

Clarke, J. I. 2000. *The Human Dichotomy: The Changing Numbers of Males and Females*. Amsterdam: Pergamon.

Clarke, S. C. 1995. Advance Report of Final Marriage Statistics, 1989 and 1990. *Monthly Vital Statistics Report* 43 (12, Supplement).

Cleland, J., and C. Wilson. 1987. Demand Theories of the Fertility Transition: An Iconoclastic View. *Population Studies* 41:5–30.

Cliff, A. D., and P. Haggett. 1996. The Impact of GIS on Epidemiological Mapping and Modelling. In *Spatial Analysis: Modelling in a GIS Environment*, eds. P. Longley and M. Batty. New York: John Wiley & Sons.

Clinton, H. R. 2010. *Remarks on the 15th Anniversary of the International Conference on Population and Development*. U.S. Department of State 2010 [cited 2010]. Available from http://www.state.gov/secretary/rm/2010/01/135001.htm.

Clough, S. 1968. *European Economic History*. New York: Walker.

Coale, A. 1973. The Demographic Transition. In *Proceedings of International Population Conference*, ed. IUSSP, Vol. 1, 53–72. Liege, Belgium: IUSSP.

———. 1974. The History of the Human Population. *Scientific American* 231 (3): 41–51.

———. 1986. Preface. In *The Decline of Fertility in Europe*, eds. A. Coale and S. C. Watkins. Princeton, NJ: Princeton University Press.

Coale, A., and J. Banister. 1994. Five Decades of Missing Females in China. *Demography* 31 (3):459–80.

Coale, A., and J. Trussell. 1974. Model Fertility Schedules: Variations in the Age Structure of Child-Bearing in Human Populations. *Population Index* 40 (2):185–256.

Coale, A., and M. Zelnick. 1963. *Estimates of Fertility and Population in the United States*. Princeton, NJ: Princeton University Press.

Cohen, B., and M. R. Montgomery. 1998. Introduction. In *From Birth to Death: Mortality Decline and Reproductive Change*, eds. M. R. Montgomery and B. Cohen. Washington, DC: National Academy Press.

Cohen, J. 1995. *How Many People Can the Earth Support*. New York: W. W. Norton.

Cohen, M. N. 1977. *TheFood Crisis in Prehistory: Overpopulation and the Origins of Agriculture*. New Haven: Yale University Press.

Cole, W. A., and P. Deane. 1965. The Growth of National Incomes. In *The Cambridge Economic History of Europe,* Vol. 6, Part 1, eds. H. H. Habakkuk and M. Postan. Cambridge, UK: Cambridge University Press.

Coleman, D. A. 2007. Demographic Diversity and the Ethnic Consequences of Immigration—Key Issues that the Commission's Report Left Out. *Vienna Yearbook of Population Research 2007*:5–13.

———. 2009. Migration and Its Consequences in 21st Century Europe. *Vienna Yearbook of Population Research 2009*:1–18.

Coleman, I. 2010. The Global Glass Ceiling. *Foreign Affairs* (May/June):http://www.foreignaffairs.com/print/66350.

Coleman, J., and T. J. Fararo eds. 1992. *Rational Choice Theory: Advocacy and Critique*. Newbury Park: Sage Publications.

Coleman, R., and L. Rainwater. 1978. *Social Standing in America*. New York: Basic Books.

Commission of the European Communities. 2006. *The Demographic Future of Europe—From Challenge to Opportunity; Commission Commuication COM (2006) 571*. European Commission 2006 [cited 2010]. Available from http://eur-lex.europa.eu/LexUriServ/LexUriServ.do?uri=COM:2006:0571:FIN:EN:PDF.

Commission on Population Growth and the American Future. 1972. *Population and the American Future*. Washington, DC: Government Printing Office.

Commonwealth of Australia. 2010. *Australia to 2050: Future Challenges* 2010 [cited 2010]. Available from http://www.treasury.gov.au/igr/igr2010/Overview/pdf/IGR_2010_Overview.pdf.

Condorcet, M. J. A. N. d. C. 1795 [1955]. *Sketch for an Historical Picture of the Progress of the Human Mind, translated from the French by June Baraclough*. London: Weidenfield and Nicholson.

Copetake, J. 2006. Where Business Is a Pleasure. *The World in 2006 (The Economist)*, 113–114.

Corder, M. 2006. Ex-Congelese Militia Leader Faces Judges. Associated Press.

Cornelius, W., S. Borger, A. Sawyer, D. Keyes, C. Appleby, K. Parks, G. Lozada, and J. Hicken. 2008. Controlling Unauthorized Immigration from Mexico: The Failure of "Prevention through Deterrence" and the Need for Comprehensive Reform. San Diego, CA: UCSD Center for Comparative Immigration Studies.

Cornelius, W., D. Fitzgerald, and P. L. Fischer eds. 2008. *Mayan Journeys: The New Migration from Yucatán to the United States*. Boulder, CO: Lynne Rienner Publishers.

Cornelius, W. A. 2002. Impacts of NAFTA on Mexico-to-U.S. Migration. In *NAFTA in the New Millenium*, eds. P. H. Smith and T. Chambers. La Jolla, CA: UCSD Center for U.S.-Mexican Studies.

Corona Vásquez, R. 1991. Confiabilidad de los Resultados Preliminares del XI Censo General de Población y Vivienda de 1990. *Estudios Demográficos y Urbanos* 6 (1): 33–68.

Council on Environmental Quality. 1980. *The Global 2000 Report to the President, Volume 1*. Washington, DC: Government Printing Office.

Courbage, Y. 2000. The Future Population of Israel and Palestine. *Population & Sociétés* 362 (November): 1–4.

Crenshaw, E. M., A. Z. Ameen, and M. Christenson. 1997. Population Dynamics and Economic Development: Age-Specific Population Growth Rates and Economic Growth in Developing Countries, 1965 to 1990. *American Sociological Review* 62:974–84.

Critchfield, R. 1994. *The Villagers: Changed Values, Altered Lives: The Closing of the Urban-Rural Gap*. New York: Anchor Books.

Crosby, A. W. 1972. *The Columbian Exchange: Biological and Cultural Consequences of 1492*. Westport, Conn: Greenwood Press.

———. 1989. *America's Forgotten Pandemic: The Influenza of 1918*. New York: Cambridge University Press.

———. 2004. *Ecological Imperialism: The Biological Expansion of Europe, 900–1900, Second Edition*. New York: Cambridge University Press.

Cross, A., W. Obungu, and P. Kizito. 1991. Evidence of a Transition to Lower Fertility in Kenya. *International Family Planning Perspectives* 17:4–7.

Crowder, K., and L. Downey. 2010. Interneighborhood Migration, RAce, and Environmental Hazards: Modeling Microlevel Processes of Environmental Inequality. *American Journal of Sociology* 115 (4): 1110–49.

Cutler, D., and G. Miller. 2005. The Role of Public Health Improvements in Health Advances: The Twentieth-Century United States. *Demography* 42 (1): 1–22.

Cutright, P., and R. M. Fernquist. 2000. Effects of Societal Integration, Period, Region, and Culture of Suicide on Male Age-Specific Suicide Rates: 20 Developed Countries, 1955–1989. *Social Science Research* 29:148–72.

Cutter, S. L., J. T. Mitchell, and M. S. Scott. 2000. Revealing the Vulnerability of Places: A Case Study of Georgetown County, South Carolina. *Annals of the Association of American Geographers* 90 (4): 713–37.

Dalla Zuanna, G. 2001. The Banquet of Aeolus: A Familistic Interpretation of Italy's Lowest Low Fertility. *Demographic Research* 4 (5): 133–62.

Daly, H. 1971. A Marxian–Malthusian View of Poverty and Development. *Population Studies* 25 (1): 25–37.

Daly, H. A. 2008. Growth and Development: Critique of a Credo. *Population and Development Review* 34 (3): 511–18.

Damassa, T. 2006. *EarthTrends Update August 2006: Water Scarcity*. World Resources Institute 2006 [cited 2007]. Available from http://www.wri.org.

Danziger, S., and P. Gottschalk eds. 1993. *Uneven Tides: Rising Inequality in America*. New York: Russell Sage Foundation.

DaVanzo, J., and A. Chan. 1994. Living Arrangements of Older Malaysians: Who Coresides With Their Adult Children? *Demography* 31 (1): 95–113.

Davidson, K., E. Mostofsky, and W. Whang. 2010. Don't Worry, Be Happy: Positive Affect and Reduced 10-year Incident Coronary Heart Disease: The Canadian Nova Scotia Health Survey. *European Heart Journal* Published online 17 February 2010.

Davis, K. 1945. The World Demographic Transition. *The Annals of the American Academy of Political and Social Science* 237 (January): 1–11.

———. 1949. *Human Society*. New York: Macmillan.

———. 1951. *The Population of India and Pakistan*. Princeton: Princeton University Press.

———. 1955a. Institutional Patterns Favoring High Fertility in Underdeveloped Areas. *Eugenics Quarterly* II (Section 2): 33–39.

———. 1955b. Malthus and the Theory of Population. In *The Language of Social Research*, eds. P. Lazarsfeld and M. Rosenberg. New York: Free Press.

———. 1963. The Theory of Change and Response in Modern Demographic History. *Population Index* 29 (4): 345–66.

———. 1965. The Urbanization of the Human Population. *Scientific American* 213 (3): 40–54.

———. 1967. Population Policy: Will Current Programs Succeed? *Science* 158: 730–39.

———. 1972. The American Family in Relation to Demographic Change. In *U.S. Commission on Population Growth and the American Future, Volume 1, Demographic and Social Aspects of Population Growth*, eds. C. Westoff and R. Parke. Washington, DC: Government Printing Office.

———. 1973. *Cities and Mortality*. Liège: IUSSP.

———. 1974. The Migration of Human Populations. *Scientific American* 231:92–105.

———. 1984. Wives and Work: The Sex Role Revolution and its Consequences. *Population and Development Review* 10 (3): 397–418.

———. 1986. Low Fertility in Evolutionary Perspective. In *Below-Replacement Fertility in Industrial Societies: Causes, Consequences, Policies*, eds. K. Davis, M. S. Bernstam and R. Ricardo-Campbell.

———. 1988. Social Science Approaches to International Migration. In *Population and Resources in Western Intellectual Tradition*, eds. M. Teitelbaum and J. Winter. New York: The Population Council.

Davis, K., and J. Blake. 1955. Social Structure and Fertility: An Analytic Framework. *Economic Development and Cultural Change* 4:211–35.

Davis, M. 2006. *Planet of Slums*. London: Verso.

de Beauvoir, S. 1953. *The Second Sex; Translated and Edited by H.M. Parshley*. New York: Knopf.

de Groot, N. G., N. Otting, G. G. M. Doxiadis, S. S. Balla-Jhagjhoorsingh, J. L. Heeney, J. J. van Rood, P. Gagneux, and R. E. Bontrop. 2002. Evidence for an Ancient Selective Sweep in the MHC Class I Gene Repertoire of Chimpanzees. *Proceedings of the National Academy of Sciences* 99 (18): 11742–47.

De Jong, G. 2000. Expectations, Gender, and Norms in Migration Decision-Making. *Population Studies* 54:307–19.

De Jong, G., and J. Fawcett. 1981. Motivations for Migration: An Assessment on a Value-Expectancy Model. In *Migration Decision Making*, eds. G. De Jong and R. Gardner. New York: Pergamon Press.

de Sandre, P. 2000. Patterns of Fertility in Italy and Factors of its Decline. *Genus* 56 (1–2): 19–54.

De Santis, S. 1996. Canada Modifies 1996 Census Form after Angry Homemaker's Campaign. *Wall Street Journal*, August 9, A5C.

de Savigny, D. 2003. Integrating Census and Survey Data. Paper read at Conference on Migration, Urbanization and Health: The Role of Remote Sensing (RS) and Geographic Information Systems (GIS) for Monitoring, Surveillance, and Program Evaluation, at Princeton University Program in Urbanization and Migration.

de Sherbinin, A., D. Carr, S. Cassels, and L. Jiang. 2007. Population and Environment. *Annual Review of Environment and Resources* 32:345–73.

DeCarlo, S. 2010. *What the Boss Makes*. Forbes, 28 April 2010 2010 [cited 2010]. Available from http://www.forbes.com/2010/04/27/compensation-chief-executive-salary-leadership-boss-10-ceo-compensation-intro.html.

DellaPergola, S. 1980. Patterns of American Jewish Fertility. *Demography* 17 (3):261–73.

Demeny, P. 1968. Early Fertility Decline in Austria-Hungary: A Lesson in Demographic Transition. *Daedalus* 97 (2): 502–22.

———. 1994. *Population and Development*. Liège: International Union for the Scientific Study of Population.

Demerath, N. 1976. *Birth Control and Foreign Policy: The Alternatives to Family Planning*. New York: Harper & Row.

Demos, J. 1965. Notes on Life in Plymouth Colony. *William and Mary Quarterly* 22 (264–86).

DeNavas-Walt, C., R. W. Cleveland, and B. H. Webster, Jr. 2003. Income in the United States: 2002. *Current Population Reports* P60–221.

Deveau, S. 2010. *China Rides: Middle Class Driving Demand for Cars*. Financial Post 2010 [cited 2010].

Available from http://www.financialpost.com/news-sectors/story.html?id=3058463.

Dharmalingam, A. 1994. Old Age Support: Expectations and Experiences in a South Indian Village. *Population Studies* 48:5–19.

Diamond, J. 1997. *Guns, Germs, and Steel*. New York: W.W. Norton.

———. 2005. *Collapse: How Societies Choose to Fail or Succeed*. New York: Viking.

Diaz-Briquets, S., and L. Perez. 1981. Cuba: The Demography of Revolution. *Population Bulletin* 36 (1).

Diekmann, A., and H. Englehardt. 1999. The Social Inheritance of Divorce: Effects of Parent's Family Type in Postwar Germany. *American Sociological Review* 64:783–93.

Diouf, J. 2009. *How to Feed the World in 2050*. United Nations Food and Agriculture Organization 2009 [cited 2010]. Available from http://www.fao.org/fileadmin/templates/wsfs/docs/expert_paper/How_to_Feed_the_World_in_2050.pdf.

Divine, R. 1957. *American Immigration Policy, 1924–1952*. New Haven, CT: Yale Univeristy Press.

Dixon, J. A., and K. Hamilton. 1996. Expanding the Measure of Wealth. *Finance & Development* 33 (4): 15–19.

Dixon-Mueller, R. 1993. *Population Policy and Women's Rights: Transforming Reproductive Choice*. Westport, CT: Praeger.

———. 2001. Female Empowerment and Demographic Processes: Moving Beyond Cairo. In *IUSSP Contributions to Gender Research*, ed. International Union for the Scientific Study of Population. Paris: IUSSP.

Dodoo, F. N.-A., and A. E. Frost. 2008. Gender in African Population Research: The Fertility/Reproductive Health Example. *Annual Review of Sociology* 34: 431–52.

Dogan, M., and J. Kasarda. 1988. Introduction: How Giant Cities Will Multiply and Grow. In *The Metropolis Era, Volume 1, A World of Giant Cities*, eds. M. Dogan and J. Kasarda. Newbury Park, CA: Sage Publications.

Domschke, E., and D. Goyer. 1986. *The Handbook of National Population Censuses: Africa and Asia*. Westport, CT: Greenwood Press.

Donaldson, P., and A. O. Tsui. 1990. The International Family Planning Movement. *Population Bulletin* 45 (3).

Donaldson, P. J. 1990. *Nature Against Us: The United States and the World Population Crisis, 1965–1980*. Chapel Hill, NC: The University of North Carolina Press.

Doornbus, G., and D. Kromhout. 1991. Educational Level and Mortality in a 32-Year Follow-Up Study of 18-Year-Old Men in the Netherlands. *International Journal of Epidemiology* 19:374–79.

Douglas, E. T. 1970. *Margaret Sanger: Pioneer of the Future*. New York: Holt, Rinehart and Winston.

Douglass, M. 2000. Mega-Urban Regions and World City Formation: Globalisation, the Economic Crisic and Urban Policy Issues in Pacific Asia. *Urban Studies* 37 (12): 2315–2335.

Drake, F. 2000. *Global Warming: The Science of Climate Change*. London: Arnold Publishers.

Dublin, L., A. Lotka, and M. Spiegleman. 1949. *Length of Life: A Study of the Life Table*. New York: Ronald Press.

Duff, C. 1997. Plans for Census 'Sampling' Anger GOP in Congress. *Wall Street Journal*, 12 June:A20.

Duggan, M., P. Singleton, and J. Song. 2007. Aching to Retire? The Rise in the Full Retirement Age and its Impact on the Social Security Disability Rolls. *Journal of Public Economics* 91:1327–50.

Duleep, H. 1989. Measuring Socioeconomic Mortality Differentials Over Time. *Demography* 26:345–51.

Dumond, D. 1975. The Limitation of Human Population. A Natural History. *Science* 232:713–20.

Dumont, A. 1890. *Depopulation et Civilisation: Etude Demographique*. Paris: Lecrosnier & Babe.

Dunlop, J. E., and V. A. Velkoff. 1999. Women and the Economy in India, Report WID/98-2. Washington, DC: U.S. Census Bureau.

Durand, J. D. 1967. The Modern Expansion of World Population. *Proceedings of the American Philosophical Society* 3 (June): 137–40.

Durkheim, E. 1893 [1933]. *The Division of Labor in Society, translated by George Simpson*. Glencoe: Free Press.

Dye, J. L. 2008. Fertility of American Women: 2006. *Current Population Reports* P20–558.

Dyson, T. 1991. On the Demography of South Asian Famines. *Population Studies* 45:5–25.

———. 1996. *Population and Food: Global Trends and Future Prospects*. London: Routledge.

Dyson, T., R. Cassen, and L. Visaria eds. 2004. *Twenty-first Century India: Population, Economy, Human Development, and the Environment*. Oxford, UK: Oxford University Press.

Easterlin, R. 1978. The Economics and Sociology of Fertility: A Synthesis. In *Historical Studies of Changing Fertility*, ed. C. Tilly. Princeton, NJ: Princeton University Press.

———. 2008. Introduction. In *The Lucky Few*, ed. E. Carlson. New York: Springer.

Easterlin, R., and E. Crimmins. 1985. *The Fertility Revolution: A Supply-Demand Analysis*. Chicago: University of Chicago Press.

Easterlin, R. A. 1968. *Population, Labor Force, and Long Swings in Economic Growth*. New York: National Bureau of Economic Research.

Eaton, J., and A. Mayer. 1954. *Man's Capacity to Reproduce*. Glencoe: Free Press.

Ebenstein, A., and S. Leung. 2010. Son Preference and Access to Social Insurance: Evidence from China's Rural Pension Program. *Population and Development Review* 36 (1): 47–70.

Eberstadt, N. 1994a. Demographic Shocks After Communism: Eastern Germany, 1989–93. *Population and Development Review* 20 (1): 137–52.

———. 1994b. What You Won't Hear at Cairo. *Wall Street Journal* 6 September.

———. 2001. The Population Implosion. *Foreign Policy* (March–April).

The Economist. 1996. Cities: Fiction and Fact. *The Economist* 8 June.
———. 1998. China: The X-Files. *The Economist* 14 February.
———. 2003. Afghanistan: The Pains of Motherhood. *The Economist* (22 November): 42.
———. 2005. Slavery: Unbroken Yokes. *The Economist*, 12 March:49.
———. 2006. Big Mac Index. *The Economist*, 12 January.
———. 2008. The Philippines: Too Many Babies. *The Economist* (26 April): 62.
———. 2009a. A Special Report on the Arab World. *The Economist*, 25 July:8.
———. 2009b. Afghanistan's Child Brides: The Unhappiest Day of Her Life. *The Economist*, 15 August:12.
———. 2009c. Lawless Roads: Mexico's Southern Border. *The Economist*, 26 September:48.
———. 2009d. Quebec's Demography: The Cradle's Costly Revenge. *The Economist*, 10 January:34–35.
———. 2010a. Are Women on Their Way at Last? The Saudis Argue About Sexual Equity. *The Economist*, 1 May:49.
———. 2010b. Longevit Swaps: Live Long and Prosper. *The Economist*, 6 February:83.
The Economist Intelligence Unit. 2010. *Global Liveability Report: Cities in Canada and Australia Are Most Liveable in the World*. The Economist Intelligence Unit 2010 [cited 2010]. Available from http://www.eiu.com/site_info.asp?info_name=The_Global_Liveability_Report&page=noads&rf=0.
Edmonston, B., and C. Schultze eds. 1995. *Modernizing the U.S. Census*. Washington, DC: National Academy Press.
Ehrlich, P. 1968. *The Population Bomb*. New York: Ballantine Books.
———. 1971. *The Population Bomb, Second Edition*. New York: Sierra Club/Ballantine Books.
Ehrlich, P., and A. Ehrlich. 1972. *Population, Resources, and Environment, 2nd Edition*. San Francisco: Freeman.
———. 1990. *The Population Explosion*. New York: Simon & Schuster.
———. 2004. *One With Nineveh: Politics, Consumption, and the Human Future*. Washington, DC: Island Press.
Ehrlich, P. R., A. H. Ehrlich, and G. C. Daily. 1997. *The Stork and the Plow: The Equity Answer to the Human Dilemma*. New Haven: Yale University Press.
Eichenlaub, S. C., S. E. Tolnay, and J. T. Alexander. 2010. Moving Out but Not Up: Economic Outcomes in the Great Migration. *American Sociological Review* 75 (1): 101–25.
Elliott, J. R. 1999. Putting "Global Cities" in Their Place: Urban Hierarchy and Low-Income Employment During the Post-War Era. *Urban Geography* 20 (2): 95–115.
Emerson, M. O., G. Yancy, and K. J. Chai. 2001. Does Race Matter in Residential Segregation? Exploring the Preferences of White Americans. *American Sociological Review* 66:922–35.
Engels, F. 1844 [1953]. *Outlines of a Critique of Political Economy, Reprinted in R. L. Meek, 1953, Marx and Engels on Malthus*. London: Lawrence and Wishart.
Environmental Fund. 1981. The Perils of Vanishing Farmland. *The Other Side* No. 23.
Epstein, P. R. 2000. Is Global Warming Harmful to Health? *Scientific American* 282 (August): 50–57.
Evans, D. K., and E. Miguel. 2007. Orphans and Schooling in Africa: A Longitudinal Analysis. *Demography* 44 (1): 35–57.
Eversley, D. 1959. *Social Theories of Malthus and the Malthusian Debate*. Oxford: Clarendon Press.
Ezzati, M., and D. M. Kammen. 2001. Indoor air pollution from biomass combustion as a risk factor for acute respiratory infections in Kenya: an exposure-response study. *Lancet* 358 (9282): 619–24.
Ezzati, M., and A. D. Lopez. 2003a. Estimates of Global Mortality Attributable to Smoking in 2000. *The Lancet* 362 (9387): 847–49.
Fagan, B. 2000. *The Little Ice Age: How Climate Made History 1300–1850*. New York: Basic Books.
Fairclough, G. 2007. China Confronts Price of its Cigarette Habit. *Wall Street Journal*, 3 January:A1.
Falkenmark, M., and C. Widstrand. 1992. Population and Water Resources: A Delicate Balance. *Population Bulletin* 47 (3).
Fan, C. C. 2000. The Vertical and Horizontal Expansions of China's City System. *Urban Geography* 20 (6): 493–515.
———. 2008. *China on the Move: Migration, the State, and the Household*. London and New York: Routledge.
Fankhouser, S. 2009. If It Warms Up, Who's Going to Pay? *Wall Street Journal* (7 December): B1.
Fargues, P. 1995. Changing Hierarchies of Gender and Generation in the Arab World. In *Family, Gender, and Population in the Middle East*, ed. C. M. Obermeyer. Cairo: The American University in Cairo.
———. 1997. State Policies and the Birth Rate in Egypt: From Socialism to Liberalism. *Population and Development Review* 23 (1): 115–38.
———. 2000a. *Générations Arabes*. Paris: Fayard.
———. 2000b. Protracted National Conflict and Fertility Change: Palestinians and Israelis in the Twentieth Century. *Population and Development Review* 26 (3): 441–82.
———. 2008. Emerging Demographic Patterns Across the Mediterranean and Their Implications for Migration Through 2030. Washington, DC: Migration Policy Institute.
Farley, R. 1970. *Growth of the Black Population*. Chicago: Markham.
———. 1976. Components of Suburban Population Growth. In *The Changing Face of the Suburbs*, ed. B. Schwartz. Chicago: University of Chicago Press.
Farley, R., S. Danziger, and H. J. Holzer. 2000. *Detroit Divided*. New York: Russell Sage Foundation.
Farley, R., and W. H. Frey. 1994. Changes in the Segregation of Whites From Blacks During the 1980s: Small

Steps Toward a More Integrated Society. *American Sociological Review* 59:23–45.

Fasenfest, D., J. Booza, and K. Metzger. 2004. *Living Together: A New Look at Racial and Ethnic Integration in Metropolitan Neighborhoods, 1990–2000*. Washington, DC: The Brookings Institution.

Fergany, A. M., and R. Santana. 2009. Immigrant-filled fishing boat sinks off Libya; hundreds feared dead. *San Diego Union-Tribune (via the Associated Press)*, 1 April:A3.

Feshbach, M., and A. Friendly. 1992. *Ecocide in the USSR: Health and Nature Under Siege*. New York: Basic Books.

Fetto, J. 2000. It Ain't Easy Eating Green. *American Demographics* 22 (5): 13.

Fields, J. 2001. America's Families and Living Arrangements: 2000. *Current Population Reports* P20–537.

Fillion, P., and K. McSpurren. 2007. Smart Growth and Development Reality: The Difficult Co-ordination of Land Use and Transport Objectives. *Urban Studies* 44 (3): 501–23.

Findlay, A. M. 1995. Skilled Transients: The Invisible Phenomenon. In *The Cambridge Survey of World Migration*, ed. R. Cohen. Cambridge, UK: Cambridge University Press.

Findley, S., and J. Ford. 1993. Reversals in the Epidemiological Transition in Harlem. Paper read at Paper Presented at the Annual Meeting of the Population Association of America, at Cincinnati, Ohio.

Findley, S. E. 1999. *Women on the Move: Perspectives on Gender Changes in Latin America*. Liege: International Union for the Scientific Study of Population.

Finkle, J., and B. Crane. 1975. The Politics of Bucharest: Population Development and the New International Economic Order. *Population and Development Review* 1 (1): 87–114.

Finkle, J. L., and C. A. McIntosh. 2002. United Nations Population Conferences: Shaping the Policy Agenda for the Twenty-first Century. *Studies in Family Planning* 33 (1): 11–23.

Firebaugh, G. 1979. Structural Determinants of Urbanization in Asia and Latin America, 1950–1970. *American Sociological Review* 44:199–215.

———. 2003. *The New Geography of Global Income Inequality*. Cambridge, MA: Harvard University Press.

Firebaugh, G., and F. D. Beck. 1994. Does Economic Growth Benefit the Masses? Growth, Dependence, and Welfare in the Third World. *American Sociological Review* 59:631–53.

Fischer, C. 1976. *The Urban Experience*. New York: Harcourt Brace Jovanovich.

———. 1981. The Public and Private Worlds of City Life. *American Sociological Review* 46:306–16.

———. 1984. *The Urban Experience, 2nd Edition*. San Diego: Harcourt Brace Jovanovich.

Fishlow, A. 1965. *American Railroads and the Transformation of the Antebellum Economy*. Cambridge, MA: Harvard University Press.

Fitzgerald, D. 2008. *A Nation of Emigrants: How Mexico Manages its Migration*. Berkeley and Los Angeles: University of California Press.

Fitzsimmons, J. D., and M. R. Ratcliffe. 2004. Reflections on the Review of Metropolitan Area Standards in the United States, 1990–2000. In *New Forms of Urbanization: Beyond the Urban-Rural Dichotomy*, eds. A. G. Champion and G. Hugo. London: Ashgate Publishing Company.

Fogel, R. W. 2004. *The Escape From Hunger and Premature Death, 1700–2100: Europe, America, and the Third World*. New York: Cambridge University Press.

Fogel, R. W., and L. A. Helmchen. 2002. Economic and Technological Development and Their Relationships to Body Size and Productivity. In *The Nutrition Transition: Diet and Disease in the Developing World*, eds. B. Caballero and B. M. Popkin. San Diego: Academic Press.

Foner, A. 1975. Age in Society: Structure and Change. *American Behavioral Scientist* 19 (2): 144–65.

Food and Agriculture Organization. 2007. The State of World Fisheries and Aquaculture 2006. Rome, Italy: Food and Agriculture Organization of the United Nations.

———. 2009a. *Growing More Food—Using Less Water: Prepared for the Fifth World Water Forum, Istanbul, Turkey*. Food and Agriculture Organization of the United Nations 2009a [cited 2010]. Available from http://www.fao.org/fileadmin/user_upload/newsroom/docs/water_facts.pdf.

———. 2009b. The State of Food Insecurity in the World 2009. Rome, Italy: Food and Agriculture Organization of the United Nations.

Foot, D. K. 1996. *Boom, Bust & Echo: How to Profit From the Coming Demographic Shift*. Toronto: Macfarlane Walter & Ross.

Ford, L. R. 2003. *America's New Downtowns: Reinvention or Revitalization*. Baltimore, MD: The Johns Hopkins University Press.

Ford, T. 1999. Understanding Population Growth in the Peri-Urban Region. *International Journal of Population Geography* 5:297–311.

Foster, G. 1967. *Tzintzuntzan: Mexican Peasants in a Changing World*. Boston: Little, Brown.

Francese, P. 1979. The 1980 Census: The Counting of America. *Population Bulletin* 34 (4).

Franklin, B. 1751. *Observations Concerning the Increase of Mankind*. Boston: S. Kneeland.

Freedman, A. 1991. Nestlé to Restrict Baby-Food Supply to Third World. *Wall Street Journal* 30 January.

Freedman, R., M.-C. Chang, and T.-H. Sun. 1994. Taiwan's Transition from High Fertility to Below-Replacement Levels. *Studies in Family Planning* 25 (6): 317–31.

Freeman, O. L. 1992. Perspectives and Prospects. *Agricultural History* 66 (2): 3–11.

Frejka, T., and W. W. Kingkade. 2001. U.S. Fertility in International Comparison: An Exploration to Aid Projections. In *The Direction of Fertility in the United States*, ed. U.S. Census Bureau. Washington, DC: Council of Professional Associations on Federal Statistics.

Frey, W. H. 1995. The New Geography of Population Shifts. In *State of the Union: American in the 1990s, Volume Two: Social Trends*, ed. R. Farley. New York: Russell Sage Foundation.

———. 2004a. The Fading of City-Suburb and Metro-Nonmetro Distinctions in the United States. In *New Forms of Urbanization: Beyond the Urban-Rural Dichotomy*, eds. A. G. Champion and G. Hugo. London: Ashgate Publishing Company.

———. 2004b. The New Great Migration: Black Americans' Return to the South, 1965–2000. Washington, DC: The Brookings Institution.

———. 2006. *Diversity Spreads Out: Metropolitan Shifts in Hispanic, Asian, and Black Populations Since 2000.* Washington, DC: The Brookings Institution.

———. 2009. *A Rollercoaster Decade for Migation.* Brookings Institution 2009 [cited 2010]. Available from http://www.brookings.edu/opinions/2009/1229_migration_frey.aspx.

Friedberg, L. 1998. Did Unilateral Divorce Raise Divorce Rates? Evidence From Panel Data. *American Economic Review* 88:608–27.

Friedlander, D. 1983. Demographic Responses and Socioeconomic Structure: Population Processes in England and Wales in the Nineteenth Century. *Demography* 20 (3): 249–72.

Friedman, T. L. 2008. *Hot, Flat, and Crowded.* New York: Farrar, Straus and Giroux.

Friedmann, J. 2005. *China's Urban Transition.* Minneapolis: University of Minnesota Press.

Frier, B. W. 1999. Roman Demography. In *Life, Death, and Entertainment in the Roman Empire*, eds. D. S. Potter and D. J. Mattingly. Ann Arbor: University of Michigan Press.

Frisch, R. 1978. Population, Food Intake, and Fertility. *Science* 199:22–30.

Frisch, R. E. 2002. *Female Fertility and The Body Fat Connection.* Chicago: University of Chicago Press.

Fuguitt, G., and D. Brown. 1990. Residential Preferences and Population Redistribution in 1972–88. *Demography* 27:589–600.

Fuguitt, G., and J. Zuiches. 1975. Residential Preferences and Population Distribution. *Demography* 12:491–504.

Furstenberg, F., and A. J. Cherlin. 1991. *Divided Families: What Happens to Children When Parents Part?* Cambridge, MA: Harvard University Press.

Fuwa, M. 2004. Macro-Level Gender Inequality and the Division of Household Labor in 22 Countries. *American Sociological Review* 69:751–67.

Galle, O., W. Gove, and J. McPherson. 1972. Population Density and Pathology: What Are the Relations for Man. *Science* 176:23–30.

Galloway, P. 1984. *Long Term Fluctuations in Climate and Population in the Pre-Industrial Era.* Berkeley: University of California.

Gao, F., E. Bailes, D. L. Robertson, Y. Chen, C. M. Rodenburg, S. F. Michael, L. B. Cummins, L. O. Arthur, M. Peeters, G. M. Shaw, P. M. Sharp, and B. H. Hahn. 1999. Origin of HIV-1 in the Chimpanzee Pan Troglodytes Troglodytes. *Nature* 397 (6718): 436–41.

Garcia y Griego, M., J. R. Weeks, and R. Ham-Chande. 1990. "Mexico." In *Handbook on International Migration*, eds. W. J. Serow, C. B. Nam, D. F. Sly and R. H. Weller. New York: Greenwood Press.

Garreau, J. 1991. *Edge City: Life on the New Frontier.* New York: Doubleday.

Gartner, R. 1990. The Victims of Homicide: A Temporal and Cross-National Comparison. *American Sociological Review* 55:92–106.

Garza, G. 2004. The Transformation of the Urban System in Mexico. In *New Forms of Urbanization: Beyond the Urban-Rural Dichotomy*, eds. A. G. Champion and G. Hugo. London: Ashgate Publishing Company.

Gaymu, J., P. Ekamper, and G. Beets. 2007. Who Will be Caring for Europe's Dependent Elders in 2030. *Population-E* 62 (4): 675–706.

Gendell, M. 2001. Retirement Age Declines Again in 1990s. *Monthly Labor Review* (October): 12–21.

Gibson, C. 1976. The U.S. Fertility Decline, 1961–1975: The Contribution of Changes in Marital Status and Marital Fertility. *Family Planning Perspectives* 8:249–52.

Gillies, A. T. 2004. Demography Plays. *Forbes* (26 July): 164–65.

Gillis, J. R., L. A. Tilly, and D. Levine eds. 1992. *The European Experience of Declining Fertility: A Quiet Revolution 1850–1970.* Oxford: Basil Blackwell.

Glass, D. V. 1953. *Introduction to Malthus.* New York: Wiley.

Glenn, E. N. ed. 2009. *Shades of Difference: Why Skin Color Matters.* Stanford, CA: Stanford University Press.

Global Aging Report. 1997. Guaranteeing the Rights of Older People: China Takes a Great Leap Forward. *Global Aging Report* 2 (5): 3.

Gober, P. 1993. Americans on the Move. *Population Bulletin* 48 (3).

———. 2000. Immigration and North American Cities. *Urban Geography* 21 (1): 83–90.

Godfrey, B. J., and Y. Zhou. 1999. Ranking World Cities: Multinational Corporations and the Global Urban Hierarchy. *Urban Geography* 20 (3): 268–81.

Godwin, W. 1793 [1946]. *Enquiry Concerning Political Justice and Its Influences on Morals and Happiness.* Toronto: University of Toronto Press.

Goldman, N. 1984. Changes in Widowhood and Divorce and Expected Durations of Marriage. *Demography* 21 (3): 297–308.

Goldscheider, C. 1971. *Population, Modernization, and Social Structure.* Boston: Little, Brown.

———. 1991. The Demographic Embeddedness of the Arab-Jewish Conflict in Israeli Society. In *Israeli Politics in the 1990s: Key Domestic and Foreign Policy Factors*, eds. B. Reich and G. Kieval. Westport, CT: Greenwood Press.

———. 1996. *Israel's Changing Society: Population, Ethnicity, and Development.* Boulder, CO: Westview Press.

———. 1999. Religious values, dependencies, and fertility: Evidence and implications from Israel. In *Dynamics of Values in Fertility Change*, ed. R. Leete. Oxford: Oxford University Press.

———. 2006. Religion, Family, and Fertility: What Do We Know Historically and Comparatively? In *Religion and the Decline of Fertility in the Western World*, eds. R. Derosas and F. van Poppel. Dordrecht: Springer.

Goldscheider, F., and C. Goldscheider. 1993. *Leaving Home Before Marriage: Ethnicity, Familism, and Generational Relationships*. Madison, WI: The University of Wisconsin Press.

———. 1994. Leaving and Returning Home in 20th Century America. *Population Bulletin* 48 (4).

———. 1999. Changes in Returning Home in the United States, 1925–1985. *Social Forces* 78 (2): 695–720.

Goldstein, A., and W. Feng eds. 1996. *China: The Many Facets of Demographic Change*. Boulder, CO: Westview Press.

Goldstein, J. R., T. Sobotka, and A. Jasilioniene. 2009. The End of "Lowest-Low" Fertility? *Population and Development Review* 35 (4): 663–99.

Goldstein, S., and A. Goldstein. 1981. The Impact of Migration on Fertility: An 'Own Children' Analysis For Thailand. *Population Studies* 35 (2): 265–84.

Goldstone, J. A. 1986. State Breakdown in the English Revolution: A New Synthesis. *American Sociological Review* 92:257–322.

———. 1991. *Revolution and Rebellion in the Early Modern World*. Berkeley: University of California Press.

———. 2002. Population and Security: How Demographic Change Can Lead to Violent Conflict. *Journal of International Affairs* 56:3–22.

———. 2010. The New Population Bomb. *Foreign Affairs* 89 (1): 31–44.

Goliber, T. 1985. Sub-Saharan Africa: Population Pressures on Development. *Population Bulletin* 40 (1).

Goode, W. J. 1993. *World Changes in Divorce Patterns*. New Haven: Yale University Press.

Goodkind, D. M. 1995. Vietnam's One-or-Two Child Policy in Action. *Population and Development Review* 21 (1): 85–112.

———. 2004. China's Missing Children: The 2000 Census Underreporting Surprise. *Population Studies* 58 (3): 281–95.

Gordon, C., and C. F. Longino, Jr. 2000. Age Structure and Social Structure. *Contemporary Sociology* 29 (5): 699–703.

Gordon, D. 2003. Area-Based Deprivation Measures—a U.K. Perspective. In *Neighborhoods and Health*, eds. I. Kawachi and L. F. Berkman. New York: Oxford University Press.

Gordon, M. 1975. *Agriculture and Population*. Washington, DC: Government Printing Office.

Goudie, A. 2006. *The Human Impact on the Natural Environment, 6th Edition*. Malden, MA: Blackwell Publishing.

Gould, W. T. S., and A. M. Findlay eds. 1994. *Population Migration and the Changing World Order*. New York: Chichester.

Gove, W. 1973. Sex, Marital Status, and Mortality. *American Journal of Sociology* 79 (1): 45–67.

Grabill, W., C. Kiser, and P. Whelpton. 1958. *The Fertility of American Women*. New York: Wiley.

Graebner, W. 1980. *A History of Retirement*. New Haven: Yale University Press.

Grammich, C., J. DaVanzo, and K. Stewart. 2004. Changes in American Opinion about Family Planning. *Studies in Family Planning* 35 (3): 197–206.

Grant, J., and S. Hoorens. 2007. Does the Commission's Report Adequately Address the Key Issues of the Demographic Future of Europe. *Vienna Yearbook of Population Research 2007*:13–19.

Grant, M. J., and J. R. Behrman. 2010. Gender Gaps in Educational Attainment in Less Developed Countries. *Population and Development Review* 36 (1): 71–89.

Graunt, J. 1662 [1939]. *Natural and Political Observations Made Upon the Bills of Mortality, Edited with an Introduction by Walter F. Willcox*. Baltimore: The Johns Hopkins University Press.

Greenhalgh, S. 1986. Shifts in China's Population Policy 1984–86: Views From the Central, Provincial, and Local Levels. *Population and Development Review* 12 (3):491–516.

Greenhalgh, S., Z. Chuzhu, and L. Nan. 1994. Restaining Population Growth in Three Chinese Villages, 1988–93. *Population and Development Review* 20 (2): 365–96.

Gregorio, D. I., S. J. Walsh, and D. Paturzo. 1997. The Effects of Occupation-Based Social Position on Mortality in a Large American Cohort. *American Journal of Public Health* 87 (9): 1472–75.

Griffin, D. H., and P. J. Waite. 2006. American Community Survey Overview and the Role of External Evaluations. *Population Research and Policy Review* 25:201–23.

Gu Baochang, Wang Feng, Guo Zhigang, and Zhang Erli. 2007. China's Local and National Fertility Policies at the End of the Twentieth Century. *Population and Development Review* 33 (1): 129–47.

Guest, A. M., G. Almgren, and J. M. Hussey. 1998. The Ecology of Race and Socioeconomic Distress: Infant and Working-Age Mortality in Chicago. *Demoraphy* 35 (1): 23–34.

Guihati, K. 1977. Compulsory Sterilization: The Change in India's Population Policy. *Science* 195:1300–1305.

Guillard, A. 1855. *Éléments de Statistique Humaine ou Démographie Comparée*. Paris: Guillaumin et Cie Libraires.

Guilmoto, C. Z. 1998. Institutions and Migrations: Short-Term Versus Long-Term Moves in Rural West Africa. *Population Studies* 52:85–103.

———. 2009. The Sex Ratio Transition in Asia. *Population and Development Review* 35 (3): 519–49.

Guinness World Records. 2008. *Most Prolific Mother Ever*. Available from http://www.guinnessworldrecords.com/news/2008/03/080304.aspx.

Gunter, C. 2005. She Moves in Mysterious Ways. *Nature* 434:279–80.

Gupta, G. R. 1998. Claiming the Future. In *The Progress of Nations: 1998*, ed. UNICEF. New York: United Nations Childrens Fund.

Gutmann, M. P., and V. Field. 2010. Katrina in Historical Context: Environment and Migration in the U.S. *Population and Environment* 31:3–19.

Guz, D., and J. Hobcraft. 1991. Breastfeeding and Fertility: a Comparative Analysis. *Population Studies* 45:91–108.

Hacker, J. D. 2003. Rethinking the "Early" Decline of Marital Fertility in the United States. *Demography* 40 (4): 605–20.

Hagan, J., and H. Foster. 2001. Youth Violence and the End of Adolescence. *American Sociological Review* 66:874–99.

Hager, T. 2006. *The Demon Under the Microscope: From Battlefield Hospitals to Nazi Labs, On Doctor's Heroic Search for the World's First Miracle Drug*. New York: Random House.

Hahn, B. A. 1993. Marital Status and Women's Health: The Effects of Economic Marital Adjustments. *Journal of Marriage and the Family* 55:495–504.

Halfon, S. 2006. *The Cairo Consensus: Demographic Surveys, Women's Empowerment, and Regime Change in Population Policy*. Lanham, MD: Lexington Books.

Hampshire, S. 1955. Introduction. In *Sketch for an Historical Picture of the Progress of the Human Mind*, ed. M. J. A. N. d. C. Condorcet. London: Weidenfield and Nicholson.

Han, S. S., and S. T. Wong. 1994. The Influence of Chinese Reform and Pre-Reform Policies on Urban Growth in the 1980s. *Urban Geography* 15 (6): 537–64.

Handwerker, P. 1986. *Culture and Reproduction: An Anthropological Critique of Demographic Transition Theory*. Boulder: Westview Press.

Handy, S. 2005. Smart Growth and the Transportation-Land Use Connection: What Does the Research Tell Us? *International Regional Science Review* 28 (2):146–67.

Hank, K., and H.-P. Kohler. 2000. Gender Preferences for Children in Europe: Empirical Results from 17 FFS Countries. *Demographic Research* 2 (1).

Hansen, J. 1970. *The Population Explosion: How Sociologists View It*. New York: Pathfinder Press.

Hansen, K. 1994. Geographic Mobility: March 1992 to March 1993. *Current Population Reports* P20–481.

Haq, M. 1984. Age at Menarche and the Related Issue: A Pilot Study on Urban School Girls. *Family Planning Perspectives* 13 (6): 559–67.

Harbison, S. F., and W. C. Robinson. 2002. Policy Implications of the Next World Demographic Transition. *Studies in Family Planning* 33:37–48.

Hardin, G. 1968. The Tragedy of the Commons. *Science* 162:1243–48.

Hardoy, J. E., D. Mitlin, and D. Satterthwaite. 2001. *Environmental Problems in an Urbanizing World*. London: Earthscan Publications.

Harkavy, O. 1995. *Curbing Population Growth: An Insider's Perspective on the Population Movement*. New York: Plenum Press.

Harlan, J. 1976. The Plants and Animals That Nourish Man. *Scientific American* 235 (3):88–97.

Harris, D. R., and J. J. Sim. 2002. Who Is Multiracial? Assessing the Complexity of Lived Race. *American Sociological Review* 67:614–27.

Harris, M., and E. B. Ross. 1987. *Death, Sex, and Fertility: Population Regulation in Preindustrial and Developing Societies*. New York: Columbia University Press.

Harris, R., P. Sleight, and R. Webber. 2005. *Geodemographics, GIS and Neighborhood Targeting*. Chichester, England: John Wiley & Sons, Ltd.

Harrison, J. R., and G. R. Carroll. 2005. *Culture and Demography in Organizations*. Princeton, NJ: Princeton University Press.

Harrison, P. 1993. *The Third Revolution: Population, Environment and a Sustainable World*. London: Penguin Books.

Hartley, L. P. 1967. *The Go-Between*. New York: Stein and Day.

Hartmann, B. 1995. *Reproductive Rights and Wrongs: The Global Politics of Population Control*. Boston: South End Press.

Harvey, W. 1986. Homicide Among Young Black Adults: Life in the Subculture of Exasperation. In *Homicide among Black Americans*, ed. D. Hawkins. New York: University Press of America.

Hatcher, R. A., J. Trussell, F. Stewart, A. Nelson, W. Cates, F. Guest, and D. Kowal. 2004. *Contraceptive Technology, 18th Edition*. New York: Ardent Media.

Hattersly, L. 2005. Trends in Life Expectancy by Social Class—An Update. *Health Statistics Quarterly* 2:533–39.

Hatton, T. J., and J. G. Williamson. 1994. What Drove the Mass Migrations from Europe in the Late Nineteenth Century? *Population and Development Review* 20 (3): 533–59.

Haub, C. 2002. How Many People Have Ever Lived on Earth. *Population Today* (November/December).

Haug, W. 2000. National and Immigrant Minorities: Problems of Measurement and Definition. *Genus* 56 (1–2): 133–47.

Hawass, Z., Y. Gad, S. Ismail, R. Khairat, D. Fathalla, N. Hasan, A. Ahmed, H. Elleithy, M. Ball, F. Gaballah, S. Wasef, M. Fateen, H. Amer, P. Gostner, A. Selim, A. Zink, and C. Pusch. 2010. Ancestry and Pathology in King Tutankhamun's Family. *Journal of the American Medical Association* 303 (7): 638–47.

Hawley, A. 1972. Population Density and the City. *Demography* 91:521–30.

Hayes, J. M., and L. E. Hill. 2008. Immigrant Pathways to Legal Permanent Residence: Now and Under a Merit-Based System. San Francisco: Public Policy Institute of California.

Hayward, M. D., E. M. Crimmins, T. P. Miles, and Y. Yang. 2000. The Signficance of Socioeconomic Status in Explaining the Racial Gap in Chronic Health Conditions. *American Sociological Review* 65:910–30.

Headey, D. D., and A. Hodge. 2009. The Effect of Population Growth on Economic Growth: A Meta-Regression

Analysis of the Macroeconomic Literature. *Population and Development Review* 35 (2): 221–48.

Hecht, J. 1987. Johann Peter Süssmilch: A German Prophet in Foreign Countries. *Population Studies* 41:31–58.

Heilig, G., T. Büttner, and W. Lutz. 1990. Germany's Population: Turbulent Past, Uncertain Future. *Population Bulletin* 45 (4).

Henry, L. 1961. Some Data on Natural Fertility. *Eugenics Quarterly* 8:81–91.

Henshaw, S. K., and K. Kost. 2008. *Trends in the Characteristics of Women Obtaining Abortions, 1974 to 2004*. Guttmacher Institute 2008 [cited 2010]. Available from http://www.guttmacher.org/pubs/2008/09/18/Report_Trends_Women_Obtaining_Abortions.pdf.

Herlihy, D., and C. Klapisch-Zuber. 1985. *Tuscans and Their Families: A Study of the Florentine Catasto of 1427*. New Haven: Yale University Press.

Herman, T. 1999. The Big Shift. *Wall Street Journal*, 29 November:R24.

Heron, M., D. L. Hoyert, S. L. Murphy, J. Xu, K. Kochanek, and B. Tejada-Vera. 2009. Deaths: Final Data for 2006. *National Vital Statistics Reports* 57 (14).

Herskind, A. M., M. McGue, N. V. Holm, T. I. A. Sorensen, B. Harvald, and J. W. Vaupel. 1996. The Heritability of Human Longevity: A Population-Based Study of 2,872 Danish Twin Pairs Born 1870–1900. *Human Genetics* 97:319–23.

Heuser, R. 1976. *Fertility Tables For Birth Cohorts by Color: United States, 1917–73*. Rockville, MD: National Center for Health Statistics.

Hill, A. G., R. Darko, J. Seffah, R. M. K. Adanu, J. Anarfi, and R. B. Duda. 2007. Health of Urban Ghanaian Women as Identified by the Women's Health Study of Accra. *International Journal of Gynaecology & Obstetrics* 99 (2):150–56.

Hill, D., and M. Kent. 1988. *Election Demographics*. Washington, DC: Population Reference Bureau.

Himes, N. E. 1976. *Medical History of Contraception*. New York: Schocken Books.

Himmelfarb, G. 1984. *The Idea of Poverty: England in the Early Industrial Age*. New York: Alfred A. Knopf.

Hinde, T. 1995. *The Domesday Book: England's Heritage, Then & Now*. London: Tiger Books International.

Hirschman, A. 1958. *The Strategy of Economic Development*. New Haven: Yale University Press.

Hirschman, C. 1999. Theories of International Migration and Immigration: A Preliminary Reconnaissance of Ideal Types. In *The Handbook of International Migration: The American Experience*, eds. C. Hirschman, P. Kasinitiz and J. DeWind. New York: Russell Sage Foundation.

———. 2005. Immigration and the American Century. *Demography* 42 (4): 595–620.

Hirschman, C., R. Alba, and R. Farley. 2000. The Meaning and Measurement of Race in the U.S. Census: Glimpses into the Future. *Demography* 37 (3): 381–93.

Hirschman, C., and M. Butler. 1981. Trends and differentials in Breast Feeding: An Update. *Demography* 18 (1): 39–54.

Hobbs, F., and N. Stoops. 2002. *Demographic Trends in the 20th Century*. Washington, DC: U.S. Census Bureau.

Hobcraft, J. 1996. Fertility in England and Wales: A Fifty Year Perspective. *Population Studies* 50 (3): 485–524.

Hockings, P. 1999. *Kindreds of the Earth: Badaga Household Structure and Demography*. Walnut Creek, CA: Alta Mira Press.

Hodell, D., J. Curtis, and M. Brenner. 1995. Possible Role of Climate in the Collapse of Classic Mayan Civilization. *Nature* 375:391–94.

Hodgson, D. 2009a. Abortion, Family Planning and Population Policy: Prospects for the Common-Ground Approach. *Population and Development Review* 35 (3):479–518.

———. 2009b. Malthus' Essay on Population and the American Debate over Slavery. *Comparative Studies in Society and History* 51 (4): 1–29.

Hoefer, M., N. Rytina, and B. C. Baker. 2008. Estimates of the Unauthorized Immigrant Population Residing in the United States: January 2007. *Population Estimates of the Department of Homeland Security*.

———. 2010. *Estimates of the Unauthorized Immigrant Population Residing in the United States: January 2009*. US Department of Homeland Security 2010 [cited 2010]. Available from http://www.dhs.gov/xlibrary/assets/statistics/publications/ois_ill_pe_2009.pdf.

Hohm, C. 1975. Social Security and Fertility: An International Perspective. *Demography* 12 (4): 629–44.

Holdren, J. 1990. Energy in Transition. *Scientific American* 263 (3): 156–63.

Hollerbach, P. 1980. Recent Trends in Fertility, Abortion, and Contraception in Cuba. *International Family Planning Perspectives* 6 (3): 97–106.

Hollingsworth, T. H. 1969. *Historical Demography*. Ithaca: Cornell University Press.

Hollman, F. W., T. J. Mulder, and J. E. Kallan. 2000. Methodology and Assumptions for the Population Projections of the United States: 1999 to 2100. Washington DC: US Bureau of the Census Population Division Working Paper No. 38.

Hookway, J. 2008. Filipinos Test Catholic Clout: Family Planning Policies Urged to Help Strengthen the Economy. *Wall Street Journal* 20 June:A9.

Horsley, G. H. R. 1987. *New Documents Illustrating Early Christianity: A Review of the Greek Inscriptions and Papyri Published in 1979*. Australia: Macquarie University.

Howell, N. 1979. *Demography of the Dobe Kung*. New York: Academic Press.

Hsu, M.-L. 1994. The Expansion of the Chinese Urban System, 1953–1990. *Urban Geography* 15 (6): 514–36.

Hu, Y., and N. Goldman. 1990. Mortality Differentials by Marital Status: An International Comparison. *Demography* 27:233–50.

Hudson, V. M., and A. M. den Boer. 2004. *Bare Branches: The Security Implications of Asia's Surplus Male Population*. Cambrindge, MA: MIT Press.

Huie, B., P. M. Krueger, R. G. Rogers, and R. A. Hummer. 2003. Wealth, Race, and Mortality. *Social Science Quarterly* 84 (3): 667–84.

Hume, D. 1752 [1963]. Of the Populousness of Ancient Nations. In *Essays: Moral, Political and Literary*, ed. D. Hume. London: Oxford.

Hummer, R. A., D. A. Powers, S. G. Pullum, G. L. Gossman, and W. P. Frisbie. 2007. Paradox Found (Again): Infant Mortality Among the Mexican-Origin Population in the United States. *Demography* 44 (3): 441–57.

Hummer, R. A., R. G. Rogers, C. B. Nam, and F. B. LeClere. 1999. Race/Ethnicity, Nativity, and U.S. Adult Mortality. *Social Science Quarterly* 80 (1): 136–53.

Hunter, L. M. 2005. Migration and Environmental Hazards. *Population and Environment* 26:273–302.

Huntington, S. P. 1996. *The Clash of Civilizations and the Remaking of the World Order*. New York: Simon & Schuster.

Hutchinson, E. P. 1967. *The Population Debate: The Development of Conflicting Theories up to 1900*. Boston: Houghton Mifflin.

Hutzler, C., and S. V. Lawrence. 2003. China Acts to Lower Obstacles to Urban Migration. *Wall Street Journal*, 22 January:A2.

Huzel, J. 1969. Malthus, the Poor Law, and Population in Early Nineteenth-Century England. *Economic History Review* 22:430–52.

———. 1980. The Demographic Impact of the Old Poor Law: More Reflexions on Malthus. *Economic History Review* 33:367–81.

———. 1984. Parson Malthus and the Pelican Inn Protocol: A Reply to Proessor Levine. *Historical Method* 17:25–27.

———. 2006. *The Popularization of Malthus in Early Nineteenth-Century England: Martineau, Cobbett and the Pauper Press*. Aldsershot, UK: Ashgate Publishing Company.

Iacoca, L. w. W. N. 1984. *Iacoca: An Autobiography*. New York: Bantam Books.

Iceland, J., and K. A. Nelson. 2008. Hispanic Segregation in Metropolitan America: Exploring the Multiple Forms of Spatial Assimilation. *American Sociological Review* 73:741–65.

Iceland, J., D. H. Weinberg, and E. Steinmetz. 2002. *Racial and Ethnic Residential Segregation in the United States: 1980–2000*. Washington, DC: U.S. Census Bureau.

Idler, J. E. 2007. *Officially Hispanic: Classification Policy and Identity*. Lanham, MD: Rowman and Littlefield.

INEGI. 2010. *Tasa Global de Fecundidad pro Entidad Federativa, 2000 a 2010*. Available from http://www.inegi.org.mx/est/contenidos/espanol/rutinas/ept.asp?t=mpob17&c=9689.

Inglehart, R., and W. E. Baker. 2000. Modernization, Cultural Change, and the Persistence of Traditional Values. *American Sociological Review* 65:19–51.

Inglehart, R., and P. Norris. 2003. *Rising Tide: Gender Equality and Cultural Change Around the World*. New York: Cambridge University Press.

International Labour Office. 2003. Stop Child Trafficking! *World of Work* 47 (June): 4–6.

International Labour Organization. 2003. *Facts on Women at Work*.. Available from http://www.ilo.org/gender/

———. 2008. *Mekong Sub-regional Project to Combat Trafficking in Children and Women*. Available from http://www.ilo.org/public/english/region/asro/bangkok/child/trafficking/downloads/buildingknowledge/meeting-thechallenge.pdf.

IPCC. 2007. Climate Change 2007: Synthesis Report. Contribution of Working Groups I, II, and III to the Fourth Assessment of the Intergovernmental Panel on Climate Change [Core Writing Team, Pachuri, R.K., and Reisinger, A. (eds.)]. Geneva, Switzerland: IPCC.

Iraq Body Count. 2010. *Iraq Body Count* 2010 [cited 2010. Available from http://www.iraqbodycount.org/.

Isaacs, S., and R. Cook. 1984. *Laws and Policies Affecting Fertility: A Decade of Change*. Baltimore, MD: The Johns Hopkins University.

Islam, M. M., and M. M. Uddin. 2001. Female Circumcision in Sudan: Future Prospects and Strategies for Eradication. *International Family Planning Perspectives* 27 (2): 71–76.

Israel Central Bureau of Statistics. 2010. *Statistical Abstract of Israel 2009*. Available from http://cbs.gov.il/reader/.

Issawi, C. 1987. *An Arab Philosophy of History: Selections from the Prolegomena of Ibn Khaldun of Tunis (1332–1406)*. Princeton, NJ: Princeton University Press.

Jain, A. 1998. Population Policies That Matter. In *Do Population Policies Matter? Fertility and Politics in Egypt, India, Kenya, and Mexico*, ed. A. Jain. New York: The Population Council.

James, E., A. Cox Edwards, and A. Iglesias. 2010. *Chile's New Pension Reforms*. National Center for Policy Analysis 2010 [cited 2010]. Available from http://www.ncpa.org/pub/st326.

James, P. 1979. *Population Malthus: His Life and Times*. London: Routledge & Kegan Paul.

Jasso, G., D. S. Massey, M. R. Rosenzweig, and J. P. Smith. 2000. The New Immigrant Survey Pilot (NIS-P): Overview and New Findings About U.S. Legal Immigrants at Admission. *Demography* 37 (1): 127–38.

Jejeebhoy, S. J. 1998. Associations Between Wife-Beating and Fetal and Infant Death: Impressions from a Survey in Rural India. *Studies in Family Planning* 29 (3): 300–308.

Jenkins, J. C., and S. Scanlan. 2001. Food Security in Less Developed Countries, 1970 to 1990. *American Sociological Review* 66 (October): 718–44.

Jeon, Y., and M. P. Shields. 2005. The Easterlin Hypothesis in the Recent Experience of Higher-Income OECD Countries: A Panel-Data Approach. *Journal of Population Economics* 18:1–13.

Johnson, A. W., and T. Earle. 1987. *The Evolution of Human Societies: From Foraging Group to Agrarian Societies*. Stanford, CA: Stanford University Press.

Johnson, K. M., and D. T. Lichter. 2008. Natural Increase: A New Source of Population Growth in Emerging Hispanic Destinations in the United States. *Population and Development Review* 34 (2): 327–46.

Johnson, N. 2000. Marital Status and Mortality: The National Longitudinal Mortality Study. *Annals of Epidemiology* 10 (4): 224–38.

Johnson, N. J., P. D. Sorlie, and E. Backlund. 1999. The Impact of Specific Occupation on Mortality in the U.S. National Longitudinal Mortality Study. *Demography* 36 (3): 355–67.

Jones, C. 2002. *The Great Nation: France from Louis XV to Napolean 1715–99*. New York: Columbia University Press.

Jones, R. 1988. A Behavioral Model for Breastfeeding Effects on Return to Menses Postpartum in Javanese Women. *Social Biology* 35:307–23.

Judis, J. B., and R. Teixeira. 2002. *The Emerging Democratic Majority*. New York: Scribner.

Kahn, J., and W. Mason. 1987. Political Alienation, Cohort Size, and the Easterlin Hypothesis. *American Sociological Review* 52:155–69.

Kalbach, W. E., and W. W. McVey. 1979. *The Demographic Bases of Canadian Society, Second Edition*. Toronto: McGraw-Hill Ryerson Limited.

Kalleberg, A. L., B. F. Reskin, and K. Hudson. 2000. Bad Jobs in America: Standard and Nonstandard Employment Relations and Job Quality in the United States. *American Sociological Review* 65:256–78.

Kanaiaupuni, S. M., and K. M. Donato. 1999. Migradollars and Mortality: The Effects of Migration on Infant Survival in Mexico. *Demography* 36 (3): 339–53.

Kannisto, V. 2001. Mode and Dispersion of the Length of Life. *Population: An English Selection* 13 (1): 159–72.

Kaplan, C., and T. Van Valey. 1980. *Census 80: Continuing the Factfinder Tradition*. Washington, D.C.: U.S. Bureau of the Census.

Kaplan, D. 1994. Population and Politics in a Plural Society: The Changing Geography of Canada's Linguistic Groups. *Annals of the Association of American Geographers* 84 (1): 46–67.

Kaplan, R., and R. Kronick. 2006. Marital Status and Longevity in the United States. *Jounral of Epidemiology and Community Health* 60:760–65.

Kaplan, R. D. 2000. *The Coming Anarchy: Shattering the Dreams of the Post Cold War*. New York: Vintage Books.

Kaplowitz, P. B., and S. E. Oberfield. 1999. Reexamination of the Age Limit for Defining When Puberty is Precocious in Girls in the United States: Implications for Evaluation and Treatment. *Pediatrics* 104 (4): 936–41.

Kasarda, J. 1995. Industrial Restructuring and the Changing Location of Jobs. In *State of the Union: America in the 1990s, Volume One: Economic Trends*, ed. R. Farley. New York: Russell Sage Foundation.

Kasinitz, P., J. H. Millenkopf, M. C. Waters, and J. Holdaway. 2008. *Inheriting the City: The Children of Immigrants Come of Age*. New York: Russell Sage Foundation.

Kazemi, F. 1980. *Poverty and Revolution in Iran*. New York: New York University Press.

Keely, C. 1971. Effects of the Immigration Act of 1965 on Selected Population Characteristics of Immigrants to the United States. *Demography* 8:157–70.

Kempe, F. 2006. Thinking Global: Demographic Time Bomb Ticks On. *Wall Street Journal*, 6 June:A10.

Kemper, R. V. 1977. *Migration and Adaptation*. Beverly Hills, CA: Sage Publications.

———. 1991. Migracion Sin Fronteras: El Caso del Pueblo de Tzintzuntzan, Michoacan, 1945–1990. In *Migración y Fronteras*, ed. S. M. d. Antropología. Mexico, DF: Mesa Redonda.

———. 1996. Migration and Adaptation: Tzintzuntzenos in Mexico City and Beyond. In *Urban Life: Readings in Urban Anthropology, 3rd Edition*, eds. G. Gmelch and W. P. Zenner. Prospect Heights, IL: Waveland Press.

Kemper, R. V., and G. Foster. 1975. Urbanization in Mexico: The View From Tzintzuntzan. *Latin American Urban Research* 5:53–75.

Kennedy, S., and L. Bumpass. 2008. Cohabitation and Children's Living Arrangements: New Estimates from the United States. *Demographic Research* 19:1663–92.

Kephart, W. 1982. *Extraordinary Groups: The Sociology of Unconventional Life-Styles, 2nd Edition*. New York: St. Martins Press.

Kertzer, D. I. 1993. *Sacrificed for Honor: Italian Infant Abandonment and the Politics of Reproductive Control*. Boston: Beacon Press.

———. 1995. Toward a Historical Demography of Aging. In *Aging in the Past: Demography, Society, and Old Age*, eds. D. I. Kertzer and P. Laslett. Berkeley: University of California Press.

Kertzer, D. I., and D. P. Hogan. 1989. *Family, Political Economy, and Demographic Change: The Transformation of Life in Casalecchio, Italy, 1861–1921*. Madison: University of Wisconsin Press.

Kertzer, D. I., M. J. White, L. Bernardi, and G. Gabrielli. 2009. Italy's Path to Very Low Fertility: The Adequacy of Economic and Second Demographic Transition Theories. *European Journal of Population* 25: 89–115.

Keyfitz, N. 1966. How Many People Have Ever Lived on the Earth? *Demography* 3 (2): 581–82.

———. 1968. *Introduction to the Mathematics of Population*. Reading, MA: Addison-Wesley.

———. 1971. On the Momentum of Population Growth. *Demography* 8 (1): 71–80.

———. 1972. Population Theory and Doctrine: A Historical Survey. In *Readings in Population*, ed. W. Petersen. New York: MacMillan.

———. 1973. Population Theory. In *The Determinants and Consequences of Population Trends, Volume I*, ed. U. Nations, Chapter III. New York: United Nations.

———. 1982. Can Knowledge Improve Forecasts? *Population and Development Review* 8 (4): 729–51.

Keyfitz, N., and H. Caswell. 2005. *Applied Mathematical Demography, Third Edition*. New York: John Wiley & Sons, Inc.

Khan, M., and C. Prasad. 1985. A Comparison of 1970 and 1980 Survey Findings on Family Planning in India. *Studies in Family Planning* 16 (6): 312–20.

Khawaja, M. 2000. The recent rise in Palestinian fertility: Permanent or transient? *Population Studies* 54 (3): 331–46.

Khawaja, M., and S. Randall. 2006. Intifada, Palestinian Fertility and Women's Education. *Genus* 62 (1): 21–51.

Kholer, H.-P., F. C. Billari, and J. A. Ortega. 2006. Low Fertility in Europe: Causes, Implications, and Policy Options. In *The Baby Bust: Who Will Do the Work? Who Will Pay the Taxes?*, ed. F. R. Harris. Lanham, MD: Rowman & Littlefield Publishers, Inc.

Kim, Y. J., and R. Schoen. 1997. Population Momentum Expresses Population Aging. *Demography* 34 (3): 421–28.

King, N., Jr., and Y. J. Dreazen. 2007. Iraqi Refugees Create Quandary. *Wall Street Journal* (24 May): A6.

Kinsella, K., and Wan He. 2009. An Aging World: 2008. Washington, DC: U.S. Census Bureau.

Kirk, D. 1946. *Europe's Population in the Interwar Years*. Geneva, Switzerland: League of Nations.

Kisker, E., and N. Goldman. 1987. Perils of Single Life and Benefits of Marriage. *Social Biology* 34 (3–4): 135–52.

Kitagawa, E., and P. Hauser. 1973. *Differential Mortality in the United States: A Study in Socioeconomic Epidemiology*. Cambridge, MA: Harvard University Press.

Klatsky, A. L., and G. D. Friedman. 1995. Annotation: Alcohol and Longevity. *American Journal of Public Health* 85 (1): 16–18.

Kline, J., Z. Stein, and M. Susser. 1989. *Conception to Birth: Epidemiology of Prenatal Development*. New York: Oxford University Press.

Knodel, J. 1970. Two and a Half Centuries of Demographic History in a Bavarian Village. *Population Studies* 24:353–69.

Knodel, J., and E. van de Walle. 1979. Lessons From the Past: Policy Implications of Historical Fertility Studies. *Population and Development Review* 5:217–45.

Knorr-Held, L., and E. Rainer. 2001. Projections of Lung Cancer Mortality in West Germany: A Case Study in Bayesian Prediction. *Biostatistics* 2:109–129.

Kohler, I., S. H. Preston, and L. B. Lackey. 2006. Comparative Mortality Levels among Selected Species of Captive Animals. *Demographic Research* 15 (14): 413–34.

Komlos, J. 1989. The Age at Menarche in Vienna: the Relationship between Nutrition and Fertility. *Historical Methods* 22:158–63.

Konner, M., and C. Worthman. 1980. Nursing Frequency, Gonadal Function, and Birth Spacing Among Kung Hunter-Gatherers. *Science* 207:788–91.

Koonin, L. M., L. T. Strauss, C. E. Chrisman, and W. Y. Parker. 2000. Abortion Surveillance—United States, 1997. *Mortality and Morbidity Weekly Report* 49 (SS11): 1–44.

Korenromp, E. L., B. G. Williams, E. Gouwa, C. Dye, and R. W. Snow. 2003. Measurement of Trends in Childhood Malaria Mortality in Africa: An Assessment of Progress Toward Targets Based on Verbal Autopsy. *The Lancet Infectious Diseases* 3 (6): 349–58.

Krach, C. A., and V. A. Velkoff. 1999. Centenarians in the United States: 1990. *Current Population Reports* (P23–199RV).

Kraly, E. P., and R. Warren. 1992. Estimates of Long-Term Immigrationto the United States: Moving US Statistics Toward United Nations Concepts. *Demography* 29 (4): 613–26.

Kranhold, K. 1999. Food Woos 'Echo Boomers' With Live TV. *Wall Street Journal*, 13 August:B8.

Kravdal, Ø. 2010. Demographers' Interest in Fertility Trends and Determinants in Developed Countries: Is it Warranted? *Demographic Research* 22 (22): 663–90.

Kravdal, Ø., and R. R. Rindfuss. 2008. Changing Relationships between Education and Fertility: A Study of Women and Men Born 1940 to 1964. *American Sociological Review* 73:854–73.

Kreager, P. 1986. Demographic Regimes as Cultural Systems. In *The State of Population Theory: Forward From Malthus*, eds. D. Coleman and R. Schofield. Oxford: Basil Blackwell.

———. 1988. New Light on Graunt. *Population Studies* 42 (1): 129–40.

———. 1993. Histories of Demography: A Review Article. *Population Studies* 47 (3): 519–39.

Kreider, R. M., and J. M. Fields. 2002. Number, Timing, and Duration of Marriages and Divorces: 1996. *Current Population Reports* P70–80.

Krellenberg, K., D. Heinrichs, and J. Barton. 2010. Climate and Adaptation Strategies in Latin American City-Regions: The Case of Santiago de Chile. *UGEC Viewpoints (Arizona State University Global Institute of Sustainability)* (3): 4–7.

Krueger, A. 2009. Support for Iraqi Immgrants "Maxed Out." *San Diego Union-Tribune* (7 November): B1.

Krunholz, J. 2006. Census Officials' Departure Revives Sampling Debate. *Wall Street Journal*, 16 November:A10.

Kuijsten, A. 1999. Households, Families and Kin Networks. In *Population Issues: An Interdisciplinary Focus*, eds. L. J. G. van Wissen and P. A. Dykstra. New York: Kluwer Academic/Plenum Publishers.

Kulu, H. 2005. Migration and Fertility: Competing Hypotheses Re-examined. *European Journal of Population* 21 (1): 51–87.

Kunitz, S. J. 1994. *Disease and Social Diversity: The European Impact on the Health of Non-Europeans*. New York: Oxford University Press.

Kunstler, J. H. 1993. *The Geography of Nowhere: The Rise and Decline of America's Man-Made Landscape*. New York: Simon & Schuster.

Lacey, R. 2009. *Inside the Kingdom: Kings, Clerics, Modernists, Terrorists, and the Struggle for Saudi Arabia*. New York: Viking.

Lalasz, R. 2006. In the News: The Nigerian Census: PRB On-Line.

Landers, J. 1993. *Death and the Metropolis: Studies in the Demographic History of London 1670–1830*. Cambridge, UK: Cambridge University Press.

Larsen, U. 2000. Primary and Secondary Infertility in sub-Saharan Africa. *International Journal of Epidemiology* 29:285–91.

Larsen, U., and S. Yan. 2000. Does Female Circumcision Affect Infertility and Fertility? A Study of the Central African Republic, Cote d'Ivoire, and Tanzania. *Demography* 37 (3): 313–21.

Laslett, P. 1971. *The World We Have Lost*. London: Routledge & Kegan Paul.

———. 1991. *A Fresh Map of Life: The Emergence of the Third Age*. Cambridge, MA: Harvard University Press.

Laxton, P. 1987. *London Bills of Mortality*. Cambridge, UK: Chadwyk-Healey Ltd.

Leasure, J. W. 1962. Factors Involved in the Decline of Fertility in Spain: 1900–1950. Doctoral thesis, Economics, Princeton University, Princeton, NJ.

———. 1982. L' Baisse de la Fecondité aux États-Unis de 1800 a 1860. *Population* 3:607–22.

———. 1989. A Hypothesis About the Decline of Fertility: Evidence From the United States. *European Journal of Population* 5:105–17.

Lee, E. 1966. A Theory of Migration. *Demography* 3:47–57.

Lee, J. Z., and Wang Feng. 1999. *One Quarter of Humanity: Malthusian Mythology and Chinese Realities*. Cambridge, MA: Harvard University Press.

Lee, R. 1976. Demographic Forecasting and the Easterlin Hypothesis. *Population and Development Review* 2:459–68.

———. 1987. Population Dynamics in Humans and Other Animals. *Demography* 24:443–65.

Lee, R. B. 1972. Population Growth and the Beginnings of Sedentary Life Among the Kung Bushmen. In *Population Growth: Anthropological Implications*, ed. B. Spooner. Cambridge, MA: MIT Press.

Leibenstein, H. 1957. *Economic Backwardness and Economic Growth*. New York: John Wiley & Sons.

Lengyel-Cook, M., and R. Repetto. 1982. The Relevance of the Developing Countries to Demographic Transition Theory: Further Lessons from the Hungarian Experience. *Population Studies* 36 (1):105–28.

Leroux, C. 1984. Ellis Island. *San Diego Union* 26 May.

Lesthaeghe, R. J. 1977. *The Decline of Belgian Fertility, 1800–1970*. Princeton: Princeton University Press.

Lesthaeghe, R. J., and J. Surkyn. 1988. Cultural Dynamics and Economic Theories of Fertility Change. *Population and Development Review* 14:1–45.

Levitt, P., J. DeWind, and S. Vertovec. 2003. International Perspectives on Transnational Migration: An Introduction. *International Migration Review* 37 (3): 565–75.

Levy, S., G. R. Frerichs, and H. L. Gordon eds. 1994. *The Dartnell Marketing Manager's Handbook*. Chicago: Dartnell Corporation.

Lewis, B. 1995. *The Middle East: A Brief History of the Last 2,000 Years*. New York: Scribner.

Lexis, W. 1875. *Einleitung ein die Theorie der Bevölkerungs-Statistik*. Strasbourg: Trubner.

Li, N., and S. Tuljapurkar. 1999. Population Momentum for Gradual Demographic Transitions. *Population Studies* 53:255–62.

Lightbourne, R., S. Singh, and C. Green. 1982. The World Fertility Survey. *Population Bulletin* 37 (1).

Lillard, L. A., and C. W. A. Panis. 1996. Marital Status and Mortality: The Role of Health. *Demography* 33 (3): 313–27.

Linder, F. 1959. World Demographic Data. In *The Study of Population: An Inventory and Appraisal*, eds. P. M. Hauser and O. D. Duncan. Chicago: University of Chicago Press.

Lindh, T., and B. Malmberg. 1999. Age Structure Effects and Growth in the OECD, 1950–1990. *Journal of Population Economics* 12:431–49.

Lingappa, J., L. McDonald, P. Simone, and U. Parashar. 2004. Wresting SARS from uncertainty. *Emerging Infectious Diseases* 10 (2):[serial online].

Livi Bacci, M. 1991. *Population and Nutrition: An Essay on European Demographic History*. Cambridge, UK: Cambridge University Press.

———. 2000. *The Population of Europe*. Oxford: Blackwell Publishers.

Livi-Bacci, M. 2001. *A Concise History of World Population, Third Edition*. Malden, MA: Blackwell Publishers, Ltd.

Lloyd, C. B., and S. Ivanov. 1988. The Effects of Improved Child Survival on Family Planning Practice and Fertility. *Studies in Family Planning* 19 (3): 141–61.

Logan, J. R., R. Alba, and W. Zhang. 2002. Immigrant Enclaves and Ethnic communities in New York and Los Angeles. *American Sociological Review* 67 (2): 299–322.

Lollock, L. 2001. Foreign-Born Population in the United States: March 2000. *Current Population Reports* (P20–534).

London, B. 1987. Structural Determinants of Third World Urban Change: An Ecological and Political Economic Analysis. *American Sociological Review* 52:28–43.

Long, L. 1988. *Migration and Residential Mobility in the United States*. New York: Russell Sage Foundation.

Longley, P., and M. Batty. 1996. Analysis, Modelling, Forecasting, and GIS Technology. In *Spatial Analysis: Modelling in a GIS Environment*, eds. P. Longley and M. Batty. New York: John Wiley & Sons.

Lopez, A. D., C. D. Mathers, M. Ezzati, D. T. Jamison, and C. J. L. Murray. 2006a. *Global Burden of Disease and Risk Factors*. New York: Oxford University Press.

———. 2006b. Measuring the Global Burden of Disease and Risk Factors, 1990–2001. In *Global Burden of Disease and Risk Factors*, eds. A. D. Lopez, C. D. Mathers, M. Ezzati, D. T. Jamison and C. J. L. Murray. New York: Oxford University Press.

Lorimer, F. 1946. *The Population of the Soviet Union: History and Prospects*. Geneva, Switzerland: League of Nations.

———. 1959. The Development of Demography. In *The Study of Population*, eds. P. M. Hauser and O. D. Duncan. Chicago: University of Chicago Press.

Lovejoy, P. E., and J. S. Hogendorn. 1993. *Slow Death for Slavery: The Course of Abolition in Northern Nigeria 1897–1936*. New York: Cambridge University Press.

Low, N., B. Gleeson, R. Green, and D. Radovic. 2005. *The Green City: Sustainable Homes, Sustainable Suburbs*. Oxfordshire, UK: Routledge.

Lu, D., M. Batistell, P. Mausel, and E. Moran. 2007. Mapping and Monitoring Land Degradation Risks in the Western Brazilian Amazon Using Multitemporal Landsat TM/ETM+ Images. *Land Degradatin and Development* 18:41–54.

Lutz, W. 2007. Adaptation Viersus Mitigation Policies on Demographic Change in Europe. *Vienna Yearbook of Population Research 2007*:19–26.

———. 2009. What Can Demographers Contribute to Understanding the Link Between Population and Climate Change. *PopNet (Population Network Newsletter of IIASA)* 41 (Winter): 1–2.

Lutz, W., B. C. O'Neill, and S. Scherbov. 2003. Europe's Population at a Turning Point. *Science* 299:1991–92.

Lutz, W., W. C. Sanderson, and S. Scherbov. 2008. *IIASA's 2007 Probabilistic World Population Projections, IIASA World Population Program Online Data Base of Results*. 2008 [cited. Available from http://www.iiasa.ac.at/Research/POP/proj07/index.html?sb=5.

——— eds. 2004. *The End of World Population Growth in the 21st Century: New Challenges for Human Capital Formation and Sustainable Development*. London: Earthscan.

Lutz, W., and M. Shah. 2002. *Population in Sustainable Development*. Global Science Panel on Population & Environment 2002 [cited 2003]. Available from http://www.iiasa.ac.at/Admin/INF/hague/GSP_final_statement.pdf

Lynch, S. M., and J. S. Brown. 2001. Reconsidering Mortality Compression and Deceleration: An Alternative Model of Mortality Rates. *Demography* 38 (1): 79–95.

Ma, L. J. C., and C. Cartier eds. 2003. *The Chinese Diaspora: Space, Place, Mobility, and Identity*. Lanham, MD: Rowman & Littlefield.

MacDonald, A. 2008. U.K. Cuts Immigration as Economy Slows Down. *Wall Street Journal*, 6 December:A6.

MacIntyre, S., and A. Ellaway. 2003. Neighborhoods and Health: An Overview. In *Neighborhoods and Health*, eds. I. Kawachi and L. F. Berkman. Oxford: Oxford University Press.

Mackie, G. 1996. Ending Footbinding and Infibulation: A Convention Account. *American Sociological Review* 61:999–1017.

Macunovich, D. J. 2000. Relative Cohort Size: Source of a Unifying Theory of Global Fertility Transition? *Population and Development Review* 26 (2): 235–61.

Makinwa-Adebusoye, P. 1994. Report of the Seminar on Women and Demographic Change in Sub-Saharan Africa, Dakar, Senegal, 3–6 March 1993. *IUSSP Newsletter* January–April:43–48.

Maloutas, T. 2004. Segregation and Residential Mobility: Spatially Entrapped Social Mobility and its Impact on Segregation in Athens. *European Urban and Regional Studies* 11 (3): 195–211.

Malthus, T. R. 1798 [1965]. *An Essay on Population*. New York: Augustus Kelley.

———. 1872 [1971]. *An Essay on the the Principle of Population, Seventh Edition*. London: Reeves & Turner.

Mandelbaum, D. 1974. *Human Fertility in India*. Berkeley: University of California Press.

Manson, G. A., and R. E. Groop. 2000. U.S. Intercounty Migration in the 1990s: People and Income Move Down the Urban Hierarchy. *Professional Geographer* 52 (3): 493–504.

Manton, K. G., and K. C. Land. 2000. Active Life Expectancy Estimates for the U.S. Elderly Population: A Multidimensional Continuous-Mixture Model of Functional Change Applied to Completed Cohorts, 1982–1996. *Demography* 37 (3): 253–66.

Manton, K. G., E. Stallard, and L. Corder. 1997. Changes in the Age Dependence of Mortality and Disability: Cohort and Other Determinants. *Demography* 34 (1): 135–57.

Marcoux, A. 2000. *Population and Deforestation (SD Dimensions Program of the FAO)*. United Nations Food and Agriculture Organization 2000 [cited 2007]. Available from http://www.fao.org/sd/wpdirect/WPan0050.htm.

Marini, M. M., and P.-L. Fan. 1997. The Gender Gap in Earnings at Career Entry. *American Sociological Review* 62:588–604.

Martin, J. A., B. E. Hamilton, P. D. Sutton, S. J. Ventura, F. Menacker, S. Kimeyer, and T. J. Mathews. 2009. Births: Final Data for 2006. *National Vital Statistics Reports* 57 (7):Hyattsville, MD: National Center for Health Statistics.

Martine, G. 1996. Brazil's Fertility Decline, 1965–95: A Fresh Look at Key Factors. *Population and Development Review* 22 (1): 47–75.

Marx, K. 1890 [1906]. *Capital: A Critique of Political Economy, translated from the Third German Edition by*

Samuel Moore and Edward Aveling and Edited by Frederich Engels. New York: The Modern Library.

Mason, A. 1988. Saving, Economic Growth, and Demographic Change. *Population and Development Review* 14 (1): 113–44.

Mason, K. O. 1997. Explaining Fertility Transitions. *Demography* 34 (4): 443–54.

Massey, D. 1996a. The Age of Extremes: Concentrated Affluence and Poverty in the Twenty-First Century. *Demography* 33 (4): 395–412.

———. 1996b. The False Legacy of the 1965 Immigration Act. *World on the Move: Newsletter of the Section on International Migration of the American Sociological Association* 2 (2): 2–3.

——— ed. 2008. *New Faces in New Places: The Changing Geography of American Immigration*. New York: Russell Sage Foundation.

Massey, D., J. Arango, G. Hugo, A. Kouaouci, A. Pellegrino, and J. E. Taylor. 1993. Theories of International Migration: A Review and Appraisal. *Population and Development Review* 19 (3): 431–66.

———. 1994. An Evaluation of International Migration Theory: The North American Case. *Population and Development Review* 20 (4): 699–752.

Massey, D., and N. Denton. 1993. *American Aprtheid: Segregation and the Making of the Underclass*. Cambridge, MA: Harvard University Press.

Massey, D., and K. Espinosa. 1997. What's Driving Mexico–U.S. Migration? A Theoretical, Empirical, and Policy Analysis. *American Journal of Sociology* 102 (4): 939–99.

Massey, D. S. 2002. A Brief History of Human Society: The Origin and Role of Emotion in Social Life. *American Sociological Review* 67:1–29.

Massey, D. S., J. Durand, and N. J. Malone. 2002. *Beyond Smoke and Mirrors: Mexican Immigration in an Era of Economic Integration*. New York: Russell Sage Foundation.

Mather, M., K. L. Rivers, and L. A. Jacobsen. 2005. The American Community Survey. *Population Bulletin* 60 (3).

Mathews, Z., S. Padmadas, I. Hutter, J. McEachran, and J. J. Brown. 2009. Does Early Childbearing and a Sterlization-Focused Family Planning Program in India Fuel Population Growth? *Demographic Research* 20 (28): 693–720.

Maume, D. 1983. Metropolitan Hierarchy and Income Distribution: A Comparison of Explanations. *Urban Affairs Quarterly* 18: 413–29.

Mayhew, B., and R. Levinger. 1976. Size and the Density of Interaction in Human Aggregates. *American Journal of Sociology* 82 (1): 86–109.

McCaa, R. 1994. Child Marriage and Complex Families Among the Nahuas of Ancient Mexico. *Latin American Population History* (26): 2–11.

McCall, L. 2000. Gender and the New Inequality: Explaining the College/Non-College Wage Gap. *American Sociological Review* 65:234–55.

McDaniel, A. 1992. Extreme Mortality in Nineteenth Century Africa: The Case of Liberian Immigrants. *Demography* 29 (4): 581–94.

———. 1995. *Swing Low, Sweet Chariot: The Mortality Cost of Colonizing Liberia in the Nineteenth Century*. Chicago: University of Chicago Press.

———. 1996. Fertility and Racial Stratification. In *Fertility in the United States: New Patterns, New Theories*, eds. J. B. Casterline, R. D. Lee and K. Foote. New York: The Population Council.

McDonald, P. 1993. Fertility Transition Hypothesis. In *The Revolution in Asian Fertility: Dimensions, Causes, and Implications*, eds. R. Leete and I. Alam. Oxford: Clarendon Press.

———. 2000. Gender Equity in Theories of Fertility Transition. *Population and Development Review* 26 (3): 427–39.

McEvedy, C., and R. Jones. 1978. *Atlas of World Population History*. New York: Penguin Books.

McFalls, J., and M. McFall. 1984. *Disease and Fertility*. New York: Academic Press.

McFarlan, D., N. McWhirter, M. McCarthey, and M. Young. 1991. *The Guinness Book of World Records*. New York: Bantam Books.

McGinnis, J. M., and W. H. Foege. 1993. Actual Causes of Death in the United States. *Journal of the American Medical Association* 270 (18): 2207–12.

McKeown, T. 1976. *The Modern Rise of Population*. London: Edward Arnold.

———. 1988. *The Origins of Human Disease*. Oxford: Basil Blackwell.

McKeown, T., and R. Record. 1962. Reasons for the Decline of Mortality in England and Wales during the 19th Century. *Population Studies* 16 (2): 94–122.

McKinnish, T., R. Walsh, and T. K. White. 2010. Who Gentrifies Low-Income Neighborhoods? *Journal of Urban Economics* 67:180–93.

McLanahan, S., and L. Casper. 1995. Growing Diversity and Inequality in the American Family. In *State of the Union: America in the 1990s, Volume Two: Social Trends*, ed. R. Farley. New York: Russell Sage Foundation.

McLanahan, S., and G. Sandefur. 1994. *Growing Up With a Single Parent: What Hurts, What Helps*. Cambridge, MA: Harvard University Press.

McNeill, W. H. 1976. *Plagues and People*. New York: Doubleday.

McQuillan, K. 2004. When Does Religion Influence Fertility? *Population and Development Review* 30 (1): 25–56.

Meade, M. S., and R. J. Earickson. 2000. *Medical Geography, Second Edition*. New York: The Guilford Press.

Meadows, D. 1974. *Dynamics of Growth in a Finite World*. Cambridge, MA: Wright-Allen Press.

Meadows, D. H., D. L. Meadows, J. Randers, and W. Bherens III. 1972. *The Limits to Growth*. New York: The American Library.

Measure DHS. 2010. *Demographic and Health Survey STATcompiler* 2010 [cited 2010]. Available from http://www.statcompiler.com/.

Meek, R. 1971. *Marx and Engels on the Population Bomb*. Berkeley, CA: Ramparts Press.

Mendes, A. B., and I. H. Themido. 2004. Multi-outlet Retail Site Location Assessment. *International Transactions in Operation Research* 11:1–18.

Mennis, J. L., and L. Jordan. 2005. The Distribution of Environmental Equity: Exploring Spatial Nonstationarity in Multivariate Models of Air Toxic Releases. *Annals of the Association of American Geographers* 95 (2): 249–68.

Mesquida, C. G., and N. I. Wiener. 1999. Male Age Composition and Severity of Conflicts. *Politics and the Life Sciences* 18 (2): 181–89.

Messersmith, L. J., T. T. Kane, A. I. Odebiyi, and A. A. Adewuyi. 2000. Who's at Risk? Men's STD Experience and Condom Use in Southwest Nigeria. *Studies in Family Planning* 31 (3): 203–16.

Metchnikoff, E. 1908. *Prolongation of Life*. New York: Putnam.

Mhloyi, M. 1994. *Status of Women, Population and Development*. Liège: International Union for the Scientific Study of Population.

Mier y Terán, M. 1991. El Gran Cambio Demográfico. *Demos* 4:4–5.

Migration News. 1998. Canada: Immigration, Diversity Up. *Migration News* 5 (1).

Migration Policy Institute. 2010. *Global City Migration Map*. Migration Policy Institute 2010 [cited 2010]. Available from http://www.migrationinformation.org/DataHub/gcmm.cfm.

Mill, J. S. 1848 [1929]. *Principles of Political Economy*. London: Longmans & Green.

———. 1873 [1924]. *Autobiography*. London: Oxford University Press.

Miller, G. T. 2004. *Living in the Environment: Principles, Connections and Solutions, 13th Edition*. Belmont, CA: Brooks/Cole Thomson Learning.

———. 2009. *Living in the Environment: Principles, Connections, and Solutions, 16th Edition*. Belmont, CA: Wadsworth/Cengage.

Millman, J., and C. Vitzthum. 2003. Changing Tide: Europe Becomes New Destination for Latino Workers. *Wall Street Journal*, 12 September:A2.

Ministry of Management Services [Canada]. 2003. How many people were missed in the 2001 census? *BC Stats, Population Section*.

Moch, L. P. 1992. *Moving Europeans: Migration in Western Europe Since 1650*. Bloomington: Indiana University Press.

Mock, G. 2000. *Domesticating the World: Conversion of Natural Ecosystems*. World Resources Institute 2000 [cited 2007]. Available from http://earthtrends.wri.org/text/agriculture-food/feature-34.html.

Moffett, S. 2005. Fast-Aging Japan Keeps Its Elders on the Job Longer. *Wall Street Journal*, 15 June:A9.

———. 2006. Abe has Remedy to Spur Japan: Open up the Economy. *Wall Street Journal*, 2 November:A4.

Mohai, P., and R. Saha. 2006. Reassessing Racial and Socioeconomic Disparities in Environmental Justice Research. *Demography* 43 (2): 383–99.

Mokdad, A. H., J. S. Marks, D. F. Stroup, and J. L. Gerberding. 2004. Actual Causes of Death in the United States, 2000. *Journal of the American Medical Association* 291:1238–45.

Moller, H. 1968. Youth as a Force in the Modern World. *Comparative Studies in Society and History* 10 (3): 237–60.

Monteverde, M., K. Noronha, A. Palloni, and B. Novak. 2010. Obesity and Excess Mortality Among the Elderly in the United States and Mexico. *Demography* 47 (1): 79–96.

Montgomery, M. 2009. Urban Poverty and Health in Developing Countries. *Population Bulletin* 64 (2).

Montgomery, M., and B. Cohen eds. 1998. *From Death to Birth: Mortality Decline and Reproductive Change*. Washington, DC: National Academy Press.

Montgomery, M., and P. C. Hewett. 2005. Urban Poverty and Health in Developing Countries: Household and Neighborhood Effects. *Demography* 42 (3): 397–25.

Montgomery, M. R., R. Stren, B. Cohen, and H. Reed eds. 2003. *Cities Transformed: Demographic Change and Its Implications in the Developing World*. Washington, DC: National Academies Press.

Moore, W. E. 1945. *The Economic Demography of Eastern and Southern Europe*. Geneva, Switzerland: League of Nations.

Morelos, J. B. 1994. La Mortalidad en México: Hechos y Consensos. In *La Población en el Desarrollo Contemporáneo de México*, eds. F. Alba and G. Cabrera. Mexico City: El Colegio de Mexico.

Morgan, S. P. 1996. Characteristic Features of Modern American Fertility. In *Fertility in the United States: New Patterns, New Theories*, eds. J. B. Casterline, R. D. Lee and K. A. Foote. New York: Population Council.

———. 2001. Should Fertility Intentions Inform Fertility Forecasts? In *The Direction of Fertility in the United States*, ed. U.S. Census Bureau. Washington, DC: Council of Professional Associations on Federal Statistics.

Morgan, S. P., Guo Zhigang, and S. R. Hayford. 2009. China's Below-Replacement Fertility: Recent Trends and Future Prospects. *Population and Development Review* 35 (3): 605–29.

Morrill, R., J. Cromartie, and G. Hart. 1999. Metropolitan, Urban, and Rural Commuting Areas: Toward a Better Depiction of the United States Settlement System. *Urban Geography* 20 (8): 727–48.

Morrison, P. A., and T. M. Bryan. 2010. Targeting Spatial Clusters of Elderly Consumers in the U.S.A. *Population Research and Policy Review* 29:33–46.

Mosher, S. W. 1983. *Broken Earth: The Rural Chinese*. New York: Free Press.

Mosher, W. D., A. Chandra, and J. Jones. 2005. Sexual Behavior and Selected Health Measures: Men and Women 15–44 Years of Age, United States, 2002. *Advance Data from Vital and Health Statistics* 362.

Mouw, T. 2000. Job Relocation and the Racial Gap in Unemployment in Detroit and Chicago, 1980 to 1990. *American Sociological Review* 65:730–53.

Muhua, C. 1979. For the Realization of the Four Modernizations, There Must be Planned Control of Population Growth. *Excerpted in Population and Development Review* 5:723–30.

Muhuri, P. K., and S. H. Preston. 1991. Effects of Family Composition on Mortality Differentials by Sex Among Children in Matlab, Bangladesh. *Population and Development Review* 17 (3): 415–34.

Mulder, T. J. 2001. Accuracy of the U.S. Census Bureau National Population Projections and Their Respective Components of Change. In *The Direction of Fertility in the United States*, ed. U.S. Census Bureau. Washington, DC: Council of Professional Associations on Federal Statistics.

Muller, P. O. 1997. The Suburban Transformation of the Globalizing American City. *Annals of the American Association of Political and Social Science* 551:44–58.

Mumford, L. 1968. The City: Focus and Funtion. In *International Encyclopedia of the Social Sciences*, ed. D. Sills. New York: Macmillan.

Muñoz-Peréz, F., and F. Prioux. 2000. Children Born Outside Marriage in France and Their Parents: Recognitions and Legitimations Since 1965. *Population: An English Selection* 12:139–196.

Murdock, S., and D. A. Swanson eds. 2008. *Applied Demography at the Beginning of the 21st Century*. Dordrecht, The Netherlands: Springer.

Murdock, S. H., and D. R. Ellis. 1991. *Applied Demography: An Introduction to Basic Concepts, Methods, and Data*. Boulder: Westview Press.

Murray, C. J. L., S. Kulkarni, and M. Ezzati. 2006. Eight Americas: New Perspectives on US Health Disparities. *American Journal of Preventive Medicine* 29:4–10.

Murray, C. J. L., and A. D. Lopez. 1996. *The Global Burden of Disease: A Comprehensive Assessment of Mortality and Disability from Diseases, Injuries, and Risk Factors in 1990 and Projected to 2020*. Cambridge, MA: Harvard University Press.

Mustelin, J., R. G. Klein, B. Assaid, T. Sitari, M. Khamis, A. Mzee, and T. Haji. 2010. Understanding Current and Future Vulnerability in Coastal Settings: Community Perceptions and Preferences for Adaptation in Zanzibar, Tanzania. *Population and Environment* 31:371–98.

Myrdal, G. 1957. *Economic Theory and Underdeveloped Areas*. London: G. Duckworth.

Nag, M. 1962. *Factors Affecting Human Fertility in Non-Industrial Societies: A Cross-Cultural Study*. New Haven: Yale University Press.

Nagata, K. 2008. *Food Self-Sufficiency: Japan Needs Imports to Keep Itself Fed*. JapanTimes.co 2008 [cited 2010]. Available from http://search.japantimes.co.jp/cgi-bin/nn20080226i1.html.

Nalin, D., R. Cash, and R. Islam. 1968. Oral Maintenance Therapy for Cholera in Adults. *Lancet* (2): 370–72.

National Population Commission [Nigeria] and ICF Macro. 2009. *Nigeria Demographic and Health Survey 2008*. Abuja, Nigeria: National Population Commission and ICF Macro.

National Research Council. 1993. *A Census That Mirrors America: Interim Report*. Washington, DC: National Academy Press.

———. 2008. *Energy Futures and Urban Air Pollution: Challenges for China and the United States*. Washington, DC: National Academies Press.

Naujoks, D. 2009. *Emigration, Immigration, and Diaspora Relations in India*. Migration Information Source 2009 [cited 2010]. Available from http://www.migrationinformation.org/Profiles/display.cfm?ID=745.

Nelson, K. L., and A. Murray. 2008. Sanitation for Unserved Populations: Technologies, Implementation Challenges, and Opportunities. *Annual Review of Environment and Resources* 33:119–51.

Netanyahu, B. 1983. West Bank Time Bomb? A Demographic Fallacy. *Wall Street Journal*, 18 October:30.

Nevins, J. 2002. *Operation Gatekeeper: The Rise of the "Illegal Alien" and the Making of the U.S.–Mexico Boundary*. New York: Routledge.

Newsweek. 1974. How to Ease the Hunger Pangs. *Newsweek* 11 November.

Newton, L. 2008. *Illegal, Alien, or Immigrant: The Politics of Immigration Reform*. New York: New York University Press.

Nicholls, W. H. 1970. Development in Agrarian Economies: The Role of Agricultural Surplus, Population Pressures, and Systems of Land Tenure. In *Subsistence Agriculture and Economic Development*, ed. C. Wharton. Chicago: Aldine.

Nickerson, J. 1975. *Homage to Malthus*. Port Washington, NY: National University Publications.

Nielsen, J. 1978. *Sex in Society: Perspectives on Stratification*. Belmont, CA: Wadsworth Publishing Co.

Nizard, A., and F. Muñoz-Pérez. 1994. Alcohol, Smoking and Mortality in France since 1950: An Evaluation of the Number of Deaths in 1986 due to Alcohol and Tobacco Consumption. *Population: An English Selection* 6:159–94.

Nobles, M. 2000. *Shades of Citizenship: Race and the Census in Modern Politics*. Stanford, CA: Stanford University Press.

Nonaka, K., T. Miura, and K. Peter. 1994. Recent Fertility-Decline in Dariusleut Hutterites: An Extension of Eaton and Mayer's Hutterite Fertility. *Human Biology* 66:411–20.

Norris, P., and R. Inglehart. 2004. *Sacred and Secular: Religion and Politics Worldwide*. New York: Cambridge University Press.

Notestein, F., I. Taeuber, D. Kirk, A. Coale, and L. Kiser. 1944. *The Future Population of Europe and the Soviet Union*. Geneva, Switzerland: League of Nations.

Notestein, F. W. 1945. Population—The Long View. In *Food for the World*, ed. T. W. Schultz. Chicago: University of Chicago Press.

Nu'Man, F. 1992. *The Muslim Population in the United States: A Brief Statement*. Washington, D.C.: American Muslim Council.

Nyce, S. A., and S. J. Schreiber. 2005. *The Economic Implications of Aging Societies: The Costs of Living Happily Ever After*. New York: Cambridge University Press.

O'Brien, R. M. 2000. Age Period Cohort Characteristic Models. *Social Science Research* 29:123–39.

O'Donnell, J. J. 2006. *Augustine: A New Biography*. Harper Perennial 2006.

O'Neill, B. C., and B. S. Chen. 2002. Demographic Determinants of Household Energy Use in the United States. *Population and Development Review* 28 (Supplement): 53–88.

O'Neill, B. C., M. F. Landis, and W. Lutz. 2004. Population, Greenhouse Gas Emissions, and Climate Change. In *The End of Population Growth in the 21st Century: New Challenges for Human Capital Formation & Sustainable Development*, eds. W. Lutz, W. C. Sanderson and S. Scherbov. London: Earthscan.

Obaid, T. A. 2009. A Message From Thoraya Ahmed Obaid, UNFPA Executive Director. In *Healthy Expectations: Celebrating Achievements of the Cairo Consensus and Highlighting the Urgency for Action*, eds. United Nations Population Fund (UNFPA) and Population Reference Bureau (PRB). New York and Washington, DC: UNFPA and PRB.

OEDC. 2009. *Educational Attainment by Gender and Average Years Spent in Formal Education*. OECD, Social Policy Division, Directorate of Employment, Labour and Social Affairs 2009 [cited 2010]. Available from http://www.oecd.org/dataoecd/56/9/37863998.pdf.

Oeppen, J. 1993. Back Projection and Inverse Projection: Members of a Wider Class of Constrained Projection Models. *Population Studies* 47 (2): 245–68.

Oeppen, J., and J. W. Vaupel. 2002. Broken Limits to Life Expectancy. *Science* 296 (10): 1029–31.

Ogawa, N., and R. D. Retherford. 1997. Shifting Costs of Caring for the Elderly Back to Families in Japan: Will It Work? *Population and Development Review* 23 (1): 41–58.

Ohlin, G. 1976. Economic Theory Confronts Population Growth. In *Economic Factors in Population Growth*, ed. A. Coale. New York: John Wiley & Sons.

Okolo, A. 1999. The Nigerian Census: Problems and Prospects. *The American Statistician* 53 (4): 321–25.

Olshansky, S. J. 2008. Longevity in the Twenty-first Century. *Population Studies* 62 (2):245–249.

Olshansky, S. J., and B. A. Carnes. 1997. Ever Since Gompertz. *Demography* 34 (1): 1–15.

Olshansky, S. J., L. Hayflick, and B. A. Carnes. 2002. No Truth to the Fountain of Youth. *Scientific American* 286 (6): 92–96.

Omran, A. 1971. The Epidemiological Transition: A Theory of the Epidemiology of Population Change. *Milbank Memorial Fund Quarterly* 49:509–38.

———. 1977. Epidemiologic Transition in the United States. *Population Bulletin* 32 (2).

Omran, A. R. 1973. The Mortality Profile. In *Egypt: Population Problems and Prospects*, ed. A. R. Omran. Chapel Hill: Carolina Population Center.

Omran, A. R., and F. Roudi. 1993. The Middle East Population Puzzle. *Population Bulletin* 48 (1).

Oppenheimer, V. K. 1967. The Interaction of Demand and Supply and Its Effect on the Female Labour Force in the U.S. *Population Studies* 21 (3): 239–59.

———. 1994. Women's Rising Employment and the Future of the Family in Industrializing Societies. *Population and Development Review* 20 (2): 293–342.

Oren, M. B. 2002. *Six Days of War: June 1967 and the Making of the Modern Middle East*. New York: Oxford University Press.

Orshansky, M. 1969. How Poverty is Measured. *Monthly Labor Review* 92 (2): 37–41.

Ortega y Gasset, J. 1932. *The Revolution of the Masses*. New York: W. W. Norton & Company, Inc.

Ortiz de Montellano, B. R. 1975. Empirical Aztec Medicine. *Science* 188:215–20.

Oster, E. 2009. Proximate Sources of Population Sex Imbalance in India. *Demography* 46 (2) 325–39.

Over, M., and O. McCarthy. 2010. *Global Health Policy: Death Toll from Haiti's Earthquake in Perspective*. Center for Global Development 2010 [cited 2010]. Available from http://blogs.cgdev.org/globalhealth/2010/02/death-toll-from-haiti's-earthquake-in-perspective.php.

Overbeek, J. 1980. *Population and Canadian Society*. Toronto: Butterworths.

Palmore, J., and R. Gardner. 1983. *Measuring Mortality, Fertility, and Natural Increase*. Honolulu: East-West Populaiton Institute.

Pampel, F. C. 1993. Relative Cohort Size and Fertility: The Socio-Political Context of the Easterlin Effect. *American Sociological Review* 58:496–514.

———. 1996. Cohort Size and Age-Specific Suicide Rates: A Contingent Relationship. *Demography* 33:341–55.

Pappas, G., S. Queen, W. Hadden, and G. Fisher. 1993. The Increasing Disparity in Mortality Between Socioeconomic Groups in the United States, 1960 and 1986. *The New England Journal of Medicine* 329 (2): 103–9.

Park, C. B., and N. Cho. 1995. Consequences of Son Preference in a Low-Fertility Society: Imbalanceof the Sex Ratio at Birth. *Population and Development Review* 21 (1): 59–84.

Passel, J. S., and D. V. Cohn. 2008. Trends in Unauthorized Immigration: Undocumented Inflow Now Trails Legal Inflow. Washington, DC: Pew Hispanic Center.

———. 2009. A Portrait of Unauthorized Immigrants in the United States. Washington, DC: Pew Hispanic Center.

Pastor, M., Jr., J. Sadd, and J. Hipp. 2001. Which Came First? Toxic Facilities, Minority Move-In, and Environmental Justice. *Journal of Urban Affairs* 23 (1): 1–21.

Peak, C., and J. R. Weeks. 2002. Does Community Context Influence Reproductive Outcomes of Mexican Origin Women in San Diego, California? *Journal of Immigrant Health* 4 (3):125–36.

Pearlman, D. N., S. Zierler, S. Meersman, H. K. Kim, S. Viner-Brown, and C. Caron. 2006. Race Disparities in Childhood Asthma: Does Where You Live Matter? *Journal of the American Medical Association* 98 (2): 239–47.

Peng, P. 1996. Population and Development in China. In *The Population Situation in China: The Insiders' View*, ed. China Population Association and the State Family Planning Commission of China. Liege, Belgium: International Union for the Scientific Study of Population.

Pennisi, E. 2001. Malaria's Beginnings: On the Heels of Hoes? *Science* 293 (5529): 416–17.

Perez, A. D., and C. Hirschman. 2009. The Changing Racial and Ethnic Composition of the US Population: Emerging American Identities. *Population and Development Review* 35 (1): 1–51.

Perlmann, J. 2005. *Italians Then, Mexicans Now: Immigrant Origins and Second-Generation Progress, 1890–2000*. New York: Russell Sage Foundation.

Perry, P. 2001. White Means Never Having to Say You're Ethnic: White Youth and the Construction of "Cultureless" Identities. *Journal of Contemporary Ethnography* 30 (1): 56–91.

Peter, K. 1987. *The Dynamics of Hutterite Society*. Canada: University of Alberta Press.

Petersen, W. 1975. A Demographer's View of Prehistoric Demography. *Current Anthropology* 16:227–46.

———. 1979. *Malthus*. Cambridge, MA: Harvard University Press.

Pew Research Center. 2004. *A Global Generation Gap*. Pew Global Attitudes Project 2004 [cited 2010]. Available from http://pewglobal.org/commentary/display.php?AnalysisID=86.

Philipov, D., and C. Berghammer. 2007. Religion and fertility ideal, intentions and behavior: A comparative study of European countries. *Vienna Yearbook of Population Research 2007*:271–305.

Phillips, D. 1974. The Influence of Suggestion on Suicide. *American Sociological Review* 39:340–54.

———. 1977. Motor Vehicle Fatalities Increase Just After Publicized Suicide Stories. *Science* 196:1464–65.

———. 1978. Airplane Accident Fatalities Increase Just After Newspaper Stories About Murder and Suicide. *Science* 201:748–50.

———. 1983. The Impact of Mass Media Violence on U.S. Homicides. *American Sociological Review* 48 (4): 560–68.

———. 1993. Psychology and Survival. *Lancet* 342: 1142–45.

Phillips, D., and D. Smith. 1990. Postponement of Death Until Symbolically Meaningful Occasions. *Journal of the American Medical Association* 263 (14): 1947–51.

Phillips, K. 1969. *The Emerging Republican Majority*. New Rochelle, NY: Arlington House.

Pimentel, D., X. Huang, A. Cardova, and P. M. 1997. Impact of Population Growth on Food Supplies and Environment. *Population and Environment* 19 (1): 9–14.

Plane, D., and P. Rogerson. 1994. *The Geographical Analysis of Population: with Applications to Planning and Business*. New York: John Wiley & Sons.

Plato. 360BC [1960]. *The Laws*. New York: Dutton.

Pol, L. G., and R. K. Thomas. 2001. *The Demography of Health and Health Care, Second Edition*. New York: Kluwer Academic/Plenum Publishers.

Polgreen, L. 2008. Court Rules Niger Failed by Allowing Girl's Slavery. 28 October:www.nytimes.com.

Pollack, R. A., and S. C. Watkins. 1993. Cultural and Economic Approaches to Fertility: Proper Marriage or Mésalliance. *Population and Development Review* 19 (3): 467–96.

Popkin, B. M. 1993. Nutritional Patterns and Transitions. *Population and Development Review* 19:138–57.

———. 2002. The Dynamics of the Dietary Transition in the Developing World. In *The Nutrition Transition: Diet and Disease in the Developing World*, eds. B. Caballero and B. M. Popkin. San Diego: Academic Press.

———. 2009. *The World Is Fat: The Fads, Trends, Policies, and Products That Are Fattening the Human Race*. New York: Penguin.

Popkin, B. M., and P. Gordon-Larsen. 2004. The Nutrition Transition: Worldwide Obesity Dynamics and Their Determinants. *international Journal of Obesity* 28 (3): S2-S9.

Population Action Council. 1985. India Seeking Two-Child Family Norm by 2000. *Popline* 7 (5):1–2.

Population Information Program. 1985. Periodic Abstinence. *Population Reports of the Johns Hopkins University* 1 (3).

Population Reference Bureau. 2009. *2009 World Population Data Sheet*. Washington, DC: Population Reference Bureau.

Portes, A. 1995. Children of Immigrants: Segmented Assimilation and its Determinants. In *The Economic Sociology of Immigration: Essays on Networks, Ethnicity and Entrepreneurship*, ed. A. Portes. New York: Russell Sage Foundation.

Portes, A., and R. G. Rumbaut. 2001. *Legacies: The Stories of the Immigrant Second Generation*. Berkeley and Los Angeles: University of California Press.

———. 2006. *Immigrant America: A Portrait, Third Edition*. Berkeley: University of California Press.

Poston, D., and B. Gu. 1987. Socioeconomic Development, Family Planning, and Fertility in China. *Demography* 24 (4): 531–52.

Poston, D. L. 1990. Apportioning the Congress: A Primer. *Population Today* 18 (7/8): 6–8.

Poston, D. L., C.-F. Chang, and H. Dan. 2006. Fertility Differences Between the Majority and Minority Nationality Groups in China. *Population Research and Policy Review* 25:67–101.

Potter, R. 1992. *Urbanisation in the Third World*. Oxford: Oxford University Press.

Potts, M., and R. Short. 1999. *Ever Since Adam and Eve: The Evolution of Human Sexuality*. Cambridge, UK: Cambridge University Press.

Prengaman, P. 2006. *Expatriate Mexicans Worry about Election*. Associated Press 2006 [cited 2006]. Available from www.ap.org.

Presbyterian Church (USA). 2008. *Religious and Demographic Profile of Presbyterians, 2008* 2008 [cited 2010]. Available from http://www.pcusa.org/research/panel/summaries/08fall-summary.pdf.

Preston, S. 1978. *The Effects of Infant and Child Mortality on Fertility*. New York: Academic Press.

Preston, S., and M. R. Haines. 1991. *Fatal Years: Child Mortality in Late Nineteenth-Century America*. Princeton, NJ: Princeton University Press.

Preston, S. H. 1970. *Older Male Mortality and Cigarette Smoking*. Berkeley: Institute of International Studies, University of California.

———. 1986. Are the Economic Consequences of Population Growth a Sound Basis for Population Policy? In *World Population and U.S. Policy: The Choices Ahead*, ed. J. Menken. New York: W.W. Norton.

Preston, S. H., P. Heuveline, and M. Guillot. 2001. *Demography: Measuring and Modeling Population Processes*. Oxford: Blackwell Publishers.

Preston, S. H., and H. Wang. 2006. Sex Mortality Differences in the United States: The Role of Cohort Smoking Patterns. *Demography* 43 (4): 631–46.

Price, D. O. 1947. A Check on Underenumeration in the 1940 Census. *American Sociological Review* 12 (1): 44–49.

Princeton University Office of Population Research. 2010. *The Emergency Contraception Website* 2010 [cited 2010]. Available from http://ec.princeton.edu/emergency-contraception.html.

Prioux, F. 2007. Recent Demographic Developments in France: Fertility at a More Than 30-Year High. *Population-E* 62 (3): 415–56.

Pumain, D. 2002. An Evolutionary Approach to Settlement Systems. Paper read at Paper prepared for the conference "New Forms of Urbanization: Conceptualizing and Measuring Human Settlement in the Twenty-first Century," organized by the IUSSP Working Group on Urbanization, at Bellagio, Italy.

———. 2004. An Evolutionary Approach to Settlement Systems. In *New Forms of Urbanization: Beyond the Urban-Rural Dichotomy*, eds. A. G. Champion and G. Hugo. London: Ashgate Publishing Company.

Pumphrey, G. 1940. *The Story of Liverpool's Public Service*. London: Hodden & Stoughton.

Qiao, X. 2001. From Decline of Fertility to Transition of Age Structrue: Ageing and its Policy Implications in China. *Genus* 57 (1): 57–81.

Raley, R. K., and L. Bumpass. 2003. *The Topography of the Divorce Plateau*. Demographic Research 8-8 2003 [cited 2004]. Available from www.demographic-research.org

Randall, S. 1996. Whose Reality? Local Perceptions of Fertility Versus Demographic Analysis. *Population Studies* 50 (2): 221–34.

Rashad, H., and E. E. Eltigani. 2005. Explaining Fertility Decline in Egypt. In *Islam, the State and Population* eds. G. W. Jones and M. S. Karim. London: Hurst & Company.

Rashed, T., and J. R. Weeks. 2003. Assessing Vulnerability to Earthquake Hazards Through Spatial Multicriteria Analysis of Urban Areas. *International Journal of Geographical Information Science* 17 (6): 549–78.

Rashed, T., J. R. Weeks, H. Couclelis, and M. Herold. 2007. An Integrative GIS and Remote Sensing Model for Place-Based Urban Vulnerability Analysis. In *The Integration of RS and GIS*, ed. V. Mesev. New York: John Wiley & Son.

Ratha, D., S. Mohapatra, and A. Silwal. 2009. *Migration and Remittance Trends 2009; Migration and Development Brief 11*. World Bank 2009 [cited 2010]. Available from http://siteresources.worldbank.org/INTPROSPECTS/Resources/334934-1110315015165/MigrationAndDevelopmentBrief11.pdf.

Ravenstein, E. 1889. The Laws of Migration. *Journal of the Royal Statistical Society* 52:241–301.

Ray, I. 2007. Women, Water, and Development. *Annual Review of Environment and Resources* 32:421–49.

Reagan, P. B., and R. J. Olsen. 2000. You Can Go Home Again: Evidence From Longitudinal Data. *Demography* 37 (3): 339–50.

Reed, H., J. Haaga, and C. Keely eds. 1998. *The Demography of Forced Migration: Summary of a Workshop*. Washington, DC: National Academy Press.

Reed, H., M. A. Koblinsky, and W. H. Mosley eds. 2000. *The Consequences of Maternal Morbidity and Maternal Mortality: Report of a Workshop*. Washington, DC: National Academy Press.

Rees, W. E. 1996. Revisiting Carrying Capacity: Area-Based Indicators of Sustainability. *Population and Environment* 17 (3): 195–215.

Reher, D., and R. Schofield. 1993. *Old and New Methods in Historical Demography*. Oxford: Clarendon Press.

Reissman, L. 1964. *The Urban Process: Cities in Industrial Societies*. New York: The Free Press.

Reitz, J. G. ed. 2005. *Ethnic Relations in Canada: Institutional Dynamics*. Montreal, CN: McGill-Queen's University Press.

Rendall, M. S. 2000. Entry or Exit? A Transition-Probability Approach to Explaining the High Prevalence of Single Motherhood Among Black Women. *Demography* 36 (3): 369–76.

Rendall, M. S., O. Ekert-Jaffé, H. Joshi, K. Lynch, and R. Mougin. 2009. Universal Versus Economically Polarized Change in Age at First Birth: A French-British Comparison. *Population and Development Review* 35 (1): 89–115.

Rérat, P., O. Söderström, and E. Piguet. 2009. Guest Editorial: New Forms of Gentrification Issues and Debates. *Population, Space and Place* Published online at www.interscience.wiley.com.

Reschovsky, C. 2004. *Journey to work: 2000, Census 2000 Brief C2KB-33*. Washington, DC: U.S. Census Bureau.

Retherford, R. D. 1975. *The Changing Sex Differentials in Mortality*. Westport: Greenwood Press.

Revelle, R. 1984. The Effects of Population Growth on Renewable Resources. In *Population Resources, Environment, and Development*, ed. U. Nations. New York: United Nations.

Riccio, B. 2008. West African Transnationalisms Compared: Ghanaians and Senegalese in Italy. *Journal of Ethnic and Migration Studies* 34(2):217–34.

Riche, M. 1997. Should the Census Bureau Use "Statistical Sampling" in Census 2000? *Insight*, 18 August.

Ricketts, T. C., L. A. Savitz, W. M. Gesler, and D. N. Osborne. 1997. Using Geographic Methods to Understand Health Issues. Rockville, MD: Agency for Health Care Policy and Research.

Riddle, J. M. 1992. *Contraception and Abortion From the Ancient World to the Renaissance*. Cambridge, MA: Harvard University Press.

Riley, J. C. 2005. Estimates of Regional and Global Life Expectancy, 1800–2001. *Population and Development Review* 31 (3): 537–43.

Riley, M. W. 1976. Social Gerontology and the Age Stratification of Society. In *Aging in America*, eds. C. S. Kart and B. Manard. Port Washington, NY: Alfred Publishing Co.

Riley, N. 2004. China's Population: New Trends and Challenges. *Population Bulletin* 59.

Riley, N., and R. W. Gardner. 1996. *China's Population: A Review of the Literature*. Liege, Belgium: International Union for the Scientific Study of Population.

Rindfuss, R. R., and P. C. Stern. 1998. Linking Remote Sensing and Social Science: The Need and the Challenges. In *People and Pixels: Linking Remote Sensing and Social Science*, eds. D. Liverman, E. F. Moran, R. R. Rindfuss and P. C. Stern, 1–27. Washington, DC: National Academy Press.

Rives, B. 1997. Strategic Financial Planning for Hospitals: Demographic Considerations. In *Demographics: A Casebook for Business and Government*, eds. H. J. Kintner, T. W. Merrick, P. A. Morrison, and P. R. Voss. Santa Monica, CA: RAND.

Robey, B. 1983. Achtung! Here Comes the Census. *American Demographics* 5 (10): 2–4.

Robinson, J. G., K. K. West, and A. Adlakha. 2002. Coverage of the Population in Census 2000: Results from Demographic Analysis. *Population Research and Policy Review* 21:19–38.

Robinson, R. V., and E. F. Jackson. 2001. Is Trust in Others Declining in America? An Age-Period-Cohort Analysis. *Social Science Research* 30:117–45.

Robinson, W. C. 1986. Another Look at the Hutterites and Natural Fertility. *Social Biology* 33:65–76.

———. 1997. The Economic Theory of Fertility Over Three Decades. *Population Studies* 51:63–74.

Rodenbeck, M. 1999. *Cairo: The City Victorious*. New York: Alfred A. Knopf.

Rodgers, J. L., H.-P. Kohler, K. O. Kyvik, and K. Christensen. 2001. Behavior Genetic Modeling of Human Fertility: Findings from a Contemporary Danish Twin Study. *Demography* 38 (1): 29–42.

Rodriguez, G. 2006. Demographic Translation and Tempo Effects: An Accelerated Failure Time Perspective. *Demographic Research* 14 (6): 85–110.

Rogers, E. M. 1995. *Diffusion of Innovations, Fourth Edition*. New York: The Free Press.

Rogers, R. G., R. A. Hummer, and C. B. Nam. 2000. *Living and Dying in the USA: Behavioral, Health, and Social Differentials of Adult Mortality*. San Diego: Academic Press.

Rogers, R. G., and E. Powell-Griner. 1991. Life Expectancies of Cigarette Smokers and Nonsmokers in the United States. *Social Science and Medicine* 32:1151–59.

Roof, W. C. 1999. *Spiritual Marketplace: Baby Boomers and the Remaking of American Religion*. Princeton, NJ: Princeton University Press.

Rosenberg, T. 2010. The Burden of Thirst. *National Geographic* 217 (4): 96–115.

Rosenhause, S. 1976. India Taking Drastic Birth Control Step. *Los Angeles Times* 25 September.

Rosental, P.-A. 2003. The Novelty of an Old Genre: Louis Henry and the Founding of Historical Demography. *Population-E* 58 (3): 97–130.

Ross, C. E., and C.-I, Wu. 1995. The Links between Education and Health. *American Sociological Review* 60:719–45.

Ross, E. B. 1998. *The Malthus Factor: Poverty, Politics and Population in Capitalist Development*. London: Zed Books.

Rossi, P. 1955. *Why Families Move*. New York: Free Press.

Roy, A., and N. Alsayyad eds. 2004. *Urban Informality: Transnational Perspectives from the Middle East, Latin America, and South Asia*. Lanham, MD: Lexington Books.

Rudel, T., O. Coomes, E. Moran, F. Achard, A. Angelson, J. Xu, and E. Lambin. 2005. Forest Transitions: Towards a Global Understanding of Land Use Change. *Global Environmental Change* 15:23–31.

Ruggles, S. 1994. The Transformation of American Family Structure. *American Historical Review* 99 (1):103–28.

———. 1997. The Rise of Divorce and Separation in the United States, 1880–1990. *Demography* 34 (4): 455–66.

Ruggles, S., and M. Heggeness. 2008. Intergenerational Coresidence in Developing Countries. *Population and Development Review* 34 (2): 253–81.

Rumbaut, R., D. S. Massey, and F. D. Bean. 2006. Linguistic Life Expectancies: Immigratn Language Retention in

Southern California. *Population and Development Review* 32 (3): 447–60.

Rumbaut, R. G. 1994. Origins and Destinies: Immigration to the United States Since World War II. *Sociological Forum* 9(4): 583–621.

———. 1995a. The New Immigration. *Contemporary Sociology* 24 (4): 307–11.

———. 1995b. Vietnamese, Laotian, and Cambodian Americans. In *Asian Americans: Contemporary Trends and Issues*, ed. P. G. Min. Beverly Hills: Sage Publications.

———. 1997. Assimilation and Its Discontents: Between Rhetoric and Reality. *International Migration Review* 31 (4): 923–60.

Russell, B. 1951. *New Hopes for a Changing World*. New York: Simon & Schuster.

Russell, C. 1999. Been There, Done That! *American Demographics* 21 (1): 54–58.

Ryder, N. 1965. The Cohort as a Concept in the Study of Social Change. *American Sociological Review* 30 (6): 843–61.

———. 1987. Reconsideration of a Model of Family Demography. In *Family Demography: Methods and Their Applications*, eds. J. Bongaarts, T. K. Burch and K. W. Wachter. Oxford: Clarendon Press.

———. 1990. What is Going to Happen to American Fertility? *Population and Development Review* 16 (3): 433–54.

Sagan, C. 1989. The Secret of the Persian Chessboard. *Parade Magazine* 5 February:14.

Salgado Mendoza, G. T. 2004. Migration of Latin American *Nikkei* and Chinese Trainees to Japan. *Papeles de Poblacion* 41: 237–51.

Salibi, K. S. 1988. *A House of Many Mansions: The History of Lebanon Reconsidered*. London: Taurus.

Samara, R., B. Bucker, and A. Tsui. 1996. *Understanding How Family Planning Programs Work: Findings From Five Years of Evaluation Research*. Chapel Hill: University of North Carolina, Carolina Population Center.

Samir, K. C., B. Barakat, A. Goujon, V. Skirbekk, W. C. Sanderson, and W. Lutz. 2010. Projection of Populations by Level of Educational Attainment, Age, and Sex for 120 Countries for 2005–2050. *Demographic Research* 22 (15): 383–472.

Sampson, R. J., and J. D. Morenoff. 2004. Spatial (Dis)Advantage and Homicide in Chicago Neighborhoods. In *Spatially Integrated Social Science*, eds. M. F. Goodchild and D. G. Janelle. New York: Oxford University Press.

Samuel, T. J. 1966. The Development of India's Policy of Population Control. *Milbank Memorial Fund Quarterly* 44:49–67.

———. 1994. *Quebec Separatism is Dead: Demography is Destiny*. Toronto: John Samuel and Associates.

Sanchez-Albornoz, N. 1974. *The Population of Latin America: A History*. Berkeley: University of California Press.

———. 1988. *Españoles Hacia America: La Emigración en Masa, 1880–1930*. Madrid: Alianza Editorial.

Sanderson, S. K. 1995. *Social Transformations: A General Theory of Historical Development*. Cambridge, MA: Blackwell.

Sanger, M. 1938. *Margaret Sanger: An Autobiography*. New York: W. W. Norton & Company.

Santana, R. 2009. Five-year Death Toll Surpasses 85,000. *San Diego Union-Tribune*, 15 October:A3.

Santelli, J. S., L. D. Lindberg, J. Abma, C. S. McNeely, and M. Resnick. 2000. Adolescent Sexual Behavior: Estimates and Trends From Four Nationally Representative Surveys. *Family Planning Perspectives* 32 (4): 156–65.

Santhya, K. G. 2003. *Changing Family Planning Scenario in India: An Overview of Recent Evidence*. New Delhi: Population Council.

Sardon, J.-P. 2002. Recent Demographic Trends in the Developed Countries. *Population: English Edition* 57 (1): 111–56.

Sassen, S. 2001. *The Global City: New York, London, Tokyo, 2nd Edition*. Princeton, NJ: Princeton University Press.

Sauvy, A. 1969. *General Theory of Population*. New York: Basic Books.

Sayre, N. F. 2008. The Genesis, History, and Limits of Carrying Capacity. *Annals of the Association of American Geographers* 98 (1): 120–34.

Schachter, J. 2001. Why People Move: Exploring the March 2000 Current Population Survey. *Current Population Reports P23–204*.

———. 2004. Geographical Mobility: 2002 to 2003. *Current Population Reports P20–549*.

Schackman, B. R., K. Gebo, R. Walensky, E. Losina, T. Muccio, P. Sax, M. Weinstein, G. Seage, R. Moore, and K. Freedberg. 2006. The Lifetime Cost of Current Human Immunodeficiency Virus Care in the United States. *Medica Care* 44 (11): 990–97.

Schapera, I. 1941. *Married Life in an African Tribe*. New York: Sheridan House.

Schiller, N. G., L. Basch, and C. S. Blanc. 1995. From Immigrant to Transmigrant: Theorizing Transnational Migration. *Anthropological Quarterly* 68 (1): 48–63.

Schmertmann, C. P., J. E. Potter, and S. M. Cavenaghi. 2008. Exploratory Analysis of Spatial Patterns in Brazil's Fertility Transition. *Population Research and Policy Review* 27: 1–15.

Schneider, P. 2003. Content and Data Quality in Census 2000. Washington, DC: US Census Bureau Census 2000 Testing, Experimentation, and Evaluation Program, Topic Report Series, No. 12.

Schnore, L., C. Andre, and H. Sharp. 1976. Black Suburbanization 1930–1970. In *The Changing Face of the Suburbs*, ed. B. Schwartz. Chicago: University of Chicago Press.

Schoen, R., and V. Canudas-Romo. 2005. Changing Mortality and Average Cohort Life Expectancy. *Demographic Research* 13 (5): 117–42.

Schoen, R., and Y. J. Kim. 1998. Momentum Under a Gradual Approach to Zero Growth. *Population Studies* 52:295–99.

Schoen, R., and N. Standish. 2001. The Retrenchment of Marriage: Results from Marital Status Life Tables. *Population and Development Review* 27 (3): 553–63.

Schofield, R., and D. Coleman. 1986. Introduction: The State of Population Theory. In *The State of Population Theory: Forward from Malthus*, eds. D. Coleman and R. Schofield. Oxford: Basil Blackwell.

Schofield, R., and D. Reher. 1991. The Decline of Mortality in Europe. In *The Decline of Mortality in Europe*, eds. R. Schofield, D. Reher and A. Bideau. Oxford: Clarendon Press.

Schumpeter, J. 1942. *Capitalism, Socialism, and Democracy, Second Edition*. New York: Harper & Row.

Schwartz, C. R., and R. D. Mare. 2005. Trends in Educational Assortative Marriage From 1940 to 2003. *Demography* 42 (4): 621–46.

Schweber, L. 2006. *Disciplining Statistics: Demography and Vital Statistics in France and England, 1830–1885*. Durham, NC: Duke University Press.

Scrimshaw, S. 1978. Infant Mortality and Behavior in the Regulation of Family Size. *Population and Development Review* 4 (3): 383–403.

Seager, J. 1993. *Earth Follies: Coming to Feminist Terms with the Global Environmental Crisis*. New York: Routledge.

——— ed. 1990. *The State of the Earth Atlas*. New York: Simon & Schuster.

Sedgh, G., S. Henshaw, S. Singh, E. Ahman, and I. H. Shah. 2007. Induced Abortion: Rates and Trends Worldwide. *Lancet* 370:1338–45.

Seghetti, L. M., S. R. Viña, and K. Ester. 2005. *Enforcing Immigration Law: The Role of State and Local Law Enforcement (Congressional Research Service, Library of Congress)*. Congressional Research Service 2005 [cited 2010]. Available from http://www.ilw.com/immigrationdaily/news/2005,1026-crs.pdf.

Sell, R., and G. DeJong. 1983. Deciding Whether to Move: Mobility, Wishful Thinking and Adjustment. *Sociology and Social Research* 67 (2): 146–65.

Serbanescu, F., L. Morris, P. Stupp, and A. Stanescu. 1995. The Impact of Recent Policy Changes on Fertility, Abortion, and Contraceptive Use in Romania. *Studies in Family Planning* 26 (2): 76–87.

Shafik, N. T., and I. Johnson. 2003. Letter from the Vice President of Environmentally and Socially Sustainable Development and from the Vice Presiden of Infrastructure. In *Environment Matters at the World Bank: Annual Review 2003*, ed. The World Bank. Washington, D.C.: The World Bank Group.

Shelton, B. A. 2000. Understanding the Distribution of Housework Between Husbands and Wives. In *The Ties That Bind: Perspectives on Marriage and Cohabitation*, ed. L. J. Waite. New York: Aldine de Gruyter.

Shkolnikov, V., F. Meslé, and J. Vallin. 1996. Health Crisis in Russia: Part I, Recent Trends in Life Expectancy and Causes of Death from 1970 to 1993. *Population: An English Selection* 8:123–54.

Short, J. F. J. 1997. *Poverty, Ethnicity, and Violent Crime*. Boulder, CO: Westview Press.

Short, J. R. 2004. Black Holes and Loose Connections in a Global Urban Network. *Professional Geographer* 56 (2): 295–302.

Shryock, H. 1964. *Population Mobility within the United States*. Chicago: University of Chicago Press.

Siegel, J. 1993. *A Generation of Change: A Profile of America's Older Population*. New York: Russell Sage Foundation.

Siegel, J. S. 2002. *Applied Demography: Applications to Business, Government, Law, and Public Policy*. San Diego: Academic Press.

Simcox, D. 2006. *Toward Negative Population Growth: Cutting Legal Immigration by Four-Fifths (An NPG Position Paper)*. Negative Population Growth, Inc. 2006 [cited 2010]. Available from http://npg.org/pospapers/cuttingimmigration.html.

Simmel, G. 1905. The Metropolis and Mental Life. In *Classic Essays on the Culture of Cities*, ed. R. Sennet. New York: Appleton-Century-Crofts.

Simmons, G. C., C. Smucker, S. Bernstein, and E. Jensen. 1982. Post-Neonatal Mortality in Rural India: Implications of an Economic Model. *Demography* 19 (3): 371–89.

Simmons, I. G. 1993. *Environmental History: A Concise Introduction*. Oxford: Basil Blackwell Publishers.

Simmons, L. 1960. Aging in Preindustrial Societies. In *Handbook of Gerontology*, ed. C. Tibbetts. Chicago: University of Chicago Press.

Simon, J. 1981. *The Ultimate Resource*. Princeton, NJ: Princeton University Press.

Simon, J. L. 1992. *Population and Development in Poor Countries: Selected Essays*. Princeton, NJ: Princeton University Press.

Simons, M. 2000. Between Migrants and Spain: The Sea that Kills. *New York Times*, 30 March.

Singer, M. 1999. The Population Surprise. *Atlantic Monthly* (August): 22–25.

Siri, M. J., and D. L. Cork eds. 2009. *Vital Statistics: Summary of a Workshop*. Washington, DC: National Academies Press.

Skinner, G. W. 1997. Family systems and demographic processes. In *Anthropological Demography: Toward a New Synthesis*, eds. D. Kertzer and T. Fricke, 53–95. Chicago: University of Chicago Press.

Slackman, M. 2008. Dreams Stifled, Egypt's Young Turn to Islamic Fervor. *New York Times* (17 February).

Smail, J. K. 1997. Population Growth Seems to Affect Everything but Is Seldom Held Responsible for Anything. *Politics and the Life Sciences* 16 (2): 231–36.

Smart Growth Network. 2010. *About Smart Growth* 2010 [cited 2010]. Available from http://smartgrowth.org/about/default.asp.

Smelser, N. J. 1997. The Rational and the Ambivalent in the Social Sciences: 1997 Presidential Address. *American Sociological Review* 63:1–16.

Smil, V. 1994. How Many People Can the Earth Feed? *Population and Development Review* 20 (2): 255–92.

———. 2000. *Feeding the World: A Challenge for the Twenty-First Century*. Cambridge, MA: The MIT Press.

Smith, A. 1776. *An Inquiry into the Nature and Causes of the Wealth of Nations*: http://www.socsci.mcmaster.ca/~econ/ugcm/3ll3/smith/wealth/wealbk01, accessed 2003.

Smith, C. A., and M. Pratt. 1993. Cardiovascular Disease. In *Chronic Disease Epidemiology and Control*, eds. R. C. Brownson, P. L. Remington and J. R. Davis. Washington, DC: American Public Health Association.

Smith, D. P. 1992. *Formal Demography*. New York: Plenum.

Smith, D. P., and B. S. Bradshaw. 2005. Rethinking the Hispanic Paradox: Death Rates and Life Expectancy for US Non-Hispanic White and Hispanic Populations. *American Journal of Public Health* 96 (9): 1686–92.

Smith, D. S. 1978. Mortality and Family in the Colonial Chesapeake. *Journal of Interdisciplinary History* 8 (3): 403–27.

Smith, G., M. Shipley, and G. Rose. 1990. Magnitude and Causes of Socioeconomic Differentials in Mortality: Further Evidence From the Whitehall Sutdy. *British Medical Journal* 301:429–32.

Smith, J. 2006. *Guatemala: Economic Migrants Replace Political Refugees*. Migration Information Source 2006 [cited 2010]. Available from http://www.migrationinformation.org/Profiles/display.cfm?ID=392.

Smith, K. R., and N. J. Waitzman. 1994. Double Jeopardy: Interaction Efects of Marital and Poverty Status on the Risk of Mortality. *Demography* 31 (3): 487–507.

Smith, R., L. Ashford, J. Gribble, and D. Clifton. 2009. Family Planning Saves Lives. Washington, DC: Population Reference Bureau.

Smith, S., J. Tayman, and D. Swanson. 2001. *Population Projections for States and Local Areas: Methodology and Analysis*. New York: Plenum Press.

Snipp, C. M. 1989. *American Indian: The First of This Land*. New York: Russell Sage Foundation.

Snow, J. 1936. *Snow on Cholera*. London: Oxford University Press.

Sontag, D. 2000. Gaza Adding Children at an Unrivaled Rate. *New York Times*, 24 February.

Sörenson, A., and H. Trappe. 1995. The Persistence of Gender Equality in Earnings in the German Democratic Republic. *American Sociological Review* 60:398–406.

Spar, E. J. 1998. Demographics: End of Year (D.C. Year, That Is) Wrap-Up. *Business Geographics* (January): 38–39.

Spengler, J. 1974. *Population Change, Modernization, and Welfare*. Englewood Cliffs, NJ: Prentice-Hall.

Spengler, J. J. 1979. *France Faces Depopulation: Postlude Edition, 1936–1976*. Durham, NC: Duke University Press.

Špidla, V. 2007. Introduction by Commissioner Vladimir Spidla to the four essay written in response to the communication on *The Demographic Future of Europe. Vienna Yearbook of Population Research 2007*:1–3.

Spooner, B. ed. 1972. *Population Growth: Anthropological Implications*. Cambridge, MA: MIT Press.

Stack, S. 1987. Celebrities and Suicide: A Taxonomy and Analysis. *American Sociological Review* 52:401–12.

Stangeland, C. E. 1904. *Pre-Malthusian Doctrines of Population*. New York: Columbia University Press.

Staples, R. 1986. The Masculine Way of Violence. In *Homicide Among Black Americans*, ed. D. Hawkins. New York: University Press of America.

Stark, O., and R. Lucas. 1988. Migration, Remittances, and the Family. *Economic Development and Cultural Change* 36:465–81.

Starr, P. 1987. The Sociology of Official Statistics. In *The Politics of Numbers*, eds. W. Alonso and P. Starr. New York: Russell Sage Foundation.

Statistics Canada. 1995. Census 1996. *Focus for the Future* 10 (1): 1–3.

———. 2007. *Urban Boundary Files*. Available from http://www.statcan.gc.ca/bsolc/olc-cel/olc-cel?lang=eng&catno=92-164-X.

———. 2008. *Difference Between Statistics Canada's Census counts and population estimates*. Available from http://www12.statcan.ca/census-recensement/2006/ref/info/estimates-estimations-eng.cfm.

———. 2009a. *2006 Census: Data Products; Topic-Based Tabulations (926)*. Available from http://www12.statcan.gc.ca/census-recensement/2006/dp-pd/tbt/.

———. 2009b. *Persons in Low Income Before Tax*. Available from http://www40.statcan.gc.ca/l01/cst01/famil41a-eng.htm.

Statistika Centralbyran [Sweden]. 1983. *Pehr Wargentin: den Svenska Statistikens Fader*. Stockholm: Statistika Centralbyran.

Staveteig, S. 2005. The Young and the Restless: Population Age Structure and Civil War. *Environmental Change and Security Program Report* 11:12–19.

Stephenson, G. 1964. *A History of American Immigration*. New York: Russell and Russell.

Stockwell, E. G., F. W. Goza, and K. S. Balistreri. 2005. Infant Mortality and Socioeconomic Status: New Bottle, Same Old Wine. *Population Research and Policy Review* 24:387–99.

Stolnitz, G. J. 1964. The Demographic Transition: From High to Low Birth Rates and Death Rates. In *Population: The Vital Revolution*, ed. R. Freedman, Chapter 2. Garden City. NY: Anchor Books.

Stone, L. 1975. On the Interaction of Mobility Dimensions in Theory on Migration Decisions. *Canadian Review of Sociology and Anthropology* 12:95–100.

Straus, M. 1983. Societal Morphogenesis and Intrafamily Violence in Cross-Cultural Perspective. In *International Perspectives on Family Violence*, eds. R. Gelles and C. Cornell. Lexington, MA: D.C. Heath.

Stub, S. T. 2009. Crisis Spurs Migration to Israel. *Wall Street Journal*, 3 December:A12.

Stycos, J. M. 1971. *Ideology, Faith and Family Planning in Latin America*. New York: McGraw-Hill.

Sullivan, T. M., J. T. Bertrand, J. Rice, and J. D. Shelton. 2006. Skewed Contraceptive Method Mix: Why it Happens, Why it Matters. *Journal of Biosocial Science* 38:501–21.

Sung, K. 1995. Measures and Dimensions of Filial Piety in Korea. *The Gerontologist* 35 (2):2 40–47.

Sussman, G. 1977. Parisian Infants and Norman Wet Nurses in the Early Nineteenth Century: A Statistical Study. *Journal of Interdisciplinary History* 7 (4): 637–53.

Sutherland, I. 1963. John Graunt: A Tercentenary Tribute. *Royal Statistical Society Journal, Series A* 126:536–37, reprinted in K. Kammeyer 1975 (ed.), *Population: Selected Essays and Research* (Chicago: Rand McNally).

Szreter, S. 1996. *Fertility, Class, Gender in Britain 1860 to 1940*. Cambridge, UK: Cambridge University Press.

Szreter, S., and E. Garrett. 2000. Reproduction, Compositional Demography, and Economic Growth: Family Planning in England Long Before the Fertility Decline. *Population and Development Review* 26 (1): 45–80.

Ta-k'un, W. 1960. A Critique of neo-Malthusian Theory. *Excerpted in Population and Development Review (1979)* 5 (4): 699–707.

Tabutin, D., and B. Schoumaker. 2005. The Demography of the Arab World and the Middle East from the 1950s to the 2000s. *Population, English Edition* 60:505–616.

Taeuber, I. 1958. *The Population of Japan*. Princeton, NJ: Princeton University Press.

Tavernise, S. 2006. The Exodus: 644,500 Iraqis Flee Ravages of War. *San Diego Union-Tribune (New York Times News Service)* (14 June): A17.

———. 2009. Survey of Pakistan's Young Predicts "Disaster" If Their Needs Aren't Addressed. *New York Times* (22 November).

Taylor, W., J. S. Marks, J. R. Livengood, and J. P. Koplan. 1993. Current Issues and Challenges in Chronic Disease Control. In *Chronic Disease Epidemiology and Control*, eds. R. C. Brownson, P. L. Remington and J. R. Davis. Washington, DC: American Public Health Association.

Teitelbaum, M. 1975. Relevance of Demographic Transition for Developing Countries. *Science* 188:420–25.

Teitelbaum, M., and J. Winter. 1988. Introduction. In *Population and Resources in the Western Intellectual Tradition*, eds. M. Teitelbaum and J. Winter. New York: Population Council.

Telles, E. E., and V. Ortiz. 2008. *Generations of Exclusion: Mexican Americans, Assimilation, and Race*. New York: Russell Sage Foundation.

Thatcher, R. 2001. The Demography of Centenarians in England and Wales. *Population: An English Selection* 13 (1): 139–56.

Thomas, H. 1997. *The Slave Trade: The Story of the Atlantic Slave Trade: 1440–1870*. New York: Simon & Schuster.

Thompson, W. 1929. Population. *American Journal of Sociology* 34 (6): 959–75.

Tietze, C., and S. Lewit. 1977. Legal Abortion. *Scientific American* 236 (1): 21–27.

Tobias, A. 1979. The Only Article on Inflation You Need to Read: We're Getting Poorer, But We Can Do Something About It. *Esquire* 92 (5): 49–55.

Tobler, W. 1995. Migration: Ravenstein, Thornthwaite, and Beyond. *Urban Geography* 16 (4):327–343.

———. 2004. On the First Law of Geography: A Reply. *Annals of the Association of American Geographers* 94 (2): 304–10.

Tolnay, S. 1989. A New Look at the Effect of Venereal Disease on Black Fertility: The Deep South in 1940. *Demography* 26:679–90.

Tolnay, S. E., K. C. White, K. D. Crowder, and R. M. Adelman. 2005. Distances Traveled During the 'Great Migration': An analysis of Racial Differences among Male Migrants. *Social Science History* 29:523–48.

Torrieri, N., and H. Jennifer. 2000. Census Scene, Part 3: Enabling an Annual Census. *Geospatial Solutions* (November): 38–42.

Torrieri, N. K. 2007. America is Changing, and So is the Census: The American Community Survey. *The American Statistician* 61 (1): 16–21.

Toulemon, L. 1997. Cohabitation is Here To Stay. *Population: An English Selection* 9:11–46.

Tu, P. 2000. Trends and Regional Differentials in Fertility Transition. In *The Changing Population of China*, eds. Z. Peng and G. Zhigang. Malden, MA: Blackwell Publishers.

Turke, P. 1989. Evolution and the Demand for Children. *Population and Development Review* 15:61–90.

Tyner, J. 2009a. *The Philipines: Mobilities, Identities, Globalization*. New York: Taylor & Francis.

———. 2009b. *War, Violence, and Population: Making the Body Count*. New York: The Guilford Press.

Tyner, J. A. 1999. The Geopolitics of Eugenics and the Exclusion of Philippine Immigrants From the United States. *The Geographical Review* 89 (1): 54–73.

U.K. National Archives. 2009. *Domesday Book*. Available from http://www.nationalarchives.gov.uk/catalogue/ RdLeaflet.asp?sLeafletID=266.

U.K. Office for National Statistics. 2009. *Centenarians: The Fastest Growing Age Group*. Available from http://www.statistics.gov.uk/cci/nugget.asp?id=1875.

U.S. Census Bureau. 1975. *Historical Statistics of the United States*. Washington, DC: Government Printing Office.

———. 1978. History and Organization. Washington, DC: U. S. Bureau of the Census.

———. 1979. Country Demographic Profiles: Mexico.

———. 1999. *Census Bureau Looks Back Over a Century of Accomplishments*. Available from http://www.census.gov/Press-Release/www/1999/cb99–250.html

———. 2002. Urban Area Criteria for Census 2000. *Federal Register* 67 (51):11663–70.

———. 2005. *TIGER Overview*. Available from http://www.census.gov/geo/www/tiger/overview.html.

———. 2007. *Statistical Abstract of the United States: 2007*. Washington, DC: U.S. Census Bureau.

———. 2008a. *U.S. National Population Projections, Released 2008 (Based on Census 2000)*. Available from http://www.census.gov/population/www/projections/downloadablefiles.html.

———. 2008b. *Wealth and Asset Ownership: Table 1. Median Value of Assets for Households, by Type of Asset Owned and Selected Characteristics*. Available from http://www.census.gov/hhes/www/wealth/2002_tables.html.

———. 2009a. *Table 6: Estimates of the Components of Resident Population Change by Race and Hispanic Origin for the United States: July 1, 2007, to July 1, 2008 (NC-EST2008-06)*. Available from www.census.gov.

———. 2009b. *Voter turnout in 2008* 2009b [cited 2010]. Available from http://www.census.gov/Press-Release/www/releases/archives/voting/013995.html.

———. 2010a. *America's Families and Living Arrangements: 2009*. Available from http://www.census.gov/population/www/socdemo/hh-fam/cps2009.html.

———. 2010b. *Current Population Survey, Alternative Measures of Income and Poverty, Table 2. Percent of Persons in Poverty, by Definition of Income and Selected Characteristics: 2008* 2010b [cited 2010]. Available from http://www.census.gov/hhes/www/cpstables/032009/rdcall/2_000.htm.

———. 2010c. *Geographical Mobility/Migration: Calculating Migration Expectancy*. Available from http://www.census.gov/population/www/socdemo/migrate/cal-mig-exp.html.

———. 2010d. *Population Estimates: Metropolitan and Micropolitan Statistical Area Estimates, Components of Population Change*. Available from http://www.census.gov/popest/metro/CBSA-est2009-comp-chg.html.

U.S. Centers for Disease Control. 2007. Chartbook on Trends in the Health of Americans/ Health, United States 2006. Atlanta: U.S. Centers for Disease Control.

———. 2010a. *2009 H1N1 Flu ("Swine Flu") and You*. Available from http://www.cdc.gov/h1n1flu/qa.htm.

———. 2010b. *Breastfeeding Among U.S. Children Born 1999—2006, CDC National Immunization Survey*. Available from http://www.cdc.gov/breastfeeding/data/NIS_data/2006/socio-demographic_any.htm.

U.S. Department of Defense. 2010. *Operation Iraqi Freedom (OIF) U.S. Casualty Status* 2010 [cited 2010]. Available from http://www.defense.gov/NEWS/casualty.pdf.

U.S. Department of Homeland Security. 2009. *Yearbook of Immigration Statistics: 2008*. Available from http://www.dhs.gov/files/statistics/publications/LPR08.shtm.

———. 2010. *Yearbook of Immigration Statistics: 2009*. U.S. Available from http://www.dhs.gov/files/statistics/publications/yearbook.shtm.

U.S. Department of State. 2010. Summary of Refugee Admissions from the Bureau of Population, Refugees, and Migration, Office of Admissions, Refugee Processing Center.

U.S. Energy Information Administration. 2010. *International Energy Outlook 2009*. Available from http://www.eia.doe.gov/oiaf/ieo/world.html.

U.S. Environmental Protection Agency. 2010. *Smarth Growth* 2010 [cited 2010]. Available from http://www.epa.gov/dced/.

U.S. Immigration and Naturalization Service. 1991. *An Immigrant Nation: United States Regulation of Immigration, 1798–1991*. Washington, DC: Government Printing Office.

U.S. Office of Management and Budget. 2000. Standards for Defining Metropolitan and Micropolitan Statistical Areas. *Federal Register* 65 (249): 82227–38.

U.S. Social Security Administration. 2010. *Annual Statistical Supplement, 2009*. Available from http://www.ssa.gov/policy/docs/statcomps/supplement/2009/index.html.

Udry, J. R. 1994. The Nature of Gender. *Demography* 31 (4):561–74.

———. 2000. Biological Limits of Gender Construction. *American Sociological Review* 65:443–57.

UN Economic Commission for Europe. 2003. *Trends in Europe and North America: Families and Households* 2003 [cited 2007]. Available from http://www.unece.org/stats/trend/ch2.htm.

UN Habitat. 2005. *Water and Sanitation in the World's Cities: Local Action for Global Goals*. London: Earthscan.

———. 2010. *State of the World's Cities 2010/2011—Cities for All: Bridging the Urban Divide*. New York: United Nations.

UNAIDS. 2009. AIDS Epidemic Update December 2009. Geneva: UNAIDS [www.unaids.org].

UNFPA. 2010. *Population Issues: ICPD/15*. Available from http://www.unfpa.org/public/icpd.

UNHCR. 2010. *Who is a refugee?* Available from http://www.unhcr.org.au/basicdef.shtml.

United Nations. 1953. *Causes and Consequences of Population Trends*. New York: United Nations.

———. 1973. *The Determinants and Consequences of Population Trends: New Summary of Findings on Interaction of Demographic, Economic and Social Factors, Volume I*. New York: United Nations.

———. 1979. *Trends and Characteristics of International Migration Since 1950*. New York: United Nations.

———. 2001. *Human Development Report 2001: Making New Technologies Work for Human Development*. Available from http://hdr.undp.org/reports/global/2001/en/

United Nations Development Programme. 2006. *Human Development Report*. New York: UNDP.

United Nations High Commissioner for Refugees. 2009. *2008 Global Trends: Refugees, Asylum-seekers, Returnees,*

Internally Displaced and Stateless Persons. Available from http://www.unhcr.org/4a375c426.html.

United Nations Population Division. 1993. *The Sex and Age Distribution of the World Populations: The 1992 Revision*. New York: United Nations.

———. 1999. *The World at Six Billion* 1999. Available from http://www.un.org/esa/population/publications/sixbillion/sixbillion.htm.

———. 2000. Replacement Migration: Is it a Solution ot Declining and Ageing Populations? New York: United Nations.

———. 2005. Living Arrangements of Older Persons Around the World. New York: United Nations.

———. 2009a. International Migration, 2009 Wallchart (United Nations publication, Sales No. E.09.XIII.8). New York: United Nations.

———. 2009b. *What Would it Take to Accelerate Fertility Decline in the Least Developed Countries? UN Population Division Policy Brief No. 2009/1*. Available from http://www.un.org/esa/population/publications/UNPD_policybriefs/UNPD_policy_brief1.pdf.

———. 2009c. *World Contraceptive Use (POP/DB/CP/Rev2009)*. Available from http://www.un.org/esa/population/publications/WCU2009/Main.html.

———. 2009d. World Fertility Data 2008 (POP/DB/Fert/Rev2008).

———. 2009e. *World Marriage Data 2008 (POP/DB/Marr/Rev2008)*. Available from http://www.un.org/esa/population/publications/WMD2008/Main.html.

———. 2009f. World Population Prospects: The 2008 Revision. New York: United Nations.

———. 2010a. *World Population Policies 2009*. New York: United Nations.

———. 2010b. *World Urbanization Prospects: The 2009 Revision*. Available from http://esa.un.org/unpd/wup/unup/.

United Nations Population Fund. 1987. *1986 Report by the Executive Director*. New York: United Nations.

———. 1991. *Population and the Environment: The Challenges Ahead*. New York: United Nations.

United Nations Statistics Division. 2008. *Principles and Recommendations for Population and Housing Censuses, Revision 2*. New York: United Nations.

———. 2010. *2010 World Population and Housing Census Programme*. Available from http://unstats.un.org/unsd/demographic/sources/census/censusdates.htm.

Uppsala Conflict Data Program. 2010. *Latest Versions of Data: UCDP/PRIO Armed Conflict Dataset v.4-2009, 1946–2008* 2010 [cited 2010]. Available from http://www.pcr.uu.se/research/UCDP/data_and_publications/datasets.htm.

Vallin, J. 1999. *Mortalite, Sexe et Genre*. Liege: International Union for the Scientific Study of Population.

———. 2002. The End of the Demographic Transition: Relief or Concern? *Population and Development Review* 28 (1): 105–20.

Vallin, J., and F. Meslé. 2009. The Segmented Trend Line of Highest Life Expectancies. *Population and Development Review* 35 (1): 159–87.

Van Cleave, J., S. L. Gortmaker, and J. M. Perrin. 2010. Dynamics of Obesity and Chronic Health Conditions Among Children and Youth. *Journal of the American Medical Association* 3030 (7): 623–30.

van de Kaa, D. J. 1987. Europe's Second Demographic Transition. *Population Bulletin* 42 (1).

———. 2004. Is the Second Demographic Transition a useful research concept: Questions and Answers. *Vienna Yearbook of Population Research 2004*:4–10.

van de Walle, E. 1992. Fertility Transition, Conscious Choice and Numeracy. *Demography* 29:487–502.

van de Walle, E., and J. Knodel. 1980. Europe's Fertility Transition: New Evidence and Lessions for Today's Developing World. *Population Bulletin* 34 (6).

Van Hook, J., Weiwei Zhang, F. D. Bean, and J. S. Passel. 2006. Foreign-Born Emigration: A New Approach and Estimates Based on Matched CPS Files. *Demography* 43 (2): 361–82.

Vanderpool, C. 1995. *Integrated Natural Resource Systems*. East Lansing, MI: Michigan Agricultural Experiment Station, Michigan State University.

Vandeschrick, C. 2001. The Lexis Diagram, a Misnomer. *Demographic Research* 4 (3).

Vaupel, J. W., and E. Loichinger. 2006. Redistributing Work in Aging Europe. *Science* 312 (5782): 1911–13.

Velkoff, V. A., and A. Adlakha. 1998. Women of the World: Women's Health in India. Washington, DC: U.S.Census Bureau.

Veyne, P. 1987. The Roman Empire. In *A History of Private Life, Volume 1: From Pagan Rome to Byzantium*, ed. P. Veyne. Cambridge, MA: Harvard University Press.

Villalvazo Peña, P., J. P. Corona Medina, and S. García Mora. 2002. Urbano-rural, Constante Busqueda de Fronteras Conceptuales. *Revista de Información y Analisis* 20:17–24.

Visaria, P., and V. Chari. 1998. India's Population Policy and Family Planning Program: Yesterday, Today, and Tomorrow. In *Do Population Policies Matter? Fertility and Politics in Egypt, India, Kenya, and Mexico*, ed. A. Jain. New York: Population Council.

Viscusi, W. K. 1979. *Welfare of the Elderly: An Economic Analysis and Policy Prescription*. New York: John Wiley & Sons.

Vishnevsky, A., and V. Shkolnikov. 1999. Russian Mortality: Past Negative Trends and Recent Improvements. In *Population Under Duress: The Geodemography of Post-Soviet Russia*, eds. G. J. Demko, G. Ioffe and Z. Zayonchkovskaya. Boulder, CO: Westview Press.

Vlassoff, C. 1990. The Value of Sons in an Indian Village. *Population Studies* 44:5–20.

Wachter, K. 2005. Spatial Demography. *Proceedings of the National Academy of Sciences* 102 (43): 15299–300.

Wackernagel, M., and W. E. Rees. 1996. *Our Ecological Footprint: Reducing Human Impact on the Earth*. Philadelphia, PA: New Society Publishers.

Wagmiller, R. L., Jr. 2007. Race and the Spatial Segregation of Jobless Men in Urban America. *Demography* 44 (3): 539–62.

Wagmiller, R. L., Jr., M. C. Lennon, L. Kuang, P. M. Alberti, and J. L. Abers. 2006. The Dynamics of Economic Disadvantage and Children's Life Chances. *American Sociological Review* 71:847–66.

Waite, L. 2004. The Demographic Faces of the Elderly. In *Aging, Health, and Public Policy: Demographic and Economic Perspectives (Supplement to Population and Development Review, Vol. 30)*, ed. L. Waite. New York: Population Council.

Waite, L. J. 2000. The Family as a Social Organization: Key Ideas for the Twenty-first Century. *Contemporary Sociology* 20 (3): 463–69.

Waite, L. J., and M. Gallagher. 2000. *The Case for Marriage*. New York: Doubleday.

Wal-Mart. 2009. *A Brief Introduction to Wal-Mart in China* 2009 [cited 2010]. Available from http://www.walmartchina.com/english/walmart/index.htm.

Waldman, P. 1991. As Acreage Erodes, Palestinians Feel Pressure to Deal. *Wall Street Journal*, 10 May:A9.

Waldorf, B., and R. Franklin. 2002. Spatial Dimensions of the Easterlin Hypothesis: Fertility Variations in Italy. *Journal of Regional Science* 42:549–78.

Waldron, I. 1986. What Do We Know About Causes of Sex Differences in Mortality? A Review of the Literature. *Population Bulletin of the United States* 18 (1995): 59–76.

Wall, R., J. Robin, and P. Laslett eds. 1983. *Family Forms in Historic Europe*. New York: Cambridge University Press.

Wallace, P. 2001. *Agequake: Riding the Demographic Rollercoaster Shaking Business, Finance and our World*. London: Nicholas Brealey Publishing.

Wallace, R. 1761 [1969]. *A Dissertation on the Numbers of Mankind, in Ancient and Modern Times, 1st and 2nd editions, revised and corrected*. New York: Kelley.

Wallerstein, I. 1974. *The Modern World System*. New York: Academic Press.

———. 1976. Modernization: Requiescat in Pace. In *The Uses of Controversy in Sociology*, eds. L. A. Coser and O. N. Larsen. New York: Free Press.

Wallis, C. 1995. How to Live to be 120. *Time*, 6 March, 85.

Walsh, J. 1974. U.N. Conference: Topping Any Agenda is the Question of Development. *Science* 185:1144.

Walsh, M. W. 2010. Social Securit to See Payout Exceed Pay-in This Year. *New York Times*, 24 March.

Ware, H. 1975. The Limits of Acceptable Family Size in Western Nigeria. *Journal of Biosocial Science* 7:273–96.

Warren, C. A. B. 1998. Aging and Identity in Premodern Times. *Research on Aging* 20 (1): 11–35.

Wasserman, I. M. 1984. Imitation and Suicide: A Reexamination of the Werther Effect. *American Sociological Review* 49:427–36.

Watkins, S. C. 1986. Conclusion. In *The Decline of Fertility in Europe*, eds. A. Coale and S. C. Watkins. Princeton: Princeton University Press.

———. 1991. *From Provinces Into Nations: Demographic Integration in Western Europe, 1870–1960*. Princeton, NJ: Princeton University Press.

Wattenberg, B. J. 2004. *Fewer: How the New Demography of Depopulation Will Shape Our Future*. Chicago: Ivan R. Dee, Publisher.

Weber, A. 1899. *The Growth of Cities in the Nineteenth Century*. New York: Columbia University Press.

Weeks, G. B., and J. R. Weeks. 2010. *Irresistible Forces: Explaining Latin American Migration to the United States*. Albuquerque: University of New Mexico Press.

Weeks, J. R. 2004a. The Role of Spatial Analysis in Demographic Research. In *Spatially Integrated Social Science: Examples in Best Practice*, eds. M. F. Goodchild and D. G. Janelle. New York: Oxford University Press.

———. 2004b. Using Remote Sensing and Geographic Information Systems to Identify the Underlying Properties of Urban Environments. In *New Forms of Urbanization: Conceptualizing and Measuring Human Settlement in the Twenty-first Century*, eds. A. G. Champion and G. Hugo. London: Ashgate Publishing Limited.

———. 2010. Unpublished data from the 2000 Ghana Census of Population and Housing. San Diego, CA: San Diego State University.

Weeks, J. R., A. Getis, A. G. Hill, M. S. Gadalla, and T. Rashed. 2004. The Fertility Transition in Egypt: Intra-Urban Patterns in Cairo. *Annals of the Association of American Geographers* 94 (1): 74–93.

Weeks, J. R., A. G. Hill, A. Getis, and D. Stow. 2006. Ethnic Residential Patterns as Predictors of Intra-Urban Child Mortality Inequality in Accra, Ghana. *Urban Geography* 27(6): 526–48.

Weeks, J. R., P. Jankowski, and J. Stoler. 2010. Who's Knocking at the Door? New Data on Undocumented Immigrants to the United States. *Population, Space and Place*.

Weeks, J. R., D. Larson, and D. Fugate. 2005. Patterns of Urban Land Use as Assessed by Satellite Imagery: An Application to Cairo, Egypt. In *Population, Land Use, and Environment: Research Directions*, eds. B. Entwisle and P. C. Stern, 265–86. Washington, DC: National Academies Press.

Weeks, J. R., Jr. 2004. *Unpopular Culture: The Ritual of Complaint in a British Bank*. Chicago: University of Chicago Press.

Weiss, K. H. 1973. Demographic Models for Anthropology. *American Antiquity* 38 (2: Part II).

Weiss, M. 1988. *The Clustering of America*. New York: Harper & Row.

Weiss, M. J. 2001. *The Clustered World: How We Live, What We Buy, and What it all Means About Who We Are*. Boston: Little, Brown and Company.

Weller, R., J. Macisco, and G. Martine. 1971. Relative Importance of the Components of Urban Growth in Latin America. *Demography* 8 (2): 225–32.

Wells, R. 1971. Family Size and Fertility Control in Eighteenth-Century America: A Study of Quaker Families. *Population Studies* 25 (1): 73–82.

———. 1982. *Revolutions in Americans' Lives*. Westport, CT: Greenwood Press.

Wendelken, S. 1996. Religiously Mapping. *Business Geographics* (September):54.

Westerhof, G. J., A. E. Barrett, and N. Steverink. 2003. Forever Young?: A Comparison of Age Identities in the United States and Germany. *Research on Aging* 25 (4): 366–83.

Westley, S. B. 2002. Assessing Women's Well-Being in Asia. *Asia-Pacific Population & Policy, East-West Center* 61.

Westoff, C. 1978. Marriage and Fertility in the Developed Countries. *Scientific American* 239 (6): 51–57.

———. 1990. Reproductive Intentions and Fertility Rates. *International Family Planning Perspectives* 16:84–89.

———. 1994. What's the World's Priority Task? Finally, Control Population. *New York Times Magazine* 6 February.

———. 1997. Population Growth: Large Problem, Low Visibility. *Politics & Life Sciences* 16 (2): 226–27.

Westoff, C., and A. Bankole. 1996. The Potential Demographic Significance of Unmet Need. *International Family Planning Perspectives* 22 (1): 16–20.

Westoff, C., and L. Bumpass. 1973. The revolution in birth control practices of U.S. Roman Catholics. *Science* 179:41–44.

Westoff, C., and R. Rindfuss. 1974. Sex Preselection in the United States: Some Implications. *Science* 184:633–36.

Westoff, C. F. 2001. *Unmet Need at the End of the Century: DHS Comparative Reports No. 1*. Calverton, MD: ORC Macro.

———. 2003. *Trends in Marriage and Early Childbearing in Developing Countries, DHS Comparative Reports No. 5*. Calverton, MD: ORC Macro.

———. 2010. Desired Number of Children: 2000–2008 (DHS Comparative Reports 25). Calverton, MD: ICF Macro.

Westoff, C. F., and T. Frejka. 2007. Religiousness and Fertility among European Muslims. *Population and Development Review* 33 (4): 785–809.

Westoff, C. F., and E. F. Jones. 1979. The end of 'Catholic' fertility. *Demography* 16:209–17.

Westoff, C. F., and J. R. Weeks. 2010. Religiousness and Reproduction in Muslim Countries, presented at the Annual Meeting of the Population Association of America. Dallas, TX.

Westoff, L., and C. Westoff. 1971. *From Now to Zero*. Boston: Little, Brown.

Whitacre, P. T., and P. Tsai eds. 2009. *The Public Health Effects of Food Deserts: Workshop Summary*. Washington, DC: National Academies Press.

White, A. A., and K. F. Rust eds. 1997. *Preparing for the 2000 Census: Interim Report II*. Washington, DC: National Academy Press.

White, K. J. C. 2002. Declining Fertility among North American Hutterites: The Use of Birth Control within a Darisusleut Colony. *Social Biology* 49 (1–2): 58–73.

Whitmore, T. M. 1992. *Disease and Death in Early Colonial Mexico*. Boulder, CO: Westview Press.

Willcox, W. F. 1936. *Natural and Political Observations Made Upon the Bills of Mortality by John Graunt*. Baltimore: The Johns Hopkins Press.

Williams, D. R., H. W. Neighbors, and J. S. Jackson. 2003. Racial/ethnic discrimination and health: Findings from community studies. *American Journal of Public Health* 93:200–208.

Williams, J. D. 1994. Using Demographic Analysis to Fix Political Geography. *Applied Demography* 8 (3): 1–3.

Williams, N., and C. Galley. 1995. Urban-Rural Differentials in Infant Mortality in Victorian England. *Population Studies* 49:401–20.

Wilmoth, J. R., and S. Horiuchi. 1999. Rectangularization Revisited: Variability of Age at Death Within Human Populations. *Demography* 36 (4): 475–95.

Wilson, A. C., and R. L. Cann. 1992. The Recent African Genesis of Humans. *Scientific American* 266 (4): 68–74.

Wilson, T. 1991. Urbanism, Migration, and Tolerance: A Reassessment. *American Sociological Review* 56:117–23.

Wimmer, A., L.-E. Cederman, and B. Min. 2009. Ethnic Politics and Armed Conflict: A Configurational Analysis of a New Global Data Set. *American Sociological Review* 74:316–37.

Winter, J. G. ed. 1936. *Papyri in the University of Michigan Collection: Miscellaneous Papyri*. Ann Arbor: University of Michigan Press.

Wirth, L. 1938. Urbanism as a Way of Life. *American Journal of Sociology* 44 (3–24).

Wolch, J., M. Pastor, Jr., and P. Dreier. 2004. *Up Against the Sprawl: Public Policy and the Making of Southern California*. Minneapolis: University of Minnesota Press.

Wolffsohn, M. 1987. *Israel: Polity, Society, Economy, 1882–1986: An Introductory Handbook*. Atlantic Highlands, NJ: Humanities Press International.

Wonacott, P., J. Whalen, and B. Bahree. 2003. China's Growing Thirst for Oil Remakes the Global Market. *Wall Street Journal*, 3 December:A1.

Wood, J. W., and M. Weinstein. 1988. A Model of Age-specific Fecundability. *Population Studies* 42 (1): 85–113.

Woodrow-Lafield, K. 1996. Emigration from the USA: Multiplicity Survey Evidence. *Population Research and Policy Review* 15 (2): 171–99.

World Bank. 1999. Gender and Law: Eastern Africa Speaks. *Human Development* (126).

———. 2000a. *World Development Indicators Database, July 2000* 2000a [cited 2001]. Available from http://www.worldbank.org

———. 2000b. *World Development Report 2000/2001: Attacking Poverty*. New York: Oxford University Press.

———. 2003. *World Development Report 2003: Sustainable Development in a Dynamic World*. The World Bank 2003 [cited 2003]. Available from http://econ.worldbank.org/wdr/wdr2003/

———. 2007. *Statistical Manual, Annex 3: Glossary*. The World Bank Group 2007 [cited 2007]. Available from http://go.worldbank.org/U0ORXRBQU0.

———. 2009. World Development Report 2010: Development and Climate Change. Washington, DC: The World Bank Group.

World Commission on Environment and Development. 1987. *Our Common Future*. New York: Oxford University Press.

World Health Organization. 2002a. *Suicide Prevention*. World Health Organization 2002a [cited 2004]. Available from http://www.who.int/mental_health/prevention/suicide/suicideprevent/en/

———. 2002b. World Report on Violence and Health. Geneva: World Health Organization.

———. 2004. Unsafe Abortion—Global and Regional Estimates of the Incidence of Unsafe Abortion and Associated Mortality in 2000. Geneva: World Health Organization.

———. 2007. *Maternal Mortality in 2005: Estimates Developed by WHO, UNICEF, UNFPA, and the World Bank* 2007 [cited 2010]. Available from http://whqlibdoc.who.int/publications/2007/9789241596213_eng.pdf.

———. 2009. Life Tables for WHO Member States.

———. 2010. *Cumulative Number of Confirmed Human Cases of Avian Influenza A/(H5N1) Reported to WHO* 2010 [cited 2010]. Available from http://www.who.int/csr/disease/avian_influenza/country/cases_table_2010_02_17/en/index.html.

World Resources Institute. 2000. *World Resources 2000/2001*. New York: Oxford University Press.

Wright, R. 1989. The Easterlin Hypothesis and European Fertility Rates. *Population and Development Review* 15:107–22.

Wrigley, E. A. 1974. *Population and History*. New York: McGraw-Hill.

———. 1987. *People, Cities and Wealth*. Oxford: Blackwell Publishers.

———. 1988. The Limits to Growth. In *Population and Resources in Western Intellectual Tradition*, eds. M. Teitelbaum and J. Winter. New York: Population Council.

Wrigley, E. A., and R. S. Schofield. 1981. *The Population History of England, 1541–1871: A Reconstruction*. Cambridge, MA: Harvard University Press.

WWF. 2008. *Living Planet Report 2008*. Gland, Switzerland: WWF International.

Yamani, M. 2000. *Changed Identities: The Challenge of the New Generation*. Washington, DC: Brookings Institution.

Yin, S. 2005. *Abortion in the United States and the World*. Population Reference Bureau 2005 [cited 2010]. Available from http://www.prb.org/Articles/2005/AbortionintheUnitedStatesandtheWorld.aspx.

York, R., E. A. Rosa, and T. Dietz. 2003. Footprints on the Earth: The Environmental Consequences of Modernity. *American Sociological Review* 68:279–300.

Yount, K. M. 2003. Gender Bias in the Allocation of Curative Heatlh Care in Minia, Egypt. *Population Research and Policy Review* 22 (3). 267–99.

Zamiska, N. 2006. China Wrestles with TB among Migrant Workers. *Wall Street Journal*, 1 November:A6.

Zelinsky, W. 1971. The Hypothesis of the Mobility Transition. *The Geographical Review* 61 (2): 219–49.

Zengwang Xu, and R. Harriss. 2010. A Spatial and Temporal Autocorrelated Growth Model for City Rank Size Distribution. *Urban Studies* 47 (2): 321–35.

Zhang, L. 2008. Religious Affiliation, Religiosity, and Male and Female Fertility. *Demographic Research* 18 (8):233–262.

Zhao, Z. 1994. Demographic Conditions and Multigeneration Households in Chinese History: Results from Genealogical Research and Microsimulation. *Population Studies* 48 (3): 413–26.

———. 2001. Chinese Genealogies As a Source for Demographic Research:A Further Assessment of Their Reliability and Biases. *Population Studies* 55:181–93.

Zhou, Y., and L. J. C. Ma. 2000. Economic Restructuring and Suburbanization in China. *Urban Geography* 21 (3): 205–36.

Zhu, Y. 2004. Changing Urbanization Processes and In Situ Rural-Urban Transformation: Reflections on China's Settlement Definitions. In *New Forms of Urbanization: Beyond the Urban-Rural Dichotomy*, eds. A. G. Champion and G. Hugo. London: Ashgate Publishing Company.

Zimmer, Z., L. G. Martin, M. B. Ofstedal, and Y.-L. Chuang. 2007. Education of Adult Children and Mortality of Their Elderly Parents in Taiwan. *Demography* 44 (2): 289–305.

Zinsser, H. 1935. *Rats, Lice and History*. Boston: Little, Brown.

Zipf, G. K. 1949. *Human Behavior and the Principle of Least Effort*. Reading, MA: Addison-Wesley.

Zlotnick, H. 1994. Expert Group Meeting on Population Distribution and Migration. *International Migration Review* 28 (1): 171—204.

Zuberi, T. 2001. *Thicker Than Blood: How Racial Statistics Lie*. Minneapolis: University of Minnesota Press.

GEOGRAPHIC INDEX

SUBJECT INDEX